ALLE ZEIT WACH 1842

Nadia Magnenat-Thalmann
Daniel Thalmann (Eds.)

New Trends in Computer Graphics

Proceedings of CG International '88

With 470 Figures, Including 120 in Color

Springer-Verlag
Berlin Heidelberg New York
London Paris Tokyo

Prof. Dr. Nadia Magnenat-Thalmann
Centre Universitaire d'Informatique
Université de Genève
12 rue du Lac
CH-1207 Genève, Switzerland

Prof. Dr. Daniel Thalmann
Laboratoire d'Infographie
Département d'Informatique
Ecole Polytechnique Fédérale de Lausanne
CH-1015 Lausanne, Switzerland

Cover: Frame of the film *Eglantine*, directed by
N. Magnenat-Thalmann and D. Thalmann

ISBN-13 : 978-3-642-83494-3 e-ISBN-13 : 978-3-642-83492-9
DOI : 10.1007 / 978-3-642-83492-9

Softcover reprint of the hardcover 1st edition 1988

2145/3140-543210

Preface

New Trends in Computer Graphics contains a selection of research papers submitted to Computer Graphics International '88 (CGI '88). CGI '88 is the Official Annual Conference of the Computer Graphics Society. Since 1982, this conference has been held in Tokyo. This year, it is taking place in Geneva, Switzerland. In 1989, it will be held in Leeds, U.K., in 1990 in Singapore, in 1991 in U.S.A. and in 1992 in Montreal, Canada.

Over 100 papers were submitted to CGI '88 and 61 papers were selected by the International Program Committee. Papers have been grouped into 6 chapters. The first chapter is dedicated to Computer Animation because it deals with all topics presented in the other chapters. Several animation systems are described as well as specific subjects like 3D character animation, quaternions and splines. The second chapter is dedicated to papers on Image Synthesis, in particular new shading models and new algorithms for ray tracing are presented. Chapter 3 presents several algorithms for geometric modeling and new techniques for the creation and manipulation of curves, surfaces and solids and their applications to CAD. In Chapter 4, an important topic is presented: the specification of graphics systems and images using languages and user-interfaces. The last two chapters are devoted to applications in sciences, medicine, engineering, art and business.

In addition to CGI '88, special events during the conference have included:

- The First Computer-generated Film Festival of Geneva, with a competition of the best films in the world
- An exhibition on how Marilyn Monroe has been synthesized by computer
- Demonstrations of the use of graphic systems for art, education, science and technology.

The conference was organized by the Computer Graphics Society (CGS) with the cooperation of le Ministère des Relations Internationales du Québec, le Ministère du Commerce Extérieur et du Développement Technologique du Québec, the Display group of the British Computer Society, the Swiss Computer Graphics Association (SCGA), l'Association Suisse pour l'Automatique (ASSPA), la Société Suisse d'Informatique Médicale (SSIM), l'Ecole des Hautes Etudes Commerciales de Montréal, L'Université de Genève, l'Ecole Polytechnique Fédérale de Lausanne et l'Université de Montréal.

Nadia Magnenat-Thalmann
Daniel Thalmann

Table of Contents

Chapter 1
Computer Animation 1

Locating Sampling Points for Cubic Splines
K. Harada, E. Nakamae (Japan) 3

Design and Implementation of the Animation Language SOLAR
T.-S. Chua, W.-H. Wong, K.-C. Chu (Singapore) 15

AVENUE: An Integrated 3-D Animation System
A. Doi, M. Aono, N. Urano, S. Uno (Japan) 27

The Use of Quaternions for Animation, Modelling and Rendering
D. Pletincks (Belgium) 44

Toward General Animation Control
G. Hégron, B. Arnaldi, G. Dumont (France) 54

3-D Facial Animation Using Image Samples
J.F.S. Yau, N.D. Duffy (UK) 64

Human Prototyping
N. Magnenat-Thalmann, H.T. Minh, M. de Angelis, D.Thalmann
(Switzerland and Canada) 74

"Occursus Cum Novo", Computer Animation by Ray Tracing in a Network
W. Leister, Th. Maus, H. Müller, B. Neidecker, A. Stösser (Germany) 83

Chapter 2
Image Synthesis 93

A General Shading Model
A. Sfarti (USA) 95

The H-Test, a Method of High Speed Interpolative Shading
K. Harrison, D.A.P. Mitchell, A.H. Watt (UK) 106

Synthetic Image Generation for Highly Defocused Scenes
Y.C. Chen (USA) 117

Particals: An Artistic Approach to Fuzzy Objects
M. Inakage (Japan) 126

VOXAR: A Tridimensional Architecture for Fast Realistic Image Synthesis
R. Caubet, Y. Duthen, V. Gaildrat (France) 135

Image Generation with an Associative Processor Array
R. Storer, A.W.G. Duller, E.L. Dagless (UK) 150

A Strategy for Mapping Parallel Ray-Tracing into a Hypercube Multiprocessor System
H. Kobayashi, T. Nakamura, Y. Shigei (Japan) 160

Parallel Space Tracing: An Experience on an iPSC Hypercube
K. Bouatouch, T. Priol (France) 170

Ray-Traced View and Visual Transparent Quality of Double Transparent Objects
M. Iizuka (Japan) 189

Antialiasing for Ray Tracing Using CSG Modeling
J. Argence (France) 199

Image Warping Among Arbitrary Planar Shapes
G.Wolberg (USA) 209

A Simple Method for Color Quantization: Octree Quantization
M. Gervautz, W. Purgathofer (Austria) 219

Chapter 3
Geometric Modeling and CAD 233

An Efficient Polygon Handling Technique in a CAAD Environment
C. Gambaro, C. Pienovi (Italy) 235

Volume and Surface Properties in CSG
G. Wyvill, P. Sharp (New Zealand) 257

A Hierarchical Model for Spatial Stacking
N.M. Aziz (USA) 267

Set Operation Evaluation Using Boolean Octree
D. Badouel, G. Hégron (France) 275

Efficiency of Uniform Grids for Intersection Detection on Serial and Parallel Machines
Wm. R.Franklin, N. Chandrasekhar, M. Kankanhalli, M. Seshan, V. Akman (USA) 288

Adjacency Finding Algorithms in a Variable-Resolution Boundary Model
L. De Floriani (Italy) 298

On Triangulating Palm Polygons in Linear Time
H. ElGindy, G. Toussaint (Canada) 308

Vertical Scan-Conversion for Filling Purposes
R.D. Hersch (Switzerland) 318

Field Functions for Implicit Surfaces
B. Wyvill, G.Wyvill (Canada and New Zealand) 328

A Cellular Array for Computing Bicubical B-Splines Coefficients
L. Ciminiera, P. Montuschi, A. Valenzano (Italy) 339

New Results for the Smooth Connection Between Tensor Product Bézier Patches
W.-H. Du, F.J.M. Schmitt (France) 351

Three-Dimensional Shape Generation Based on Generalized Symmetry
T. Tanaka, S. Naito, T. Takahashi (Japan) 364

Geometric Modeling with Euclidean Constructions
N. Fuller, P. Prusinkiewicz (Canada) 379

Using GT/CAPP to Enhance Product Data Exchange Standard - Key to CAD/CAM Integration
I. Al-Qattan, J.R. Rose (USA) 392

Chapter 4
Graphics Systems and Languages 401

Drawing Input Through Geometrical Constructions: Specification and Applications
T. Noma, T.L. Kunii, N. Kin, H. Enomoto, E. Aso, T.Yamamoto (Japan) 403

On the Construction of Constrained Circles, an Unified Approach
P.J. Zsombor-Murray, K. Linder (Canada) 416

A Model for Image Structuration
A. Braquelaire, P. Guitton (France and Canada) 426

An Object-Oriented Interface for Network-Based Image Processing
B.G. Nichol (USA) 436

Applying Direct Manipulation to Geometric Construction Systems
R.M. White (Switzerland) 446

Implementing a Definitive Notation for Interactive Graphics
M. Beynon, E. Yung (UK) 456

GRAFLOG: Programming with Interactive Graphics and PROLOG
L.A. Pineda, N. Chater (UK) 469

Modelling and Building Graphics Systems: GKS
M. Boano, R. Brazioli, S.M. Fisher, P. Palazzi, W.R. Zhao
(Switzerland, UK and China) 479

The Choice of a Graphics System; Standard, Emerging Standard or De-facto-Standard
M. Jern (Denmark) 488

Chapter 5
Computer Graphics in Medicine and Sciences 497

Molecular Graphics: A New Tool in Computer-Assisted Chemistry
J. Weber, P.-Y. Morgantini, J.-P. Doucet, J.-E. Dubois (Switzerland and France) 499

Molecular Graphics and Modeling on the PC
H. van de Waterbeemd, P.-A. Carrupt, N. Huijsmans (Switzerland) 509

MOPIC: An Advanced Molecule Rendering Program for Microcomputers
F.T. Marchese, S. Reda (USA) 519

Computer Graphics and Complex Ordinary Differential Equations
F. Richard (France) 527

Approximation of Missing Sections of CT-Image Sequences Using Binary Interpolation
V. Heyers, J. Dengler, H.-P. Meinzer (Germany) 537

Computer Graphic Techniques Applied to Medical Image Analysis
O. Ratib (USA) 546

Three-Dimensional Reconstruction Procedure Using GKS Primitives and Software Transformations for Anatomical Studies of the Nervous System
J.-P. Hornung, R. Kraftsik (Switzerland) 555

The Use of Three-Dimensional Dynamic and Kinematic Modelling in the Design of a Colonoscopy Simulator
A. Poon, C. Williams, D. Gillies (UK) 565

Chapter 6
Applications of Computer Graphics 575

A Hierarchical Simulation Environment for VLSI
M. Bourgault, J. Cloutier, C. Roy, S. Fauvel, E. Cerny (Canada) 577

3-D Geometric Modelling in Design and Manufacturing of Furniture Parts
F. Zhang, S. Cai, Y. Wang, Z. Ju (China) 584

Computer-Assisted Color Conversion
D.M. Geshwind (USA) 593

Analysis of Urban Geographic Queries
P. Boursier (France) 601

GQL: A Graphical Database Language Using Pattern Images
H. Du, M. Azmoodeh (UK) 611

Computer-Aided Sail Section Drawing
L.P. Vidal (Spain) 621

The Effect of Format on Information Processing Using Graphics
L. Gingras, L. Harvey, M.-C. Roy, F. Cloutier (Canada) 631

Development of an Integrated Computer Art System
M. King (UK) 643

Improving the Programmability of Robotic Workcells
G. Carayannis, A. Malowany (Canada) 653

Simulation and Teaching Techniques for Interactive Robot Programming: ROPSE
S. Elbaba, A. Troncy, M. Martinez (France) 663

Conference Committees 673

Authors' Addresses 675

Chapter 1

Computer Animation

Locating Sampling Points for Cubic Splines

K. Harada and E. Nakamae (Japan)

ABSTRACT

Locating sampling points for cubic splines is investigated in this paper. The direct application of the proposal is for designing motion of objects for computer animation. The method consists of two parts: (i) obtaining the relative position of the sampling points, and (ii) mapping the sampling points on the cubic spline interpolant based on the relative position sequence obtained in (i).

The obtained results may be used for design of motion for phenomena described parametrically.

Key words; interpolation, imparametrization, sampling points and cubic splines

1. INTRODUCTION

Cubic spline interpolants[1)] have been widely used in the field of computer animation, computer aided geometric design (CAGD), and similar applications because the interpolants may be obtained by relatively simple calculation, and their mathematical background has been well investigated[2)]. Among various cubic splines, parametric cubic splines[1)] have been used traditionally because they are applicable to data of any dimensional. Moreover, the chord length parametrization[3)] is known to be better than others since calculation experience has shown that the parametrization method offers better results than others in the sense that the obtained interpolants exhibit less wiggle.

In this paper, we focus on the application of cubic splines with chord length parametrization for design of motion in computer animation. For creating computer animation, splines have traditionally been used for keyframing.[4),5)] Keyframing is one of the movement design techniques. There are two spline interpolations for two types of control in keyframe design[6)], kinetic and positional control. In keyframing, control is the main purpose to use splines, thus B-splines rather than cubic splines have been used. The kinetic B-spline is defined as the interpolant which gives the keyframe number as a function of time, and the positional B-spline is defined as the interpolant which gives the value of the parameter as a function of keyframe number. Composition of these two splines gives the final interpolant which gives the value of the parameter of time (that specifies the position of each object), and the movement of each object is determined. Once all key frames have been established frames that are inserted (if required) between two successive keyframe images are generated in linear manner with respect to time.

Another type of motion design for computer animation has recently been proposed by Reynolds[7]. Instead of scripting the paths (with interpolant) of each object individually, the movement is generated based on the laws of simulated physics that rule each motion. There is no need to interpolate positional data because each movement is calculated step by step.

In this paper, these two ideas are combined. The movement of each object is supposed to be determined by some pre-defined rule (constant acceleration, for example). Unlike the Reynolds' approach, each path of movement is supposed to be defined. Therefore, the interpolation technique is implemented, but no control is activated: cubic splines rather than B-splines are used. Paths of each object's movement are defined by cubic spline interpolants, and the position of each object at a frame time is specified on the interpolant. The specification of the location of each frame is the point which differentiates our method from the widely used linear frame generation method.

Cubic spline interpolants consist of curve segments that are defined between each consecutive data point. Except in random-vector type equipments the obtained interpolants are recorded and/or displayed by using a finite number of points. Let us call such points sampling points, i.e., the set of sampling points is regarded as the interpolant to the given data set, and the position of an object at one keyframe time corresponds to one such sampling point. The simplest and widely used method to generate sampling points on the interpolants is that a pre-defined number of sampling points are specified in parametric space by setting their parameter values. Though the parameter value difference between each consecutive sampling points is specified to be constant in this simple method, when they are displayed, the distance between consecutive sampling points is not constant in general. This is because the mapping between parametric and display spaces is not linear.

In order to locate an object in computer animation motion design at a desired position, we have to specify its position coordinate. In the application here, each object moves along a cubic spline interpolant. However, there is no direct way to calculate the position of a sampling point (corresponding to the position of an object on the interpolant) at a given distance from the previous sampling point.

Practical solutions for the problem can be obtained by investigating the relation between the parametric space and the actual display space. Sederberg et al[8] reported an imparametrization method. The inverse transformation is always possible. They suggested the application of the method to the problem of calculating the intersection between parametric curves and/or surfaces. The imparametrization method is applied here to derive the mapping between parameter and display spaces.

Discussion in this paper starts out with the parametric form of the cubic splines. Therefore, we first follow Sederberg's method. Relative position between each sampling points is first specified for later processing. A simple method that defines the relative position is offered. Then, the relative position is used to solve the equation; the solution is a parameter value and specifies the position of a sampling point. For demonstration, the proposal is applied to calculate the position of a moving object in a simple computer animation.

2. IMPLICITIZATION OF CUBIC SPLINES

Let us assume that n data points P_1, $P_2, \ldots, P_n$ are given in two-dimensional space. The widely used parametric planar cubic splines for these data points are described by the following equations[1]:

$$
\begin{aligned}
x(t) &= a_3^i t^3 + a_2^i t^2 + a_1^i t + a_0^i \ , \\
y(t) &= b_3^i t \ + b_2^i t \ + b_1^i t + b_0^i \ , \\
&\emptyset \leqq t \leqq t_i, \quad i = 1,2,\ldots,n-1.
\end{aligned}
\tag{1}
$$

i is the segment number, and a_0^i through b_3^i are defined on the interval between P_i and P_{i+1}. Since the chord length parametrization is adopted here, t_i is chosen as the Euclidean distance between P_i and P_{i+1}.

The actual display of the cubic spline interpolants is performed using the set of points generated on each segment. The traditional method to display the cubic spline interpolant defined by Eq.(1) is as follows:

Sampling Method

> Set the number of sampling points to be generated on each segment. Let this number be m. Divide t_i (i=1,2,...n-1) by m+1, and calculate the coordinate of each sampling point. The parameter value t of each sampling point is $t_i*j/(m+1)$, j=Ø,1,2,...,m; i={1,2,...,n-1}. Sampling points are generated by using the parameter value and calculating the coordinates using Eq.(1).

When displayed, the spacing of two consecutive sampling points is uneven in general though their spacing in parameter space is even. This is due to the fact that the mapping between parameter and display spaces in not linear. To investigate the relation between display and parameter spaces, the introduction of implicitization is required.

For implicitization, Sederberg et al[8] have exploited the classical fundamental theory of elimination, a related theorem, the resultant, and Sylvester's method. By following Sederberg's procedure the parametric cubic spline in Eq.(1) that represents a planar curve is rewritten as $a^i_3t^3 + a^i_2t^2 + a^i_1t + a^i_0 - x = 0$ and $b^i_3t^3 + b^i_2t^2 + b^i_1t + b^i_0 - y = 0$. Then, the implicitization of Eq.(1) is obtained by:

$$\begin{vmatrix} a^i_3 & a^i_2 & a^i_1 & a^i_0-x & 0 & 0 \\ 0 & a^i_3 & a^i_2 & a^i_1 & a^i_0-x & 0 \\ 0 & 0 & a^i_3 & a^i_2 & a^i_1 & a^i_0-x \\ b^i_3 & b^i_2 & b^i_1 & b^i_0-y & 0 & 0 \\ 0 & b^i_3 & b^i_2 & b^i_1 & b^i_0-y & 0 \\ 0 & 0 & b^i_3 & b^i_2 & b^i_1 & b^i_0-y \end{vmatrix} = 0 \qquad (2)$$

Eq.(2) is a bicubic equation with respect to x and y. With the aid of a symbolic math program, it may be expanded. Table 1 shows the number of coefficients of each term. The total number of coefficients is 102.

Table 1: Number of coefficients of Eq.(2)

Symbol	Variable	No. of terms
A	x^3	1
B	y^3	1
C	x^2y	1
D	xy^2	1
E	x^2	7
F	y^2	7
G	xy	8
H	x	21
I	y	21
J	Constant	34

3. LOCATING SAMPLING POINTS

For locating sampling points on an interpolant, two procedures have to be established. First, the inter relation among sampling points has to be specified. The relation determines the relative position of a sampling point to other sampling points. Then, the obtained point sequence is mapped to an interpolant. To implement the mapping the relation between Eqs.(1) and (2) has to be investigated.

3-1 Relative Position of Sampling Points

Relative position among sampling points, which reflects the

speed of the object, is defined by some rule. In computer animation, there are several factors that determine the movement of each object[3]. If an object is getting bigger, its speed should be reduced to obtain realistic appearance. Curvature of the path is another factor that determines the speed. Objects move slowly where the curvature is blarge and vice versa. For simplicity the curvature of the interpolant is supposed to be the only factor that dominates the movement of an object. The curvature of the function y=f(x) is given by

$$k = y'' / (1 + y'^2)^{3/2} \tag{3}$$

where ' denotes the derivative with respect to x. Cubic splines (more specifically linear cubic splines) have been derived under the condition that $1+y'^2$ is very close to one. Thus, the curvature is considered y", instead of Eq.(3). In parametric form, the approximated curvature may be written as

$$y'' = (d^2y/dt^2 * dx/dt - dy/dt * d^2x/dt^2) / (dx/dt) \tag{4}$$

dx/dt through d^2y/dt^2 in this equation can be easily calculated by using Eq.(1). However, when the absolute value of dx/dt is small the numerical calculation of Eq.(4) causes problems. For defining movement based on the curvature, its sign is not important. Thus, the practically useful pseudo K is defined as follows:

$$K = \sqrt{(d^2x/dt^2)^2 + (d^2y/dt^2)^2} \tag{5}$$

Eq.(5) has been derived under the observation that two approximated curvatures defined in parameter space, i.e. d^2x/dt^2 and d^2y/dt^2, are mutually orthogonal in the display space, and the magnitude of the total pseudo curvature defined by these two values is obtained as their vector sum.

Various rules can be considered to describe the relation between K and the relative position. A natural rule would be that the speed of an object is proportional to the reciprocical value of the curvature. The assumption is adopted in the later application.

Figure 1 shows a coordinate system which is useful to show the relation between K and the relative position on the curve. The horizontal and vertical axes are the relative position and K, respectively. A method to simply derive the motion of an object based on K is as follows: (a) Integrate K along the curve throughout the interpolant (throughout one period if the

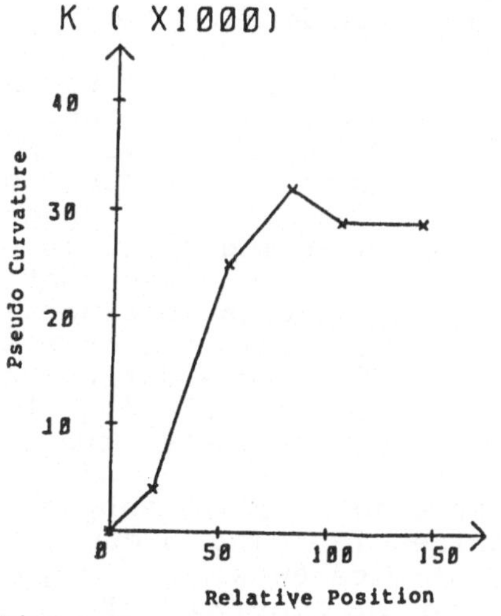

Figure 1:

Relation between K and relative position on the interpolant.

interpolant is periodic). (b) Divide the integrand by the number of sampling points to be generated on the interpolant. (c) Calculate the position of each sampling point on the horizontal axis of Figure 1 such that the integrand between two successive sampling points is equal to the value calculated in step (b).

The obtained sequence applies when the motion of each object is totally determined by the approximated curvature. Suppose an object is stationary at a keyframe time, and then begins to move with constant acceleration. The movement may be simulated by controlling the vertical coordinate of K in Figure 1. If the value K of the start point is large, the initial speed of the object is low and vice versa. A typical example is offered in section 4.

This procedure produces only the relative position of each sampling point. Their actual coordinates on the interpolant are calculated in the following section.

3-2 Mapping to the Interpolant

The aim of this section is to investigate the relation between Eqs.(1) and (2). More specifically, the goal may be described with the following problem:

Problem

> How can we set a total of m sampling points based on the relative position sequence given in the previous section?

Practical solution of this problem is the target of this paper. Therefore, neither the exact curve length nor the iterative method to control the spacing along the curve will not be considered. Two types of solution may be considered:

> (a) Set the first sampling point on P_1, i.e. the first data point, and calculate the second sampling point by solving Eq.(2). Then, the second sampling point is treated as the new start point from which the new sampling point is calculated, and the third sampling point is obtained by again solving Eq.(2). The procedure continues until the mth sampling point is obtained.
> (b) The procedure flow is the same as in (a) except for the equation solving step. Now, the equation for calculating the next sampling point is set up in parameter space.

Procedure (b) is adopted in this paper because procedure (a) requires handling bicubic equations. Moreover, procedure (a) is complicated since the paths (or the interpolants) are multi-valued in general. To execute (b), on the other hand, the relation between Eqs.(1) and (2) should first be clarified. To this aim, the following theory found in many mathematics text books is useful:

Theorem

Let $F(x,y)$ be continuously differentiable inside a region that contains a point (p,q). Furthermore, let $F(p,q)=0$. If the partial derivative $F_y(p,q)\neq 0$, then there exists a single valued continuous function $f(x)$ that satisfies $F(x,f(x))=0$ and $q=f(p)$. The function $y=f(x)$ is differentiable and,

$$dy/dx = -F_x(x,y) / F_y(x,y). \quad (6)$$

Let (p,q) and (p',q') be two sampling points on the curve of Eq.(2). The Euclidean distance between these points ($\sqrt{(p-p')^2+(q-q')^2}$) is a good approximation to the distance between these points along the curve. By applying Taylor expansion,

$$q - q' \simeq (dy/dx)_{x=p} (p - p'), \quad (7)$$

is obtained. Therefore, the Euclidean distance is described by the simple difference $|p - p'|$.

The problem in this section is solved if each spacing between two successive sampling points is set to its desired value. The desired distance is derived by using the sequence obtained in the previous section. Let $\ell_1, \ell_2 \ldots, \ell_m$ be the sequence obtained in the previous section on the horizontal axis of Figure 1. Suppose α be the distance between P_1 and P_n along the curve to $(\ell_m - \ell_1)$. A new useful sequence is defined by $L_1 = P_1$, $L_{i+1} - L_i = (\ell_{i+1} - \ell_i)\alpha$; $i=1,2,\ldots,m-1$. The sequence defines the desired distance of the sampling point on the interpolant.

The equation to calculate the parameter value of each sampling point is:

$$|p - p'| \sqrt{1 + \{(F_x/F_y)_{x=p,\ y=q}\}^2} = T_k, \quad (8)$$
$$k = 2,3,\ldots,m$$

where $T_k=L_k-L_{k-1}$. F_x and F_y in Eq.(8) is calculated by using the coefficient of the segment where T_k exists. For better numerical behavior, the values of F_x and F_y in Eq.(8) are compared prior to solving the equation. If the absolute value of the denominator is smaller than that of the numerator the following equation is used instead of Eq.(8):

$$|q - q'| \sqrt{1 + \{(F_y/F_x)_{x=p,\ y=q}\}^2} = T_k. \quad (9)$$

The final locating method is given by:

<u>Locating Method</u>

Calculate the parameter value of each sampling point by solving Eq.(8) (or Eq.(9) depending on the situation; the latter description is only for Eq.(8) for briefness). The outline of the proposed method is depicted in Figure 2.

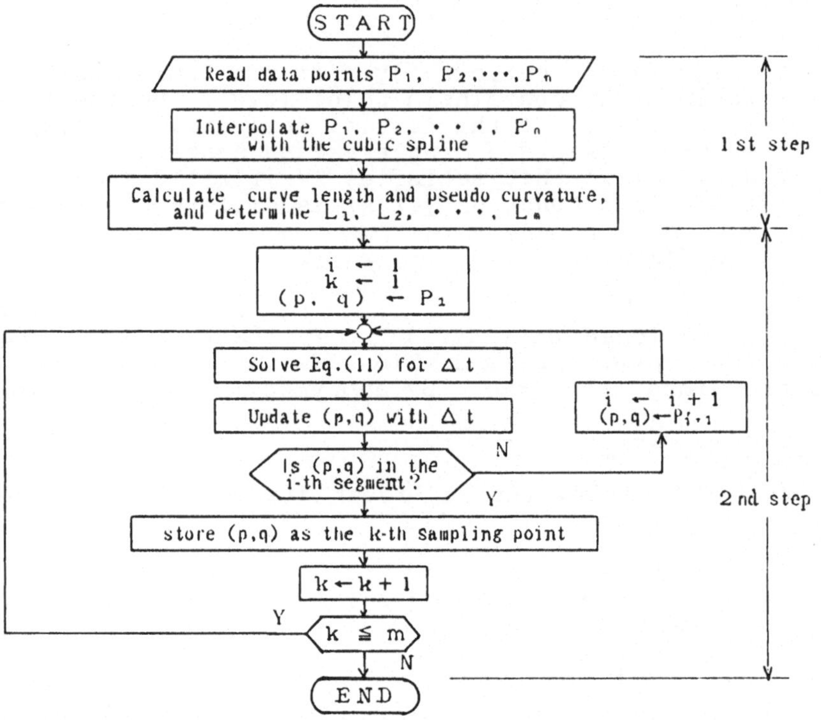

Figure 2: Algorithm of the proposed method.

In the algorithm, Eq.(8) is solved sequentially for each segment starting from the first sampling point (therefore the first data point) through the last sampling point. When solving Eq.(8) for the second sampling point, the coordinate of the first sampling point, which is already known, is used as the coordinate of (p,q). Then, (p,q) is replaced with the coordinate of the second sampling point, and the calculation for the third sampling point continues. The procedure continues until the calculation for the last sampling point completes.

$F_x(p,q)$ and $F_y(p,q)$ in Eq.(8) are calculated by the following equations:

$$F_x(p,q) = 3Ap^2 + 2Cpq + Dq^2 + 2Ep + Gq + H,$$
$$F_y(p,q) = 3Bq^2 + Cp^2 + 2Dpq + 2Fq + Gp + I. \qquad (10)$$

The capital letters A through I indicate the coefficients listed in Table 1. Note that these coefficients are calculated only once in the processing of each segment. Furthermore, the constant J composed of 34 terms (a_0 through b_3) need not be considered when solving Eq.(8).

The term $|p - p'|$ is evaluated by assuming the parameter value of p and p' to be t_p and $t_p + \Delta t$, respectively. By definition, $\emptyset \leq t_p \leq t_i$. Then, we can rewrite Eq.(8) to obtain the final cubic equation to calculate the coordinate (p',q'):

$$a_3^i \Delta t^3 + (3a_3^i t_p + a_2^i)\Delta t^2 + (3a_3^i t_p^2 + 2a_2^i t_p + a_1^i)\Delta t - |J_i| = \emptyset , \qquad (11)$$

$$|J_i| = T_k \sqrt{1 + \{(F_x/F_y)_{x=p,\, y=q}\}^2} .$$

The bisection method is appropriate to solve this cubic equation because a good initial guess $\Delta\overline{t}$ for the desired solution of Eq.(11) is given by:

$$\Delta\overline{t} = T_k . \qquad (12)$$

The sequence of parameter values $\overline{T_k}$ (k=2,...,m) obtained by solving Eq. (11) is the solution for the sampling point locating problem. Note that the first sampling point (k=1) is the first data point. Due to the characteristics of the bisection method, convergence to the root is very fast. Calculation experience has shown, however, that Newton's method for Eq.(11) sometimes results in one of the two unwanted roots.

There are two approximations that cause the spacing between consecutive sampling points in the display space not to conform exactly to the characteristic (equal spacing or equal acceleration, for example) specified in the parameter space. First, Eq.(11) (or originally Eq.(8)) is a linear approximation of the mapping equation between parameter and display spaces. The second approximation is in the case when the consecutive sampling points are located in different curve segments.

Let the kth sampling point be on the ith curve segment, with the (k+1)st sampling point known to be located on the (i+1)st curve segment. The data point at the junction is P_{i+1}. We first have to calculate the distance between the kth sampling point and P_{i+1} along the curve (not along the parameter). The Euclidean distance between these points is used as the approximate distance; this causes approximation error especially when the distance between the kth sampling point and P_{i+1} is large.

The error due to these approximations decreases as the number of sampling points increases. For small numbers of sampling points, a simple technique is offered to counter this problem. The major problem in this situation is that the last sampling point does not coincide (as is often required) in general to the last data point. This happens because the calculation of the proposed method proceeds in one direction from the first data to the last data, and calculation error accumulates. A simple cure is to adjust the parameter value of the last sampling point to that of the last data point. The parameter value of other sampling points is also modified by a linear transformation.

4. EXAMPLES

For demonstration, the proposed method has been applied to the "figure eight shaped" planar data shown in Figure 3. There are nineteen data points for this curve. The first data is on the intersection of the curve. The data number increases first turning along the curve counter-clockwise beginning from the intersection point to the tenth data point which coincides with the first data point. The number increases then moving clockwise to the nineteenth data which again coincides with the same point as the first data point. Since the first and the last data point are the same, this is a closed curve.

In the actual calculation, a pseudo point is introduced as the twentieth data. It is intended to coincide with the second data point. The reason extending the data is that the last sampling point calculated may fall short of the last data. Adjustment of the last sampling point, as described in foregoing section, solves the unwanted problem, and is applied in all the following applications.

In Figure 4, 41 sampling points were generated on the curve. Spacing between consecutive sampling points is constant in the relative position definition. Except where curvature does not change gradually, the sampling points are also almost evenly spaced. The twenty-first sampling point, however, does not locate on the intersection due to the accumulation of calculation error. The same problem also occurs in the subsequent examples.

Figure 5 is a simple simulation of a car moving on a curved road. The relative positions of sampling points were calculated by using K in Figure 1. A total of 41 sampling points is shown on a cubic spline interpolant. The speed is slow before entering a curved region, and it is high when entering straight road.

Figure 6 is a three-dimensional representation of the car's motion. A z coordinate is added to the data in Figure 3 so that the 1st data is the lowest and the nineteenth or the last data is the highest. (a) corresponds to the example in Figure 5, after the speed of the car has been stabilized. (b) shows the case where the initial speed of the car is nearly zero. Moderate initial speed is supposed when calculating the movement in (c). Nineteen positions of a car is shown in each picture. The difference among pictures is well observed in the earlier stage of the car movement.

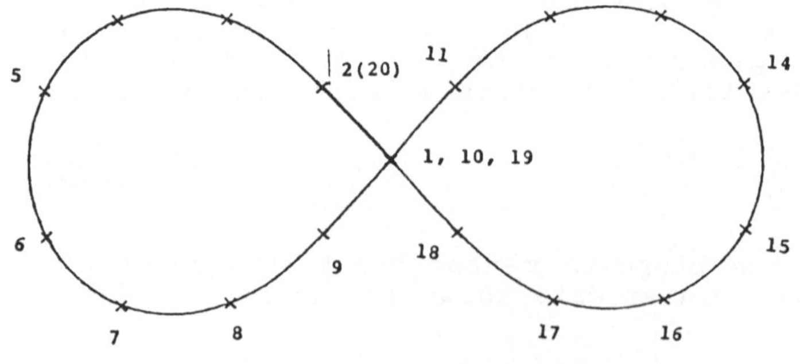

Figure 3:
Cubic spline interpolant forthe eighteen data points. Data points are shown with X symbols.

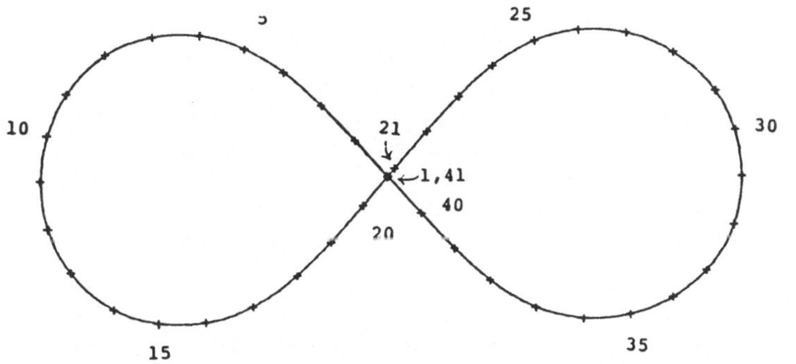

Figure 4:
41 sampling points generated on the cubic spline interpolant. Spacing between consecutive sampling points (+ mark) is constan in the parametric space.

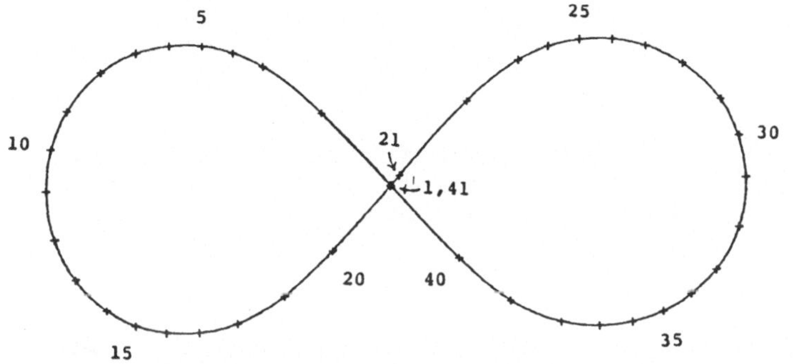

Figure 5:
41 sampling points generated on the cubic spline interpolant. The motion was determined by using Figure 1. Car motion along a curved road is simulated with the location of each sampling point. The speed exhibits a stable pattern, the speed distribution attained long after the initial state.

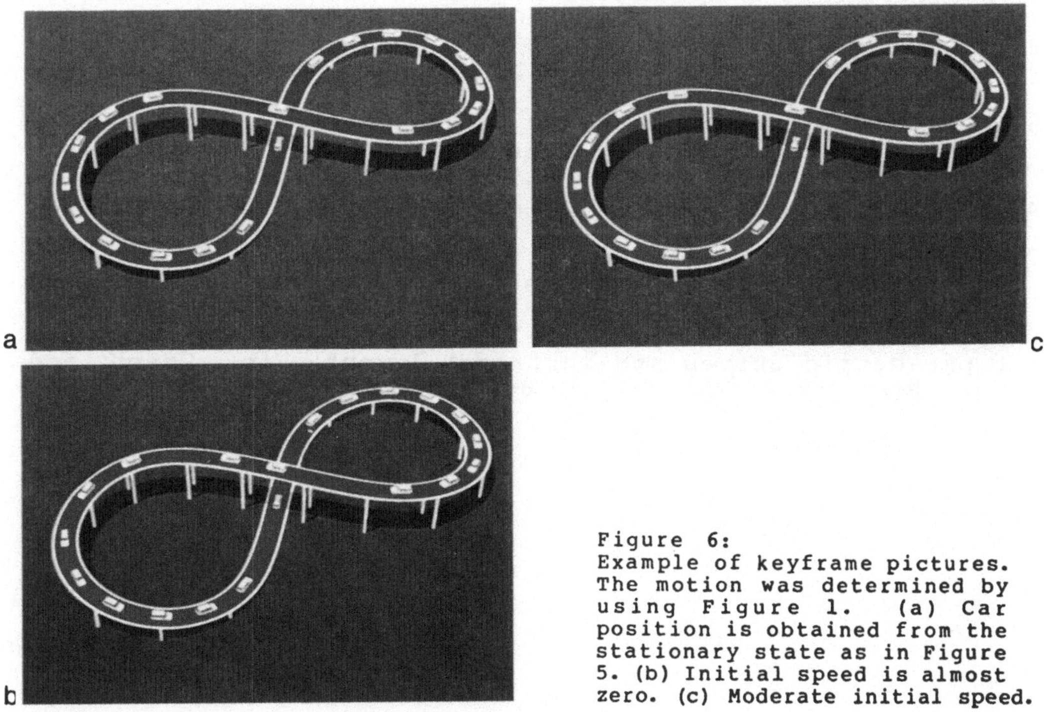

Figure 6:
Example of keyframe pictures. The motion was determined by using Figure 1. (a) Car position is obtained from the stationary state as in Figure 5. (b) Initial speed is almost zero. (c) Moderate initial speed.

CONCLUSIONS

A method has been proposed to improve the spacing of sampling points. The essential part of the new method consists of solving cubic equations. $\overline{T}_k$ (k=2,3,...,m) are the obtained sequence values. The bisection method is very useful for this numerical calculation because a good initial guess for the calculation is available.

The proposed method provides a good approximation for setting the position of each sampling point at its required position on the curve with a relatively small amount of calculation effort. One of the main applications of the proposal is for computer animation.

ACKNOWLEDGMENTS

We are grateful to Bonnie G. Sullivan for her discussions and preparing the manuscript. Special thanks to Toshio Akinobu for his skillful computer operation to obtain Figure 6.

REFERENCES

1 Rogers, D F and Adams, J A , Mathematical elements for computer graphics McGraw-Hill (1976)
2 de Boor, C, A practical guide to splines Springer-Verlag (1978)
3 Lasseter, J 'Principles of traditional animation applied to 3D computer animation' Comput. Gr (1987) Vol.21 No.4 pp.35-44
4 Kochanek, D H U and Bartels, R H 'Interpolating splines with local tension, continuity, and bias control' Comput. Gr. (July 1984) Vol.18 No.3 pp.33-41
5 Steketee, S N and Badler, N I 'Parametric Keyframe Interpolation Incorporating Kinetic Adjustment and Phrasing Control' Comput. Gr. (1985) Vol.19 No.3 pp.255-262
6 Reynolds, C W 'Flocks, herds, and schools: a distributed behavioral model' Comput. Gr. (1987) Vol.21 No.4 pp.25-34
7 Brodlie, K W 'A review of methods for curve and function drawing'(in Mathematical Methods in Computer Graphics and Design, K.W.Brodlieed.) Academic Press (1980)
8 Sederberg, T W and Anderson, D.C. 'Implicit representation of parametric curves and surfaces' Comput. Vis., Graph. and Image Proc.(1984) Vol.28 pp.72-84

Design and Implementation of the Animation Language SOLAR

T.-S. Chua, W.-H. Wong, and K.-C. Chu (Singapore)

Abstract

One of the biggest problem in computer animation is the enormous amount of specification necessary to produce an animation sequence. Our animation language, SOLAR, is designed to enable us to specify animation easily and efficiently. SOLAR achieves this through the use of object-oriented paradigm and abstractions. Supports for high-level abstractions and adaptive motion are provided through its class-inheritance and message-passing mechanisms. Five kinds of abstractions are supported, i.e. structural, motion, functional, character and world modeling. Together, they provide good support for programming animation. All interactions between graphical objects are achieved through its message-passing mechanism. This paper describes the main features of SOLAR and its implementation.

Keywords: *Computer Animation, Object-oriented Language, Animation Language, Abstraction, Inheritance Mechanism.*

1. Introduction

Computer animation involves the rapid updating of images on the computer screen to give the illusion of motion. While traditional computer graphics rely solely on static images to convey information, computer animation conveys much more information in the form of motion. Because of this, computer animation has become an essential part of future information systems.

Although much work has been done in the area of image rendering [MAGNE85c], the field of motion control and specification for computer animation is still in its early stage of development [WILHE87]. Commonly used approaches for motion control are fairly low-level and require considerable amount of user input to specify the motion. To facilitate the task of generating animation information, an animation system is developed as part of a public information system [CHANG86]. The goal of the animation system is to provide an easy-to-use interactive environment for the relatively novice users to compose and modify animation information. The input into the system can be specified through graphical means or via programming. The animation information specified is then stored and used as part of the public information database. The details and design of the animation system is described in [CHUA87a].

As with the design of all man-machine interaction systems, there are the elements of textual input language and interactive action language to be considered [FOLEY74]. This paper is concerned only with the design and implementation of the textual language called SOLAR (stands for Structured Object-oriented Language for

AnimatoRs). The design of SOLAR aims at facilitating the generation of the language through a sequence of graphical interactions. To permit real-time playback of the animation using most existing display hardware, only 2-D graphics is considered. The restriction to only 2-D graphics means that relatively low-cost hardware can be used for display and no expensive film making equipment is needed to produce the animation. This, however, demands that powerful language features be available in SOLAR to support most useful animation features such as those described in [REYNO82]. Object priority is also used to allowed for overlaying of multiple images to achieve two-and-half-D animation. It is felt that this is sufficient for most commercial applications where the system is designed for.

This paper describes the main features of the animation language, SOLAR, and its implementation.

2. Review of Language Support of Animation Languages

The specification of an animation sequence is generally carried out in two distinct phases - the modeling phase, that defines the structural outlook of the objects involved in the animation, and the dynamic phase, which describes the behavior of these objects. The latter is the most important and difficult phase in computer animation. The description of object behavior in dynamic phase requires the abilities to define individual object motion, coordinate multiple object actions and specify adaptive motions [MAGNE85c]. Adaptive motion capabilities enable an object to use information about itself and the environment to adjust its motion accordingly. In addition, camera and other special effects [SATO84] must also be included in the dynamic phase to enhance the animation sequence. The challenge in the design of an animation language is to enable these actions to be specified clearly and easily.

The biggest problem in animation control and specification is the tremendous amount of information necessary to produce an animation sequence. One technique that has been widely used in programming community to tackle such problems is the use of abstraction [SHAW80]. Different levels of abstractions, representing increasing degree of details, is used to specify complex ideas in a step-wise manner. The five kinds of abstractions useful in computer animation are structural, motion, functional, character and world modeling [ZELTZ85]. The structural abstraction outlines the modeling of the graphical object. Motion abstraction defines motion independent of the graphical object that it controls. Functional abstraction permits the grouping of a set of motions with a structural element to effect a particular class of motion (called skill in [ZELTZ85]). At the higher level, character abstraction associates a collection of skills with a class of object structures. Adaptive motion capability is usually built-in at this level to enable the object to make decision on which skill to perform in a particular circumstance. Lastly, world modeling defines the environment in which all objects operate.

The five kinds of abstraction enable an animation sequence to be defined in steps; starting from the simple object structure and motion descriptions, to a more complex level of functional definition, object character building with adaptive skills and world modeling of interacting objects. The level of an animation language is determined largely by the level of abstractions that it provides, and whether it supports adaptive motion. The higher the level of the language, the easier it is for the user to define complicated animation with interacting objects.

For low level language such as GRAMPS [DONNE81], facilities are provided only in the form of primitive verbs and macro verbs for defining motions. Although GRAMPS permits the direct control of interactive device through motion abstraction, it provides only up to the functional level of abstractions. Similar level of abstractions can also be identified for notational languages such as [FEINE82], which uses musical notation, or [SINGH83], which uses Benesh notation, for defining motions.

High level animation languages, such as ASAS [REYNO82], tend to support the full level of abstractions with some form of adaptive motion control. ASAS is developed based on the actor paradigm of [HEWIT79]. It uses the notion of actors to perform dynamics on hierarchical graphical objects. More than one actor may be applied concurrently to handle different aspects of dynamics of a graphical object. Actors may pass messages to other actors for synchronization. The message passing mechanism makes it possible for ASAS to express adaptive motion. The actor paradigm in ASAS facilitates the definition of transformation hierarchies (structural abstraction) and behaviors (functional and character abstractions) with adaptive motion control.

The MIRA-SHADING language [MAGNE84] provides the level of abstractions similar to those provided by ASAS. Although the language does not support message passing, synchronization between different objects can be provided through the use of common parameters. The language is used in the implementation of an interactive director-oriented animation system called MIRANIM [MAGNE85a]. Extensive facilities are provided through MIRANIM for defining complicated motions based on the evolution laws [MAGNE85b] and manipulating camera effects [MAGNE86].

Motion control languages are also of interests in robotics [NAGEL84]. A similar classification of language level based on abstractions can also be applied to robotics languages. Low-level robotics languages such as VAL [SHIMA79] and AL [FINKE75] require explicit instructions to control each stage of robot motions. Higher level robotics languages such as AUTOPASS [LIEBE77] or AML [TAYLO82] permit the user to program the system in user domain terms, with support for character building and world modeling. One common feature of robotics languages that is absent in conventional animation languages is the extensive use of sensory feedback information to access the world model. The use of sensory feedback such as vision [SHIMA79], to locate and/or track the position of an object, provides an elegant way of implementing automatic adaptive motion for an object in an unknown environment.

3. The Main Features of Animation Language SOLAR

It is evident from the previous discussions that abstractions and adaptive motion are keys to the expressive power of an animation language. In addition, the animation language must support concurrency and permit controlled access to the world environment for high-level decision making with learning capabilities.

One programming model that has been widely recognized as the natural model for concurrency and data abstraction is the object-oriented programming model [OOPSL86]. A number of high-level animation languages reviewed, such as the ASAS and MIRA-SHADING, are based on the variants of this model. The object-oriented approach originated with Simula [DAHL66] and was made popular by Smalltalk [GOLDB83]. The design of our animation language SOLAR is influenced largely by the superclass-class-instance hierarchical structure of Smalltalk. The general syntax of SOLAR class definition is outlined in Fig 1.

All objects in the system operate independently and concurrently. The behavior of the object is described in terms of a set of methods. A method consists of mainly message passing statements and other statements to modify the local variables of the object. In order to provide a convenient time interval for executing the methods and performing system operations such as the updating of screen contents, SOLAR uses a master clock

```
CLASS <class_name> IS
(Superclass := <class_name>)
[(Local: [<var>]^{1-n} )]
    [ <method_description>; ]^{1-n}
END <class_name> {class_definition};

<method_description> ::=
    <selector> : [ <argument_list> ]
    BEGIN
        [syn_animation_statement>; ]^{0-n}
        [ EXCEPTION
        [asyn_animation_statement>; ]^{0-n} ]
    END <selector>;

<syn_animation_statement> ::= <statement_part> WHEN (CLOCK = <t>);

<asyn_animation_statement> ::= <statement_part> WHEN (boolean_expression);

<statement_part> ::= <message_passing_stmt> | <assignment_stmt> | <loop_stmt> | <return_stmt>

<message_passing_stmt> ::= [<var> :=] '[' <object_name> <= [<message>]^{1-n} ']'

<message> ::= <message_name> : [<parameter>]^{0-n}
```

Figure 1 - General Syntax of SOLAR

to synchronize all operations. There are two types of statements in SOLAR - synchronous and asynchronous statements. Synchronous statements are executed at a specific clock cycle relative to the time that the method containing the statements is activated. Asynchronous statements are executed when a boolean condition is satisfied. In SOLAR, all asynchronous statements in a method are grouped together under the EXCEPTION section. At the beginning of every clock cycle, these asynchronous statements are checked and, if necessary, executed before the synchronous ones. The EXCEPTION section is used mainly to implement automatic adaptive motion control. The system automatically updates the contents of the screen at the end of every clock cycle.

A single inheritance structure is used to organize the objects into classes and superclasses. Under this structure, an object instanced under a class can only inherit methods from that class. This forces the behavior of the object to be static. In order to model the dynamic and changing behavior of objects and environment in computer animation, it is necessary to inject some dynamic features into the language. In SOLAR, we adopt the approach of [HENDL86] where the functionality of an instanced object can be enhanced by using the mixin class independent of the object's class definition. The methods of the mixin class(es) has priority over those defined under the object's class. In this manner, the dynamic behavior of an object can be added easily at run-time and thus enabling an object to acquire skill dynamically. Examples on the use of mixin-class can be found in [CHUA87b].

The highest class in SOLAR is the class OBJECT. Below the class OBJECT, five system sub-classes are defined. They are the GRAPHICAL_OBJECT, BACKGROUND, MOTION, UTILITY and CAMERA classes. The class hierarchy is shown in Fig 2. The GRAPHICAL_OBJECT class contain all dynamic objects that appear on the screen. The dynamics of these graphical objects are defined using the MOTION class objects. Difficult computation based on, for example, the law of physics can be defined using the UTILITY class objects. For efficiency, all static graphical objects that make up the background scene are defined as BACKGROUND class objects. CAMERA class objects are used to manipulate the view of the world model.

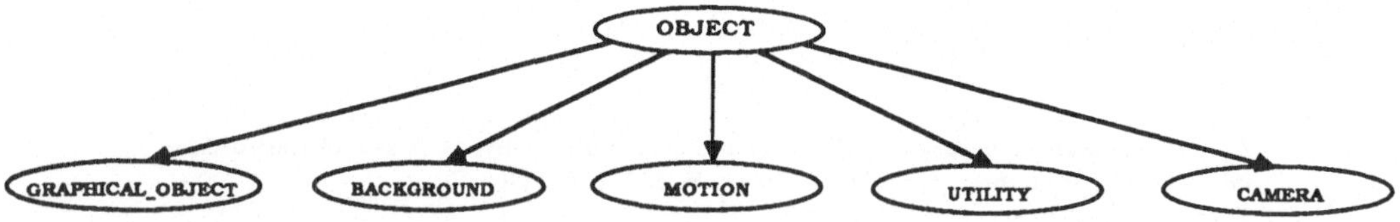

Figure 2 - SOLAR Class Hierarchy

The GRAPHICAL_OBJECT and BACKGROUND are known as display classes since objects instanced under these classes possess a structure definition and a set of display attributes that defines the outlook of these objects on the screen. The set of display attributes includes the x-position, y-position, orientation, priority, visibility, x-scaling, y-scaling as well as the hue, saturation and value components of its color. These attributes are stored as local variables in the object. The dynamics of a display object can be defined as the variations of these display attributes. GRAPHICAL_OBJECT class objects may be combined or detached dynamically to model hierarchical objects and motions.

For each class, a set of pre-defined methods are available to perform certain common operations. Under the class OBJECT, there are pre-defined methods for creating an object (*new:*); destroying an object (*kill:*); and, assigning and enquiring the values of local variables within the object. Each sub-class also has its own set of pre-defined methods. For example, the class CAMERA provides methods to define the SIZE, and to ZOOM, PAN, SPIN etc the world window. In addition, a set of UTILITY subclasses, such as the VISION class, are also pre-defined to provide controlled access to the world model for decision making. The use of these classes and features will be illustrated in next section.

4. An Example Script in SOLAR

In this section, we follow through an example on modeling the dynamics of a human figure to highlight the language features. No attempt is made to explain the language syntax in details. Interested readers are referred to [CHUA87b] for details.

4.1. The Definition of MOTION Objects

Motion in SOLAR is achieved by varying the display attributes of the graphical objects over time. The variation of an attribute over time is defined compactly using an attribute curve, similar to the p-curve of [BAECK69]. The role of MOTION objects is similar to that of ACTORs in ASAS [REYNO82]. More than one MOTION object may be applied concurrently to handle different display attributes of the same graphical object. The MOTION object selects an attribute curve and associates it with a display attribute. It also defines the transformations necessary to map the attribute curve to the actual scales of display attribute and time interval. The definition of attribute curve and MOTION object for swinging motion is given by:

```
/*   Define the curve as a parametric equation in t          */
CURVE Sine_Curve IS EQUATION [sine(t)];
     .....
     Swing[1] := [Motion <= new:] WHEN (CLOCK = 0);
     [Swing[1] <= set_motion_type: ORIENTATION set_motion_curve: Sine_Curve, 0, 360
                              set_attribute_scale: 30 set_motion_interval: 6] WHEN (CLOCK = 0);
End Swinging;
```

In this example, we initialize the MOTION object to be of type Orientation (to perform rotational motion) and map the specified part of Sine_Curve into a duration of 6 clock cycles (the time interval of the motion). The value of attribute is scaled to 30 which means a 30 degree swinging motion.

```
CLASS Man IS
(Superclass := GRAPHICAL_OBJECT)
init:       []
      Begin
            /*    define main structure type for Man and attach other objects as sub-objects of Man       */
            [Me <= Set_structure_type: Man_Body] WHEN (CLOCK = 0);
            Vision1 := [Vision <= new:] WHEN (CLOCK = 0);
            Head1 := [Head <= new:] WHEN (CLOCK = 0);
            [Me <= Attach_sub_object: Head1, (0, 30), 0] WHEN (CLOCK = 0);
            FOR i := 1 TO 2
                  Arm[i] := [Arm <= new:] WHEN (CLOCK = 0);
                  Leg[i] := [Leg <= new:] WHEN (CLOCK = 0);
            ENDFOR;
            /*    Arm and Leg are themself hierarchical objects consisting of two joints          */
            [Me <= Attach_sub_object: Arm[1], (0, 25), +1] WHEN (CLOCK = 0);
            [Me <= Attach_sub_object: Arm[2], (0, 25), -1] WHEN (CLOCK = 0);
            [Me <= Attach_sub_object: Leg[1], (0, -25), +1] WHEN (CLOCK = 0);
            [Me <= Attach_sub_object: Leg[2], (0, -25), -1] WHEN (CLOCK = 0);
      END init;

Walk:       [WSwing, XYWalk, JSwing, JBend, XYJump]
      Begin
            [Me <= add_motion: XYWalk[1], XYWalk[2]] WHEN (CLOCK = 0);
            [Me.Arm[1] <= add_motion: WSwing[1]] WHEN (CLOCK = 0);
            [Me.Leg[1] <= add_motion: WSwing[2]] WHEN (CLOCK = 0);
            [Me.Leg[2] <= add_motion: WSwing[1]] WHEN (CLOCK = 0);
            [Me.Arm[2] <= add_motion: WSwing[2]] WHEN (CLOCK = 0);
      EXCEPTION
            [Me <= jump: WSwing, XYWalk, JSwing, JBend, XYJump]
                  WHEN ([Vision1 <= dist_of_nearest_obj: Me, (1,0), 30] < 40);
      END Walk;

Walk_and_Jump:    [WSwing, XYWalk, JSwing, JBend, XYJump]
      Begin
      EXCEPTION
            [Me <= Walk: WSwing, XYWalk, JSwing, JBend, XYJump]
                  WHEN ([Vision1 <= dist_of_nearest_obj: Me, (1,0), 30] >= 40);
            [Me <= jump: WSwing, XYWalk, JSwing, JBend, XYJump]
                  WHEN ([Vision1 <= dist_of_nearest_obj: Me, (1,0), 30] < 40);
      END Walk_and_Jump;

Jump:       [WSwing, XYWalk, JSwing, JBend, XYJump]
      Begin
            [Me <= add_motion: XYJump[1], XYJump[2]] WHEN (CLOCK = 0);
            [Me.Arm[1] <= add_motion: JSwing[1]] WHEN (CLOCK = 0);
            [Me.Arm[1].Lower_Arm <= add_motion: JBend[1]] WHEN (CLOCK = 0);
            [Me.Arm[2] <= add_motion: JSwing[2]] WHEN (CLOCK = 0);
            [Me.Arm[2].Lower_Arm <= add_motion: JBend[1]] WHEN (CLOCK = 0);
            [Me.Leg[1] <= add_motion: JSwing[2]] WHEN (CLOCK = 0);
            [Me.Leg[1].Lower_Leg <= add_motion: JBend[2]] WHEN (CLOCK = 0);
            [Me.Leg[2] <= add_motion: JSwing[1]] WHEN (CLOCK = 0);
            [Me.Leg[2].Lower_Leg <= add_motion: JBend[2]] WHEN (CLOCK = 0);
      EXCEPTION
            [Me <= Walk_and_Jump: WSwing, XYWalk, JSwing, JBend, XYJump] WHEN (CLOCK = 10);
      END Jump;
END Man;
```

Figure 3 - The Definition of Class Man

4.2. The Definition of Class Man

We shall define a class Man which has the capability to walk and jump when encountering an obstacle. The definition of class Man is given in Fig 3. In SOLAR, the special method named *init:* is used to initialize an instanced object; it is executed whenever an object is instantiated under a class. The *init:* method in the definition of Man creates five additional objects and attach them as sub-objects to Man. For example, Arm[1] is attached to Man_Body at position (0, 25) with a relative priority of +1. When an object is attached to other object, all its display attributes are interpreted in relation to its parent object. In fact, motions of all objects in SOLAR are performed relative to their higher level objects.

The methods *Walk:*, *Jump:* and *Walk_and_Jump:* of class Man use 5 sets of MOTION objects as their parameters. These MOTION objects are assumed to have been defined before hand to perform the necessary motions. The *add_motion:* message attaches a MOTION object to a graphical object. A number of MOTION objects may be added to control different attributes of a graphical object simultaneously. The MOTION object, once assigned, will remain in force until it is destroyed.

The EXCEPTION sections of these methods use an UTILITY subclass object called *Vision1* to access the world model. The object *Vision1* returns the distance of the nearest obstacle from the calling object in a particular direction when it receives a *dist_of_nearest_obj:* message. If the nearest obstacle is less than 40 units in front of the calling object, then the calling object sends a *jump:* message to itself to perform a jump motion across the obstacle. The use of VISION class objects permits automatic adaptive motion control to be implemented elegantly.

The set of methods defined in the class, together with those inherited from its superclass and mixin classes, represents the capability of an instanced object to perform dynamics.

4.3. The Main Animation Script

Once the necessary structure types, attribute curves and object classes have been defined, the main animation script can be defined. The script shown in Fig 4 sets up the scene and world window for the main object named *John*, of class Man, to operate. The sequence shows *John* jumping across an obstacle when walking from the left to the right of the screen. The sequence is terminated when *John* reaches the end of the screen. The result of the animation is illustrated in Fig 5 and 6.

```
ANIMATION Human_Motion IS
Begin
/*   Create the necessary MOTION and BACKGROUND objects (with obstacle - i.e. having same priority as Man) */
/*   Create the Camera and set the World Window */
     Camera1 := [CAMERA <= new:] WHEN (Clock = 0);
     [Camera1 <= set_window: -150, 150, -150, 100] WHEN (CLOCK = 0);
     ...
     /* Create man and set it into motion      */
     John := [Man <= new:] WHEN (Clock = 0);
     [John <= set_x_position: -140 set_y_position: 0
               Walk: WSwing_Obj, Walk_Obj, JSwing_Obj, Bend_Obj, XYJump_Obj] WHEN (CLOCK = 0);
     END_ANIMATION WHEN ([John <= x_position:] >= 150);
END Human_Motion;
```

Figure 4 - The Main Animation Sequence

Figure 5 - Object John walking towards the obstacle

Figure 6 - Object John jumping across the obstacle

5. The Implementation of The SOLAR Interpreter

The animation sequence defined in SOLAR can either be compiled or interpreted to generate the desired animation on the computer display. Although the compilation approach can result in a very efficient implementation, it requires considerable implementation effort and was not considered feasible at this stage. Furthermore, as SOLAR was designed to be used as part of an animation system capable of real-time playback, an interpretive approach to implementing SOLAR is more suitable as it permits better interactive use.

Although the use of object-oriented paradigm greatly enhances the expressive and modeling power of SOLAR, it is difficult to produce an efficient implementation of the language especially on a conventional serial machine. The need for real-time playback capability demands that the interpreter be able to update the screen at the rate of at least 24 times per second in order to produce smooth animation. To meet such stringent performance requirement, minimum work, possibly restricting to only updating of screen, should be carried out during the display phase. All object-oriented processing, such as the execution of message passing statements and methods, checking of asynchronous actions etc, must be resolved before the final display.

Our current implementation divides the Interpreter into three passes as shown in Fig 7. The first two are the pre-processing passes; the actual updating of screen is carried out only at the third pass.

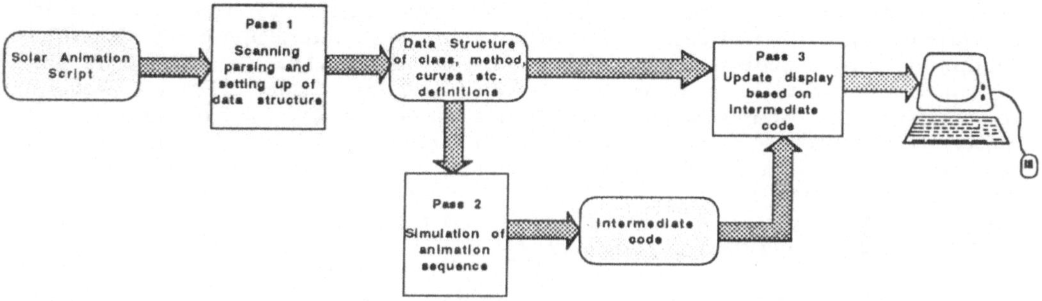

Figure 7 - Structure of SOLAR Interpreter

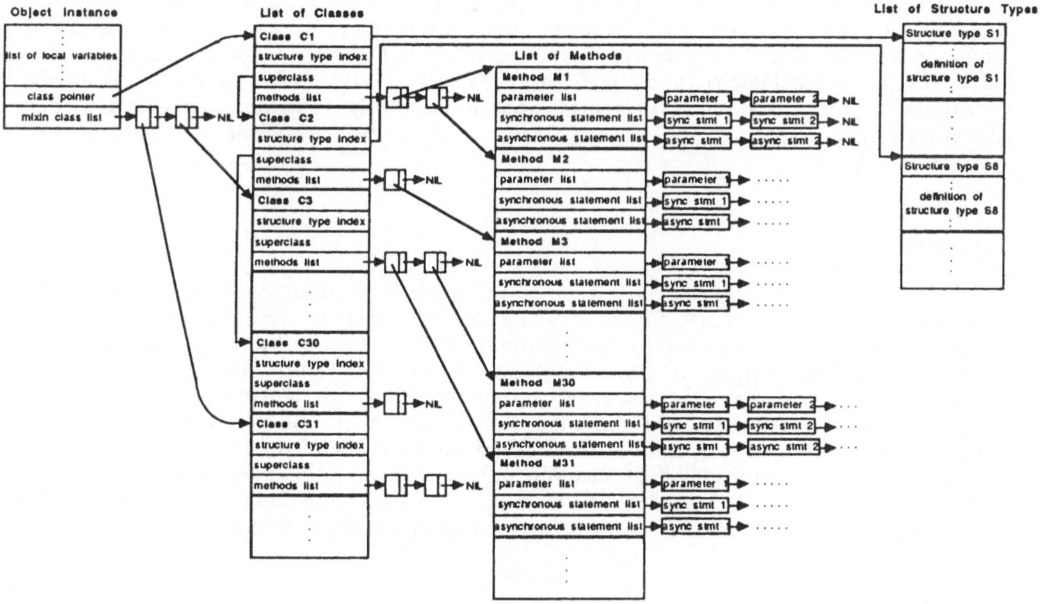

Figure 8 - Data Structure for Object Class Hierarchy

The first pass performs the scanning, parsing, resolution of the identifiers as well as the initialization of the main data structures. The scanning and parsing processes are implemented using the combination of the LEX [LESK75] and YACC [JOHNS75] software tools. The data structures shown in Fig 8 have been designed to store the definitions of objects, classes, methods and attribute curves etc. All methods defined in the script are maintained in a common linked list. Each class contains pointers to the list of methods under its definition. The object instance maintains its own list of local variables, class pointer and, if necessary, a list of mixin pointers. With this data structures, any change in the object's class or mixin class can be easily reflected by modifying the appropriate class pointer. The use of mixin class could potentially produce name clashes in method definitions, SOLAR handles this by simply giving priority to mixin classes, with the most recently acquired mixin class having the highest priority. When a message is received by the object, the object first searches for the method through its mixin class list, and then proceed to its class hierarchy until the method is found.

Once the data structures have been set up, the second pass performs a simulation of concurrent object interactions in SOLAR to produce an intermediate representation containing only a sequence of serial events. All message passing statements and asynchronous event invocations are resolved at this stage. The intermediate representation that we have chosen consists of a list of (low-level) updates of graphical objects' attributes at every clock cycle. In order to reduce the size of this representation, only those objects whose attributes change during the clock cycle will appear in the update list. Although the use of low-level update list would result in a very bulky intermediate representation, it enables the animation to be generated at a very high speed during the actual display.

From the intermediate representation, the third pass simply transfers the updates directly on to the screen at each clock cycle. As only simple matrix and vector computations are performed at this stage, it is felt that sufficiently fast updates of screen can be produced even for reasonably complicated animation sequences.

A prototype version of the Interpreter for SOLAR has been implemented on an APOLLO DN580 graphics workstation. The Interpreter is implemented using C language and the CGI-like graphics standard [CG&A86]. CGI is adopted because it is more flexible and efficient than PHIGS and GKS especially on low-end systems. Initial testing show that the 3-pass interpretation approach is feasible. Current effort is concentrated on implementing a full version of the Interpreter on the IBM RT/PC systems.

6. Summary

This paper discusses the design and main implementation considerations of the animation language SOLAR. The language is designed to be object-oriented and contain dynamic features which enable animation sequences to be specified easily. The efficient implementation of the language is possible only through the 3-pass interpretation process as discussed in the paper. Work is continuing to refine the definition of the language, to enhance the language in modeling knowledge and handling interactive inputs, and to provide an efficient (real-time) implementation of the language on a range of machines for public information applications. In parallel with this effort, work is also done to develop suitable action language for generating the animation sequence interactively using graphical pointing device.

Acknowledgement

We appreciate the support of Telecommunication Authority of SINGAPORE.

References

[BAECK69] R.M. Baecker - "Picture-Driven Animation", AFIPS Conf. Proc. , Vol 34, Spring Joint Computer Conf 1969, pp 273-288.

[CHANG86] I.F. Chang - "Sharing Information via Intelligent Public Information System (IPIS)", (Keynote address), in Proceedings of 'South East Asia Regional Computer Conference', Thailand, 1986.

[CHUA87a] T.S. Chua, W.H. Wong and K.C. Chu - "The Design of an Animation Package for Public Information Applications", in Proc of Inter-Faculty Symposium on 'Computer Graphics and Image Processing', NUS, Sep 87.

[CHUA87b] T.S. Chua, W.H. Wong and K.C. Chu - "SOLAR - a Structured Object-Oriented Language for Animators", Technical Report No 39, Institute of Systems Science, Nov 1987.

[CG&A86] IEEE Computer Graphics and Applications, 6 (8), Aug 1986.

[DAHL66] O. Dahl and K. Nygaard - "Simula, an Algol-based Simulation Language", Comm. ACM, 9, 1966, pp 671-678.

[DONNE81] T.J. O'Donnell and A J. Olson - " GRAMPS - A Graphics Language Interpreter for Real-Time, Interactive, Three-Dimensional Picture Editing and Animation", Computer Graphics (Proc. SIGGRAPH), Vol 15, No 3, 1981, pp 133-142.

[FEINE82] S. Feiner, D. Salesin and T.F. Banchoff - "DIAL : A DIagrammatic Animation Language", IEEE CG&A, Sep 82, pp 43-54.

[FINKE75] R. Finkel, R. Taylor, R. Bolles, R. Paul and J. Feldman - "An Overview of AL, a Programming System for Automation", Proc of 4th Int'l Joint Conf on AI, 1975, pp 758-765.

[FOLEY74] J.D. Foley, V.L. Wallace - "The Art of Natural Graphic Man-Machine Conversation", Proceedings of IEEE, April 1974.

[GOLDB83] A. Goldberg and D. Robson - "Smalltalk-80: The Language and its Implementation", Addison Wesley, 1983.

[HENDL86] J. Hendler - "Enhancement for Multiple Inheritance", SIGPLAN Notices, 21(10) Oct 1986, pp 98-106.

[HEWIT79] C. Hewitt - "Control Structures as Pattern of Message-Passing", Brown RH (ed) Artificial Intelligence : an MIT Perspective, MIT Press, Cambridge, MA, pp 443-465, 1979.

[JOHNS75] S. C. Johnson, "Yacc - Yet Another Compiler Compiler, Comp. Sci. Tech. Rep. No. 32, 1975, Bell Laboratories, Murray Hill, New Jersey.

[LESK75] M. E. Lesk - "Lex - A Lexical Analyzer Generator", Comp. Sci. Tech. Rep. No. 39, Bell Laboratories, Murray Hill, New Jersey, October 1975.

[LIEBE77] L.I. Lieberman and M.A. Wesley - "AUTOPASS: An Automatic Programming System for Computer Controlled Mechanical Assembly", IBM Journal of Research and Development, 21(4), 1977, pp 321-333.

[MAGNE84] N. Magnenat-Thalmann, D. Thalmann, M. Fortin and L. Langlois - "MIRA-SHADING: A Language for the Synthesis and Animation of Realistic Images", Proc Computer Graphics Tokyo '84, pp T2-2, 1-13.

[MAGNE85a] N. Magnenat-Thalmann, D. Thalmann and M. Fortin - "Miranim : An Extensible Director-Oriented System for the Animation of Realistic Images", IEEE CG&A, March 85, pp 61-73.

[MAGNE85b] N. Magnenat-Thalmann and D. Thalmann - "3-D Computer Animation: more an Evolution than a Motion Problem", IEEE CG&A, Oct 1985, pp47-57.

[MAGNE85c] N. Magnenat-Thalmann and D. Thalmann - "Computer Animation: Theory and Practice", Springer-Verlag, Tokyo, 1985.

[MAGNE86] N. Magnenat-Thalmann and D. Thalmann - "Special Cinematographic Effects with Virtual Movie Camera", IEEE CG&A, Apr 1986, pp 43-50.

[NAGEL84] R.N. Nagel - "State of Art and Prediction for AI and Robotics", in 'Robotics and AI', Ed. by M. Brady et al, NATO ASI Series, Vol F11, 1984, pp 3-45.

[OOPSL86] OOPSLA '86 Proceedings, September 1986

[REYNO82] C.W. Reynolds - "Computer Animation with Scripts and Actors", Computer Graphics, 16(3), Jul 82, pp 289-296.

[SATO84] Hidemaru Sato - "Standardization of Computer Animation Commands for Computer Animation System", Frontiers in Computer Graphics, Proc. of Computer Graphics Tokyo '84.

[SHAW80] M. Shaw - "The Impacts of Abstractions Concern on Modern Programming Languages" Proc of IEEE '68, 1968, pp 1119-1130.

[SHIMA79] B. Shimano - "VAL: A Versatile Robot Programming and Control System", COMPSAC 97 Conference Proceedings, 1979, pp 878-883.

[SINGH83] B. Singh, J.C. Beatty, K.S. Booth and R. Ryman - "A Graphics Editor for Benesh Movement Notation", Computer Graphics, 17(3), Jul 1983, pp51-62.

[TAYLO82] R.H. Taylor, P.D. Summers and J.M. Meyers - "AML: A Manufacturing Language", Int'l J. of Robotics Research, 1(3), 1982, pp 19-41.

[WILHE87] J. Wilhelms - "Towards Automatic Motion Control", IEEE CG&A, 7(4), Apr 1987, pp 11-22.

[ZELTZ85] D. Zeltzer - "Towards an integrated view of 3-D computer animation", The Visual Computer, Springer-Verlag, 1, 1985, pp 249-259.

AVENUE: An Integrated 3-D Animation System

A. Doi, M. Aono, N. Urano, and S. Uno (Japan)

Abstract

The present paper emphasized a total approach to 3-D computer animation, based on AVENUE. An integrated animation system needs to support all kinds of animation, and AVENUE has this potential, since it supports smooth object modeling, motion specification, and rendering. The authors describe the system concept[1], a modeling method using a geometry language, and a motion specification method using a 3-D interactive parametric keyframe and rule based motion analysis. They also explain a rendering technique that uses sub-division technique for CSG(Constructive Solid Geometry) with deformation.

Key Words Computer graphics, 3-D computer animation, CSG, texture mapping, keyframe, interpolation, deformation, raytracing

INTRODUCTION

Computer animation is an effective tool for presentation, entertainment, education, and simulation, and offers numerous advantages for still pictures. This is especially true of 3-D computer animation, which tends to produce more realistic images than those limited to 2-D, primarily because the model and its motion can be more precisely represented in 3-D space.

3-D computer animation generally follows three processes:

1. Object modeling
2) Motion specification
3) Rendering

We have developed an integrated 3-D animation system, AVENUE, which smoothly supports these three processes, and aims eventually to support all kinds of animation. This paper describes the system concept [1] and a method for modeling, animating, and displaying articulated figures for use with AVENUE.

SYSTEM CONCEPT

- Flexible animation

Our animation method involves not only shift, rotation, and scaling, but also attribute change and geometrical and topological deformation. Simple deformations, such as "stretch","squash","bend","twist", etc., are indispensable to make animation aesthetically pleasing, though they need not follow physical laws. Such deformations have been achieved by various methods including, fractals, meta ball, surface patches, and high-order equations. However, it is difficult to use these methods to construct articulated objects in object modeling. Instead, we introduce deforming operations utilizing transformation functions. This method does not rely on geometrical changes in the shape of object, is unrelated to object modeling, yet it allows a user to treat a solid as if it were made of clay.

- Separation of objects and motions

Our method makes it possible to perform object modeling and motion specification concurrently. By thus separating objects and motions, the user can independently build up object and motion databases. Animation with several combinations of objects and motions is also possible.

- Extended CSG model

The incorporation of surface information such as color, reflection, texture mapping, bump mapping and transparency is indispensable for computer animation. To define objects, we use an extended CSG model with surface information. With this model, it is easy to input data, and at the same time memory is saved. Moreover, the added surface information makes it possible to improve the realism of objects.

- Integration of keyframed system and scripted system

Current 3-D Animation systems can be classified into two categories: key-frame systems and scripted systems. While key-frame systems (e.g.,**GRAMPS**[2] and **BBOP**[3]) are very easy to learn, they have certain weak points in their specification of regular motions. Conversely, in scripted systems (**ASAS**[4], **MIRA-3D**[5], and **CINEMIRA**[6]) it is easy to specify regular motions, but beginners usually find it difficult to get the desired animation results using the animation language, since these systems require the novice to remember both how to write and how to specify the complicated motions. We have considered the advantages of both methods, and have designed a 3-D animation system with an interactive mode for beginners and an animation language (**SCRIPT**) offering rendering capability for experts. Thus, when the user does not know how to program, and the desired motion is complex, the key-frame system, which is based on the interactive mode can produce the required animation by using the graphic display. The specified motion is automatically transferred to the **SCRIPT** program.

- **Continuous and discontinuous motions**

  Specified motions are defined in the system by continuous function forms. The transformation from continuous to discontinuous is archived during rendering. The merit of this procedure is that the same motion can be displayed at different speeds by changing the time interval.

- **Motion analysis**

  To allow the user to input motions easily, the system calculates the trajectory of objects from the data of previously defined objects and environments.

- **Rendering**

  The defined objects and the specified motions are sent to the rendering sector. The rendering function has both wire-frame and surface display (list-priority method[7], scan-line method, and ray-tracing method) facilities. The user can select one of these rendering methods, taking into consideration the trade-off between time and image quality.

OBJECT DESCRIPTION

Figure 1 is a schematic diagram showing the relationship among "geometry description", "attribute description", and "structure description." We provide two languages: **ORDL** for "structure description" and **CSGDDL** for "geometry description" and "attribute description."

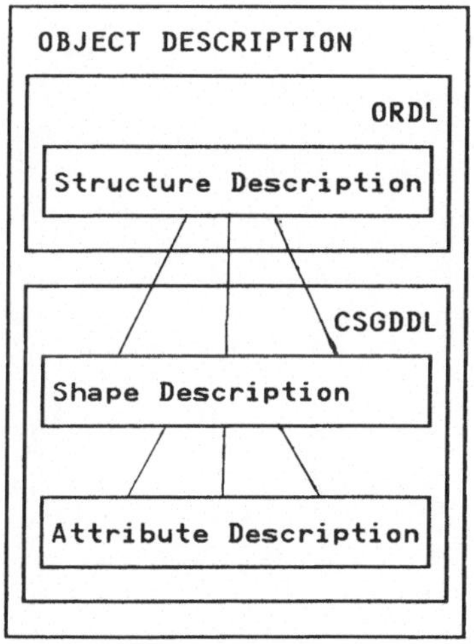

Fig. 1 Concept of Shape, Structure, and Attribute Description

GEOMETRY DESCRIPTION AND ATTRIBUTE DESCRIPTION IN AVENUE

A three-dimensional object is described by **CSGDDL** (CSG Data Description Language). As the name implies, this treats the CSG model as a fundamental three-dimensional object. In practice, the model is enhanced to allow some specific processing, which we will discuss later. The shape and the location of objects are determined by combining set operations (AND,OR,NOT) and affine transformation operations. There are two reasons why we adopt a CSG model: (1) It is much easier and more strictly controllable to represent quadratic curves such as the ellipsoid, cylinder, and cone by CSG models than by boundary representation or octtree models, and (2) CSG models generally require less storage than other methods. The reason we adopt a procedural language is that it enables us to specify the attributes of an object more strictly than in interactive processing. Indeed, attributes such as optical reflection or refraction are quite difficult to specify through interactive processing.

The CSG modeling primitives we used in AVENUE are infinite plane, finite plane, cuboid, polyhedron, ellipsoid, cylinder, cone, paraboloid, hyperboloid and torus. In **CSGDDL**, the geometry is specified by the "geometry" block in each "define primitive" statement. The greatest difference separating our CSG model from ordinary others CSG models is that each primitive has associated surface information, which in turn is used for attribute mapping [8,9]. The surface information is specified by the "surface" block in the "define primitive" statement. Figure 2 shows an example of an object description written in **CSGDDL**. In the "surface" block, attributes are specified by "optics", "color", "pattern", and "bump" orders, respectively.

```
$rfl = 0.8 ; $hil = 5; .........
#i = 1
while(#i <= 3) {
  define primitive(cylinder) "cylind1".#i{
    solid { stuff compact; color @col.#i;}
    surface (front,common) {
      optics (metallic) { reflect $rfl;
                          hilight $hil; }
    }
    geometry (inside) {
      shift <<0,0,0>>; rotate <<0,0,0>>;
      size @siz.#i from 0 to $len.#i;
    }
  }
  define primitive (plane) "cylind2".#i {
    . . . . . . . . . . . . . . .
  }
  define primitive (plane) "cylind3".#i {
    . . . . . . . . . . . . . . .
  }
  define and "CAND".#i { "cylind1".#i,
             "cylind2".#i, "cylind3".#i }
   #i += 1
}
define primitive (ellipsoid) "sphere" {
  . . . . . . . . . . . . . . . . .
}
define and "SAND" { "sphere" }
define or "COR1"  { "CAND.1" }
define or "COR2"  { "CAND.2" }
define or "COR3"  { "CAND.3" }
define or "SOR"   { "SAND"   }
define object "arm_parts" { "SOR","COR3" }
define object "foot_parts"{ "SOR","COR2" }
define object "leg_parts" { "SOR","COR1" }
```

Fig. 2 Example of **CSGDDL**

STRUCTURE DESCRIPTION IN AVENUE

Articulated objects, such as robots and parts of the human body, naturally have link structures, which can be represented by N-array tree structures, which is represented by the following expression:

$$C_{i+1} = M_i * C_i$$

where Ci and Ci+1 are coordinate systems, and Mi a matrix of the link relation. Ci is the parent coordinate of Ci+1.

Each coordinate system corresponds to the name of an object defined by **CSGDDL**. The relational structure of coordinate systems is specified by **ORDL** (ORientation Description Language)[10]. An example of **ORDL** is given in Fig. 3, which shows a robot link structure.

The "coordinate" statement defines a coordinate system, which is also a unit for animation in AVENUE. The name specified within a pair of curly brackets corresponds to that of the CSG object. Figure 5 shows a ray-traced image generated from the **ORDL** file and the associated **CSGDDL** file.

```
/*call ROBOT CSGDDL file */
CSG { ROBOT };
COORDINATES rarm { arm_parts };
COORDINATES larm { arm_parts };
COORDINATES rfoot{ foot_parts};
COORDINATES rleg { leg_parts };
 . . . . . . . . . . . . . . . .
STRUCTURE Robokun {/*Robot structure
                     link relation */
  trunk {
    rarm shift  << 10, 10,   0>>
         rotate <<  0,  0,-120>>
    larm shift  <<-10, 10,   0>>
         rotate <<  0,  0, 120>>
    hip {
      rleg shift  <<8,-10,   0>>
           rotate <<0,  0,-180>>
        {
          rfoot shift <<0, 8, 0>>
        }
          . . . . . . . . . . .
    }
    head shift   <<0, 14, 0>>
  }
}
```

Fig. 4 Example 1

◁ Fig. 3 Example of **ORDL**

CAMERA AND LIGHT DESCRIPTION IN AVENUE

Cameras and lights are defined by "camera" and "light" statements, respectively. Multiple cameras and lights are allowed, each with an associated name. In a camera description, parameters are given defining the volume of a three-dimensional view, and the type of view can be specified as either parallel or perspective projection. Since we currently support only a single-point light source, the position and intensity of the source are sufficient as "light" parameters. During rendering, one of the cameras and one or more lights are selected for actual calculation.

MOTION SPECIFICATION

Introduction

There are two main types of animation. One type allows the animator to describe the desired motions. For this type of animation, AVENUE supports 3-D keyframe animation. The user can specify the motions of objects interactively by using an interactive motion generator, called KEYFRAMER (KEY FRAME motion generatoR). Motion is created by interpolation between keyframes. The second type is animation done in conjunction with scientific and engineering simulations. While the motions generated by simulation programs would in some cases produce realistic motions, AVENUE does not currently include a simulation program. In fact, it would be impossible for it to support all the kinds of simulation programs that will be developed by users in many different fields. However, the output of simulations can be transformed into the AVENUE motion format and visualized. If this done, AVENUE may be used as a rendering tool for simulation.

Although we have described two types of animation, we aim at a third type. Occasionally a user requires very realistic motions: however it is highly time-consuming to specify these. In order to solve this problem, AVENUE supports a rule-based motion system, ROMA (Rigid Objects' Motion Analyzer). Although ROMA has strict constraints, it can generate motions automatically using by environmental information and user-specified rules.

In the following section, we describe the motion specification of AVENUE.

3-D KEYFRAME ANIMATION

AVENUE has a 3-D interactive motion generator, KEYFRAMER , to allow the user to input a motion interactively. Keyframe animation in AVENUE is like parametric keyframe animation based on a parametric model[11]. A keyframe of KEYFRAMER is a set of parameters {p1,p2,p3,....,pn}, including a position vector, color, reflection, angles of the x,y,z axes,..etc. The parameters between keyframes are generated by the interpolation facilities of KEYFRAMER. The transition of these parameters results in animation.

We classify this kind of parametric animation according to the following two types of motions:

1. Motions of coordinates (involved deformation, camera & light motion)
2. Changes in the shape and attributes (color, reflection, etc.) of objects.

In the first type, the coordinates are independent of the shapes and attributes of objects; thus the user does not have to consider the last two factors, and can begin inputting the shape and the motion simultaneously.

The coordinates are defined by coordinate statements of **ORDL**. The commands for coordinates are as follows:

- shift
- rotate by x,y,z-axis
- scale by x,y,z-axis
- bend by x,y,z-axis
- twist by x,y,z-axis
- taper by x,y,z-axis.

Introducing coordinates allows us to create a set of objects whose coordinates are shifted, rotated, or deformed.

When we handle shape-changing deformations, we must change numerous parameters, even for simple operations (e.g.,bend, twist, and taper). A deformation of coordinates is a transformation function **F**, which explicitly modifies the coordinates of points in space. When **p** is a point in the undeformed coordinates, **P** is a point of the deformed coordinates; this is represented by the equation, **P = F(p)**[12]. In this method, the user can animate global and local deformations. For example, the "Twist on Y-axis" command is produced by the following equations.

Twist on Y-axis

$$Ct = COS(f(y)) \; ; \quad St = SIN(f(y))$$

$$| x' \ y' \ z' \ 1 | = | x \ y \ z \ 1 | \begin{vmatrix} Ct & 0 & St & 0 \\ 0 & 1 & 0 & 0 \\ -St & 0 & Ct & 0 \\ 0 & 0 & 0 & 1 \end{vmatrix}$$

Finally, a set of points is transformed by the following transformation,

Transformation Function

P = **p** * |Bend||Twist||Taper||Rotate||Scale||Shift|

where
P is a point of the animated coordinates
p is a point of the un-animated coordinates

Since the animation resulting from the second type of motion is dependent on the shapes and attributes of objects, it may be somewhat different from the animation resulting from the first type. If so, the parameters of shapes and attributes of objects are interpolated directly. The two types of animations are integrated on the screen in the rendering stage.

Interactive Motion Specification

The 3-D interactive motion generator, KEYFRAMER, starts by positioning the objects written in **CSGDDL** and **ORDL** and then generates their motions interactively. To specify the objects' motions, we control their parameters. This is done with physical input devices. The relationship between the parameters and the physical input devices (a set of 8 dials) is set up by the "assignment" statements.

First, the user specifies the coordinate that he wants to animate, either directly or by selecting the coordinate name defined by the **ORDL** coordinate statement on the terminal. Next, by using the dial devices, he can get feedback while changing these parameters. It is an important feature of this system that the user can modify these parameters continuously by connecting their values to numeric input devices. The modified output is displayed on the IBM 5080 graphic display system. The parameter sets modified by KEYFRAMER and the time information are saved in the database as a "Keyframe". The user may save some or all of the parameters, and generates animation by interpolating between the keyframes. A group of parameters can be controlled by a single device, or a single parameter can be a function of several devices. This flexibility can also be used to group the control of related parameters or to establish alternative control modes for the same set of parameters.

Camera and light motion are independent of the objects' motions, although they are defined in the same manner, after the objects' motions have been specified. The user can specify the camera and the light while monitoring the motions of the objects.

These parameters and time information saved as keyframes are transferred to the interpolation process.

Though interpolation is an extremely versatile tool, it is difficult for an animator to control the in-between frames and to get the motion he desires. KEYFRAMER overcomes this problem in two ways: by supporting many interpolation methods, and by supporting effective key-frame manipulation facilities.

Our system supports the following interpolation functions:

- Beta spline (3 degree)[13]
- Cardinal spline (3 degree)[14]
- Interpolated spline using B-spline (3 degree)[16]
- Linear interpolation

Another way to control the in-between frames is to add more key frames. KEYFRAMER provides motion editing facilities. An animator can add, delete, modify, and copy keyframes. In addition to editing, the animator can specify interpolation spline parameters between keyframes, such as tension and bias[15]. He can also register the interpolated state as a keyframe.

The parameters between keyframes, which may include position vectors, colors, reflections, angles of x,y,z axis, light motions, and camera motions are interpolated, and parameter lists for all the frames are generated. These lists are sent to the rendering sector.

SIMULATION

In order to visualize a simulation of H2O molecules in a closed box, we need to make plastic models of the molecules before beginning the animation.

In AVENUE, the H2O plastic molecules are defined by **CSGDDL**. An H2O molecule is constructea from three ellipsoids and two cylinders. We assign the models to a closed box in the initial state. The description is written in **ORDL**. The simulation program calculates the new positions, directions, and speeds. These motions are transferred to the AVENUE motion format and AVENUE visualizes the simulation.

Figure 5 shows a ray-traced image extracted by this animation method.

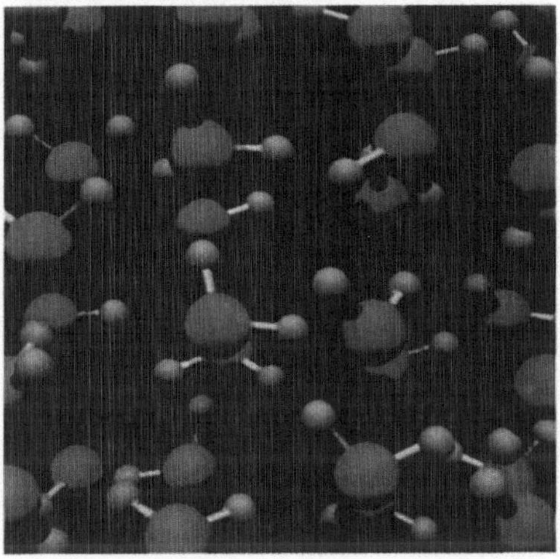

Fig. 5 Example 2

MOTION ANALYSIS

Introduction

There is a lot of controversy about 3-D animation. When we look back over the history of computer graphics, most research into rendering has been concentrated on how to abstract the states of objects and their environments at specific space-time coordinates. The space-time coordinate system represents 4-dimensional regions of time and space. We call it **location**. From this point of the view, 3-D animation is an abstraction of transitions in the state of affairs with respect to location.

A major point of difference among the many 3-D animation systems that have been proposed is the way they represent 3-D animation. We can basically categorize the methods of representation into the following three approaches:

- Explicit representation
- Programmed representation
- Implicit representation

One system that takes the first approach is keyframing animation. In this system, a user specifies key frames one by one, and the system interpolates the pictures between the key frames. The second category includes such animation systems as **MIRA**[5] and **CINEMIRA**[6]. Users program the motions of objects by an animation language such as SCRIPT. In systems which take one of these two approaches, the user can generate desirable motions according to his mental animation scenarios. However, it requires a lot of work to make the key frames or to program the scenarios. In the third approach, events and the relations between them are described in such a way as to represent the animation implicitly.

Now let us reconsider the nature of 3-D animation. If we state that the nature of 3-D animation is **the abstraction of transitions in the state of affairs with respect to location**, as proposed at the beginning of this section, the third approach is the most suitable. Note that we are not saying the first two approaches are inappropriate for 3-D animation, but that we also need the third approach. **Director**[18] and **ASAS**[4], which are based on **ACTOR**[17], fall in this third category. The authors of those papers concentrated on how the system should be. In this paper, however, we describe not only the system, but also how to represent 3-D animation implicitly.

Representations

Approach

One of our purposes is to find a flexible method of abstracting transitions in the state of affairs with respect to the location. If users are interested in only one special application - for example, the kinetics of a robot - there must exist a suitable representation for it. In this paper, however, we provide a general paradigm for 3-D animations. For this reason the abstraction should be more general, so that it can incorporate many applications and combinations of applications; for example, both kinetic and general problem solving. Note that we are not saying this approach is efficient, but that it is more user-friendly in that it provides a homogeneous environment.

Representation of Events

If we assume, as was previously proposed, that representation of events refers to the changes in objects and their environments with respect to place and time, then the abstraction should incorporate such representation. Here, we describe a method of abstraction that does so. The representations should be powerful enough to cover various events and environments. There is a method of representing events and the relations between them as a situation(situate). We will explain how to apply the method to 3-D animation. We assume the world consists of individuals with their own properties and of the relation among them. If (x1,x2,x3,...,xn) are the individuals, their relation is r and i represents whether this relation is true or false, the **situation type** is represented as the following tuple.

<r,(x1,x2,x3,....,xn),i>

The above representation lacks the concept of location, which, as we mentioned before, is very important for 3-D animation. We add this as **L** to the above tuple and represent an **EVENT** as the following tuple

<**L**,r,(x1,x2,x3,....,xn),i>

where
L is time-space location
r is n-array relation
(x1,x2,x3,....,xn) are individuals
i determines whether the event is true or false

Let us consider the following example.

In location l1 :
There exist the sun and a sunflower located at m1 and m2
respectively at time t0.
It is a sunny day.

The above statements can be represented as the following events:

<l1,is_at,(sun,m1,t0),yes>
<l1,is_at,(sunflower,m2,t0),yes>
<l1,sunny_day,(),yes>

where
l1 is a specific location.
m1 and m2 are specific positions in l1.
t0 is the specific time in l1.

Note that the first two events are the two array relations, and that the third one is the zero array relation.

An event always has specific values as the entities of the tuple. This is often inconvenient, because some specific events have many similarities. For example, an event "e1" and an event "e2" may be identical except for their locations, but some relations are still retained in both "e1" and "e2". Therefore, variables should be allowed in the representation in order to relax the constraint. An **EVENT TYPE** is the same as a set of events, except that location relation, object, and true-false variables are allowed. Thus the event type in the above example can be represented as follows:

E(L,M1,M2,T) =
{<L,is_at,(sun,M1,T),yes>
<L,is_at,(sunflower,M2,T),yes>
<L,sunny_day,(),yes> }

In the above, variables start with a capital letter. If the user wants a specific set of events, he substitutes specific values for those variables, such as E(l1,m1,m2,t0).

Representation of Rules

A rule is defined as a special case of events and has a two array relation. All rules are represented as follows:

```
<l,if_then,(e1,e2),yes>

where
  e1 and e2 are events
```

The above representation means that if the event "e1" is true then the event "e2" is true. For example, if we would like to represent a rule,

> The sunflower faces the sun when it is a sunny day
> in location l1.
> (let this rule be valid in location l2)

then the rule is represented as follows.

```
<l2,if_then, (E1(l1),E2(l1)),yes>
where
 E1(L) = {<L,sunny_day,(),yes>}
 E2(L) = {<L,face,(sunflower,sun),yes>}
```

Of course, types of rules are allowed as event types, as mentioned before. Thus the above type of rule is represented as follows:

```
R(L1,L2) = <L2,if_then, (E1(L1),E2(L1)),yes>
```

All the rules and rule types are represented in this manner.

System Configurations

Data Flows

The system configurations are explained in this section. Currently the system can only interpret the translations and rotations of rigid objects. That is why we call the system ROMA (Rigid Object Motion Analyzer). If we include other transitions in the animation, we will have much more to implement. For example, if we include the deformations of objects, the object model must take care of them. Although our final goal is to include all representations as events and to develop a complete animation system, it will take more time to include abstractions of the entire world - for example, models of objects for the purpose of implementation.

Figure 6 shows the system configurations and the data flows of ROMA. The input is represented as a set of event types. After some event types have been converted to events by substituting values for the variables of event types, the events and event types are separated by the system into **FACTS** and **RULES**. **FACTS** are all events except special events; **RULES** are described in the section on representations. By using and updating these data the system infers the transitions of **FACTS** and analyzes the motions of objects. As a result of this process, motion data are generated as output.

The rendering component interprets for display the motion data together with the object data defined by CSG. The user views the result in a wireframe display to confirm the motion, and when he is satified, the image generation component generates images one by one.

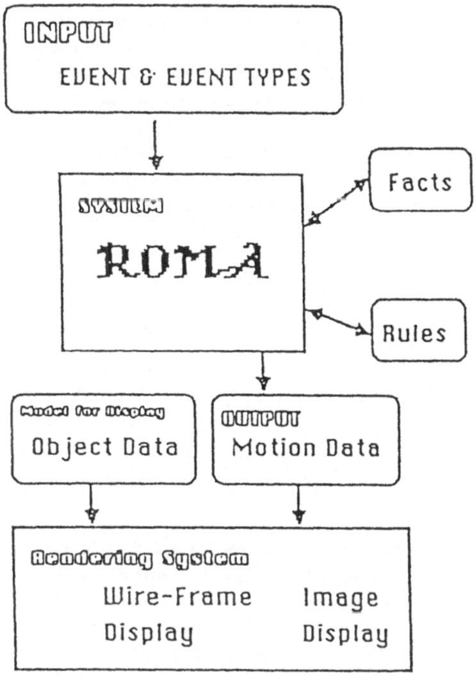

Fig. 7 Sun and Sunflower

◁ Fig. 6 System Overview of ROMA

Motion Generation

The system has its own clock, and by updating this, it generates motions for each instance of time. At a certain time, the system chooses applicable rules from the rule set, examining whether the rules can be applied at that time based on the locations of the rules. After obtaining the applicable rule set, the system selects a rule and determines whether it is valid. If so, the system applies the rule and adds a new fact to the set of facts. This process is repeated until there are no more applicable rules. The binding of the variables occurs dynamically at the time when the rules are evaluated.

ROMA produces Fig. 7 by implementing the events and the relation between the sun and the sunflower. The user specifies only the events and the rules, and ROMA then automatically generates the motions of objects.

RENDERING

In this section, we describe our rendering technique for CSG with deforming operations[19]. A detailed description of ray-tracing with attribute mapping is given in [8,9].

Though a ray-tracing method can directly render CSG with deforming operations, it takes a lot of CPU time for each picture. Furthermore, it is not adequate for interactive manipulations or in an animation environment. It is preferable to approximate CSG with deforming operations on polygons. This is because generated polygons are widely used in computer graphics, and many methods are available for rapid image synthesis. Animation needs a particularly large number of pictures, and rapid image synthesis is important.

Our algorithm handles all C1 continuous surfaces defined by a rectangular parameterization. Our CSG primitives have both implicit equation form and parametric form. For example, we define a standard cylinder by

```
x**2 + z**2  = r**2
```

and we can construct the parameterization

```
x =  r * cos(PI*(2.0*u-1.0))
y =  top*v + bot*(1.0-v)
z =  r * sin(PI*(2.0*u-1.0))
0.0 <= (u,v) <= 1.0
```

where PI = 3.14, top, bot = each coordinate of the y-axis

First, we sample with a raw grid of parametric u-v values from the (u,v) plane for each of the primitives. Next, we use the rectangular subdivision method[20] (subpieces are subdivided into rectangules). This rectangular parametric sampling of the surface is refined by using the normal vector criterion of flatness. When adjacent normal vectors diverge too greatly, the surface is recursively subdivided. Deforming operations are represented mathematically by X=F(x), where X is a set of points in the deformed solids, and x is a set of points in the undeformed solids. The Jacobian matrix J for the transformed function, F(x), is

```
Ji(x) =  F(x)/ x
```

The new normal vector N(X) is calculated by using the following equation[12]:

```
N(X) = (det(J))*J  *N(x)
```

In other words, the new normal vector N(X) is expressed as the product of matrix J and the old normal vector N(x). The subdivision process continues until the dot products are within normal vector tolerances. After first-level subdivision, these subpieces are used in set operations between primitives. From Table 1, each subpiece's four corner points are calculated for related primitives, which are found by traversing the CSG tree. If all four points are outside for related primitives, the subpiece is OUTside. If they are inside for related primitives, the subpiece is INside. Otherwise, the subpice is Unknown, and is divided until an intersection tolerance (second-level subdivision) is reached. The divided subpieces are similarly

Table 1 Region Classification of a CSG Solid

A+B(OR)			
A\B	in	on	out
in	in	in	in
on	in	on	on
out	in	on	out

A-B(DIFF)			
A\B	in	on	out
in	out	on	in
on	out	on	on
out	out	out	out

A*B(AND)			
A\B	in	on	out
in	in	on	out
on	on	on	out
out	out	out	out

classified as INside, OUTside and Unknown. The Unknown subpieces of an intersection tolerance are forcibly divided into INside or OUTside by linear interpolation. All INside subpieces are registered and transferred to the polygon data. Figure 8 shows this algorithm.

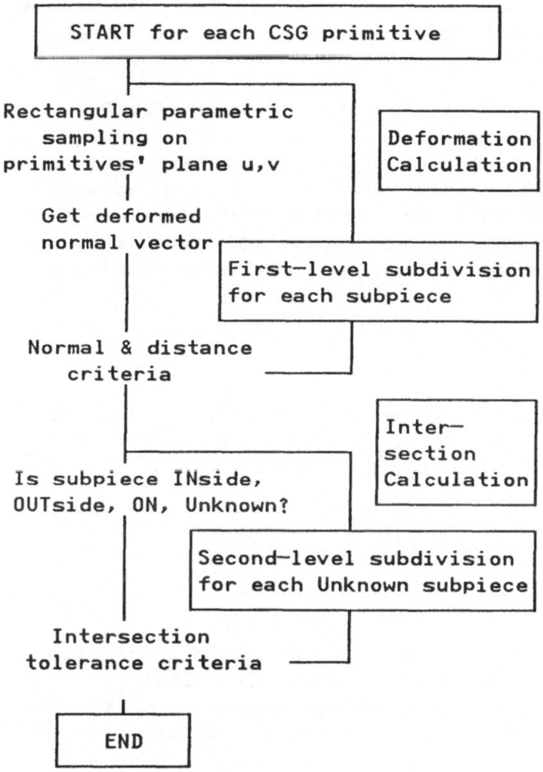

Fig. 8 Rendering Algorithm Using the Subdivision Technique

SYSTEM OVERVIEW OF AVENUE

The host computer is an IBM 3081 running on VM/CMS. The graphic device is the IBM 5080 Graphics System, which has local three-dimensional clipping, viewing transformation, and an area-filling facility. The color monitor, an IBM 5083 with 1024*1024 pixels, can display 256 colors simultaneously from a pallet of 4096 possible colors. The purpose of the IBM 5080's vector display is to support real-time, smooth rotation and translation of animated objects input by a user through the valuators (dials) of the graphics work-station. The computer-generated image and natural image captured by a RGB camera are saved on an optical disk. There is a video recording sub-system which records the images generated by AVENUE on video film frame by frame. AVENUE is written in C-language and Prolog, with a small part in Assembler. The graphics application program interface is graPHIGS[21].

CONCLUSION

The present paper emphasizes a total approach to 3-D computer animation based on AVENUE. An integrated animation system needs to support all kinds of animation, and AVENUE has this potential, since it supports smooth object modeling, motion specification, and rendering. AVENUE has the following proven qualities:

- Complex objects can be precisely input by using **ORDL** and **CSGDDL**.
- In general, motions are easy to input as a result of the interactive approach based on a 3-D keyframe method.
- Motions can be easily and precisely input under strict conditions by using ROMA.
- Realistic images can be rapidly rendered by attribute mapping[8,9].

We are currently continuing work on this system. Ultimately we intend to develop the following items: (1) An interactive object-modeling system (2) Extension of **ORDL** and **CSGDDL** (3) Extension of the ROMA system (4) An improved ray tracing method for rapid image synthesis (5) Application of AVENUE to fields such as education, presentation, and the film industry.

ACKNOWLEDGEMENTS

The authors are indebted to Dr. Akio Koide, Mr. Kazutoshi Sugimoto, Mr.Kazuya Shimizu, and Mr.Shinichi Iwai for discussion of the 3-D computer animation system, the system concept, the motion specification, and the rendering methods.

REFFERENCE

[1] A.Doi, M.Aono, N.Urano, S.Uno, "3-D Animation System-object description, motion specification, interpolation," graphics and CAD, JIPS, 1986.
[2] O'Donnell TJ, Olson AJ, "GRAMPS-A graphical language interpreter for real-time, interactive, 3-D picture editing and animation," Computer Graphics, Vol.15(3), 1981.
[3] Stern G., "Bbop - a program for 3-dimensional animation," NICOGRAPH '83 Proceedings Tokyo, Japan, 1983.
[4] Reynolds,C.W., "Computer Animation with Script and Actors," Computer Graphics, Vol.16(3), 1982.
[5] Magnenat-Thalmann N,Thalmann D., "The Use of High level 3-D Graphical Types in the Mira Animation System," IEEE Computer Graphics & Application, Vol.3, Num.9, 1983.
[6] Magnenat-Thalmann N,Thalmann D., "Actors and camera data types in computer animation," Graphics Interface '83 Conference Proceedings, pp 203-210, 1983.
[7] Henry Fuchs, Gregory D.Abram, and Eric D.Grant, "Near Real- Time Shaded Display of Rigid Objects," Computer Graphics, Vol.17(3), 1983.
[8] Masaki Aono and Tosiyasu L.Kunii, "Attribute Mapping," TRL report, TR87-1010, 1987.
[9] Masaki Aono, "Rendering Method using Attribute Mapping," JIPS, Vol.33, 1986.
[10] A.Doi, M.Aono, N Urano and S.Uno, "AVENUE : A 3-Dimensional Animation System," TRL report, TR871016, 1987.
[11] Pat Hanrahan and David Sturman, "Interactive Animation of Parametric Models," Visual Computer, Vol.1, Num.4, Dec.1985.
[12] Alan H.Barr, "Global and Local Deformations of solid PRIMITIVES," Computer Graphics, Vol.18(3), 1984.

[13] B.Barsky and J.Beatty, "Local Control of Bias and Tension in Beta-Splines," Computer Graphics, Vol.17(3), 1983.
[14] A.Smith, "Spline Tutorial Notes-Technical Memo No.77," SIGGRAPH '83 Tutorial Notes: Introduction to Computer Animation, pp.64-75, July, 1983.
[15] Doris H.U.Kochanek, R.H.Bartels, "Interpolating Splines with Local Tension, Continuity, and Bias Control," Computer Graphics, Vol.18(3), 1984.
[16] deBoor, C., A **Practical Guide to Spline**, Springer-Verlag, NewYork, 1978.
[17] Hewitt,C., "Viewing Control Structures as Paterns of Passing Messages," Artificial Intelligence, Vol.8, pp323-364, 1977.
[18] Magnenat-Thalmann N, Thalmann D., **Computer Animation**, Springer-Verlag, Tokyo, 1985.
[19] A.Doi, M.Aono, N.Urano, "A Fast Rendering Method for CSG with Deforming Operation," JIPS, Vol.35, 1987.
[20] Wayne E. Carlson, "An Algorithm and Data Structure for 3D Object Synthesis Using Surface Patch Intersection", Computer Graphics, Vol16.(3), 1982.
[21] IBM,Programmer's Reference for graPHIGS

The Use of Quaternions for Animation, Modelling and Rendering

D. Pletincks (Belgium)

Abstract

Quaternions, although not well known, provide a solid base to describe orientation of an object or a vector. They are efficient and well suited to solve rotation and orientation problems in computer graphics and animation. This paper describes a new method for splining quaternions so that they can be used with keyframe animation. We also show that quaternions, although up to now solely used for animation purposes, can be used succesfully in the field of modelling and rendering and we prove that we can construct a significantly faster rendering algorithm with the use of quaternions.

1. Origin and properties of quaternions

Quaternions were discovered by Sir William Rowan Hamilton in October of 1843, while trying to extend the complex plane to the three dimensional space. After failing for 14 years to find a way to multiply triples so that the norm was preserved, Hamilton suddenly realised that quadrupels would work [HANK80]. By an odd quirk of mathematics only systems of 2, 4 or 8 components will be norm preserving. Soon after their discovery, quaternions were shown to be good representations of orientation [CAYL]. James Clerk Maxwell, in his classic "Treatise on Electricity and Magnetism" used quaternion differentials. Dot and cross products of vectors were discovered as part of the quaternion product.

As may seem from this short introduction, quaternions are supprisingly old and supprisingly unknown. In the world of aerospace engineering and robotics although they linger around already for some years. Quaternions can have many faces, but the most easy to visualise and comprehend is the quaternion of unit lenght which can represent orientation. Let's approach the quaternion world from an animator's point of view.

Positioning a rigid body in 3D space, as we all know, can be done with 6 degrees of freedom : some fixed point of the object can be placed anywhere in space with a translation, while every orientation of the object can be achieved by rotating it about that fixed point (Euler proved this in 1752). When rotating the object, one can observe that one line of points remains fixed, namely the "rotation axis" (which passes through the fixed point). So one way to describe orientation is a rotation about an axis **(X, Y, Z)** over a certain angle **2** θ (fig. 1).

The unit quaternion who represents this rotation is

$$\mathbf{Q} = (\mathbf{w}, \mathbf{x}, \mathbf{y}, \mathbf{z}) = (\cos\theta,\ \mathbf{X}\sin\theta,\ \mathbf{Y}\sin\theta,\ \mathbf{Z}\sin\theta)$$

or written in some handier way

$$\mathbf{Q} = (\cos\theta, \sin\theta\ (\mathbf{X}, \mathbf{Y}, \mathbf{Z})) \qquad [1]$$

with $w^2 + x^2 + y^2 + z^2 = 1$ (with the presumption $X^2 + Y^2 + Z^2 = 1$). Note that a unit quaternion only has three degrees of freedom (because of its normalisation).

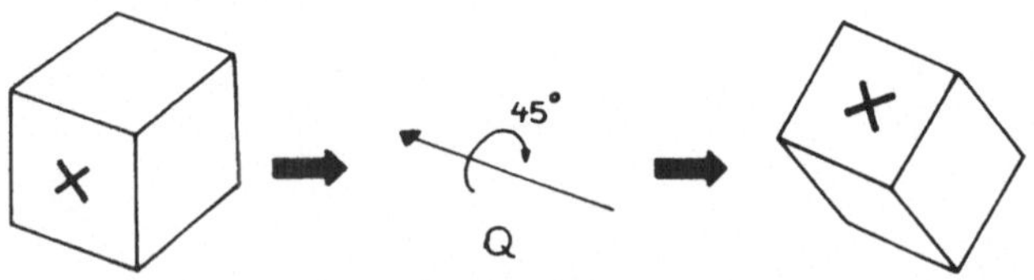

fig. 1 : quaternion acting upon a cube

One can show [SHOE85] that there is a great deal of analogy between quaternions and rotation matrices (which are orthonormal matrices). Both form a non-communicative group under their muliplication. Both are easily converted one into the other [SHOE85]. Although simular, composing (multiplicating) quaternions is much more efficient than composing rotation matrices. This comes from the fact that rotation matrices are a redundant way to describe rotations, while quaternions aren't. Hamilton defined quaternions in such a way that the product of two unit quaternions remains a unit quaternion, i.e. the multiplication of quaternions is norm preserving. A quaternion describes the rotation an object should make from its begin position to its new orientation. When a second quaternion is applied on this last position, the object rotates towards a new orientation. The overall quaternion, being product of the two quaternions, depicts the rotation from the begin position to the last orientation (see fig. 2).

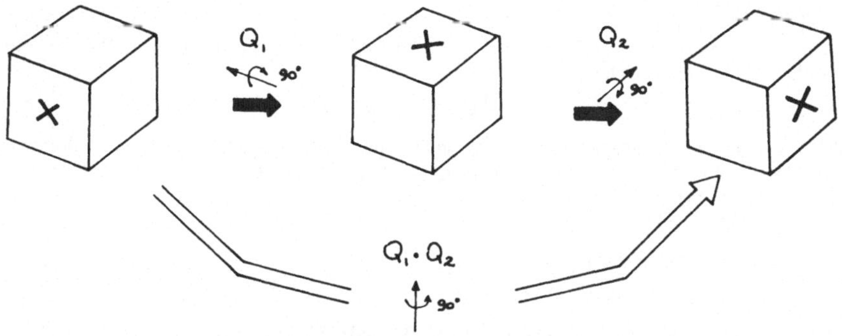

fig. 2 : composition of quaternions

Although quaternions have everything a proper rotation description should have, so many animators use Euler angles. And are bothered with it ! One has to apply the Euler rotations in a certain order (because rotations do not commute !). Changing the order alters the whole animation (and there are about a dozen ways to specify Euler rotations). Euler angle animation suffers also from gimbal lock (loosing a rotational degree of freedom) and from non-uniformity (a fixed change in Euler angles does not always give the same amount of rotational change). In their defense, it must be said that they are handy to specify keyframes with (and for solving differential equations - which is what Euler designed them for). But, we're lucky : Euler angles are easily converted to quaternions [SHOE85]. Quaternions on the other hand do not suffer from singularities, like gimbal lock, and provide a uniform description of all possible orientations.

Vectors $\bar{v}$ can also be described as quaternions, by eliminating the rotational part ([BLAK87], [SHOE85]) (i.e. $\cos\theta = 0$ and $\sin\theta = 1$) :

$$\bar{v} = (0, (X, Y, Z)) \quad [2]$$

Vectors can be rotated by a quaternion Q like this ([SHOE87]) :

$$\bar{v}' = Q^{-1} \cdot \bar{v} \cdot Q \quad [3]$$

An indepth overview of the mathematical properties of quaternions can be found in [SHOE87].

2. Linear interpolation of quaternions

From equation [1] it can be seen that all unit quaternions occupy the surface of a sphere in the 4-dimensional space. It is not trivial to do linear interpolation on such a hypersphere. Therefore we will develop quaternion interpolation intuitively from an analogy with the 3D vector space.

3D vectors form an additive group, quaternions form a multiplicative group. The inverse of a vector $\bar{v}$ is $-\bar{v}$ while the inverse of a quaternion Q is Q^{-1} with

$$Q^{-1} = (w, -x, -y, -z) \quad [4]$$

Scaling a vector $\bar{v}$ is done by $\alpha \cdot \bar{v}$ (α being a scalar) while scaling a quaternion Q goes like

$$Q' = Q^{\alpha} = (\cos\theta,\ \sin\theta\ (X, Y, Z))^{\alpha} = (\cos\alpha\theta,\ \sin\alpha\theta\ (X, Y, Z)) \quad [5]$$

The vector $\Delta\bar{v}$ which brings $\bar{v}_1$ to $\bar{v}_2$ is

$$\Delta\bar{v} = \bar{v}_2 - \bar{v}_1 = -\bar{v}_1 + \bar{v}_2 \quad [6]$$

while the quaternion ΔQ which transforms Q_1 into Q_2 is by analogy

$$\Delta Q = Q_1^{-1} \cdot Q_2 \qquad [7]$$

Linear interpolation between $\bar{v}_1$ and $\bar{v}_2$ can be written as

$$\bar{v} = \bar{v}_1 + \alpha \cdot (\bar{v}_2 - \bar{v}_1)\ ;\ 0 \le \alpha \le 1 \qquad [8]$$

where $\bar{v}$ goes from $\bar{v}_1$ to $\bar{v}_2$ as α goes from **0** to **1**. As this is a frequently used function, we define a function "**lerp**" (from "LInear intERPolation") :

$$\bar{v} = \mathbf{lerp}\ (\bar{v}_1, \bar{v}_2, \alpha) = \bar{v}_1 + \alpha \cdot (\bar{v}_2 - \bar{v}_1) \qquad [9]$$

From the analogy we can define a "spherical linear interpolation" function or "**slerp**" in the unit quaternion space (remember this is a sphere) like this

$$Q = \mathbf{slerp}\ (Q_1, Q_2, \alpha) = Q_1 \cdot (Q_1^{-1} \cdot Q_2)^{\alpha}\ ;\ 0 \le \alpha \le 1 \qquad [10]$$

The interpolated vector $\bar{v}$ goes along a straight line and the interpolated quaternion **Q** goes along a great arc on the 4D sphere, which is the shortest way between Q_1 and Q_2. For $\alpha = 0.5$, we get a special case for **lerp**() and **slerp**(), because the result is the midpoint between $\bar{v}_1$ and $\bar{v}_2$ or Q_1 and Q_2 (the appendix shows how easily **slerp**() and **smid**() are put into code [SHOE87]) :

$$\mathbf{mid}\ (\bar{v}_1, \bar{v}_2) = \mathbf{lerp}\ (\bar{v}_1, \bar{v}_2, 0.5) \qquad [11]$$

$$\mathbf{smid}\ (Q_1, Q_2) = \mathbf{slerp}\ (Q_1, Q_2, 0.5) \qquad [12]$$

If α lies outside the range [0,1], we extrapolate $\bar{v}$ or **Q** on a straight line or great arc. Extrapolation doesn't give any problems in vector space and it is easy to see it doesn't give problems in quaternion space either. As α grows, we keep running on a great circle on the hypersphere.

3. Spline subdivision

Most splines used nowadays can be written in the

$$S_i\ (t) = [t^3\ t^2\ t\ 1] \cdot \mathbf{P} \cdot \begin{bmatrix} D_i \\ D_{i+1} \\ D_{i+2} \\ D_{i+3} \end{bmatrix} \qquad [13]$$

where S_i (t), $(0 \le t \le 1)$ is the **i**-th polynomial segment of the spline and D_i, $(0 \le i \le m)$ are the control points (there are **m + 1** of them) [DUFF86]. **P** is a matrix holding the polynomial coefficients and incorporates the properties of the spline [FOLE84].

The class of splines, covered by the above representation, is local, linear and uniform. A local spline is one for which changing the value of a single control point D_j, $(0 \le j \le m)$ affects only a bounded number (in this case 4) of spline segments in the control point's vicinity. A linear spline is one for which linear transformations of the spline can be reduced to (the same) linear transformation of the control points. A uniform spline is one for which each polynomial segment is defined along a parameter interval of lenght 1. Generalisation to non-uniform control point spacing is quite straight forward [DUFF86]. The properties of the spline are fully controlled by the matrix **P**. For instance the family of uniform cardinal splines (with first order continuity) are represented by ([CLAR81]) :

$$P_C = \begin{bmatrix} -c & 2-c & c-2 & c \\ 2c & c-3 & 3-2c & -c \\ -c & 0 & c & 0 \\ 0 & 1 & 0 & 0 \end{bmatrix}\ ;0 \le c \le 1 \qquad [14]$$

An interesting member of the cardinal spline family is the Catmull-Rom cubic spline for which **c = 0.5** [CATM78]. Most computer animation systems use cardinal splines for interpolation between keyframes. The behaviour of cardinal splines for varying **c** can be found in [DUFF86]. Given the above formulation, it is easy to find the beginpoint (**t = 0.0**), the midpoint (**t = 0.5**) and the endpoint (**t = 1.0**) of a polynomial segment of a spline. In doing so, we subdivide each spline segment in two halves. For the cardinal spline there comes :

beginpoint $B_i\ (t = 0.0) = D_{i+1}$

midpoint $M_i\ (t = 0.5) = -0.125\, c\, D_i + (0.5 + 0.125\, c)\, D_{i+1} + (0.5 + 0.125\, c)\, D_{i+2} - 0.125\, c\, D_{i+3}$

endpoint $E_i\ (t = 1.0) = D_{i+2} = B_{i+1}$

Let's now apply this subdivision method for cardinal splines. The only point we have to construct is $\mathbf{M_i}$. It is easy to see that

$$\mathbf{M_i = lerp\ (mid\ (D_i, D_{i+3}),\ mid\ (D_{i+1}, D_{i+2}), 1 + 0.25\,c\,);\ 0 \leq c \leq 1} \qquad [15]$$

We construct this midpoint $\mathbf{M_i}$ graphically with $\mathbf{c = 0.5}$ (Catmull - Rom spline), (see fig. 3).

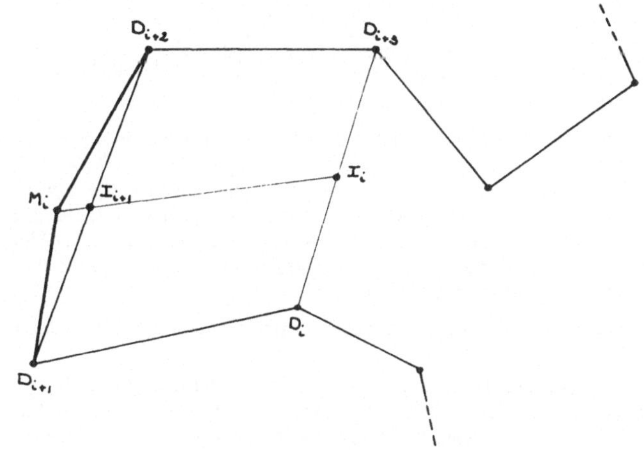

$\mathbf{I_i = mid\ (D_i, D_{i+3});\ I_{i+1} = mid\ (D_{i+1}, D_{i+2});\ d\ (M_i, I_{i+1}) = 0.125\ d\ (I_i, I_{i+1})}$

fig. 3 : graphical construction of the Catmull-Rom spline

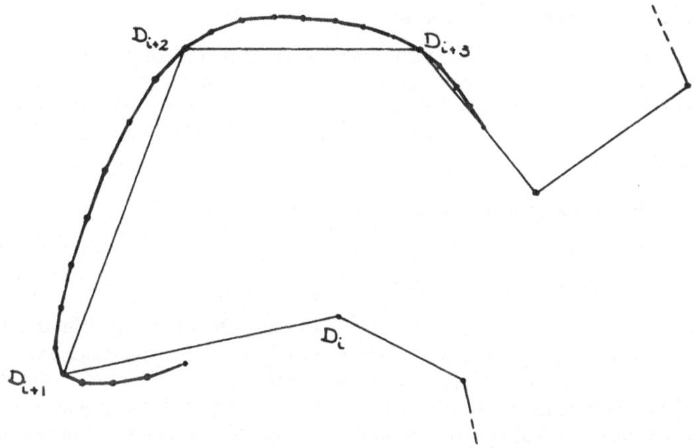

fig. 4 : approximated cardinal spline after 3 subdivisions

If we construct these points for each segment $\mathbf{i}$ and draw straight lines in between them, we get some piecewise linear approximation of the spline we want to construct (see bold line in fig. 3). The original set of control points $\mathbf{\{D_i\}}$ plus the set of constructed points $\mathbf{\{Mi\}}$ form a new set of control points on which we can apply the same subdivision scheme. After a limited number of subdivisions we get a fairly good approximation of the spline we wanted to construct (fig. 4).

Although this way of working is very attractive, we have to point out that the constructed points of the second or more generation are not guaranteed to lie on the spline itself. This stems from the fact that in most cases the boundary conditions, imposed on $\mathbf{S_i\ (t)}$ in $\mathbf{t = 0.0}$ and $\mathbf{t = 1.0}$ do not hold exactly in $\mathbf{t = 0.5}$ (but they do approximately for most splines [PLET87], so the result is a good approximation of the spline itself).

The scheme we proposed here, is also applicable to other types of splines [PLET87] and is used succesfully in a real time digital paint system to interpolate the position of brush dots in a brush stroke. Tom Duff uses an approximation of this scheme with B-splines [DUFF86]. An important difference between a B-spline and a cardinal spline is the former does not pass always through the control points while the latter does. In the next section, we will use this subdivision method for splining quaternions. Each control point D_i will correspond to a keyframe quaternion. To find the quaternion for a certain in-between frame, we locate the proper linear segment and use linear interpolation to obtain the corresponding quaternion.

4. Splining quaternions

The piecewise linear approximation of a spline can also be applied in the quaternion space by using the simularity of "**lerp**" in the Cartesian space with "**slerp**" in the quaternion space. This means that a straight line in Cartesian space is replaced by a great arc in quaternion space.

Already three algorithms have been proposed to spline quaternions : a Bezier interpolation scheme by Ken Shoemake [SHOE85], an approximate B-spline interpolation scheme by Tom Duff [DUFF86] and a Boehm quadrangle spline by Ken Shoemake [SHOE87]. The scheme by Tom Duff has the advantage of (extreme) smoothness because B-splines have a continuity of second degree but consequently the disadvantage of not passing through the control points. The schemes by Ken Shoemake have the advantage of local control of the spline, but as this is accomplished by placing and/or moving quaternion control points, it can be cumbersome to do this interactively and it is not transparent to the user.

From a practical point of view, the use of quaternions in an interactive system should have the following properties:

1. Keyframes need to be respected (i.e. the motion has to pass through the keys exactly).
2. As quaternions are not easily visualised on a 2D screen, they should be transparent to the user. Keyframes can easily be defined by means of Euler angles, which are readily transformed to quaternions for internal use within the interpolation software [SHOE87].
3. There should be some control on the behaviour of the interpolation. This behaviour should, if necessary, be different for every part in between the keyframes or can be the same for the whole animation.
4. The generation of the motion has to be fast and robust.

As cardinal splines pass through the control points, don't need additional control points which are not associated with a keyframe, and have spline behaviour control via the c-parameter (which can differ for each spline segment), they are most suited for interpolating quaternions in a keyframe animation system. Out of a set $\{Q_i ; i = 0, 1, ..., m\}$ of keyframes quaternions, one can generate a more elaborate set $\{Q'_j ; j = 0, 1, ..., 2m\}$ by cardinal spline subdivision with

$$Q_j' = \text{slerp}\,(\text{smid}\,(Q_{i-1}, Q_{i+2}), \text{smid}\,(Q_i, Q_{i+1}), 1 + 0.25\,c)$$
$$\text{with } j = 2i + 1 ; 0 \le i \le m ; 0 \le c \le 1 \qquad [16]$$

$$Q_j' = Q_i \qquad \text{with } j = 2i ; 0 \le i \le m \qquad [17]$$

In practice, this subdivision scheme has to be repeated only 3 or 4 times. Out of the resulting set, the quaternions for each frame can be calculated by a single **slerp()**. As the transformations from Euler angles to quaternions and from quaternions to rotation matrices (for use in the visualisation software or hardware) are well defined, the algorithm is robust. If we compare the efficiency of the four proposed interpolation schemes with each other (see table 1) we see that the B-spline algorithm is the most efficient, closely followed by the cardinal spline algorithm. In table 2, timings of the two basic functions "slerp()" and "smid()" are given for three different computers.

table 1 : number of function calls/segment

	subdivision level		
scheme	1	2	3
Bezier	6 S	18 S	42 S
B-spline	3 M	9 M	21 M
Boehm	3 S	9 S	21 S
Cardinal	1S + 2M	3S + 6M	7S + 14M

(S = slerp(), M = smid())

table 2 : time/function call for different computers

computer	slerp()	smid()
Celerity C1230	98 µs	61 µs
Iris 4D/60T	31 µs	20 µs
Iris 3130	396 µs	85 µs

5. Quaternions for modelling

Some modelling tasks become quite simple when working with quaternions. As an example, we take the "propagation control graph" (PCG) of the MIRALAB modelling program [MAGN85]. A PCG is a set of control polygons, which defines a mesh of control points. With this mesh, one can construct a spline surface with beta-splines, Bezier splines or some other spline type. A PCG is constructed by repeating a control polygon along a path (fig. 5). While repeating, the control polygon can be rotated, scaled or interpolated to another control polygon (fig. 6).

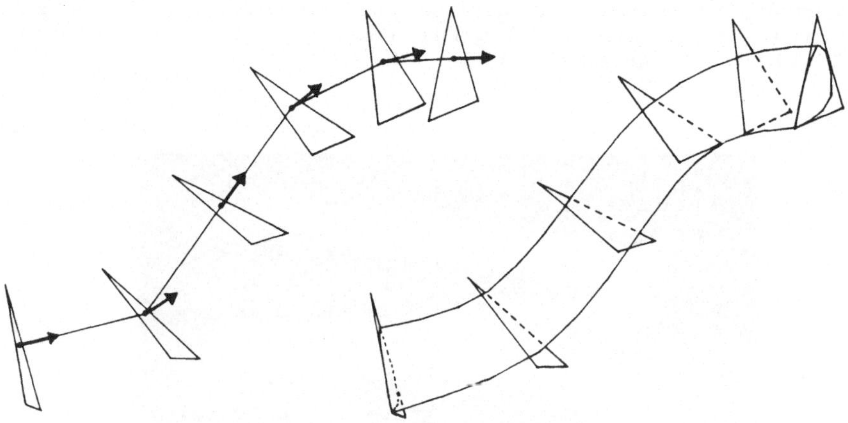

fig. 5 : PCG and resulting surface (β-splines)

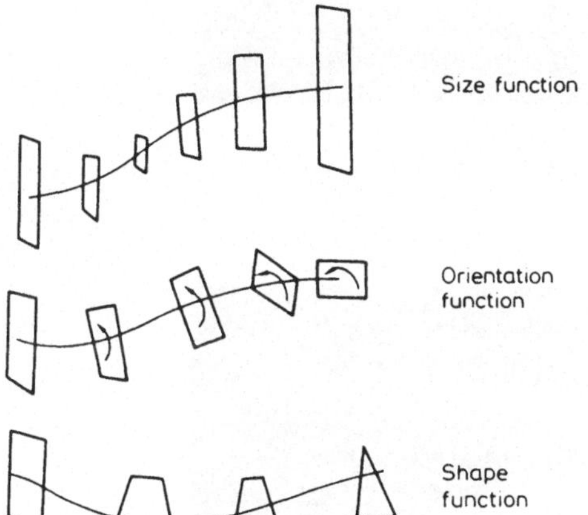

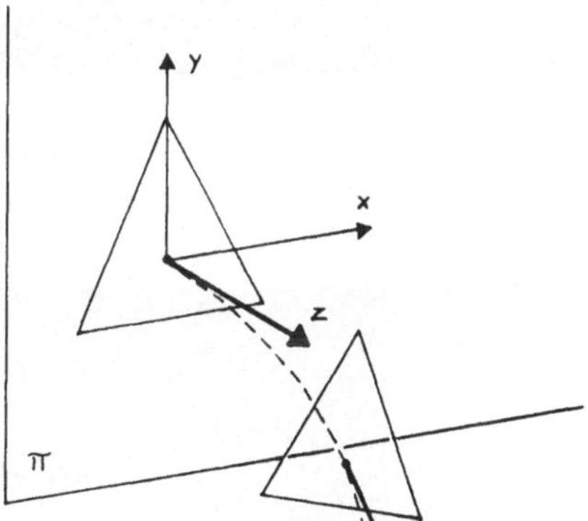

fig. 6 : scaling, rotating and interpolating the control polygon [MAGN85]

fig. 7 : construction of a 3D PCG

The control polygon is a 2-dimensional figure, connecting a set of control points. The path or "backbone" of the PCG is perpendicular to the plane of the control polygon at the point of intersection of both (fig. 5). If the backbone is a 2-dimensional curve, there is no problem in finding the 3-dimensional orientation of the control curve. If the backbone is a 3-dimensional curve, we can make the normal of the control polygon coincide with the tangent of the backbone, but we need a criterion to decide on the orientation of the control polygon. A good criterion is that, when no rotation around the backbone is specified, the orientation of the control polygons should vary as less as possible with respect to the initial orientation of the control polygon (i.e. at the beginning of the backbone).

We can solve the problem with quaternions. Suppose we use the orientation of the first control polygon (at the beginning of the backbone) as reference position, to which we connect coordinate axes **xyz**, **z** being the normal of the first control polygon and Π being the plane of the **xy** axes. Rotating the control curve, so that the normal $\bar{n}$ of the control polygon matches the tangent of the backbone at some point, can be done with a quaternion whose rotation axis lies in the plane π of the first control polygon (fig. 7). This leaves one degree of freedom to specify the rotation around the backbone (rotation around **z**). As the quaternion we use to match the tangent, only has two degrees of freedom, the orientation variation is minimal, which proves our criterion.

Figures 8 and 9 show three dimensional rendered propagation control graphs, with a triangular control polygon, resulting in a teardrop shaped section. In fig. 8, no rotation around the backbone is specified. In fig. 9, a rotation of 2π per turn of the spiral makes the resulting surface twist around the backbone. Rendering was done with the BODYBUILDING program of MIRALAB.

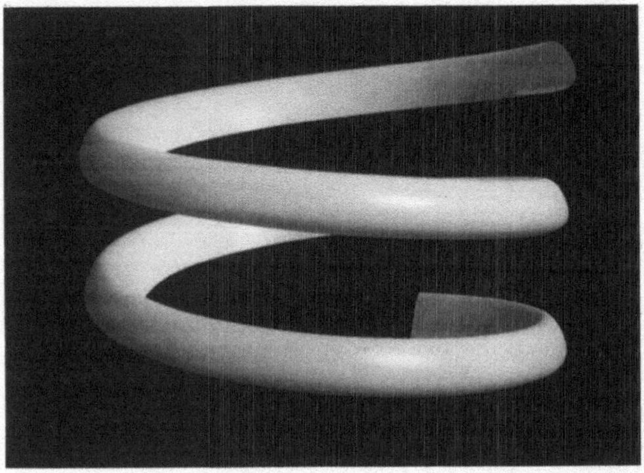

fig. 8 : rendered 3D PCG without torsion

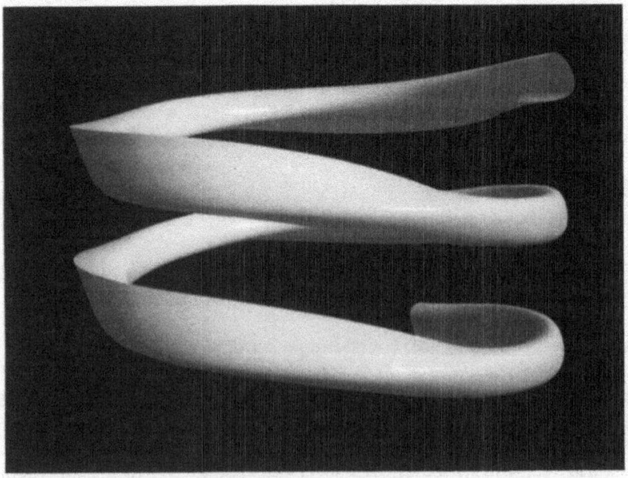

fig. 9 : rendered 3D PCG with torsion

6. Quaternions for rendering.

At the beginning of this paper, we proved that vectors also can be written in quaternion format. In analogy to vertex normals, we can construct vertex quaternions (sum all adjacent quaternions and normalise the result). Figure 10 shows a polygon where each vertex has his corresponding quaternion. If we go along the edge **AB**, $Q_A^{-1} \cdot Q_B$ will be the quaternion which transforms Q_A into Q_B. If we go along the edge in **n + 1** steps,

$$\Delta Q_{AB} = (Q_A^{-1} \cdot Q_B)^{1/n} \qquad [18]$$

will be the quaternion who transforms Q_D into the Q_D of the next scanline. The same holds for the quaternion Q_E along the edge **AC** where

$$\Delta Q_{AC} = (Q_A^{-1} \cdot Q_C)^{1/m} \qquad [19]$$

and where there are **m + 1** scanlines from **A** to **C**. Interpolation along the scanline **DE** (over **k + 1** pixels) gives

$$\Delta Q_{DE} = (Q_D^{-1} \cdot Q_E)^{1/k} \qquad [20]$$

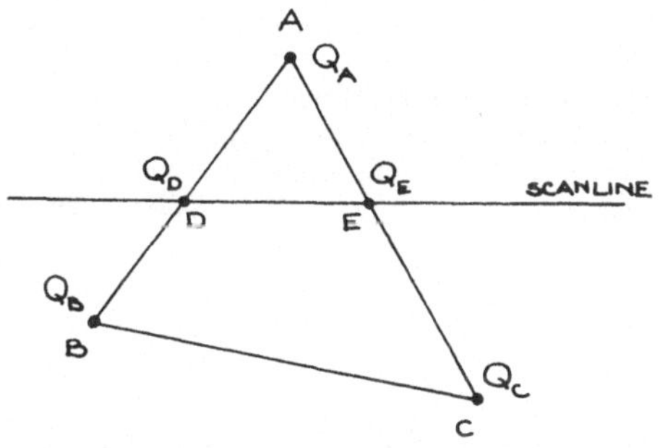

fig. 10 : vertex quaternions

So one can calculate the appropriate quaternion **Q** for each pixel, which represents the interpolated normal in that pixel. The following piece of pseudocode gives the structure of a rendering program with quaternion interpollation :

$\Delta Q_{AB} = (Q_A^{-1} \cdot Q_B)^{1/n}$
$\Delta Q_{AC} = (Q_A^{-1} \cdot Q_C)^{1/m}$
$Q_D = Q_E = Q_A$
for each scanline over k + 1 pixels
{
  $Q = Q_D$
  $\Delta Q_{DE} = (Q_D^{-1} \cdot Q_E)^{1/k}$
  for each pixel on the scanline
    {
    shading calculations
    $Q = Q \cdot \Delta Q_{DE}$
    }
  $Q_D = Q_D \cdot \Delta Q_{AB}$
  $Q_E = Q_E \cdot \Delta Q_{AC}$
}

One can see that there is no need for normalising the quaternions (as intended by Hamilton), they stay normalised all the time. As normalising and incrementing a normal along a scanline can take up to 50 % of the time spent in the inner loop of a normal renderer (a great deal of the time is spent in calculating a square root [EARN87]), and as quaternion multiplication is quite efficient and easy, we can save time per pixel we render. Tabel 3 shows how much faster the quaternion incrementation works in comparison with incrementation and normalisation of normals (code was written in C) table 3 : speed up comparisons

computer	incrementation speedup	max. rendering speedup
Iris 3130	1.81	1.29
Iris 4D/60T	2.05	1.35
Celerity C1230	1.25	1.11

7. Conclusion

In this paper we showed the advantages of using quaternions in animation, modelling and rendering. We proposed a keyframe animation system, which uses quaternions internally for better orientation representation, and which is capable of generating smooth orientation changes with preservation of the keyframes, and with high efficiency. We indicated that orientation problems in modelling can be solved by the use of quaternions and we developped a new solution to the normalisation problem of normals in rendering and showed the speed up which goes with this.

Acknowledgments

I would like to thank Jean Despaey, Jef Vandenberghe, Bruno Vermeulen and Peter De Mangelaere for reading and commenting this paper. Thanks also to Marianne Gryson, Erwin Keustermans and Veerle Delange for the text and the illustrations. I would like to acknowledge Luc De Simpelaere for creating the opportunity and the environment to explore computer graphics and for stimulating the development of new ideas in this field.

References

[BLAK87] Blake E.H.
"A metric for Computing Adaptive Detail in Animated Scenes using Object Oriented Programming"
Proc. Eurographics 87, pp. 295-307

[BOEH84] Boehm W. et al.
"A survey of curve and surface methods in CAGD"
Computer Aided Geometric Design 1 (1984), pp. 1-60

[CATM74] Catmull E. & Rom R.
"A Class of Local Interpolating Splines"
Computer Aided Geometric Design, pp. 317-326, 1974

[CAYL] Cayley A.
"On certain results relating to quaternions"
Philosophical Magazine xxvi, pp. 141-145, Feb. 1845

[CLAR81] Clark J.
"Parametric Curves, Surfaces and Volumes in Computer Graphics and Computer-Aided Geometric Design", Techn. Rep. 221, Computer Systems Laboratory, Stanford Univ., Palo Alto, California, nov. 1981

[DUFF86] Duff T.
"Splines in Animation and Modelling"
Siggraph 86 Course #15 : "State of the Art in Image Synthesis"

[EARN87] Earnshaw R.A.
"The mathematics of computer graphics"
The Visual Computer (1987) 3, pp. 115-124

[FOLE84] Foley J.D. & Van Dam A.
"Fundamentals of Interactive Computer Graphics"
Addison Wesley, 1984

[HANK80] Hankins T.L.
"Sir William Rowan Hamilton"
The John Hopkins University Press, 1980

[MAGN85] Magnenat-Thalmann N. & Thalmann D.
"Area, spline-based and structural models for generating and animating 3D characters and logos"
The Visual Computer (1985) 1, pp. 15-23

[PLET87] Pletinckx D.
"The use of spline subdivision in computer animation and digital painting"
Barco Industries Creative Systems technical memo #TM.03DEC87.DP
[SHOE85] Shoemake K.
"Animating Rotation with Quaternion Curves"
Computer Graphics, 19(3), pp. 245-254, Proc. Siggraph 85
[SHOE87] Shoemake K.
"Quaternion Calculus and Fast Animation"
Siggraph 87 Course # 10 : "Computer Animation : 3D Motion specification and control", pp. 101-121

Appendix : C code to implement quaternion interpollation

```
#define W 0
#define X 1
#define Y 2
#define Z 3

typedef double quaternion;

smid (q1, q2, q)

quaternion q1[], q2[], q[];

{
    double sqrt(), sum, factor;

    sum = q1[W] * q2[W] + q1[X] * q2[X] + q1[Y] * q2[Y] + q1[Z] * q2[Z];
    factor = 1.0 / sqrt (2.0 * (1.0 + sum));

    q[W] = (q1[W] + q2[W]) * factor;
    q[X] = (q1[X] + q2[X]) * factor;
    q[Y] = (q1[Y] + q2[Y]) * factor;
    q[Z] = (q1[Z] + q2[Z]) * factor;

    return;
}

slerp (q1, q2, alfa, q)

quaternion q1[], q2[], q[];
double alfa;

{
    double acos(), sin(), sum;
    double beta1, beta2, teta;

    sum = q1[W] * q2[W] + q1[X] * q2[X] + q1[Y] * q2[Y] + q1[Z] * q2[Z];
    teta = acos (sum);

    if (teta ≤ EPSILON)
        {
        beta1 = 1.0 - alfa;
        beta2 = alfa;
        }
    else
        {
        beta1 = sin ((1.0 - alfa) * teta) / sin (teta);
        beta2 = sin (alfa * teta) / sin (teta);
        }
    q[W] = beta1 * q1[W] + beta2 * q2[W];
    q[X] = beta1 * q1[X] + beta2 * q2[X];
    q[Y] = beta1 * q1[Y] + beta2 * q2[Y];
    q[Z] = beta1 * q1[Z] + beta2 * q2[Z];

    return;
}
```

Toward General Animation Control

G. Hégron, B. Arnaldi, and G. Dumont (France)

Abstract

In this paper we present an analysis of animation control processes. The design of an animation system is strongly coupled with the considered application. So these systems are specialized, some of them in audiovisual production, in C.A.D. or in mechanical computation. We are working on the design of a general animation system with the capability to generate motion resulting from mechanical laws in an audiovisual environment. The heart of this system is a structured graph used to store a hierarchical description of the objects and the mechanical joints linking them together to build a multibody mechanical system. Motion control can also be specified by key-framing techniques or explicit trajectories for the objects which are not submitted to mechanical laws. The dynamical formalism takes into account holonomic and nonholonomic constraints using the principle of virtual works associated with LAGRANGE's multipliers. Symbolical equations of motion are automatically built by the system and solved for each time step (frame) to give object locations and orientations.

1 Introduction

The specification of a computer animation system is broadly defined according to three main interdependent criteria [20] :

- the system's motion control,
- the animation model,
- the application.

In the relevant literature, the various proposed animation systems favour one of these criteria to the detriment of the others. Either the human interface is more or less animator dependent, or the animation model uses kinematic or dynamic data, or the application is film or simulation oriented. These restrictions lead the system's creator to define ad hoc 3D object geometric models and scene structures, the specifications of which are not suitable for general animation purpose.

Our goal at IRISA is to conceive a more general system of animation which would not only include kinematics and dynamics (forward and inverse) but would also be able to welcome high level motion description. The use of kinematics and dynamics provides explicit control of the motions on the one hand and capability to simulate the realistic appearance of forces acting on the bodies which frees the animator of the description of real phenomena on the other hand.

After a short look at previous work in the field, we describe the design and implementation of a first version. A survey of the system structure is firstly presented. Thereafter each subsystem is discussed, especially the scene modelling which includes general multibody structures, the motion generation method, and the mechanical animation kernel which derives the equations of motion from the principle of virtual works and the lagrangian formalism.

2 Survey

There are different ways to achieve 3D computer animation [1].

According to the system's motion control Zeltzer [31] defined three levels of autonomy of the systems. In the guiding systems the animator should know a priori the values of the different parameters of the mobile objects and specify them to the computer [13]. In the programme level systems the computer is loaded with sufficient knowledge to interpret elementary commands specified in a script (programme) by the animator [17]. In the task level systems the animator gives only information such as initial positions and forces to be applied, and the computer generates itself the movements following physical or mechanical laws, extracting the necessary new information from the geometric data base [30].

According to the animation model, three approaches may be distinguished by imposing and solving kinematic, dynamic or geometric constraints. The kinematics can be explicitly specified by the description of "keyframes" which are automatically interpolated by "in-between" frames [24]. Implicit methods are based for instance on the "inverse kinematics" where the motion of end links in a chain is specified by the user, but the motion of interior links is algorithmicly computed [4]. In order to render the reality of natural phenomena the animator can be provided with physical laws such as the movement of the waves [11] or of particles [21], or dynamic models for which the user specifies forces and torques [1,27]. The incorporation of both kinematic and dynamic techniques within a single coherent system is still at the experimental stage [15]. Implementation of closed three-dimensional kinematic chains was also rarely presented in the literature on computer animation. Closed chains were rather studied for the dynamic control of robots [16]. But in this case assumptions are strong, solutions are specific and not suitable for general mechanism animation. A simple but general approach which provides an effective means of building and animating parameterized models by solving geometric constraints, was introduced by Witkin and al. [28].

According to the application, two fields may be distinguished. The first one is the production of films (cartoons, teaching films, advertisements) where the rendering is very important and where the motions can be fancy. The second one is simulation which aims at describing what happens, whatever happens [14,18](for example in robotics: control of robot arm, collision detection, path planning). The simulation objective is especially numerical results.

With regard to this short survey, we state that the animation model jointly with the object geometric models are the of computer animation systems heart, on which both upstream, the user interface ergonomics and downstream, the application fields are strongly dependent.

The methods presented in this paper give a first attempt to animate the geometry or the rendering of a 3D scene with any types of animation techniques simultaneously. The moving

[1] As the computer animation bibliography is increasing considerably, the references of this short survey are not exhaustive but just indicative.

objects are general multibody systems containing open or closed chains. A general dynamic formulation which may incorporate kinematic and dynamic constraints and processes forward and inverse dynamics is presented and tested on a complex model.

3 Presentation of our own animation system

We are working on the definition of a general animation system which takes into account all the previous remarks. The animation process can be split into three logical steps: scene modelling, motion generation and visualization. The heart of this system is a structured graph where step by step and class by class informations are added. *Topological* graphs of objects and "general motion parameters" are stored in this data structure. When an object is used, control is handed to the object administrator which collects the informations such as internal parameters, geometric models, etc ...

3.1 Scene modelling

In this part we present the way to achieve a hierarchical description of a scene. A scene is made up of some independent objects in the modelling point of view (ex: a table, a wall, a chair,...). An object consists possibly in elementary bodies linked together by mechanical joints, some of them can be rigid, the other ones express the internal degrees of freedom of this object. This arrangement of bodies can be considered as a representation of the object *topology*, in the sense that it is an essential information about the object structure without any assumption on its geometric modelling (figure 1). For one *topology*, we define the object *style*, by specifying its geometry and colour(ex: blue garden chair, red kitchen chair, ...). The basic structure used to store this representation is a graph.

To completely define an object *morphology*, it is necessary to specify all the object attributes. They can be classified in :

- geometric representation (geometric modelling),
- texture and photometry informations,
- mechanical properties.

We can use several techniques to express the geometric representation for one body. *LGRC* [7] is a compiled language, developed at IRISA, which gives a representation of the geometric modelling by a CSG tree [22,25]. We can also use a polygonal representation, interactively built or derived from the CSG tree [5], according to the visualization algorithm. The photometry informations describe the interactions between light sources and object surfaces. Several illumination models [9,19,26] can be used depending on the wished rendering quality. The mechanical properties are expressed by the mass, the inertia center and the inertia matrix for each body, and a class of joints between the bodies with the location of axis and special points. All the inertia and mass properties are computed by a ray-tracer algorithm. These attributes are not independent: generally, joints axis and photometry attributes depend on accurate locations resulting from geometric modelling. The way to achieve the connections between these different entities is shown in the next section.

3.2 Motion generation

For an animation, a sequence is a well-ordered frame series derived from a scene. During the sequence, each object can move, change scale or change rendering. For a given object there are two classes of parameters: internal parameters described in the previous part and external

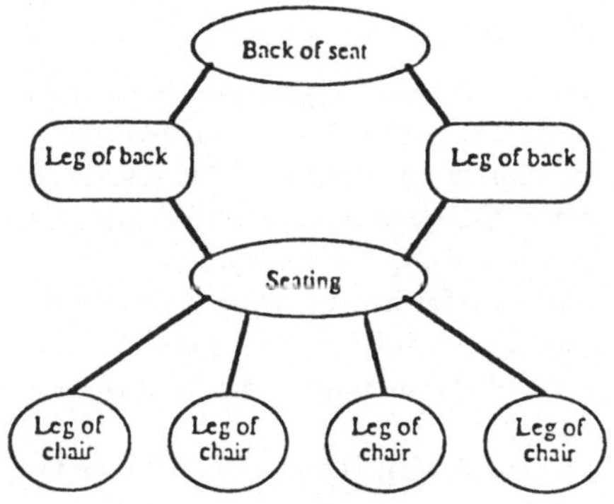

Figure 1: Chair topology

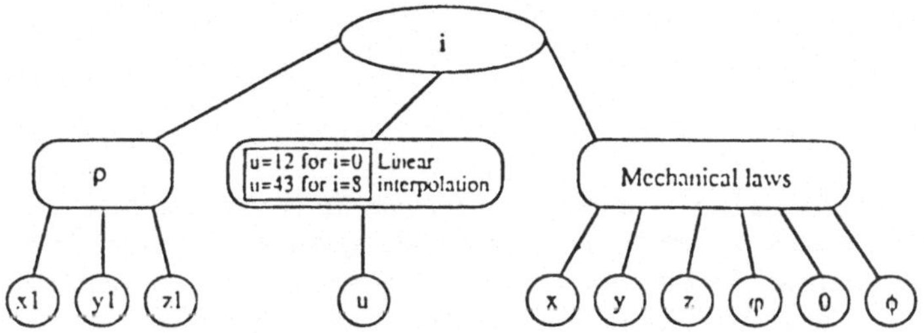

Figure 2: Motion production

parameters which are the six degrees of freedom resulting from the location and orientation of this object. The motion, in the general meaning, is obtained by the evolution of these parameters over the time. We can point out that, in a sequence, time is implicitly defined by the well-ordered frame series: the frame number i coincides with an absolute time for this sequence. A parameter open to motion is named a "general motion parameter". A sequence is completely defined when the motion of all the parameters is well-defined as follows: if a is such a parameter, then $a = f(i)$ is known. The way to achieve this assignment is important for the ergonomics of the system.

The chosen method is to link together the "general motion parameters" step by step and to supplement it with extra "general motion parameters" if necessary. A given trajectory is a link between the three location parameters of an object: for instance, let x, y and z be the coordinates of a point constrained to follow an helical trajectory in the absolute coordinate system. We have the set of equations: $x = \cos\rho$, $y = \sin\rho$, $z = \rho$ which links ρ to x, y and z. Here ρ is the only motion parameter needed to describe the effective trajectory. The next step consists in linking ρ to i (frame number or time) in order to build the object temporal behaviour as shown in figure 2. The sequence is entirely defined when i is the last general motion parameter. This technique builds a tree step by step with i being the root and all initial parameters being the leaves.

The goal is to supply as complete a tool as possible to give the user facility in complex trajectory description. The use of such a method results in several aspects in motion generation being possibly employed (figure 2) :

- Explicit trajectory: the use of explicit function to link parameters together, as explained in the previous section, lies in this class.
- Key framing: a link is created between a parameter a and the frame number i by giving to a key values associated with some frame numbers and using an interpolation method (linear, quadratic, spline,...) to compute a in between.
- Mechanical laws: we can consider "mechanical laws" as a special link which implicitly joins a set of parameters to time: the mechanical module solves motion equations with respect to time.

3.3 Visualization

We dispose of several visualization algorithms. We can use a ray-tracer algorithm, developed at IRISA, which operates under space subdivision principle [2,3,8] with a CSG modelled scene. Space is divided in an irregular fashion to fit the objects as closely as possible. This results in a set of 3D regions named "cells" being created. A boolean CSG tree is distributed into the cell structure to form in each cell the minimal boolean CSG tree using the relevant primitives. The searching process for the "next cell" along the ray path is performed by using a local data structure associated with each cell. Frames are now computed on a Intel's *IPSC* parallel computer with 64 processors. Scan-line method can be employed when the objects are represented by polygonal faces, or after a CSG to polygonal face conversion.

Frame rendering can be either in black and white or in colour with the use of 24 bytes for each pixel graphic display monitor (IRIS 3130).

4 Mechanical module

4.1 Mechanical model

We have to deal with the dynamical formalism to animate our models. In the general case the multibody systems that we take into account are "general multibody systems" [23,29]: we find holonomic and nonholonomic constraints. We will use the principle of virtual works associated with LAGRANGE's multipliers to treat our problem[6,12]. This formalism appears to be general and systematic enough to be implemented on a computer. It can be expressed as: let $q = (q^i)_{i=1,n}$ be the lagrangian parameters of one multibody system (S), submitted to p holonomic constraints: $f_h(q,t) = 0 \ \ , h = 1,2,...,p$, and to $p\prime$ nonholonomic constraints: $g_l(q,\dot{q},t) = 0 \ \ , l = 1,2,...,p\prime$. This nonholonomic constraints could be expressed as: $a_{li}(q,t)\cdot\dot{q}^i + b_l(q,t) = 0$ where $\dot{q}^i = \frac{dq^i}{dt}$ is the derivative of q^i with respect to time and where the EINSTEIN's compact notation is used:

$$a_{li}(q,t)\cdot\dot{q}^i = \sum_{i=1}^{n} a_{li}(q,t)\cdot\dot{q}^i.$$

The principle of virtual works is as follows: there exists at least one reference frame in which, for all virtual displacements of (S) and at any moment, the amount of virtual works that exert upon (S) is zero. That is to say: $\delta\mathcal{W}_d + \delta\mathcal{W}_l + \delta\mathcal{W}_j = 0$
where:

$\delta\mathcal{W}_d$ is virtual work of given effects,
$\delta\mathcal{W}_l$ is virtual work of binding effects,
$\delta\mathcal{W}_j$ is virtual work of inertia effects.

For one system with the generalized coordinates $q = (q^i)_{i=1,n}$ the principle of virtual works can be written as: $\mathcal{Q}_i + \mathcal{L}_i + \mathcal{J}_i = 0 \ \ , i = 1,2,...,n$.
where $\mathcal{Q}_i$(resp. $\mathcal{L}_i$, $\mathcal{J}_i$) is the generalized given(resp. binding, inertia)effect relative to q^i.
Let $\mathcal{C}$ be the kinetic energy of (S), the LAGRANGE's formula gives:

$$\mathcal{J}_i = -\frac{d}{dt}\left(\frac{\partial\mathcal{C}}{\partial\dot{q}^i}\right) + \frac{\partial\mathcal{C}}{\partial q^i} \quad , i = 1,2,...,n.$$

We have now the set of equations(with application of the LAGRANGE's multipliers principle):

$$\begin{cases} \mathcal{Q}_i - \dfrac{d}{dt}\left(\dfrac{\partial\mathcal{C}}{\partial\dot{q}^i}\right) + \dfrac{\partial\mathcal{C}}{\partial q^i} + \lambda^h\dfrac{\partial f_h}{\partial q^i} + \mu^l a_{li} = 0 & , i = 1,2,...,n \\ f_h(q,t) = 0 & , h = 1,2,...,p \\ g_l(q,\dot{q},t) = 0 & , l = 1,2,...,p\prime . \end{cases}$$

This system is a general non-linear differential equation system that we have to solve.

The algorithm we are working on, is based on this approach. Let us consider a modelled system of objects submitted to bindings and external forces. The kinetic energy of the whole system is firstly symbolically computed, then the work of binding effects and the work of external forces. Then, by application of the virtual works principle, one systematic symbolical derivation is done that produces the system of movement equations. This method has the advantage of being very general for solving mechanical problems. It is also systematic and allows an efficient implementation on computers. More details are to be found on in reference [10].

4.2 Examples

This section presents two examples of the use of the mechanical model. The first, a simple one, is described in details as an illustration of the resolution method. The second accounts for the generality of the model we use.

bipendulum

The method is now explained according to the system represented on figure 3.Let us consider the planar bipendulum represented on figure 3. It is made of two bars of respective lengths l_1 and l_2 and of respective masses m_1 and m_2. The first one is linked at A with a joint of axis orthogonal to the plan (x, y), the link at B is of the same type. The chosen parameters are $(x_1, y_1, x_2, y_2, \theta_1, \theta_2)$ where (x_i, y_i) is the location of the inertia center of the bar and θ_i is the angle between the bar and the vertical line. We present here the input data and the motion equations of this system.

****Input data for bipendulum model****

kinetic

$0.5 * m1 * (sqr(ddt(x1)) + sqr(ddt(y1)))\ +$

$0.5 * m2 * (sqr(ddt(x2)) + sqr(ddt(y2)))\ +$

$(m1 * l1 * sqr(l1)/12) * sqr(ddt(teta1))\ +$

$(m2 * l2 * sqr(l2)/12) * sqr(ddt(teta2))\ \#$

holonomic

$\{link\, at\, A\}$

$x1 - (l1/2) * sin(teta1)\#$

$y1 + (l1/2) * cos(teta1)\#$

$\{link\, at\, B\}$

$x2 - l1 * sin(teta1) - (l2/2) * sin(teta2)\#$

$y2 + l1 * cos(teta1) + (l2/2) * cos(teta2)\#$

nonholonomic

$\{there\, is\, no\, nonholonomic\, constraint\}$

work

$\{work\, of\, gravity\}$

$-m1 * g * y1 - m2 * g * y2\#$

const

$\{defining\, constants\}$

$m1 = 1.0$

$m2 = 1.0$

$l1 = 1.0$

$l2 = 1.0$

$g = 9.8$

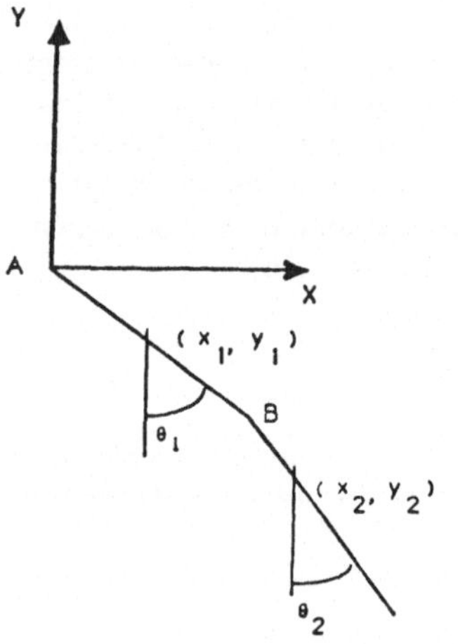

Figure 3: Bipendulum

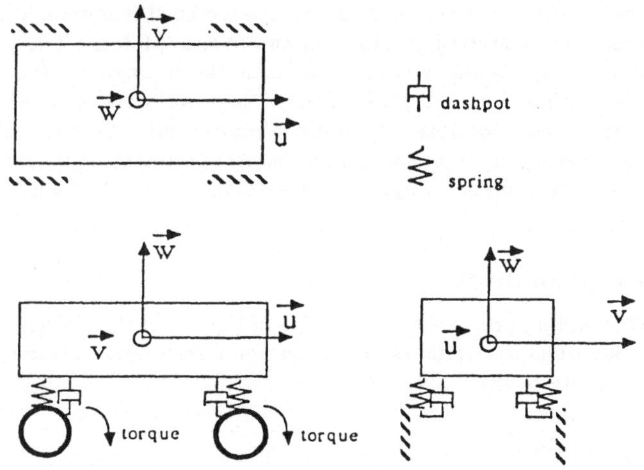

Figure 4: Model of a car

init

{initialization of parameters for n − 1 and n − 2 respectively}

$x1$	=	0.78541, 0.78541
$x2$	=	0.78541, 0.78541
$y1$	=	0.78541, 0.78541
$y2$	=	0.78541, 0.78541
$teta1$	=	0.78541, 0.78541
$teta2$	=	0.78541, 0.78541

****Output data produced by the computer****

list of equations

−	$ddt2(teta1)/6$	−	$holo0 * cos(teta1)/2$	−	$holo1 * sin(teta1)/2$		
		−	$holo2 * cos(teta1)$	−	$holo3 * sin(teta1)$		#
−	$ddt2(teta2)/6$	−	$holo2 * cos(teta2)/2$	−	$holo3 * sin(teta2)$		#
−	$ddt2(x1)$	+	$holo0$				#
−	$ddt2(x2)$	+	$holo2$				#
−	$ddt2(y1)$	+	$holo1$	−	9.8		#
−	$ddt2(y2)$	+	$holo3$	−	9.8		#
	$x1$	−	$sin(teta1)/2$				#
	$y1$	+	$cos(teta1)/2$				#
	$x2$	−	$sin(teta1)$	−	$sin(teta2)/2$		#
	$y2$	+	$cos(teta1)$	+	$cos(teta2)/2$		#

A car

We describe now a model of a car that we have chosen because of its interest in animation and of its mechanical complexity.

The model presented on figure 4 is a right parallelepiped on four couple spring-absorbers and wheels: their effects will be taken into account in the writing of the work. If l_0 is the rest length of the spring and l its current length, the work of deformation of the spring-absorber system is: $+\frac{1}{2}\cdot k\cdot(l-l_0)^2+\frac{1}{2}\cdot\nu\cdot(\dot{l})^2$ where k and ν are respectively the spring and the absorber constants.

The system is animated by exerting a torque on each wheel(this car is a "four wheel drive"!) mimicing the engine. The guiding is assumed to be produced by a torque too, and regulated by a spring-absorber system. The wheels are rolling without sliding on the ground. Such a link can be modelled as: let (O, x, y) be a referential and let us consider a wheel of radius r rolling without sliding on the Ox axis. The contact condition is written as $y_c = r$ (where c is the center of the wheel) and the associated nonholonomic constraint as $r \cdot \dot{\theta} + \dot{x} = 0$. One other introduced condition is the relation between the orientation of the two guiding wheels(the front wheels), in order to assume that they roll on concentric circles(that is compatible with the conditions of rolling without sliding and with the reality).

As we said, this model is of great interest, not only because of the kind of animation we can plan, but also in the mechanical scope where we have to face non-coarse problems.
After this short survey of the problems we may have to deal with, when using mechanical laws to animate our models, let us describe the stages of modelling. We first define a geometric model of the multibody system(with positions and dimensions); if the density of one solid(or its mass) is given, the data are used to compute the inertia center and the inertia matrix J of this solid, then by choice of a parameter system(three translational and three rotational degrees of freedom for one solid) the calculation of the kinetic energy becomes very simple to achieve, by using the formula: $C = \frac{1}{2} \cdot m \cdot \vec{V}^2 + \frac{1}{2} \cdot {}^t\vec{\Omega} \cdot J \cdot \vec{\Omega}$
where $\vec{V}$ is the speed vector of the inertia center of the solid and $\vec{\Omega}$ the instantaneous rotational vector of the solid. We can now take the links into account and derive binding equations from the binding models. The calculation of work is directly linked to the applied forces(or torques) and to the parameters. From all these equations can the symbolical equations of motion be written.

5 Conclusion

An animation system draft incorporating the simultaneous cooperation of different animation controls as key framing, kinematics and dynamics laws in a coherent way has been presented. Such an animation system provides a powerful tool to easily describe complex and realistic motions. The mechanical model was chosen in order to animate general multibody systems including open and closed chains. Not only does it allow the specification of behaviour functions as forces, torques, damping and springiness, but also it might welcome keyframed paths, kinematic trajectories and energy constraints. Besides, it will help design complex mechanical systems which require to specify the initial values of all the parameters. With our mechanical model this initialization which may be an impossible task for the animator, especially for multiple closed loops, can be solved from both joint constraints and limited number of parameter values which are sufficient to define for instance locations and/or orientations of some system parts. The mechanical equations can give an equilibrium state of the system or detect any incoherency. Future developments as event handler will provide the user goal directed animation.

Acknowledgements

This research was partially supported by NATO Grants n^0 0436/87, and partially conducted under MECANIM project jointly defined with SESA(Rennes) and SOGITEC(Rennes) and supported by the "Ministère de l'Industrie" and by the "Conseil Régional de Bretagne".

References

[1] W.W. Armstrong and M.W. Green. The dynamics of articulated rigid bodies for purposes of animation. *The Visual Computer*, 1(4):231–240, December 1985.

[2] B. Arnaldi and T. Priol. *Synthèse d'image par lancer de rayon, subdivision spatiale, algorithmes et architecture.* Technical Report, Université de Rennes I, Juin 1986.

[3] B. Arnaldi, T. Priol, and K. Bouatouch. A new space subdivision method for ray tracing csg modelled scenes. *The Visual Computer*, 3(2):98–108, August 1987.

[4] N.I. Badler and al. Multi-dimensional input techniques and articulated figure positionating by multiple constraints. Workshop on Interactive 3D Graphics. Chapel Hill, North Carolina, October 1986.

[5] D . Badouel. *Opérations Booléennes sur les Solides.* Technical Report, Université de RENNES 1, June 1987.

[6] Y. Bamberger. *Mécanique de l'ingénieur 1: systèmes de corps rigides.* Volume 1, Hermann, 293 rue Lecourbe 75015 Paris, 1981.

[7] K. Bouatouch, B. Arnaldi, and T. Priol. Lgrc: un langage pour la synthèse d'images par lancer de rayons. *T S I*, 6:475–489, November 1986.

[8] K. Bouatouch, M.O Madani, T. Priol, and B. Arnaldi. A new algorithm of space tracing using a csg model. In *EUROGRAPHICS'87 Conference Proceeding*, pages 65–78, Centre for Mathematics and Computer Science, August 1987.

[9] R.L. Cook and K.E. Torrance. A reflectance model for computer graphics. *ACM transactions on graphics*, 1(1):7–24, January 1982.

[10] G. Dumont. *Application de la mécanique des systèmes de corps rigides à l'animation d'images de synthèse.* Technical Report, Ecole Nationale des Ponts et Chaussées et Université de PARIS 6, PARIS, June 1987.

[11] A. Fournier and W.T. Reeves. A simple model of ocean waves. *Computer Graphics (Siggraph Proc. '86)*, 20(4):75, August 1986.

[12] P. Germain. *Mécanique.* Volume 1, Ecole Polytechnique, 91128 Palaiseau Cedex, 1986.

[13] J. Gomez. Twixt: a 3-d animation system. *Computer and Graphics*, 9(3):291–298, 1985.

[14] C.F. Hoffmann and J.E. Hopcroft. Simulation of physical systems from geometric models. In *IEEE Journal of Robotics and Automation*, pages 194–206, IEEE, June 1987.

[15] P.M. Isaacs and M.F. Cohen. Controlling dynamic simulation with kinematic constraints, behavior functions and inverse dynamics. *Computer Graphics (Siggraph Proc. '87)*, 21(4):215–224, July 1987.

[16] J.F. Kleifinger. *Modélisation dynamique de robots à chaîne cinématique simple, arborescente ou fermée, en vue de leur commande.* PhD thesis, ENSM, Université de Nantes, Mai 1986.

[17] N. Magnenat-Thalmann and D. Thalmann. The use of high level 3-d graphical types in the mira animation system. *IEEE Computer Graphics and Applications*, 3(9):9–16, 1983.

[18] N. Orlandea. *Development and Application of Node-Analogous Sparsity-Oriented Methods for Simulation of Mechanical Dynamic System.* PhD thesis, University of Michigan, 1973.

[19] B.T. Phong. Illumination model for computer generated images. *Communications of the ACM*, 18:311–317, June 1975.

[20] X. Pueyo and D. Tost. *A survey of Computer Animation.* Technical Report DMI01-87, DMI of ETSEIB, Poly. Univ. of Barcelona, May 1987.

[21] W.T. Reeves. Particle systems. a technique for modelling a class of fuzzy objects. *Computer Graphics (Siggraph Proc. '83)*, 17(3):359–376, July 1983.

[22] A.A. Requicha. Representation for rigid solids : theory, methods, and systems. *ACM Computing Surveys*, 12(4):437–464, December 1980.

[23] W.O. Schielen. Computer generation of equations of motion. In E.J. Haug, editor, *Computer Aided Analysis and Optimisation of Mechanical System Dynamics*, pages 183–215, Springer-Verlag, 1984.

[24] S.N. Steketee and N.I. Badler. Parametric keyframe interpolation incorporating kinetic adjustement and phrasing control. *Computer Graphics (Siggraph proc. '85)*, 19(3), July 1985.

[25] R.B Tilove and A.A.G Requicha. Closure of boolean operations on geometric entities. *Computer Aided Design*, 12(5):219–220, September 1980.

[26] T. Whitted. An improved illumination model for shaded display. *Communications of the ACM*, 23:343–349, June 1980.

[27] J. Wilhems and B. Barsky. Using dynamic analysis to animate articulated bodies such as humans and robots. pages 197–204, Graphics interface'85, May 1985.

[28] A. Witkin, K. Fleischer, and A. Barr. Energy constraints on parameterized models. *Computer Graphics (Siggraph Proc. '87)*, 21(4):225–232, July 1987.

[29] J. Wittenburg. *Dynamics of Systems of Rigid Bodies.* Teubner, Stuttgart, 1977.

[30] D. Zeltzer. Motor control techniques for figure animation. *IEEE Computer Graphics and Applications*, 2(9):53–59, November 1982.

[31] D. Zeltzer. Towards an integrated view of 3d computer animation. *The Visual Computer*, 1(4):249–259, December 1985.

3-D Facial Animation Using Image Samples

J. F. S. Yau and N. D. Duffy (UK)

ABSTRACT

Most established methods using three dimensional (3-D) computer graphics for human facial animation fall short of achieving truly realistic images, due to the lack of sufficient surface detail for the eyes, mouth and skin/hair textures. A new method is presented here, combining 3-D computer graphics with texture mapping techniques to synthesise and animate facial images which are convincing enough to be comparable with real video images. Animation is achieved by manipulation of a 3-D model of the subject's face in conjunction with a set of pre-stored digitised image samples.

KEYWORDS: Computer graphics, facial animation, texture mapping, image synthesis, rendering, illumination, keyframe animation.

1. Introduction

Much progress has been made in the field of computer animation, but the task of animating the human face has always remained a major challenge. In using computer graphics to achieve realistic facial animation, the two major goals that have to be satisfied are that of achieving sufficient static and dynamic realism. By static realism we mean that a synthesised image of a motionless face looks realistic from any view-point. Dynamic realism concerns accurate modelling of head, eye and mouth movements and other relevant motions associated with changes in facial expression.

We present in this paper a new approach to facial animation capable of achieving a high degree of both static and dynamic realism. A hybrid technique is adopted, combining a 3-D shaded polygon facet representation of the face with texture mapped digitised image samples selected from a pre-stored library. Texture mapping is a relatively efficient way to create the appearance of complex surface detail without having to go through the tedium of modelling and rendering every 3-D detail of a surface [6],[7],[8],[9]. The technique essentially involves the projection of some pattern or image stored as a flat two dimensional picture onto the surface of a three dimensional object. The use of real image samples, as derived from captured video pictures of the subject, enables synthesis of highly realistic images since the subject's skin, hair and facial feature textures are accurately reproduced.

2. Background

Attempts to classify facial expression were made by [1],[2],[3]. The main outcome of such work in classification of facial dynamics was the development of The Facial Action Coding System (FACS) by Ekman [2]. This was a notation based system which described about fifty independent facial action units. These action units were closely related to the muscle structure which were responsible for causing changes in facial expression. Many such action units are required to encode even the simplest of facial expressions. In fact, from the set of fifty action units, there are as many as seven thousand different muscle combinations, making expression analysis a non-trivial task. Even so, the FACS system is still incomplete. The system gives no indication of how the surface of the face will distort due to flesh deformation over the bone structure caused by activation of facial action units.

Early work on facial dynamics used 3-D wire-frame models drawn on vector graphics terminals. Changes in facial expression were achieved by either stretching or contracting appropriate areas of the wire-frame net representing the facial surface. Although such display techniques served to illustrate facial animation dynamics, they were incapable of being statically realistic, due to the fact that image composition comprised of line segments only. The next stage in the move towards static realism was the application of shading, so that the face appeared as an actual surface rather than a mesh of line segments. This approach was adopted by Parke [4,5], who applied continuous shading to a polygon model derived from measurements from a real person's face. Features such as eye-balls, eye-brows, mouth and lips were all modelled using appropriately coloured polygon facets and animated by applying rotation & translational 3-D transformations. The resultant images offered a significant improvement in static realism due to the fact that one was now seeing a facial surface, with basic eye & mouth features, being animated within a simulated light source environment.

Although Parke's shaded polygon model approach proved to be a major step forward towards the goal of achieving computer generated 3-D facial animation, its limitations were also clear. Synthesised images could never hope to approach the point where they resemble camera images of a real person. This is due to the fact that the only data pertaining to the subject modelled upon is 3-D coordinate data describing his or her face, there is absence of any skin or hair texture information. As a consequence of lack of this information, synthesised faces will always adopt a cartoon-like appearance. A further difficulty is that a relatively large number of polygon facets are required for adequate representation of features such as the eye-lashes, eye-balls or teeth.

3. Applications

The design of any new system or scheme is almost invariably dictated by its targetted application, the facial animation method presented in this paper is no exception. Its intended application is for use within a model-based image coding scheme, where *a priori* knowledge is utilised to achieve extremely low bit-rate transmission of head & shoulder video phone images. The scheme at the transmitter end of the communications channel involves analysis of video pictures of the subject at frame rate. Cues concerning head motion, eye and mouth shape are derived and sent down the channel. Since there is absence of any image data, very little bandwidth is needed to convey the handful of motion cues at frame rate.

At the receiver end, images are synthesised at frame rate by applying the received motion cues to data from a stored data-base of the subject. The output stage of this image coding scheme is therefore that of a computer generated head that closely follows the eye, mouth and global head dynamics of the original real video sequence as analysed at the transmitter end of the channel. Clearly the success of the model-based image coding scheme hinges on two critical factors, the frame by frame analysis for motion cues and secondly, the acceptability of the synthetically generated images at the receiver end.

Although this paper presents one method of generating the synthetic facial images, there are two different strategies that may be pursued when animating the face . The first is specifically intended for the model-based image coding application. This strategy involves attempting to duplicate a real video animation sequence frame by frame, so that the synthetic sequence's dynamics follows that of the original, with perfect lip synchronisation to the original audio track. Whilst the latter approach uses very little inter-frame correspondence, the contrary holds for the second animation strategy, where there is extensive use of parametric keyframe animation. Here the animation sequence is assembled by concatenating smaller keyframed animated sequences in accordance to some story-board plan. Both approaches will be explained in more detail in the 'facial animation' section of this paper.

4. Obtaining the initial data

The information required for the image synthesis process consists of data relating to the structure of the face and a single frontal facial image together with a number of sub-images derived from a code-book of alternative mouth shapes and eye orientations.

The facial image information was obtained from capturing suitable frames from a video tape sequence of the subject. Captured images were required to be as diffusely illuminated as possible, so as not to contend with the lighting model in the rendering stage of the image synthesis. The use of two spot lamps on either side of the subject's face gave sufficiently uniform illumination when recording the video sequence. Once a suitable full face image was chosen, the code-book of sub-pictures was constructed by accumulating mouth and eye pictures taken from a video sequence of the subject going through the motions of speech.

A laser light striping technique was used to obtain the 3-D coordinates of the subject's face. Light from a low powered helium-neon laser is dispersed by a cylindrical lens to a thin line which falls horizontally across the subject's face. A video camera is mounted at an oblique angle relative to the plane of the laser light. The image seen by the camera is that of the laser line following the contour of the face. This image is captured and processed to yield a set of 3-D coordinates. Further contours are obtained by stepping the laser line down the subject's face by means of deflection from a galvanometer mounted mirror. A complete 3-D depth map of the face is built up by processing 128 line positions.

Use of laser light always calls for careful consideration of safety aspects. In the described 3-D data capture set-up, the apparatus used was a Class II 0.5 mW HeNe laser. The beam was dispersed to a line of 800mm x 2mm (giving a radiant exposure of 0.312 Wm^{-2}) before being cast upon the subject's face. Assuming a pupil diameter of 7mm and that the eye region accounts for 2cm of the head scan distance, the total eye exposure time for a scan time of five seconds is 400mS. BS4803 table 3, part 3, pp11 defines a maximum permissible exposure as $MPE_{eye}=18t^{-0.25}Wm^{-2}=22.6Wm^{-2}$. In any case, even exposure to the direct non-dispersed beam for up to 0.25S (longer than blink reflex time) is not considered hazardous.

5. Data Reduction

The depth map data obtained from the laser scan of the subject's face contains much redundant information, particularly for those areas of the face which do not cover complex surface features. In order to reduce the amount of information to manageable proportions for subsequent processing, a 3-D polygon model of the facial surface is created by using a triangulation algorithm [10]. The algorithm creates large triangles for areas of low surface detail and smaller ones for more complex areas. In practice, around 400 polygon facets were sufficient to represent the surface of the face. The data reduction converts the raw data into a compact data structure more suitable for real-time processing and image synthesis. Each polygon is defined by a set of edges, each edge refers to two cartesian vertices for its definition. The topology of the data structure is such that each edge or vertice is defined only once, even though they may be referred to many times. This storage structure plays a key role in both the animation and image synthesis of the reconstructed image.

6. Image Synthesis

The resultant output image, for a given 3-D polygon model, is dependent upon an input parameter file and also the texture map image. The latter is a full face image which is to be projected over the 3-D facial surface during the rendering process, whilst the former holds a set of parameters determining the view-point, target-point, head position & orientation, lighting parameters, jaw movement data and also the clipping plane definitions.

Much of processing required for the image synthesis is that of the path followed for conventional shaded 3-D computer graphics. The initial 3-D polygon model is specified in absolute or world coordinates. Geometric transformations are performed on the vertices of the polygon model in order to obtain the desired orientation, head and jaw positions. This is followed by a transformation from the world to the eye coordinate system, where each vertex point is specified in a new coordinate system that is centred around the selected view-point. The polygon model is clipped against the specified view-port before hidden surface removal is performed on the polygon facets. Visible parts of the polygons undergo a final perspective transformation before they are rendered with smooth shading and texture in screen space. In order to facilitate the texture mapping process, there are a number of extensions that need to be incorporated.

Since it is required that the image used for the texture mapping be effectively pasted onto the facial surface, there has to be some form of mapping function that allows the visible parts of the polygon facets to address the 2-D space of the texture map image. It is crucial that the texture map image is always correctly aligned for all synthesised image frames, i.e. the eyes, nose and mouth image components are texture mapped to the correct locations on the 3-D facial surface with no mis-alignment or scaling error. A method that satisfies the latter criteria to a good approximation is the technique where the texture map image is orthographically projected onto a correctly scaled and positioned 3-D facial surface polygon model. Using such a method, the 2-D texture map image is in a plane parallel to that of the facial surface. Assuming correct positional and scaling alignment of the polygon model over the texture map image, each (x,y,z) point lying on the polygon surface addresses the texture map image pixel element I(x,y) (see fig.1). This pixel element is used as an additional coefficient when the shading for the final synthesised image is calculated.

The procedure for mapping visible polygon coordinates to the correct 2-D texture map image space as described so far only works if the polygon model of the face is always in correct alignment with the texture map image. Consequently, if the polygon model's orientation or position were changed, the correct registration between the polygon coordinates and the texture map image space would be lost. To overcome this problem, the concept of static and dynamic polygon models was introduced.

In order to ensure that the texture mapping process is invariant to 3-D animation of the facial polygon model, we hold a copy of the polygon model data structure which is correctly aligned with respect to the texture map image, this data structure is termed the static model. A second copy of the facial polygon data structure is set up, termed the dynamic polygon model. It is the latter data structure that undergoes all the 3-D and perspective transformations required for the generation of the final output image. Throughout the whole processing chain followed in achieving the final output image, constant toplogy is always maintained between the static and dynamic polygon model data structures. By this we mean that there is always a one to one mapping of vertices and polygon edges between the two data structures. The philosophy behind this arrangement is that instead of a single facial polygon model with a mapping function to the texture map image, a scheme that does not permit 3-D animation of the face, we have a scheme where the dynamic model maps to the texture map image indirectly through the static model. This technique allows 3-D animation of the face without effecting the texture mapping process. No matter what the orientation or position of the dynamic model, the texture mapping is dictated by the relationship between the static model and the texture map image space.

Fig. 6 shows the general outline of the image synthesis scheme. The dynamic model, once transformed into screen space coordinates, is subjected to a Watkins type scan line hidden surface removal algorithm [13][14]. For each raster scan line of the screen, the Watkins algorithm scan converts any polygons that may possibly appear within that scan line. The subsequent visible line segments are then quantised into pixels and shaded according to the simulated light source and texture map image. In order to maintain the one to one mapping between the static and dynamic models right down to the pixel coordinate level, the polygon scan conversions have to be performed on the static model as well, this is termed slave scan conversion.

The remaining problem is to break the visible line segments for each scan line into pixels and decide the intensity of each one. The intensity of each pixel is determined by combining the coefficient obtained from an illumination model with the coefficient derived from the texture mapping. For the illumination model, Phong shading [11] was implemented. This involves determining the vector normals to the dynamic 3-D model at the end-points of each visible segment. The illumination coefficients along a visible segment are obtained by applying the lighting model at each pixel position, using a vector normal interpolated between those at the segment end-points. For each visible segment, the texture mapping coefficients are obtained by traversing along the corresponding static line segment and using the XY coordinates to address the texture map image pixel elements.

Depending on the orientation of a polygon facet with respect to the view-point, the texture map image may be over-sampled or under-sampled when the polygon is rendered, leading to inevitable aliasing effects. If a visible line segment is longer than its corresponding static model line segment the texture map image gets over-sampled, since as the visible segment is traversed, duplicate mapping coefficients are encountered due to the shorter length of the static model line segment. This effectively results in a stretching of texture map image in the final output image. If however the visible segment is shorter than its static segment, under-sampling of the texture map image occurs and the process becomes prone to aliasing effects. The latter can cause degradation in image fidelity but its effect when mapping facial images is only slight. This is due to the fact that images of people's faces tend to have a relatively low spatial frequency content.

7. Facial Animation

Implementation of the facial animation comprises of two components, 3-D manipulation of the facial polygon model and secondly, selection of the image samples that are to be used. By 3-D manipulation we mean the performance of 3-D geometric transformations required to set the face to the desired orientation and position in 3-D space. In addition, any necessary distortions to the polygon surface are performed. In the authors' present implementation, the only such distortions are the flexing of the jaw area of the face in order to simulate jaw movement. It is anticipated however, that more basic facial surface distortions are required if extreme expressions such as a grin or a frown are to be handled realistically.

The selection of image samples for every facial image generated in the frame sequence is particularly important for correct animation of the eyes and mouth. If the same image data were texture mapped onto the 3-D polygon model of the face for every frame the result would be a moving head, but with complete absence of any eye or mouth dynamics. As mentioned previously, there are two different animation strategies, these apply to both the 3-D manipulation and texture map selection components. In the case where the model-based image coding application is intended, the 3-D orientation parameter set and image sample selection are both explicitly derived from analysis of each frame of the original video. In the case where general story-board animation is desired, the 3-D transformations are keyframed whilst the image samples are taken from pre-stored sequences of discrete facial actions such as eye blinks and shifts, or mouth utterances.

The keyframing used to implement story-board animation interpolates between the parameter sets defining the end-point frames in order to generate intermediate frames. This technique is much more efficient than conventional keyframing, where interpolation is performed between the actual images, since generating parameter sets for intermediate frames involves operations on a mere handful of data. The parameter set of the authors' current implementation of the software comprises of the following:

n	ID number
alpha	Field of view angle
D	Hither clipping plane position
F	Yonder clipping plane position
vx,vy,vz	Viewing position
tx,ty,tz	Target position
amb	Proportion of ambient light
lum	Intensity of simulated light source
Kd	Constant in lighting model equation
lx,ly,lz	Light source position in screen coordinates
y1,z1,y2,z2	Jaw region definition
ry,rz	Jaw axis of rotation
ang	Jaw rotation angle
mx,my,mz	Head global move
theta,psi,phi	Head orientation

3-D manipulation of the face for a story-board animation sequence is therefore achieved by specifying particular parameter sets along the time axis and allowing keyframing to account for intermediate frames. The remaining task is to choose the image sample data that is to be texture mapped for each generated image. The following description of how the image sample data is assembled holds true for both facial animation strategies. In the present implementation of the animation system, the image samples are stored in the form of eye and mouth sub-picture files. In addition to the parameter set, a texture map image is required for each synthesised frame. This texture map image is assembled by overlaying the desired eye and mouth sub-pictures over a complete full face image of the subject (to be known as the base picture).

Each sub-picture has three parameters written into its file header. The first is an identification code, this is followed by two integers giving the xy coordinates of a fixed reference point within the image. The latter parameters are used in conjunction with a second xy coordinate pair from the full face base picture in order to obtain the position at which the sub-picture is to be overlayed. There are several xy coordinate pairs held within the base picture header file, the actual one chosen for use in the overlaying of a particular sub-picture depends on the sub-picture's identification code. This scheme ensures correct location of sub-picture groups, e.g. left eye, right eye, mouth etc.

When overlaying the sub-pictures over the full face base picture, there will inevitably be discontinuities over the sub-picture boundaries. In order to eliminate this, a surrounding margin was set up around each sub-picture and a cross-fading function implemented along this margin. Hence when one traverses across this margin, the pixels cross-fade from the sub-picture to the base picture. It was found that a margin of only 6 pixels width was sufficient to eliminate any boundary discontinuities.

Once the resultant mapping image has been constructed from the base picture and the selected sub-pictures, it is ready to be mapped onto the facial surface to form the output image. A further measure was undertaken in order to improve the realism of the mouth animation. This involved rotating the lower part of the facial surface around a fixed axis to simulate jaw motion. The amount of jaw rotation imparted was made to be dependent upon the mouth shape used to generate the image. For each mouth sub-picture there is an additional parameter written into the header file indicating the amount of jaw rotation associated with that particular mouth shape. Note that that jaw area rotation of the 3-D facial surface is performed prior to the texture mapping, so that the full face image is projected onto the revised facial surface.

8. Results

Figures 1-5 illustrate typical results obtained from using the described techniques. Fig. 1 shows a projection of the 3-D static polygon model over the texture map image. Results showing typical synthesised images with variations in lighting, sub-picture entry and viewing parameter changes are illustrated in figures 2-5. Processing was performed by a Perkin Elmer 3230 and the resultant images were displayed using a Gresham Lion S214 framestore. Typical processing times are 3-4 mins for a Phong shaded, texture mapped 256 x 256 24-bit RGB colour image. The images shown were generated without any pre-filtering in the texture mapping process or anti-aliasing. With real-time applications in mind, the chosen working screen resolution was considered to offer a good compromise between image quality and processing requirements.

The model-based image coding application demands that facial images be synthesised at frame rate, i.e. 25 times per second. The lower the working screen resolution, the more feasible real-time operation becomes. It was found that even with resolution as low as 256 x 256, aliasing was minimal and was restricted to some edges around the nose and eyes. Even the effect of temporal aliasing was slight, with evidence of some shimmering at the edges where aliasing was present. The reason that good results are still obtained when texture mapping at such resolutions can be attributed to the fact that facial images generally do not have a high spatial frequency content. In any case, for the image coding application it is more important that the facial dynamics are accurately represented. As long as the images are adequate and free of excessive aliasing the quality of individual frames in the pixel scale is not of paramount importance.

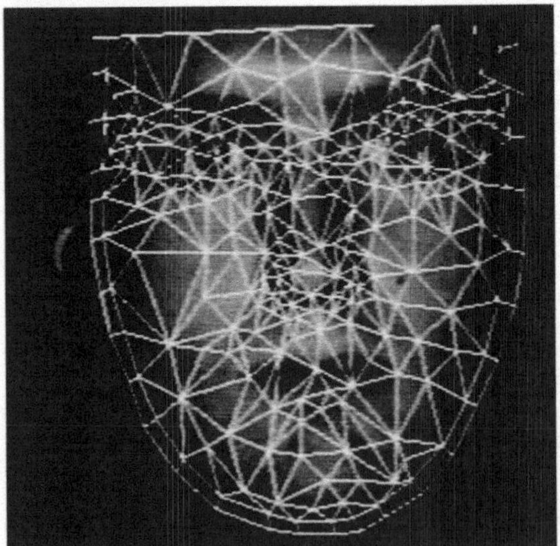

Fig. 1 3-D Static Polygon Model Projection

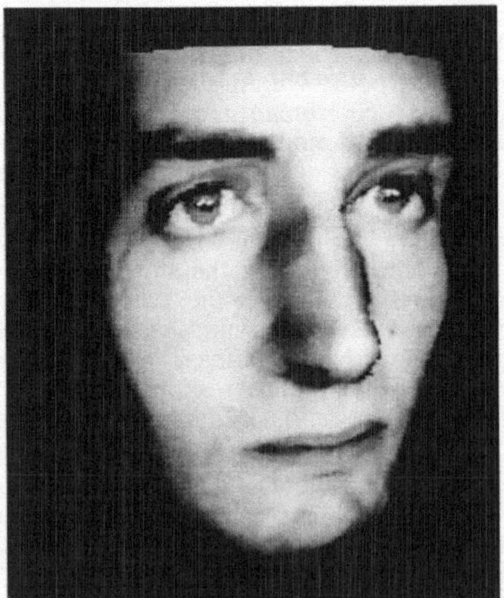

Fig. 2 Texture Mapped View

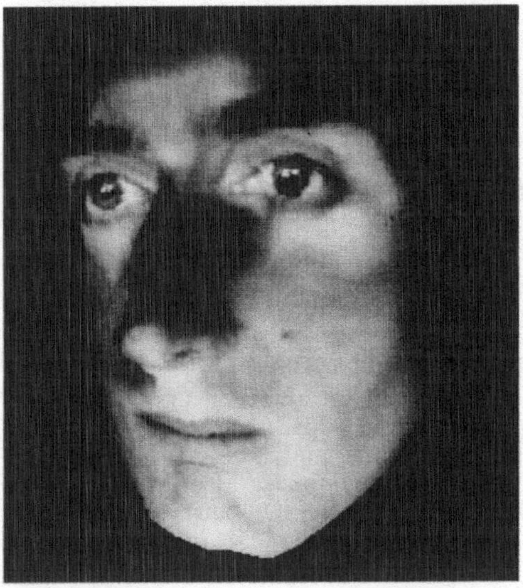

Fig. 3 Light Source Position Change

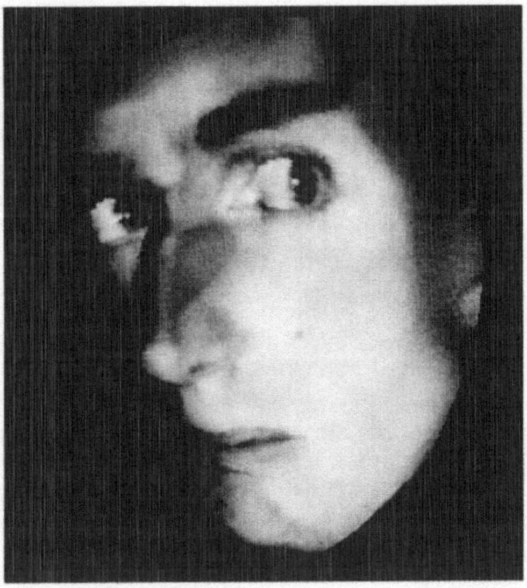

Fig. 4 Eye Sub-picture Entry

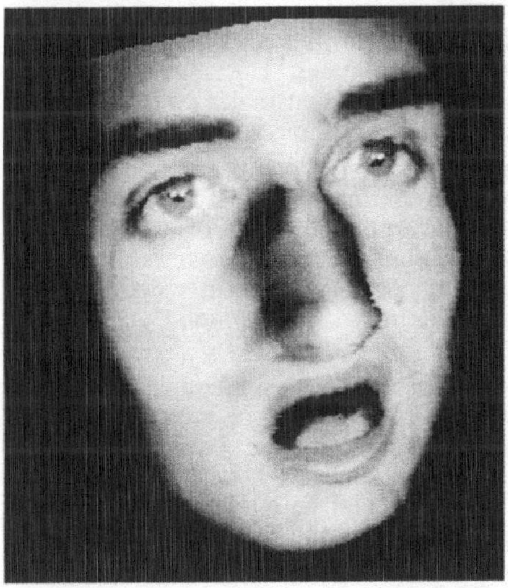

◁ Figure 5 Mouth Sub-picture Entry

Figure 6 Image Synthesis Process Structure

▽

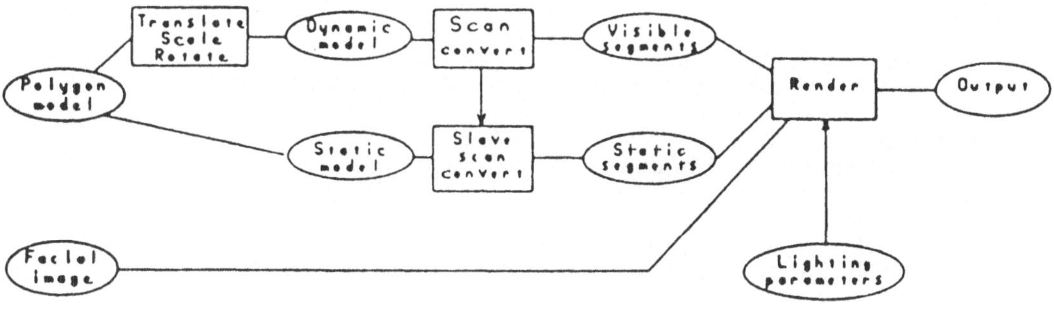

9. Conclusions

The combination of texture mapping photographic images and manipulation of a 3-D model of the subject's face proved to be a very effective method of generating synthesised facial animation of a real person. The technique of using image samples in the image synthesis can be compared with using sound sampling in the synthesis of natural instrument sounds. It is now fairly well established that the best way to synthesise a complex sound such as that of a concert piano is to use real piano sound samples as building blocks for the sound synthesis. The task of synthesising a piano voice from first principles, i.e. from fourier analysis and synthesis, is impractical for real-time processing due to the sheer complexity of the problem. The same philosophy holds for facial image synthesis. There is no need to model every little surface detail on a person's face in terms of polygons and lighting models if one can simply by-pass the task by using image samples.

When making comparisons between the texture mapping approach and others, it is important to note how the different approaches fare within a particular application. The texture mapping approach was intended for use within the model-based image coding scheme, several features make it particularly suitable for this application. Since less than 500 polygons are needed to represent the facial surface, real-time animation prospects are excellent. Within the front-end of the image coding application, it is intended that the frame by frame analysis of the real video be such that the eyes and mouth are located within the image and referenced into a pre-stored code-book of sub-pictures. If such a code-book is also held at the receiver end of the communications channel, the sub-picture entries themselves can be utilised as texture map components, hence keeping much of the processing within the image domain. If the Parke or Waters approach were adopted one would have to analyse each video frame, derive and convey the necessary muscle states and then at the receiver, reconstruct the face from the muscle states. The stumbling block lies mainly within the frame analysis end, deriving muscle states that make up a particular facial expression from a single 2-D video image is a somewhat arduous task.

However if one were to consider the more general case of storyboard animation where only synthesis is involved, then the FACS or muscle state approach comes more into play. The quantification of facial actions and expressions make the planning of an animated sequence a relatively easy task. Difficulties still arise if the animated sequence is to be lip-synced to real speech. Such problems can be overcome if one analyses real video pictures of mouth positions of someone performing the speech utterances, a technique taken from the model-based image coding application.

It was found that although the present system implementation was adequate for a face going through the motions of speech, further extensions would be necessary if facial expression is to be conveyed. For example, further sub-picture code book entries are required for the eye-brows and for the cheek distortions associated with expressions such as a smile or grin. In fact, it is envisaged that the optimal facial animation system would be one which uses the muscle state model to perform any underlying facial distortions pertaining to a particular expression, with the texture mapping approach used for the image rendering and animation of the eye and mouth facial features.

REFERENCES

[1] S.M.Platt, N.I. Badler "Animating Facial Expressions"
ACM Computer Graphics, Vol.15 No.3 August 1981.

[2] P. Ekman, W.V. Friesen "Facial Action Coding System"
Human Interaction Laboratory, Dept. of Psychiatry,
University of California Medical Centre, San Francisco.

[3] M. Rydfalk "Candide, a Parameterised Face"
PCS 1987 Stockholm, Sweden.

[4] F.I.Parke "Computer Generated Animation of Faces", Proceedings of the ACM, Vol.1 Aug 1972 pp.451-457.

[5] F.I.Parke "Parameterized Models for Facial Animation", IEEE Computer Graphics and Applications Vol 12 Nov 1982.

[6] P.S.Heckbert "Survey Of Texture Mapping", IEEE Computer Graphics and Applications November 1986 pp.56-67.

[7] J.F.Blinn, M.E.Newell "Texture and Reflection in Computer Generated Images", Communications of the ACM, Oct 1976 Vol 19 No.10 pp.542-547

[8] S.McEwan "Achieving Texture in Computer Graphics", presentation at Online Computer Graphics '86 Conference, London.

[9] J.Amanatides "Realism in Computer Graphics: A Survey", IEEE Computer Graphics and Applications, Jan 1987 pp.44-56.

[10] J.F.S.Yau "An Automatic Algorithm for Generating an Optimum Polygon Representation of a 3-D Surface" Research Memorandum RM/87/3 Heriot-Watt University.

[11] B.T.Phong "Illumination for Computer Generated Pictures" Communications of the ACM, June 1975 vol 8 No.6 pp.311-317

[12] G.P.Philip "Data Acquisition for the Talking Heads Project" Final Year Project Report 1986, Heriot-Watt University.

[13] D.F.Rogers Procedural Elements for Computer Graphics McGraw-Hill, New York 1985. pp.279-292

[14] W.M.Newman, R.F.Sproull Principles of Interactive Computer Graphics, 1st edition, McGraw-Hill 1973. pp.313-321, pp.537-552.

[15] J.D.Foley, A.V.Dam Fundamentals of Interactive Computer Graphics, Addison-Wesley 1982.

[16] Waters K. "A Muscle Model for Animating Three-Dimensional Facial Expression", Proc. SIGGRAPH '87

[17] Waters K. "'Laugh, I Almost Cried' - Expressive Three-Dimensional Facial Animation", presentation at Online Computer Graphics '86 Conference.

Human Prototyping

N. Magnenat-Thalmann, H. T. Minh, M. de Angelis, and D. Thalmann
(Switzerland and Canada)

Abstract

Creation of new synthetic actors is a tedious and painful task. The situation may be improved by introducing tools for the creation. Three approaches are discussed in this paper: modification and edition of an existing synthetic actor using local transformations; generation of new synthetic actors obtained by interpolation between two existing actors; creation of a synthetic actor by composition of different parts. Animation of synthetic actors is also discussed.

Keywords: synthetic actor, computer animation, local transformation, inbetweening

Introduction

The problem of constructing human characters from a geometrical point of view is mainly a problem of entering free-form shapes, as shown in Fig.1. Essentially, two general approaches have been used until now: digitizing methods and parametric-surface approaches. The first class of methods is time-consuming and suffers of a lack of creativity. The second class is convenient for creating human characters, as already shown by M.Nahas [1] except when these characters have to be like well-known personalities.

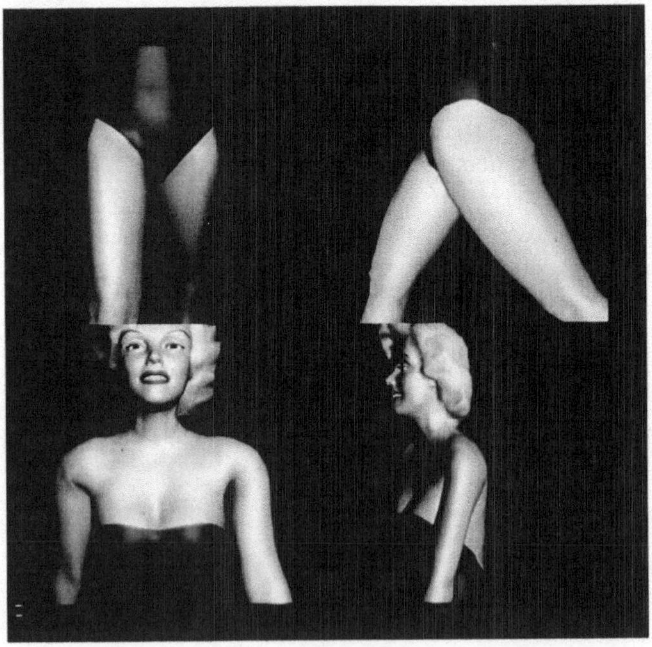

Fig.1 Human characters are essentially based on free-form surfaces

The most direct 3D digitizing technique [2] [3] is simply to enter the 3D coordinates using a 3D digitizer. Three types of such devices are now available: devices based on orthogonal magnetic fields, devices based on sound captors, devices based on laser light. Another common way of creating 3D objects is by 3D reconstruction from 2D information. Several techniques are possible: 3D reconstruction from 2D plans, 3D reconstruction from several photographs and lofting methods. For the two first methods, two or three orthogonal projections (plans) are entered and the computer is used to derive 3D coordinates. With photographs, the method works as follows:

1. Interesting points or grids are drawn onto the object
2. Several pictures are taken of the object.
3. An appropriate coordinates system is drawn for each picture
4. Each point is identified by a number. Points have to be identified in at least two pictures to compute the X-, Y- and Z-coordinates of each point
5. After placing the pictures on the digitizer, the user marks points that determine the boundaries of the pictures and those that identify the coordinate systems
6. For each point, two different positions are successively marked
7. Connections between the points are identified by numbers: this defines the strokes of points in wire-frame models and grids in facet-based models

Lofting methods are popular methods consisting of reconstructing an object from a set of serial cross sections, like tracing the contours from a topographic map. Several reconstruction methods are possible.

As described in other papers [4] [5], the creation of new synthetic actors is a tedious and painful task. For example, there are seven steps in the construction of a synthetic object by digitizing:

1. Planification and document search
2. Creation of plaster models
3. Selection of facets and vertices
4. Photo taking
5. Photo preparation
6. Digitizing
7. Object composition, generation and edition

The situation may be improved by introducing tools for the creation. Three approaches are possible and will be discussed in this paper:

1. Modification and edition of an existing synthetic actor using local transformations
2. Generation of new synthetic actors obtained by interpolation between two existing actors
3. creation of a synthetic actor by composition of different parts.

Local transformations of existing synthetic actors

A local transformation (LT) is a transformation applied to a part of a figure and not the whole as a global transformation. Generally a local transformation consists in two steps:

1. selection of a region to be affected
2. selection of the transformation and its parameters

We may distinguish 5 ways of selecting a facet-based region :

1. by indicating the vertex numbers
2. by selecting the vertices inside a box; which means the selection of a region bounded by six 3D vectors, which are threshold values.
3. by percentage and angle on a circle; in this case the region is defined by two anchor points that are used as extremas and two percentage bounds. It selects a region which is like a slice of pie or a slice of a virtual cylinder.
4. by color selection, e.g. all vertices with a given hue value
5. by a set-theory operation between two regions already selected using one the previous methods.

Four methods of transformations may be found:

1. **percentage to a vertex**
Each vertex is moved towards a reference vertex according to a specified percentage of the distance between both vertices.

2. **guided translation**
A translation is first calculated to move a vertex A towards a vertex B according to a given percentage; then this translation is applied on all vertices included in the selected region. For instance, a percentage of 0 does not affect any vertex; a percentage of 1 makes all vertices move according to the distance between A and B in the direction A towards B.

3. **scale according to a plane**
A scale is applied on the current figure. The amplitude of the scaling is proportional to the distance between a vertex and a specified plane.

4. **variable translation**
The transformation is applied according to a variation degree and a possibility of an acceleration/deceleration [6] factor on the selected region. The variation degree is defined relatively to the distance between any vertex and the center of the region. A variation of 0 indicates that all vertices will be affected in the same way. A variation of 1 indicates that the center vertex will be the more affected and the peripherical vertices of the area won't be affected at all.

Results of local transformations are shown in Fig.2.

Shape interpolation between human faces

Two solutions to this problem are possible:

1. Make facets and vertices in one object appear or disappear in order to obtain a good correspondence
2. Reorganize both figures by creating a new structure of facets common to both human faces.

Our approach is based on the second solution, because any inbetween human face should be animated as both original faces.

Grid generation

The technique consists of extracting profiles of a digitized object from selected planes and generating a grid which corresponds to the original object. The designer provides an original figure (human face or body part) and a series of N planes; each plane is given by a point and the normal to the plane.

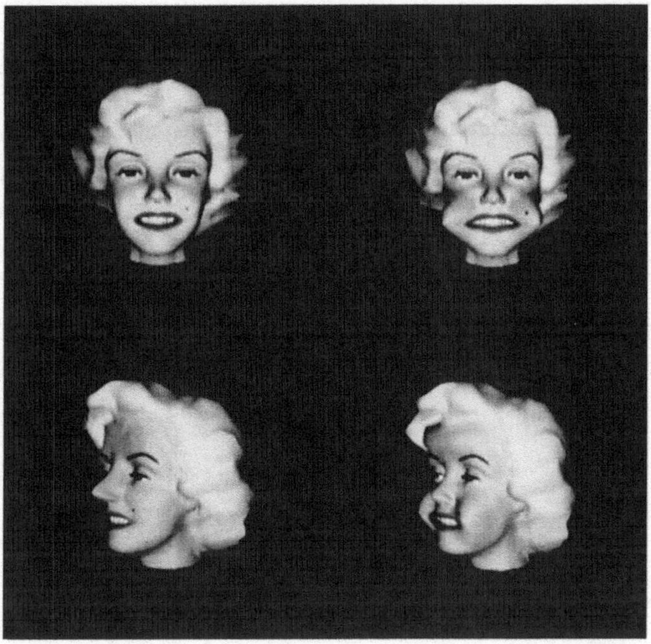

Fig.2 Local transformations to the actress face. Left-top: same inflation for both cheeks; right-top: hyper inflation of both cheeks; left-bottom: light inflation of the nose; right-bottom: inflation of the cheeks and the forehead

The designer also selects the number M of profiles. He/she also indicates a point A which is the approximate location of the starting point for each profile and a threshold value to suppress the connection between the initial and the final points for an open surface. The simplest algorithm could be to cut the object by a series of horizontal and vertical planes; however, this introduces ambiguities as shown in Fig.3. Basically, the method works in two steps:

1) profile determination by finding the intersection points between the human face and each plane and then creating object profiles by connecting the intersection points
2) grid generation.

Consider the face to be preprocessed and a series of planes; the larger the number of profiles, the more the grid will be accurate; however, there is a price to pay in memory. The types of element of the generated surface may be also selected; the two most popular surfaces are based on triangles and quadrilaterals. Note that the method works for surfaces with holes (e.g. eyes). The principle of the method is shown in Fig.4.

Inbetween calculation

For example, consider now two human faces F_1 and F_2 obtained using the grid generation algorithm. Because the topology of two different human faces may be very different, the dimensions of the grids will probably be different. There are two steps in the method:

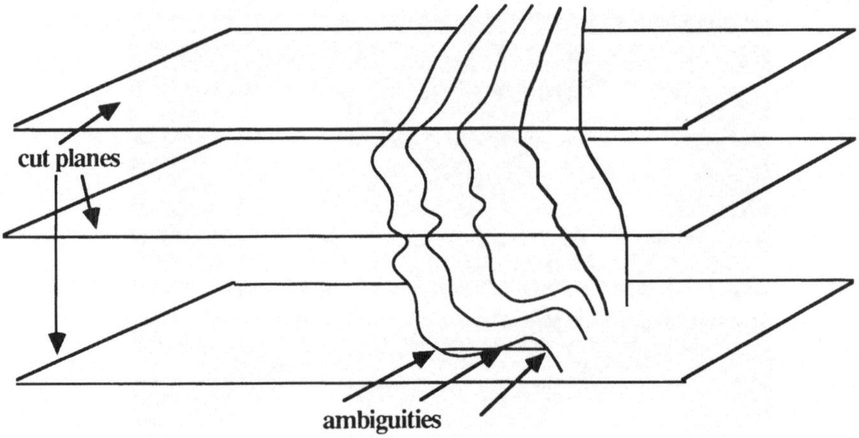

Fig.3. Ambiguities in selecting intersection points

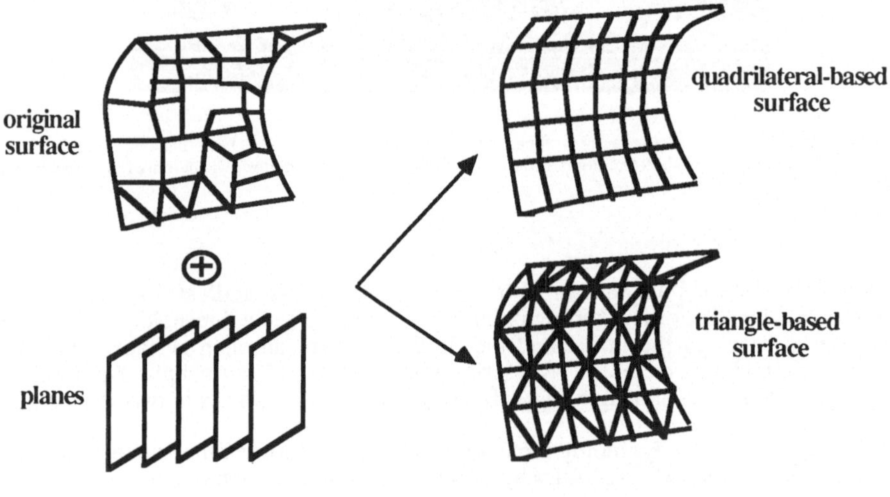

Fig.4 Principle of grid generation

Step 1: search for correspondences

Establish a correspondence between the profiles, then find the correspondence between the parallel sections using a similar method. Now, the correspondence between points is straightforward.

Step 2: Generation of the inbetween object

An inbetween human face is just obtained by linear interpolation. As our purpose is to animate inbetween human faces, it is essential to have a correspondence between similar physical regions. For this reason, we separate both human faces into 7 regions by cutting the 3D face using horizontal planes and applying the algorithm for each pair of regions. Regions must be selected so that their borders occur at the level of the mouth, and the eyes as shown in Fig.5.

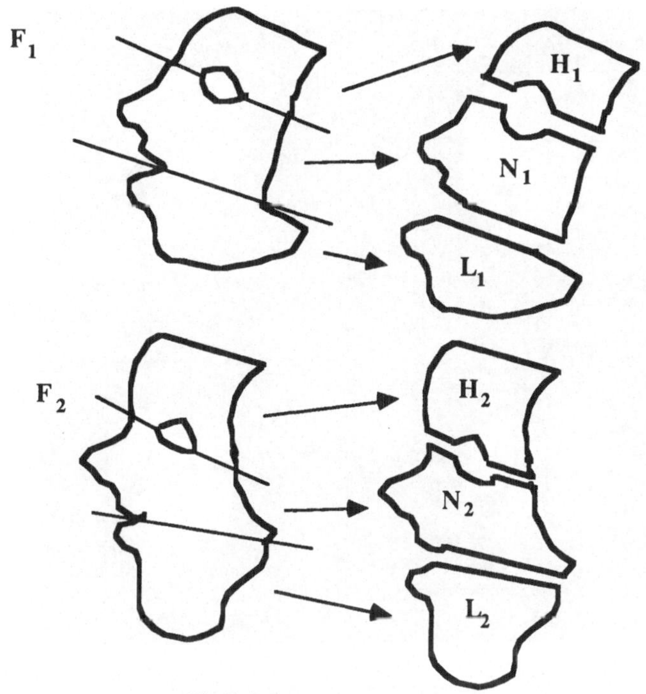

Fig.5. Selection of regions

Although, the algorithm processes surfaces with holes, it is easier for the animation process to consider a closed mouth and eyes. Therefore, it is easier if the extremities of the mouth and the eyes are on the borders of the regions.

Fig.6 and Fig.7 show examples of interpolation between two synthetic actors.

Composition

A synthetic actor may be also composed from primitive parts. Composition is an operation consisting of assembling two irregular figures in one unique coherent figure; for example, the torso may be joined to an arm. Generally both figures to be composed do not have the right position, orientation or size for a direct assembly. This implies the use of common elements to both figures to allow them to be assembled. These common elements are vertices located on the border of both figures, where they are to be joined; these vertices are called **brothers**. Because of the shading process, each vertex on the border of the first figure must have a brother on the border of the other figure; otherwise, shading discontinuities will appear.

The figures to be composed do not necessarily have the same border, especially when they have been separately digitized. To perform the composition operation, it is necessary to define a master figure and a slave figure and to indicate three non-linear vertices on both borders. The result of the composition of both figures is a new figure which has the following vertices:

1. all vertices of the master figure
2. all vertices of the slave figure except the vertices of the border, which are replaced by the brothers of the master figure.

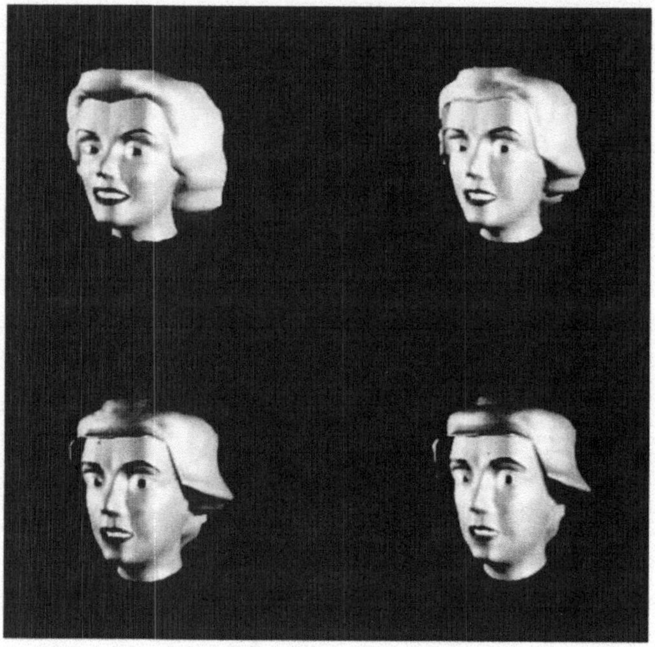

Fig.6 Interpolation between two synthetic actors: 0%, 20%, 40%, 50%

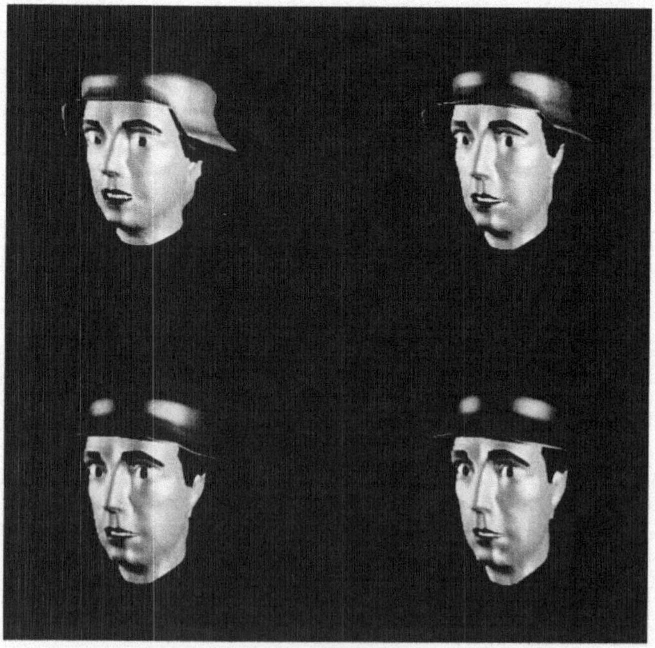

Fig.7 Interpolation between two synthetic actors: 60%, 80%, 90%, 100%

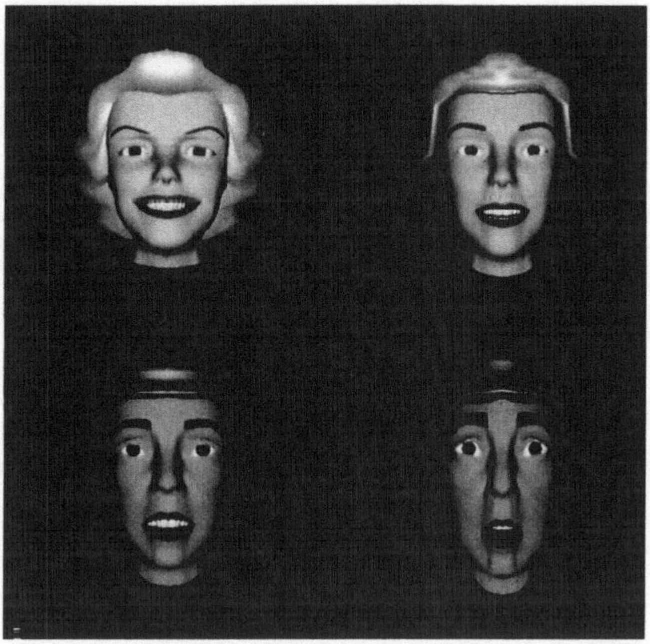

Fig.8 Animation of inbetween synthetic actors. Four views: 0%, 33%, 66% 100%
Expression interpolation: from smile to opened mouth and eyebrow motion

Translation, rotation and scale operations are performed to make the three non-linear points of both figures correspond. When both figures have been digitized very similarly: the composition is straightforward. When important differences exist between the digitized figures, it is necessary to rearrange vertices on the border.

The reverse operation of composition is called decomposition; this separates the composed figure into parts, even when vertices of the complete figure have been modified.

Animation techniques

The above techniques may be extended to the human animation process. For example, it is possible to transform one character into another one and also transform the animation at the same time. It implies an interpolation at several levels:

1. the shape level (already discussed)

2. the facial-parameter level

As already discussed in [5], expressions are based on facial parameters. For an inbetween actor A_I at the percentage λ between two actors A_1 and A_2, the basic parameter p_I is computed as:

$$p_I = p_1 + \lambda\,(p_2 - p_1)$$

3. the expression level

If the actor A_1 is smiling (expression E_1) and the actor A_2 is crying (expression E_2), any inbetween actor A_I at the percentage λ must have an inbetween expression E_I. The expression E_I is obtained as the collection $\{FP_{kI}\}$ where each FP_{kI} is calculated as the result of the corresponding AMA procedure using basic parameters p_{jI} obtained themselves as above by a linear interpolation:

$$p_{jI} = p_{j1} + \lambda\ (p_{j2} - p_{j1})$$

4. the script level

A unique script may be provided for an actor A_1 transformed into another actor A_2. In this case the action is performed on all inbetween actors. A more general and interesting case is when the actor A_1 plays a role according to a script S_1 and the actor A_2 plays another role according to the script S_2. An inbetween actor A_I should play a role according to an inbetween script S_I. This means that the expressions of the inbetween actors are calculated as inbetween expressions according to the current value of the percentage between actors.

Fig.8 shows a complete example.

Acknowledgements

The authors would like Ross Racine and Denis Rambaud for their collaboration. The research was supported by the Natural Sciences and Engineering Council of Canada, and the FCAR foundation (Government of Quebec).

References

[1] Nahas M, Huitric H and Saintourens M (1987) **Animation of a B-spline Figure**, The Visual Computer, Vol.3, No4

[2] Smith AR (1983) Digital filmmaking. Abacus 1(1):28-45

[3] Blum R (1979) **Representing three-dimensional objects in your computer**. BYTE, May Issue, pp14-29

[4] Magnenat-Thalmann N, Thalmann D (1987) **The Direction of Synthetic Actors in the film Rendez-vous à Montréal**, IEEE Computer Graphics and Applications, Vol. 7, No 12.

[5] Magnenat-Thalmann N, Primeau E. and Thalmann D (1987) **Abstract Muscle Action Procedure for Human face Animation**, The Visual Computer, Vol.3, No4

[6] Magnenat-Thalmann N, Thalmann D (1985) **Computer Animation: Theory and Practice**, Springer, Tokyo New York Berlin Heidelberg, p.49.

"Occursus Cum Novo" - Computer Animation by Ray Tracing in a Network

W. Leister, Th. Maus, H. Müller, B. Neidecker, and A. Stösser (Germany)

Abstract. The goal of the project *"Occursus Cum Novo"* was to generate a complex photo-realistic animation of nontrivial length in reasonable time at reasonable costs. Photographic realism comprises complex geometric models as well as simulation of several optical effects. This paper starts with an introduction to the *"Occursus Cum Novo"* modeling environment. Following the toolkit approach, it offers a set of tools for textual, graphical interactive, and simulative modeling, embedded in the UNIX programming environment. The second part is devoted to rendering. Photo-realistic pictures generated by raytracing are still those of highest quality. However, due to the tremendous time of computation, raytraced animations are rather rare. An organization scheme for rendering on a network of work stations is described which enabled us to generate a 5-minutes raytraced animation within 2 months without affecting any of the regular users of the work stations. The results of the project are of general interest since they show a way for efficient high quality photo-realistic animation synthesis for the future.

1. The Project *"Occursus Cum Novo"*

The computer graphics group at the computer science department of the University of Karlsruhe has been working for years in the area of photo-realistic computer graphics, and, in particular, on optimizing the raytracing image synthesis technique. An efficient raytracing package, VERA (**V**ery **E**fficient **R**aytracing **A**lgorithm), was developed which is suitable for rendering extensive scenes of several ten-thousands of geometric primitives. For VERA, independent of other researchers [Gla86,FTI86], the grid technique including grid traversal by a DDA was developed. A difference to the other approaches is the marriage of hierarchical scene specification with the grid structure. This alliance allows to render large scenes, since the grid structure adapts to the spatial distribution of the geometric primitives. More details on VERA are beyond the scope of this paper. They are outlined in [SML87].

Knowing about the quality of the images generated by VERA, a committee of the Austrian Television (ORF) decided to give a grant for computer animation for the "Prix ARS Electronica '87" in Linz, Austria. They asked for a computer-generated animation of three minutes at U-matic highband video resolution. The time available for the project was about ten months. Although it was not quite clear at that time whether the job could be done solely by raytracing, our group decided to face the challenge.

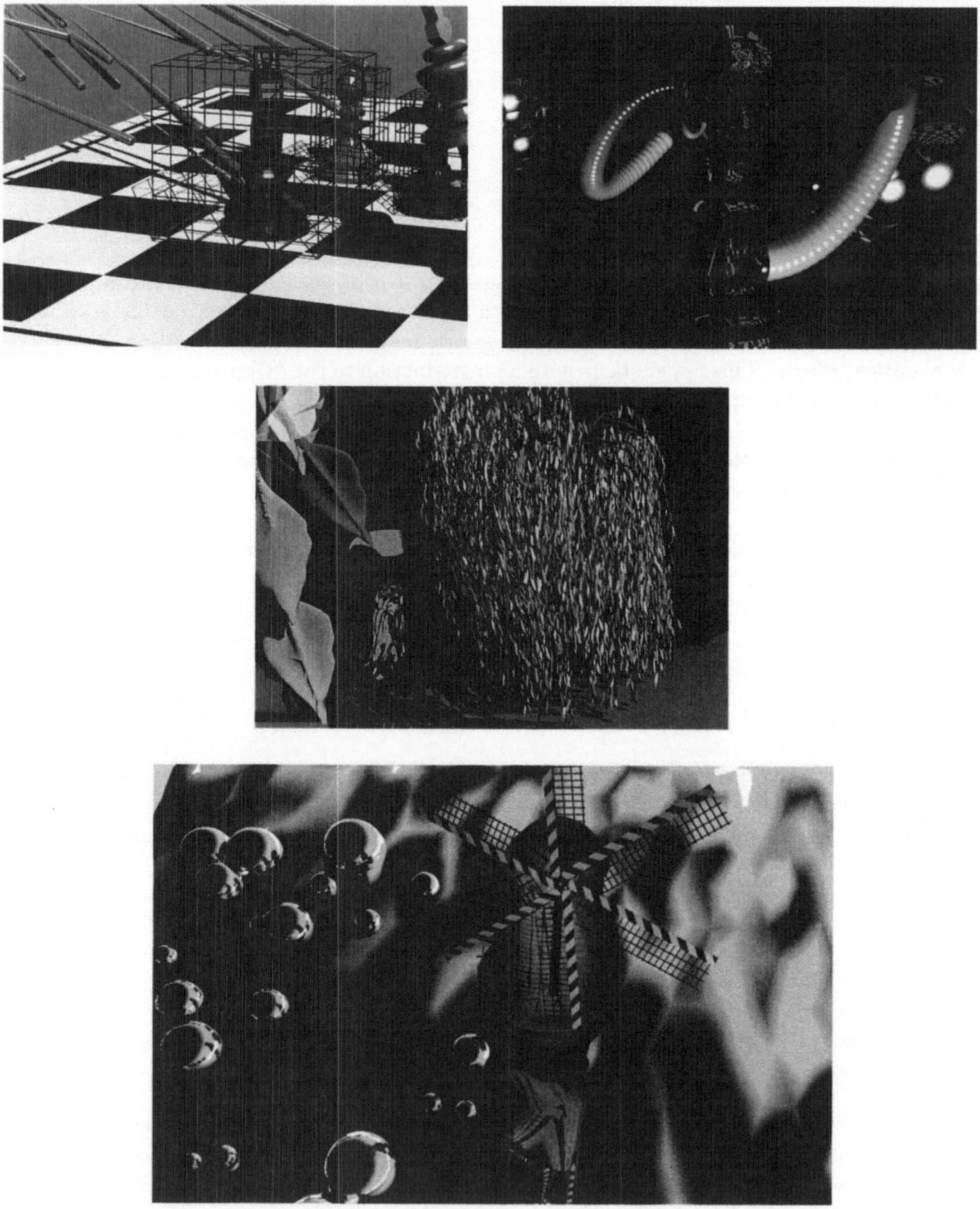

Figure 1: Some typical frames of the animation "Occurso Cum Novo"

The process of generating a computer animation consists of the phases script writing, modeling, rendering, and postprocessing [MT85]. The script of *"Occursus Cum Novo"* tries to plot out an amalgamation of four realms: science, technics, nature and art. This is realized by citing various "real" objects like a clock watch, chess men, trees, wind mills, a painting by MONDRIAN, a sculpture which looks like one of JEAN ARP etc. and on the other hand by the intrusion of some of the objects in one of the main movie scenes into the other, from the "hard" to the "soft" world. Some typical frames are shown in Fig. 1.

The following sections are devoted to modeling and rendering. In section 2, the modeling philosophy applied for *"Occursus Cum Novo"* is outlined. The emphasis is on modeling complex scenes and motions satisfying the aspect of realism from the viewpoint of geometry. Rendering by ray tracing is the content of section 3 where the usage of a computer network for this purpose is described.

2. Modeling

There are three mainstreams of modeling philosophies: textual modeling, graphical interactive modeling, and generative simulation. A powerful modeling environment has to integrate these methods. The question arises how to include them into one system. In the *"Occursus Cum Novo"* project, the toolkit approach was chosen. The toolkit technique is en vogue in other areas of modeling and design in computer science too, for example in software engineering. Famous in this area is the UNIX operating system. Several researchers have realized the usefulness of UNIX in geometric modeling and animation [Se85,PH87,Wav85], and so we did in the *"Occursus Cum Novo"* project.

Textual Modeling. The tools in a toolkit have to operate on a common basis. In the *"Occursus Cum Novo"* modeling environment, the major objects to be manipulated are files of scene descriptions written in the input language of the VERA-renderer. The VERA scene specification language was originally designed for static scenes. An example is shown in Fig. 2. The geometric primitives are triangles including Phong interpolation technique, spheres and cone segments. They are specified by keywords (e.g. `Ph`, `Sph`) followed by geometric parameters. Materials have a textual identifier (`Mat`) which is used to assign them to the geometric primitives (`Col`). Further, the VERA language allows to assign names to scenes in order to call them as subscenes in other scene definitions, under transformations composed of rotations, translations, and scaling. To animate static scenes, variables identifiable by the leading character '#' are introduced into the static format. In principle, variables can replace any item in a static scene thus defining a framework for animation. The variables are bound by textually substituting the actual values. These current frame parameters are calculated by special Pascal programs specifying the animation by simulating the effects of the modeled world. The dancing worms and the water in *"Occursus Cum Novo"* were animated by special purpose programs. A more general tool, the motion simulator METAMORPHOSIS, is described below.

```
Name Galilei                                                    name in pixel file header
Size 780 576                                                                   frame size
Anti-Alias                                                             alias treatment on
RayTrDepth 3                                                   maximum ray tracing depth
Camera 0 -500 300 0 0 25 0 10 140     view point / point of interest / top edge point
EyeLight 300000 1 1 1                                   white light source in view point

Col white                                               stone (for test: white sphere
Sph 0 0 92 12                                         with center 0; 0; 92 and radius 12)
Col metal                                                     table: reflecting square
P4 -200 -200 0    -200 200 0    200 200 0    200 -200 0

Id white
   Drf 1 1 1                                                  diffuse reflection white
Id metal
   Drf 0 0.5 0.7                                          diffuse reflection sea green
   Spd 0.3 0.3 0.8                                                       bluish mirror
```

Figure 2: Example of a VERA scene specification.

The VERA language for static scenes and and the general purpose language Pascal for animation are simple enough to specify complex motions quickly, at least for people somewhat experienced in writing programs. The capabilities of the given software environment can be used, ranging from text editors over compilers to version control. In addition, tools for visually judging the quality of a design are necessary, in particular for such time-consuming rendering techniques like ray tracing. For example, a sequence of frames is raytraced at low resolution, typically 128×128 pixels, and reduced to bitmap quality by color reduction and dithering. The frames are held in the main memory of a work station, and written at a frequency of 12 to 25 frames per second onto the bitmap display.

Graphical interactive modeling. Complex modeling was supported by different tools. As a graphical interactive tool, we mention the contour reconstruction program REPROS [MG87]. REPROS (**Re**construction from **P**lanar **Cro**ss **S**ections) allows to build 3-d-solids from parallel plain cross sections. Fig. 3 shows a sequence of contours and the reconstruction of the corresponding surface. The contours are interactively edited using a data tablet. The software was developed together with J.D. BOISSONNAT, INRIA, France, based on improvements of earlier work in [Boi84]. A remarkable feature of REPROS is that several contours are allowed on a cross section, and that branchings and holes can be reconstructed. In the *"Occursus Cum Novo"* -animation, REPROS was used for designing landscapes and sculptures.

Generative simulation. Interactive systems like REPROS require considerable user input. The advantage of generative simulators is their ability to generate impressive scenes on a sparse input. The program WAXI generates complex scenes by a recursive building mechanism. The input consists of segments. A segment possesses a base point

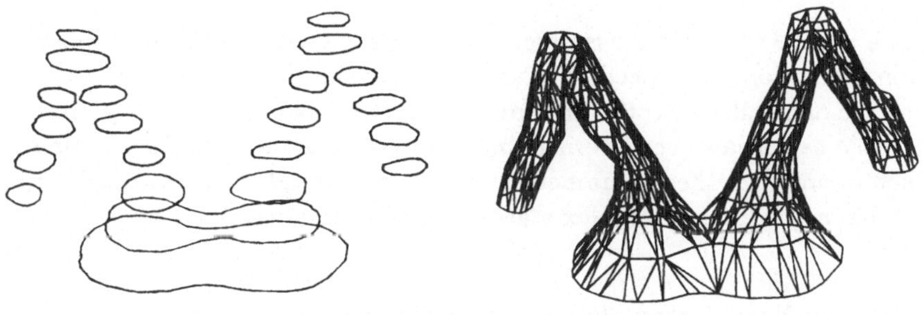

Figure 3: A sequence of contours and the corresponding reconstruction.

and some growth points. These are specified by local coordinate systems controlling the place and direction of growth. For each growth point, a segment to be attached is specified. The main growing strategy is successively attaching segments at the growth points, starting at a root segment, so that the growing direction and the base point direction given by the local coordinate systems fit together. Besides exact fitting, random aberrations and aberrations induced by "magnetic sources" are possible. Magnetic sources are defined by points located in the scene, possibly attached to segments. The size of the resulting scene can be either influenced by bounding the number of iterations, or by bounding-volumes restricting the space geometrically in which the object is allowed to grow. If the growing process is stopped according to some bounding condition, it can switch to an exception segment specified at the growing point. The exception segment is the root of a new growing process. This mechanism allows for example to fix leaves or fruits at a tree.

Similar generators are known in literature with special emphasis on trees [AK84,Sm84, Pru86]. In *"Occursus Cum Novo"* too, WAXI was used for tree generation. Special properties of WAXI are the concept of external control by the concepts of magnetism and pruning volumes, and the concept of visibility. These properties helped to animate weeping willows in the wind.

Another program is METAMORPHOSIS. It simulates the motion of a set of geometric primitives. The output generated by METAMORPHOSIS is a sequence of scenes in the VERA format corresponding to the frames of the animation. Each geometric primitive of METAMORPHOSIS has an individual time of birth and time of death. During its life time, its state changes according to a set of laws of the world model. The main components of METAMORPHOSIS are the creator BRAHMA, the maintainer VISHNU, and the destroyer SHIVA[1]. They iterate over a dynamic data structure M describing the current state of the world of primitives. Within an iteration, Brahma creates new primitives and inserts them into M. Vishnu maintains the world in a consistent state according to the model rules and reports the current state for rendering. Shiva determines the life time of each primitive and removes it in case of death.

[1]In Hinduism, Brahma, Vishnu und Shiva are assigned the roles of the creator, the maintainer and the destroyer, respectively.

The state of a geometric primitive is described by parameters like the location in space, the direction of motion, the speed, the acceleration, the mass, the visibility, and the behavior in case of a collision with other primitives (transparent, reflecting, absorbing). There is a basic set of laws considering simple physical properties, for example gravitation, which operate on these parameters. It can be extended arbitrarily by the user writing suitable procedures. Complex state transitions are described by a combination of these laws.

In *"Occursus Cum Novo"* , examples are rays attacking chess pieces, a wall constructed from flying bricks, and the metamorphosis of a statue into a cloud of spheres and vice versa. Particularly helpful were the different concepts of visibility in case of collision. For example, the observer could be protected from flying bricks and spheres by introducing invisible reflecting and absorbing primitives.

3. Rendering by raytracing in a network

Raytracing an animation requires considerable computer power. One way to get enough floating point operations is to use a super-computer. Although a Cyber 205 was accessible, and a vectorized version of VERA exists [MC86], there was not enough free time available on this machine. We decided to use the network of about 30 SUN work stations of our department, interconnected by Ethernet. The idea was to use the idle time of these work stations, bothering none of the other users. This also meant to minimize the disk space permanently used by the rendering process on all but one machine.

The calculation of an animation is partitioned into jobs. Each job is the calculation of one frame. The jobs are organized in a queue which is held on one machine acting as a server. All other machines are client machines, getting jobs from the server, executing them, and reporting the results back to the server. The organization of the network queue is totally decentralized with respect to crash safeness. If one of the clients has crashed, there is no need for manual operating. Communication is done using the SUN Network File System (NFS) [Net86]. All demon-programs are written in the C programming language using the capabilities of the Unix operating system.

Our approach differs from other implementations known in the graphics community [Pet87] in various points:

- In contrast to APOLLO's strategy with the raytraced computer animation "Quest", our network is totally automatized.
- A centralized method implemented by MATTHEW MERZBACHER, UCLA, assumes the availability of computers at fixed time periods. Interruption is hardly to carry out with this system.
- The method of MIKE MUUSS of the Army Ballistic Research Lab using "chunks" of scanlines leads to relatively high overhead and would have caused severe changes in our rendering software.

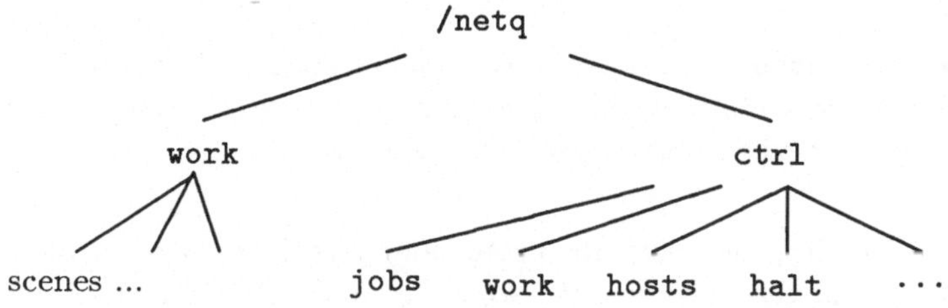

Figure 4: The directory structure of the network queue.

- PAUL HECKBERT'S solution at NYIT is totally decentralized and uses disc capacity on all machines. Further he mentioned problems in synchronization.
- JOHN W. PETERSON in Utah had a heterogeneous network. This required more overhead in controlling the different machines, in particular when a system crashes.

Now let us have a look at the organization of the network queue on the *server* in more details. The network queue is part of the file system of the server. It resides in a subdirectory named `/netq`, of Fig. 4. The directory `work` contains all input-, output- and intermediate files required for frame rendering. The directory `ctrl` contains all data necessary to control the network queue. Fig. 4 shows the subdirectories of `ctrl`. These subdirectories are used as follows:

- `jobs`

  This subdirectory contains all jobs waiting for execution. Each job is a file containing a shell-script to be executed. The files in the Unix operating system are sorted alphabetically, and it is this arrangement according to which the jobs are processed. Three types of jobs are distinguished, `a-`, `b-` and `h-`jobs. Class `a` contains fast jobs, usual previews. Class `b` contains usual jobs, while `h-`jobs are those requiring large main memory (8 MB).

- `work`

  Contains all jobs currently running. When a client picks up a job it moves the file for this task from `jobs` to `work`.

- `done`

  All files are moved to `done` when they are processed. The directory `done` is used for documentation and error recovery.

- `bad`

  All jobs leading to an error which cannot be solved automatically are moved to `bad`. This happens if the job goes down or is killed by a `kill -9` command. After error analysis such a job can be moved to `jobs` again for another attempt.

- `hosts`

  In the subdirectory `hosts` all work stations are mentioned that are ready for work. For each work station a file with the station's name exists, in which the status of the machine is given (executing, dispatching, idle, ...).

There are further directories, necessary for protocoling, statistics, and error recovery. So in one directory we find the most recently executed jobs. This directory allows the controlling demon to decide whether a machine has gone down. In another directory we can put all hosts to be stopped because of administrative reasons. Finally statistics on job interruptions and computational times are protocoled.

New jobs are initiated by the command `nq [-f] [-l] [-8] file` on a machine. `file` contains a shell script or a bundle of shell scripts for animation. With the parameters we can decide whether we have a preview or a huge job, whether we have one shell script or a bundle of them.

On each *client* a demon (background process) is installed during boot time, by the command `netqd [-u time] [-r] [-8] [-w workdir]`. The demon asks every five minutes whether the machine is idle. If idle, a job is accepted and a child process is initiated to execute this job. Then the demon continues to check every 10 seconds whether the machine is still idle. If not, the child process is killed and the corresponding file is moved from `work` to `jobs`. Process killing requires that VERA can continue at any time independent of the location of the interrupt. Further, the status of the child process is supervised every 10 seconds. If an accident happens, the job is moved to `bad`. If the job is finished, it is moved to `done`. Other controlling demons are running on the server machine to supervise if some machines were going down without coming up again.

4. Results

The calculated frames are collected on the server and then stored on magnetic tape. *"Occursus Cum Novo"* required 40 high density magnetic tapes. The data volume was about nine Gigabytes which were reduced to less than 35 % by Unix-compress. The network queue is totally automatized. Even the crash of client work stations can be handled automatically. The only operating requirements are saving frames on magnetic tapes and error handling for jobs in the directory `bad`. Fig. 5 shows a brief statistics of the *"Occursus Cum Novo"* project. Almost three years of SUN cpu time were required for rendering, delivered by the network in about two months real time. On the average, 90 % of the whole computational power of the network was used for *"Occursus Cum Novo"* . This rises from the fact that the work stations were mostly used interactively by other users, and not for number-crunching jobs in the background.

Bad jobs did not appear very often (maximally 1 %). Their reasons were unforeseen errors in the raytracer (numerical problems or missing main storage capacity with large scenes) or inoperable machines. Some of the scenes had to be calculated on machines

What	Σ
tasks	6454
dispatches	9544
interrupted runs	3090
previews	3137
frames	3317
cpu-hours	23307
cpu-month	≈ 32
actual number of machines	22 – 34

Figure 5: Statistics of the calculation in the network.

with 8 MB minimum only. Other problems occurred with some misconfigured machines. So in some cases the Unix kernel had too small text and procedure tables.

On machines where some SUN specific software was running, our demon did not recognize that keys had been pressed on the keyboard. So the raytracer could not be interrupted when an user started working. When the disks were full the network queue stopped automatically. This happened about once a day. Since shipping out files on tape required human operating, this caused a problem on weekends leading to machines running idle. Another problem was that we had to convert the image files into the wavefront file format [Wav85] for recording. Because of the great amount of data (ca. 1.3 MB per image) this task produced much traffic on the network and maximum disk shift rate. Due to network overload sometimes the format change failed.

5. Conclusion

The project *"Occursus Cum Novo"* showed that animation by raytracing has come to maturity for commercial use. The overall project duration was less than half a year. The result could only be obtained by the optimized raytrace software VERA, and a network of work stations mainly used for interactive work, i.e. with a lot of idle time for number-crunching. Networks of work stations are a cost efficient alternative to super-computers and even mini-super-computers at least for animation. Our Unix-based approach also demonstrated how to build a super-computer that works at once by compacting the computer network to a number of boards in a rack, connected by an Ethernet-cable. A relatively inexpensive piece of hardware may be obtained immediately, comparable in power with many specialized raytracing machines in the literature. Currently, insufficient modeling tools are the main bottleneck in the entire process of creating a computer animation. In our opinion, the toolkit approach combined with textual facilities is quite useful. More tools are necessary in order to open high quality in computer animation to artists too.

References

[**AK84**] Aono, M., Kunii, T.L.: Botanical Tree Image Generation, IEEE Computer Graphics & Appl. 4(5) (1984) 10-34

[**Boi84**] J.-D. Boissonnat, Geometric Structures for 3-Dimensional Shape Representation, ACM Transactions on Graphics 4 (1985) 266-286

[**FTI86**] A. Fujimoto, T. Tanaka, K. Iwata, ARTS: Accelerated Ray Tracing System, IEEE Computer Graphics & Appl., April 1986, 12-25

[**Gla86**] A.S. Glassner, Space Subdivision for Fast Raytracing, IEEE Computer Graphics & Appl., October 1986, 15-22

[**MT85**] N. Magnenat-Thalmann, D. Thalmann, Computer Animation: Theory and Practice, Springer-Verlag, Berlin, 1985

[**MC86**] H. Müller, A. Christmann, Realistic Image Synthesis on Vectorial Super Computers (in German), it-Informationstechnik 5 (1986) 275-280

[**MG87**] H. Müller, B. Geiger, Reconstruction of Complex Solids from Planar Cross Sections and their High-Quality Display (in German), in: Proceedings GI-Jahrestagung 1987, Informatik-Fachberichte 127, Springer-Verlag, 1987

[**Net86**] Network File System Protocol Specification, Revision B, Sun Micro Systems, February 1986

[**Pet87**] J.W. Peterson, Distributed Animation Summary, electronic mail peterson@cs.utah.edu, May 1987

[**PH87**] M. Potmesil, E.M. Hoffert, FRAMES: Software Tools for Modeling, Rendering and Animation of 3D Scenes, Computer Graphics 21 (1987) 85-93

[**Pru86**] P. Prusinkiewicz, Graphical Applications of L-Systems, Proceedings of Graphics Interface '86 - Vision Interface '86, 247-253

[**SML87**] A. Schmitt, H. Müller, W. Leister, Ray Tracing Algorithms - Theory and Practice. to appear in NATO ASI Series: Theoretical Fundamentals of Computer Graphics, Springer-Verlag

[**Se85**] C. Sequin, The Berkley UNIGRAFIX Tools, Version 2.5, Technical report UCB/CSD 86/281, Berkeley, University of California, 1985

[**Sm84**] Smith, A.R.: Plants, Fractals, and Formal Languages, Computer Graphics 18 (1984) 1-10

[**Wav85**] Wavefront Technologies, 1421 State Street, Santa Barbara, CA 93101

Chapter 2

Image Synthesis

A General Shading Model

A. Sfarti (USA)

ABSTRACT

This paper attempts to generalize and to unify the shading models described by Gouraud [1] and Phong [2]. The major effort in this direction is to produce a model that exhibits the following features:

1. It is incremental in an arbitrary scan direction across a two dimensional polygon.
2. The increments in the x and y directions are constant across the elementary polygon to be shaded.
3. It maintains continuity of the intensity I or of the normals N when traversing the edges that bound the elementary polygons.
4. In the case of the shading process following the projection it considers the contribution of the z coordinate.
5. The shading is invariant with respect to rotation.

The first three features are satisfied by the models proposed by Gouraud and Phong whereas the last two are not. It is the purpose of this paper to introduce a general model that is invariant with respect to rotation, can be applied either before or after projection and is insensitive to the presence of concave vertices.

Keywords: shading model, rotation-invariance, perspective projection.

INTRODUCTION

Despite their shortcomings, the Gouraud and Phong shading models are very widely used by commercial systems for rendering realistic three-dimensional objects. Tom Duff [4] has pointed out that the shading rules are not invariant with respect to rotation and as a consequence, as the orientation of an object changes from frame to frame, its shade also changes. Duff corrects this problem by proposing a parametrical model that interpolates simultaneously among the four vertices of a four-sided polygon by using two independent parameters u and v. The purpose of this paper is to present an alternate rotation-invariant model that lends itself to incremental rendering.

The elementary polygons used by the present algorithm are planar in the sense of being contained into a hyperplane determined in a space of geometric and intensity coordinates. The rotation-invariance of the model is the direct result of the construction that replaces the sequential linear interpolation along polygon edges with the global properties of hyperplanar surfaces. The method is explained for triangle-mesh surfaces with the observation that polygon-mesh surfaces can be reduced to triangle-mesh if triangles can be inscribed into the polygons.

The proposed model reduces the shading process to an incremental algorithm that allows shading across spans of constant X or constant Y or even across lines of arbitrary direction. The increments need to be computed as part of the algorithm set-up. Since the model is global rather than local the increments are independent of the number of polygon edges that intercept a particular scanline. The model does not require any edge or vertex sorting and it is insensitive to the presence of concave vertices.

A very simple example demonstrates that for the models proposed by Phong or Gouraud in order to use a purely incremental algorithm one needs to continually adjust the values obtained by the linear interpolation along the edges. In Figure 1 the intensity values along the edges V_2V_1 and V_2V_3 need to be adjusted to correspond to the center of the pixels. This adjustment requires the derivation of the parameter s from the Bresenham decision element E (see paragraph 6). This is an expensive process because it has to be executed separately for each edge and for every scanline and because it requires division followed by multiplication:

$$I_{center} = I_{edge}\ (1+s.dI)$$

where $s = .5\ (1 \pm E/dy)$ or $s = .5\ (1 \pm E/dx)$

depending on the orientation of the edge and $dy = abs\ (y_2 - y_1)$

For the commercially available floating point processors division is five to ten times more expensive than multiplication. For a database constructed from triangles that span 10 scanlines the overhead amounts to 2*10*10 multiplications, that is, very high. Multiplication by 1/dy is not an option since it introduces error.

The discussion of the new model will be limited to "flat" hyperpolygons in the (x,y,z,I) space or in the (x,y,z,Nx,Ny,Nz) space. Here I stands for intensity and Nx, Ny, Nz stand for the x,y,z components of the normal. A hyperpolygon is "flat" if all the vertices

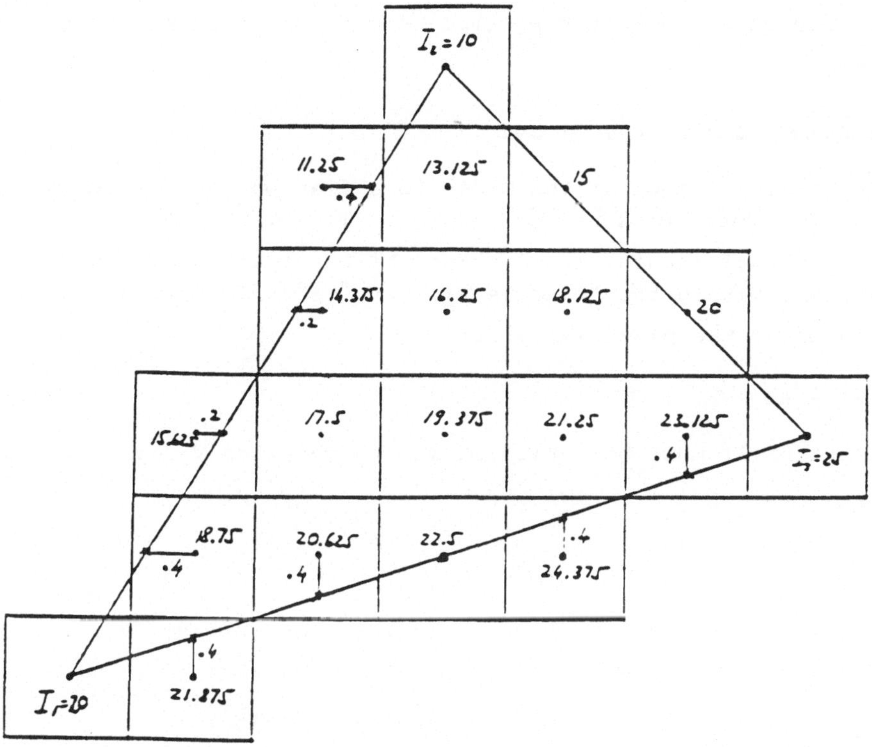

Figure 1. Adjustment of intensity values at the polygon edges

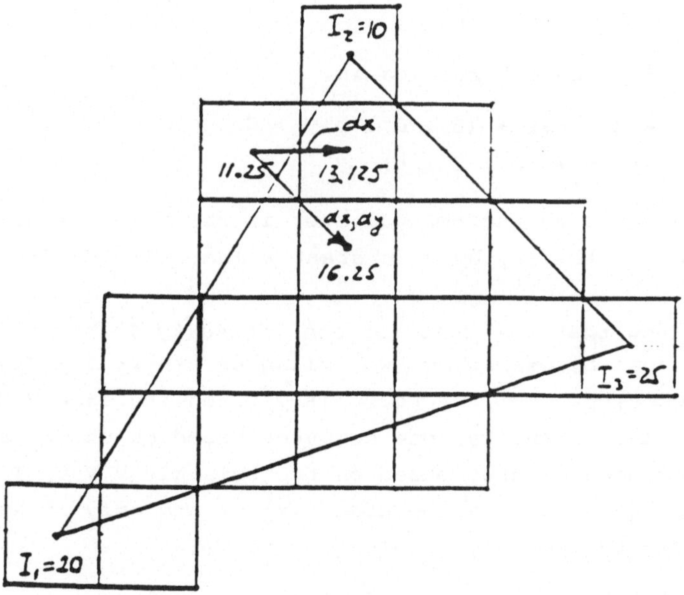

Figure 2. Incremental computation of intensity values
(dI/dx = 1.875, dI/dy = 3.125)

satisfy the equation of the hyperplane determined by any of the three vertices.

1. General Intensity Model

The basic element of the model is a flat polygon determined by three of its vertices $V_i = (x_i, y_i, z_i, I_i)$ i=1,2,3.

The general shading model makes the assumption that the intensity of any pixel within the triangle $V_1 V_2 V_3$ is a linear function of the coordinates of the pixel (x, y, z).

$$I(x,y,z) = Ax + By + Cz \tag{1}$$

The relation (1) must be satisfied in the vertices $V_1 V_2 V_3$. Thus:

$$\begin{aligned} Ax_1 + By_1 + Cz_1 &= I_1 \\ Ax_2 + By_2 + Cz_2 &= I_2 \\ Ax_3 + By_3 + Cz_3 &= I_3 \end{aligned} \tag{2}$$

(2) determines uniquely A, B and C as functions of (x_i, y_i, z_i, I_i) i = 1,2,3.

(x_i, y_i, z_i) i=1,2,3 determine a plane of equation:

$$z = ax + by + c \tag{3}$$

a, b, c are uniquely determined by the relations:

$$ax_i + by_i + c = z_i, \; i = 1,2,3 \tag{4}$$

Substituting (3) into (1) results in:

$$I(x,y,z) = (A + C \,.\, a)x + (B + C \,.\, b)y + C \,.\, c \tag{5}$$

$$dI = (A + C \,.\, a)\, dx + (B + C \,.\, b)\, dy \tag{6}$$

It follows that for an incremental step in the x (or y) direction ($dx\pm 1$, $dy=\pm 1$) I will vary by a constant value: A + Ca (respectively B + Cb).

We may show that the value of the intensity I is continuous across the polygon edges by examining two triangles $V_1V_2V_3$ and $V_1V_2V_4$ that share the edge V_1V_2. For any point (x,y,z) on the edge V_1V_2 there are two values of the intensity, one computed based on the triangle $V_1V_2V_3$: $I=Ax+By+Cz$ and one computed based on the triangle $V_1V_2V_4$ $I'=A'x + B'y + C'z$. I is continuous across the edge V_1V_2 if and only if $Ax + By + Cz = A'x + B'y + C'z$ for any x,y,z belonging to V_1V_2 (7)

$$\begin{aligned} x &= x_1 + (x_1 - x_2) \,.\, u \\ y &= y_1 + (y_1 - y_2) \,.\, u \\ z &= z_1 + (z_1 - z_2) \,.\, u \end{aligned} \tag{8} \quad 0 \le u \le 1$$

By substituting (8) into (7) we obtain:

$(A-A')\ [x_1 + (x_1-x_2)u] + (B-B')[y_1 + (y_1-y_2)u] + (C-C')\ [z_1 + (z_1-z_2)u]$ $= 0$ for any u. This happens if:

$$(A-A')\ x_1 + (B-B')\ y_1 + (C-C')\ z_1 = 0 \text{ and} \quad (9)$$
$$(A-A')(x_1-x_2) + (B-B')(y_1-y_2) + (C-C')(z_1-z_2) = 0 \quad (10)$$

Substituting (9) into (10) we obtain:

$$(A-A')\ x_2 + (B-B')\ y_2 + (C-C')\ z_2 = 0 \quad (11)$$
$$\text{or } Ax_2 + By_2 + Cz_2 = A'x_2 + B'y_2 + C'y_2 \quad (12)$$

But (9) and (12) are automatically satisfied since they represent the vertex intensities I_1 and I_2, respectively. The next question to be answered is: are the derivatives of I continuous? The answer is no, since in general:

$$A + C\ .\ a \neq A' + C'\ a' \text{ and } B + C\ .\ b \neq B' + C'\ b'$$

Therefore the general intensity model, though more precise than the Gouraud model, will still exhibit Mach banding. If we take:

$$D = \begin{vmatrix} x_1 & y_1 & z_1 \\ x_2 & y_2 & z_2 \\ x_3 & y_3 & z_3 \end{vmatrix} \quad D_A = \begin{vmatrix} I_1 & y_1 & z_1 \\ I_2 & y_2 & z_2 \\ I_3 & y_3 & z_3 \end{vmatrix} \quad D_B = \begin{vmatrix} x_1 & I_1 & z_1 \\ x_2 & I_2 & z_2 \\ x_3 & I_3 & z_3 \end{vmatrix} \quad D_C = \begin{vmatrix} x_1 & y_1 & I_1 \\ x_2 & y_2 & I_2 \\ x_3 & y_3 & I_3 \end{vmatrix}$$

then $A=D_A/D$ $B=D_B/D$ $C=D_C/D$

$$e = \begin{vmatrix} x_1 & y_1 & 1 \\ x_2 & y_2 & 1 \\ x_3 & y_3 & 1 \end{vmatrix} \quad d_a = \begin{vmatrix} z_1 & y_1 & 1 \\ z_2 & y_2 & 1 \\ z_3 & y_3 & 1 \end{vmatrix} \quad d_b = \begin{vmatrix} x_1 & z_1 & 1 \\ x_2 & z_2 & 1 \\ x_3 & z_3 & 1 \end{vmatrix}$$

then $a = d_a/e$ $b=d_b/e$.

The computation of a general 3 x 3 determinant takes 9 multiplications and 5 additions. Therefore the computation of A, B, C will take 36 multiplications, 20 additions, and 3 divisions. The computation of a 3 x 3 determinant having a column of all ones takes 2 multiplications and 5 subtractions. Therefore a and b will take 6 multiplications, 15 subtractions and 2 divisions. Therefore the computation of the derivatives of I will take 44 multiplications, 37 additions and 5 divisions. Certain processors are capable of executing a floating point operation in 100 ns. This implies a set-up time for the shading algorithm of about 8.6 microseconds. This figure limits to 4000 the number of shaded triangles per frame, assuming animation at the 30 frames per second rate.

In the general case the system of equations (1) can have more than three equations and it is not solvable because the vertices are not in the same hyperplane. The system can be still solved by using a least-square method. A very good algorithm is described in [5] and makes use of the Moore-Penrose pseudoinverse matrix.

The rotation invariance can be demonstrated by observing that a 90° rotation in the (x,y) plane corresponds to replacing x with y and viceversa in the equations that define dI/dx and dI/dy:

$$dI/dx = D_A/D + D_C/D \cdot da/e$$

If we replace x with y and viceversa we obtain:

$$-D_B/(-D) + (-D_C)/(-D) \cdot (-d_b)/(-e) = dI/dy$$

In other words, dI/dx and dI/dy exchange roles when the observer and the light source are rotated together. According to Duff [4] this is proof of the rotation-invariance of the model.

2. General Normal Model

In this model the vertices of the elementary triangles are described by $(x_i, y_i, z_i, Nx_i, Ny_i, Nz_i)$ $i = 1,2,3$ where (Nx_i, Ny_i, Nz_i) is the vector normal. If we assume a linear dependence between the normal and x, y, z then the components of the normal can be expressed as:

$$\begin{aligned} Nx_i &= A_1 x_i + B_1 y_i + C_1 z_i \\ Ny_i &= A_2 x_i + B_2 y_i + C_2 z_i \\ Nz_i &= A_3 x_i + B_3 y_i + C_3 z_i \end{aligned} \qquad (13)$$

The system (13) determines uniquely (A_j, B_j, C_j) $j = 1,2,3$. Because (x_i, y_i, z_i) $i = 1,2,3$ determine a plane as described by (3) we obtain:

$$\begin{aligned} Nx &= (A_1 + C_1 a)\ x + (B_1 + C_1 b)\ y \\ Ny &= (A_2 + C_2 a)\ x + (B_2 + C_2 b)\ y \\ Nz &= (A_3 + C_3 a)\ x + (B_3 + C_3 b)\ y \end{aligned} \qquad (14)$$

for any point inside the triangle $V_1V_2V_3$.

3. Intensity Shading and Perspective Projection

The models presented previously can be applied for shading in object space or for shading following parallel projection. We will present in this paragraph an approximative model for shading following perspective projection. If shading is executed after perspective projection then we must replace the spatial differentials dx and dy by dx_p and dy_p where x_p and y_p represent the coordinates (x,y) post projection. We will introduce a variation of the perspective projection equations presented in [3] (page 275) that applies to the intensity as well as to x, y and z.

$$x_p = x \cdot d/z$$
$$y_p = y \cdot d/z \tag{16}$$
$$z_p = - d/z \tag{17}$$
$$I_p = I \cdot d/z \tag{18}$$

where d is the distance between the center of projection and the projection plane. This type of projection foreshortens not only x and y but also I, according to (18). This represents an approximation to the point source intensity relation that states that intensity varies inversely proportional to the square of the distance. This projection maintains relative depth as well. If $0 < z_1 < z_2$ then $z_{p1} < z_{p2}$ because $-d/z_1 < -d/z_2$.

By inverting (16), (17), (18) we get:

$$z = -d/z_p$$
$$x = -x_p/z_p \tag{19}$$
$$y = -y_p/z_p$$
$$I = -I_p/z_p$$

Substituting (19) into (1) we obtain

$$I_p = Ax_p + By_p + Cd \tag{20}$$

Here A and B are the same as the A and B determined for the general intensity model. We can regard (20) as a simplified Gouraud model.

4. Shading and Time Varying Models

In this model we take into consideration the fact that the vertices are known functions of time: $(x_i, y_i, z_i, N_i)=(x_i(t), y_i(t), z_i(t), N_i(t))$. If we assume that the normals in a point inside the triangles do not depend explicitly of t (i.e., the surface is rigid) we can write that the normals in the vertices V_1 V_2 V_3 satisfy $N_{ij} = A_j(t)$ $x_i(t) + B_j(j)\ y_i(t) + C_j(t)\ z_i(t)$ (21)

Relations (21) determine $A_j(t)$ $B_j(t)$ and $C_j(t)$. Since x_i, y_i, z_i vary in time, so do a, b, c from eq (4).

$$a\ x_i(t) + b\ y_i(t) + c_i = z_i(t) \qquad (22)$$

then:

$$N_j(t) = (A_j(t) + C_j(t) * a(x_i(t), y_i(t), z_i(t)) * x(t) + (B_j(t) + C_j(t) * b(x_i(t), y_i(t), z_i(t)) * y(t) \qquad (23)$$

where:

$$Aj(t) = \begin{vmatrix} N_{1j}(t) & y_2(t) & z_1(t) \\ N_{2j}(t) & y_2(t) & z_2(t) \\ N_{3j}(t) & y_3(t) & z_3(t) \end{vmatrix} \text{ div } \begin{vmatrix} x_1(t) & y_1(t) & z_1(t) \\ x_2(t) & y_2(t) & z_2(t) \\ x_3(t) & y_3(t) & z_3(t) \end{vmatrix} \qquad (24)$$

$$\text{and } a\ (t) = \begin{vmatrix} z_1(t) & y_1(t) & 1 \\ z_2(t) & y_2(t) & 1 \\ z_3(t) & y_3(t) & 1 \end{vmatrix} \text{ div } \begin{vmatrix} x_1(t) & y_1(t) & 1 \\ x_2(t) & y_2(t) & 1 \\ x_3(t) & y_3(t) & 1 \end{vmatrix} \qquad (25)$$

5. Generalization of the General Models

The models introduced by this paper function identically if we replace the triangles with arbitrary polygons with the only restriction that the polygons must be planar. The direction of shading is not restricted to be parallel to the x axis; shading along any direction is feasible. The generalization can be pushed even further by generating a general shading model for bicubic patches or any other general surfaces. The only complication is that these models are not going to have constant derivatives for I or N but rather complex functions of x, y, z.

6. Edge Effects

Due to the incremental nature of the above presented algorithms, the edges could present an annoying effect of "dove-tail joint". That is, at the intersection of the surfaces the value of the z coordinate derived from the formula: $z = z + dz$ (where $dz = adx + bdy$) is not correct. As the ideal edge passes between pixels, the computed value of z "zig-zags" between values computed based on the equations of the two surfaces that determine the edge. The two surfaces determine different values for z (with the exception of the points located exactly on the ideal edge). By choosing the z value based on z - buffering comparison one can seriously distort the altitudes along the edges, resulting in objects that have either blunter or sharper edges (depending on the object orientation). The "dove-tail joint" can be observed in Fig. 3.

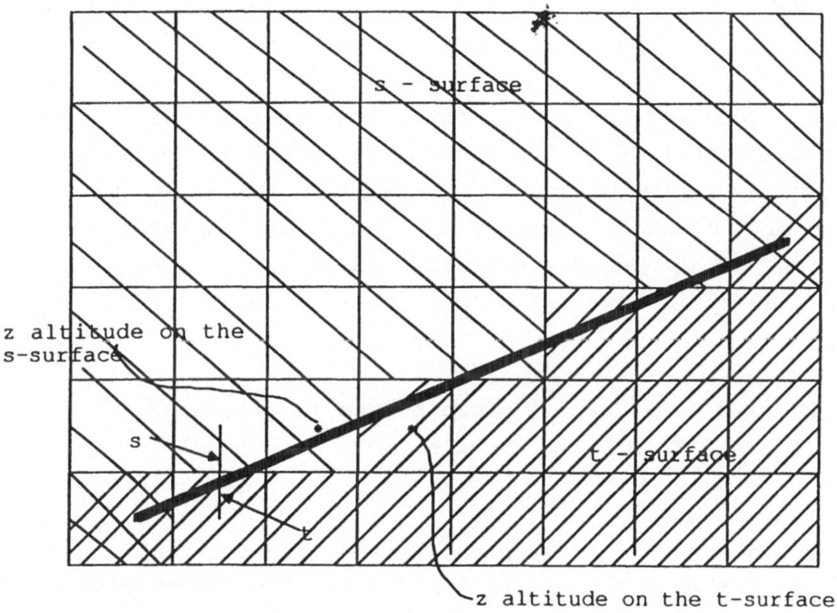

Figure 3. Effects of sampled computation of z

The algorithm presented below suggests a correction step that must be executed along the edges of each newly shaded polygon. Each edge needs to be interpolated and the z values in the z - buffer need to be replaced with the exact values. Assume that the two surfaces determining the edge in Fig. 2 are described by the equations:

$$z_s = a_s x + b_s y + c_s \quad (26)$$
$$z_t = a_t x + b_t y + c_t \quad (27)$$

along the edge $(x, y, z_s) = (x, y, z_t)$. Here s and t refer to the parameters introduced in [3] for the description of the Bresenham line algorithms (page 434).

Inside the polygons the z values are computed based on the sampled integer coordinates:

$$Z_s = a_sX + b_sY + c_s \quad (29)$$
$$Z_t = a_tX + b_tY + c_t \quad (30)$$
$$dZ_s = a_sdX + b_sdY \quad (31)$$
$$dZ_t = a_tdX + b_tdY \quad (32)$$

where dX = -1, 0 +1 and dY = -1, 0, +1. Along the edge we compute exact values for z according to the expressions (26), (27):

$$z_s = a_sx + b_sy + c_s = a_sX + b_s\ (Y - s) + c_s = Z_s - b_s * s \quad (33)$$
$$z_t = a_tx + b_ty + c_t = a_tX + b_t\ (Y + t) + c_t = Z_t + b_t * t \quad (34)$$

Since s - t = E/dx and s + t = 1, it follows that s = .5(1 + E/dx) and t = .5(1 - E/dx) where E is the error term and dx = $abs(x_2-x_1)$.

We can write now a modified Bresenham algorithm that allows the computation of the exact values of z. The following example treats only the first octant but the extension is trivial. Note that the meaning of s and t is inverted with respect to [3].

```
Begin
        X = X + 1               ;step in the +X direction
        If E < 0 Then           ;s < t
    Begin
        E = E + incrl
        Y = Y + 1               ;step in the +Y direction.
        Z = Z + as + bs         ;Z is used for the incremental algorithm
        z = Z - bs * s          ;z is used for the edge only.
        Replace (z)
    End Else
    Begin
        E = E + incr2           ;s >= t.
        Z = Z + at              ;Step in the Y direction.
        z = Z + bt * t          ;z is used for the edge only.
        Replace (z)
    End
End.
```

The algorithm can be used not only for computing the exact z values but also to compute the pixel area partially covered by each of the polygons determining the edge. The variable E determines uniquely the amount of partial coverage. This makes possible the correct blending of the two intensities I_s and I_t computed from the incremental algorithm presented in the previous paragraphs.

7. Conclusion

The algorithms presented generalize the Gouraud and the Phong shading models. They also minimize the amount of computation for setting up the incremental algorithms of shading since the increments for I and N are constant across the triangle of interpolation.

Bibliography

[1] H. Gouraud, "Continuous Shading of Curved Surfaces", IEEE Transactions on Computers, C-20(6), June 1971, pp 623-628.

[2] Bui-Tuong Phong, "Illumination for Computer Generated Pictures", Communications of the ACM, 18(6), June 1975, pp 311-317.

[3] J. D. Foley and A. VanDam, "Fundamentals of Interactive Computer Graphics".

[4[] T. Duff, "Smooth Shaded Renderings of Polyhedral Objects on Raster Displays", Computer Graphics, Vol. 13, pp. 270-279, 1979 (Proc. SIGGRAPH 79).

[5] J. Stoer and R. Bulirsch, "Introduction to Numerical Analysis", Springer-Verlag, pp 210-213.

The H-Test, a Method of High Speed Interpolative Shading

K. Harrison, D. A. P. Mitchell, and A. H. Watt (UK)

Abstract. In computer graphics curved surfaces are commonly represented by a mesh of polygons. When these objects are rendered, the 'visibility' of the polygonal definition is diminished by using an interpolative shading algorithm. The two algorithms used for this are Phong shading (Phong 1975) and Gouraud shading (Gouraud 1971). Phong shading is capable of producing more realistic specular highlights, but is more expensive than Gouraud shading.

In general for an object, the number of specularly highlighted polygons is small compared to the number of non-highlighted polygons, especially for a single light source. We describe a reliable and consistent method which allows objects to be Gouraud shaded, with Phong shading used only to add the specular highlights. Thus, images of the quality associated with Phong shading can be produced with little more computation than that needed for an equivalent Gouraud shaded image.

Introduction. The current de-facto reflection model used in computer graphics is the Phong model. This computes the intensity of light reflected from a surface element due to one or a number of (usually distant) point light sources. Three terms being evaluated:

$$I = I_{ambient} + I_{diffuse} + I_{specular}$$

$$= I_{ambient} + I_l(k_d(\mathbf{L}.\mathbf{N}) + k_s(\mathbf{N}.\mathbf{H})^n)$$

N is the unit surface normal, **H** is the vector bi-sector of **L** and **V** (where **L** is the unit light vector and **V** is the unit view vector). I_l is the intensity of the light source. k_d is a diffuse reflection coefficient and k_s is a specular reflection coefficient.

This model is usually incorporated in a bi-linear interpolation scheme to efficiently shade polygon mesh models. The two common interpolative methods are Gouraud interpolation and Phong interpolation.

Gouraud shading is effective for shading surfaces which reflect light diffusely. Specular reflections can be modelled using Gouraud shading, but the shape of the specular highlight produced is dependent on the relative positions of the underlying polygons. The advantage of Gouraud shading is that it is computationally the less expensive of the two models, only requiring the evaluation of the intensity equation at the polygon vertices, and then bi-linear interpolation of these values for each pixel.

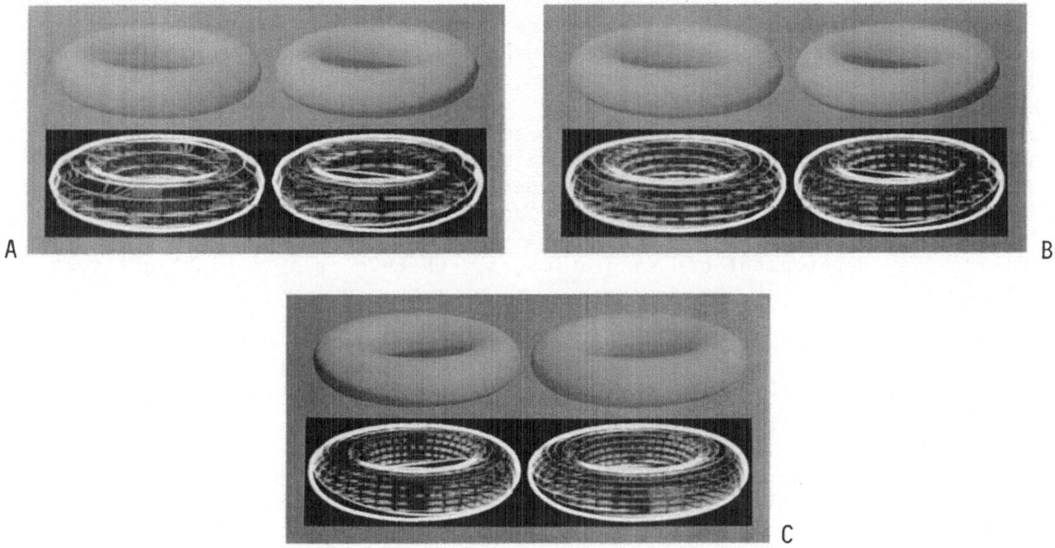

Fig. 1A-C. Gouraud diffuse shaded (left) and Phong diffuse shaded (right) torii, together with their second order spatial differentials. A 10x20 polygons, B 15x30 polygons and C 20x40 polygons.

Phong shading produces highlights which are much less dependent on the underlying polygons. But, more calculations are required involving the interpolation of the surface normal and the evaluation of the intensity function for each pixel.

Even if we consider just the diffuse term, there is some noticeable difference between the two methods. This difference is manifested in the visibility of Mach bands. The visibility of Mach bands depends strongly on the 'polygonal resolution', this is illustrated in Fig. 1. The thin white lines give an estimation of the 'strength' of the Mach bands (which are generally difficult to reproduce photographically). Note that the difference between the two differentiated images becomes less as the toroid is more accurately defined.

Generally, an object will have relatively few such highlighted polygons. So, it would be computationally more efficient to Phong shade the highlighted polygons, and to Gouraud shade the remainder. In practice, the diffuse components produced for a particular pixel by the two interpolation methods differ slightly, and it is necessary to Gouraud shade the entire object. The Phong specular term is then evaluated on the highlighted polygons, and combined with the Gouraud diffuse value.

To enable the implementation of the combined shading algorithm, a test has to be determined in order to ascertain which of the polygons are partially or fully within an area of specular highlight. This test will be known as the highlight test or H-test.

Similar geometric approaches are to be found in (Phong 1975a) and (Bergman 1986). Phong's method is based on the reflection vector and an extra coordinate transformation to align the light source (assuming there is only one) along the z axis. Bergman uses a simple test which compares the directions of the polygon's vertex normals with the direction of maximum highlight. This will detect only those specular highlights which correspond to the simplest case (case 1) given below. Although most highlighted polygons fall into this category the remainder are aesthetically significant. It is particularly important in animated sequences to detect all highlighted polygons otherwise highlights may 'switch' on and off. The emphasis in (Bergman 1986) is on the high speed interactive development of single images, where a simple highlight test will suffice.

A completely different approach to efficient shading has been investigated in (Duff 1979) and (Bishop 1986). These are mathematical optimisations of the basic Phong method. Bishop, for example, uses a two-dimensional Taylor series to approximate the Phong equation.

Theory. The H-test is based on a hierarchy of simple tests that predict the value of the highlight function between two vertices. For there to be a contribution from the specular term, we can say:

$\mathbf{N.H} \geq T$, a threshold term.

The value of this term is examined at pairs of vertices to predict the variation in its magnitude along the edge. A hierarchy of five simple tests performs this prediction.

A) To determine whether **N.H** at any vertex is greater than the threshold value.
B) Determines if **N.H** reaches a maximum along any polygon edge.
C) Determines whether the maximum of test B is greater than zero.
D) Determines if this maximum is greater than the threshold value.
E) Is performed once per polygon, and determines if a polygon has a maximum along each of its edges.

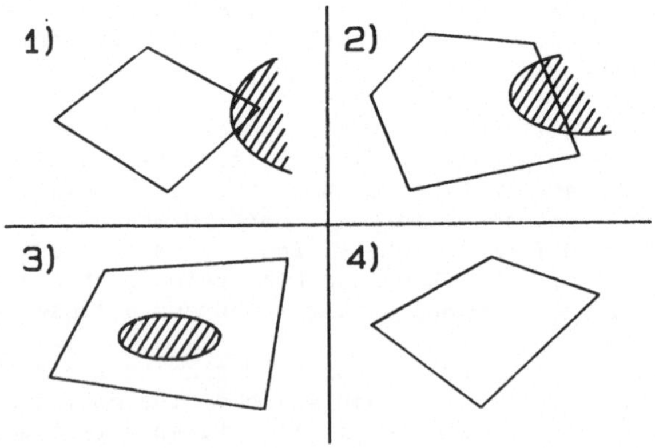

Fig. 2. The four distinct cases of specular highlights possible on a polygon.

From these tests, it is possible to determine which of the four cases shown in Fig. 2 is applicable to the current polygon. The tests are now described in more detail.

Test A. This test simply evaluates **N.H** at a polygon vertex and compares this with the threshold value. IF **N.H** is greater than the threshold, then the current vertex is within the visible region of a specular highlight. This test is sufficient to determine all polygons matching case 1) of Fig. 2.

Test B. This checks to see if the intensity of the specular highlight reaches a point of maximum along the current edge. In fact it will find any stationary point, but points of minimum and inflection will be rejected by the subsequent tests. Let the unit normals at the two vertices be **A** and **B**. During Phong shading, the normal is linearly interpolated along an edge. ie.

$$\mathbf{N}(u) = (1-u)\mathbf{A} + u\mathbf{B} \text{ for some } u \ (0 \leq u \leq 1) \qquad \text{Let } \phi(u) = \frac{\mathbf{N}(u).\mathbf{H}}{|\mathbf{N}(u)|}$$

A specular contribution should be considered if $\phi(u)$ is greater than the threshold T for some u $(0 < u < 1)$.

Since test A has failed, and $\phi(0) = \mathbf{A.H}$ and $\phi(1) = \mathbf{B.H}$ are both less than the threshold, if $\phi(u) > T$ for some u $(0 < u < 1)$ a point of maximum must occur in $\phi(u)$ between the two vertices. Now,

$$\phi(u) = \frac{\mathbf{N}(u).\mathbf{H}}{|\mathbf{N}(u)|} \qquad = \frac{a + u(b-a)}{\sqrt{(pu^2-pu+1)}}$$

Where $a = \mathbf{A.H}$, $b = \mathbf{B.H}$, $c = \mathbf{A.B}$ and $p = 2(1-c)$.

Differentiating, setting $\phi'(u) = 0$ and letting $d = bc-a$ and $e = ac-b$ gives

$$u = \frac{e}{e+d}$$

There are now four possibilities to consider:

1) $d = 0$ & $e = 0$
   then $\phi(u) =$ constant.
   Thus there is no maximum along that edge.

2) $de = 0$
   if $d = 0$ and $e \neq 0$ then $u = 1$,
   if $e = 0$ and $d \neq 0$ then $u = 0$.
   Thus there is no maximum along that edge.

3) $de < 0$
   implies that d and e are of opposite signs. So, either $u < 0$ or $u > 1$.
   So there is no maximum on the edge.

4) $de > 0$
   implies that d and e are of the same sign, and so $0 < u < 1$.
   Thus there is a maximum along the edge.

Thus, $de > 0$ is a necessary and sufficient condition for the intensity of the specular highlight to reach a maximum between the two vertices.

Test C. This test determines whether the value of the maximum located by test B is greater than zero. This is a less expensive preliminary to test D, and is also necessary to ensure the validity of subsequent tests.

From test B we have that

$$\phi(u) = \frac{a + u(b-a)}{\sqrt{(pu^2-pu+1)}}$$

Now, at the point of maximum we require

$$\phi(u) > 0 \quad \text{ie.} \quad a+u(b-a) > 0$$

Re-arranging gives $\quad d(ad+be) > 0$

Setting $g = ad+be$ gives $\quad dg > 0$

Thus, if $dg > 0$ then the value of the maximum from test C is greater than zero.

Test D. All that now remains to be determined is whether the maximum is greater than the threshold.

ie. $\phi(u) \geq T$ or $a+u(b-a) \geq T\sqrt{(pu^2-pu+1)}$

From the previous test, we know that $a+u(b-a) > 0$, and $T > 0$ by definition, thus

$$[a+u(b-a)]^2 \geq T^2(pu^2-pu+1)$$

Re-arranging and setting $f = de$ gives

$$g^2 \geq T^2(d^2+2cf+e^2).$$

Thus, if this condition is satisfied, then the value of **N.H** at the point of maximum is greater than the threshold and there is a visible highlight crossing the edge.

We can now discuss the way in which these tests detect the cases shown in Fig. 2:

Case 1) - one or more of the polygons vertices are within the visible area of the highlight. Test **A** is applied to each vertex in turn.

Case 2) - one or more of a polygons edges are within the visible area of a specular highlight. This is found by sequential application of Tests B, C and D.

Case 3) - will only occur on large polygons, with very tight specular highlights. This usually means that the object has been defined by insufficient polygons. This will result in very noticeable Mach bands together with non-smooth silhouette edges. Although this case was not considered to be very important, an extra test

(Test E) was added. If a maximum occurs on every polygon edge (each such maximum being less than the threshold) then there is a completely enclosed highlight on that polygon. This inexpensive test will trap many such highlights.

Test E. This final test determines whether a polygon completely contains the visible region of a specular highlight.

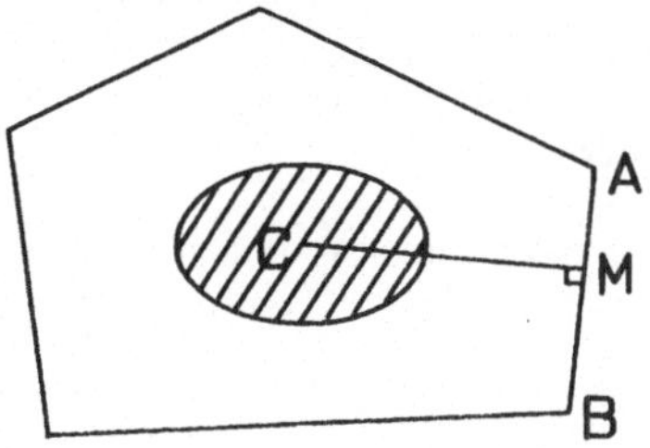

Fig. 3. The position of one of the maximums formed by a completely enclosed specular highlight.

Consider the polygon of Fig. 3, where the specular highlight is completely contained within the polygon, and centred on C. Along the edge AB the intensity will reach a maximum (with **N.H** less than the threshold) at M. Where M is the point of intersection of the edge AB and the line perpendicular to AB and passing through C. This assumes that the specular highlight is bounded by a convex curve. If there is a maximum on each of the polygon edges then there is a specular highlight present on that polygon.

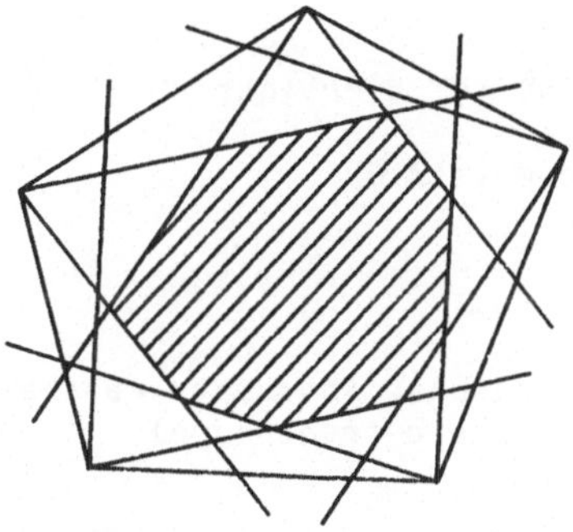

Fig. 4. The area of a polygon on which a totally enclosed specular highlight must be centred for test E to be effective.

Test E will only detect specular highlights centred within the shaded area of Fig. 4. This area is defined by the perpendiculars to the edges at each of the vertices.

In general for a reasonably 'regular' polygon (ie. all the sides and angles are of a similar size), this area will lie towards the centre of the polygon. Now, as tests A-D detect all specular highlights crossing a vertex or an edge, test E will trap all the remaining highlights, except for those that are centred on the unshaded portion of Fig. 4 and do not cross the polygon boundary.

Thus, the H-test will trap the vast majority of highlights, and in general will only fail on large (or irregularly shaped) polygons with small highlights near but not touching the polygon's boundary.

Case 4) - If all the above five tests have failed then the polygon is assumed to have no visible specular highlight, and thus no Phong shading is required.

The H-test Algorithm. The algorithm is now given in the form of a pseudo Pascal function:

```
FUNCTION H_test : boolean;

  VAR
    a,b,c,d,e,f,g : real;
    all_edges_max : boolean;
    highlight : boolean;

BEGIN
  all_edges_max := true;
  highlight := false;
  WHILE more_vertices AND NOT highlight DO
  BEGIN
    get_next_normal(A);
    IF A.H > T THEN        {the current vertex is within the visible}
      highlight := true    {region of a specular highlight}
  END;

  reset_polygon_data;
  WHILE more_vertices AND NOT highlight DO
  BEGIN
    get_next_pair_of_normals(A,B);
    a := A.H; b := B.H;
    c := A.B;
    d := b*c-a; e := a*c-b;
    f := d*e;
    IF f > 0 THEN {the specular intensity reaches a maximum}
    BEGIN          {along the current edge}
      g := a*d + b*e;

      IF d*g > 0 THEN {the maximum is greater than zero}

        IF g² ≥ T²*(d²+2*c*f+e²) THEN {the maximum is greater}
          highlight := true            {than the threshold}
    END
    ELSE {the current edge did not have a maximum}
      all_edges_max := false
  END;

  H_test := highlight OR all_edges_max;
END {H_test};
```

Analysis of the Algorithm. Each test was analysed, as shown in Table 1, where '+' refers to addition, subtraction and comparison operations. Square operations are listed separately because with suitable hardware/software, it is possible to perform them more efficiently than by using a call to multiply.

Table 1. The calculations required to perform each of the four basic tests (A-D) on a polygon edge.

	+	*	x^2
A	3	3	0
B	5	6	0
C	2	3	0
D	3	3	4

The calculations needed to fully determine the case applicable to a particular polygon edge are given in Table 2. Note, that the letters indicate which of the tests have to be performed to determine the given result. Upper case letters indicate that the test was successful, lower case letters that it failed.

Table 2. The five possible results of applying the H-test to a polygon edge.

Tests performed	Result for single edge	Possible results for parent polygon (Cases)	Total calculations		
			+	*	x^2
A	highlight	1	3	3	0
ab	no highlight	1,2,4	8	9	0
aBc	no highlight	1,2,3,4	10	12	0
aBCd	no highlight	1,2,3,4	13	15	4
aBCD	highlight	2	13	15	4

In general, most polygons will not have a highlight, so the most common result will be 'ab'. Unfortunately, the H-test will have to be applied to each polygon edge before the polygon can be recorded as having no highlight. For most well defined objects, any highlighted polygons will be determined by test A alone. This test is performed as a separate preliminary on each vertex in turn until it either succeeds, or fails for every vertex.

Tests C and D will be performed on very few polygons (generally only on objects defined by insufficient polygons).

If the result is 'aBc' or 'aBCd' for each edge (ie. a maximum on every edge) then test E will succeed, indicating that the current polygon corresponds to case 3), and thus there is a highlight present.

Example Timings. The time taken to evaluate the H-test and to perform the rendering are given, Table 3, for the test torii as defined above. Also provided are the timings for the same objects rendered using Phong shading and Gouraud shading using diffuse reflection only. As well as the time taken to perform hidden surface removal but without any shading calculations or interpolation.

Table 3. Rendering times for various shading methods.

Object:		10x20	15x30	20x40
Number of polygons:	Visible:	99	223	393
	Highlighted:	24	50	74
Time (seconds) for shading:	None:	69	87	109
	Gouraud:	123	146	172
	Phong:	327	357	389
	Fast Phong:	278	314	349
	H-test:	187	209	232

The Phong shading algorithm (used for both the combined shading and the fast Phong shading timings given below), uses efficient incremental calculations which combine the interpolation of the polygon normals with the evaluation of the dot products **L.N** and **N.H.** The row labelled Phong gives the timings for a standard Phong shading implementation. In this context 'standard' means a direct or 'lazy' implementation of the Phong equation.

Table 4. Timings expressed relative to Gouraud shading

	10x20	15x30	20x40
Gouraud	1.00	1.00	1.00
Phong	4.78	4.58	4.44
Fast Phong	3.87	3.85	3.81
H-test	2.19	2.07	1.95

Table 5. Timings expressed relative to Phong shading

	10x20	15x30	20x40
Gouraud	0.21	0.22	0.23
Phong	1.00	1.00	1.00
Fast Phong	0.81	0.84	0.86
H-test	0.46	0.45	0.44

Relative timings are given in Tables 4 and 5. Note, these timings only compare the time taken for actual shading calculations, the relative time for 'None' would be zero.

Applicability to Multiple Light Sources. The visual attraction of many images can be significantly increased by the use of multiple light sources, compare Figs. 5A and 5B. Unfortunately, with Phong shading the rendering time increases dramatically. Gouraud shading is not usually

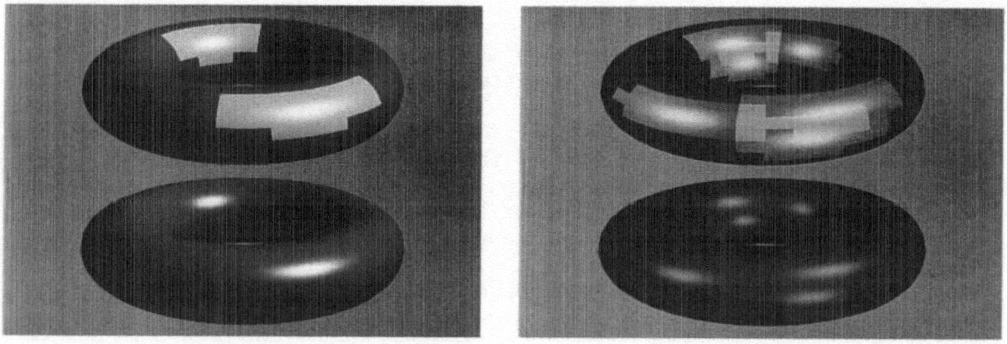

A B

Fig. 5A-B. The highlighted polygons (yellow) as determined by the H-test together with the appearance of the final image. A one light source, B three light sources.

suitable as it is the extra specular highlights which generally add to the aesthetics of the image.

In a Phong shading environment the use of multiple light sources requires the intensity equation to be evaluated for each light source for every visible pixel of the object. This significantly increases the overall rendering time. Gouraud shading only requires extra intensity calculations to be performed at the polygon vertices, the interpolation time remaining constant.

The extra rendering time needed, when using combined shading, will not be as significant as that needed for Phong shading. This assumes that a large proportion of the polygons remain free of specular highlights. The efficiency of this technique can be guaranteed by recording which light sources are producing a specular highlight on a particular polygon (rather than simply recording the polygon as being highlighted). Fig. 5B shows few polygons which are highlighted by more than one light source. In this case it is only necessary to evaluate the Phong specular term for a subset (possibly none) of the light sources.

Conclusions. Using the new combined shading algorithm, images of a similar quality to those rendered using Phong shading can be produced in significantly less time. The H-test also allows the efficient implementation of multiple light sources, thus giving greater flexibility in the production of aesthetically pleasing images.

A useful side effect of this method, is that it separates the specular component from the ambient and diffuse components. As the ambient and diffuse components are produced by Gouraud shading, the image can be stored as a sequence of line segments of linearly changing intensity, with the specular information stored at the end of the file. In this way the storage requirements for such images can be significantly reduced. The algorithm has also shown itself to be relatively simple to implement within a Phong shading environment, requiring two minor changes to the rendering program:

1) The addition of the H-test function and a tag field for each polygon in the database. The H-test function then needs to be evaluated for each polygon, the polygon being tagged according to the result.

2) Modification of the rendering section of the program. This involves evaluating and saving the sum of the ambient and diffuse terms of the intensity equation at each polygon vertex. These values are then used by a Gouraud shader, which checks the tag field to see if a specular highlight is present on the current polygon. If this is the case then the simplified Phong shader (which evaluates the specular term only) is run in parallel with the Gouraud shader.

References

1. Bergman L, Fuchs H, Grant E and Spach S (1986) Image Rendering by Adaptive Refinement. Computer Graphics 20(4):29-37

2. Bishop G (1986) Fast Phong Shading. ACM Computer Graphics 20(4):103-106

3. Duff T (1979) Smoothly Shaded Renderings of Polyhedral Objects on Raster Displays. ACM Computer Graphics 13(2):270-275

4. Gouraud H (1971) Continuous Shading of Curved Surfaces. IEEE Transactions on Computers C-20(6):623-629

5. Phong BT (1975) Illumination for Computer Generated Pictures. Communications of the ACM 18(60):311-317.

6. Phong BT (1975a) Improved rendition of polygonal models of curved surfaces. Proceedings Second USA-Japan Computer Conference:475-480.

Synthetic Image Generation for Highly Defocused Scenes

Y. C. Chen (USA)

ABSTRACT

The algorithm for synthetic image generation with the lens effect consists of two consecutive processors: the hidden-surface processor and the focus processor (Potmesil and Chakravarty 1981). This algorithm was revised by Chen (1987) using simple light particle theory instead of the wave theory to avoid the complicated calculation and the huge memory consumption. However, from the experimental observation, the algorithm based on hidden-surface processor and focus processor can only serve as an approximation formula for the slightly defocused scenes. The purpose of this paper is to present a new algorithm for the highly defocused scenes. An image generated using this new algorithm was compared to the real photograph captured by a camera, and no noticeable difference of the defocused effect between the image and the photograph can be detected.

Keywords: computer graphics, synthetic image generation, lens effect,blurry image, defocused scene, light particle theory, camera model

1. INTRODUCTION

Blurring is a factor affecting the realism of the visual system (Newman 1973; Foley 1982). Blur on objects provides the viewers with the three-dimensional feeling of the objects. The blurring effects on the synthetic image can be simulated by an image captured through a lens and an aperture.

The usefulness of blurring effect on the synthetic image generation is several folds. Through the blurring effect one can select highlighting and direct the viewer's attention to a particular portion of the image. It is also useful for many commonly used cinematographic techniques for animated sequences, such as fade-in and fade-out. Furthermore, it provides the viewers with three-dimensional feeling by the effect of the depth of field.

One of major works in simulating the lens and the aperture is to calculate the light intensity distribution coefficient f_{ij}, between pixels i and j. The coefficient f_{ij} can be obtained from either the diffraction of light wave (Potmesil 1981, 1982) or the propagation of particle (Chen 1987).

Based on light intensity distribution coefficients f_{ij}, the processor of generating the synthetic image under the lens and the aperture effects can be decomposed into two independent sub-processors: the hidden-surface processor and the focus processor (Potmesil 1981, 1982). The hidden-surface processor uses any ray-tracing algorithm (Whitted 1980; Kay 1979) to create a temporary intermediate image plane. The focus processor, which combines the data created by the hidden-surface processor and the coefficients of light intensity distribution f_{ij}, generates the synthetic image. However, the algorithm based on focus processor and the hidden-surface processor is only an approximate approach. For the highly defocused scene, the algorithm is unable to produce reasonable image of the scene, because the pin-hole camera model used in hidden-surface processor eliminates all the information of the scene behind the objects. In the highly defocused case, part of the scene behind objects can be clearly seen from the image plane. In other words, the object can not completely block the scene behind it. In an image with clear background, a new coefficient b_{ij}, called blocking coefficient, is defined to describe the amount of light intensity in pixel i on the image plane blocked by the small object j. Similar to the coefficient f_{ij}, b_{ij} can be obtained from the light particle theory. The new algorithm, which I developed, is suitable for the general highly defocused sences.

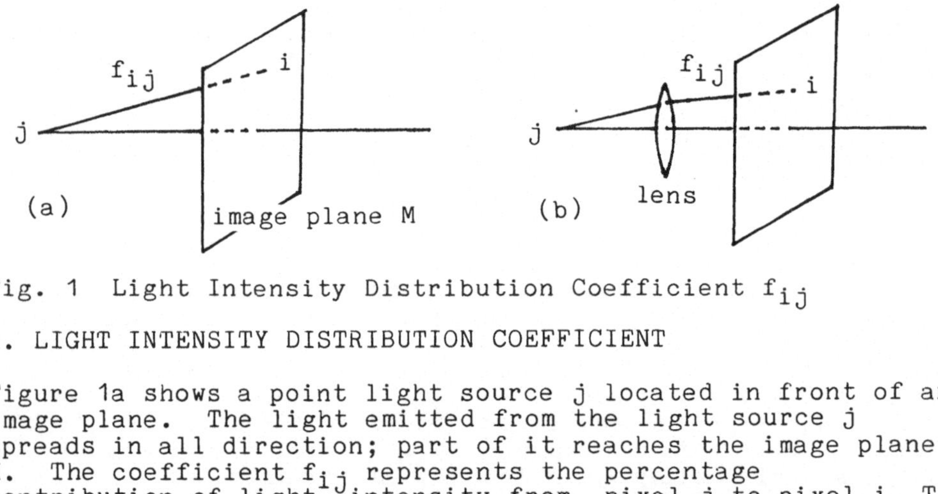

Fig. 1 Light Intensity Distribution Coefficient f_{ij}

2. LIGHT INTENSITY DISTRIBUTION COEFFICIENT

Figure 1a shows a point light source j located in front of an image plane. The light emitted from the light source j spreads in all direction; part of it reaches the image plane M. The coefficient f_{ij} represents the percentage contribution of light intensity from pixel j to pixel i. The same definition is used in the case a lens and an aperture are present between the point light source j and the image plane M (Fig. 1b). While the light intensity of the light source at pixel j is set to be 1 (one), the light intensity found at pixel i on the image plane is equivalent to the coefficient f_{ij}. The light intensity at pixel i can be calculated by two different theories: wave theory (Potmesil 1981; 1982; Beiser 1964; Born 1970) and light particle theory (Chen 1987).

The conventional treatment of lens effect is based on the wave theory of light. The calculations involved are tedious and time consuming. The detail formula for f_{ij} can be found in Potmesil's papers (1981;1982). It was found that the intensity distribution coefficients derived from the particle theory (Chen 1987) can give an adequate represention of the exact formula derived from the wave theory. The f_{ij} can be found in terms of the object length p, the diameter of the lens d, the focal length of the lens F, and the defocused distance z', as described below:

$$f_{ij} = 4\Delta/\pi G^2 \text{ if i is inside the geometry image circle,}$$
$$= 0 \text{ if i is outside the geometry image circle,} \quad (1)$$

where Δ is the pixel area and G, the diameter of the geometry image circle, which is d.z'.(1/F+1/p).

3. THE ALGORITHM FOR SLIGHTLY DEFOCUSED SCENES

The algorithm for rendering slightly defocused scene (Potmesil 1981, 1982) consists of two independent processors: the hidden-surface processor and the focus processor.

(a) The Hidden-surface Processor

The hidden-surface processor calculates the information of each sample point on the intermediate image plane by using a geometric pin-hole camera model.

The hidden-surface processor traces the ray from each sample point through the pin-hole to the object and then to the background. Many ray-tracing and hidden-surface algorithms (Whitted 1980; Kay 1979) can be used in this processor.

(b) The Focus Processor

The focus processor generates the synthetic image on the graphic raster display by using the information of each pixel on the intermediate image plane P. The information contains RGB intensities and the depth z of the sample point on the object. Each pixel on the intermediate image plane can be considered an imaginary point light source q_j located at distance z from the lens with three intensities for the three primary colors (RGB). Q_{ij}, the intensity of the ith pixel on the raster display contributed by the imaginary light source q_j, can be expressed as

$$Q_{ij} = f_{ij} \cdot q_j,$$

where the coefficient f_{ij} is the percentage of light intensity of the pixel j contributed to the pixel i. The final intensity Q_i of pixel i is computed as the weighted average of all the input sample points (Potmesil 1982). Thus,

$$Q_i = \sum_j f_{ij} \cdot q_j / \sum_j f_{ij} ,$$

where the index j sums over all pixels on the intermediate image plane.

Fig. 2 Scene with Highly Defocused Object

4. ALGORITHM FOR HIGHLY DEFOCUSED SCENE WITH CLEAR BACKGROUND

In the hidden-surface processor, only a very small amount of light can pass through the infinitesimal pin-hole; therefore, the hidden objects are invisible. The results produced by the processor are different from the real photographs (Fig. 2) taken by cameras. The scene consisting of a white wall with blue strips in Fig. 2 is behind a small red disk. While the disk is highly defocused, the whole wall can be seen through the blurred disk. Therefore, the rendering algorithm using the pin-hole model is considered as a very rough approximate method. In the slightly defocused scene, the partial visibilty of the hidden object is difficult to detect by the human perception system. Thus, the algorithm with the pin-hole model is acceptable in the slightly defocused scene.

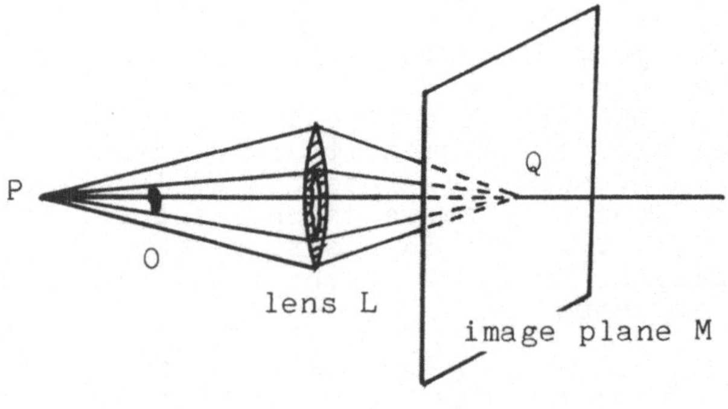

Fig. 3 Partial Visibility of Hidden Object

In the highly defocused image, on the other hand, the partial visibility for the scene behind an blurred object is obvious. The reason for the partial visibility of a hidden object is illustrated in Fig. 3. The part of light emitted from the point P is blocked by the object O. The remaining light rays (shaded area), reaching the lens L are bent toward point Q on the image plane M by the lens L. Because the part of light from P can form a image point Q, P is visible from the image plane M.

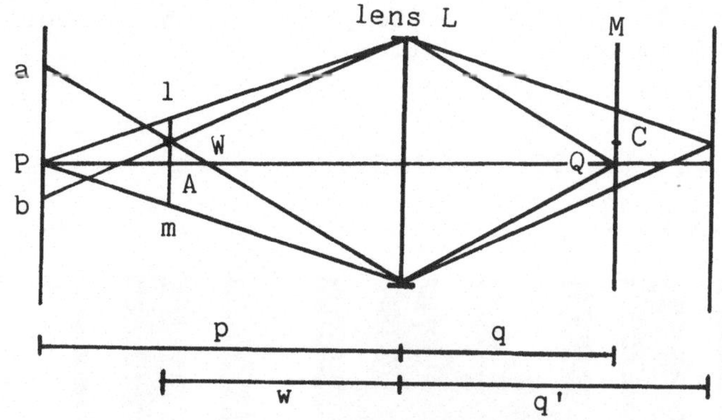

Fig. 4 Coordinate System for Blocking Coefficient b_{ij}

A scene consisting of two small objects P and W is used to test the blocking effect. The distance p and w are measured from the lens L to the objects P and W, respectivly (Fig. 4). An image plane M is placed at the distance q behind the lens, where q satisfies the equation $1/p + 1/q = 1/F$, so that the object P can form a sharp image on the image plane M. Without the object W, all the light rays from the object P reaching the lens are bent toward the image point Q on the image plane M. While the object W is present between P and L, a fraction Δ/A of light is blocked by the object W, and the light intensity in Q is reduced by the same fraction Δ/A, where Δ is the area of the object W and A is the cross section area of the cone of which the vertice and the base are at the positions of P and L, respectively. Notice that the fraction is not a function of the vertical coordinates of the object W. All the objects located inside the circle of which the diameter denoted $\overline{ab}$ are blocked by the object W by a factor of Δ/A; the objects outside the circle are not blocked by the object W. The image of the circular area denoted $\overline{ab}$ is also a circular area, C, on the image plane. The center of the circular area C is at the forward direction of the object W. From the formula that the length ratio of the object P to the image Q is equal to the ratio of p to q, the diameter D of the circular area C can be obtained as

$$D = (\overline{ab}.q)/p = (d.(p-w).q)/(w.p) = (1/w+1/p).q.p. \qquad (2)$$

The right hand side of the above equation is equivalent to the diameter G of the geometry image circle of the object W on the image plane M, because

$$G = (q'-q).d/q = (1/q-1/q').q.p = ((1/F-1/p)-(1/F-1/w)).q.d$$

$$= (1/w-1/p).q.d = D,$$

where q' is the image distance of W. In other words, the object W has two effects to any pixel i inside the geometry image circle of W: (1) Pixel i receives f_{iw} of light intensity from W, and (2) The intensity, obtaining from the objects on the plane at position of P, of pixel j is reduced by a factor of Δ/A, which can be proven to be proportional to f_{iw}. The proof is shown as follow:

$$\Delta/A = 4\Delta/(\pi\overline{Im}^2) = 4\Delta/(\pi\overline{ab}^2).p^2/(p-w)^2$$

$$= 4\Delta/(\pi D^2).q^2/(p-w)^2 = 4\Delta/(\pi G^2).q^2/(p-w)^2$$

$$= f_{ij}.q^2/(p-w)^2.$$

Fig. 5 Photograph of Blue Strip Wall behind Blurred Red Disk

Fig. 6 Computer Generated Image of Wall and Disk

The blocking effect on a sharp image can be described by a simple coefficient b_{ij}, which is proportional to f_{ij}. Therefore, the algorithm for rendering the scene consisting of a clear background and blocking objects located on a vertical plane becomes quite simple: Rendering the sharp images first and then the blocking objects, which is blurred on the image plane, by the formula

$$I_i = I^o_i \left(1 - \sum_w b_{iw}\right) + \sum_w I_w.f_{iw}, \qquad (3)$$

where I^o_i is the original light intensity in pixel i, I_i is the new light intensity in pixel i, I_w is the light intensity of the wth pixel of blocking objects, and the index w sums over all the blocking objects.

A scene with a white and blue strips background located 4.5 meter from a camera and a red disk with 0.3 meter diameter located 2 meters in front of the camera is used to check the validity of the algorithm. Figure 5 is the photograph of the scene taken by the camera with a 50mm lens having 135mm focal length. Figure 6 shows the same scene generated by the computer using the above algorithm. There are some differences between Fig. 5 and Fig. 6 in color, texture, and brightness. However, the blurring effects in the both pictures are almost alike, showing that the formula (3) is very close to the real situation.

Fig. 7 Geometry Image Circle and Shadow

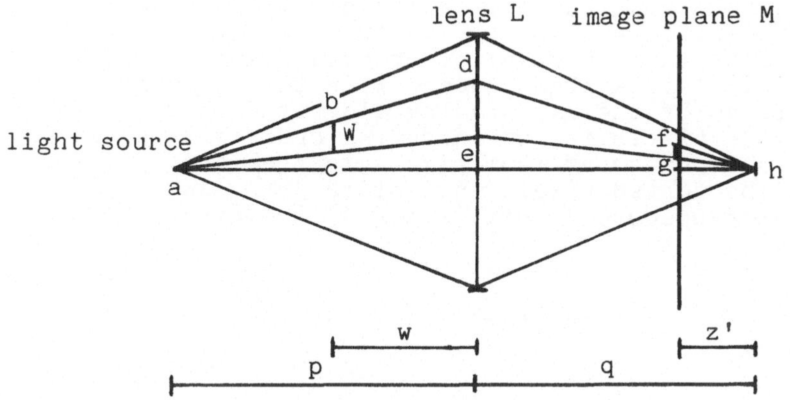

Fig. 8 Coordinate System of Defocused Scene

5. ALGORITHM FOR GENERAL DEFOCUSED SCENES

The blocking effect can be expanded to generate the general defocused scene. The image of a point light source on an image plane with defocused distance z' is a circular area (Fig. 7a). From equation (1), the diameter of the circular area is d.z'/q. If a small circular object W with diameter t is present between the light source and the lens (Fig. 8), then part of light from the light source is blocked by the object W. The amount of light blocked is proportional to the area of the object W. The image of the light source on the image plane M is shown in Fig. 7b. The small circle is the shadow of the object W. The diameter and the center of the shadow are K.t and (K.x, K.y), respectively. The distance w is measured from the object to the lens, (x,y) is the Cartesian coordinate of the object W, and K=z'.p/(p-w).q. This is due to the similarities between triangles abc and ade, and triangles hfg and hde. Thus, the light intensity distribution function f_{ij} in equation (1) is modified as

$$f_{ij} = 4\Delta/\pi G^2 \text{ ...if is i in the geometry image circle of j and not in the shadows of objects before j,}$$
$$= 0 \text{ .....elsewhere.}$$

Hence, the revised f_{ij} is not only a function of the coordinate of pixel i and pixel j, but also a function of the coordinates of objects before j. The rendering algorithm for the defocused scene must contain a step to check whether pixel i is located inside the shadows of all the objects closer to the lens than pixel j. The details of the algorithm is described as follow:

ALGORITHM

0. main procedure
   a. Subdivide the surfaces of all the objects in the scene into small units, called pixels. Using any ray-tracing algorithm to find the light intensity in each pixel of objects. Assume that each pixel is a light source with the intensity I_j, found by the ray-tracing alogrithm.
   b. Sort the pixels in the ascending order of the distances measured from pixels to the lens.
   c. Push the sorted pixels into stack 1.
   d. Repeat procedure 1 until stack 1 is empty.
   e. Stop.

1. Procedure 1
   a. Pop a pixel j from stack 1 and call procedure 2.
   b. Return.

2. Procedure 2
   a. Compute the geometry image circle of pixel j on the image plane.
   b. Push all the pixels inside the circle into stack 2.
   c. Repeat procedure 3 until stack 2 is empty.
   d. Return.

3. Procedure 3
   a. Pop a pixel i from stack 2.
   b. If pixel i is ouside the shadows of all the pixels in stack 1, then add $I_j \cdot 4 \cdot \Delta/\pi G^2$ to the light intensity I_i of pixel i.
   c. Return.

4. End.

The algorithm for the general highly defocused scene is very time consuming, because for each pixel i inside the geometry image circle of j, the algorithm searchs every pixel left in stack 2 to determine whether pixel i is in its shadows. Fortunately, most scenes people interested are either with a clear background, such as a wedding photograph through a blurred heart shaped gate or with a background which is already rendered. In the first case, the simpler algorithm with blocking coefficient b_{ij} discussed in the last section can be applied directly. In the second case, the rendered background can be approximated by an image of a photograph located at a distance F.q/(q-F) in front of the lens, where q is the distance from the image plane to the lens. The final image can be considered as the image of the object with the clear background, formed by the imaginary photograph. Consequently, the image can be handled by the algorithm discussed in the last section.

6. CONCLUSION

In this paper, the previous work on the blurred image has been briefly reviewed. An algorithm for highly defocused scene with clear background was developed in section 4. Another algorithm is proposed to render general highly defocused scenes. Since the blocking factor is a function of positions of the light source, pixels on the image plane, and the blocking objects, is makes the algorithm time consuming. Fortunately, most defocused scenes can be tranferred to the case which can be handled by the algorithm in section 4, such as wedding photograph through a blurred heart shaped gate.

7. BIBLIOGRAPHY

Beiser A (1964) The Science of Physics. Addison-Wesley, Reading, MA

Born M, Wolf E (1970) Principles of Optics, 4th ed. Pergamon, London

Chen Y. (1987) Lens Effect on Synthetic Image Generation Based on Light Partical Theory. Computer Graphics 1987: 347-366; also in The Visual Computer 3(3):125-136

Cook L, Porter T, Carpenter L (1984) Distributed Ray-Tracing. Computer Graphics 18(3):137-145

Foley J, Van Dan A (1982) Fundamentals of Interactive Computer Graphics. Addison-Wesley, Menlo Park, CA

Kay D, Greenberg D (1979) Transparency for Computer Synthesied Images. Computer Graphics 13(2):158-164

Newman W, Sproull R (1973) Principles of Interactive Computer Graphics. McGraw-Hill, New York, NY

Potmesil M, Chakravarty I (1981) A Lens and Camera Model for Synthetic Image Generation. Computer Graphics 15(3):297-305

Potmesil M, Chakravarty I (1982) Synthetic Image Generation with a lens and Aperture Camera Model. ACM Transaction on Graphics 1(2):85-108

Whitted T (1980) An Improved Illumination Model for Shaded Display. CACM 23(6):343-349

Particals: An Artistic Approach to Fuzzy Objects

M. Inakage (Japan)

ABSTRACT

An artistic approach for modeling fuzzy objects called Particals is presented. The method unifies the modeling and rendering process. Particals treat fuzzy objects as a cluster of miniscule particles. The distribution of particles is defined by a stochastic function. Particles are generated during the rendering process by referencing the stochastic function. Ray tracing is used for rendering so that intersection, reflection, refraction, and shadow calculations can be incorporated. The algorithm is efficient and it produces impressionistic images with very intricate textures. However, it suffers from the stobing effect in animation sequences because the method does not maintain frame to frame coherence. The particles appears to be equal in size because the size is fixed to the size of the pixel on the image screen.

Keywords: computer art, ray tracing, stochastic modeling, texture

1. Introduction

Three dimensional computer graphics modeling has been focused on the solid objects. Various texture mapping techniques are used to add textures onto a surface to provide visual complexity [1,6,7]. These image synthesis methods are appropriate for modeling solid objects, but they are not suited for handling a class of "fuzzy" objects. In many cases, methods for modeling fuzzy objects are adopted to the visual simulation of natural phenomena.

Blinn [2] introduced a method for simulating light reflections from dusty surfaces. This method treated clouds as thin layer of surfaces such as rings of Saturn. Kajiya and von Herzen [4] and Nomura et al. [5] presented a volume density approach to simulate thick layers of clouds. The volume density approach suffers from its computational cost. Gardner [3] developed an algorithm for visual simulation of clouds. Reeves [8] introduced particle systems to model fuzzy objects as a collection of miniscule particles. Particle systems can easily become computationally and memory intensive because particles must be pre-generated in a spherical volume. The rendering of particles are treated separately from the other objects. The separately rendered images are composited during the postrendering process. Hence, fuzzy objects defined by the particle systems cannot intersect with other objects, nor can they be reflected or cast shadows onto other objects.

This paper introduces a method for modeling "fuzzy" objects which consist of miniscule particles. The method is called Particals. The goal of this paper is to achieve the esthetic quality of natural phenomena represented by fuzzy objects, and not the physical characteristics of these phenomena. The algorithm does not generate photo-realistic imagery because it is based on the esthetic interpretation of natural phenomena. Particals produces impressionistic images with intricate textures which resembles the painting technique developed by the postimpressionist painters.

2. Particals

Dusts and fogs are composed of minute particles which are scattered stochastically inside a finite volume. There are two ways to model such volume. One approach is to actually generate millions of particle inside a defined volume. The other approach is to functionally define the distribution of particles for a given volume. Particle systems use the former aprroach while particals take the latter approach. The particals method is a functional based modeling method which integrates the modeling and rendering processes. Fuzzy objects are defined by a stochastic function which is later used by the renderer. This approach eliminates the necessity to pre-generate the particles, both saving computational cost and memory space.

2.1 The Basic Model

The basic model of particals is a stochastically defined spherical volume. The equation of a sphere for a radius r is

$$r = \sqrt{a(x-x_0)^2 + b(y-y_0)^2 + c(z-z_0)^2}$$

where a,b,c are scale parameters, and x_0,y_0,z_0 are the coordinates for the center of sphere.

The surface of sphere is considered to be a collection of points. In order to stochastically distribute the particles, the surface of sphere is fragmented into minute fragments. Each surface fragment represents a particle. A stochastic function is applied to the radius r to define fuzzy objects. Figure 1 illustrates the particals. The two radii $r1$ and $r2$ corresponds to the solid and fuzzy surfaces repectively. The degree of fragmentation depends on the ratio between the radii $r1$ and $r2$. The radius of fuzzy objects is a sum of the two radii $r1$ and $r2$:

$$R = r1 + r2$$
$$r2 = random()$$

where R is the radius of fuzzy objects, and *random()* is a stochastic function. Since $r1$ does not vary while $r2$ is varied, the radius of fuzzy objects is $r1 \leq R \leq (r1 + r2)$.

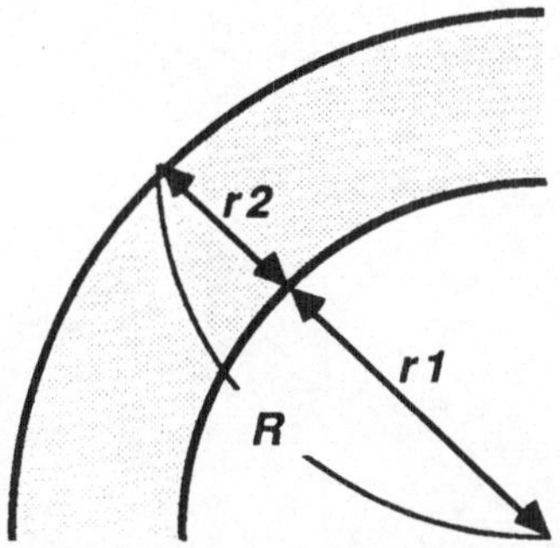

Fig.1 Stochastically defined fuzzy objects

2.2 Rendering

Ray tracing is used to render the particals so that reflections, refractions and shadows can be included. Rendering the particals relies on the point sampling process of ray tracing algorithm. Rays are shot from the eye point and extended to the object space via a screen. The screen point samples the rays. For each ray, the ray is traced and tested for an intersection with objects. To test for an intersection with particals, the radius is determined by the stochastic function for each sampled ray. The result is a decomposition of the spherical surface at the screen resolution. Fuzzy objects defined by the particals are further compared with other intersecting objects along the extended eye ray. The closest intersecting object is used to calculate the intensity of reflecting light. Hence, particals can intersect with other objects and other particals.

Figure 2 shows the ray intersection with the particals. The sphere is positioned at point C, and it has a fixed radius AC and a stochastically varied radius AB. The total radius of a "fuzzy" sphere varies between $AC \leq R \leq BC$. Depending on the size of radius R, the ray intersects with the particals. If the ray intersects with particals, shading model is applied to calculate the intensity of reflecting light at the fragmented surface. Figures 3 and 4 show the particals with different ratio of fixed and varying radii. Note that the highlight is distorted in fig. 4 due to the fragmented surface.

Particals can be reflected onto other objects, refracted by lenses, and cast shadows. These effects are the features of ray tracing renderer. The reflected particals and shadows rely on the self-similarity of the stochastic modeling. When the ray is reflected by a reflective surface, the reflected ray is extended to be tested for intersections. To test for ray-surface intersection with the particals, the stochastic function is used to determine the radius. Similarly, the stochastic function is used to generate the particals for the shadow test. Figure 5 shows that the particals can be reflected and cast shadows. These particles are not actually casting shadows nor are reflected onto the solid sphere. They only have similar appearances.

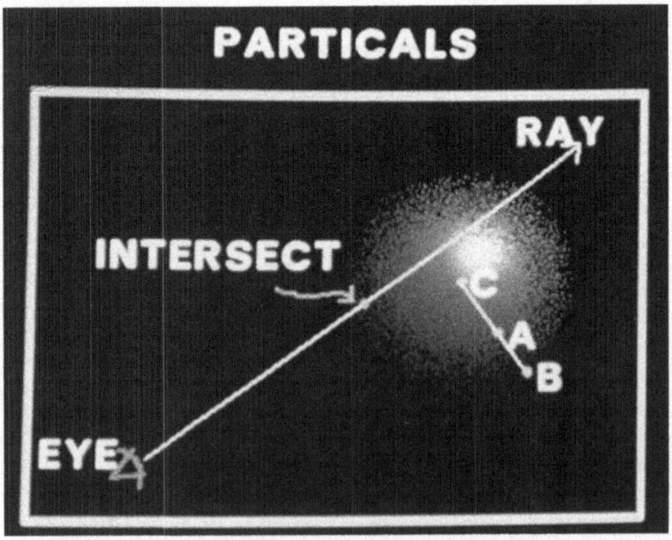

Fig. 2 Eye ray intersecting with the particals

The stochastic modeling have another feature, the levels of detail. As the particals occupy larger area of the screen, more rays intersect with the stochstically varying surface. Hence, more particles are rendered. Since the distribution characteristics of the particals follows the self-similarity law of stochastic modeling, it appears that more detail is becoming visible. Figure 6 illustrates the levels of detail. It is a closer view of fig. 5. The camera is positioned closer to the particals which is covering larger area on the screen.

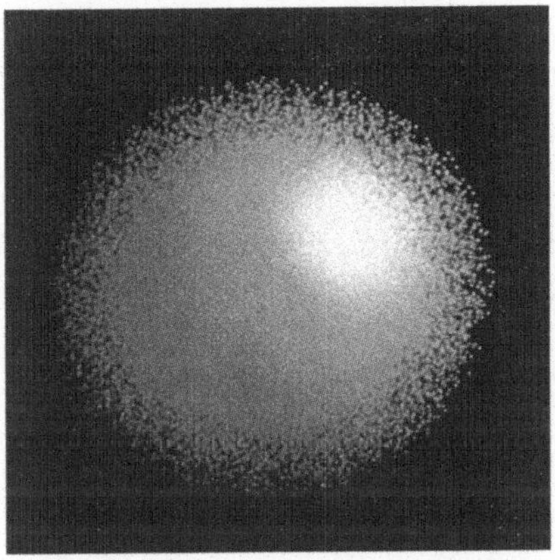

Fig. 3 Particals with small stochastic radius

Fig. 5 Reflected and shadow particals

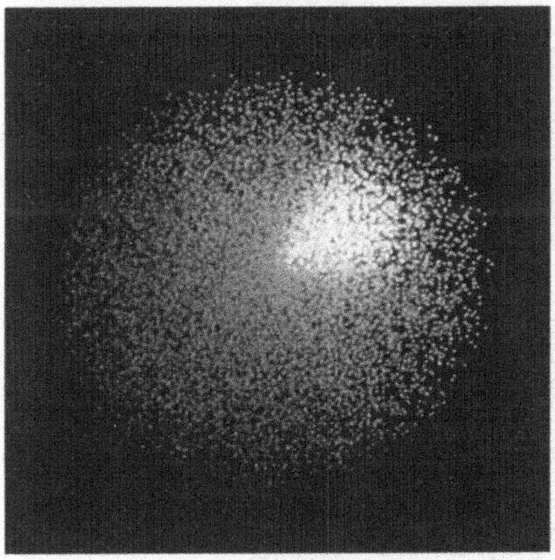

Fig. 4 Particals dominated by stochastic function

Fig. 6 Closer view of particals

3. Artistic Applications

Particals provide impressionistic images of "fuzzy" objects. In addition, the images possess visually intricate and delicate three dimensional textures. Figure 7 ("Fogbow") and fig. 8 ("Evolution") are examples of particals that are used to generate intricate textures. Many intersecting particals objects are positioned near the camera to cover the entire screen. This technique resembles the technique called the pointillism, which is used in the paintings by Seurat, a French postimpressionist painter. The colored points are blended in the eye.

Figure 9 ("POP") shows the particals with reflectance mapping. For the ray that intersects with the particals, the reflectance map is referenced using the radius as an index to the map. Both fig. 8 and 9 are rendered on a 16 bit personal computer. The particals method is computationally inexpensive because only a stochastic function is added to the standard ray tracing renderer.

Figures 10 and 11 ("Sandstorm" and "Dream Cloud" respectively) are examples of particals intersecting with solid objects and particals. The advantage of particals over other methods is that the particals are not treated as a special case by the renderer. Hence, the method can be easily incorporated into the existing renderer. The three dimensional quality of clustered particles and its intricate texture extend the possibility of expression by ray tracing. The contrast of photo-realistic rendering and the impressionistic rendering can be combined in three dimensional space.

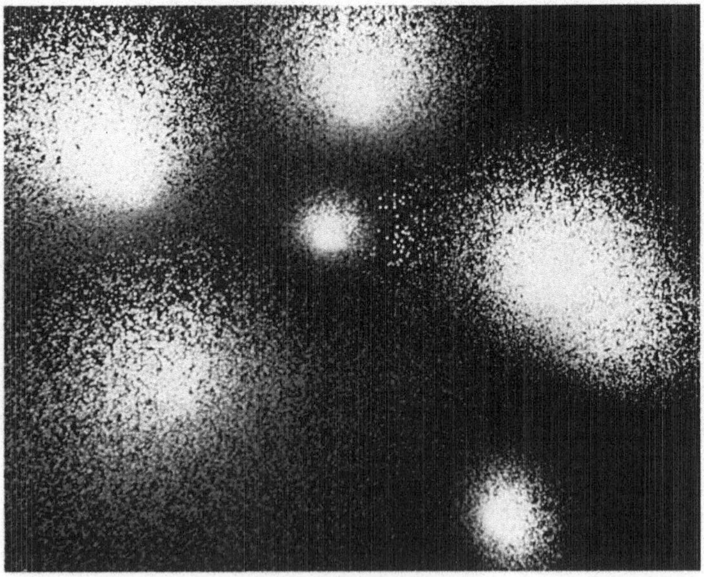

Fig. 7 "Fogbow"

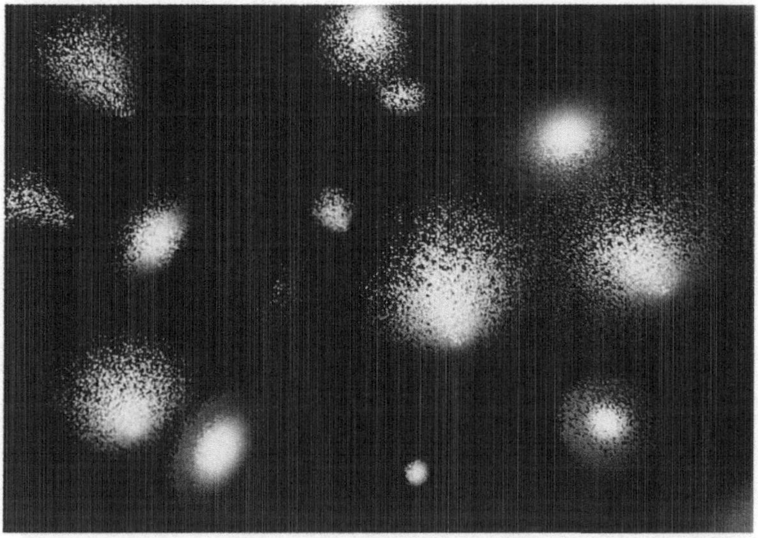

Fig. 8 "Evolution"

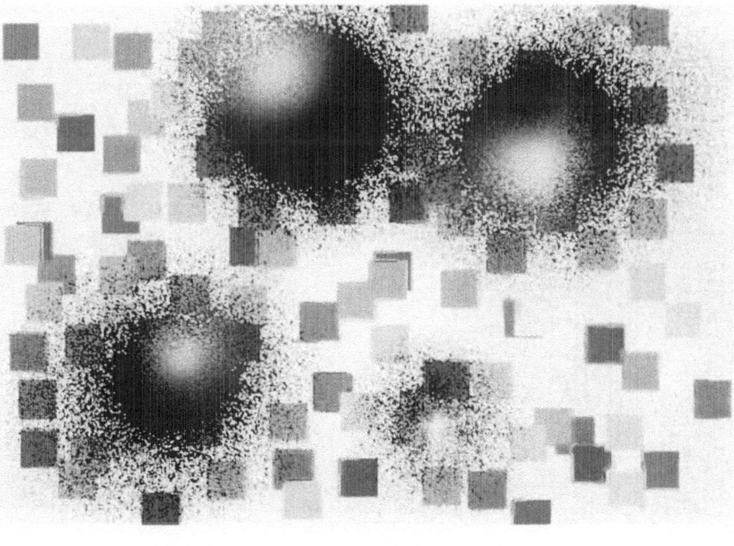

Fig. 9 "POP"

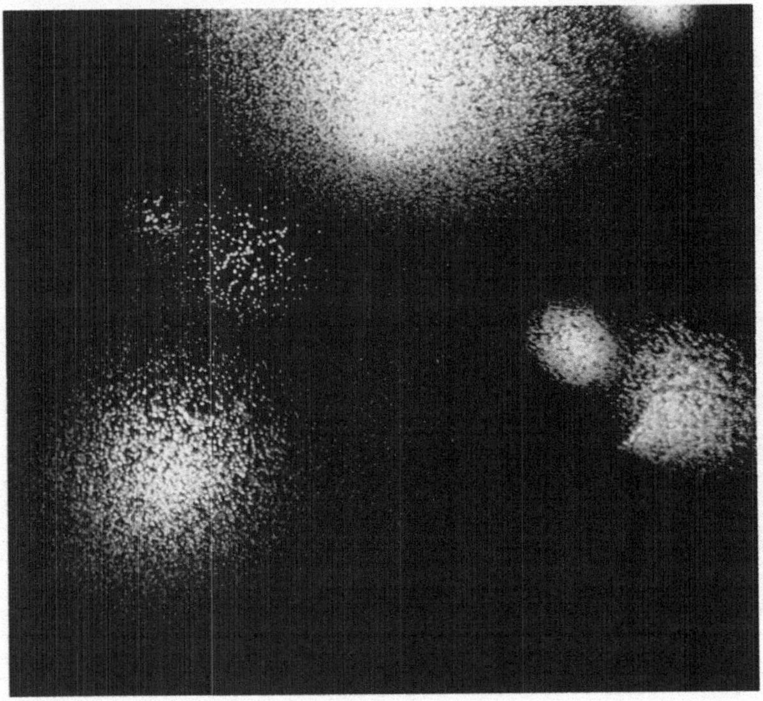

Fig. 10 "Sandstorm"

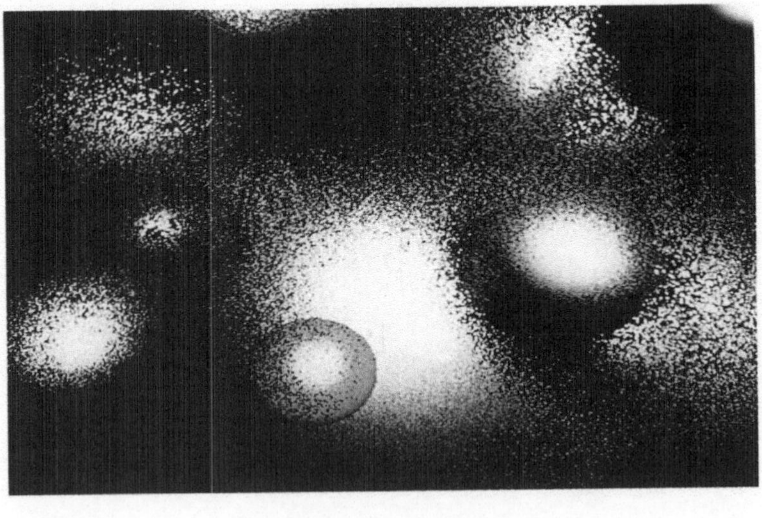

Fig. 11 "Dream Cloud"

4. Discussion

One of the problems with the particals method is the size of particles. Particles are generated by testing for an intersection with an eye ray and a sphere. If the ray intersects with the surface, a pixel is rendered. Hence, the size of particles is exactly the size of screen pixel regardless of its distance. The levels of detail is increased by moving closer to the particals, but the size of particles is unchanged.

Another drawback of this method is the frame to frame coherence. The model does not track the positions of rendered particles of the previous frame. This causes the strobing effect when the particals are animated. From the experiment, the strobing effect may not be disturbing for certain purposes because the particles in the sandstorm and fog are constantly moving, which have similar visual effect.

To examine the efficiency of the algorithm, a timing test is performed. The test was performed on a NEC PC-9801 VM2 personal computer. It uses 8086 16 bit CPU and 8087 floating point co-processor. A 36-bit frame buffer was connected directly to the I/O bus. The data used for this timing test were:

eye point:	0,0,-600
screen:	0,0,-200
screen size:	640 x 480
center of particals:	0,0,0
radius of solid sphere:	150
radius of particals:	r1:0 r2:150
light source:	800,-600,-600 (point light source)
highlight coefficient:	10
calculation window:	-150,-150 to 150,150 (screen resolution)

The results were:

solid sphere:	4 minutes 10 seconds
particals:	3 minutes 30 seconds

The rendering time for particals is faster because there are fewer intersections for the particals than the solid sphere. For the intersecting pixel, the light intensity calculation must be performed.

5. Conclusions

The particals method is presented to model "fuzzy" objects. The algorithm is based on the esthetic interpretation of natural phenomena. It produces impressionistic images with intricate three dimensional textures. The method integrates the modeling and rendering processes. Particals are defined as a spherical volume with stochastically varying radius. By varying the radius, the spherical surface is fragmented into miniscule particles. This functionally defined model is referenced by the ray tracing renderer. Particals can be reflected onto other surfaces and cast shadows by using the self-similarity characteristics. This algorithm is efficient and it can be easily adopted to the standard ray tracing renderer.

Acknowledgements

The author would like to thank the Visible Language Workshop/the Media Laboratory,MIT for the use of Perkin-Elmer system (figures 5,6,7,10,11). Figures 2,3,4,8,9 used YDK,Inc. IM-9800 36-bit frame buffer. Noriyoshi Tezuka provided photographic support.

References

[1] Blinn,J.F. and Newell,M.E.,"Texture and Reflection in Computer Generated Images," *Comm. ACM, 19,*10,1976, p.542-547

[2] Blinn,J.F.,"Light Reflection Functions for Simulation of Clouds and Dusty Surfaces," *Computer Graphics, 16,*3,1982, p.21-29

[3] Gardner,G.Y.,"Visual Simualtion of Clouds," *Computer Graphics, 19,*3,1985, p.297-303

[4] Kajiya,J.T. and Von Herzen,B.P.,"Ray Tracing Volume Density," *Computer Graphics, 18,*3,1984, p.165-173

[5] Nomura,S., Yokoi,S., and Toriwaki,J.,"Study on Techniques for Rendering Foggy Objects," *NICOGRAPH 86*, p.126-135 (in Japanese)

[6] Peachey,D.R.,"Solid Texturing of Complex Surfaces," *Computer Graphics, 19,*3,1985, p.279-286

[7] Perlin, K.,"An Image Synthesizer," *Computer Graphics, 19,*3,1985, p.287-296

[8] Reeves,W.T.,"Particle Systems--A Technique for Modeling a Class of Fuzzy Objects," *Computer Graphics, 17,*3,1983, p.359-376

VOXAR: A Tridimensional Architecture for Fast Realistic Image Synthesis

R. Caubet, Y. Duthen, and V. Gaildrat (France)

Abstract :

The ray-tracing algorithm was up to now the origin of the most beautiful synthesised images. Yet, it was penalized by the great number of intersection computations required, due to the non-exploitation of the spatial coherency.

In order to decrease the cost of image production, architectures were proposed, based on the ray-tracing algorithm parallelism.

We propose a volumic architecture model traced over reality, using the parallelism due to the scene coherency.

This architecture is based on the object decomposition into voxels and on the incremental integer logic. This allows the suppression of the intersection computations at the rendering step.

During the object decomposition into voxels, the texture is included into the material features. Thus, the objects are not created plain but textured just as if they were sculptured into the material.

The object decomposition into voxels allows the generation of composite scenes where the objects modelled by different methods will be rendered by the same technique.

Key words : Ray-tracing, Parallelism, Voxels, Incremental integer logic, Transputer.

INTRODUCTION

Realistic image synthesis is a fascinating field which requires at present a maximum of innovations in modeling and rendering the natural world, and in parallel algorithmic and multi-processors architecture.

To get high quality images, the algorithms of hidden surface removing such as those of Warnock and Watkins [PROCG] gave place to the ray-tracing algorithm [WHI80].
The images it gives integrate special effects such as :

- shading and shadowing
- transparency with refraction
- multiple reflections
- colored light sources
- various modelings

But ray-tracing requires a huge computation power and needs great improvements. Though important means are developped, computation times are still counted in hours, or even into days for complex scenes.
A solution to decrease these computation times is to do some compromises.

For example :

- an image will not include reflects or shading.
- the object modeling will be simple and the scene will not be too complex.
- shading is not affected by reflects.

These compromises satisfy synthesis images producers for the moment.
Yet, as the cost of high quality images decreases and makes the image synthesis possible, the wish to get fine images is felt.

Now the aim is a "fast" rendering of high quality images.

The approach may be a software one [GLA84,FUJ86] :
One tries to speed-up the intersection computations between a ray and and object or to reduce the number of intersection computations.

The approach may also be a hardware one [BOU84,DIP84,BRU86] :
Because of the parallelism of the ray-tracing algoritm due to the fact that each pixel can be independently computed, it is obvious that parallel processing can be made during the image computation.

Our research aims at designing a parallel machine model which will not only allow a fast computation of realistic synthesised images but will also be efficient for modeling and animation.

1 THE RAY-TRACING ALGORITHM : PROBLEMS AND EXISTING SOLUTIONS

1.1 PRINCIPLE OF THE RAY-TRACING ALGORITHM

The principle of the ray-tracing algorithm can be described as follows :
For each point of the screen, a ray is cast from the observer towards the scene. From the first point met by this ray, other rays, reflected and/or refracted, are cast. These new rays will in turn be reflected and/or refracted until all the rays go out of the scene.

To compute the pixel color, the required information is returned along the rays according to a shading model, the lighting conditions, and the objects material features.

1.2 WHAT MUST BE IMPROVED ?

- The most common inconvenience of the ray-tracing algorithm is the great number of intersection computations made for each ray.
Actually, when a ray is cast, the intersection between this ray and all the objects of the scene wherever they are must be computed. There is no exploitation of the spatial coherency at all.
Whitted has shown that over 90 % of the computing time is spent during the intersection calculations for a complex scene.
- To compute the color of a pixel, a tree of reflected and refracted rays is built. But this tree is built absolutely sequentially, which corresponds to a depth first construction of the tree.
Even if several pixels are simultaneously computed, there is no inter-ray parallelism.
- According to the type of modeling used to generate the objects, the intersection computations with a ray will be entirely different.

Actually, the computation of the intersection between a ray and a polygon is much more simple than the computation of the intersection with a free form surface.

- The antialiasing, to get proper results, requires pre or post processings, expensive in time and memory.

1.3 TECHNIQUES TO SPEED UP THE RAY-TRACING

If we sum up the techniques to speed-up the ray-tracing , we can see that three main methods are developped :

1.3.1 SCREEN PARTITION (CRISTAL-TPX) [BOU84,BRU86]

A supervisor divides the screen into areas, each of them being computed by an independent processor.
This parallelism is entirely exterior to the scene structure.
Each processor executes the initial ray-tracing algorithm. For each ray, the processor computes the intersection with all the objects of the scene in order to find the visible point.

1.3.2 ADAPTATIVE SUBDIVISION [DIP84]

The volume of the scene is divided into subvolumes. A processor and a list of its own objects are allocated to each subvolume.
The division is adaptative in order to get a better distribution of the objects within the volume.

When a ray is cast, the intersection is first computed with the objects of the first subvolume crossed.
If no intersection is found, the ray goes to the next subvolume and so on, until either an intersection is found or the ray goes out of the scene.

The improvement of the computation time compared to the usual method is also proportionnal to the number of processors used.

1.3.3 CELLULAR DECOMPOSITION (ARTS) [FUJ86]

The scene is divided into elementary cells, each of them including the list of the surfaces (and not the objects) which cross it.

To cast a ray, an incremental calculation of its path is made. When the ray reaches an occupied cell, the intersections with the concerned surfaces are computed.

If CRISTAL-TPX and ARTS computation times are compared, it appears that, in sequential processing, ARTS computes an image three or four times faster than CRISTAL-TPX with 128 processors.

2 PRESENTATION OF THE VOXAR PROJECT

We based our approach on the building of "perfect" images by trying to take into account all -at least the maximum possible- of the affecting factors (light, heat, ...).

In all the animation films, when an object is touched by light, it casts it again according to its opacity, rugosity, and transparency features.

But we can also imagine that, when it is touched by a small stone, it gives a sound due to the shock, as well as a heat source that can influence the reflective qualities of an object.

As a summary, we can say that an object within its space reacts to all the sollicitations by a behavior that , a priori, only the object knows. It has the physical features which enable it to react.

To simulate this behavior in the best way, we decided to study this problem from two points of view :

1_ Algorithmic : Parallel programming is the main point. To improve efficiently the processing time parallelism must be used.

2_ Machine architecture : It must be as close as possible to the organization of a real scene.

From the specific problems laid by the ray-tracing algorithm and the existing speeding-up techniques, we defined a solution to the problem of fast generation of realistic synthesis images.

We are going to present the advantages of this solution for different points :
incremental calculation, modeling, shading computations, textures, antialiasing, screen processing.

Then, we will deal with the bases of the architectures of our parallel machine model.

3 SOLUTION

Considering the ray-tracing speeding-up techniques, one might think of implementing ARTS's technique on each processor of the CRISTAL-TPX machine to improve the computation time (from 384 to 512 compared to this machine).

This would be nowadays quite difficult, because the data structure required by ARTS is so large that one could not afford to copy it 128 times in order for each processor to know it.

Yet the principle of the cellular decomposition and incremental calculation of the ray path is very interesting and can even be deepened.

We thus thought of a more accurate decomposition than that used by ARTS :
We take the voxel as the scene elementary decomposition unit. A voxel is equivalent to a basic cell. A scene composed with objects is coded into a voxels 3D matrix.

In order for each voxel to have a behavior (for example reflecting or refracting the light it receives) one processor for each voxel should be necessary. But a "good" image to the eye might require 1000 x 1000 x 1000 voxels that is GIGA processors. This doesn't seem possible at the present time.

The expended results could be interesting because the scene would be animated or would "live" through a billion of active cells ...

Our project, less ambitious, is based on this idea reduced to more realistic data.
We will define the term "Metavoxel" as a cube of voxels.
Instead of associating a processor with each voxel, we associate one with each cubic matrix of voxels : with each Metavoxel.
A scene of 1000 x 1000 x 1000 voxels is transformed into 10 x 10 x 10 = 1000 connected processors to make a cube.

The scene to render is now a set of voxels, occupied or not by objects.
Only the voxels crossed by the surface of an object are occupied. Thus only those voxels are stored.
Each of these voxels contains :

- color information,
- specular exponent,
- specular reflection coefficient,
- absorption coefficient (if it is transparent),
- refraction index,
- object identifier.

In fact, all the physical features required by the simulation. These features can be completed in Object-oriented programming style.
The global management of the scene (message sending through our tridimentional network and processes handling) still remains the same.
Now let us see the voxels contribution to the solving of technical problems.

3.1 INCREMENTAL INTEGER LOGIC AND RAY TREE MANAGEMENT

With a scene decomposition into voxels, ray-tracing is reduced to incremental calculation which determine the voxels successively crossed by the ray (or by the message associated with that ray).

During the incremental calculation, as soon as the ray meets an occupied voxel (i.e occupied with a small part of the object surface), the intersection between the ray and an object of the scene is detected without really calculating the intersection between this ray and this object.

The ray-tracing algorithm implies the generation of a ray tree to calculate a pixel color. In the classic way this tree is built by the depth first method, whereas with the Metavoxels scene decomposition, the tree is built by the breadth first method :

The tree is built recursively.

When a ray meets an occupied voxel (thus there is an intersection), a reflected ray and a refracted one are cast from the intersection point.

To a given tree depth, all the rays are simultaneously cast.
Thus there are not only an inter-pixels parallelism but also an inter-ray parallelism.
This latter is much closer to reality, where the rays cast by a real light source rebound independently one from another on the shining surface they meet.

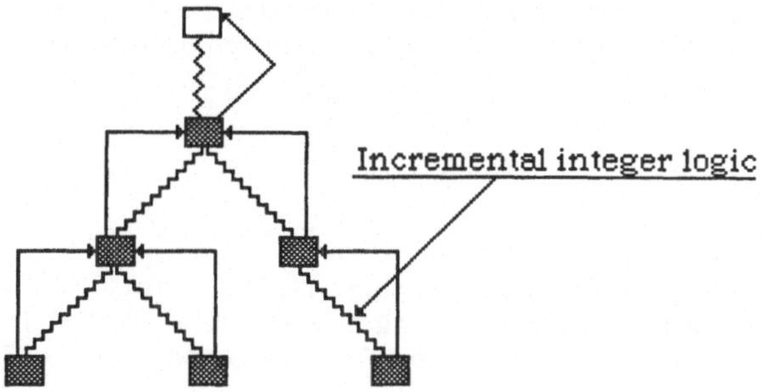

Figure 1 : **Binary ray tree**

By convention :

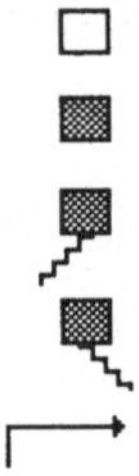

= initial voxel from where the primary ray is cast

= occupied voxel met

= reflected ray

= refracted ray

= information returned

Once the tree is built (the last rays cast are out of the scene without meeting a full voxel), the color informations are returned and processed at each node to give the pixel color.

The ray tree management must not be centralized but distributed to the Metavoxels which share the scene processing

The Metavoxel processor has two main tasks :

1_ The incremental calculation.
For each ray crossing the Metavoxel, the Metavoxel processor makes the incremental calculation to look for all the voxels successively crossed by the ray until it finds an occupied voxel.
If it doesn't, it transmits the ray to the following concerned voxel which takes over the task.

2_ Tree management.
When, within a Metavoxel, a ray meets an occupied voxel, the Metavoxel goes on building the ray tree.
For this, it stores the origin Metavoxel identification and according to the normal and the material features (refractive and reflective coefficients) it computes and casts into the scene the reflected and refracted rays.
These two new messages now include the last Metavoxel identification and the processor can proceed to another ray. It will later receive the color information returned from the refracted and reflected rays.
Once it has all the required information, it computes the partial color in this tree node with a shading model and transmits it to the requiring Metavoxel.

Thus a Metavoxel must manage two queues :

- The first one includes the rays which are to cross the Metavoxel.
- The second one stores, for all the rays which met an occupied voxel, the Metavoxel waiting for the returned color information.

3.2 MODELING

The scene to be rendered is composed of empty and occupied voxels. A voxel includes informations characterizing the material that it is composed of.

color, reflective coefficient, absorption coefficient, ...

A problem remains :

How to determine the normal at the surface at the intersection point. This is a non trivial problem. The best way to avoid it is to include the normal at the surface into the information associated with the voxels.

This implies that the normals have been determined before the rendering. Thus the normal is now included into the voxel structure at the modeling step. An object is once and for all decomposed into voxels at this step.

Modeling means creating objects shapes from basic elements which can be :

- polygons
- C.S.G. (Constructive Solid Geometry) primitives
- free form surfaces
- fractals
- voxels

In the usual modeling, each coding type requires its own rendering algorithm. For example :

The computation of an intersection between a ray and a polygon is quite different from that of an intersection between a ray and a C.S.G. object.

That's why only one type of modeling is usually found.
At the very most there are algorithms working both on curved surfaces (i.e BEZIER surfaces) and planar surfaces (i.e polygons).

Since our rendering algorithm works on a data structure which is the object decomposition into voxels, it becomes independent from the modeling used.

The voxel data structure is actually the single structure on which the various modelings are projected before producing a set of images.

For instance : A desk generated by polygons, a bottle made with B-splines and an ashtray composed with C.S.G. primitives could be present in the same scene because of their voxels coding.

So the modelization becomes a crucial step :

When a user creates an object, the surface of the object is decomposed into voxels including information about the color and the material features, and the normal at the surface.

Thus, whatever the type of modeling chosen is, a file of voxels is generated for each object, this file is then used at the rendering step.

Once the object has been divided into voxels, it becomes possible to interactively deform it by "sculpting" the voxels, thus to generate objects with a totally free form shape without refering to the initial modelizations.

When the scene has been combined, i.e when its objects have been chosen and located, a data structure must be generated, which includes all the voxels occupied by the objects.

This data structure could be a 3D voxels matrix, but as the percentage of actually occupied voxels is very low, this structure is not possible.

We chose to store the occupied voxels in the form of a sparse matrix.
But to minimize the loss of time due to the research in a sparse matrix, we defined a device which enables us to immediately know if a given voxel is in the matrix.

3.3 SHADING COMPUTATION

In the ray-tracing algorithm, when a ray meets a point in the scene, the lighting of the point must be determined.

For this a ray is cast towards each light source from the intersection point. Then the reflected and the refracted rays are cast, which will make possible the calculation of the exact color of the point.
Example : For three ligth sources we cast five rays at each node of the ray tree.

However the shading is independent of the point of view.

If we integrate the shading when generating the scene, only two rays will be cast to each node of the tree.

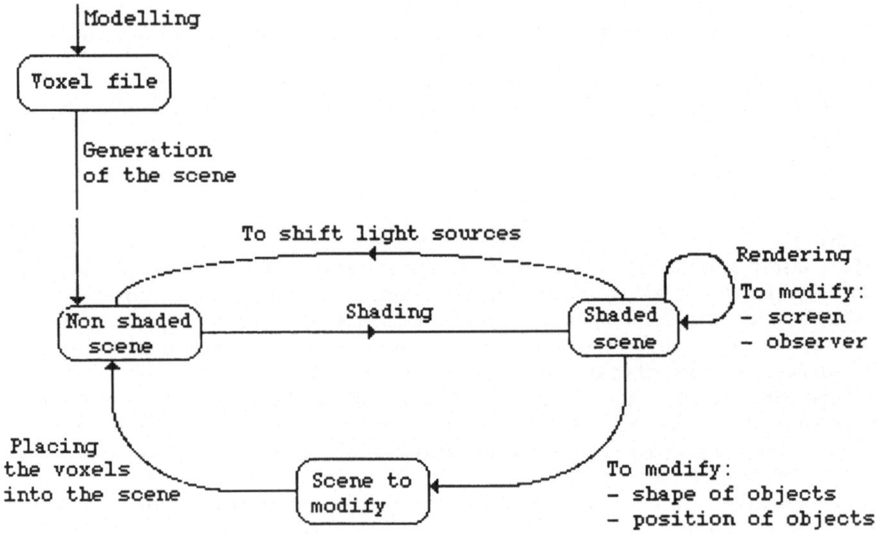

Figure 2 : **States of the scene when generating an animation**

Evaluation for three light sources :

1_ Totally flat and opaque objects:

For a single view of the scene :

If the shading is computed in the usual way, three rays are cast towards the light sources in every visible point.

For a scene with n visible voxels, we cast : **n + 3 x n** rays.

The shading during the scene generation is made for all the voxels of the scene.

We cast **3 x m** rays to compute the scene lighting (**m** = number of voxels in the scene). Then a primary ray is cast in each visible point : **n** visible points.

Total : **n + 3 x m** rays.

For ß views of the same scene : (if we move the screen and/or the observer position)

Usual shading : ß x (n + 3 x n) = **4n x ß** rays

Scene shading : **3 x m + n x ß** rays

2_ Totally specular objects :

For a single view of the scene :

Usual shading : For the **n** primary rays meeting a specular object surface, the trees are constructed at a depth of 14. The number of rays cast is :

$$n \times \left(\left(\sum_{i=0}^{13} 2^i \right) \times 5 + 1 \right) = n \times \left((2^{14} - 1) \times 5 + 1 \right)$$

Scene shading : To compute the shading of the m voxels of the scene, $3 \times m$ rays are cast towards the light sources. Then to built the binary ray tree we cast :

$n \times ((2^{14} - 1) \times 2 + 1)$ rays.

The total is : $3 \times m + n \times ((2^{14} - 1) \times 2 + 1)$ rays.

For ß views of the same scene :

Usual shading : $\beta \times n \times ((2^{14} - 1) \times 5 + 1)$ rays.

Scene shading : $3 \times m + \beta \times n \times ((2^{14} - 1) \times 2 + 1)$ rays.

Results :

We see that for scenes including specular objects computed at a tree depth of 14, the usual shading cast **twice and a half** more rays that the shading in the scene, and this from the first view on.

For scenes composed with flat objects, computed with a depth of 1, the shading in the scene becomes more efficient than the usual way only for several images of the same scene. (see : Fig 3)

Conclusion on shading :

the shading when generating the scene, for scenes with multiple reflects, divides by a factor 2.5 the number of rays to be cast.

But for scenes with a flat dominant character, where there are few rebounds, the shading in the scene is better only if several views are computed with the same configuration of the scene (if the objects or the light sources are not modified).

The origin of this penalization lies in the fact that shading is computed also for voxels never touched by a ray.

For a scene with flats objects where $m = 2 \times n$, we compute twice the voxels shading that is needed because half of them are not visible.

This inconvenience disappears when a small number of views are computed (less than 10) without modifying the scene (remember that 24 images are necessary to make one second of film).

But the possibility to store the shading in the voxels can always be an advantage.

There is a problem when we compute a small number of views of a scene. To avoid this, the shading of all the voxels must not automatically be computed.

When generating the scene, the occupied voxels are placed into the Metavoxels; each of them have a flag to indicate if the shading has already been computed.

The first time a ray meets this voxel, the shading is computed and stored. The flag now indicates that the shading has already been done.

Then, each time a ray meets this voxel, it knows that the shading must not be computed again.

Thus, the number of rays cast towards the light sources will be minimized. The shading is computed only once for voxels met by at least a ray.

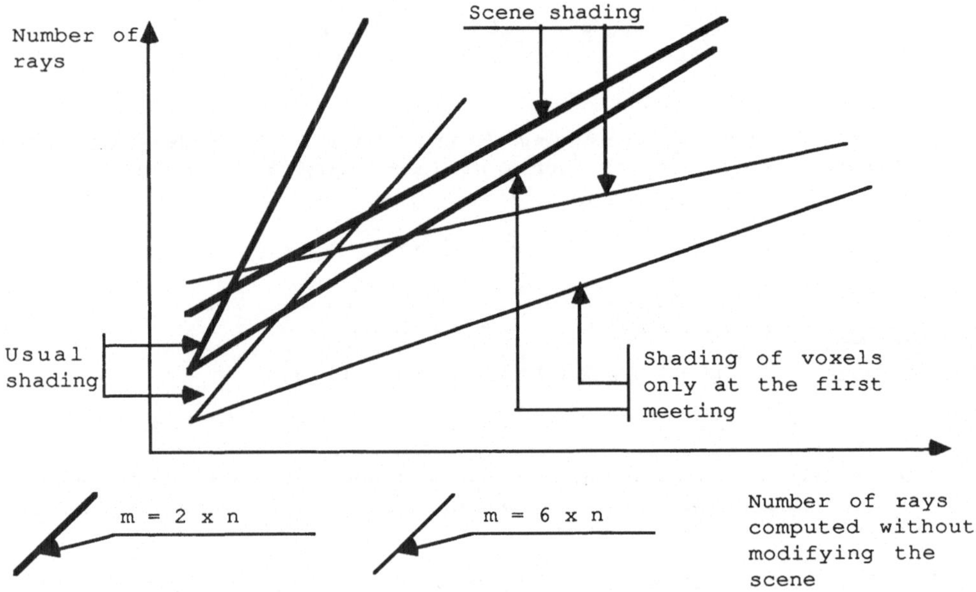

Figure 3 : **Number of rays cast for scenes composed with flat objects**

Number of rays cast for a scene with shading computed once, and only once, considering that 5% non shaded voxels appear at each view.
(number compared with the scene shading and usual shading)

Thus we can affirm that the objects decomposition into voxels enables us to decrease the number of rays cast to render a scene, whatever its composition is.

3.4 TEXTURES

Textures are very important for image quality. They can be planar ones or solid ones, but the surface texturing is made only at the rendering step.

The texture is mapped point by point on the object at each intersection point between a ray and the object.

Moreover it is not stored; thus each time a ray intersects the surface of a textured objects, the texture must be computed.

With the decomposition into voxels, the texture is applied a priori on the surface of the object at the modeling step.

We no longer create uniform objects which are "wrapped" when we want to see them, but objects sculptured into material are generated.

The texture is stored into the color and the features of the surface, and does not oblige any further processing when rendering.

The use of solid textures [PEA85,PER85,CIP87] eliminates any processing of antialiasing due to the compression of planar textures applied to curved surfaces.

3.5 ANTIALIASING

The aliasing is a non-wanted impairment of the image due to the insufficient definition.

The image creation supposes a regular sampling corresponding to the pixels composing the screen.

The pixel size limits the high frequencies which can be rendered. This limit to one cycle every two pixels is called the Nyquist limit. [ROB86]

Trying to render frequencies beyond this limit will give aliasing.
This aliasing produces jagged edges and moiré patterns in texture.

The aliasing can be accepted for fixed images or for applications where speed is more important than realism, but cannot be accepted for animated images.

The ray-tracing algorithm beeing discrete by definition, it is very sensitive to aliasing.

·For an entire suppression of the aliasing it is necessary to know for a given pixel all the informations which contribute to its color.
All that the "observer" sees through a pixel (the vision area) should be determined.

Casting a ray enables us to pick up a punctual color information in the vision area.
In a scene composed with voxels, it is possible to really try to determine all the voxels seen through the pixel. Then the application of a filter can give the exact color of the point to be displayed.

But this would be very expensive and it is likely that the improvement of the image quality would not be much better than with other antialiasing techniques.

To supply this image impairment, we kept two methods which can be used in a voxel environnement.

a_ Oversampling :

It can be adaptative or not.

If not, 4 to 256 rays for a pixel are cast, according to a regular grid and the results are combined by filtering all the colors obtained for a pixel.

If it is adaptative : if the i pixel color is very different from that of the pixel i+1, a ray is cast half way between those two pixels. If the result is much more different from the previous ones, an intermediate ray is cast, and this down to a lower limit of distance between two samplings.

b_ Stochastic oversampling :

The oversampling is no longer made according to a regular grid but at random locations on the pixel surface.

This irregular oversampling, combined with a more or less complex filter replaces aliasing by noise. And this noise is not a nuisance to an human observer (contrary to aliasing).
We will now see how oversampling is applied to voxels :

a_ Modeling :

To decompose objects into voxels, it is possible to cast parallel rays going through the pixel center, in order to determine the occupied voxels, and this towards three directions : x, y, z.

This type of regular sampling will give aliasing.
To solve this problem, the pixels will be oversampled and 4, 9, 16 or 25 rays for a pixel will be cast.

We will get a voxel divided into sub-voxels :

For pixels oversampled at 4 .sub-pixels, the voxels are divided into 8 sub-voxels

For pixels oversampled at 16 .sub-pixels, the voxels are divided into 64 sub-voxels

Each sub-voxel is occupied or not. If it is occupied it has the features of the surface, the color, the normal, and an object identifier.

Because of the problems of available memory, we cannot have a great oversampling : for 64 sub-voxels, 64 times more informations must be stored for an occupied voxel.

b_ At the rendering step :

The image is oversampled at 4 rays a pixel, in an irregular way. The rays are not cast at the center of each sub-pixel but at any point of the sub-pixel surface.

The scene incremental calculation unit will not be the voxel but the sub-voxel.
Once the color of each sub-voxel has been determined, the resulting color to be displayed must be found.
For this, the average of the 4 colors is computed (a complex filter is not necessary for only 4 sub-pixels).

3.6 SCREEN - OBSERVER :

a_ The screen is within the scene :

The place for each pixel in the scene will be determined, and thus the corresponding voxel.

The Metavoxel to which the voxel belongs cast the primary ray and waits for the returned color.
The Metavoxel remains loaded with all the rays that cross it.

b_ The screen is out of the scene (totally or partly) :

A pixel is projected according to the direction given by the observer position until it meets a voxel. The pixel is processed by the Metavoxel to which the voxel belongs .

If the observer is at infinity :

Two contiguous pixels will remain contiguous :

If the observer is not at infinity :

Two contiguous pixels will not be projected on two contiguous voxels.

If the image is computed in this way, an important aliasing phenomenon will occur.

To solve this problem, each pixel must be oversampled when computing the image, and the rays must be irregularly cast.

Each ray from a sub-pixel will be projected on a sub-voxel on the sides of the scene volume. The Metavoxel to which the sub-voxel belongs will cast the primary ray and will wait for the returned color.

The task which will recover the colors will compute the average of the colors of four sub-pixels. This average will give the final color of the pixel.

4 ARCHITECTURE

The VOXAR machine will be composed with a tridimentional processors network, each processor storing a Metavoxel.

Each cube side is connected to a neighbour one (a cube has 6 sides, thus 6 neighbours). Each processor manages a metavoxel and must have 6 priviliged connections with its neighbours.

To code a real scene, the complete description of the features of all the voxels belonging to the processor Metavoxel must be stored into the local memory of each processor.

If we consider a network of 10 x 10 x 10 processor s for a scene of 1000 x 1000 x 1000 voxels with an 10% voxel occupation rate; 100 Mega "information-for-a-voxel" (I.V.) to share out between 1000 processors must be stored (i.e 0.1 Mega I.V. for a processor).

To be able to design this network, we turned to existing VLSI technology to build parallel machines, and specifically Transputer.

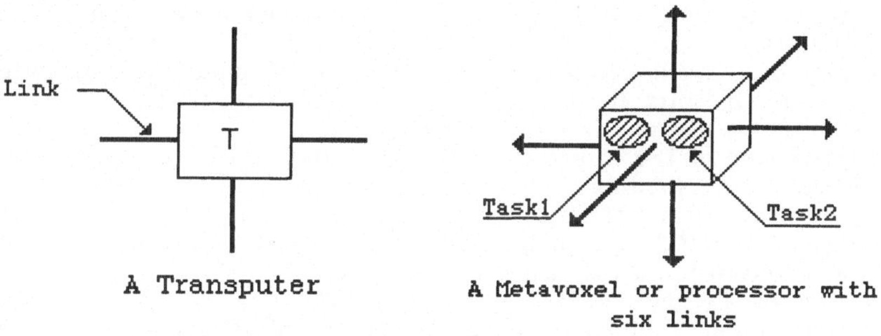

Figure 4 : **The four communication links of a Transputer**

A processor has two main tasks to execute :
tree management and incremental calculation,
and each Metavoxel has six neighbours; so the cell could be constructed by:

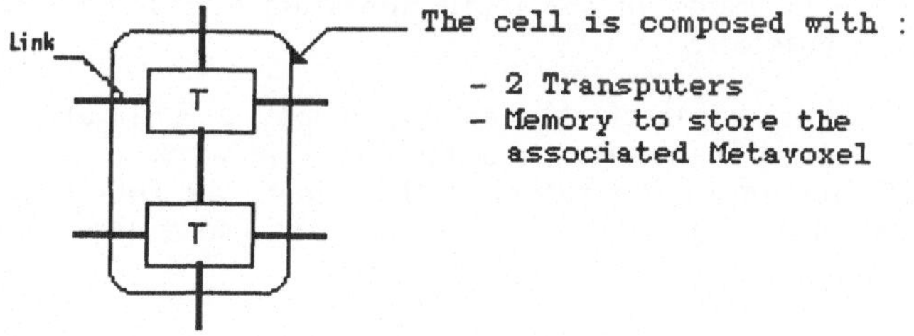

Figure 5 : **Composition of a cell**

We will get 10 x 10 x 10 cells that is 2000 Transputers to create a machine. In this machine the rays will go through the scene under the form of messages. The messages are transmitted from one cell to the following one through the network.

This communication is simultaneously done on all the parts of the scene divided into voxels. Hence a parallelism close (although limited) to the real word.

This prototype must be evaluated to study the effects of this very important communication on the machine behavior.

A system out of the machine must be defined to assume the loading of the voxels into the memory of each cell and to recover the image once it has been computed.

CONCLUSION

The study of the existing parallel machines enabled us to define the concepts used to solve the problems laid by the ray-tracing algorithm.
We chose the scene partition and the incremental integer logic.

A further study of these approches led us to a decomposition of the scene into voxels.
The decomposition into voxels allows :

- The independence of the rendering software towards the differents types of modeling.
- The application of surface texture to objects at the modeling step (without aliasing using solid texturing).
- The exploitation of the spatial coherency.
- The suppression of the intersection computations at the rendering step.
- The storage of the shading .

The research now deals with differents aspects :

- The study of the VOXAR machine kernel : specification and detailed design of the scheduler and the tasks it will manage.
- The writing of the low levels software in OCCAM.
- The definition of a library of solid textures and study of the textures parallelism in the VOXAR machine.
- The study of the contribution of artificial intelligence to the interactive 3D modeling. [DJE87]
- The generation of textured voxels from various modelizations.
- The rendering of free form surfaces by ray-tracing. [SAN87]
- The implementation in Oriented Object Language of the ICC principle (Inverse Cone Casting). [RAI87]
  The images given by the ray tracing algorithm have lighting errors which can be avoided by casting the rays from the light sources.
  The study of the implementation of this new technique on the VOXAR machine.

All these research themes should lead to a simulation of the voxar machine in OCCAM on a Transputer tridimentional network.

If this simulation validates the model, the following step will be to build a prototype of 3 x 3 x 3 Metavoxels that is 54 Transputers.

BIBLIOGRAPHY

[BOU84] BOUVILLE CH., BRUSQ R., DUBOIS J.L., MARCHAL I.
"Synthèse d'images par lancer de rayons : algorithme et architecture"
Premier colloque image, Biarritz 1984

[BRU86] BRUSQ R.
"Synthèse d'images par lancer de rayons : la machine CRISTAL, résultats et perspectives"
Deuxième colloque image, Nice 1986

[CAU86] CAUBET R., PUJADO R., SAUR S.
"Textures et synthèse d'images"
Deuxième colloque image, Nice 1986, Vol 2

[CIP87] CIPRES P.
"Textures solides : extraction d'un objet à partir d'un volume de textures"
Rapport de D.E.A. informatique, L.S.I., 1987

[DIP85] DIPPE A.Z., WOLD E.H.
"Aliasing through stochastic sampling"
SIGGRAPH 85

[DIP84] DIPPE M. SWENSEN J.
"An adaptative subdivision algorithm and parallel architecture for realistic image synthesis"
SIGGRAPH 84, pp149,158

[DJE87] DJEDI N.
"Synthèse d'images :Etude de la contribution des techniques de l'intelligence artificielle"
Rapport de D.E.A. informatique, L.S.I., 1987

[FUJ86] FUJIMOTO A., TANAKA T., IWATA K.
"ARTS : Accelerated Ray-Tracing System"
IEEE Computer Graphics & Applications, Avril 1986, pp 16,26

[GAI86] GAILDRAT E.
"L.S.I. : Logiciel de Synthèse d'Images"
Rapport de D.E.A. informatique, L.S.I., 1986

[GAI86] GAILDRAT E., INGUIMBERT-GAILDRAT V.
"Proposition d'architecture parallèle pour le lancer de rayons"
Convention Informatica Llatina, Barcelone 1986

[GLA84] GLASSNER A.S.
"Space subdivision for fast ray-tracing"
IEEE Computer Graphics & Applications, Octobre 1984, pp 15,22

[HIL85] HILLIS D.
"The connection machine"
MIT Press 1985

[ING85] INGUIMBERT-GAILDRAT V.
"Les ombres portées et la transparence"
Rapport de D.E.A. informatique, L.S.I., 1985

[PEA85] PEACHEY D.R.
"Solid texturing of complex surfaces"
SIGGRAPH 85

[PER85] PERLIN K.
"An image synthesizer"
SIGGRAPH 85

[RAI87] RAINJONNEAU S., LOUCHET T.
"Nouvelle approche: l'Inverse Cone Casting par langages objets"
Rapport de D.E.A. informatique, L.S.I., 1987

[PROCG] ROGERS D.F.
"Procedural elements for computer graphics"
Mac Grow Hill book compagny

[ROB86] ROBERT, COOK
"Stochastic sampling in computer graphics"
ACM Transaction on graphics, Vol 5 n°1, janvier 1986, pp 51-72

[SAN87] SANDOUK Z.
"Lancer de rayons appliqué aux surfaces de forme libre : B_spline"
Rapport de D.E.A informatique, L.S.I., 1987

[WHI80] WHITTED R.
"An improved illumination model for shading display"
CACM 1980, n°23, pp 343,349

Image Generation with an Associative Processor Array

R. Storer, A. W. G. Duller, and E. L. Dagless (UK)

ABSTRACT

Associative processor arrays are described in relation to a VLSI processor array currently being designed at Bristol University. Its application to a number of image generation tasks is considered. Some performance estimates are given for a processor-per-pixel system incorporating this chip

1. Introduction

This research is the result of experience gained as part of a SERC/Alvey project (with additional funding from MOD) MMI 043: SCAPE based image processing and pattern recognition. SCAPE (Single Chip Array Processing Element) is a VLSI associative processor array developed at Brunel University [Lea 1985].

A number of SIMD image processing architectures have been examined, and conclusions drawn as to the optimum architecture for a class of image related tasks. To this end a flexible simulation of a complete image processing system has been implemented on Apollo workstations to allow investigation into the effects of altering the design parameters of such architectures [Duller et al 1987].

To evaluate and finalise the current design for a new associative processor array (working name GLITCH[1]) [Storer 1987] and various supporting hardware configurations, its use in a variety of applications is being investigated. This paper describes the application of the design to a number of image generation problems.

A trial associative processor array is currently being designed in conjunction with the SERC Design Centre at UMIST.

2. Image generation hardware

The problem of image generation, and in particular polygon rendering, is one in which a large number of very simple calculations need to be performed in real-time. Thus SIMD type computers are ideally suited to such tasks. The problem has been addressed at length by Fuchs et al [1988], where an architecture (known as Pixel-planes 4) is described which performs a number of image generation tasks in real-time. The approach used is to produce a "smart" framestore which performs the simple pixel based operations in situ. In this way an extremely fast dedicated system has been produced.

The approach described by Fuchs et al [1988] differs considerably from that of GLITCH. The most important difference is the way in which memory is addressed in the two machines. In the Pixel-planes machine, the memory is addressed conventionally by position, whereas in GLITCH all memory references are by contents. Thus for "search" type operations associative processors such as GLITCH are very efficient. In addition GLITCH has a much more complex ALU and is therefore a more general purpose processor than Pixel-planes. In the following section the GLITCH architecture is described in general terms.

3. Associative Processor Arrays

The associative processor array or more correctly, the parallel associative processor array is an example of a SIMD architecture. The term associative is taken to mean that memory is addressed in terms of its contents rather its position. An associative processor array is an array of Content Addressable Memory (CAM) each "word" of which has a simple arithmetic and logic unit (ALU) associated with it. The combination of memory word and ALU will be referred to as a processing element (PE) (see Fig. 1).

An instruction broadcast to the array is followed by a description of the pattern which identifies the required processors. The PEs which are to perform an operation are identified

1 Goes LIke The Clappers, Hopefully !

by matching all or part of their contents to the given ternary pattern (0, 1 or x for "don't care"). All other processors will be inactive for that operation. For example, the instruction:

WRITE [byte0 11xx0100] [] byte1 = 11110000

would modify the contents of CAM byte 1 in all the processors with a matching pattern in byte 0.

In addition, a processor can be further identified as belonging to a given subset. The subset bits (four in GLITCH) can be used as a further condition for matching, eg:

WRITE [byte0 11xx0100] [1xx0] byte1 = 11110000

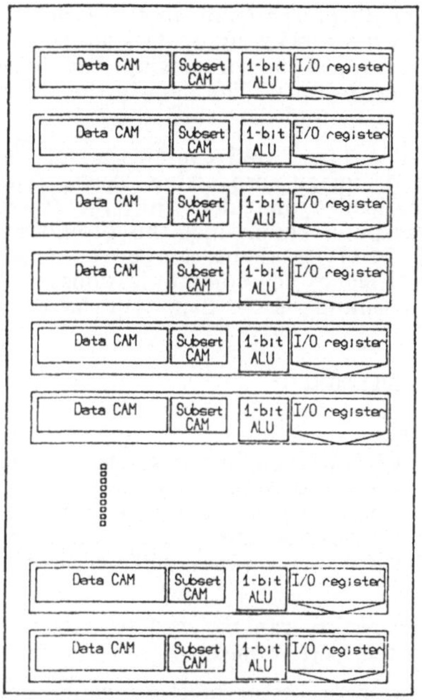

Figure 1

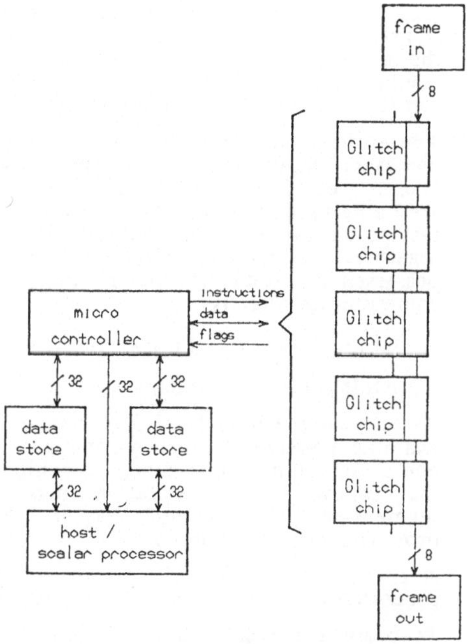

Figure 2

Unlike machines such as the DAP [Flanders et al 1979] in which pattern matching and data writing is performed one bit at a time, the content addressable memory allows a whole word to be matched or written back to each activated PE in a single cycle.

Once a number of processors have been tagged a number of ALU functions can be used to perform the required operations. One such operation is that of bit-serial arithmetic.

3.1 Bit Serial Arithmetic

Due to the 1-bit nature of the ALU in each PE it is necessary to perform arithmetic in a bit serial manner. Thus one bit from each operand is considered at a time in every PE. The effect of this type of arithmetic is to make high precision calculations costly, however, it is possible to tailor the precision of the arithmetic to the requirements of the algorithm.

3.2 Bit Serial comparison

With conventional CAM designs, processors can provide inequality information about their contents ('greater than' or 'less than') by carrying out a bit-serial comparison with the broadcast pattern. The use of magnitude comparing CAM [Kohonen 1980] which would produce inequality and equality information in a single cycle is being considered. The extra silicon area that is required use to implement this type of CAM will have to be balanced against the increase in speed in this type of operation.

4. The GLITCH Architecture

A single GLITCH chip consists of 128 PE's each containing 64 bits of content addressable data store, 4 content addressable subset bits and a one-bit arithmetic and logic unit. The

ALU contains two single bit registers known as the tag and carry registers. The tag register also functions as a one bit accumulator. The chip has a 100ns cycle time in which time a complete search and write operation can be performed or one bit of a bit-serial arithmetic, logic or comparison operation.

As in the SCAPE design, chips will be cascaded together to form a linear chain, thus allowing easy extensibility. The problem of long shifts along the chain for communication between distant PEs has been alleviated to some extent by the provision of a barrel shifter mechanism within each chip. This will allow arbitrary distances to be shifted within each chip in unit time. A mechanism to cascade the barrel shift into neighbouring chips is being examined.

GLITCH has an 8-bit shift register running the entire length of the chain to facilitate the transfer of data to and from framestores concurrently with the processing of data already in the chain. Once the shift register is full with new data and all processing has been completed on the data in the CAM, the two sets of data are swapped. The data in the CAM can then be processed while a new data set is shifted in and the old data shifted out.

The entire GLITCH system under investigation is shown in Fig. 2 and contains all of the necessary hardware to perform image generation and image processing tasks. The framestores will be double-buffered to allow one set to be loaded/unloaded while the others are being processed. The host shown in Fig. 2 will be transputer based since this provides a fast scalar processor as well as allowing a number of GLITCH chains to be connected together. The task of programming several chains is simplified by the communications links possessed by each transputer since it is only the transputer hosts that will have to communicate directly.

5. Using Associative Processor Arrays for Image Generation

5.1 An Intelligent Framestore

As an example of a high performance processor array for real-time image generation we examine a system comprising enough GLITCH chips to store and process all the pixels in one image frame in parallel, 512 chips for a 256 x 256, eight-bit image in the examples that follow. Higher resolution images can be processed on the same size system by segmenting the image into areas of 256 x 256 pixels, the processing times will be directly proportional to the number of segments needed.

A single video shift register threaded through all the processors can be used to extract a processed image in about 4ms, in parallel with processing the next frame.

To perform the calculations described in the examples, each processor must know the co-ordinates of the pixel it is generating, using sixteen of the CAM data bits for this and eight for the pixel intensity leaves forty bits of workspace for each processor. If this is not enough for a particular processing task, two or more processors can work together on the same pixel each being used to hold different parts of the intermediate calculations and each identified by a different subset bit pattern.

Twenty four bit, colour images can be generated in a similar way by allocating the same address to three processors, one to handle each of the red, green and blue components of the pixel.

5.1.1 Circles

All the processors calculate the distance in pixels (D) of the centre of their pixel (X_p, Y_p) from the edge of the circle whose radius (R) and centre (X_c, Y_c) are broadcast by the host machine:

$$D = R - \sqrt{(X_p - X_c)^2 + (Y_p - Y_c)^2}.$$

Those with a zero result lie on the edge of the circle, those with a positive result lie within it. If a solid disc is required, all those pixels whose centre is 0.5 pixel, or more, within the circle will be activated and take on the broadcast intensity for the disc (I). Any pixels now having $-0.5 < D < 0.5$ are sufficiently covered by the edge of the disc that their intensity (I_p) should be altered to avoid aliasing effects (Fig. 3). They take on a change in intensity approximately proportional to the area of the pixel covered by the disc (as detailed in section 4.1.3 below) and given by:

$$I_p := (I - I_p)(D + 0.5) + I_p.$$

This value is of course calculated by all such pixels simultaneously.

If an annulus of width W is required (this includes the case of a one pixel wide circular line) the distance is modified to give the pixel's distance from the edge of the annulus:

$$D := W/2 - |D|,$$

and the pixel intensities calculated in the same way.

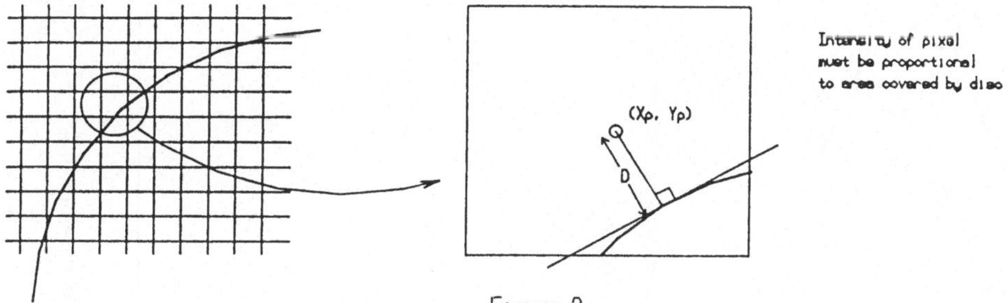

Figure 3

5.1.2 Ellipses

The locus of pixels lying on an ellipse is given by:

$$D_a + D_b = R,$$

where D_a and D_b are the distances of the pixel centre from the the foci and R is a constant. In the same way as for circles, the distances from the foci and thus a measure of the pixel's distance from the ellipse (D) is calculated by each pixel:

$$D = R - D_a + D_b,$$

and the pixel intensities for either solid or annular ellipses are calculated in the same way as above.

5.1.3 Straight Lines

The perpendicular distance (D) of a point (X_p, Y_p) from a straight line is given by:

$$D = (Y_p - Y_0) \operatorname{Cos} \theta - (X_p - X_0) \operatorname{Sin} \theta$$

where (X_0, Y_0) is a point on the line and θ is the angle the line makes with the x-axis:

$$-\pi/2 \leq \theta < \pi/2.$$

Points on the clockwise side of this ray (decreasing θ) will have negative distances. To generate a line between two points (X_0, Y_0) and (X_1, Y_1), the host machine calculates:

$$\operatorname{Cos} \theta = (X_1 - X_0)/h$$

$$\operatorname{Sin} \theta = (Y_1 - Y_0)/h$$

where $h = \sqrt{\{(X_1 - X_0)^2 + (Y_1 - Y_0)^2\}}$,

and then broadcasts the values of Cos θ, Sin θ, X_0 and Y_0 so that each pixel can calculate the perpendicular distance of its centre from the line. For a line of width W, this value is modified to give the distance from the edge of the line:

$$D := W/2 - |D|,$$

pixels now having $0.5 \leq D \leq W/2$ are considered completely covered by the line and take on the intensity of the line, I. Those with $D \leq -0.5$ are far enough away from the line to remain at their original intensity I_p. Pixels with $-0.5 < D < 0.5$ are partly covered by the line and must have their intensity modified in proportion to the area covered, to avoid aliasing effects.

If the line is horizontal (Fig. 4) the area covered is directly proportional to D and is half the pixel area when D = 0. Thus the correct pixel intensity is given by:

$$I_p := (I - I_p)(D + 1/2) + I_p. \qquad (1)$$

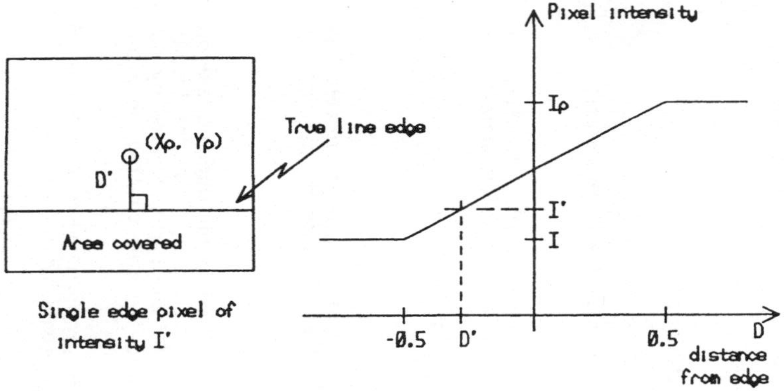

Single edge pixel of intensity I'

Figure 4

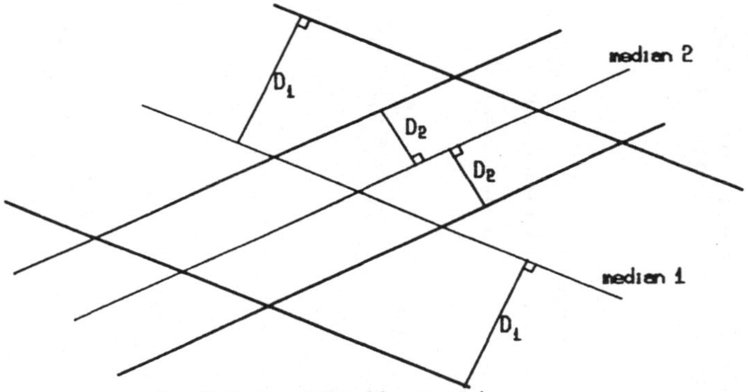

Parallelogram defined by its medians

Figure 6

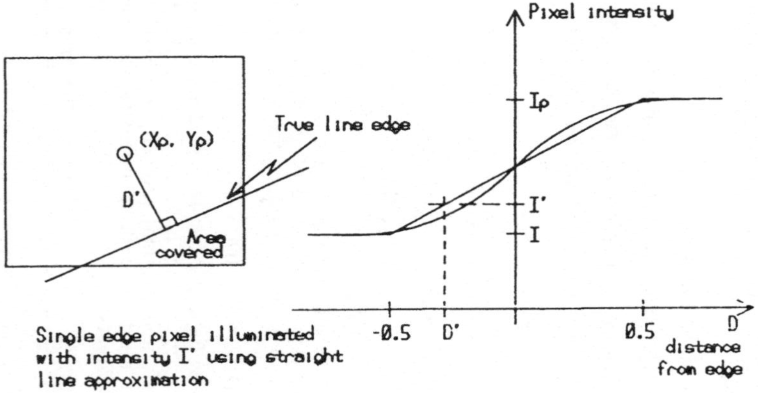

Single edge pixel illuminated with intensity I' using straight line approximation

Figure 5

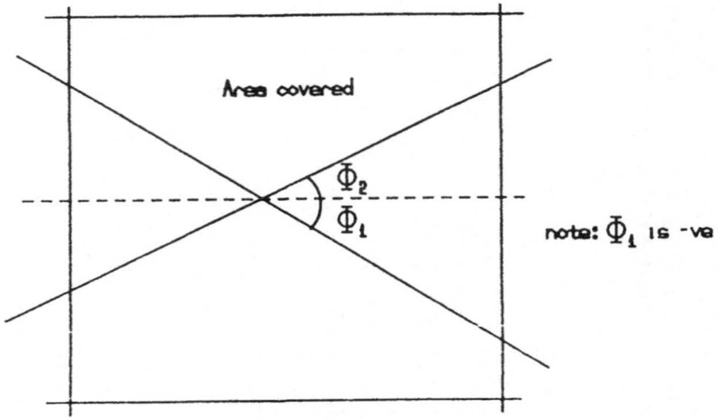

Area covered at vertex pixel $\simeq \dfrac{\pi - (\Phi_2 - \Phi_1)}{2\pi}$

Figure 7

With other than horizontal lines, this becomes an approximation to the true pixel value, the worst case being a line at forty five degrees (Fig. 5) when the true intensity is proportional to D^2. However, the results obtained with this approximation agree well with those of the often quoted Modified Bresenham's Algorithm [Pitteway 1980] used by sequential machines for anti-aliasing straight lines.

This technique generates a line across the whole image frame. For single pixel wide line segments, pixels beyond the endpoints can be disabled by defining a processing window with the end points as opposite corners. Broader line segments can be treated as rectangles and produced as described in the following section.

5.1.4 Parallelograms

The pixels within a parallelogram can be identified as those lying within a given perpendicular distance of the two medians (Fig. 6).

Pixels are identified as being inside, outside or on the edge of a band around, first one median and then the other as for straight lines. Pixels within both bands are within the shape, those outside either band are discarded and the remaining edge pixel intensities are calculated in the same way as already described. Pixels found to be on the edge of both bands will be the vertices and take on an intensity (I_p) proportional to the difference in angle between the two medians (Fig. 7):

$$I_p := (I/2 - I_p/2)\{1 - (\theta_2 - \theta_1)/\pi\} + I_p, \qquad (2)$$

where I is the required intensity of the parallelogram. Any polygon composed of pairs of parallel sides can be constructed in this way.

5.1.5 Polygons

More general polygons can be generated from a list of vertices. If the distance of each pixel from an edge of a convex polygon is calculated from two vertices, as for straight lines, taken in anticlockwise order around the polygon then those pixels outside the polygon will have a negative result and the corresponding processors can be de-activated. After all the edges have been treated in this way, only those inside the polygon will still be active and can take on the appropriate intensity value.

The order of operations is as follows:

```
classify all pixels as 'inside'.
for each pair of vertices
        {
        host calculates Cos θ and Sin θ.
        calculate distance (D) from line.
        classify pixels as outside, vertex or edge.
                {
                if D ≤ -0.5 classify as 'outside'.
                if D < 0.5 and pixel is classed 'edge' classify as 'vertex'
                and modify intensity according to (2).
                if D < 0.5 and pixel is classed 'inside' classify as 'edge'
                and calculate temporary intensity value according to (1).
                }
        }
all pixels still classed as 'edge' take on their temporary intensity.
all pixels still classed as 'inside' take intensity of polygon.
END
```

An example of the progress of this algorithm is shown in Fig. 8. Concave polygons can be generated by combining information about two or more convex polygons. In Fig. 9, pixels within polygon A but not in polygon B form the concave polygon C. Similarly, compound shapes and shapes with holes can be generated.

5.1.6 Windowing and Clipping

With the techniques described, it is not necessary for the host machine to modify the data broadcast to the array to allow for shapes which are partly off the screen ie: no clipping calculations are required; only pixels which actually exist take part in the calculations. In addition, shape generation can easily be confined to a screen window by de-activating all pixels outside the window.

3D Polygon drawing algorithm (20 x 20 image, 0,0 is bottom left), vertices at: (3,5,50) (17,2,0) (18,18,50) (18,18,70) (3,10,67)

Distance from line connecting 3,5 to 17,2 in 0.1 pixels.

131	133	135	137	139	141	143	145	147	149	152	154	156	158	160	162	164	166	168	170
121	123	125	127	129	131	133	135	138	140	142	144	146	148	150	152	154	156	159	161
111	113	115	117	119	122	124	126	128	130	132	134	136	138	140	142	145	147	149	151
101	103	105	108	110	112	114	116	118	120	122	124	126	129	131	133	135	137	139	141
91	94	96	98	100	102	104	106	108	110	112	115	117	119	121	123	125	127	129	131
82	84	86	88	90	92	94	96	98	101	103	105	107	109	111	113	115	117	119	122
72	74	76	78	80	82	85	87	89	91	93	95	97	99	101	103	105	108	110	112
62	64	66	68	71	73	75	77	79	81	83	85	87	89	91	94	96	98	100	102
52	54	57	59	61	63	65	67	69	71	73	75	78	80	82	84	86	88	90	92
43	45	47	49	51	53	55	57	59	61	64	66	68	70	72	74	76	78	80	82
33	35	37	39	41	43	45	47	50	52	54	56	58	60	62	64	66	68	71	73
23	25	27	29	31	34	36	38	40	42	44	46	48	50	52	54	57	59	61	63
13	15	17	20	22	24	26	28	30	32	34	36	38	41	43	45	47	49	51	53
3	6	8	10	12	14	16	18	20	22	24	27	29	31	33	35	37	39	41	43
-6	-4	-2	0	2	4	6	8	10	13	15	17	19	21	23	25	27	29	31	34
-16	-14	-12	-10	-8	-6	-3	-1	1	3	5	7	9	11	13	15	17	20	22	24
-26	-24	-22	-20	-17	-15	-13	-11	-9	-7	-5	-3	-1	1	3	6	8	10	12	14
-36	-34	-31	-29	-27	-25	-23	-21	-19	-17	-15	-13	-10	-8	-6	-4	-2	-0	2	4
-45	-43	-41	-39	-37	-35	-33	-31	-29	-27	-24	-22	-20	-18	-16	-14	-12	-10	-8	-6
-55	-53	-51	-49	-47	-45	-43	-41	-38	-36	-34	-32	-30	-28	-26	-24	-22	-20	-17	-15

Classification of pixels as Inside, Outside, Edge or Vertex after first edge.

I	I	I	I	I	I	I	I	I	I	I	I	I	I	I	I	I	I	I	I
I	I	I	I	I	I	I	I	I	I	I	I	I	I	I	I	I	I	I	I
I	I	I	I	I	I	I	I	I	I	I	I	I	I	I	I	I	I	I	I
I	I	I	I	I	I	I	I	I	I	I	I	I	I	I	I	I	I	I	I
I	I	I	I	I	I	I	I	I	I	I	I	I	I	I	I	I	I	I	I
I	I	I	I	I	I	I	I	I	I	I	I	I	I	I	I	I	I	I	I
I	I	I	I	I	I	I	I	I	I	I	I	I	I	I	I	I	I	I	I
I	I	I	I	I	I	I	I	I	I	I	I	I	I	I	I	I	I	I	I
I	I	I	I	I	I	I	I	I	I	I	I	I	I	I	I	I	I	I	I
I	I	I	I	I	I	I	I	I	I	I	I	I	I	I	I	I	I	I	I
I	I	I	I	I	I	I	I	I	I	I	I	I	I	I	I	I	I	I	I
I	I	I	I	I	I	I	I	I	I	I	I	I	I	I	I	I	I	I	I
I	I	I	I	I	I	I	I	I	I	I	I	I	I	I	I	I	I	I	I
E	I	I	I	I	I	I	I	I	I	I	I	I	I	I	I	I	I	I	I
O	E	E	E	E	E	I	I	I	I	I	I	I	I	I	I	I	I	I	I
O	O	O	O	O	O	E	E	E	E	E	I	I	I	I	I	I	I	I	I
O	O	O	O	O	O	O	O	O	O	E	E	E	E	E	I	I	I	I	I
O	O	O	O	O	O	O	O	O	O	O	O	O	O	O	E	E	E	E	E
O	O	O	O	O	O	O	O	O	O	O	O	O	O	O	O	O	O	O	O
O	O	O	O	O	O	O	O	O	O	O	O	O	O	O	O	O	O	O	O

Distance from line connecting 17,2 to 18,18 in 0.1 pixels

180	170	160	150	140	130	120	110	100	90	80	70	61	51	41	31	21	11	1	-9
180	170	160	150	140	130	120	110	100	90	80	70	60	50	40	30	20	10	0	-10
179	169	159	149	139	129	119	109	99	89	79	69	59	49	39	29	19	9	-1	-11
178	168	158	148	138	128	119	109	99	89	79	69	59	49	39	29	19	9	-1	-11
178	168	158	148	138	128	118	108	98	88	78	68	58	48	38	28	18	8	-2	-12
177	167	157	147	137	127	117	107	97	87	77	67	57	47	37	27	17	7	-2	-12
177	167	157	147	137	127	117	107	97	87	77	67	57	47	37	27	17	7	-3	-13
176	166	156	146	136	126	116	106	96	86	76	66	56	46	36	26	16	6	-4	-14
175	165	155	145	135	125	115	105	95	85	75	65	56	46	36	26	16	6	-4	-14
175	165	155	145	135	125	115	105	95	85	75	65	55	45	35	25	15	5	-5	-15
174	164	154	144	134	124	114	104	94	84	74	64	54	44	34	24	14	4	-6	-16
173	163	153	143	133	124	114	104	94	84	74	64	54	44	34	24	14	4	-6	-16
173	163	153	143	133	123	113	103	93	83	73	63	53	43	33	23	13	3	-7	-17
172	162	152	142	132	122	112	102	92	82	72	62	52	42	32	22	12	2	-7	-17
172	162	152	142	132	122	112	102	92	82	72	62	52	42	32	22	12	2	-8	-18
171	161	151	141	131	121	111	101	91	81	71	61	51	41	31	21	11	1	-9	-19
170	160	150	140	130	120	110	100	90	80	70	61	51	41	31	21	11	1	-9	-19
170	160	150	140	130	120	110	100	90	80	70	60	50	40	30	20	10	0	-10	-20
169	159	149	139	129	119	109	99	89	79	69	59	49	39	29	19	9	-1	-11	-21
168	158	148	138	128	119	109	99	89	79	69	59	49	39	29	19	9	-1	-11	-21

Classification of pixels as Inside, Outside, Edge or Vertex after second edge

I	I	I	I	I	I	I	I	I	I	I	I	I	I	I	I	I	I	E	O
I	I	I	I	I	I	I	I	I	I	I	I	I	I	I	I	I	I	E	O
I	I	I	I	I	I	I	I	I	I	I	I	I	I	I	I	I	I	E	O
I	I	I	I	I	I	I	I	I	I	I	I	I	I	I	I	I	I	E	O
I	I	I	I	I	I	I	I	I	I	I	I	I	I	I	I	I	I	E	O
I	I	I	I	I	I	I	I	I	I	I	I	I	I	I	I	I	I	E	O
I	I	I	I	I	I	I	I	I	I	I	I	I	I	I	I	I	I	E	O
I	I	I	I	I	I	I	I	I	I	I	I	I	I	I	I	I	I	E	O
I	I	I	I	I	I	I	I	I	I	I	I	I	I	I	I	I	I	E	O
I	I	I	I	I	I	I	I	I	I	I	I	I	I	I	I	I	E	E	O
I	I	I	I	I	I	I	I	I	I	I	I	I	I	I	I	I	E	O	O
I	I	I	I	I	I	I	I	I	I	I	I	I	I	I	I	I	E	O	O
I	I	I	I	I	I	I	I	I	I	I	I	I	I	I	I	I	E	O	O
E	I	I	I	I	I	I	I	I	I	I	I	I	I	I	I	I	E	O	O
O	E	E	E	E	E	I	I	I	I	I	I	I	I	I	I	I	E	O	O
O	O	O	O	O	O	E	E	E	E	E	I	I	I	I	I	I	E	O	O
O	O	O	O	O	O	O	O	O	O	E	E	E	E	E	I	I	E	O	O
O	O	O	O	O	O	O	O	O	O	O	O	O	O	O	E	E	V	O	O
O	O	O	O	O	O	O	O	O	O	O	O	O	O	O	O	O	O	O	O
O	O	O	O	O	O	O	O	O	O	O	O	O	O	O	O	O	O	O	O

Figure 8a

Classification of pixels as Inside, Outside, Edge or Vertex for whole polygon

O	O	O	O	O	O	O	O	O	O	O	O	O	O	O	O	O	O	O	O
O	O	O	O	O	O	O	O	O	O	O	V	E	E	E	E	E	E	V	O
O	O	O	O	O	O	O	O	O	O	E	I	I	I	I	I	I	I	E	O
O	O	O	O	O	O	O	O	O	E	I	I	I	I	I	I	I	I	E	O
O	O	O	O	O	O	O	O	E	I	I	I	I	I	I	I	I	I	E	O
O	O	O	O	O	O	O	E	I	I	I	I	I	I	I	I	I	I	E	O
O	O	O	O	O	O	E	I	I	I	I	I	I	I	I	I	I	I	E	O
O	O	O	O	O	E	I	I	I	I	I	I	I	I	I	I	I	I	E	O
O	O	O	O	E	I	I	I	I	I	I	I	I	I	I	I	I	I	E	O
O	O	O	V	I	I	I	I	I	I	I	I	I	I	I	I	I	E	E	O
O	O	O	E	I	I	I	I	I	I	I	I	I	I	I	I	I	E	O	O
O	O	O	E	I	I	I	I	I	I	I	I	I	I	I	I	I	E	O	O
O	O	O	E	I	I	I	I	I	I	I	I	I	I	I	I	I	E	O	O
O	O	O	E	I	I	I	I	I	I	I	I	I	I	I	I	I	E	O	O
O	O	O	V	E	E	I	I	I	I	I	I	I	I	I	I	I	E	O	O
O	O	O	O	O	O	E	E	E	E	E	I	I	I	I	I	I	E	O	O
O	O	O	O	O	O	O	O	O	O	E	E	E	E	E	I	I	E	O	O
O	O	O	O	O	O	O	O	O	O	O	O	O	O	O	E	E	V	O	O
O	O	O	O	O	O	O	O	O	O	O	O	O	O	O	O	O	O	O	O
O	O	O	O	O	O	O	O	O	O	O	O	O	O	O	O	O	O	O	O

Updated z-buffer

0	0	0	0	0	0	0	0	0	0	0	0	0	0	0	0	0	0	0	0
0	0	0	0	0	0	0	0	0	0	0	70	67	64	61	59	56	53	50	0
0	0	0	0	0	0	0	0	0	0	70	67	64	61	58	55	52	50	47	0
0	0	0	0	0	0	0	0	0	69	66	63	61	58	55	52	49	46	43	0
0	0	0	0	0	0	0	0	69	66	63	60	57	54	52	49	46	43	40	0
0	0	0	0	0	0	0	68	65	63	60	57	54	51	48	45	43	40	37	0
0	0	0	0	0	0	68	65	62	59	56	54	51	48	45	42	39	36	33	0
0	0	0	0	0	67	65	62	59	56	53	50	47	44	42	39	36	33	30	0
0	0	0	0	67	64	61	58	56	53	50	47	44	41	38	35	33	30	27	0
0	0	0	67	64	61	58	55	52	49	46	44	41	38	35	32	29	26	24	0
0	0	0	63	60	57	55	52	49	46	43	40	37	35	32	29	26	23	0	0
0	0	0	60	57	54	51	48	46	43	40	37	34	31	28	26	23	20	0	0
0	0	0	57	54	51	48	45	43	40	37	34	31	28	25	23	19	17	0	0
0	0	0	53	50	48	45	42	39	36	33	30	28	25	22	19	16	13	0	0
0	0	0	50	47	44	41	39	36	33	30	27	24	21	19	16	13	10	0	0
0	0	0	0	0	0	38	35	32	30	27	24	21	18	15	12	9	7	0	0
0	0	0	0	0	0	0	0	0	0	23	20	18	15	12	9	6	3	0	0
0	0	0	0	0	0	0	0	0	0	0	0	0	0	0	6	3	0	0	0
0	0	0	0	0	0	0	0	0	0	0	0	0	0	0	0	0	0	0	0
0	0	0	0	0	0	0	0	0	0	0	0	0	0	0	0	0	0	0	0

Updated pixel intensities

0	0	0	0	0	0	0	0	0	0	0	0	0	0	0	0	0	0	0	0
0	0	0	0	0	0	0	0	0	0	0	38	50	50	50	50	50	50	24	0
0	0	0	0	0	0	0	0	0	0	50	100	100	100	100	100	100	100	44	0
0	0	0	0	0	0	0	0	0	50	100	100	100	100	100	100	100	100	38	0
0	0	0	0	0	0	0	0	50	100	100	100	100	100	100	100	100	100	31	0
0	0	0	0	0	0	0	50	100	100	100	100	100	100	100	100	100	100	25	0
0	0	0	0	0	0	50	100	100	100	100	100	100	100	100	100	100	100	19	0
0	0	0	0	0	50	100	100	100	100	100	100	100	100	100	100	100	100	13	0
0	0	0	0	50	100	100	100	100	100	100	100	100	100	100	100	100	100	6	0
0	0	0	38	100	100	100	100	100	100	100	100	100	100	100	100	100	100	0	0
0	0	0	50	100	100	100	100	100	100	100	100	100	100	100	100	100	94	0	0
0	0	0	50	100	100	100	100	100	100	100	100	100	100	100	100	100	87	0	0
0	0	0	50	100	100	100	100	100	100	100	100	100	100	100	100	100	81	0	0
0	0	0	50	100	100	100	100	100	100	100	100	100	100	100	100	100	75	0	0
0	0	0	26	71	92	100	100	100	100	100	100	100	100	100	100	100	69	0	0
0	0	0	0	0	0	15	36	57	78	99	100	100	100	100	100	100	62	0	0
0	0	0	0	0	0	0	0	0	0	1	22	43	64	85	100	100	56	0	0
0	0	0	0	0	0	0	0	0	0	0	0	0	0	0	8	29	25	0	0
0	0	0	0	0	0	0	0	0	0	0	0	0	0	0	0	0	0	0	0
0	0	0	0	0	0	0	0	0	0	0	0	0	0	0	0	0	0	0	0

Figure 8b

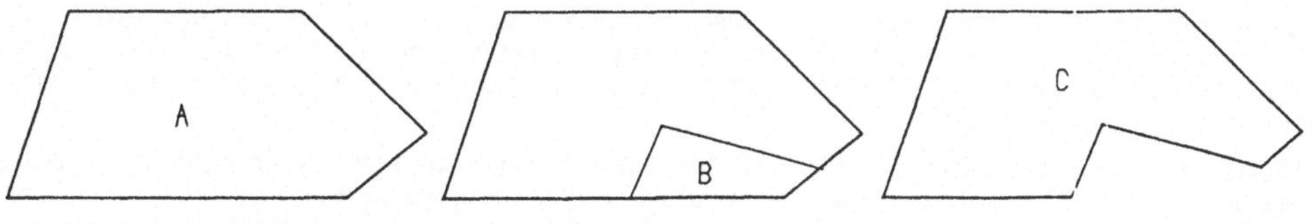

Figure 9

Simple rectangular windows are achieved by broadcasting the co-ordinates of opposite corners. Each processor compares its address with these and decides if it is inside or outside the window. Those outside then do not take part in any further processing until re-activated.

Membership of more complex polygonal or circular windows is calculated in exactly the way described above for generating those shapes.

5.1.7 Three Dimensional Polygon Rendering

A common method of rendering three dimensional surfaces is the use of polygonal facets. When displaying the surface from a chosen viewpoint, those facets which are totally or partly hidden by others must be displayed accordingly. The GLITCH architecture is particularly suited to implementing the z-buffer solution to this problem [Newman 1979][Rogers 1985].

The host machine will have calculated the x, y and z co-ordinates of the vertices of the polygon. Pixels can be classified as inside, outside, edge or vertex of this polygon as above and new intensity values calculated for each class but without modifying any pixels. Meanwhile, the host machine solves the plane equation,

$$ax + by + cz + d = 0$$

for any three vertices, using:

$$a = (Y_1 - Y_2)(Z_1 + Z_2) + (Y_2 - Y_3)(Z_2 + Z_3) + (Y_3 - Y_1)(Z_3 + Z_1)$$

$$b = (Z_1 - Z_2)(X_1 + X_2) + (Z_2 - Z_3)(X_2 + X_3) + (Z_3 - Z_1)(X_3 + X_1)$$

$$c = (X_1 - X_2)(Y_1 + Y_2) + (X_2 - X_3)(Y_2 + Y_3) + (X_3 - X_1)(Y_3 + Y_1)$$

$$d = -(aX_1 + bY_1 + cZ_1).$$

The values: a/c, b/c and d/c are broadcast to the array so that each pixel (X_p, Y_p) classified as inside, edge or vertex can calculate the z co-ordinate of the polygon at its centre:

$$Z = -a/c\, X_p - b/c\, Y_p - d/c$$

Where this value is closer to the viewer than the existing value Z_p, the polygon will be visible, the pixel takes on its previously calculated intensity value and updates its z-buffer value, $Z_p := Z$.

Note that if c is zero, all the points in the polygon will be co-linear in the plane of the display and there will not be a unique value of Z for each pixel. An alternative method must be used to update the z-buffer, by calculating the Z values along those edges nearest the viewer. Other pixels within the polygon must be hidden by some previously drawn facet and remain unchanged.

Where the images of overlapping facets meet in the display plane there will be an edge requiring anti-aliasing, a simple spatial filter can be used to achieve this. Each pixel within the most recent polygon interrogates its nearest neighbours and takes on an average of their values.

6. Results

The following are very rough estimates of the times taken by a GLITCH system to perform the tasks described in section 4.1. The accuracy of these estimates is being improved constantly as the simulation software is refined. Given that bit-serial operations such as addition and comparison execute at the rate of 100ns per bit, we estimate that the calculation of perpendicular distance of every pixel from a line, as described in section 4.1.3, will complete in about 20μs and calculation of intensities for edge pixels (equation 1) about 7μs. This means that a line of any width can be produced in about 30μs.

Parallelograms require two distance calculations, two edge intensity calculations and a vertices calculation (equation 2, about 6μs), making a total time of 60μs. Polygons can be produced at a rate of about 35μs per vertex, allowing time for the distance, classification and intensity calculations.

Windows of processors can be set up in the time it takes to classify the pixels as being inside or outside the shape given as the window. For a rectangular window with edges parallel to the axes, this is about 4μs. For polygonal windows, about 20μs per vertex. Assuming simple Lambertian shading, three dimensional polygons are produced at the same rate as two dimensional ones, 35μs per vertex, but an additional 20μs is required per polygon for updating the z-buffer.

At the time of writing, confident estimates of the time to produce circles or ellipses, perform spatial filtering for anti-aliasing or polygon rendering with more complex shading algorithms have not yet been produced.

7. Conclusions

Generation of computer graphics images is one of the image processing related tasks we believe are suitable for associative array processors due to the large number of simple local computations. The results above have been produced for an early version of the proposed architecture. Evidence on design data so far developed suggests that instruction cycle times of 50ns may be feasible. In the first prototype design 64 PEs will be accommodated on a chip about 6mm by 7mm using relaxed design rules.

8. Acknowledgements

We gratefully acknowledge the financial support of SERC and the Alvey directorate.

9. References

Duller A.W.G., Morgan A.D. and Storer R., 1987
Associative Processor Arrays: Simulation and Performance Estimates for Image Processing.
Proc. Alvey Vision Conference, Cambridge, Sept 1987

Flanders P.M., Hunt D.J., Reddaway S.J. and Parkinson D., 1979
Efficient high speed computing with the Distributed Array Processor
High Speed Computer and Algorithm organisation Ed. Kuck D.J., Lawrie D.H. and Sameh A.H. (Academic Press)

Fuchs H., Poulton J., Eyles J. and Greer T, 1988
Coarse-Grain and Fine-Grain Parallelism in the Next Generation Pixel-planes Graphics System.
Int. Conf. Parallel Processing for Computer Vision and Display, Leeds UK.

Kohonen, T., 1980
Content Addressable Memories.
Springer-Verlag, 1980

Lea R.M., 1985
A VLSI array processor for image processing
Algorithmically Specialised Parallel Computers, (Academic Press) pp 159-168

Newman W.M. and Sproull R.F., 1979
Principles of Interactive Computer Graphics
McGraw-Hill, 1979

Pitteway M and Wattkinson D, 1980
Bresenham's Algorithm with Grey Scale
Communications of ACM, vol. 23 (11), pp 625-626 November 1980

Rogers D.F., 1985
Procedural Elements for Computer Graphics
McGraw-Hill, 1985

Storer R., 1987
An Instruction Set for an Associative Array Processor
University of Bristol internal report

A Strategy for Mapping Parallel Ray-Tracing into a Hypercube Multiprocessor System

H. Kobayashi, T. Nakamura, and Y. Shigei (Japan)

ABSTRACT

We present a systematic and efficient strategy for mapping an adaptively/ regularly subdivided object space (a set of subspaces) into the nodes of the hypercube. The property of this mapping is that the distance between the neighbouring subspaces on the hypercube is proportional to the difference between the sizes of these subspaces. Especially, if neighbouring subspaces are of equal size, these subspaces are allocated to the neighbouring processors. As a result, we can realize a communication-effective implementation of parallel ray-tracing on the hypercube multiprocessor system. The mapping is derived from the byproduct of octree encoding of an object space.

1. INTRODUCTION

A ray-tracing algorithm can be an efficient tool to synthesize very realistic images (Whitted 1980). However, ray tracing is very time-consuming since ray-object intersection calculations exponetially increases as the complexity of the scene increases. Fast image synthesis using ray tracing is one of the most important topics in computer graphics.

Several parallel ray tracing algorithms have been proposed to reduce the execution time of the computation (Nishimura et al. 1983; Dippe and Swensen 1984; Kobayashi et al. 1987a,1987b). These parallel processing schemes are classified into two categories: <u>pixel-oriented parallel processing and object-oriented parallel processing</u>.

<u>Pixel-oriented parallel processing</u> is based on only pixel parallelism of a screen. Processing elements (PEs) of a parallel system create subimages of a screen. PEs require pixels of subimages to be calculated and the object description related to given pixels to a host computer. This approach is very simple and effective in a small scale multiprocessor system. However, as the number of PEs increases, this control scheme causes a large amount of communications between PEs and the host computer. Increase of this kind of global communications makes PEs ineffective.

On the other hand, in <u>object-oriented parallel processing</u>, only a small part of object description of a space, called a subspace or subvolume, is stored in each PE. Intersection calculations and intensity calculations on the intersecting object for given rays are processed by the PE having the description of the intersecting object. Therefore, ray information is transferred from one PE to the next PE as if rays are propagated through an object space. Ray propagation is achieved by inter-PE communications. If locally communicating tasks are mapped into the neighbouring PEs in a parallel architecture, the communication overhead can be kept at a minimum. Under the above condition, there is no global communications within the system even though a large scale multiprocessor system is constructed.

In this paper, we present a strategy for mapping parallel ray-tracing based on object-oriented parallel processing into a hypercube multiprocessor system. The outline of the paper is as follows. In Section 2, we briefly describe the hypercube-connected parallel architecture, and in Section 3, we describe the essential features of parallel ray tracing based on object-oriented parallel processing. In Section 4, we propose a strategy for mapping an adaptively/regularly subdivided object space into the nodes of the hypercube in a communication-effective way. Finally, we present some concluding remarks in Section 5.

2. A HYPERCUBE MULTIPROCESSOR SYSTEM

A hypercube is a multiprocessor array with powerful interconnection features (Saad and Schultz 1985; Seitz 1985). An n-dimensional hypercube consists of 2^n nodes (PEs) that are numbered by n-bit binary numbers, from 0 to 2^n-1. The PEs are interconnected so that there is a link between two processors if and only if their binary representation differs by only one bit. There are many reasons for the recent growing interest in the hypercube configurations. To reach the PE from any other PE in the hypercube, one needs to pass at most n links. Another appealing feature of the hypercube is its homogeneity and symmetrical properties. Unlike many other architectures, no PE plays a particular role. These features facilitate algorithm design as well as programming. Moreover, each PE has n links, which is a logarithmically increasing function of the total number of PEs. From these reasons, the hypercube seems to be a good candidate for a general purpose parallel architecture.

A multiprocessor system for parallel ray-tracing is shown in Fig. 1. The system consists of PEs interconnected by the hypercube network. The PE consists of a processor and local memory. Each PE is connected to the hypercube network via a communication switch (CSs). The CS is a dedicated communication processor that maintains connections to other switches. Communication links (CLs) interconnect the CSs. There is no global memory and global bus in the system. Communications between PEs are locally done by message passing. The separation of communications by the CSs and computations by the PEs allows each PE to achieve computational efficiency.

3. A PARALLEL RAY TRACING ALGORITHM BASED ON OBJECT-ORIENTED PARALLEL PROCESSING

In image synthesis using ray tracing, calculations of the local intensity, reflection and refraction at any point of an object are carried out on each object in a space. Thus, computational efforts for image synthesis occurs on each object, and can be localized. As a result, we proposed an object-oriented parallel processing approach to image synthesis by ray tracing (Kobayashi et al. 1987a, 1987b), as opposed to a conventional pixel-oriented parallel processing approach.

In an object-oriented parallel processing system, the objects in a space are allocated to the PEs, and rays travel within the multiprocessor system by interprocessor communications. Thus, the processor space as a geometrical configuration of the multiprocessor system corresponds to the object space. The PE determines the intersecting object for a given ray and calculates the local intensity of the intersecting object. If a ray does not intersect an object, or rays are newly generated after reflection/transmission process, the PE transfers these rays to the next PEs according to their directions.

The main problem of this approach is how to allocate objects to PEs. It is necessary to clarify the positional relationship between the objects since propagation of rays is achieved by interprocessor communications. To this end, we study a space subdivision method (Glassner 1894; Fujimoto et al. 1986) A space subdivision method regularly or adaptively divides an object space into many subspaces. Since each subspace is geometrically continuous, it is easy to develop the locality between subspaces, namely parallel tasks. Thus, we can achieve effective parallel processing regarding communications between tasks when the locally communicating tasks are allocated to the neighbouring PEs of a parallel system.

4. A SCHEME FOR MAPPING A SUBDIVIDED OBJECT SPACE INTO A HYPERCUBE MULTIPROCESSOR SYSTEM

4.1 SPACE SUBDIVISION

A space subdivision is classified into two categories: regular and adaptive subdivisions. In the former, an object space is divided into regular subspaces without regard to existence of objects in a space. In the latter, an object space is divided into irregular subspaces. The space including surfaces of objects is finely divided so that boundaries of subspaces may be close to surfaces of objects. When there are a few objects in a space, an adaptive subdivision suits for a space subdivision method since it avoid generating lots of empty subspaces. However, in the regularly subdivided object space, it is easy to determine the subspaces pierced by a given ray (Fujimoto et al. 1986). We study a recursive octal subdivision of an object space (Jackins and Tanimoto 1980; Meager 1982) suiting for both regular and adaptive subdivisions.

4.2 A SCHEME FOR MAPPING A SUBDIVIDED OBJECT SPACE INTO A HYPERCUBE MULTIPROCESSOR SYSTEM

To achieve highly effective parallel processing, a communication-effective implementation of parallel tasks is required. In object-oriented parallel processing of ray tracing, subspaces correspond to parallel tasks and communications between them are caused by ray propagation from one subspace to its neighbouring subspace. Dependence between parallel tasks is represented by positional relationship between neighbouring subspaces. Thus, it is necessary to map neighbouring subspaces into the neighbouring PEs of the hypercube as much as possible. Here, the neighbouring subspaces mean face-neighbouring subspaces along three coordinate axes.

In an adaptive subdivision, it is impossible to map all neighbouring subspaces into the neighbouring PEs except the case of a complete connected multiprocessor system. Thus, we define the nearly optimum mapping as follows:

- When neighbouring subspaces are at the same level in a recursive octal subdivision, these subspaces are allocated to the neighbouring PEs of the hypercube.

- When neighbouring subspaces are at different levels in a recursive octal subdivision, these subspaces are allocated to the PEs whose communication distance is proportional to the difference between the levels of the neighbouring subspaces. Here, communication distance means traversed intermediate communication switches between two communicating PEs.

In the hypercube multiprocessor system, the PEs are interconnected if and only if the Hamming distance between their processor numbers is one. Therefore, neighbouring subspaces at the same level should be assigned to the PEs whose Hamming distance is one. To derive the processor numbers from the byproduct of a recursive octal subdivision, we define node numbers for eight sibling subspaces as shown in Fig. 2. Notice that the Hamming distance of node numbers of subspaces faced in one of x, y, and z directions is one. We call each bit of node number a direction bit.

In node numbers sequences at the same level in the specific direction, the direction bit alters in turn. For example, one of the sequences in the x direction is as follows:

000 100 000 100 000 100 ···

Neighbouring numbers marked by solid lines and dashed lines are the node numbers of neighbouring sibling nodes and neighbouring cousin nodes of an octree, respectively. Thus, by exchanging node numbers between specific sibling nodes, we can generate numbers sequence so that the Hamming distance of numbers between neighbouring sibling nodes is one and that between neighbouring cousin nodes is zero.

000 100 100 000 000 100 ···

We call these numbers processor numbers of each node of an octree. Finally, processor numbers of the PEs of the hypercube for leaf nodes (subspaces) of an octree are generated by combining whole processor numbers of ancestor nodes (including the leaf node) of the leaf node. By this mapping, neighbouring leaf nodes are allocated to the neighbouring PEs of the hypercube. Processor numbers of each node of an octree are easily obtained by calculating a exclusive-OR operation of the node number of a given node and the node number of its parent node.

The algorithm for determining the PEs of the hypercube for each leaf node of an octree is briefly described as follows:

1. Let level of an octree be n, the n-th node at level i be n(i,n), $i=0,1,\cdots,n$, $m=0,1,\cdots,8^{n-i}-1$, and the node number of n(i,m) be o(i,m). Here, for a root node n(n,0), o(n,0)=0.
2. For an arbitrary node n(i,m), a processor number p(i,m) of n(i,m) is obtained as follows:

$$p(i,m) = o(i,m) \oplus o(i+1,m'),\ m' \in \{0,1,\cdots,8^{n-i-1}-1\}$$

where, $\oplus$ means an exclusive-OR operation and n(i+1,m') is the parent node of n(i,m).
3. For all nodes of an octree, generate processor numbers by step 2.
4. For leaf node $n(0,\ell)$, namely subspace, the PE number $P(\ell)$ of the hypercube is determined as follows:

$$P(\ell) = p(n-1,k_{n-1})\cdot 8^{n-1} + p(n-2,k_{n-2})\cdot 8^{n-2} + \cdots + p(1,k_1)\cdot 8 + p(0,\ell)$$
$$= \sum_{j=1}^{n-1} p(j,k_j)\cdot 8^j + p(0,\ell)$$

where, $n(j,k_j)$, $j=0,1,\cdots,n-1$, $k_j \in \{0,1,\cdots,8^{n-j}-1\}$ is a set of ancestor nodes of the leaf node $n(0,\ell)$.

Figure 3 shows a mapping example. Figure 3(a) shows a complete octree representing a regularly subdivided object space and node numbers of each node. Figure 3(b) shows processor numbers of nodes obtained by above mapping algorithm. Finally, Figure 3(c) shows mapping subspaces (leaf nodes of an octree) into the PEs of a six-dimensional hypercube system.

In general, the mapping algorithm can map neighbouring leaf nodes represented by a complete n-tree to the neighbouring PE of the hypercube. Figures 4 and 5 show mapping examples for n=2 (a binary tree) and 4 (a quadtree). Therefore, for n=2, 4, and 8, ring, torus, and wraparounded 3D grid structures of neighbouring leaf nodes can be constructed in the hypercube, respectively.

When the number of processors is limited and is smaller than that of subspaces, several subspaces are allocated to a single processor. To this end, we show two mapping methods: block and distributed allocations. Here, the 3k-dimensional hypercube is assumed.

A. Block allocation (Fig. 6)

This mapping is to allocate a block of neighbouring subspaces to the single PE. Part of local communications between neighbouring subspaces is achieved within the single PE. The block allocation is obtained by using processor numbers at upper k levels of an octree.

B. Distributed allocation (Fig. 7)

This mapping is to allocate subspaces at certain interval apart to a processor. Neighbouring subspaces are allocated to the neighbouring PEs, respectively. Since the computational load in an object space tends to concentrate in a local, the distributed allocation are able to distribute much heavier load existing in a local space to the PEs approximately uniformly. The allocation is obtained by applying the mapping algorithm to nodes of an octree up to level k.

When space subdivision stops at level m (>0) in an adaptive subdivision, processor numbers of nodes from level m-1 to level 0 is undefined. By filling undefined processor numbers with a specific number (e.g. 111 or 000), neighbouring subspaces at different levels can be allocated to the PEs whose communication distance is proportional to the difference between the levels of neighbouring subspaces. However, this mapping produces the PEs not allocated to subspaces. To avoid this and achieve effective parallel processing, we extend a condensed octree obtained by adaptive subdivision to a complete octree. In order to keep the features of an adaptive subdivision, we create a complete octree of an adaptive subdivision by copying the subspace at level k to subspaces at level 0 instead of subdividing a space finely (Fig. 8).

By applying the mapping algorithm to the complete octree of an adaptive subdivision, several same subspaces are allocated to the different PEs. When the PE (source) transfer a given ray to the next PE (destination) and some destinations having the same subspace exist, the source selects the nearest PE as its destination. The selection can be carried out by filling undefined processor numbers of the destination with the processor numbers used in the source. Thus, communication distances between the PEs having neighbouring subspaces at different levels are remarkably reduced without spoiling the advantages of an adaptive subdivision.

4.3 TRANSFORMATION OF PARALLEL PROCESSING FORMS

In the mapping mentioned in Section 4.2, three-dimensional parallel processing is performed for each subspaces. However, when the number of PEs is limited and an object spaces is dense, one- or two-dimensional parallel processing parallel to a screen is more effective than three-dimensional parallel processing (Kobayashi et al. 1987b). Figure 9 shows one-, two-, and three-dimensional parallel processing forms in object-oriented parallel processing. Here, subspaces represented by solid lines are unit subspaces to be allocated to the PEs as parallel tasks.

In order to achieve one- and two-dimensional parallel processing forms in the hypercube, we perform the following procedure. Firstly, we select slices of an object space along the specific direction(s) from an octree. And then we connect the slices with a relation tree representing the positional relationship between them. Figure 10 shows new data structures for one- and two-dimensional parallel processing forms with an octree for a three dimensional parallel processing form. For one-dimensional parallel processing, the new data structure consists of two-dimensional slices represented by a quadtree and the relation tree represented by a binary tree. On the other hand, the data structure for two-dimensional parallel processing consists of one- dimensional slices represented by a binary tree and the relation tree represented by a quadtree.

The new data structures are easily constructed from an octree by using the features of the node numbers of each node of an octree. After the new data structure is constructed from an octree, the appropriate processing form is constructed in the hypercube by applying the mapping algorithm, described in Section 4.2, to the relation tree. Finally, leaf nodes of the relation tree, namely slices are allocated to the PEs of the hypercube according to the processor numbers.

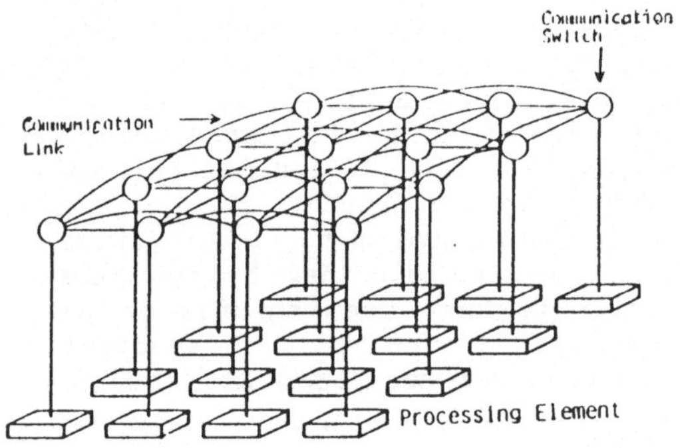

Fig. 1. Hypercube-connected multiprocessor system.

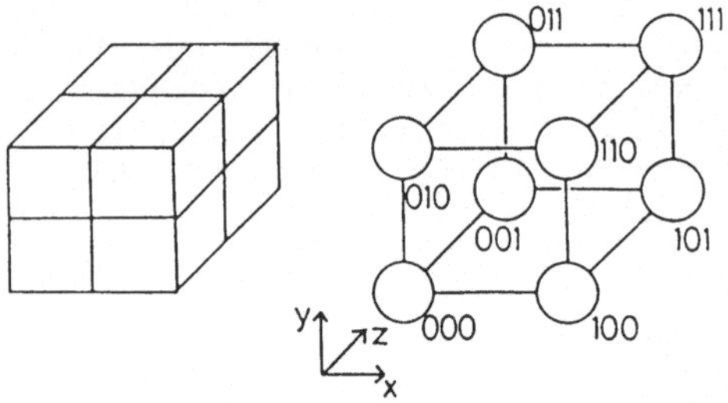

Fig. 2. Octants and the node numbers.

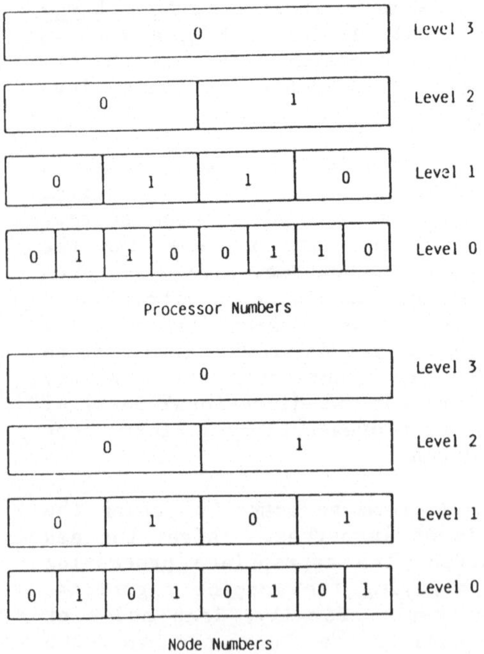

Fig. 4. Mapping neighbouring leaf nodes of a binary tree into the neighbouring PEs of hypercube.

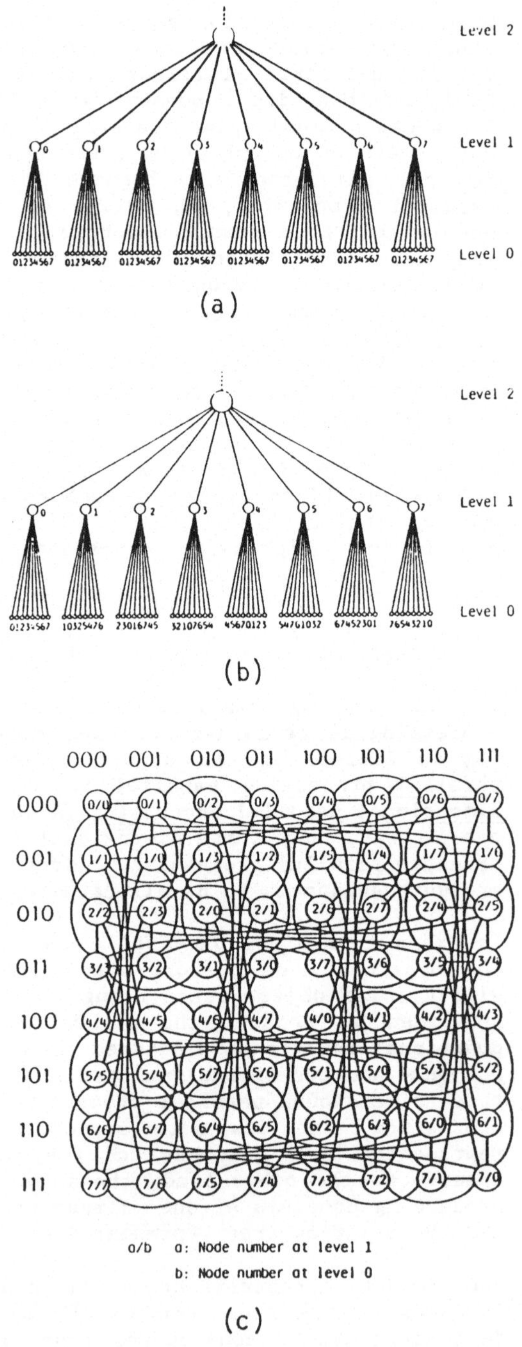

Fig. 3. Mapping neighbouring leaf nodes of an octree into the neighbouring PEs of hypercube. Node numbers (a), processor numbers(b), and mapping subspaces into the PEs (c).

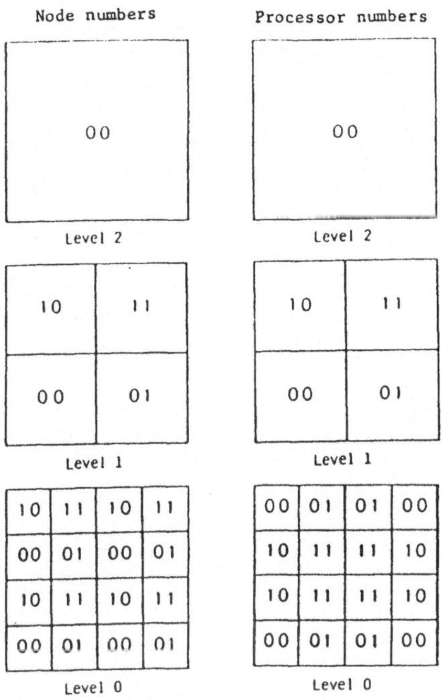

Fig. 5. Mapping neighbouring leaf nodes of a quadtree into the neighbouring PEs of hypercube.

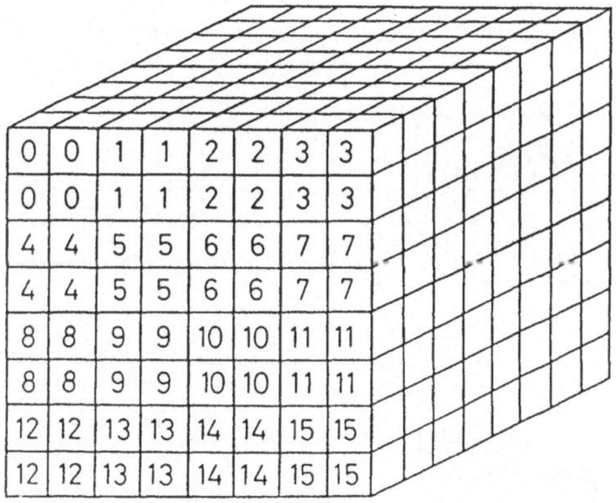

Fig. 6. Block allocation.

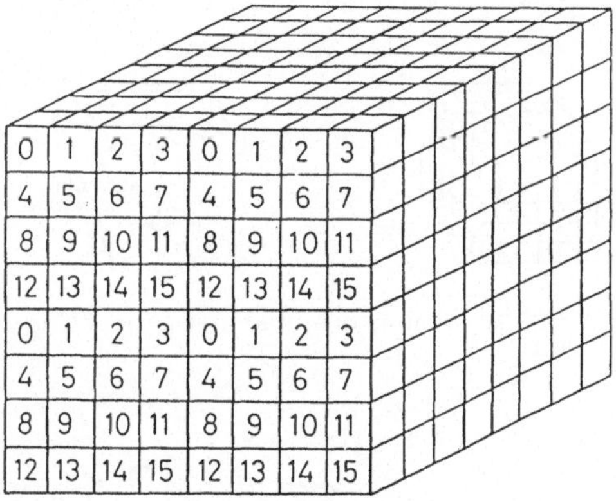

Fig. 7. Distributed allocation.

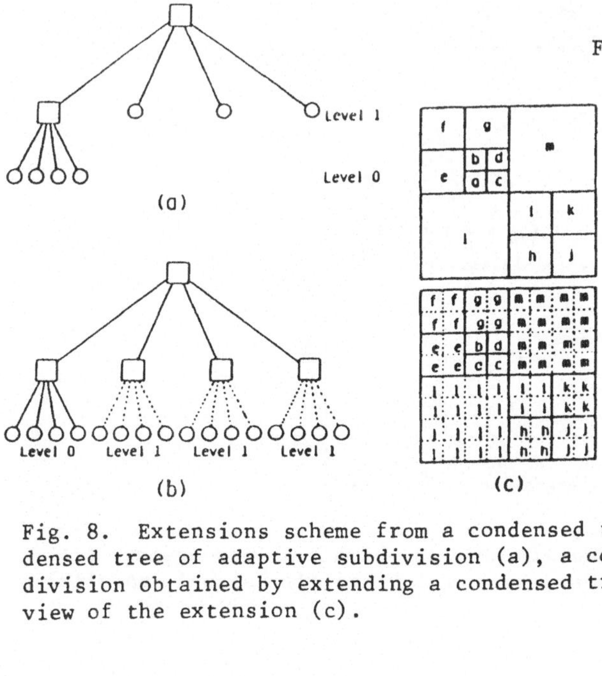

Fig. 8. Extensions scheme from a condensed tree to a complete tree. A condensed tree of adaptive subdivision (a), a complete tree of adaptive subdivision obtained by extending a condensed tree (b), and a two-dimensional view of the extension (c).

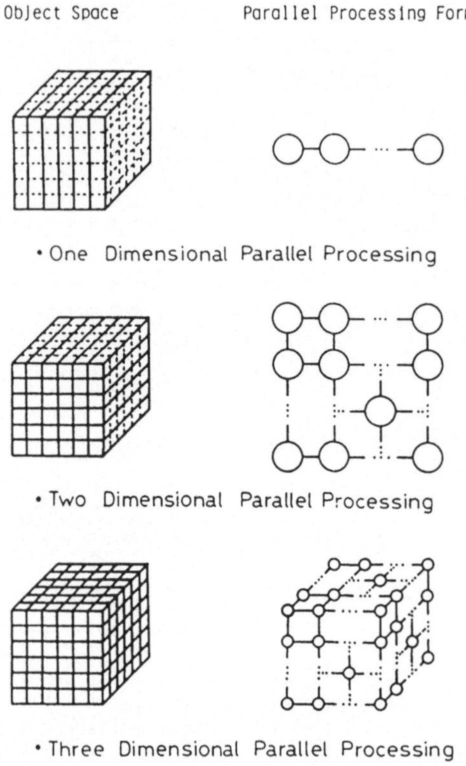

Fig. 9. Parallel processing forms for one-, two-, and three-dimensional object-oriented parallel processing.

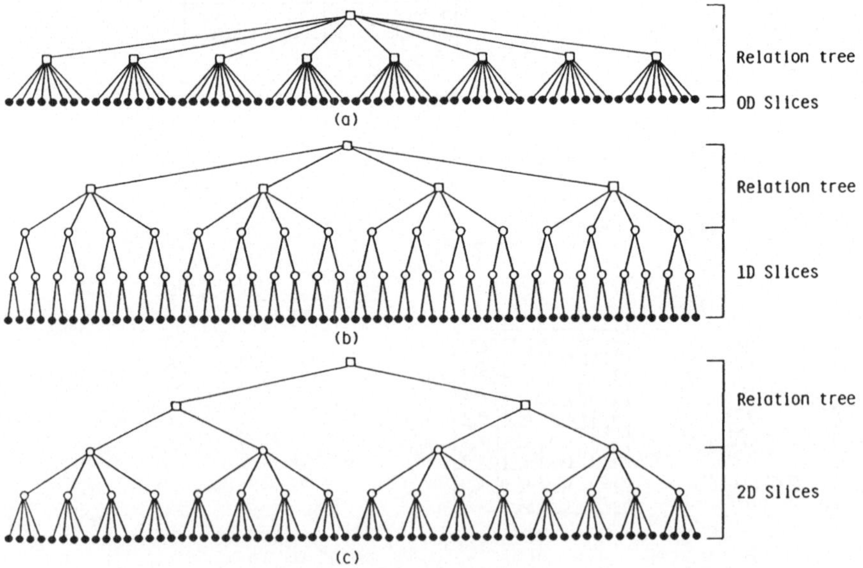

Fig. 10. Data structures for one-dimensional parallel processing (c), two-dimensional parallel processing (b), and three-dimensional parallel processing (a).

5. CONCLUSION

In this paper, we have presented a systematic and efficient strategy for mapping an adaptively/regularly subdivided object space into the nodes of the hypercube. The property of this mapping is that the distance between the neighbouring subspaces on the hypercube is proportional to the difference between the sizes of these subspaces. As a result, we can realize a communication-effective implementation of parallel ray-tracing on the hypercube multiprocessor system. Mapping is derived from the byproduct of octree encoding of an object space.

ACKNOWLEDGEMENTS

The authors are grateful to Professor Tosiyasu L. Kunii of the University of Tokyo for motivating them to do this research and for helpful conversations.

6. REFERENCES

Deppe M, Swensen J (1984) An Adaptive Subdivision Algorithm and Parallel Architecture for Realistic Image Synthesis. Computer Graphics, 18:3:149-158

Fujimoto A, Tanaka T, Iwata K (1986) ARTS: Accelerated Ray-Tracing System. IEEE Computer Graphics and Applications 6:4:16-26

Glassner AS (1984) Space Subdivision for Fast Ray Tracing. IEEE Computer Graphics and Applications 4:10:15-22

Jackins CL, Tanimoto SL (1980) Oct-Trees and Their Use in Representing Three-dimensional Objects. Computer Graphics and Image Processing :4:249-270

Kobayashi H, Nakamura T, Shigei Y(1987a) Parallel Processing of an object space for image synthesis using ray tracing. The Visual Computer 3:13-22

Kobayashi H, Kubota H, Nishimura S, Nakamura T, Shigei Y(1987b) Load balancing strategies for a parallel ray tracing system based on constant subdivision. Submitted to The Visual Computer

Meagher D (1982) Geometric Modeling Using Octree Encoding. Computer Graphics and Image Processing :19:123-147

Nishimura H, Ohno H, Kawata T, Shirakawa I, Omura K (1983) LINKS-1:A Parallel Pipelined Multimicrocomputer System for Image Creation. Proceedings of 10th Ann Int Symp Comput Archi:387-394

Saad Y, Schultz MH(1985) Topological Properties of Hypercubes. Dept. Comput. Sci., Yale Univ., New Haven, CT, Res. Rep. 389

Seitz CL(1985) The Cosmic Cube. Comm of the ACM 28:22-33

Whitted T(1980) An Improved Illumination Model for Shaded Display. Comm ACM 23:343-394

Parallel Space Tracing: An Experience on an iPSC Hypercube

K. Bouatouch and T. Priol (France)

Abstract

A parallel space tracing algorithm is presented. It subdivides the scene into regions. These latter are distributed among the processors of a 2D array architecture which is mapped onto an iPSC hypercube machine designed by Intel company. Each processor subdivides its own region into cells to accelerate the ray tracing algorithm. Processors communicate by means of messages. The pyramidal shape of the regions allows to delete the primary ray messages. An efficient termination algorithm is described. A method of performing a roughly uniform load distribution is proposed.

Key Words : image synthesis, parallel ray-tracing, hypercube.

1 Introduction

It is acknowledged that ray tracing is the most effective technique for the rendering of high quality images [13,18,21]. Ray tracing simulates the operation of a camera, following light rays in reverse order. It consists in shooting rays from an observer through a simulated screen plane towards the objects of a scene (primary rays). The program computes the intersection of each ray with each object, and determines which intersection is closest. Light sources contributions to the pixel intensity are computed by shooting rays from the intersection point to each light source and determining if the rays are occluded by some solid objects (light rays). If this is the case, the relevant point is shadowed. According to the photometric properties of the objects, new rays are shot from the closest intersection point, in order to take into account the contribution to the pixel intensity of the neighboring objects [6,14,21]. Indeed, if the object is transparent, then a new ray is shot in the refracted direction and if in addition it is reflective, then a new ray is shot in the reflected direction (secondary rays). Consequently, the number of rays is very important. This yields a lot of computations of intersections between rays and objects, and makes then the ray-tracing technique extremely time-consuming.

Two approaches have been attempted in order to overcome this large number of intersections: algorithmical and architectural.

This work has been supported by C^3 and by the CCETT (Centre Commun d'Etudes de Télédiffusion et Télécommunications) under contract 86ME46

1.1 Algorithmical approach

Two classes of algorithms have been proposed in the literature. The methods of the first class involve a creation of a tree of bounding volumes whose leaves are the extents of the objects and the nodes represent the bounding volumes of parts of the scene [18,19]. If a new ray fails to intersect the extent of an object, then it cannot intersect the object itself. This allows the saving of a lot of computations.

As for the methods of the second class, they involve a 3D subdivision of the bounding volume of the scene which is generally a parallelepiped whose faces are perpendicular to the view coordinate axes [2,3,10,11,15,22]. Indeed, this bounding volumes is subdivided into 3D regions containing a small number of objects. A ray which enters a region, intersects only those objects lying in this region. If no intersection is found or the intersected objects are all transparent (in the case of light rays), a computation of the next region traversed by the ray is performed.

These subdivision methods have proved their efficiency since they can reduce considerably the synthesis time, but at the expense of a more important memory requirement.

1.2 Architectural approach

All the parallel machines which have been completed or proposed can be classified in three groups. Those of the first group [4,17] use the fact that each pixel may be processed independently, thereby the pixels are divided evenly among the processors. There is no problem of interprocessor communication since the database is duplicated in each processor's memory. Even in the case of scenes of moderate complexity (several hundreds of objects) the performance is degraded due to the large amount of ray-objects calculations. One solution is to subdivide the space containing the scene and duplicate the data base associated with this subdivision, in each processor's memory. Unfortunately this would require a very large memory.

As for the machines of the second group [12], the objects of the scene are distributed among the processors. The method involves a tree of extents used for intersection computation. Only the top levels of this tree are replicated in every processor. The leaves of the subtree constituted by these top levels, enclose the parts of the database distributed among the processors. One or more parts of the database and a subset of the pixel array are controlled by each processor. The drawback of this technique relies on the fact that the criterion of distribution is not easy to determine automatically, and in addition, a lot of time is spent in the traversal of the tree of extents.

The machines of the last group are based on the subdivision of the space into 3D regions. Each of the processors is assigned one or more regions and each region contains a part of the database. This latter is then distributed among the processors. Neighbouring processors contain adjacent regions and communicate locally via messages. A very important source of inefficiency, inherent in these machines, is the load imbalance problem. Indeed, the processors near the light sources and those controlling the regions located in the middle of the scene, are more solicited than the processors near the edges. To overcome this problem, some attempts have been proposed in the literature [8,16]. They consist of a dynamic redistribution of the load among the processors, in order to make it uniform. We will see in the next section that theses techniques present many artifacts.

In spite of these remarks, we think that the machines of the third group would be the most interesting if we could resolve all (or a part of) the problems due to this kind of machines. These machines are presented in the next section and parallel space tracing is described in the third section. The last section is reserved to the conclusion.

2 Machines based on space subdivision

Firstly, in this section, we describe three machines based on the distribution of 3D regions among the processors and which have been proposed by Cleary [5], Dippe [8] and Nemoto [16]. Then we make remarks about some aspects of their implementation and raise some problems which have not been emphasized by their simulation and which influence considerably the efficiency of these machines.

2.1 Description

To our knowledge, three machines have been proposed in the literature but none has been completed.

- Cleary's machine

  This machine consists of an array of processors. The authors proved that a 2D array is better than a 3D one, since it reduces the number of messages exchanged by the processors. We approve of them since our experience on an iPSC hypercube has shown that even with a 2D array, the number of messages is so large that the associated queues are rapidly saturated. In this machine, each processor is connected to its four neighbors by means of dual port memories. It may happen that several processors contribute to the final intensity of a pixel. These contributions are passed from processor to processor back to the processor where the ray started. This is one of the drawbacks of this implementation since the overhead of messages is increased.

- Dippe's machine

  The architecture is a 3D array of processors, each one is assigned one or more regions. The shape of these regions are general cubes which are general hexahedra. A set of tetrahedra is constructed with groups of six tetrahedra forming a cube, which are then arranged to fill the space occupied by the scene. The boundaries of the regions are moved to assure a roughly uniform distribution of load. When a region's load is higher than those of its neighbors, some load is transferred to them. This is done by moving the corners of a region. The redistribution of load is performed by means of messages called redistribution messages. Each ray resulting from a ray-object intersection contains its contribution to the intensity of a pixel; that reduces messages.

- Nemoto's machine

  The regions resulting from the space subdivision, are orthogonal parallelepipeds which consist of several unit cubes. A unit cube has a size equal to one, and edges parallel to each axis. The architecture is a 3D array of processors; each one has six connections to its six neighbors and is assigned one region. In order to avoid a load imbalance, the loads of two neighboring regions are compared by the associated processors. If the load of one region is lower than the one of another region, and the lower load is under the given threshold value, the separating face is slid by one unit along the axis perpendicular to this face.

2.2 Remarks

Among the three machines described previously, those of Nemoto and Dippe seem the most realistic because they try to solve the problem of load imbalance. Nevertheless, many problems remain in suspense. That leads us to make remarks concerning the questions of space subdivision, dynamic load redistribution, distributed algorithmic and overhead of interprocessor messages.

- Space subdivision

  In Dippe's machine, the movement of a ray (or objects in case of load redistribution) from a region to its neighbor involves a very expensive boundary intersection. This is due to the subdivision of the space into tetrahedra. As for Nemoto's machine, the regular space partition becomes irregular after a dynamic redistribution load. Indeed, a region may become adjacent to several other regions. This makes it expensive to rout the messages on an 2D array.

- Load redistribution

  The load redistributions proposed are interesting but involve a lot of messages, whereas messages associated to primary, secondary and light rays are yet very numerous. This load redistribution is not quite simple because the movement of a corner or a face affects all the adjacent regions. Which corner or face is selected first ? What is the behaviour of the algorithm when all the processors are adjusting their load at the same time ? What is the periodicity of the load redistribution ? This latter may be a source of oscillations. How to avoid it ? Due to these non-answered questions we prefer a static load redistribution which will be described in the next section.

- Distributed algorithmic

  Due to the large number of messages, some processors may be in a situation of deadlock. How to avoid it ? This is a crucial problem which has never been evoked by the authors quoted previously. A second question which may be asked is: what is the algorithm of termination which does not affect the efficiency of the distributed machine. An efficient termination algorithm will be given in the next section.

- Messages overhead

  It is clear that if we try successfully to reduce the number of messages, we can improve the efficiency of these machines and avoid the problems evoked previously. For example light rays involve a lot of messages and make the processor near them, very busy. Finding a means for suppressing them would be very effective. We will propose en efficient one in the next section.

The following section presents some solutions for the evoked problems. We have chosen to implement these solutions on an existing parallel machine which is an iPSC hypercube designed by Intel Company, because simulation does not raise the problems inherent in a distributed machine.

3 Implementation of our algorithm an an iPSC hypercube

Our algorithm is based on the distribution of the database among the processors of a multiprocessor machine. It is implemented on an iPSC hypercube which is a multiprocessor system constituted by 64 processors. Each processor is a 80286 microprocessor supplied with a 80287 coprocessor and a 4.5 Mbytes of local memory. The topology of this machine is a hypercube. It allows a large choice of architectures (2D or 3D array, ring, etc...).

For our implementation, we have chosen a 2D array due to the reasons evoked previously. Each processor is connected to its four neighbors and is assigned one region containing a part of the database which is a CSG tree. These regions result from a space subdivision technique which is described below.

3.1 Space subdivision into regions

The method is illustrated by figures 1 and 3. The screen is subdivided into a 2D grid. All the elements of the grid (called pixels area) contain roughly the same number of pixels. A 3D region controlled by a processor is a pyramid whose back face lies on the back face of the extent of the scene, and whose front face is a pixel area. The shape of the region is such that a primary ray which is shot in a region, does not leave it. This decreases the messages overhead since the transmission of primary ray messages is avoided.

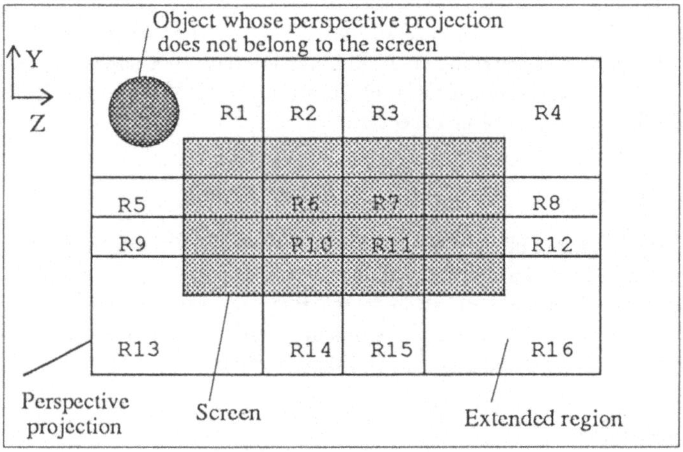

Figure 1: Subdivision in regions.

The regions at the edges of the screen are made larger in order to take into account the secondary rays intersecting the objects whose perspective projection do not lie on the screen. Indeed, they are extended up to the edges of the perspective projection of the front face of the scene extent.

This subdivision does not resolve sufficiently the problem of load imbalance since it is just based on an uniform distribution of pixels. It is just implemented to raise the problems evoked previously and to solve a part of them. A more efficient subdivision method performing a roughly uniform distribution load, is being implemented. It is described later in this paper.

3.2 Overview of our algorithm

The algorithm consists mainly of four phases:

1. The host processor of the iPSC subdivides the space into 3D regions as described above. Then it affects to each processor a region and a part of the data base which results from a *CSG tree pruning* technique [2,3,20].

2. Each processor subdivides in its turn its own 3D region into subregions called cells [2]. The result is a set of cells which are linked together by means of four pointers associated with the cells corners.

3. When all the processors have accomplished their subdivision, they notify (by messages) the host processor which sends to them a message to allow them to start the synthesis phase.

4. Synthesis phase: each process shoots primary rays through its pixel area. These rays remain in the associated region and are not transmitted to the neighboring regions since the shape of a region is a pyramid. These primary rays yield light rays which may be transmitted to the neighboring regions by the sending of messages. It is the case in our present implementation. It will be seen later that these messages can be avoided. Primary rays generate also secondary rays whose associated messages are passed to the neighboring processors. Each processor is assigned one FIFO queue in order to save the messages which come from the neighboring processors. When a processor receives a ray, it computes its contribution to the intensity of the associated pixel and then transmits it to the host processor to cumulate it to the contents of the frame buffer location associated with the relevant pixel. This is possible since the computation of the final intensity of a pixel is distributed among several processors.

These different phases are detailed below.

3.3 Subdivision of a region

Let us show now how each of the processors subdivides its own region. The subdivision method is well described in [2]. We recall briefly the main aspects of this method.

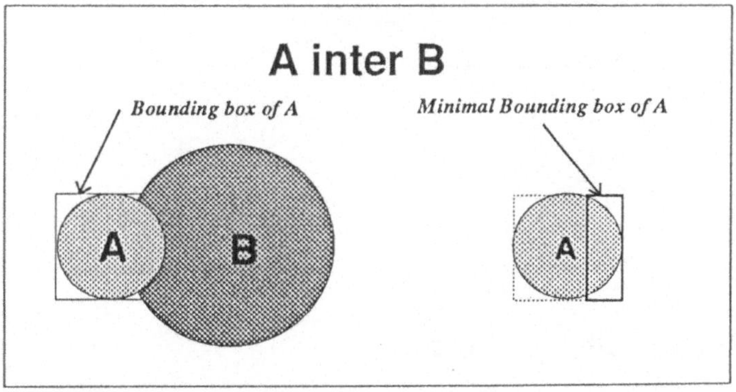

Figure 2: Minimal bounding box perspective projection.

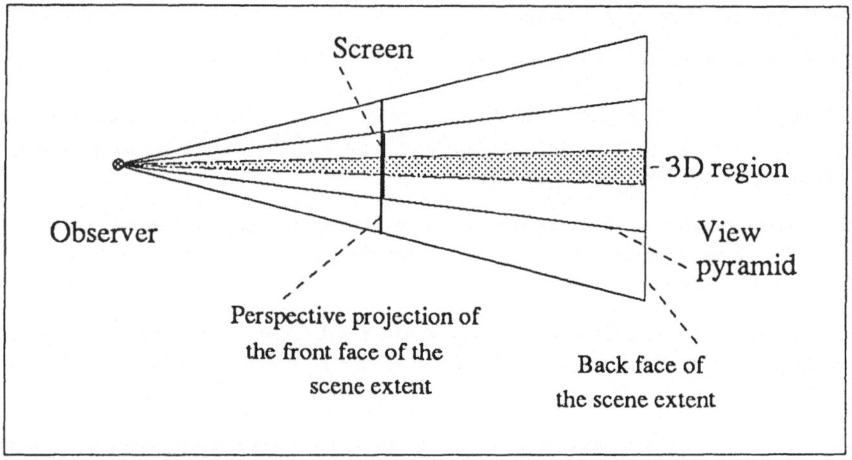

Figure 3: Projection of the 3D regions on a XZ plane.

With each region, is associated a subtree which is the restriction of the whole CSG tree representing the scene, to the objects lying in this region. With each object is associated a minimal bounding box which bounds the part of the object effectively used. These minimal bounding boxes are projected in perspective on the screen plane (Fig. 2). The result is a set of rectangles lying on the screen. Each rectangle is then decomposed into its four segments, used to perform a binary space partioning [9].

The way to carry out the BSP is to choose one segment among the available segments list. The line containing this segment, separates the plane into two regions. According to the segment's location, the segments list is broken into two other lists, each one is associated with a region. The line extension of the chosen segment, may intersect other segments. In this case

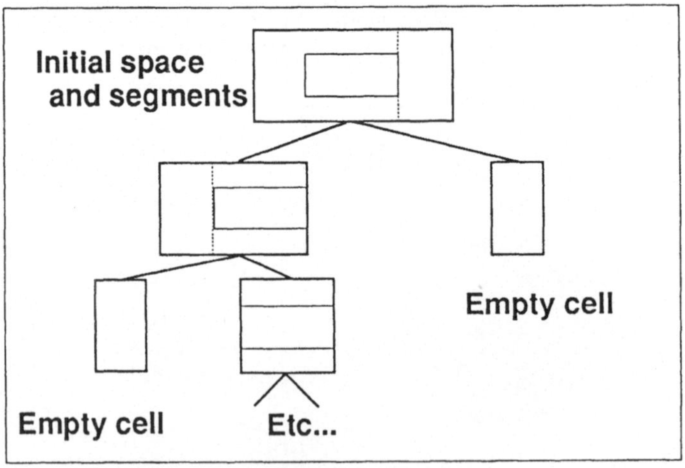

Figure 4: Binary space partitioning

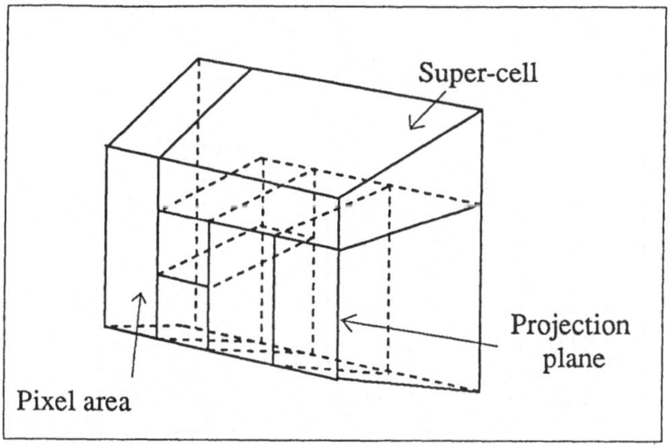

Figure 5: Super cells structure

they are split and put in the two new lists. The same process is applied recursively to these regions, until the associated lists become empty (Fig. 4). Terminal 2D boxes, containing or not a subset of primitives are then created. The BSP process results in a 2D partition of the screen plane, whose extension along the depth axis gives 3D cells, called super-cells (Fig. 5).

Each of them may be empty or may contain some primitive objects. A non empty super-cell projection defines a "pixel sub-area", in the sense that they are the only screen areas which are ray-traced. To take advantage of the spatial coherence of the scene, a spatial subdivision is accomplished on the super-cell structure that we call ***depth partitioning***.

3.3.1 Depth partitioning

The goal of this step is to refine the subdivision in the third dimension for each super-cell which contains some primitives, distributed along the Z axis. Indeed, the faces of the minimal bounding boxes which are perpendicular to the Z axis, are used to subdivide each super-cell into cells (Fig. 6). A region associated with each processor is then a set of cells. The cell connectivity is assured by means of four pointers.

3.3.2 Cell connectivity

To accomplish the task of searching the next cell along the ray path, a local information is added to each cell, named connectivity information, to provide a means for localizing its neighboring cells. For one cell, we use a fixed set of pointers associated with the cell corners. The meaning of one pointer, is to link cells by their corners. The 3D extension is made from the particular connectivity relation between cells on the Oz axis. Only one pointer is necessary to cover all the cells lying in the direction of this axis (Fig. 7).

PTLU, PTRU, PTRD, PTLD name each corner used in our method and up, down, front, back, left and right are the names of the associated pointers according to the direction of the adjacency relation. With this technique, we can follow the path of a ray across the cell structure. Figure 8 shows a 2D projection of this structure and the path of a ray using pointers. Arrows indicate pointers effectively used and straight lines the other pointers.

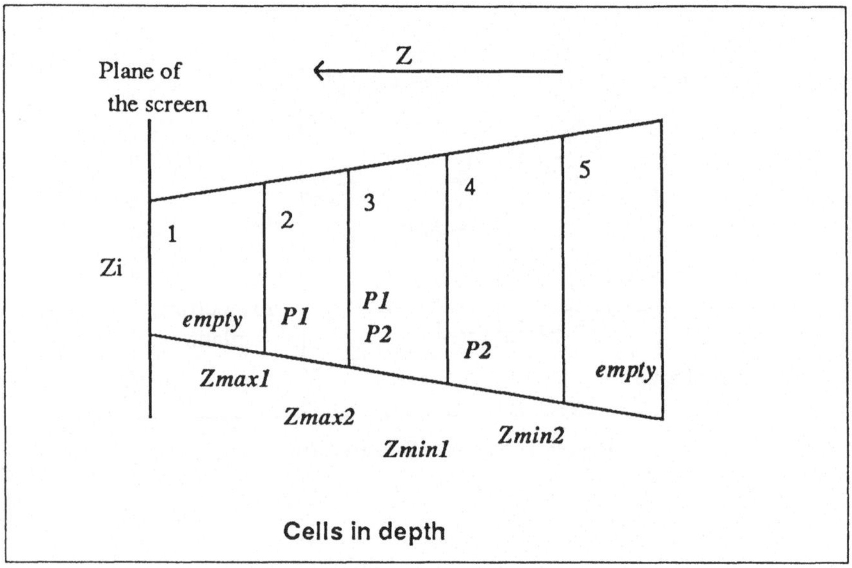

Figure 6: Depth subdivision along the Oz axis

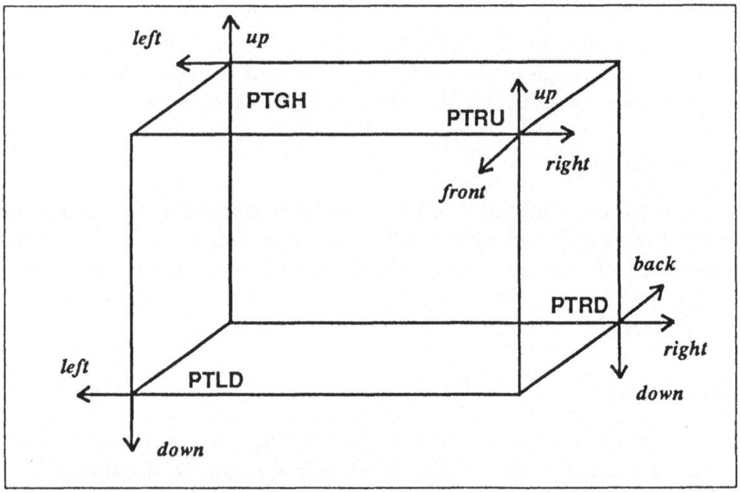

Figure 7: Connectivity using corner pointers

3.3.3 Searching the next cell along the ray path

The search of the next cell along a ray path involves the computation of intersections of this ray with the faces of a cell. Since cells are polyhedra, this may be time consuming. We have resolved this problem by expressing a ray in two coordinate systems. The first one is the eye

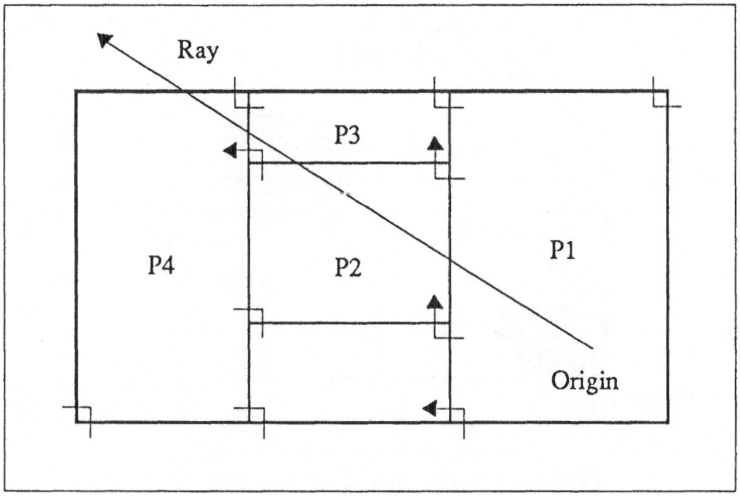

Figure 8: Ray path across the structure

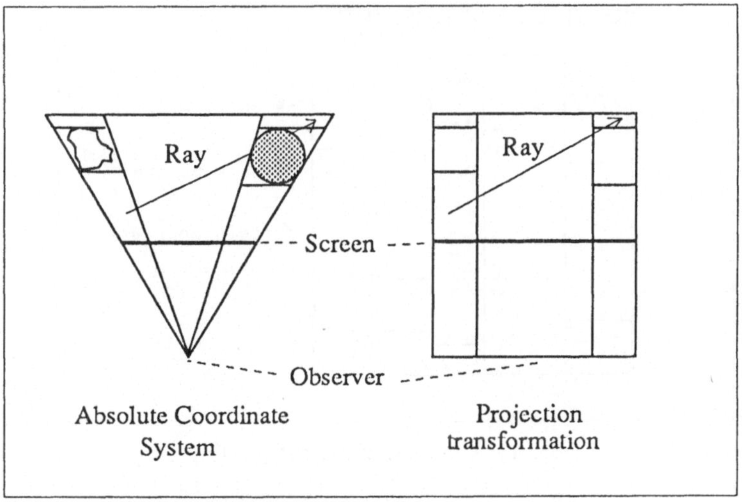

Figure 9: Coordinate system

coordinate system and the second is such that a cell becomes a rectangular parallelepiped whose faces are perpendicular to the axes (Fig. 9). This solution is also used by a processor, to know the one controlling the next region along the ray path.

3.3.4 Determining the entry cell

When a processor receives a ray, it must be able to determine the cell of its own region, which is pierced by this ray. To do that, each processor localizes two particular cells during the phase of subdivision into cells of its own region. These are the right-up an left-low cells as shown in

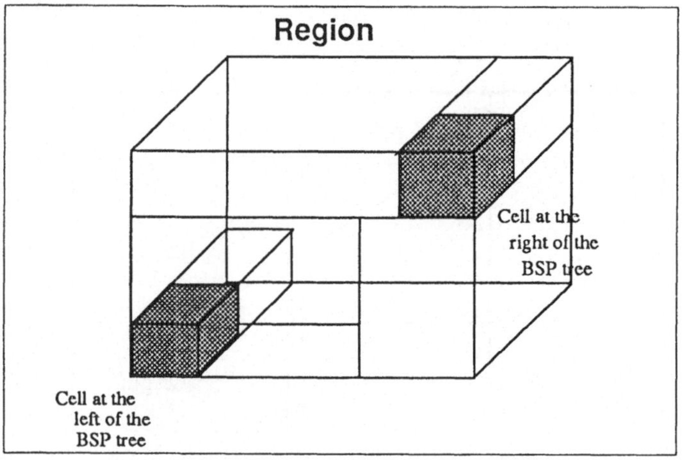

Figure 10: Right-up and left-low cells

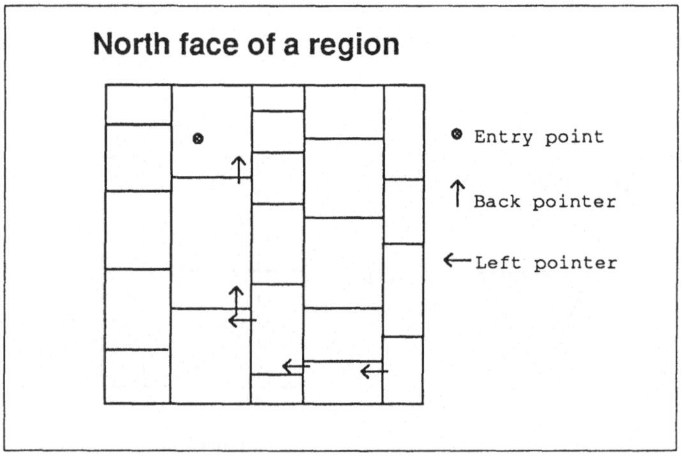

Figure 11: Computing the entry cell

figure 10. Thanks to their connectivity pointers, these two cells allow the determination of the cell pierced by the received ray (Fig. 11).

3.4 Distributing the computation of the pixels intensity

For the sake of simplicity, we use the illumination model proposed by Whitted [21]. The contribution of each ray to the intensity of a pixel is computed by each of the processors and transmitted to the host processor which uses it to update the frame memory. To do that, the data structure of a ray message must contain the cumulated product of the specular reflection and transparency coefficients K_s and K_t of the objects intersected by all the intermediary rays generated by a primary ray. This avoids the return messages of intensity contribution.

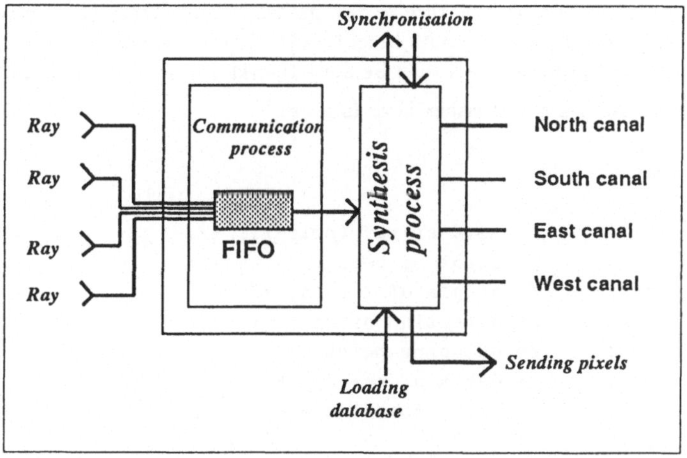

Figure 12: Communication between the two processes.

3.5 Interprocessors communication

Our algorithm uses a set of processes. Each process communicates with another one by means of messages. These processes are located on each node of the iPSC and on the host processor. The process associated with this latter controls all the input/output operations. Whereas, two processes are associated with each node processor:

1. Synthesis process.
2. Communication process.

3.5.1 Process associated with the host processor

This process controls all the input/output operations as for example the reading of the database. It subdivides the space into regions and distributes them among the node processors. It synchronizes the running of the synthesis process of the node processors. After doing that, it waits for the reception of the messages of intensity contribution, coming from the node processors, to update the frame buffer.

3.5.2 Process associated with the Node processors

Figure 12 illustrates the communication between the two processes associated with each node processor.

- **Communication process**

  Its role is to receive the ray messages generated by the synthesis process of the four neighbouring processors. These messages are stored in a *FIFO* queue. As soon as the communication channel between the two process of a node is free, 8 ray messages are at once sent to the synthesis process in order to avoid the latency-time due to the communication mode of the iPSC. The operating system resident in each node processor, schedules the processes in a time-slicing fashion. The periodicity of the scheduling is 50ms. If the communication process does not receive ray messages and cannot send ray messages to the synthesis process, it interrupts its execution (before the 50ms are passed) to allow the one of the synthesis process. This may be done thanks to the system command *flick()*.

The data structure of a ray message is as follows :

```
typedef struct
  {
  type      kr;      /* kind of ray (primary, */
                     /* light or secondary ray */
  point     ori;     /* origin of the ray */
  vecteur   dir;     /* direction of the ray */
  point     end;     /* outgoing point */
  short     depth;   /* depth of the ray */
  short     ipix;    /* pixel coordinate */
  short     jpix;    /*    "           "   */
  short     face;    /* face containing the */
                     /* outgoing point */
  double    maxlum;  /* distance between the origin */
                     /* of the ray and the light source */
  double    coeff;   /* Cumulated product of the Ks, Kt */
  double    att;     /* Attenuation factor */
  } ray;
```

- **Synthesis process**

The first task of this process is to receive its region and its associated subtree, transmitted by the host processor, and to subdivide it into 3D cells. It then shoots its own primary rays. Some rays may be sent to the processors controlling the regions lying along their path. This sending is performed asynchronously in order to avoid the locking of the synthesis process. But if the channel is already used for the sending of a previous message, the synthesis process remains locked until the releasing of this channel. To avoid the saturation of the FIFO queue, the synthesis process computes the rays sent by the communication processor in priority.

Once, the fraction of the pixel intensity is computed by the synthesis process, this latter stores it in a queue. As soon as this queue becomes full, it is transmitted to the host processor. This allows to save time since communication between a node and the host processor is time-consuming. The synthesis process is described by the following algorithm:

```
main()
{
  while(image_not_finished()) {

      /* Processing of primary rays */

      generate_primary_ray(r)
      evaluate_ray(r);
```

```
        /* Processing of rays coming from */
        /* the neighbouring processors    */

        while(ray_to_read())
           read_ray(r);
           compute_entry_cell(r)
           evaluate_ray(r);
        }
    }
}
```

where :

evaluate_ray(r) processes a ray according to its type. Secondary or light rays may be shot.

compute_entry_cell(r) computes the entry cell according to the entry point in the region.

image_not_finished() this procedure corresponds to the implementation of the termination algorithm.

3.6 Termination algorithm

We have chosen to implement the termination algorithm proposed by Dijkstra [7]. To do that, we configurate the iPSC into a virtual ring on which moves a token whose color may be white or black. At the initialization phase, the processor 0 has the token. After having completed a tour round the ring, if the token remains white the termination algorithm is then effective. Otherwise, processor 0 must emit another white token. This latter is not immediately passed from a processor to its neighbour. Indeed, the synthesis process consists of two phases. In the first phase, the primary rays and the received rays are simultaneously processed. The second phase starts when all the primary rays are treated. During this phase, a node processor has to consume only the rays coming from its neighbouring processors. It is in the second phase that the token moves from processor to processor. A processor transmits the token (whatever its color) to its neighbor only if it has nothing to do. When a processor P receives the token, two cases have to be considered:

1. If the token is black, processor P transmits it to the next processor in the ring.

2. If the token is white, it is transmitted to the next processor in the ring, only if processor P has not sent a message to a previous processor in the ring before receiving the token. Otherwise processor P modifies the color of the token before transmitting it to the next processor in the ring.

Each processor transmits the token to the next processor only if it has finished to compute its primary rays. The goal of this technique is to minimize the number of tokens. First results have shown that only a dozen is enough to detect the termination of our parallel algorithm.

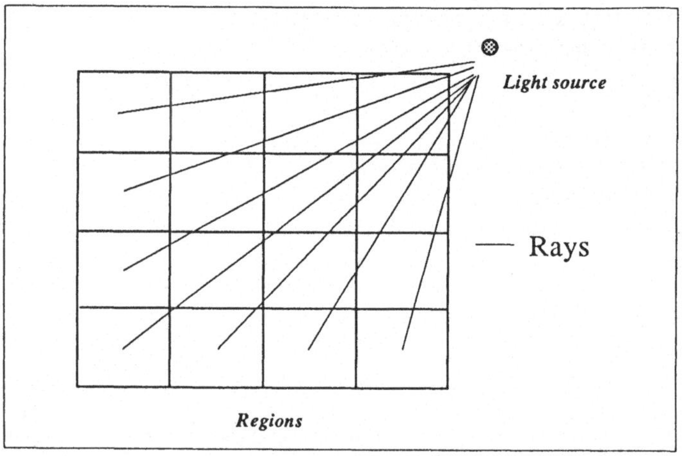

Figure 13: Light rays path.

3.7 Load distribution

The first tests have been performed with a scene of one hundred objects and with a resolution of 256 x 256 pixels. Our present parallel algorithm seems slower than Roth's (where the database is duplicated in each processor and the pixels are distributed among all the processors). In fact, the algorithm is very performant at the beginning of the synthesis phase. After that, its efficiency decreases rapidly. The state to which converges the algorithm is such that 75 percent of the process are locked due to the saturation of the FIFO queues. This means that the load is not uniformly distributed. This load imbalance is mainly due to the processing of the light rays which all converge to the light sources, yielding then a lot of messages (Fig. 13). In the following, on the one hand, we propose a means of deleting the light ray messages and on the other hand a method of uniform load distribution which is performed before the starting of the synthesis phase.

3.7.1 Deleting the light ray messages

The aim is to allow each node processor to process locally its light rays. To do that, it must know all the objects potentially intersected by the light rays which originate from its own region. These light rays form a cone whose apex is a light source and which contains the spherical bounding box of the relevant regions (Fig. 14). A small part of the database (which is a subtree in our case) is then associated with a cone which is henceforth called light cone. Thus at each region, correspond as many light cones as light sources.

In fact each light cone is truncated by a plane which subdivides the space into two half-spaces. A leaf of the subtree associated with a light cone is such that its spherical bounding box intersects both the light cone and the half space containing the light source (Fig. 15). Spherical bounding boxes are used since sphere-cone intersection is easy to compute [1].

3.7.2 Static load distribution

As mentioned previously, dynamic load redistribution [8,16] yields a lot of messages and consequently a lot of computations of ray-boundary intersection. This degrades dramatically the

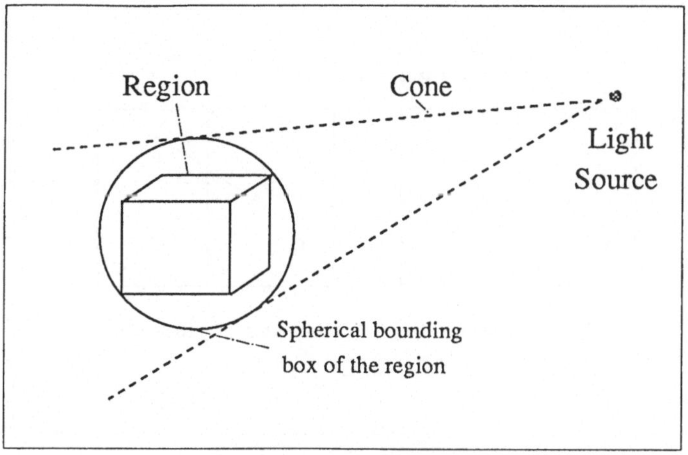

Figure 14: Light cone.

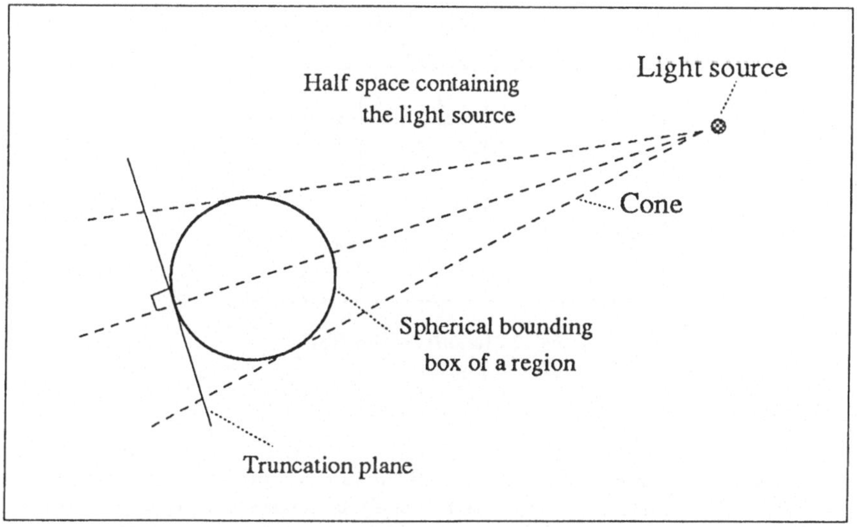

Figure 15: Truncated light cone.

performance of a distributed machine. We think it is more realistic to perform a load distribution staticly, that is before starting the synthesis phase. The proposed redistribution method consists in sub-sampling the image in order to represent a set of coherent rays by only one ray generated by ray-tracing the sub-sampled image. The algorithm consists of two steps. In the first step, the primary rays corresponding to this sub-sampling and all the derived secondary and light (in case of non use of light cones) rays are computed. In the second step, the pyramidal bounding box of the scene is adaptively subdivided into regions; each one contains roughly the same number of rays. In fact this subdivision is accomplished by means of a 2D BSP technique

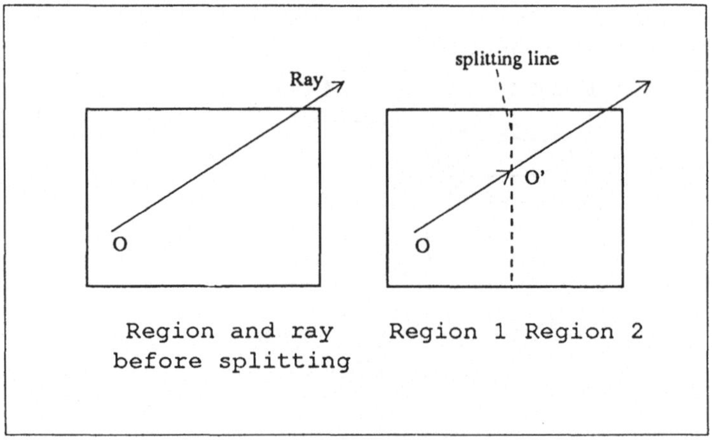

Figure 16: Splitting a ray into two rays.

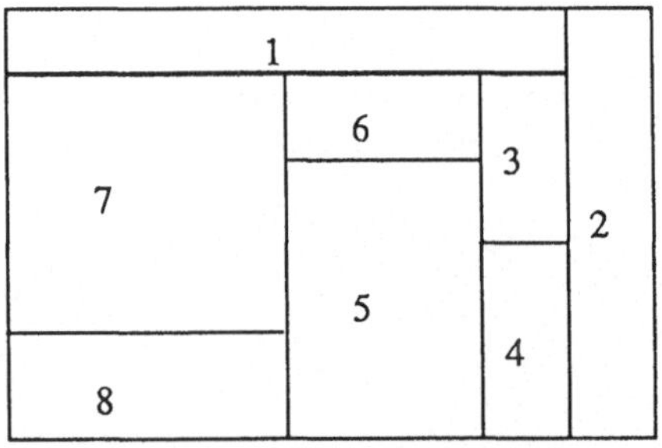

Figure 17: Result of the BSP.

which is performed on the screen plane. Indeed, all the rays are projected in perspective on the screen plane and the 3D regions are represented by their associated pixels areas described in the previous section. During the BSP step, a ray may belong to two adjacent regions created by a BSP splitting line. This ray is then split into two rays (Fig. 16).

The result of the BSP subdivision is firstly a set of rays including the original rays computed in the first step and secondly a set of regions containing roughly the same number of rays. We can now define the load metric. It is only determined by the number of rays to be processed, since objects are supposed to be of the same kind and since ray tracing in a 3D region is nearly independent of the number of objects [2]. Since a region may be adjacent to several others (Fig. 17), we obtain an adjacency graph which represents the interprocessors communications. It is important to suitably map this graph on the hypercube topology in order to minimize the messages routing. An other important point is the choice of a good sub-sampling. This latter is not obvious. For example, it must be regular and must depend on the image resolution. This choice is under investigation.

4 Conclusion

We have presented a parallel space tracing algorithm whose implementation on an iPSC hypercube has allowed us to raise all the problems due to a distributed machine. Only one part of the solutions of these problems have been implemented whereas the other part (static load distribution, light cones) is being implemented. Our main goal was to reduce considerably the number of messages in order to accelerate the algorithm and to avoid the crucial problem of deadlock. Indeed, primary ray messages have been deleted and light cones have been proposed to avoid light ray messages. Load redistribution messages can also be avoided if a static load distribution is used.

References

[1] J. Amanatides. Ray tracing with cones. *Computer Graphics*, 18(3):129–135, July 1984.

[2] B. Arnaldi, T. Priol, and K. Bouatouch. A new space subdivision method for ray tracing csg modelled scenes. *The Visual Computer*, 3(2):98–108, August 1987.

[3] K. Bouatouch, M.O Madani, T. Priol, and B. Arnaldi. A new algorithm of space tracing using a csg model. In *EUROGRAPHICS'87 Conference Proceeding*, pages 65–78, Centre for Mathematics and Computer Science, August 1987.

[4] C. Bouville, R. Brusq, J.L. Dubois, and I. Marchal. Synthèse d'images par lancer de rayons: algorithmes et architecture. In *Premier Colloque Image*, pages 683–696, May 1984.

[5] J.G Cleary, B.M Wyvill, G.M. Birtwistle, and R. Vatti. Multiprocessor ray tracing. *Computer Graphics Forum*, 5(1):3–12, March 1986.

[6] R.L. Cook and K.E. Torrance. A reflectance model for computer graphics. *ACM transactions on graphics*, 1(1):7–24, January 1982.

[7] E.W Dijkstra, W.H.J Feijen, and A.J.M Van Gasteren. Derivation of a termination detection algorithm for distributed computation. *Inf. Proc. Letters*, 16:217–219, June 1983.

[8] M. Dippe and J. Swensen. An adaptive subdivision algorithm and parallel architecture for realistic image synthesis. *Computer Graphics*, 18(3):149–158, July 1984.

[9] H. Fuchs. On visible surface generation by a priori tree structure. In *SIGGRAPH'80 Conference Proceeding*, pages 149–158, July 1980.

[10] A. Fujimoto, T. Tanaka, and K. Iawata. Arts : accelerated ray tracing system. *IEEE Computer Graphics and Applications*, 6(4):16–26, April 1986.

[11] A. Glassner. Space subdivision for fast ray tracing. *IEEE Computer Graphics and Applications*, 4(10):15–22, October 1984.

[12] J. Goldsmith and J. Salmon. *A Ray Tracing System for the Hypercube.* Technical Report, California Institute of Technology, 1985.

[13] R.A. Goldstein and R. Nagel. 3d modeling with synthavision simulation. *Simulation*, 16(1):25–31, January 1971.

[14] A. Roy Hall and Donald P. Greenberg. A testbed for realistic image synthesis. *IEEE Computer Graphics and Applications*, 3(8):10–20, November 1983.

[15] M. R. Kaplan. Space-tracing, a constant time ray tracer. In *SIGGRAPH'85 tutorial on the uses of spatial coherence in ray tracing*, 1985.

[16] K. Nemoto and T. Omachi. An adaptative subdivision by sliding boundary surfaces for fast ray tracing. *Graphics Interface*, 43–48, 1986.

[17] H. Nishimura, H. Ohno, T. Kawata, I. Shirakawa, and K. Omuira. Links-1: a parallel pipelined multimicrocomputer system for image creation. In *Proc. of the 10th Symp. on Computer Architecture*, pages 387–394, 1983.

[18] S.D Roth. Ray casting for modeling solids. *Computer Graphics and Image Processing*, 18(2):109–144, February 1982.

[19] S. Rubin and T. Whitted. A three-dimensional representation for fast rendering of complex scenes. *Computer Graphics*, 14(3):110–116, July 1980.

[20] R.B Tilove and A.A.G Requicha. Closure of boolean operations on geometric entities. *Computer Aided Design*, 12(5):219–220, September 1980.

[21] T. Whitted. An improved illumination model for shaded display. *Communications of the ACM*, 23:343–349, June 1980.

[22] G. Wyvill and T.L. Kunii. A functional model for constructive solid geometry. *The Visual Computer*, 1(1):3–14, July 1985.

Ray-Traced View and Visual Transparent Quality of Double Transparent Objects

M. Iizuka (Japan)

ABSTRACT

A constructive solid geometry for simulation models is composed of fundamental primitives in a ray tracing algorithm. Only a ray of light from two components of specular reflection and refraction is simply traced backwards according to the value of depth level and threshold of energy attenuation. Ray traced images of a main transparent object enclosed with another transparent object are displayed on a color CRT. Complex color rendering view of double transparent objects is discussed from a viewpoint of the color shift and visual transparent quality of computer-generated images.

Keywords. Full color rendering, Constructive solid geometry model, Ray tracing method, Depth level, Color shift of transparent objects

1. Introduction

Computer graphics, including computer art and computer animation, is concerned with image synthesis of real or imaginary objects. The book " 3 - D Computer Graphics " published by E. Nakamae and T. Nishita [1] includes the contents of the state of the art on important areas of computer graphics. S. Yokoi and J. Toriwaki [2] explained a role of the ray tracing method in the area of computer graphics, the computation techniques of intersection point, and the high speed technology for computation. N. M. Thalmann and D. Thalmann [3] published a valued book completely dedicated to the numerous techniques of image synthesis. The book is very useful as a unique handbook of mathematical formulae for image synthesis and its application, and contains a bibliography of over 500 literatures.

Ray tracing techniques have been known as one of the most powerful means for displaying 3-D objects in the field of computer graphics. The main attraction of this technique is hidden line or hidden surface removal as a set of many intersection points. Although there are the merits and demerits in a conventional (or reverse) ray tracing method on the basis of the position of a viewer, i.e., point of sight, it is possible to simply display opaque and/or transparent images in quasi or full color.

A new approach and many modified application techniques are proposed according to the aim of ray traced images with good quality. For example, radiosity method [4], rendering integral method [5], bi-directional ray tracing method [6], etc. have been used in order to positively demonstrate the effects of ambient or global illumination arising out of complex interreflections in an open or closed environment system. On the other hand, the drawbacks of ray tracing techniques usually take a long computation time for carrying out the fine color rendering with good resolution. A new idea of bounding volumes has been introduced by H. Weghorst et al. [7] in order to decrease the number of intersection point within an effective domain of a CRT in advance.

When using a color CRT for 8 colors, quasi-fine color images may be generated by means of R•G•B bit expansions and the photographic multiple exposure techniques in place of using a random dither method. M. Iizuka et al. [8] had a discussion for and against the simulation results of opaque 3-D objects. It is impossible to observe the final images generated on a color CRT directly in this method. There is inconvenience of taking a photo of multiple exposure contrary to expectaion. M. Morikawa [9] made a survey of ray tracing techniques for opaque and/or transparent objects composed of fundamental primitives, and showed an elaborate and useful program list coded in BASIC and many quasi-color images displayed by the random dither method on a standard color CRT device. Recently, various frame buffer modules for displaying simultaneously many colors have been developed and supplied at a low price. A 16 bit multipurpose microcomputer with a frame buffer board will soon be spread in Japan as full color CG systems for CG, CA, CAD/CAM etc.

In this study, a complex of reflected scene with reality at the boundary surfaces may be simulated in connection with constructive solid geometry models which contain a combination of some or many primitives. The color shift and transparency of transparent objects, the computation time and depth level based on effects of reflection and refraction at the boundary surface are discussed from a practical viewpoint of color rendering techniques for double transparent models.

2. Basic Expression of Opaque and/or Transparent Materials

It is known that the reflected light received by a viewer from any point on an object depends on the angle between the direction of sight and the reflected light vector at that point. The quantitative formulation for intensity computation has been proposed in many different ways in order to display computer-generated images of opaque objects by H. Gouraud [10], B. T. Phong [11], and J. F. Blinn [12]. T. Whitted [13], R. A. Hall and D. P. Greenberg [14] added the specular and refractive components to the fundamental expression for the express purpose of intensity computation of transparent objects.

The basic expression of opaque and/or transparent materials is formulated as follows assuming that the reflective characteristics from objects are independent of the wavelengh λ.

$$\begin{bmatrix} R \\ G \\ B \end{bmatrix} = \left[a \cdot \begin{bmatrix} Rd \\ Gd \\ Bd \end{bmatrix} + A \cdot \left\{ \{ \rho_d \cdot \cos\theta \} \cdot \begin{bmatrix} Rd \\ Gd \\ Bd \end{bmatrix} + \{ w(\theta) \cdot \cos^g \alpha \} \cdot \begin{bmatrix} IRp \\ IGp \\ IBp \end{bmatrix} \right\} \right] \cdot Li$$

$$+ Ks \cdot \begin{bmatrix} Rs \\ Gs \\ Bs \end{bmatrix} + Kt \cdot \begin{bmatrix} Rt \\ Gt \\ Bt \end{bmatrix} \quad (1)$$

where, ρ_d : diffuse reflectance of object

$w(\theta) = \rho_s$: specular reflectance of object

θ : angle between incident light and surface normal

α : angle between halfway direction and surface normal for Blinn model (angle between viewing line and specular direction of incident light for Phong model)

a : attenuation coefficient of ambient light

g : glossy index

Li : intensity coefficient of light source (0.0 to 1.0)

A : shadow coefficient (0 or 1)

IRp, IGp, IBp : intensity of light source (0 to 255)

R, G, B : RGB color intensity of arriving at viewer (or at CRT screen)

Rd, Gd, Bd : RGB color intensity of objects

Rs, Gs, Bs : RGB color intensity from direction of specular reflection

Rt, Gt, Bt : RGB color intensity from transparent direction

$$Ks = \frac{1}{2} \left\{ \left[\frac{\sin(p-q)}{\sin(p+q)} \right]^2 + \left[\frac{\tan(p-q)}{\tan(p+q)} \right]^2 \right\} = \frac{1}{2} \left\{ \left[\frac{Ci - n \cdot Cr}{Ci + n \cdot Cr} \right]^2 + \left[\frac{n \cdot Ci - Cr}{n \cdot Ci + Cr} \right]^2 \right\}$$

$$Kt = 1 - Ks$$

Ci = cos(p) ; p : incident angle
Cr = cos(q) ; q : refractive angle
n : refractive index [n = sin(p)/sin(q)]

The third term in Eq.(1) corresponds to the highlight component to a viewer from a light source. The forth and fifth terms have an important role for simulating the effects of reflection and refraction for transparent objects in connection with an idea of the depth level, i.e., a tree construction for shading models. The component of specular reflectance : $w(\theta)$ for opaque objects is uniform over the surface. The specular reflectance : Ks for transparent objects is not constant in the ray tracing algorithm. The two squared terms in Ks called Fresnel formula represent reflection of the "s" and "p" polarizations, respectively.

Table 1 Typical modeling techniques for simulating transparent objects

Technique	Characteristics	Note
(a) Simplified technique for transparent effects	τ : uniform irrespective of n	M.E.Newell & R.G.Newell,[1] D.Kay [2]
(b) Standard technique for reflection & refraction effects	Snell law, Fresnel formula, Index of refraction	T.Whitted [3]
(c) Advanced technique for considering effects of wave length	$\rho(\lambda)$: $\tau(\lambda)$	R.A.Hall & D.P. Greenberg [4]
	Direction of refraction related to λ	S.W.Thomas [5]
(d) Modified technique for spectrum absorption model	Lambert & Bouguer law : $\tau(x) = \exp[-\alpha x]$	T.Yasuda et al. [6]

[Notes]
(1) Proc. ACM, Nat.Conf., (1972) 443
(2) Computer Graphics, Vol.13, No.3 (1979) 158
(3) Comm. ACM, Vol.23, No.6 (1980) 343
(4) IEEE CG&A, Vol.3, NO.8 (1983) 10
(5) Visual Computer, Vol.2, No.1 (1986) 3
(6) Trans. Inf. Pro. Society of Japan, Vol.26, No.4 (1985) 591 [in Japanese]

For simplicity, the effect of multiple reflection is neglected between diffuse objects, and a ray of light passing through transparent objects is not absorbed depending on the pass length of light. But T. Yasuda et al. [15] proposed a ray tracing algorithm based on the Lambert-Bouguer law, i.e., the simplified spectrum absorption model. Table 1 shows the typical modeling techniques for simulating 3-D transparent objects. We use a modified notion of Whitted algorithm through this study.

Generally, the color intensity with relation to the viewing line and intersection point in an illumination model is formulated as the recurrence expression by means of bottom-up procedure.

$$\left.\begin{aligned} I &= Ii + \rho_i \cdot Si + \tau_i \cdot Ti \\ Si &= Ij + \rho_j \cdot Sj + \tau_j \cdot Tj \\ Ti &= Ik + \rho_k \cdot Sk + \tau_k \cdot Tk \end{aligned}\right\} \qquad (2)$$

$$(i < j < k \text{ or } i < k < j : i;\ j;\ k = 1,2,3, \ldots\ldots, m)$$

where,
- m : node point (intersection point)
- N : maximum depth level ($0 \leq N \leq m$ or $0 < m \leq N$)
- I : RGB color intensity of light arriving at a viewer
- Ii : reflected RGB color intensity at node point i by ambient light and direct light
- Si : incident RGB color intensity at node point i by secondary reflected light component
- Ti : incident RGB color intensity at node point i by refracted (or transmitted) light component
- ρ_i : average specular reflectance on surface containing node point i
- τ_i : average transmittance on surface containing node point i

It is very important to choose properly the value of depth level in connection with the computation time and its transparent quality of ray traced images as one of main parameters in a ray tracing algorithm. The maximum depth level is not always equivalent to the number of node point on the surface. The second and third terms in Eq.(2), i.e., the forth and fifth terms in Eq.(1) at each node, may be computed after the tree is completely grown or when arrived at till the specified maximum depth level. In Eq.(2), the terms : Ii, Ij, and Ik are often omitted in the simulation model, when the color intensity of direct light at the points : Pi , Pj, and Pk does not exsit owing to the shadow or obstruction objects.

Note that Eq.(2) changes together with the geometrical relationships between the direction of a viewing line and the intersection point of objects, even though the position of a viewer and a light source, and the surface property of a model are fixed as the constant parameters in the ray tracing algorithm. The suffixs i ; j ; k are not equal to the number of fundamental objects composed of a few basic primitives, but correspond to the node point, i.e., the position of intersection point based on the ray tracing line at the boundary surface.

3. Fine Color Rendering using SuperFrame Module Board

A primary consideration for the display of computer-generated or reconstructed images is the information density, i.e., pixel or dot resolution of the image. Quasi color images are simply generated as the dot combination of R, G and B primary colors in a random dither method when using a standard color CRT device which may display simultaneously 8 colors containing black and white.

The treatment of full color for computer graphics is possible by a commercially available microcomputer (or workstation), for example, a 16 (or 32) bit computer system with frame buffer boards. See the technical report as for the specifications of the typical frame buffer board for a 16 bit microcomputer which is extensively used in Japan [16].

An input/output type interface board called SuperFrame developed of late by Sapience Co. may be set up in a part of the extension slot for a 16 bit PC-9801 microcomputer. This interface board is a frame memory of I/O type, and it is composed of four types of registers, i.e., control registers; x and y registers; R, G, and B registers; and mode registers. The three kinds of R·G·B registers are used for reading and writing the current position of each pixel within the color intensity level : $0 \leq IR$; IG ; $IB \leq 255$. The dot resolution has 640 x 400 in this microcomputer system, and the memory size of this module board is 640 x 400 x 24 bits. Accordingly, it is possible to display $2^8 \times 2^8 \times 2^8$ colors. Full color images may be displayed simply and directly without using a random dither method. Usually, look-up tables are used in conjunction with a frame buffer memory, and can be updated quickly for altering displayed colors under program control from the CPU. But this microcomputer system has no the look-up table. As a result, it is impossible to quickly and freely modify displayed colors on a color CRT with the analog terminal. The two control registers are used for initializing the superframe board. The x and y registers are used for writing data only on a CRT screen, and the bit size of register construction differs from between the two.

For effectively using the SuperFrame module board, two types of computer languages : (i) display routines by the machine language for N88-BASIC and (ii) graphic library routines for C language under the program control by by MS-DOS are available at a 16 bit PC-9801 microcomputer.

4. Three Dimensional View of Transparent Objects

In this study, the problems of color shift and transparency of ray traced images, which are composed of typical primitive models expressed by a quadratic equation, are discussed from the color rendering simulation results.

Figure 1 (a) and (b) shows a complex of reflected color rendering view of ray traced transparent objects under the condition of 320 x 200 pixels. Each value of depth level is fixed as N = 5 and 10, respectively. The main transparent object : a wineglass with two opaque spheres is enclosed with another outer transparent object : parallelepiped made of glass. A part of the striped board is clearly reflected in the bottom part of the opaque spheres and the wineglass in Fig.1 (b). In Fig.1 (a), it seems to us as if the 3-D reflected view of a ray-traced image of the wineglass had become translucent under the same CSG model.

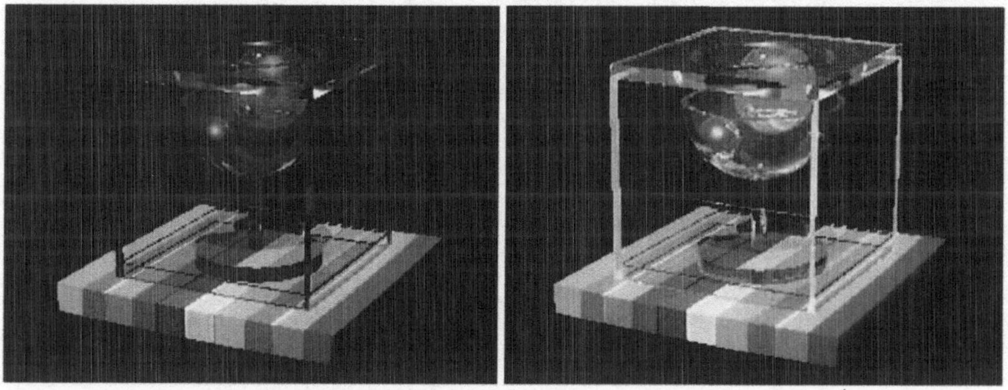

(a) Depth level : N = 5 (b) Depth level : N = 10

Fig.1 Ray-traced images with double transparent objects under number of resolution : 320 x 200 pixels

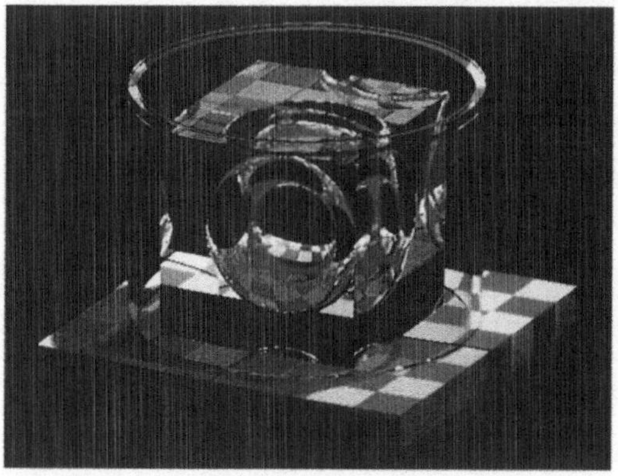

Fig.2 Ray-traced image with double transparent objects Depth level : N = 10 Pixel resolution : 640 x 400

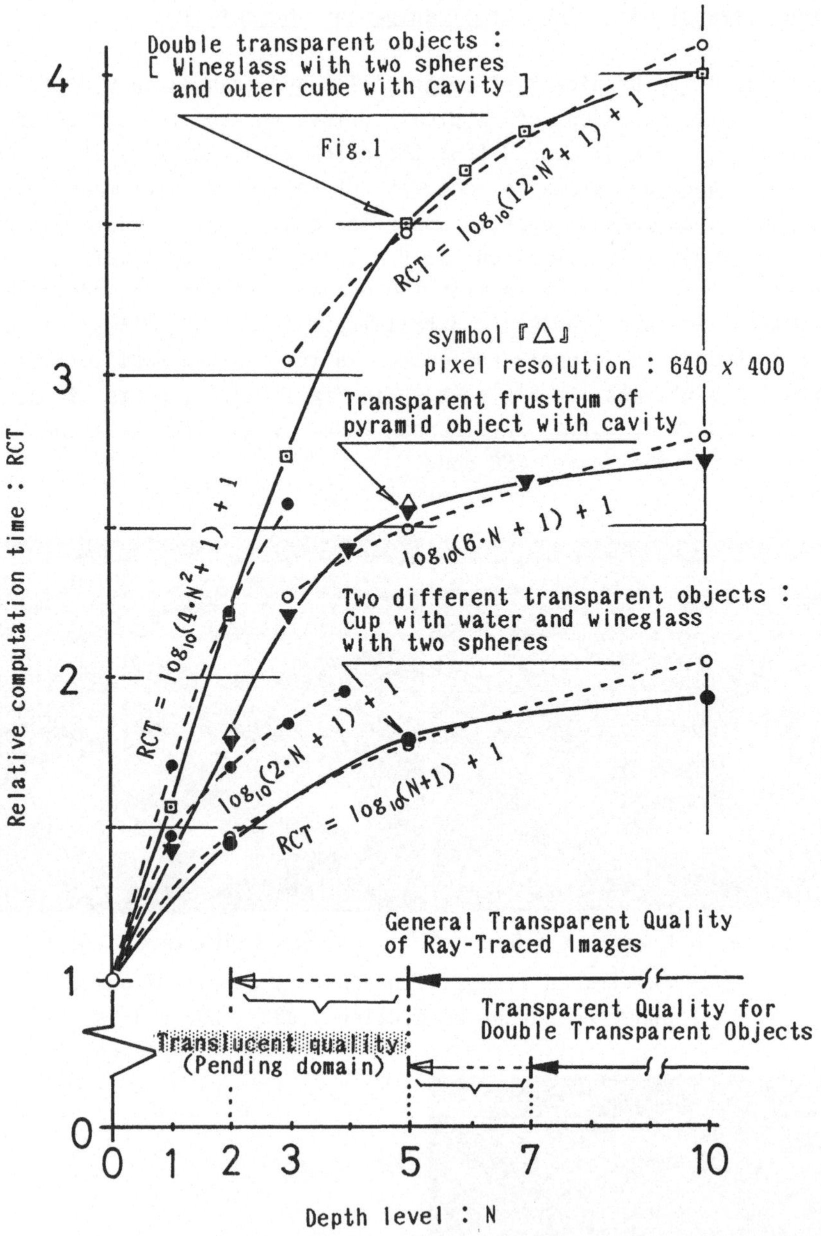

Fig.3 Relative computation time and value of depth level under the pixel resolution : 320 x 200

Figure 2 demonstrates a complex reflected view of double transparent objects in the case of the high resolution of 640 x 400 pixels. The outer object is constructed from a clear and hollow cylindrical glass : n = 1.5, and the inner object is made of transparent glass cube with a spherical hollow : n = 2.4.

Figure 3 shows, in the full color rendering method, the characteristic curves for the relative computation time vs. the value of depth level. Note that computation time is not always in proportional to the depth level. The result of color rendering, in particular, the translucent (or semi-transparent) quality of computer-generated color images appears clear except for a part of the special perspective domain. It is rather difficult to estimate a proper value of depth level for multiple transparent objects in advance.

Figures 4 and 5 show the ray-traced images of transparent objects under the condition of middle resolution : 320 x 200.

Fig.4 Ray-traced image with specular reflectance at two non-checker boards

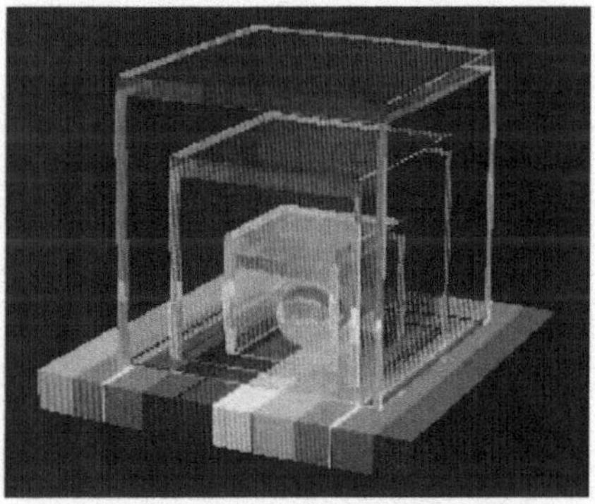

Fig.5 Ray-traced image in the case of multiple transparent objects

5. Conclusions

The visual color appearance and 3-D reflected view of transparent objects become translucent or transparent under the same CSG model and refractive index owing mainly to the value of depth level. The color shift and transparency of ray traced images are affected by the threshold value for energy attenuation, i.e., the synthetic coefficients of intensity level : $\Pi\ (\rho_i \tau_j)$. When the value of depth level is specified as more than 4 ~ 5 in consideration of computation time, fairly good transparent quality of ray traced images is demonstrated intuitively in the case of double transparent objects.

Acknowledgement

A ray tracing algorithm and its software program have been provided and published by M. Morikawa, and continuously modified by the author and research members. Many ray traced images were produced using a 16 bit microcomputer (PC-9801) with a 640 x 400 X 24 bit frame buffer (Sapience Co.) and a color CRT.

References

(1) E.Nakamae and T.Nishita : "3-D Computer Graphics " , Shokode Co. Ltd., (1986) [in Japanese]

(2) S.Yokoi and J.Toriwaki : Ray tracing method for computer graphics, p.145 -157, in M. Takagi et al. Eds. "Recent Trend of Image Processing Algorithm " , New Tech. Conmmunication Co. Ltd.,(1986) [in Japanese]

(3) N.M.Thalmann and D.Thalmann : "Image Synthesis ", Springer-Verlag (1987)

(4) M.F.Cohen and D.P.Greenberg : The Hemi-Cube : a Radiosity Solution for Complex Environments, SIGGRAPH'85, C.G.,Vol.19, No.3 (1985) 31

(5) J.T.Kajiya : The Rendering Equation, SIGGRAPH'86, Vol.20, No.4(1986) 143

(6) S.Chattopadhyay and A.Fujimoto : Bi-Directional Ray Tracing, p.335-343, in T.L.Kunii ed. " Computer Graphics 1987 " , Springer-Verlag (1987)

(7) H.Weghorst et al. : Improved Computational Methods for Ray Tracing, ACM Trans. on Graphics, Vol.3, No.1 (1984) 52

(8) M.Iizuka et al. : Generation of quasi-fine colour images by random dither techniques and photographic multiple exposure techniques, DISPLAY, Vol.8, No.2 (1987) 79

(9) M.Morikawa : "PC-9801 Introduction to 3-D Graphics" , ASC Pub., (1986) [in Japanese]

(10) H.Gouraud : Continuous Shading of Curved Surfaces, IEEE Trans. on Computer, C-20, No.6 (1971) 623

(11) B.T.Phong : Illumination for Computer Generated Pictures, CACM, Vol.18, No.6 (1975) 311

(12) J.F.Blinn : Simulation of Wrinkled Surfaces, SIGGRAPH'78, Vol.12, No.3 (1978) 286

(13) T.Whitted : An Improved Illumination Model for Shaded Display, CACM, Vol.23, No.6 (1980) 343

(14) R.A.Hall and D.P.Greenberg : A Testbed for Realistic Image Synthesis, IEEE CG&A, Vol.3, No.8 (1983) 10

(15) T.Yasuda et al. : An Improved Ray Tracing Algorithm for Rendering Transparent Objects, Trans. Inform. Pro. Society of Japan, Vol.25, No.6 (1984) 953 ; Vol.26, No.4 (1985) 591 [in Japanese]

(16) A.Ishizuka : A New Epoch in Personal Computer Graphics, NIKKEI COMPUTER GRAPHICS, No.7 (1987) 10 [in Japanese]

Antialiasing for Ray Tracing Using CSG Modeling

J. Argence (France)

Abstract

Aliasing is a decisive problem in realistic image producing. Since ray tracing is a rather slow algorithm of visualization, antialiasing an image by systematically oversampling its pixels is quite costly. We suggest a local adaptive oversampling algorithm for antialiasing ray tracing. We use space coherence to determine which pixels on the screen need be oversampled. The C.S.G. model is used to define the scene, and also to limit it, for each pixel, to objects of concern only. To minimize memory space needs, we work on a window over the screen .

CR Categories and Subject Descriptors: I.3.3 [Computer Graphics]: Picture/Image Generation; I.3.5 [Computer Graphics]: Computational Geometry and Object Modeling; I.3.7 [Computer Graphics]: Three-Dimensional Graphics and Realism.

Keywords: computer graphics, ray tracing, constructive solid geometry, antialiasing.

1 INTRODUCTION

For several years, ray tracing has been developed for the high quality realistic images it produces, even if this has to be balanced by a large amount of computation. Like other visualization algorithms, ray tracing generates pictures whose quality is spoiled by aliasing. As its aim is to produce realistic images, it is crucial to solve aliasing problems when using this method.

Since aliasing is the result of undersampling during display, one usual method to solve aliasing problems without any loss of quality is to oversample the image. Amanatides [1] introduces a method for anti-aliasing ray tracing : the definition of a ray is extended to a cone by including information on the spread angle and the virtual origine. But as this makes the ray-object intersections procedures more complex, the only cases considered involve the sphere, the plane and the planar polygon. Although beautiful, the output images include only very few simple objects (Kirk [9]). Cook [4] introduces a distributed ray tracing method wich allows many effects like motion blur, depth of field, penumbras, transculency, fuzzy reflections. This method requires oversampling for each effect. Dippé[6], Lee[10], Mitchell[11], Purgathofer[14], combined this method with statistical technics to choose the pattern or the rate of sampling. But oversampling is very costly, if we are working on a n^2 pixels image (for example n = 512), and we divide each pixel into p (p = 4) subpixels then n^2p (= 2^{20}) ray-object intersection tests have to be performed. Let m be the number of aliased pixels. Only $m(p-1) + n^2$ ray-object intersection tests are actually necessary. If m is very much smaller than n^2, the method we suggest will help cut greatly the number of pixels to be treated, namely from n^2 to m. If, as Rubin and Whitted[17] pointed out, their algorithm spends most of its time computing ray-object intersections, any systematic oversampling of the image increases the number of ray-object intersections and therefore is very costly : we are assured to save a lot of time if we detect only those pixels that need processing. Whitted[18] introduced a detecting method in which one looks for abrupt changes of intensity on neighboring pixels, because aliasing is most apparent in areas of abrupt intensity changes. Roth[16] only tests the difference between pointers to visible surface on a line drawing. If the visible surface at pixel (i,j) is different from the visible surface at pixel (i,j+1) then a ray is generated halfway between them.

Furthermore, the rendering of complex scenes requires a large amount of computation. This is why we suggest a local adaptive oversampling algorithm (L.A.O.) for antialiased ray tracing. We claim that our algorithm, as Whitted's and Roths's, is adaptive because it only oversamples pixels areas when a certain condition is met. The adjective local refers to the fact that any additional computation consecutive to oversampling in the case of ray-object intersections is minimized by restricting the scene to objects of concern only. For each oversampled pixel, we build a sub-scene for the primary ray, another for the shadow ray, and so on for refraction rays... Furthermore, we do not need much memory space since we only work on a window over the screen to determine if a pixel needs be oversampled.

We first present the characteristics of the C.S.G. model we use in our algorithm. Then, in paragraph 3, we describe the procedure of antialiasing. Finally, we give the result tests.

2 C.S.G. MODELING

In the last few years, the constructive solid geometry method has become a very popular alternative to surface-based models[15]. In a C.S.G. system, objects are constructed with primitive objects connected by set operations, such as union, difference, intersection, on the space. Usually, the primitive objects are spheres, cylinders, cubes, cones, half-spaces, tori... etc...

Our ray tracing system ([8],[13]) is working on a binary tree structure where a leaf represents a primitive object to which a linear matrix is associated and a node is a set operation between sub-objects. A scene is a tree structure containing all the objects to be visualized. We call sub-scene a part of the scene composed of selected objects; the structure this sub-scene inherits is strictly the same as that of the scene.

The primitive objects were chosen as follows :

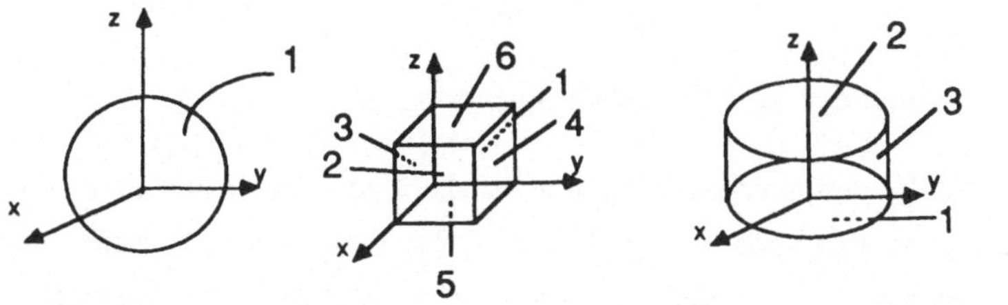

sphere number 1. cube number 1,2,3,4,5,6. cylinder number 1,2,3

Fig. 1 a few primitives

A number is associated with each C^1 surface of a primitive. Spheres only have one C^1 surface, cubes have six, cylinders three, cones two and so on... Indeed, between two or more C^1 surfaces (patches) with different number, there is a discontinuity on the normals, and an aliasing risk.

Each node contains more information to speed up ray tracing: we keep a couple of bounding orthogonal rectangular boxes with standard orientation, one for the primary ray and one for the shadow ray and a bounding sphere for other secondary rays. Boxes were chosen for primary rays, because we use a very fast procedure to compute ray-box intersections ; we thus gained nearly 42 per cent over bounding spheres for image number 1 [2].

3 THE ANTIALIASING ALGORITHM

The primitive-ray intersection procedures do not only return usual results, such as intersection points (in, out), normal vectors, color..., but also the associated primitive patch number and a flag if the primitive is smaller, on the screen, than the size of a pixel. Small objects are determined by a preprocessing step for primary rays. We only have to test if the side of the projection surface of their bounding boxes is more than one pixel wide. For secondary rays, things are much more complicated. We choose to approximate by creating a virtual eye and a virtual screen. The position of the virtual eye is defined by the incident ray and the distance covered by light between the "real" eye and the intersection point (cf. Fig. 2).

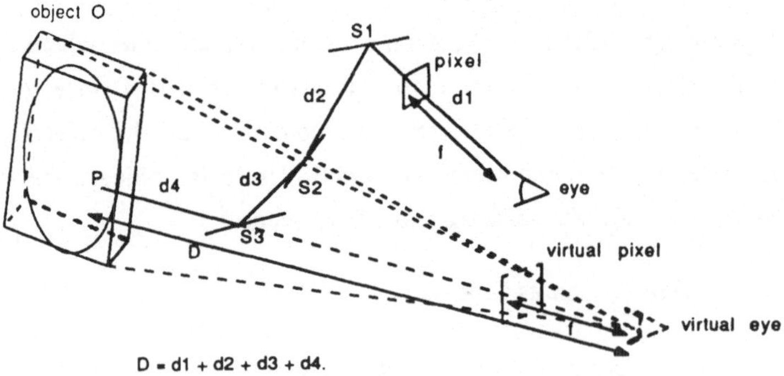

Fig. 2 definition of a vitual eye to detect small objects

The size of an object is computed as a fraction of the size of a virtual pixel. For example in Fig. 2, object O is small for the incident ray. We may thus infer either that the surfaces are planes or have very small curvature. The ray-CSG tree intersection procedure returns, in addition to the associated patch number, the number of the primitive in the scene tree, the list of pointers to "simple" objects intersected, a shadow boolean, a list of pointers to the shadow-producing objects, and a list of all information for reflection and refraction rays.

By "simple" object pointer, we mean a pointer to the first node whose parents are only unions but not intersections nor differences. If all the parent nodes of the primitive are unions we can keep one pointer on this primitive only, but if there is at least one difference operator (or one intersection operator) there is no way to know exactly how much "matter" we have without keeping all the information for the operator (Fig. 3).

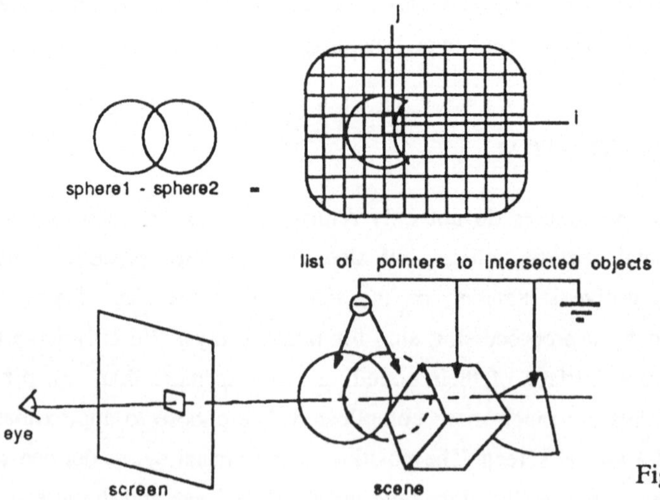

Fig. 3 list of "simple" objects

Here is now all the information that is necessary to keep :

- the number of the intersected primitive
- the number of the intersected primitive patch
- the list of pointers to the intersected objects
- a boolean whose value is true if the intersected primitive is not lighted by the source
- the list of pointers to the shaded objects
- the list of light sources
- the list of pointers to very small objects being tested
- the list of the previous information for refraction rays
- the list of the previous information for reflection rays

We only keep, for each pixel, information relative to three lines. On line i we calculate the information for line (i+1). Then, we work on a 3x3 window on these three lines to readjust the color of the pixels on the line i by oversampling them if necessary.

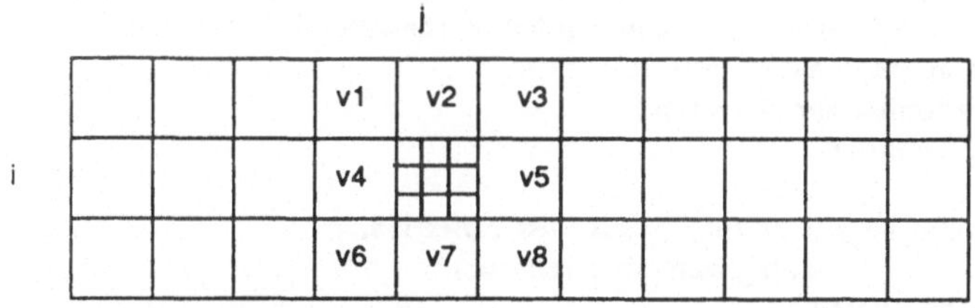

Fig. 4 window on the screen

A sketch for antialiasing program is presented below:

```
 procedure main(scene)       {
/**********************/
  compute the first two lines and keep information in two arrays Info1, Info2;
  for each line i, i superior or equal to 2 and i lower than  MAX_LINES  {
      for each column j
          compute line (i+1)  and keep information in array Info3;
      for each ray (i,j) , j superior or equal to 2 and j lower than MAX_COLUMNS
        antialiasing(Info1[j-1],Info1[j],Info1[j+1],Info2[j-1],Info2[j],Info2[j+1],
              Info3[j-1],Info3[j],Info3[j+1]);
   swap Info1 and Info2 , then Info2 and Info3.
   }
 }
 procedure  antialiasing(Info_pixel1,Info_pixel2,...,Info_pixel9)  {
/*****************************************************************/
  to_be_aliased = false;
  test_aliasing(to_be_aliased,Info_pixel1,Info_pixel2,...,Info_pixel9);
  if (to_be_aliased) {
    create a sub-scene for the primary ray whith the union of every intersected objects
    and small objects tested found in Info_pixel1,Info_pixel2,...,Info_pixel9;
```

```
    create a sub-scene for the shadow ray;
    create a sub-scene for the reflection ray;
    create a sub-scene for the refraction ray;

    call a procedure which recursively oversamples (i,j) pixel into p
    sub-pixels, computes 8 intersection whith sub_rays and sub_scenes,
    and uses the same tests as procedure test_aliasing(...) but
    without re-creating sub-scenes (it would be a waste of time);

    color of pixel(i,j) is the mean value of the nine sub-pixels color;
  }
  else
    there is nothing to do, since color of pixel(i,j) has already been
        computed;
}
procedure test_aliasing(to_be_aliased,Info_pixel1,Info_pixel2,...,Info_pixel9)
/******************************************************************************/
/* To determine the final color of  pixel (i,j), compare the nine
   values ( the value of the eight neighbors  and that of (i,j) ) */

  if  (there is at least one intersection or a small object test)
   if (all nine pixels have the same primitive number) and (they have the
       same patch number) and (they are all lighted by the same light sources)
       and (there is no small object test)
    if (there is no reflection nor refraction)
        to_be_aliased = false;
    else  {
         test_aliasing(to_be_aliased,Info_pixel1->list_reflection,...,
                              Info_pixel9->list_reflection);
         if (NOT(to_be_aliased))
            test_aliasing(to_be_aliased,Info_pixel1->list_refraction,...,
                              Info_pixel9->list_refraction);
    }
   else  to_be_aliased = true;
  else   to_be_aliased = false;
}
```

Obviously, antialiasing is more complicated when modeling transparencies and specularities, because there are many recursive calls to the procedure test_aliasing. It can be improved by just keeping the leaves of the reflection-refraction tree and the tree path associated with each leaf.

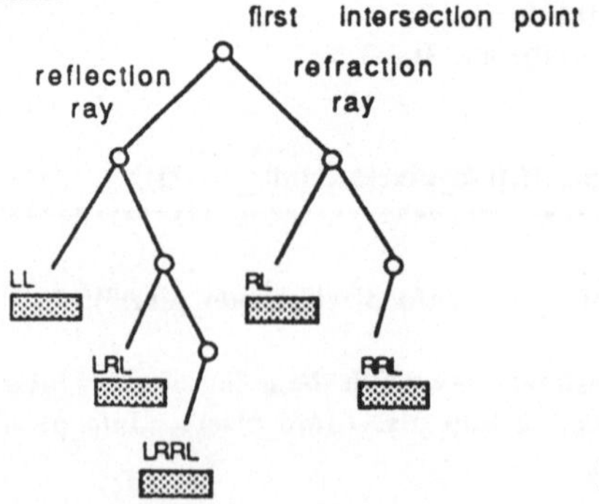

Fig. 5 reflection-refraction tree

If all nine pixels do not have the same tree path for each leaf, aliasing is detected. If all the nine pixels do not have the same number of leaves and the same tree path for each correspondent leaf, aliasing is detected. Else we have to call test_aliasing on the values of the leaves. This simplification is merely an approximation, but troubles rarely appear.

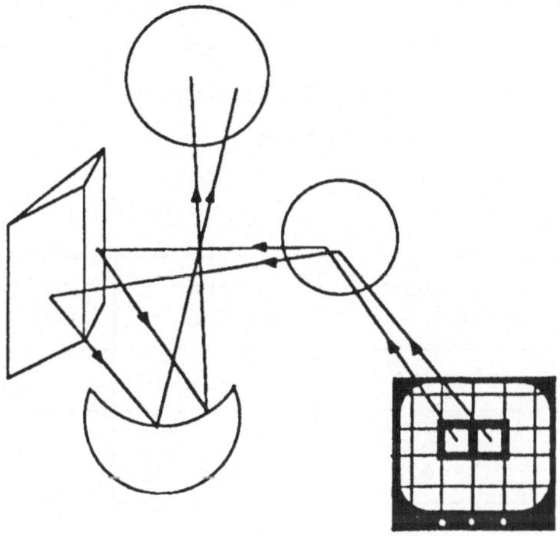

Fig. 6 a case of wrong approximation

4 RESULTS AND CONCLUSION

Instead of Whitted's method, we need not calculate the difference of intensity between two pixels; as we only have to compare a few values, a lot of computation time is saved. Besides, we do not rely on arbitrary decisions based on human eye sensitivity to determine, for a picture, which pixels are to be oversampled; obviously we sometime oversample non-aliased pixels. As the following table shows, the number of oversampled aliased pixels is smaller than that found for Whitted's method. For the latter, the RGB colour components are values between 0 and 255, and the threshold is taken to be 16, the maximal value for which visual effects were found to be identical to those of LAO algorithm.

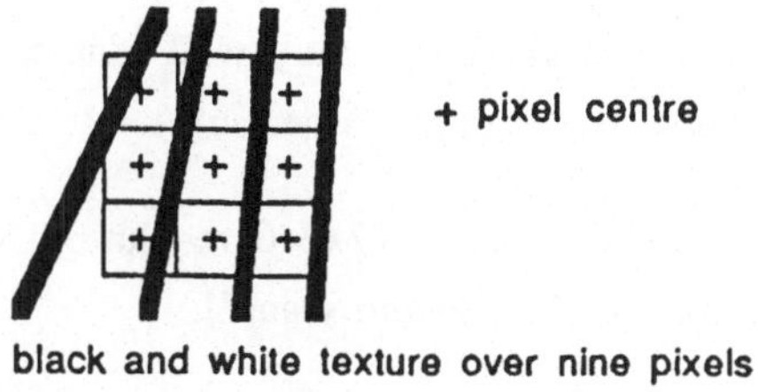

Fig. 7 "moiré" problems unsolved

Moreover, our method does not oversample textured pixels. Actually, oversampling is not very good for tartan-like textures in highly compressed areas. Nine neighboring pixels may have one unique color while their subpixels have different ones, thus, occasionally leaving "moiré" problems unsolved.

For mathematical texturing functions, texture patterns antialiasing can be achieved simply by testing their frequencies, and dropping those exceeding half the frequency of image sampling [12]. Stored texture maps can be antialiased with methods similar to those suggested by Williams[19], Crow[5], Ghazanfarpour[7].

methods:	no treatment image 1	Whitted's method	LAO algorithm image 2
number of pixels:	327,680	327,680	327,680
number of primary rays intersecting objects:	39,475	183,836	76,652
number of all intersections of primary rays with objects:	54,353	264,055	214,725
number of shadow rays intersecting objects:	5,053	23,932	24,053
number of all intersections of shadow rays with objects:	5,271	25,194	24,413
number of undersampled pixels	0	23,904	17,824
number of primitives	43	43	43
relative time increase	1	3.45	1.33

Our algorithm seems to be an efficient answer to aliasing problems in ray tracing. It has be developed in C.S.G. modeling because it is a very well-adapted environment. It can be used with any scan-line algorithm, for example Atherton[3].

The following images were computed for a 512x640 resolution, with 2^{12} colors chosen over 2^{24} colors by an algorithm based on Peano scan[2].

Image 1: Aliased flower

Image 2: Antialiased flower by LAO algorithm

Image 3: Oversampled pixels by LAO algorithm (zoom x12)

Image 4: Reflection-refraction : two spheres.

Image 5: Textured room

REFERENCES

[1] AMANATIDES, J. Ray tracing with cones. *Computer Graphics 18*, 3 (July 1984), 129-136.

[2] ARGENCE, J. Tracé de rayon, un peu mieux, un peu plus vite. *Rapport Interne*, Ecole des Mines de Saint-Etienne.

[3] ATHERTON, P. R. A scan-line hidden surface removal procedure for constructive solid geometry. *Computer Graphics, 17*, 3 (July 1983), 73-82.

[4] COOK, R. L., PORTER, T., CARPENTER, L. Distributed ray tracing. *Computer Graphics 18*, 3 (July 1984), 137-145.

[5] CROW, F.C. Summed-area tables for texture mapping. *Computer Graphics 18*, 3 (July 1984), 207-212.

[6] DIPPE M. A. Z., WOLD E. H. Antialiasing through stochastic sampling. *Computer Graphics 19*, 3 (July 1985), 69-78.

[7] GHAZANFARPOUR, D. Synthèse d'images et antialiassage. *Thèse de Docteur-Ingenieur*, Ecole des Mines de Saint-Etienne, (Nov. 1985).

[8] KAJIYA, J.T. SIGGRAPH83 Tutorial on ray tracing.

[9] KIRK, D. B. The simulation of natural features using cone tracing. *Visual Computer 3*, (1987),63-71.

[10] LEE, M. E., REDNER, R. A., USELTON, S. P. Statistically optimized sampling for distributed ray tracing. *Computer Graphics 19*, 3 (July 1985), 61-67.

[11] MITCHELL, D. P. Generating antialiased images at low sampling densities. *Computer Graphics 21*, 4 (July 1987),65-72.

[12] NORTON, A., ROCKWOOD, A.P., SKOLMOSKI, P.T. Clamping: a method of antialiasing textured surfaces by bandwidth limiting in object space. *Computer Graphics 16*, 3 (July 1982), 1-8.

[13] PEROCHE, B., ARGENCE J., GHAZANFARPOUR, D., MICHELUCCI, M. La synthèse d'images *Hermes*, (1988), 199-238.

[14] PURGATHOFER, W. A statistical method for adaptive stochastic sampling. *Eurographics*, (1986),145-152.

[15] REQUICHA, A.A.G. Representation for rigid solids: theory, methods and systems. *ACM Computing Surveys 12*, (Dec. 1980), 110-116.

[16] ROTH, S.D. Ray casting for modeling solids. *Computer Graphics and Image Processing 18*, (1982), 109-144.

[17] RUBIN, S.M., WHITTED, T. A 3-dimensional representation for fast rendering of complex scenes. *Computer Graphics 14*, (1980), 110-116.

[18] WHITTED, T. An improved illumination model for shaded display. *Com. ACM 23*, (June 1980), 343-349.

[19] WILLIAMS, L. Pyramidal parametrics. *Computer Graphics 17*, (jul 1983), 1-11.

Image Warping Among Arbitrary Planar Shapes

G. Wolberg (USA)

ABSTRACT

Image warping refers to the 2D resampling of a source image onto a target image. Despite the variety of techniques proposed, a large class of image warping problems remains inadequately solved: mapping between two images which are delimited by arbitrary, closed, planar curves. Such problems are typified by the requirement to derive a spatial transformation given only boundary correspondence information.

This paper describes a novel algorithm to perform image warping among arbitrary planar shapes whose boundary correspondences are known. A generalized polar coordinate parameterization is introduced to facilitate an efficient mapping procedure. Images are treated as collections of interior layers, extracted via a thinning process. Mapping these layers between the source and target images generates the 2D resampling grid that defines the warping. This mapping is shown to be decomposable into three 1D transformations, thereby highlighting the primary benefit of the new parameter space. Applications include fast nonrectangular convolution, elastic matching, quantification of shape deformation, and visual effects.

1. INTRODUCTION

Image warping is a geometric transformation that maps a source image onto a target image. It has proven to be an important tool in image processing and computer graphics. The two roles that it has played in these fields has dichotomized the research in this area [Smith87]. The common ground, however, is found in two areas — fast spatial transforms ([Catmull 80], [Fant 86], [Fraser 85], [Oka 87]) and filtering ([Burt 81], [Crow 84], [Heckbert 86], [Williams 83]).

Despite the considerable attention that image warping has received, a large class of image warping problems has been neglected: mapping between two images which are delimited by arbitrary closed curves, e.g., hand-drawn curves. In this instance, the mapping is driven by the correspondence of boundary points. The spatial transformation of the interior points must be computed by the image warping algorithm.

The lack of attention to this class of problems can be easily explained. In image processing, there is a well-defined 2D rectilinear coordinate system. Correcting for distortions amounts to mapping the four corners of a nonrectangular patch onto the four corners of a rectangular patch. In computer graphics, a parameterization exists for the 2D image, the 3D object, and the 2D screen. Consequently, warping amounts to a change of coordinate system (2D to 3D) followed by a projection onto the 2D screen. The problems considered in this paper fail to meet the above properties. They are neither parameterized nor are they well suited for four-corner mapping.

The algorithm described in this paper treats an image as a collection of interior layers. Informally, the layers are extracted in a manner similar to peeling an onion. A radial path emanates from each boundary point, crossing interior layers until the innermost layer, the skeleton, is reached. Assuming correspondences may be established between the boundary points of the source and target images, the warping problem is reduced to mapping between radial paths in both images. Note that the layers and the radial paths actually comprise a sampling grid.

This algorithm uses a generalization of polar coordinates. The extension lies in that radial paths are not restricted to terminate at a single point. Rather, a fully connected skeleton obtained from a thinning operation may serve as terminators of radial paths directed from the boundary. This permits the processing of arbitrary shapes.

2. BACKGROUND

The use of control grids and analytic expressions accounts for the majority of image warping techniques. Unfortunately, they fail to handle our problem of mapping an image, of arbitrary shape, onto a second arbitrary shape. This is a consequence of their inappropriateness for boundary value problems, the class with which we are dealing.

Boundary value problems have long been addressed in heat conduction, electrostatic potential, and fluid flow theory. Conformal mapping and relaxation techniques are commonly used to evaluate such mappings. In [Fiume 87], conformal mapping is used to map images among arbitrary simple polygons. Conceptually, this approach can be applied to arbitrary shapes. In practice, however, the Schwarz-Christoffel transformation which constructs the conformal maps are analytically complicated and the implementation is limited to polygons with only a few vertices.

In a recent paper, Greene and Lamming [Greene 86] describe a relaxation algorithm to propagate the boundary mapping information to interior points. The user specifies two polygons, and a mesh relaxation is used to derive a mapping from the first polygon onto the second polygon. Typically, the algorithm requires 200 iterations to converge. Tailored for interactive use, not attempt is made to prevent artifacts caused by sampling irreproducibly high spatial frequencies. In addition, the image folds upon itself when radical transformations are made near the margin of the figure. Nevertheless, their system, designed for visual art applications, represents the closest effort to the work described in this paper.

In related approaches, relaxation or finite element analysis techniques may be utilized to propagate the boundary information while satisfying some constraint. A typical constraint may be the minimization of the pixels' "spring energies." Unlike such methods, which are constrained by physical models and require many iterations to converge, the technique proposed here is not tied to a physical model and allows mapping values to be computed at once. There is no need for iterative refinement.

3. STATEMENT OF THE PROBLEM

We desire to map a source image, S, onto a target image, T, each with arbitrary boundaries. Both S and T are actually subimages which may be extracted with the use of a mouse and digitizing tablet, thresholding, or other segmentation method. Pixels lying in the extracted subimage are designated as foreground. The remaining pixels are assigned a background value with the boundaries defined as the interface between foreground and background pixels.

The mapping will effectively treat S as if it were printed on a sheet of rubber, and stretch it to take the shape of T. The only constraint is that topological equivalence be maintained — that is, S may be stretched and squeezed but not torn. Also, the mapping must allow for the specification of corresponding points between the boundaries. The mapping of noncontrol points along the boundaries is derived through interpolation of adjacent control points. Control point adjustments tailor the warping results.

4. OVERVIEW

This section illustrates the algorithm in terms of its functional units. The remainder of the paper elaborates upon the basic components listed here. The warping algorithm described herein has three stages:

1) Reparameterize S and T using a transformation function g. This yields S' and T', respectively. The new parameter space facilitates a convenient solution to our boundary value problem.

2) Apply a second transformation, h, to map (resample) S' onto T'. This stage requires filtering to avoid artifacts arising from severe compression or expansion.

3) Apply an inverse mapping, g^{-1}, to convert T' into T, the desired result.

Figure 1 depicts the homomorphism outlined above. The transformation functions g, h, and g^{-1} are elaborated in the following sections.

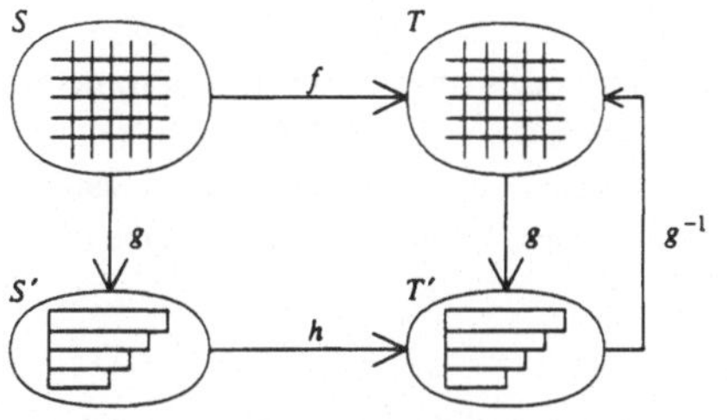

Figure 1: Chain of transformations to map S onto T.

5. REPARAMETERIZATION INTO THE (U,V) PARAMETER SPACE

This section describes the function that transforms images S and T into a new parameter space. This reparameterization corresponds to function g in Fig. 1. Its purpose is to allow the mapping process to operate upon a coordinate system that is more amenable to the boundary value problem presented here.

5.1 Introduction

A function, f, that maps S onto T requires that a parameterization exist for both images, such that a correspondence may be established. Unfortunately, the rectilinear (x,y) coordinate system imposed by the input image is not ideally suited for boundary value problems because it lacks the means of conveniently expressing a relation between the boundary and interior points. We seek to impose a parameterization more closely tied to the boundary.

In the absence of a suitable parametric representation for both images, the algorithm decomposes a 2D image into an alternate representation consisting of layers of interior pixels. The layers are extracted in a manner akin to peeling an onion. This imposes a (u,v) parameterization in which u runs along the boundary, and v runs radially inward across successive interior layers.

5.2 The (u,v) Coordinate System

Since the mapping information is only defined along the boundary, it is reasonable to first consider the mapping of adjacent points. These points comprise the adjacent layer. This data can then propagate further until the innermost layer is assigned a correspondence. Two problems arise. Firstly, how may we derive the positions of interior layers? Note that these layers actually define a sampling grid within the shape. Secondly, how is the mapping information transformed from layer to layer? Clearly there are many possible solutions. However, we shall see that a convenient metric may be expressed as a result of solving the first problem.

The algorithm poses a formulation based on the radial influence of each boundary point. This measure is defined by the path spanned between the boundary point and a corresponding point on the innermost layer. These radial paths are analogous to orthogonal grid lines (v direction) with respect to the interior layers (u direction). The innermost layer will be referred to as the *skeleton*. Figure 2 illustrates some (u,v) grid lines superimposed upon an arbitrary shape. The skeleton is highlighted in boldface.

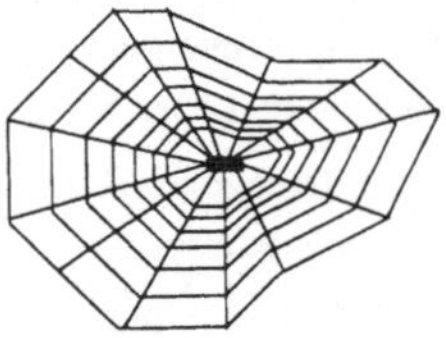

Figure 2: Arbitrary shape with superimposed sampling grid.

5.3 Extracting Interior Layers

The positions at which each layer must sample the image can be defined by an "eroding boundary." In convex shapes, an eroding boundary coincides with shrinking (scaling down) the boundary positions about the centroid. Problems arise, however, if scaling is applied to shapes containing concavities. The reduced boundary does not lie entirely within the larger adjacent boundary, and the centroid is no longer guaranteed to lie within the shape.

5.3.1 Thinning

The difficulty of expressing erosion analytically for shapes containing concavities is bypassed with a discrete approximation — a thinning algorithm. Thinning has long been a tool in the computer vision field for shape analysis applications. In this context, thinning, together with boundary traversal, is used to erode foreground pixels along the boundary while satisfying a necessary connectivity constraint. This helps us impose the (u,v) coordinate system upon the S and T images.

Classical thinning algorithms operate on binary raster images. They scan the image with a window (usually 3×3), labeling all foreground pixels lying along the boundary with one of two labels. The first label, *DEL*, is designated to deem the foreground pixel as deletable. This designation is issued if the foreground pixel is not found essential in preserving the mutual connectivity of neighboring foreground pixels in the window. If, however, it must be retained in order to preserve neighborhood connectivity, the pixel is said to lie on the shape's symmetric axis, or *skeleton*, and labeled *SKL*. Skeletons typically resemble a stick-figure of the image. They have the property of being fully connected (no gaps).

A thinning algorithm is used to assure that the shape is unraveled into closed layers. This constraint is imposed in order to avoid tearing the eroding shape, thereby maintaining topological equivalence over all scales. That is, the deletion of boundary pixels in one layer must not introduce holes in the next layer. For example, consider a dumbbell shape. As outer layers of the shape are peeled off, the thin center bar will eventually erode away, isolating the circles at each end. No simple closed path would remain to traverse the resulting shape. Skeletons are therefore generated for the purpose of "bridging the gaps" between remaining boundary pixels. This translates into a guarantee that subsequent layers will remain closed. Consequently, the two ends of the dumbbell remain connected even after the center bar would have been eroded by normal means. A detailed description of the thinning algorithm used in this work is given in [Wolberg 85]. Further references may be found in [Arcelli 85], [Pavlidis 82], and [Rosenfeld 82].

5.3.2 Boundary Traversal

The boundary is traversed following each thinning pass. The preceding thinning iteration imposed a connectivity constraint on the boundary pixels and labeled them accordingly. Consequently, they are traversed while concurrently initializing the appropriate layer list and deleting those pixels labeled *DEL*. *SKL* pixels remain intact and are guaranteed to appear in all subsequent layers. Note that interior pixels, not having been labeled by the thinning algorithm, are not traversed in the same pass.

5.3.3 Layer Alignment

Unwrapping the shape into consecutive layers presupposes that the first traversed point may be accurately mapped from layer to layer. An error in this correspondence yields misalignment problems. Therefore, the starting point for traversal is initially chosen to be the top-leftmost boundary point. This choice offers the least ambiguity for correspondence in subsequent levels. The ambiguity is diminished by the fact that at most four of the eight adjacent neighbors are foreground pixels. Furthermore, since at least two of the four candidates are in direct contact with the background, they are likely to be designated as *DEL* by the thinning algorithm and deleted during the traversal. A better scheme consists of starting at a boundary point of high curvature.

Clearly the most reliable choice for a starting point is one which is known to be contained in all subsequent layers. Since skeletal points satisfy this property, we may choose the first encountered skeletal point to take on this role. Therefore, the top-leftmost point is used as the starting point for traversal until a skeletal point is found. All subsequent traversals will then begin from that skeletal point.

5.3.4 An Example

Consider the shape given in Fig. 3. All foreground pixels are labeled with a number. The format used is *layer/pos*, where *layer* denotes the layer in which that pixel is contained, and *pos* represents its position in the layer. For example, the first element in the outermost layer is pixel 0/00, the top-leftmost boundary point. The label 0/00 is interpreted as layer 0, position 00. In addition, all skeletal pixels are highlighted with a double-edged border.

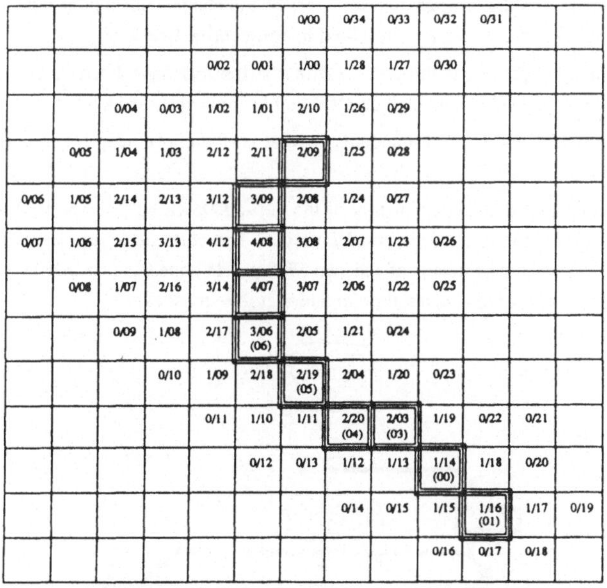

Figure 3: An arbitrary shape with labeled pixels.

The shape is processed in p passes, where p is the maximum distance between an interior point to the closest boundary point. This represents the number of iterations needed to yield the entire skeleton and terminate the peeling operation.

In Fig. 3, notice that pixels 0/00 and 1/00 lie on the top-leftmost points of the image in the first and second pass, respectively. In the second pass, when pixel 1/14 is traversed and is found to be labeled *SKL*, layer 1 is realigned using a circular shift. This places pixel 1/14 at the start of the list and assures proper alignment in all subsequent passes (section 5.3.3). The new role of pixel 1/14 is denoted in Fig. 3 with a (00) entry. Similarly, its neighboring skeletal points will also appear in subsequent traversals and are numbered appropriately in parentheses.

5.4. Layer Correspondence

Tracking the position of each point on the boundary as it makes its way to the skeleton is a central idea of this algorithm. By iteratively establishing correspondence across successive interior layers, we define the ν grid lines in our (u,v) coordinate system. Due to the list representation that the unraveled layers have taken, the desired mapping across layers may be achieved by exploiting the 1D nature of lists.

In the absence of *SKL* points along the boundary, the 1D sampling grid of the extracted layer may be mapped onto its adjacent interior layer by uniform scaling. This means that the pixels are sampled from the adjacent layer at positions dictated by their location in the current layer and the ratio of both layers' lengths. However, the introduction of *SKL* points complicates the matter. Since they are present in all subsequent traversals, their correspondences are fixed across layers and must therefore not be imposed by scaling. Instead, *SKL* pixels partition *DEL* intervals into subintervals. These segments, in turn, remain subject to uniform scaling. Their corresponding subintervals in the next layer are found by identifying the same delimiting *SKL* points which originally partitioned the intervals. Finally, when all the pixels in the outer layer are found to be skeletal, the innermost layer has been reached, and the peeling procedure terminates.

5.5 Data Structure: L-trees

The recursive subdivision of layers gives rise to a tree representation. We shall refer to the resulting data structure as an L-tree, for layer tree. An L-tree has the following properties.

1) Each level of the tree coincides with an interior layer of the shape. Beginning with the outermost layer stored in the root, successive layers are represented in consecutive tree levels.

2) The vertices in each level represent the non-*OLDSKL* strips that have been subdivided by intervening *OLDSKL* pixels. Non-*OLDSKL* pixels include *DEL* and first-generation *SKL* pixels.

3) Leaves denote strips which have no descendants — that is, the entire strip maps onto an *OLDSKL* segment in the next layer.

Figure 4 illustrates a tree with nodes consisting of the non-*OLDSKL* strips. The root, denoting the outermost layer, has only one child since it contains no *SKL* pixels. The child node represents the second exposed layer. It gives rise to two children as a result of the two *SKL* pixels appearing in that layer. The subdivision continues until a node's strip maps onto a skeletal point and thereby vanishes.

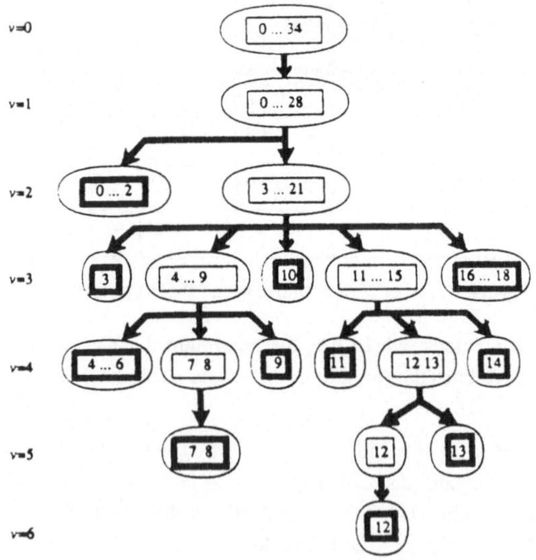

Figure 4: An L-tree representation.

5.6 The (u,v) Parameters

Our (u,v) parameterization is conveniently obtained from L-trees. The (u,v) coordinates are indices into the layer lists stored in the tree vertices. The v coordinate runs from 0 to v_{max}, where v_{max} is the height of the tree. The v coordinate of a pixel is given by its level in the tree (see Fig. 4). The u coordinate runs from 0 to u_{max}, where u_{max} is the length of the outermost layer. Since interior layers have fewer pixels than u_{max}, the successive levels must necessarily be supersampled in order to evaluate the pixels along the radial paths. The (u_i,v_j) value is determined by descending from the ith boundary pixel, stored in the root, onto the jth level. Clearly, since the distances between boundary points and their corresponding skeletal points vary, (u,v) is defined only over a finite, but irregular range.

The subsequent mapping stage requires the image pixels, currently stored in the layers of the tree vertices, to be restored into an image of conventional format. Therefore, the (u,v) and (x,y) axes are aligned and the (u_i,v_j) points are collected from the distinct tree vertices into a single reparameterized image, S', as depicted in Fig. 5. Notice that each column in that figure represents a radial path.

6. MAPPING BETWEEN THE (U,V) PARAMETER SPACES

This section describes the function that resamples S' onto T'. This mapping corresponds to function h in Fig. 1. The mapping solution in the (u,v) space is now more tractable than its counterpart in the rectilinear coordinate system.

6.1 Introduction

The primary benefit of the (u,v) parameterization is that the image may now be considered as a collection of radial paths defined between each boundary point and its corresponding skeletal point. Furthermore, decomposing the image in this manner facilitates efficient referencing of interior image information using an orthogonal coordinate system. Since the range of valid (u,v) values for S' and T' is generally different, the problem becomes one of resampling S' so that its dimensions match that of T'. As a result, we describe a resampling scheme which is decomposed into three simple 1D transforms: the first pass in the v direction, the second in the u direction, and the third pass in the v direction again (see Fig. 5).

6.2 First Pass: Normalizing the v-axis

Unlike standard rectangular images lying on the (x,y) plane, the (u,v) space is defined over an irregular domain. The first pass of the mapping function is responsible for normalizing the v-axis in S' so that the (u,v) space is defined over a rectangular domain. This serves to establish correspondence between radial paths and facilitates a straightforward 1D scaling operation along the u-axis, a property required for the second pass.

The normalization is achieved as follows. For each u, resample the column of pixels along the v-axis so that v_{max} samples are used for the corresponding radial path. v_{max} is the height of the L-tree used to store the layers for S'. This is an appropriate choice since it coincides with the number of samples used to represent the longest radial path. This forces all columns to be supersampled at a rate dictated by v_{max} and the height of the respective column. The resulting sampling rate properly exceeds the Nyquist rate below which the highest frequency (the samples in the longest radial path) would be irreproducible.

6.3 Second Pass: Resampling the u-axis

The second pass of the mapping function scales the u-axis in S' so that its dimension matches that of T'. This serves to equate the number of radial paths in both images. Due to the first pass, a simple 1D scaling operation may be applied to each row in S'. This is a consequence of the fact that the (u,v) space is now defined over a rectangular domain. Since the boundaries of S and T are also their longest layers, respectively, the scale factor used is simply the ratio of the number of pixels in their boundaries.

6.4 Third Pass: Resampling the v-axis

Now that the (u,v) parameter spaces for S and T have identical dimensions in the u direction, the information in the v direction must be made identical as well. For each u, resample the column of pixels along the

v-axis in S' so that its resulting dimension matches that of the corresponding column in T'. The sampling rates are dictated by the heights of the corresponding columns in S' and T'.

The three passes are depicted pictorially in Fig. 5. Notice that the first pass supersamples all columns so that they have dimensions v_1, the height of the tree. This now allows us to apply a 1D scale operation to match the number of radial paths between S and T. As a result, the u_1 columns in S' are resampled to map onto the u_2 columns in T'. Finally, each of the u_2 columns are resampled to take on the dimensions given by T'. The intensity data in S' has now been fully mapped onto T'.

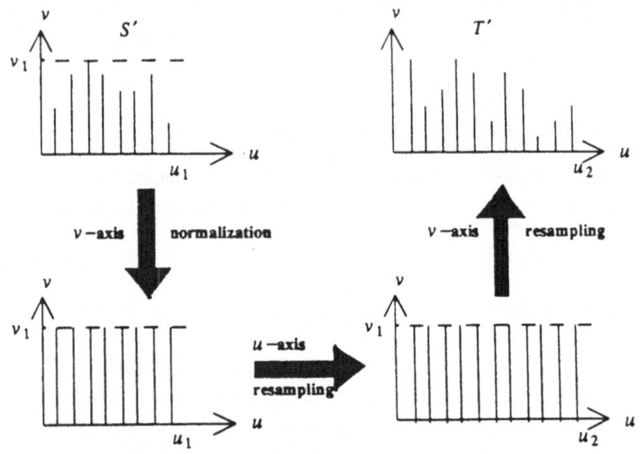

Figure 5: Three passes are required to map S' onto T'.

7. REPARAMETERIZATION FROM (U,V) TO (X,Y)

Having already initialized the content of T' with the resampled data of S', we must now reapply it onto T. This coincides with function g^{-1} in Fig. 1. Not surprisingly, this stage is the reverse sequence of operations described in section 5 that reparameterized (x,y) into (u,v). The following two steps are required.

1) Scale appropriate intervals along the rows of T' to update the layers in T's L-tree.
2) Traverse shape T while concurrently updating the traversed pixels with the values stored in the L-tree. The traversal consists of the same cycle of thinning and boundary traversal described in section 5.

8. RESULTS

The algorithm is written in C and runs on an EDGE 1200 super-minicomputer under the UNIX operating system. The execution time for the 256×256 images shown was approximately 30 seconds. Note, however, that segments of the code are subject to large speedups. For instance, the thinning passes are subject to parallel processing. In addition, the 1D scaling operations are ideally suited for simple hardware implementation.

Several warping examples are given below. Figure 6 shows four images. S and T are displayed in the upper left and lower left quadrants, respectively. The lower right quadrant shows S mapped onto the shape defined by the foreground pixels of T. The mapping of T onto S is shown in the upper right quadrant. In both cases, only one boundary correspondence point is used: the upper leftmost point of S maps onto that of T.

Figure 7 shows the effect of adding additional boundary correspondence points. In the upper right quadrant only the top-leftmost points of S and T are used. In the lower right quadrant the central topmost and bottommost points are used. Notice that the checkerboard pattern is less severely skewed along the boundary in the latter case. A similar result is shown in Fig. 8, where the face is mapped onto a square. Note that the ear lies near a skeletal point and so radial paths in that area undergo severe expansion when mapped to the larger radial paths of the square. The distribution of these paths is limited in the lower right quadrant by an appropriate choice of boundary correspondence points.

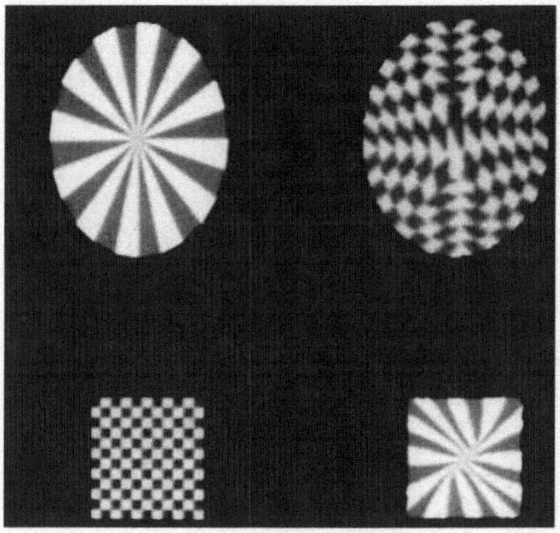

Figure 6

Figure 9

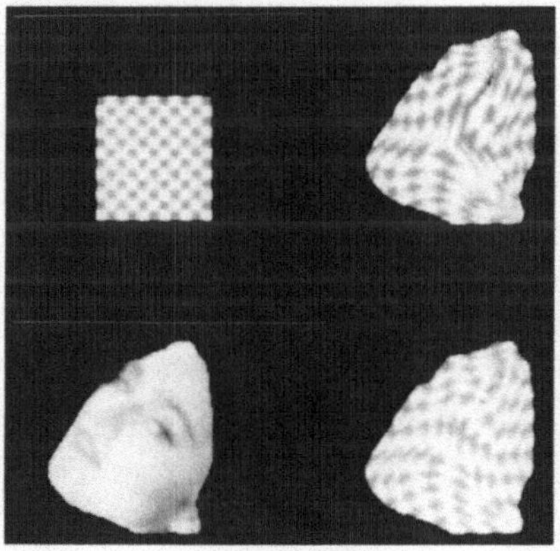

Figure 7

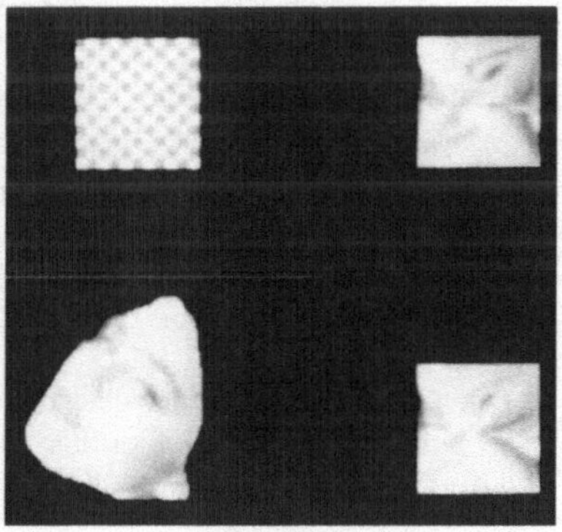

Figure 8

9. SUMMARY AND CONCLUSIONS

This paper describes an efficient algorithm to perform image warping among arbitrary shapes. The resulting spatial transformation is derived using boundary correspondence specified by control points. These points serve to clamp the effect of the warp perturbation to specified intervals.

The algorithm formulates a convenient homomorphism to yield a tractable solution to this problem. The chain of transformations begins with the reparameterization of the source and target images. This consists of initializing two L-trees with values that are peeled off both shapes, one layer at a time. A thinning algorithm supplements this procedure to assure that *closed* layers are extracted, thereby guaranteeing that all interior pixels are considered. Once the L-trees are initialized for the source and target images, the warping problem becomes one of mapping one L-tree onto another. Since the pixels are now scattered in a tree, we supersample the tree and collect the data into a standard image format. This facilitates the application of three 1D transformations to map the reparameterized source image onto that of the target. Having done this, we simply restore the target's L-tree and reapply the updated pixel values onto the target image. This sequence yields the desired result.

Aside from the obvious visual effects application, this algorithm is well-suited for warping an arbitrary shape into a rectangle, a shape suited for FFT filtering. This enables fast convolution without incorporating neighboring background pixels. More studies remain to be done on the effectiveness of this method for this purpose. Finally, an extension of this algorithm from the current discrete implementation to a continous domain offers promising possibilities for increased accuracy and control. This would prove valuable for the mapping, analysis, and registration of 2D and 3D data useful in a variety of applications.

ACKNOWLEDGEMENTS

I wish to thank Professors Terry Boult, Steve Feiner, John Kender, Peter Allen, and Gerald Maguire for many scintillating discussions and constant feedback. This work was carried out at Fantastic Animation Machine, New York City, where Jim Lindner originally suggested the problem to me. I thank him for his patience and continual support. The author is supported by a National Science Foundation Graduate Fellowship.

REFERENCES

[Arcelli 85] Arcelli, C. and G.S. di Baja, "A Width-Independent Thinning Algorithm," *IEEE Trans. Pattern Anal. Machine Intell.*, vol. PAMI-7, pp. 463-474, July 1985.

[Burt 81] Burt, P.J., "Fast Filter Transforms for Image Processing," *Computer Graphics and Image Processing*, vol. 16, 1981, pp. 20-51.

[Crow 84] Crow, F.C., "Summed-Area Tables for Texture Mapping," *Computer Graphics*, (SIGGRAPH '84 Proceedings), vol. 18, no. 3, July 1984, pp. 207-212.

[Catmull 80] Catmull, E. and A.R. Smith, "3-D Transformations of Images in Scanline Order," *Computer Graphics*, (SIGGRAPH '80 Proceedings), vol. 14, no. 3, July 1980, pp. 279-285.

[Fant 86] Fant, K.M., "A Nonaliasing, Real-Time Spatial Transform Technique," *IEEE Computer Graphics and Applications*, vol. 6, no. 1, January 1986, pp. 71-80.

[Fiume 87] Fiume, E., A. Fournier, and V. Canale, "Conformal Texture Mapping," Proceedings of *Eurographics '87*, pp. 53-64.

[Fraser 85] Fraser, D., R.A. Schowengerdt, and I. Briggs, "Rectification of Multichannel Images in Mass Storage Using Image Transposition," *Computer Vision, Graphics, and Image Processing*, vol. 29, no. 1, January 1985, pp. 23-36.

[Greene 86] Greene, D., and M. Lamming, "Interactive Distortion of Images," Xerox Palo Alto Research Center, 1986.

[Heckbert 86] Heckbert, P., "Survey of Texture Mapping," *IEEE Computer Graphics and Applications*, vol. 6, no. 11, November 1986, pp. 56-67.

[Oka 87] Oka, M., K. Tsutsui, A. Ohba, Y. Kurauchi, and T. Tagao, "Real-Time Manipulation of Texture-Mapped Surfaces," *Computer Graphics*, (SIGGRAPH '87 Proceedings), vol. 21, no. 4, July 1987, pp. 181-188.

[Pavlidis 82] Pavlidis, T., "An Asynchronous Thinning Algorithm," *Comput. Graph. Image Processing*, vol. 20, pp. 133-157, 1982. pp. 263-272.

[Rosenfeld 82] Rosenfeld, A. and A. Kak, *Digital Picture Processing*, Volume 2, NY: Academic Press, 1982.

[Smith 87] Smith, A.R., "Planar 2-Pass Texture Mapping and Warping," *Computer Graphics*, (SIGGRAPH '87 Proceedings), vol. 21, no. 4, July 1987, pp. 263-272.

[Williams 83] Williams, L., "Pyramidal Parametrics," *Computer Graphics*, (SIGGRAPH '83 Proceedings), vol. 17, no. 3, July 1983, pp. 1-11.

[Wolberg 85] Wolberg, G., "An Omni-font Character Recognition System," M.E.E thesis, Cooper Union School of Engineering, Oct. 1985. (Available from UMI, Ann Arbor, Michigan.) Also appears in Proceedings of *IEEE Computer Vision and Pattern Recognition*, June 1986.

A Simple Method for Color Quantization: Octree Quantization

M. Gervautz and W. Purgathofer (Austria)

Abstract

A new method for filling a color table is presented that produces pictures of similar quality as existing methods, but requires less memory and execution time. All colors of an image are inserted in an octree, and this octree is reduced from the leaves to the root in such a way that every pixel has a well defined maximum error. The algorithm is described in PASCAL notation.

Keywords: color quantization, image display, color table, raster graphics, octree.

Introduction

The human eye is able to distinguish about 200 intensity levels in each of the three primaries red, green, and blue. All in all, up to 10 million different colors can be distinguished. The RGB-cube with 256 subdivisions on each of the red, green, and blue axes, as it is very often used, represents about 16.77 million colors and suffices for the eye. It enables display of color shaded scenes without visible color edges, and is therefore well suited for computer graphics (Fig. 1).

Color devices (mainly frame buffers) that allow for the projection of those 16 million colors at the same time are complicated and therefore expensive. On the other hand, even good dithering techniques produce relatively poor quality pictures on cheap devices //Jar76//. Therefore devices with color tables are produced that allow the use of a small contingent K (e.g. K=256) of colors out of a larger palette (e.g. 16 million colors).

When displaying images that contain more than K colors on such devices, the problem arises of which K colors out of the possible colors shall be selected and how the original colors are mapped onto the representatives to produce a satisfying picture. Such a selection is also needed for some other algorithms, such as the CCC-method for image encoding //Cam86//. The question is how much expense can or shall be invested in

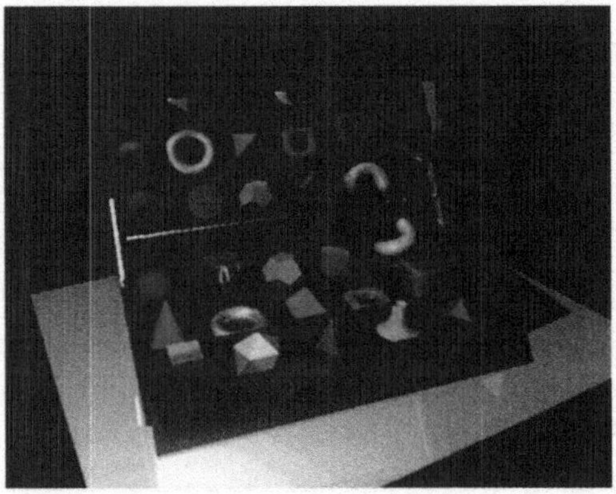

Figure 1: Computer generated image displayed with 16 million colors

this job. This paper first describes existing methods for the solution of this problem, and then presents a new algorithm we called "octree quantization" in detail.

Existing Solutions

The simplest way to handle the problem is to divide the RGB-cube into equal slices in each dimension and use the cross product of these (few) color levels of every primary for the color table. This "uniform quantization" could, e.g., devide the red axis and the green axis into 8 levels each, and the blue axis (our eye is less sensitive to blue) into 4 levels, so that 8.8.4=256 colors are available. The mapping of an image value into this selection is simply done by rounding each of the components (Fig. 2).

Figure 2: The same image as Fig. 1 displayed with 64 colors obtained from uniform quantization

The "popularity algorithm" chooses the K most frequently occurring colors for the color table. Therefore, in a first pass the whole image is explored, and all its colors are stored in a color histogram with their frequencies. The required memory for this histogram is quite large. Then the K colors with the highest frequencies are extracted. After the color table entries have been selected, the problem of mapping the original colors onto the available representatives remains. For this //Hec82// presents a method for finding the nearest color table neighbour for every point within the RGB-cube (Fig. 3). Although this "locally sorted search" lies significantly below the primitive solution to the problem (comparison with all color table entries) in terms of execution time, still a relatively high effort remains.

Figure 3: The same image as Fig. 1 displayed with 64 colors obtained from the popularity algorithm

The "median cut algorithm" //Hec82// tries to select K colors in such a way that each of these colors represents approximately the same number of pixels. To achieve this the color cube is subdivided into K rectangular boxes. In each of the K-1 subdivision steps the rectangular box with the most points in it is split into two parts along the longest dimension with about the same numbers of points in each half. The set of color table entries is obtained by calculating the mean value of points in each of the K boxes. For this, again, a color histogramm is needed and additionally radix lists for the subdivision steps. If the boxes are organized as a k-d-tree, this structure can be used very well for the mapping of the actual colors onto the color table (Fig. 4).

Figure 4: The same image as Fig. 1 displayed with 64 colors obtained from the median cut method

The new Method: Octree Quantization

Principle of the Method

The image is read sequentially. The first K different colors are used as initial entries to the color table. If another color is added, which means that the already processed part of the image has K+1 different colors, some very near neighbours are merged into one and substituted by their mean. For every further color this step is repeated, so that at any moment no more than K representatives are left. This, of course, is also true when the image is completely processed.

The Octree

For this method a data structure has to be used that enables quick detection of colors that lie close together in the color space. An octree is well suited for this problem //Jak80, Mea82//. The RGB-cube can easily be administered by an octree.

```
const  MaxDepth = 8;  (* maximum depth of the octree *)

type Color  = record  R,G,B : integer end ;

     Octree = ↑ Node;
     Node   = record
                 Level       : integer;
                 case  Leaf : boolean of
                   false : (Next : array [0..7] of Octree);
                   true  : (ColorCount : integer;
                            ColorIndex : integer;
                            RGB        : Color);
              end ;
```

It suffices to use an octree of depth 8 (two in the eighth is 256 levels in red, green, blue; eight in the eighth gives 16 million colors) to represent all possible colors. The red, green, and blue components (each between 0 and 255) are the coordinates within the octree:

```
function Branch (RGB : Color; Depth : integer) : integer;

(* evaluates the branch of the octree for the color RGB
   in depth Depth *)

begin
  Branch:= Bit (MaxDepth-Depth, RGB.R) * 4 +
           Bit (MaxDepth-Depth, RGB.G) * 2 +
           Bit (MaxDepth-Depth, RGB.B);
end ;
```

Every exact color is represented by a leaf in depth 8. Intermediate nodes represent subcubes of the RGB space. The greater the depth of such a node, the smaller is the color subcube represented by it, therefore the depth of a node is a measure for the maximum distance of its colors.

The Algorithm

Just as for the median cut algorithm, the octree quantization is done in three phases:

- evaluation of the representatives
- filling the color table
- mapping the original colors onto the representatives

These three steps are now described in detail using the color octree.

Evaluation of the Representatives

The octree is only constructed in those parts, that are necessary for the image of interest. At the beginning, the octree is empty. Every color that occurs in the image is now inserted by generating a leaf in depth 8, thereby the color is represented exactly.

```
var Size        : integer; (* number of leaves *)
    OctreeDepth : integer; (* depth of the octree *)

procedure InsertTree ( var Tree : Octree; RGB : Color;
                       Depth : integer);

(* inserts the color RGB into the subtree Tree
   in depth Depth *)

  procedure NewAndInit ( var Tree : Octree; Depth : integer);

  (* produces and initializes a new octree node *)

  var i : integer;

  begin (* NewAndInit *)
    new (Tree);
    with Tree↑ do
      begin
        Level:= Depth;
        Leaf:= Depth = OctreeDepth;
        if Leaf
        then
          begin
            Size:= Size+1;
            ColorCount:= 0;
            RGB:= (0,0,0);
          end
        else for i:=0 to 7 do Next[i]:= nil ;
  end ;

begin (* InsertTree *)
  if Tree = nil
  then  NewAndInit (Tree,Depth);
  with Tree↑ do
    if Leaf
    then
      begin
        ColorCount:= ColorCount + 1;
        AddColors (Tree↑.RGB, RGB)
      end
    else InsertTree (Next[Branch(RGB,Depth)], RGB, Depth+1);
end ;
```

In this way an incomplete octree is created, in which many branches are missing. Actually, this octree does not have to be filled with all the colors because every time the number of colors reaches K+1, similar colors are merged into one, so that there are never more than K colors left. We will call this action a reduction of the octree.

```
procedure ReduceTree;
(* combines the successors of an intermediate node
   to one leaf *)

var Tree         : Octree;
    Children, i  : integer;
    Sum          : Color;

begin (* ReduceTree *)
  GetReducible (Tree); (* finds a reducible node *)
  Sum:= (0,0,0);
  with Tree↑ do
    begin
      for i:=0 to 7 do
        if  Next[i] <> nil
        then
          begin
            Children:= Children+1;
            AddColors (Sum, Next[i]↑.RGB)
          end ;
      Leaf:= true;
      RGB:= Sum;
    end ;
  Size:= Size-Children+1;
end ;
```

Every time the number of leaves (that is the number of representatives found up to the moment) exceeds K, the octree is reduced. The reduction begins at the bottom of the octree by always substituting some leaves by their predecessor.

Reducing the octree, the following criteria are relevant:

- From all reducible nodes, those that have the largest depths within the octree shall be chosen first, for they represent colors that lie closest together.

- If there is more than one node in the largest depth, additional criteria could be used for an optimal selection (for simplicity, none of them was considered in the following program).

  e.g.: Reduce the node that represents the fewest pixels up to now. In this way the error sum will be kept small.

  Reduce the node that represents the most pixels up to now. In this case large areas will be uniformly filled in a slightly wrong color, and detailled shadings (like antialiasing) will remain.

To construct the color octree, the whole image has to be read once.

```
var K : integer;

procedure GenerateOctree ( var Tree : Octree);
(* constructs an incomplete octree Tree
   from all colors of the image in RGBfile *)

var RGB : Color;

begin (* GenerateOctree *)
  Size:= 0;
  Tree:= nil ;
  RGBread (RGBfile,RGB);
  while not RGBeof (RGBfile) do
    begin
      InsertTree (Tree, RGB, 1);
      while Size > K do ReduceTree;
      RGBread (RGBfile,RGB)
    end ;
end ;
```

Filling the Color Table

At the end the K leaves of the octree contain the colors for the color table. They can be written into the color table by recursively examining the octree:

```
procedure InitColorTable (Tree : Octree;
                          var Index : integer);
(* fills the color table with the means of the colors
   represented by the octree leaves *)

var i : integer;

begin (* InitColorTable *)
  if Tree <> nil
  then
    with Tree↑ do
      if Leaf
      then
        begin
          ColorTable[Index]:= Mean (RGB,ColorCount);
          ColorIndex:= Index; (* the color index is also
                                written into the octree leaf *)
          Index:= Index+1;
        end
      else
        for i:=0 to 7 do InitColorTable (Next[i], Index);
end ;
```

Mapping onto the Representatives

The mapping of the original colors onto their representatives can now be managed easily with the octree, too. Trying to find any original color in the reduced octree will end at a leaf in some depth. This node contains a color very similar to the one in search, and is therefore its representative. Since the index of the color table is stored there too, no further search has to be carried out.
If the original image used less than K colors, no reduction will have taken place, and the found color table index will contain exactly the correct color. Otherwise, only the path to the leaf in depth 8 was shortened by the reduction, so that the color will be displayed less exactly by the mean of all the colors that had their pathes over this node. Since the octree contains only K leaves, all original colors are mapped onto valid color table entries. For this the image has to be read a second time.

```
procedure ImageOutput (Tree : Octree);
(* displays the whole image; every original color is
   mapped onto a color table index *)

  procedure Quant (Tree : Octree; Orig : Color) : integer;
  (* for the original color Orig its representative
     is searched for in the octree, and the index of
     its color table entry is returned *)

  begin (* Quant *)
    with Tree↑ do
      if Leaf
      then Quant:= ColorIndex
      else Quant:= Quant (Next[Branch (Orig, Level)], Orig)
  end ;

begin (* ImageOutput *)
  RGBread (RGBfile,RGB);
  while not RGBeof (RGBfile) do
    begin
      PixelOutput (Quant (Tree, RGB));
      RGBread (RGBfile, RGB);
    end ;
end ;
```

The visual result using this octree quantization is of similar quality as the result using the median cut method (Fig. 5).

Improvements

A significant portion of the execution time is spent with the search for an optimal reducible node every time a reduction of the octree has to take place. These nodes can be collected during the construction of the tree easily in an appropriate structure. They have to be sorted by depth to ensure quick

Figure 5: The same image as Fig. 1 displayed with 64 colors obtained from octree quantization

access. An appropriate structure for this purpose has proved to be 8 linear lists (one for every depth level) containing all reducible nodes. All nodes of one depth level are elements of the same list. The node with the largest depth can then be found quickly for reduction. For this, the declaration of the node of the octree has to be expanded:

```
type Node = record
              ...
              NextNode : Octree;
              (* next node in the same depth level *)
              ...
            end ;

var ReduceList : array [0..MaxDepth] of Octree;
     (* one list for every depth level in the octree *)
```

The procedure MakeReducible is activated when a new intermediate node (Leaf = false) is created in NewAndInit.

```
procedure MakeReducible (Level : integer; Node : Octree);

(* inserts the node Node with depth Level into the
   right list *)

begin (* MakeReducible *)
  Node↑.NextNode:= ReduceList[Level];
  ReduceList[Level]:= Node;
end ;
```

```
procedure GetReducible ( var Node : Octree);
(* finds the best reducible node of the octree *)

begin (* GetReducible *)
  while ReduceList[OctreeDepth-1] = nil do
    OctreeDepth:= OctreeDepth-1;
  Node:= ReduceList[OctreeDepth-1];
  ReduceList[OctreeDepth-1]:=
                   ReduceList[OctreeDepth-1]↑.NextNode;
end ;
```

At any given moment one level of the octree will be the depth in which the reductions take place. This depth is the level of the deepest intermediate nodes. At the beginning, this is level 7 and it moves towards the root during the octree construction. This "reduction level" states what the minimal distance between two representatives will already have to be. This minimal distance can never again decrease by adding even more colors to the octree. Therefore, nothing beneath this level + 1 will ever again be relevant, so that the insertion of colors can also stop at that depth. The depth of the octree is not constant, but decreases with lifetime (see NewAndInit).

Memory and Computational Expense

Let N be the number of pixels of the original image. If the image is run-length encoded, N can also be the number of runs of the image. The algorithm has to be modified slightly by using runs instead of pixels in the octree.

Let K be the number of representatives, that is the size of the color table.

Let D be the number of different colors in the original image.

In general the following equations hold:

$$N > D > K \quad \text{and} \quad N \gg K.$$

An upper bound for the memory used by the octree is 2*K-1 nodes, because there are K leaves and at the most (in the case of a bintree) K-1 intermediate nodes. The algorithm needs very little memory! It is also independent of N and D, that is, of the image. Only the color table size is relevant.

Upper bounds for the number of steps for the insertions, for the generation of the color table, and for the quantization are:

Insertion : N * MaxDepth

N insertions take place, each of them not deeper than MaxDepth.

Color table generation : 2 * K

To fill the color table the incomplete octree has to be examined once, for every node there is exactly one call to the procedure InitColorTable.

Mapping : N * MaxDepth

For every pixel the color index of its representative is found not deeper than in the maximum tree depth.

Thus the octree quantization algorithm is of O(N), the larger part of the execution time is spent by I/O-operations.

Comparison with the other Methods

The following Table 1 gives a short comparision with the other mentioned methods.

	memory	search for representatives	mapping	picture quality
Uniform Quant.	0	O(K)	O(N)	bad
Popularity algorithm	O(D)	O(K*N)	at least O(N)	depends on data
Median Cut	O(D)	O(N*ld(K))	O(N*ld(K))	good
Octree Quant.	O(K)	O(N)	O(N)	good

Conclusion

A new method was presented to find a color table selection for displaying an image on a screen. The picture quality of this "octree quantization" is as good as that for existing methods. The expense in terms of memory and execution time, however, lies significantly below the expense of those algorithms, especially the memory occupied is independent of the image complexity. The method is therefore well suited for microcomputers, too. The implementation is described completely so that it is easy to adapt it.

Acknowledgements

This project was sponsored by Digital Equipment Inc. and the Foschungsförderungsfonds der gewerblichen Wirtschaft and developed on a minicomputer VAX 11/730. We want to thank our colleagues for valuable discussions, especially Mr. Eduard Gröller and Mr. Michael Zeiller.

References

//Cam86// G.Campbell, T.A.De Fanti, et.al.: Two Bit/Pixel full Color Encoding. In Computer Graphics, ACM-SIGGRAPH, Vol.20, No.4, 1986, pp.215-223.

//Hec82// P.Heckbert: Color Image Quantization for Frame Buffer Display. In Computer Graphics, ACM-SIGGRAPH, Vol.16, No.3, July 1982, pp.297-307.

//Jak80// C.L.Jakson, S.L.Tanimoto: Octrees and Their Use in Representing Three-Dimensional Objects. In Computer Graphics and Image Processing, Vol.14, No.3, 1980, pp.249-270.

//Mea82// D.Meagher: Geometric Modelling Using Octree Encoding. In Computer Graphics and Image Processing, Vol.19, No.2, 1982, pp.129-147.

//Jar76// J.F.Jarvis, N.Judice, N.H.Nike: A Survey of Techniques for the Display of continous tone Pictures on bilevel Displays. In Computer Graphics and Image Processing, Vol.5, No.1, 1976, pp.13-40.

Chapter 3

Geometric Modeling and CAD

An Efficient Polygon Handling Technique in a CAAD Environment

C. Gambaro and C. Pienovi (Italy)

ABSTRACT

In this paper, we present a polygon handling technique for two-dimensional applications, based on a boundary representation, namely a winged-edge data structure. First, properties of boundary models modified to represent planar elements are analyzed, by extending the Euler formula to the case of faces lying in a plane.
The concept of history is used as a connection between the produced output polygons and the input polygons, so providing a powerful retrieval tool.
Finally, a simplified data structure is presented, as a friendly interface between the user and the internal polygon representation.

1. INTRODUCTION

Polygon handling is a typical computational geometry problem which arises in a number of applications, dealing both with two-dimensional data and three-dimensional data whose projections in a plane are particularly meaningful.
Examples include many computer graphics applications involving clipping and hidden line and surface management, point-in-polygon techniques for retrieval in an image or in a geometric data base, Computer Aided Design, and cartography. Most of these applications require highly efficient techniques for data storage and manipulation, so allowing interactive and real-time operations.

Several mathematical representations and the corresponding data structures have been proposed in the literature, able to deal with 2-D or 3-D objects. Many of them are particularly intended for CAD applications. Boundary representations, which conceptually represent an object by storing a collection of polygons defining its faces, are among the most widely used mathematical models in CAD. Such a collection of geometric data is sufficient for a complete description of an object, and, in fact, it has been proven to be convenient, together with local information about vertex neighborhood, for computation of several polygon and polyhedron properties [9]. However, some other information is usually stored to increase the efficiency, depending on the application.
Thus, besides the <u>geometric data</u> including vertex coordinates and surface or curve equations, <u>topological data</u> describing the relationships between the geometric entities, such as edge and face adjacency, are usually stored [1,3,4,6].

Research in efficient handling of polygons or polyhedra has also been recently stimulated by developments in the field of robotics and industrial automation. A crucial problem arising there is that of collision avoidance among moving polygons and polyhedra. A typical example of this class of applications is given by an object moving from a start point to a final point among a set of obstacles in a 2 or 3-dimensional space. The problem is that of finding a collision-free trajectory if one exists, or concluding that such a trajectory does not exist [7].

We approached the polygon handling for a Computer Aided Architectural Design application. The problem was that of designing an interactive system for a fast check of existing public housing and new building projects against the current building codes, which establish precise requirements, nearly all 2-dimensional, to be met. To this aim, a library of 2-dimensional standard polygonal elements representing pieces of furniture and fixtures was assumed to be predefined, and the problems of their interactive allocation on a plane, intersection check, and retrieval was considered. It has to be noted that the standard polygonal elements may belong to different categories having a different architectural meaning, such as polygons describing a physical object and polygons corresponding to the space extension required for its use, thus increasing the number of possible types of polygon intersections [5]. Moreover, since the retrieval of previously introduced polygons should be provided at any time, some kind of label must be associated with any polygon P given in input, and stored together with P and with every subpart of P deriving from intersections.

In this paper, we present a polygon handling technique, based on a boundary data structure, namely a planar winged-edge structure, proposed by Weiler [2] and able to meet the requirements imposed by the application.
Section 2 describes the application environment, and introduces the main operations which are usually required. Section 3 presents the data structure storing the geometrical and topological information, and shows some examples of the allowed polygons, i.e. concave simple polygons which can have multiple disconnected nested components. We will also describe a substructure used as an interface with the outside, and similar to the conventional polygon representations. This substructure has proven useful for an easy exchange of information with the user and to give the output of our system as an input to other systems such as graphics packages.
Finally, Section 4 presents the algorithms which realize the main operations presented in Section 2, including a description of how the data structure is built up and of how the conversions between the internal data structure and the interface data substructure are performed.

2. THE CAAD SYSTEM

The presented Computer Aided Architectural Design system was thought of with the aim of performing a fast check of the existing public housing, and evaluating new building projects awaiting for approvation. It was also a matter of great interest to verify the suitability and completeness of the tentative building code, in order to finally define powerful building regulations.
A system was then designed based on the assumption that a library of two-dimensional standard planning elements representing pieces of

furniture and fixtures were predefined, with each element related to a physical dimension and to a user's space extension required by its use.
Operations are provided at two levels, namely a global (flat) level and local (room) level. Going up and down through the two levels is a capability provided at any time during a session. The operations allowed at flat level are the definition of the plan of the house as a union of rooms, the placement of fixtures on it, and the assignment of an activity function to each room. At room level, however, each room may be worked up selecting the pieces of furniture from the standard catalogue. At this time, overlappings between the user's space of different objects or even between an object and the user's space of another one may happen; in this case, the system should provide facilities for pointing out these situations, for example filling the intersection regions with different patterns, according to the category of the overlapping.
Moreover, editing capabilities for data erasing and modifying and new data inserting are available at each step.
The output of the process is the final plan of the house, or a set of different architectural solutions to be compared.

3. THE DATA STRUCTURE

A data structure convenient for the described application is asked to meet the following requirements:

- it should be able to deal with polygons of complicated shape, such as concave and multiply connected polygons;
- it should provide the necessary efficiency for interactive manipulation;
- it should keep the necessary information to perform retrieval operations;
- it should allow an easy computation of the mass properties which are useful to the architectural project.

From this point of view, a particularly interesting data structure is the one proposed by Weiler [2] for the composition of a set of polygons, with the goal of performing boolean operations on them. This structure, integrated with a suitable interface towards the user and the conventional graphics packages, has proven to be convenient for many other operations, such as retrieval, delete and query.
The main facilities provided by this structure include an efficient handling of polygons with a complex shape, and the definition of a history associated with each element in the image, so providing an easy retrieval of previously introduced information.
Moreover, the separation between geometrical and topological data permits to operate only on the data which are relevant for the required operation.

3.1 The representation scheme

The representation scheme described in [2] is a boundary representation, i.e. it is based on the technique of describing an object by means of the elements which bound it. Thus, it belongs to the category of representations depending on the object features (object-space representations), in opposition to the image-space representations.
Building up such a structure is an iterative process which merge a set of input polygons P1, P2,...,Pn, where every Pi is a polygon of the kind usually accepted in they CAD modelers, i.e. is a simple polygon, generally

concave, which may include non connected nested components. Hence, every Pi is generally represented by a set of closed contours B(i,j), $j \geq 1$, which do not intersect (see Fig. 1a).

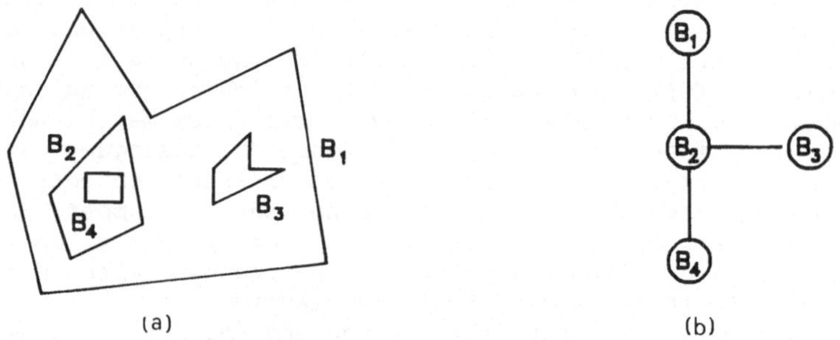

Fig. 1 a) Example of input polygon.
b) Corresponding boundary hierarchy representation.

Given a set of n input polygons:

P1, P2, ...Pn

the comparison algorithm proposed by Weiler produces a set of m output polygons:

X1, X2, ...Xm

where every Xj is simple, simply connected and generally concave.
The output polygons are constructed so as to satisfy the following properties:

1) $Xi \cap Xj = 0$ for every pair (i,j), $i \neq j$
2) for every Xi, there exists at least one Pj such that:
   $Xi \cap Pj = Xi$
3) for every pair (r,s), $1 \leq r \leq m$, $1 \leq s \leq n$, either one of the following relations is satisfied:
   a) $Xr \cap Ps = 0$
   or: b) $Xr \cap Ps = Xr$

In other words, the output polygons Xj do not overlap each other, and they are homogeneous with respect to the input polygon areas. More formally, this property can be expressed as follows:

given any two points p and p' such that:
$p \in Xi$ and $p' \in Xi$
if $p \in Pj$, then also $p' \in Pj$.

It has to be noted that property 3 permits the definition of an ownership relation between polygons Pi and polygons Xj.

3.2 The data structure

The data structure adopted to encode the described representation scheme stores separately the geometrical and the topological relationships between the processed polygons.
Hence, two data structures are used: a higher level structure, which is in the form of a binary tree encoding the geometrical information corresponding to inclusion or coexistence of the polygons, and a lower level structure, which organizes the topological relationships between the polygon single elements in the form of a planar graph.

The data organization is essentially the same all through the steps of the process, from the input definition to the extraction of a set of polygons (or a combination of polygons) according to the user's queries.
However, while the above tree and graph structures are complete of all the information required by the efficiency constraints, a simplified representation, called boundary hierarchy structure, is used to communicate with the outside.
The boundary hierarchy structure is easier to define by the user than the complete structure, and constitutes an interface towards the generally employed polygon representations. Input polygon definition and modeling of set of polygons as an answer to a specific query are the typical moments in which the boundary hierarchy structure is employed in the CAAD system.
In the boundary hierarchy representation, each polygon is described by a set of closed boundaries, whose geometrical relations of inclusion or coexistence in the same physical space are organized in a binary tree. This binary tree represents a geometrical inclusion as a father-son relationship, and a geometrical independence as a brother-brother relationship.

Figure 1b shows how the input polygon depicted in Fig. 1a is represented by the boundary hierarchy structure.

The boundary hierarchy structure is augmented with other information to produce the internal structure used by our CAAD system. As we will see in more detail in the following, the internal structure integrates the description of the geometrical relationships with the definition of a set of external contours, which bound the part of the plane that is complementary to the union of the polygons introduced so far. Moreover, the topological relationships among the polygon elements are organized in a graph structure, which is essentially based on the winged-edge structure defined by Baumgart [1], but is modified to represent polygonal elements all lying in the same plane.
In the following, we will refer to the complete data structure as the planar winged-edge (denoted as pw-e).

Faces, edges and vertices are considered as the basic elements of a winged-edge data structure, both three-dimensional and planar.
The edges, in particular, represent the reference elements, from which the adjacency relationships with respect to elements of a different type are derived. Hence, the edge structure encompasses all the information needed to reconstruct the topology of the whole graph which represents the model. As a consequence, the faces are modeled as a sequence of edges, while the vertices are defined by means of their geometrical coordinates, without any explicitly stored relationship between them.
Then, for every edge e, the following information is stored (see Fig. 2):
1) two adjacency relationships corresponding to the two vertices V1 and V2 which are the endpoints of e;
2) four adjacency relationships corresponding to the four edges adjacent to e along the two loops of edges to which e belongs, traversed in clockwise (CW) and counterclockwise (CCW) order respectively.

In addition to that, for some of the edges further information is stored to connect them to the faces. More precisely, one edge is chosen in the loop of edges bounding a face as an entry-point, and a back relation is stored as a return-entry-point.

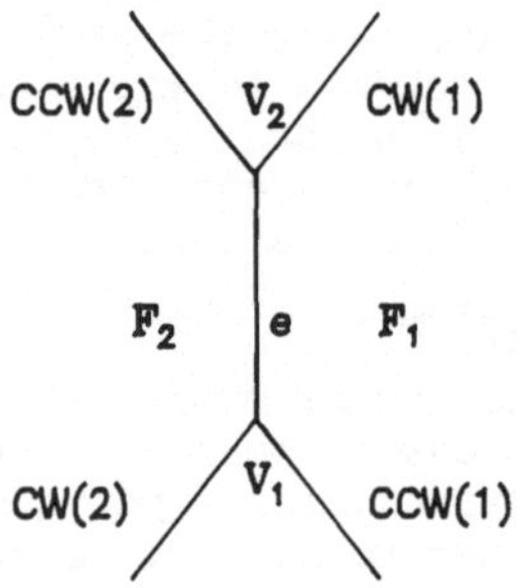

Fig. 2 - Representation of a winged-edge.

It can be noted that the possibility of defining the relationship 2) assumes that the following property be valid:

Property 1
In a three-dimensional winged-edge representation, every edge e belongs to two and only two closed contours, which bound two faces Fi and Fj, $1 \leq i \leq n$, $1 \leq j \leq n$, of the solid, which are adjacent along edge e.

Adopting a winged-edge like representation in the plane, as our application requires, leads to the following modified formulation of Property 1:

Property 2
In a planar winged-edge representation, every edge e either belongs to two closed contours which define two complanar adjacent faces Fi and Fj, $1 \leq i \leq n$, $1 \leq j \leq n$, or it belongs to a closed contour bounding a face Fi, $1 \leq i \leq n$, and to a closed contour bounding an area not belonging to any face of the model.

Then, adapting the winged-edge representation to a planar context leads to introduce a further face F0, which we will call the outer face, defined as the face containing the part of the plane which does not belong to any of the input polygons. Like the other faces, F0 may be described by means of a set of closed contours as well, each of which is called an outer contour.

Properties of a pw-e can be better seen by thinking of it as a generalized case of the plane model of a solid.

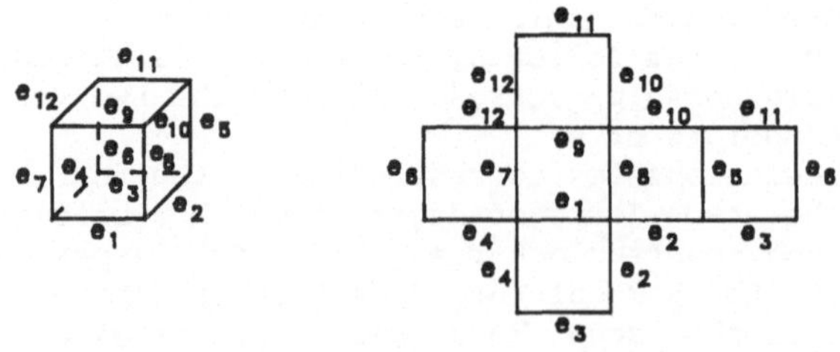

a) b)

Fig. 3 - A solid object S (a) and its plane model (b).

Let S be a three-dimensional solid object, modeled by a boundary representation and bounded by a set of n faces {F1,F2,...Fn}.
The plane model of S is a planar graph σ having labelled regions, arcs and nodes, corresponding to faces, edges and vertices respectively. A set of nodes of σ or a pair of arcs of σ may have the same label, and then they are thought as <u>topologically coincident</u>, in the sense that they must overlap in the three-dimensional reconstruction of S.
Graph σ is said to be properly labelled if:

1) every arc e of σ either separates two labelled regions, or separates a labelled and an unlabelled region, and is topologically coincident with another arc e' which separates a labelled and an unlabelled region;

2) the nodes which are endpoints of topologically coincident arcs are topologically coincident as well [4].

Requirement 1 is quite close to Property 2 stated in the case of the pw-e representation, which may be seen as an extension σ' of the plane model σ to the case in which the graph elements cannot be topologically coincident.

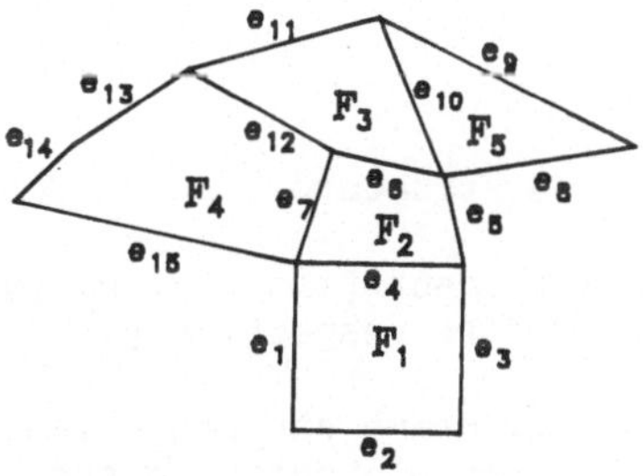

Fig. 4 - An example of σ'

Furthermore, if S is a topologically valid solid, the following relation holds, that establishes a constraint on the number of elements which define the boundary representation of S:

$$f + v - e = 2 ,$$

where f, e and v represent the number of faces, edges and vertices of S respectively. This relation, which is known as the Euler formula, maintains its validity under the operation of mapping from S to its plane model σ, provided that the topologically coincident elements of σ are considered only once.

Introducing the outer face F0 in σ', as well as making the set of adjacency relationships between the faces of σ' complete, guarantees that the Euler formula still holds.
Then, the boundary representation of σ' will include the following set of (n+1) faces [8]:

{F0, F1,...,Fn}

We can now reformulate Property 2 in a form symmetric to the terms of Property 1:

<u>Property 2bis</u>

In a planar winged-edge, every edge e belongs to two and only two closed contours, which bound two faces Fi and Fj, $0 \le i \le n$, $0 \le j \le n$, of the solid, which are adjacent along edge e.

In the pw-e structure, every face Fi, $0 \le i \le n$, is represented by a set of closed contours C(i,j), $j \ge 1$. Figure 5a shows an example of a planar graph σ ' containing the following faces:

F0 represented by contours C0 e C0'
F1 " " " C1 e C1'
F2 " " contour C2.

While Fig. 5b shows the corresponding tree structure.

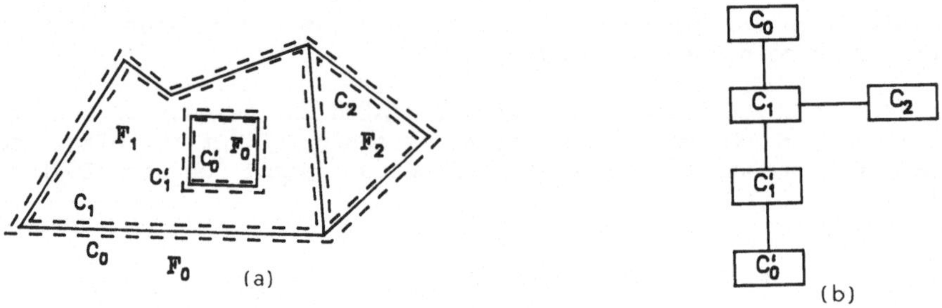

Fig. 5 a) Examples of σ'.
b) Corresponding tree structure.

As a consequence, two faces are identified by a polygon Pi, which contain the interior and the exterior of Pi respectively.

On the contrary, the winged-edge graph structure contains the topological relationships between the polygon elements. In the graph structure, every edge e is represented by a non-ordered pair of distinct vertices, so that every edge has a different pair of vertices, and between two vertices there exists at most one edge. Since any edge e belongs to two distinct contours (see Fig. 5a), two sides are considered for every edge e, and on each side a travelling direction is established and the corresponding adjacency relationships are defined.
A contour C is then represented by a loop of edges, from which the information related to the vertices can be derived whenever necessary.
In a pseudo-Pascal form, the pw-e structure may be described as follows:

```
side = 1..2;
direction = (CW, CCW);

cptr = ↑ contour;
eptr = ↑ edge;
vptr = ↑ vertex;

contour = record
            entry_edge : eptr;
            entry_side : side;
            coexisting_contour : cptr;
            contained_contour : cptr
          end;
```

```
edge    = record
            adj_vertices: array[side] of vptr;
            adj_edges: array[side,direction] of eptr;
            return_contour: array[side] of cptr
          end;

vertex  = record
            x,y: real
          end;
```

Figure 6 graphically shows the data structure associated with a contour. We refer, as an example, to contour C2 of Fig. 5a.

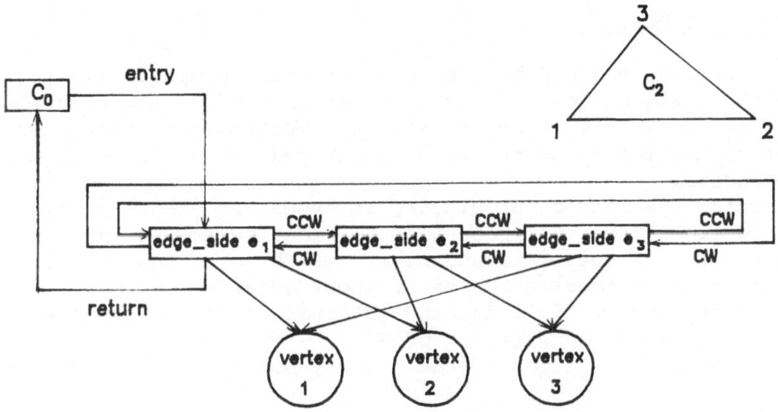

Fig. 6 - Data structure representing a contour.

Figure 7 visualizes the adjacency relationships explicitly stored in the pw-e structure.

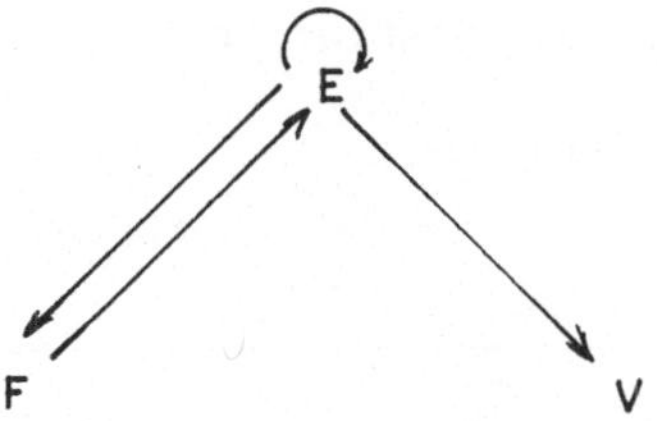

Fig. 7 - Adjacency relationships stored in the pw-e.

The corresponding boundary hierarchy structure, on the contrary, includes a binary tree which stores the geometrical relationships among the boundaries, and a set of loops of vertices which represent the boundaries. Its pseudo-Pascal description is as follows:

```
bptr = ↑boundary
lptr = ↑vertex_list;

boundary = record
              coexisting_boundaries : bptr;
              contained_boundaries : bptr;
              boundary_vertices : lptr
           end;

vertex_list = record
                 x,y : real;
                 adj_vertex : lptr
              end;
```

3.3 The concept of history

An original aspect introduced by the data structure proposed in [2] with respect to the classical w-e is given by the idea of a history associated with every edge of the structure, so that the information about from which of the input boundaries a current edge is derived is available at any time during the process.

The idea on which the concept of history is based is that every output polygon Xj obtained from the process of combination of the input polygons Pi is represented by a set of boundaries, which are the result of a recombination of input edges or parts of input edges.

Furthermore, every edge e of Pi has an internal and an external side, facing the interior and the exterior of Pi.

Hence, the following definition of the history associated with an edge can be given:

The edge-history associated with an edge e on one of its sides is the set of identifiers of the input polygons to whose contours e belongs:

$$He = \{k \mid e \in B(k,j) \text{ of } Pk\}$$

In particular, 0 is the identifier of the outer face F0.

As a consequence a history may be defined associated with every contour C:

The contour-history associated with a contour C, having e1, e2,...en as the loop of edges, is the union of the edge-histories of its edges on the side corresponding to the interior of C:

$$Hc = \cup He(i), \quad i=1,n.$$

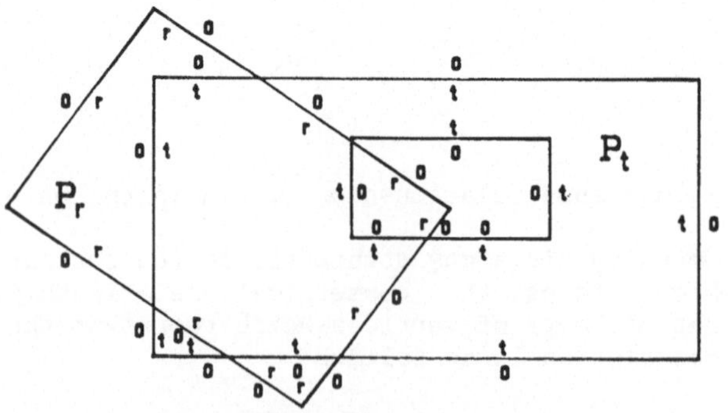

Fig. 8 - History of edges.

Storing the histories associated with edges and contours introduces the following further information into the pseudo-Pascal description of the pw-e given above:

```
                        history = set of owners;

in record edge:         edge_history: array[side] of history

in record contour:      contour_history: history
```

4. FUNDAMENTAL ALGORITHMS

In this section we investigate how the main operations introduced in section 2 can be realized making use of the proposed data structure. In fact, efficient algorithms can be built up, based on the separation between geometrical and topological data and taking advantage of the information of history.

The fundamental algorithms required by the described application can be classified in the following categories:

- conversion algorithms, which provide an interface towards and from the usual data structures adopted to store polygons;
- manipulation algorithms, which are necessary to insert new polygons into the structure or to delete polygons from the structure;
- query algorithms, which allow retrieval operations, such as recomposition of input polygons, or extraction of a substructure corresponding to the result of an operation among the input polygons;
- geometric transformation algorithms;
- computation algorithms, which evaluate dimensional parameters, such as linear and area data corresponding to the produced output.

In the following, we will give an idea of the more widely employed techniques, providing a detailed description of the most interesting algorithms.

4.1 Conversion algorithms

As it has been said in section 3, the pw-e structure requires an interface towards the outside, called the boundary hierarchy structure. The reason for that is to give the user an easier tool, and, on the other hand, to interface with traditional data structures for the description of planar polygons, so as to be able to include library drawing and computational geometry facilities in the CAAD system.

Both kind of conversion have been investigated, i.e. from pw-e to boundary hierarchy structure and from boundary hierarchy structure to pw-e.

The input conversion, i.e. from the boundary hierarchy structure to pw-e, can be regarded as a preprocessor performed on the input data before they are handled by the manipulation algorithms.

Let Pi be an input polygon described, in the boundary hierarchy structure, by a set of boundaries B(i,j) organized in a binary tree, as described in section 3.

The steps through which the conversion algorithm operates are the following:

1) every boundary B(i,j) is converted into two contours C(i,j,int) and C(i,j,ext) lying on it "internally" and "externally" respectively;
2) for every boundary element B(i,j) in the boundary binary tree, two contour elements are created in the contour binary tree. The relation between the pair of contours themselves is always an inclusion relationship, and the order of the inclusion must be checked for every pair. Two contours derived from two different input boundaries maintain the same inclusion or coexistence relationships which related the boundaries.
3) the loop of edges corresponding to C(i,j,int) and C(i,j,ext) is built up starting from the list of vertices of B(i,j). It has to be noted that C(i,j,int) and C(i,j,ext) share the same loop of edges, but they correspond to the two sides of the edges.

An example of the produced structure is given in Fig. 9, which refers to the input polygon of Fig. 1a, whose boundary hierarchy structure was shown in Fig. 1b.

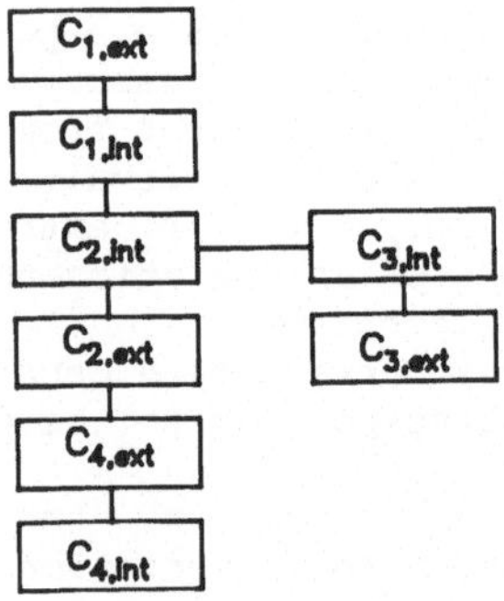

Fig. 9 - Pw-e structure corresponding to the boundary hierarchy structure of Fig. 1b.

The output conversion, i.e. from pw-e to boundary hierarchy structure, is a postprocessor with respect to query algorithms, which extract a part of the structure from the complete pw-e as an answer to the user's query. The extracted substructure is composed by a set of faces which define a partition of the polygonal region corresponding to the query. Thus, the output conversion algorithm needs to perform a simplification step before the structure conversion itself can be accomplished.
The two steps are described below:

1) Simplification step.
   The set of contours representing the extracted faces, although they define a valid partition of the required area and enclose an area which correspond to the user's query, are generally redundant in the number of extracted contours, in the sense that the set of their edges does not coincide with the set of edges of the desired boundaries (see Fig. 10). More precisely, some completely internal edges, which do not lie on any boundary of the required polygonal

element, may be present in the extracted substructure. Then, the algorithm performs a reduction of edges by eliminating all those edges which belong to two distinct contours and suitably joining the interrupted contours. The final result is a set of contours which is in a one-to-one correspondence with the required boundaries.

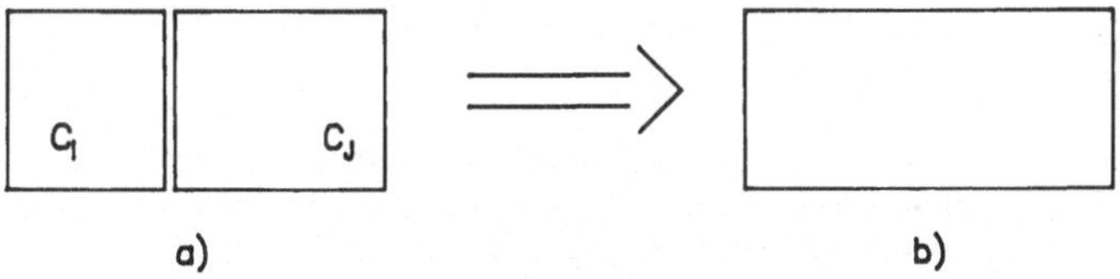

Fig. 10 - Simplification step: a) before; b) after.

2) Conversion step.
   Every contour C of the binary tree of the pw-e structure is converted into a boundary B of the binary tree of the boundary hierarchy structure. At the same time, the circular list of vertices of B is created from the loop of edges of C.

4.2 Manipulation algorithms

The basic manipulation operations include insertion of new elements and deletion of previously inserted elements.

The insertion of a new polygon Pn in a pw-e structure S already containing a combination of a set of (n-1) polygons is performed by means of the comparison technique described in [2]. Thus, we will limit our description to the main steps of the process, referring to the mentioned paper for a more detailed discussion of the algorithm:

1) Merging the pw-e graph structure of Pn into structure S.
   The contours are merged into a single graph structure whenever they intersect. This can be accomplished by contour edge comparisons to discover the intersections. The contours are then joined together at each intersection.
   At the end of this step, a unique graph structure is obtained, which is topologically up-to-date, but contains redundant and disorganized information related to the contours and their mutual geometrical relationships.
2) Traversing the resulting graph, contour by contour, so that the redundant information is eliminated and the data about the contour history is collected.
3) Organizing the binary tree, by checking the geometrical relations among the contours.

The deletion of a polygon Pi from a pw-e structure containing Pi is quite a challenging problem, because Pi is generally embedded in S as a set of separate contours. The information about which of the current contours are derived from Pi is stored in S as an edge-history.

The deletion algorithm takes advantage of this information to identify the edges which may possibly be eliminated. On the other hand, a contour generally derives from more than one input polygon, so that its contour-history may contain other identifiers besides i. Therefore, the algorithm has to delete the identifier i all over the structure, and all the structure elements which derive from and only from the input polygon Pi.

A brief description of the steps performed by the deletion algorithm is given below:

1) eliminate identifier i from the edge-histories of the edges belonging to the contours whose contour-history contains i. If an edge assumes an edge-history 0 on both sides as a consequence of this elimination, then the edge itself is eliminated, and the corresponding loop of edges is suitably joined;
2) eliminate identifier i from the contour-histories, and update the contours which have had at least one edge eliminated;
3) perform step 2) and 3) of the insertion algorithm, since the number of contours and their mutual geometrical relationships may have changed.

A more detailed pseudo-Pascal description of steps 1) and 2) is given below:

```
Algorithm DELETE_POLYGON (i:polygon_id;C:cptr)
//At the first activation, C is the first contour in the
  binary tree structure//
  if C ≠ nil then
  if i in history(C) then
          SEARCH_DELETE (i,C);
          DELETE_CONTOUR_HISTORY(i,C)
  end;
  let C' be the son of C;
  DELETE_POLYGON (i,C');
  let C' be the brother of C;
  DELETE_POLYGON (i,C')
  end
end DELETE_POLYGON.
```

```
Procedure SEARCH_DELETE (i:polygon_id,C:cptr)
  let versus be an arbitrary traversal versus;
  let e' be the first edge of C having i in its history;
  while there exists e' do
     e <--- e';
     repeat
         int <--- INT_SIDE(e,C);
         ext <--- EXT_SIDE(e,C);
         e" <--- NEXT_EDGE(e,int,versus);
         if i in history (e,int) then
             DELETE_EDGE_HISTORY(e,int,i);
             if history(e,int)=0 and history (e,ext)=0 then
                  UPDATE_ENTRY(C,e);
                  C' <--- GET_CONTOUR (e,ext);
                  UPDATE_ENTRY(C',e);
                  if e=e' then
                      UPDATE_END_LOOP (e',versus)
                  end;
                  DELETE_EDGE(e)
             end
         end;
         e <--- e"
     until e=e'
  end
  DELETE_CONTOUR_HISTORY(i,C)
end SEARCH_DELETE.
```

In Algorithm DELETE_POLYGON the following primitive functions and procedures have been used:

INT_SIDE(e,C), which returns the side of edge e corresponding to the interior of contour C;

EXT_SIDE(e,C), which returns the side of edge e corresponding to the exterior of contour C;

NEXT_EDGE(e,side,direction), which returns the edge following e in the specified direction and on the specified side of e;

GET_CONTOUR(e,side), which returns the contour to which e belongs on the specified side;

DELETE_EDGE_HISTORY(e,side,i), which deletes the polygon identifier i from the edge-history of the specified side of edge e;

DELETE_CONTOUR_HISTORY(C,i), which deletes the polygon identifier i from the contour-history of contour C;

DELETE_EDGE(e), which deletes edge e from the pw-e structure;

UPDATE_END_LOOP(e,direction), which updates the loop control variable e in the specified direction;

UPDATE_ENTRY(C,e), which moves the entry-edge of contour C to another edge of the loop if edge e is the current entry-edge of C.

4.3 Query algorithms

As we have seen, every input polygon is represented in the pw-e by a set of contours, each enclosing a part of the area belonging to the original polygon. Thus, a reconstruction operation is required to answer the query of retrieving an initial polygon.

On the other hand, a typical request advanced by the user is the result of a boolean operation made between two or more of the initial polygons. Most boolean operations can be performed efficiently by simply traversing the structure and analysing the edge-history and contour-history information. Clearly, the corresponding algorithms will become much faster as the contour-history information becomes sufficient for the query, because working on the history corresponds to a high level interaction with the structure, namely performing a conditioned visit of a binary tree.
In the following we give examples of both the approaches, presenting reconstruction and boolean operation algorithms.

The reconstruction algorithm gives an answer to the query of extracting an old input polygon Pi from the pw-e. Although this query might be regarded as a particular case of a boolean operation (for example as the union Pi $\cup$ Pi), we provide a specific solution for this operation, due to its great utility and frequent use.

Exctracting the edges of Pi from a pw-e structure S containing Pi requires a search for edges having identifier i in their history. After an edge belonging to the boundary of Pi has been recognized, a search can be performed by exploiting the coherence property of the boundary (see Fig. 11).

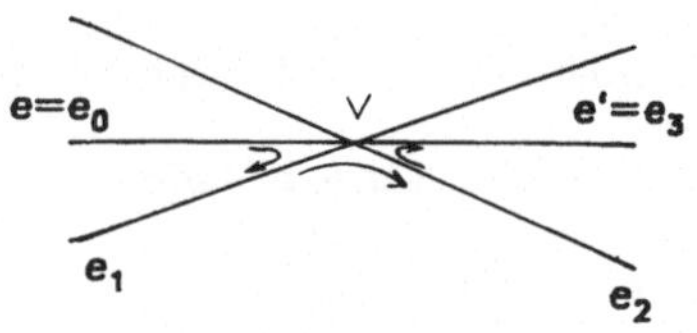

Fig. 11 - Reconstructing an edge.

Let e' be the edge of S following e along the boundary of Pi to which e belongs, and V be their common vertex. Then, there must exist a chain of angularly ordered edges from e to e', all having one endpoint in V and such that:

$$e = e0 < e1 < e2 < \dots < en = e'$$

where every pair ei, e(i+1) have one side belonging to the same loop, and:

$$ek \not\in Pi \qquad \text{for every } 0 < k < n.$$

Thus, the reconstruction algorithm starts searching S for a contour C having i in its contour-history, and for an edge e of C having i in its edge-history and not yet considered. Then, the graph is searched along the chain of edges starting from e.

A pseudo-Pascal description of the reconstruction algorithm is given below:

```
Algorithm SEARCH_BUILD (i:polygon_id; C:cptr);
//At the first activation, C is the first contour in the
  binary tree structure;
  S' is the output structure//
  if C ≠ nil then
      if i in history(C)  then
          BOUNDARY (i,C,S')
      end;
      let C' be the son of C;
      SEARCH_BUILD (i,C');
      let C' be the brother of C;
      SEARCH_BUILD (i,C')
  end
end SEARCH_BUILD.

Procedure BOUNDARY(i:polygon_id; C:cptr; S':cptr)
  let versus be an arbitrary traversal versus;
  C' <--- C;
  let e' be the first edge of C' with i in its history;
  while  there exists an e' not yet visited do;
      INSERT_NEW_CONTOUR (e',S');
      e  <--- e';
      repeat
          int <--- INT_SIDE (e,C);
          ext <--- EXT_SIDE (e,C);
          if i in history (e,int) then
              INSERT_EDGE (e,S');
              e <--- NEXT_EDGE (e,int,versus)
          else
              C <--- GET_CONTOUR (e,ext);
              e <--- NEXT_EDGE (e,ext,versus)
          end
      until e = e'
  end
end BOUNDARY.
```

The two following further procedures have been used:

INSERT_NEW_CONTOUR (e,S), which inserts a new contour containing the edge e into the output structure S;

INSERT_EDGE (e,S), which inserts a new edge e into the output structure S.

Let's now examinate how boolean operations can be performed on the pw-e.

In general, the extraction of the contours which bound polygonal regions resulting from boolean operations requires that the contour-histories are examined, and those satisfying a condition depending on the specific operation are selected.

The following are examples of the conditions imposed by the different boolean operations:

global_union, i.e. the union of all the polygons given in input; in this case the condition is that the selected contours are the outer contours, identified by a contour-history containing only 0;

partial_union, i.e. the union of all the polygons whose identifiers are included in a set R; the selected contours have in their contour-history one, at least, of the elements of R;

intersection between two or more polygons whose identifiers are included in a set R; every selected contour has in its history all the elements of R;

difference between two or more polygons whose identifiers are included in a set R1, and two or more polygons whose identifiers are included in a set R2; every selected contour has in its history one, at least, identifier belonging to R1, while it does not have any of the identifiers belonging to R2.

Thus, every contour history has to be checked against an identifier (in the case of global_union), a reference set (in the cases of partial_union and intersection) or two reference sets (in the case of difference). Although the conditions above are necessary to determine the requested output, they are not generally sufficient. In fact, the contour-history, deriving from the edge-history, only contains edge ownership, and does not explicitly contain the global area inclusion information, i.e. the area ownership.
However, while coexisting contours do not contain global information about area ownership, in the case of contained contours the area ownership, though not explicitly stored, can be derived from the ancestors's contour-histories.

To this aim, a <u>dynamic history set</u> Hd is built up during the traversal of the structure, which contains at any moment the identifiers of all the input polygons owning the area under examination, so that if an included contour is met, we can automatically recognize its owners. The mechanism by which contour identifiers are treated is a parity check technique, i.e. an identifier k is activated or deactivated every time it is encountered during the traversal process.
This means that a polygon identifier is inserted into Hd if it is not yet there, or it is discarded from Hd if it is already there.
For simplicity, in the following algorithms a subset of Hd will be used, which contains only the identifiers of interest for the requested operation, namely the identifiers which are present in the reference set R (or in the reference sets R1 and R2).
Moreover, an extended concept of the history of a contour C is introduced, which takes in account the contour-history of C and the histories propagated from the brothers of C.
Therefore, the boolean operations listed above can be translated as follows making use of the reference and dynamic history sets.

Global_union: a contour C belongs to the global_union if its history is 0 and set Hd is empty when C is traversed.

Partial_union: a contour C belongs to the required partial_union if its history contains elements of R, and set Hd is empty when C is traversed or after the history of C has been discarded from Hd.

Intersection: a contour C belongs to the required intersection if its history contains elements of R, and Hd = R when C is traversed.

Difference: a contour C belongs to the difference if its history contains elements of R1, does not contain element of R2, and Hd is empty when C is traversed or after the history of C has been discarded from Hd.

The substructure extracted from the pw-e according to a query defines a geometrical partition of the area corresponding to the requested polygonal region.

A detailed description of the algorithms performing the considered boolean operations is given below.

```
Algorithm SEARCH_GLOBAL_UNION (C:cptr)
//At the first activation, C is the root contour
  of the binary tree structure;
  Hd is the set of active histories;
  at the first activation Hd is empty;
  S' is the extracted structure//
  if C ≠ nil then
       PUSH (Hd);
       extended_history <--- EXTENDED_HISTORY (C);
       if extended_history  = 0 then
            if Hd = 0 then
                 INSERT_STRUCTURE (C,S')
            end
       else
            if extended_history ∩ Hd = 0 then
                 INSERT_ACTIVE (extended_history,Hd)
            else
                 DELETE_ACTIVE (extended_history,Hd)
            end
       end
       let C' be the son of C;
       SEARCH_GLOBAL_UNION (C');
       POP (Hd);
       let C' be the brother of C;
       SEARCH_GLOBAL_UNION (C')
  end
end SEARCH_GLOBAL_UNION.
```

The following primitives have been used in the above algorithm:

PUSH (H), which saves the current set of active histories H;
POP (H), which restores the previously saved set of histories in H;
INSERT_ACTIVE (H,H'), which inserts the set of histories H into the current set of active histories H';
DELETE_ACTIVE (H,H'), which deletes the set of histories H from the current set of active histories H';
INSERT_STRUCTURE (C,S), which inserts contour C into the output structure S.
EXTENDED_HISTORY (C), which returns the union of history(C) and the histories propagated from its brothers.

```
Algorithm SEARCH_PARTIAL_UNION (C:cptr)
//At the first activation, C is the root of the binary tree structure;
  Hd is the current set of active histories,  at the first activation,
  Hd is empty;  S' is the  extracted  structure;  R is the reference
  set of the polygon identifiers involved in the union operation//
   if C ≠ nil then
      PUSH (Hd);
      extended_history <--- EXTENDED_HISTORY (C);
      if extended_history ∩ R ≠ 0 then
          if extended_history ∩ Hd = 0 then
              if Hd = 0 then
                  INSERT_STRUCTURE (C,S')
              end
              INSERT_ACTIVE (extended_history ∩ R,Hd)
          else
              DELETE_ACTIVE (extended_history ∩ Hd,Hd);
              if Hd = 0 then
                  INSERT_STRUCTURE (C,S')
              end
          end
      end
      let C' be the son of C;
      SEARCH_PARTIAL_UNION (C');
      POP (Hd);
      let C' be the brother of C;
      SEARCH_PARTIAL_UNION (C')
  end
end SEARCH_PARTIAL_UNION.
```

```
Algorithm SEARCH_INTERSECTION (C:cptr)
//At the first activation, C is the root of the binary tree structure;
  Hd is the current set of active histories,  at the first activation,
  Hd is empty; S'is the extracted structure; R is the reference set of
  the polygon identifiers involved in the intersection operation//
  if C ≠ nil then
      PUSH (Hd);
      extended_history <--- EXTENDED_HISTORY (C);
      if extended_history ∩ R ≠ 0 then
          if extended_history ∩ Hd = 0 then
              INSERT_ACTIVE (extended_history ∩ R,Hd);
              if Hd = R then
                  INSERT_STRUCTURE (C,S')
              end
          else
              if Hd = R then
                  INSERT_STRUCTURE (C,S')
              end
              DELETE_ACTIVE (extended_history ∩ R,Hd)
          end
      end
      let C' be the son of C;
      SEARCH_INTERSECTION (C');
      POP (Hd);
      let C' be the brother of C;
      SEARCH_INTERSECTION (C')
  end
end SEARCH_INTERSECTION.
```

```
Algorithm SEARCH_DIFFERENCE (C:cptr)
//At the first activation, C is the root contour
  of the binary tree structure;
  Hd is the current set of active histories;
  at the first activation, Hd is empty;
  S' is the extracted structure;
  R1 and R2 are the reference sets of the polygon
  identifiers involved in the difference operation//
  if C ≠ nil then
      PUSH (Hd);
      extended_history <--- EXTENDED_HISTORY (C);
      if extended_history∩ R1 ≠ 0 and extended_history∩ R2=0 then
          if extended_history∩ Hd = 0 then
              if Hd = 0 then
                  INSERT_STRUCTURE (C,S')
              end
              INSERT_ACTIVE (extended_history∩ R1,Hd)
          else
              DELETE_ACTIVE (extended_history∩ R1,Hd);
              if Hd = 0 then
                  INSERT_STRUCTURE (C,S')
              end
          end
      end
  else
      if extended_history∩R2 ≠ 0  then
          if extended_history∩ Hd = 0 then
              INSERT_ACTIVE (extended_history ∩ (R1 ∪ R2),Hd)
          else
              DELETE_ACTIVE (extended_history ∩(R1 ∪ R2),Hd)
          end
      end
      let C' be the son of C;
      SEARCH_DIFFERENCE (C');
      POP (Hd);
      let C' be the brother of C;
      SEARCH_DIFFERENCE (C')
  end
end SEARCH_DIFFERENCE.
```

5. CONCLUSION

We have presented and discussed a polygon handling technique which was designed for applications in Computer Aided Architectural Design.
The basic requirements imposed by the application have been met, since the proposed technique is able to deal with input polygons of complicated shape (concave and multiply connected polygons) and permits the retrieval of previously inserted polygons.
The data structure on which this technique is based is a winged-edge representation, which has been modified to represent elements in a plane, their mutual relationships, and a history associated with them and containing the history of their construction.
A fundamental feature of the proposed method is the separation between the structure construction and interrogation steps. This feature allows the user to define the structure and perform the necessary manipulation

at the beginning, and then to interrogate it with as many queries as desired, thus achieving a good interaction efficiency.
A boundary hierarchy structure has been designed as well, to the aim of facilitating the exchange of information between the user and the system.
A set of algorithms for conversion, manipulation and query on the structure have been given. However, other operations can be easily realized, such as algorithms which compute dimensional parameters (e.g. area and perimeter) corresponding to an input polygon embedded in the data structure, or to a boolean combination of a set of input polygons. Since the proposed representation is an object-space model, it has the property of being invariant under geometric transformations. Furthermore, a geometric transformation operates only on a part of the geometrical information stored in the structure, namely on the vertex coordinates. The other geometrical information, such as inclusion relationships, and the topological information remain unchanged through a geometrical transformation.

6. REFERENCES

[1] Baumgart,B.G., "A polyhedron representation for Computer Vision", National Computer Conference, 1975, pp.589-596.

[2] Weiler,K., "Polygon comparison using a graph representation", Computer Graphics, vol.14, n.3, 1980, pp.10-18.

[3] Mantyla,M., Sulonen,R., "GWB: A solid modeler with the Euler operators", Computer Graphics and Applications, vol.2, n.7, 1982, pp.17-31.

[4] Mantyla,M., "A note on the modeling space of Euler operators", Computer Vision, Graphics and Image Processing, vol.26, 1984, pp.45-60.

[5] Gambaro,C., Gambaro,P., Pienovi,C., "An interactive graphical system for CAAD applications", Proc. VII Int. Symposium on CAD/CAM, Zagreb, 1985, pp.159-164.

[6] Weiler,K., "Edge-based data structures for solid modeling in curved surface environments", Computer Graphics and Applications, vol.5, n.1, 1985, pp.21-40.

[7] Whitesides,S., "Computational geometry and motion planning", in Computational Geometry, Ed. G.Toussaint, North-Holland, 1985.

[8] Preparata,F.P., Shamos,M.I., Computational Geometry - An introduction, Springer-Verlag, 1985.

[9] Franklin,W.R., "Polygon properties calculated from the vertex neighborhoods", Proc. 3rd Symposium on Computational Geometry, 1987, pp.110-118.

Volume and Surface Properties in CSG

G. Wyvill and P. Sharp (New Zealand)

Abstract

If we use a red drill to make a hole in a blue block, the inside of the hole will still be blue. To simulate this process in a CSG system, we subtract a red cylinder from the blue block. The hole's surface belongs to the cylinder but it takes its colour from the block.

We present algorithms for elucidating the correct colours from CSG models and describe an application in design for wood turning.

Keywords: CAD, CSG, Geometric modelling, Ray tracing, Texture mapping.

Introduction

Constructive Solid Geometry (CSG) is a technique of geometric modelling. In a CSG system, all objects are regarded as sets of points in space and more complicated objects are constructed from simpler ones by applying the operations of set theory. Addition can be used to glue objects together and subtraction can be used to simulate cutting operations such as drilling, milling and turning. Because any object can be added to (or subtracted from) any other, it is convenient to represent a compound object by a tree structure where each node represents an addition or subtraction of its sub-nodes. The simplest (primitive) objects are elementary planes, spheres, cones and similar objects with simple and precise mathematical definitions, and these are represented by the leaves of the tree. It is important to appreciate that these primitive objects represent *volumes*. The plane, for example, is defined as the semi-infinite volume bounded by a plane surface. For further background on CSG, see Myers (1982), Requicha (1977, 1982) and Roth (1982).

Because CSG systems use sets of points in 3D space, the representation of objects is truly volumetric. In principle, CSG gives us a full representation of a shape and not just its bounding surfaces. It is frequently claimed that this complete representation makes CSG superior to other modelling techniques and we agree.

But this completeness of description is of no use unless it is exploited to provide information not available from other kinds of model. We are particularly interested in cases where an object, made of several pieces glued together, is cut or shaped so that the inner structure is revealed at the surface of the cut. Figure 1 shows such an object: A bowl has been turned out of a workpiece made by joining differently coloured pieces of wood.

The most elegant way of making pictures from a solid model is by ray tracing. The basic algorithm for this was described by Roth (1982) and this has been developed in various ways to improve efficiency (Fujimoto 1985, 1986, Woodwark 1986a, Wyvill 1986, 1987). Woodwark (1986b), Laidlaw (1986) and others have described alternative methods of rendering, but none of these algorithms appears to be able to deal with pictures like Fig. 1.

We explain why this is so and present algorithms to display colours that reveal the internal structure of CSG models. We have applied our methods to create practical designs for wood turning.

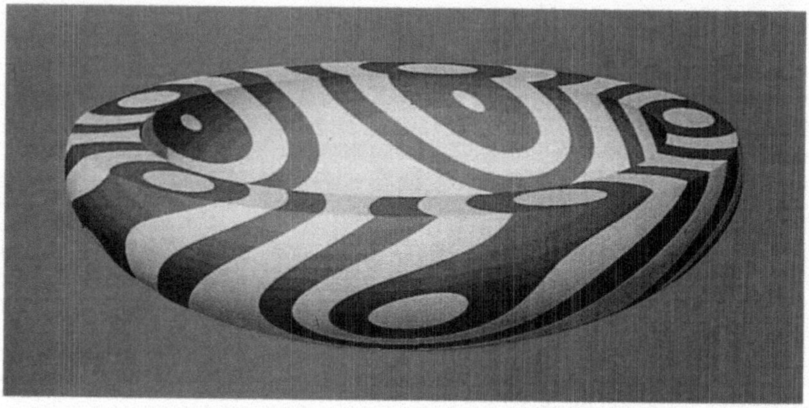

Fig. 1. Design for a bowl made from layered wood

Fig. 2. A red drill makes a red hole – We expect it to be blue.

Colour: a property of volumes

Published algorithms do not produce the correct colours from CSG models. This is not a criticism of these algorithms. The problem simply does not seem to have been addressed. The reason is that rendering algorithms have concentrated on identifying surfaces. In the case of CSG models represented by polygons (Laidlaw 1986), the algorithms given find a set of polygons that correctly describes an object's boundary. Internal boundaries are deliberately eliminated to simplify the model. Ray tracing algorithms seek to find the surface which first intercepts a given ray. Figure 2 shows the simple example of a block from which a cylinder has been subtracted to make a hole. We would expect the inside of the hole to have the same colour as the block. But the inside of the hole is a surface of the subtracted cylinder and has taken its colour from the cylinder.

We expect the inside of the hole to have the colour of the block because we think of colour as a property of the material of the block. If the colour is merely painted on, we would expect the inside of the hole to be different. Some properties are logically inherited from surfaces. We could, for example, texture the cylinder to represent surface scratches made by a drill. We would think it logical for the surface to acquire such a texture from the cylinder. In our application, we want to treat colour as a property of volumes rather than surfaces. This is why we need to extend the rendering algorithms.

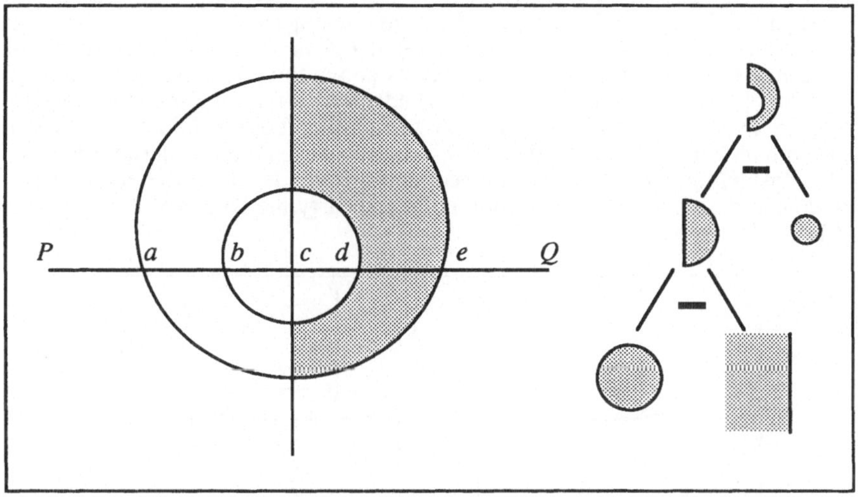

Fig. 3. Ray intersection with a CSG tree

Intersection algorithm

The kernel of a ray tracer for CSG models is an algorithm to find the correct, first intersection of a ray with the surface of the object in question. Roth (1982) explains how to do this, but the following description is based on that of Wyvill (1986). Start with the example of Fig. 3. The shaded area in the centre represents a cross section of an object made by subtracting a plane and a cylinder from a second cylinder. The tree structure on the right shows the construction. The ray *PQ* intersects the various primitive objects at *a, b, c, d* and *e*. The correct point of intersection is *d*. Points *a, b,* and *c* are closer, but *a* and *b* are contained in the volume of the subtracted plane space, and *c* is contained in the volume of the subtracted cylinder.

To find the correct intersection, in the general case, we find all the intersections and sort them by distance from the ray origin. The first intersection not outside the object is the one we are seeking. To find whether a particular intersection is inside or outside the object, we perform a simple, recursive traversal of the CSG tree:

```
function csgin(point, tree): boolean;
begin
    if tree is a leaf node then
        csgin := tree.inside(point)
    else if tree.type = PLUS then
        csgin := csgin(point, tree.left) or csgin(point, tree.right)
    else csgin := csgin(point, tree.left) and not csgin(point, tree.right)
end;
```

Here, we have assumed that each node of the CSG tree represents an addition or subtraction of sets and that a primitive routine, tree.inside, is available to tell us whether a particular point is inside or outside each primitive object.

Inside/outside is not enough

Even without the complications of objects with internal structure, the simple inside/outside test does not guarantee to find the right surface. In Fig. 4 we see two cylinders, whose top surfaces are coplanar. A ray (arrow) strikes cylinder B. The corresponding CSG tree is shown in Fig. 5. Each cylinder is actually built from three primitive objects: a primitive cylinder and two primitive planes named *base* and *top*. Remember that a plane is the collection of all points on one side of a plane surface. In this case, all points above the plane are subtracted from the primitive (infinitely long) cylinder to create a cylinder with a flat top. The ray shown in Fig. 4 intersects with the planes that form the top surfaces of both cylinders, but clearly the intersection with the top of A is not valid. This surface exists only in the definition of A. Yet in terms of the inside/outside test, this intersection is valid. If the cylinders, A and B, are differently coloured, this wrong intersection point can carry the colour of A to a point on the surface of B.

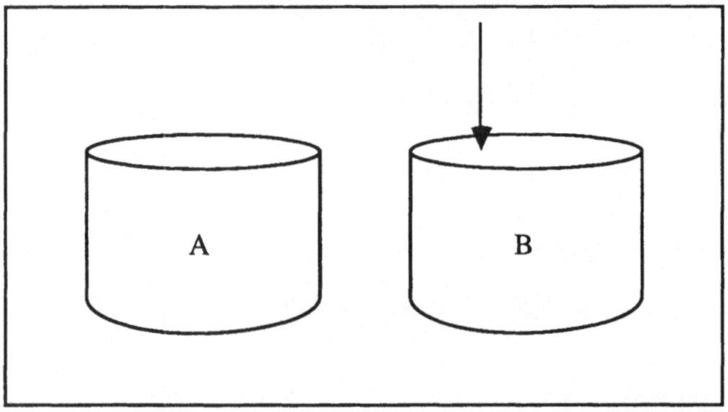

Fig. 4. Coincident surfaces produce wrong colours. Although the top of A doesn't extend beyond the sides of A, the subtracted primitive plane does, and a false intersection can occur on the surface of B.

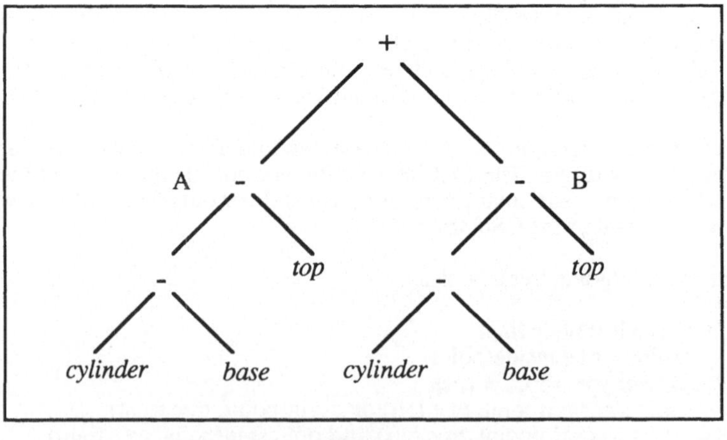

Fig. 5. The CSG tree for Fig. 4

In practical cases, this problem with coplanar surfaces occurs quite often. Designs in engineering tend to use many parts that line up in one way or another. To find the right intersection in all cases, we have to alter the basic logic of the algorithm to take into account the special association of the point of intersection and the particular surface intersected.

This can be done with a single traversal of a CSG tree but instead of looking for the inside/outside property, we define a new property of provisional intersection points. This has a value IN, OUT or BORDER. Each intersection point has the property BORDER with respect to the primitive object that it actually intersects. Even if the point happens to lie on the boundary of another primitive object, it is not given the value, BORDER. To find the value (IN, OUT or BORDER) of a point with respect to a CSG tree, we use a table of rules for combining the values at each node. Table 1 sets out these rules.

PLUS Node

	Right branch		
Left branch	IN	OUT	BORDER
IN	IN	IN	IN
OUT	IN	OUT	BORDER
BORDER	IN	BORDER	

MINUS Node

	Right branch		
Left branch	IN	OUT	BORDER
IN	OUT	IN	BORDER
OUT	OUT	OUT	OUT
BORDER	OUT	BORDER	

Table 1. Rules for intersections

Now see what happens to the ray in Fig. 4 when its intersection with the top of A is checked with the tree of Fig. 5. When the ray intersects with the top of A, it has the property BORDER with the top of A. However, at the MINUS node, this point will be seen to be OUT with respect to the left branch of the subtree and cannot be recognised as an intersection point. The following algorithm implements these rules as it traverses the tree.

```
type logic3 = (IN, OUT, BORDER);

function elucidate(point, tree, leaf): logic3;
{ Point is the intersection of the ray and the surface represented by the leaf node, leaf.}
   begin
      if tree is a leaf node then
         begin  if tree = leaf then elucidate := BORDER
                else elucidate := tree.inside(point)
         end
      else if tree.type = PLUS then
         case elucidate(point, tree. right, leaf) of
            IN:         elucidate := IN;
            OUT:        elucidate := elucidate(point, tree.left, leaf);
            BORDER: if elucidate(point, tree.left, leaf) = IN then elucidate := IN;
                        else elucidate := BORDER
         end {case}
      else {tree.type = MINUS}
         case elucidate(point, tree.right, leaf) of
            IN:         elucidate := OUT;
            OUT:        elucidate := elucidate(point, tree.left, leaf);
            BORDER: if elucidate(point, tree.left, leaf) = IN then
                              elucidate := BORDER;
                        else elucidate := OUT
         end {case}
   end;
```

Algorithm 1. Identification of intersection surface

This description is not quite complete. There are still some problems associated with rounding errors and the meaning of IN and OUT for points on the surface of an object. But this is beyond the scope of this paper. For the moment, it is sufficient to show that we can eliminate false intersections and that when we have an intersection, we can always say which primitive object was intersected.

Correct colour for subtraction

Having established the correct identity of a primitive component, the colour can be found from the description of that component. However, in the case where we have a subtracted primitive, the colour must be taken from the primitive volume from which it was subtracted.

In our system, each instance of a primitive object is represented by a record containing information about colour, texture, and position and orientation in space. The argument *leaf* in Algorithm 1 is actually a pointer to one of these records. We must extend the algorithm to find a pointer to identify the primitive from which the volume properties must be taken. In many cases, these two pointers will be the same.

When the elucidate function returns a value IN, it must also return a pointer to say which primitive it is in. Then, when the values IN and BORDER are combined at a MINUS node, the correct pointers are available.

Asymmetric addition operator

The earliest version of our system, (Wyvill 1985), did not permit the general addition (union) of sets. We tried to model nature and did not allow two objects to occupy the same space. In the present system we permit this, for reasons explained below. But this means that a given point can be inside more than one primitive in the CSG tree and the colour, or other properties would then be defined ambiguously. We resolve this ambiguity by defining an asymmetric addition operator, ⧺.

By definition: A ⧺ B ≡ (A - B) + B

This means that in the case of addition, the colour of the right operand is used over any shared volume. Inside the object, A ⧺ B, any point in B has the colour of B. Only points in A but not in B will have the colour of A.

Elucidation algorithm

We can now present the elucidation algorithm for correct colour recognition. Note carefully, in each recursive call, whether *colour* or *tempcolour* is passed.

```
function elucidate(point, tree, leaf, colour): logic3;
{ Colour is an output parameter to carry back the colour information.}
var tempcolour;
    begin
        if tree is a leaf node then
            begin  if tree = leaf then elucidate := BORDER;
                   else elucidate := tree.inside(point);
                   colour := tree
            end
        else if tree.type = PLUS then
            case elucidate(point, tree. right, leaf, colour) of
                IN:         elucidate := IN;
                OUT:        elucidate := elucidate(point, tree.left, leaf, colour);
                BORDER: if elucidate(point, tree.left, leaf, tempcolour) = IN then
                            begin
                                elucidate := IN;
                                colour := tempcolour
                            end
                        else elucidate := BORDER
            end {case}
        else {tree.type = MINUS}
            case elucidate(point, tree.right, leaf, colour) of
                IN:         elucidate := OUT;
                OUT:        elucidate := elucidate(point, tree.left, leaf, colour);
                BORDER: if elucidate(point, tree.left, leaf, colour) = IN then
                            elucidate := BORDER;
                        else elucidate := OUT
            end {case}
    end;
```

Algorithm 2. Complete colour elucidation

Space division

To make ray tracing efficient, it is necessary to separate the components of the model in some way, to avoid having to test every object against every ray. We use a system of regular space division (Fujimoto 1985, Cleary 1987). The ray tracer works within a volume that is divided into cubical voxels in a regular 3D grid. Each voxel is described as full, empty or compound. A compound voxel contains:

- a part of the surface of some primitive object *or*
- a part of the surface of a primitive being subtracted from full space *or*
- something more complex: a reduced CSG tree (RCSG).

An RCSG is a CSG tree extracted from the original tree. It contains only those primitives that actually have some effect in the voxel concerned. How these are built from the original tree has been described previously (Wyvill 1986).

Fujimoto (1986) describes a fast way to identify all the voxels intersected by the surface of a given primitive. But to handle CSG subtractions, we need to find the inner (full) voxels as well. For this reason, although we use a regular space division for our ray tracer, we create the data structure by means of a recursive algorithm based on octrees (Wyvill 1985, Brown 1987). In the case where an object is subtracted from full space, we have to record the colour and other properties of the full voxel. In other words, it is no longer sufficient to know that a voxel is full, we have to know of what it is full.

To create our space division, we first create an octree and then flatten it by further dividing any voxels that are not of minimum size. Any primitive on its own can be considered to be an octree at level zero of space division. Thus the process of creating the octree can be described in terms of adding or subtracting two existing octrees. This is an adaptation of our earlier method (Wyvill 1986).

To subtract two octrees, a - b:

1. If a is empty, return empty.
2. If b is empty, return a.
3. If b is full, return empty.
4. If the limit of the octree depth has been reached, create an RCSG node.
5. Otherwise, it is time to subdivide. If either a or b is already divided, access its children, otherwise create the subvoxels.
6. Recursively subtract the eight children.

To add two octrees, a ⇷ b:

1. If a is empty, return b.
2. If b is empty, return a.
3. If b is full, return b.
4. If the limit of the octree depth has been reached, create an RCSG node.
   If a is full, set the full flag for this RCSG node.
5. Otherwise, it is time to subdivide. If either a or b is already divided, access its children, otherwise create the subvoxels.
6. Recursively add the eight children.

When we subdivide a voxel, we test each of the eight subvoxels to see whether it is full, empty or still contains a boundary of the primitive. Full subvoxels still contain a pointer to a record describing the primitive but they are flagged to indicate that they are full. RCSG nodes can also be full, although they contain boundaries between primitives.

The purpose of subdivision is to make ray tracing efficient. By reducing the number of primitives in any one voxel, we avoid many expensive intersection calculations. Any solid defined using asymmetric addition can also be defined using the equivalence:

A ⇷ B ≡ (A - B) + B

But A ⇷ B is a single operation whereas (A - B) + B creates two coincident surfaces. This is why we now permit union of sets. By introducing the operator, ⇷, we simplify our descriptions and improve efficiency.

An application: laminated wood turning

If we turn a bowl or cup from a composite block of wood, the finished article displays a surface pattern showing its internal structure. The use of this technique is quite popular among amateur turners because the results are pleasing and the composite workpiece can be made from offcuts too small for other work. Most often, we see bowls made with a checker-board pattern in which all the joints are flat.

More interesting patterns can be made if we laminate the wood in concentric cylinders. This would be difficult on an ordinary wood lathe, but on a metal lathe with sliding carriage and micrometer tool feeds, it is quite easy.

Unfortunately, it takes a long time to do this kind of work. Each piece must be glued in place and the glue set, before a hole can be bored for the next insert. Only when all this is done can the work be turned into its final form.

It is not easy to design these articles. The curves that appear on the surface are difficult to predict, and it can take days to make something, only to find that the pattern is unsatisfactory.

Using our solid modeller, we created the eggcup shown in Fig. 6. It takes only five minutes or so for the system to make a prototype picture, so we were able to adjust the dimensions and angles many times in simulation before attempting to make the eggcup itself.

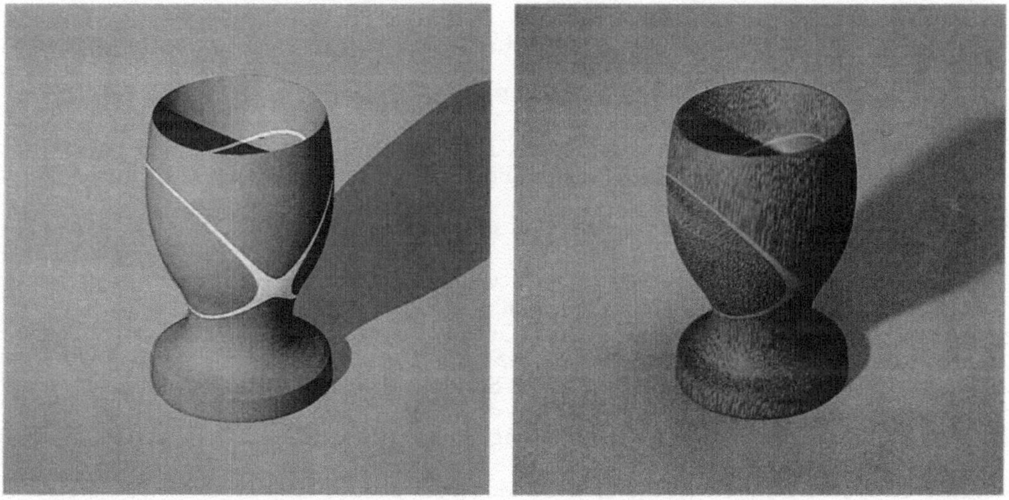

Fig. 6. (a) CSG design, (b) The actual eggcup turned from balau and holly

Conclusion

We have designed a solid modelling system that handles volume properties consistently and allows us to display internal structure from a CSG definition. Using our system, we have created designs for wood turning that would have been almost impossible otherwise.

The 'correct colour' algorithm uses a 3-value logic instead of a simple inside-outside test.

We have introduced an asymmetric addition operator that simplifies our descriptions and makes ray tracing a little faster.

In solving this problem, we have become aware of a more general question in CSG modelling. It should be possible for the user to choose how colours, or other properties, are transferred from one component to another. It is easy to find an example where a surface should acquire its colour from one object and its texture from another. We are currently refining the system to handle cases like this.

Acknowledgement

The computer graphics project at Otago has been jointly funded by Otago University and the University Grants Committee.

References

Brown, T. 1987: Efficient Ray Tracing of Solid Models, *MSc thesis,* University of Otago

Cleary, J. G. et al. 1983: Multiprocessor Ray Tracing, *Research Report No. 83/128/7,* Dept. Computer Science, University of Calgary

Cleary, J. G. and Wyvill, G. 1987: Analysis of an Algorithm for Fast Ray Tracing Using Uniform Space Subdivision, *The Visual Computer* (in press)

Fujimoto, A. and Iwata, K. 1985: Accelerated Ray Tracing, *Computer Graphics Visual Technology and Art* (Proc. of CG Tokyo '85), 41-65

Fujimoto, A., Perrott, C. G. and Iwata, K. 1986a: Environment for Fast Elaboration of Constructive Solid Geometry, *Advanced Computer Graphics* (Proc. CG Tokyo '86), 20-33

Fujimoto, A., Tanaka, T. and Iwata, K. 1986b: ARTS: Accelerated Ray Tracing System, *IEEE CG&A,* Vol. 6, No. 4, 16-26

Glassner, A. S. 1984: Space Subdivision for Fast Ray Tracing, *IEEE CG&A,* Vol. 4, No. 10, 15-22

Laidlaw, D. H., Trumbore, W. B. and Hughes, J. F. 1986: Constructive Solid Geometry for Polyhedral Objects, *Computer Graphics* (Proc. SIGGRAPH '86), Vol. 20, No. 4, 161-170

Myers, W. 1982: An industrial perspective on solid modeling, *IEEE CG&A,* Vol. 2, No. 2, 86-97

Ohta, M. and Maekawa, M. 1987: Ray Coherence and Constant Time Ray Tracing Algorithm, *Computer Graphics 1987* (Proc. CG International '87, Karuizawa), 303-314

Requicha, A. A. G. and Voelker, H. B. 1977: Geometric Modelling of Mechanical Parts and Processes, *Computer,* Vol. 10, No. 12, 48-57

Requicha, A. A. G. and Voelker, H. B. 1982: Solid Modeling: A Historical Summary and Contemporary Assessment, *IEEE CG&A,* Vol. 2, No. 2, 9-24

Roth, S. D. 1982: Ray Casting for Modeling Solids, *Computer Graphics and Image Processing,* Vol. 18, 109-144

Whitted, T. 1980: An Improved Illumination Model for Shaded Display, *Comm. ACM,* Vol. 23, No. 6, 343-349

Woodwark, J. and Bowyer, A. 1986a: Better and faster pictures from solid models, *Computer-Aided Engineering Journal,* February, 17-24

Woodwark, J. 1986b: Generating wireframes from set-theoretic solid models by spatial division, *Computer Aided Design,* Vol. 18, No. 6, 307-315

Wyvill, G. and Kunii, T. L. 1985: A functional model for constructive solid geometry, *The Visual Computer,* Vol. 1, No. 1

Wyvill, G., Kunii, T. L. and Shirai, Y. 1986: Space Division for Ray Tracing in CSG, *IEEE CG&A,* Vol. 6, No. 4, 28-34

Wyvill, G., Ward, A. and Brown, T. 1987: Sketches by Ray Tracing, *Computer Graphics 1987* (Proc. CG International '87, Karuizawa), 315-333

A Hierarchical Model for Spatial Stacking

N. M. Aziz (USA)

Abstract

Building larger objects out of smaller rectangular parallelepipeds may be called a stacking operation. A modeling technique is developed for stacking a given number of parallelepipeds in a predefined arrangement. The technique uses the method of spatial occupancy and takes advantage of the specific properties of the stacking order for obtaining a solid model with hidden lines/surfaces removed. The algorithm uses efficient methods for handling huge databases and large computation time needed for solid modeling on microprocessors.

Introduction

This paper explains the methods used in the generation of a three dimensional graphics display for certain parallelopiped (PP) stacking patterns. These patterns are used in the actual loading or stacking of boxes or books into cuboidal spaces such as trucks, warehouses, bookshelves and in pallets. The overall flowchart of the algorithm is shown in Fig. 1.

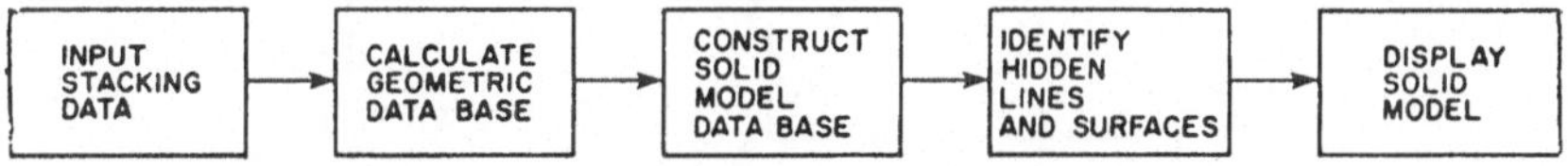

Figure 1. Flowchart of the algorithm

Several terms that appear frequently in the paper are introduced at this stage to provide clarity. A pattern is a certain predefined arrangement of N rectangular parallelepipeds of dimensions (L,W,D). In general, a pattern is a multi-layer arrangement in which the number of PPs in any direction can be more than one. Each PP can be placed in six different orientations, as shown in Fig. 2.

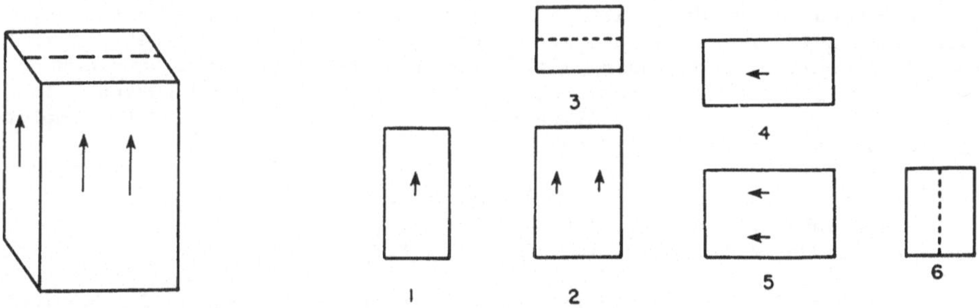

a) Definition sketch of parallelepiped faces

b) Front view of the six possible orientations of a parallelepiped

Figure 2

The shape of a pattern is determined by the arrangement of the PPs in the pattern and is reflected in the database. The vertices of all PPs are numbered 1 through 6 as shown in Fig. 3. This numbering scheme is independent of PP orientation as shown in the examples of Fig. 4. Vertex 1 is the front-left node and 5 is the top-left node. Vertex numbering is done in a counter-clockwise fashion beginning with the bottom vertices.

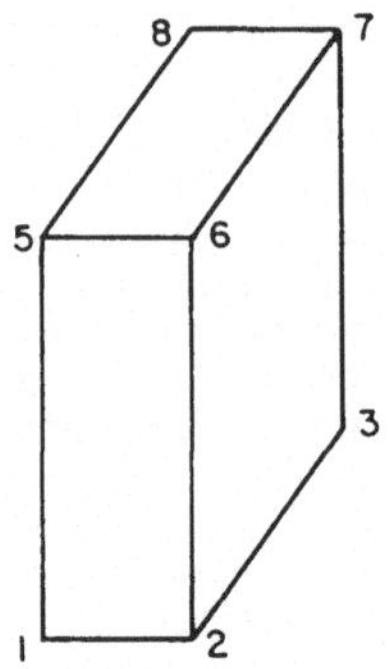

Figure 3. Vertex numbering of a parallelepiped.

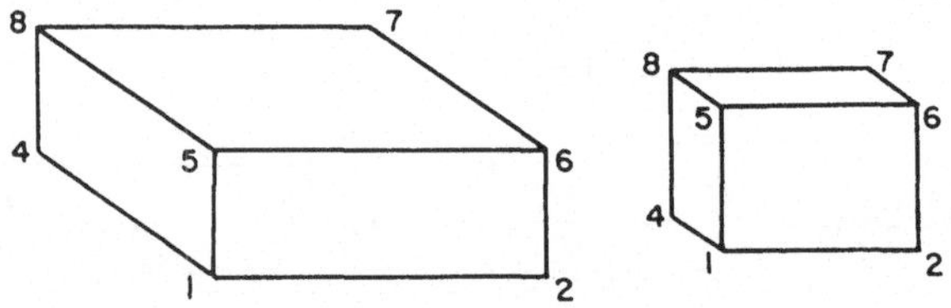

Figure 4. Numbering scheme for different PP orientations.

Topological Database Generation

To simplify the algorithm, a pattern is considered to be made up of the same size PPs. These PPs can be in one or in all six different orientations. As a first step towards building pattern topology, a freehand sketch of the pattern can be used as a guide for constructing the database. The PPs in a pattern are then numbered sequentially, beginning with the one at the lower left hand corner.

The next step is to perform actual PP stacking. For this purpose, in addition to PP dimensions, the minimum number of information needed to completely define a pattern are the following:

a. PP orientation code, O_i, such that $1 \le O_i \le 6$
b. Reference PP code, R_i, such that $1 \le R_i \le N$
c. Reference vertex code, V_i, such that $1 \le V_i \le 6$

where subscript i refers to the PP number. Reference PP number, R_i, indicates the PP that will be used to determine the location of the current PP in the pattern. The reference PP must be one that is in contact with the current PP. In addition, R_i is independent of orientation codes. The third piece of information needed to determine the location of a PP in a pattern is the set of coordinates $<x_j,y_j,z_j>$ where $j = V_i$. Here, the coordinates of vertex 1 of a certain PP say PP_i are the same as the coordinates of V_i of R_i. The reference vertex V_i, is therefore, never equal to 1, and theoretically speaking, can be any other vertex of the R_i. In a one layer pattern, V_i is usually equal to 2 or 5. For a multi-layer pattern, the typical V_i values are 2, 4 or 5. As an example, refer to Fig. 5, and consider the following conditions:

a) If V_i=2, then PP_i (reads PP number i) is to the right of R_i
b) If V_i=5, then PP_i is on top of R_i
c) If V_i=4, then PP_i is behind R_i.

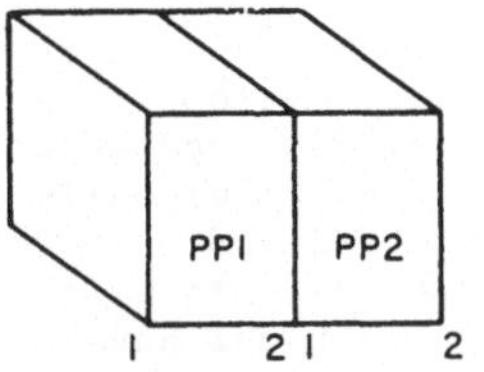

a) V_i=2, i.e. PP2 is to the right of PP1

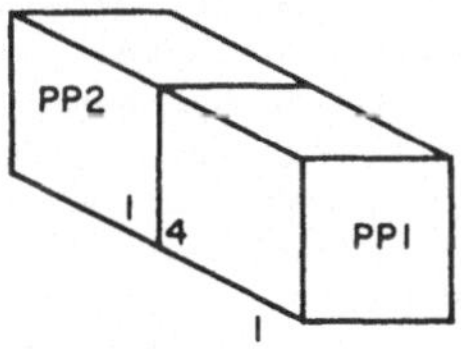

b) V_i=4, i.e. PP2 is behind PP1

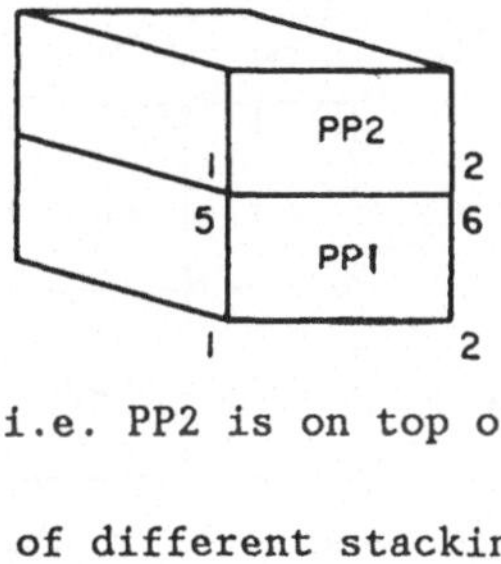

c) V_i=5, i.e. PP2 is on top of PP1

Figure 5. Illustration of different stacking and reference vertices

The hierarchical database just established is that needed for solid modeling of the stacking pattern. This database is then converted to boundary representation for display purposes. The algorithm calculates the coordinates of the vertices of all the PPs from the topological database of the pattern.

According to the vertex numbering scheme, the coordinates of any vertex can be calculated from the (x,y,z) coordinates of any other vertex. This information is readily available from the pattern database since vertex 1 for each PP is always defined through the connectivity information supplied in the topological data of the pattern. The coordinates of node 1 of any PP in the pattern, say PP_i, are the same as the coordinates of the reference vertex V_i. Therefore, by adding the respective PP dimensions to the coordinates of vertex 1, the coordinates of the other vertices are obtained. These coordinates, as well as the connectivity data are used by the solid modeling and hidden line removal components of the project.

Solid Modeling of Patterns

There are several methods of solid modeling that have been used for various application in CAD/CAM/CAE [6,7]. One method, however, that lends itself directly to applications such as stacking of PPs is the spatial occupancy enumeration method [1,3]. This method yields a unique and geometrically complete solid model and is very popular for the calculation of integral properties of solids [4,5] and for finite element mesh generation. In this enumeration method the 3D space is divided into a number of cells, and each cell is tested as to whether it occupies a portion of the model. Only the cells that occupy the object are considered as part of the whole model.

The first step in this method as applied to stacking rectangular parallelepipeds is the generation of cuboidal envelopes. A cuboidal envelope is defined here as a cube or a rectangular parallelopiped that encloses one or more PPs. Beginning with the first PP, a cuboidal envelope is created. The size of this envelope is the same as the size of PP#1 and is made up of only one occupied cell. The second PP is then introduced and if it is of the same type as the first one (i.e. $R_2=1$ and $O_2=O_1$), the original cuboidal envelope is updated to contain it. The envelope is now made up of 2 full cells. Suppose that PP 3 is on top of the first PP and has the same orientation (i.e $R_3=1$ and $O_3=O_1$). In this case the original cuboidal envelope is updated to include the third PP. The cuboidal envelope is now made up of 4 cells, each being of the same shape and size. Three of these cells are fully occupied and the fourth cell, which is above PP number 2, is empty, see Fig. 6. If the fourth PP is of the same shape as the previous three, and is located above the second PP, it will occupy the cell above PP#2 and the cuboidal envelope is again updated so that all the cells are full. However, in the event that $R_4=2$ but $O_4=O_2$, then PP#4 cannot fill a cell of the original envelope exactly. In other words, PP#4 will not fit in a cell of the original cuboidal envelope. In this case, another cuboidal envelope is generated with a cell size and shape to match PP#4 exactly.

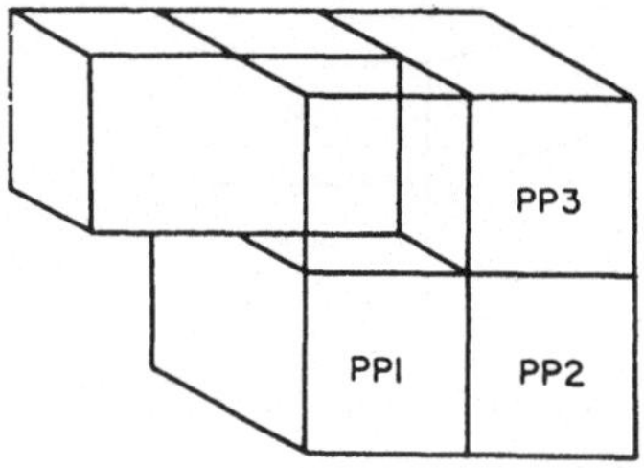

a) Cuboidal envelope with 4 cells, 3 of which are occupied

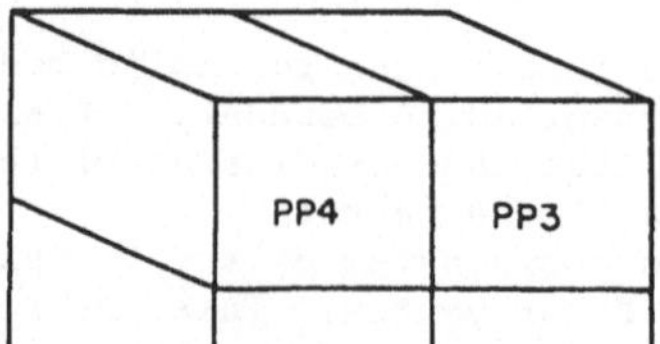

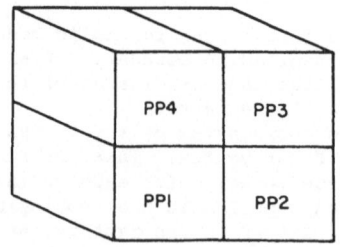

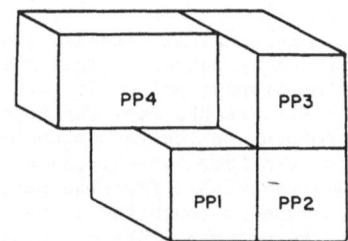

b) possible 4 th cell occupied with the same PP.

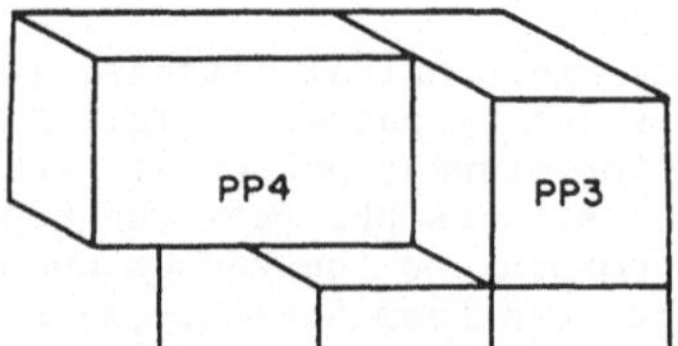

c) Possible new envelope created with a different PP.

Figure 6. Cuboidal envelopes demonstration

Every additional PP will be tested to determine whether it would fit in one of the existing cuboidal envelopes. In addition, each cuboidal envelope is expanded in 3D and contains cells of equal size. The fitting test continues until all the PPs of the pattern are accounted for. In general, the solid modeling technique implemented here takes care of the PPs as follows: Since the pattern contains PPs of the same dimensions, the algorithm builds six original cuboidal envelopes that account for the six orientation of a PP. Therefore, whenever a PP is considered, it is tested as to whether it can fit in the cuboidal envelope whose cell size is of the same orientation as the PP itself. If the PP fits exactly in a cell, then that cuboidal envelope is updated to include the current PP. All other PPs of the same orientation are tested to determine the possibility of their filling exactly a cell in the existing envelope, if not, a new envelope is added and is used in later testing.

The preceding method generates the information necessary to define the pattern as a solid model. In order to display the pattern as one solid model, which is a combination of other solids (PPs), a hidden line detection algorithm is developed and used to eliminate the hidden lines from the model.

Detection of Hidden Lines

Three dimensional models of wireframes yield cluttered and ambiguous object representations [2,9]. However, solid models that are developed by the method of spatial occupancy enumeration give an unambiguous and unique representation of the object if hidden lines are removed [6,7]. Therefore, in order to render the solid model complete, a hidden line algorithm is developed to detect hidden lines in the pattern.

In general, the hidden line detection and removal process is computationally very expensive. However, an efficient hidden line detection method can be developed for the specific application at hand which ensures that computational needs are kept to a minimum.

A sure method of hidden line removal is ray tracing [8]. This method detects hidden lines or points by issuing an imaginary ray (line) of light from the viewer to the object. If the ray intersects a part of the object or if it intersects another object before reaching the point of interest, then that point is not seen by the viewer, or in other words, it is hidden. On the other hand, a point is considered visible if the ray from the viewer to the point is not intercepted.

For the application at hand, the hidden line algorithm first tests the visibility of all vertices in the pattern. Testing takes place in several stages:

a. First the algorithm tests whether the vertex is visible with respect to all the cuboidal envelopes. If the point is visible by the envelopes, then it is visible and no more testing is needed with regard to this point. If the test indicates that the point is hidden by the envelopes, then more testing is needed.
b. If test (a) indicates that the point is hidden, the algorithm then tests whether the point is hidden by all the cubes that are located between the point and the viewer. The result of this test determines the correct and final visibility of the point.

Since this method of visibility detection is time consuming, the algorithm utilizes a unique property of the pattern topological data to reduce such computations. Since the pattern data base is built in such a way to indicate the adjacency properties of the PPs in the pattern, the visibility of several vertices can be trivially determined according to the following:

a. If two identical PPs (O_i=O_i-1) are placed one to the right of another (V_i=2), then vertex 1 of the current PP and vertex 2 of R_i have the same visibility condition. In addition, vertices 4, 5 and 8 of the current

PP have the same visibility as corners 3, 4 and 7 of the reference PP, respectively.

b. If one PP is placed on top of another PP of the same orientation (V_i=5 and O_i=$O(R_i)$ then the visibility of vertices 1, 2, 3 and 4 of the top PP are the same as the visibility of vertices 5, 6, 7 and 8 of the bottom PP, respectively.

c. If one PP is placed behind another PP of the same orientation (V_i=4 and O_i=$O(R_i)$, then vertices 1, 2, 5 and 6 of the rear PP have the same visibility as that of vertices 3, 4, 7 and 8 of the front PP, respectively.

d. If the PPs are of different orientations, then only vertex 1 of the current PP and the V_i have the same visibility.

It was observed that this visibility test reduces the number of points to be tested by step one significantly, and leads to a more efficient algorithm.

Another property of the pattern arrangement is utilized to reduce the computational time needed for the detection of hidden points. This property applies efficiently to multi-layered patterns by declaring that the PPs that are completely internal to the pattern are hidden.

Once the visibility of all the vertices of the PPs in the pattern are determined, the visibility of the edges of all PPs must be determined. An edge of a PP may be completely hidden, completely visible, or partially visible. The determination of the visibility of the edges is based upon the following criteria:

1. If the two vertices that are the end points of an edge are visible, then the edge is completely visible.
2. If the two vertices that are the end points of an edge are hidden, then the edge is completely hidden.
3. If one of the vertices that is an end point of the edge is visible and the other end point is hidden, then the line could be totally hidden or partially visible. In order to determine the visibility of the line in this PP, the following is considered:

   a) If a point on this line that is a very small distance from the visible end point is hidden, the entire line is then declared hidden.
   b) If (a) above is false, then the point at which the line changes from visible to hidden is located. The method of mid-point subdivision is used to determine this point of visibility transition.

The hidden line algorithm just described, provides the last step in the solid modeling operation. Figures 7 through 9 are examples of the patterns modeled during this project. The examples are for a variety of combinations of stacking patterns in order to show the versatility of the model. These models are generated on a microcomputer and are part of a larger PC-based modeling package.

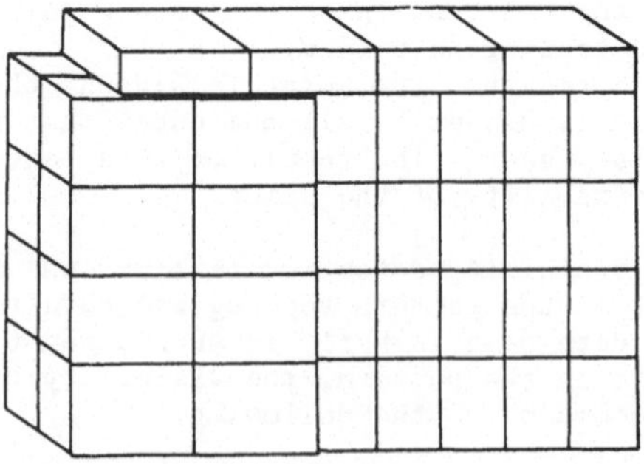

Figure 7. PP stacking with 3 different orientations

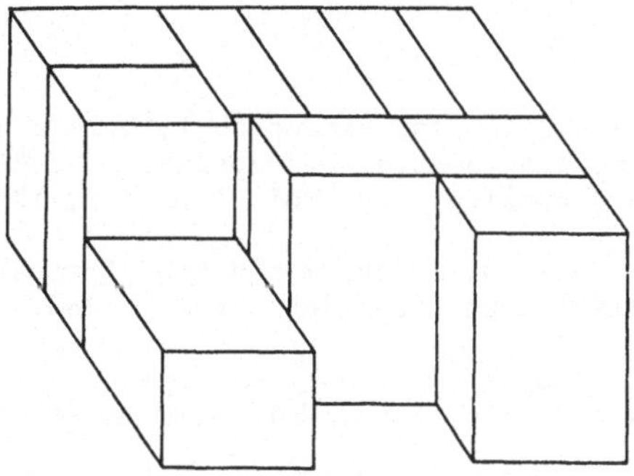

Figure 8. PP stacking with 3 different orientations illustrating the capabilities of the algorithm.

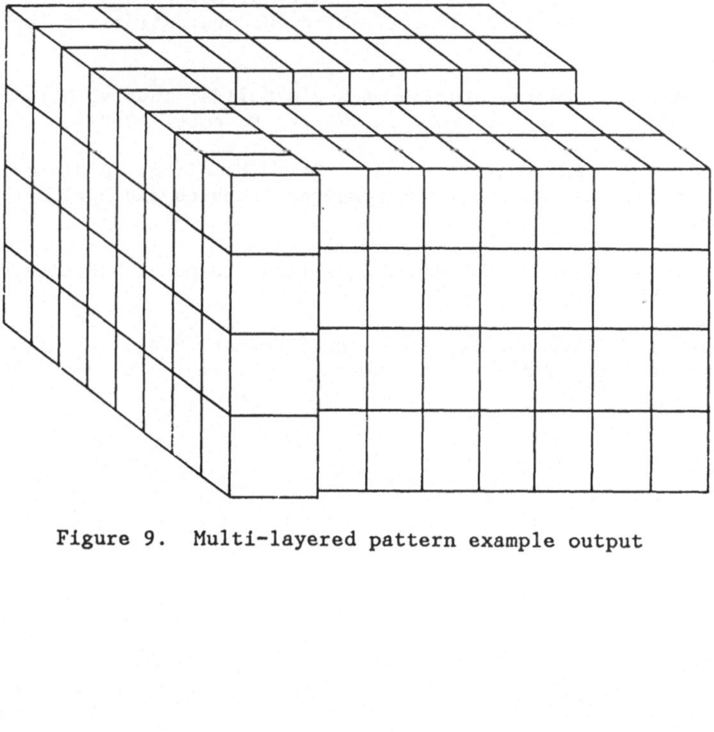

Figure 9. Multi-layered pattern example output

Conclusions

The use of a hierarchical model for constructing a pattern made by stacking a number of parallelepipeds as described in this paper is user friendly. The algorithm follows the same steps that are usually executed during loading boxes in a truck or books in boxes.

The applicability of the model has far reaching effects since most manufactured products are packaged in rectangular-shaped boxes and are usually stacked in warehouses, in pallets or loaded on trucks. The technique explained above also provides simple means for building new pattern structures, for determining engineering properties of the stack, and for studying the stability of a given stacking pattern.

References

1. Carlbom I., Chakravarty, I., and Vanderschel, D.: A Hierarchical Data Structure for Representing Spatial Decomposition of 3-D Objects, IEEE Computer Graphics and Applications, Vol. 5, April, 1985.

2. Foley, J.D., and Van Dam, A.: Fundamentals of Interactive Computer Graphics, Addison-Wesley Publishing Co., Reading, Mass., 1983.

3. Franklin, W.R.: Building an Octree from a set of Parallelepipeds, IEEE Computer Graphics and Applications, Vol. 5, October, 1985.

4. Lee, Y.T., and Requicha, A.A.G.: Algorithms for Computing Volume and Other Integral Properties of Solids. I. Known Methods and Open Issues, Communications of The ACM, Vol. 25, No. 9, 1982.

5. Lee, Y.T., and Requicha, A.A.G.: Algorithms for Computing Volume and Other Integral Properties of Solids. II. A Family of Algorithms based on Representation and Cellular Approximation, Communications of The ACM, Vol. 25, No. 9, 1982.

6. Requicha, A.A.G.: Representation of Rigid Solids: Theory, Methods, and Systems, Computing Surveys, Vol. 12, No. 4, December 1980.

7. Requicha, A.A.G., and Voelcker, H.B.: Solid Modeling: A Historical Summary and Contemporary Assessment, IEEE Computer Graphics and Applications, Vol. 2, No. 2, 1982.

8. Roth, S.D.: Ray Casting for Modeling Solids, Computer Graphics and Image Processing, Vol. 18, No. 2, 1982.

9. Sutherland, I.E., and Sproull R.F., and Shumaker, R.A.: A Characterization of Ten Hidden Surface Algorithms, Computing Surveys, Vol. 6, 1974.

Set Operation Evaluation Using Boolean Octree

D. Badouel and G. Hégron (France)

Abstract

Set operation evaluation is an important component of Geometric Modeling System (GMS). Input data can be a CSG (Constructive Solid Geometry) representation with solid primitives approximated by polyhedra. This representation is a powerful tool for solid object description. Output data will be the unique resulting polyhedral object which provides an efficient data structure in display field. With no use of spatial coherency, computational complexity of set operation is quadratic. In this paper, we are introducing a new space subdivision scheme called *Boolean Octree* which performs set operations on polyhedra in an efficient way. This structure aims at limiting set operation evaluation in a 'minimal space of calculation' where primitive boundaries intersect each other and where resulting evaluation participates in the construction of the final resulting object. *Boolean Octree* computes set operations in a local level providing a linear complexity for geometric calculations. During space subdivision, *Boolean Octree* has a global view on *local* CSG tree (projection of the CSG tree in local space) taking into account simplifications of the boolean expression , avoiding evaluation and subdivision for the object parts out of the 'minimal space of calculation'.

1 Introduction

The problem of set operation evaluation is the following : given a boolean expression, represented by a CSG tree, how can we produce as a result the unique regular solid object ? A set is *regular* if it is the closure of its interior (see [RT78]).
In Boundary representation (B_reps), an object is represented by segmenting its boundary into bounded subsets called *Faces* delimited by their bounding *Edges*. When polyhedral structure is chosen, *Faces* are polygons and *Edges* line segments. With a B_reps, the following property formally proved in [RT78] can be used :

The boundary of A<op>B is a subset of the boundaries bA and bB cf the operands A and B. Generalizing, the boundary of any object composition is included into the union of the primitive boundaries.

Thus, set operation evaluation can be treated as a problem of 'split and merge' of boundary primitives: boundary splitting when primitives intersect each other and selecting and merging the resulting sub_boundaries to make up the new solid object. Polygons of each object are split so that no two polygons 'intersect'. Two non_coplanar polygons 'intersect' if a bi_point of one of them is an interior bi_point of the other. Polygons that share a Vertex or an Edge, or that are coplanar, do not intersect. 'Split and Merge' problem can be expressed with a 'Set Membership Classification' function (see [Til80] for a general and complete description). The classification of a set A with respect to a set B divides A into subsets (called A*in*B, A*out*B, and A*on*B).

The solid A<op>B can be made up with the merging of some of the subsets resulting of the classification of B wrt A and the classification of A wrt B (different classification schemes are detailed in Section 2).

In the brute_force approach, each polygon from one polyhedron must be compared with each polygon of other polyhedra to find all possible intersections. In this case, algorithm has a quadratic complexity for geometric calculations. By the way, we lay emphasis on space subdivision. In regard of current realizations (*Exact Octree* particularly), one of our purpose was to better delimit a 'minimal space of calculation' (see Section 3): this notion leads us to define the *Boolean Octree*. As for *Exact Octree*, algorithms using this structure have a linear complexity. All methods using *Octrees*, *Exact Octrees* (or *Polytrees* which are very similar), first subdivide the set of object primitives, and then, evaluate these operations by an incremental way without taking care global simplifications.

Boolean Octree is a dynamic structure which represents a solid object. No preliminary subdivision of the solid primitives is necessary. At the beginning of the process, a Boolean Octree is the CSG tree of the operand B_reps located in the parallelepipedic enclosure of the scene. Process ending, this box has been subdivided and each resulting sub_volume (each leave of the octree) contains a description of the resulting object in this local space. Between these both states, each node of the octree contains a description of the local CSG tree : the primitive of which boundary intersect the local volume, and the polygons of each ones which intersect this volume.

Two kinds of operation can reduce a local CSG tree :

1. the evaluation of a set operation: if the configurations of both operands are 'simple' (for a local description of an object there is only one vertex, one edge, or one face) the set operation is computed.

2. the cell subdivision : if no 'simple' configuration is detected , no evaluation is made, the volume is subdivided in eight sub_boxes (*Octant*) and the CSG tree is projected in these sub_volumes.

The process ends when there is no more CSG tree in the sub_volumes. This means, each CSG tree is reduced to only one leave (one local object description).

After a short look at previous set operation evaluation methodologies, the boolean octree scheme is described. Thereafter, the local evaluation principle is presented and before the conclusion examples and results are discussed.

2 From Classification to Subdivision

To evaluate boolean combinations various methods are used in current Geometric Modeling Systems. Common aim is the splitting of solid object entities to make up the new resulting solid. Set operation methodologies can be characterized by :

1. what classification scheme is used to resolve A<op>B ?

2. what kind of structure is used to take into account space coherency ?

A presentation of different classification schemes used in Geometric Modeling System follows :

- the Geometric WorkBench (GWB) of Helsinki university uses an EDGE/FACE classification scheme (see [MS82]). Each Edge/Face intersection is evaluated and new edges are created to close the truncated polygons. Classification result is four temporary objects A*in*B, A*out*B, B*in*A, and B*out*A. The result of set operations is formed by :

- $A \cup B$: 'gluing' *AoutB* and *BoutA*
- $A - B$: 'gluing' *AoutB* and *BinA*
- $A \cap B$: 'gluing' *AinB* and *BinA*

Closure of the solid object is provided with Euler Operators. An advantage of Mäntylä's method is that the topological description of the objects is independant from the geometrical description. On the other hand, specific situations like vertices belonging to the intersection plane of two objects are not taken into account (see [MM87]). The Euler operator can make up all valid B_reps for manifold objects but cannot model all non_manifold objects.

- Requicha and Voelcker [RV85] use a EDGE/SOLID classification scheme in PADL_2 system to generate and evaluate B_reps from a CSG description. Solid/Solid intersections are evaluated to generate tentative edges. Edge/Solid classification is made on CSG with a 'divide_and_conquer' algorithm. Tentative edges that belong to the common boundary of two objects need a neighborhood information to resolve 'on/on' ambiguities. If the resulting neighborhood information is 'full' or 'empty', the edge is either inside or outside the solid and must be discarded. Otherwise, the edge is a part of the resulting object boundary. The updating of the neighborhood information can be quite complex.

- FACE/FACE classification scheme is used by Laidlaw and al. [LTH86], and Ayala and al. in the DMI system [ABJN85]. The polygons which are on the boundary of two objects are classified SAME if they have the same orientation in both objects. Otherwise, they are classified OPPOSITE. Classification of A wrt B produces four subsets of bA: A*in*B, A*on*B(SAME), A*on*B(OPPOSITE), and A*out*B. Set operation evaluation merges subsets resulting from the classification of A wrt B and the classification of B wrt A as follows :

  - $A \cup B$: *AoutB, AonB (SAME)* and *BoutA*
  - $A \cup B$: *AoutB, AonB (OPPOSITE)* and *BinA*
  - $A \cap B$: *AinB, AonB (SAME)* and *BinA*

The FACE/FACE classification is well suitable for polyhedral data structure. The basic item for classification is a polygon and neighborhood information is the orientation of the embedding plane. Closure of the resulting object can be ensure without using Euler Operators. We have chosen this classification scheme and we present its local implementation in Section 4.

Two main *location schemes* are used for geometric entities (objects, polygons ...). First by adding to each entity an information (Volume enclosure) about its location. Volume enclosures are first compared, and then entities intersection is computed if necessary. A second approach is in transforming the data structure into a hierarchical data structure like Exact Octree [BN85,Nav86], Polytree [CCV85,Car87], or BSP tree [TN87]. Then, set operations are evaluated from this new data structure.

To reduce the number of geometric calculations in their algorithm, Laidlaw and al. [LTH86] use box enclosures for the objects and for each polygon. In spite of cheaper comparison tests, a set operation complexity is still quadratic (in O(n*m) where n and m are the number of faces of both objects) . Linear complexity could be reached by hierarchizing box enclosures. This method has been advocated by Mäntylä and al. .
Mäntylä and Tamminen describe in [MT83] a 3D 'Spatial Directory' where each box enclosure

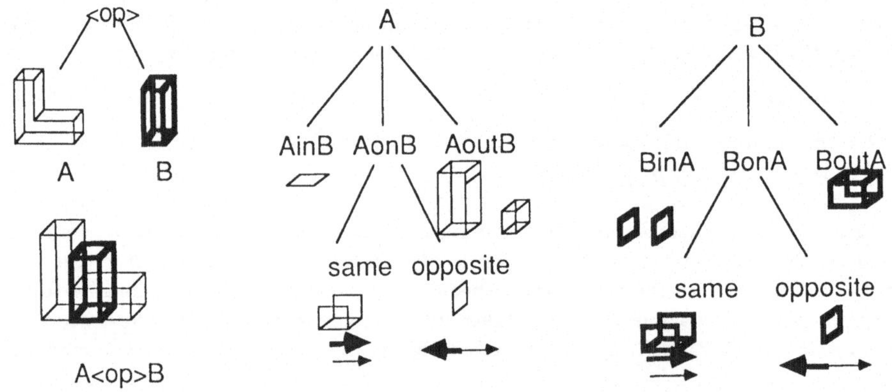

Figure 1: An example of FACE/FACE classification.

is put into cells of the directory. When adding a box in a full cell, the cell is halved to insure a maximum of entities for each cell. This is the first method which provides a linear complexity for set operations evaluation. However to compute the box enclosure for each geometric entity and to put it into the *Spatial Directory* entails a systematic pre_processing. This pre_processing could be convenient and efficient if all the applications of the Solid Modeling System used the Geometric Workbench structure(Mäntylä and Sulonen 1982).

A classical data structure used to study spatial location is the *Octree*. Nevertheless, exact representation of polyhedron is lost when the object is transformed into an Octree. To preserve polyhedral data structure *Exact Octree* or *Polytree* can be used. This kind of Octree was first suggested by Yamaguchi [YKFT84] and used for set operation evaluation by Navazo and al. [NAB86,Nav86] and Carlbom [Car87]. In addition to the classical node types of the Octree (BLACK, WHITE and GREY nodes), three new node types are defined: FACE, EDGE and VERTEX nodes which contain only one Face, one Edge, or one Vertex of the polyhedron. One difference between Exact Octree and Polytree (and also Boolean Octree) is that Exact Octree does not take into account specific situations like these :

1. case of an edge belonging to more than two polygons.

2. case of a vertex being connected to more than one cycle of polygons.

To avoid 'maximal' subdivision these specific situations have to be recognized as a unique edge and a unique vertex. In our implementation specific situations are treated in the location process and in the set operation evaluation process.
The main point of this structure is the definition of the terminal nodes which define a simpleness criterion. Complexity of a set operation using an Octree is proportionnal to the number of Octants necessary to represent each object. I. Navazo has proved in [Nav86] that with Exact Octree this number is lineary depending on the polygons in the Octants. Resulting complexity for a set operation is in O(n + m) (where n and m are the face numbers of both objects).

3 A subdivision and evaluation scheme : the Boolean Octree

Polytree (and Exact Octree) permits to delimit local spaces where the number of polygons is limited. The *Boolean Octree* is inspired by this method. In order to reduce the 'space of calculation' the construction is dynamic and consists of two alternating stages : subdivision and

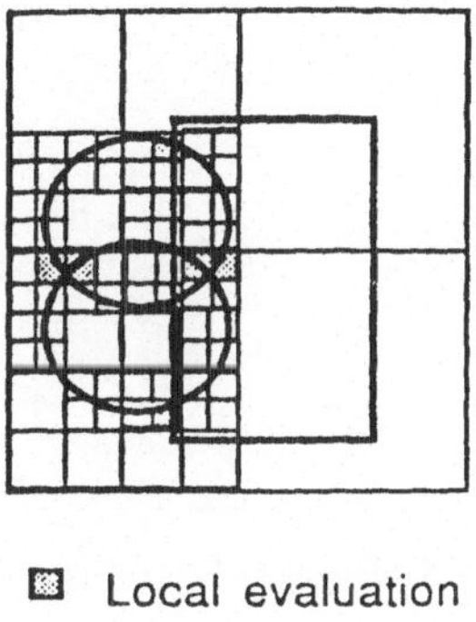

Figure 2: Space subdivision with a Polytree.

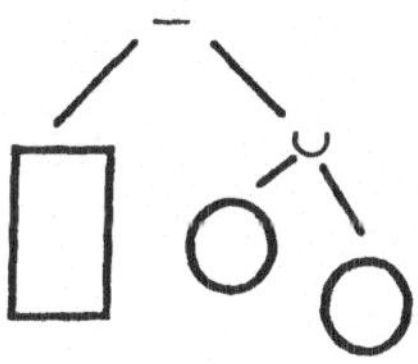

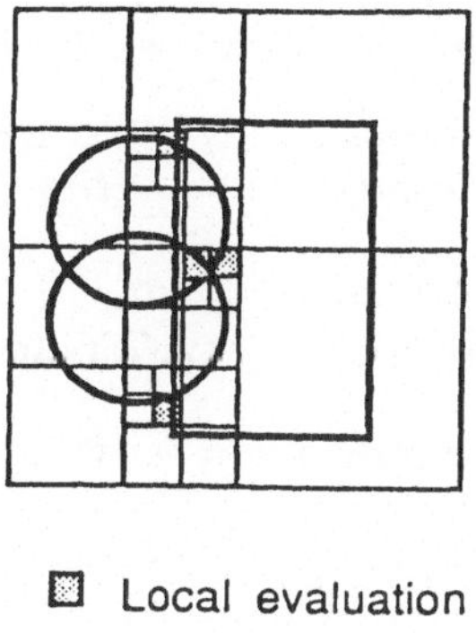

Figure 3: Space subdivision with a Boolean Octree.

evaluation. We define different spaces to delimit volumes where geometric calculations are not necessary.

- the *definition space* of an object corresponds to the volume enclosure of its boundaries. When boolean expression is evaluated, all resulting polygons are members of the *global definition space*. No evaluation out of this volume is necessary.
- the *interaction space* for an operation is the common space between its both operands. Whatever the operation may be used, no subdivision is necessary out of this space : we are out of the *definition space* of one (or both) operand. The result out of this space for the operation would be empty or reduce to the non_empty operand.
- the *calculation space* takes into account the global nature of the boolean expression (represented by the CSG tree). For each operation, it would be defined as the intersection between the *interaction space* of the operation and the *global definition space*. In this volume, geometric computations ('Split and Merge' process) are necessary, i.e. the interaction between two objects out of *calculation space* does not require evaluation.

Our choice is not the *explicit* calculation of these spaces with a structure like box enclosure. The use of an octree allows, in an adaptative way, to bring us nearer to these volumes. Decomposition level depends on the complexity of the data in a local volume.
Our purpose is to reduce as much as possible the primitive decomposition in the *interaction spaces*, and the polygon classification in the *calculation space*.
With Polytree, primitives are first converted in a polytree data structure and a set operation is made on this representation. Evaluation of the whole boolean expression is made in an ascending way. Thus, a set operator uses two polytrees as operands and the result is a new polytree which can be used in its turn as operand. Figure 2 gives a 2D example of space subdivision using a polytree. Operands are performed systematically, even if some object parts do not occur in the final object.

We formally define a Boolean Octree in BNF as follows :

$$Octree ::= CSG\_tree \mid (Octant_0, \ldots, Octant_7)$$
$$Octant_i ::= Octree$$

$$CSG\_tree ::= Item \mid (Operation,\ Subtree_{left},\ Subtree_{right})$$
$$Subtree_x ::= CSG\_tree$$

$$Operation ::= \cup, \cap, -$$

$$Item ::= \{Type,\ edge\ list,\ vertex\ list,\ polygon\ list,\ [Draught\ of\ Construction]\}$$

$$Type ::= BLACK \mid WHITE \mid GREY \mid FACE \mid EDGE \mid VERTEX$$

A 2D example of space subdivision with a Boolean Octree is shown in Fig. 3. The Boolean Octree subdivision is analogous to other Octree subdivision schemes : the box enclosure of the scene is recursively subdivided into eight Octants as far as a stopping criterion is reached. Differences with other Octree subdivisions are the data structure used in the Octants (see the BNF description) and the stopping criterion (CSG tree reduced to an Item).
Each Octant contains the projection of the CSG tree in its local volume. A CSG tree projected in an Octant is the boolean expression made of primitives, the boundary of which does not intersect the local volume are discarded. An Item contains the local description of a primitive.

When a local CSG tree is reduced to an Item, we have a local description of the final object : the evaluation is over for this volume. Otherwise, subdivision goes on and an evaluation is done for the set operations with both 'simple' operands (Item with type FACE, EDGE or VERTEX). BLACK and WHITE Items contribute to the simplification of the CSG tree. Depending on the set operator, if one of both operands is BLACK or WHITE, the corresponding sub_tree is substituted either for the other operand (or its complementary), or for a BLACK or WHITE Item (see Fig. 5).

The main procedure executes the processing from a boolean expression on polyhedra (represented by a CSG tree) as follows :

- first, executing *Subdivide* routine to make up the Boolean Octree corresponding to the boolean expression.
- then, going all over this Octree to mark which polygons are members of the final object boundary.

Space subdivision (i.e. box enclosure of the CSG tree) is 'normalized' : vertex coordinates are transformed with an ***affinity*** [1] and a ***translation*** to get values in the $0 \leftrightarrow 1024$ interval.
At the first execution of the *Subdivide* recursive routine, Items of the CSG tree have GREY Type. A space subdivision level corresponds to a recursivity level. The parameters transmitted to the *Subdivide* routine are :

- a boolean expression (CSG tree) of Items representing the final object (or a part of).
- the description of the space subdivision (Octant). An Octant is defined with the coordinates of its zero point (x, y, z) and its size.

[1] Changing scale in a different way for each of the three dimensions.

Subdivide routine cuts the transmitted Octant into eight regular sub_boxes. Zero point coordinates of each sub_Octant are computed with the three vectors VX, VY, and VZ. For each sub_Octant, the routine makes up the projection of the CSG tree in the sub_space executing the *Build_tree* routine. This new tree (CSG_tree1) is reduced when possible by the *Reduce_tree* routine. At last, if this CSG tree is reduced to only one Item, it is not be necessary to go on the subdivision process : it is the stopping criterion for the recursivity. Else, this sub_space will be also subdivided. The result of the *Subdivide* routine is a Boolean Octree reduced to an Item. Figure 4 gives the pseudocode of the *Subdivide* routine.

```
                 Vectors used to compute the zero point of the sub_Octants.
                           VX = { 0, 1, 0, 1, 0, 1, 0, 1 }
                           VY = { 0, 0, 0, 0, 1, 1, 1, 1 }
                           VZ = { 1, 1, 0, 0, 1, 1, 0, 0 }

call: Subdivide ( 0, 0, 0, 1024, CSG_tree )


procedure Subdivide ( x, y, z, size, CSG_tree ) result Octree
|   sz := size / 2 ;
|   for i=0 to 7 do
|   |   x1 := x + VX[i] * sz ;
|   |   y1 := y + VY[i] * sz ;
|   |   z1 := z + VZ[i] * sz ;
|   |
|   |   CSG_tree1 := build_tree(x1,y1,z1,sz,CSG_tree) ;
|   |   reduce_tree (CSG_tree1) ;
|   |
|   |   if CSG_tree1 is a LEAVE then
|   |   |   Octree.Octant_i := CSG_tree1.Item ;
|   |   else
|   |   |   Octree.Octant_i := Subdivide(x1,y1,z1,sz,CSG_tree1) ;
|   |   endif
|   done
end
```

Figure 4: Subdivide routine.

For each Item of the CSG tree parameter, the *Build_tree* routine selects vertices, edges, and polygons stepping into the new sub_Octant. The chosen data structure organisation is the symmetrical following data structure :

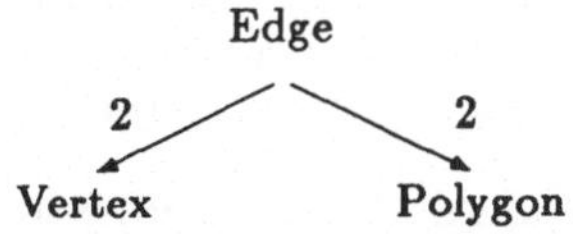

The symmetrical data structure allows faster data accesses than data structure where edges are not explicitly represented and it is less storage consuming than the winged edge data structure [Woo85]. Because of this choice, first tests in the *Build_tree* routine are realised with the edges :

1. for each edge, we determine if one of both end points is in the Octant.

Union $A \cup B$	
A	$A \cup B$
BLACK	BLACK
WHITE	B

Intersection $A \cap B$	
A	$A \cap B$
BLACK	B
WHITE	WHITE

Difference $A - B$	
A	$A - B$
BLACK	$\neg$ B
WHITE	WHITE

B	$A \cup B$
BLACK	BLACK
WHITE	A

B	$A \cap B$
BLACK	A
WHITE	WHITE

B	$A - B$
BLACK	WHITE
WHITE	A

Figure 5: Simplifications of CSG trees with BLACK or WHITE nodes.

2. if both end points of an edge are out of the Octant, we determine if this edge passes through the Octant by using a SUTHERLAND and SPROULL three_dimensionnal encoding of the vertices (see [SS68]). For a sub_Octant (decomposition level *i*), the code can be partially inherited from Octant of the *i* – *1* level as three boundary planes are common to these two Octants. If the edge crosses the Octant it is conserved, and the end points and the polygons sharing this edge too.
   The following tests are accomplished on polygons not yet selected by the previous tests. Having no edge intersecting the Octant, these polygons either are out of the Octant or pass right through the Octant.

3. does the plane embedding the polygon pass through the Octant ? The answer is given by classifying the end points of the Octant diagonals with respect to the plane.

4. if (3) is true, then the intersection Plane/Diagonal is computed and classified with respect to the polygon. If the intersection point belongs to the polygon this one crosses the Octant. As convex polygons are used, the chosen classification algorithm is the DAHAN and LE TUAN ones (see [Heg85]). The last test is the most time_consuming, consisting in the computation of the distance sign digit between the point and each edge.

Build_tree routine ending, it remains to evaluate the Octant type depending on the selected data :

- no polygon has been selected : the Type is BLACK or WHITE. The classification of an Octant point (zero point for example) with respect to the configuration of the planes in the upper_Octant allows us to conclude. Configuration of the planes in an Octant is represented with a 'Draught of Construction' (see next section).

- only one polygon and no edge : FACE Type.

- only one edge and the polygons sharing this edge. After an evaluation of a set operation, more than two polygons can share an edge. In fact in the data structure there are two (or more) edges which are equals (same end points). In the 'Split and Merge' process they are chained and considered here as a unique edge.

- there is only one vertex in the Octant, there is neither an edge nor a polygon which pass right through the Octant : VERTEX Type.

- otherwise : GREY Type.

The *Reduce_tree* routine performs a recursive simplification of the CSG tree. When BLACK or WHITE Items are present, *Reduce_tree* routine uses tables of the Fig. 5. For each set operation, if both operands are FACE, EDGE, or VERTEX Items, *Reduce_tree* calls 'Split and Merge' routine for the effective evaluation of a set operation.

4 Local evaluation

The following presentation of the 'Split and Merge' routine is succinct. More details are given in [BH88]. The routine steps are :

- the polygon splitting of both objects.
- the classification of each polygon with respect to the other object.
- the merging of the classified polygons depending on the set operation (see Tables 5).

During the set operation evaluation, a polygon can be split several times in one or more Octants. A polygon must be cut effectively only once, and further its sub_polygons will be cut. To ensure data base coherency between two different Octants, and to make splitting processing easier, a polygon is chained to its sub_polygons. With this link, accesses to the polygons not yet split (actives ones) is facilitated. This chain allows us to keep for each polygon the list of the polygons already compared with it avoiding same computation several times in different Octants.

D.H. Laidlaw [LTH86] uses a 'ray_casting' method to determine the position of a PolygonA relative to the SolidB. A ray is cast from the barycenter of polygonA in the direction of the normal vector of the embedding plane. If no PolygonB is intersected, PolygonA is classified OUTSIDE SolidB. Otherwise, the classification of PolygonA is depending on the PolygonB which intersects the ray closest to barycenter. This technique can not be used with a subdivision scheme where local description needs an information concerning the local configuration of the object. This technique acts on a global description of the objects, and thus, requires a lot of calculations for Polygon/Line intersection.
I. Navazo [Nav86] realizes classification (in an Exact Octree), using an encoding of the various potential configurations of EDGE and VERTEX nodes. To ensure an exhaustive encoding, the polygon number sharing a vertex is limited to four. This must be respected by primitive definitions. Unfortunately, during the construction of a new object, if two sub_objects intersect on a vertex, more than four polygons can shared a vertex. With these specific situations, VEXTEX configurations can not be represented by an exhaustive encoding.
We have implemented a general method which can resolve specific situations. Polygon/Solid classification is made using a 'Draught of Construction' which represents the solid configuration in an Octant. A 'Draught of Construction' is a boolean expression of half_spaces (see Fig. 6).

The half_spaces are represented by the embedding planes of polygons present in this Octant (in the Item description). Our purpose is to define, for each octant, the solid configuration as an union of convex parts (this is a canonical form). Thus, a PolygonA/SolidB classification is made using PointA/Half_spaceB classifications where the PointA is an interior point of PolygonA and Half_spaceB a half_space referenced by the 'Draught of Construction' of SolidB.
The elaboration of the 'Draught of Construction' is made as late as possible. As we use convex primitives, when the information has not been drawn up, the planes form a convex part. Nevertheless, after each operation evaluation, the 'Draught of Construction' must be made up and transformed into a canonical form (using a system of transformation rules).

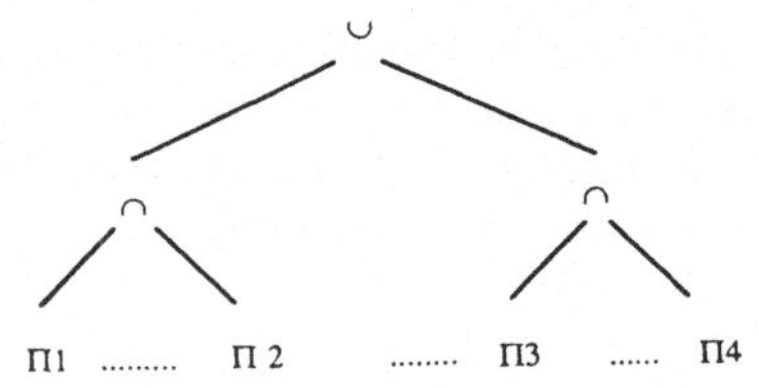

Figure 6: Draught of Construction: a union of convex parts.

5 Results and discussion

This set operation evaluation algorithm has been implemented in C language on a SUN3/160 running under Unix. The CSG description is supported by LGRC [BAP86] which is a language for geometric solid modeling, developed at IRISA. Few results are given in the Fig. 7,8,9,10. These numbers are not minimal, we do not pretend to have the fastest implementation.

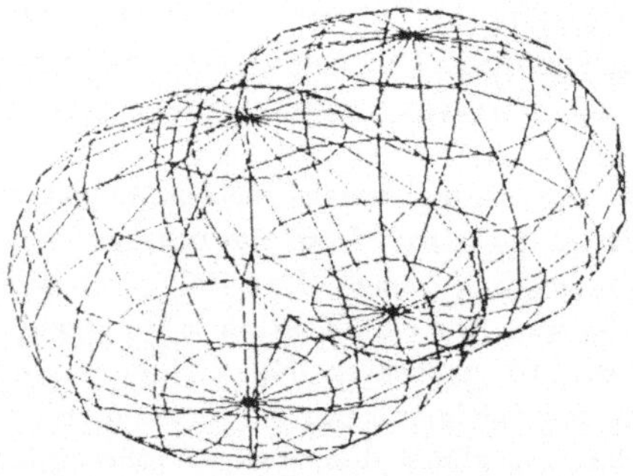

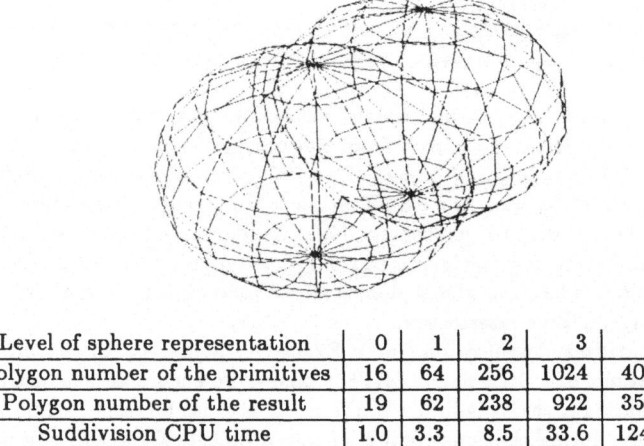

Level of sphere representation	0	1	2	3	4
Polygon number of the primitives	16	64	256	1024	4096
Polygon number of the result	19	62	238	922	3544
Suddivision CPU time	1.0	3.3	8.5	33.6	124.4
Evaluation CPU time	0.6	1.7	4.9	10.4	21.3
Total CPU time	1.6	5.0	13.4	44.0	145.7

Figure 7: An example of execution times (in sec.) depending on the number of polygons used.

Our purposes are illustrated with these three examples. Figure 8 shows us a specific configuration where primitives intersect themselves on a common edge. An other example concerns the study of the subdivision computation time relative to the terminal calculation ones (set operation evaluations with terminal Items). Figure 10 gives us CPU times of an execution depending on the minimal size of the smallest octants. A minimal size of 1024 means that no space subdivision is used and a minimal size of 1 is the smallest size. The smallest one is not the most efficient because redundant tests in neighboring Octants increase the terminal intersection computation times despite of the test avoiding the comparisons of two polygons twice. The subdivision computation time increases in an logarithmic way while the evaluation one decreases in an

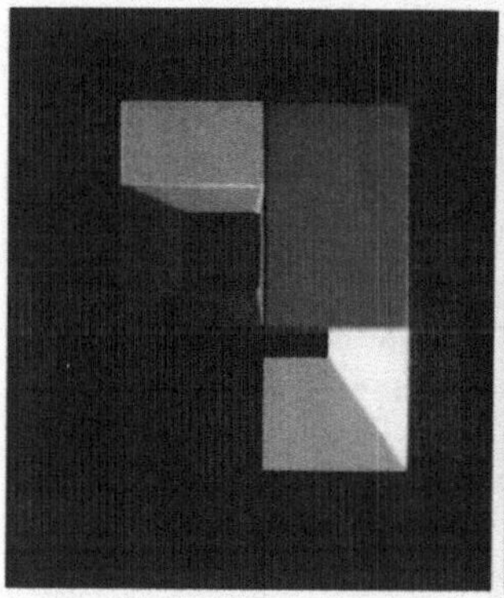

CPU time for the subdivision	0.2 sec.
CPU time for the evaluation	0.6 sec.

Figure 8: A specific situation.

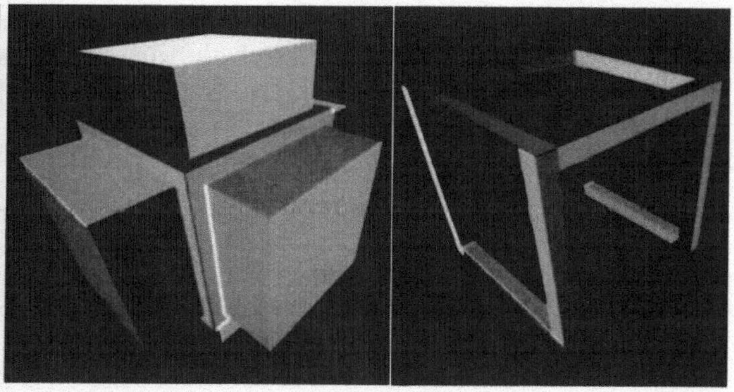

CPU time for the subdivision	0.2 sec.
CPU time for the evaluation	2.7 sec.

Figure 9: An openning block.

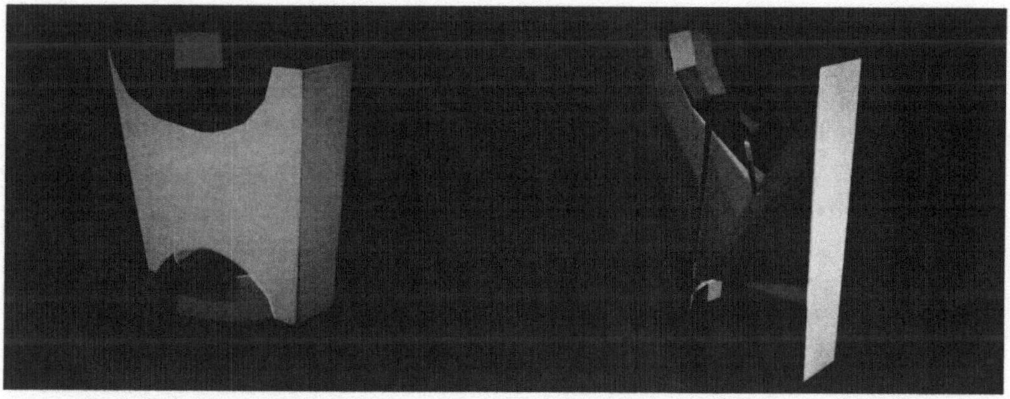

Minimal size	1024	512	256	128	64	32	16	8	4	2	1
Subdivision CPU time	0	2.2	5.5	11.5	15.0	21.2	23.9	24.1	25.0	25.5	25.6
Evaluation CPU time	1535.7	362.3	92.9	24.7	32.8	37.2	38.5	39.0	38.7	34.1	35.1
Total CPU time	1535.7	364.5	98.4	36.2	47.8	58.4	62.4	64.6	63.7	59.6	60.7

Figure 10: An example of execution times (in sec.) depending on the min_size.

exponential way. The example Fig. 7 illustates the linearity of our algorithm. With the same situation (the union of two spheres), we modify the number of polygons used with a parametric construction of the sphere.

6 Conclusion

In this paper, we have introduced a method to acheive set operation evaluation with polyhedral objects. Our current implementation uses convex primitives, but general polyhedra can be also traited adding a convexity information for the edges. We have chosen an octree structure instead of a box enclosure hierarchy to have a better knowledge on polygon location, and thus to decrease the calculation for the polygon intersections.
Future work would be an assessing study between different subdivision schemes and a study to acheive our set operation evaluation on parallel architectures. A parallel subdivision can be envisaged, but a parallel implementation of the splitting does not seem very realistic because of the data base coherency between the adjacent octants which requires data sharing between local splitting processes. This last remark leads to improve the splitting algorithm which always remains a critical point.

Acknowledgement We would like to thank Jean Luc CORRE for the software environment concerning polyhedral object description and visualization.

References

[ABJN85] D. Ayala, P. Brunet, R. Juan, and I. Navazo. Object representation by means of non minimal division quadtrees and octrees. *ACM transactions on graphics*, 4(1), 1985.

[BAP86] K. Bouatouch, B. Arnaldi, and Thierry Priol. LGRC: un langage pour la synthèse d'image par lancer de rayon. *T.S.I.*, 5(6), 1986.

[BH88] D. Badouel and G. Hégron. *Modélisation géométrique : opérations booléennes sur les polyèdres.* Technical Report, INRIA, Rennes France, 1988. à paraître.

[BN85] P. Brunet and I. Navazo. *Geometric Modelling using Exact Octree Representation of Polyhedral Objects*, page 159. EUROGRAPHICS'85, North Holland, 1985.

[Car87] I. Carlbom. An algorithm for geometric set operations using cellular subdivision techniques. *IEEE Computer graphics and applications*, may 1987.

[CCV85] I. Carlbom, I. Chakravarty, and D. Vanderschel. A hierarchical data structure for representing the spatial decomposition of 3D objects. *IEEE Computer graphics and applications*, april 1985.

[Heg85] G. Hégron. *Synthèse d'image: algorithmes élémentaires.* Dunod informatique, août 1985.

[LTH86] D.H. Laidlaw, W.B. Trumbore, and J.F. Hughes. Constructive solid geometry for polyhedral objects. *Communication of the ACM*, 20(4), august 1986.

[MM87] D. Martin and Ph. Martin. *Difficulties and errors that could occur in intersecting algorithms, for edges solids modeling.* CESTA – MARI87, Paris, La Villette, 1987.

[MS82] M. Mäntylä and R. Sulonen. GWB: a solid modeler with euler operators. *IEEE Computer graphics and applications*, september 1982.

[MT83] M. Mäntylä and M. Tamminen. Localized set operations for solid modeling. *ACM Computer Graphics*, 17(3), july 1983.

[NAB86] I. Navazo, D. Ayala, and P. Brunet. *A Geometric Modeller Based on the Exact Octtree Representaion of Polyhedra*. Computer Graphics Forum5, North Holland, 1986.

[Nav86] I. Navazo. *Contribució a les tèchniques de modelat geomètric d'objectes polièdrics usant la codificació amb arbres octals*. PhD thesis, Universitat politècnica de Catalunya, Barcelone, 1986.

[RT78] A.A.G. Requicha and R.B. Tilove. *Mathematical Foundations of Constructive Solid Geometry: General Topology of Regular Closed Sets*. Production automation project 27, University of Rochester, New_York, march 1978.

[RV85] A.A.G. Requicha and H.B. Voelcker. Boolean operations in solid modeling: boundary evaluation and merging algorithms. *Proceedings of the IEEE*, 73(1), january 1985.

[SS68] I.E. Sutherland and R.F. Sproull. *A clipping divider*, page 765. FICC Thompson books, Washington, D.C., 1968.

[Til80] R. B. Tilove. Set membership classification: a unified approach to geometric intersection problems. *IEEE Transactions on computers*, 29(10), october 1980.

[TN87] W.C. Thibault and B.F. Naylor. Set operations on polyhedra using binary space partitioning trees. *Computer Graphics*, 21(4), july 1987.

[Woo85] T. C. Woo. A combinational analysis of boundary data structure shemata. *IEEE Computer graphics and applications*, 5(3), march 1985.

[YKFT84] K. Yamaguchi, T.L. Kunii, K. Fujimura, and H. Toriya. Octree_related data structures and algorithms. *IEEE Computer graphics and applications*, 4(1), January 1984.

Efficiency of Uniform Grids for Intersection Detection on Serial and Parallel Machines

Wm. R. Franklin, N. Chandrasekhar, M. Kankanhalli, M. Seshan, and V. Akman (USA)

Abstract

The uniform grid data structure is a flat (non-hierarchical) grid whose resolution adapts to the data. An exhaustive analysis of the uniform grid data structure for determining intersections in a set of many small line segments is presented. Databases from cartography, VLSI, and graphics with up to 115,973 edges are used. For each data set the intersection time, the ratio of edge pairs tested to pairs found to intersect, and size of intermediate data structures was measured as a function of grid resolution. The execution time was relatively insensitive to the grid size over a range of up to a factor of 10. 115,973 edges were processed to find 135,050 intersections in 683 seconds on a Sun 3/50 workstation. This data structure is also ideally suited for implementation on a parallel machine. When executing on a 16 processor Sequent Balance 21000, total times averaged ten times faster than when using only one processor. Finding all 81,373 intersections in a 62,045 edge database took only 28 seconds elapsed time. This research shows that more complicated, hierarchical data structures, such as quadtrees, are not necessary for this problem.

Introduction

In diverse disciplines such as graphics, cartography, and VLSI design there are problems, such as hidden surface detection, map overlaying, and interference detection, respectively, where the fundamental, low level, operation that consumes most of the time is edge intersection. Some applications are described in Brown [3], Eastman and Yessios[6], Levin [17], Maruyama [18], Ottman, Widmayer, and Wood [20], Nievergelt and Preparata [19], Six and Wood [22], Tilove [23], and Bentley and Wood [2].

We are given from thousands to millions of small edges, very few of which intersect, and must determine the pairs of them that do intersect. Clearly, a quadratic algorithm comparing all $\binom{N}{2}$ pairs is not acceptable. A worst case solution that finds all K intersections of N edges in time $T = \theta\left(K + \frac{N\log^2 N}{\log\log N}\right)$ is presented in Chazelle [5]. However, this method has some limitations. First, it cannot find all the red-blue intersections in a set of red and blue edges without finding (or already knowing) all the red-red and blue-blue intersections. Second, it is inherently sequential, and is more difficult to parallelize. Chazelle has recently improved the time to $T = \theta(K + N\log N)$.

Alternative data structures, based on hierarchical methods such as quadtrees, have also been used extensively, Samet [21]. They are intuitively reasonable data structures to use since they subdivide to spend more time on the complicated regions of the scene. A criticism of their overuse in Geographic Information Systems in given in Waugh [24].

This paper concentrates on an alternative data structure, ***the uniform grid***. Here, a flat, non-hierarchical grid is superimposed on the data. The grid adapts to the data since the number of grid cells, or resolution, is a function of some statistic of the input data, such as average edge length. Each edge is entered into a list for each cell that is passes through. Then, in each cell, the edges in that cell are tested against each other for intersection. The grid is completely regular and is not finer in the denser regions of the data.

The uniform grid (in our use) was first presented in Franklin[7] and was later expanded by Franklin, Akman, and Wu [8, 9, 10, 11, 12, 13, 14]. In these papers the uniform grid was called an ***adaptive*** grid. However, there is another, independent and unrelated, use of the term adaptive grid in numerical analysis in the iterative solution of partial differential equations. Our papers present an expected linear time object space hidden surface algorithm that processed 10,000 random spheres packed ten deep in 383 seconds on a Prime 500. The idea was extended to a fast haloed line algorithm that was tested on 11,000 edges. The concept was applied to other problems such as point containment in polygon testing. Finally it was used, in Prolog and with multiple precision rational numbers in the map overlay problem in cartography.

However, an objection has been repeatedly raised to the uniform grid. Although it is proven theoretically and demonstrated experimentally that the grid is fast for random data, real world data appears much worse than random. Frequently some parts of a real scene are much denser than other parts so that an evenly spaced grid would appear not to work. A hierarchical technique, such as a quadtree, appears to be necessary.

However, even a quadtree cannot efficiently process all data sets. If we have N parallel edges separated by distances of N^{-p} for $p>1$, then it will take more than quadratic time to build either a uniform grid or a quadtree with cells fine enough to distinguish the edges. The plane sweep algorithm would work well in this case. However, the plane sweep cannot handle the red-blue intersection case mentioned above.

There are good reasons for assuming that data sets with one region exponentially denser than another are not common. If there are relatively sparse regions in the data, people then tend to put anything at all in to fill the vacuum. We could also define such data sets out of existence as numerical analysts do with partial differential equations. Just as they consider only equations that satisfy a Lipschitz condition where the greatest slope of a curve is bounded, we might restrict ourselves to sequences of data sets where the densest region's density, relative to the average density, remains bounded as $N \rightarrow \infty$.

This present paper presents experimental evidence that the uniform grid is an efficient means of finding intersections between edges in real world data also. The uniform grid is similar to a quadtree is the same sense that a relational database schema is similar to a hierarchical schema. The power of relational databases, derived from their simplicity and regularity, is also becoming apparent.

The uniform grid data structure is also ideally suited to execution on a parallel machine because of the simpler data structures. Also, it is more numerically robust than sweepline algorithms that have problems

In the following sections, we will review a theoretical development of the uniform grid, see the databases used to testing, and learn the test results.

Intersection Algorithm

Assume that we have N edges of length L independently and identically distributed (i.i.d.) in a 1×1 screen. We place a $G \times G$ grid over the screen. Thus each grid cell is of size $\frac{1}{G} \times \frac{1}{G}$. The grid cells partition the screen without any overlaps or omissions. The intersection algorithm proceeds as follows.

1. For each edge, determine which cells it passes through and write ordered pairs *(cell number, edge number)*.
2. Sort the list of ordered pairs by the cell number and collect the numbers of all the edges that pass through each cell.
3. For each cell, compare all the edges in it, pair by pair, to test for intersections. To determine if a pair of edges intersects, we test each edge's endpoints against the equation of the other edge. We ignore calculated intersections that fall outside the current cell. This handles the case of some pair of edges occurring together in more than one cell.

Theoretical Analysis

Let $N_{c/e}$ be the number of cells that an average edge passes through. Then, approximately,

$$N_{c/e} = (1+2LG)$$

Then N_p, the total number of (cell, edge) pairs is

$$N_p = N(1+2LG)$$

The average number of edges per cell is

$$N_{e/c} = \frac{N_p}{G^2}$$
$$= \frac{N}{G^2}(1+2LG)$$

The time to calculate the (cell, edge) pairs is

$$T_1 = N_p$$

The time to test the edges for intersections is about

$$T_2 = G^2 N_{e/c}{}^2$$
$$= \frac{N^2}{G^2}(1+2LG)^2$$

and the total time is

$$T = T_1 + T_2$$
$$= N + 2LGN + \frac{N^2}{G^2} + \frac{2LN^2}{G} + 4L^2N^2$$

This is minimized if the 2 fastest terms in the sum grow at the same speed, which occurs throughout the range from $N_{c/e} = 2$ to $N_{e/c} = 4$, i.e.

$$\frac{1}{2L} < G < \frac{2NL + \sqrt{4N^2L^2 + 16N}}{8}$$

The flatness of the time curve from about $N_{c/e} = 2$ to $N_{e/c} = 4$ is also observed experimentally. If the average is used for N then the grid is quite insensitive to nonuniform data.

What about some cells being denser since the edges are randomly distributed? Since the time to process a cell depends on the square of the number of edges in that cell, an uneven distribution might increase the total time. However, since the edges are assumed independent, the number of edges per cell is Poisson distributed, and the expected value of the square of the number of edges equals the square of the expected number of edges. Therefore the expected time doesn't increase.

Test Data

We used four different types of data sets, as follows [4].

1. The Risch Ukranian Easter egg, projected onto a plane. The multiple coincidences make this a hard case, especially for a sweep-line algorithm that must keep all the active edges ordered.
2. The state boundaries of the coterminous USA, shifted and overlaid on themselves. The multiple near correlations make this a bad case also.
3. The USGS (United States Geological Survey) DLG (Digital Line Graph) sampler tape. This represents a quadrangle around Chikamauga Tennessee that is split into 8 rectangles. Each rectangle has 4 overlays, for a total of 32 files. The overlays are
   a) hydrography,

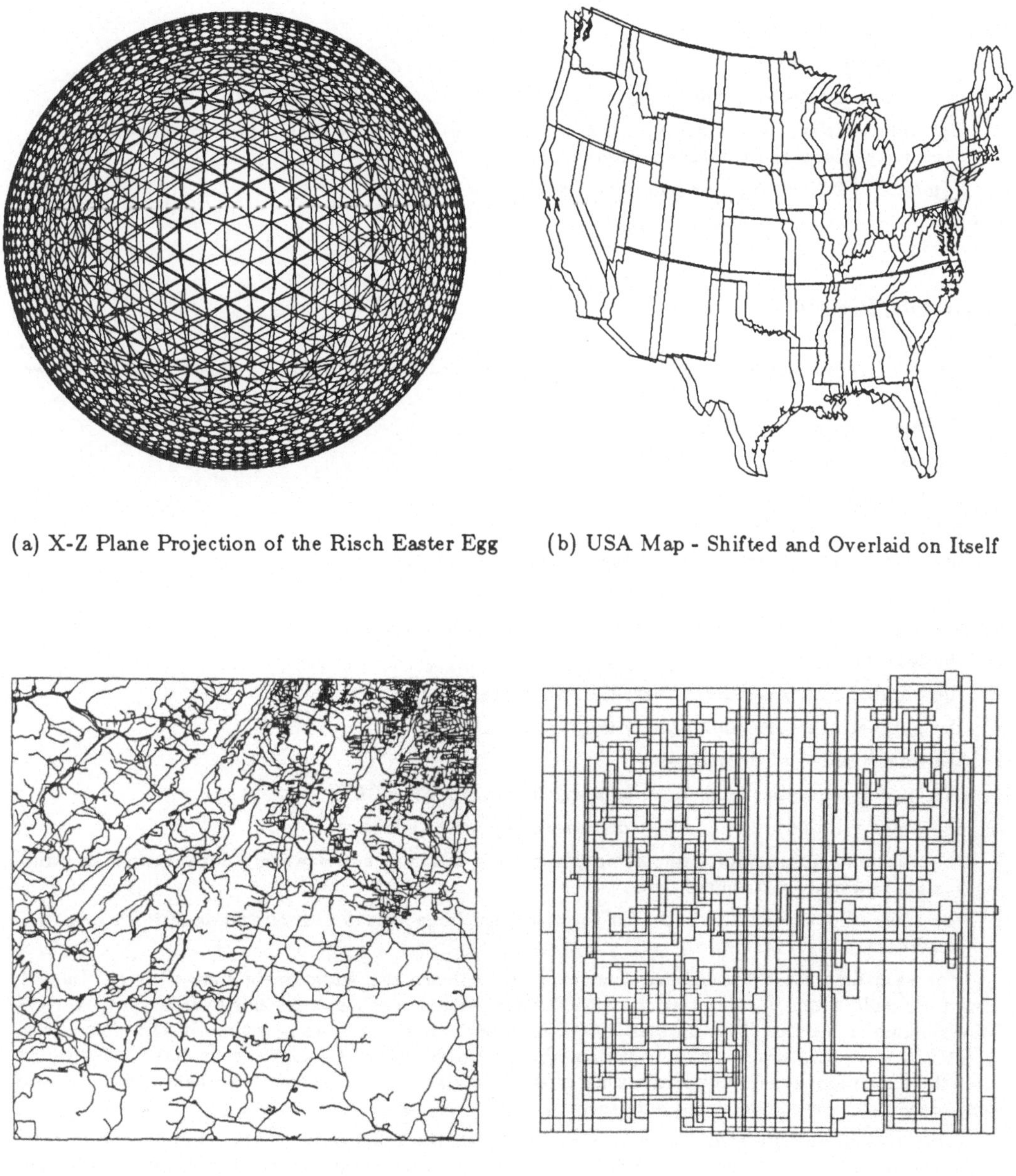

(a) X-Z Plane Projection of the Risch Easter Egg

(b) USA Map - Shifted and Overlaid on Itself

(c) Chikamauga Area 3/8 - Hydrography vs Roads & Trails

(d) CIF Data - XFACE11.MAG

Figure 1: Test Data Sets

b) roads and trails,

c) railroads, and

d) pipes and transmission lines.

Each file overlay was divided into 8 sections by USGS. These data files were sometimes processed separately and sometimes combined.

4. Some CIF (Caltech Intermediate form) VLSI data.

Sample plots of this data is shown in figure 1.

Experimental Results

For each data set, we tried different grid sizes to find the optimum. For each experiment, we measured

a) the standard deviation of edge length,

b) the number of (edge, cell) pairs,

c) the number of pairs per cell,

d) the number of pairs per edge,

e) the time in seconds to determine the pairs on the Sun 3/50,

f) the time to sort the pairs by cell number,

g) the time to pair up the edges in each cell and calculate intersections,

h) the total time,

i) the number of intersections where the two edges shared an endpoint,

j) the number of intersections where they didn't,

k) the total number of intersections,

l) the expected number of intersections, calculated from .2 N^2L^2,

m) the observed number of comparisons between pairs of edges,

n) the expected number of comparisons, assuming that the edges were independently and uniformly randomly distributed, and

o) the ratio of observed and expected comparisons; large values indicating nonuniform or correlated data.

For each data set we tried many values of G to learn the variation of time with G. Table 1 shows the results from intersecting the 18,092 edges in the roads & trails and hydrography overlays of the Chikamauga DLG. There are 23,586 intersections in all, and the best time is 93 seconds with a 275 ×275 grid. The time is within 50% of this for grids from 115 ×115 up to 800 ×800, which shows the extreme insensitivity of the time to the grid size. This is why real scenes with dense and sparse areas can be accommodated efficiently.

The economy of the grid structure is shown by the fact that only 40,031 comparisons of pairs of edges were needed to isolate the 23,586 intersections. This behavior was also observed in hidden surface algorithm described in earlier publications. There is not much room for further improvement by a hierarchical method.

Figure 2 graphs the time versus G for the USA state boundaries shifted and overlaid on themselves. The execution time is within 20% of the optimum from about $G=40$ to $G=400$ and is within a factor of two of the optimum from about $G=20$ to $G=700$. Outside these limits, the execution time starts to rise quickly.

Table 2 shows the results from processing each data set. Our biggest example overlaid all four parts of the DLG, totaling 115,973 edges of average length 0.0022. It found the 135,050 intersections in 683 seconds with a 650 ×650 grid.

The size of the grid, 422,500 cells, may appear inefficient. However, most cells are empty and, unlike in a tree data structure, an empty cell does not occupy even one word of storage, not even for a nil pointer.

Table 1: Chikamauga Area 3 - Hydrography, Roads & Trails

No. of edges	18092
Avg. edge length	0.0044
Standard deviation	0.0061
Xsects. by end pt. coincidence	23007
Xsects. by actual equation soln	579
Total intersections	23586

Grids	Pairs	P/Cell	P/Edge	Grid Time	Sort Time	Xsect Time	Total Time
10	18988	189.880	1.050	15.45	4.60	3060.15	3080.20
13	19235	113.817	1.063	15.43	4.62	2486.20	2506.25
15	19421	86.316	1.073	17.15	7.55	2101.47	2126.17
20	19959	49.898	1.103	15.58	4.75	1370.98	1391.31
25	20420	32.672	1.129	16.17	5.17	927.71	949.05
30	20888	23.209	1.155	15.83	4.92	689.41	710.15
40	21931	13.707	1.212	15.78	4.92	421.88	442.58
50	22862	9.145	1.264	15.88	5.10	308.15	329.14
65	24378	5.770	1.347	16.18	5.50	217.57	239.26
80	25841	4.038	1.428	16.50	5.80	168.63	190.93
100	27713	2.771	1.532	16.95	6.27	131.89	155.11
115	29187	2.207	1.613	17.47	6.53	114.10	138.09
125	30131	1.928	1.665	17.72	6.70	105.30	129.71
140	31572	1.611	1.745	18.22	7.15	95.23	120.60
150	32496	1.444	1.796	18.47	7.20	89.38	115.05
160	33514	1.309	1.852	18.77	7.47	84.50	110.73
175	35005	1.143	1.935	19.33	8.07	79.40	106.80
200	37340	0.933	2.064	20.15	8.38	72.06	100.60
275	44483	0.588	2.459	22.63	10.03	60.61	93.28
325	49373	0.467	2.729	24.68	11.42	57.48	93.58
400	56617	0.354	3.129	28.72	13.37	55.01	97.10
500	66222	0.265	3.660	30.92	16.03	56.05	103.00
625	78304	0.200	4.328	36.22	19.25	56.70	112.16
800	95143	0.149	5.259	45.91	24.13	61.85	131.89
1000	114419	0.114	6.324	61.35	30.20	69.01	160.56

Execution in Parallel

The uniform grid method is ideally suited to execution on a parallel machine since it mostly consists of two types of operations that run well in parallel: applying a function independently to each element of a set to generate a new set, and sorting. Determining which cells each edge passes through is an example of the former operation.

We implemented several versions of the algorithm on a Sequent Balance 21000 computer, which contains 16 National Semiconductor 32000 processors [1, 15], and compared the elapsed time when up to 15 processors were used to the time for only one processor [16]. The speedup ratios ranged from 8 to 13. Figure 3 shows the results from processing 3 overlays of the United State Geological Survey Digital Line Graph, totaling 62,045 edges. 81,373 intersections were found. The

Table 2: Summary of Results from Processing All the Data Sets

Serial Computation						
Database	Edges	Length	Std Dev	Xsects	Grid Size	Time
Risch Egg - YZ Projection	5897	0.0355	0.0124	39666	100	194.24
XZ Projection	5897	0.0391	0.0132	37415	115	193.18
XY Projection	5897	0.0352	0.0131	40177	80	183.83
USA Map	915	0.0186	0.0245	1078	125	4.97
Shifted by 2% and overlaid on itself	1830	0.0184	0.0243	2430	140	14.38
Shifted by 10% & overlaid	1830	0.0180	0.0237	2348	125	12.57
Chikamauga Area 1 - Hydrography, Roads & Trails	13712	0.0044	0.0084	15039	275	68.50
Area 2, HR&T	14145	0.0049	0.0080	16595	275	71.11
Area 3, HR&T	18092	0.0044	0.0061	23586	275	93.28
Area 4, HR&T	16425	0.0048	0.0076	20335	200	88.58
Area 5, HR&T	12869	0.0053	0.0103	14978	275	62.93
Area 6, HR&T	13871	0.0050	0.0080	16072	275	69.40
Area 7, HR&T	13579	0.0134	0.0518	16640	160	188.76
Area 8, HR&T	11937	0.0048	0.0098	13283	275	58.86
All sections - Railroads	1122	0.0159	0.0543	1316	150	8.10
Pipe & Transmission Lines	850	0.0277	0.0523	1211	115	7.95
Railroads, Pipe & Transmission Lines	1972	0.0206	0.0533	2745	115	22.28
Railroads, Pipe & Transmission Lines Overlaid on itself	3944	0.0206	0.0533	13268	115	84.15
Hydrography, Railroads, Pipe & Transmission Lines	55973	0.0023	0.0162	53426	500	323.09
Roads & Trails, Railroads, Pipe & Transmission Lines	62045	0.0026	0.0106	81373	500	436.35
Hydrography, Roads & Trails, Railroads, Pipe & Trans. Lines	115973	0.0022	0.0115	135050	650	682.51
VLSI Data - XFACEA.MAG	436	0.0314	0.0908	1403	150	5.22
VLSI Data - XFACELL.MAG	1960	0.0467	0.0852	6488	65	16.87
VLSI Data - XFACELL.MAG - Rotated by 30 deg.	1960	0.0352	0.0643	6488	125	32.48
VLSI Data - XFACELL.MAG - Rotated by 90 deg.	1960	0.0467	0.0852	6488	65	18.67

Parallel Computation							
Database	Edges	Xsects	Grid Size	Time Taken For			
				1 Proc	5 Procs	10 Procs	15 Procs
Risch Egg - YZ Projection	5897	39666	100	98.91	24.02	14.19	11.96
XZ Projection	5897	37415	115	97.88	23.55	14.83	11.81
XY Projection	5897	40177	80	92.33	20.33	12.36	10.40
Roads & Trails, Railroads, Pipe & Transmission Lines	62045	81373	250	273.11	62.98	39.42	27.77
Random Edges of Size 0.01	50000	45719	100	521.06	108.90	57.88	40.15

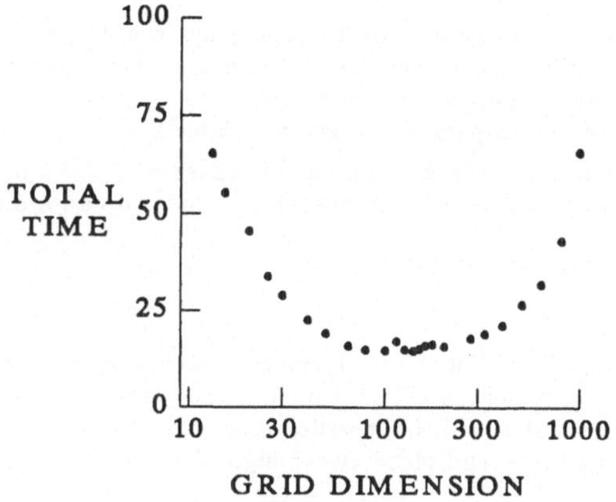

Figure 2: Graph of Time vs Grid Resolution for the USA Overlaid on Itself

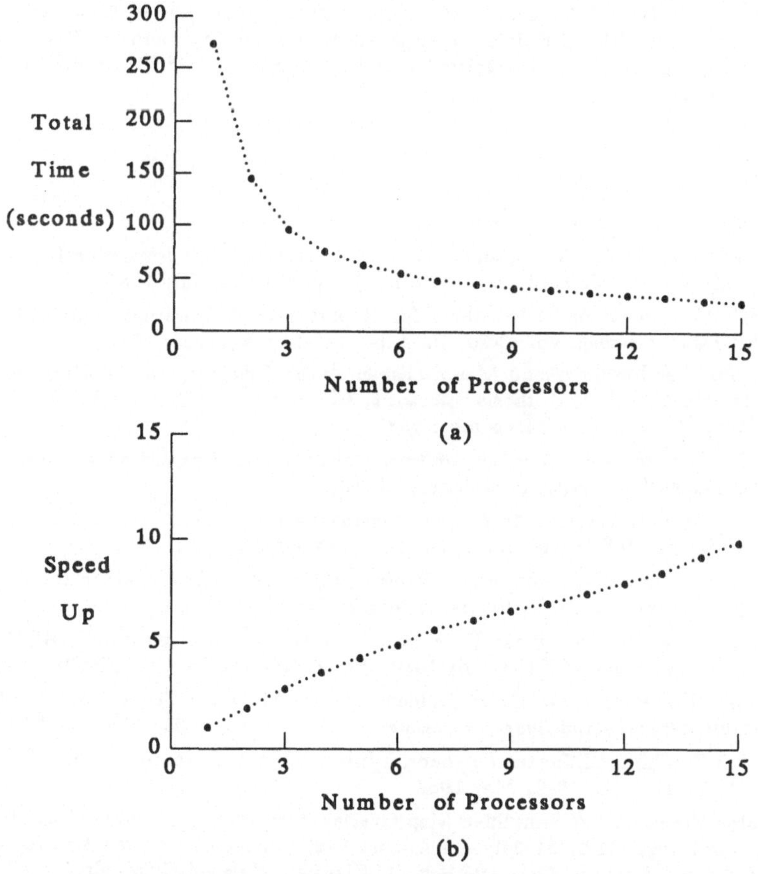

Figure 3: Time and Speedup When Intersecting the 62045 Edges in the Roads & Trails, Railroads, and Pipes and Transmission Lines Overlays of the Chikamauga DLG in Parallel on 1 to 15 Processors. Grid Size = 250. 81,373 Intersections Found.

time for one processor was 273 seconds, and for 15 processors was 28 seconds, for a speedup of about 10. This is a rate of 7.9 million edges and 10.5 million intersections per hour. For other data sets, these extrapolated times would depend on those data sets' number of intersections per edge. Times for intersecting other data sets in parallel are given in table 2.

Finally, the speedup, as a function of the number of processors, was still rising smoothly at 15 processors. This means that we should achieve an even bigger speedup on a more parallel machine.

Conclusion

We have answered the objection that the uniform grid is suitable for only evenly spaced data by showing experimentally that it is just as efficient on unevenly spaced, real data. Since it is also very easy to implement, and executes well on parallel machines, there is now no need for more complicated methods such as quadtrees and plane-sweep algorithms.

Acknowledgements

This work was supported by the National Science Foundation under PYI grant no. DMC-8351942. Don Porter of RPI's Information and Technology Services allowed us to drag down his Suns running the time tests. The CIF data was supplied by Jim Guilford, and the Risch Easter Egg by Julian Gomez. Their assistance is appreciated especially since it is surprisingly difficult to obtain large real graphic databases.

References

1. Sequent Computer Systems Inc., *Balance Technical Summary,* 1986.
2. J.L. Bentley and D. Wood, "An Optimal Worst Case Algorithm for Reporting Intersections of Rectangles," *IEEE Trans. Comput.*, vol. C-29, no. 7, pp. 571-576, July 1980.
3. K.Q. Brown, "Comments on 'Algorithms for Reporting and Counting Geometric Intersections'," *IEEE Trans. Comput.*, vol. C-30, no. 2, pp. 147-148, February 1981.
4. Narayanaswami Chandrasekhar and Manoj Seshan, "The Efficiency of the Uniform Grid for Computing Intersections," M.S. thesis, Electrical, Computer, and Systems Engineering Dept., Rensselaer Polytechnic Institute, December 1987.
5. B.M. Chazelle, *Reporting and Counting Arbitrary Planar Intersections,* CS-83-16, Dept. of Computer Science, Brown University, Providence, RI, 1983.
6. C.M. Eastman and C.I. Yessios, *An Efficient Algorithm for Finding the Union, Intersection, and,* Sept. 1972. Carnegie-Mellon University, Dept. of Computer Science
7. W. Randolph Franklin, *Combinatorics of Hidden Surface Algorithms,* Center for Research in Computing Technology, Harvard University, June 1978. Ph.D. thesis
8. Wm. Randolph Franklin, "A Linear Time Exact Hidden Surface Algorithm," *ACM Computer Graphics,* vol. 14, no. 3, pp. 117-123, July 1980. Proceedings of SIGGRAPH'80
9. Wm. Randolph Franklin, "An Exact Hidden Sphere Algorithm That Operates In Linear Time," *Computer Graphics and Image Processing,* vol. 15, no. 4, pp. 364-379, April 1981.
10. Wm. Randolph Franklin, "Efficient Polyhedron Intersection and Union," *Proc. Graphics Interface'82,* pp. 73-80, Toronto, 19-21 May 1982.
11. Wm. Randolph Franklin, "A Simplified Map Overlay Algorithm," *Harvard Computer Graphics Conference,* Cambridge, MA, 31 July - 4 August 1983. sponsored by the Lab for Computer Graphics and Spatial Analysis, Graduate School of Design, Harvard University.
12. Wm. Randolph Franklin, "Adaptive Grids For Geometric Operations," *Proc. Sixth International Symposium on Automated Cartography (Auto-Carto Six),* vol. 2, pp. 230-239, Ottawa, Canada, 16-21 October 1983.

13. Wm. Randolph Franklin and Varol Akman, *A Simple and Efficient Haloed Line Algorithm for Hidden Line Elimination,* Univ. of Utrecht, CS Dept., Utrecht, October 1985. report number RUU-CS-85-28

14. Wm. Randolph Franklin and Peter Y.F. Wu, *A Polygon Overlay System in Prolog,* Autocarto 8 Conference, Baltimore, March-April 1987.

15. Marta Kallstrom and Shreekant Thakkar, "Programming three Parallel Computers," *IEEE Software,* vol. 5, no. 1, pp. 11-22, January 1988.

16. Mohan Kankanhalli, "Uniform Grids for Lines Intersection in Parallel," M.S. Thesis, Electrical,Computer & Systems Engineering Dept., Rensselaer Polytechnic Institute, Troy, NY, February 1988.

17. J.Z. Levin, "Mathematical Models For Determining the Intersections of Quadric Surfaces," *Computer Graphics and Image Processing,* vol. 11, pp. 73-87, 1979.

18. K. Maruyama, "A Procedure to Determine Intersections Between Polyhedral Objects," *Int. J. Comput. Infor. Sc.,* vol. 1, no. 3, pp. 255-266, 1972.

19. J. Nievergelt and F.P. Preparata, "Plane-Sweep Algorithms for Intersecting Geometric Figures," *Comm. ACM,* vol. 25, no. 10, pp. 739-747, October 1982.

20. Thomas Ottmann, Peter Widmayer, and Derick Wood, "A Fast Algorithm for the Boolean Masking Problem," *Computer Vision, Graphics, and Image Processing,* vol. 30, pp. 249-268, Academic Press, 1985.

21. H. Samet, "The Quadtree and Related Hierarchical Data Structures," *ACM Computing Surveys,* vol. 16, no. 2, pp. 187-260, June 1984.

22. H.-W. Six and D. Wood, "The Rectangle Intersection Problem Revisited," *BIT,* vol. 20, pp. 426-433, 1980.

23. R.B. Tilove, "Set Membership Classification: A Unified Approach to Geometric Intersection Problems," *IEEE Trans. Comput.,* vol. C-29, no. 10, pp. 874-883, October 1980.

24. T.C. Waugh, "A Response to Recent Papers and Articles on the Use of Quadtrees for Geographic Information Systems," *Proceedings of the Second International Symposium on Geographic Information Systems,* pp. 33-37, Seattle, Wash. USA, 5-10 July 1986.

Adjacency Finding Algorithms in a Variable-Resolution Boundary Model

L. De Floriani (Italy)

Abstract

A variable-resolution boundary model of three dimensional objects provides a representation of the surfaces enclosing it at successively finer levels of specification. A hierarchical graph structure, called a structured edge-face graph (SEFG) is described, which encodes the boundary of a solid object at variable resolution is described. The structured edge-face graph is based on a face-oriented relational description of the object boundary. The concept of adjacency relation between pairs of primitive boundary entities at fixed accuracy is introduced, and adjacency finding algorithms which operate on a structured edge-face graph object representation are presented.

1. Introduction

Object representation plays an important role in computer graphics, where object models are used to produce digital images of the real world, and in computer vision, where object models are used to achieve an automatic understanding of real world shapes represented by digital images. Boundary (or surface-based) representations have been widely used for surface rendering and seem also to be the natural choice for detailed general-purpose object models in the 3D vision problem, where input data are usually related to visual surface information [Bes85]. Classical boundary schemes have the advantage of producing detailed descriptions of objects of arbitrary shape, but they cannot represent objects at different levels of abstraction as required to achieve data reduction when dense samples of points defining the object surface are given.

Variable-resolution object representations, on the other hand, provide efficient tools for 3D vision and graphics, since they allow the manipulation of objects at increasingly higher levels of detail and the application of efficient algorithms based on a divide-and-conquer approach [Fau83, Sam84]. Examples of hierarchical object representations are the octree [Mea82], the prismtree [Fau83], the hierarchical triangulations [DeF84, Dut83, Gom79], or the Delaunay tree [Boi86],

Variable-resolution models based on boundary representation provide strictly object-dependent polyhedral descriptions of the surfaces enclosing an object and allow both a fast surface rendering by the application of ray tracing algorithms, and an efficient detection of object intersection [Dob83]. A variable-resolution boundary representation can be regarded as a tree structure in which the root provides a polyhedral description of an object at the highest level of abstraction, whereas any other node describes a segmentation of a face belonging to its parent in the tree. An approximation error is usually associated with any face further refined into a connected set of faces. A variable-resolution boundary model (VRBM) can be viewed as a generalization of hierarchical curve representations like the striptree [Bal81]. In the most general case, such a surface model will be based on faces of arbitrary shape, and, thus, it cannot be described by a segmentation tree like quadtree-based surfaces [Sam84] or hierarchical triangulations [DeF84]. The possibility of having arbitrarily-shaped faces relaxes the constraints imposed by the fixed splitting rules of triangle-based models, and allows the application of general split-and-merge strategies based on suitable approximation criteria to any initial surface segmentation or to any set of points defining the object boundary. Note that a VRBM id different from the hierarchical boundary model described in [DeF88] for CAD/CAM applications, since this latter represents the decomposition of the boundary of a solid object into its form features, and, like the CSG tree [Req81], is a fixed-resolution model.

Crucial problems of any object representation are the choice of an efficient encoding structure and the definition of suitable structure accessing algorithms which allow the complete reconstruction of the object. In the paper, we describe a graph-based structure for representing the three primitive entities defining the boundary of an object (i.e., its faces, edges and vertices), and a subset of their mutual adjacency relations at variable levels of abstraction. The resulting hierarchical structure, called a <u>structured edge-face graph</u> [DeF86], is a hierarchy of edge-face graphs, each describing a portion of the object boundary.

In the remainder of this paper, we define algorithms which reconstruct the adjacency relations between pairs of primitive entities at different levels of accuracy. For instance, given a face f of an object S, we show how to retrieve from the model those faces sharing an edge with f and having an error associated which is less or equal to a predefined threshold value. In a polyhedral environment, nine mutual adjacency relations can be defined over the three primitive boundary entities [Wei85]. Here, we define the nine relations at finite precision, thus taking into account the approximation error associated with the object faces, and we concentrate on those relations which connect the three primitive entities to the object faces. The structured edge-face graph, together with the algorithms for reconstructing the nine adjacency relations at any fixed precision, provides a complete variable-resolution description of the boundary of a solid object.

2. <u>The structured edge-face graph</u>

A <u>boundary representation</u> (Brep) B of a solid object S is a segmentation of its boundary into a collection of quasi-disjoint subsets, called <u>faces</u>, where each face is in turn represented by its bounding <u>edges</u> and <u>vertices</u> [Wei85, Woo85]. A <u>variable-resolution boundary model</u> (VRBM) of the boundary of an object S defines a set of approximations of the surfaces enclosing it at different levels of abstraction. An approximation of the boundary B of S will be a surface-based representation of an object S', the boundary of which is sufficiently "close" to that of S.

If V is the set of points in the 3D space defining the boundary of an object S, an approximation B' of the boundary B of S will be a planar-faced polyhedron consisting of a set of faces with vertices at a subset V' of V. The accuracy of any approximation can be evaluated by computing a distance-based error. The error associated with an approximation B' of B is defined as the maximum approximation error at the faces forming B'.

Each face f of B' will have an error associated which is evaluated as the maximum distance of the points in V-V', whose orthogonal projections fall within f, from the surface defining f. Hence, B' and its approximation error define a three-dimensional strip which encloses S.

A variable-resolution boundary model is described by a tree, in which the root gives the boundary description of S at the highest abstraction level, while any other tree node defines a boundary specification of a face in its parent at a higher resolution. The portions Bi of the boundary of S described by the various tree nodes are called components. The root component is denoted B0, whereas any other component Bi will be the expansion component of a face fi, called a macroface, belonging to the parent Bj of Bi. Figure 1b shows a variable-resolution representation of the object in Fig. 1a. The root component B0 describes the cube, which defines the representation of the object at the highest abstraction level. B1 and B2 define a boundary specification of f1 and f2 respectively: B1 and B2 are thus expansion components of macrofaces f1 and f2 respectively. Each arc of the tree describes the association between a macroface fi and its expansion graph Bi, and is labeled fi. From a variable-resolution boundary model it is possible to extract approximations of the object boundary at fixed accuracy by recursively replacing macrofaces with their expansion components [DeF86]. Only the root component describes the boundary of a valid three dimensional object (see, for instance, the example in figure 1). To transform any other component Bi into a boundary representation of a valid object, we complete Bi with a dummy face, which is bounded by the boundary edges of Bi, i.e., by the edges of Bi belonging to only one face of Bi. The dummy face of Bi will correspond to the macroface in its parent component Bj expanded into Bi. Thus, we denote the dummy face of Bi by fi' and the "completed" variable-resolution model by B*.

A VRBM B* of an object S can be described by a hierarchical graph-based structure in which each node is a relational description of a component of B*. A relational boundary model of a polyhedral object with a single shell and simply-connected faces is defined in terms of the three primitive topological entities describing its boundary, i.e., faces, edges and vertices, and of a suitably chosen subset of their nine mutual adjacency relations [Woo85]. Examples of relational boundary models are the winged-edge structure and its variants [Wei85], the symmetric structure [Woo85], or the face-based boundary graphs [Ans85], which differ in the number and in the kind of relations they explicitly store.

The graph-based model we propose, called a structured edge-face graph, is a combination of a hierarchical structure describing the different levels of abstraction and of a relational model representing portions of the object boundary, called an edge-face graph [Ans85]. The edge-face graph (EFG) representing the boundary of an object S is defined as a pair G=(N,A), where N denotes the set of nodes of G and A the set of its arcs such that

(i) Each node of N represents exactly one face f of S.

(ii) For every edge e shared by two faces f' and f" and connecting two vertices v' and v", there exists exactly one arc in A joining nodes f' and f" and labeled (v',v").

The face-edge and the edge-face relations are represented in the EFG by the incidencies of the arcs of G into its nodes, while the edge-vertex relation is encoded into the labels attached to the arcs of G. The face-edge relation has been shown to be individually sufficient to provide an unambiguous description of the boundary of a solid object [Wei85]. The other two relations are encoded for efficiency.

Given a VRBM B* of an object S and denoted the edge-face graph describing a component Bi of B* by Gi=(Ni,Ai), then the family {G0,G1,...,Gn} defines a hierarchy of edge-face graphs, called a structured edge-face graph (SFEG) and denoted by G*. The root G0 of G* describes the root component B0 of B*, while any other component Gi of G* is the relational representation of a component Bi of B*. If Bi is the boundary specification of a macroface fi in its parent component Bj, then Gi will be the expansion graph of node fi belonging to its parent graph Gj. Node fi is called a macronode. Figure 2 shows the SEFG describing the variable resolution model depicted in Fig. 1. The root graph G0 contains two macronodes f1 and f2, which correspond to the two faces of B0 further refined in the hierarchical model. Graphs G1 and G2 describe B1 and B2, and thus are the expansion graphs of f1 and f2 respectively.

The connection between a boundary component Bi of B* and its parent component Bj is defined by the macroface fi of Bj expanded into Bi and by the dummy face fi' which completes Bi. Such an association is established by mapping the edges bounding fi into those bounding fi'. Hence, the parent-child relation between the corresponding components Gi and Gj in the SEFG G* describing B* is defined by the pair (fi, fi'), where fi is the macronode of Gi corresponding to macroface fi and fi' is the dummy node of Gi corresponding to the dummy face fi': every arc e of Gj incident to node fi is associated with that arc e' of Gi incident to node fi' which corresponds to the edge e' of Bi associated with edge e.

3. Face-based adjacency relations at finite precision

The structured edge-face graph represents the faces, edges and vertices of an object together with three of their mutual adjacency relations in a hierarchical form. The basic problem in connection with any boundary data structure is to retrieve the possible adjacency relations from the structure without errors or ambiguities [Wei85]. Once a model has been shown to be sufficient to represent the boundary of a solid object unambiguously, suitable structure accessing primitives must be provided to reconstruct those relations not explicitly stored in the model. In a VRBM, structure accessing algorithms capable of retrieving any adjacency information at any predefined degree of accuracy must be defined. Such algorithms combine suitable tree traversing strategies with the techniques used to extract adjacency information from the edge-face graph.

Since in our model the error value is associated with the object faces, we consider first the three adjacency relations which connect each of the three primitive entities to the object faces, namely the Face-Face, the Edge-Face and the Vertex-Face relations, that we term face-based adjacency relations, for brevity. Note that the edge-face relation is the only one encoded in the EFG. The model gives, however, only the two faces sharing a given edge in a single component.

Given a variable-resolution representation B* of an object S and an accuracy value Eps, the queries corresponding to the face-based relations at degree Eps of accuracy can be defined as follows.

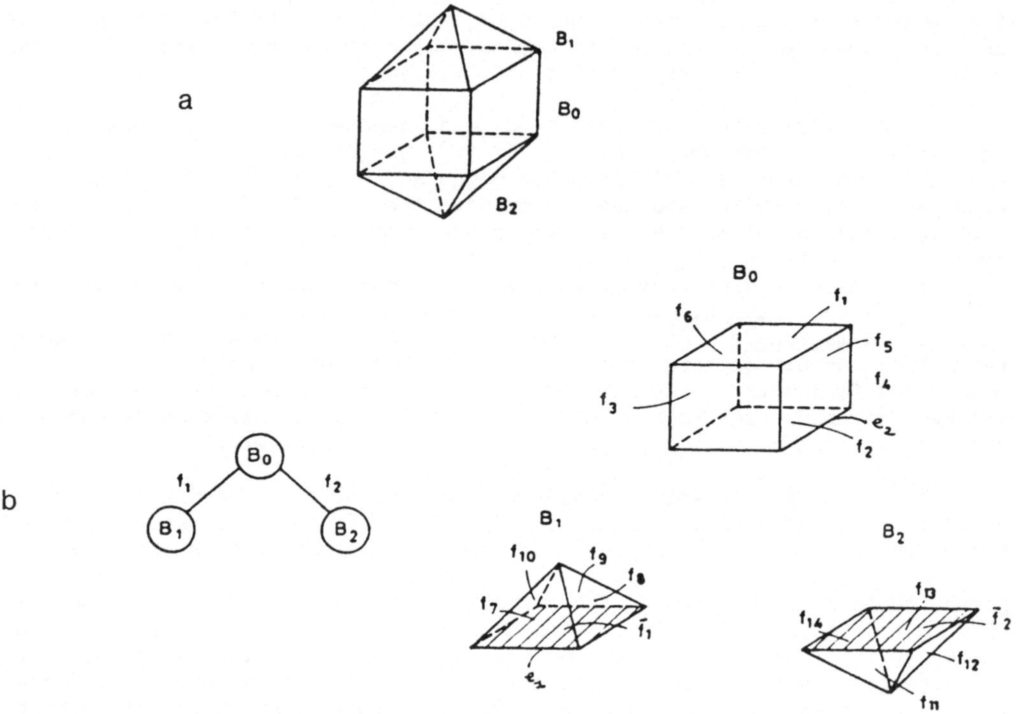

Figure 1: An example of variable-resolution boundary model of an object.

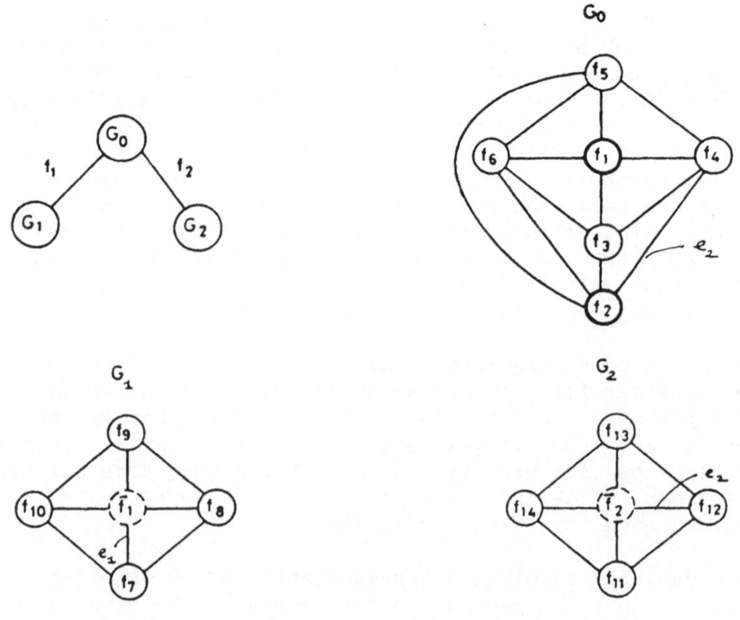

Figure 2: Structured edge-face graph description of the variable-resolution model of Fig. 1.

Face-Face query
Given a face f of S, find all the faces f' of S such that
(i) There exists an edge e in S shared by f and f'
(ii) Error(f)<=Eps
(iii) If Bk is the component of B* containing f', then, for every face f" belonging to the parent of Bk in B* and sharing edge e or a part of it with f, Error(f")>Eps.

Edge-Face query
Given an edge e of S, find all the faces f' of S such that
(i) f' is bounded by e or by a part of e
(ii) Error(f')<=Eps
(iii) If Bk is the component of B* containing f, then, for every face f" bounded by e or by a part of it and belonging to the parent of Bk in B*, Error(f")>Eps.

Vertex-Face query
Given a vertex v of S, find all the faces f' of S such that
(i) v is a bounding vertex of f'
(ii) Error(f')<=Eps
(iii) If Bk is the component of B* to which f' belongs, then, for every f" belonging to the parent of Bk in B* and satisfying condition (i), Error(f")>Eps.

Both the Face-Face and Edge-Face queries can be expressed in terms of a single edge-adjacency query, which consists of retrieving the collection of the faces of S sharing a given edge e with a given face f and having an error associated less or equal to the given threshold value Eps. The edge-adjacency query at degree Eps of accuracy can be defined as follows. Given a face f of S and an edge e bounding f, find all the faces f' of S such that (i) f' and f share edge e or a part of e; (ii) Error(f')<=Eps; and (iii) If Bk is the component of B* containing f', then, for every f" belonging to the direct ancestor of Bk in B* and satisfying condition (i), Error(f")>Eps.

In the following two subsections, we define algorithms for answering the edge adjacency and the Vertex-Face queries on a VRBM B* at fixed accuracy by assuming the SEFG as basic encoding structure of B*.

3.1 An edge-adjacency finding algorithm

In terms of the SEFG representation, the edge-adjacency query at degree Eps of accuracy can be stated as follows. Given a node f of a component Gi of G* and an arc e of Gi incident into f, find all the nodes f' of G* such that (i) if Gk is the component of G* to which f' belongs and e' an arc of Gk corresponding to e, then f' is an extreme node of e' in Gj; (ii) Error(f')<=Eps; and (iii) for every node f" belonging to a direct ancestor Gj of Gk such that there exists an arc e" in Gj corresponding to arc e and incident to node f", Error(f")>Eps.

Algorithm EDGE_ADJACENT_FACES described below returns the list of the faces adjacent to a given face f along an edge e of f at degree Eps of accuracy. It locates the faces which are adjacent to f by ascending the tree describing the SEFG until a common ancestor to the component containing f and to those containing its edge-adjacent faces is located, and then descending the tree by looking for those adjacent faces which have an error less or equal to Eps. A similar approach is used in neighbor finding algorithms which operate on regular decompositions like the quadtree and related structures [Sam84]. The basic difference with respect to such algorithms is that the search direction cannot be established in our case by looking at the position of the face in the boundary decomposition. A Pascal-like description of algorithm EDGE_ADJACENT_FACES and of the recursive procedure EXPAND_NODE is presented below. The description is referred to the SEFG G*. The names of the procedures and functions used as primitives are self explanatory.

```
Function EDGE_ADJACENT_FACES(G*,Gi,f,e,v1,v2,Eps);
(* It returns the list of the nodes of a component Gi of G* which
   correspond to the faces adjacent to f along edge e=(v1,v2)
   at level Eps of accuracy *)
   f':= OTHER_EXTREME_NODE(Gi,e,f);
   if IS_DUMMY_NODE(Gi,f') then
      Gj:= PARENT(G*,Gi);
      e':= ARC_CORRESPONDING_TO(e,Gj);
      fi:= MACRONODE_EXPANDED_INTO(Gj,Gi);
      AF:= EDGE_ADJACENT_FACES(G*,Gj,fi,e',v1,v2,Eps)
    else
      AF:= EXPAND_NODE(G*,Gi,f',v1,v2,Eps);
    return(AF)
end EDGE_ADJACENT_FACES.


Function EXPAND_NODE(G*,Gi,f',e,v1,v2,Eps);
(* It returns the list of the nodes adjacent to node f at
   degree Eps of accuracy which are obtained by recursively
   expanding the other extreme f' of arc e in Gi *)
   A:= 0;
   if Error(f') <=Eps or not IS_MACRO(G*,Gi,f') then
     A:= A U {f'}
   else
      Gk:= EXPANSION_GRAPH(G*,Gi,f');
      f*:= DUMMY_NODE(Gk);
      for every e" in IA(Gk,f*) do
      (* IA(Gk,f*) denotes the set of the arcs of Gk
         incident to node f* *)
         if IS_BOUNDARY_TIE(Gk,e",Gi,e) and
            IS_A_SUBSEGMENT(e",v1,v2) then
         (* IS_BOUNDARY_TIE returns the value True if arc e" of Gk
            is mapped into arc e of Gi, the value False otherwise.
            IS_A_SUBSEGMENT returns the value True if e" is a
            subsegment of the segment joining v1 to v2, the value
            False  otherwise *)
         f":= OTHER_EXTREME_NODE(Gk,e",f*);
         A:= A U EXPAND_NODE(G*,Gi,f",e",v1,v2,Eps)
      end for;
   return(A)
end EXPAND_NODE.
```

The time complexity of algorithm EDGE_ADJACENT_FACES depends on the number N of the components of G* and on the number of boundary arcs of each component. In fact, each component Gi of G* is examined exactly once in the worst case, and the arcs incident into the dummy node of each component are considered once (see the for loop in algorithm EXPAND_NODE). Thus, the worst-case time complexity of algorithm EDGE_ADJACENT_FACES is O(N+BA), where BA is the total number of arcs incident to the dummy nodes of the components of G*.

Algorithms for answering the Face-Face and the Edge-Face queries at degree Eps of accuracy are straightforward applications of algorithm EDGE_ADJACENT_FACES. In the first case, given an arc e belonging to a component Gi of G*, the above algorithm is applied twice, once for each extreme node of Gi. In the second case, given a node f of Gi, algorithm EDGE_ADJACENT_FACES is applied once for each of the arcs of Gi incident into f. In this way, the faces adjacent to face f at degree Eps of accuracy are retrieved. The resulting worst-case time complexity will be O((N+BA)*Ef), where Ef denotes the number of edges bounding a face f.

3.2 A vertex adjacency finding algorithm

Algorithm VERTEX_FACE described below answers the Vertex-Face query on a VRBM B* of an object S at degree Eps of accuracy, by applying a top-down searching strategy to the SEFG representation G* of S. First, given a vertex v of S, the lowest level component Gi of G* containing nodes corresponding to faces incident to vertex v is located. In other words, if Gj is an ancestor of Gi in G*, there cannot exist any face described by a node in Gj which is incident to v. Those faces of Gi, which share vertex v and are encoded into the nodes of Gi, are considered, and any of such faces having an error associated greater than Eps is expanded by a recursive application of algorithm VERTEX_ADJACENT_FACES. This algorithm employs a preorder traversal of the tree describing G*, since it is recursively activated each time a node f is found which does not satisfy the stopping condi(i.e., Error(f)>Eps). A Pascal-like description of algorithms VERTEX_FACE and VERTEX_ADJACENT_FACES is reported below. The names of the functions and procedures used as primitives in the description are self explanatory.

```
Function VERTEX_FACE (G*,v,Eps);
(* It returns the list of the nodes of G* corresponding
   to the faces of the object incident into vertex v
   and having an error value less or equal to Eps *)
   Gi:= LOWEST_LEVEL_COMPONENT(G*,v);
   return (VERTEX_ADJACENT_FACES(G*,Gi,v,Eps))
end VERTEX_FACE.


Function VERTEX_ADJACENT_FACES (G*,Gi,v,Eps);
   LIF:= O;
   LIFi:= FACES_SHARING_VERTEX(Gi,v);
   f:= FIRST_NODE(LIFi);
   while f<>nil do
      if not IS_DUMMY_NODE(Gi,f) then
         if Error(f)<=Eps or not
            IS_MACRO(Gi,f) then
            LIF:= LIF U {f}
         else
            LIF:= LIF U VERTEX_ADJACENT_FACES(G*,
                        EXPANSION_GRAPH(G*,Gi,f),v,Eps);
      f:= NEXT_NODE(LIFi,f)
   end while;
   return (LIF)
end VERTEX_ADJACENT_FACES.
```

In algorithm VERTEX_FACE, each component of G* is examined exactly once in the worst case. Hence, the top-down traversal of G* requires O(N) steps. The traversal of G* is performed by LOWEST_LEVEL_COMPONENT first and then by algorithm VERTEX_ADJACENT_FACES. In each component Gi, all the nodes corresponding to the faces incident to vertex v are examined. Such nodes must be retrieved from the internal data structure since the Vertex-Face relation is not encoded into the edge-face graph. Hence, the worst-case time complexity is O(N+F), where F is the total number of object faces.

4. Edge- and vertex-based relations at fixed accuracy

The remaining six adjacency relations can be grouped into two categories, called edge-based and vertex-based relations. The Face-Edge, Edge-Edge and Vertex-Edge relations belong to the former class, the Face-Vertex, Edge-Vertex and Vertex-Vertex to the latter. Since the approximation error is associated with the object faces, the edge-based queries at degree Eps of accuracy are defined in terms of the face-based ones, and the corresponding structure accessing algorithms are completely similar to those presented in the previous section.

Vertex-based relations deserve a separate treatment. It makes no sense defining the Edge-Vertex query at fixed accuracy, being an edge unambiguously identified by its two extreme vertices and by the two faces sharing it. The Face-Vertex and Vertex-Vertex relations can be expressed as the combination of the Face-Edge and Vertex-Edge relations with the Edge-Vertex one respectively. Given the set Ef of the edges bounding a given face f at degree Eps of accuracy, the set of the vertices bounding f at the same resolution are simply the extreme vertices of the edges belonging to Ef. Similarly, given the set Ev of the edges incident to a vertex v at degree Eps of accuracy, the set of the vertices adjacent to v at the same resolution are the extreme vertices of the edges belonging to Ev which are different from v.

5. Concluding remarks

A hierarchical data structure has been presented, which provides a topological description of variable-resolution boundary models based on faces of arbitrary geometric shape. Being surface-based, a VRBM is capable of describing arbitrary objects to any desired level of accuracy, and hence it seems to be the right choice as a detailed general-purpose object model [Bes85]. Also, it provides a reduction in the number of points needed to represent the object shape and a fast rendering of objects by means of ray tracing algorithms as well as an efficient detection of object intersections [Dob83]. Being object-centered, VRBMs are also invariant through rigid transformations.

In our topological model, the edge-face graph has been chosen as basic relational representation of objects composed of a single shell and of simply-connected faces since it provides a face-oriented description of its boundary, which is topologically sufficient and stores a restricted number of adjacency relations between pairs of boundary entities.

Algorithms for retrieving the nine possible adjacency relations between pairs of primitive topological entities at fixed precision have been described. Such algorithms work on an SEFG representation of an object, and are based on suitable traversing strategies of its tree description. Primitive operations for defining a VRBM have been introduced in [DeF86] together with their inverse ones. These operations allow a stepwise manipulation of the structured model by using either a bottom-up or a top-down approach, or a combination of the two, as well as the construction of a one-level detailed description of the object boundary from its SEFG.

References

[Ans85] Ansaldi,S., De Floriani,L,, Falcidieno,B., Geometric modeling of solid objects by using a face adjacency graph representation, Computer Graphics (SIGGRAPH'85), 19, 3, 1985, pp.131-139.

[Bal81] Ballard,D.H., Striptrees: a hierarchical representation for curves, Comm. ACM, 214, 5, 1981, pp.310-321.

[Bes85] Besl,P.J., Jain,R.C., Three-dimensional object recognition, Computing Surveys, 17, 1, 1985, pp.75-145.

[Boi86] Boissonat,J.D., Tellaud,M., A hierarchical representation of objects: the Delaunay tree, Proceedings 2nd ACM Symposium on Computational Geometry, Yorktown Heights, New York, 1986, pp.260-268.

[DeF84] De Floriani,L., Falcidieno,B., Nagy,G., Pienovi,C., A hierarchical structure for surface approximation, Computer and Graphics, 8, 2, 1984, pp.183-193.

[DeF86] De Floriani,L., A Hierarchical Boundary Model for Variable-Resolution Representation of Three-Dimensional Objects, Proceedings 8th Int. Conference on Pattern Recognition, Paris, 1986.

[DeF88] De Floriani, L., Falcidieno, B., A Hierarchical Boundary Model for Solid Object Representation, ACM Trans. on Graphics, 7, 1, January 1988 (in print).

[Dob83] Dobkin,D.P., Kirkpatrick,D.G., Fast detection of polyhedral intersections, Theoretical Computer Science, 27, 1983, pp.241-253.

[Dut83] Dutton,G., Geodesic modeling of planetary relief, Proceedings AUTOCARTO, 1983, pp.186-201.

[Fau83] Faugeras,O.D., Ponce,J., Prismtrees: a hierarchical representation for 3D objects, Proceedings 8th International Conference on Artificial Intelligence, Karlsruhe, 1983, pp.982-988.

[Gom79] Gomez,D., Guzman,A., Digital model for three dimensioanl surface representation, Geo-Processing, 1, 1979, pp.53-70.

[Mea82] Meagher,D., Geometric modeling using octree encoding, Computer Graphics and Image Processing, 19, 2, 1982, pp.129-147.

[Req80] Requicha,A.A.G., Representations of rigid solids - theory, methods and systems, Computing Surveys, 12, 4, 1980, pp.437-464.

[Sam84] Samet,H., The quadtree and related hierarchical data structures, Computing Surveys, 16, 2, 1984, pp.187-260.

[Wei85] Weiler,K., Edge based data structures for solid modeling in curved surface environments, IEEE Computer Graphics and Applications, 5, 1, 1985, pp.21-40.

[Woo85] Woo,T.C., A combinatorial analysis of boundary data structure schemata, IEEE Computer Graphics and Applications, 5, 3, pp.19-27.

On Triangulating Palm Polygons in Linear Time

H. ElGindy[1] and G. Toussaint[2] (Canada)

ABSTRACT

No one has yet been able to triangulate a simple polygon of n vertices in $O(n)$ time. The fastest algorithm to date, due to Tarjan and van Wyk, runs in $O(n \log\log n)$ time. On the other hand several classes of simple polygons do admit linear-time triangulation. Some examples of such famous classes are: star-shaped, monotone, spiral, edge visible, and weakly externally visible polygons. In this paper the notion of geodesic paths is used to characterize all the classes of polygons for which linear time triangulation algorithms are known. First we introduce a new class of polygons, termed *palm polygons*, which subsumes *many* known classes of polygons for which linear time triangulation algorithms are known, and present an algorithm for triangulating *palm polygons* in $O(n)$ time. Then a class of polygons termed *crab polygons* is defined and shown to contain *all* classes of existing polygons for which linear time triangulation algorithms are known. As a by product of this characterization we obtain a new very simple linear time algorithm for triangulating star-shaped polygons.

1. INTRODUCTION

Since Garey et al [1] presented an $O(n \log n)$ running time algorithm for triangulating simple polygons, the problem has received a lot of attention. Tarjan and van Wyk [2] presented an $O(n \log\log n)$ time algorithm for triangulating such polygons. Chazelle and Incerpi [3] presented an adaptive algorithm whose complexity depends on the sinuosity of the polygon, where the sinuosity of a polygon is the number of times the boundary alternates between spirals of opposite orientation. Other researchers directed their attention to identifying the classes of polygons which can be triangulated in linear, and thus optimal, running time [4-10]. Famous examples of such classes are: star-shaped, monotone, and spiral polygons. Recently, a linear time algorithm for triangulating weakly externally visible polygons has been presented in [11]. This algorithm unifies and generalizes the results in [4,6,7,10] since such polygons are known to belong to the class of weakly externally visible polygons [12]. Recall that a polygon is weakly externally visible if for every point x on the boundary of P there exists an infinite half line that intersects P only at x.

The main contribution of this paper is the use of shortest paths to characterize all the classes of polygons for which linear triangulation algorithms are known. We reach this objective in two steps. First we introduce a new class of polygons, called *palm polygons*, which contains many known classes of polygons for which linear time triangulation algorithms are known, and present a linear time

[1]Research supported by the Faculty of Graduate Studies and Research (McGill University) grant 276-07.

[2]Research supported by FCAR grant EQ-1678 and NSERC grant A9293.

algorithm for triangulating such polygons. We then describe the class of polygons, called *crab polygons*, and show that it contains all classes of polygons for which linear triangulation algorithms exist. We also describe a simpler algorithm for triangulating star-shaped polygons. Unlike all existing algorithms [5,6,10], the algorithm does not require computing a point in the kernel using the involved algorithm in [13].

2. DEFINITIONS AND NOTATION

A polygon P with n distinct vertices is a closed path $p_1, p_2, \ldots p_n, p_{n+1}$ ($p_{n+1} = p_1$) where p_i has (x_i, y_i) as its x- and y-coordinates. The ith edge (or side) of P, denoted by e_i, is the closed line segment joining the pair of vertices p_i and p_{i+1}. The boundary of P, denoted by BD(P), is the sequence of edges $e_1, e_2, \ldots e_n$. A polygon is said to be simple when no two edges intersect other than at their end points. We assume that the vertices are given in clockwise order so that the interior of the simple polygon always lies to the right as its boundary is traversed. Between a pair of points u and v on BD(P), we define the chain CN(u,v) to be the subset of BD(P) so that the interior of P always lies to the right as CN(u,v) is traversed from u to v.

Let s and t be a pair of points in P. We define the chain SIP(s,t) to be the shortest internal path between the points s and t. SIP(s,t) is said to be left (right) turning if at every point x $\in$ SIP(s,t) the interior of P lies to the right (left) of x as edges of the chain are traversed from s to t. If SIP(s,t) consists of the line segment $\overline{st}$, t is said to be visible from s. The visibility polygon from a point s, denoted by VP(s), is defined as the subset of P that is visible from s.

3. LINEAR TIME ALGORITHM FOR TRIANGULATING PALM POLYGONS

A simple polygon P is said to be palm-shaped with respect to an interior point O if SIP(O,x), for every x $\in$ P, is a convex chain, and is called a palm polygon if it is palm-shaped with respect to some interior point (refer to Fig. 1 for an illustration.) A well known subclass of palm polygons is the class of star-shaped polygons. A polygon P is said to be star-shaped if there exists a point K such that SIP(K,x), for every x $\in$ P, consists of the line segment $\overline{Ox}$. We also say that P is a left-palm polygon if there exists an interior point O such that SIP(O,x), for every x $\in$ P, are left turning chains. A right-palm polygon is defined similarly. In this section we present a linear time algorithm for triangulating palm polygons. The algorithm is based on the use of an algorithm for solving the two-dimensional hidden-line problem to decompose a palm polygon into a collection of left- and right-palm polygons which can then be triangulated using a simple linear running time triangulation algorithm.

Before we present the algorithm, we describe the properties of palm polygons which led to its development.

Lemma 1 Given a simple polygon P that is palm-shaped with respect to an interior point O. The removal of VP(O) decomposes P into a collection of left- and right-palm polygons.

Lemma 2 Given a polygon P that is left-palm with respect to the jth vertex, the algorithm TR-POL [9] (also refer to Appendix) correctly triangulates P.

Proof. It follows from P being a left-palm polygon with respect to p_j that SIP(p_j, q), for every q $\in$ BD(P), consists only of a subset of the vertices of CN(p_j, q). Therefore edges added at Step 2(d) (when p_{k+1} is convex) lie in the interior of P, and the reduced polygon (obtained by deleting p_{k+1}) remains left-palm with respect to the jth vertex. Since the algorithm terminates when the jth vertex is reached, T will contain the edge list of the triangulation. ■

The case of right-palm polygons is similar. We now describe the algorithm:

ALGORITHM TriPalm(P,O)

1. Use an algorithm for solving the hidden-line problem in simple polygons [14,15] to compute the visibility polygon VP(O).
2. Connect the adjacent vertices on the boundary of VP(O), which are not adjacent on the boundary of P, to create a star-shaped polygon with respect to O, and a collection of left- and right-palm polygons.
3. Triangulate the star-shaped polygon using any of the algorithms in [5,6,10].
4. Use the algorithm TR-POL to triangulate each of the left- and right-palm components separately.

END TriPalm.

Theorem 1 Algorithm TriPalm triangulates a palm polygon correctly in linear running time.

Proof. Correctness of the algorithm follows from lemmas 1-2 and the correctness of the algorithms in [14,15]. It is easy to see that each step of the algorithm runs in linear time, and thus the theorem follows. ■

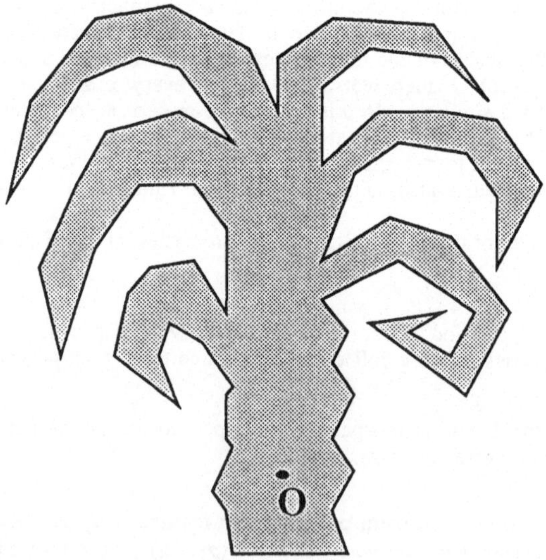

Fig. 1: A palm-shaped polygon with respect to O.

4. TRIANGULATING A STAR-SHAPED POLYGON WITHOUT A KERNEL POINT

In this section we describe a new linear running-time algorithm for triangulating star-shaped polygons. Unlike the algorithms in [5,6,10], our algorithm does not require knowledge of a point in the kernel, and is much easier to implement.

Before presenting the main ideas that led to the development of the algorithm, we introduce two additional definitions. A vertex $p_i \in$ BD(P) is said to be *maximal* with respect to a point X if both edges e_{i-1} and e_i lie on the same side of the directed line joining X to p_i. A vertex $p_i \in$ BD(P) is said to be *convex left maximal* with respect to a point X if p_i is a convex vertex and both edges e_{i-1} and e_i lie to the right of the directed line joining X to p_i. *Convex right*, *reflex left*, and *reflex left* vertices are defined similarly (refer to Fig. 2 for illustrations.)

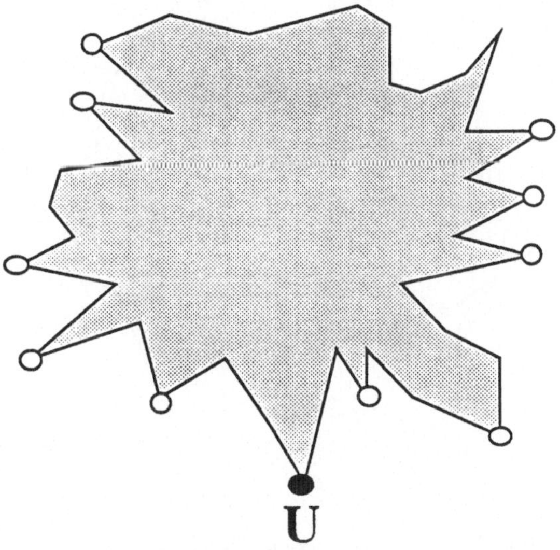

Fig. 2: A star-shaped polygon. The convex maximal vertices with respect to U are marked with a circle.

Lemma 3 For each vertex U of a star-shaped polygon P there exists a point Z on BD(P) such that convex maximal vertices in CN(U, Z) with respect to U are *left* and convex maximal vertices in CN(Z, U) with respect to U are *right*.

Proof. Let p_i and p_k be two consecutive left convex maximal vertices in CN(U, Z), and let p_j be a right convex maximal vertex such that $i < j < k$. Let Y be the intersection of the line passing through U and p_j with BD(P) that is closest to U. The existence of such point follows from the simplicity of P.

Assume that the vertices p_i, p_j and p_k are in sorted angular order around U (as shown in Fig. 3.) Since P is star-shaped, there exists a point $X \in$ P such that VP(X) = P (i.e., each of the vertices must be visible from X and none of them is maximal with respect to X.) Therefore, the point X must lie in the region enclosed by the chain CN(U, Y) and the line segment $\overline{YU}$ A contradiction.

The different cases when the vertices p_i, p_j and p_k are not in sorted angular order around U can be analyzed in a similar way. Thus the lemma follows. ■

Corollary 1. SIP(U, v), for every vertex $v \in$ CN(U, Z), is left turning.

Corollary 2. SIP(U, v), for every vertex $v \in$ CN(Z, U), is right turning.

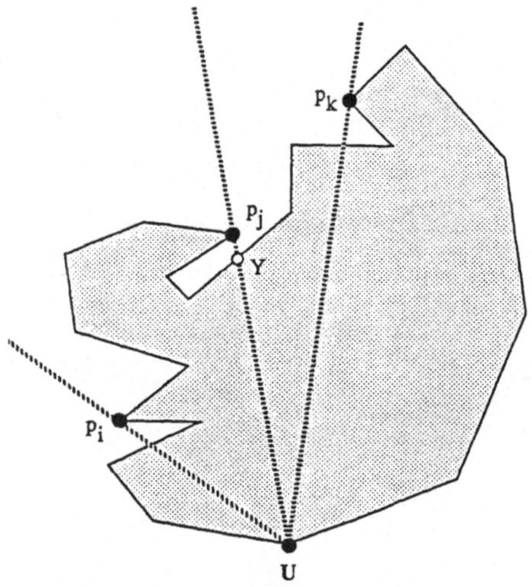

Fig. 3: Illustrating the proof of lemma 3.

Lemma 4 Let U be a convex vertex of a star-shaped polygon P, p_i be the convex left maximal vertex that is furthest away from U in the clockwise order, and p_k be the convex right maximal vertex that is furthest away from U in the counterclockwise order. The vertices in CN(p_i, p_k), other than p_i or p_k, are not maximal with respect to U and occur in sorted angular order around it.

Proof. Let $p_j \in$ CN(p_i, p_k) be a left reflex maximal vertex with respect to U. Due the simplicity of P, the chain CN(p_{i+1}, p_{j-1}) must contain a right convex maximal vertex contradicting the definition of p_k. Therefore, the chain CN(p_{i+1}, p_{k-1}) does not have maximal vertices with respect to the vertex U and is thus sorted with respect to it.

The case of right reflex maximal vertex can be handled in a similar way. Thus the lemma follows. ■

We now present the algorithm.

ALGORITHM TriStar(P)

1. Label the vertices such that p_1 is convex, and find the convex left maximal vertex p_i that is furthest away from p_1 in the clockwise order, and the convex right maximal vertex p_j that is furthest away from p_1 in the counterclockwise order.

2. Apply the algorithm TR-POL (see Appendix) to triangulate each of the chains CN(p_1, p_i), and CN(p_j, p_1) separately.

3. The polygon enclosed by the chains SIP(p_1, p_i), CN(p_i, p_j), and SIP(p_j, p_1) is *radially monotonic* with respect to p_1 and therefore can be triangulated as in [7, lemma 12].

END TriStar.

Theorem 2 Algorithm TriStar triangulates a star-shaped polygon correctly in linear running time.

Proof. Correctness of the algorithm follows from lemmas 3-4 and the correctness of the algorithms in [7] and [9]. It is easy to see that each step of the algorithm runs in linear time, and thus the theorem follows. ■

5. A HIERARCHY OF POLYGONS WITH LINEAR TIME TRIANGULATION ALGORITHMS

The design of linear time algorithms for triangulating polygons has been mainly confined to isolated classes of polygons. Recent efforts have been directed towards unifying and generalizing these isolated results [5,7,11]. As a result the classes of weakly externally visible, radially monotone and palm polygons emerged as the largest independent classes for which linear time algorithms exist (refer to the diagram in Fig. 4 for the relations between the different classes of simple polygons.) Recall that a polygon P is *radially monotone* if there exists a point r in the plane such that every infinite half line emanating from r that intersects P does so only in a single line segment. Clearly star-shaped polygons are radially monotone with r a point in the kernel of P. In this section we show that the three classes belong to a single class of polygons, termed *crab* polygons.

A simple polygon P is said to be a *crab* polygon if there exists a point O in the plane such that the shortest path between O and x, for all x $\in$ BD(P), not properly intersecting BD(P), is a convex chain. The class of palm polygons is clearly a specialization of crab polygons when the point O is restricted to lie in P.

Theorem 3 A weakly externally visible polygon P belongs to the class of crab polygons.

Proof. We will prove that the shortest paths from every point O in the exterior of P to every point x $\in$ BD(P) are convex.

First assume O be a point in the exterior of the convex hull of P, denoted by CH(P), and let s and t be the intersection of the two half lines emanating at O and tangent with CH(P) (refer to Fig. 5.) There are two cases to be considered:

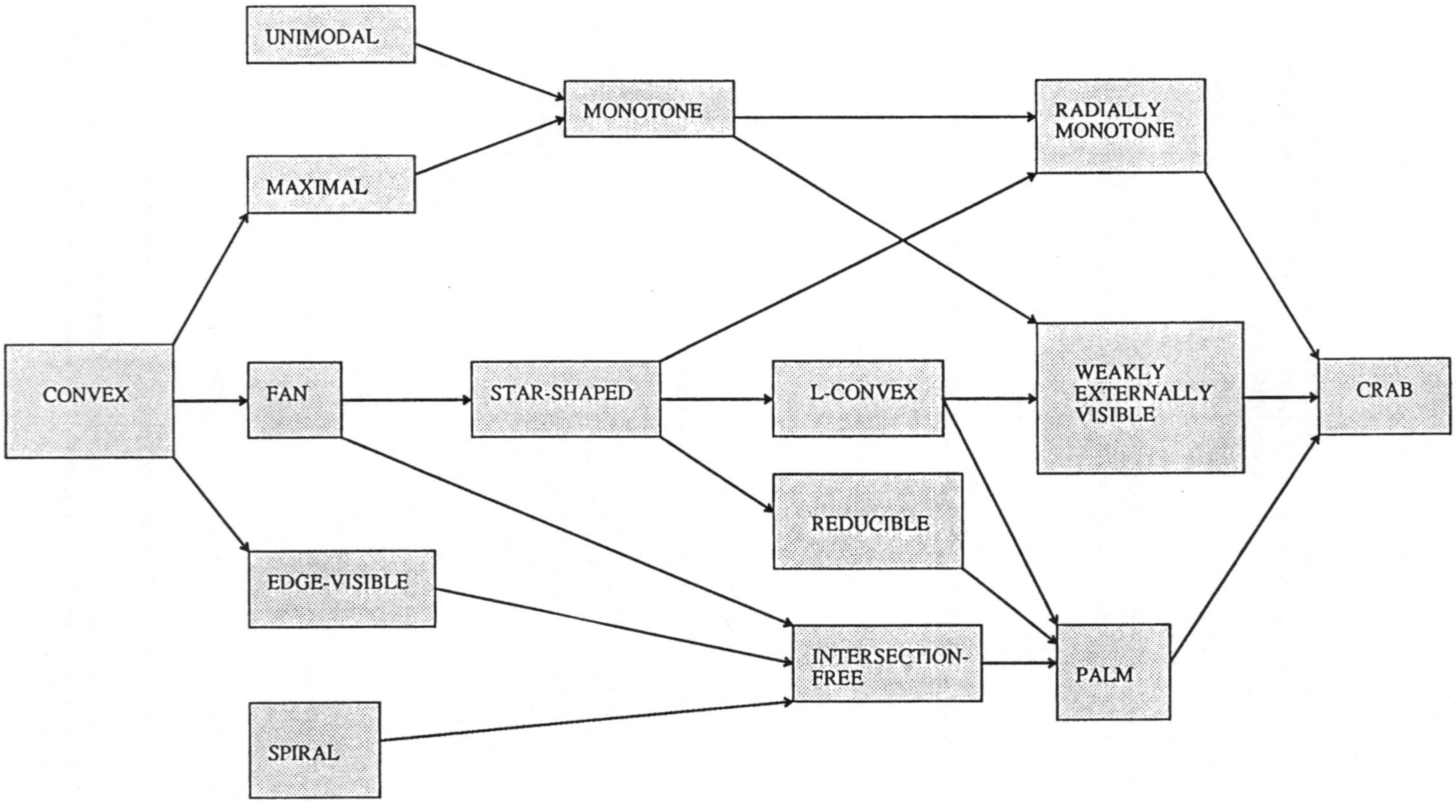

Fig. 4: A hierarchy of simple polygons for which linear time triangulation algorithms are known.

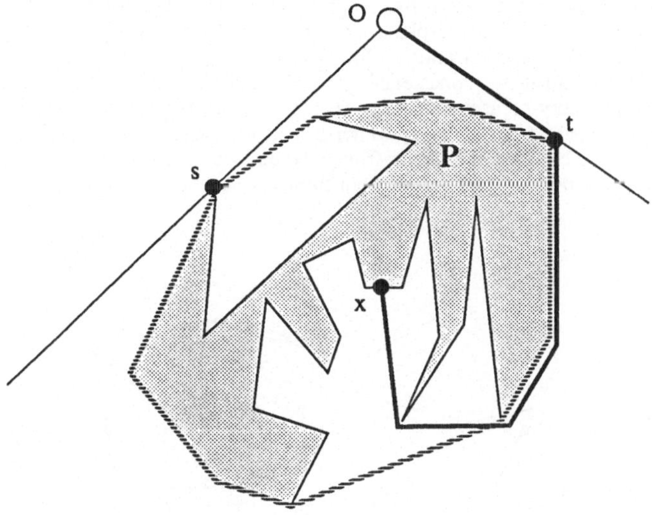

Fig. 5: Illustrating the proof of theorem 3.

Case 1: If x ∈ CH(P) and x ∈ CN(s,t), then SEP(O, x), the shortest external path from O to x, is a line segment. If x ∈ CH(P) and x ∈ CN(t,s), then SEP(O,x) is the shorter of the following two paths:

(1) concatenation of $\overline{O s}$ and the portion of CH(P) from s to x.
(1) concatenation of $\overline{O t}$ and the portion of CH(P) from t to x.

In each situation SEP(O, x) is a convex chain.

Case 2: If x is not in CH(P), then it must lie in the interior of some "pocket" of P. A *pocket* of P is a simply connected region exterior to P and interior to CH(P). A *pocket-lid* is an edge of CH(P) that is not an edge of P. Since P is weakly externally visible it follows that SEP(x,y), for every point y lying in the *lid* of the *pocket* containing x, is either left turning or right turning. Therefore SEP(O, x) is the concatenation of two chains both of which is either jointly left turning or jointly right turning.

The situation when O is a point in the interior of or on CH(P) can be analyzed in a similar way and thus the theorem follows. ■

Theorem 4 A radially monotone polygon belongs to the class of crab polygons.

Proof. Let P be radially monotone with respect to a point r. If r ∈ P, then P is a star-shaped polygon. It is well known that star-shaped polygons are weakly externally visible and thus it follows from theorem 3 that P is a crab polygon. Therefore let r lie in the exterior of P.

Since P is radially monotone, there exist two supporting half lines emanating at r which intersect P at two vertices a and b, and partition the plane into two closed wedges W_{in} and W_{out} such that the interior of P, int(P), lies in W_{in} and no point in int(P) lies in W_{out} (refer to Fig. 6.) It is important to remark that the polygon obtained by concatenating $\overline{br}$, $\overline{ra}$, and CN(a,b) is weakly externally visible. Let $O \in W_{out}$ and consider any point x $\in$ BD(P). If x $\in$ CN(b,a), then both x and O are visible from r. Therefore the shortest path from O to x, which lies in the exterior of P is either left turning or right turning. If x $\in$ CN(a,b), then it follows from theorem 3 that the shortest path from O to x is either left turning or right turning. Thus the theorem follows. ■

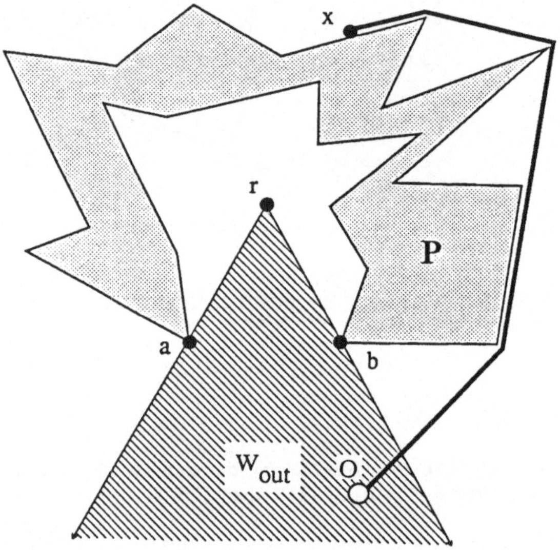

Fig. 6: Illustrating the proof of theorem 6.

6. CONCLUDING REMARKS

In this paper we used the notion of shortest path to define a new class of polygons, termed *crab polygons*, which subsumes all the classes of simple polygons for which linear triangulation algorithms are known. Avis and Toussaint [16] presented a linear algorithm for checking whether a simple polygon is weakly externally visible which can then be triangulated in linear time [11]. It remains to be shown whether a *crab polygon* can be identified efficiently.

Based on this characterization, we also presented a new linear time algorithm for triangulating a star-shaped polygon which does not require computing a point in the kernel. Another open problem is to develop a linear time algorithm for triangulating a *palm polygon* which does not require knowledge of an interior point with respect to which the polygon is palm-shaped. Finally no algorithm is yet known for computing the *palm-kernel* of a simple polygon, i.e., the largest subset of P from which the polygon is palm-shaped. The *star-kernel* on the other hand is known to be computable in linear time [13].

APPENDIX

Algorithm TR-POL (P, j)

Step 1. Create edge list T and put in T all edges of P.

Step 2. Starting with the jth vertex do (a)-(f) below for every three consecutive points k, $k+1$, $k+2$ until j is reached.

(a) $S = (y_{k+1} - y_k)(x_{k+2} - x_{k+1}) + (x_k - x_{k+1})(y_{k+2} - y_{k+1})$

(b) If $S \geq 0$ and $k+2 = j$, STOP.

(c) If $S \geq 0$ move one point forward and go to (a).

(d) Delete point p_{k+1} and add edge $p_k\ p_{k+2}$ to T.

(e) If $k \neq j$ move one point backward; else move one point forward.

(f) Go to (a).

end TR-POL

REFERENCES

[1] M. Garey, D. Johnson, F.P. Preparata, and R. Tarjan, "Triangulating a simple polygon," *Information Processing Letters* 7 (1978), pp. 175-179.

[2] R.E. Tarjan and C. van Wyk, "An $O(n\log\log n)$ time algorithm for triangulating simple polygons," manuscript, July 1986.

[3] B. Chazelle and J. Incerpi, "Triangulation and shape complexity," *ACM Transactions of Graphics* 3 (1984), pp. 135-152.

[4] H. ElGindy, D. Avis, and G.T. Toussaint, "Applications of a two-dimensional hidden-line algorithm to other geometric problems," *Computing* **31** (1983), pp. 191-202.

[5] S.H. Lee and K.Y. Chwa, "A new triangulation linear class of simple polygons," *Intern. J. Computer Math.* **22** (1987), pp. 135-147.

[6] A. Schoone and J. van Leeuwen, "Triangulating a star-shaped polygon," Technical Report No. RUV-CS-80-3, University of Utrecht, April 1980.

[7] G.T. Toussaint, "Shortest path solves translation separability of polygons," Technical Report No. SOCS-85-27, School of Computer Science, McGill University, October 1985.

[8] G.T. Toussaint, "A new linear algorithm for triangulating monotone polygons," *Pattern Recognition Letters* 2 (1984), pp. 155-158.

[9] G.T. Toussaint and D. Avis, "On a convex hull algorithm for polygons and its application to triangulation problems," *Pattern Recognition* **15** (1982), pp. 23-29.

[10] T.C. Woo and S.Y. Shin, "A linear time algorithm for triangulating a point-visible polygon," *ACM Transactions on Graphics* **4** (1985), pp. 60-70.

[11] H. ElGindy, "A linear algorithm for triangulating weakly externally visible polygons," Technical Report No. 86-75, Department of Computer and Information Science, University of Pennsylvania, September 1986.

[12] G.T. Toussaint, "A hierarchy of simple polygons," manuscript.

[13] D.T. Lee and F.P. Preparata, "An optimal algorithm for finding the kernel of a polygon," *J ACM* **26** (1979), pp. 415-421.

[14] H. ElGindy and D. Avis, "A linear algorithm for computing the visibility polygon from a point," *Journal of Algorithms* 2 (1981), pp. 186-197.

[15] D.T. Lee, "Visibility of a simple polygon," *Computer Vision, Graphics, Image Processing* **22** (1983), pp. 207-221.

[16] D. Avis and G.T. Toussaint, "An optimal algorithm for determining the visibility of a polygon from an edge," *IEEE Transaction on Computers* **C-30** (December 1981), pp. 910-914.

Vertical Scan-Conversion for Filling Purposes

R. D. Hersch (Switzerland)

ABSTRACT

Conventional scan-conversion algorithms were developed independently of filling algorithms. They cause many problems, when used for filling purposes. However, today's raster printers and plotters require extended use of filling, especially for the generation of typographic characters and graphic line art. A new scan-conversion algorithm, called *vertical scan-conversion* has been specifically designed to meet the requirements of parity scan line fill algorithms. Vertical scan-conversion ensures the selection of exactly one pixel per intersecting scan line between a local minimum and a local maximum of the shape outline. Pairs of selected pixels define horizontal spans. All horizontal spans contain the full set of pixels interior to the original shape. Vertical scan-conversion greatly simplifies traditional edge-tracking filling algorithms, such as ordered edge fill, flag fill and descriptive contour fill, removing the need for testing and processing special cases.

Keywords

raster graphics, scan-conversion, filling

1. Introduction

The world of Computer Graphics is synthetic and artificial. Definitions and algorithms should help to represent and display selected real world items in the best possible way. Binary raster printing devices require the selection of configurations of discrete pixels to represent analog shapes like typographic characters or graphic line art.

Scan-conversion and filling algorithms are the basic tools used for the generation of any two-dimensional shape. Despite the fact that some algorithms are well known [BRESENHAM65], only few computer graphics specialists have real experience with them. These algorithms are generally implemented in firmware and are available to users as library calls. Recently, several researchers have pointed to limitations and side effects of existing scan-conversion algorithms [BRESENHAM87], [PITTEWAY85], [HERSCH87].

The various algorithms for scan-conversion and filling are the result of independent research. Therefore, traditional scan-conversion [BRESENHAM65] is not fully compatible with the requirements of most filling algorithms. Filling algorithms like ordered edge fill [NEWMAN79], flag fill [ACKLAND81] or descriptive contour fill [HERSCH86] require the detection and separate processing of special cases.

The purpose of this paper is to provide the basis for a new scan-conversion algorithm suiting the needs of edge tracking parity fill algorithms like ordered edge fill, flag fill and descriptive contour fill.

2. Lack of coherence of previous filling algorithms, due to inadequate scan-conversion techniques

Conventional straight line segment, circular and conic arc scan-conversion is defined for integer departure and arrival points. Corresponding departure and arrival pixels belong to the scan-converted segment. Scan conversion of several connected segments leads to a duplication of pixels at junctions between segments (Fig. 1).

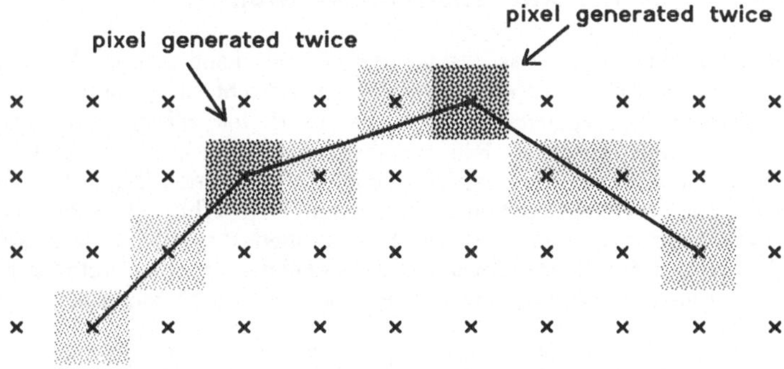

Fig. 1 Traditional scan-conversion of connected segments

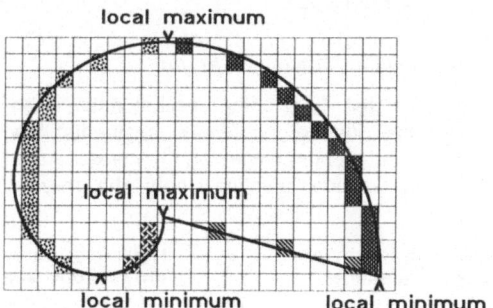

Ordered edge lists as well as edge-flag fill require that scan-conversion of contour segments lying between a local minimum and a local maximum (walls) should generate exactly one pixel on each intersected scan line (Fig. 2). This requirement is derived from the basic topological property stating that a straight line intersects a closed shape in an even number of points. Integer scan-conversion of connected segments does not meet this requirement. Therefore, implementors of filling algorithms have to analyze junctions between segments and rasterize them as two pixels or one pixel, after establishing whether the junction point is a local extrema or not. Furthermore, horizontal segments have to be detected and discarded [ROGERS85].

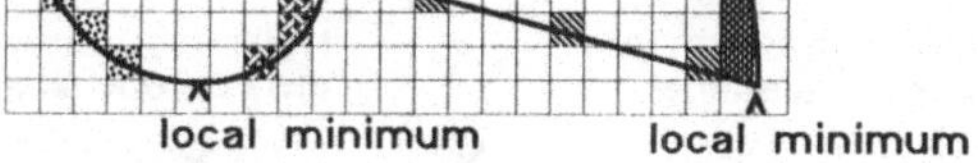

Fig. 2 Scan conversion of contour parts (walls) lying between local minimas and local maximas

The problem of selecting exactly one pixel at intersections between contour parts (walls) and scan lines becomes even more intricate for the scan-conversion of cubic parametric splines. In such cases, recursive subdivision or forward differencing techniques are generally used [BARTELS87]. Recursive subdivision and forward differencing lead to a series of closely spaced points having real-number coordinates.

To obtain one simple discrete pixel on each intersection between walls and scan lines, heuristic methods are generally used [NEWMAN79]. Contour intersections with ordinates through pixel centers are calculated and coverage percentages of pixel surfaces are evaluated.

These coverage evaluation procedures are cumbersome and inefficient. There is a need for a scan-conversion algorithm able to scan-convert polysegments with real vertices and to produce exactly one pixel per scanline intersection.

3. First octant real-number scan-conversion

A previous approach [HERSCH87] has demonstrated the importance of *fixed-point real number scan-conversion* for the scan-conversion of straight line, circular arcs and spline segments. Real number scan-conversion can be used for filling, although it was not developed primarly for this purpose. Real number scan-conversion generates those pixels with pixel centers closest to the original continuous outline (Fig. 3). Selected pixel centers lie within the original segment´s bounding box. This algorithm is called *first octant real-number scan conversion*, since it is defined for straight line and circular arc segments in the first octant. Scan-conversion of segments in other octants is obtained by applying interoctant transformations (concatenation of symmetries along x, y or y=x axis).

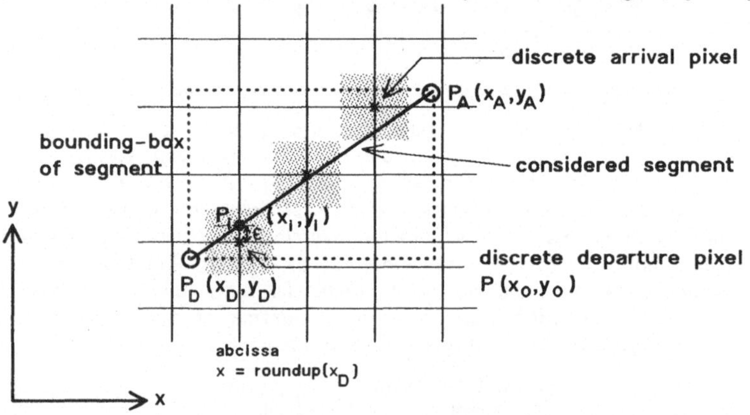

Fig. 3 First octant real number scan conversion

It has also been shown [HERSCH87] that first octant real-number scan-conversion does not ensure 8-point connectivity at the junction between segments having different primary directions. Furthermore, first octant scan-conversion generates many more pixels than necessary. Among all pixels lying on one scanline, only the leftmost or rightmost pixels are kept (Fig. 4) for later filling.

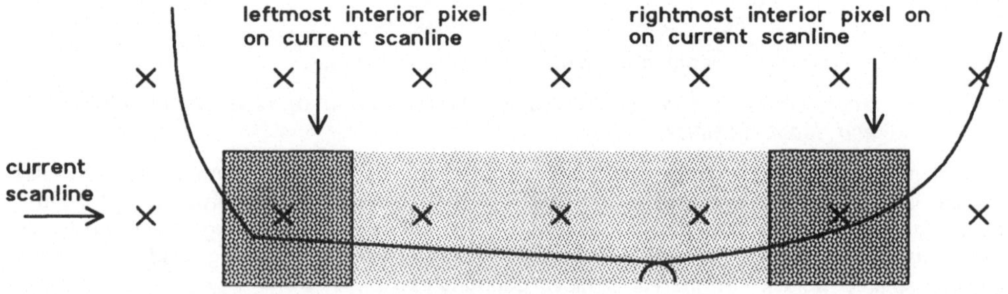

Fig. 4 Keeping leftmost and rightmost pixels

The aim of the new *vertical scan-conversion* algorithm is to generate directly, without ambiguity, leftmost or rightmost interior pixels.

4. Requirements for a new vertical real-number scan-conversion algorithm

The definition of a new vertical scan-conversion algorithm is directly derived from the requirements of scanline parity fill algorithms. These requirements can be expressed with the help of the following definitions.

Definition 1

The set of discrete pixels representing a closed continuous shape contains all pixels, whose pixel centers lie within the shape boundary (Fig. 5)

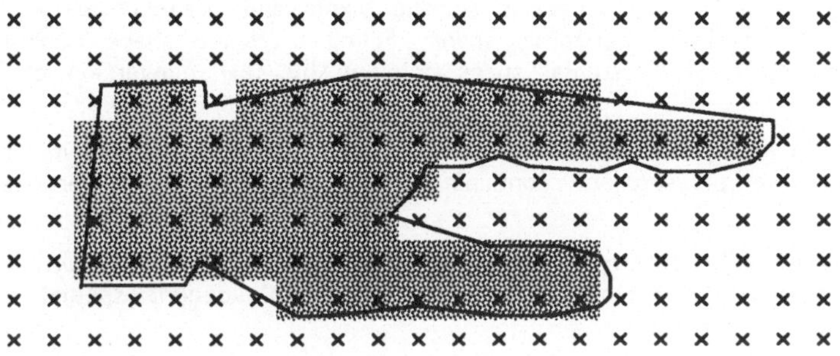

Fig. 5 Closed shape rendered by its interior pixels

Definition 2

The part of a closed contour outline lying between a local minimum and a local maximum in scanning direction is called a *wall*. A *left wall* is part of the left border of a closed shape. A *right wall* is part of the right border of a closed shape (Fig. 6).

Definition 3

A horizontal span is defined as the set of pixels lying on one scanline and whose pixel centers lie between a left wall and the following right wall (Fig. 6). A horizontal span is given by the coordinates of its starting pixel and by the coordinates of the pixel following its last pixel (afterlast pixel). A span with identical coordinates for starting and afterlast pixel is a null-span containing an empty set of pixels.

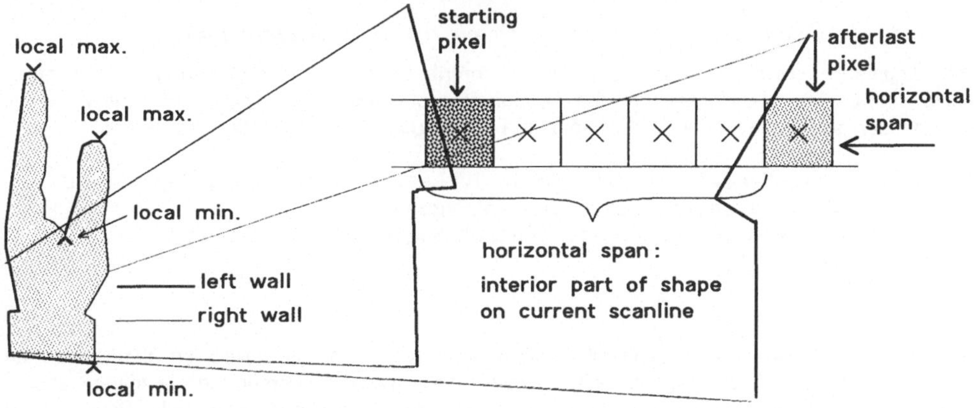

Fig. 6 Closed shape with left and right walls

A scan line has an even number of intersections with a closed shape. Intersections with left walls and right walls provide horizontal spans. The set of all spans contains all pixels interior to the shape outline.

These statements enable us to derive the basic requirement for scan-conversion:

Requirement :	Scan-conversion of a wall should lead to the selection of exactly one pixel on each scan line. The closest pixel to the wall, lying on its right side, should be selected.

Scan-conversion of left walls generates starting pixels and scan-conversion of right walls generates afterlast pixels of horizontal spans. Filling a closed shape consists of marking all pixels belonging to all horizontal spans obtained by scan-conversion of left and right walls.

Each wall is given, after subdivision or forward differencing of its original spline description, by one polysegment containing many closely spaced vertices having real coordinates.

To fulfill the previously described requirement for *wall scan-conversion*, we should be able to scan-convert polysegments without taking into account special orientations or sizes of individual segments.

5. Vertical real-number scan-conversion

Let us analyze the problems we face when scan-converting a polysegment representing a shape wall (Fig. 7).

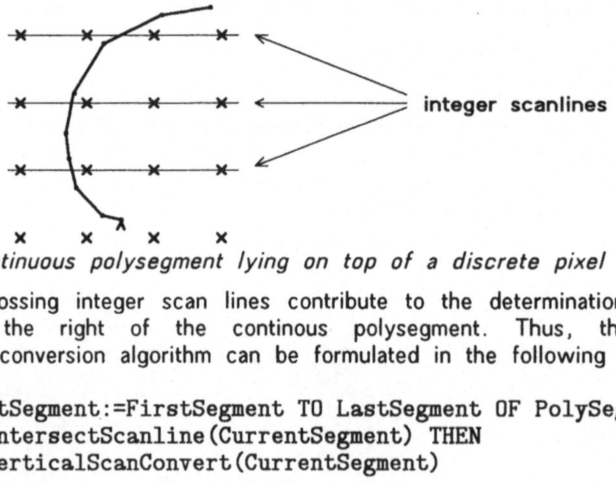

Fig. 7 Continuous polysegment lying on top of a discrete pixel grid

Only segments crossing integer scan lines contribute to the determination of the closest pixels lying to the right of the continous polysegment. Thus, the new vertical real-number scan-conversion algorithm can be formulated in the following way :

```
FOR CurrentSegment:=FirstSegment TO LastSegment OF PolySegment DO
     IF  IntersectScanline(CurrentSegment) THEN
         VerticalScanConvert(CurrentSegment)
     ENDIF
ENDFOR
```

Vertical scan-conversion of segments intersecting scan lines is based on the computation of the intersection of the segment with the lowest intersecting scanline and on incremental calculation of intersections with the next scanlines (Fig. 8). Pixels to the right of scanline-segment intersections are chosen as discrete pixels defining either starting or afterlast pixels of spans.

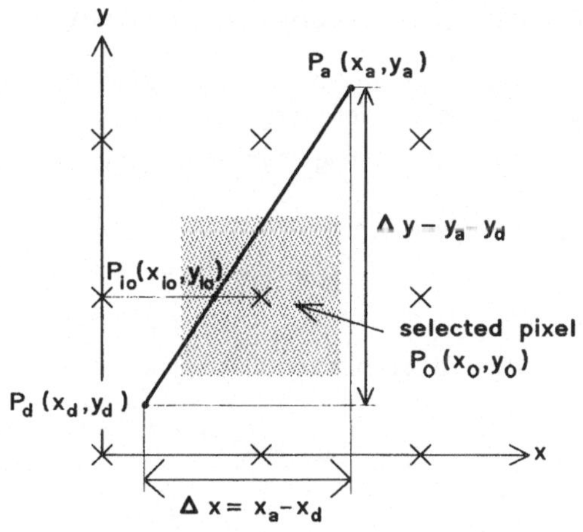

Fig. 8 Vertical scan-conversion of segment P_dP_a

In mathematical terms :

Intersection point $P_{io}(x_{io}, y_{io})$ with scanline above real departure point:

$$y_{io} = \text{roundup}(y_d)$$

$$x_{io} = x_d + \frac{\Delta x}{\Delta y}(y_{io} - y_d)$$

Selected first discrete pixel $P_o(x_o, y_o)$:

$$y_o = y_{io}$$

$$x_o = \text{roundup}(x_{io})$$

Recurrent formulation for the next real intersection points P_{ik+1}

$$y_{ik+1} = y_{ik} + 1$$

$$x_{ik+1} = x_{ik} + \frac{\Delta x}{\Delta y}$$

and for the selection of pixel P_{K+1}

$$y_{k+1} = y_{ik+1}$$

$$x_{k+1} = \text{roundup}\ (x_{ik+1});$$

The number of pixels to be scan-converted :

$$\text{nbpixel} = \text{trunc}(y_a) - \text{roundup}(y_d) + 1$$

This scan-conversion algorithm guarantees the selection of one discrete pixel on each intersection between walls (polysegments) and integer scanlines.

Let us analyze the behaviour of vertical scan-conversion in the cases which create problems with conventional scan-conversion.

6. Behaviour of vertical real-number scan conversion

When conventional scan-conversion algorithms are used for filling, one needs to recognize and appropriately process the following situations:

1) Existence, within a wall, of a long horizontal polysegment going through pixel centers
2) Local maximum lying on a pixel center
3) Vertex point of a polysegment wall lying exactly on a pixel center
4) Partly degenerated shape

Case a: vertical scan-conversion of horizontal segment P_0P_1

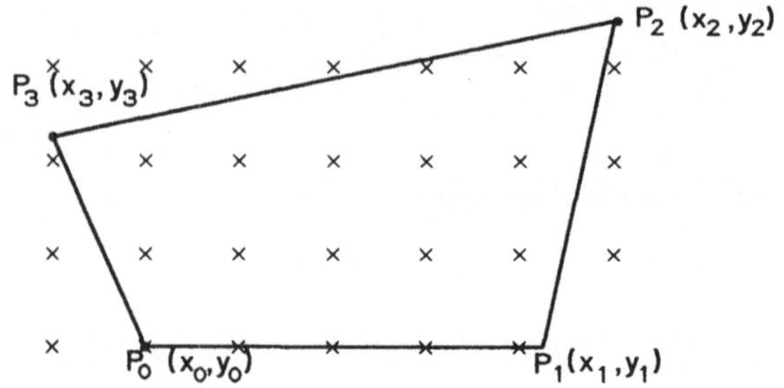

Fig. 9 Long horizontal segment through pixel centers

$$nbpixel(P_0P_1) = trunc(y_1) - roundup(y_0) + 1 = 0$$

Line segment P_0P_1 does not generate discrete pixels. Horizontal segments need not to be treated as special cases.

Case b: local maximum on a pixel center

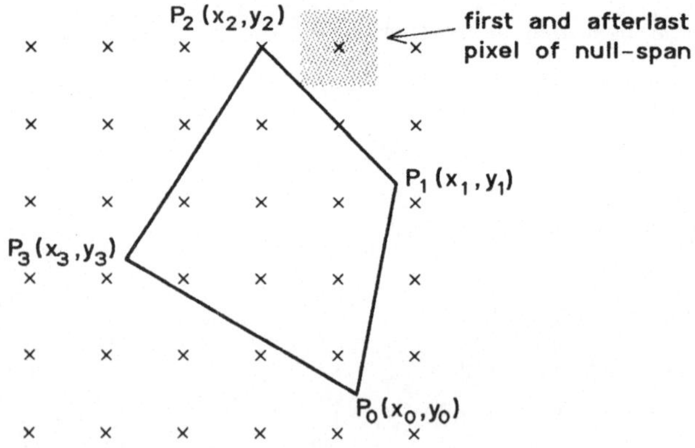

Fig. 10 Vertex at local maximum lying on pixel center

Vertical scan-conversion of segment P_3P_2 :

$$nbpixel(P_3P_2) = trunc(y_2) - roundup(y_3) + 1 = y_2 - trunc(y_3+1) + 1$$

P_3P_2 intersects scanline $y=y_2$ at (x_2,y_2).

The selected discrete pixel on scanline $y=y_2$ is (x_2+1,y_2). The same pixel is selected by vertical scan-conversion of segment P_1P_2. Therefore, pixel (x_2+1,y_2) is both the first and the afterlast pixel of a horizontal null-span.

Case c: intermediate vertex points on pixel centers

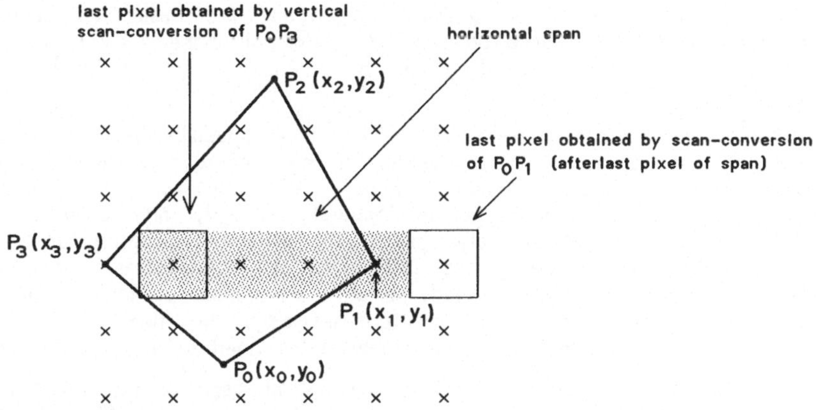

Fig. 11 Polysegment vertices P_3 and P_1 lying on pixel centers

Vertical scan-conversion of P_0P_3 leads to the selection of pixel (x_3+1, y_3). The first pixel obtained by scan-conversion of P_3P_2 lies on scanline y_3+1. Therefore, pixel (x_3+1,y_3) is the only pixel selected on scanline y_3 by scan-conversion of wall $P_0P_3P_2$.

Pixel (x_3+1,y_3) is the first pixel of a horizontal span. Pixel (x_1+1, y_1) is the afterlast pixel of a horizontal span. If $y_3=y_1$, the span contains the set of pixels $\{(x_3+1,y_3), (x_3+2,y_3),\ldots, (x_1,y_1)\}$.

Due to the mathematical definitions of vertical scan conversion and horizontal spans, pixels having non-extremal polysegment vertices on their pixel centers belong to the interior of the shape if they belong to a right wall. Pixels with non-extremal vertices on their pixel centers obtained by scan-conversion of a left wall do not belong to the interior pixel set.

Case d: partly degenerated shape

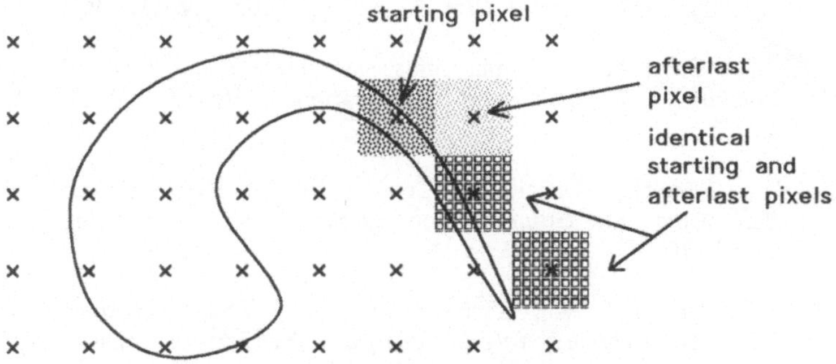

Fig. 12 Null-spans given by identical starting and afterlast pixels

The definition of *starting* and *afterlast* pixels as being the first pixels lying on the right respectively of a left or of a right wall allows null-segments to be generated when there are no discrete pixel centers between a left and a right contour part (Fig. 12). Vertical scan-conversion therefore provides a basis for generating shapes scaled down by any factor.

7. Conclusion

In the synthetic world of computer graphics, algorithms are based on appropriate definitions. Filling algorithms are based on scan-conversion of shape outlines. Restrictive definition of scan-conversion leads to filling algorithms requiring tests to be carried out for many special cases.

A new algorithm called *vertical scan-conversion* has been specially developed to meet the requirements of shape filling. It is very useful for the generation of figures described by spline outlines. During scan-conversion, splines are subdivided into polysegments having real vertices. Vertical scan-conversion generates exactly one pixel for each intersection between scanlines and the polysegment. The generated pixel represents either the first pixel or the pixel following the last pixel of a horizontal span. Vertical scan-conversion of contour polysegments leads to an even number of selected pixels on each scanline. Conventional filling algorithms (ordered edge fill, flag fill, descriptive contour fill) can be used in a simplified form, removing the need to test special cases.

Vertical scan-conversion does not suit the requirements of seed or tint fill algorithms [ROGERS85], due to the fact that vertically scan-converted contour walls (Fig. 2) do not form 8-connected discrete shape boundaries.

The future of 2-d imaging devices lies in more general algorithms which cover all possible cases without exceptions. Only such algorithms can be efficiently integrated in sillicium to produce very fast raster drawing devices.

References:

[ACKLAND81] B.D. Ackland, N.H. Weste, "The Edge Flag Algorithm - A Fill Method for Raster Scan Displays," *IEEE Trans. on Computers,* Vol 30, No 1, January 1981, pp. 41-48

[BARTELS87] R.H. Bartels, J.C. Beatty, B.A. Barsky, *An Introduction to the Use fo Splines in Computer Graphics*, Morgan Kaufmann Publ., 1987

[BRESENHAM65] J.E. Bresenham, "Algorithm for computer control of a digital plotter," *IBM Systems Journal,* Vol 4, No 1, 1965, pp 25-30

[BRESENHAM87] J.E. Bresenham, "Ambiguities in Incremental Line Rastering," *IEEE Computer Graphics and Applications*, Vol 7, No 5, May 1987, pp. 31-43

[HERSCH86] R.D. Hersch, "Descriptive Contour Fill of Partly Degenerated Shapes," *IEEE Computer Graphics and Applications,* Vol 6, No 7, July 1986, pp.61-70

[HERSCH87] R.D. Hersch, "Real Scan-Conversion of Shape Contours," *Proceedings Computer Graphics International 87,* Karuizawa, Japan, Ed. T.L. Kunii, Springer Verlag, 1987, pp. 207-220

[NEWMAN79] W.M. Newman, R.F. Sproull, *Principles of Interactive Computer Graphics,* McGraw-Hill, 1979

[PITTEWAY85] M.L.V. Pitteway, "Algorithms for Conic Generation", *Fundamental Algorithms for Computer Graphics*, (Ed. R. Earnshaw), Nato Asi Series, Vol. F17, Springer-Verlag Berlin, 1985, pp.219-237

[ROGERS85] D.F. Rogers, *Procedural Elements for Computer Graphics*, McGraw-Hill, 1985

Appendix

Shapes described by cubic splines, subdivided and generated with vertical scan-conversion

(resolution: 150 dots/inch)

Field Functions for Implicit Surfaces

B. Wyvill and G. Wyvill (Canada and New Zealand)

Abstract

The use of 3D computer generated models is a rapidly growing part of the animation industry. But the established modelling techniques, using polygons or parametric patches, are not the best to define characters which can change their shape as they move. A newer method, using iso-surfaces in a scalar field, enables us to create models that can make the dynamic shape changes seen in hand animation. We call such models, Soft Objects. From the user's point of view, a soft object is built from primitive key objects that blend to form a compound shape. In this paper, we examine some of the problems of choosing suitable keys and introduce some new field functions that increase the range of shapes available as keys.

Key words: soft objects, geometric modelling, computer animation.

Introduction

The use of 3D computer generated models in the animation industry has increased dramatically over the last ten years. The animator has the problem of designing and animating 3D characters and backgrounds. The most popular primitives for building such models in commercial systems are spline surfaces (e.g. B spline patches, Alias Research and polygon meshes, Vertigo Imagery). Primitive operations such as extrusion and surfaces of revolution aid the building of such meshes. However these techniques do not lend themselves to the creation of flexible objects such as 3D cartoon characters or the surface of a liquid. Even if polygons or patches are used as part of the rendering process, they are not usually convenient as a tool for describing 3D shapes. A technique more suited to the representation of flexible surfaces was developed by Blinn to model constant energy surfaces in molecules.(see [Blinn, 82]). A somewhat different approach to producing blended surfaces is provided by volume modelling systems. A good technique for providing blending in such systems is given in [Middleditch, 85]. In this paper the technique of building 3D models from an iso-surface in a scalar field is referred to as the Soft Object or implicit surface method. About the same time new algorithms for finding these implicit surfaces, along with field functions based on a cubic, were developed in Japan [Nishimura, 85] and in Canada [Wyvill, 86]. In the latter work the surface is sampled by uniformly subdividing space into cubic regions. Each cube can then be replaced by polygons which form an approximation to the surface. This process is referred to as polygonisation [Bloomenthal, 87]. Blinn rendered the surface directly from the function. Using the polygonisation technique enables surfaces to be prototyped. This is particularly important in an interactive environment where the surface is required in real time, see [Jevans 88]. By altering the size of the cubic cells the effective sampling rate is altered. Surface accuracy can thus be traded for speed for fast prototyping. Another advantage for polygonising the surface is that many manufacturers (e.g. Silicon Graphics) produce special purpose hardware with display lists, geometry pipelines and fast rendering oriented towards polygon primitives. Soft Object modelling can be easily integrated into these systems at the polygon level.

More recently interest has been shown by several researchers in polygonising an implicit surface. An adaptive subdivision algorithm is presented in [Von Herzen, 87]: Where the surface is changing rapidly the cubic cells are subdivided until certain criteria are satisfied. Von Herzen indentifies one major problem in his algorithm, when polygons replace adjacent cells of different size then "Cracks" between the polygons can be left in certain cases. An elegant solution to this problem is presented in [Bloomenthal 87]. After finding the cubic grid, by whatever method, each cube has to be replaced by a set of polygons. An algorithm for doing this was described in [Wyvill, 86] and a slightly more efficient algorithm given in [Lorensen 87]. A third, yet more efficient algorithm is presented in [Wyvill, 88a]. Work on implicit surfaces has led to more efficient implementation than in Blinn's original paper, although in most subsequent work a single key is used to generate a spherical surface.

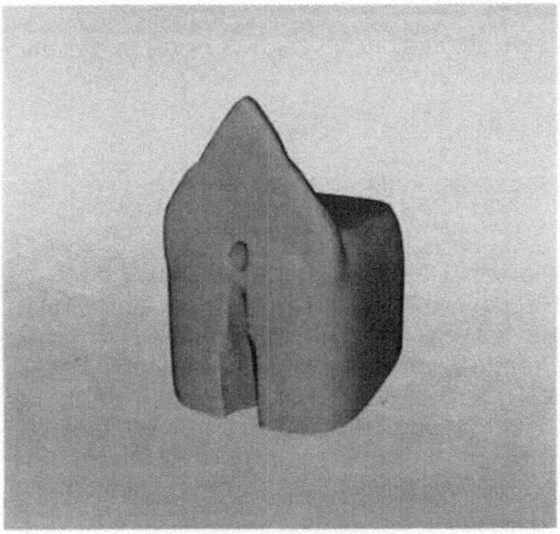

Figure 1: (Left) Iron age Bloomery furnace.

Figure 2: (Right) Soft Letters

In this paper we introduce a new family of field functions that lead to implicit surfaces of various shapes which have so far proved to be more useful for modelling than previous field functions. We also show how a single model can be built using more than one field function, giving rise to some models that would be extremely difficult to build by other techniques. We show that the new field functions are useful for modelling and we examine some of the outstanding problems in using this technique. Fig. 1 shows an example of a model built from several different field functions. It represents an iron age bloomery furnace which was reconstructed in cooperation with archaeologist Nick David at the University of Calgary. The real structure is built from clay and the computer model from Soft Objects provides a simple and appropriate model.

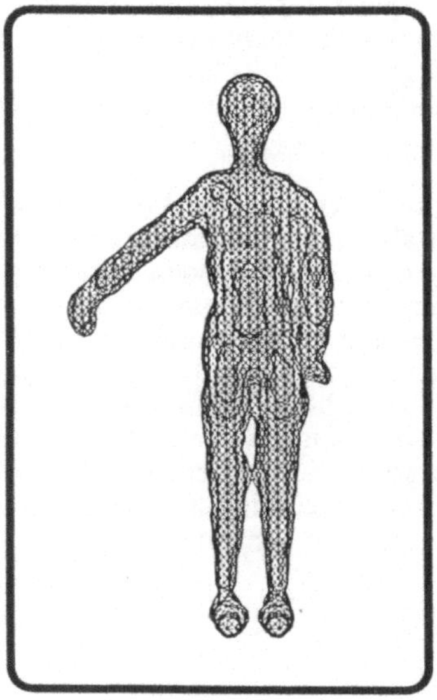

Figure 3

Problems with Soft Object Techniques for Modelling

Over the last three years we have gained some experience with using the soft object for modelling. The major problems are as follows:

a) Primitive Shape: A modeller's view of the Soft Object technique is that each key is a building block of some primitive shape, such as a sphere. Primitives can be made to blend by placing keys close together. A spherical primitive has severe limitations when flat surfaces are desired. A large number of primitives are required to produce a given effect. Fig. 2 shows the letters SFOT made from primitive spheres. The letter S has insufficient primitives (22 spheres) to describe the constantly changing curve and the underlying spheres may be observed as undesirable bulges. The T (22 spheres) requires fewer sphere primitives to manufacture the cylindrical vertical section so that it appears to be smooth. Many objects are best built from a variety of primitives rather than relying on one shape. A technique for doing this is described in this paper.

b) Undesirable Blending: A common problem with Soft Objects is that it is often required to blend certain groups of objects but not others. Consider the crude man in Fig. 3. When the arms bend they should not blend with the body although the upper arm should blend with the shoulder, as shown by the right arm of the figure. The left arm of the crude man blends both with the shoulder and unfortunately with the hips. The knees also blend undesirably. A technique for solving a sub-set of such blending problems is presented in this paper.

c) Under Sampling Effects: As a Soft Object model is moved through space in an animation sequence it is also moving through the 3D cubic grid from which the surface is sampled. If the grid is too large the surface will appear to ripple as it makes moves the grid. This is a form of aliasing characteristic of undersampling the surface.

It should be noted that these problems are inherent in this approach to modelling, they are not artefacts of our earlier implementation.

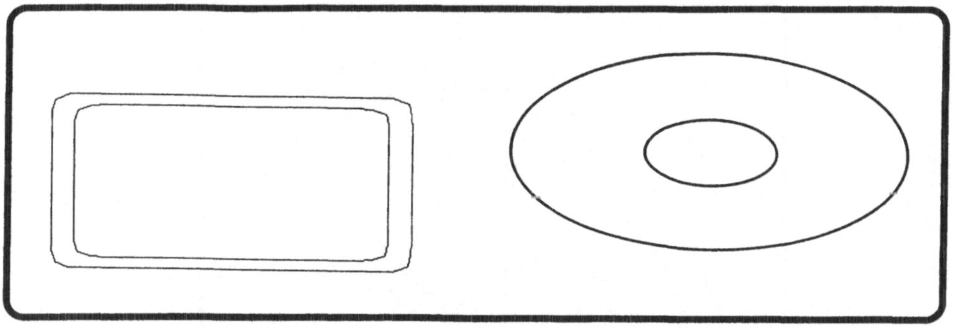

Figure 4:
An ellipsoid and a hyperellipsoid are shown in cross section. The outer contour represents the limit of influence of the field function and the inner one represents the surface. The ellipsoid function produces a large region between the contours and these shapes blend well. In the smaller region between the contours of the hyperellipsoid, the field drops rapidly to zero and the shapes blend only locally. The actual functions are:

$C((0.5 * x)^2 + y^2)$ and $C((0.5 * x)^{16} + y^{16})$ where $C(r)$ is our cubic. The contours show the function for f=0 and f=magic (0.5)

Previous Field Functions

In Blinn's system, [Blinn, 82], the principal field function used was an exponential function:

$$D(x, y, z) = \exp(-ar^2)$$

where r is the distance from the key point. But he also generalised the exponent for non spherical keys. The function:

$$-ar^2 = (x-x_i)^2 + (y-y_i)^2 + (z-z_i)^2$$

is a special case of a quadric in x,y,z and he showed how this could be replaced by a general quadric to obtain a range of primitive shapes to blend. He also suggested using hyperellipsoids by allowing exponents larger than 2 in the quadric forms.

Blinn's choice of an exponential function was suggested by the electron density fields he was modelling. But it had the disadvantage that, in principle, every key point affected the field at all points in space. We [Wyvill, 86] replaced it by a cubic function of similar shape. We chose the cubic coefficients so that the field and its derivative (with respect to r) dropped to zero at a known distance R . Beyond this 'radius of influence' the field was defined to be zero. This enabled us to combine fields, efficiently and without approximation, using large numbers of key points, because the field at any point depends only on key points in that locality. Blinn was clearly aware of the limitations of his method. He suggested using alternative decay functions but he did not include any demonstration of their effect. Replacing the r squared by a general quadric, turns out to be a very clever generalisation. The combined function: exp(Q(x,y,z)) where Q(x,y,z) is a general quadric works very well. So does our cubic approximation: C(Q(x,y,z))

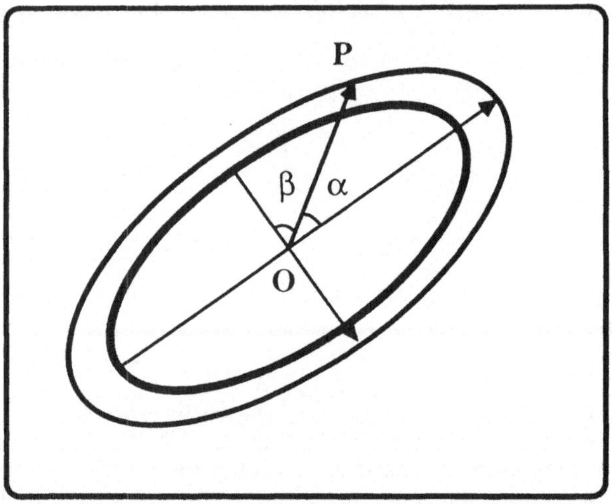

Figure 5: 2D representation of the iso-surface (in bold) due to a single key and the surface at which the force falls to zero (outer light faced ellipse)

The coefficients of the cubic, C , can be chosen to approximate the exponential over the relevant range of Q. Problems arise, however, as soon as we depart from the quadric function. This is illustrated in Fig. 4. Field functions are shown as a sequence of contour lines. The one on the left is from a simple ellipsoid represented by a quadric. The one on the right is from a hyperellipse. The quadric provides a neat generalisation of the idea of radius, but the super ellipsoid does not. The result is that the function falls off far too quickly. The close contours show this. We need to be able to use arbitrary shapes for our primitives and yet keep the controlled decay of the field with distance. Our method is not as elegant as Blinn's quadrics but it is more general.

A New Family of Field Functions

In order to find the position of the iso-surface formed by a generalised version of the field function presented in [Wyvill, 86], a few concepts have to be defined:

The primitive shape is defined by the field function. The field function is calculated from a key, given by 3 vectors normal to each other, which intersect at the origin of the key. These can be thought of as the axes of the primitive. The field function defines the surface due to the key. At the origin of the key the field has a fixed value, due to that key, known as the "force" [Nishimura, 85]1. In most of our examples, this value is fixed at plus or minus one. The contribution to the field due to the key decreases with distance from the origin, until the radius of influence is reached when the contribution is deemed to be zero.

Given a point P at distance r from the origin O of the key the contribution of that key is determined as follows:

1. Calculate the distance R where the field value turns to zero along the line OP due to the key by solving the field function.
2. If $r >= R$ then the contribution is zero.
3. Else the field is found from r and R . (Decay function).

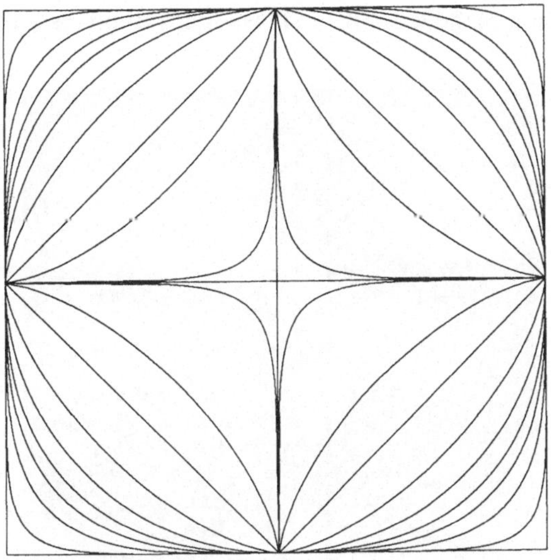

Figure 6: Piet Hein Function $x^n + y^n = 1$ From the centre n = 0,0.3, 0.7, 1.0, 1.5, 2, 2.5, 3, 4, 8,∞ The function was calculated in the positive quadrant then duplicated by symmetry.

The field function must provide a continuous closed surface. A useful family of such functions called super ellipsoids was made popular by the Danish scientist and poet, Piet Hein, see [Gardner, 65]. Other functions that could be used are the family of super quadrics [Barr, 81]. The super ellipsoids are found from the equation of the ellipsoid:

$$\frac{x^2}{a^2} + \frac{y^2}{b^2} + \frac{z^2}{c^2} = 1 \qquad \text{--------(1)}$$

Piet Hein observed that some pleasing shapes can be made by changing the power from 2 to some real power, n . Fig. 6 shows a family of these function in 2D for various values of n . To make this useful for building soft objects the field function must provide a means of calculating R (see step 1 above). The following function is formed by replacing x, y,z in (1) with Rcos(alpha) , Rcos(beta) and R cos (gamma) where alpha , beta and gamma are the angles made by the axes of the key and the vector OP. (See Fig. 5).

$$\frac{R^n\cos^n(\alpha)}{a^n} + \frac{R^n\cos^n(\beta)}{b^n} + \frac{R^n\cos^n(\gamma)}{c^n} = 1 \qquad \text{--------(2)}$$

where n is a real value.This form of the super ellipsoid provides a primitive defined by a key oriented at an arbitrary angle. The axes a, b, c can be used to alter the aspect ratio of the primitive. Since the axes are orthogonal, gamma can be found in terms of alpha and beta . Also since OP and the key axes' vectors are known, the cosine can be evaluated with a few multiplications. The value of the field can now be found from the values of r and R . It has been found empirically that substituting r and R into the cubic function given in [Wyvill, 86] provides good results. Reasonable results can also be obtained with fewer floating point calculations using:

$$F = 1 - \frac{r^2}{R^2} \qquad \text{--------(3)}$$

The contribution to the field F , of some key can be scaled by the force characteristic of that key. The force can be positive or negative providing the user with further control on the shape of the objects being modelled. Fig. 7 shows four primitives with values of n at 2 (an ellipsoid) 2.5, 3 and 4.

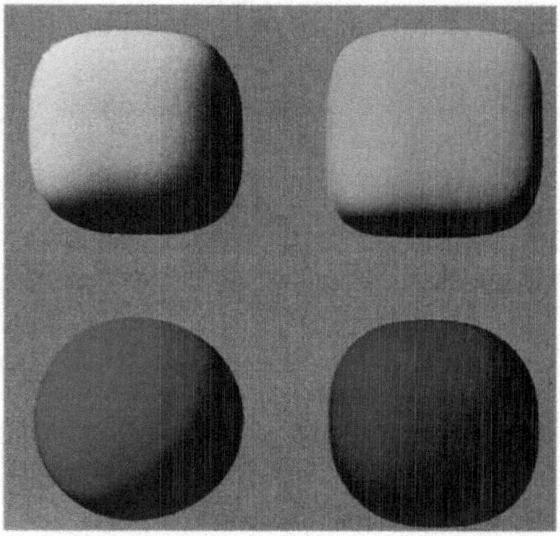

Figure 7: n = 3 (yellow) n = 4 (cyan) n = 2 (magenta) n = 2.5 (red)

Using Several Field Functions Simultaneously

Each key is identified with a number n , that refers to the n th power in equation (2). When the field at some point in space is evaluated the contribution from each key is calculated using the appropriate value of n and added into the total. Fig. 8a shows a key with n = 4 merging with a key with n = 2 . Keys can have a negative contribution to the field. Fig. 9 shows the result of combining two primitives. The block is made from a single key with n = 4 and the depression is made by adding a second primitive with n = 2.5 but with negative force. Blinn showed this effect using a spherical shape function for both positive and negative primitives [Blinn, 82]. Figure 10 shows a crude human shape constructed out of keys with n = 2 sitting on a mattress (a single key with n=4). The human figure is polygonised on a separate pass and therefore does not blend with the bed.(See section on hierachical clothing.) The imprint of the body is made by using the same human figure constructed out of negative keys and allowed to interact with the bed.

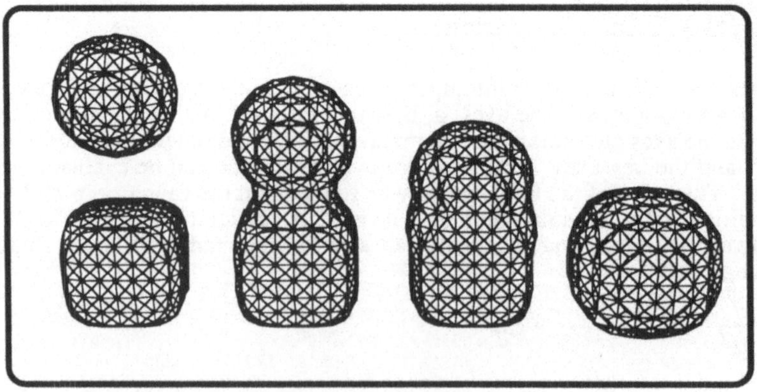

Figure 8a: Key (n=2) merging with key (n=4)

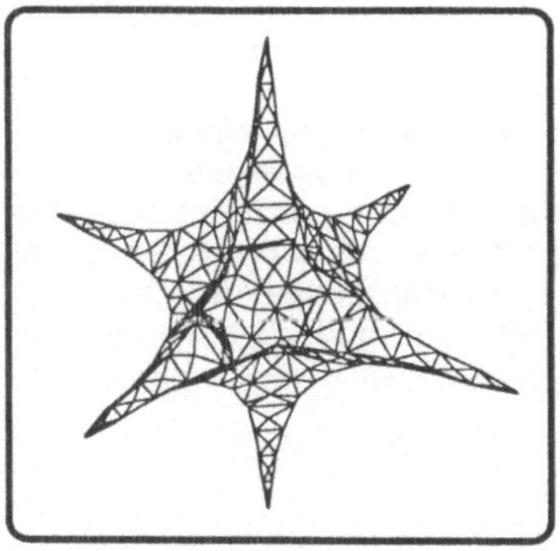

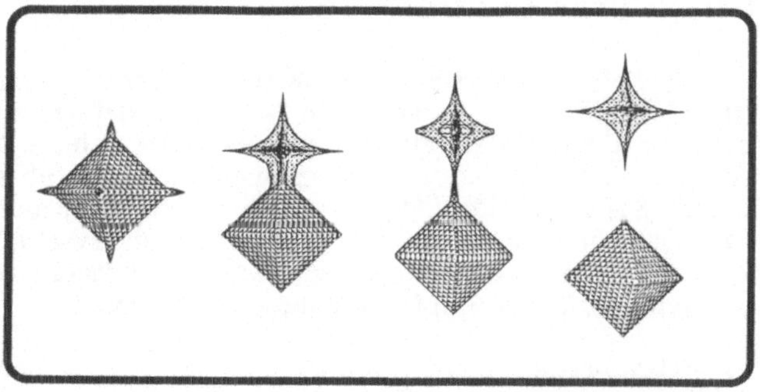

Figure 8b(left): Key (n = 0.5) Showing the effect of inadequate resolution in the space grid. The six points should have the same form.
Figure 8c (right) shows Key (n = 0.5) merging with key (n = 1)

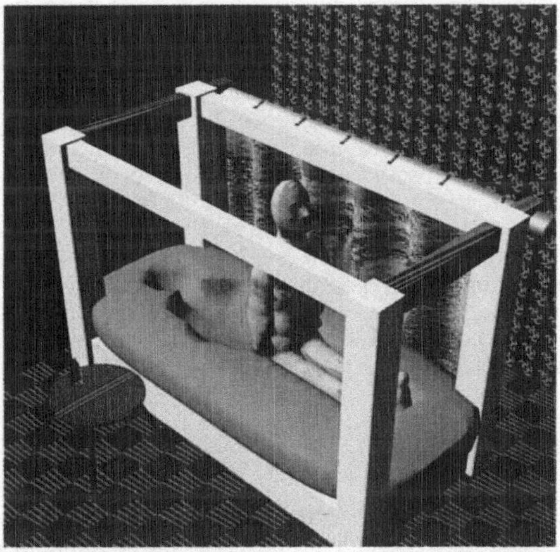

Figure 9: Positive key (n = 4) merging with (-)ve key (n = 2.5)

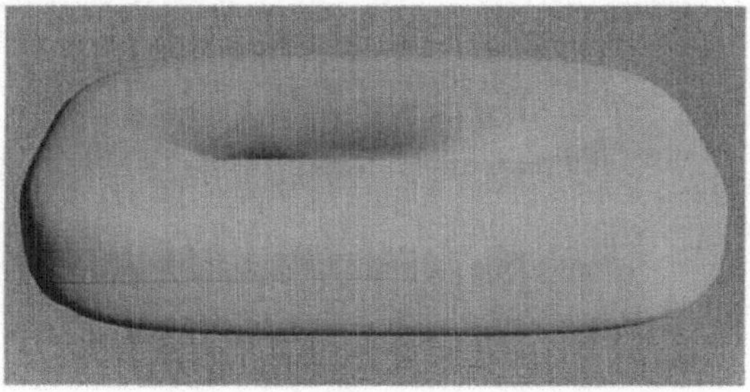

Figure 10: Monday Morning

Hierarchical Control

The Soft Object system we have built has been integrated into the Graphicsland animation system [Wyvill, 86c]. In the system, a model is defined as a list of instances of other models. Recursive references are allowed and controlled using a numerical limit. Primitives in the system can be of a variety of types which may be sub-systems such as a particle system [Reeves, 81] or the Soft Object system. Attributes needed to control the way in which the surface is to be produced are inherited through the system. Fig. 11 provides an overview of the modelling data structure. Details of the data structure and the traversal algorithm are given in [Wyvill, 86c]. For Soft Objects the attributes are:

Function type
Group
Quality
Surface attributes (colour, texture etc.)

Function type refers to the field function that is to be used to evaluate the contribution due to this soft primitive. Currently we use a float which becomes the power N in the super ellipsoid equation. This could be extended to include an integer selector to choose a class of function to be used, with the float selecting a member of that class. This allows for experimentation with new classes of function by altering the Soft Object sub-system without changing the testbed. When the data structure is traversed, each primitive is passed to its respective sub-system. A model in the system can be given a Group attribute. All Soft primitives which share the same group are passed to the Soft Object sub-system together. Each new group causes a new version of the sub-system to be executed. Only the primitives within a group will be blended together. An example is shown in Fig. 12. The letter T is made from two primitives using the super ellipsoid function with N=4 for the horizontal section and N=2 for the vertical. Fig. 12a shows the result of blending the two objects. Figure 12b shows a version where the two parts of the model have been created and given different group attributes and therefore do not blend but intersect when one is placed on top of the other. The Quality attribute governs the density of the polygon mesh approximating the surface of a group. The higher the quality the smaller the size of the cubic grid described earlier. Fig. 12b also illustrates this feature. The horizontal bar has been given a lower quality attribute (fewer polygons) than the vertical section.

Conclusions & Further Work

We have described further work in our "Soft Object" modelling system. Certain problems with this technique have been identified. The introduction of new primitive shapes gives some choice to the user, however a method of allowing the user to define the primitives would be more general. We have only provided this to the limited extent that the user may choose a real power to define a hyper ellipsoid. To make this approach to modelling practical we are developing fast interactive techniques to allow the user real time editing of implicit surfaces. [Jevans 88]. The blending problem stated earlier is also difficult to solve generally. We have found that many of these problems can be overcome with a creative use of the hierarchical group structure. However there is still a problem when model A must blend with model B and C, but B must not blend with C. This is exemplified in Fig. 3. In such a situation, when calculating the field at a point between a B key and a C key, only the higher of the two contributions should be considered. The third problem mentioned has been addressed by others, [Von Herzon 87, Bloomenthal 87], and also by our research group, [Jevans 88]. One view is that the polygon mesh is merely an intermediate test stage. A more precise surface can be obtained by ray tracing. Our current work includes a fast parallel ray tracer which uses a combination of uniform and adaptive space sub-divison. Figures 9 and 7 were produced with a prototype version of this algorithm.

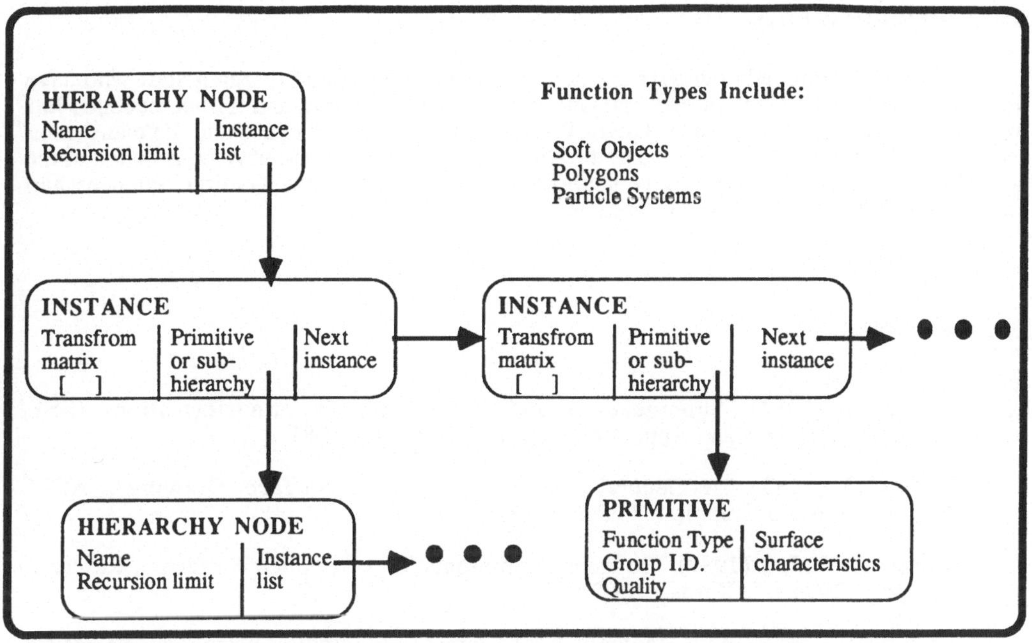

Figure 11: Basic Data Structure of Graphicsland Modelling System.

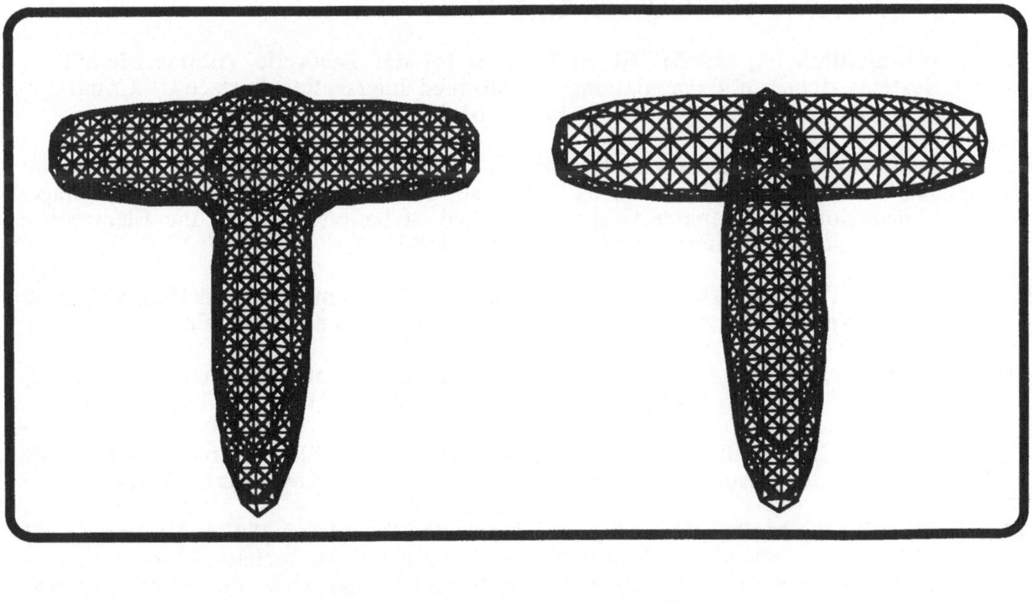

Figure 12a: Shows blending while 12b does not.

Acknowledgements

We would like to acknowledge the help of all the students and research staff who have worked on the Graphicsland project and soft objects, also the current and former students; Jeff Allan, Angus Davis, Dave Jevans, Trevor Paquette and Craig McPheeters and the many other graduate and undergraduate students at the University of Calgary who have contributed to the project. This research is partially supported by grants from the Natural Sciences and Engineering Research Council of Canada.

References

1. **Barr, A, (1981)** "Superquadrics and angle preserving transformations IEEE Comput. Graphics and Appl. Vol. 1 pp. 11-23, January 1981

2. **Blinn J (1987)** "A Generalization of Algebraic Surface Drawing", ACM Transactions on Graphics, (1) P 235, 1982

3. **Bloomenthal, J (1987)** "Boundary Representation of Implicit Surfaces", Research Report CSL-87-2, Xerox PARC.

4. **Gardner, M, (1965)** "Mathematical Games," Computer Graphics, Scientific American (July)

5. **Jevans, D, Wyvill, B, and Wyvill, G (1988)** "Speeding Up 3D Animation For Simulation", Proc. SCS Conference .

6. **Lorensen,W, (1987)** "Blend Surfaces for Set Theoretic Volume Modelling Systems Accurate Triangulations of Deformed Intersecting Surfaces," Computer Graphics, (Proc. SIGGRAPH 85) 21 (4) 163-169

7. **Middleditch, A, (1985)** "Blend Surfaces for Set Theoretic Volume Modelling Systems Accurate Triangulations of Deformed Intersecting Surfaces," Computer Graphics, (Proc. SIGGRAPH 85) 19 (3) 161-170

8. **Nishimura, H ,Hirai, A, Kawai, T, Kawata, T, Shirakawa, I, Omura, K (1985)** "Object Modeling by Distribution Function and a Method of Image Generation," Computer Graphics, Journal of papers given at the Electronics Communication Conference '85 (in Japanese) J68-D (4)

9. **Reeves, William, (1983)** "Particle systems - A Technique for modelling a class of fuzzy objects," Computer Graphics, (Proc. SIGGRAPH 83) 2 91-108

10. **Von Herzen, B, (1987)** "Accurate Triangulations of Deformed Intersecting Surfaces," Computer Graphics, (Proc. SIGGRAPH 87) 21 (4) 103-110

11. **Wyvill, G, Wyvill, B, and McPheeters, C, (1986)** "Data Structures for Soft Objects," The Visual Computer, 2 (4) 227-234. published by Springer-Verlag.

12. **Wyvill, B, McPheeters, C, and Garbutt, R., (1986)** "The University of Calgary 3D Computer Animation System," Journal of the Society of Motion Picture and Television Engineers. Vol. 95. No. 6. pp 629-636 (Awarded SMPTE journal award 1987)

A Cellular Array for Computing Bicubical B-Splines Coefficients

L. Ciminiera, P. Montuschi, and A. Valenzano (Italy)

Abstract

Two cellular arrays are presented in this paper that are able to compute bicubical B-spline polynomial coefficients. The first array can be used to compute in parallel all the coefficients for a given surface and as well as providing a speedup factor of 256 compared to the single processor computation. The second array allows to partition the computation of the coefficients so that a smaller size of the array is required. This allows the user to reach a reasonable tradeoff between the speed needs and the VLSI implementation requirements.

1 Introduction

The recent progress in technology has enabled the quality of the graphics workstations to reach such degree of sophistication as to make object visualization not only a necessary instrument for a wide range of applications, but it has also introduced a new art form which can be used to represent the real world.

While the rendering algorithms have made consistent advances, the modeling techniques have to be improved further so that the quality of object representation can be enhanced. Splines provide a powerful mathematical tool for the modelization of shapes by means of a set of parameters as well as Bezier and Hermite [1], [2] polynomials. Each of these representations offers the user some specific properties which are not included in the other and the choice of one form instead of the other, reflects the user's need for certain qualities rather than others. Available solutions include B-splines, which cover a wide range of applications, and whose success is due mostly to their definition of parametric continuity of the first and second derivative. Since the human eye is not able to identify discontinuities in the third derivative, the B-splines offer an interesting modeling which provides smooth shapes and excellent aesthetic results. Since the publication of de Boor's work [3], much research has been done and new splines have been studied and defined, including the β-splines [4], [5], [6], which guarantee geometric continuity by introducing new parameters of tension and polarization, and the ν-splines [7], which are used mostly for interpolation problems. However, the B-splines require the smallest number of parameters and they still provide an interesting and simple modeling in certain graphical environments such as the ray-tracing procedure [8].

B-spline algorithms are highly computation intensive, because they make use of rather simple calculations which are to be performed on a large number of points. This results in the time required to generate a non trivial surface being in the order of tens of minutes even for the most powerful graphic workstations, and, therefore, the development of hardware units dedicated to the speeding up of such computations would be very valuable.

Recently, systolic arrays [10]-[15] have emerged as one of the most promising approaches to the implementation of special processors for highly computation intensive algorithms, because the simplicity of each processing element and the regularity of the array structure make them suitable for cost effective implementation using VLSI circuits.

Although they have been applied to a number of algorithms for engineering and scientific applications, systolic arrays have not been used in implementation of algorithms for graphic applications. This paper presents a systolic array for the computation of coefficients of the bicubic B-spline polynomial [1].

The paper is organized as follows. Section 2 reviews the algorithm used, with an explicit derivation of the coefficients involved in the computations. Section 3 presents the array used to compute the coefficients of the bicubic B-spline polynomial while section 4 discusses the architecture of the processing elements in the array. Section 5 deals with a slightly different array, that allows the computation of the coefficients to be partitioned according to the size of the cellular array. Finally, section 6 presents some comments on the performance of the array, i.e. considerations regarding the time required to compute all the coefficients for a given surface.

2 The Algorithm

The use of the B-splines to construct curves and surfaces mostly derives from the work of Riesenfeld [9]. It has been demonstrated that cubic splines provide the continuity of the first and second order derivatives of the surface in correspondence with the *knots*. In this paper we assume that we are dealing with cubic splines. A surface is expressed as

$$S(\bar{u},\bar{v}) = \sum_{i=-3}^{m} \sum_{j=-3}^{n} P_{i,j} B_{i,3}(\bar{u}) B_{j,3}(\bar{v}) \tag{1}$$

where $B_{i,3}(\bar{u})$ and $B_{j,3}(\bar{v})$ represent the B-splines of order 3, and $\{P_{i,j}\}$ a $(m+4)\cdot(n+4)$ set of three dimensional points referred to as *control vertices*. For equally spaced *knots* [1] the form of the cubic B-spline is well known [1], [2].

Let $\bar{u}_{-3} \leq \ldots \leq \bar{u}_0 \leq \bar{u}_1 \leq \ldots \leq \bar{u}_{m+1}$ and $\bar{v}_{-3} \leq \ldots \leq \bar{v}_0 \leq \bar{v}_1 \leq \ldots \leq \bar{v}_{n+1}$ be the two sequences of distinguished values representing the knots. With no loss of generality we can assume there is a unit distance between any two consecutive knots.

Therefore, within the two parametric intervals $\bar{u}_i \leq \bar{u} < \bar{u}_{i+1}$ and $\bar{v}_j \leq \bar{v} < \bar{v}_{j+1}$ the substitutions $u = \bar{u} - \bar{u}_i$ and $v = \bar{v} - \bar{v}_i$ (with $0 \leq u, v < 1$) into the expression (1) yield, for $i = 0..m, j = 0..n$

$$S_{i,j}(u,v) = \sum_{\theta=i-3}^{i} \sum_{\phi=j-3}^{j} P_{\theta,\phi} B_{\theta,3}(u) B_{\phi,3}(v) \tag{2}$$

By defining

$$\Pi_{i,j} = \begin{bmatrix} P_{i-3,j-3} & P_{i-3,j-2} & P_{i-3,j-1} & P_{i-3,j} \\ P_{i-2,j-3} & P_{i-2,j-2} & P_{i-2,j-1} & P_{i-2,j} \\ P_{i-1,j-3} & P_{i-1,j-2} & P_{i-1,j-1} & P_{i-1,j} \\ P_{i,j-3} & P_{i,j-2} & P_{i,j-1} & P_{i,j} \end{bmatrix}, \quad K_3 = \begin{bmatrix} -1 & 3 & -3 & 1 \\ 3 & -6 & 3 & 0 \\ -3 & 0 & 3 & 0 \\ 1 & 4 & 1 & 0 \end{bmatrix}$$

and

$$U = [\, u^3 \;\; u^2 \;\; u \;\; 1 \,] \;, \quad V = [\, v^3 \;\; v^2 \;\; v \;\; 1 \,]$$

equation (2) can be rewritten

$$S_{i,j} = \frac{1}{36}\, U \, K_3 \, \Pi_{i,j} \, K_3^T \, V^T \tag{3}$$

The same approach can be followed when the Bezier polynomials are considered instead of the B-splines. It is sufficient to substitute in formula (3) the matrix K_3 with the matrix R_3, where

$$R_3 = \begin{bmatrix} -1 & 3 & -3 & 1 \\ 3 & -6 & 3 & 0 \\ -3 & 3 & 0 & 0 \\ 1 & 0 & 0 & 0 \end{bmatrix}$$

is the characteristic matrix of the Bezier polynomials, and to delete the factor $\frac{1}{36}$.

Let us now express the surface $S_{i,j}$ in terms of the coefficient of the bicubic polynomial resulting from equation (3).

$$S_{i,j} = \frac{1}{36} \sum_{f=0}^{3} \sum_{g=0}^{3} c_{i,j}^{f,g} u^f v^g$$

In this case, it is possible to solve the product $K_3\ \Pi_{i,j}\ K_3^T$ and to determine the 16 coefficients $c_{i,j}^{f,g}$ of the bicubic polynomial. It is clear that each coefficient $c_{i,j}^{f,g}$ depends on the grid of control vertices which appear in the matrix $\Pi_{i,j}$. Therefore, the coefficient $c_{i,j}^{f,g}$ can be expressed in terms of a set of values which weight the control vertices of $\Pi_{i,j}$. In formulae,

$$c_{i,j}^{f,g} = \sum_{h=1}^{4} \sum_{k=1}^{4} w_{h,k}^{f,g} P_{i+h-4,j+k-4} \tag{4}$$

An explicit formulation of the 256 values $w_{h,k}^{f,g}$ is reported in Table 1, where they have been grouped in the 16 matrices corresponding to the coefficients $c_{i,j}^{f,g}$ by means of the notation

$$\begin{bmatrix} w_{1,1}^{f,g} & w_{1,2}^{f,g} & w_{1,3}^{f,g} & w_{1,4}^{f,g} \\ w_{2,1}^{f,g} & w_{2,2}^{f,g} & w_{2,3}^{f,g} & w_{2,4}^{f,g} \\ w_{3,1}^{f,g} & w_{3,2}^{f,g} & w_{3,3}^{f,g} & w_{3,4}^{f,g} \\ w_{4,1}^{f,g} & w_{4,2}^{f,g} & w_{4,3}^{f,g} & w_{4,4}^{f,g} \end{bmatrix} \tag{5}$$

For example, the expression of the coefficient $c_{i,j}^{0,1}$ of $u^0 v^1$ is

$$c_{i,j}^{0,1} = -3P_{i-3,j-3} + 3P_{i-3,j-1} - 12P_{i-2,j-3} + 12P_{i-2,j-1} - 3P_{i-1,j-3} + 3P_{i-1,j-1}$$

However, the coefficients of the bicubic polynomial resulting from the Bezier approach can be deduced in a similar manner.

3 Array structure

When bicubic B-splines are considered, 16 coefficients $c_{i,j}^{f,g}$ for each coordinate x, y, z, must be computed for each basic area element forming the resulting surface. For our purposes a basic area element is a rectangular surface portion $S_{i,j}(u,v)$ delimited by four control vertices. Figure 1 shows a possible arrangement for a general basic area element and the vertices affecting the computation of the 16 B-spline coefficients associated to $S_{i,j}(u,v)$.

Table 1: The coefficients $c_{i,j}^{f,g}$

terms $w^{3,3}$				terms $w^{3,2}$				terms $w^{3,1}$				terms $w^{3,0}$			
1	-3	3	-1	-3	6	-3	0	3	0	-3	0	-1	-4	-1	0
-3	9	-9	3	9	-18	9	0	-9	0	9	0	3	12	3	0
3	-9	9	-3	-9	18	-9	0	9	0	-9	0	-3	-12	-3	0
-1	3	-3	1	3	-6	3	0	-3	0	3	0	1	4	1	0
terms $w^{2,3}$				terms $w^{2,2}$				terms $w^{2,1}$				terms $w^{2,0}$			
-3	9	-9	3	9	-18	9	0	-9	0	9	0	3	12	3	0
6	-18	18	-6	-18	36	-18	0	18	0	-18	0	-6	-24	-6	0
-3	9	-9	3	9	-18	9	0	-9	0	9	0	3	12	3	0
0	0	0	0	0	0	0	0	0	0	0	0	0	0	0	0
terms $w^{1,3}$				terms $w^{1,2}$				terms $w^{1,1}$				terms $w^{1,0}$			
3	-9	9	-3	-9	18	-9	0	9	0	-9	0	-3	-12	-3	0
0	0	0	0	0	0	0	0	0	0	0	0	0	0	0	0
-3	9	-9	3	9	-18	9	0	-9	0	9	0	3	12	3	0
0	0	0	0	0	0	0	0	0	0	0	0	0	0	0	0
terms $w^{0,3}$				terms $w^{0,2}$				terms $w^{0,1}$				terms $w^{0,0}$			
-1	3	-3	1	3	-6	3	0	-3	0	3	0	1	4	1	0
-4	12	-12	4	12	-24	12	0	-12	0	12	0	4	16	4	0
-1	3	-3	1	3	-6	3	0	-3	0	3	0	1	4	1	0
0	0	0	0	0	0	0	0	0	0	0	0	0	0	0	0

The spatial relation between the 16 vertex point matrix and the basic area element depicted in Fig. 1 mainly depends on the boundary conditions selected for the whole surface. In other words, by suitably choosing the starting values during the initialization step of the computation it is possible to totally or partially overlap the computation matrix and the space of definition of $S_{i,j}(u,v)$ in Fig. 1.

On the one hand, for a given basic area element and for each spatial coordinate each coefficient $c_{i,j}^{f,g}$ is obtained as shown in equation 4. These 16 coefficients can be computed fully in parallel since they depend on the same set of control vertices, whilst on the other hand, the computation of each $c_{i,j}^{f,g}$ requires the sum of 16 vertices with the weights w shown in (5).

A square array of 16×16 cells can then be used to compute all the coefficients $c_{i,j}^{f,g}$ in parallel. Each column of the array in Fig. 2 is devoted to the computation of a different coefficient $c_{i,j}^{f,g}$.

At the $t-th$ time step each cell in the array inputs two data i_1 and i_2 and outputs two results o_1 and o_2 given by:

$$o_1(t) = i_1(t-1) \tag{6}$$

$$o_2(t) = i_2(t) + i_1(t) * w \tag{7}$$

where w is the weight coefficient hardwired in each cell. Different cells hold different coefficients w.

As can easily deduced from Fig. 2 the output line o_2 of each cell in a column is directly connected to the input i_2 of the cell immediately below it. The input lines i_1 of the first four cells in the first column are connected to the external inputs and are used to bring the values of the vertices into the array. These data are then propagated downwards and rightwards in the structure so that it is not necessary to read the same value twice until the array is processing the same group of data rows. The value of the $c_{i,j}^{f,g}$ is then computed while data are passed downwards in the column.

Data vertices are input into the array by columns four at a time. However, so that the whole structure can work properly, data must be arranged as shown in Fig. 3 when they enter the array. In other words, it is necessary to have an initialization phase at the beginning of the first time step, i.e. when $i = 0$ and $j = 0$, so that the first datum $P_{-3,-3}$ enters the first cell in the first column of the array and at the end of the step the product $w_{1,1}^{3,3}P_{-3,-3}$ is placed on the o_2 line of the same cell. During the second step, $P_{-2,-3}$ enters the second cell in the first column, while $P_{-3,-2}$ is read into the first cell. At the end of the second step the partial result $w_{2,1}^{3,3}P_{-2,-3} + w_{1,1}^{3,3}P_{-3,-3}$ is output from the second cell while the product $w_{1,1}^{3,3}P_{-3,-2}$ is obtained from the first cell. This sequence continues so that at the n-th step the vertices $P_{i-3,n}$,$P_{i-2,n-1}$,$P_{i-1,n-2}$ and $P_{i,n-3}$ enter the first four cells respectively. Then, after the first 16 steps the result $c_{0,0}^{3,3} = w_{4,4}^{3,3}P_{0,0} + \ldots w_{2,1}^{3,3}P_{-2,-3} + w_{1,1}^{3,3}P_{-3,-3}$ exits the array from the o_2 line of the bottom cell in the first column.

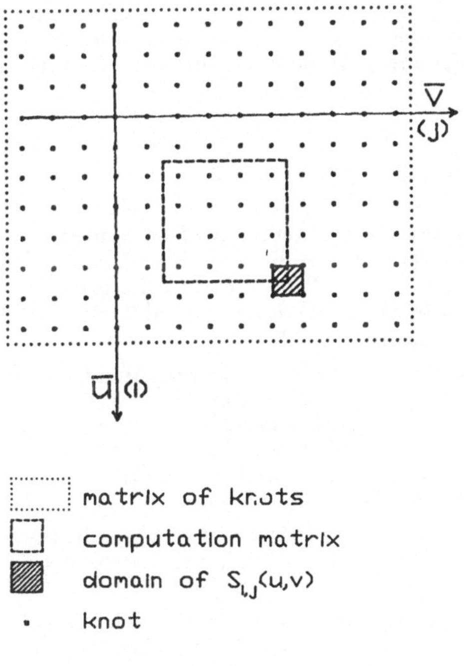

Figure 1: The computation of the $S_{i,j}(u,v)$

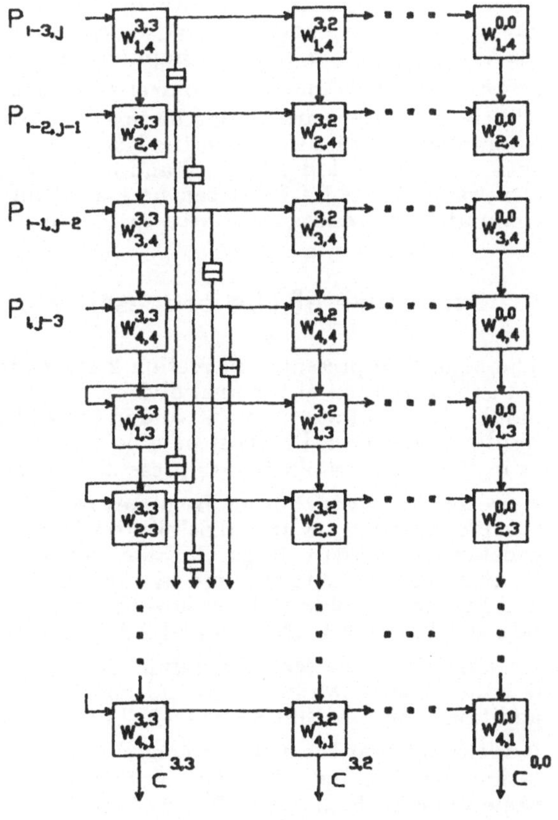

Figure 2: The structure of the cellular array

Data propagation inside the array makes use of delay elements (shown by rectangular boxes in Fig. 2) so as to guarantee the proper timing when distributing the different values among the cells. For this purpose the input line o_1 of each cell (except for the first four leftmost cells) is connected to the input i_1 of its right neighbor as well as to the same input of the the cell placed in the fourth row below the one that is being considered. In this way data are passed rightwards with a delay of one clock cycle and downwards with a delay of three clock cycles and so reach the cells in the array with the proper timing.

The last row of cells in the array is responsible for outputting the coefficients $c_{i,j}^{f,g}$ from the lines o_2. It is worth noting that because of the scheme adopted for inputing the data, the 16 coefficients $c_{i,j}^{f,g}$ obtained from the array at the end of a given step are not associated to the same basic area element $S_{i,j}(u,v)$. In fact, at the end of the 16-th step $c_{0,0}^{3,3}$ is obtained from the bottom cell in the first column, then at the end of the next step the second column completes the computation of $c_{0,0}^{3,2}$ while the first column outputs $c_{0,1}^{3,3}$. After the 32-nd step a steady state is reached where each column produces a coefficient c at each step. Hence, at the end of the n-th step the coefficients $c_{0,n-16}^{3,3}, c_{0,n-15}^{3,2}, \ldots c_{0,n}^{0,0}$ are obtained in parallel from the array.

If the whole matrix of the control vertices consists of $m+4$ rows and $n+4$ columns and a steady state condition is assumed, a group of four rows of input data is processed by the array in m steps and $16m$ coefficients $c_{i,j}^{f,g}$ are produced.

After processing data rows with indexes $i-3, i-2, i-1, i$ the array is fed with a new group of rows with indexes $i-2, i-1, i, i+1$, so that the coefficients related to $S(i+1,j), j = 1..m$ can be computed. In fact, $n(m+15)+15$ steps are required to process the whole matrix of control vertices and produce the nm coefficients $c_{i,j}^{g,f}$. The additional 15 steps are needed because at the end of the computations the array has to be emptied in order to obtain the last 15 results. This is required only when data rows with indexes $n+1, n+2, n+3$ and $n+4$ are processed, since, in general, a new group of rows $i-2, i-1, i, i+1$ can be loaded into the array while the cells are still busy computing the results associated to the row indexes $i-3, i-2, i-1, i$.

4 Structure of the processing element

The algorithm presented in section 2 shows that the elementary step of computation, with the exception of the final division by 36, consists in the multiplication of an input number by a suitable constant, and in the addition of the result obtained to the previous results. Thus, each PE must be able to perform a multiplication and an addition, just as in the other systolic arrays presented in the literature [10]-[15].

However, the algorithm for B-splines shown in section 2 allows some simplification of the PE structure, as the multiplication involves only an external datum, and a small constant. The first column of Table 2 shows in all the possible types of multiplication for positive constants required by the algorithm, with x indicating the external datum and the second column shows how the multiplication may be actually computed. It can be seen that only 1 addition and 2 shift operations are required, at most.

An analysis of the second column of Table 2 shows that one operand of the addition is either x or 0, while the second operand is either 0, 2x or 8x and the result of the addition should be shifted by 0, 1, 2 or 3 positions left.

It turns out that the arithmetic circuit shown in Fig. 4 is able to carry out the computations required for a PE. The block S/C is able to produce a result of either 0 or the same value as the input shifted by 0 or 2 positions left; since the outputs are connected to the adder circuit by introducing a further left shift, S/C is able to generate the values 0, 2x and 8x.

Table 2: Types of multiplications to be performed during the algorithm

1x	x
3x	2x+x
4x	2(2x)
6x	2(2x+x)
9x	8x+x

12x	4(2x+x)
16x	8(2x)
18x	2(8x+x)
24x	8(2x+x)
36x	4(8x+x)

The block SH produces the same value as its input s shifted by 0, 1, 2 or 3 positions left, so that it is able to generate 0, 2s, 4s and 8s. In this way, all the multiplications in Table 2 can be performed. However, the algorithm presented in section 2 requires some of the coefficients appearing in Table 2 to be used in the negative form. Therefore, the final adder/subtractor circuit is able to either add or subtract the locally computed multiplication to or from the partial result which comes from the other cells. With this device negative coefficients are implemented too.

Each PE contains programmable blocks, such as SH, S/C, C and the adder/subtractor, although it does not require any actual control unit which can manage such devices. In fact, each PE is assigned one of the specific coefficients presented in Table 1, which means that the value of the coefficient can be "hardwired" in the cell.
In order to specialize a cell, it is necessary to make the following choices:

- the wiring implementing either the constant 0 or the number of left shifts to be performed on the value of x before entering the left input of the adder;
- the wiring implementing the number of left shifts (if any) to be performed on the output of the adder;
- the wiring implementing either the constant 0 or connecting the output of the register holding x to the right input of the adder;
- the operation (addition or subtraction) to be performed by the adder/subtractor.

The result is that the blocks S/C, SH and C do not require any active device, because they can be implemented by a suitable wiring of signals, if each cell is designed individually, starting from the general structure of Fig. 4. This choice minimizes the complexity of the final circuit, but increases the complexity of the design, because the number of cells to be designed increases.

In order to simplify the design process, another implementation can be devised. The blocks SH, S/C and C can be implemented by using programmable circuit, where the word *programmable* is used in the same sense as for PLAs, that has the potentiality of performing different types of shift and clear operations, as shown in the example of Fig. 5. The same approach can be used for the adder/subtractor, by using the well known circuit which is able to perform both addition and subtraction.

5 Partitioned array

The rapid advances of integration technology make it possible for circuits of ever increasing size to be integrated in single chip; however, in some cases, a single monolithic circuit would be not sufficient to implement the whole array presented in sections 3 and 4. Moreover, it is possible that, in specific circumstances, the designer would prefer to implement a more compact array, even though the decreased complexity would have to be paid for by accepting an increased computation time.

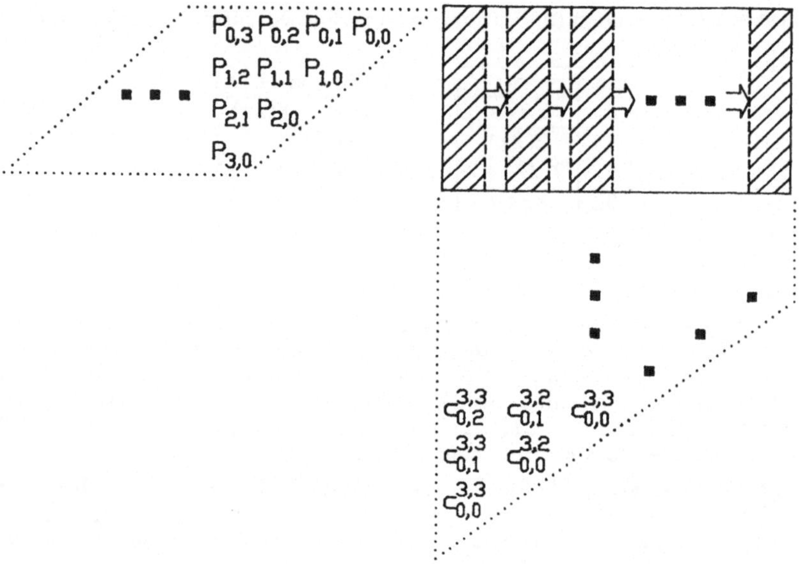

Figure 3: The input of data into the cellular array

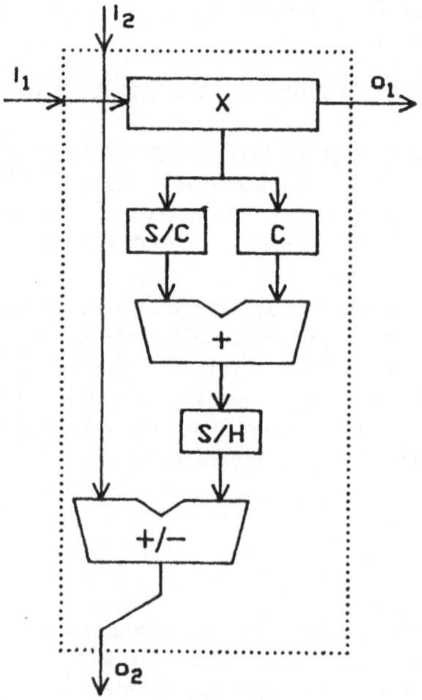

Figure 4: The basic cell

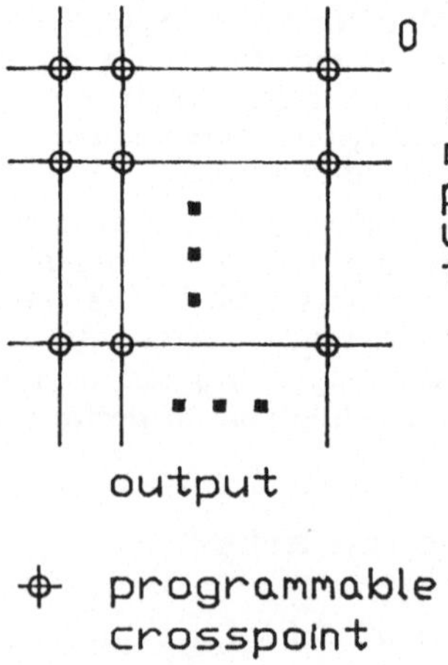

Figure 5: The programmable array for implementing the blocks S/C, C and S/H

The most obvious way to partition the whole array is by columns; in fact, each column in Fig. 2 is devoted to the computation of a single coefficient of the bicubic B-spline. In this case, the partitioned array is the one presented in Fig. 6; note that the layout is the same as for the first column of the whole array in Fig. 2, therefore the data are input and processed in the way as in the first column of the array in Fig. 2.

The real difference between the partitioned array and a column of the unit in Fig. 2 lies in the fact that the latter has to compute only one coefficient $c_{i,j}^{f,g}$ while the former must be able to compute any of the 16 coefficients.

The result is that it is not possible to use a hardwired operand in this reduced array, as in the PEs of the whole array. Fortunately, the decomposition of each multiplication required by the algorithm, shown in Table 2, is still valid, hence it is not necessary to implement a real multiplication circuit within each cell, but the computations are obtained by using only additions and shifts.

The block diagram of each PE in the reduced array is presented in Fig. 7. As it can be seen, it is quite similar to the one shown in Fig. 4, as the registers and the blocks performing arithmetic operations are unchanged.

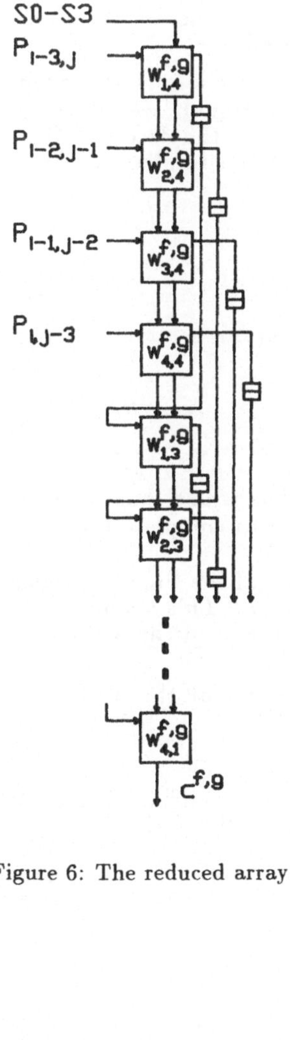

Figure 6: The reduced array

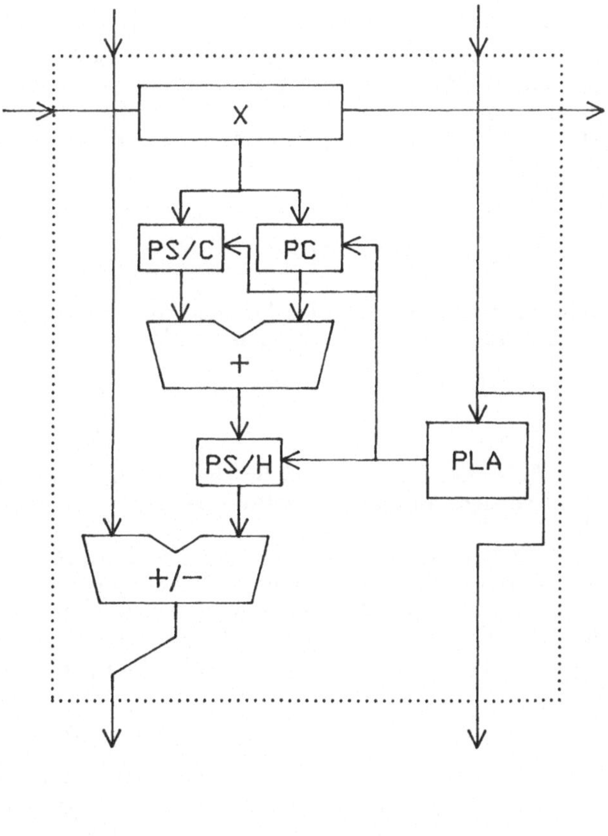

Figure 7: The single processing element of the reduced array

The blocks SH, C, and S/C are now replaced by PSH, PC and PS/C, whose function is determined by the value of 4 control signals S0-S3, as follows:

PSH performs a shift of 0, 1, 2 or 3 positions left, according to the values of S0-S3;

PS/C performs either a shift of 1 or 3 positions, or outputs a 0 value, according to the values of S0-S3;

PC replicates the input or outputs a 0 value, according to the values of S0-S3.

Note that each PE in Fig. 6 has a different decoding PLA, because S0-S3 are identical for all the array, as they carry the encoded value of the column of the whole array to be implemented by the reduced unit. Thus, the value of $w_{h,k}^{f,g}$ implemented within each PE depends on the position of the PE within the reduced array, hence the need to have different decoding circuits for each PE.

As the reduced array presented above is able to compute only one coefficient, it is necessary for the whole set of control vertices to be passed through the array 16 times, with different values of the signals S0-S3, in order to compute all the 16 coefficients of bicubic B-spline.

The full sized array represents the fastest and most expensive implementation, while the reduced array is much cheaper and slower; a range of solutions exists between these two end configurations. In fact, it is possible to implement more than one but not all the columns, decreasing the complexity of the array with respect to the full sized one, and enhancing the computation speed with respect to the reduced one.

Assuming that the implemented array includes $K = 2^k$ $(0 \leq k \leq 3)$ columns, the layout is the same as for the leftmost 2^k columns, but only $4 - k$ control signals are needed to indicate which group of coefficients has to be computed. Of course, the decoding PLA within each PE has to be programmed according to both the columns implemented and the position within the array.

6 Array performance

A relevant performance index for the arrays presented in the previous sections is represented by the speedup factor S_p defined as

$$S_p = \frac{T_s}{T_p} \tag{8}$$

where T_p is the time required by the cellular array to process the whole matrix of the control vertices and T_s is the time needed by a single processor to complete the same task.

In the following we will assume that a computation step consists of the time t_{st} needed to compute the partial result $ab + c$ where a,b,c are input numbers. This enables us to compare T_p and T_s independently of the number representation and of the arithmetic algorithms chosen.

As indicated in section 3 the time needed by the full array to compute all the coefficients $c_{i,j}^{f,g}$ in parallel is given by

$$T_p = (n(m + 15) + 15)t_{st} \tag{9}$$

where $m + 4$ and $n + 4$ are the dimensions of the control vertices matrix. If a single processor is used to process the same matrix a time T_s is required given by

$$T_s = (nm(16)(16))t_{st} = 256nm\ t_{st} \tag{10}$$

It follows that the speedup factor for the full array is given by

$$S_p = \frac{256nm}{n(m+15)+15} \tag{11}$$

while the efficiency $E_p = S_p/p$ where p is the number of cells in the array is given by

$$E_p = \frac{nm}{n(m+15)+15} \tag{12}$$

When n and m are large, as in many practical applications, $S_p \rightarrow 256$ and $E_p \rightarrow 1$; in other words when the number of control vertices is high all the 256 processing elements in the array work in parallel and the overheads for loading and unloading the cells are very small.

If a partitioned array is used consisting of K columns, where $16/K$ is an integer, the control vertices matrix must be loaded in the array $16/K$ times. In this case T_p is given by

$$T_p = \left(\frac{16n(m+15)+K}{K}\right) t_{st} \tag{13}$$

and the speedup factor can be expressed as

$$S_p = \frac{256nmK}{16n(m+15)+K} \tag{14}$$

that is S_p is about $16K$ when m and n are large.

7 Conclusions

Two new systolic arrays to compute the coefficients of B-spline bicubic polynomial have been presented in this paper.

Given the simplicity of the computations required and the regularity of their structure, the arrays lend themselves to a cost effective implementation, by means of suitable VLSI circuits.

The first array facilitates the parallel computation of all the bicubical coefficients affecting a given surface. The array structure has been introduced and the structure of the basic processing element has been presented. The solution proposed also takes into account the problem of distributing the input data among the different cells in the array.

The second array is a slightly modified version of the first one. In this case, however, the array size can be selected according to the implementation requirements since it is possible to partition the problem of computing the coefficients in smaller pieces according to the dimension of the array.

Formulae have been derived expressing the speedup factors which can be achieved with the proposed arrays. It has been shown that, when a large matrix of control vertices is considered, a speed up factor of 256 is obtained with the full array, while a speed up factor of 16K can be reached by using a partitioned array consisting of 16K cells.

References

[1] T. Pavlidis, "Graphics and Image Processing," Springer-Verlag, New York, 1982.

[2] J.D. Foley and A. Van Dam, "Fundamentals of Interactive Computer Graphics", Addison Wesley, 1981.

[3] C. de Boor, "A Practical Guide to Splines," Applied Mathematical Sciences, Vol.27, Springer-Verlag, New York, 1978.

[4] B.A. Barsky, "The Beta-Spline: A Local Representation Based on Shape Parameters and Fundamental Geometric Measures," PhD thesis, Dept. of Computer Science, University of Utah, Dec. 1981.

[5] B.A. Barsky and J.C. Beatty, " Local Control of Bias and Tension in Beta-spline," Computer Graphics, Vol.17, No.3, 1983, pp.193-218.

[6] B.A. Barsky "Computer Graphics and Geometric Modeling Using Beta-splines," Springer-Verlag, Tokyo, 1986.

[7] G.M.Nielson "Rectangular ν-splines," IEEE Computer Graphics & Applications, February 1986, pp.35-40.

[8] M.A.J. Sweeney and R.H. Bartels, "Ray Tracing Free-Form B-spline Surfaces," IEEE Computer Graphics & Applications, February 1986, pp.41-49.

[9] R.F. Riesenfeld, "Applications of B-spline Approximation to Geometric Problems of Computer Aided Design," PhD dissertation, Dept. of Systems and Information Science, Syracuse University, 1973.

[10] H.T. Kung and C.E. Leiserson, "Systolic Arrays (for VLSI)," Sparse Matrix Proc., 1978, 1979, Academic Press, Orlando, Fla., PP.256-282.

[11] C. Mead and L. Conway, eds., "Introduction to VLSI," 1980, Addison-Wesley, Reading, Mass., pp.271-292.

[12] H.T. Kung, "Why Systolic Architectures ?," Computer, Vol.15, No.1, Jan. 1982, pp.37-46

[13] D.I. Moldovan and J.A.B. Fortes, "Partitioning and Mapping Algorithms Into Fixed-Size Systolic Arrays," IEEE Trans. Computers, Vol.C-35, No.1, Jan 1986, pp.1-12.

[14] S.Y. Kung, VLSI Array Processors, Prentice-Hall, Englewood Cliffs, N.J., 1987.

[15] IEEE Computer, Special Issue on Systolic Architectures, Vol.20, No.7, July 1987.

New Results for the Smooth Connection Between Tensor Product Bézier Patches

W.-H. Du and F. J. M. Schmitt (France)

Abstract

The tensor product Bézier patch is one of the most widely used models for the representation of surfaces in CAGD. The shape of the objects to be designed is often complex so a piecewise representation is needed in most cases. If the resulting piecewise surface is to present a smooth aspect of its shape, then the geometric continuity between adjacent surface patches is essential.

Much research has been devoted to this problem, and diverse solutions have already been published. Nevertheless, various problems remain, especially the smooth connection between a non-four-number of patches meeting at a common corner. In this paper, we first study the general behaviour of the G^1 continuity constraints around an N-patch corner, which leads to useful results concerning the propagation of these constraints according to the parity of N. Then we present the conditions which allow a local determination of the surface patches, and analyze the remaining degrees of freedom which can be used to modify locally the surface shapes. These results are very useful for the design of a piecewise representation of smooth complex surfaces using Bézier patches where various configurations must be used for the connection at a corner of a different number of patches.

1. Introduction

Since the introduction of parametrical representations for the mathematical modelling of free-form curves and surfaces, diverse models have been developed, such as Coons patches, Bézier and B-splines curves and surfaces [5, 11, 20]. Several comprehensive surveys on the surface models used in CAGD (Computer Aided Geometric Design) can be found in [2, 3, 8, 15].

Most of the surface models developed in CAGD use tensor product representation, one of the most popular is the Bézier patch which presents attractive geometric properties, simple calculations, and is frequently used in free-form surface modelling.

The objects encountered in practical applications often present complex surfaces which possess some geometric continuities such as the continuity of the position, of the tangent plane, even of the curvature and torsion. When a complex surface is designed by using the tensor product Bézier representation, it is necessary, in most cases, to subdivide the surface into several pieces, and to represent each piece by a Bézier patch. The shape of the resulting piecewise representation will only present a smooth aspect if some continuity exists in its geometric properties. Thus, the control of the geometric continuity between adjacent surface patches becomes a fundamental problem.

Much research has been devoted to this problem, and diverse solutions have already been proposed. Nevertheless, various problems remain, especially the smooth connection between a non-4 number of patches meeting at a common corner. In this paper, we will study the general behaviour of the constraints allowing the continuity of the tangent plane (or G^1 continuity) around a corner where N patches meet. This will lead to useful results concerning the propagation of the continuity constraints around an N-patch corner according to the parity of N. To be tractable, the propagation of the continuity constraints must be limited in order to allow a local determination of the surface patches. We will give the conditions permitting such a local determination, and will analyze the remaining degrees of freedom which can be used to modify locally the surface shape while respecting the G^1 continuity property. These results are very useful for the design of a piecewise representation of smooth complex surfaces using Bézier patches where various configurations of connection between patches must be used.

Section 2 recalls the Bézier patch representation and Section 3 the geometric continuity between adjacent patches. In Section 4 we analyze the G^1 continuity constraints between only two adjacent patches, and in Section 5 the general behaviour of these constraints around an N-patch corner.

2. Tensor Product Bézier Patch Representation

Let us here briefly recall the mathematical expression of the tensor product Bézier patch and its main geometric properties, more detailed description can be found in [3, 5, 6, 7, 8, 14, 15].

A tensor product Bézier patch of degree $m \times n$ is defined by a control graph composed of $(m+1) \times (n+1)$ points in a 3D space, located on a topologically rectangular mesh. It is expressed as the tensor product of two Bézier curves of degree m and n as follows:

$$\mathbf{Q}\,(u,v) = \sum_{i=0}^{m} \sum_{j=0}^{n} \mathbf{P}_{ij}\, B_i^m(u)\, B_j^n(v), \qquad 0 \le u,\ v \le 1, \tag{1}$$

where $B_k^L(t) = \dfrac{L!}{k!(L-k)!}\, t^k (1-t)^{L-k}$ is the k-th term of a L-th degree univariate Bernstein polynomial, and $\mathbf{P}_{ij}$ are the 3D control points.

The Bézier patch defined by expression (1) can be seen as a mapping of the parametric domain $0 \le u,\ v \le 1$ into the 3D space. As an example, Fig. 1 shows a bicubic Bézier patch with its associated control graph.

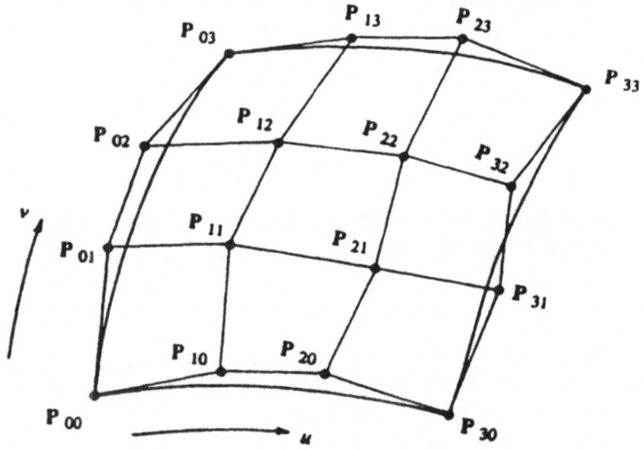

Figure 1. A bicubic Bezier patch with its associated control graph.

The Bézier patch possesses numerous interesting geometric properties. For example, the surface patch lies within the convex hull of its defining control points and mimics the shape of the control graph. This is a very useful property for shape design. Moreover, a boundary curve of a Bézier patch is obtained by setting the corresponding parameter value to 0 or 1. For instance, taking $u = 0$ in expression (1) gives:

$$\mathbf{Q}\,(0,v) = \sum_{i=0}^{m} \sum_{j=0}^{n} \mathbf{P}_{ij}\, B_i^m(0)\, B_j^n(v) = \sum_{j=0}^{n} \mathbf{P}_{0j}\, B_j^n(v), \quad 0 \le v \le 1, \tag{2}$$

which is a Bézier curve of degree n, uniquely determined by the control points belonging to the corresponding side of the control graph. Similar results hold for the three other boundaries.

Furthermore, the cross-boundary derivative vector along the boundary $\mathbf{Q}\,(0,v)$ is given by[1]:

1 We use $\mathbf{Q}^{(a,b)}(u,v)$ to denote the value of the parametric derivative vector $\dfrac{\partial^{a+b}\mathbf{Q}\,(u,v)}{\partial u^a \partial v^b}$.

$$Q^{(1,0)}(0,v) = \sum_{i=0}^{m}\sum_{j=0}^{n} \mathbf{P}_{ij} \frac{dB_i^m(u)}{du}\Big|_{u=0} B_j^n(v) = m \sum_{j=0}^{n} (\mathbf{P}_{1j} - \mathbf{P}_{0j})\, B_j^n(v), \quad 0 \le v \le 1, \tag{3}$$

which is similar to expression (2) with the vectors formed by the difference vectors between the two rows of control points $\mathbf{P}_{0j}$ and $\mathbf{P}_{1j}$, located on and immediately near the boundary $\mathbf{Q}(0,v)$. Similar results can be found along the three other boundary curves.

3. Smooth Connection Between Adjacent Patches

Consider now the smooth connection problem between adjacent patches where specific continuity properties are required. These properties will be satisfied by applying some constraint equations, called *continuity constraints*, to the patches concerned. The constraints traditionally considered correspond to the equality of the parametric derivatives along the common boundary between adjacent patches. The resulting continuity is called *parametric continuity*. For example, two adjacent patches are said C^0 continuous if they share a common boundary, and C^1 (or C^2) continuous if, in addition, the first (or the first and second) parametric derivatives are identical along their common boundary. It is obvious that the parametric continuity depends on the parametrization of the surfaces, and consequently is less significant geometrically; it is too restrained and of little use for the modelling of free-form surfaces. Less strong and geometrically more significant constraints must not depend on the parametrization of the surfaces. The continuity obtained by application of these constraints is called *geometric continuity* or *visual continuity* according to the manner of interpreting the nature of such a continuity [1,12-13,16]. For example, two adjacent patches are said G^1 (or VC^1) continuous, if the tangent plane (or equivalently the normal vector to the surface) is continuous along their common boundary, and G^2 (or VC^2) continuous if, in addition, the curvature vectors (or equivalently: the osculating paraboloid, the Dupin indicatrix, or the second fundamental form) is identical along this boundary.

In practice the G^2 continuity is difficult to control in a piecewise surface representation due to very intricate constraints. However, for many applications the G^1 continuity is sufficient. We will limit our attention to the G^1 continuity problem for the smooth connection between adjacent Bézier patches. We first describe the G^1 continuity constraints between only two adjacent patches. These results will serve as a basis for the study of the G^1 continuous connection between N patches meeting at a common corner.

4. G^1 continuity constraints between two adjacent patches

Consider two adjacent patches $\mathbf{Q}_L(u_L,v_L)$ and $\mathbf{Q}_R(u_R,v_R)$ of degree $m \times m$ (see Fig. 2). $\mathbf{Q}_L$ and $\mathbf{Q}_R$ are positionally continuous if they share a common boundary $\Gamma(v)$, that is,

$$\Gamma(v) = \mathbf{Q}_L(u_L{=}1, v_L{=}v) = \mathbf{Q}_R(u_R{=}0, v_R{=}v), \qquad 0 \le v \le 1.$$

In Section 2, we recalled that a boundary of a Bézier patch is uniquely determined by the control points belonging to the corresponding side of the control graph. So, the constraint of continuous position between patches $\mathbf{Q}_L$ and $\mathbf{Q}_R$ is equivalent to requiring that they share the same control points along their common boundary. Let $[\mathbf{P}^L]$ and $[\mathbf{P}^R]$ denote the matrices of control points of the patches $\mathbf{Q}_L$ and $\mathbf{Q}_R$, respectively, and $\mathbf{C}_i$, $i = 0, 1, 2, ..., m$, the common control points, we have then:

$$\mathbf{C}_i = \mathbf{P}^L_{m\,i} = \mathbf{P}^R_{0\,i}, \qquad i = 0, 1, 2, ..., m. \tag{4}$$

The tangent plane of a parametric surface $\mathbf{Q}(u,v)$ includes the two derivative vectors with respect to u and v, denoted by $\mathbf{Q}^{(1,0)}(u,v)$ and $\mathbf{Q}^{(0,1)}(u,v)$, respectively. The two patches $\mathbf{Q}_L$ and $\mathbf{Q}_R$ meet with G^1 continuity if the tangent plane is continuous at their common boundary. If we assume that the parametric derivative vectors of each patch are well-defined with non-null magnitude, and are non-collinear, we have the following necessary and sufficient condition for the G^1 continuity: the first derivative vector along the common boundary and the cross-boundary derivative vectors of both patches are coplanar at each point of this boundary (see Fig. 2), i.e. the determinant formed by these three vectors is zero:

$$det[\ \Gamma^{(1)}(v),\ \mathbf{Q}_L^{(1,0)}(u_L{=}1, v_L{=}v),\ \mathbf{Q}_R^{(1,0)}(u_R{=}0, v_R{=}v)\ ] = 0, \qquad 0 \le v \le 1. \tag{5}$$

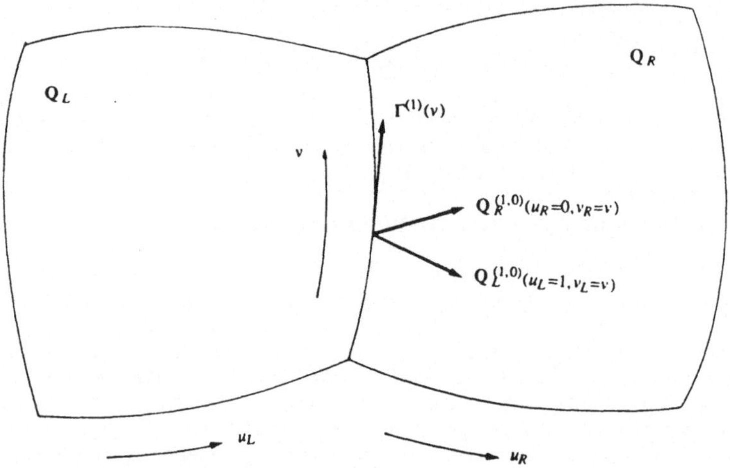

Figure 2. Two adjacent Bézier patches $\mathbf{Q}_L$ and $\mathbf{Q}_R$ meeting with the continuity of the tangent plane (or G^1 continuity) along their common boundary $\Gamma(v)$.

The above condition can be rewritten under another equivalent and more convenient form as a linear combination of the three vectors:

$$\alpha(v)\,\mathbf{Q}_R^{(1,0)}(u_R{=}0,v_R{=}v) + \beta(v)\,\mathbf{Q}_L^{(1,0)}(u_L{=}1,v_L{=}v) + \gamma(v)\,\Gamma^{(1)}(v) = 0, \quad 0 \le v \le 1, \tag{6}$$

where $\alpha(v)$, $\beta(v)$ and $\gamma(v)$ are polynomial functions of v.

From equation (3), we know that $\mathbf{Q}_L^{(1,0)}(u_L{=}1,v_L{=}v)$ and $\mathbf{Q}_R^{(1,0)}(u_R{=}0,v_R{=}v)$ are both an m*-th* degree polynomial of v, given by:

$$\mathbf{Q}_L^{(1,0)}(u_L{=}1,v_L{=}v) = m\sum_{i=0}^{m}(\mathbf{C}_i - \mathbf{P}_{m-1\,i}^{L})\,B_i^m(v), \tag{7.1}$$

$$\mathbf{Q}_R^{(1,0)}(u_R{=}0,v_R{=}v) = m\sum_{i=0}^{m}(\mathbf{P}_{1i}^{R} - \mathbf{C}_i)\,B_i^m(v), \tag{7.2}$$

By differentiating the expression of $\Gamma(v)$, as given in equation (2), we obtain the following expression of $\Gamma^{(1)}(v)$ which is an $(m-1)$*-th* degree polynomial of v:

$$\Gamma^{(1)}(v) = m\sum_{i=0}^{m-1}(\mathbf{C}_{i+1} - \mathbf{C}_i)\,B_i^{m-1}(v). \tag{7.3}$$

In order to balance the degree of the three polynomials in equation (6), we take $\alpha(v)$ and $\beta(v)$ as constant, and $\gamma(v)$ as a linear function of v. Without loss of generality, we can set the value of $\alpha(v)$ to 1, and for later convenience, we note the value of $\beta(v)$ by $-\beta$:

$$\alpha(v) = 1, \qquad \beta(v) = -\beta, \qquad \gamma(v) = \gamma_0\,(1-v) - \gamma_1\,v. \tag{8}$$

Substituting equations (7) and (8) into equation (6) yields:

$$\sum_{i=0}^{m}(\mathbf{P}_{1i}^{R} - \mathbf{C}_i)\,B_i^m(v) - \beta\sum_{i=0}^{m}(\mathbf{C}_i - \mathbf{P}_{m-1\,i}^{L})\,B_i^m(v) + (\gamma_0\,(1-v) - \gamma_1\,v)\sum_{i=0}^{m-1}(\mathbf{C}_{i+1} - \mathbf{C}_i)\,B_i^{m-1}(v) = 0.$$

Using the following identities:

$$(1-v)\sum_{i=0}^{m-1}(\mathbf{C}_{i+1} - \mathbf{C}_i)\,B_i^{m-1}(v) = \sum_{i=0}^{m}\frac{m-i}{m}(\mathbf{C}_{i+1} - \mathbf{C}_i)\,B_i^m(v)$$

$$v\sum_{i=0}^{m-1}(\mathbf{C}_{i+1} - \mathbf{C}_i)\,B_i^{m-1}(v) = \sum_{i=0}^{m}\frac{i}{m}(\mathbf{C}_i - \mathbf{C}_{i-1})\,B_i^m(v)$$

where the fictitious points $\mathbf{C}_{m+1}$ and $\mathbf{C}_{-1}$ appear only for convenient notations, we finally obtain:

$$\sum_{i=0}^{m}\left[(\mathbf{P}_{1i}^{R} - \mathbf{C}_i) + \beta\,(\mathbf{P}_{m-1\,i}^{L} - \mathbf{C}_i) + \gamma_0\,\frac{m-i}{m}(\mathbf{C}_{i+1} - \mathbf{C}_i) + \gamma_1\,\frac{i}{m}(\mathbf{C}_{i-1} - \mathbf{C}_i)\right]B_i^m(v) = 0, \quad 0 \le v \le 1.$$

The $m+1$ terms $B_i^m(v)$, $i = 0, 1, ..., m$ being the m–*th* degree univariate Bernstein polynomial, they form a basis of the m–*th* degree polynomial space. So, the above expression means that each composite term before $B_i^m(v)$ must be zero. We obtain then the following G^1 continuity constraints between $\mathbf{Q}^L$ and $\mathbf{Q}^R$ (see Fig. 3):

$$(\mathbf{P}^R_{1i} - \mathbf{C}_i) + \beta\,(\mathbf{P}^L_{m-1\,i} - \mathbf{C}_i) + \gamma_0\,\frac{m-i}{m}\,(\mathbf{C}_{i+1} - \mathbf{C}_i) + \gamma_1\,\frac{i}{m}\,(\mathbf{C}_{i-1} - \mathbf{C}_i) = 0, \qquad (9)$$

$$i = 0, 1, 2, ..., m.$$

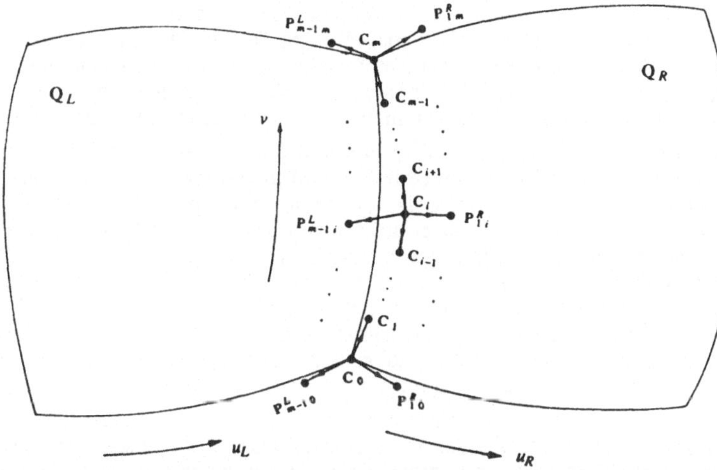

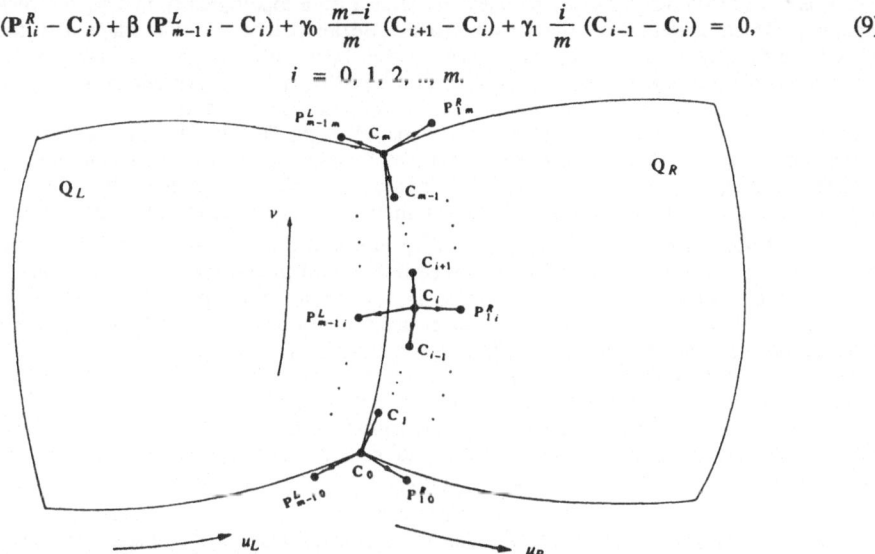

Figure 3. Geometric interpretation of the G^1 continuity constraints (9) between the two adjacent patches $\mathbf{Q}_L$ and $\mathbf{Q}_R$, expressed with the control points situated at the neighbourhood of their common boundary curve.

Farin [13] first gave this solution with a geometric interpretation. The $m+1$ linear equations (9) involve the three columns of control points located in the immediate neighbourhood of the boundary Γ common to the two adjacent patches. They form the *geometric* constraints guaranteeing the G^1 continuity. Because they control *only* the geometric properties of the connection between two adjacent patches they are intrinsically independent of the parametric directions u_L, u_R and v which we have arbitrarily chosen for the derivation of constraints (9). This is directly apparent when interpreting each equation (9) as a barycentric combination of the 4 difference vectors formed between $\mathbf{C}_i$ and its 4 adjacent control points (the barycentric combination is reduced to 3 difference vectors at the two ends of Γ for $i = 0$ and $i = m$). However, the definition of the constants β, γ_0 and γ_1 are dependent on *the chosen orientation* of the common boundary Γ inherited from the previous parametric direction v: β weights the difference vectors oriented towards the *left* side of Γ, γ_0 weights the difference vectors $(\mathbf{C}_{i+1} - \mathbf{C}_i)$, oriented from $\mathbf{C}_0$ to $\mathbf{C}_m$ in the control graph, while γ_1 weights the difference vectors $(\mathbf{C}_{i-1} - \mathbf{C}_i)$, oriented from $\mathbf{C}_m$ to $\mathbf{C}_0$.

If we consider the reverse orientation of Γ from $\mathbf{C}_m$ to $\mathbf{C}_0$, we can rewrite the G^1 continuity constraints (9) by introducing 3 new constants β', γ_0' and γ_1'. γ_0' and γ_1' now weight the difference vectors oriented from $\mathbf{C}_m$ to $\mathbf{C}_0$ and from $\mathbf{C}_0$ to $\mathbf{C}_m$ respectively. The constant β' weights the difference vectors opposite to those weighted by β. To guarantee identical G^1 continuity properties, we must have the following relations:

$$\beta' = \frac{1}{\beta}, \qquad \gamma_0' = \frac{\gamma_1}{\beta}, \qquad \gamma_1' = \frac{\gamma_0}{\beta}.$$

The particular case where $\beta = \beta' = 1$ is very attractive because it gives an equal weighting of the difference vectors on the two sides of the boundary curve Γ. However, we still need to specify the orientation of Γ together with the two constants γ_0 and γ_1 (or γ_0' and γ_1'), γ_0 (or γ_0') weighting the difference vectors oriented from the beginning to the end of the boundary curve and the reverse for γ_1 (or γ_1').

The smooth connection between only two adjacent patches has already been studied in a general setting by several authors [4-7, 9-10, 13-14, 17-19, 21-22, 24]. But, the smooth connection between several patches meeting at a common corner is much more complex because of the intertwining of the continuity constraints along their boundary curves meeting at this corner. In numerous CAGD applications, the patches are defined on a topologically rectangular mesh. The rectangular parametric domain of the tensor product Bézier patches is well adapted to this topology, and it allows a relatively simple, smooth connection between these patches [4-7, 18, 22-23]. However, diverse surface shapes can not be represented just by a set of patches defined on a rectangular mesh. Typical examples include the so-called suitcase corners and the branches of a treelike volume. To represent such particular surface shapes using Bézier patches, we have two possible approaches: either by permitting three, five or more patches to meet at a common corner, or by degenerating one, two or more boundaries of a patch [5,7]. But this degeneration produces an asymmetrical treatment of the patch whereas the symmetry of the surface shapes is often required.

Several authors have studied the smooth connection problem at a non-4 patch corner. Bézier sketches a theorical solution in [5,7], expressed in terms of the polynomial coefficients. Sarraga [21] extends Bézier's work to interpolate a generally unrestricted network of cubic Bézier curves where three, four or five curves are allowed to meet at an interior network node. Chiyokura and Kimura [9-10] propose another method to interpolate smoothly an irregular network of cubic Bézier curves by using the Gregory patch, a modified Bézier patch. Hosaka and Kimura [17-18] connect three, five or six bicubic Bézier patches at a common but isolated corner to construct an agglomerated patch having three, five or six sides. Beeker [4] considers the smooth connection problem at a three- or five-patch corner inside a mesh of bicubic patches, and surrounded by four-patch corners. Schmitt and Du [23] refine and extend the approach proposed by Beeker.

Up until now, the smooth connection problem between a non-4 number of patches meeting at a common corner has been considered either in an isolated manner, or in some special cases. In the following section, we study in a general setting how the G^1 continuity constraints (9) intertwine when any number N of patches meet at a common corner. We state explicitly the resulting constraints to be satisfied. We then describe how the control points can be determined under these constraints and analyze the remaining degrees of freedom which can be used to control the surface shape in the neighbourhood of the common corner.

5. G^1 continuity constraints around an N-patch corner

Consider a corner $\mathbf{O}$ where N Bézier patches $\mathbf{Q}_j$, $j = 1, 2, ..., N$ of degree $m \times m$ meet together, as shown in Fig. 4. The indices are taken cyclically around the corner $\mathbf{O}$. These patches are positionally continuous, if they all share the corner point $\mathbf{O}$, and if each of them shares the same control points with its adjacent patches along their common boundary curves Γ_j, $j = 1, 2, ..., N$. We assume that the orientation of these boundary curves is from the common corner towards the outside. For each boundary curve Γ_j, we can thus define unambiguously the associated constants β, γ_0 and γ_1 which will be noted by β_j, γ_j^0 and γ_j^1. Any other choice for the orientation could be taken, but would lead to equivalent results as seen in Section 3. We can then simply renote the control points in the neighbourhood of $\mathbf{O}$: on each boundary curve Γ_j, $\mathbf{C}_0$ is the common corner $\mathbf{O}$; $\mathbf{C}_1$ and $\mathbf{C}_2$ are renoted by $\mathbf{C}_j$ and $\mathbf{E}_j$ respectively; the nearest interior control point of the patch $\mathbf{Q}_j$ from the corner $\mathbf{O}$ is renoted by $\mathbf{I}_j$.

The G^1 continuity around the corner point $\mathbf{O}$ is obtained if the G^1 continuity constraints (9) along each boundary curve Γ_j are satisfied. From Fig. 4, we see that these constraints intertwine around the corner point $\mathbf{O}$. The control point $\mathbf{C}_j$ ($j = 1, 2, ..., N$) appears in the first G^1 continuity constraints (9) (where $i = 0$) along the three adjacent boundary curves Γ_{j-1}, Γ_j and Γ_{j+1} (the indices being taken cyclically, the indice $N+1$ is equivalent to the indice 1 and the indice -1 equivalent to the indice N). Similarly the control point $\mathbf{I}_j$ ($j = 1, 2, ..., N$) appears in the second G^1 continuity constraints (9) (where $i = 1$) along the two adjacent boundary curves Γ_j and Γ_{j+1}. The remaining G^1 continuity constraints (9) (where $i = 2,..., m$) along any boundary curve Γ_j no longer share common control points with those along its adjacent boundary curves Γ_{j-1} and Γ_{j+1}, so there is no longer any interaction between them. This means that around the N-patch corner $\mathbf{O}$, the interaction between the G^1 continuity constraints (9) along the N boundary curves Γ_j is limited only to the first two G^1 continuity conditions (9) ($i = 0, 1$).

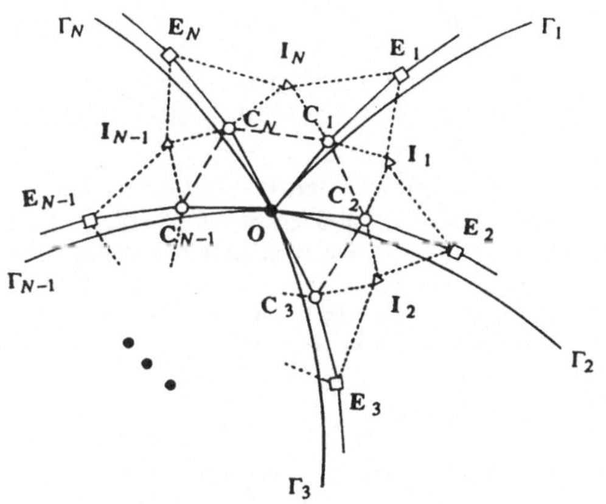

Figure 4. N Bézier patches meeting at the common corner $\mathbf{O}$.

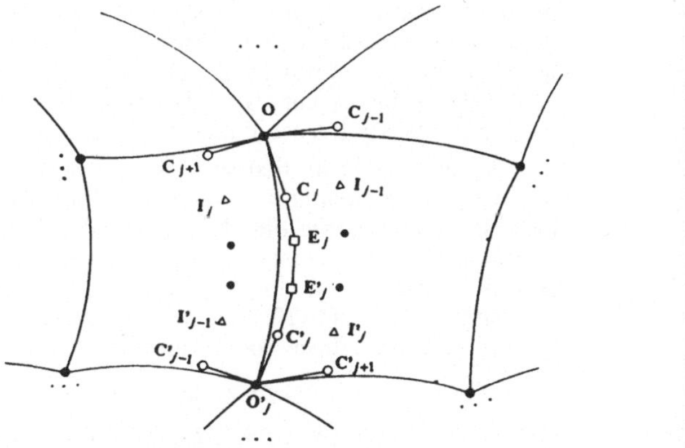

Figure 5. Determination of the control points around the even-number patch corner $\mathbf{O}$ in the case of biquintic patches.

These intertwined G^1 continuity constraints can be easily regrouped into two sets. The first set consists of the first constraints (9) (where $i = 0$) which control the G^1 continuity at the corner point $\mathbf{O}$, and which involve with $\mathbf{O}$ the control points $\mathbf{C}_j$, $j = 1, 2, ..., N$, located on the boundary edges. With the new notations and according to equations (9), we obtain the following system:

$$(\mathbf{C}_2 - \mathbf{O}) + \beta_1 (\mathbf{C}_N - \mathbf{O}) + \gamma_1^0 (\mathbf{C}_1 - \mathbf{O}) = 0 \qquad (10.1)$$

....

$$(\mathbf{C}_{j+1} - \mathbf{O}) + \beta_j (\mathbf{C}_{j-1} - \mathbf{O}) + \gamma_j^0 (\mathbf{C}_j - \mathbf{O}) = 0 \qquad (10.j)$$

....

$$(\mathbf{C}_1 - \mathbf{O}) + \beta_N (\mathbf{C}_{N-1} - \mathbf{O}) + \gamma_N^0 (\mathbf{C}_N - \mathbf{O}) = 0 \qquad (10.N)$$

The second set consists of the second constraints (9) (where $i = 1$) acting on the G^1 continuity along each boundary curve and in which are involved the control points $\mathbf{I}_j$ and $\mathbf{E}_j$, $j = 1, 2, ..., N$:

$$(\mathbf{I}_1 - \mathbf{C}_1) + \beta_1 (\mathbf{I}_N - \mathbf{C}_1) + \gamma_1^0 \frac{m-1}{m} (\mathbf{E}_1 - \mathbf{C}_1) + \gamma_1^1 \frac{1}{m} (\mathbf{O} - \mathbf{C}_1) = 0 \qquad (11.1)$$

....

$$(\mathbf{I}_j - \mathbf{C}_j) + \beta_j (\mathbf{I}_{j-1} - \mathbf{C}_j) + \gamma_j^0 \frac{m-1}{m} (\mathbf{E}_j - \mathbf{C}_j) + \gamma_j^1 \frac{1}{m} (\mathbf{O} - \mathbf{C}_j) = 0 \qquad (11.j)$$

....

$$(\mathbf{I}_N - \mathbf{C}_N) + \beta_N (\mathbf{I}_{N-1} - \mathbf{C}_N) + \gamma_N^0 \frac{m-1}{m} (\mathbf{E}_N - \mathbf{C}_N) + \gamma_N^1 \frac{1}{m} (\mathbf{O} - \mathbf{C}_N) = 0 \qquad (11.N)$$

In order to satisfy the G^1 continuity constraints expressed by system (10) and (11), the involved control points $\mathbf{O}$, $\mathbf{C}_j$, $\mathbf{I}_j$ and $\mathbf{E}_j$, $j = 1, 2, ..., N$, must be defined in a compatible way. We will consider that the corner point $\mathbf{O}$ is first fixed after having freely chosen its position in the 3D space. In the following sub-sections, we will first describe how the control points $\mathbf{C}_j$, $j = 1, 2, ..., N$, can be defined under the constraints of system (10), and then the control points $\mathbf{I}_j$ and $\mathbf{E}_j$, $j = 1, 2, ..., N$, under the constraints of system (11).

5.1. Determination of the control points $\mathbf{C}_j$ under constraints (10)

It can be observed that with constraint (10.j), the control points $\mathbf{C}_{j-1}$, $\mathbf{C}_j$, $\mathbf{C}_{j+1}$, and the corner point $\mathbf{O}$ must be coplanar. We immediately deduce that the N control points $\mathbf{C}_j$ must be coplanar with the corner $\mathbf{O}$. This plane is the tangent plane of the piecewise surface at the corner $\mathbf{O}$. We will note the normal vector of this plane by $\vec{n}$. We observe also, from system (10) and Fig. 4, that if any two adjacent control points $\mathbf{C}_j$ and $\mathbf{C}_{j+1}$ are fixed, the remaining control points $\mathbf{C}_k$, $k \neq j$, $j+1$, are then successively defined by the G^1 continuity constraints in system (10) when crossing one after another the boundary curves Γ_k. But in order to obtain a compatible solution, the values of the β_j and γ_j^0 must satisfy the conditions shown below.

We first freely fix two successive control points, for example, $\mathbf{C}_1$ and $\mathbf{C}_2$. To determine the remaining control points $\mathbf{C}_j$, we begin from the boundary curve Γ_2 and cross successively, in a clockwise direction (see Fig. 4), the boundary curves $\Gamma_2, \Gamma_3, ..., \Gamma_{N-1}$. We then obtain successively, by system (10), the vectors $\mathbf{C}_3 - \mathbf{O}$, $\mathbf{C}_4 - \mathbf{O}$, ..., $\mathbf{C}_N - \mathbf{O}$, all expressed as a linear combination of the two vectors $\mathbf{C}_1 - \mathbf{O}$ and $\mathbf{C}_2 - \mathbf{O}$. When we cross the boundary curves Γ_N and Γ_1, the continuity constraints (10.N) and (10.1) define a new value for the vectors $\mathbf{C}_1 - \mathbf{O}$ and $\mathbf{C}_2 - \mathbf{O}$, respectively, expressed also as a linear combination of $\mathbf{C}_1 - \mathbf{O}$ and $\mathbf{C}_2 - \mathbf{O}$:

$$(\mathbf{C}_1 - \mathbf{O}) = F_1(\beta_j, \gamma_j^0, j = 1, 2, ..., N)\,(\mathbf{C}_1 - \mathbf{O}) + G_1(\beta_j, \gamma_j^0, j = 1, 2, ..., N)\,(\mathbf{C}_2 - \mathbf{O}), \quad (12.1)$$

$$(\mathbf{C}_2 - \mathbf{O}) = F_2(\beta_j, \gamma_j^0, j = 1, 2, ..., N)\,(\mathbf{C}_1 - \mathbf{O}) + G_2(\beta_j, \gamma_j^0, j = 1, 2, ..., N)\,(\mathbf{C}_2 - \mathbf{O}), \quad (12.2)$$

where $F_1(\,.\,)$, $F_2(\,.\,)$, $G_1(\,.\,)$ and $G_2(\,.\,)$ are all polynomial functions in which the degree of the variables β_j and γ_j^0 is 0 or 1.

In the general case where the points $\mathbf{O}$, $\mathbf{C}_1$ and $\mathbf{C}_2$ are not chosen colinear, equations (12) are equivalent to the following constraints to be satisfied by the β_j and γ_j^0, $j = 1, 2, ..., N$:

$$F_1(\beta_j, \gamma_j^0, j = 1, 2, ..., N) = 1, \qquad G_1(\beta_j, \gamma_j^0, j = 1, 2, ..., N) = 0, \quad (13.1)$$

$$F_2(\beta_j, \gamma_j^0, j = 1, 2, ..., N) = 0, \qquad G_2(\beta_j, \gamma_j^0, j = 1, 2, ..., N) = 1. \quad (13.2)$$

These four constraints can be rewritten into four others from which one is particularly simple and can be directly found as follows. By taking on the right the vector product of equation (10.j) with $(\mathbf{C}_j - \mathbf{O})$, and then the scalar product with the normal vector $\vec{n}$, we obtain:

$$[(\mathbf{C}_{j+1} - \mathbf{O}) \times (\mathbf{C}_j - \mathbf{O})] \cdot \vec{n} + \beta_j\,[(\mathbf{C}_{j-1} - \mathbf{O}) \times (\mathbf{C}_j - \mathbf{O})] \cdot \vec{n} = 0$$

and,

$$\beta_j = \frac{[(\mathbf{C}_{j+1} - \mathbf{O}) \times (\mathbf{C}_j - \mathbf{O})] \cdot \vec{n}}{[(\mathbf{C}_j - \mathbf{O}) \times (\mathbf{C}_{j-1} - \mathbf{O})] \cdot \vec{n}},$$

where β_j is geometrically interpreted as the ratio of the area of the triangle $\mathbf{O}\ \mathbf{C}_j\ \mathbf{C}_{j+1}$ and the area of the triangle $\mathbf{O}\ \mathbf{C}_{j-1}\ \mathbf{C}_j$. With the cyclical notation of the indices j we finally deduce the following constraint involving only the constants β_j:

$$\prod_{j=1}^{N} \beta_j = \prod_{j=1}^{N} \frac{[(\mathbf{C}_{j+1} - \mathbf{O}) \times (\mathbf{C}_j - \mathbf{O})] \cdot \vec{n}}{[(\mathbf{C}_j - \mathbf{O}) \times (\mathbf{C}_{j-1} - \mathbf{O})] \cdot \vec{n}} = 1. \quad (14)$$

The β_j can be chosen and fixed according to the constaint (14). Among the four constraints (13), three remain acting on the γ_j^0, $j = 1,2,..., N$. The values of $(N-3)$ γ_j^0 can be freely chosen, the remaining 3 γ_j^0 are then determined by the constraints (13).

Thus, at an N-patch corner where the G^1 continuity is required, we have 3 degrees of freedom for the free positionning of the corner point $\mathbf{O}$, and 6 for the free choice of any two adjacent control points $\mathbf{C}_j$ and $\mathbf{C}_{j+1}$. At this fixed total number of 9 degrees of freedom for the determination of the control points $\mathbf{O}$ and $\mathbf{C}_j$, $j = 1, 2,..., N$, must be added the $N-3$ degrees of freedom for the choice of the N γ_j^0 when the β_j have been fixed according to (14). All these degrees of freedom can be used to control the surface shape in the neighbourhood of the corner $\mathbf{O}$.

5.2. Determination of the control points $\mathbf{I}_j$ and $\mathbf{E}_j$ under constraints (11)

Consider now system (11) and the determination of the control points $\mathbf{I}_j$ and $\mathbf{E}_j$, $j = 1, 2, ..., N$, the control points $\mathbf{O}$ and $\mathbf{C}_j$ having already been chosen as described above. We can perform this determination in different ways. However, it is in general desirable that the continuity constraints propagate as little as possible. We consider the following solution which satisfies this property. We first freely fix the N control points $\mathbf{E}_j$ and then determine the interior control points $\mathbf{I}_j$ under the constraints system (11).

To do this, we rewrite system (11) under the following equivalent matrix product form:

$$\begin{bmatrix} 1 & 0 & \dots & 0 & \beta_1 \\ \beta_2 & 1 & \dots & 0 & 0 \\ 0 & \beta_3 & \dots & 0 & 0 \\ \vdots & \vdots & & \vdots & \vdots \\ 0 & 0 & \dots & 1 & 0 \\ 0 & 0 & \dots & \beta_N & 1 \end{bmatrix} \begin{bmatrix} \mathbf{I}_1 \\ \mathbf{I}_2 \\ \mathbf{I}_3 \\ \vdots \\ \mathbf{I}_{N-1} \\ \mathbf{I}_N \end{bmatrix} = \begin{bmatrix} \mathbf{H}_1 \\ \mathbf{H}_2 \\ \mathbf{H}_3 \\ \vdots \\ \mathbf{H}_{N-1} \\ \mathbf{H}_N \end{bmatrix}, \tag{15}$$

where

$$\mathbf{H}_j = (1+\beta_j)\,\mathbf{C}_j + \gamma_j^0 \frac{m-1}{m} (\mathbf{C}_j - \mathbf{E}_j) + \gamma_j^1 \frac{1}{m} (\mathbf{C}_j - \mathbf{O}), \quad j = 1, 2, \dots, N. \tag{16}$$

The above $N \times N$ matrix has a diagonal structure and its rows and columns contain only two non-nul elements. Its determinant is:

$$Det[\,.\,] = 1 + (-1)^{N+1} \prod_{j=1}^{N} \beta_j\,.$$

When the β_j have been chosen according to the constraint (14), we obtain:

$$Det[\,.\,] = 1 + (-1)^{N+1} = \begin{cases} 2 & \text{if } N \text{ is odd,} \\ 0 & \text{if } N \text{ is even.} \end{cases}$$

When N is odd, we can thus inverse the $N \times N$ and find a unique solution to $\mathbf{I}_j$, $j = 1, 2, \dots, N$, the control points $\mathbf{E}_j$, $j = 1, 2, \dots, N$ having been freely chosen.

When N is even, the determinant of the $N \times N$ matrix equals zero. Due to the nature of this matrix, it can be easily verified that its rank is $N-1$. This means that for the control points $\mathbf{I}_j$, $j = 1, 2, \dots, N$ to have a solution, the N elements $\mathbf{H}_j$ must satisfy a particular linear equation whose coefficients correspond to the linear dependence of the rows of the $N \times N$ matrix. We then obtain the following supplementary constraint:

$$\sum_{j=1}^{N} (-1)^{j-1} \Big[\prod_{k=1}^{j} \beta_k\Big]^{-1} \mathbf{H}_j = 0. \tag{17}$$

When this constraint is satisfied 3 degrees of freedom are thus released for the determination of the interior control points $\mathbf{I}_j$.

In order to provide a better geometric interpretation for the difference between N even and N odd, we can use the simplified analogy of a closed chain made of N spokes (the extremities of which would the $\mathbf{I}_j$), the middle of each spoke being placed on a fixed pivot (the pivots would be the $\mathbf{C}_j$). If the number N of the spokes is odd (as N=3) a unique and fixed postion for the chain can be found. If N is even a position would be found only when the pivots respect certain relative positions, and in this case the chain can be articulated like a ring of synchronized see-saw. To illustrate the G^1 continuity around an N-patch corner according to the parity of N, two numerical examples are given in the Appendix.

The linear constraint (17) can be rewritten by replacing $\mathbf{H}_j$ by its expression (16): a linear constraint is then obtained with the corner point $\mathbf{O}$ and the $2N$ control points $\mathbf{C}_j$ and $\mathbf{E}_j$. The existence of this new constraint (17) in the case of an even-number patch corner increases the difficulty of the determination of the control points. In the next section, we study in which circumstances the constraint (17) propagates and impedes a local determination. We will first consider the general case where the constants γ_j^0 and γ_j^1 are non-nul and then discuss the partcular case where these constants are nul.

5.3. Case of the even-number patch corner

(1) In the case of biquintic (or higher degree) patches ($m \geq 5$), we can impose the linear constraint (17) solely on the choice of the control points $\mathbf{E}_j$, $j = 1, 2, ..., N$. This will not affect the local determination of the homologous control points around the patch corners $\mathbf{O'}_j$ adjacent to $\mathbf{O}$ and situated at the ends of the curves Γ_j, $j = 1, 2, ..., N$ (see Fig. 5), i.e. in this case, the control points around each patch corner are defined in a local manner.

(2) In the case of biquartic patches ($m = 4$), the control point $\mathbf{E}_j$ located on the boundary curve Γ_j in the neighbourhood of the corner $\mathbf{O}$ also become the homologous point $\mathbf{E'}_j$ for the corresponding adjacent patch corner $\mathbf{O'}_j$ (see Fig. 6). In this case, two situations have to be considered. In the first situation, all the adjacent corners $\mathbf{O'}_j$ are odd-number patch corners. The linear constraint (17) required at the even corner $\mathbf{O}$ can then be imposed solely on the choice of the control points $\mathbf{E}_j$, $j = 1, 2, ..., N$. This will not affect the local determination of the control points around the adjacent patch corners $\mathbf{O'}_j$. In the second situation, there is at least one of the adjacent corners $\mathbf{O'}_j$ which is an even-number patch corner. The corresponding linear constraint (17) required at this adjacent patch corner intertwines with the linear constraint (17) required at the corner $\mathbf{O}$ because they share the common control point ($\mathbf{E}_j = \mathbf{E'}_j$). This means that, in this situation, the linear constraint (17) propagates and it is no longer possible to have a local determination of the control points $\mathbf{E}_j$ and $\mathbf{I}_j$ around the corner $\mathbf{O}$.

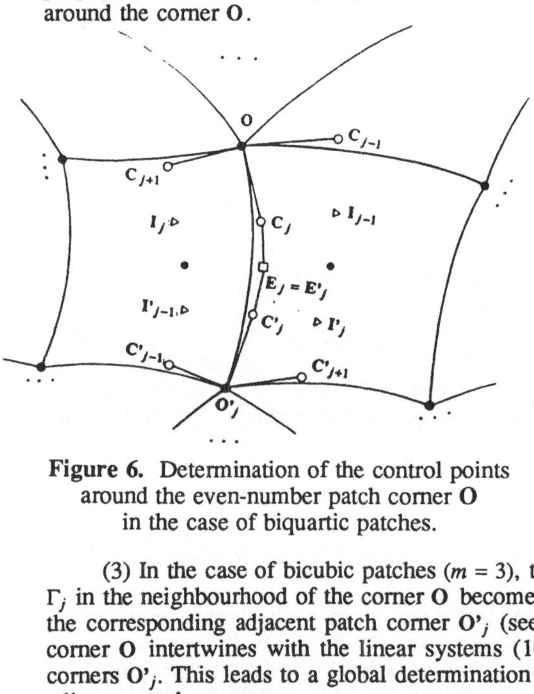

Figure 6. Determination of the control points around the even-number patch corner **O** in the case of biquartic patches.

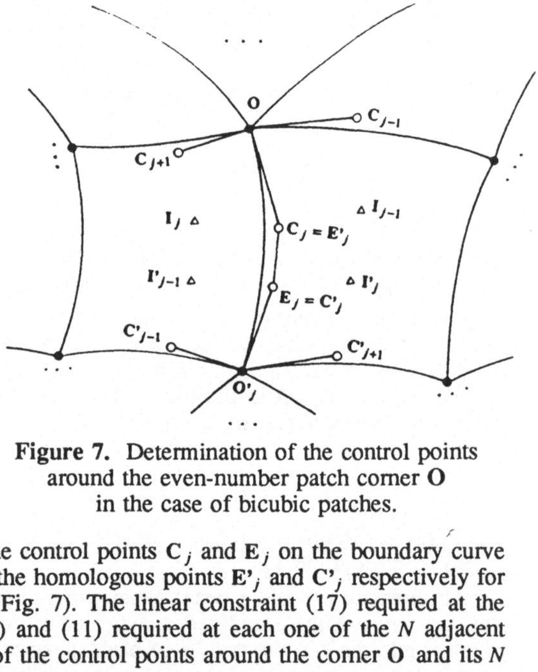

Figure 7. Determination of the control points around the even-number patch corner **O** in the case of bicubic patches.

(3) In the case of bicubic patches ($m = 3$), the control points $\mathbf{C}_j$ and $\mathbf{E}_j$ on the boundary curve Γ_j in the neighbourhood of the corner $\mathbf{O}$ become the homologous points $\mathbf{E'}_j$ and $\mathbf{C'}_j$ respectively for the corresponding adjacent patch corner $\mathbf{O'}_j$ (see Fig. 7). The linear constraint (17) required at the corner $\mathbf{O}$ intertwines with the linear systems (10) and (11) required at each one of the N adjacent corners $\mathbf{O'}_j$. This leads to a global determination of the control points around the corner $\mathbf{O}$ and its N adjacent patch corners.

Up until now in this analysis we have considered the general case where the values of γ_j^0 and γ_j^1 are non-nul. Indeed, the propagation of the linear constraint (17) is due to the presence of non-nul γ_j^0 and γ_j^1. In the case of a piecewise surface defined on a rectangular mesh, we can set the values of all the γ_j^0 and γ_j^1 to zero at each 4-patch corner. From this specific choice the control points $\mathbf{E}_j$ disappear from the equation (16) and the constraint (17) concerns then only the control points $\mathbf{O}$ and $\mathbf{C}_j$. When these points satisfy system (10), it can be verified that the constraint (17) on the control points $\mathbf{O}$ and $\mathbf{C}_j$ is automatically satisfied and thus vanishes. So, in this particular case, the continuity constraints remain localized around each 4-patch corner. To obtain a local determination of the control points, the use of bicubic patches is then sufficient. This is the solution generally used [4,5,7,17,18,22,23]. However, when N is different from 4, it is no longer possible to set all the γ_j^0 and γ_j^1 to zero (the choice of zero value will produce degenerated surface patches [23]). In this case, to be sure of obtaining a local determination of the control points around each patch corner, we can use the biquintic Bézier patches which offer sufficient degrees of freedom to limit the propagation of the G^1 continuity constraints around the even-number patch corners, as seen previously.

5.4. Remaining degrees of freedom

We now analyze the number of degrees of freedom remaining in the intertwined G^1 continuity constraints around an N-patch corner. These degrees of freedom will permit the control of the shape of the G^1 continuous surface around the corner $\mathbf{O}$. As we have already seen, for any N, either odd or even, there are 9 degrees of freedom for the free positionning of the corner point $\mathbf{O}$ and of any two adjacent control points $\mathbf{C}_j$ and $\mathbf{C}_{j+1}$. The remaining control points $\mathbf{C}_k$, $k \neq j, j+1$ are then fully determined by system (10) when the set of constants β_j and γ_j^0 have been fixed. The β_j must be chosen under the constraint (14), i.e. their product is equal to 1. But this constraint (14) intertwines with the full set of the similar constraints corresponding to the other piecewise surface corners. The β_j must then be chosen in a global way. However, a simple and homogeneous solution exists: we choose for any β_j the value 1. We still dispose of $N-3$ degrees of freedom for the choice of the constants γ_j^0 according to the constraints (13). So, we finally have $9 + (N-3) = N + 6$ degrees of freedom in the determination of the set of the control points $\mathbf{O}$ and $\mathbf{C}_j$, $j = 1, 2, ..., N$.

When N is odd, we can freely choose the control points $\mathbf{E}_j$, situated on the boundary curve Γ_j, $j = 1, 2, ..., N$. Thus we have $3N$ degrees of freedom for their determination. The interior control points $\mathbf{I}_j$, $j = 1, 2, ..., N$, are then totally determined by system (15).

When N is even, for the interior control points $\mathbf{I}_j$, $j = 1, 2, ..., N$ to have a solution, we must impose the compatibility linear constraint (17) on the control points $\mathbf{E}_j$, $j = 1, 2, ..., N$. We have now, only $3(N-1)$ degrees of freedom for their determination. However, due to the rank $N-1$ of the $N \times N$ matrix in equation (15), 3 degrees of freedom are released for the determination of the interior control points $\mathbf{I}_j$, $j = 1, 2, ..., N$.

From there, we observe that there are $3N$ degrees of freedom remaining in the determination of the set of the $2N$ control points $\mathbf{I}_j$ and $\mathbf{E}_j$, but these degrees are distributed in different manners according to the parity of N. More globally, when N is odd, all the degrees of freedom can be used to determine the control points situated on the boundary edges: $\mathbf{O}$, $\mathbf{C}_j$, $\mathbf{E}_j$, $j = 1, 2, ..., N$. When N is even, 3 degrees of freedom are removed from the determination of the control points $\mathbf{E}_j$ situated on the boundary edges, and used to determine the interior control points $\mathbf{I}_j$, $j = 1, 2, ..., N$. This transfer provokes, around an even-number patch corner, the propagation of the intertwined G^1 continuity constraints one control point further along each boundary curve towards the adjacent corners.

The above discussions deal with the general case where the values of γ_j^0 and γ_j^1 are non-nul. In the case of a piecewise surface defined on a rectangular mesh, all the γ_j^0 and γ_j^1 can be set to zero at each 4-patch corner and, as we have already mentioned in Subsection 5.3, this specific choice permits us to localize the G^1 continuity constraints in the neighbourhood of each 4-patch corner. In this particular case of an even-number patch corner, we then have 9 degrees of freedom to define the corner point $\mathbf{O}$ and any two adjacent control points $\mathbf{C}_j$ and $\mathbf{C}_{j+1}$, 12 degrees of freedom for the $\mathbf{E}_j$, and finally 3 degrees of freedom for determining the four interior control points $\mathbf{I}_j$, $j = 1, 2, 3, 4$.

6. Conclusion

We have studied, in this paper, the general behaviour of the G^1 continuity constraints in a piecewise representation of a surface using Bézier patches. We have explicitly stated the linear constraints arising around an N-patch corner and we have shown how they intertwine. The analysis has led to interesting conclusions concerning the propagation of these constraints around an N-patch corner according to the parity of N. We have then given the conditions under which this propagation does not impede a local determination of the surface patches. We have also analyzed the degrees of freedom which remain under the G^1 continuity constraints and which can be used to control the surface shape in the neighbourhood of the patch corner. All these new results are very useful for the design of smooth complex surfaces by using a piecewise representation with Bézier patches and where various configurations are necessary for the connection at a corner of an even or an odd number of patches.

Appendix

To illustrate the G^1 continuity around a common corner where odd or even number N Bézier patches meet, we present here two specific examples with bicubic Bézier patches: a 3 (odd number) patch corner and a 6 (even number) patch corner. In each case, we give the control graphs of all the patches, the coordinates of the control points $\mathbf{C}_j$, $\mathbf{E}_j$ and $\mathbf{I}_j$ around the patch corner $\mathbf{O}$, and shaded raster image of the resulting surface. One can verify that the continuity constraints (10) and (11) around each patch corner are satisfied, and in the case of the 6-patch corner, the linear constraint (17) can also be verified.

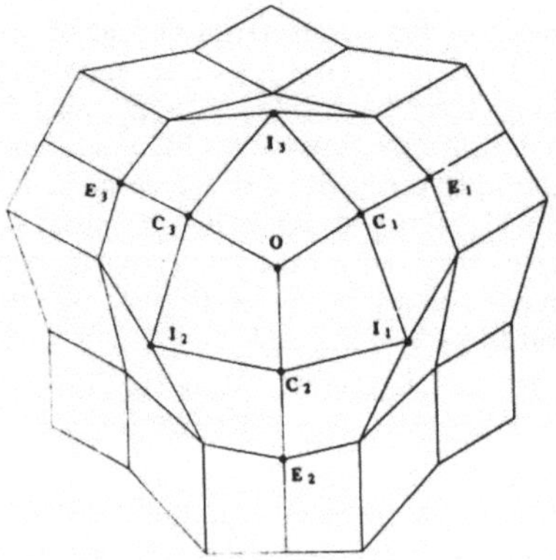

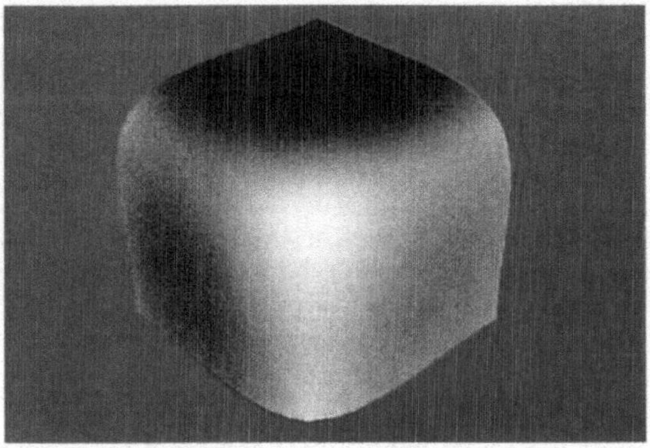

Control graphs | shaded raster image

A 3-patch corner

$\beta_j = 1,\ \gamma_j^0 = 1,\ \gamma_j^1 = 0,\ j = 1, 2, 3.$

$\mathbf{O}$ (1.0000,1.0000,1.0000),

$\mathbf{C}_1$(0.7500,1.1250,1.1250), $\mathbf{E}_1$(0.3333,1.0000,1.0000), $\mathbf{I}_1$(0.8890,1.4443,0.8890),

$\mathbf{C}_2$(1.1250,1.1250,0.7500), $\mathbf{E}_2$(1.0000,1.0000,0.3333), $\mathbf{I}_2$(1.4443,0.8890,0.8890),

$\mathbf{C}_3$(1.1250,0.7500,1.1250), $\mathbf{E}_3$(1.0000,0.3333,1.0000), $\mathbf{I}_3$(0.8890,0.8890,1.4443),

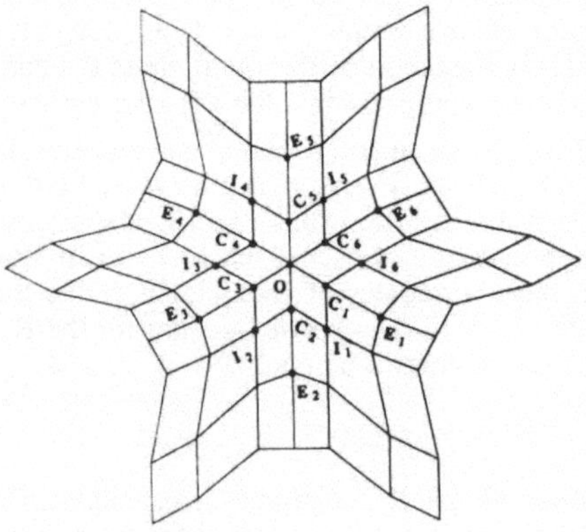

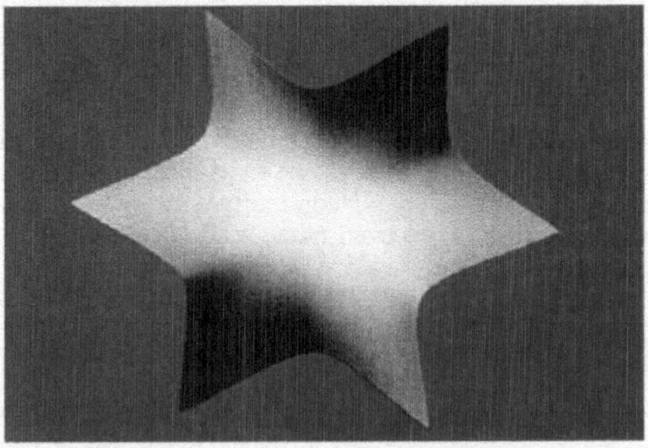

Control graphs | shaded raster image

A 6-patch corner

$\beta_j = 1,\ \gamma_j^0 = -1,\ \gamma_j^1 = 0,\ j = 1, 2, 3, 4, 5, 6,$

$\mathbf{O}$ (1.0000,1.0000,1.0000),

$\mathbf{C}_1$(0.8333,1.3333,0.8333), $\mathbf{E}_1$(0.5833,1.8333,0.5833), $\mathbf{I}_1$(1.0000,1.5000,0.5000),

$\mathbf{C}_2$(1.1667,1.1667,0.6667), $\mathbf{E}_2$(1.4167,1.4167,0.1667), $\mathbf{I}_2$(1.5000,1.0000,0.5000),

$\mathbf{C}_3$(1.3333,0.8333,0.8333), $\mathbf{E}_3$(1.8333,0.5833,0.5833), $\mathbf{I}_3$(1.5000,0.5000,1.0000),

$\mathbf{C}_4$(1.1667,0.6667,1.1667), $\mathbf{E}_4$(1.4167,0.1667,1.4167), $\mathbf{I}_4$(1.0000,0.5000,1.5000),

$\mathbf{C}_5$(0.8333,0.8333,1.3333), $\mathbf{E}_5$(0.5833,0.5833,1.8333), $\mathbf{I}_5$(0.5000,1.0000,1.5000),

$\mathbf{C}_6$(0.6667,1.1667,1.1667), $\mathbf{E}_6$(0.1667,1.4167,1.4167), $\mathbf{I}_6$(0.5000,1.5000,1.0000),

References

[1] B. A. Barsky: *The Beta-spline: A Local Representation Based on Shape Parameters and Fundamental Geometric Measures*, Ph.D. Thesis, University of Utah, Salt Lake City, Utah, December, 1981.

[2] B. A. Barsky: "A Description and Evaluation of Various 3-D Models," *IEEE Computer Graphics & Applications*, Vol. 4, No. 1, January, 1984, pp. 38-52.

[3] R. H. Bartels, J. C. Beatty and B. A. Barsky: *An Introduction to the Use of Splines in Computer Graphics*, to be published by Morgan Kaufmann Publishers, Inc., Los Altos, California, 1987.

[4] E. Beeker: "Smoothing of Shapes Designed with Free-Form Surfaces," *Computer-Aided Design*, Vol. 18, No. 4, May, 1986, pp. 224-232.

[5] P. E. Bézier: *Emploi des machines à commande numérique*, Masson et Cie., Paris, 1970. Translated by R. A. Forrest and A. F. Pankhurst as: *Numerical Control -- Mathematical and Applications*, John Wiley and Sons Ltd., London, 1972.

[6] P. E. Bézier: "Mathematical and Practical Possibilities of UNISURF," in *Computer-Aided Geometric Design*, edited by R. E. Barnhill and R. F. Riesenfeld, Academic Press, New York, 1974, pp. 127-152.

[7] P. E. Bézier: *Courbes et surfaces*, Mathématiques et CAO, Volume 4. Hermès Publishing 1986.

[8] W. Boehm, G. Farin and J. Kahmann: "A Survey of Curve and Surface Methods in CAGD," *Computer Aided Geometric Design*, Vol. 1, 1984, pp. 1-60.

[9] H. Chiyokura and F. Kimura: "Design of Solids with Free-Form Surfaces," *Computer Graphics (SIGGRAPGH'83 Conference Proceedings)*, Detroit, 1983, pp. 289-298.

[10] H. Chiyokura and F. Kimura: "A New Surface Interpolation Method for Irregular Curve Models," *Computer Graphics Forum*, Vol. 3, 1984, pp. 209-218.

[11] S. A. Coons: "Surfaces for Computer-Aided Design of Space Forms," Report MAC-TR-41, Massachusetts Institute of Technology, June, 1967.

[12] T. A. DeRose: *Geometric Continuity: A Parametrization Independent Measure of Continuity for CAGD*, Report No. UCB/CSD 86/255, UC Berkeley.

[13] G. Farin: "A Construction for the Visual C^1 Continuity of Polynomial Surface Patches," *Computer Graphics and Image Processing*, Vol. 20, 1982, pp. 272-282.

[14] I. D. Faux and M. J. Pratt: *Computational Geometry for Design and Manufacture*, Ellis Horwood Ltd., 1979.

[15] R. A. Forrest: "On Coons and Other Methods for the Representation of Curved Surfaces," *Computer Graphics and Image Processing* Vol. 1, No. 4, December 1972, pp. 341-359.

[16] G. Herron: "Techniques for Visual Continuity," In G. Farin ed., *Geometric Modelling*, SIAM, Philadelphia, 1987. pp. 163-174.

[17] M. Hosaka and F. Kimura: "Synthesis Methods of Curves and Surfaces in Interactive CAD," *Proceedings of the International Conference on Interractive Techniques in Computer Aided Design*, Bologna, 1978, pp. 151-156.

[18] M. Hosaka and F. Kimura: "A Theory and Methods for Three Dimensional Free-Form Shape Construction," *Journal of Information Processing*, Vol. 3, No. 3, 1980. pp. 140-151.

[19] J. Kahmann: "Continuity of Curvature between Adjacent Bézier Patches," in R. E. Barnhill and W. Boehm edited *Surfaces in CAGD*, North-Holland, Amsterdam, 1983, pp. 65-75.

[20] R. F. Riesenfeld: *Applications of B-Splines Approximation to Geometric Problems of Computer-Aided Design*, Ph.D. Thesis, Syracuse University, Syracuse, New York, May, 1973.

[21] R. F. Sarraga: " G^1 Interpolation of Generally Unrestricted Cubic Bézier Curves," *Computer Aided Geometric Design*, Vol 4, No. 1-2, 1987. pp. 23-39.

[22] F. J. M. Schmitt, B. A. Barsky and W.-H. Du: "An Adaptive Subdivision Method for Surface-Fitting from Sampled Data," *SIGGRAPH'86 Conference Proceedings*, ACM, Dallas, Texas, August 18-22, 1986. pp. 179-188.

[23] F. J. M. Schmitt and W.-H. Du: "Bézier Patches with Local Shape Control Parameters," *Proceedings of EUROGRAPHICS'87*, Amsterdam, 24-28 August 1987, pp. 261-274.

[24] M. Veron, G. Ris and J.-P. Musse: "Continuity of Biparametric Surface Patches," *Computer Aided Design*, Vol. 8, No. 4, October 1976, pp. 276-273.

Three-Dimensional Shape Generation Based on Generalized Symmetry

T. Tanaka, S. Naito, and T. Takahashi (Japan)

Abstract

A new principle of generating three-dimensional shapes from two-dimensional images based on generalized symmetry is presented. Generalized symmetry is an extended concept of symmetry and represents the symmetrical characteristics of an object in terms of its curvilinear symmetry axis. This paper first develops the definition and the constraint of the generalized symmetry, and then describes an algorithm which generates the three-dimensional shape of an object from a line-drawing. This assumes that the line-drawing is an orthographic projection of an object which exhibits generalized symmetry. Several experiments by computer simulation verify that the algorithm can generate three-dimensional shapes from line-drawings.

1 Introduction

The recent progress in software and hardware technology for image rendering has made it possible to synthesize images of very complex scenes. However, modeling of objects still remains a great problem that demands a lot of effort from graphic designers. In a typical system, designers have to estimate and input the three-dimensional positions of a great number of surface points for the intended object using data tablets or key boards. Furthermore, this task involves a lot of trial and error. This is one of the stumbling blocks which limit the productivity of computer image-creation as well as application areas of computer graphics.

Many attempts have been made to improve modeling systems, and several useful techniques for manipulating certain classes of three-dimensional objects have been developed. Barr[1] and Sederberg[2] proposed methods of deforming solid geometric models. Pentland[3] proposed a method which constructs natural forms with deformed primitive shapes. In addition many methods describing natural objects, such as trees, mountains, and waves, have been proposed[4][5][6]. However, those methods do not seem to be suitable for establishing a user-friendly modeling system, since they can only handle limited classes of shapes. Thus, a variety of techniques are necessary to model a variety of classes of three-dimensional shapes.

One of the most useful approaches, we believe, to realize a user-friendly man-machine interface is to create the three-dimensional shape of an object from a sketch, since sketches are often used to represent three-dimensional shapes and since sketches can represent quite extensive classes of three-dimensional shapes.

Kanade[7] has proposed a recovery method for a symmetrical planar shape when it is to be mapped into three-dimensional space. This method recovers the original shape from its projected line-drawing if the shape consisted of symmetrical planar surfaces. However, this method cannot be applied to objects with curved surfaces.

In order to recover a more general class of shapes, we propose a generation method for objects whose three-dimensional surfaces satisfy the constraints of "generalized symmetry". As the two-dimensional representation of an object, we adopted line-drawings, from which an object's shape may be generated.

Generalized symmetry is a property of a pair of three-dimensional curves and it is an extended concept of planar-symmetry, where the property of its symmetrical axis is extended to include three-dimensional curves. Generalized symmetry is a useful property of objects, since there are a lot of generalized symmetrical objects in nature and industrial environments.

It is possible to extend of this method to the generation of another class of objects represented by the generalized cylinder which is introduced in Computer Vision to extensively represent three-dimensional volumes[9]. This is discussed in this paper, and it is shown that various kinds of objects can be created from line-drawings using a slightly modified property of generalized symmetry.

This paper develops (1) a generalized symmetry, (2) a generation algorithm based on the generalized symmetry constraint, and (3) applications for generalized cylindrical object modeling.

2 Principle of Shape Generation

2.1 Generalized Symmetry

Figure 1(a) shows an example of symmetrical line-drawings, which are planar and symmetrical about a straight symmetry axis. The line-drawing shown in Fig. 1(b) is not strictly symmetrical, however, it can be regarded as a projection of a symmetrical shape in three-dimensional space and viewed from an oblique angle. This property of the line-drawing is called skewed symmetry and has been proposed by Kanade[7]. Kanade has proposed a method of recovering the three-dimensional shape based on the skewed symmetry constraint.

On the other hand, the line-drawing in Fig. 1(c) is neither symmetrical nor skewed symmetrical. However, one can understand that it depicts a leaf, and recognize it as a symmetrical object whose symmetrical axis is a curve in three-dimensional space. This kind of symmetry is named generalized symmetry. Generalized symmetry is a property of a pair of three-dimensional smooth curves, where their symmetrical axis is also a three-dimensional smooth curve. The pair of three-dimensional curves can twist around the generalized symmetry axis.

In natural and industrial scenes, there are many generalized symmetrical shapes. Thus, generalized symmetry is expected to be a useful technique for modeling a three-dimensional object and provides a basis for the inverse problem of generating the three-dimensional object from its two-dimensional view.

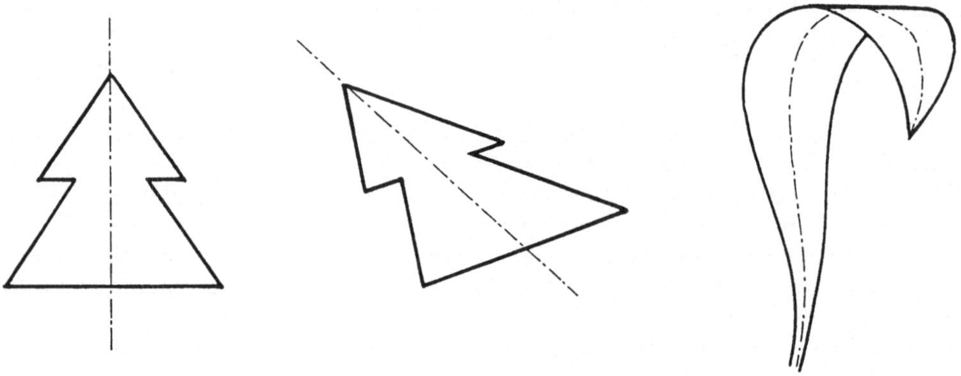

(a) Real symmetry (b) Skewed symmetry (c) Generalized symmetry

Figure 1: Three types of Symmetry.

2.2 Definition of Generalized Symmetry

The mathematical definition of generalized symmetry is described as follows. In Fig. 2, B_1 and B_2 are three-dimensional smooth curves, which are first-order differentiable. If curve C satisfies the following condition and it is first order differentiable, the pair of curves B_1 and B_2 are generalized symmetrical. The curve C is named generalized symmetry axis.

[Condition]

> A vector $\boldsymbol{l}$ is a unit tangent vector at any point P on curve C. Plane S is perpendicular to vector $\boldsymbol{l}$ and passes through point P. Curves B_1 and B_2 intersect with plane S at points P_1 and P_2, respectively. Finally the pair of points P_1 and P_2 are symmetrical about point P.

2.3 Generalized Symmetry Constraint

Figure 3 shows the geometry of the object space in which x-y plane is a projection plane. In this figure, it is assumed that the pair of curves B_1 and B_2 are generalized symmetrical and curve C is the generalized symmetry axis. A straight line M is the tangent line at point P on curve C. The points P_1 on B_1 and P_2 on B_2 are symmetrical

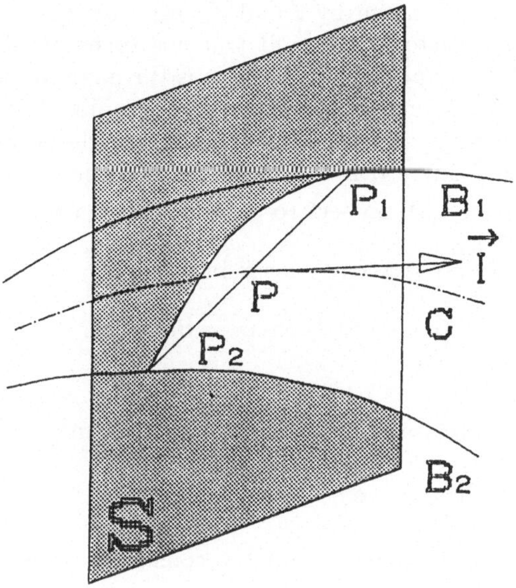

$$\overline{P_1P} = \overline{P_2P}$$

Figure 2: The definition of generalized symmetry.

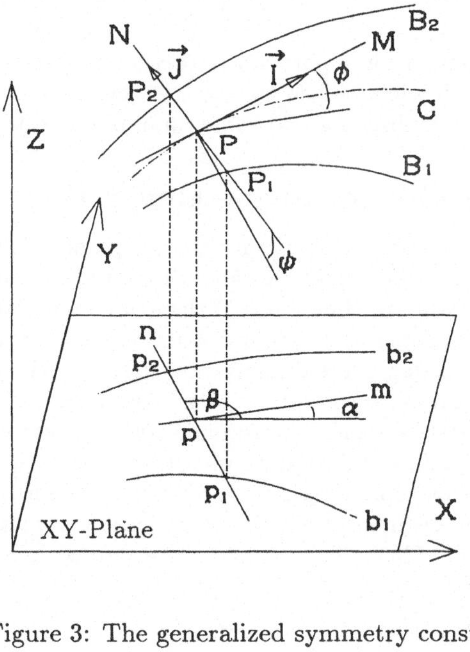

Figure 3: The generalized symmetry constraint.

about point P. A straight line N connects the points P_1, P and P_2. The unit direction vectors of lines M and N are denoted by $\boldsymbol{I}$ and $\boldsymbol{J}$, respectively. Let vector $\boldsymbol{I}$ be called the unit tangent vector and vector $\boldsymbol{J}$ the unit transverse vector. Angle ϕ is the angle between the line M and the x-y plane, and angle ψ is the angle between the line N and the x-y plane. The straight lines m and n are the orthographical projections of lines M and N onto the x-y plane, respectively. Angle α is the angle between line m and the x-axis of the x-y plane, and angle β is the angle between line n and the x-axis. The vectors $\boldsymbol{I}$ and $\boldsymbol{J}$ are described with respect to α, β, ϕ, and ψ as

$$I = (\cos\phi\cos\alpha,\ \cos\phi\sin\alpha,\ \sin\phi), \tag{1}$$

$$J = (\cos\psi\cos\beta,\ \cos\psi\sin\beta,\ \sin\psi). \tag{2}$$

Since the pair of curves B_1 and B_2 satisfies the definition of generalized symmetry, vector $\boldsymbol{I}$ is perpendicular to vector $\boldsymbol{J}$, that is, $I \cdot J = 0$. Using this fact and Eq.1 and Eq.2 we obtain

$$\cos(\beta - \alpha) + \tan\phi\tan\psi = 0. \tag{3}$$

This equation is called the generalized symmetry constraint, which gives the relation among α, β, ϕ, and ψ.

When a projection of a generalized symmetrical object is given by a two-dimensional line-drawing, angles α and β are known from the line-drawing. Therefore, if either ϕ or ψ is known, the other is obtained from Eq.3, so that the vectors $\boldsymbol{I}$ and $\boldsymbol{J}$ are recovered. The generation algorithm is discussed in the next section.

3 Shape Generation from Line-Drawing

In this section, the shape generation algorithm is presented. On the assumption that an intended shape satisfies the generalized symmetry, the three-dimensional shape is created its two-dimensional line drawing and some nominated vectors.

3.1 Information Needed for Shape Generation

As discussed in section 2.3, in order to generate the shape of an object, we use three kinds of information about the object: (1) a pair of two-dimensional curves which are projections of generalized symmetrical curves, (2) the symmetrical relation between the curves, and (3) vector information at any point (i.e. angle ϕ or ψ). Our purpose is to develop a method for modeling three-dimensional shapes with sketches. Therefore, the three kinds of information are to be put into the computer in the form of sketches drawn on a data-tablet. First, a pair of two-dimensional curves is drawn on a data-tablet. Since the curves represent the outline of a three-dimensional shape, they are called contours. Then, the corresponding points of symmetry on the two contours are indicated by transverse line segments, whose interpolation points with the contours correspond with each other. These line segments are named auxiliary vectors. The symmetrical relation can alternatively be given by numerical functions, though this is not very practical for our purpose. The angle between each auxiliary vector and x-y plane (i.e. angle ψ) is given, at present these are input from a key board.

Thus, the following is the final information necessary to generate three-dimensional shapes from two-dimensional line-drawings,

(1) contours,

(2) auxiliary vectors,

(3) angles between the auxiliary vectors and x-y plane.

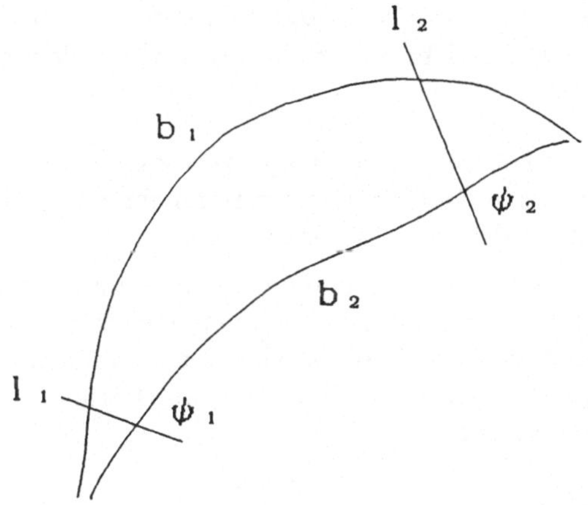

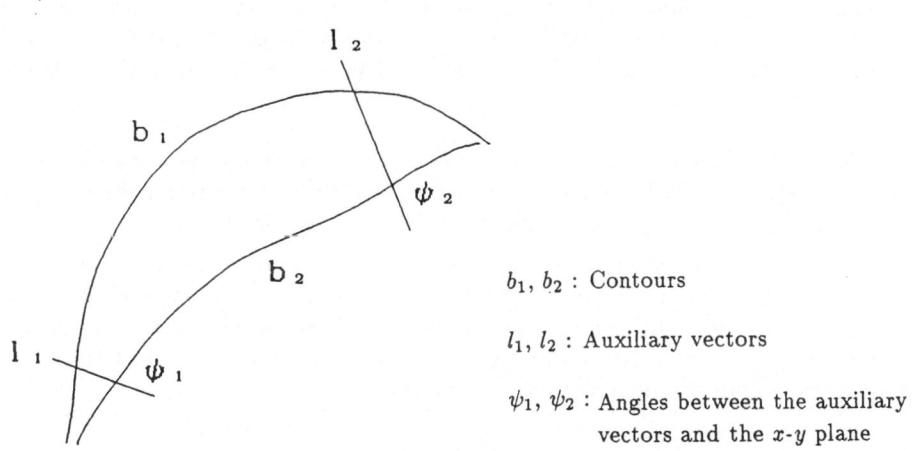

b_1, b_2 : Contours

l_1, l_2 : Auxiliary vectors

ψ_1, ψ_2 : Angles between the auxiliary vectors and the x-y plane

Figure 4: An example of line-drawing information.

Figure 4 shows an example of input information. Curves b_1 and b_2 are contours, line segments l_1 and l_2 are auxiliary vectors, and angles ψ_1 and ψ_2 are the angles between l_1 and x-y plane and l_2 and x-y plane, respectively. Because l_1 and l_2 are not parallel, the shape is expected to be twisted.

3.2 Surface Generation Algorithm

The algorithm explained here generates the three-dimensional shape of a curved surface from a line-drawing, based on the assumption that contours b_1 and b_2 are the results of an orthographical projection of three-dimensional smooth curves which satisfy the generalized symmetry. Since the contours are curves projected onto the x-y plane, reconstruction of the three-dimensional shape is reduced to the determination of the z-coordinates of each contour point. The generation algorithm consists of the following steps:

Step1: Determination of symmetrical relation
Step2: Determination of projected axis c
Step3: Calculation of angles α and β
Step4: Interpolation of angle ψ
Step5: Determination of vector $\boldsymbol{I}$ and $\boldsymbol{J}$
Step6: Generation of generalized symmetry axis C
Step7: Generation of three-dimensional shape

Each step is discussed in the following sections.

3.3 Step1: Determination of Symmetrical Relation

The symmetrical relationship between the two contours, and therefore the three dimensional surface, is determined by the auxiliary vectors. Contour points and their fill vectors between the auxiliary vectors are created by interpolation in the following process.

(1) If both contours have points where the contour curvature is greatest and these points are approximately aligned then a new auxiliary vector is generated by the computer to connect the two points of maximum curvature.

(2) The contour lines between auxiliary vectors are divided into equal numbers of units of suitable size. Corresponding points (symmetrical points) on each contour are connected to form fill vectors. In regions outside the auxiliary vectors, it must be assumed that the shape is not twisted hence all fill vectors are parallel and extrapolated from the nearest auxiliary vector.

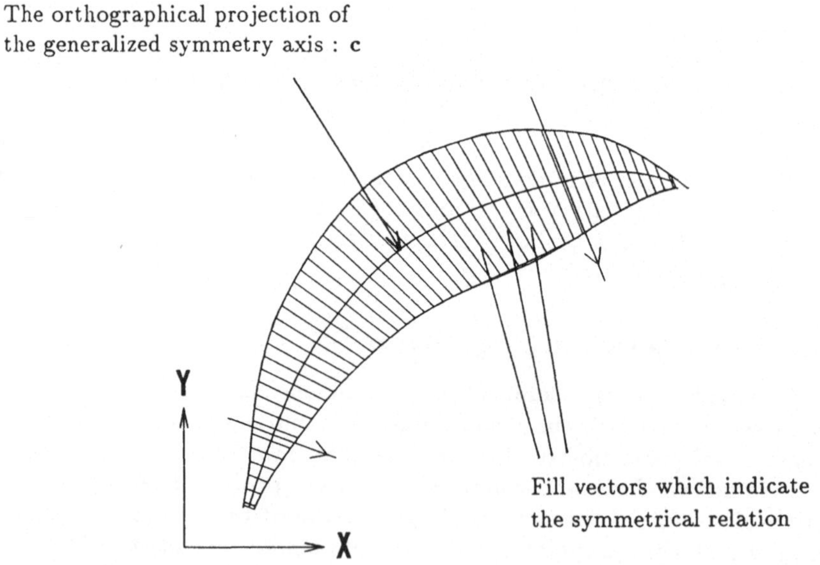

Figure 5: The symmetrical relation created by interpolation and the symmetry axis **c**.

Through this interpolation, the symmetrical relation is determined at every point on the contours, and every point on contour b_1 is paired with a point on contour b_2. Figure 5 shows the symmetrical relation determined by interpolating between the auxiliary vectors shown in Fig. 4.

3.4 Step2: Determination of Projected Axis c

The generalized symmetry axis passes through the mid-point of corresponding symmetrical points. This relation holds even after orthographic projection. Thus, curve c, which goes through the mid-point of every pair of symmetrical points determined in Step 1, is the orthographic projection of the generalized symmetrical axis. Figure 5 shows curve c obtained from Fig. 4.

3.5 Step3: Calculation of Angles α and β

At each point on curve c, angles α and β are calculated. α is the angle between the tangent line of curve c at the point and the x-axis. β is the angle between the fill vector and the x-axis.

3.6 Step4: Interpolation of Angle ψ

In order to generate the three-dimensional shape, angle ψ must be given for fill vectors obtained in Step 1. However, angle ψ has been given only for the original auxiliary vectors input by the user. Therefore, it is necessary to interpolate angle ψ. The interpolation is executed with the following assumptions.

(1) Angle ψ for fill vectors between auxiliary vectors varies smoothly along curve c.

(2) In areas where angle β changes sharply, angle ψ also changes sharply.

(3) Angle ψ is equal to ψ_1 at l_1 and equal to ψ_2 at l_2 (refer to Fig. 4).

(4) Angle ψ for fill vectors beyond the auxiliary vectors is the same as the closest auxiliary vector.

3.7 Step5: Determination of Vector $\boldsymbol{I}$ and $\boldsymbol{J}$

Angle ψ is obtained from the generalized symmetry constraint by substituting the values of α, β, and ϕ into Eq.3. Consequently, vectors $\boldsymbol{I}$ and $\boldsymbol{J}$ at any point on curve c are determined by substituting the four angles at that point into Eq.1, where vector $\boldsymbol{I}$ is the unit tangent vector of the generalized symmetry axis C at the point, and vector $\boldsymbol{J}$ the unit transverse vector.

3.8 Step6: Generation of Generalized Symmetry Axis C

Since curve c determined in Step 2 is the orthographic projection of the generalized symmetry axis C onto the x-y plane. The x- and y-coordinates of every point on axis C are equal to those of the corresponding point on axis c. Thus, reconstructing axis C is equal to determining z for every point on axis C. The z can be determined by the unit tangent vector.

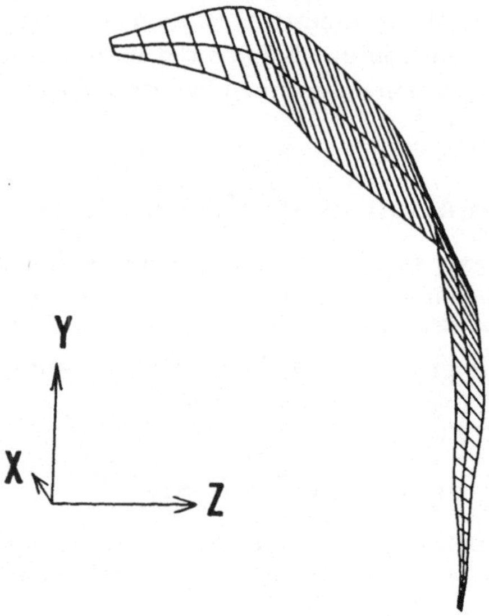

Figure 6: Surface generated from Fig.4.

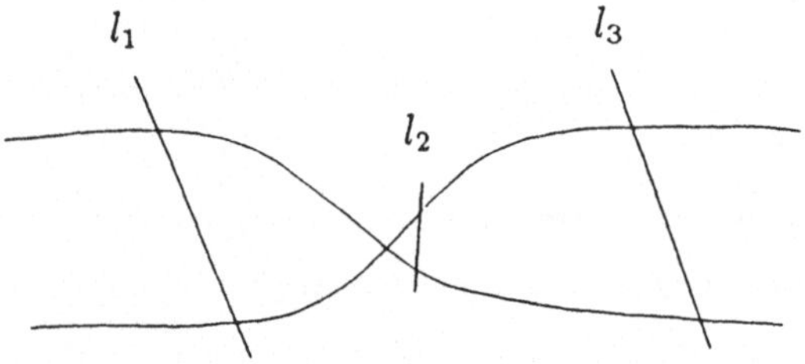

(a) Line drawing of a curved surface

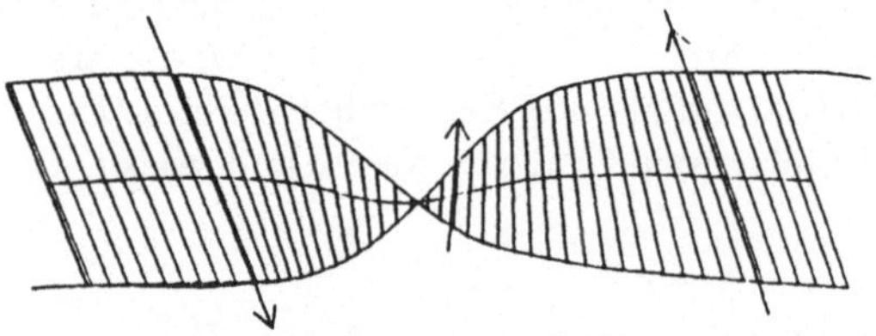

(b) The symmetry axis and fill vectors

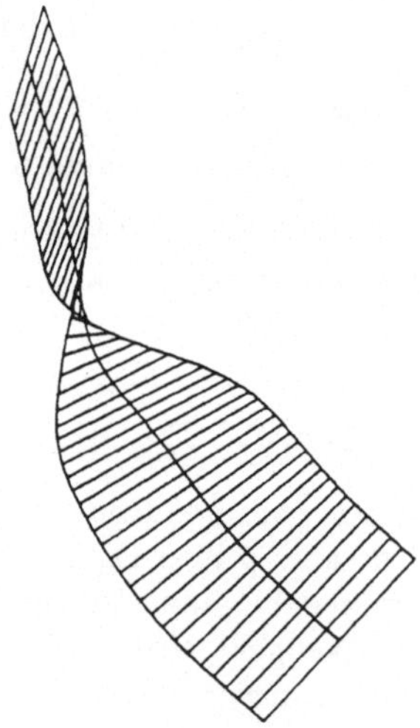

(c) The generated 3D shape

Figure 7: Generation of a curved surface which satisfies generalized symmetry.

3.9 Step7: Generation of Three-Dimensional Shape

Since the projection of curves B_1 and B_2 on the x-y plane are contours b_1 and b_2, the three-dimensional shape of B_1 and B_2 can be generated, if the z of each point on B_1 and B_2 are known. The z for those curves are obtained from the generalized symmetry axis C and the unit transverse vectors $\boldsymbol{J}$. Thus, the curved surface whose edges are the curves B_1 and B_2 is generated. Figure 6 shows the surface generated from the sketch shown in Fig. 4.

An experimental result is shown in Fig. 7. Figure 7(a) shows a line-drawing of a twisted surface used in the experiment. The symmetrical relation is determined by interpolating between the given auxiliary vectors l_1, l_2 and l_3. The result is shown in Fig. 7(b). The generated three-dimensional shape is shown in Fig. 7(c). From this example, we see that twisted curved surfaces can be designed from simple line-drawings.

3.10 Generation of Planar-Symmetrical Object

It was explained in section 3.3 and 3.6 that the symmetrical relation and the angle ψ are determined by interpolation. However, when the three-dimensional shape is symmetrical about a plane, its shape can be generated without interpolation. This is a special case of generalized symmetry. In this case, the generalized symmetry axis is a planar curve and the fill vectors are parallel to each other. Thus, the unit transverse vector $\boldsymbol{J}$ is the same everywhere on the generalized symmetry axis. Consequently, if only one auxiliary vector and its angle to the x-y plane are given, the transverse vector $\boldsymbol{J}$ and tangent vector $\boldsymbol{I}$ are the same at any point on the generalized symmetry axis, thus generating the three-dimensional shape.

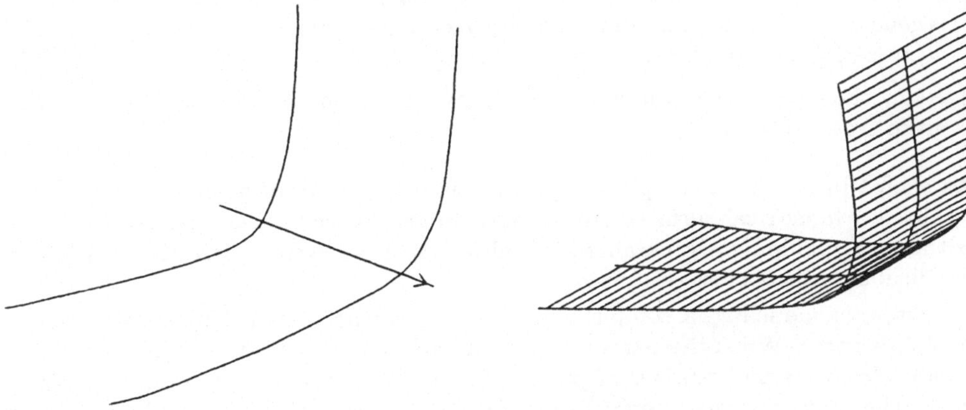

(a) A line drawing of a curved surface (b) 3D shape generated from (a)

Figure 8: Generation of a curved surface which is symmetrical about a plane.

Figure 8 shows the experimental result of generating a shape which is symmetrical about a plane. Figure 8(b) shows the curved surface generated from the line-drawing of Fig. 8(a).

4 Application to Generalized-Cylindrical Object Modeling

In this section, a method for modeling generalized-cylindrical objects from their line-drawings by utilizing the generalized symmetry constraint is presented. According to Shani[8], a generalized-cylindrical object is defined by an axis, some cross sections, their coordinate systems, and a sweeping rule. When cross sections are given at separate positions, the sweeping rule becomes an interpolation scheme between the cross sections. The generalized symmetry method provides all the information for defining the generalized-cylindrical objects except for cross sections. The generalized symmetry axis substitutes for the axis of the generalized cylinder. Unit tangent vector $\boldsymbol{I}$ and unit transverse vector $\boldsymbol{J}$ at a point on the axis give a coordinate system for the cross section at the point. And also the differential of vector $\boldsymbol{I}$ along the axis can be used as the parameter for interpolating between the cross sections.

Therefore, if cross sections are given, a generalized cylindrical shape can be generated by the generalized symmetry constraint. In our experimental system, cross sections are given at the auxiliary vectors.

The generation algorithm mentioned in section 3.2 can be used as follows in the generation of generalized-cylindrical objects.

(1) According to the algorithm mentioned in section 3.2, the three-dimensional surface is generated from the contours, auxiliary vectors, and angles between the auxiliary vectors and the x-y plane.

(2) Along the generalized symmetry axis, cross sections are interpolated between the given cross sections.

As shown in Fig. 9, a complicated chair was designed from a plain line-drawing. Generalized symmetrical surfaces are included in generalized-cylindrical objects. The algorithm can manipulate generalized-cylindrical shapes except where the axis is not perpendicular to their cross sections.

In computer modeling, a complicated object is usually designed by constructing a lot of simple parts. When the parts are created with our method, the object shape can be created from a small number of patrs. Figure 10(a) shows a wire-frame image of a plant. The plant consists of only 13 generalized cylinderical shapes, and all of them were easily created with our method. Its shaded image is shown in Fig. 10(b).

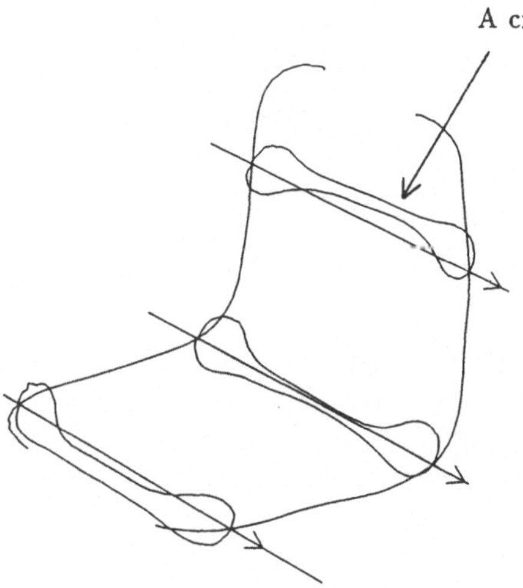

(a) A line drawing of a chair

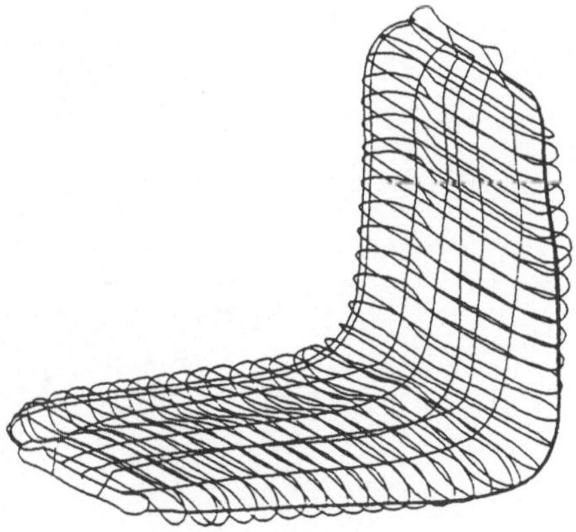

(b) Generated 3D shape

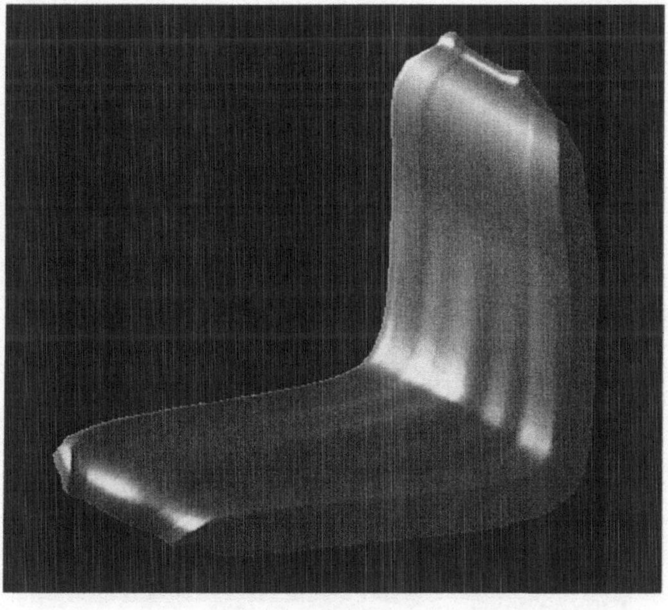

(c) Shaded image

Figure 9: Generation of a generalized-cylindrical object.

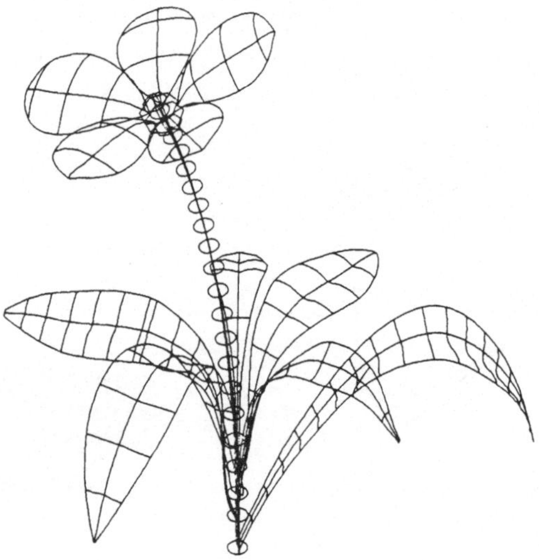

(a) A wire-frame image of a plant

(b) Shaded image

Figure 10: An object designed by constructing generalized cylindrical surfaces.

5 Conclusion

We proposed a method for generating three-dimensional shapes from line-drawings by the generalized symmetry constraint. It is obvious that the generation is easier when the shape is bounded by curved lines that are symmetrical about a plane to be mapped into three-dimensional space.

We have also proposed an algorithm that can generate bulky generalized-cylindrical shapes by adding information about cross sections to line-drawings. As an example, a complicated chair was generated from a simple line-drawing.

There exists a need for a process to modify generated shapes, since the shapes obtained will not be necessarily what was intended. There should be a method by which users can view and directly modify generated shapes by manipulating their projected contour lines.

Our method can manipulate a class of objects satisfying generalized symmetry criteria. Although, it can cover quite extensive shapes of objects, there are classes of objects which the method cannot handle. Additional modeling techniques are necessary to manipulate those classes of objects in order to establish a complete and user-friendly man-machine interface. There are many properties, other than line-drawings and sketches, such as images themselves, which may be useful in generating three-dimensional shapes. To determine which properties are suitable is a future problem.

Acknowledgement We would like to thank Dr. Hiroshi Yasuda, Dr. Isao Masuda and Dr. Kei Takigawa for their continuous support. We would also like to thank Mr. Mikio Shinya, Mr. Takafumi Saito and Mr. Tadashi Naruse for their advice and encouragement. We are greatly indebted to Dr. Noriyoshi Osumi for editing this paper.

References

[1] A.H.Barr, "Global and local deformations of solid primitives", Computer Graphics, Vol.18, No.3, pp.21-30(1984)

[2] T.W.Sederberg, "Free-form deformation of solid geometric models", Computer Graphics, Vol.20, No.4, pp.151-160(1986)

[3] A.P.Pentland, "Perceptual organization and the representation of natural form", Artificial Intelligence, Vol.28, No.3, pp.293-331(1986)

[4] A.R.Smith, "Plants, fractals, and formal languages", Computer Graphics, Vol.18, No.3, pp.1-10(1984)

[5] P.E.Oppenheimer, "Real time design and animation of fractal plants and trees", Computer Graphics, Vol.20, No.4, pp.55-64(1986)

[6] W.T.Reeves, "Particle system - a technique for modeling a class of fuzzy object", Computer Graphics, Vol.17, No.3, pp.359-376(1983)

[7] T.Kanade, "Recovery of the 3-dimensional shape of an object from a single view", Artificial Intelligence, Vol.17, pp.409-460(1980)

[8] U.Shani, "Spline as embeddings for generalized cylinders", Computer Vision, Graphics, and Image Processing, Vol.27, pp.129-156(1984)

[9] G.J.Agin and T.O.Binford, "Representation and recognition of curved objects", IEEE Trans. Comput., Vol.C-25, pp.439-449(1976)

Geometric Modeling with Euclidean Constructions

N. Fuller and P. Prusinkiewicz (Canada)

ABSTRACT

This paper presents an interactive graphics system called L.E.G.O. The purpose of L.E.G.O. is to model two- and three-dimensional objects using Euclidean geometry constructions. Constructions are described by programs in the L.E.G.O. language, based on LISP. These programs can be entered in textual form or developed using a graphical interface in a multiple-window environment. Both interface styles can also be used concurrently. Applications of L.E.G.O. include computer-assisted instruction of geometry, geometric modeling, and kinematic analysis. The use of imperative constructions and the powerful interface based on the idea of graphical programming are the most distinctive features of the system.

Key words: constraint-based graphics systems, geometric constructions, graphical programming, iconic interfaces, LISP.

1. INTRODUCTION

Computer-assisted instruction of geometry has been largely influenced by the LOGO project [1,18]. However, its central concept, turtle geometry, makes LOGO of little use in teaching classical Euclidean ideas whose educational value have been known since ancient times. Consequently, with educational applications in mind, we have created a computer graphics system called L.E.G.O., based on the Euclidean notions and operations. The educational aspects of L.E.G.O. are described in [9]. A survey of applications is given in [8]. In this paper we describe the interface design for L.E.G.O. Specifically, we address the problem of defining geometric constructions without textual programming and we solve it using the visual programming approach.

The paper is organized as follows. Section 2 introduces the concept of construction-based modeling. In Section 3 constraint-based systems known from the literature are surveyed and contrasted with L.E.G.O. The essential aspects of L.E.G.O. are described in the next two sections. They present the L.E.G.O. language, the graphics interface, and the use of the system in a multiple-window environment. Possible applications of L.E.G.O. are outlined in Section 6. Finally, in Section 7 we summarize the obtained results.

L.E.G.O. is written in Franz LISP [7,25]. The LISP language was used because it allows the programmer to interactively build, write and read in geometric constructions defined as functions. The version described in this paper runs on an IRIS 3130 workstation. A number of routines written in C are used to access the IRIS graphics library [23] from LISP. Additionally, the mex window management system [23] provides the rudiments for man-machine interaction.

2. CONSTRUCTION-BASED MODELING

Modeling using geometric constructions is distinctively different from other modeling techniques. This difference can be best presented by referring to an example. Thus, consider the object shown in Fig. 1. Some methods for describing it are illustrated in Fig. 2, and can be expressed as follows:

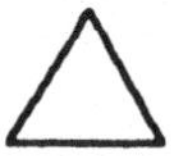

Fig. 1. An object.

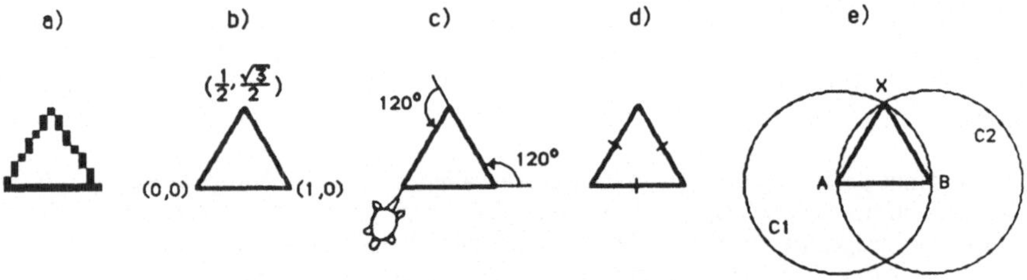

Fig. 2. Some interpretations of the object from Fig. 1.

(a) Figure 1 is a set of pixels.

(b) Figure 1 is a plot of three lines, with the Cartesian coordinates of the endpoints equal to (0,0), (1,0) and $(\frac{1}{2},\frac{\sqrt{3}}{2})$.

(c) Figure 1 is the trace of a turtle moving forward a unit distance, turning left by 120°, moving forward a unit distance, turning left by 120°, and moving forward a unit distance again.

(d) Figure 1 is an equilateral triangle.

(e) Figure 1 is the result of the following construction:

- Given line *AB*, draw circles *C*1 and *C*2 with radius *AB* and centers *A* and *B*, respectively.
- Intersect circles *C*1 and *C*2. Denote a point of intersection by *X*.
- Draw lines *AX* and *BX*.

Descriptions of type (a) and (b) are widely used in computer graphics. In case (a) a picture is thought of as a bitmap, i.e., a set of pixels defined in a system of coordinates. In case (b) the graphics primitives are not limited to pixels; they include lines and, possibly, also other simple figures, such as circles, ellipses and filled polygons. These primitives are defined with respect to a system of coordinates. A description of type (c), made popular by LOGO [1,18], differs from type (b) in that polar coordinates (relative to the current position of the turtle) are used instead of Cartesian coordinates. All three cases, however, reflect the analytic approach to geometry. Geometric figures are denied existence independent of a system of coordinates. They are conceptualized as plots of analytic relations.

Descriptions (d) and (e) belong to a totally different family. They describe Fig. 1 directly in geometric terms. In case (d) the figure is specified using a set of declarative constraints, or geometric *relations* between elements of the picture. These constraints impose equal length on all sides of the triangle. In case (e), the figure is described using a sequence of imperative constraints, or Euclidean geometry *constructions* (with a straightedge and a compass). This is the type of object description used in L.E.G.O. (Throughout this paper, the term "object" is used to denote both two-dimensional figures and three-dimensional objects.)

The idea of applying geometric constructions to object modeling is a relatively new one in computer graphics. This is rather surprising, given the fundamental role of constructions in Euclidean geometry. One system, other than L.E.G.O., which does use geometric constructions is a two-dimensional illustrator Gargoyle [3]. In contrast to L.E.G.O., however, the Gargoyle constructions are forgotten as soon as they are used, rather than becoming a part of the data structure. Consequently, the behaviour of L.E.G.O. and Gargoyle is essentially different. Other constraint-based systems reported in the literature use declarative constraints.

3. CONSTRUCTION-BASED MODELING AND CONSTRAINT-BASED SYSTEMS

This section places L.E.G.O. in the context of previous work in the area of constraint-based graphics systems. Attention is focused on the techniques for constraint solving and the design of man-machine graphical interfaces.

3.1. Constraint Solving Techniques

Constraint-based graphics systems described in the literature [4,5,14,17,20,22,24] accept object definitions expressed in terms of geometric relations between object elements. These definitions are subsequently transformed into analytical descriptions of graphical primitives to be displayed or plotted. Many fundamental relations lead to nonlinear equations. For example, relations "lines *L*1 and *L*2 are congruent" or "lines *L*1 and *L*2 are perpendicular to each other" are represented by quadratic equations.

Various techniques for solving systems of nonlinear equations have been used to satisfy sets of constraints. The most straightforward approach relies on general-purpose numerical methods. For example, Sketchpad [22] used the relaxation method, and Juno [17] used the Newton-Raphson method. Unfortunately, these methods are adequate only when applied to relatively small sets of constraints (a few tens of equations). For larger sets it is difficult to find initial conditions which let the system of equations converge to the desired solution. In addition, numerical methods tend to be too slow for interactive applications.

The difficulties related to the use of general-purpose numerical methods can be overcome using two approaches. One technique, implemented in METAFONT [14] and IDEAL [24], restricts admissible constraints to those which can be expressed by linear equations. For example, specifying a distance between two arbitrary points is not allowed, since it leads to a quadratic equation. On the other hand, a vertical or horizontal displacement is expressed by a linear equation and therefore can be specified.

Another technique relies on dividing the set of constraints into smaller subsets, which can be solved in succession. The constraint solver may attempt to perform this partitioning automatically, using heuristic algorithms [4]. This leads to a purely declarative type of object description, since the user lists constraints without indicating how to solve them. Alternatively, the user may be required to explicitly partition the set of constraints, by describing the object as a hierarchy of components [17,20,22]. By this means, he indicates the order in which the constraints should be solved. This introduces an imperative element to the object definition.

Construction-based object descriptions used in L.E.G.O. are purely imperative. They specify geometric objects by algorithms expressed in geometric terms. These algorithms never require solving more than two quadratic equations simultaneously. The solutions can always be found analytically without ever resorting to numerical methods.

3.2. Graphical Interfaces

The objects modeled in constraint-based systems can be described textually, in an appropriate programming language [14,20,24], or visually, using a graphical interface. In the case of declarative constraints, the interface is straightforward. The type of constraint is determined by selecting an icon or menu item, and the arguments are picked directly on the graphics screen. This type of interface originates from Sketchpad [22]. Unfortunately, it cannot be easily extended to geometric constructions, for they require a mechanism for defining complete algorithms. A systematic approach to designing a graphical interface for this purpose can be based on the idea of graphical programming, i.e., creating programs by manipulating graphical objects on the screen.

Two approaches to graphical programming can be distinguished. In the explicit (algorithmic [11]) programming case, the user manipulates a graphical representation of the program, for example a flowchart [11] or a Nassi-Shneiderman diagram [19]. In the case of implicit programming (implicit editing [17], demonstrational programming [11]) images on the screen represent an example of the solution of the given problem. The program is created, to some extent, as a "side effect" of constructing the object on the screen. Implicit graphical programming is the cornerstone of the graphical interface of L.E.G.O. It was also fundamental to the design of the graphical interface in Juno [17]. L.E.G.O. removes many limitations of this earlier system.

4. THE L.E.G.O. LANGUAGE

The L.E.G.O. language [10] is a graphical extension of Franz LISP [7,25] and it preserves the LISP syntax. L.E.G.O. and LISP functions can be interleaved in the same program. However, L.E.G.O. maintains its own symbol table and therefore cannot be considered simply as a library of LISP functions. This symbol table contains information about primitive graphical objects: points, lines, circles, planes and spheres. Associated with these primitives is a set of predefined functions which make it possible to define new objects in terms of the objects already specified. This set is based on fundamental operations with straight-edge and compass. The following functions are essential for developing two-dimensional constructions:

(**point** *x y new_name*)

Creates a point given coordinates *x* and *y*, and calls it *new_name*. (The term "create" means to produce a new graphic primitive by recording its features in the L.E.G.O. symbol table and by drawing it on the screen.)

(**line** *point1 point2 new_name*)

Creates a line from a previously defined *point*1 to a previously defined *point*2, and calls it *new_name*.

(**circle** *center radius new_name*)

Creates a circle given a previously defined point *center*, with the radius equal to the length of a previously defined line *radius*. The circle is called *new_name*.

(**intersection** *primitive1 primitive2 new_name1* [*new_name2*])

Creates the points of intersection between two-dimensional primitives - points, lines or circles. Intersections with a point can be used to check whether it coincides with another point, or whether it lies on a line or a circle. The actual number of intersections is returned as the value of the function. The value of −1 is returned when intersecting two identical lines or circles.

In order to illustrate key features of the L.E.G.O. language, let us consider some simple programs. They can be developed noninteractively (using a text editor) or interactively. In the latter case, each statement entered to the system is immediately executed to provide visual feedback [9]. The first program creates line *L* defined by points *A* and *B*, and bisects *L* with line *P* perpendicular to *L*.

Program 1.

```
1   (point 400 370 A)
2   (point 600 470 B)
3   (line A B L)
4   (circle A L C1)
5   (circle B L C2)
6   (intersection C1 C2 X1 X2)
7   (line X1 X2 P)
```

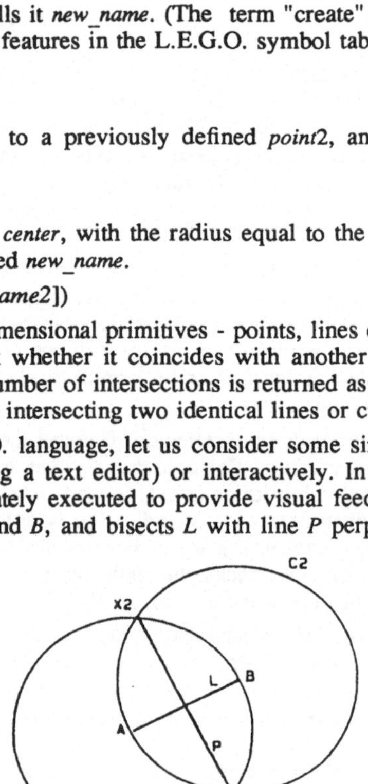

Fig. 3. Bisecting a line in L.E.G.O.

A geometric construction can be specified as a function using function definition functions **define_function** and **end_function**. For example, in order to specify the construction to bisect a line as a function, the statements:

```
(define_function bisect (A B) (P))
...
(end_function)
```

should have been typed after lines 2 and 7 of Program 1, respectively. The statements in lines 3-7 would then constitute the function body. Parameters of the **define_function** function indicate that the new function **bisect** shall be called with two arguments referring to previously defined primitives (*A* and *B*), and will create a new primitive *P* as a result. Note that line *L* will become local to the function **bisect** and therefore should not be referred to outside the body of this function. The function **bisect** can be used, for example, to construct the circumcircle of a given triangle *ABC* (Program 2 and Fig. 4).

Program 2.

```
(bisect A C P)
(bisect  B C Q)
(intersection P Q X)
(line X C R)
(circle X R Z)
```

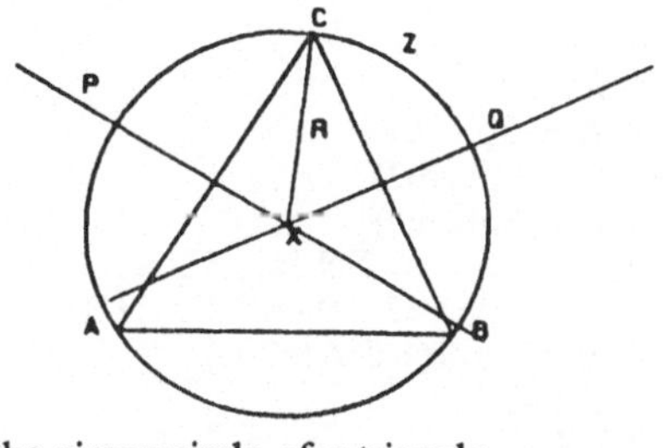

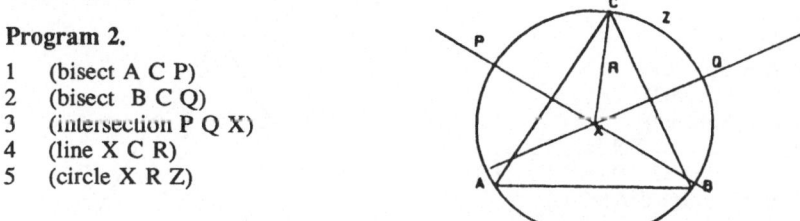

Fig. 4. Construction of the circumcircle of a triangle

L.E.G.O. functions can be called recursively. Assume that the user-defined function (**midtriangle** *A B C D E F*) creates a triangle given vertices *A,B,C*, and returns the midpoints of the edges: *D,E,F*. Using **midtriangle**, the Sierpiński gasket [16] (Fig. 5) can be defined as follows:

Program 3.

```
1   (point 220 150 A)
2   (point 790 150 B)
3   (point 505 643 C)
4   (define_function gasket (A B C))
5   (midtriangle A B C D E F)
6   (write_function)
7   (if (> (distance A B) 40) then
8           (gasket A D F)
9           (gasket B E D)
10          (gasket C F E))
11  (end_function)
```

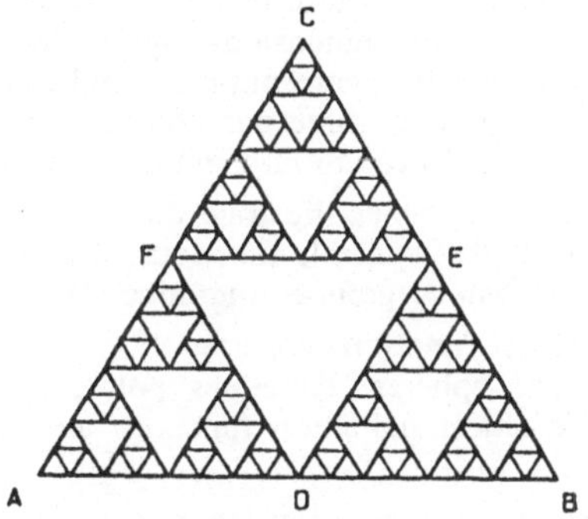

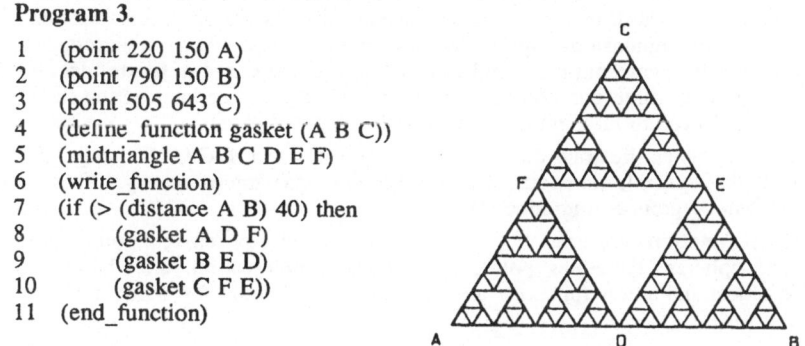

Fig. 5. The Sierpiński gasket.

Line 6 calls function **write_function** which temporarily writes the function currently being defined. This is a necessary statement before this function can call itself. Line 7 illustrates the mixing of LISP and L.E.G.O. functions. A predefined L.E.G.O. function **distance** is used in conjunction with the LISP macro **if...then** to control the termination of the recursive calls.

In order to develop three-dimensional constructions, the functions **point, line** and **intersection** described before are extended to operate on three-dimensional primitives. Additionally, the following functions are defined:

(**ppp_plane** *point1 point2 point3 new_name*)

(**pl_plane** *point line new_name*)

(**ll_plane** *line1 line2 new_name*)

Each of these functions enters plane *new_name* to the L.E.G.O. symbol table. The plane is specified by three non-collinear points, a line and a point not on the line, or two intersecting or parallel lines, respectively. Generally, the plane is not drawn.

(**circle** *center radius plane new_name*)

Creates a circle on a previously defined *plane*, given the *center* and the *radius* of the circle. The circle will be called *new_name.*

(**sphere** *center radius new_name*)

Creates a sphere given a previously defined point *center*, with the radius equal to the length of a previously defined line *radius*. The sphere is called *new_name*.

An example of a three-dimensional construction is given by Program 4. It creates a wire-frame model of a regular tetrahedron, given an equilateral triangle *ABC* (Fig. 6).

Program 4.

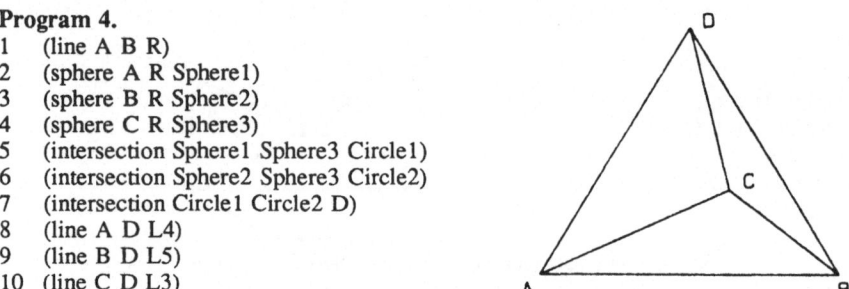

```
(line A B R)
(sphere A R Sphere1)
(sphere B R Sphere2)
(sphere C R Sphere3)
(intersection Sphere1 Sphere3 Circle1)
(intersection Sphere2 Sphere3 Circle2)
(intersection Circle1 Circle2 D)
(line A D L4)
(line B D L5)
(line C D L3)
```

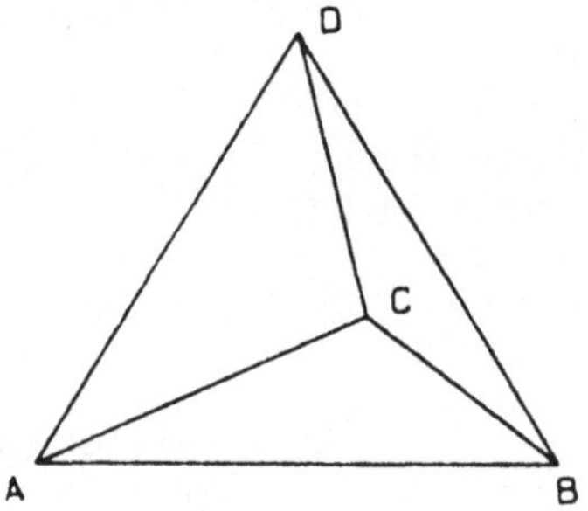

Fig. 6. Construction of a regular tetrahedron.
(The spheres used for construction are not displayed.)

Within the L.E.G.O. symbol table two- and three-dimensional objects are represented in the same way. In order to place two-dimensional objects (specifically, circles and points created using the **point** function) in three-dimensional space, the notion of *current plane* is introduced. By default it is the z=0 plane. The current plane can be changed using the **current_plane** function. The arguments of this function are three non-collinear points, or two parallel or intersecting lines. The current plane can be also forced to align with any previously specified plane.

While the above examples illustrate the essential features of the L.E.G.O. language, they use but a small fraction of the available functions. In total, L.E.G.O. has approximately 100 predefined functions [10], which can be grouped into nine classes.

1. **Object definition functions** are used to create L.E.G.O. graphics primitives: points, lines, circles, planes and spheres. Functions **point, line, sphere, intersection**, etc. belong to this category. The object definition functions are the fundamental tools for modeling geometric objects in L.E.G.O.

2. **Query functions** provide information about graphical primitives. Two subclasses can be distinguished:
   - *Functions which return a numerical value* (e.g. coordinate of a point, distance between points, length of a line). They are used primarily in conditional statements.
   - *Functions which return a graphic primitive* (e.g. endpoint of a line, center of a sphere, plane containing a circle). They are useful when arguments other than points are passed to functions.

3. **Drawing functions** are used to display simple figures such as alphanumerical symbols, arcs of circles and filled polygons. They are not considered L.E.G.O. primitives and, consequently, cannot be passed as arguments to the function **intersection**.

4. **Presentation definition functions** are used to control the appearance of graphical objects on the screen. Examples of controlled features are listed below:
   - *Visibility of primitives.* Auxiliary construction lines may be removed from the final picture.
   - *Display of primitive names.* In some applications, such as the presentation of geometric constructions for educational use, primitives should be labeled. In other cases, such as the modeling of realistic scenes, display of names should be suppressed.
   - *Color, width and style of lines.*
   - *Color, size and type of fonts.*

5. **Function definition functions** form a class which contains **define_function** and **end_function**, already described.

6. **Viewing functions** are used to define parameters of the projection, rotate objects in space, etc.

7. **Interaction supporting functions** make it possible to remove or modify previously defined primitives. These functions are particularly useful when developing constructions interactively, since each statement entered to the system is immediately executed and it cannot be subsequently altered by editing.
8. **System functions** are used for file manipulation (such as function loading), to configure the system for a particular type of graphics output device (such as a plotter), etc.
9. **Debugging functions** provide information about primitives stored in the symbol table, actual viewing parameters, etc.

5. VISUAL PROGRAMMING

5.1. General Principles

The visual interface is built on top of the textual interface. This means that it is used to build a textual L.E.G.O. program statement by statement. However, it supersedes typing by more intuitive operations based on the direct manipulation paradigm [21]. This is achieved using several graphics input techniques. Thus, function names are selected from a menu. Coordinates are located using the mouse. Graphical objects (passed as arguments to functions) are identified by picking using the mouse rather than by referring by name. (Usually the user need not even know object names.) The appearance of objects (color, line width, point size) and the viewing parameters are controlled by manipulating the appropriate icons. In order to make the visual interface complete (i.e. superseding all functions of the textual interface) a method for defining functions and condition statements in the graphics mode is also available. Using graphical operations we build a L.E.G.O. statement, then execute and append it to the program under construction.

5.2. Implementation

The screen is partitioned into windows (Color Plate 1). The actual construction is created in a window called the *working area*. The second window displays the icon associated with the current geometric *operation*. The third graphics window contains icons which change the *presentation* of objects such as the color, linewidth, etc. Three textual windows contain system and error *messages*, the textual form of the L.E.G.O. *statement* being built and the listing of the *program* constructed so far.

In order to build a L.E.G.O. statement, the user first selects a function name from a pop-up menu. The icon associated with this choice will appear in the operation window and a skeleton of the L.E.G.O. statement will appear in the statement window. The fields of the statement are filled by selecting primitives in the working area, by locating a position in the working area, by manipulating the icon in the operation window or by selecting parts of the icons in the presentation window. The statement window is updated as each field is filled. Once a complete L.E.G.O. statement has been built, it can be executed by selecting the **enter** item from the pop-up menu. If the statement is successfully executed it is appended to the program being built and displayed in the program window. Some statements are automatically executed and added to the program by selecting an item in the presentation window (e.g. changing the current drawing color). The **cancel** item aborts the definition of the statement.

Let us consider the building of a L.E.G.O. statement which draws a circle. It is assumed that the point which will become the center of the circle and a line equal to its radius are already on the screen. For this example, let us assume that their names are A and B respectively. The user starts the construction by selecting the word **circle** in a pop-up menu (Color Plate 2a). "(circle nil nil nil nil)" appears in the statement window. This indicates that there are four arguments to the circle function. The circle icon is drawn in the operation window and its central point changes color from red to yellow (Color Plate 2b). This informs the user that the system expects him to pick (by pointing with the cursor) the point to become the circle center. After this has been done, "(circle A nil nil nil)" appears in the statement window and the colors of the icon change to indicate that a centre has now been established and that a line defining the circle radius should be picked next (Color Plate 2c). The primitive B is selected and "(circle A B nil nil)" in the statement window indicates that the radius will be the length of line B. At this point the icon no longer prompts the user for there is now sufficient information in order to draw a circle.

The third argument to the circle function is the plane on which it lies. If this is not given, by default it is the current plane. The fourth argument is the name that will be assigned to the circle. If the user does not specify the name, it will be automatically assigned by the system. In order for the user to enter the name of the plane, he clicks into the square shown in the icon. The square will change color to yellow indicating that the plane can now be selected (Color Plate 2d). Similarly the name of the circle can be entered by selecting the "N" in the circle icon and typing the name (Color Plate 2e).

The user can alter the default sequence of actions by clicking into an appropriate element of the icon. For example, by clicking into the line depicting the circle radius the user brings the icon to the state shown in Color Plate 2c. This allows for defining the radius before choosing the center of the circle, or for redefining the radius in the case of a mistake.

In principle, icons represent functions of the L.E.G.O. language. However, this is not a one-to-one correspondence and calls to different L.E.G.O. functions may result from manipulating the same icon. In the terminology of Lodding [15], most icons are representational. They depict an instance of the general class of objects they refer to. Thus, the icon shown in Fig. 7a is used to create a line given its endpoints, and the icon shown in Fig. 7b is used to select line width. The representational icons become slightly less intuitive when they refer to large classes of objects. The icon shown in Fig. 7c presents the points of intersection between two circles, but it can also be applied to intersect other primitives, such as a sphere and a plane. The icons used to specify actions such as moving a point (Fig. 7d) or removing a primitive (Fig. 7e) are abstract. Their design emphasizes an action to be performed rather than a concrete graphical object.

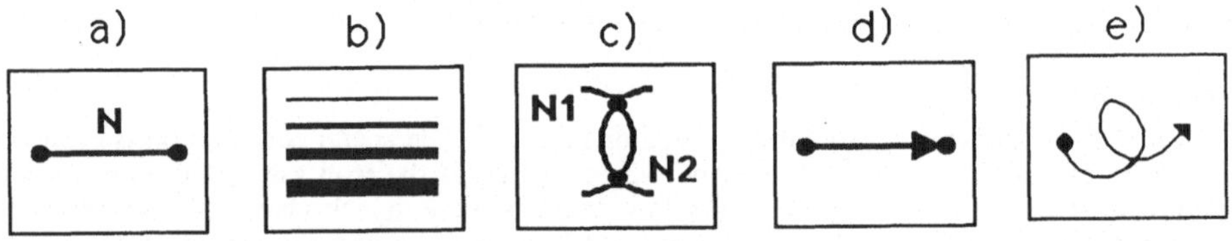

Fig. 7. Examples of L.E.G.O. icons.

Three of the icons are slightly less intuitive and require further explanations. The icon shown in Fig. 8a is used to define conditional statements. The only test available in the graphical programming mode compares the lengths of two lines. The user picks these lines and specifies, in succession, the alternative constructions to be performed depending on the result of the comparison. After the definition of the conditional statement is completed, the construction displayed on the screen corresponds to the actual relation between the compared lines.

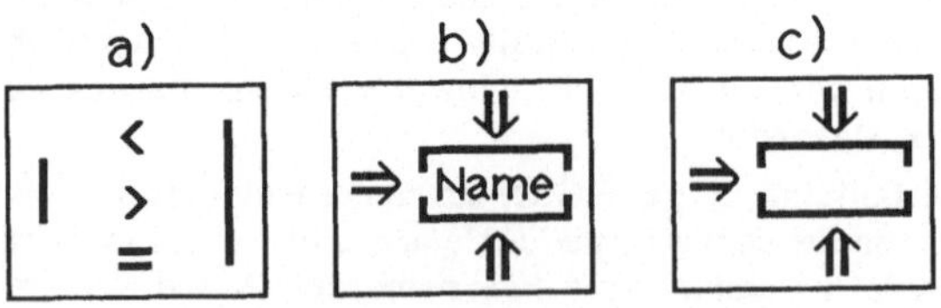

Fig. 8. Examples of L.E.G.O. icons.

The above method for defining conditional statements may seem slightly strange. What is the point of comparing lines which are already on the screen and the result of the comparison is known in advance? The answer to this question is that the result of the comparison may change. Specifically, this may happen if the starting points of the construction are moved on the screen, or if the conditional statement is defined within a function which can be called with different arguments.

In order to define functions, a section of the program must be selected as a function body. One way of doing this in the graphical programming mode is to rerun the program and click into elements ┌─┐ and └─┘ in the function-definition icon (Fig. 8b) when the relevant portion of the construction starts and terminates. Items in a pop-up menu make it possible to step through the program (forwards and backwards), thus facilitating this task. Alternatively, the user can enter the numbers of the first and the last lines of the program section to become the function body. Referring to the program in the textual form, while inconsistent with the graphical programming approach, is convenient for users familiar with the L.E.G.O. language. Newly created functions can be added to the menu of user-defined functions. They can be used in the same way as the predefined functions with the exception that they are all represented by the same generic icon (Fig. 8c).

The name of the function being defined is entered from the keyboard. The list of its input primitives is specified by selecting the top arrow in the function-definition icon (Fig. 8b) and picking the desired primitives in the working area of the screen. The list of primitives to be returned is formed in an analogous way, after selecting the bottom arrow in the icon. The left arrow can be optionally used to declare numerical parameters.

Two problems that arose in designing the graphical interface to develop three-dimensional constructions were the location of three-dimensional points and the picking of planes. At the present time, three-dimensional points may be specified in two ways. The coordinates of the point may be typed by choosing the **type** option in the menu or the point may be located on the current plane. The location selected by the cursor defines a line of points that are projected onto the screen at that location. The point of intersection between that line and the current plane will be the three-dimensional point. In order to solve the second problem, some way was needed to clip planes since if they were represented in their entirety they would generally cover the entire working area. They are intersected with the sides of a box and the resulting lines of intersection are picked for the plane (Color Plate 3).

A user may prefer the graphical interface for some operations, and the textual interface for others. Consequently, in L.E.G.O. both interface types can be used concurrently in a multiple-window environment provided by mex [23]. Mixing graphical and textual operations within a single statement is possible.

L.E.G.O. programs can also be considered as text files and edited outside the L.E.G.O. system. This mode of operation is particularly useful when making substantial changes to an existing program. For the purpose of file editing, it is convenient to run a text editor (vi) concurrently with L.E.G.O., in a separate window. The modified program can be then quickly loaded into the L.E.G.O. system and rerun.

6. APPLICATIONS OF L.E.G.O.

This section presents selected applications of L.E.G.O.

6.1. Computer assisted instruction of Euclidean geometry.

The fundamental concept of L.E.G.O., mimicry of constructions with straightedge and compass, makes the system suitable for teaching Euclidean geometry [9]. The educational applications of L.E.G.O. fall roughly in two categories: "the computer as a blackboard" and "the computer as a virtual laboratory". In the first case, L.E.G.O. is used by the instructor to prepare illustrations of geometric objects and constructions. Such illustrations are more precise and visually more attractive than those drafted on a traditional blackboard. Pictures created using L.E.G.O. can be captured using a camera and presented as slides, distributed to students in the form of plots or prints, or shown directly on the computer screen. Stepping through a L.E.G.O. program makes it possible to present a construction in progress (Fig. 9).

Use of L.E.G.O. as a virtual laboratory assumes interaction between the system and the students. Specifically, they can look at the L.E.G.O. objects from different angles and change data for constructions. Object manipulation reveals the general properties of the objects and constructions, and helps formulate them in the form of hypotheses. For example, moving vertices of a quadrangle (Fig. 10) brings to the student's attention that the figure created by connecting the midpoints of the edges of an arbitrary quadrangle is always a parallelogram.

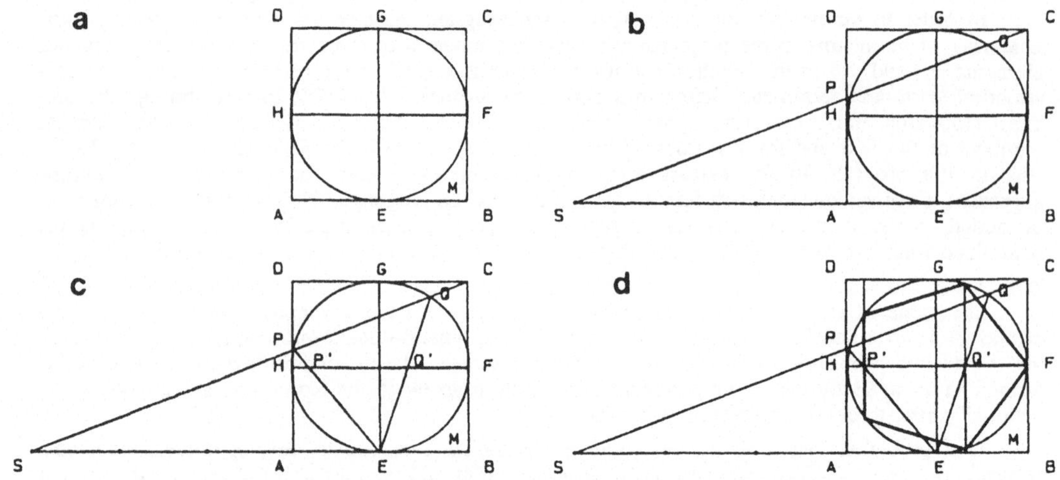

Fig. 9. Von Staudt's construction of a regular pentagon [2].

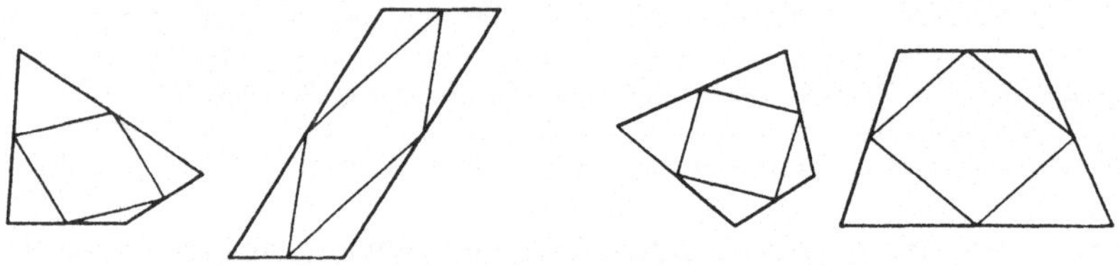

Fig. 10. Manipulating an object reveals its general properties.

6.2. Geometric modeling.

L.E.G.O. constructions can be used for modeling three-dimensional objects. For example, Color Plate 4 shows a dodecahedron inscribed in a sphere constructed using L.E.G.O. Repetitive (recursive or iterative) geometric constructions can also be used to model curved surfaces. Figure 11 illustrates the L.E.G.O. construction of a polygon mesh of a vase. The vertices of the vase lie at the intersections of four vertical planes with a sequence of horizontal circles.

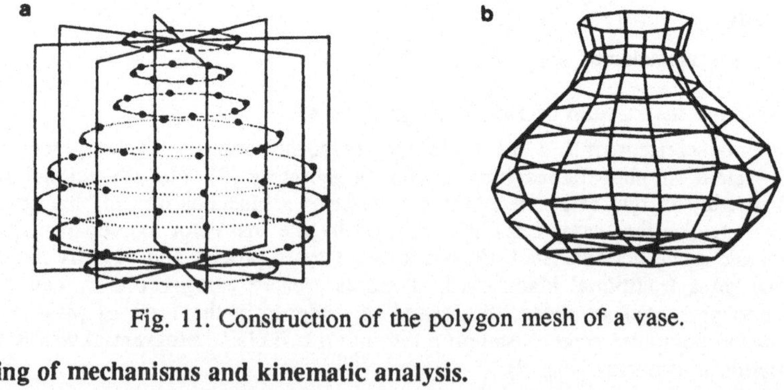

Fig. 11. Construction of the polygon mesh of a vase.

6.3. Modeling of mechanisms and kinematic analysis.

Mechanisms consist of movable elements (links) connected together in kinematic pairs which put constraints on the motion of the links. The essential problem of kinematic analysis is to determine the relationship between the input and the output motion of a mechanism. This relationship can be very complex and difficult to grasp. Consequently, working models of mechanisms are often necessary to gain a full understanding of the motion [12]. Alternatively, mechanisms can be represented as computer models. The possibility of modeling mechanisms using constraint-based graphics systems was recognized by Sutherland [22] and described as the most interesting application of Sketchpad. Various types of mechanisms can also be modeled using L.E.G.O. They can be interactively manipulated by the user, or put in motion by a "virtual motor", i.e., a function which moves the input links without user intervention. As an example of a mechanism consider James Watt's linkage [6] (Fig. 12a). If it is put in motion by rotating the left link, the midpoint of the middle link traces a Bernoulli's lemniscate. A "stroboscopic picture" of the linkage reveals that the velocity of the midpoint of the middle (red) link varies while the left (blue) link rotates at a constant speed (Color Plate 5). A film animating the movement of this mechanism has been made using L.E.G.O. Another mechanism, called Peaucelier's linkage, is shown in Fig. 12b. It is interesting from the historical perspective, as it is the first exact solution to the straight-line motion problem. (This problem consists of converting a circular motion at the input into a linear motion at the output of the linkage [6].)

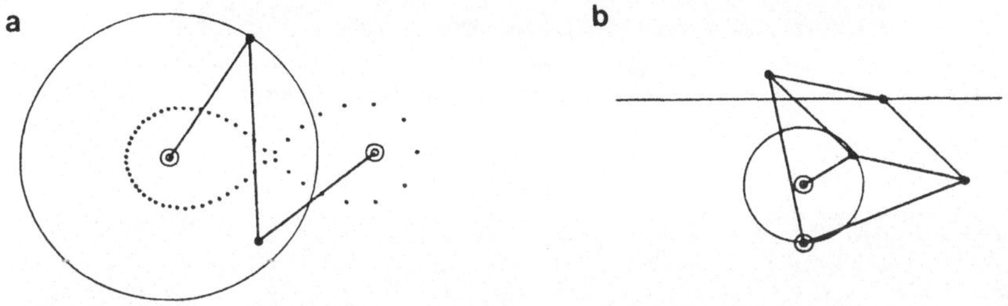

Fig. 12. Examples of linkages: (a) James Watt's linkage, (b) Peaucelier's linkage.

7. CONCLUSIONS

L.E.G.O. is an interactive object modeling system based on geometric constructions. Objects are described directly in geometric terms and can be manipulated interactively. A graphical interface is extensively used for man-machine communication. These features are not unique to L.E.G.O. and can also be found in declarative constraint-based systems. However, the use of geometric constructions eliminates the need for solving large systems of nonlinear equations inherent in declarative constraint-based systems. Consequently, L.E.G.O. can be used to model comparatively more complex objects.

The man-machine interface is an important feature of L.E.G.O. It is based on the concept of graphical programming. The graphical interface can be used concurrently with the textual interface, and the user is allowed to change the type of interface even when specifying a single statement.

Construction-based modeling is ideally suited for some applications, such as the teaching of Euclidean geometry, and the modeling and analysis of mechanisms. The construction-based approach can also be used in less obvious applications, such as the modeling of curved surfaces.

Since the beginning of 1985, various versions of L.E.G.O. have been available to computer graphics students at the University of Regina. They found the system very attractive, easy to use, and applicable to many practical problems. Although these opinions were not formally surveyed, they reinforce our conclusion that geometric constructions and implicit graphical programming provide a viable basis for an interactive object modeling system.

ACKNOWLEDGMENT

This research was supported in part by grant No. A0324 and a scholarship from the Natural Sciences and Engineering Research Council of Canada.

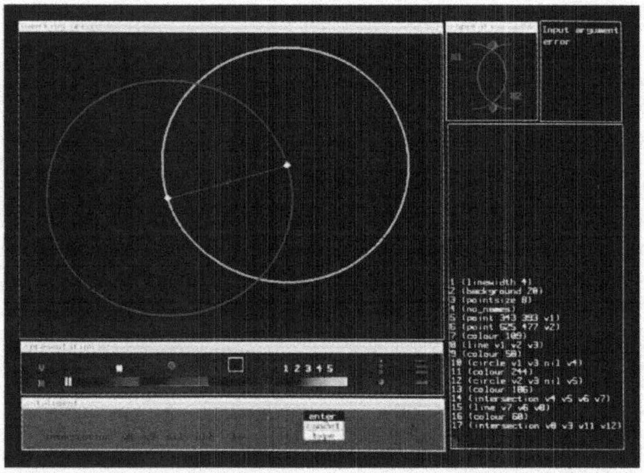

Plate 1:

Example of the L.E.G.O. screen in graphical programming mode. Windows from left to right top to bottom are: working area, operation window, messages window, representation window, program window and statement window.

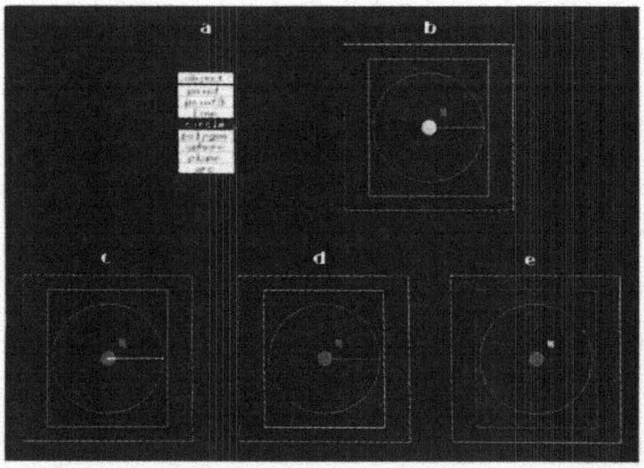

Plate 2: Menu and icon states while creating a circle

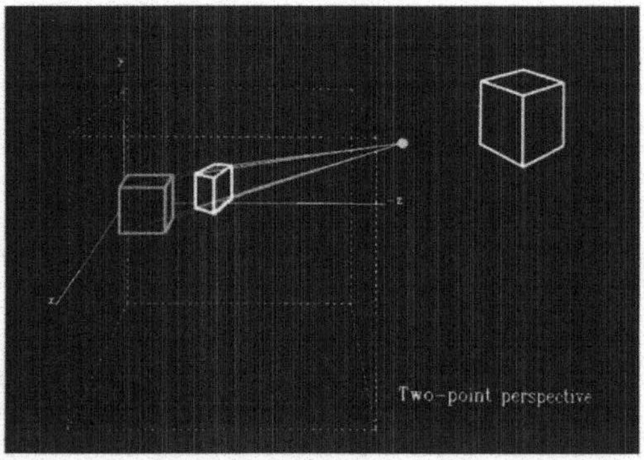

Plate 3: Representation of a plane clipped by a box

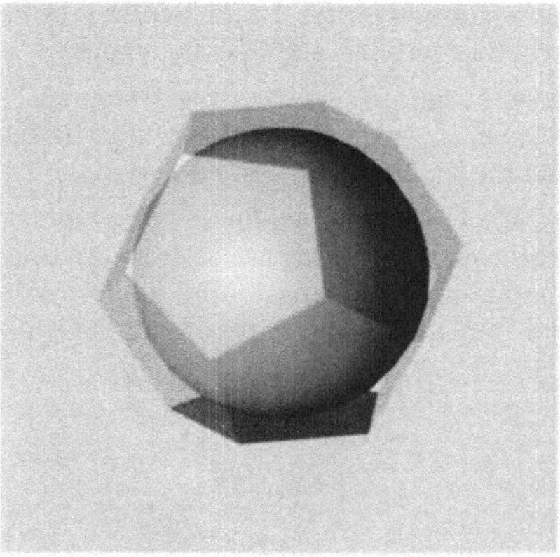

Plate 4: A sphere inscribed in a dodecahedron, constructed using L.E.G.O.

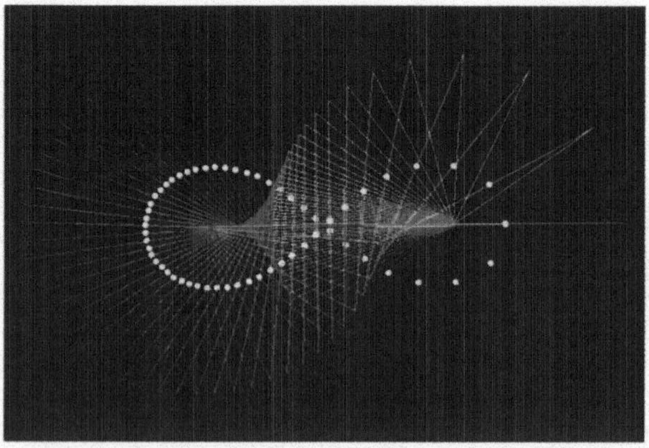

Plate 5: A stroboscopic view of James Watt's linkage

REFERENCES

[1] Abelson, H., and diSessa, A.: *Turtle Geometry: The computer as a medium for exploring mathematics*. MIT Press, Cambridge, 1980.

[2] Behnke, H., Bachmann, F., Fladt, K., and Kunle, H. (Eds.): *Fundamentals of Mathematics. Vol II: Geometry*. MIT Press, Cambridge, 1983.

[3] Bier, A., and Stone, M., Snap-Dragging. *Computer Graphics* **20** (4), 1986, pp. 233-240.

[4] Borning, A.: The programming language aspects of Thinglab, a constraint-oriented simulation laboratory. *ACM Trans. on Programming Languages* **3** (4), Oct. 1981, pp. 353-387.

[5] Borning, A., and Duisberg, R.: Constraint-based tools for building user interfaces. *ACM Transactions on Graphics* **5** (4), pp. 345-374.

[6] Cundy, H. M., and Rollet, A. P.: *Mathematical Models*. Oxford University Press, London, 1961.

[7] Foderaro, J.: *The Franz LISP Manual*. University of California, Berkeley, 1979.

[8] Fuller, N., Prusinkiewicz, P.: L.E.G.O. – An interactive graphics system for teaching geometry and computer graphics. *Proceedings of CIPS Edmonton '86*, pp. 75-84.

[9] Fuller, N., Prusinkiewicz, P., Rambally, G.: L.E.G.O. - An interactive computer graphics system for teaching geometry. *Proceedings, 4th World Conference on Computers In Education, 1985*, pp. 359-364.

[10] Fuller, N.: *User's Guide to L.E.G.O. - Version 1.0*. Techn. Rep. CS-85-19, Department of Computer Science, University of Regina, 1985.

[11] Glinert, E. P., and Tanimoto, S. L.: Pict: An interactive graphical programming environment. *Computer* **17** (11), Nov. 1984, pp. 7-25.

[12] Hain, K.: *Applied Kinematics*. McGraw-Hill, New York, 1967.

[13] Johnson, T. E.: Sketchpad III: A computer program for drawing in three dimensions. In *1963 Spring Joint Computer Conference,* reprinted in Freeman H. (Ed.): *Interactive Computer Graphics,* IEEE Computer Soc. 1980, pp. 20-26.

[14] Knuth, D. E.: *TEX and METAFONT*. Digital Press and American Mathematical Society, Bedford, 1979.

[15] Lodding, K. N.: Iconic Interfacing. *IEEE Computer Graphics and Applications* **3** (2), March/April 1983, pp. 11-20.

[16] Mandelbrot, B.B.: *The Fractal Geometry of Nature*. W.H. Freeman, San Francisco, 1982.

[17] Nelsen, G.: Juno, a constraint-based graphics system. *Computer Graphics* **19** (33), July 1985, pp. 235-243.

[18] Papert, S.: *Mindstorms: Children, computers, and powerful ideas*. Basic Books, New York, 1980.

[19] Pong, M. C., and Ng, N.: PIGS - A system for programming with interactive graphical support. *Software - Practice and Experience* **13** (9), Sept. 1983, pp. 847-855.

[20] Prusinkiewicz, P., and Streibel, D.: Constraint-based modeling of three-dimensional shapes. *Proceedings of Graphics Interface '86 – Vision Interface '86*, pp. 158-163.

[21] Schneiderman, B.: Direct Manipulation: A Step beyond Programming Languages. *Computer* **16** (8), August 1983, pp. 57-69.

[22] Sutherland, I. E.: Sketchpad: A man-machine graphical communication system. In *1963 Spring Joint Computer Conference,* reprinted in Freeman H. (Ed.): *Interactive Computer Graphics,* IEEE Computer Soc. 1980, pp. 1-19.

[23] *User's Guide for IRIS Graphics Programming (Version 3.0)*. Silicon Graphics, Inc., Mountain View, California, 1986.

[24] Van Wyk, C. J.: A high-level language for specifying pictures. *ACM Transactions on Graphics* **1** (2), April 1982, pp. 163-182.

[25] Wilensky, R.: *LISPcraft*. W.W. Norton, New York, 1984.

Using GT/CAPP to Enhance Product Data Exchange Standard - Key to CAD/CAM Integration

I. Al-Qattan and J. R. Rose (USA)

ABSTRACT

The ability to exchange standard data among various computer-aided design (CAD) and computer-aided manufacturing (CAM) tools used in discrete parts manufacturing provides an important key with regard to the full implementation of computer-integrated manufacturing (CIM). This paper will discuss two coding techniques which will enhance the process of data transfer on two levels. This approach involves the creation of product codes which are used on the production planning level and feature codes which are used on the operational level. "C" language computer programs have been written to create an interactive procedure which places the designer in the manufacturing loop. The impact of group technology integrated with computer-aided process planning (GT/CAPP) on the generation of a product data exchange standard (PDES) will be demonstrated.

INTRODUCTION

Using the computer as a tool for data acquisition, transfer and display is one of the most exciting and rapidly growing fields in manufacturing technology today. There is virtually no area in which computers can not be used to some advantage. Two dimensional computer-aided design (CAD) software packages have been available for a number of years and have gained widespread use. More recently, highly sophisticated three dimensional solid modeling packages have been developed which greatly extend the usefulness of the computer as a design tool. On the other end of the computer-aided design/manufacturing (CAD/CAM) spectrum, computer numerical control (CNC) programming systems have been used since the 1960's. Unfortunately, CAD and CAM systems have advanced independently of one another. Thus, this lack of integration of CAD and CAM systems has been recognized as the main obstacle facing the full implementation of computer integrated manufacturing (CIM). One of the major problems associated with CIM implementation has to do with gaining the ability to exchange data and information among CIM tools. The initial sections of this paper will define CIM tools and present the evolution of data exchange standards. A proposed GT/CAPP scheme which will enhance product data exchange specifications will then be discussed.

CIM FUNCTIONS

To remain competitive in the world market, manufacturers are highly motivated to implement computer-integrated manufacturing. These powerful CIM tools are; computer-aided design (CAD), computer-aided manufacturing (CAM), computer-aided process planning (CAPP), manufacturing resource planning (MRP), automated material handling (AMH), computer numerical control (CNC), group technology (GT), and robotics. While the application of each of these individual tools will help to increase productivity, the integration of all of them will lead to an exponential growth in productivity and cost reduction.

Figure 1 shows CIM functions[1]. CAD can simply be described as "using computers in the design process." In the design phase, computers are used to conceptualize,

---

[1] Peter Marks, "CIM Directions - Report and Guidelines from a Survey of CIM Directors in U.S. Companies," Fall Industrial Engineering Conference Proceedings (December 7-10, 1986), pp. 1-17.

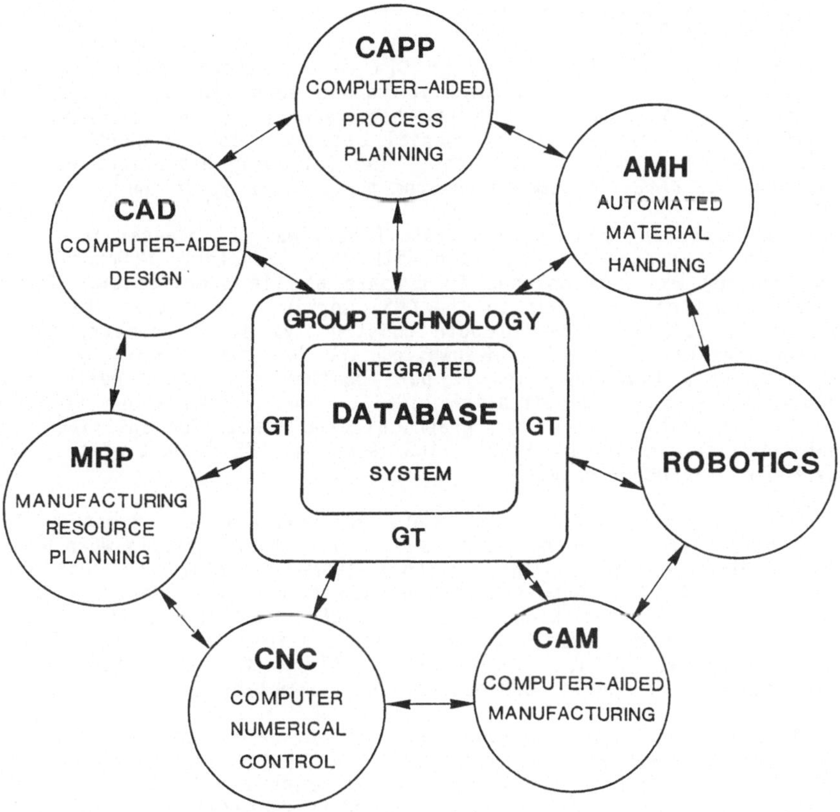

Figure 1. CIM Functions

design, draft, analyze, modify, and generate necessary data for manufacturing. CAM is concerned with the computer control of the manufacturing processes involved. CAPP deals with the major tasks to be performed after the design phase, and it establishes the vital link between CAD and CAM. CAPP generates all the technical documents necessary to manufacture a part as per the design and specifications. The document developed in this stage is called a process plan or route sheet. MRP primarily deals with a computer-based plan for optimizing the use of manufacturing resources. GT is a manufacturing philosophy that helps to identify the similarities among parts in order to form part families or groups. AMH and robotics deal with the use of material handling equipment and industrial robots for programmable moving and loading/unloading of workpieces for different manufacturing applications[2]. Effective database systems (DBS) must be structured in a systematic manner such that they contain all necessary manufacturing information and can be accessed by any CIM function. The proposed bi-level coding system will create an environment where the cross-referenced data files may be accessed very rapidly and simply through the use of a product code, and the information required to be conveyed from one level to the other will be minimized by the use of a feature code.

---

[2] I. Al-Qattan and M. Sundaram, "CAPP-Vital to CAD and CAM Integration," National Computer Graphics Association Proceedings - Computer Graphics Association, 1987, pp. 207-216.

THE EVOLUTION OF DATA EXCHANGE STANDARDS

As the number and sophistication of CIM tools systems increases, so does the need for a way to transfer information among these tools. The ability of CIM to dramatically improve productivity has recently become a driving force which is compelling industry to pay special attention to the need to transfer data and information among CIM functions. The following historical development of data exchange standards is summarized from the article by Wilson[3].

The American National Standards Institute (ANSI) was the pioneer in establishing the first draft standards associated with data transfer. McDonnell Douglas Automation (McAuto) was commissioned to prepare a file specification for solid modeling data based on the ideas in the ANSI working documents. This contract was completed in 1979 and covered both constructive solid geometry (CSG) and boundary representation (B-rep). Meanwhile, the National Bureau of Standards (NBS) commissioned a few industries to put together a standard referred to as Initial Graphics Exchange Specification (IGES). The initial scope of IGES was restricted to the typical geometric, graphical, and annotation entities required to draw a blueprint. In the mid 1980's, ANSI adopted IGES as part of the standard for the exchange of product data.

A series of modifications, improvements and extensions ultimately led to the publication of IGES-3.0 in April of 1986. While these efforts were underway, Computer-Aided Manufacturing - International (CAM-I) decided to test some of the concepts developed by McAuto within the IGES framework. The resulting document, entitled "Experimental Boundary File" (XBF), was published in 1982. A joint effort by the CAM-I and IGES communities has resulted in the IGES Experimental Solids Proposal (ESP). ESP is essentially a subset of XBF. Both are designed to handle B-rep models, CSG models, and assemblies.

Aerospatiale in France had also developed a set of data exchange specifications called "Standard d'Exchange et de transfert" (SET) which was based on IGES-2.0 files. The SET specifications were seen as a major advancement in that they produced significant reduction in file size when compared with IGES and also achieved processing times which were approximately three times faster.

The US Air Force has introduced the Product Data Definition Interface (PDDI) in two stages. The first was completed in 1983, and the second was completed at the end of 1985. The PDDI was based on the transfer needs for four types of parts that were considered to be typical of the airframe industry. One of the important factors related to this project was that it enhanced and facilitated the data exchange between designer and manufacturer.

German automobile manufacturers have developed the Verband der Deutschem Automobilindustrie Flachen-Schnittstelle (VDAFS) standard. VDAFS is based on IGES-1.0 and, unlike the other standards, can handle only a narrow section of the CIM spectrum, but, within its limited confines, it functions well.

The International Standards Organization (ISO) was created as a technical committee with the responsibility to attempt to unify all data exchange standard efforts in a unique standard called STEP (Standard for the Exchange of Product Model Data). Figure 2 illustrates the evolution of data exchange standards.

Recently, the IGES community and other researchers realized that a major effort should be devoted to the information modeling of the entire manufacturing area - in other words, attempting to determine the information exchange needs that would be required by future CIM systems and network transfer standards.

---

3 Peter Wilson, "A Short History of CAD Data Transfer Standards," IEEE Computer Graphics and Applications, Vol. 7(June 1987), pp. 64-67.

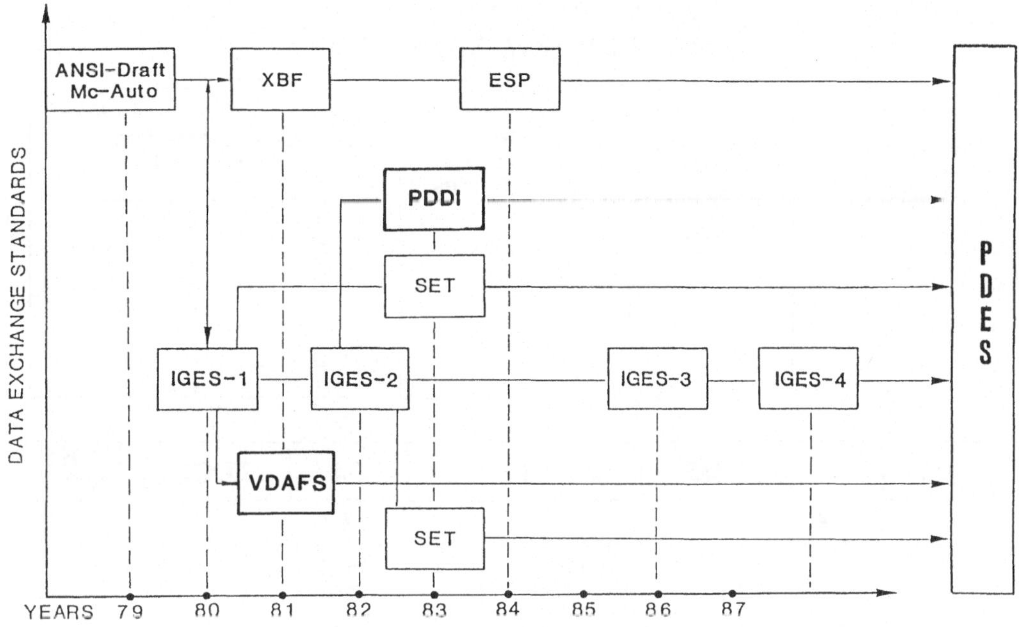

Figure 2. The Evolution of Data Exchange Standards

The Product Data Exchange Specification (PDES) has been proposed and accepted as the basis for the future ISO exchange standard (STEP).

Group Technology Scheme

Group technology (GT) is a manufacturing philosophy used in production planning in which similar products or parts are identified and grouped together to take advantage of their similarities in design and manufacturing characteristics. GT does not include a classification and coding scheme only. It also contains a technique for developing methods for grouping parts into part families (PF) and machines into machine cells (MC). Therefore, a product family is a collection of products which are similar, either because of their geometric shape and/or size or because similar machining steps are required in their production. Grouping helps to decompose a complex manufacturing system into a series of smaller and simplier subsystems. Two GT schemes are proposed in this paper. The first, called Product Code (PC), is used for product design specifications. The second, called feature code (FC), is used for decomposing a product into features. Figures 3 and 4 illustrate the product and feature codes, respectively[4]. The product code contains general information such as geometric shape, material, dimensional ratio, number of internal/external features, the machines to be used, part number (which includes all features), and the batch size of the product to be produced. The product code system provides a sort of horizontal level communication to facilitate access to the database at the functional level, thereby enabling the transfer of data and information among CIM tools. The

---

4 Thomas Gunn, Computer Application in Manufacturing (Industrial Press, 1984), pp. 156-159.

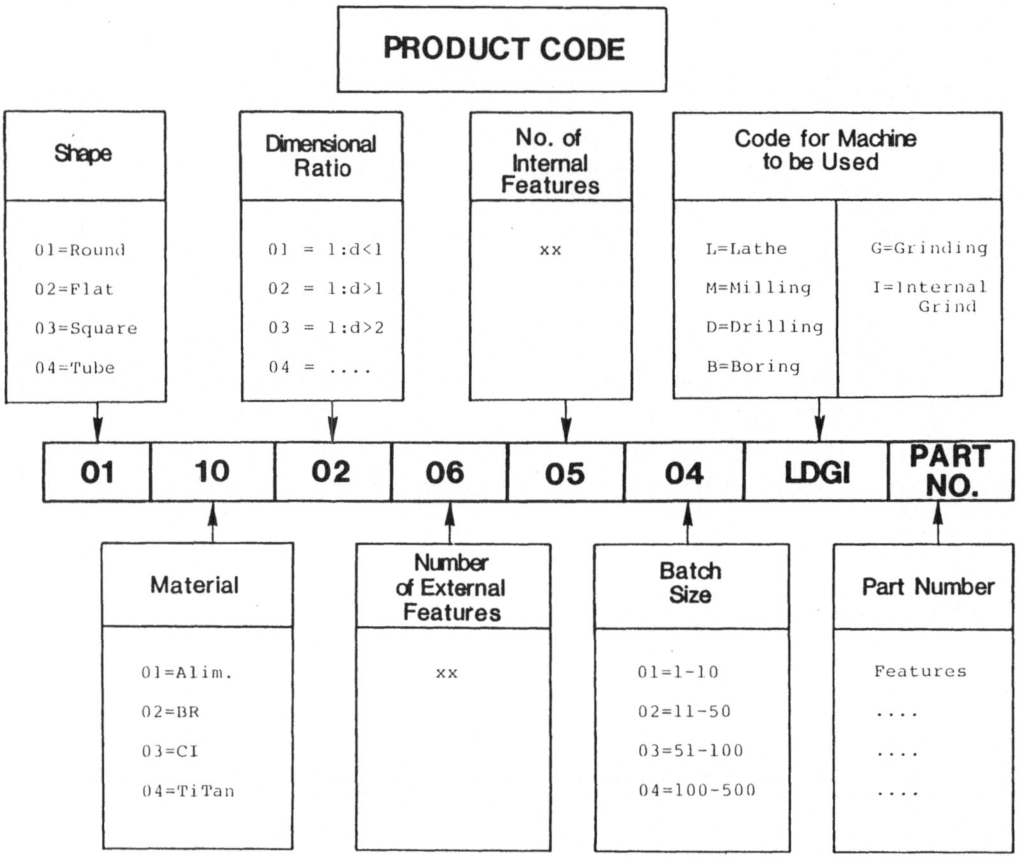

Figure 3. Product Code System

feature code information includes tolerance level, surface finish, machining operations, setup and processing time, and special fixtures required for feature extraction. The feature code provides, at the operational level, vertical communication which enables easy access to the database system in order to implement the search for optimization parameters. The proposed method dissects the data and information into two parts. One part is used for generating the NC cutter path and contains information associated with the configuration of the solid model to be fabricated. The other part is used for production planning, such as forming GT cells, the sequence of machining operations, tooling and fixtures selection, and searching for optimization parameters. The proposed method will help to reduce the amount of information transfer from one tool to another and expedite the communication of information through the product code. "C" language computer programs have been written to create an interactive environment to generate both the product and features codes. The interactive procedure presented here places the designer in the manufacturing loop and requires the CAD user to input special manufacturing information which is then transferred to the database system for further utilization.

THE LINK BETWEEN GT/CAPP AND PDES

The basic idea behind group technology is using coding and classification methods to group together similar parts into part families and similar machines

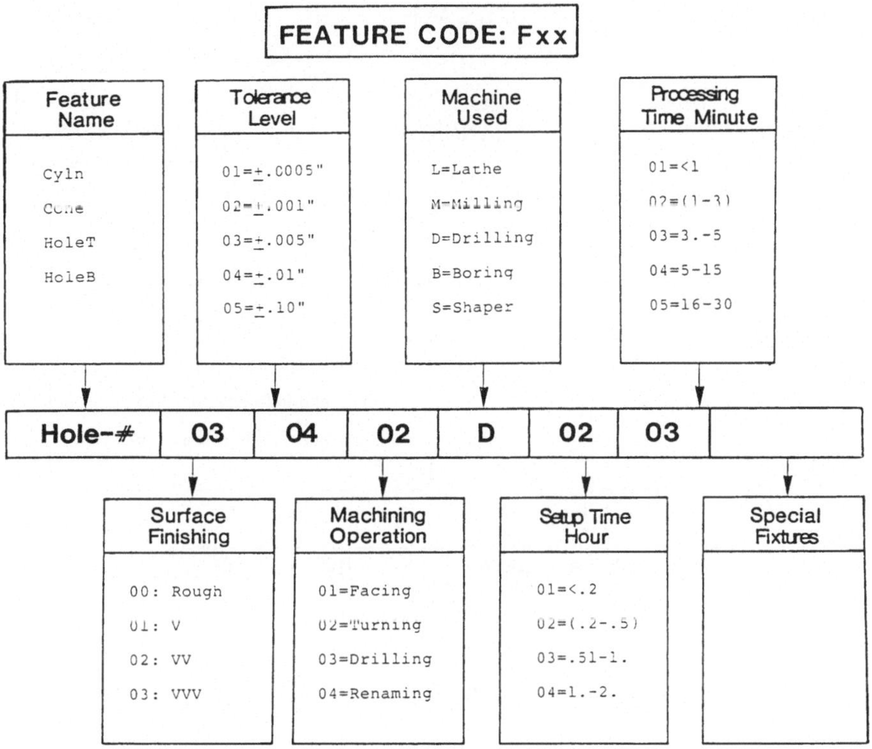

Figure 4. Feature Code System

into machine cells. Grouping allows for the decomposition of a manufacturing system into a number of smaller subsystems. Dealing with a number of subsystems will simplify the flow of the information and will minimize the amount of data to be managed. The main problem in process planning is the complexity of scheduling required for machining operations. GT cells provide a tool to reduce the complexity of this problem because parts with the similar process plans (routes) are grouped into part families and corresponding machines are grouped into machine cells. The scheduling of each part family is far easier than scheduling all parts together. Computerized process planning involves using the computer to perform all instructions required to produce a part as per the design and specifications. There are two approaches to implementing CAPP, variant and generative. Variant process planning is interactive and uses the computer for sorting, retrieving, editing, and modifying data to obtain a process plan. Generative process planning is fully automated. Each plan obtained is unique and there are no predefined plans stored in the database. The generative approach requires an expert knowledge-based system (KBS). The KBS must contain decision logic in the form of production rules (condition-action), decision trees, or artificial intelligence (AI)[5].

The concept of product data exchange specifications (PDES) as defined by the National Bureau of Standard (NBS) is "aimed to communicating a complex product model with sufficient information content as to be interpretable directly by advanced CAD/CAM application. These applications include generative process planning, CAD directed inspection, and automatic generation and verification of NC cutter

---

5 I. Al-Qattan and Robert Mabrey, "Demonstration of Geomod/CAPP Integration," I-DEAS and International Users' Conference, pp. 105-109, 1987.

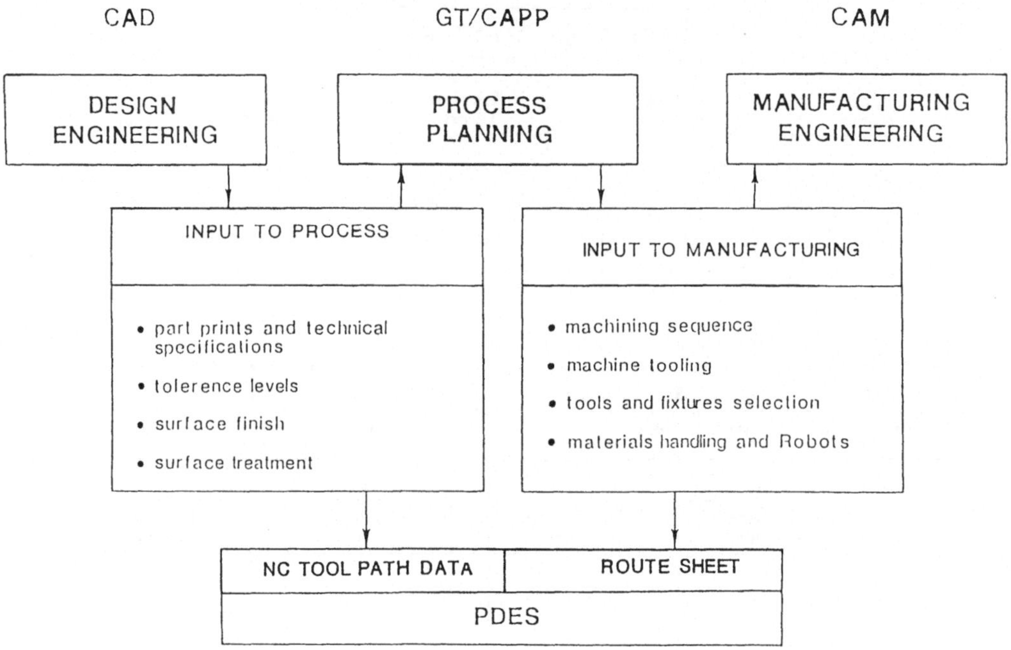

Figure 5. Relationship among Design, GT/CAPP, CAM and PDES

path data,"[6]. Integrating GT and CAPP will provide the ability to minimize the amount of information transfer. This will result in the obtainment of cutter path information much more quickly and also provide an excellent vehicle for computerized process planning. Figure 5 describes how the design function is linked with the manufacturing function through the integration of GT and CAPP. The designer, after designing and testing a part using appropriate CAD software, establishes a database to produce a part print and technical specifications which will be used as input data required by the process planner. The result of the work done in process planning will be a route sheet that can be used as a manufacturing method to fabricate a product.

Figure 6 illustrates a flow diagram of the link between the CIM tools associated with producing the PDES. After completing the design phase, the designer will interact with two "C" computer programs, one to generate product codes and the other to generate feature codes. Each coded feature is extracted from the CAD tool and will include all necessary information about the geometrical shape of the feature. This information will be assigned to a single feature code. Data for obtaining the NC tool path can be accessed easily by calling the feature code. Each encoded product includes its features which will be used to form GT cells. Many researchers have developed methods to solve the problem of GT cells. For example, Burbidge used the Production Flow Analysis (PFA) approach, King used Rank Order Clustering Algorithm (ROCA), Purcheck used combinatorial and hueristic method, and Kumar applied Graph Theory to deal with GT cell problems. As a further attempt in their direction Al-Qattan developed a method using network

---

6 Brad Smith, "PDES - Product Data Exchange Specification," <u>Autofact</u> 87 Conference, (Detroit, Michigan), 1987.

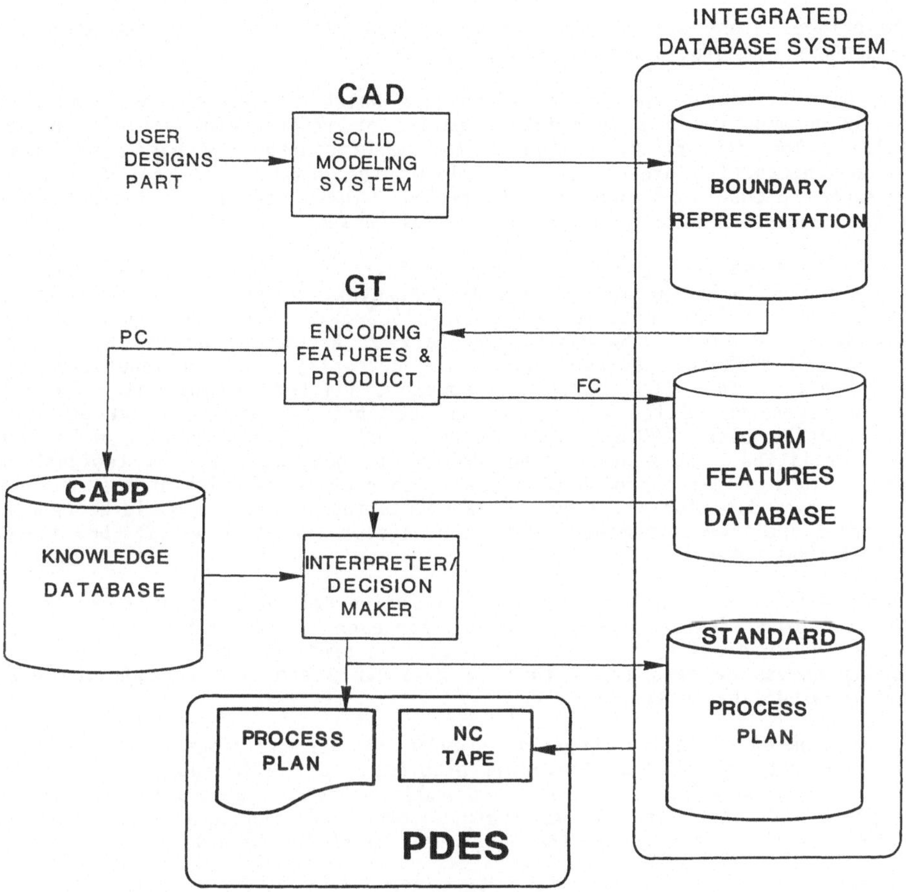

Figure 6. System Flow Diagram for "Expert System"
GT/CAPP Enhance PDES

analysis in conjunction with branching and bounding techniques[7]. A "C" computer program was developed to form GT cells using this method is available. A significant advantage of this technique is that each GT cell will be treated as an independent system, and the relevant cell information will be provided through the use of expert knowledge-based system (KBS). The output of the KBS will be the necessary sequence of machining operations, the sequencing of tools and fixtures, the determination of machining parameters (feed rate, cutting speed, and depth), and, finally, the issuance of a process plan for each product. The process plan and the information obtained from CAD system for each feature for NC toolpath correspond to the PDES standard.

CONCLUSIONS AND SUMMARY

The ability to exchange standard data among various computer-aided design and manufacturing tools used in discrete parts manufacturing provides the opportunity

---

[7] I. Al-Qattan, "An Efficient Method of Designing GT Cells Using Network Analysis," to be published in International Journal of Production Research.

to build bridges among the "islands of automation" and results in the achievement of true computer-integrated manufacturing.

This paper introduced two coding techniques which improve the process of data transfer by decomposing a system into a series of smaller and simpler subsystems (GT cells). The concept of designing for manufacturability has been used by creating an interactive procedure which places the designer in the manufacturing loop to encode product and feature information. The impact of GT integrated with CAPP on the generation of a PDES database was discussed in detail.

Over the past several years, a massive effort has been directed toward the development of an IGES standard. There are, however, several significant problems associated with the implementation of IGES. IGES data files are huge and require extremely long run times. Secondly, the task of accommodating the wide variety of CAD and CAM software packages which are currently used in manufacturing is immense. Finally, the IGES concept is somewhat limited in that it only yields information regarding NC toolpath data and does not aid in the generation of an automated process plan. PDES, on the other hand, is more powerful with regard to its capabilities. It provides the ability to generate both NC toolpath data and process plans. This approach also has a major drawback. The process of encoding all necessary data for all types of manufacturing industries would be unacceptablely complex and time consuming. Thus, the development of universal PDES standard appears to be impractical.

The problems inherent in creating a single universal PDES standard can be overcome by developing a separate PDES standard for each of the several types of manufacturing. The complexity of the problem would be greatly reduced, and the process of encoding necessary data could then be reasonably achieved through the use of an expert knowledge based system.

The formation of GT cells appears to provide another significant means of reducing the complexity of the manufacturing problems. GT cells coupled with product codes will reduce scheduling problems and will enable the generation of automated process plans. Further, the use of feature codes will reduce the amount of data to be managed and will accelerate the obtainment of NC toolpath data.

REFERENCES

Al-Qattan, I., "An Efficient Method of Designing GT Cells Using Network Analysis." to be published in International Journal of Production Research.

Al-Qattan, I., and Robert Mabrey, "Demonstration of Geomod/CAPP Integration," Structural Dynamics Research Corporation, I-DEAS International Users' Conference, October 26-29, 1987, Cincinnati, Ohio.

Al-Qattan, I., and Sundaram, M., "CAPP-Vital to CAD and CAM Integration," National Computer Graphics Association, Proceedings - Computer Graphics '87, March 22-26, 1987, Philadelphia, Pennsylvania.

Gunn Thomas, COMPUTER APPLICATION IN MANUFACTURING," Industrial Press, pp. 156-159, 1984.

Marks, Peter, "CIM Directions - Report and Guidelines from a Survey of CIM Directors in U.S. Companies.", proceedings Fall Industrial Engineering Conference, December 7-10, 1986, Boston, Massachusetts.

Smith, Brad, "PDES - Product Data Exchange Specification," AUTOFACT 87 Conference, Nov. 9-12, 1987, Detroit, Michigan.

Wilson, Peter, "A Short History of CAD Data Transfer Standards," IEEE Computer Graphics and Applications, Vol. 7, No. 6, pp. 64-67 (June 1987).

Chapter 4

Graphics Systems and Languages

Drawing Input Through Geometrical Constructions: Specification and Applications

T. Noma, T. L. Kunii, N. Kin, H. Enomoto, E. Aso, and T. Yamamoto (Japan)

ABSTRACT

This paper proposes a novel approach to 2D picture description. In this approach, points essential to specify pictures are defined through repetitive geometrical constructions, and the final image is drawn by referring to those points. The method fulfills the requirements for picture description: easiness, intuitiveness, and universality. In addition, to clarify the mechanism of drawing input, we formulate the specification of a drawing input system. To represent the relationships among points, lines, and circles, the specification uses the geometrical operations. We show the validity of drawing input through three applications: engineering drawing, apparel pattern-making, and Tibetan mandala image generation.

Keywords: drawing input, geometrical construction, picture description

1. Introduction

Input of shape is one of the most important problems in computer graphics. In the case that the object space is two-dimensional (2D) and the input is performed noninteractively, the shape input problem comes to the problem of picture description.

This paper proposes a novel approach to picture description: drawing input through geometrical constructions. This approach is summarized as follows: we define new geometrical objects such as new lines, circles, and points, from the geometrical objects which have already been defined. After defining necessary geometrical objects step by step, we draw the final picture segments using those objects, especially points.

For example, the steps of defining new geometrical objects include: (1) draw a straight line l through point $p1$ and point $p2$; (2) draw a circle c with center point p and radius r; (3) name an intersection point where line $l1$ and $l2$ intersect; (4) name two intersection points where line l and circle c intersect. These operations resemble the steps in drawing with a ruler and a pair of compasses. Because of this resemblance, we call our approach "drawing input".

However, we need not follow elementary geometry faithfully. It is also legal to define the middle point between two points in a single step. In addition, we are free from some constraints of plane geometry, such as the impossibility of trisection of an angle. The operation drawing trisection lines of an angle can be realized, if necessary.

Our drawing input method has three advantages: easiness, intuitiveness, and universality. In Chapter 2, we analyze the requirements for picture description systems, propose our solution: drawing input through geometrical constructions, and compare our solution with related works. To clarify the semantics of a drawing input mechanism, a formal specification of an example drawing input system is described in Chapter 3. In this specification, we use the geometrical operations based on formal elementary geometry, Our drawing input method can be used in a variety of application areas. In Chapter 4, we present three example applications. The first example is the definition of parametric shapes in engineering drawing. The second example is making basic patterns in computer-aided apparel pattern-making. The third example is displaying a Tibetan mandala image as a purely artistic work on a graphic device. These three examples show the universality of our drawing input method. Chapter 5 concludes this paper with some comments on future research directions.

2. Drawing Input through Geometrical Constructions

2.1. Requirements for Picture Description

2.1.1. Direct Coordinate Value Specification

In general, the most common method of picture description is specifying coordinate values of output primitives. We call this method *direct coordinate value specification.* The method has several advantages.

First of all, a few types of output primitives are enough to produce varieties of shapes, whose display resolution depends on the available graphics device capability including the memory space. For example, depending on the number of points and their coordinate values, any polygon can be described including triangle, quadrilateral, or hexagon. Moreover, if the length of the edges is sufficiently short, smooth-curved shapes such as circles and ellipsoids can also be displayed as approximations.

Secondly, this method has universality regarding application areas and implementation styles. In other words, there are few areas where the method is unapplicable, and it can be realized as an independent picture description language and/or graphics library software for common high-level programming languages such as Fortran, Pascal, and C.

Lastly, this method reflects the architecture of most of the current graphics devices, and enables us to use the devices efficiently.

Because of the above advantages, all the graphics standards such as CORE, GKS, and PHIGS use direct coordinate value specification, and in most of the graphics systems, picture description is converted to this type of description at the final stage of output.

However, this direct coordinate value specification has a disadvantage. Every geometrical information is translated into the coordinate values or formulae representing them. If a picture includes many oblique lines and/or dimensional specification in oblique directions, the formulae include square roots and/or trigonometrical functions and can be very complex for users.

2.1.2. Requirements for Picture Description

Based on the discussions in the previous subsection, the development of picture description is not for the improvement of graphical outputs but for the ease of use. Therefore, a picture description system needs to fulfill the following requirements:

(1) *Ease of Description.* More and more people want to use computer graphics, and simple and plain description of pictures is useful for the non-specialists. Conversely, if the system assumes that the user has a knowledge of difficult mathematical functions such as square roots and trigonometrical functions and of how to handle formulae including such functions, the system can be used by a small number of people.

(2) *Intuitiveness.* Originally, a picture is visually represented and appeals to our intuition on spatial data handling. The process of making the picture should also be handled in accordance with the intuition. Such intuitive picture description decreases data input costs, while non-intuitive description causes unexpected input errors and makes them undetectable.

(3) *Universality in Implementation Styles.* Even for the same application, processing styles vary depending on the situations. If a variety of processing styles of the same picture description method are supported, we can use one of them appropriately. Otherwise, the system has difficulties in the sharing of data.

2.2. Drawing Input through Geometrical Constructions

This section introduces our drawing input method. First of all, we consider direct coordinate value specification again. Because of its disadvantage, requirement 1 and 2 are not met, while requirement 3 is fully satisfied. If there is an alternative way to specify point locations which provides easy and intuitive description, then a better picture description method can be obtained. Therefore, we should concentrate on the positional specification of the points essential to define a given picture.

Now we propose a drawing input through geometrical constructions. Most of the people learn elementary geometry and/or drawing in their school days. They know how to draw a line perpendicular to a specified line and to draw a equilateral triangle when one of its edges is given. This kind of knowledge is the core of our geometrical and spatial intuition, and picture description based on this knowledge fulfills requirement 2.

Let us suppose that we are to draw an equilateral triangle one of whose edges is line segment AB (Fig. 1). In case of direct coordinate value specification, we have to calculate the coordinate value of the other point:

$$\left(\frac{x_A+x_B-\sqrt{3}(y_B-y_A)}{2},\ \frac{\sqrt{3}(x_B-x_A)+y_A+y_B}{2}\right) \qquad \begin{array}{l} A:(x_A, y_A) \\ B:(x_B, y_B) \end{array}$$

On the other hand, let us consider the case of drawing input method. Originally, drawing input method has no standard style. The operation sets and implementation styles vary depending on the application and other conditions. Table 1 shows an example operation set of drawing input method.

Operation LINE is used to draw a line. Every line in a drawing input method is supposed to be *directed,* from $p1$ to $p2$ (Fig. 2). For any line to have a direction is one of the features of our drawing input. Operation CIRC draws a circle. The relationship among c, p, and r is shown in Fig. 3. Operation P1LL defines the intersection point of two lines (Fig. 4). Operation P1PL is used to define a point $p1$ on the line l so that the

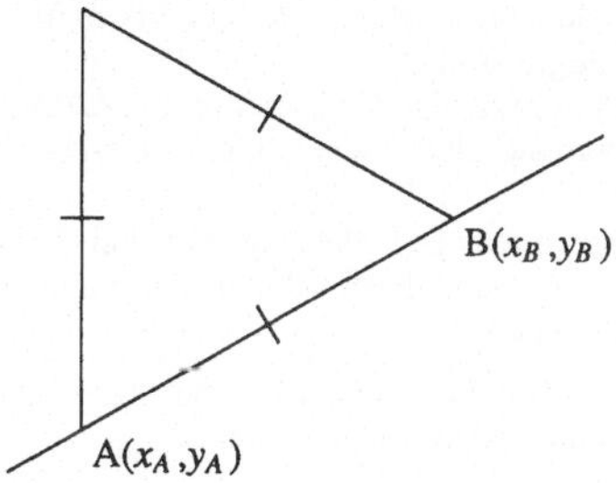

Fig. 1. Drawing an Equilateral Triangle

Table 1. An Example Operation Set of Drawing Input

Operation	Meaning
LINE l $p1$ $p2$	draw line l through points $p1$ and $p2$
CIRC c p r	draw circle c with center p and radius r
P1LL p $l1$ $l2$	define point p where lines $l1$ and $l2$ intersect
P1PL $p1$ $p2$ l d	define point $p1$ at a distance of d from point $p2$ along line l
P2CL $p1$ $p2$ c l	define points $p1$ and $p2$ where circle c and line l intersect
P2CC $p1$ $p2$ $c1$ $c2$	define points $p1$ and $p2$ where circles $c1$ and $c2$ intersect
LTTK $p1$ $p2$	put the length from point $p1$ to $p2$ into the queue

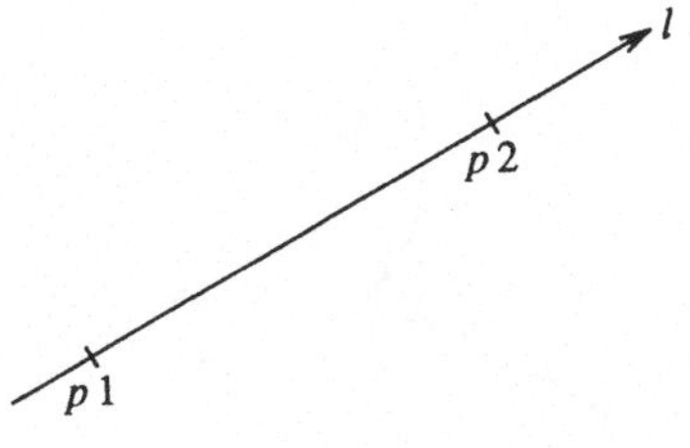

Fig. 2. Operation LINE

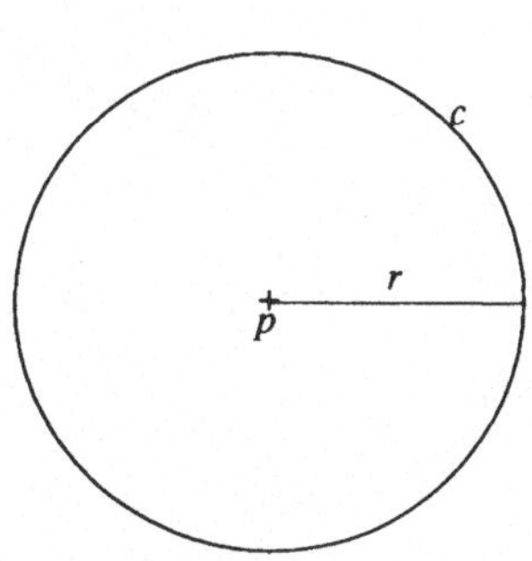

Fig. 3. Operation CIRC

distance from the reference point $p2$ to $p1$ is d. The distance d can be a negative value. The sign of d represents the direction from $p2$ to $p1$. If d is positive, the direction is the same as that of l (Fig. 5). The two intersection points of a circle and a line are defined by operation P2CL. $p1$ and $p2$ are defined so that the direction of l is from $p1$ to $p2$ (Fig. 6). If line l and circle c do not intersect, point $p1$ and $p2$ is undefined. If line l and circle c intersect only at one point, this means points $p1$ and $p2$ are identical. Operation P2CC defines two intersection points of two circles. Viewing from the center of $c1$ to that of $c2$, the point on the left hand is defined as $p1$, and the right-hand point is $p2$ (Fig. 7).

Operation LTTK differs from the above operations. In our drawing input method, it is important to use the lengths between points and the angles between lines. Variables are often used to share and hold these values. However, we consider that the use of variables is too difficult for ordinary users. Therefore, a data queue is used to hold these values. Operation LTTK puts the length from point $p1$ to point $p2$ into the queue, and in a formula part of an operation, the entry on the top is poped and referenced by an ampersand (&). Note that every command except LTTK is accompanied by naming the defined geometrical objects.

With these operations, we can specify point C of the equilateral triangle:

LTTK A B	put the length from A to B
CIRC e A &	draw circle e with center A and radius & (the length from A to B)
LTTK A B	put the length from A to B
CIRC f B &	draw circle f with center B and radius & (the length from A to B)
P2CC C D e f	define points C and D where circles e and f intersect

These operations can be specified either in a short notation on the left column or in a natural language subset on the right column. Usually, users start from the natural language version, and gradually shift to the short notation version as they are accustomed.

Obviously, the description of drawing input method is much more intuitive and easier than that of direct coordinate value specification, and the method fulfills requirement 1.

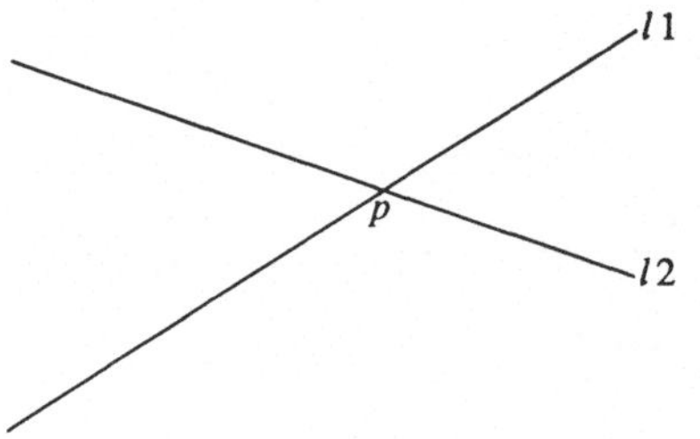

Fig. 4. Operation P1LL

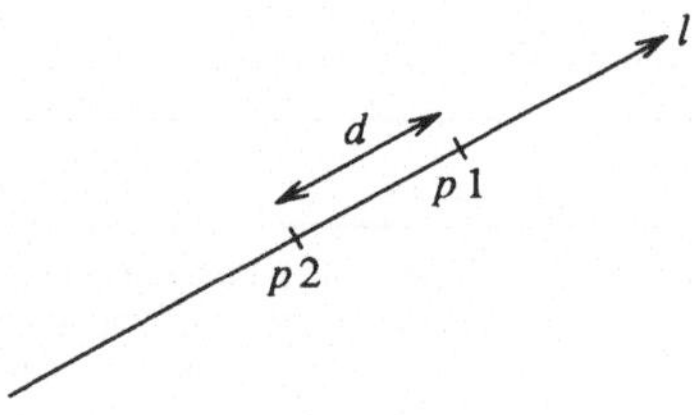

Fig. 5. Operation P1PL

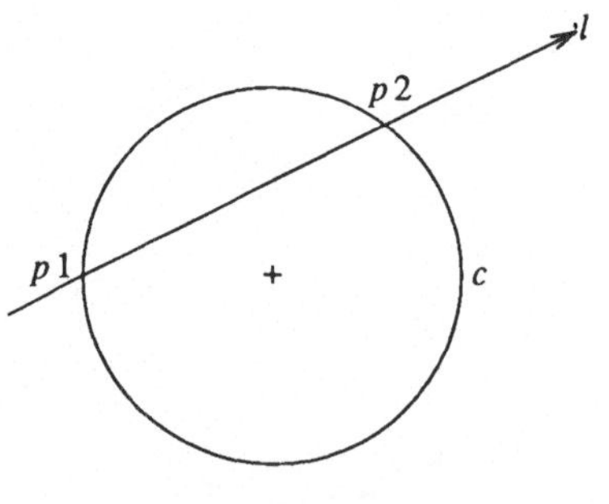

Fig. 6. Operation P2CL

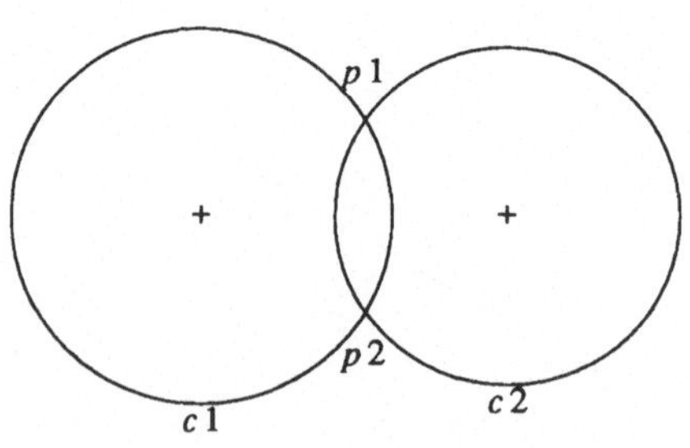

Fig. 7. Operation P2CC

Our drawing input method can be implemented in a variety of styles. First of all, we can develop an independent picture description language. To realize it, we have only to add necessary operations for output primitives.

It is also possible to append our drawing input mechanism to common high-level programming languages, as a software library or as a preprocessor.

In the case of the former, if we provide (1) a graphics library based on a direct coordinate value specification, and (2) optional operations returning the coordinate values of the specified points, then we can display primitives of the graphics library by referring to the points specified by the drawing input method.

Although dynamic manipulation of geometrical data cannot be performed in the latter case, a preprocessor is also useful in some cases, for example, drawing a menu on the screen. Of course, an application-oriented system can also be developed.

2.3. Comparisons with Related Works

In case of Turtle Graphics in Logo[1], a cursor with a direction, called *turtle*, moves from the current position by a specified distance in the current turtle direction. Since we can specify the turtle direction explicitly, it is easy to draw an equilateral triangle of the specified edge length. However, there still exists the difficulty resulting from directly specifying the distance of movement. For example, to draw the oblique side of a right-angled triangle, we have to move the turtle by a distance which is formulated with square roots or trigonometrical functions. Therefore, concerning ease of description, our drawing input method is superior to Turtle Graphics. As for intuitivity (requirement 2), we cannot determine their superiority because of their qualitative difference.

An alternative approach to picture description is the constraint-based specification of essential points[2-4]. The constraints are given by equations and/or other conditions. METAFONT[2] is originally developed for the production of high-quality typefaces using mathematical type design, and is also applied to the production of more general pictures.

IDEAL[3] also adopts a constraint-based approach and is developed for drawing pictures. In IDEAL, picture element procedures named *boxes* are defined as simultaneous equations which represent relationships among essential points, and the procedures are called by a *put* statement with some equations. Such a mechanism enables us to call the same box in different ways. For example, in [3], the box representing a simple rectangle is called in five different ways: (1) giving the height, width, and one of the corners, (2) giving one corner, height, a relation between the height and width, (3) giving two adjacent corners and the width, (4) giving two diagonal corners and a relation between the height and width, and (5) giving three corners.

In Juno[4], the constraint types are: (1) the equality of the distance between points (CONG), (2) the parallelism of two lines between points (PARA), (3) the horizontality of two points (HOR), and (4) the verticality of two points (VER). These descriptions are more intuitive than those used in METAFONT and IDEAL, and thus satisfies requirement 2 to a higher degree.

The above constraint-based descriptions are of course better than the direct coordinate value specification. In spite of their merits, they have two disadvantages.

First, in general, it takes large computation time to obtain a solution which fulfills all the constraints. Especially, when the number of constraints such as simultaneous equations is large, this approach may become impractical. This is why the systems based on this approach are mainly used for typesetting document preparation, where computation time and interactivity is seldom considered. Conversely, they are hardly applicable to such areas as build-in functions of interactive systems and software development.

Secondly, specifying consistent and sufficient conditions (constraints) for a desired picture is a difficult task. In other words, the uniqueness of all positions is not guaranteed. For example, the box for a rectangle in [3] has 7 variables: the four corners, the center, the height, and the width. It is not easy for users to verify the consistency and sufficiency of the equational specification appended to the box by a *put* statement. As another example, the problem of constructing an equilateral triangle on a given line is introduced in [4]. To specify the desired triangle ΔABC, one of whose edges is AB, we have to know the fact that the condition "AB = BC = CA" is insufficient for the uniqueness of the vertex C. Casual users cannot easily decide such things.

Let us compare our drawing input method with the constraint-based specifications.

In our drawing input, the operations are executed individually and sequentially, and execution time of each operation is fairly small. Even if the number of operations is large, the total computation time grows linearly with the number of operations. Therefore, our drawing input method overcomes the first disadvantage of the constraint-based approaches.

The second disadvantage of the constraint-based approach, the difficulty to check if the specification is consistent and sufficient, is also solved in our drawing input approach. In our approach, the uniqueness of defined geometrical objects is guaranteed by elementary plane geometry. In the next chapter, the relationship between our drawing method and elementary geometry is described in detail.

3. A Formal Specification of an Example Drawing Input System

In this chapter, to clarify the mechanism of drawing input, we give a formal specification of an example drawing input system. As described above, depending on applications, the operation sets and implementation styles vary. Therefore, we take the operation set of Table 1 as an example, and describe its formal specification.

This formal specification is given in algebraic specification, and the syntax presented here is based on that in [5]. The definitions of MAP, TRIPLET, and GEOMETRY are used in the construction of the drawing input system, described in the final section of this chapter.

What should be most emphasized in this specification is the treatment of geometrical concepts in drawing input. To specify them, we define the mathematical object, the GEOMETRY, which reflects the elementary geometry formulated in [6].

3.1. MAP

Figure 8 shows the specification of MAP, which represents the correspondence mechanism between a name and the information identified by the name, for example, a point name and the location of the point called under the name.

This definition of MAP, which uses the definition of BOOLEAN[1], is the loose closure of the set of equations, that is indicated by the keyword **Loose** at the top of the specification in Fig. 8. This definition is parameterized by two sorts: *name* and *info*. Both of them should have the equivalence relation operation (==), and *info* requires a constant, *undef*.

Sorts, Constants, and **Ops** (Operations) indicate the syntax of the specification, and they provide:

```
Loose
      MAP   (name with {–==–: name, name →Bool},
             info with {–==–: info, info →Bool; undef: →info})
Uses BOOLEAN
Sorts Map
Constants
      undef              : →Map
Ops   if–then–else–      : Bool, Map, Map →Map
      <–,–>*–            : name, info, Map →Map
      –[–←–]             : Map, name, info →Map
      retrieve           : Map, name →info
Eqns  if true then a else b = a
      if false then a else b = b
      undef [s←t] = if t == undef then undef else <s, t>*undef
      (<s, t>*b)[s'←t'] = if s==s' then if t' == undef then b else <s, t'>*b else <s, t>* (b [s'←t'])
      retrieve(undef, x) = undef
      retrieve(<s, t>*b, x) = if s==x then t else retrieve(b, x)
End
```

Fig. 8. The Specification of MAP

---

[1] The specification of BOOLEAN is not described in this paper. Readers who are interested in this definition are referred to [5].

- *Map*, the sort being defined;
- a constant, *undef*, the undefined value of Map;
- four operations: (1) **if–then–else–** for the conditional selection, (2) '<–,–>*–' for the constructor operation, (3) '–[–←–]' for the editing operation, and (4) **retrieve** for the retrieval operation from name.

The semantics of these operations is defined by the relations in **Eqns** (Equations). Informally, we can regard Map as an ordered list, and by $<s,t>*b$, the pair $<s,t>$ is appended to b. The operation $b[s \leftarrow t]$ replaces the *info* of a given *name* s with t. The current *info* of the specified *name* is returned by **retrieve**.

3.2. TRIPLET

TRIPLET is used for combining three types of data. In our example, they are the *name–info* pairs of points, lines, and circles. The definition of TRIPLET is shown in Fig. 9.

Syntax and semantics of the specification are much easier than those of MAP. The operations, **first**, **second**, and **third**, extract the first, second, and third values, respectively. Conversely, **triplet** constructs a value of *Triplet* from the specified values of its 'components': a, b, and c.

3.3. The Specification with Plane Geometry

The purpose of a formal specification is to provide a precise characterization of a software system at a convenient level of abstraction[7]. Therefore, the formal specification of a system should include all the information which characterizes the system. In case of our drawing input method, the geometrical concepts on a 2D plane form the core of our method and essential to the specification of an example drawing input system.

To specify the system with the geometrical concepts, we first define the geometrical operations which are based on geometry, and next specify the system by using the operations. In our case, the object space is 2D, and the desired geometry is formal 2D geometry.

In addition, we decide to use 2D geometry without the notion of the Cartesian coordinate system. Defining our drawing input system based on such a type of geometry means that our method is based on the elementary plane geometry, which is more intuitive than Cartesian geometry.

Although plane geometry is intuitive, its formal treatment is not easy. There are two approaches to formal plane geometry: the synthetic approach and the metric approach[6]. In this paper, we take the metric approach, which is adopted in [6] for ease of discussion.

Although we define the operations based on formal plane geometry, it is next to impossible to give their full specification in this paper. This is because giving the full specification means the full reconstruction of plane geometry. Therefore, we define geometrical operations following the discussions in [6].

Point, *Line*, and *Circle* represent entries of points, lines, and circles. Formally, plane geometry is discussed from a postulational point of view. First of all, we pay attention to the following postulate[6, p. 37].

I-1. Given any two different points, there is exactly one line containing them.

Based on the above postulate, we can define the operation **makeline**, which uniquely determines a line from an ordered pair of points.

Loose
    TRIPLET (A, B, C)
Sorts *Triplet*
Ops **first** : $Triplet \to A$
    second : $Triplet \to B$
    third : $Triplet \to C$
    triplet : $A, B, C \to Triplet$
Eqns **first(triplet(**a,b,c**))** $= a$
    second(triplet(a,b,c**))** $= b$
    third(triplet(a,b,c**))** $= c$
End

Fig. 9. The Specification of TRIPLET

makeline: *Point*, *Point* →*Line* (1)

If the two points are the same, **makeline** returns the value *undef*.

Next, we introduce a distance function **d** which satisfies the postulates of distance described in [6, p. 47].

d: *Point*, *Point* →*Real* (2)

Let P be a point of a plane E, and let r be a positive number. The *circle with center P and radius r* is defined as the set of all points Q of E whose distance from P is equal to r [6, p. 186]. From the definition of a circle, the operation **makecirc** uniquely determines a circle.

makecirc: *Point*, *Real* →*Circle* (3)

If the radius is less than 0, **makecirc** returns the value *undef*.

From the postulate **I-1**, it is easily proved that two different lines intersect in at most one point. Therefore, the operation **intrp**, which returns the intersection point of two lines, is defined.

intrp: *Line*, *Line* →*Point* (4)

When the two lines are parallel, **intrp** returns *undef*.

In Section 2.2, we suppose that every line is directed. The direction of a line is discussed below. First of all, we define a coordinate system for a line and describe a postulate relating to the coordinate system[6, p. 49].

Definition.

Let $f: L \leftrightarrow \mathbf{R}$ be a one-to-one correspondence between a line L and the real numbers. If for all points P, Q of L, we have $PQ = |f(P) - f(Q)|$, then f is a *coordinate system* for L. For each point P of L, the number $x = f(P)$ is called the *coordinate* of P.

D-4. *The Ruler Postulate.* Every line has a coordinate system.

Next, we introduce the Ruler Placement Theorem[6, p. 50].

The Ruler Placement Theorem.

Let L be a line, and let P and Q be any two points of L. Then L has a coordinate system in which the coordinate of P is 0 and the coordinate of Q is positive.

Based on the above theorem, we define the fixed coordinate system on the line define by **makeline**(P, Q), and define the direction of the line so that the coordinate of the point Q is more than that of P on the line defined by **makeline**(P, Q). *Line*, the information of a line, includes this direction as well as the information of an undirected line. To access the directional information, we define the following two operations:

codtopnt: *Line*, *Real* →*Point* (5)

pnttocod: *Line*, *Point* →*Real* (6)

As for the relationships between a line and a circle, the Line-Circle theorem[6, p. 189] should be noticed.

The Line–Circle Theorem.

If a line intersects the interior of a circle, then it intersects the circle in exactly two points.

The two points, where the circle C and the line L intersect, are distinguished by the direction of L. The operations which return *Point* of intersection are as follows:

lessp: *Circle*, *Line* →*Point* (7)

morep: *Circle*, *Line* →*Point* (8)

If L intersects C in two points,

pnttocod(L, **lessp**(C, L)) < **pnttocod**(L, **morep**(C, L))

If the intersection point of L and C is exactly one, **lessp**(C, L) = **morep**(C, L). If there is no intersection point, both of them return *undef*.

In case of the intersection between two circles, the Two-Circle Theorem[6, p. 198] plays an important role.

The Two–Circle Theorem.

Let C and C' be circles of radius a and b, and let c be the distance between their centers. If each of the numbers a, b, c is less than the sum of the other two, then C and C' intersect in two points. And the two points of intersection lie on opposite sides of the line of centers.

In Section 2.2, we discriminate the two intersection points by the sides of the directed line between the two centers, that is, the left point and the right point. This distinction, however, is informal, and there is no natural way to decide which of the half planes should be mentioned first[6, p. 62]. From the viewpoint of plane geometry, if we define for one line L and one point P not on L that P lies on the left (or right) side of L, then we can consistently determine on which side of a line a point lies.

The operations, **leftp** and **rightp**, are defined based on the discussions concerning *left* and *right* of a directed line.

leftp: *Circle* , *Circle* →*Point* (9)

rightp: *Circle* , *Circle* →*Point* (10)

Lastly, in Fig. 10, we show the syntax of the geometrical operations defined in this section.

3.4. Drawing Input System

Figure 11 shows the specification of the whole drawing input system except for LTTK operation. (Although appending the specification of LTTK operation needs much extra work, but it is of little value in this context.) The operations of an example drawing input system, LINE, CIRC, P1LL, P1PL, P2CL, and P2CC, are defined in the specification as **line**, **circ**, **p1ll**, **p1pl**, **p2cl**, and **p2cc**, respectively.

4. Applications of Drawing Input

4.1. Engineering Drawing

In general, manual drawing consists of two steps: (1) drawing lines including guide lines with a pencil, and (2) inking final lines. Our drawing input method exactly corresponds to the first step. Set squares, a T square, a pair of compasses, and a protractor are replaced with a drawing input system in a computer.

```
        GEOMETRY
Uses BOOLEAN, Real
Sorts Point, Line, Circle
Constants
        undef   : →Point
        undef   : →Line
        undef   : →Circle
Ops     _==_            : Point, Point →Bool
        _==_            : Line, Line →Bool
        _==_            : Circle, Circle →Bool
        makeline        : Point, Point →Line
        d               : Point, Point →Real
        makecirc        : Point, Real →Circle
        intrp           : Line, Line →Point
        codtopnt        : Line, Real →Point
        pnttocod        : Line, Point →Real
        lessp           : Circle, Line →Point
        morep           : Circle, Line →Point
        leftp           : Circle, Circle →Point
        rightp          : Circle, Circle →Point
End
```

Fig. 10. The Syntax of GEOMETRY

```
Loose
    DRAWSYS      (Pointname with {-==-: Pointname, Pointname →Bool },
                  Linename with {-==-: Linename, Linename →Bool },
                  Circlename with {-==-: Circlename, Circlename →Bool })
Uses System = TRIPLET(MAP(Pointname, Point), MAP(Linename, Line), MAP(Circlename, Circle))
     GEOMETRY
Ops  line   : System, Linename, Pointname, Pointname →System
     circ   : System, Circlename, Pointname, Real →System
     p1ll   : System, Pointname, Linename, Linename →System
     p1pl   : System, Pointname, Pointname, Linename, Real →System
     p2cl   : System, Pointname, Pointname, Circlename, Linename →System
     p2cc   : System, Pointname, Pointname, Circlename, Circlename →System
Eqns line(s, ln, pn, pn') = triplet(first(s),
            second(s)[ln ←makeline(retrieve(first(s), pn), retrieve(first(s), pn'))], third(s))
     circ(s, cn, pn, r) = triplet(first(s), second(s), third(s)[cn ←makecirc(retrieve(first(s), pn), r)])
     p1ll(s, pn, ln, ln') = triplet(first(s)[pn ←intrp(retrieve(second(s), ln), retrieve(second(s), ln'))],
            second(s), third(s))
     p1pl(s, pn, pn', ln, d) = triplet(first(s)[pn ←codtopnt(retrieve(second(s), ln),
            pnttocod(retrieve(second(s), ln), retrieve(first(s), pn'))+d)], second(s), third(s))
     p2cl(s, pn, pn', cn, ln) = triplet(if pn == pn' then first(s)
            else first(s)[pn'←morep(retrieve(third(s), cn), retrieve(second(s), ln))]
                   [pn ←lessp(retrieve(third(s), cn), retrieve(second(s), ln))],
            second(s), third(s))
     p2cc(s, pn, pn', cn, cn') = triplet(if pn == pn' then first(s)
            else first(s)[pn'←rightp(retrieve(third(s), cn), retrieve(third(s), cn'))]
                   [pn ←leftp(retrieve(third(s), cn), retrieve(third(s), cn'))],
            second(s), third(s))
End
```

Fig. 11. The Specification of Drawing Input System

In engineering drawing, drawing input method can be used as a means to define parametric shapes. For example, to draw a regular hexagon of an arbitrary diameter, which often appears as a head of bolt or a nut, we need to determine the positions of its six corners. In our drawing input method, they can be defined as the intersection points between a circle and three lines passing through the center of the circle with an angle of 60 degree, while in direct coordinate value specification, their positions are specified by formulae including square roots.

Examples of basic operations for engineering drawing extracted from [8] are listed below:

- construction of parallel and perpendicular lines
- dividing a line into equal parts
- proportional division of a line
- bisectors for lines and angles
- solving for the center of a known circle
- construction of a circle from three given points
- construction of a line tangent to a circle through a point

4.2. Apparel Pattern-Making

To make apparel patterns, there exists two types of techniques: draping and flat pattern-making[9]. In draping, muslin is draped on a model form and patterns are developed in three-dimensional space. On the other hand, in flat pattern-making, patterns are developed by transforming the basic patterns called *basic slopers*.

Since basic slopers represent the size of human bodies, they should be prepared depending on the body size. To make the basic slopers for a given body size, apparel educational institutions offer the rules for making basic slopers[10-15]. Although these rules vary depending on the institutions, they are all described as a 2D drawing process, and our drawing input method can be adapted to formulate the rules.

Such a *rule-based basic sloper development* by drawing input is a part of our computer-aided apparel pattern-making system VIRGO[16]. Table 2 shows the drawing input command set for the development of basic slopers. Note that, compared to [16], the number of operations increased. With these operations, we have formulated several rules for developing basic slopers including Bunka-type[10], Doreme-type[11], Ito-type[12], Percent-type[13], Sugaya-type[14], and Tanaka-type[15]. Figure 12 is an example of basic slopers on the graphic display screen, a back waist of Doreme-type basic slopers. Guide lines and reference points are drawn in red, and white lines represent the final shape of the basic sloper. In Fig. 13, to show the parametric development of basic slopers, three basic slopers for small, medium, and large sizes are developed from the rule of Bunka-type back waist.

4.3. Tibetan Mandala Image Generation

A mandala is a graphic symbol of the universe in Buddhism. It is usually drawn on a sheet of paper or cloth. In Thibet, however, it is also drawn with sand on a clay mound. In case of a *sand* mandala, before laying dyed sand, essential lines and points are determined, and based on them, sand is placed so as to represent a mandala. The determination of essential lines and points, described above, is a kind of 2D drawing process with some instruments: thread, a simple paper ruler, etc. Therefore, with our drawing input method, we reproduce a sand mandala on a graphic display as a part of our activity for preservation of traditional arts.

Table 3 shows an operation set for the sand mandala image generation. Note that it is very simple, and faithfully follow the traditional drawing with a ruler and a pair of compasses.

Figure 14 is the result of determining the essential points and lines. Figure 15 is the final image of a Tibetan mandala. To determine the points and lines, the description of about 2,500 lines is necessary. 200 out of about 250 patterns placed are different. Of course, with integrated commands, this number of lines can be decreased, but in this case, it is important to follow the classical method for the purpose of traditional art preservation.

Table 2. The Operation Set for Basic Sloper Development

Operation	Meaning
DEFC *c v*	define constant *c* as value *v*
CDEFP *p x, y*	define point *p* at coordinate (x, y)
XDEFP *p*1 *p*2 *d*	define point *p*1 at a distance of *d* from point *p*2 parallel to the x axis.
YDEFP *p*1 *p*2 *d*	define point *p*1 at a distance of *d* from point *p*2 parallel to the y axis.
DIV2P *p*1 *p*2 *p*3	define point *p*1 as a middle point of the line segment between points *p*2 and *p*3
DIV3P *p*1 *p*2 *p*3 *p*4	define points *p*1 and *p*2 as trisection points of the line segment between points *p*3 and *p*4
GDEFP *p*1 *p*2 *l d*	define point *p*1 at a distance of *d* from point *p*2 along line *l*
GLPA *l p a*	draw line *l* which has angle *a* and passes point *p*
GLPP *l p*1 *p*2	draw line *l* which passes points *p*1 and *p*2
LTTK *p*1 *p*2	put the length from point *p*1 to *p*2 into the queue
ATKPP *p*1 *p*2	put the angle from point *p*1 to *p*2 into the queue
SSDEFP *p l*1 *l*2	define point *p* where lines *l*1 and *l*2 intersect
XSDEFP *p*1 *p*2 *l*	define point *p*1 as the point which has the same x coordinate value as point *p*2 and intersect line *l*
YSDEFP *p*1 *p*2 *l*	define point *p*1 as the point which has the same y coordinate value as point *p*2 and intersect line *l*
XYDEFP *p*1 *p*2 *p*3	define point *p*1 as the point which has the same x coordinate value as point *p*2 and has the same y coordinate value as point *p*3
SMDEFP *p*1 *p*2 *l d*	define point *p*1 as the point which lies on line *l* and whose distance from point *p*2 is *d*
XMDEFP *p*1 *p*2 *p*3 *d*	define point *p*1 as the point whose distance from point *p*2 is *d* and whose x coordinate value is the same as that of point *p*3
YMDEFP *p*1 *p*2 *p*3 *d*	define point *p*1 as the point whose distance from point *p*2 is *d* and whose y coordinate value is the same as that of point *p*3

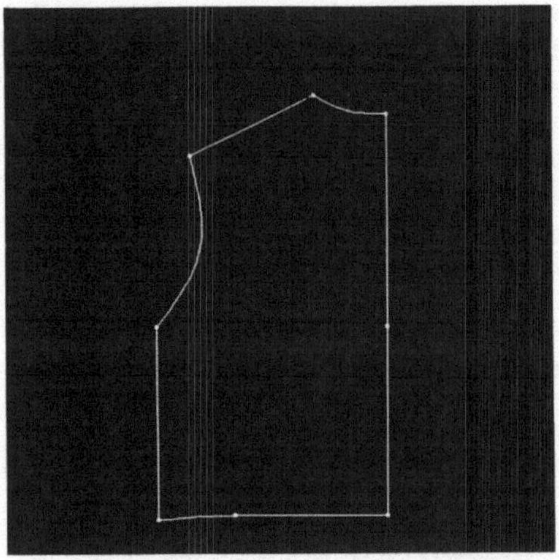

Fig. 12. Doreme-Type Basic Sloper (Back Waist)

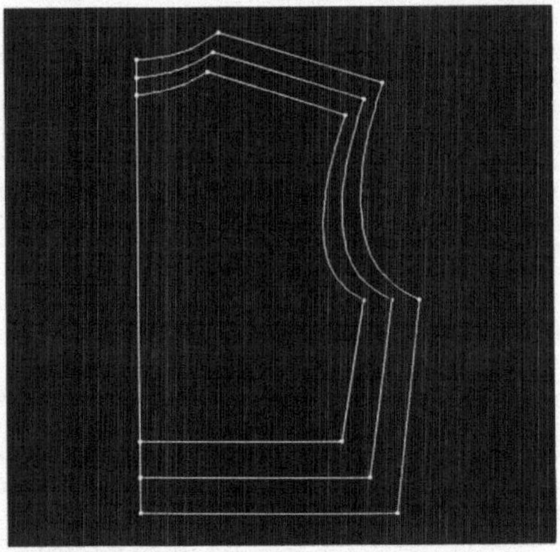

Fig. 13. Bunka-Type Basic Slopers (Back Waist) for Different Sizes

Table 3. The Operation Set for the Determination of Essential Points and Lines of a Mandala

Operation	Meaning
LINE l $p1$ $p2$	draw line l which intersects points $p1$ and $p2$
CIRC c p r	draw circle c whose center is p and radius is r
P1LL p $l1$ $l2$	define point p where lines $l1$ and $l2$ intersect
P1PL $p1$ $p2$ l d	define points $p1$ at a distance of d from point $p2$ along line l
P2CL $p1$ $p2$ c l	define points $p1$ and $p2$ where circle c and line l intersect
P2CC $p1$ $p2$ $c1$ $c2$	define points $p1$ and $p2$ where circles $c1$ and $c2$ intersect
PDIV $p1$ $p2$ n $p3$ ... pn+1	divide line segment from $p1$ to $p2$ into equal n parts and define the n-1 boundary points $p3$ through $pn+1$

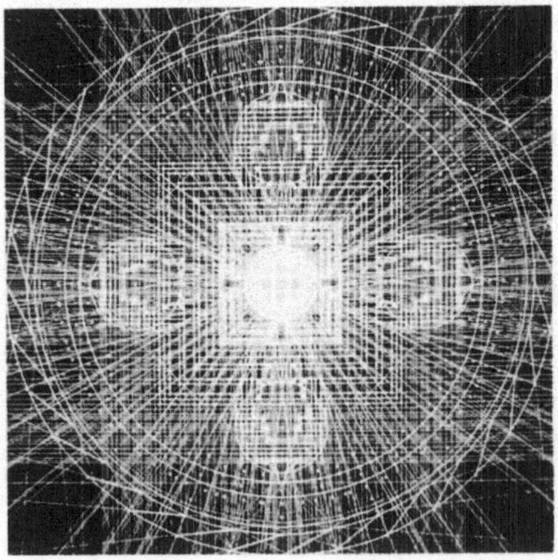

Fig. 14. The Result of Determination of Essential Points and Lines

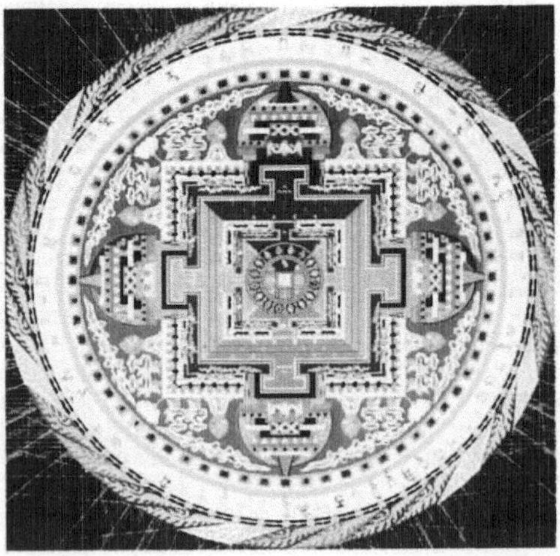

Fig. 15. The Final Image of Tibetan Mandala

5. Conclusions

Drawing input through geometrical constructions is a novel approach to picture description and has the advantages of easiness, intuitiveness, and universality. The usability of this method is shown by the three examples. We believe that drawing input is a basis of future picture description, and various tools are being developed and tested for varieties of applications.

Acknowledgements

We are grateful to Mr. Ranjit Makkuni of Xerox Palo Alto Research Center for inviting us to the world of mandala as a research topic. We are also grateful to Mr. Kojun Terai for his technical support in the development of our software. Our further gratitude goes to Mr. Issei Fujishiro, Mr. Yasuto Shirai, and Mr. Martin J. Dürst for their thoughtful comments. This work has been partially supported by Software Research Center (SRC) of Ricoh Co., Ltd.

References

1. Harold Abelson, "A Beginner's Guide to Logo," *BYTE* 7(8) pp. 88-112 (August 1982).
2. Donald E. Knuth, *The METAFONTbook*, Addison-Wesley (1986).
3. Christopher J. Van Wyk, "A High-Level Language for Specifying Pictures," *ACM Trans. on Graphics* **1**(2) pp. 163-182 (April 1982).
4. Greg Nelson, "Juno, A Constraint-Based Graphics System," *Computer Graphics* **19**(3) pp. 235-243 (July 1985).
5. B. Cohen, W. T. Harwood, and M. I. Jackson, *The Specification of Complex Systems*, Addison-Wesley (1986).
6. Edwin E. Moise, *Elementary Geometry from an Advanced Standpoint (2nd ed.)*, Addison-Wesley (1974).
7. William R. Mallgren, *Formal Specification of Interactive Graphics Programming Languages*, MIT Press (1983).
8. Louis Gary Lamit, *Descriptive Geometry*, Prentice-Hall (1983).
9. Ernestine Kopp, Vittorina Rolfo, Beatrice Zelin, and Lee Gross, *Designing Apparel through the Flat Pattern (Revised 5th Edition)*, Fairchild Publications (1981).
10. Bunka Woman's University and Bunka Fashion College (eds.), *Bunka Apparel Seminar (Bunka Fukusou Kouza)*, Bunka Publishing Bureau.
11. Yoshiko Sugino, *Introduction to Doreme Dressmaking (Doremeshiki Yousai Nyuumon)*, Kamakura Shobou (1980).
12. Hideyoshi Ito (ed.), *Mode et Mode*, Mode et Mode Co., Ltd. (1987).
13. Kimie Yoshimura, *Percent-Type Dressmaking (Wariaijakushiki Yasashii Yousai)*, Nihon Housou Shuppan Kyoukai (1978).
14. Kiyo Sugaya and Fumiko Sugaya, *Sugaya Cutting (Sugayashiki Saidan Kisohen)*, Sugaya Fukusou Gakuin Shuppan-Bu (1967).
15. Chiyo Tanaka, *Dress (Fukusou)*, Tokyo Tanaka Chiyo Fukushoku Senmon Gakkou (1987).
16. Tsukasa Noma, Kojun Terai, and Tosiyasu L. Kunii, "VIRGO: A Computer-Aided Apparel Pattern-Making System," pp. 379-401 in *Advanced Computer Graphics, Proc. Computer Graphics Tokyo '86*, ed. Tosiyasu L. Kunii,Springer-Verlag (1986).

On the Construction of Constrained Circles, an Unified Approach

P. J. Zsombor-Murray and K. Linder (Canada)

Abstract

A method to find a circle, $c(x,y,r)$, discriminates among up to eight possible solutions. Given a sufficient set of radius, centre line(s) and/or tangent line(s) the solution is the point of intersection among three planes. Including tangent circle(s) it is a piercing point of the line of two planes with a cone.

Introduction

This general problem[1] is solved with ancient geometric procedures. Implemented piecemeal[2] on CAD systems, often not all are provided, the problem being regarded as one of "myriad ... instances and exceptional cases". A systematic treatment is due. The method uses three classical descriptive geometry problems[3]. *I.e.*, to find the intersection between plane-plane, line-plane and line-cone pairs. What follows treats constraint classification, the method and choosing among solutions.

TABLE I

Classification

Four types of constraints will include

1. A given radius, R,
2. One or two given centre lines, L,
3. One, two or three given tangent lines, T, and
4. One, two or three given tangent circles, C.

Constraint	Number of Each Constraint Type Given														
R	1	1	0	0	0	1	1	0	0	0	1	0	0	1	0
L	0	0	0	0	0	1	0	1	1	0	1	2	1	2	2
T	1	0	2	1	0	0	2	1	0	3	1	0	2	0	1
C	1	2	1	2	3	1	0	1	2	0	0	1	0	0	0
Solutions	8	8	8	8	8	4	4	4	4	4	2	2	2	1	1

Point constraints are not tabulated above because they are implied by either the intersection between two centre lines or by a tangent circle of zero radius. Figure 1 shows classification by constraint intersection topology. Regions common to any of the circles are dealt with. There are seven regions and Fig. 1 shows fourteen ways these can be combined. This is a state diagram where transitions occur between regions adjacent in a binary Gray coded sequence. This shows some intricacies of three-circle patterns. It does not contribute much to a general solution of the problem posed by Table I, though.

Method

The problem is to find a circle, $c(x,y,r)$. The solution of simultaneous linear equations, the quadratic formula and analytic and descriptive geometry of conic sections will be used. It is a two-dimensional problem in three orthogonal variables and linear, L and T constraints can be written

$$Ax + By = C \quad \text{1.)}$$

or as

$$Ex + Fy + Gr = H \quad \text{2.)}$$

which is a plane with intercepts

$$x = H/E,\ y = H/F,\ r = H/G \quad \text{3.)}$$

Sometimes three equations of the form, 2.) exist to yield (x,y,r). A specified radius, R, is the trivial, canonical form

$$r = R \quad \text{4.)}$$

Where the linear coefficients are

$$E = 0,\ F = 0,\ G = 1,\ H = R \quad \text{5.)}$$

This is shown in Fig. 2, as the set of points $r = 4$. A centre line can describe a circle of any radius and yields an equation of form 2.) such that

$$G = 0 \quad \text{6.)}$$

Figure 3 represents such a vertical plane. Now a circle specified $c(R,L_1,L_2)$ may be described. *E.g.*, the usual definition of $c(x,y,r)$ is the canonical set

$$r = R,\ x = X,\ y = Y \quad \text{7.)}$$

illustrated by Fig. 4.

The two previous constraint definition planes contain the desired circle's centre. Generally, a tangent *line* does not. The plane of a tangent line is completed by *any* point in the proposed plane, *not* on this line. Choosing a circle tangent to $Ex + Fy = H$ centred at (0,0) as shown in Fig. 5 gives

$$R/a = (H/F)/(H/E) = E/F \quad \text{8.)}$$

and

$$R^2 + a^2 = (H/E)^2 \quad \text{9.)}$$

and

$$|R| = |H/(E^2 + F^2)^{1/2}| \quad \text{10.)}$$

a tangent line in form 2.) where

$$G = +or-(E^2 + F^2)^{1/2} \quad \text{11.)}$$

The sign of G determined as shown in Fig. 6 where

$$sgn[G] = sgn[(\mathbf{p}_1 - \mathbf{p}_0)x(\mathbf{w} - \mathbf{p}_0)\cdot\mathbf{k}] \quad \text{12.)}$$

given that **k** is the unit vector in the r-direction.

A parity convention between $\mathbf{w}(W_1,W_2)$, and $Ex + Fy = H$ is given, in Fig. 6, by implicitly ordered end point position vectors $\{\mathbf{p}_0(X_0,Y_0),\mathbf{p}_1(X_1,Y_1)\}$ which are assumed to produce

$$E = Y_1-Y_0,\ F = X_0-X_1,\ H = X_1Y_0-X_0Y_1 \quad \text{13.)}$$

not

$$E = Y_0-Y_1,\ F = X_1-X_0,\ H = X_0Y_1-X_1Y_0 \quad \text{13.')}$$

The signs of E, F and H are taken as given by 13.)

$$IF(\mathrm{E} > 0)\mathrm{or}((\mathrm{E} = 0)\mathrm{and}(\mathrm{F} > 0)) = \mathrm{TRUE} \quad \text{14.)}$$

If 14.) is FALSE these signs are given by 13'.) and

$$\mathrm{sgn}[\mathrm{G}] = \mathrm{sgn}[f] = \mathrm{sgn}[\mathrm{D}(\mathrm{H} - \mathrm{W}_1\mathrm{E} - \mathrm{W}_2\mathrm{F})] \quad \text{15.)}$$

where D = E unless E = 0 in which case D = F. The geometry of 15.) is described in Fig. 7.

Tangent circles cannot become planes. The equation of a circle centred at (U,V) with a radius R is the quadratic

$$(x - \mathrm{U})^2 + (y - \mathrm{V})^2 = \mathrm{R}^2 \quad \text{16.)}$$

16.) is linear in squares[4]. Let it be augmented to

$$(x - \mathrm{U})^2 + (y - \mathrm{V})^2 = (r - \mathrm{R})^2 \quad \text{17.)}$$

which is a right rectangular conical surface, apex at (U,V,-R), the set of circles tangent to the one at (U,V,R). Notice that C is related to c in one of three ways, 1) The two can be external or "kissing", 2) A "pregnant" C can enclose or contain c or 3) Conversely, c can be pregnant. Its radius cannot be negative. Case 1) is a conical surface, above the plane $r = 0$, with its apex at $r = -\mathrm{R}$. Case 2) is a conical surface between the plane $r = 0$ and the apex at $r = +\mathrm{R}$, *i.e.*, the radius of c must be in the range $r = [0,|\mathrm{R}|)$. Case 3) is the region $r > \mathrm{R}$ of the same conical surface. Figures 8a and 8b illustrate case 1) while Fig. 9 shows cases 2) and 3). These last two are topological equivalent. The procedure below cannot discriminate between *contained* and *containing* states. However, differentiation between *gravid* and merely *amorous* state is indicated by specifying negative radii for the latter.

Figure 10 shows a cone pair, apex at $(\mathrm{U}_1,\mathrm{V}_1,\mathrm{R}_1)$ and $(\mathrm{U}_2,\mathrm{V}_2,\mathrm{R}_2)$, replaced by their plane of intersection in form 2.)

$$\mathrm{E} = (\mathrm{U}_2-\mathrm{U}_1),\ \mathrm{F} = (\mathrm{V}_2-\mathrm{V}_1),\ \mathrm{G} = (\mathrm{R}_1-\mathrm{R}_2)$$

$$\mathrm{H} = {}^1/_2\{(\mathrm{R}_1{}^2-\mathrm{R}_2{}^2)+(\mathrm{U}_2{}^2-\mathrm{U}_1{}^2)+(\mathrm{V}_2{}^2-\mathrm{V}_1{}^2)\} \quad \text{18.)}$$

Problems with at least one tangent circle, require two linear and one quadratic equations. The example in Fig. 10 shows how 18.) and 14.) are used in this regard. Figure 11 shows a typical reduced problem. If there are two valid roots, (u_1,v_1,r_1) and (u_2,v_2,r_2), then

$$(u,v) = \min[(u_1-\mathrm{W}_1)^2+(v_1-\mathrm{W}_2)^2,(u_2-\mathrm{W}_1)^2+(v_2-\mathrm{W}_2)^2] \quad \text{19.)}$$

Solution of the general case proceeds as

$$\mathrm{E}_1x + \mathrm{F}_1y + \mathrm{G}_1r = \mathrm{H}_1$$

$$\mathrm{E}_2x + \mathrm{F}_2y + \mathrm{G}_2r = \mathrm{H}_2$$

$$(x - \mathrm{U})^2 + (y - \mathrm{V})^2 = (r - \mathrm{R})^2 \quad \text{20.)}$$

yielding

$$r = +\mathrm{or}-(\mathrm{A})^{1/2} - \mathrm{K}_6/2\mathrm{K}_5,\ x^+ = \mathrm{K}_1r^+ + \mathrm{K}_2,\ x^- = \mathrm{K}_1r^- + \mathrm{K}_2$$

$$y^+ = \mathrm{K}_3r^+ + \mathrm{K}_4,\ y^- = \mathrm{K}_3r^- + \mathrm{K}_4$$

where

$$\mathrm{A} = \mathrm{K}_6{}^2-4\mathrm{K}_5\mathrm{K}_7,\ \mathrm{K} = \mathrm{E}_1\mathrm{F}_2-\mathrm{E}_2\mathrm{F}_1,\ \mathrm{K}_1 = (\mathrm{G}_1\mathrm{F}_2-\mathrm{G}_2\mathrm{F}_1)/\mathrm{K}$$

$$\mathrm{K}_2 = (\mathrm{H}_1\mathrm{F}_2-\mathrm{H}_2\mathrm{F}_1)/\mathrm{K},\ \mathrm{K}_3 = (\mathrm{E}_1\mathrm{G}_2-\mathrm{E}_2\mathrm{G}_1)/\mathrm{K}$$

$$K_4 = (E_1H_2-E_2H_1)/K,\ K_5 = K_1{}^2+K_3{}^2-1$$

$$K_6 = 2\{K_1(K_2-U)+K_3(K_4-V)-R\}$$

$$K_7 = K_2{}^2+K_4{}^2+U^2+V^2-R^2-2(K_2U+K_4V) \quad \text{......... 21.)}$$

Solutions where $r < 0$ or $A < 0$ are rejected. Equation 19.) selects between two valid solutions. $K = 0$, a condition easy to visualize graphically, arises, given a parallel L T pair separated by r, a parallel T-T pair separated by $2r$ or a concentric C-C pair separated by $2r$. r is found immediately, from 20.).

$$r = (E_1H_2 - E_2H_1)/(E_1G_2 - E_2G_1)$$

$$x = (H_1-F_1y-G_1r)/E_1 \text{ or } y = (H_1-E_1x-G_1r)/F_1$$

or otherwise

$$x = (H_2-F_2y-G_2r)/E_2 \text{ or } y = (H_2-E_2x-G_2r)/F_2 \quad \text{......... 22.)}$$

The computation shown below is optimally conditioned

$IF(|E_1|<|E_2| and |F_1|<|E_2|) or (|E_1|<|F_2| and |F_1|<|F_2|) THEN\ i = 2\ ELSE\ i = 1$

$IF(|E_1|<|F_1| and |E_2|<|F_1|) or (|E_1|<|F_2| and |E_2|<|F_2|) THEN\ switch = TRUE$

IF switch = TRUE THEN

$$e = F_i,\ f = E_i,\ e_2 = F_{3-i},\ u = V,\ v = U$$

ELSE

$$e = E_i,\ f = F_i,\ e_2 = E_{3-i},\ u = U,\ v = V$$

$$g_1 = G_i,\ g_2 = G_{3-i},\ h_1 = H_i,\ h_2 = H_{3-i},\ G = g_1e_2-g_2e$$

$$r = (eh_2-e_2h_1)/G,\ K_1 = (f/e)^2+1,\ Q = e(Rg_1+h_1)$$

$$K_2 = 2\{f(u-Q)/e-v\},\ K_3 = u^2+v^2+Q^2-2uQ-(r+R)^2$$

$$A = K_2{}^2-4K_1K_3,\ P = +or-(A)^{1/2},\ t^+ = 2(P^+-K_2)/K_1$$

$$s+ = Q-t^+f/e,\ t^- = 2(P^--K_2)/K_1,\ s^- = Q-t^-f/e$$

IF switch = TRUE THEN

$$x^+ = t^+,\ x^- = t^-,\ y^+ = s^+,\ y^- = s^-$$

ELSE

$$x^+ = s^+,\ x^- = s^-,\ y^+ = t^+,\ y^- = t^- \quad \text{......... 23.)}$$

Figure 12 shows a three branch algorithm which implements all solution procedures. The right branch treats Table I where $C = 0$. The left one computes instances, $C > 0$, with no parallel L-T or T-T or concentric C-C combination. The middle branch handles cases where there are.

Figures 13.a to 13.o are tests of this algorithm applied to every case in Table I. Multiple solutions were generated selectively by designating $sgn(R)$ and w.

-13.e.i is State (9) in Fig. 1. The second smallest and the largest dark, solution circles are differentiated with w.

-13.e.ii is State (10). The constraints intersect in double convex lens-shaped regions. The three pairs of three-leaf-clover, internal solution circles are differentiated with w.

-13.e.iii is State (14). All solutions depend on $sgn(R)$ alone.

-13.e.iv is State (5), with a concentric C-C pair, $sgn(R)$ and w are required.

All graphics hardcopy was produced with PRODESIGN II[5].

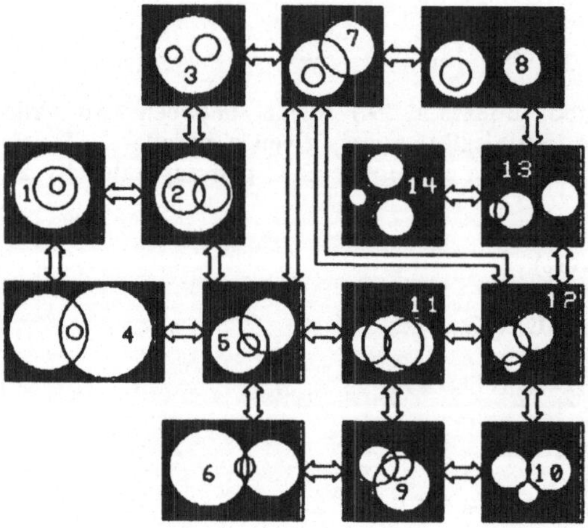

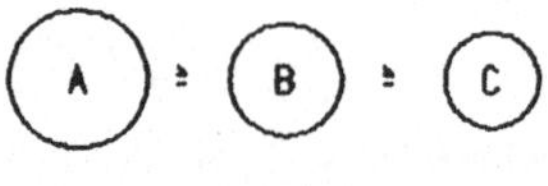

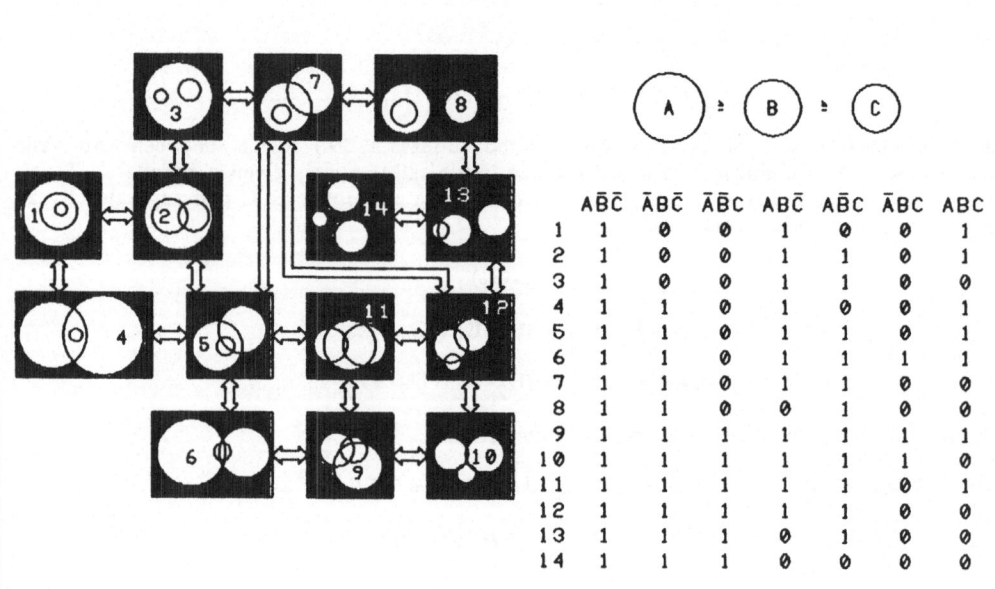

	$A\bar{B}\bar{C}$	$\bar{A}B\bar{C}$	$\bar{A}\bar{B}C$	$AB\bar{C}$	$A\bar{B}C$	$\bar{A}BC$	ABC
1	1	0	0	1	0	0	1
2	1	0	0	1	1	0	1
3	1	0	0	1	1	0	0
4	1	1	0	1	0	0	1
5	1	1	0	1	1	0	1
6	1	1	0	1	1	1	1
7	1	1	0	1	1	0	0
8	1	1	0	0	1	0	0
9	1	1	1	1	1	1	1
10	1	1	1	1	1	1	0
11	1	1	1	1	1	0	1
12	1	1	1	1	1	0	0
13	1	1	1	0	1	0	0
14	1	1	1	0	0	0	0

Figure 1

A specified radius R becomes a plane Ex+Fy+Gr=H where E=0, F=0, G=1 and H=R; a horizontal plane with r-intercept=R.

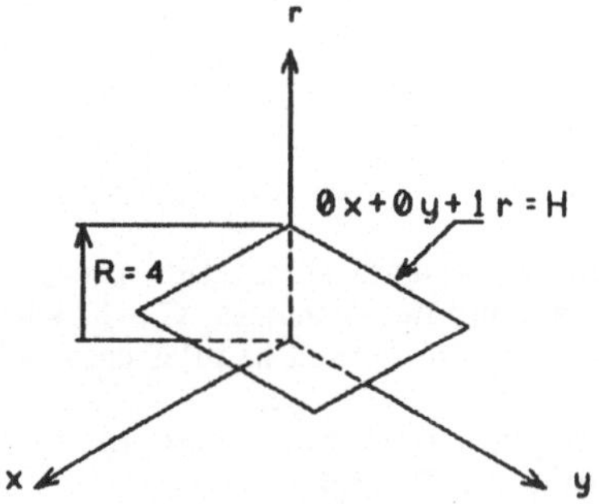

Figure 2

A centre line becomes a plane Ex+Fy+Gr=H where G=0; a vertical plane with x-intercept=H/E and y-intercept=H/F.

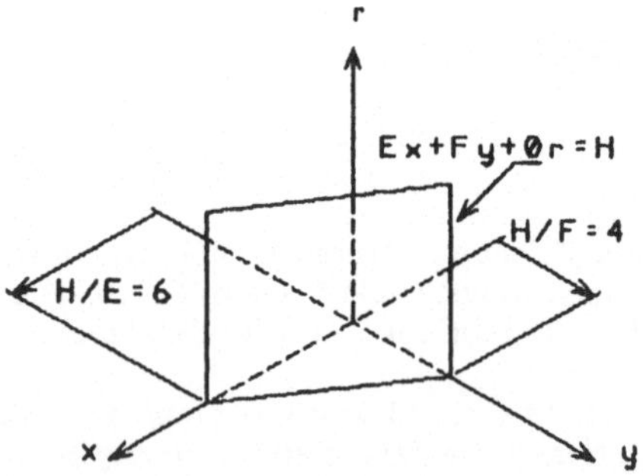

Figure 3

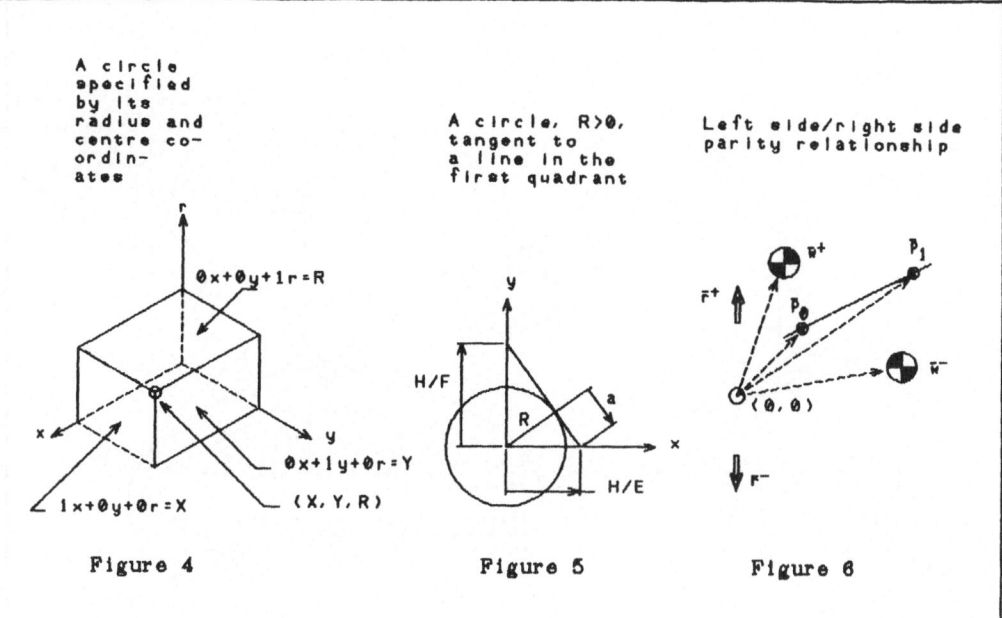

A circle specified by its radius and centre co-ordinates

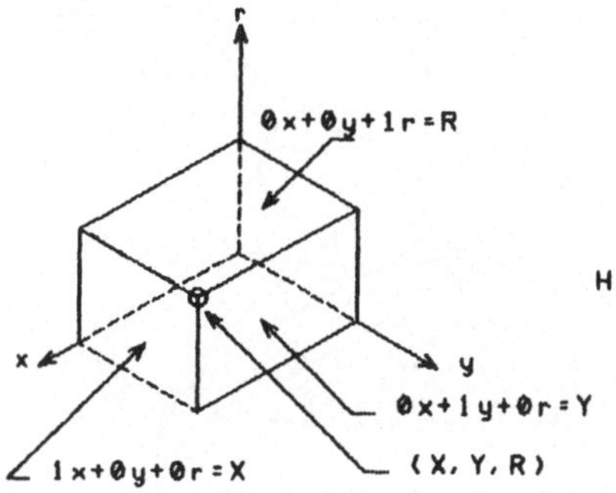

Figure 4

A circle, R>0, tangent to a line in the first quadrant

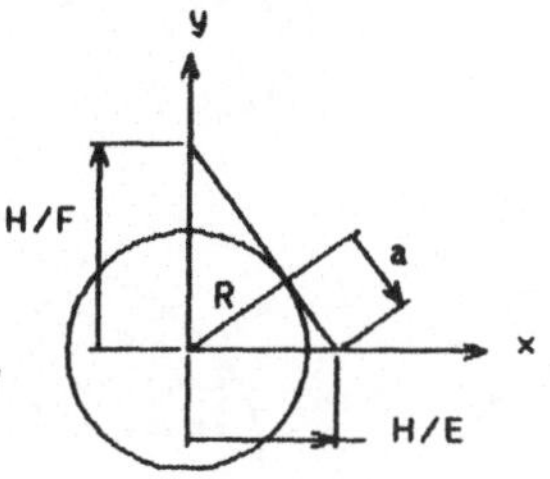

Figure 5

Left side/right side parity relationship

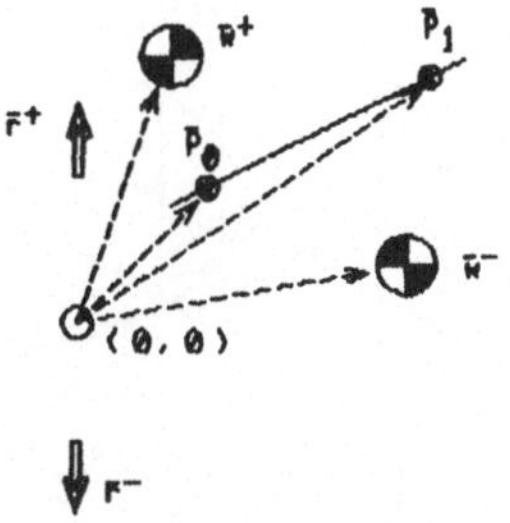

Figure 6

A tangent line Ex+Fy=H becomes the plane:- Ex+Fy±Gr=H where $G=\pm\sqrt{E^2+F^2}$

The sign is supplied by the sign of the function $f(W_1, W_2)=D(h-W_1E-W_2F)$ D=E if E≠0. If E=0 then D=F.

(W_1, W_2) are coordinates of a point on the desired circle side of the given tangent line.

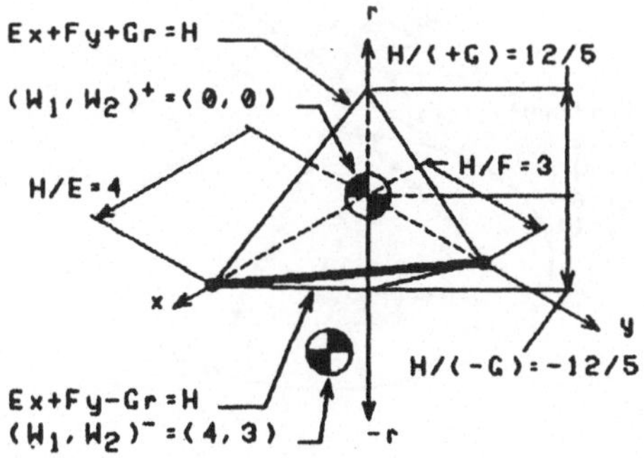

Figure 7

The locus of the set of external, "kissing" circles tangent to a circle centered at (U,V) with radius R becomes the rectangular cone:-

$(x-U)^2+(y-V)^2=(r-R)^2$

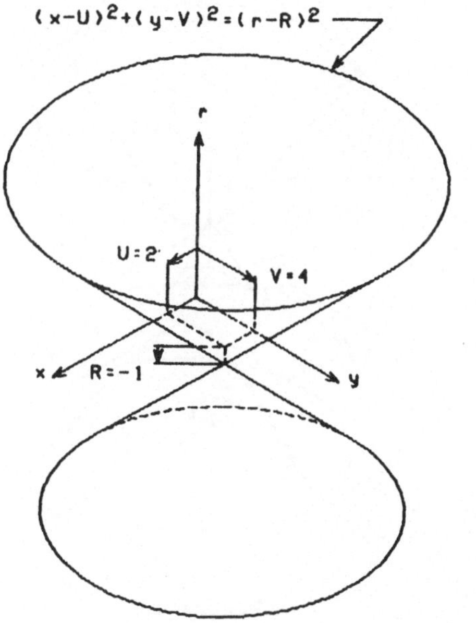

Figure 8a

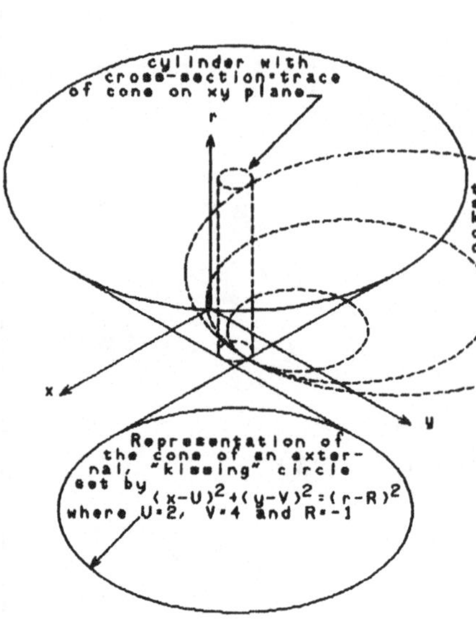

Figure 8b

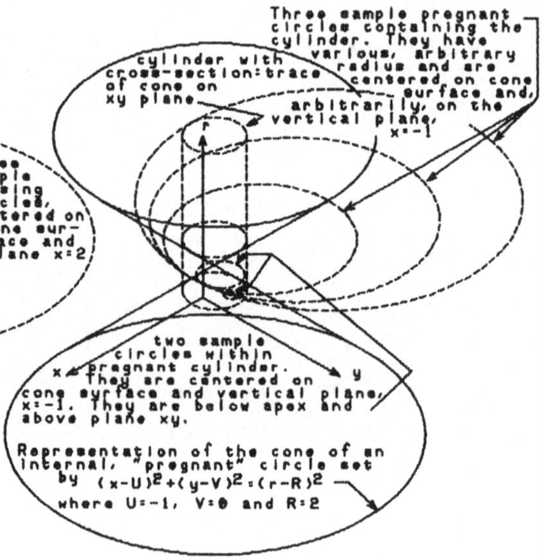

Figure 9

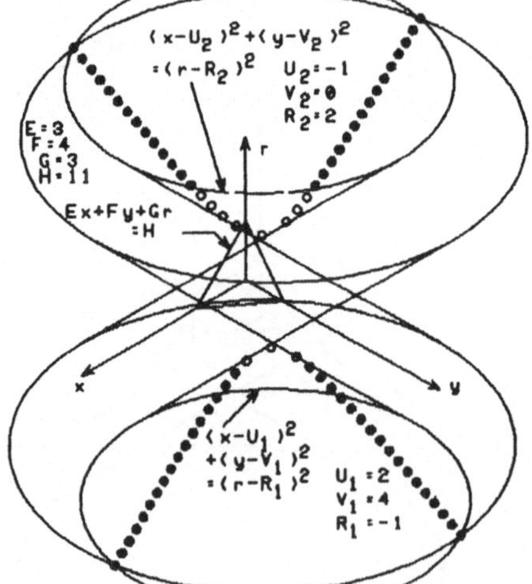

Figure 10

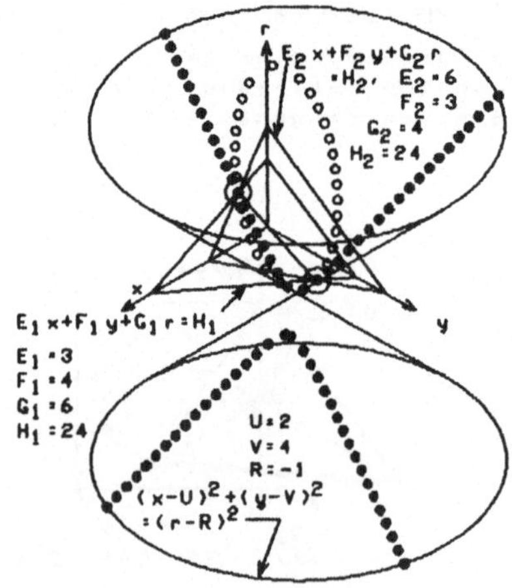

Figure 11

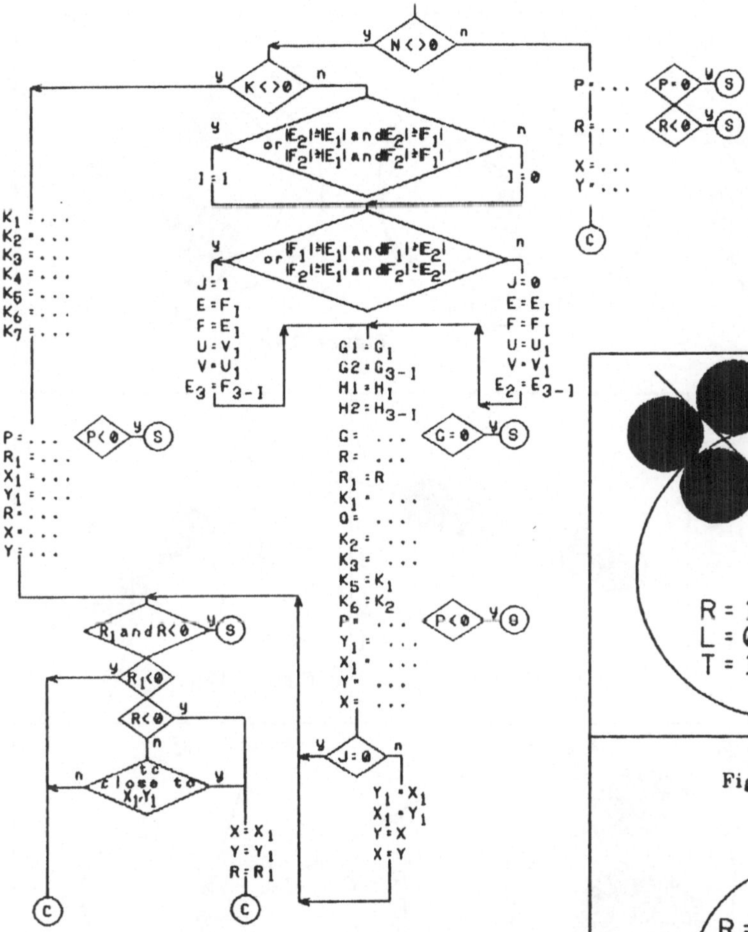

Figure 12

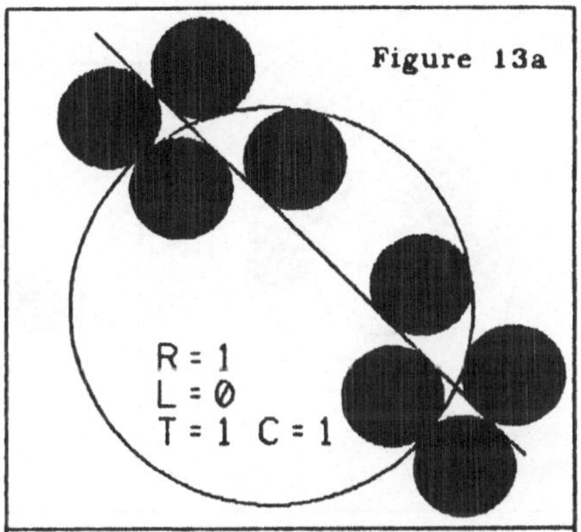

Figure 13a

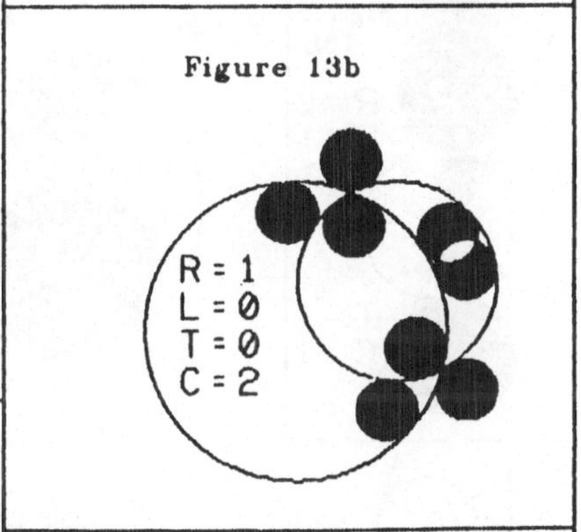

Figure 13b

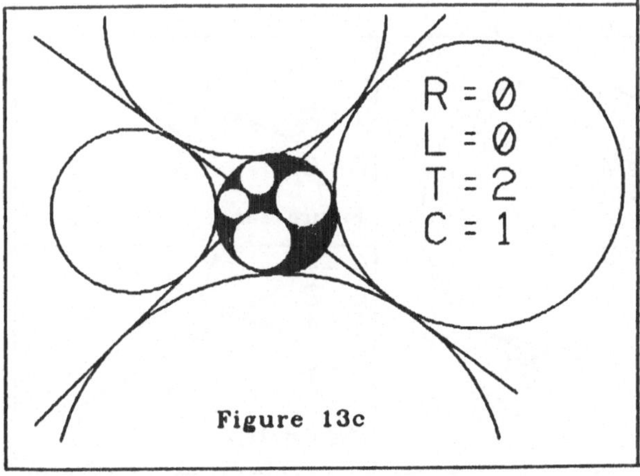

Figure 13c

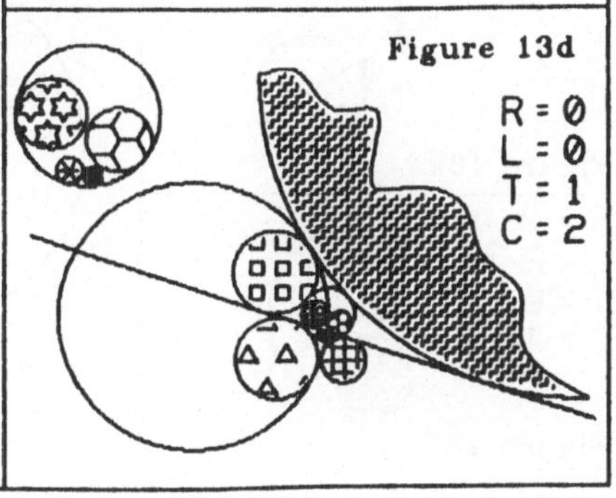

Figure 13d

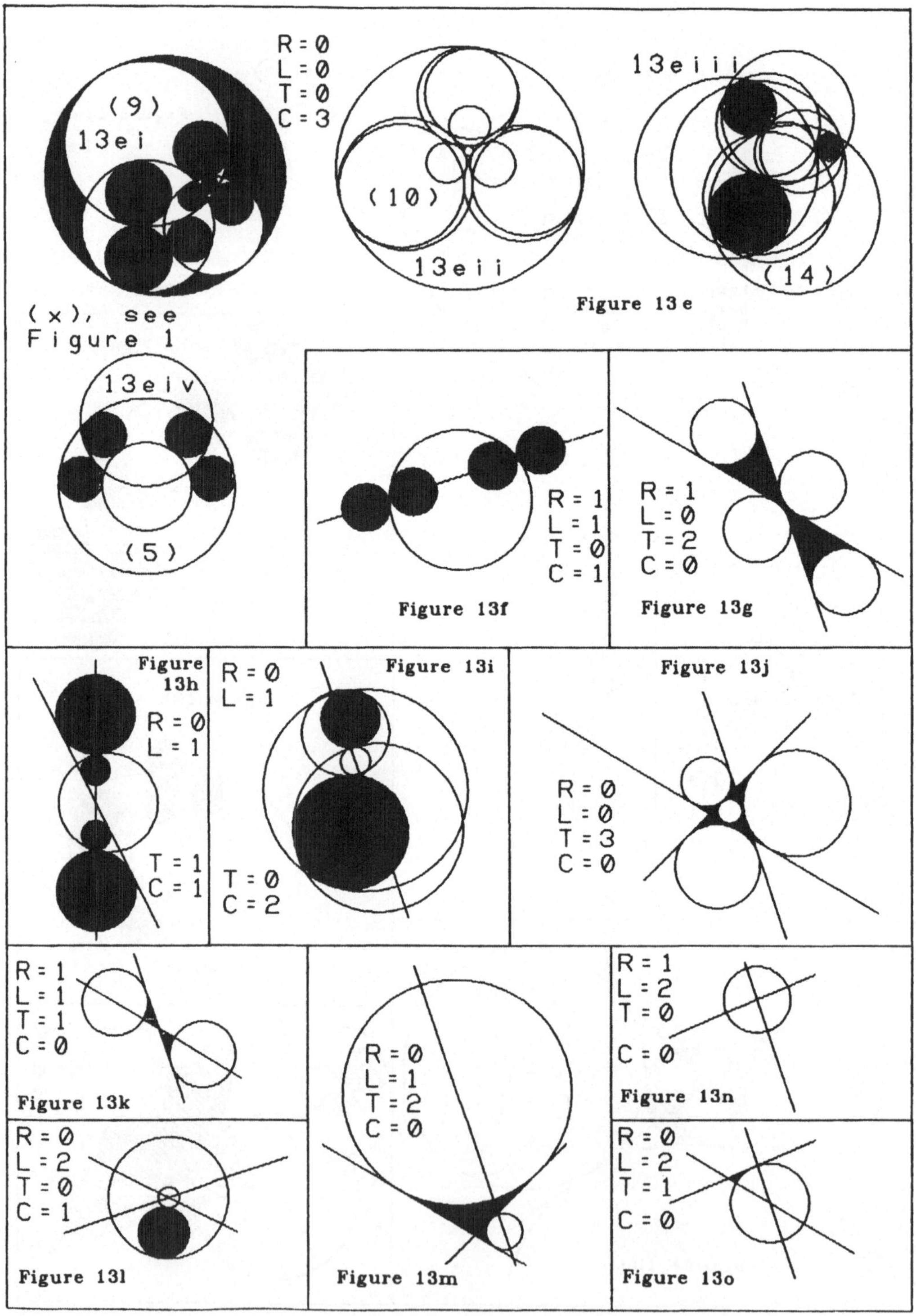

Figure 13e

Figure 13f

Figure 13g

Figure 13h

Figure 13i

Figure 13j

Figure 13k

Figure 13l

Figure 13m

Figure 13n

Figure 13o

Conclusion

This procedure is adaptable to commercial CAD systems. Aside from universality, it can be coded very compactly. This method would find use in applications such as the layout of extensive, internal/external compound spur gear trains or the design of intricate pocket-milled parts in a 2.5-D, NC environment. Consider some extensions of this work.

1. Circular arcs constrained by plane polynomial curves and splines,
2. Integration with various forms of spiral blending,
3. Extension to three dimensions for, say, piping layout and a
4. Similar, general treatment of spheres; ideally, comprehending the elements of 1.-3., above. The descriptive geometry of four-dimensions[6] might be useful in this regard.

A fifth, whimsical possibility; even application, would be to investigate cellular automata based on circle triplet constraints. One might propose birth/death rules analogous to physical laws governing, say, the development and decay of fluid vortex sheets. An introduction of a certain degree of randomness might result in, who knows, fractal-like circle patterns.

Acknowledgement

This research was supported by Natural Sciences and Engineering Research Canada grant #A4219 and Fonds pour la formation de Chercheurs et l'Aide à la Recherche (Québec) grant #EQ3072.

References

[1] Freund, D.D., "An Interactive Procedure for Constructing Line and Circle Tangencies", IEEE Comp. Graph. & Appl., v.6, n.4, 86-4, pp.59-63.

[2] Chasen, S.H., "Geometric Principles and Procedures for Computer Graphic Applications", Prentice-Hall, ISBN 0-13-352559-7, 1978, pp.50-103, pp.195-221.

[3] Slaby, S.M., "Fundamentals of Three-Dimensional Descriptive Geometry", John Wiley, ISBN 0-471-79621-2, 1976, pp.107-115, pp.104-107, pp.163-165.

[4] Hart, W.L., "Algebra, Elementary Functions and Probability", D.C Heath, LCCC 65-12574, 1965, pp.171-176.

[5] Webster, R., "PRODESIGN II (The Easy to Use CAD System)", American Small Business Computers, 118 South Mill St., Pryor OK 74361, ©1985,1986.

[6] Lindgren, C.E.S. and Slaby, S.M., "Four-Dimensional Descriptive Geometry", McGraw-Hill, LCCC 68-11931, 1968, 129pp.

A Model for Image Structuration

A. Braquelaire and P. Guitton (France and Canada)

1 - INTRODUCTION

The use of graphic paintboxes is widely spread in the domain of artistic graphics. As opposed to CAD programs which are intended for engineers for the conception of objects using equations and exact values, paintboxes are builted for graphists (publicity, video, fashion...) ([WIL 84]). This distinction has lead to the introduction of the class of 2D 1/2 images. This class of images integrates notions like hidden surface elimination (according to the relative positions of objects together) without numeric data. The user has only to put the new object in relation to the other ones (for example, one can say that: "the square is in front of the circle and behind the polygon").

In order to correctly perform these features, we need 2D 1/2 image structuration tools. In the structuration model we use, an image is a set of objects linked together by order relations. An object is defined by its frontier (the external contour), its texture (uniform color, pattern, shading...) and its relative position in the scene.

In this paper, we present a model based on contours and the data structures which are required to easily achieve interactive treatment of contours in a 2D 1/2 image. In paragraph 2 we give an intuitive approach of this problem and we briefly describe the LUMIERE project which aroused this work. In paragraph 3, we present the data model and in paragraph 4, the data structures.

2 - PROBLEM PRESENTATION

The aim of this project is to achieve a realistic 2D image manipulation and programming environment: the LUMIERE system. The development of LUMIERE is composed of three major steps: the graphic kernel, specialized graphic functions and the programming environment.

2.1 - LUMIERE project

In the graphic kernel, we define the basic object classes (contour, shape, color, brush...) which are manipulated by the system and the methods applied to each class (intersection for contours, mixing for colors, dragging for brushes...). The terms "objects", "classes" and "methods" come from the object oriented programming terminology. In this paper, we focus on the 2D 1/2 application of contours, i.e. the superposition of surfaces.

We further distinguish a special object class: the menus which provide the instanciation of new objects and the destruction or the manipulation of existing objects. A menu is created from syntactic and lexical specifications (icons are defined with a menu editor).

Contours make up another important object class. They are hierarchically defined with subobjects, the basic objects being lines, curves, circles... The contours constitute the basis of 2D image structuration, enabling sophisticated filling, 2D 1/2 effects...

In this way, we study various rendering methods, one of which is based on line and curve moves. For instance, it is easy to obtain a realistic cylinder by moving the ends of a vertical segment along circular contours; the color of the line is modified according to its position.

Another rendering method is provided by modifiing the color of each point during the filling (like in 3D synthesis). For instance, we can colour a circle using a classic filling algorithm, in which the color of each point depends on its distance from a given point. This modified filling algorithm (which is not uniform) imitates a 3D bowl display and is nearly as fast as the uniform filling algorithm. Our purpose is to specify and to mix such basis filling algorithms.

A programming environment is essential to fully manage this basic tools, providing the definition of new objects or methods. The environment we develop is based on IPL standard (Image Processing Language, [CHA 85]), flow and coroutine notions, and on object oriented and functionnal programming.

Consequently, the LUMIERE environment will be divided in two differents parts:
- a set of basic classes of graphic objects, composing the system kernel, wich is writen with the C language,
- an interpreted functionnal programming language (close to Scheme) providing the building of new classes and methods, and the instanciation of the basic objects defined in the kernel.

The communication between high and low level is based on message sending mechanism.

2.2 - The 2D 1/2 image concept

A new notion appears in graphics area: the 2D 1/2 image. This model inherits some features of 3D (like hidden surface elimination), while preserving the 2D image simplicity (simple object definitions). A major advantage of this concept is its processing speed (realistic 3D images are now, too expensive in time for interactive paint system). There is another important reason for the emergence of 2D 1/2 image: they leave a great part of freedom to the graphists; in opposite, 3D modeling systems are too exacting for artists.

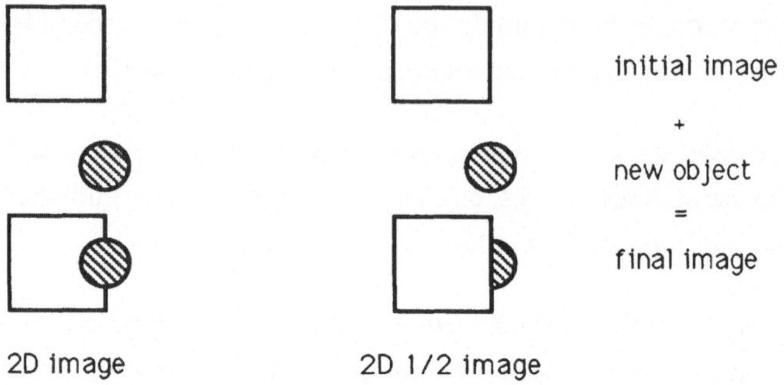

(Fig 2.1)

For the 2D 1/2 image, the user has to precise: "I put the circle behind the square". The storage of the new object (circle) allows the modification of object positions and then the display of the new image.

For example, "I put the square behind the circle" produces a new 2D 1/2 image:

(Fig 2.2)

The 2D 1/2 images solve another problem : the 2D image filling. In some configurations (like a pattern made up from the same color than the boundary) the object frontier is lost; then it is impossible to recover the initial object or to modify the pattern, by a fast way.

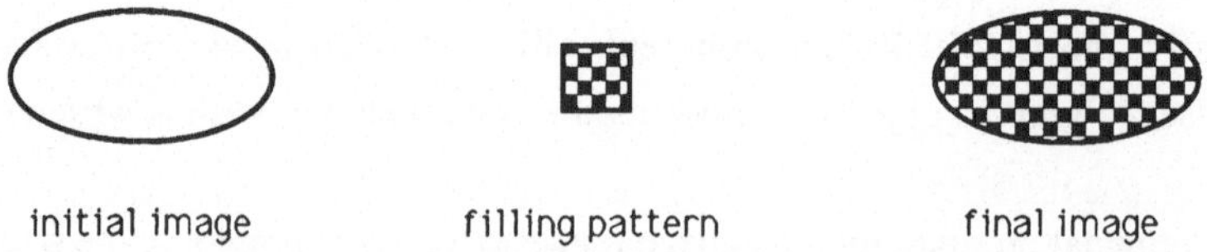

(Fig 2.3)

It is not possible to modify the pattern with classic filling algorithms.

Moreover the knowledge of an object contour allows simple object manipulations like translations or rotations. Some special effects can also be performed with the aid of the boundary storage (by example the duplication of an object with perspective computation).

To sum up, we consider an object like a list of components. These components may be made up themselves by a list of elementary components, for example contours are composed by a list of edges (notion of object oriented programming). This paper presents the contour component, while colour component is described in [CAS 88].

3 - DATA MODEL

3.1 - Model presentation

With this model, a planar map ([COR 75]) (the contour map) is associated with a scene made up of superposed objects. The vertices represent the intersection points between the object contours. Every time an object is created or modified, the new intersection points are computed and the graph is updated.

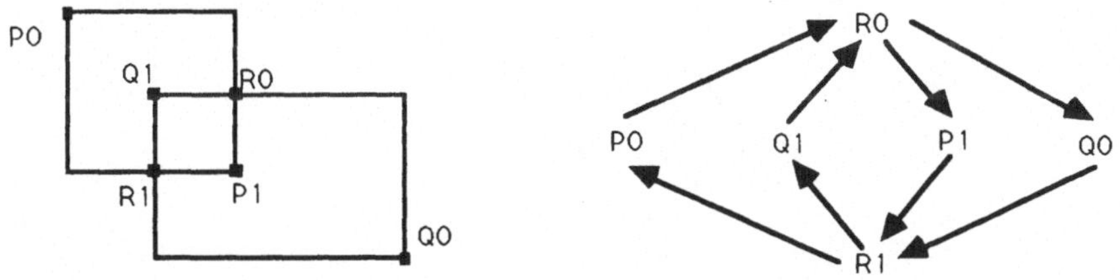

(Fig 3.1)

An object is composed of several regions and each region is surrounded by an elementary contour.

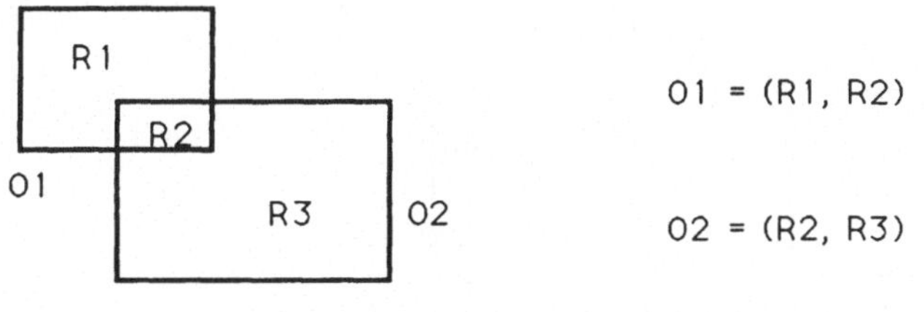

(Fig 3.2)

A travel clockwise of the external contour leads to the internal face of a region. This orientation is produced during the region creation by an internal point. This point is specified manually and may be also used for future filling.The object definition also includes other attributes like its color and its position in the scene.

For example, in Fig 3.1, ((P^0,R^0), -(Q^1,R^0), -(R^1,Q^1), (R^1,P^0)) defines the internal face of region R1.

A contour is composed of a list of monotone edges: it is important to store each point of edges to perform fast intersection computation.

3.2 - Problems

The model consistency is based on the contour graph connexity. Yet sometimes the addition of a new object does not produce any intersection point; without additional treatments the graph would become not connex.

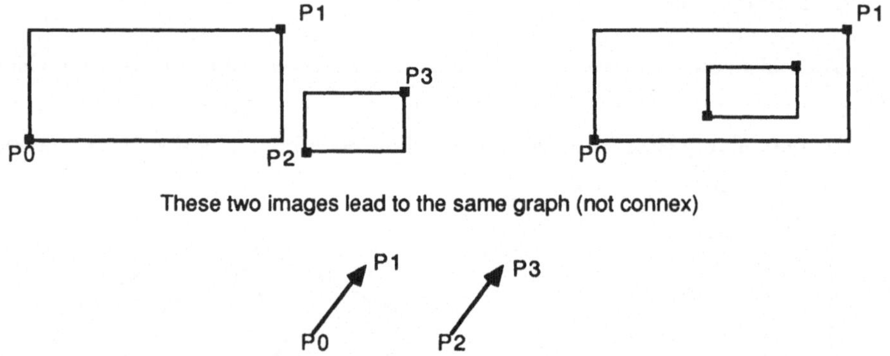

(Fig 3.3)

To avoid this situation, we add a pseudo contour which delimits an empty region and links the new contour to the current scene. The contour graph is initialized with a first contour coinciding with the image limits, the position of the region is set to infinite.

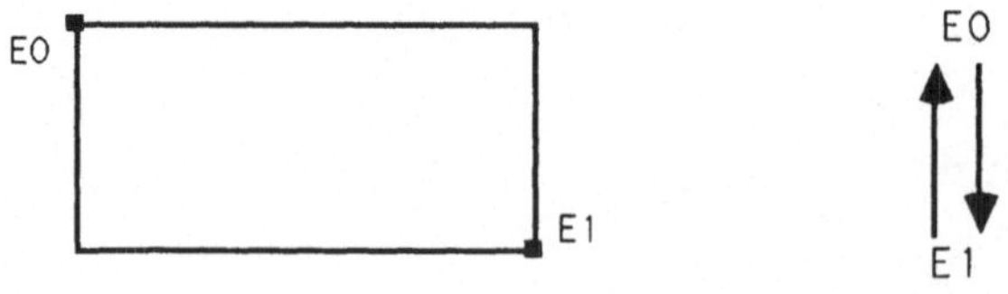

(Fig 3.4)

Then every time an object is added without producing intersection points, a vertical line is dragged starting from the "higher" point of the new contour towards the up of the screen, until an intersection point is performed (with a contour or with the screen boundary).

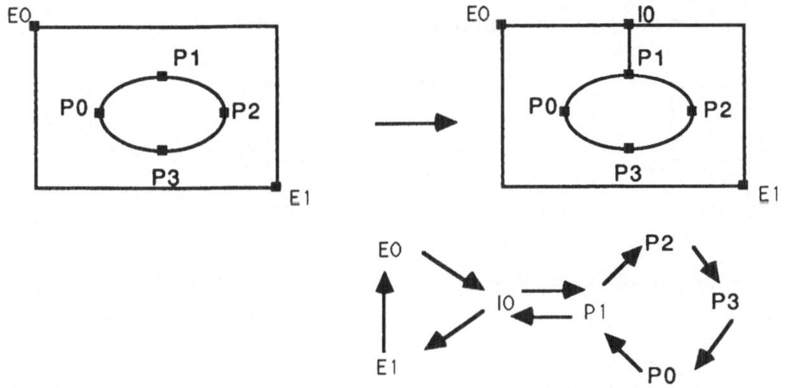

(Fig 3.5)

This extension allows the gestion of holed objects and preserve the definition of regions (consequently of objects). To obtain the region which defines an holed object, the whole set of contours (including pseudo contour) is used clockwise.

For example, in Fig 3.5, (E^0, I^0, P^1, P^0, P^3, P^2, P^1, I^0, E^1, E^0) shows the inside area of the first region, while (P^0, P^1, P^2, P^3) defines a second region.

3.3 - Definitions

Def 3.1 We distinguish four elementary moves (due to 4connexity) in an image: South, North, West and East. Couples (S,N) and (W,E) are said opposite while all other are said adjacent.

Def.3.2 An edge is an ordered sequence of adjacent points: E = (P^i; i = 0...n).
E is defined by P^0, P^n and a list of elementary moves which build a path starting from P^0 and ending with P^n.

Def.3.3 An edge E = (Pi ; i=0...n) is called monotone if and only if: it contains at the most two different elementary moves which must be adjacent

Def.3.4 A contour C = (E^i; i=0...p) is a closed sequence of contiguous monotone edges

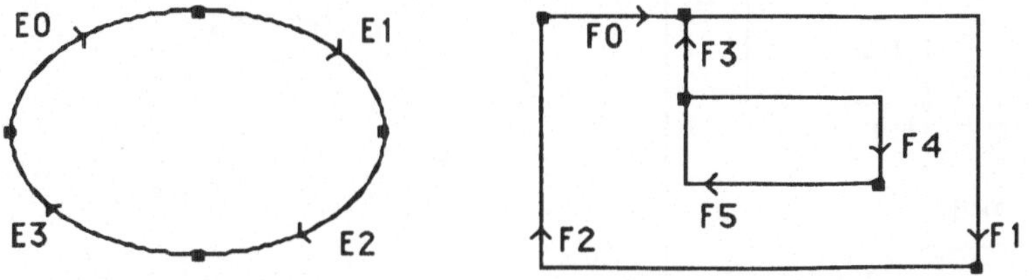

C1 = (E0, E1, E2, E3) C2 = (F0, -F3, -F5, -F4, F3, F1, F2)

(Fig 3.6)

The decomposition of a contour in an edge sequence is not always unique:

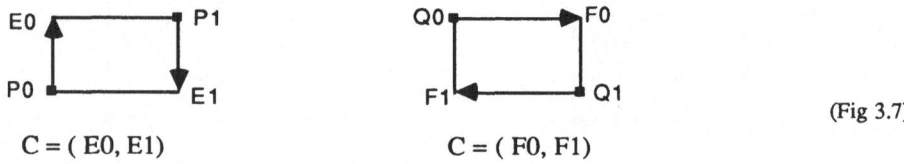

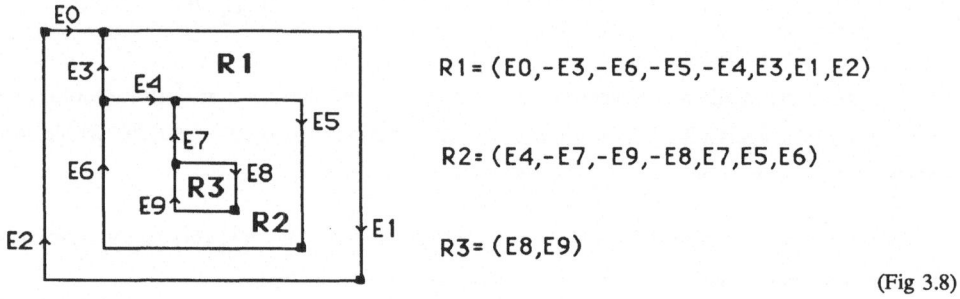

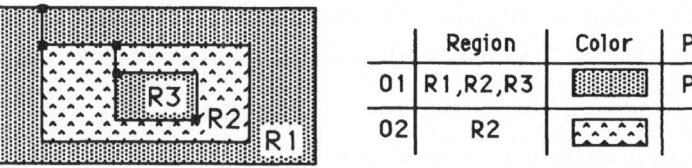

C = (E0, E1)　　　　C = (F0, F1)

(Fig 3.7)

Def.3.5 A region is the part of the plane which is surrounded by a contour. A region does not include any other edge or contour.The region set is a partition of the plane.

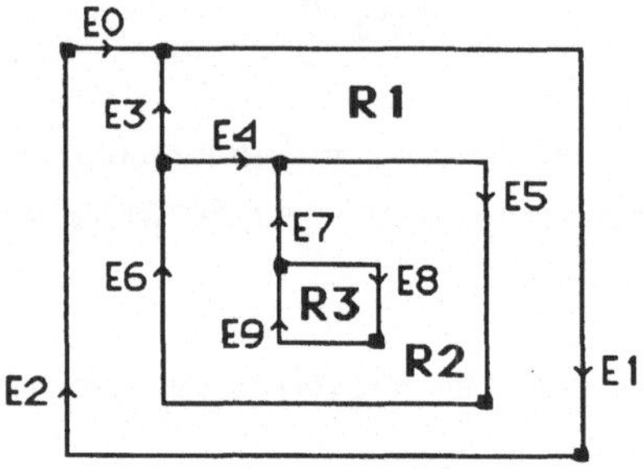

R1 = (E0,-E3,-E6,-E5,-E4,E3,E1,E2)

R2= (E4,-E7,-E9,-E8,E7,E5,E6)

R3= (E8,E9)

(Fig 3.8)

Def.3.6 An object is a set of regions and of component values.

	Region	Color	Plane
01	R1,R2,R3		P+1
02	R2		P

(Fig 3.9)

Def.3.7 A scene is a set of objects. It is represented by a planar graph (contour graph) where the vertices are, on the hand: the limits of edges making up object contours, on the other hand: the intersection points between the contours.

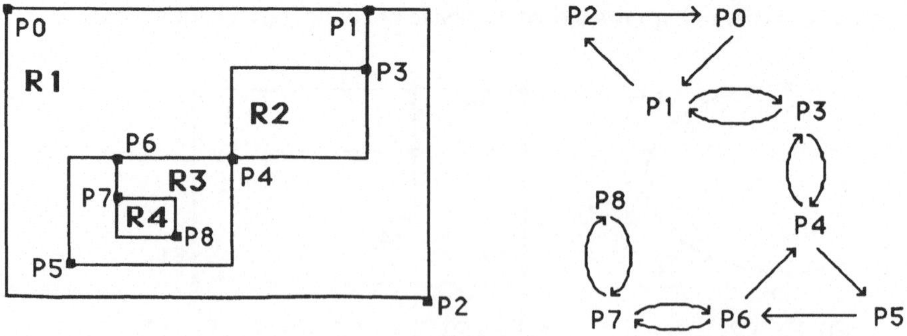

(Fig 3.10)

4 - DATA STRUCTURES

4.1 - Edges

The contour may be produced by two ways: on the one hand, an elementary figure is selected from a menu, on the other hand, the contour is drawn using a tablet and a stylus (or a mouse). In the first case, the contour decomposition is included in the figure definition. In the second case, monotone edges are extracted from the coordinate list (x,y) sent by the tablet. This processing is very fast and it does not delay the following steps.

Because edges are monotone, all the points belong to the same plane quarter. So the position of a point in relation to the precedent can be stored by one bit (4 connexity). The points starting and ending the edge are described by their coordinates. This storage allows a simple travel of the contour in every direction.

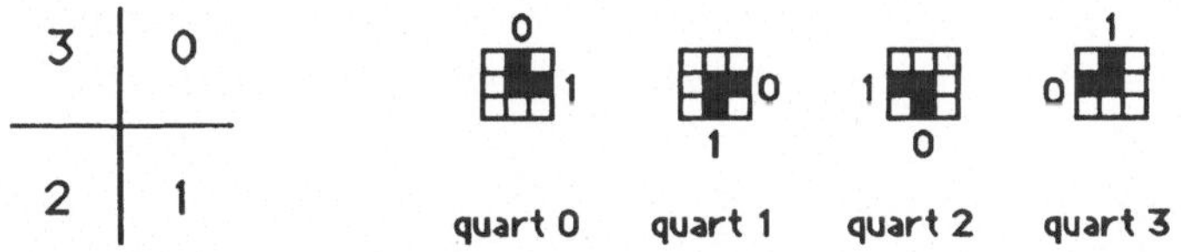

(Fig 4.1)

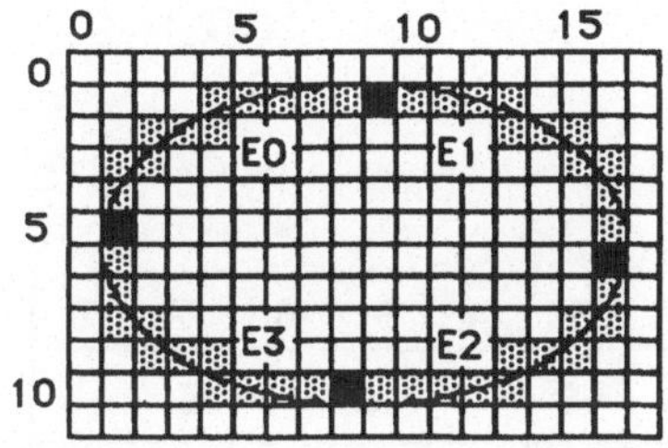

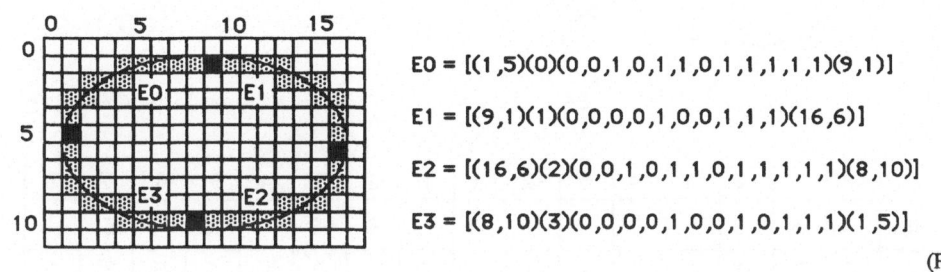

E0 = [(1,5)(0)(0,0,1,0,1,1,0,1,1,1,1,1)(9,1)]

E1 = [(9,1)(1)(0,0,0,0,1,0,0,1,1,1)(16,6)]

E2 = [(16,6)(2)(0,0,1,0,1,1,0,1,1,1,1,1)(8,10)]

E3 = [(8,10)(3)(0,0,0,0,1,0,0,1,0,1,1,1)(1,5)]

(Fig 4.2)

One of the most important algorithms is the computation of intersection points between contours. To produce these points, we use two steps. First, we perform an intersection test on the rectangles which include contours. If there is no intersection point between the rectangles, the same property remains true between contours. Second, we perform the same test for the rectangles which include edges (because they are monotone). The rectangles are defined by the ending and starting points of edges. If there exists an intersection between rectangles, each edge must be used point by point to detect intersection points. If severall adjacent intersection points are detected, they are replaced with an edge starting from the first intersection point and ending with the last one.

4.2 - Contours

The scene is described by the contour graph stored using a matrix. It performs edge linkages which made up contours. We use two conventions to build this matrix. First, we associate two numbers to an edge: a minus (resp. plus) sign and the edge number at the start (resp. the end) of the edge. Second, we define an ordered list (unclockwise) of edges which issue or terminate on the same vertex.

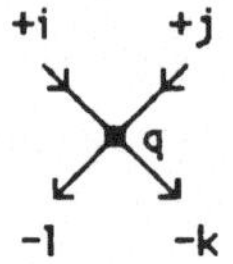

is stored

	...	-k	...	-l	...	+i	...	+j
NE		+j		-k		-l		+i
VER		q		q		q		q

+i ⟶ -l ⟶ -k ⟶ +j ⟶ +i

(Fig 4.3)

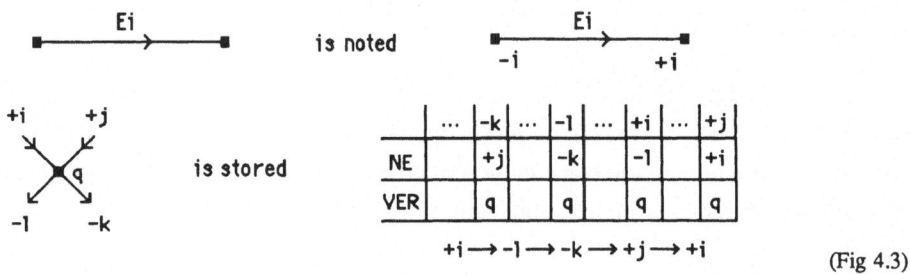

For example, let consider the scene composed of two objects and three regions:

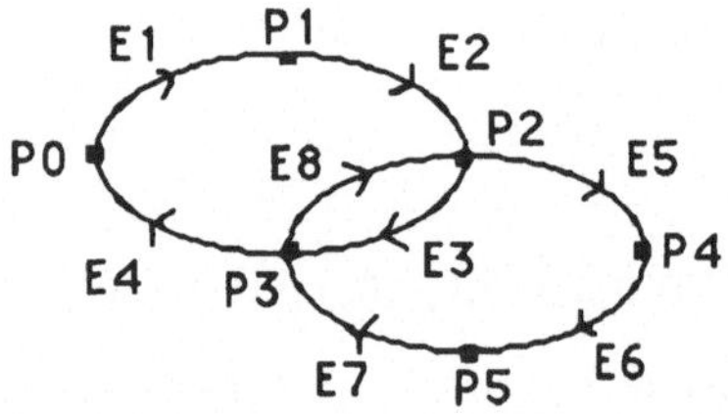

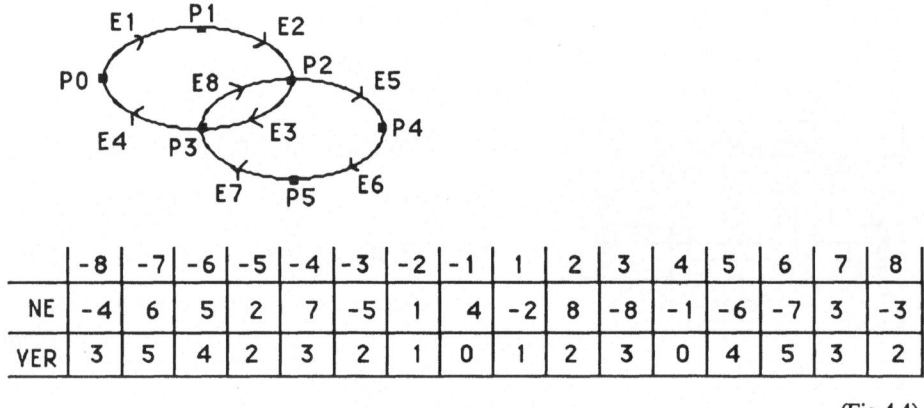

	-8	-7	-6	-5	-4	-3	-2	-1	1	2	3	4	5	6	7	8
NE	-4	6	5	2	7	-5	1	4	-2	8	-8	-1	-6	-7	3	-3
VER	3	5	4	2	3	2	1	0	1	2	3	0	4	5	3	2

(Fig 4.4)

With the aid of a matrix giving the first edge of a contour, it is possible to find any contour (consequently any region) by using the NE structure:

REGION	FE
1	-1
2	-8
3	3

FE[1]=-1, 1—>-2,2—>8,-8—>-4,4—>-1 (==FE[1])

FE[2]=-8, 8—>-3,3—>-8 (==FE[2])

FE[3]=3, -3—>-5,5—>-6,6—>-7,7—>3 (==FE[3])

(Fig 4.5)

5 - CONCLUSION

To sum up, this paper presents the basis to use this model. More details can be found in [WIR 87]. The main procedures which are required in an implementation, are described in [GUI 88]. More precisely, we defined elementary operations like creation, modification (shape, color, position) or suppression of an object in a scene. Finally we show the way to process some special effects by using this model .

We think that this model can be used in many applications. Because of its simple interface and its small storage, classic algorithms (line drawing, filling ...) may be implemented on this basis.

6 - BIBLIOGRAPHY

[CAS 88] P. CASTERAN & J.C. ROYER
Un environnement pour la couleur
Eurographics'88 - Nice - 12.16 septembre 88 (Soumis a publication)

[CHA 85] S.K. CHANG, E. JUNGERT,S. LEVIALDI,G. TORTORA & T. ICHIKAWA
An image processing language with icon assisted navigation
IEEE trans. on software engineering - vol SE 11 - p.811.819 - aug 85

[COR 75] R. CORI
Un code pour les graphes planaires et ses applications
Asterisque no 27 - Soc. math. de France - 75

[GUI 88] P. GUITTON
Un systeme de gestion interactive d'image 2D1/2
Universite du Quebec a Montreal - Rapport interne - Avril 88

[WIL 84] P.J. WILLIS
A paint program for the graphic arts in printing
Eurographics'84 - p 109.120 - North Holland

[WIR 87] L.J. WIRTH
Gestion de contours interactive
Universite de Bordeaux I - Rapport de DEA - juin 87

An Object-Oriented Interface for Network-Based Image Processing

B. G. Nichol (USA)

1 Abstract

In this paper we present a distributed image processing system that exploits a network of workstations, a network-based windowing system, and an object-oriented user interface. Image processing involves large amounts of both data storage and computation. Traditionally, image processing systems have been based on special purpose hardware specifically designed for imaging applications. However, the recent advances in workstation technology and networking make it possible to have the compute power and storage needed for imaging applications in a distributed environment. The network model, in conjunction with network based windowing systems, object-oriented programming techniques, and device independent image processing software, has been used to design the distributed imaging system described in this paper.

2 Introduction

Imaging has been a growing field of computer science and engineering for many years. More and more scientists are discovering that imaging is the best way to present and interpret their data whether it be medical, geophysical, or satellite data. However, the old model of a host/frame-buffer imaging system is expensive and restrictive. In this paper we present an image processing system that provides a less-expensive and more distributed environment by exploiting several new technologies.

Previously, the most common type of imaging system configuration, which we will refer to as the "old model", consisted of two parts: (i) the "imaging box" and (ii) the host computer. The "imaging box" refers to special purpose imaging hardware that ranges from a simple frame-buffer memory bank to a sophisticated display processor system including a bit-slice micro-processor for fast local processing, program memory, and color-lookup table memory. The more sophisticated systems are able to do special purpose operations such as 3 by 3 convolutions at refresh rates (30 times/second). Examples of the simple systems include the Raster Technologies RT 160 and the Ramtek 9400. The more complex systems include the Ikonas/Adage RDS 3000 and the Vicom. The host computer is typically a general purpose super-mini computer such as a VAX. This configuration offers a single user system that is quite fast, however it is expensive, hard to program, and restrictive in the sense that it is difficult to distribute the display and computing. For example in [Sherman 85], an experiment was performed using an old model imaging system, hosted by a VAX 11/750 with a DECNET connection to a CRAY. The purpose of the experiment was to install an image processing package on the CRAY and use the remote display for viewing. The result was that over 90 % of the total time was spent in the overhead of transferring the data to the CRAY for computing and then back to the general purpose computer for display, which far outweighed the advantage of the speed gained by doing the processing on the CRAY!

The old model imaging system is suitable for most types of imaging applications. However, recent gains in technology have made the old model somewhat obsolete. These advances include networking, integrated workstations, and device independent software. Recently the concept of a network of workstations has become very popular. The workstation is a single user system that integrates the old model components of host processor and frame-buffer. The network is made up of single user desktop workstations with varying compute and display capabilities, general purpose compute servers, and shared file servers that are common to all computers on the network. This "network model" has also had an effect on window system technology. Rather than just having several windows into one processor, windows must now be able to communicate with several different devices on the network. Since there can be several types of processors, the concept of device independent programming plays an important role. In order for the system to be integrated, it is very important that software be able to run on different processors on the network.

The network model, in conjunction with network based windowing systems, object oriented programming techniques, and device independent image processing software, has been used to design the distributed imaging system described in this paper.

In the next section we will discuss the capabilities that are necessary in order to have a practicable scientific imaging workbench. In section 4 the individual software components of our system are described: the operating system and network file system, the image processing substrate, and the network based windowing system. In section 5, the object-oriented facilities are presented and section 6 describes the actual implementation of our image processing workbench. Finally, in section 7, we show several examples of the system.

3 System Requirements

The overall goal of our network based imaging system is to provide a flexible image processing workbench. By a workbench we mean a place where a scientist is able to display an image, apply algorithms to images, and develop new algorithms. The major goals are (i) device independence, (ii) iconic specification of the processing chain, and (iii) aids for managing the images and processing. Device independent software is necessary to fully exploit the compute power of the network processors as well as the display capabilities. Both the processors and the displays on the network may have a wide range of capabilities. The concept of having icons that correspond to image processing tasks, and setting up a data-flow path is a very natural way of specifying the processing. Since such a large amount of time can be spent by the user managing their work (image file names, processing history, etc.), it is useful to provide facilities to aid the user in management such as audit trails and easy parameter modification.

Although device independent software may be slightly harder to program, it is necessary for integrating a network of different display and compute servers. The workbench should take advantage of all capabilities of the local workstation and of the available compute power and storage on the network. For example, when displaying a full-color image, the local workstation should display the image in full-color if available, or dither the image appropriately to 8-bit pseudo color or black-and white depending on the characteristics of the local workstation that the scientist using. Similarly, any non-display processing should take place not necessarily on the local workstation, but on the fastest available compute server on the network.

Although we want to distribute the computational processing on the network, at the same time we also want to integrate the image display with the processing specification. In old model architectures, the processing would typically be specified on a host console and take place on the host computer. When the processing was completed, the image would be displayed on the framebuffer. Integration of computer graphics and image processing was tried quite successfully in [Chakravarty 86] on an old model system, however this system offers no means for distributed processing. For easy of user interaction, we would like to see the processing specification take place right where the image is displayed. Furthermore, we would like to see the processing specified in a more iconic manner. This means that the user can associate certain icons to represent processing steps, and manipulate the icons depending on the order of operations and computations that they desire. Rather than running a program on an image, the user should be able to set up a processing chain of symbolic icons that can be interactively edited.

Very often a scientist will iterate a particular algorithm on an image many times, and simply modify some parameters before each iteration in an attempt to converge on the optimum results. We would like our workbench to aid in this process. The problems that arise are due to managing a large set of images, each with a different set of parameters and processing history. Our workbench must aid the user by (i) making it easy to modify parameters, (ii) making it easy to rerun a processing chain on an image, and (ii) keep track of the processing and parameter history for each displayed image. Furthermore, by taking advantage of the system file hierarchy, the user has access to their own logical file organization.

4 System Components

The workbench presented here is made up of many component parts. The major component parts are shown in Figure 1. Here we see at the lowest level the Unix [1] operating system. Above Unix is TIPC which contains the basic library functions for imaging. The C and Unix system provides a primitive access to the imaging library. Next to C we have the PostScript [2] code which is used for the graphical interface. On top of this we have the NeWS [3] windowing system which includes PostScript and extensions for interactive use. Finally on top we have the Image Editor which is the user interface to the imaging system. Each component part is discussed in the following sections.

Software Component	Purpose	Requirement Addressed
Image Editor	user interface	all
NeWS	windowing system	client/server network support
PostScript	programming language for interface and windowing system	device independent standard
C	image processing routines (TIPC)	device independent, standard
Unix	operating system (NFS)	supports shared file management and remote process execution standard

Figure 1: Software Component Hierarchy.

4.1 Unix

Unix [Kernighan 81] has become a very popular operating system for workstations and has many properties which makes it suitable for use in our imaging workbench. The most obvious is that it has become a standard operating system, however it also provides a very productive environment conducive to writing tools. Unix aids in writing programs quickly and the *make* facility helps manage program dependencies. Since there are no file types, image input and output can be done using the piping facilities which is a very powerful way of connecting components and also promotes modularity. Additionally NFS [4], the Network File System, runs on Unix. NFS hides all the low-level networking protocols and provides a transparent means of accessing the file systems of networked workstations. One advantage of NFS is that once a remote system's file system is mounted on the local system, the semantics of accessing the files are identical to accessing local files.

4.2 TIPC

An important component in any image processing system is the ability to access and process data. TIPC (from Tools for Image Processing in C, pronounced tipsy) has been designed to provide commonly used routines, the tools to build new ones, and to separate out device dependencies. The objective of TIPC is to provide these capabilities from standard software components. It is only recently that these standards have been generally accepted. Some are explicitly specified as an ANSI standard, subject to committees and public reviews, and others are *de facto* standards that have been adopted by the community because they satisfy a certain need. Image processing computing in general involves a wide range of devices (host computers, graphic display devices, array processors, image file formats, etc.) hence it is even harder to conform to standards. TIPC was written in an attempt to take advantage of as many available standards as possible so as to be easily portable to different computing environments. Where standards are not available, TIPC defines simple and general substitutes.

The standards that TIPC use relate to a variety of different devices. TIPC is written in the C programming language, which provides useful structure definitions as well as efficient compilation. C provides a mechanism for dynamic memory allocation so that a program uses only as much memory as it needs. Although TIPC

[1] Unix is a trademark of AT&T Bell Laboratories.

[2] PostScript is a registered trademark of Adobe Systems Incorporated.

[3] NeWS is a registered trademark of Sun Microsystems, Incorporated.

[4] NFS is a product of Sun Microsystems, Incorporated.

will run on any computer that has a C compiler, it was written in the Unix operating system. Probably the hardest standard to define is one for image display devices, however Adobe's PostScript page description language is rapidly being accepted as a standard for both hardcopy devices and interactive displays. TIPC uses standards such as C, Unix, and PostScript in an attempt to be as portable as possible.

An image file structure is defined in TIPC which contains an image header, an image lookup table, and the actual data. The header contains information such as image size, number of bits per pixel, data format, and some comment information. The lookup table describes the mapping from image values to color displayed. The data can be stored pixels or coded in some form such as run length encoding.

TIPC has two major software components: *imgutl* and *IPPL*. Imgutl is the image utility library which contains routines for opening image files, reading in the header, lookup table, and data, writing out the information. IPPL refers to the Image Processing Program Library, a set of C programs that use the standards and utilities set up by TIPC. Typical IPPL programs take an input file and an output file and some optional parameters. For example to low-pass filter an image one could run the IPPL program "blurr" by typing

blurr in.im8 out.im8

this would run a 3 by 3 moving average window over the image. To specify the optional arguments and change the window size one would type

blurr -x 4 -y 5 in.im8 out.im8

This runs a 4 by 5 neighborhood average over the image named in.im8 and puts the result in the file out.im8. Note that parameters are specified in a standard Unix fashion and that piping is supported. For example to run the low-pass filter over an image twice one could type

blurr in.im8 | blurr > out.im8

which is equivalent to (and more efficient than)

blurr in.im8 temp.im8

blurr temp.im8 out.im8

IPPL is a burgeoning set of programs and it currently contains routines for spatial domain filtering, histogram equalization, color look-up table manipulation, mathematical operations, etc.

4.3 NeWS/PostScript

The previous section described the C based tools that do the image processing computation. In this section we describe the system that is used as the interface between the user and the C processing routines.

For the user interface we take advantage of a network based windowing system called NeWS (Network extensible Window System) from Sun Microsystems [Sun 87]. The client/window server paradigm, where applications running on one computer can access the display of another, was previously investigated at Carnegie-Mellon University (Andrew) [Morris 86] and Massachusetts Institute of Technology (X Window System [5]) [Scheifler 86]. NeWS is a distributed window system that acts as a window server managing input and output on its host machine. Client application programs may reside anywhere on the network and send messages causing NeWS to render images on the local display. For example, a client program may be running on a network supercomputer and send the display results to the local workstation.

NeWS is written in the PostScript [Adobe 85] language which was developed by Adobe Systems and is based on a new imaging model described in [Warnock 82]. PostScript, which was originally designed as a page description language for printers, is a high-level, stack based programming language which provides powerful graphics primitives. PostScript code is interpreted so that device-independent programs are transmitted which are locally interpreted on the printer or by the window server.

One feature of PostScript that makes it especially useful for the imaging workbench is its imaging model. This model allows the programmer to describe text, graphics, and images in a device-independent and uniform way. For example, just as a vector in any traditional graphics system is subject to a transformation

[5] X Window System is a registered trademark of Massachusetts Institute of Technology

for scaling, rotation, and translation, so is an image. Text and images are treated as another graphical object and are subject to the same transformations that vectors are. Similarly, the PostScript interpreter knows how to render an image taking full advantage of the display device. Just as a color line might print as black on a black and white monitor, an 8-bit image would be dithered for 1-bit display.

The implementers of NeWS have made some extensions to PostScript to make it suitable for interactive use. For example, they have added the canvas as a drawing surface, a light-weight process mechanism, cursors, and mouse capabilities.

5 Object-Oriented Techniques

The use of object oriented techniques have been useful in obtaining several of our system goals. One of the goals of the workbench is to be very flexible. The use of object oriented techniques have enabled us to rapidly prototype this system. The inheritance properties have been useful to modify the system it for specific applications. Another goal is to support iconic representations. We define an object class that has properties useful for symbolic representation and we specialize that class for every instance.

5.1 Objects

The Image Editor utilizes a Smalltalk-like [Goldberg 84] mechanism that NeWS/PostScript provides for object oriented programming. The component concepts of this mechanism are object, class, message, method, and inheritance:

- *Object* The object is the basic construct and made up of both data and procedures (methods) to operate on the data.
- *Class* The template for the object is describe in a class definition. The class contains instance-specific information (instance variables) and class wide information (class variables and methods).
- *Message* A message is the basic communication mechanism. To cause an action, a message is sent to an object which is handled by the appropriate method.
- *Method* The method is a procedure which is invoked via a message.
- *Inheritance* This object-oriented system allows a hierarchy of classes (subclassing and superclassing) where the behavior of a subclass can be inherited from its superclass. Inherited methods and variables can also be overridden in the subclass.

6 Implementation

The image editor defines a class called *Command* (since each instance of this class contains information corresponding to one image processing command). The *Command* class has instance variables for a command name, forward and reverse links, input and output file names, and a submenu stub for instance specific parameter setting. The command name variable is simply the name (or an icon representing the name) of the processing function. The forward and reverse links point to either null or the previous and next object instances as specified by the user during execution. The input and output file names hold either actual file names or piping information, and the submenu is for parameter selection specific to this command. As an example, an instance of the *Command* class object labeled c1 would be define (in pseudo-PostScript) by:

```
/c1 /new Command send def % create a new object labeled c1

(blurr) setcommand c1 send % the command will be the low-pass filter blurr
null forward_link c1 send  % initialize links
null reverse_link c1 send
(/local/test.img) setinputfile c1 send  % set input and output file names
(/local/blurr.im8) setoutputfile c1 send
```

```
/submenu  windowsize => [                % initialize the submenu
     2 by 2
     3 by 3
     5 by 5
 ] def
```

The *Command* class also has class variables that are shared by all instances. These class variables include a current working directory, an execution host, and a display host. The current working directory specifies the current local directory path and is automatically appended to the beginning of the input and output file names. The execution host specifies which computer on the network to execute on and the display host specifies which computer to display the results on.

The methods associated with the *Command* class include procedures for class related operations and *Command* specific operations. The class related operations set up inheritances and take care of new instantiations. The *Command* specific methods manage the links, set variables, and fork jobs to Unix. Examples of *Command* specific methods include *insertanode, deleteanode, forkinfo* and *setinfile.*

As an example of the inheritance capabilities, consider the way we use the *TextBox* class. *TextBox* is a class that supports labeled boxes and arrows. It is responsible for proper box sizing depending on the size of the text, properly drawing the arrows, etc. Since we wanted to take advantage of these facilities we define the *Command* class as a subclass of the *TextBox* class. The *Command* class inherits from the *TextBox* class all the box and arrow management facilities.

6.1 Distributed Processing

To fully take advantage of the available network compute power, the system should be able to look at the current state and load average of all processors and execute jobs on the best machine available. Currently, the composed image processing job is executed on any network machine specified by the user. However, since each object can contain instance variables for an execution processor, the capability to execute sections of the job on different machines are available and the incorporation of a system like The Butler [Nichols 87] would be simple. Such systems maintain a list of workstations that are in the pool of available machines and executes a job on the most appropriate (unloaded) machine.

7 Example

In this section we will describe several examples of image processing jobs set up using the image editor. Figure 2 shows the image editor display in its default state after it starts up. There are two instances of the *Command* class in the window. The top one has the name of the default input image file and the bottom one has the name of a display option. Each object has its own background menu and the window itself has a background menu. Each object can be repositioned by using the left mouse button. All menus pop up upon right buttoning on the appropriate object. The background menu for *Command* objects have 4 options: (1) set parameters (object specific), (2) insert an object, (3) delete an object, (4) edit object. The first option is always object specific. For example, the first submenu item for the file name node is a list of other possible file names, or for the *blurr* filter, you can set the window size. The other three options are to insert an object after this object, delete this object, or edit this object. The insert option has a menu hierarchy of all the different image processing operations (filters, enhancers, math operations, etc.). The delete option simply removes the current object from the linked list. The edit object option brings up an object editor which allows you to inspect and edit the object values and send messages.

The window background menu has several options that pertain to the system in general: *Fork job, set display host, set execution host,* and *print image.* When the *fork job* option is selected, the system compiles all the current processing and parameter information and forks the job off to Unix for execution. The *set display host* and *set execution host* options bring up lists of machines on the network that are available for display and execution. The system defaults to use the user workstation as the display device and the fastest available machine on the network as the execution device

Choosing the *fork job* option in the default setup will simply display the named image in a separate window.

Figure 2: The Image Editor Upon Startup

The user can set up a processing chain, as shown in figure 3. This chain can be interactively edited, objects deleted, inserted or moved, by using the mouse and submenus. When the user wants to run the current processing chain, they select the fork job option. While the job is executing the objects corresponding to the processing steps are highlighted (via messages sent from the execution processor the the workstation host) as they are started up and unhilighted when completed. While the job is executing the local processor is available for inspecting images, editing objects, or setting up a new processing chain.

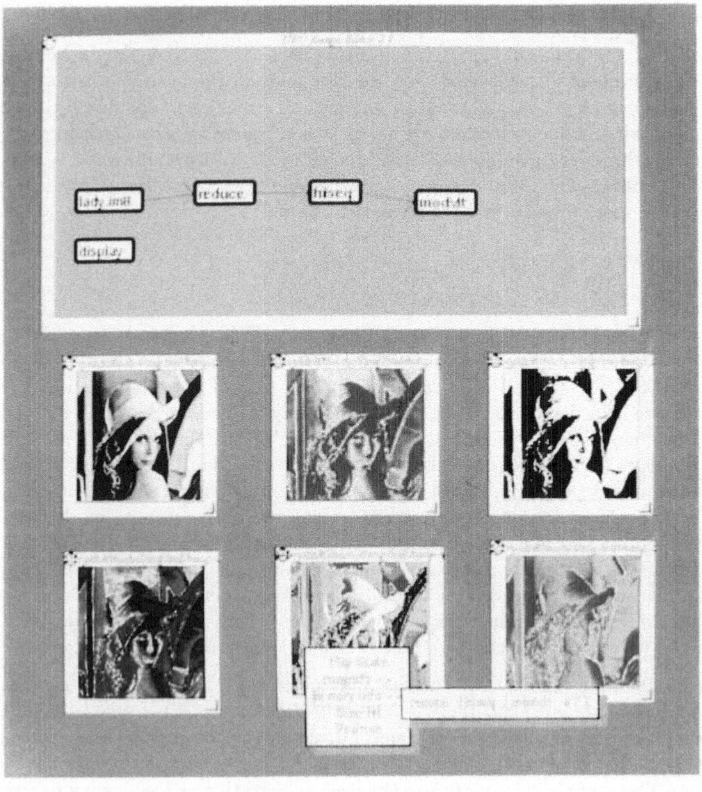

Figure 3: Processing chain showing the results of image resolution reduction, histogram equalization, and color lookup table modification. Six different color tables are shown.

When the job is complete the users cursor changes shape, prompting for positioning information for the processed image. The background menu for this image contains the history information.

Figure 3 shows a processing chain that takes the input image, reduces the resolution, equalizes the histogram, and modifies the color look-up table. The same processing chain was run 6 times with a parameter change to *modvlt* each time. Note the history information being recalled for one of the images.

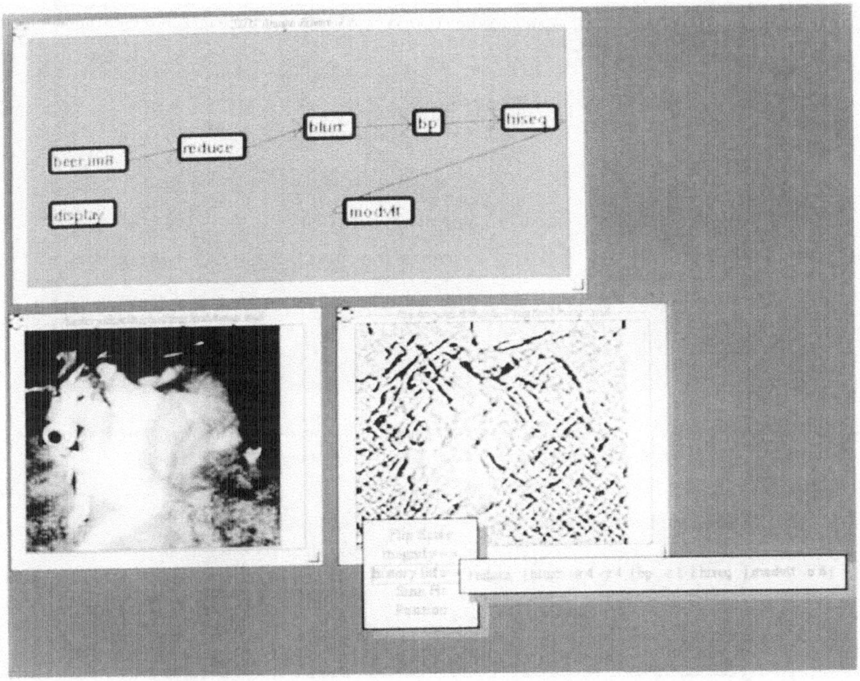

Figure 4: Here we show an example of filtering an image to extract edges.

In Figure 4 we see an example of edge extraction. Here the input image (shown on the left) has gone through a resolution reduction, a low-pass filter, a band-pass filter, a histogram equalization, and the look-up table has been binarized. Note the history information of the processed image.

Figure 5 shows several different representations of an image. First we see the standard grey-level image. Next to this the image has been converted to waveform plots. (Each column of the input image has been plotted as a wave form with negative amplitudes set to black and positive set to red. This is the way seismic interpreters often like to view seismic data.) We also see a software magnifying glass where a round portion of the image has been expanded for closer examination. Note the red object highlighted telling the user that the job is executing. And finally we see the image plotted as a histogram.

Figure 6 shows the Object Editor, which allows the user to interactively send messages to objects and inspect and modify object variables. Here the *infile* instance variable is being edited.

8 Conclusion

With the recent trends in computer technology toward desktop workstations, window servers, and networks of computers and file servers, the idea of a distributed image processing workbench becomes very desirable. With these new technologies come the ability to remotely process but locally display imagery. Utilizing

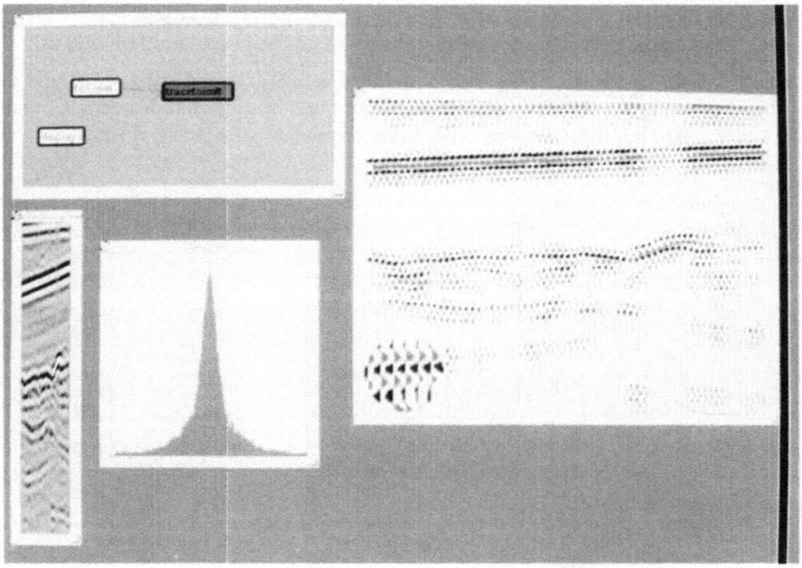

Figure 5: Seismic data in grey-level form, histogram form, and converted to wiggle-plot format. Note the use of the software "magnifying glass" in the bottom left of the wiggle-plot image.

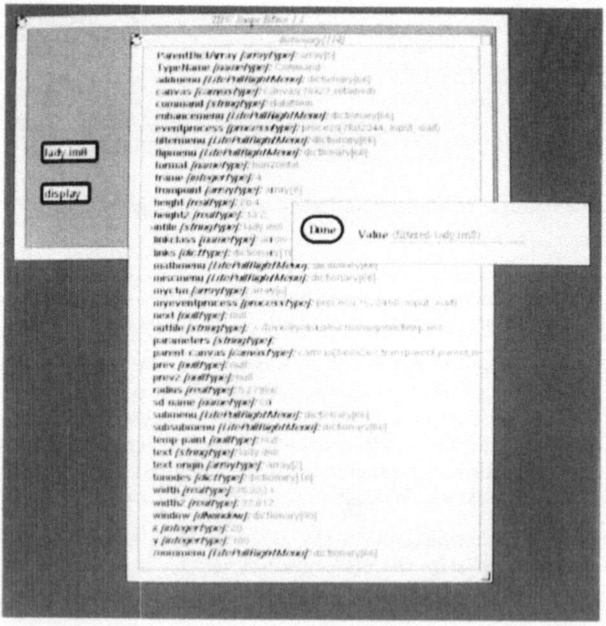

Figure 6: Using the Object Editor. Changing the value of the *infile* instance variable.

a standard such as PostScript gives us the device independence to display on a large number of output devices including hardcopy units. We have exploited these recent trends to come up with a distributed, object oriented system for image processing which allows us to more efficiently utilize our network. We believe that the trend toward networked systems will continue and become more popular and distributed software systems, such as the one presented here, are the most efficient way to make use of all the available computing power.

9 Acknowledgments

The author wishes to thank Stanley C. Vestal, Director, Systems Science for his support on this project and Indranil Chakravarty for beta testing the software and making valuable comments on both the software and this document. Thanks also to Dave Singer at Schlumberger Palo Alto Research for providing the object editor software.

10 Bibliography

References

[Adobe 85] *PostScript Language Reference Manual*, Addison-Wesley, 1985.

[Chakravarty 86] I. Chakravarty, Bruce Nichol, T. Ono, "The Integration of Computer Graphics and Image Processing Techniques for the Display and Manipulation of Geophysical Data", proceedings of Computer Graphics Tokyo '86, appearing in *Advanced Computer Graphics*, T. Kunii, Ed. Springer-Verlag 1986.

[Scheifler 86] Robert W. Scheifler, James Gettys, "The X Window System", *ACM Transactions On Graphics*, Volume 5, Number 2, April 1986.

[Goldberg 84] Adele Goldberg, *Smalltalk-80, The Interactive Programming Environment*, Addison-Wesley, Reading Massachusetts, 1984.

[Kernighan 81] Brian W. Kernighan, John R. Mashey, "The UNIX Programming Environment", it IEEE Computer, 14:4, April 1981; reprinted in *Interactive Programming Environments*, D. Barstow, H. Shrobe, and E. Sandewall, Eds. McGraw-Hill, New York, 1984.

[Morris 86] J. Morris et. al., "Andrew: A Distributed Personal Computing Environment", Communications of the ACM, Vol. 29, No. 3, March 1986.

[Nichols 87] David A. Nichols, "Using Idle Workstations in a Shared Computing Environment", ACM, 1987.

[Sherman 85] Arthur Sherman, Indranil Chakravarty, "Transporting the SPIDER Package to the Cray", Schlumberger-Doll Research Note SYS-85-32, Schlumberger-Doll Research, Ridgefield, CT, 1985.

[Sun 87] *NeWS Technical Overview*, Sun Microsystems, Inc.

[Warnock 82] John Warnock, Douglas Wyatt, "A Device Independent Graphics Imaging Model for Use with Raster Devices", *Computer Graphics*, Volume 16, No. 3, July 1982.

Applying Direct Manipulation to Geometric Construction Systems

R. M. White (Switzerland)

Abstract

The application of a direct manipulation interface to geometric construction programs has been hindered primarily because of the "ruler and compass" approach employed in these systems. This approach limits the types of geometric tasks which can be handled, and is suitable only for a procedural interface language. It is shown that the use of a least squares adjustment for geometric computations overcomes these problems. A prototype program is presented which demonstrates the generality and usefulness of such a system.

1. Introduction

The application of direct manipulation techniques [Shneiderman 1983] to program interfaces has had a profound effect upon the quality of some software - witness the transformation taking place in the publishing field with the advent of "Desktop Publishing" software. However, in the area of geometric construction only limited research and development is taking place in which direct manipulation is being applied. This is primarily for two reasons. First, geometric construction tasks are only treated from a traditional, analog ruler and compass, approach which we are all familiar with from our schooling. Second, problems exist in the displaying of multiple instances of relationships between geometric objects. This paper will focus on the first of the two problems, and present a prototype system which successfully treats geometric construction tasks using a constraint-based language instead of the ruler and compass metaphor.

The paper has two main parts. First, I present an overview of the types of problems encountered in geometric construction, with emphasis placed on the suitability of different mathematical solutions to these tasks. This section demonstrates that the mathematical methods chosen influence the choice of interface to be applied in a geometric construction system. In the second section I present a prototype which we have developed. This prototype demonstrates that the computation and interface problems can be solved.

2. Analysis of Geometric Construction Tasks

Most geometric construction programs, often referred to as Coordinate Geometry programs, or COGO for short, use traditional techniques both for the user interface, and for the numerical solution of problems. I will discuss the mathematical aspects, and show that

- ruler and compass techniques employed are only sufficient for handling a limited number of geometric construction tasks types, and
- the procedural aspect of these techniques is inappropriate for a direct manipulation interface.

2.1. Limited Geometric Construction Types

COGO programs employ analytical geometry and trigonometry to process a specified, ordered, sequence of steps describing a path to the solution. The program merely performs the computations in the order that the user would if he had to perform the task by hand. We call this the "ruler and compass" metaphor since the mathematics simulate the use of a ruler and compass to perform the construction. Figure 1 lists the commands needed to construct an equilateral triangle whose sides are 3/4 inch long, and whose base is inclined at 15° to the horizontal axis.

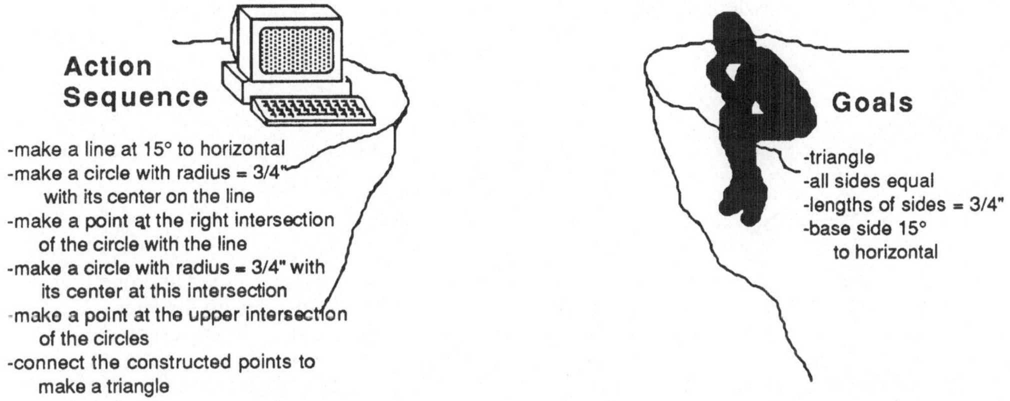
Action Sequence
-make a line at 15° to horizontal
-make a circle with radius = 3/4" with its center on the line
-make a point at the right intersection of the circle with the line
-make a circle with radius = 3/4" with its center at this intersection
-make a point at the upper intersection of the circles
-connect the constructed points to make a triangle
Goals
-triangle
-all sides equal
-lengths of sides = 3/4"
-base side 15° to horizontal

Figure 1. The sequence of commands needed to construct an equilateral triangle whose sides are 3/4 inch, and titled at 15°. Note that the user's goals are expressed in a language which is completely different from that offered by the system. This example was presented in [Bier and Stone 1986]. The drawing was adapted from [Norman 1986].

While the ruler and compass approach is sufficient to adequately handle most ordinary cases, it cannot handle more complex (but no less desirable) cases. Geometric problems can be classified according to the degree to which the solution is determined from the given constraints:

- Under-determined: The constraints do not completely determine the unknown quantities
- Exactly determined: The constraints are sufficient to determine all of the unknown quantities
- Over-determined: The constraints are more than sufficient to determine the unknown quantities.

A constraint is defined as a geometric relation which must hold between a set of objects (points, lines, areas, etc). As an example, consider a distance between two points. This is a constraint since it specifies a relation between the two points which must hold in a solution.

2.1.1. Exactly-determined Cases

For the exactly-determined case, we can employ ruler and compass techniques which will handle most cases without problem. Notable exceptions would be situations where coordinates are not specified (for example, the case of the equilateral triangle mentioned above), but these can usually be simulated by arbitrarily assigning coordinates to some points in the construction.

2.1.2. Under-determined Cases

For the under-determined case, a ruler and compass approach cannot provide a solution without making assumptions. For example, consider the task of constructing a triangle when only the lengths of two sides are known (Fig. 2). In order to solve, an assumption as to the length of the unspecified side, or as to an angle between two sides must be made. With very simple examples, some ad hoc solution can probably be found, but with much more complex sets of relations there may be contradictory solutions of this type. How would the system decide which methods to use, and which to ignore? A better solution might be to use a pseudo-inverse to solve the system of equations for the unknown values, or (as in the case of the prototype presented in this paper) to introduce a priori knowledge about coordinates into a least squares adjustment.

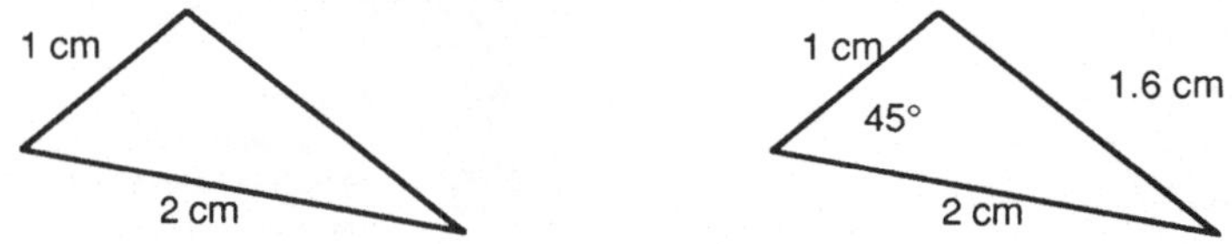

Figure 2. Example of a geometric construction task which is under-determined and one that is over-determined. In the left-hand figure, only the lengths of the two sides are known. Under-determined cases often occur as intermediate steps in the construction of complete objects. In the right-hand figure, more information is given than can be used for a trivial solution. Geometric construction tasks of this type are common when existing objects are measured and must be modelled.

2.1.3. Over-determined Cases

In the third category, over-determined situations, a ruler and compass approach again cannot provide a solution without ignoring vital information. It would have to ignore explicit relationships as specified by the user. Problems of this type are very often the case in engineering, especially when an existing object has been measured, and must be modelled. As a simple example, take the case of a triangle where all sides are known, as well as one angle (Fig. 2). A ruler and compass solution would have to ignore either the length of one side or the angle in order to arrive at a solution. However, with a least squares adjustment, we can arrive at a 'best fit' solution, ie, the squares of the differences between the observed known values, and the adjusted values is a minimum. Statistically we can ensure that this is an optimum solution.

2.2. Human Interface Aspects

Geometric construction systems to date can be classified in two categories. First there are the traditional COGO programs which, evaluate a specified sequence of functions (normally a number of distance and angle tuples for successive points starting from some initial points), to arrive at a solution for the coordinates of all points. The second category are graphics drawing systems, where various geometric objects can be specified, but have no specific constraints (ie relationships) between each other. For this paper we concern ourselves primarily with programs of this sort which employ direct manipulation. In this type of system we can specify through drawing tools, and with the help of some metric aides such as on-screen rulers, what we observe to be the situation of the geometry at one point in time. It is important to note that we can create geometry, but the graphic objects created have no inter-relations, other than their current relative locations. No method exists by which we can specify relationships between objects which must hold at all times.

We have seen that COGO systems can at least handle the most common geometric construction cases. Why then has there not been a marriage between COGO type programs, which to a limited extent can handle momentary constraints between objects, and the excellent graphic capabilities of MacDraw type programs? The remainder of the answer lies primarily in the difference between the interface language which direct manipulation programs use, and that which is suitable for COGO programs.

2.2.1. Procedural versus Declarative Languages

Note that we stated that COGO programs need a *sequence* of functions in order to solve for the unknowns (understood to be coordinates). The solution for the coordinates of point P_k is dependent upon the adequate solution of the coordinates of point P_{k-1}, where a function F_k describes the relationship between P_k and P_{k+1}. Thus, a *procedural* language (usually a command line or menu interface) is most appropriate for COGO type programs since it enforces the sequential notion of the mathematical method.

We can model the ruler and compass method at each epoch in time t as

$$t_1 : P_2 = F_1(P_1), t_2 : P_3 = F_2(P_2), ... t_k : P_{k+1} = F_k(P_k), ...$$

or, generally,

$$t_k : P_{k+1} = F_k(P_k).$$

At time t_k the system only processes the function F_k between P_k and P_{k+1}. Functions which operate over more than two points are possible, for example as in the function which returns the intersection of two lines (bounded by four points). Not that the only geometric objects explicitly used in the ruler and compass approach are points.

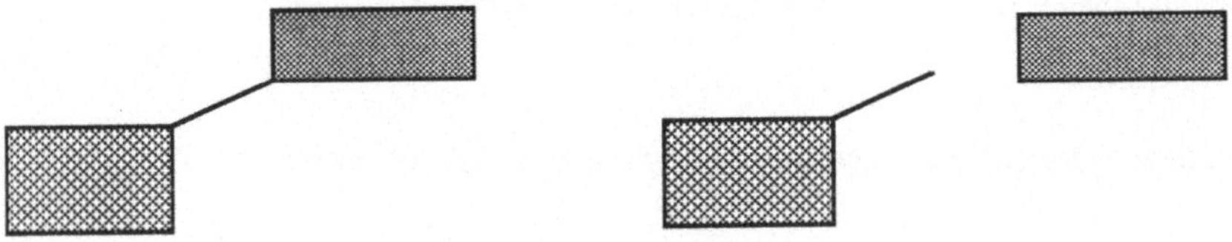

a) b)

Figure 3. Geometric (in this case, only topological) relationships are not declarable in some direct manipulation geometric construction programs such as MacDraw [Apple 1984b]. In a) there are two rectangles which are connected at their corners by a line. After selecting and dragging one of the rectangles, the line no longer connects the rectangles. There is no means by which the line can be constrained to connect the rectangles.

In some graphic drawing programs (a good example of which is MacDraw [Apple 1984b]), a *declarative* language is used. In these, the user declares what the geometry is in three ways:

- creating an object by selecting the appropriate tool on the screen and then clicking on the drawing area,
- locating an object by dragging it within the drawing area,
- dimensioning an object by dragging at the selection indicators.

(The appearance of an object can also be declared, for example, by selecting a fill pattern, but this is not of concern in this paper.) The user may declare the objects of the geometric model in any order, and alter previously declared objects at any time. Objects can be grouped together to form new objects, but when a particular object is altered other objects are not affected. For example, when a rectangle is dragged to a new location, a line which had originally terminated at one corner of the rectangle remains in its original location (Fig. 3). Metric relations between multiple objects are not possible in the absence of a method to satisfy them.

2.3. The Method/Language Disparity

Experience with direct manipulation interfaces clearly demonstrates that they have great potential for geometric construction systems. However, a system designer cannot hope to adequately combine such a language if inherent discrepancies
between the mathematical model and the interface model exist. Thus, I formulate the current problem which has been encountered in these systems as the following conclusion:

It is the disparity between the interface language which is desired and the mathematical model which is commonly used which prevents the incorporation of the two into a successful direct manipulation, geometric construction program.

2.4. Previous Attempts to Solve the Problem

A small number of attempts have been made to combine a direct manipulation interface with a general constraint solving mechanism. Among the most notable are SketchPad [Sutherland 1963], and ThingLab [Borning 1979]. SketchPad is especially remarkable considering the early date at which it was implemented. ThingLab is a very general constraint based system, but may not be appropriate for some geometric construction tasks. It uses three different methods when it attempts to solve a system of constraints, the last of which is 'relaxation', which is in effect a least squares adjustment. It is important to note that in our work, we envision the least squares adjustment as the first (and only) method to be applied in order to satisfy exactly determined, under-determined, and over-determined sets of geometric constraints.

2.5. Applying a Direct Manipulation Interface to a Least Squares Adjustment

By employing a least squares adjustment as the underlying constraint satisfying mechanism in a direct manipulation system we can solve not only the procedural versus declarative problem, but also allow the solution of a wider range of sets of constraints. The model of such as system at time t is

$$t_n : \Sigma\, C_k(S_k)$$

where S_k is a selection from the set of objects O, and C_k is a constraint tuple from the set of all constraints C. At time t_n the system knows not only the entire set of constraints $C_{1..k}$, but can satisfy multiple instances of metric constraints which involve one or more objects.

3. The HILS Prototype

The name HILS is short for "Human Interface to Least Squares". The program combines a Direct Manipulation Human Interface with a rigorous Least Squares numerical solution. In this prototype, the user sketches the topology of a geometric construction with the aid of a mouse. He then adds a number of metric constraints to this topology, and finally, requests a solution from the system.

3.1. Development

The program was initially developed on a DEC MicroVAX workstation in Precompiled Pascal [Frank 1986] at the University of Maine at Orono, but was later transferred to the Apple Macintosh in TML Pascal [TML 1985], where the current version is maintained. At present it uses no database management system, rather employs a network data structure which simulates the PANDA [Frank 1982] database management system.

3.2. Description of Use

After opening the HILS icon to start a new construction, the user is presented a dialog in which he enters information which is used to define the scale and horizontal and vertical ranges for the coordinate system of the drawing window. This may be changed at any time using **Zoom In**, **Zoom Out** commands, by specifically setting these values again, or by requesting that scale and ranges are chosen by the system which show all of the constructed geometry.

After defining the coordinate system and several points, the screen appears as in Fig. 4. In the center of the window is a viewport with world coordinate grid scales on its vertical and horizontal axes. At the upper left are two tools (in the MacDraw [Apple 1984b] sense). The upper one with the square is a tool for setting new points. The lower one with the diagonal line is for setting lines between points, currently for illustrative purposes. Both of these tools are used by clicking first on the tool, then clicking at the desired location for the object in the viewport (once to set a point, twice to select two points which are to be connected by a line). When setting a point, the user is asked to provide a name for it in a dialog box.

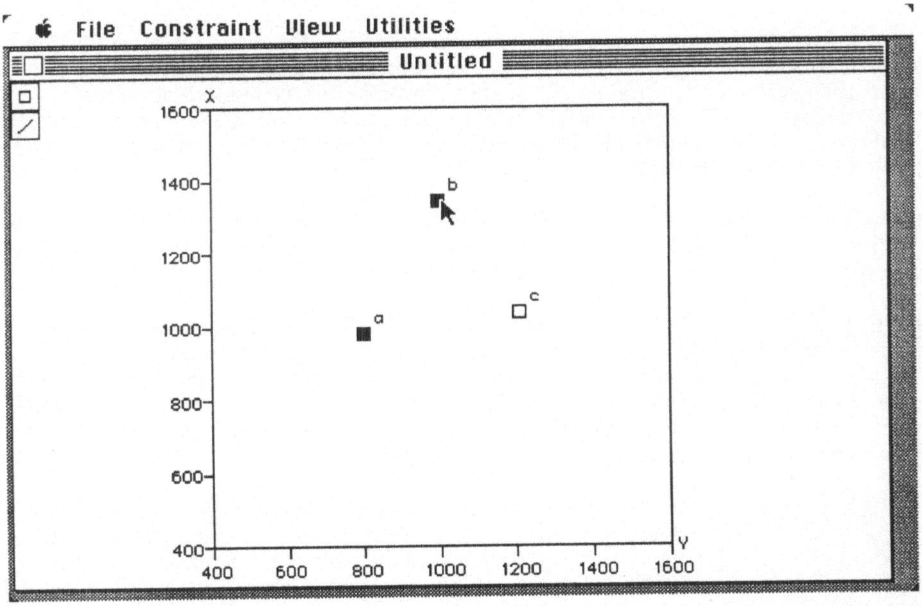

Figure 4. After setting a number of points in HILS, the user has selected two, indicated by a solid black square.

After setting some points the user may then select a point by clicking on its symbol in the viewport with the mouse. The symbol is then changed to indicate that it is selected. Additional points may be selected by holding down the Shift key and clicking. If the Shift key is not held down, the previous points will be deselected, and the one clicked on will be selected.

To add a constraint the user selects the appropriate number of points, and then chooses the type of constraint desired from the **Constraint** menu. A dialog is then presented in which the user enters the value for the constraint (eg, the desired distance between two points), and a value for the standard deviation of the constraint, which can be a measure of the estimated precision of a physical measurement (Fig. 5). The user then adds the constraint by clicking on the Constrain button in the dialog.

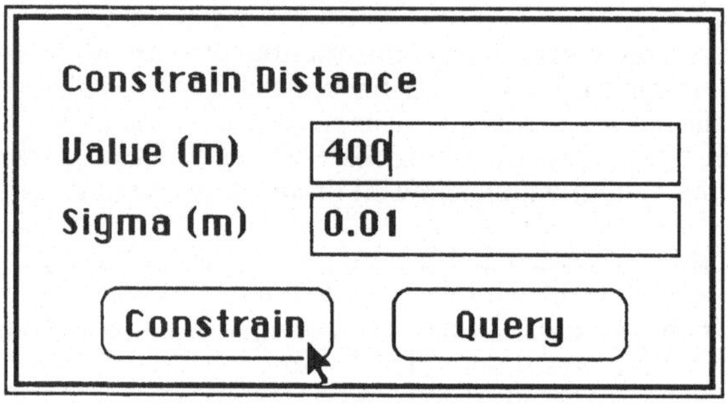

Figure 5. A constraint dialog box in HILS. In the 'value' box, the user types in the metric value needed for the constraint. In the 'sigma' box, the user may type in a value for the estimated standard deviation of the constraint, or may use the default value (shown).

It should be noted that in the true sense of direct manipulation, and following the principles set forth by such authors as Nievergelt [Nievergelt and Weydert 1979] and Shneiderman [Shneiderman 1986], only the constraints which are appropriate for the number of points currently chosen may be selected from the Constraints menu. This eliminates a potential source of errors, and provides a simple method of feedback from the system to the user about the current state of the system [Nievergelt 1982].

After setting a number of constraints, the user may wish to update the geometry. This is done by choosing **Adjust** from the Constraint menu. The system performs a least squares adjustment, and then redraws the screen to reflect the changed geometry (Fig. 6).

It is notable that the system does not require the user to add points, constraints, and lines, or adjust in a predefined sequence. The user could, for example, set two points, a distance, between the two points, tell the system to adjust, then add more points, and so on. Thus, the user can choose a path to the result which he finds convenient or natural. This is in contrast to COGO systems where the user is required to add information in a very restricted manner, such that each new point is computed from previously computed points.

HILS also offers a query mechanism by which the user can see what the existing values for coordinates, distances between points, etc are. This is done by again selecting the appropriate number of points and choosing the type of constraint from the constraint menu, as if he were going to add a new constraint. In the dialog box which is presented, the current value of, for example, the distance between the two selected points is displayed. Instead of clicking the Constrain button, the user clicks the Query button; the dialog is removed, and no constraint is added.

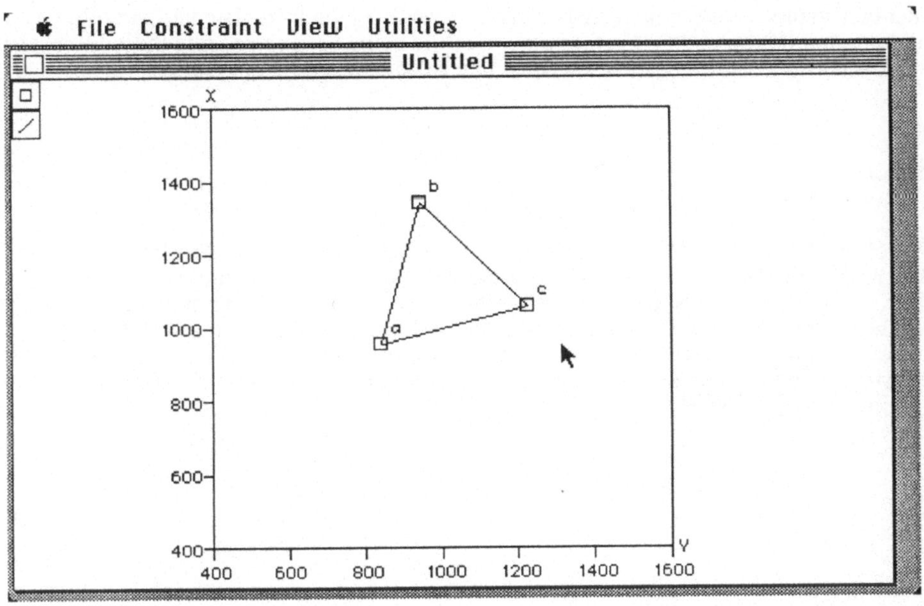

Figure 6. The HILS screen after the addition of all points and constraints, and adjusting. The geometry has been updated on the screen to show the solution for the collection of constraints.

Collections of points and constraints can be saved in the normal Macintosh manner by choosing **Save** or **Save As...** from the File menu. The geometry is stored as text in a file, in an easy to read (and most important, edit) command line format. The user could then use MacWrite [Apple 1984c], MDS Edit [Apple 1984a], or any other editor which can save the file in Text format to edit or print the point, line and constraint information. He can also open this file directly from the Finder (desktop), which starts HILS automatically, processes the file, and draws the geometry. The user may then continue with all of the previously mentioned functions of the system.

3.3. Further Research and Development

This system is currently in use in surveying classes at the Swiss Federal Institute of Technology, where some of the work to complete the prototype was accomplished. However, it is primarily a research tool used to explore the potential and limitations of interactive geometric construction.

In the future we plan to continue both research and development in this direction. With some work, the current demonstration version of HILS could be expanded such that is satisfactorily applicable in surveying and engineering offices. For further research we envision two main areas.

First, much more research must be done to solve the problems of graphical representation of multiple constraints, and likewise, interactive editing of constraints. Bertin presents theoretical reasons from the theory of graphics why these problems have no easy solutions [Bertin 1983].

The second main research topic is to develop the theoretical basis for a Geometric Constraint Calculus [Kuhn and White, 1988]. Such a calculus would provide basic constraints from which higher order constraints can be constructed. This is currently being formulated as part of a doctoral dissertation [Kuhn 1988]. Furthermore, HILS is being used to validate those ideas, and will be employed as a basis for a geometric constraint calculus system in the future.

4. Conclusions

An analysis of the the types of problems encountered in geometric construction systems leads to the conclusion that ruler and compass techniques can solve only a limited number of cases. Furthermore, the application of a least squares adjustment can provide a solution to the inherent disparity between the direct manipulation interface desired, and the mathematical techniques currently used. A prototype system, HILS, clearly demonstrates the feasibility of building a complete system which incorporates a declarative, direct manipulation interface in a general geometric construction program.

References

[Apple 1984a]:
Apple Computer Inc., Macintosh 68000 Development System User's Manual, Cupertino, CA, 1984.

[Apple 1984b]:
Apple Computer Inc., MacDraw User's Manual, Cupertino, CA, 1984.

[Apple 1984c]:
Apple Computer Inc., MacWrite User's Manual, Cupertino, CA, 1984.

[Bertin 1983]:
Bertin, Jacques, Semiology of Graphics, The University of Wisconsin Press, Madison, WI, 1983.

[Bier & Stone 1986]:
Bier, E.A., Stone, M.C, "Snap-Dragging", ACM SIGGRAPH '86, Computer Graphics, vol. 20, No. 4, August 1986.

[Borning 1979]:
Borning, Alan, "ThingLab: A Constraint-Oriented Simulation Laboratory", XEROX Palo Alto Research Center, Palo Alto, CA, 1979.

[Frank 1982]:
Frank, Andrew U., "PANDA: A Pascal Network Data Base Management System", Proceedings of the Fifth Symposium on Small Systems, Association of Computing Machinery SIGSMALL, Colorado Springs, CO, 1982.

[Frank 1986]:
Frank, Andrew U., Class Notes for Carto I, University of Maine Surveying Engineering, 1986.

[Kuhn and White 1988]:
Kuhn, W., "Formalizing the Domain of Geometric Constructions", Submitted to ACM SIGCHI Conference on Human Factors in Computing Systems, Washington DC, 1988.

[Kuhn 1988]:
Kuhn, W., "Konstrutkion und Speicherung geometrischer Modelle in räumlichen Informationssystemen", Dissertation (in preparation), ETH Zürich, Institut für Geodäsie und Photogrammetrie, 1988.

[Nievergelt and Weydert 1979]:
Nievergelt, J. and J. Weydert, "Sites, Modes, and Trails: Telling the User of an Interactive System Where He Is, What He Can Do, And How To Get Places", Institut für Imformatik Report No. 28, Swiss Federal Institute of Technology (ETH), Zürich Switzerland, 1979.

[Nievergelt 1982]:
Nievergelt, J., "Errors In Dialogue Design And How To Avoid Them", Institut für Informatik Report No. 47, Swiss Federal Institute of Technology (ETH), Zürich, Switzerland, 1982.

[Norman 1986]:
Norman, D.A., "Cognitive Engineering", D.A.Norman and S.W.Draper (Eds.): User Centered System Design, Lawrence Erlbaum Assoc., Hillsdale, NJ, 1986.

[Shneiderman 1983]:
Shneiderman, Ben, "Direct Manipulation: A Step Beyond Programming Languages", in Computer, Vol. 16, No. 8, 1983.

[Shneiderman 1986]:
Shneiderman, Ben, Designing the Human Interface: Strategies for Effective Human-Computer Interaction, Addison-Wesley, 1986.

[Sutherland 1963]:
Sutherland, I.E., "SKETCHPAD: A Man-Machine Graphical Communication System", Proc. of the Spring Joint Computer Conference, 1963.

[TML 1985]:
TML Systems, TML Pascal: User's Guide and Reference Manual, TML Systems, Jacksonville, FL, 1985.

Implementing a Definitive Notation for Interactive Graphics

M. Beynon and E. Yung (UK)

ABSTRACT

This paper describes the application of a definitive (definition-based) programming paradigm to graphics software. The potential merits of using definitive principles for interactive graphics were considered from a theoretical perspective in [Be87]; this paper is complementary, in that it describes the insights gained through practical experience in implementing a prototype system. The main characteristics of the prototype implementation are illustrated by simple examples. Analysis of the abstract machine model underlying this implementation suggests a general purpose programming paradigm based on definitive principles that can be applied to more ambitious applications.

Introduction

This paper describes the application of a novel programming paradigm to graphics software. The programming paradigm - "definitive programming" - is based upon the use of definitions for interaction. The potential merits of using definitive principles for interactive graphics were considered from a theoretical perspective in [Be87]; this paper is complementary, in that it describes the insights gained through practical experience in implementing a prototype system.

The notion of using definitive notations for interaction was first described in [Be85]. The essential principle in developing such a notation is to devise an "underlying algebra" of data types and operators which reflects the universe of discourse, and to introduce appropriate variables to represent values in the underlying algebra, either explicitly or implicitly, through a defining formula. In such a system, a **pure** definitive notation, a program - or **dialogue** - essentially consists of a sequence of variable definitions and evaluations. Perhaps the simplest example of such a notation is obtained by choosing the underlying algebra to be traditional arithmetic, when the dialogue resembles the use of a spreadsheet, stripped of its tabular interface.

As explained in [Be85], definitive notations appear to be very well-suited for dialogue. They make it possible to represent the state of a dialogue effectively, since the combination of implicit and explicit definitions allows both persistent relationships, and transient values, to be recorded. An important feature of a dialogue over a definitive notation is that all the information needed to determine the current state of the dialogue is automatically stored, and can be recovered by interrogating the variables to obtain their current definitions.

It is not our purpose in this paper to describe the detailed design of programming notations based on definitive principles; the illustrative examples below make use of abstract notations adapted from DoNaLD ("a definitive notation for line drawing"), and EDEN ("an evaluator for definitive notations"), and the interested reader is referred to [Be86a] and [Yu87] for more details. Our emphasis is upon introducing general principles and techniques that can be used to implement definitive notations for graphics, and - pursuing the directions suggested in [Be87] - can be developed to support much more sophisticated systems and applications than are illustrated here.

The paper is in two main sections. §1 introduces the principal features of the graphics notation DoNaLD, and illustrates how it may be used to describe a room layout so as to allow interactive experimentation with furniture configurations and room dimensions. §2 introduces the programming language EDEN, intended for the implementation of definitive notations. It also includes some program fragments showing how a DoNaLD dialogue is translated into EDEN. An examination of the abstract machine model underlying EDEN suggests a general purpose programming paradigm based on definitive principles. The paper concludes with a brief comparison between our approach and the use of constraint-based methods supported by object-oriented principles. Some future research directions are also outlined.

§1 DoNaLD: a definitive notations for line drawings

1.1 Basic principles

The DoNaLD notation (a "Definitive Notation for Line Drawings") is intended for the interactive display and manipulation of planar diagrams comprising points and lines. As a definitive notation, it is based upon an underlying algebra comprising five data types: **integers**, **reals**, **points**, **lines** and **shapes**, and a variety of simple geometric operators. Scalar values are represented by **integer** or **real** variables, points in the plane by **point** variables, directed line segments (that is, lines defined by an appropriate pair of endpoints) by **line** variables, and line drawings comprising a multiset of **points** and **lines**, together with a set of **real** and **integer** attributes by **shape** variables. Following the usual pattern, a DoNaLD dialogue then consists of a sequence of declarations of variables, definitions of variables of the form:

variable = formula

specifications of user-defined operators, and evaluations of variables. For this purpose, realising the line drawing represented by a **shape** variable is viewed as a special kind of evaluation.

The full details of the operators in the underlying algebra appear in [Be86a]. In brief, there are standard arithmetic operators, vector operators acting upon **points** viewed as 2-dimensional vectors, and a variety of operators on points and lines. The latter include constructors to synthesise a point in the plane from its component coordinates, and a line segment from its endpoints, and selectors to extract coordinates from **points** and endpoints from **lines** in the usual fashion. There are also geometric operators for rotating and scaling **shapes**, and an operator for combining two or more **shapes**.

1.2 Dealing with complex data types

The introduction of complex data types into the underlying algebra poses some problems for the definition and reference of variables (cf [Be85] and [Be87]). The solution to the reference problem for **shapes** adopted in DoNaLD is based upon a representation of a line drawing by a **shape** variable resembling that of a file system directory as a union of files and subdirectories. Such a representation corresponds to an abstract view of a line drawing as a union of points, lines and sub-drawings. In effect, it is based upon a recursive specification of the **shape** data type, viz:

shape = set of **real** / **integer** attributes + set of **points** + set of **lines** + set of **shapes**.

There are two kinds of variable of type **shape**; these are declared as "**shape**" and "**openshape**" variables, and are broadly analogous to "abstract" and "explicit" variables as described in [Be85]. The value of a **shape** variable is to be defined implicitly by means of an expression of type **shape**. An **openshape** variable, which resembles a directory, is composed of constituent **real, integer, point, line, shape** and **openshape** variables, and its value is defined componentwise by associating values with its constituent scalar attributes, points, lines and subshapes.

Each variable is either declared globally, or denotes a constituent of an **openshape** variable, which may itself be a variable of type **shape**. The value of a **shape** or **openshape** variable which is declared as a constituent of an **openshape** variable X is a *subshape* of the value of X, comprising a subset of the set of **points** and **lines** associated with X. The authentic variable name is that used to reference the variable from the global context, and is in general specified by a sequence of openshape variable names separated by '/''s to identify the enclosing openshape, followed by a local name to identify the appropriate constituent. (The syntax resembles filenames in UNIX directories.) A variable declaration thus takes the form

type var_name

where *type* is **integer, real, point, line, shape** or **openshape**, and *var_name* is of the form

context loc_var_name

where *context* is a concatenation

(*loc_var_name* '/')*

in which each *loc_var_name* references an **openshape** variable.

The semantics of **integer, real, point** and **line** variables is straightforward. A declaration of the form

openshape S

identifies S as an *explicit* **shape** variable, which is not itself an *l*-value, but enables the subsequent declaration of attributes and components of S. The subshape S can then be defined componentwise according to the normal semantic rules. In contrast, a declaration of the form

shape V

identifies V as a *virtual* **shape** variable, whose value and component structure must be defined by means of a **shape** expression, and, in particular, cannot be defined componentwise.

1.3 Changing contexts

The syntax of a DoNaLD dialogue is simplified by introducing an analogue of "changing the directory" in a file system; the hierarchical view of a line drawing as incorporating sub-drawings can then be reflected in the manner in which it is defined and referenced.

Formally, the set of variables associated with the **openshape** variable V consists of the points and lines of V, together with local scalar variables and all variables associated with subshapes of V. Definitions of the constituents of **openshape** variables are governed by a single *scope rule*: each subshape V/S of V, and all variables associated with V/S must be defined in terms of variables associated with V. Conceptually, the actions in a DoNaLD dialogue can be viewed as taking place in the context of a single universal **openshape** variable U, whose constituents are the **point, line, shape** and **openshape** variables not contained in any user specified **openshape** variable.

The construct used to specialise the dialogue to a particular context, and provide for all references to variables to be interpreted relative to an **openshape** other than U is:

within *context* { .... }

where a general sequence of actions, possibly including further **within**-clauses, is specified between the braces.

The scope rules permit a variable v within the openshape S (and necessarily not within any **openshape** subshape of S) to be defined in terms of variables defined in the enclosing context for S, rather than within S itself. To avoid having to leave the context of S in order to make such a definition, each variable associated with the enclosing context for S in the expression defining v can be prefixed by an escape symbol "\", to indicate that it is to be interpreted with reference to the enclosing context for S.

1.4 The user interface

A typical DoNaLD dialogue includes many definitions, not all of which can be conveniently displayed at once, reflecting different levels of abstraction in the description of a picture. The user-interface for DoNaLD is designed to reflect the way in which relationships at each level of abstraction are captured by a set of definitions, and is based upon a family of windows associated with **openshape** variables.

With each **openshape** variable, there is an associated context window, in which the appropriate local definitions are displayed together with the names of any local **openshape** variables, and through which the relationships within that context can be viewed and manipulated. The context windows are organised in a tree structure reflecting the hierarchical relationships between contexts. At the highest level of abstraction, and the root of the tree, there is a global window, in which all the declarations and definitions of variables at the outermost level are displayed. Each **openshape** variable in the global context defines a subcontext at the next level of abstraction, and its associated window is a child of the global window.

At any given stage in a DoNaLD dialogue, a number of windows can be open, but only one window is currently active. In general this is the window associated with the current context. In effect, all declarations and definitions made whilst a particular context window is active are interpreted as being in the scope of a **within** *current_context* clause. Each context window has a header to specify the **openshape** variable name relative to the universal context, and a footer comprising a set of "buttons" which are used for interrogation of variables or to change the current context, together with a dialogue box in which new declarations and definitions can be entered. Figure 2 illustrates how the definitions in Figure 1 might be presented via such an interface (for more details, see [Be86a].)

1.5 An illustrative example

The form of the basic notation introduced above is illustrated in the abbreviated dialogue depicted in Figure 1 below. A dialect of DoNaLD has been used; this makes use of a simple subset of the DoNaLD operators, but incorporates additional features for handling simple geometrical constraints. Figure 2 gives full details of the definitions in the context window associated with the **openshape** *room*, and the corresponding graphical display. (The dotted lines are used to indicate the extent of the geometric objects defined by the variables *door* and *desk.*) Figure 3 depicts the context windows of the **openshapes** that are introduced in the dialogue of Figure 1.

In Figure 1, the global context for the dialogue is the **openshape** *room*. The room is defined to be rectangular. The definitions used for this purpose include implicit definitions of the wall represented by the **lines** *E*, *S*, and *W* in terms of the corners of the room (the **points** *NW*, *NE*, *SW* and *SE*), and of the four corners in terms of the explicitly defined width, length and centre of the room. The remaining wall, represented by the pair of lines *N1* and *N2*, is implicitly defined in terms of the corners *NW* and *NE* and the location and dimensions of the door.

Figure 1 also illustrates the use of simple constraints. In DoNaLD, three types of constraint handling are envisaged; these are syntactically expressed in the form:

impose *B*, **monitor** *B*, **maintain** *B*

where *B* is a boolean variable defined to represent a condition expressed in terms of primitive arithmetic and geometric relationships. Each of the above constructs is to be read as the

```
int             width, length
point           centre, NW, NE, SW, SE
line            S, E, W, N1, N2

openshape       door
within door {
    boolean     open
    int         size
    point       hinge , lock
    line        door
    open = true
    size = 200
    hinge = \WW + {10, 0}
    lock = if open then hinge - {0, size} else hinge+{size, 0}
    door = [hinge,lock]
}

width = 800
length = 800
centre = {500, 500}
.
.
N1= [NW, door/hinge]
N2= [door/hinge + {door/size, 0}, NE]
.
.
openshape       desk
within desk {
    int         width , length
    point       centre, NW, NE, SW, SE
    line        N, S, E, W
    . . .
    width = 200
    length = 600
    . . .
    openshape drawer
    within drawer {
        int     width, length
        . . .
        length = \length div 4
        width = \width;
        . . .
    }
}
.
.
impose desk_in_room
desk_in_room = contains(room, desk)
monitor door_hits_desk
door_hits_desk = intersects(door, desk)
.
.
```

Figure 1: A sample DoNaLD dialogue

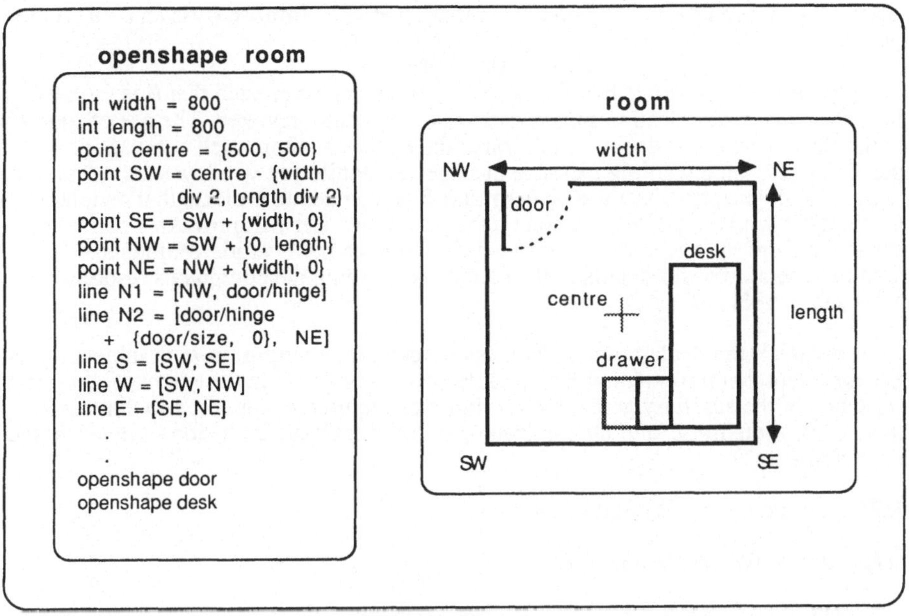

Figure 2: A context window and the corresponding display.

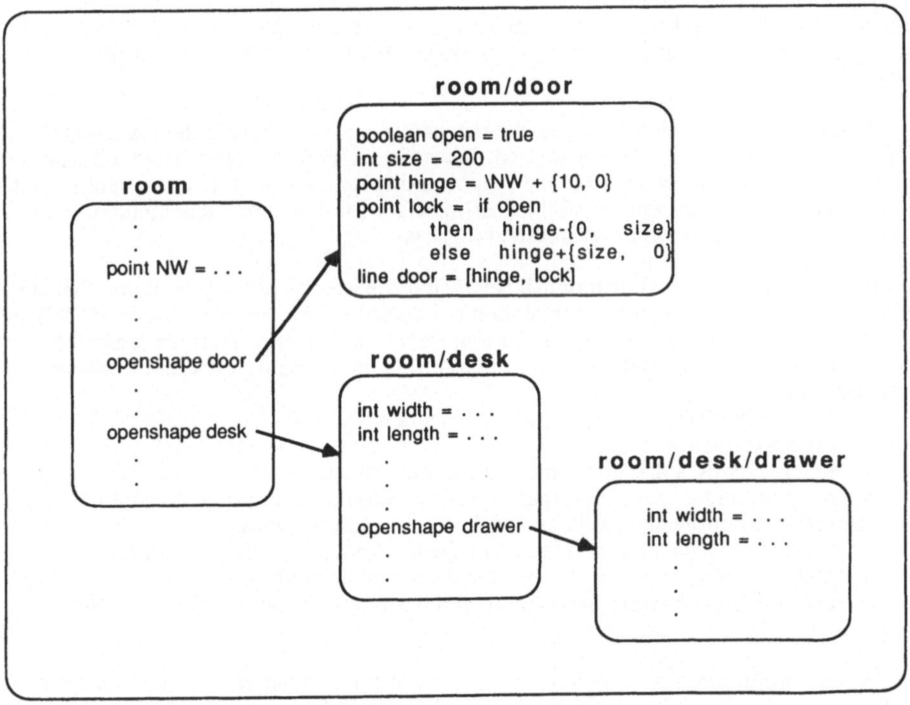

Figure 3: Context windows associated with Figure 1

declaration of a particular type of boolean variable: in effect, "**impose** *B*" is an abbreviation form of:

imposed constraint *B*

Semantically, **impose** *B* ensures that the state of dialogue is never such that *B* is violated; a dialogue action that would lead to such a state is automatically revoked. The use of **monitor** *B* on the other hand permits violation of the constraint *B*, but monitors such a violation - for example, by displaying a warning message in a special monitoring window whilst *B* is violated in the current dialogue state. The use of **maintain** *B* is intended to indicate that a violation of the constraint C through a dialogue action on the part of the user will provoke a computer response that restores a state of dialogue in which C is once more valid. (Maintenance of a constraint in general requires details of the actions prescribing the computer's response to a violation - see [Bo86] and §2.2 below.)

In Figure 1, the declaration of *desk* as an **openshape** within *room* is subject to the imposed constraint that the extent of the variable *desk* is contained in the extent of the variable *room.* (Details of the auxiliary geometrical primitives required to support **subshapes** - such as the extent of an **openshape**, and the boolean operators for **shape** inclusion - are left to the reader's imagination.)

§2 EDEN: an evaluator for definitive notations

2.1 Background to the implementation

The system of definitions and constraints in Figure 1 describes the semantic content of the user's interaction in a direct and simple fashion. The virtue of using a medium such as DoNaLD is that "the semantics of the current dialogue state" has an unambiguous interpretation, and the user-computer interaction can be conceived as a sequence of transitions from one system of definitions to the next. In effect, the procedural elements of the dialogue are encapsulated in dialogue actions, such as updating the parameter *door/open*, at a high level of abstraction. (Compare the representations of current state of the interface described in [Fo87b].)

In implementing such a dialogue, the mechanisms used to handle the textual and graphical displays also have to be considered. Just as in a spreadsheet the displayed values of variables must be continously updated, the graphical display must be kept consistent with the current dialogue state. Other aspects of the user-interface must also be implemented, such as the management of the context windows outlined in §1.4.

It will be convenient to distinguish between those aspects of the interaction that are concerned with the semantics of the application (eg does the door currently hit the desk?), and the more ephemeral issues concerning the current state of the display interface (eg is the context window for the **openshape** *desk* currently open?). In general, many different kinds of interaction must be supported:

user actions that affect the application semantics
(eg *door/open* = true)
computer responses that affect the application semantics
(eg revoking a user action that causes violation of an imposed constraint)
computer responses that are linked to the application semantics
(eg updating the current position of the door on the graphical display)
computer responses that are independent of the application semantics
(eg opening a context window when the user enters the context of another **openshape**)

In our present prototype implementation, the distinction between interaction involving the application semantics and interaction concerned with interface management is reflected in the mode of implementation. For modelling the semantics of the interaction in the application, we translate the DoNaLD dialogue into a lower level definitive notation that forms part of the implementation language. This means in particular that the current state of the semantic dialogue is explicitly modelled (albeit in a modified form) in the implementation. For dealing with the dynamic behaviour of the display interface, we then use conventional procedural programming techniques, linked - where appropriate - to the current state of the semantic dialogue.

In §2.2 below, we examine the advantages of our implementation strategy from a pragmatic perspective. In particular, we outline the main features of the programming language EDEN that has been developed as an evaluator for definitive notations, and illustrate how the dialogue in Figure 1 can be translated into EDEN. In §2.3, we consider the abstract machine model underlying EDEN, and propose a simplification that represents a new general purpose programming paradigm based on a direct generalisation of pure definitive notation. Some of the ramifications are briefly examined in §2.4. A key idea is that definitive principles can be used to describe all aspects of the interaction, not only the semantics of interaction in the application.

2.2 The EDEN language

The EDEN language (an "Evaluator for DEfinitive Notations") is intended as a general purpose software tool to assist the implementation of definitive notations [Yu87]. EDEN includes the traditional features of a procedural language: in this case, a subset of C. It also supports a definitive notation over an underlying algebra comprising **lists** (as in Lisp) whose atoms are either scalars or strings. The dependencies between the variables in this definitive notation are monitored at all times, and the current values of variables are selectively updated as required. Within EDEN, the user can define **list** functions to augment the underlying algebra, so that form of the **list** definitions can be very general. For convenience, variable type checking is handled automatically in EDEN, and no declarations of variables are required.

EDEN has an additional feature whereby procedural actions, whether in the form of redefinitions of explicitly defined **list** variables, or more traditional invocations of C-like procedures, can be linked to the semantics of the "internal dialogue" in the definitive notation. To this end, the user can specify a procedural action to be triggered when the value of a variable in the internal dialogue is altered, whether directly or as a result of the redefinition of another variable. (For a fuller account of the semantics of EDEN see §2.3 below.)

There are clear advantages in adopting EDEN as the implementation language. If a traditional procedural language is used, the simplicity of the definitive model of the current state of dialogue is obscured by the procedural mechanisms that must be invoked to effect state transitions, and great care is needed to ensure that other procedures (such as display procedures) operate in consistent dialogue states. These problems can be ameliorated by using an object-oriented programming paradigm for information hiding, but the synchronisation of update and display must still be specified explicitly. An EDEN implementation considerably simplifies the prescription of display actions linked to the semantics of the underlying application. It can also treat simple constraint management in an appropriate manner viz as direct manipulation of the state of the dialogue by the computer. (As a simple illustration, maintenance of the constraint "x==y" can be conveniently handled by introducing actions ensuring that if the value of x - respectively y - changes between one dialogue state and the next, then the dialogue action "**if** (x!=y) **then** y=|x|" - respectively "**if** (x!=y) **then** x=|y|" - is performed. Here "|x|" denotes "the current value of the variable x".)

A potential problem with EDEN is that it supports methods of programming that may be powerful but can be obscure and difficult to analyse. There is the possibility of interference between actions, and of non-termination through recursive invocation of actions. Triggering of display procedures still means that reasoning about the current state of the display during an interaction entails knowledge of the history of a complex sequence of events. These concerns motivate a closer examination of the abstract machine model underlying EDEN.

The above discussion can be illustrated by some simple fragments indicating how the DoNaLD dialogue in Figure 1 is translated into EDEN:

DoNaLD input	EDEN translation
int *width, length*	_ **is** [OPENSHAPE, _width, _length,
point *centre*	_centre, _NW, _NE, _SW, _SE,
point *NW, NE, SW, SE*	_N, _S, _E, _W];
line *N, S, E, W*	new_object(_centre, _NW, . . .);
.	**proc** P_centre: _centre { plot_point(_centre);
}	
.	**proc** P_NW: _NW { plot_point(_NW); }
.	. . .
.	
width = 800	_width **is** 800;
length = 800	_length **is** 800;
centre = {500, 500}	_centre **is** [POINT, 500, 500];
.	
.	
N1= [*NW, door/hinge*]	_N1 is [LINE, _NW, _door_hinge]
N2= [*door/hinge* + {*door/size*, 0}, NE]	_N2 is [LINE, vector_add(_door_hinge,
	[POINT, _door_size, 0]), NE];
.	.
.	.
openshape *desk*	_room_desk **is** [OPENSHAPE, _desk_width,
...];	
monitor *door_hits_desk*	
door_hits_desk = **intersects**(*desk,door*)	**proc** monitor_door_hits_desk: _door, _desk
	{ **if** intersects(_door, _desk)
	then print("door hits desk") }
within *desk* {	
int *width*	_desk_width **is** 200;
. . .	
}	

Note that in translating DoNaLD definitions to EDEN definitions, the translator prefixes object names with underscores (the identifier associated with the root shape *room* is suppressed). The EDEN definition "_ **is** [OPENSHAPE, . . .]" is equivalent to the sequence of variable declarations in the DoNaLD input; it defines the value of the variable "_" as a **list** whose first element is the type code OPENSHAPE, and whose subsequent elements are implicitly specified by the variables _width, _length, _centre etc whose definitions are introduced at a later stage.

The procedure *newobject* initializes the graphics segments. The syntax

proc *procedure_name* : *trigger* { *procedure_body* }

is used in EDEN to designate a procedure to be executed when the value of a trigger variable is altered. The triggered actions *P_centre*, *P_NW*, . . . are generated by the translator, and serve to update the graphics segments when the values of the DoNaLD variables *centre*, *NW*, ... are altered. (The procedure *plot_point* is a graphics display procedure written in EDEN.)

The EDEN definitions "_N **is** [LINE, ...]" and "_width **is** 800" are direct analogues of the corresponding DoNaLD definitions.

In the DoNaLD dialogue, the variables *width* and *length* act as two parameters of the room. The EDEN translation guarantees that the new shape of the room is automatically redisplayed when these parameters are changed. The triggered action associated with monitoring the constraint *desk_in_room* in DoNaLD behaves similarly.

2.3 The abstract machine model

Designing a medium for implementation is in effect designing an appropriate abstract machine code. The abstract machine model we have adopted solves the problem of representing the state of a general definitive dialogue by incorporating a low-level definitive notation as part of the machine code. In our case, the underlying algebra for this low-level notation is essentially based upon **lists** (as in Lisp) whose atoms are **integers**. The abstract machine can be then be viewed as having auxiliary definitive registers (DRs) that represent explicitly or implicitly defined **lists** and **integers**, and auxiliary machine instructions simulating the effect of redefinitions. The "hardware support" for the DRs includes a component that records the tree of dependencies between DRs, together with a mechanism whereby updating one DR automatically - ie as an indivisible action - selectively updates all dependent DRs. To implement a dialogue over an arbitrary definitive notation **D** on such a machine, the definitions in **D** are compiled into definitions in the low-level definitive notation in such a way that the updating of values of variables in **D** is carried out automatically. It will be convenient to refer to the "state of dialogue" within the abstract machine, as represented by the current definitions of the DRs, as the **internal dialogue state** (IDS), and the auxiliary machine instructions that update the IDS as the **internal transitions** (ITs).

As described, our machine model has the limitations of a pure definitive notation. It passively supports a user dialogue consisting of a sequence of variable definitions by recording and maintaining the functional relationships between variable values, but has no independent capability for contributing to the dialogue (ie changing the dialogue state autonomously) or invoking "external actions" such as are required to display updated values, or declare error conditions.

To elaborate our model further, we must provide a way to program autonomous action contingent upon current dialogue state. Since activities such as constraint processing require responses to user dialogue actions that directly affect the dialogue state (eg actions that restore the table to its original position if it is placed outside the room), it must be possible to program our abstract machine to perform actions that can conditionally update the IDS. To achieve this, a trigger mechanism is introduced whereby updating (ie altering the value of) a DR conditionally schedules a sequence of machine instructions for execution. An action queue is included as a component of the machine for this purpose; "scheduling a sequence of instructions" is then interpreted as "pushing the given sequence of instructions in order into the action queue". Programming the abstract machine can be viewed as associating a (possibly empty) set of rules with each DR. A typical rule for the DR v is then denoted v ~> p, read "v triggers p", where p takes the form of a guarded command **if** g **then** s. Such a rule is interpreted:

when *the DR v is updated by an internal transition*
  if g *is true in the current internal dialogue state*
    then *schedule the execution of the sequence of machine code instructions* s.

To summarise: a typical IT comprises the redefinition of a DR that automatically causes all dependent registers to be updated, all triggers associated with updated registers to be activated, and all sequences of machine code instructions associated with true guards to be scheduled. No guarantee is given about the order in which instructions within distinct guarded commands are scheduled; the only assurance is that the next instruction will be executed only when there are no pending instructions for scheduling.

At this stage, the full exploitation of the trigger mechanism has not been seriously investigated; nor does this appear to be necessary in the present application. To reassure the reader that there is some prospect of effective use of queues of triggered actions, a few comments are in order. In the first place, interference between definitions in a dialogue is easily identified: it occurs only between two or more definitions of the same variable, or when a variable dependent upon a variable redefined in one definition appears in an evaluated expression in another. In the second place, subject to non-interference between the ITs triggered by an IT, the IDS reached after execution of all the triggered ITs will be unambiguously determined irrespective of the precise order of execution.

2.4 An abstract machine model for definitive programming

Although the system of DRs and associated hardware has been presented above as a way of extending a conventional Von Neumann machine, it is clearly sufficiently powerful in its own right to merit consideration as an independent machine model. We propose to adopt this novel abstract machine model as an appropriate computational model for supporting definitive programming systems (cf [Be86b], which describes a closely related model incorporating concurrency). As might be expected, this abstract machine has very much the same characteristics as the EDEN language. On the one hand, it can be readily programmed to perform complicated tasks. On the other hand - even though the elimination of conventional machine instructions from our model leads to a considerable simplification - the possibility of interference between triggered actions and of pathological non-terminating behaviour remains.

At first sight, programming in the definitive machine model is problematical. Without the support of the conventional procedural framework, it is not immediately clear how a satisfactory complete implementation of DoNaLD is possible, for example. There are two main areas in which the current implementation relies on conventional programming techniques: the parsing of DoNaLD for translation into EDEN, and the user-interface management.

The problem of writing a parser using a definitive machine model has yet to be seriously addressed, though there seem to be prospects for using suitably defined dialogue states to simulate the states of a parser, and EDEN actions to perform the appropriate "semantic actions". (For the time being, conventional syntax-directed translation techniques are being used to convert DoNaLD input into EDEN.)

Our proposed solution to the problem of handling the display interface is to devise an appropriate definitive notation to describe the screen display. The triggered EDEN actions that formerly invoked procedures to display error messages, or to open a new context window, will then be replaced by dialogue actions in the display dialogue. The form of the definitive notation required is the subject of current research, but it is anticipated that there will be many advantages in adopting this approach. From the interface implementor's perspective, the format of the display interface can be partially described declaratively, and it will readily become possible to modify the display to reflect dynamically changing characteristics of the screen data. In effect, the current state of the screen display will be viewed as a system of definitions, rather than as a result of the cumulative effect of many procedure calls (cf [Fo87ab] and [Ha87]).

The reader who is apprehensive at the potential complexity of the abstract machine may take comfort from the fact that - as the EDEN fragments in §2.2 illustrate - its elementary use will suffice to implement most of the DoNaLD environment. It seems likely that constraint management is the only aspect that will call for more sophisticated use of the trigger mechanisms eg in using iteration for constraint satisfaction (cf [Bo86]).

§3 Retrospect and prospect

Though the practical development of definitive programming systems is as yet at an early stage of development, it is instructive to compare our approach with the object-oriented approach described in [Bo86]. The combination of declarative and procedural elements referred to in [Bo86] is itself a characteristic ingredient of programming with definitions. The role of SmallTalk as an implementation medium - in particular, the use of trigger mechanisms for the maintenance of constraints, and for animation - is in some respects similar to the use of the EDEN, as described in §2 above. (See also [Le87], where similar principles are applied in a different style.)

At present, our prototype system gives very limited support for constraints, but this does not reflect any difficulty of implementation other than that inherent in constraint manipulation as described in [Bo86] and [Ne85]. It should be possible to implement methods for constraint handling quite as sophisticated as these - by plagiarising [Bo86], and programming in EDEN rather than SmallTalk, for instance! Though there might be some virtue - perhaps eg some simplification - in translating techniques from an object-oriented to a definitive framework in this fashion, the development of definitive programming is not primarily aimed at simpler or more efficient implementation. The main advantage we anticipate in using the definitive programming paradigm lies rather in the conceptual grasp over the current state of an interactive dialogue that it provides [Be85]. At present, it is unclear how complex functional dependencies and the transparent acyclic system of functional dependencies provided by a pure definitive notation can be most effectively integrated to this end. In this connection, it should be noted that a simple functional relationship can sometimes obviate the need for a complex constraint. The parametrised definition of the door in Figure 1, for example, ensures that it is always within the room.

There are a number of important issues to be further explored. Our experience so far indicates that the use of definitive principles offers good performance, primarily because the information required to support incremental updating of images is stored in the form of dependencies between variables. It is also possible to envisage implementations that exploit parallel processing to maintain the current values of implicitly defined variables. To determine whether these advantages can be generally realised in practice, it will be necessary to investigate the most effective interfaces between our graphical models and graphical standards such as GKS. (We might alternatively attempt to specify graphical standards using our definitive approach, but this lies beyond the scope of our current programme.) Though all input to our system is at present textual, it would be clearly be more convenient to allow some direct input through the graphics interface. The only technical difficulty here is that the acyclic nature of our definitions restricts the choice of free parameters that can be explicitly changed. One solution might be to give the user visual cues to these parameters; an alternative solution would involve the development of interface routines to interpret direct references to the graphical images as oblique references to particular explicitly defined variables whose values can then be appropriately updated. For instance, pointing to the drawer of the desk in Figure 2 might be construed as referencing the integer parameter that determines how far the drawer is open.

This research forms part of a broader programme concerned with the application of definitive principles to the design and implementation of CAD software; an area in which the problem of developing interfaces within which to integrate many different representations for a geometric object is particularly acute (cf [La87] and [Ta87]). The graphical notation DoNaLD is much simpler than the notations envisaged for CAD applications [Be87], but our use of the definitive programming paradigm outlined above is equally elementary. It will be of particular interest to determine whether the use of functional programming concepts for specifying higher-order user-defined functions, or the use of symbolic manipulation to transform and simplify definitions, can be helpful in more sophisticated applications. The conspicuous absence of an explicit data base is also thought provoking.

Acknowledgements

We are much indebted to David Angier, Tim Bissell and Steve Hunt for contributions to the design of DoNaLD. We also wish to thank Mike Slade for helpful comments and suggestions.

References

[Am86] J Amsterdam, *Build a spreadsheet program*, BYTE July 1986, p97-108
[Be85] W M Beynon, *Definitive notations for interaction*, Proc hci'85, CUP 85
[Be87] W M Beynon, *Definitive principles for interactive graphics*, Proc NATO ASI: Theoretical Foundations of Computer Graphics and CAD, Il Ciocco, July 1987
[Be86a] W M Beynon, D Angier, T Bissell, S Hunt, *DoNaLD: a line drawing system based on definitive principles*, University of Warwick RR#86, 1986
[Be86b]W M Beynon, *The LSD notation for communicating systems*, University of Warwick RR#87, 1986
[Bo86] A Borning and R Duisberg, *Constraint-based tools for building user interfaces*, ACM Transactions on Graphics, Vol 5, No 4, October 1986, 345-374
[Ha87] P ten Hagen, R van Liere, *A model for graphical interaction*, Proc NATO ASI: Theoretical Foundations of Computer Graphics and CAD, Il Ciocco, July 1987
[Fo87a] J Foley, C Gibbs, W C Kim, S Kovacevic, *Formal specification and transformation of user computer interfaces*, Report GWU-IIST-87-10, Dept of Electrical Engineering and Computer Science, George Washington University, 1987
[Fo87b] J Foley, *Models and tools for the designing of user-computer interfaces*, Proc NATO ASI: Theoretical Foundations of Computer Graphics and CAD, Il Ciocco, July 1987
[La87] J Lansdown, *Graphics, Design and Artifical Intelligence*, Proc NATO ASI: Theoretical Foundations of Computer Graphics and CAD, Il Ciocco, July 1987
[Le87] C Lewis, *Using the NoPumpG Prototype*, University of Boulder, 1987
[Ne85] G Nelson, *Juno, a constraint-based graphics system*, SIGGRAPH '85, p235-243
[Ta87] T Takala, C D Woodward, *Industrial design based on geometric intentions*, Proc NATO ASI: Theoretical Foundations of Computer Graphics and CAD, Il Ciocco, July 1987
[Yu87] Y W Yung, *EDEN: an evaluator for definitive notations*, Final Year Project, Dept of Computer Science, University of Warwick , July 1987

GRAFLOG: Programming with Interactive Graphics and PROLOG

L. A. Pineda and N. Chater (UK)

Abstract

GRAFLOG is an experimental graphical and logical programming language. The system supports bidirectional mappings from graphical structures into logical structures, and the meaning of a complex graphical object is a regular function of the meanings of its constituent parts. Graphic scenarios are composed interactively from primitive graphical objects and relations, formally described by an underlying graphical grammar. Graphical symbols are introduced by deictic expressions, and represent *individuals* with their corresponding *properties*. Deictic expressions are used to impose semantic interpretations upon graphical symbols. Through logical expressions more complex interpretations are given to drawings. GRAFLOG is illustrated by an example in which the end-user is a cognitive psychologist. His view of the problem domain and the way he relates with the system are presented. GRAFLOG is programmed in PROLOG and GKS.

1. Introduction

Designers and programmers of interfaces, in particular interactive graphical interfaces for CAD applications, require a considerable amount of knowledge about graphic interaction, graphical software, geometry and topology to build these systems. Using high level tools, like GKS [6] eases the programmer's task; however, there is still a substantial set of concepts and tools which programmers have to grasp [5]. One of the issues involved in the design of interactive graphic applications is the relationship between the graphical functions and the user application. We support the view that user applications can be highly independent of the dialogue manager and the underlying graphic interactive software.

In our view, the semantics of graphic interaction plays an essential role. We stress the analogy between computer graphic interaction and linguistic interaction [8]. In this analogy, the design of graphic interactive interfaces involves the following stages: the lexical design, the syntactic design, the semantic design and the conceptual design. Lexical design involves the choice of the primitive tokens involved in graphical interaction, and the syntactic design involves the definition of the rules relating these tokens. There is common agreement in using this analogy in referring to these two design levels, and several models have been formalised. Techniques for formalisation include the use of BNF based specifications, state-transition-diagram-based specifications, programming-language-based specification, frames, flow diagrams, etc [9]. The semantic design stage is traditionally associated with the functions attached to grammatical rules. In some approaches the design of graphic interactive systems is composed of a set of functional building blocks, which are chosen by the end user to compose his own graphic interface [7]. These functions are related both with the interface design and with the end user model, or conceptual model, of the system as a whole. In our view these are two different layers of *semantics*. The design of the former set of functions involves specialised knowledge of graphics, but the latter should not. The tokens involved in graphic interaction, the syntax of the system, and the interaction mechanics should be given by the specialised programmer, because, as has been mentioned, the creation of this layer involves specialised knowledge. Graphics programming also involves the use of geometrical and topological knowledge which implies a great deal of specialisation. This kind of knowledge should be given in advance by specialists. On the other hand, the user model is used in directing the whole design effort. A user model can be thought of as the interpretation given to graphical symbols and their geometrical relations in drawings. These interpretations can be thought of as the linguistic concepts [2], or the intentions of users when graphics are created and they can be captured, and productively used, in a proper representational structure. In GRAFLOG, such a structure is the PROLOG programming language [3].

The role of PROLOG and GKS for programming complex graphical applications is a current research enterprise and some syntactic ideas have been advanced[1, 11] and a PROLOG binding to GKS has been developed [17]. In GRAFLOG the semantics of graphics is considered for this enterprise. In Section two, a typical interaction with the system is shown. Through the example, the theoretical features of the system are introduced. In Section three, the concepts of graphical grammar and its semantic interpretation are formally discussed. In Section four, a simple real application is shown, and the application is presented from the point of view of the end user, a cognitive psychologist.

2. A Graphical and Logical Coordinated dialogue

The system is an experimental interactive graphic interface for creating graphical representations and for giving them a logical, or conceptual, interpretation. The graphical interaction is driven by a linguistic facility, and when instances of primitive graphical symbols are incorporated in drawings, they receive a linguistic interpretation. The linguistic facility consists of a set of deictic expressions [12] such as *This is a mouse* or *What is this?*.

2.1. Introducing Graphical and Logical Representations

For adding a graphical symbol on the screen deictic expressions have to be typed in, for example: *Now this is a mouse* and *This is mickey*. When the first expression is typed in, a symbol from the icons menu is chosen with a pick device, and through the second an individual instance of that kind of symbol is inserted somewhere in the screen. The linguistic information given through the deictic expressions is captured by a logical representational system, and the graphical symbols themselves are represented in an analogical representational system. In the PROLOG notation the logical representation for the example is

mouse(mickey).

That is, there is an individual whose name is Mickey and he has the property of being a mouse. The linguistic name and the graphical symbol belong to different representative systems, but both kinds of symbols are related through the individual in reality that they are representing. This concept is illustrated in Figure 1.

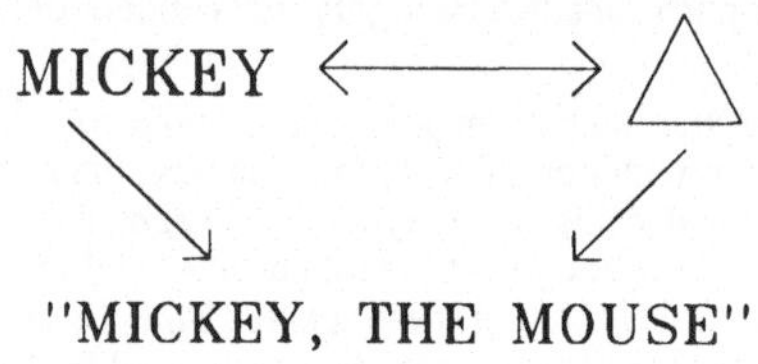

FIGURE 1: RELATION BETWEEN SYMBOLS AND REALITY.

The graphical symbol is represented by a relation in which a symbol identifier, the symbol type, and the parametric description of the symbol are held. The relation is defined and maintained by the graphical kernel, and the particular instance of the example looks like:

symbols_kb(symbol_1, triangle, PARAMETERS).

The association between both kinds of symbols is captured by a *representation function*, and for the example this function is:

represents(symbol_1, mickey).

The graphical kernel manages the identifiers of graphical symbols used in the representation function, and these identifier are also used as the reference of the GKS segment[10] in which each symbol is graphically stored.

Throughout the coordinated linguistic and graphical dialogue a representation of some state of affairs can be given. In the Figure 2, the triangle represents "Mickey" the mouse and the rectangle represents his house "Mickey's home". Each time a graphical symbol is introduced with the mechanism shown above, the system's kernel updates the logical representation, the representation function and the data-base of graphical objects. The encoding of the logical representation for the symbols in Figure 2 is as follows :

mouse(mickey).
house(home).

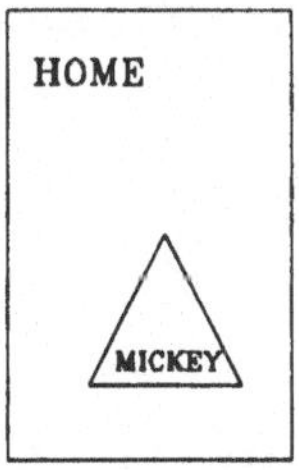

FIGURE 2: MICKEY AND HIS HOUSE.

The names depicted on the figures are shown for ease of explanation.

2.2. The Interpretation of Geometrical Knowledge

In Figure 2 there is additional knowledge that can be inferred from the graphical representation, such as the location of the graphical symbols, or the fact that the symbol representing Mickey is *in* the symbol representing his home. These facts are purely geometrical, but they can be named linguistically and used for drawing logical deductions. Natural language expressions referring to spatial notions are easy to find, for example, spatial linguistic prepositions, or comparative adjectives [12]. In the system, the graphical grammar consist of a set of rules for linking the linguistic to the graphical knowledge. These rules are primitive relations in GRAFLOG. The mentioned relations are defined as:

```
at(NAME, POSITION) :-
        represents(SYMBOL, NAME),
        g_position(SYMBOL, POSITION).

in(NAME_1, NAME_2) :-
        represents(SYMBOL_1, NAME_1),
        represents(SYMBOL_2, NAME_2),
        g_in(SYMBOL_1, SYMBOL_2).
```

In these rules, the functions prefixed with *g_* encode the predefined procedural geometrical knowledge that is asserted by the corresponding graphical grammar rule, that is, the knowledge needed for finding the position of the symbol for the *at* relation, or the geometrical predicate asserted through the *in* relation.

Given the primitive interpretations of graphical symbols and the rules provided by means of the graphical grammar, further complex interpretations can be introduced in the logical representation for expressing the user's linguistic concept of the drawing [2]. A very simple concept that the user might have in mind could be:

```
warm(mickey) :- in(mickey, home).
```

That is, if Mickey is in his home then he is warm. The PROLOG rule can be thought of as the semantic representation of the corresponding natural language sentence. In the current implementation of GRAFLOG, the natural language parser is restricted to analysing deictic expressions, and formulas like this have to be typed in PROLOG form. Although this is an over-simplification of the natural language parsing problem, the point to see is that the linguistic interaction can be interrelated to the graphical interaction through the graphical grammar. On the other hand, it is worth recalling that the sentence is an example of a linguistic interpretation that the user might have of the drawing and that this interpretation can be represented in the system, and as will be shown, used in modelling user's intentions when they are modelling or simulating problems to be solved. Given this state of affairs, users can ask for the concepts represented through the system, such as *mouse(NAME)?* or *warm(mickey)?* with the corresponding answers *NAME is mickey* and *yes.*

2.3. Modifying Drawings through their interpretations.

Through the interactive session, users can pick the symbol representing Mickey, and then change its position on the screen, as is shown in Figure 3.

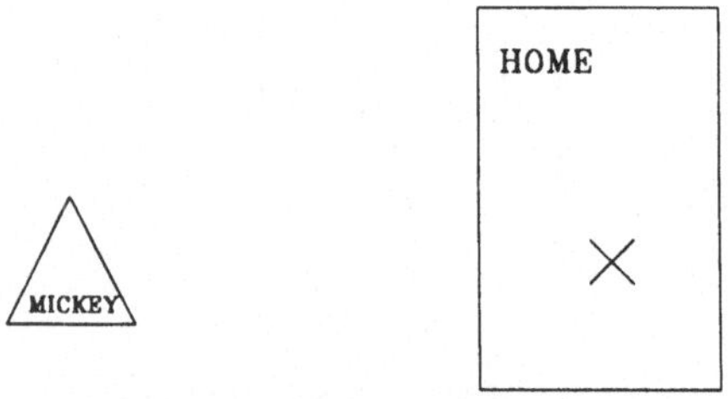

FIGURE 3: MICKEY IS OUT.

When users perform such graphical editing they have some intention in terms of what drawings mean for them [14] and such intentions can be formally represented and used by computer programs. When the transition is produced by this simple editing operation, the change from Figure 2 to Figure 3 is "blind" from the point of view of the system. In Figure 2 some facts were known to be true, and these facts are different from what can be known to be true in Figure 3, but the system has been given neither the knowledge of the relation between the states nor the reason for the transition. However, in users minds these states might be interrelated, for example, they can be thought of as two possible ways Mickey might be related to his "warmness". This kind of knowledge can be given to the system and used in the programming task.

Transitions between states can be modelled in the system if a set of functions is defined for modifying the graphics. For this purpose the relations *add, update, delete and query* have been defined. The forms of these relations are:

add(NAME, PROPERTY, TYPE, PARAMETERS).
update(NAME, PARAMETERS).
delete(NAME).
query(NAME, TYPE, PARAMETERS).

Through these relations users relate to graphical symbols with their linguistic interpretation, their names, and the system kernel links the two representational systems through the representation function. However, the user needs to know the form of the parameters of the corresponding graphical types; for example, triangles are parameterised by position and size, and rectangles by their bottom-left and top-right corners. Instances of these relations might be:

add(mickey, mouse, triangle, [POSITION, SIZE]).
add(home, house rectangle, [PO, P1]).

These functions are called by the system kernel when the parser recognises the natural language declarative deictic expression in the course of the linguistic and graphical coordinated dialogue, and they can also be directly requested by users through the logical representation, and then they can be used for building up the transformation functions reflecting the user intentions mentioned above.

If the user has the desire of Mickey getting warm, and the situation is as shown in Figure 3, then Mickey has to go home. There are two ways to achieve this state: editing the graphics, as already was shown, or telling the intention to the system. Assuming that this intention can be stated by the natural language sentence: *A mouse gets warm when he walks until he is in his house*, then we can state the imperative command *Mickey get warm.* The intention in the previous natural language sentences can be modelled with the following logical program:

```
get_warm(NAME) :-
        mouse(NAME),
        go_home(NAME).

go_home(NAME)  :- warm(NAME).
```

```
go_home(NAME) :-
                walk(NAME),
                go_home(NAME).

walk(NAME)    :-
                at(NAME, POSITION),
                one_step(POSITION, NEW_POSTION),
                update(NAME, [NEW_POSITION, ]).
```

The *get_warm* and *go_home* clauses are the representation of the natural language expression shown above. The *walk* clause can be though of as a procedural piece of code with domain specific knowledge, or if the graphical grammar is rich enough, as a piece of linguistic information referring to spatial relations that are interpreted in the context of the application. The *one_step* clause is a function which given the initial position of the symbol returns its new position and in the example it simply increments the value of the parametric position of the symbol in the horizontal direction. The clause *get_warm(mickey)* corresponds with the representation of the imperative command, and when the user requests the evaluation of this clause the system produces the set of states shown in Figure 4.

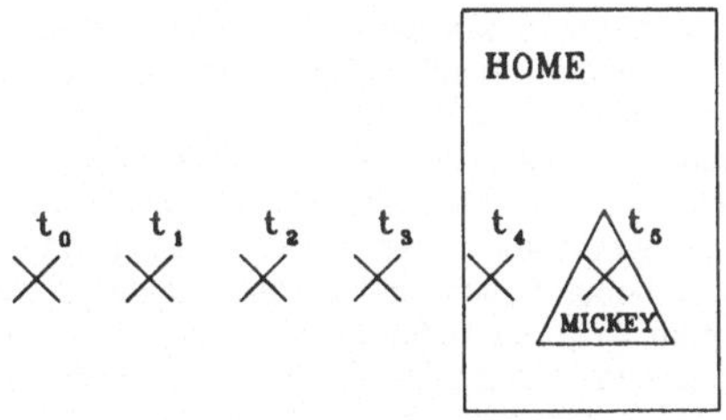

FIGURE 4: MICKEY GETTING WARM.

2.4. The States of the interaction.

In interactive computer graphics, models are constructed incrementally. For graphics used in simulation programs, different graphical states might represent the model at different times; for graphics used in the design process, different states might represent different possible descriptions, or models, of the object being designed. Then interpretations of drawings, understood through the graphical grammar, can be referred to the time or to the possible world in which they are representing the model.

In Figure 4 Mickey gets warm walking step by step until he is in his home. However, each time he walks one step, what is known to be true from the representation varies as well. The spatial properties computed through the graphical grammar are different, and then the facts asserted through the semantic interpretation imposed upon the drawing are not necessarily the same. In fact, given the nature of the "walk" process, we can say that pictures in different states are representations of the process which are true at different times. In other words, drawings can be thought of as representations of reality referring to a particular time instant, in a particular way the world could be in the model they are representing. This approach reflects a *modal theory* [4] for modelling the semantics of graphics. However, there is no need to make these indices explicit in the representational system because they are just a theoretical tool to establish a clear distinction between the meaning of graphics in the different graphical states in the interactive session. The transition of the time index in Figure 4 is caused by the *update* relation of the *walk* clause. In fact, the semantics of the functions *add, update* and *delete* is just to update the indices of time and world of the representation, because they produce representations that reflect the model in a different situation or at a different time.

2.5. The System's Initiative

In the situation modelled by the program of the example, the clause *warm(mickey)* is a fact which becomes true whenever the function *get_warm(mickey)* is satisfied by the PROLOG interpreter. In the situation shown in Figure 3, the satisfaction of this clause was requested by the user; however, the evaluation of the clause might be requested by the GRAFLOG interpreter itself. The GRAFLOG interpreter can be given a set of facts that must remain true through all the interaction session. For each one of these conditions a transformation function must be defined. These functions must have the knowledge for mapping any state in which its associated condition does not hold, to some state in which this condition is satisfied. The interpreter checks these conditions at the end of any interaction cycle. If the clause *warm(mickey)* is given as one such condition, when the user edits the drawing shown in Figure 2 to produce the drawings shown in Figure 3 the interpreter will call the evaluation of the transformation function *get_warm(mickey)*, before returning control of the interaction to the user. These rules are called by the interpreter not only after some graphical editing operation has taken place, but also after the evaluation of any transformation function that has been requested by the user. When the condition and its associated transformation function are given to the system they are incorporated in a structure called the *background set*. For the condition *warm(mickey)*, and its corresponding transformation function *get_warm(NAME)*, the entry in the background set is of the following form:

```
get_warm(NAME) :- warm(NAME).
get_warm(NAME) :- mouse(NAME), go_home(NAME).
```

The structure shown is a small recursive program built up from two clauses; the first rule links the transformation function with the condition, and then plays the role of final condition for the recursion, and the second rule produces the transition whenever the condition does not hold. At the end of any interaction cycle, the system kernel adds these two rules to the current evaluation environment and then it traits to satisfy the condition *get_warm(mickey)* defined in the background set. Of course if the transformation function does not produce the final condition the program will loop; however, these rules are very strong and they might be used just for bounding the semantic space of the model being represented by the drawings. For example, to state conceptual knowledge about the application domain. With the definition of this kind of rule, a notion of *system equilibrium* arises. The system is in equilibrium just in case the current graphical representation satisfies all the conditions given in the background set. In a sense, we can think of the system as taking the initiative when it is not in equilibrium, and trying to reach this state through the transformation functions. This knowledge stands in the background of the system and it guides the linguistic and graphical dialogue in which the user is engaged in the course of the programming session.

3. The Graphical Grammar

In the current implementation of GRAFLOG, there are five primitive types, and a set of graphical grammar relations. The graphical types are *dot, line, triangle, rectangle* and *circle* [15]. The only relation for symbols of type dot is:

```
at(NAME, POSITION).
```

The relations for symbols of type line are:

```
origin_of(NAME, SEGMENT, ORIGIN).
angle_of(NAME, SEGMENT, ANGLE).
length_of(NAME, SEGMENT, LENGTH).
```

The relations for symbols of type triangle, rectangle and circle are:

```
area_of(NAME, AREA).
at(NAME, PARAMETRIC_POSITION).
```

There are a set of graphical grammar relations which refer to "complex graphical types". They assert geometrical relations between instances of different symbols of a certain graphical type. These relations are:

in(NAME_1, NAME_2).
distance_between(NAME_1, NAME_2, DISTANCE).
links(NAME_1, NAME_2, NAME_3).

This concept of graphical grammar is rather similar to the concept of grammar in the theoretical study of natural language. The basic symbols can be thought of as analogous to words, and their geometrical properties can be thought of as the phonological components of words[12] because they can be given semantic interpretations and then they perform a function in the system. Combinations of graphical symbols can be given semantic interpretations, in the same way words of different grammatical categories combine to form sentences, and then they might be related to reality through the semantic value, true or false, of the assertion they make in drawings [16].

Regular syntactic structures can be given semantic interpretations as functions of their primitive components and their mode of grammatical relation. The interpretation of drawings is then a function of the interpretation of the graphical symbols, of their graphical properties and of their geometrical relations. This is Frege's compositionality principle[4] applied to graphical representations [16]. Frege's principle has been used implicitly throughout this paper for understanding and transforming drawings.

The concepts of graphical grammar and semantic interpretation of drawings are useful because there is a distinction that has to be made between the nature of the geometrical knowledge itself and the way it used or interpreted when drawings are created and understood. Geometry is a set of axiomatic truths that are independent of any application. But the way geometry is used in drawings implies application domain interpretations. The concept of graphical grammar allows the establishment of a clear demarcation for these two layers of knowledge, and then, graphical systems can be given in advance the knowledge of geometry. Besides, though no research has yet been done it is easy to foresee a graphical grammar incorporating topological knowledge as well. The concept of interpretation allows the use of the geometrical knowledge in the particular problem domain in which users are interested. An advantage offered by this programming paradigm is that systems can be given a rich set of specialised geometrical and topological knowledge, defined by experts, and users just have to make use of what they need in the context they are interested in.

4. An Application: the end user perspective.

Firstly let us characterise the paradigm problem which we must address. A rat is placed in a milky tank of water. Somewhere just beneath the surface is a platform upon which the rat may stand. On his first immersion the rat swims about until he chances on the platform, and stands upon it. This becomes the goal. When the rat is reimmersed at some later time he must remember the location of the platform. He is able to do this by using the various landmarks that have been carefully placed around the pool. The computational question that we must address is "How does the rat use the landmarks to relocate the platform?". This paradigm has been the subject of much experimental [13] and theoretical [18] interest.

Let us first put aside some important questions. First, we do not intend to model the workings of the rat's visual system. We shall merely take some appropriate output from this system as the input to our model. For example, we may merely assume that such information as the distance of each landmark from the rat is available. Second, we do not intend to model pattern landmark recognition - we merely assume that landmarks *L1*, *L2*, *L3*, of the learning phase, may be uniquely and correctly matched up with landmarks *L1'*, *L2'*, *L3'*, of the goal location phase. This is important because much experimental work in the area has used landmarks which are visually indistinguishable. Hence, a significant computational problem for the rat is making the appropriate mapping between the *L* and *L'* landmarks. We shall present the basic model, which is based on an analogy with the dynamics of systems of springs in physics.

4.1. The Model

Let us imagine that the rat is at goal *G* and that the landmarks are *L1*, *L2*... How is the rat to remember *G* so that he can find it again? The analogy is this (see Figure 5). Imagine that the rat constructs a linear spring from his location, *G*, to each of the landmarks, where this spring is of the length of the path from the goal to the landmark. Imagine further that all of these springs are connected at the rat's location (currently *G*). Of course, the system of springs is in equilibrium at this point, as none of the springs are in tension. There will, in general be just one other stable state if we have just two landmarks, and no other stable states at all if we have more than two landmarks.

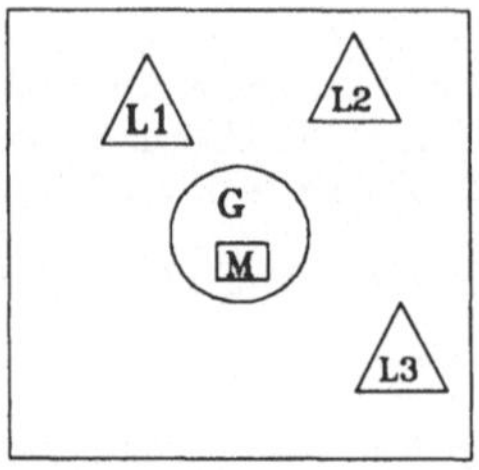

FIGURE 5: THE RAT'S GOAL.

Now imagine that the rat is displaced to location *A*. Hence the springs will be in tension (some will be stretched, others will be compressed). The system of springs will, of course, tend to pull the rat back to the stable location *G*. This is, in outline, the mechanism for goal location. The rat implements an algorithm which makes it follow the trajectory prescribed by the physics of linear springs. The direction of motion at any given point is determined by the vector sum of the "forces" acting on the rat. The force exerted by each spring is in the direction of that spring, and of a magnitude proportional to the amount that the spring has been stretched. This is just the disparity between the distance of a given landmark from *G* and the distance of that landmark from *A*.

The algorithm is written as a standard GRAFLOG program, which specifies the appropriate direction of movement for the rat give the landscape. Scenarios are known by the program through the primitive relations available in the graphical grammar. The updated location is passed to the graphics component, and the rat's new location is graphically represented, as shown below. The importance of the system, as a research tool in theoretical psychology, is that i) the landmark, goal and rat positions may be specified interactively, using the "mouse"; ii) the algorithm by which the rat updates its position may be changed straightforwardly. The output gives us the path that will be generated in a given landscape, with a given algorithm. Thus it is easy to test the plausibility of one's algorithm and derive experimental predictions from it. Thus it becomes possible to rapidly develop and test new algorithms. For example, an interesting experimental result is that if the whole landscape is uniformly scaled up by, say, a factor of two, then the rat will head for the location corresponding to the image of the goal under the transformation. Our simulation shows that the present algorithm will not give this behaviour.

The applications development is reduced to describing the graphics scenario and writing the GRAFLOG code. The graphic scenario is interactive described through the deictic expressions and graphic interaction. The condition of *in(mickey, platform)* is stated in the background set, and the model is described as its associated transformation function *find_goal(NAME)*. In the scenario, the rat is inserted inside the platform because it is the only state the system is in equilibrium. For the simulation, the rat is picked and moved to the desired starting position. At the end of the interactive cycle the interpreter checks and evaluates the background rule for mapping the rat unto the platform. The path of the rat is recalled as a graphical symbol of type line. When the rat reaches its goal the system is equilibrated and the interactive control is retuned to the user, who can create as many paths as are needed. The simplicity of the program shows that the end user need not pay attention to the graphic interaction, because he need merely deal with the logical interpretations that he imposes upon the graphical symbols rather than the symbols themselves. The code is:

```
find_goal(NAME) :-
        rat(NAME),
        new_path(NAME, PATH_NAME),
        swim(NAME).

new_path(NAME, PATH_NAME) :-
        at(NAME, POSITION),
        get_name(PATH_NAME),
        add(PATH_NAME, path, dot, POSITION).
```

```
swim(NAME,_) :- in(NAME, platform).

swim(NAME, PATH_NAME) :-
        query(PATH_NAME, dot, POSITION),
        delete(PATH_NAME),
        swimming_step(NAME, NEXT_POSITION),
        append(POSITION, NEXT_POSITION, PATH_DESCRIPTION),
        add(PATH_NAME, path, line, PATH_DESCRIPTION),
        swim(NAME, PATH_NAME).

swim(NAME, PATH_NAME) :-
        swimming_step(NAME, NEXT_POSITION),
        query(PATH_NAME,_,_,OLD_PATH),
        append(OLD_PATH, NEXT_POSITION, NEW_PATH),
        update(PATH_NAME, NEW_PATH),
        swim(NAME, PATH_NAME).
```

The clause *new_path* is an instantiation function which creates the graphical entity standing for a path. The path is created as a symbol of type dot located "at" the current position of the symbol standing for the rat. The *swim* rule consist of three clauses: the first is the final condition for the recursive transformation function; the second is called when the rat moves its first *swimming_step* through the platform, and it deletes the path that has been created as a dot, and adds the same entity but now defined as a symbol of type line; and finally, the third instances of the *swim* clause finds the next point in the rat's path, updates the rat's position, updates the path's description and calls the recursion. The clause *swimming_step* is the application model, and for its definition the user has available the logical representation of the symbols in the scenario and the primitive geometrical knowledge defined through the graphical grammar relations; for example, he makes use of the *at*, and *distance_between* relations, and then his programming task is very simple. Besides, when the paths have been created, the user can query and impose interpretations to their characteristics through the *length_of*, *angle_of* and *origin_of* relations, that is, the graphical grammar relations for symbols of type line.

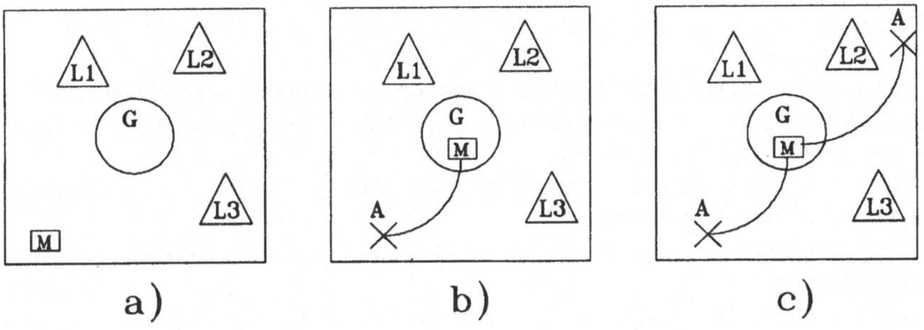

FIGURE 6: MICKEY SWIMMING TO GET HOME

5. Conclusions

GRAFLOG provides an example of a practical programming paradigm. PROLOG is itself a very high level programming language, but its power is strongly enhanced by giving the user, through graphics, a better grasp of the ontology of the individuals represented in programs, and of their primitive properties and relations. The paradigm is also recommended by the clear demarcation established between primitive geometrical knowledge and the application dependent interpretation given to geometrical symbols and relations. This programming paradigm further suggests a long term research goal in which intentions of users might be given to programs with natural language expressions instead of their corresponding logical representations, and then the programming task would be as human conversation, that is, through words and pictures.

Acknowledgements

The authors acknowledge the support and encouragement of Ewan Klein at Cognitive Science, and Aart Bijl, John Lee and Ramesh Krishnamurti at EdCAAD. We also acknowledge the helpful comments made by the anonymous referees of the paper. Luis Pineda is supported by a grant from the Mexican National Council for Science and Technology (CONACYT-44722), and by the Instituto de Investigaciones Eléctricas (IIE), México.

References

1. W Huebner and Z I Markov, "GKS Based Graphics Programming in PROLOG", pp. 277-292 in *GKS Theory and Practice*, ed. P. R. Bono & I. Herman,Springer-Verlag, Berlin (1987).
2. A Bijl, "Making Drawings Talk: Pictures in Mind and Machines", *Computer Graphics Forum* **6**(4) pp. 289-298 (1987).
3. W F Clocksin and C S Mellish, *Programming in Prolog*, Springer-Verlag, Berlin Heidelberg (1981).
4. D R Dowty, R E Wall, and S Peters, *Introduction to Montague Semantics*, D Reidel Publishing Company, Dordrecht, Holland (1981).
5. J Encarnacao, "Incorporating Knowledge Engineering and Computer Graphics for Efficient and User-Friendly Interactive Graphic Applications", pp. 9-11 in *Eurographic'85 Conference Proccedings*, ed. C. E. Vandoni,Elsevier Science Publishers B. V., North-Holland (1985).
6. G Enderle, K Kansy, and G Pfaff, *Computer Graphics Programming: GKS - The Graphics Standard*, Springer-Verlag, Berlin Heidelberg (1984).
7. G Fischer, "An Object-oriented Construction and Tool Kit for Human-Computer Communication", *Computer Graphics* **21**(2) pp. 105-109 (1987).
8. J D Foley and A van Dam, *Fundamentals of Interactive Computer Graphics*, Addison-Wesley, Reading, Massachusetts (1984).
9. R Jacob, "A Specification Language for Direct-Manipulation User Interfaces", *ACM Transactions on Graphics* **5**(4) pp. 283-317 (1986).
10. R Krishnamurti, "PROLOG/GKS Reference Manual", EdCAAD, University of Edinburgh (1987).
11. J Lee, "A Simple Picture Description System in PROLOG", *Edinburgh Architecture Research* **13** pp. 78-90 (1986).
12. J Lyons, *Introduction to Theoretical Linguistics*, Cambridge University Press, Cambridge (1968).
13. R G M Morris, P Garrud, J N P Rawlins, and J O'keefe, "Place navigation impaired in rats with hippocampal lesions", *Nature*, (297) pp. 681-683 (1982).
14. L A Pineda, E Klein, and J Lee, "GRAFLOG: Understanding Graphics Through Natural Language", *UKEurographic's 88 conference*, (1988).
15. L A Pineda, *GRAFLOG: A Graphical and Logical Programming Language*, Centre for Cognitive Science, University of Edinburgh (1988).
16. L A Pineda, *A Compositional Semantic for Graphics*, Centre for Cognitive Science, University of Edinburgh (1988).
17. P Sykes and R Krishnamurti, "GKS Inquiry Functions within PROLOG", pp. 269-276 in *GKS Theory and Practice*, ed. P. R. Bono & I. Herman,Springer-Verlag, Berlin (1987).
18. D Zipser, "Biologically plausible models of place recognition and goal location", in *Parallel Distributed Processing: Explorations in Microstructures of Cognition*, ed. McClelland & Rumelhart, (1986).

Modelling and Building Graphics Systems: GKS

M. Boano, R. Brazioli, S. M. Fisher, P. Palazzi, and W. R. Zhao
(Switzerland, UK and China)

ABSTRACT

The GKS-2D standard specifications were expressed by a combination of the Entity-Relationship (ER) model with Dataflow and State Transition diagrams. Our description was not only precise and complete, but also easier to understand than the original standard, mainly because of the use of diagrams. Starting from this description a GKS system was rapidly constructed making use of a general purpose subroutine package for ER data definition and manipulation. The performance of this GKS was found to be similar to that of commercially available products. Our description was extended to GKS-3D and is generally applicable to any graphics system. We suggest that such an approach would lead to more rapid convergence in the design of graphics standards and the construction of the corresponding systems.

INTRODUCTION

The Graphical Kernel System (GKS) is registered as an ISO Standard for computer graphics programming. It is specified in the Standard by words - with a few informal diagrams to aid understanding.

GKS provides a set of low level functions for graphics programming that can be used by applications to produce computer generated pictures. It provides a functional interface between an application program and a configuration of graphical input and output devices at a level of abstraction that hides the peculiarities of device hardware.

The standard took a long time to produce. GKS may be considered to have been started at the Seillac I meeting in May of 1976, and GKS 7.2 was a Draft ISO standard ISO/DIS 7942 in 1983. It became a full standard in 1986. Commercial packages were slow to appear. Tektronix produced a level 2b version in 1984, and Digital a 0b version in 1985.

To shrink this enormous time span, which results in obsolescent products, one must move rapidly from first specification to a working system. For this to be possible the specification must be clear to allow wide exchange of ideas and there must be a simple way to construct the system from its specification.

EXISTING SPECIFICATIONS

GKS <ISO82> is specified in the standard mostly by words and a few diagrams. Figure 9 of the standard, for example, attempts to provide an overview of a GKS system. It looks plausible, but, when examined in detail, it is not possible to check the diagram in any formal way because it uses symbols in an inconsistent manner.

Definitions of objects are widely scattered. For example, the polyline is first mentioned in the GKS standard in the list of definitions near the beginning (page 9):

"polyline: A GKS output primitive consisting of a set of connected lines".

This is not a complete description. The fact that a polyline has attributes (for example LineWidth) is only mentioned much later in section 4.4.3. Objects are generally understood much better when their attributes are identified. Chapter 6 of the standard describes the data objects of GKS but not their inter-relationships.

The Vienna development method (VDM) has been recently applied to GKS specification <DUCE86>. This is an algebraic method, which though precise, takes time to understand. This would reduce the value of the specification at the earliest design stage, where free exchange of ideas is vital. We also know of no simple path from a VDM specification to a working system.

SPECIFICATION WITH ER, DATA FLOW AND STATE TRANSITION DIAGRAMS

Our specifications make use of the Entity-Relationship (ER) model, coupled to the dataflow diagrams (DFD) of Structured Analysis <DEMARCO78> and state transition diagrams. Mathematical transformations were specified using FORTRAN statements.

Entity-Relationship

A data model consists of the definition of data structures, of operations on the data and integrity constraints. The ER model <CHEN76> organises data as entities which are objects characterised by their properties (known as attributes) and their relationship to other entities. An ER diagram is a pictorial representation of sets of entities (denoted by a rectangle) and their relationships (shown by an arrow). The attributes of the entity set are not shown on these diagrams, but are present in the complete description represented by the Data Definition Language (DDL).

The complete GKS-2D is described by 32 Entity Sets, which have been grouped into four ER diagrams. Figure 1 shows one of the four: the 'PICTURE'.

In GKS, pictures are constructed from a number of basic blocks, called output primitives, which are abstractions of the basic actions that a graphical output device can perform (e.g. drawing a line). There are six output primitives in GKS: polyline, polymarker, text, fill area, cell array and generalized drawing primitive (GDP), each of which has associated with it a set of parameters, for a particular instance of the primitive.

GKS allows output primitives to be grouped together into units known as segments which are stored and may be manipulated as a single object.

A segment may contain many graphics primitives; it may also be empty. This is shown by the word 'Segment' inside a rectangle representing the entity set 'Segment'. The relationship between 'Segment' and 'Primitive' is shown by the arrow. The 2 arrow heads indicate that there may be more than one instance of 'Primitive' in a 'Segment', and the bar by the arrow heads shows that there may be none.

A 'Segment' may be drawn many times on a workstation 'Ws', but must always be drawn at least once. Work Station Independent Segment Storage - the WISS is regarded as a workstation. A workstation may exist with no segment or it may have many drawn on it. Each instance of a 'Segment' being drawn on a workstation 'Ws' corresponds to an entity in the entity set 'Draw'.

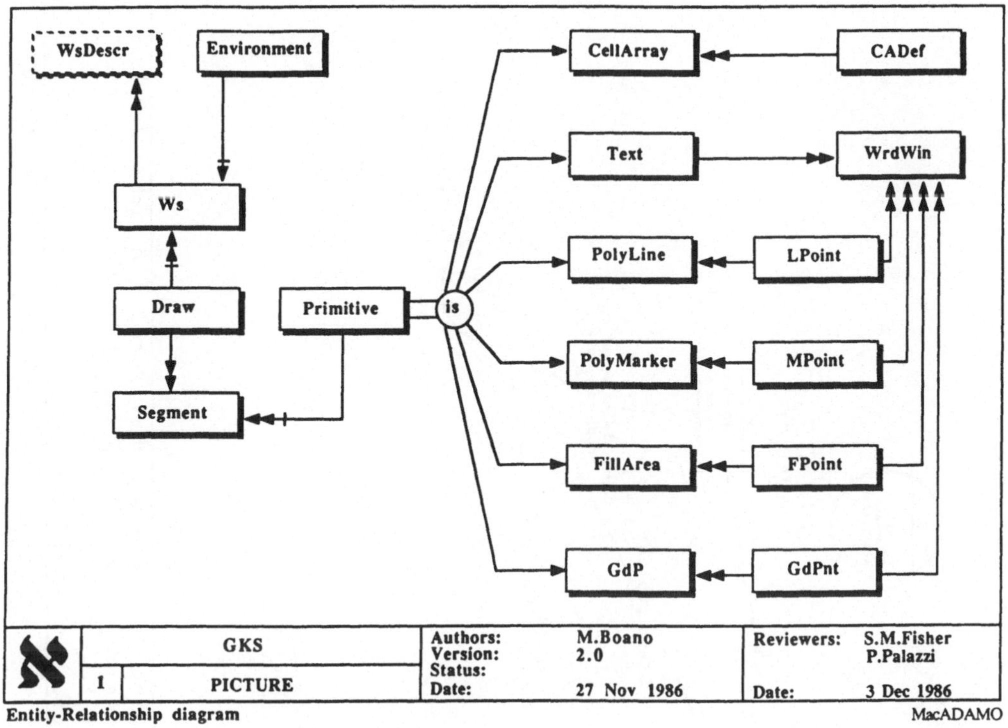

Figure 1: The 'PICTURE' ER diagram

```
DEFINE ESET

  PolyLine : 'a 2-D graphical point for Polyline primitive'
           = (Index = INTE            : 'Index in a GKS sense',
              LType = INTE [1,4]      : 'linetype : GLSOLI=1
                                                    GLDASH=2
                                                    GLDOT =3
                                                    GLDASD=4',
              LWidth= REAL            : 'width scale factor relative
                                          to WS standard line width',
              LnCol = INTE            : 'individual colour');


  LPoint   : 'a 2-D graphical point for Polyline primitive'
           = (P(2)  = REAL            : 'x = P(1), y = P(2)');


DEFINE RSET

  (LPoint [1,1] -> [2,*] PolyLine )
           : 'each polyline is related to at least 2 points';
```

Figure 2: An extract from the DDL

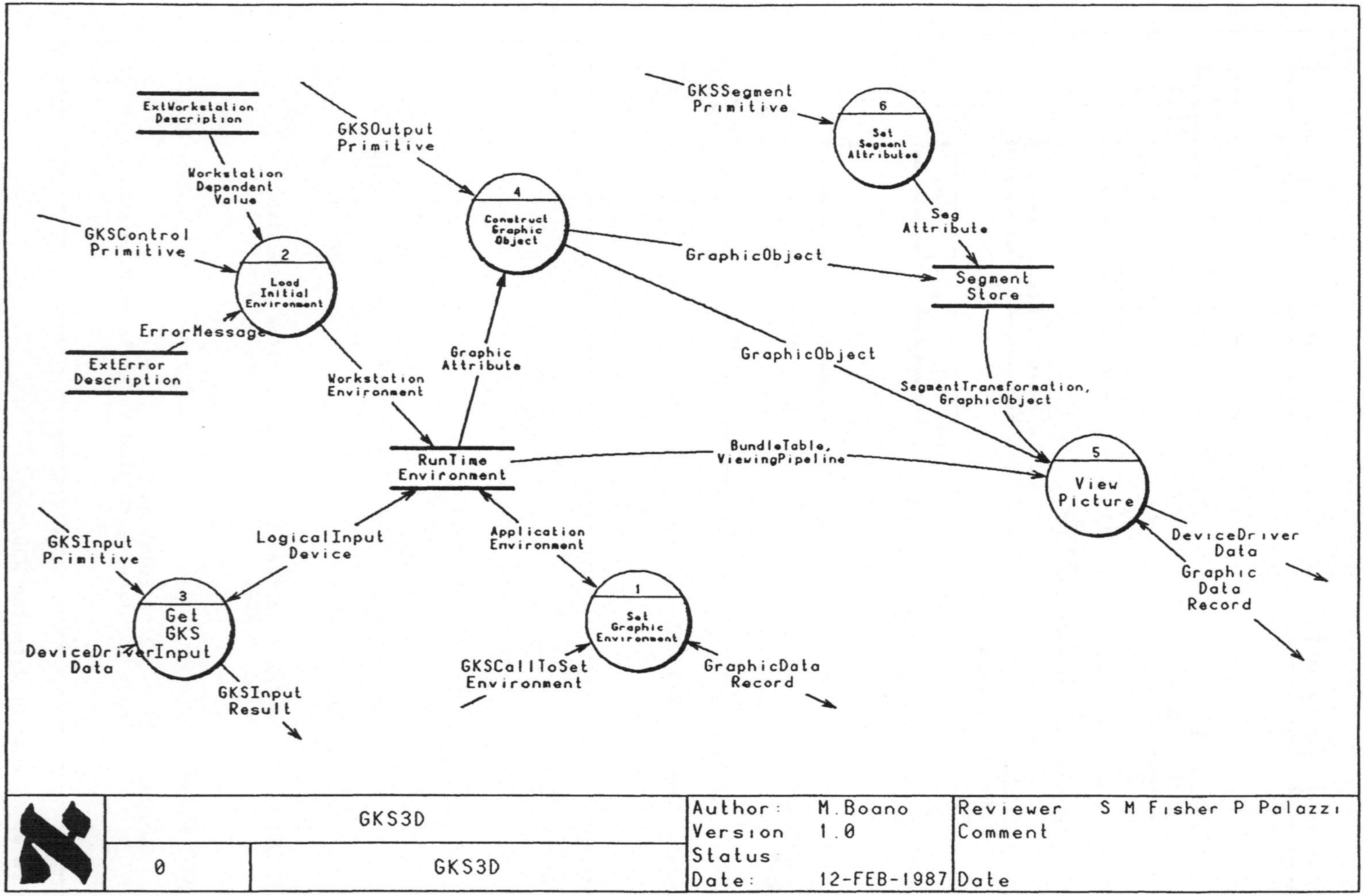

Figure 3: Top level GKS data flow diagram

ADAMO/DFP

The word 'is' appearing in a circle denotes a form of generalised relationship and here indicates that a 'Primitive' 'is' a 'CellArray' or 'Text' or a 'PolyLine' etc.

The diagram is described in detail by our data definition language (DDL). The complete DDL for the four diagrams of GKS is about 20 pages long and contains detailed comments, many of them taken from the original standard document. An extract from the DDL for the 'PICTURE' diagram describing two entity sets and a relationship between entities in those sets is shown above in Fig. 2.

Dataflow diagrams

A Dataflow diagram shows a system in terms of its active components (processes) as circles and the data interfaces between them (dataflows) as arrows. Each process may be decomposed into a further diagram to an arbitrary depth in order to reveal more detail. Dataflows may similarly be expanded in terms of their components <DEMARCO78>.

To couple DFDs and ER we require that data flows are ultimately expanded down to ER components i.e. entity-sets, attributes and relationships.

Figure 3 shows the top level diagram. Consider process 5 'View Picture', which represents the viewing pipeline. Its basic function is to take 'GraphicObjects' and 'SegmentTransformations' from the 'Segment Store', and 'GraphicObjects' directly from process 4 along with 'ViewingPipeline' information and 'BundleTables' from another store to produce 'DeviceDriverData'. Four further diagrams were drawn showing details of the system.

State Transition Diagrams

State transition diagrams are used to describe the states of a system, what event triggers a transition between states and what happens during that transition. For GKS only two such diagrams were needed. One is Fig. 13 of the GKS standard and deals with the five States of GKS itself and the other shows the setting of the Aspect Source Flags. To each diagram corresponds one state variable - itself part of the data model.

Algorithms

Transformations, such as the calculation of normalized device coordinates, are adequately described by a section of the FORTRAN code making use of variables corresponding to attributes of entities described in the data model, as shown in figure 4 below.

```
C   PROCESS  5.1 - Map to NDC space
C
C                Input  : REAL  WC_X,WC_Y     point in WC
C                Output : REAL  NDC_X,NDC_Y   point in NDC
C
    NDC_X = ( (WC_X-WrdWin_W(1,1) ) * WrdWin_Tn(1)) + WrdWin_N(1,1)
    NDC_Y = ( (WC_Y-WrdWin_W(2,1) ) * WrdWin_Tn(2)) + WrdWin_N(2,1)
```

Figure 4: Normalisation transformation - specification by code

BUILDING A GKS SYSTEM FROM THE SPECIFICATIONS

An almost complete GKS-2D system was built from our specification, making use of ADAMO <QIAN87>. ADAMO is a software system to define ER data structures, map them onto tables and manipulate them from FORTRAN programs. The TAP (TAble Package), the kernel of the ADAMO system, is a package of FORTRAN callable subroutines to manipulate ER and/or tabular data residing in memory. The TAP refers to special FORTRAN variables, that are automatically derived from the description contained in the DDL.

The manipulation of the data objects using the TAP takes place at the same level of abstraction as in the data definition, using about 15 subroutines corresponding to the elementary operations of the ER model. Object names are retained from DDL to code, and the programmer continues to think in terms of entities and relationships, following a simple path from the specification to the code.

A full level 2b system with FORTRAN binding was built, with the following omissions:

- Only those inquiry functions required by the test programs and benchmarks were written

- The only input routines coded are for locator input

A full metafile driver was written as well as a partial device driver for the Tektronix 4014. The specifications occupied a junior programmer for about 6 weeks and coding took a further four weeks.

Approximately half of the 201 external GKS subroutines deal with setting and inquiring individual attributes. They are completely trivial. For example, the routine GSPLI (Set Polyline index) has just two lines of normally executed code. The first line of executable code checks that the attribute 'State' of the 'Environment' is at least GGKOP (GKS open), and takes the form:

```
IF (.NOT.(Environment_State .GE. GGKOP))   GOTO error
```

The other line sets the current PolyLine bundle index to 'INDEX', the argument of the routine.

```
Environment_LnId = INDEX
```

The precise meaning of 'Environment_State', GGKOP and 'Environment_LnId' are defined in the DDL. The code of the corresponding inquiry function GQPLI (Inquire polyline index) is equally trivial.

The section of code shown in figure 5 is from the routine GPL (Polyline). GPL checks that the GKS state is at least Workstation active, and stores the polyline attributes if a segment is open. The device driver is then called.

In the extract below, after checking the GKS state the 'Primitive' is inserted into the entity set 'Primitive' by 'CALL INSENT(Primitive)'. INSREL relates the 'Primitive' to the open 'Segment' The 'Primitive' is then inserted, and the call to INSGEN records that the 'Primitive' 'is' a 'PolyLine'.

Figure 6 was produced by the printing routines of the TAP and shows an example of data held in the entity sets 'PolyLine' and 'LPoint'. The first five 'LPoint's belong to 'PolyLine' 1 and the other two to 'PolyLine 2'.

```
              SUBROUTINE GPL (N,PX,PY)
.
.
C
C check current GKS state
C
      IF(.NOT.(Environment_State .GE. GWSAC))GOTO error
      IF(Environment_State .EQ. GSCOP)THEN
C
C create a  Primitive and relate it to the current segment
C
              Primitive_ID = NEXT
              CALL INSENT (Primitive)
              CALL INSREL (Primitive,Primitive_Segment,Segment)
C
C create PolyLine and relate it to the new Primitive
C
              IF(Environment_Asf(1) .EQ. GINDIV)THEN
                     PolyLine_LType = Environment_LType
              ELSE
                     PolyLine_LType = INULL
              ENDIF
.
.
              PolyLine_ID = NEXT
              CALL INSENT (PolyLine)
              CALL INSGEN (Primitive,Primitive_Is,PolyLine)
      ENDIF
.
.
```

Figure 5: Extract from code - GPL

Table : PolyLine ADAMO/TAP

ID	Index	LType	LWidth	LnCol
1	=====	1	1.0	1
2	=====	1	1.0	1

Table : LPoint ADAMO/TAP

ID	P(1)	P(2)	#PolyLine	#WrdWin
1	0.0	0.1	1	2
2	0.0	0.24	1	2
3	0.142857	0.24	1	2
4	0.142857	0.1	1	2
5	0.0	0.1	1	2
6	0.0	0.1	2	2
7	0.0	0.24	2	2

Figure 6: PolyLine and LPoint tables

Timing tests were performed using a test program of our own which made use of the metafile and the WISS, a benchmark <DU86>, and our own data flow diagram plotting tool (no segments). As a result of these tests, minor changes were made to the ER schema and to the code to eliminate the obvious hot spots. This work took about 4 man weeks.

It then becomes difficult to quote figures and compare them with those of commercial packages, because each package executes rapidly for some operations, and slowly for others. Some packages also have tuning parameters which makes the study more complex. On average the execution speed of our GKS is comparable with the fastest commercial package we could find.

EXTENDING THE MODEL TO GKS-3D

The specifications were later extended to GKS-3D by adding four entity sets and changing the dimension of some attributes from 2 to 3. The dataflow diagrams for the viewing pipeline (process 5 and its expansion) were heavily modified by inserting the 'View transformation' and the 'Projection transformation'. See for example the paper presented at Eurographics '86 <SINGLET86>. The code was extended to test the viewing pipeline by drawing 3 dimensional wire frames.

CONCLUSIONS

With our approach:

- all data are described consistently in the DDL corresponding to the Entity-Relationship diagrams
- essential processing is shown in the data flow diagrams, where the data processed appears in the DDL
- distinct states are identified by state transition diagrams
- algorithms are defined by sections of code

This combination of Entity-Relationship, Data flow and state transition diagrams (and for transformations the code) is a powerful specification method which, partly because it makes much use of diagrams, makes these specifications easy to communicate and leads rapidly to a good design.

With an ER data manipulation language, the path from specification to a complete working system is straightforward and the result is not a throwaway prototype, but, as our timing results indicate a real program.

This approach has been tried for a range of applications and gives consistently good results. Its adoption by graphics systems designers would dramatically reduce development time and would allow standards to keep up with and thus be able to exploit new hardware.

ACKNOWLEDGEMENTS

We profited much from discussions with Ursula Berthon, Irene Seis, Jenny Tweed, Jurgen Bettels, David Myers, Andries Van Dam and Albert Werbrouck.

We are grateful to Friedrich Dydak and Mike Metcalf for their encouragement and support.

REFERENCES

CHEN76 Chen, P. P., The Entity-Relationship Model - Toward a Unified View of Data. ACM Trans. Database Syst. 1 (1997), 9-36

DEMARCO78 DeMarco, T., Structured Analysis and System Specification. YOURDON Press (1978)

DU87 Du, S. GKS benchmark. Private communication

DUCE86 Duce, D.A., Fielding, E.V.C., Better Understanding through Formal Specification. Comput. Graphics Forum 4 (1985) 333-348

ISO82 ISO/DIS 7942 Information Processing - Graphical Kernel System (GKS) - Functional Description: GKS Version 7.2. ISO/TC97/SC5/WG2 N163 (1982)

QIAN87 Qian, Z. et al., Use of the ADAMO data management system within ALEPH. Comput. Phys. Comms. 45 (1987) 283-298

SINGLET86 Singleton, K., An Implementation of the GKS-3D/PHIGS Viewing Pipeline Eurographics '86

The Choice of a Graphics System; Standard, Emerging Standard or De-facto-Standard

M. Jern (Denmark)

Abstract

The emergence of conflicting and competing standards is causing confusion for users and vendors alike. The Graphics Kernel System GKS may be an approved standard, but it is not perfect. Proposals for enhanced standards would need to include additional primitives and attributes to support the modern engineering workstations, which can have sophisticated image processing and advanced 3D capabilities. Though it will take some years to define, PHIGS+ may be the way of the future.

Graphics standards can all too easily become an intricate jigsaw where no one really knows where the pieces are or quite how they should fit together.

Today we have two final approved graphics standards:

- GKS (Graphical Kernel System)
- CGM (Computer Graphics Metafile)

Graphics standard committees within both ISO and ANSI are also working on several emerging standards:

- GKS-91 (Revision to the GKS standard)
- GKS-3D (Three Dimensional Extensions to GKS)
- PHIGS (Programmers' Hierarchical Interactive Graphics System)
- PHIGS+ (Extension to PHIGS)
- CGI (Computer Graphics Interface)
- CGM-3D (Three Dimensional Extension to the CGM standard)

The various GKS and PHIGS standards are application programmers' interface standards, the CGI and CGM belong to the category of graphics device interface standards.

Throughout the 70's and 80's a large number of general purpose graphics packages have been written and are today commonly used. Many of these packages have now emerged as de-facto standards. Examples are:

- GDDM (IBMs graphics application programming package)
- PLOT-10 (Tektronix graphics programming package)
- CALCOMP (The de-facto pen plotter standard)
- POSTSCRIPT (Documentation graphics language)
- REGIS (Digital Equipment's graphics system)
- DI-3000 (PVI's fundamental graphics package)
- DISSPLA (Computer Associates graphics package)
- UNIRAS (Device independent raster graphics)

GKS, imposition "from above"

With the introduction of GKS, there is the first major and internationally agreed specification of a target set of functions for computer graphics programs. However, unlike a very precisely defined programming language Pascal which is relatively well established, GKS has major differences in performance of different GKS implementations, and even of the same implementations on different machines.

The manner in which GKS became a standard is indeed quite unusual. Firstly, it was decided that a standard was needed, and then (over a ten year period) one was defined. In the case of Pascal, for instance, Pascal was first invented, and it was only many years later in the light of the great popularity that it became an international standard. In other words, by the time Pascal became a standard it had already been in use for many years.

With GKS and the whole suite of emerging standards (PHIGS, CGI, CGM) it is very much a case of imposition "from above". Whereas other standards have often reached standardization after many years of experience. This is not the case of GKS. Consequently, for some time to come, implementation must remain something of an unknown quality.

Graphics packages like PostScript, X-window and GDDM are emerging as "de-facto" standards because of their quality and therefore, because people wish to use them, they are emerging as standards from the bottom up.
PostScript represents one of the most important and exciting developments in graphics for several years. It provides a dynamic language for the control for graphical output devices, in addition to very powerful functions for the generation of graphical output.

Portability is not guaranteed by the graphics standards

Graphics standards are intended to be a means of communication between application programs and graphic devices. As such all implementations should behave in a similar manner. In reality, however, an application program cannot be transferred from one implementation to another without serious problems, because the intelligent service functions provided by various implementations are different.

Examples for important intelligent functions not prescribed in GKS are:

- Closed figures

  Many applications require a fill-area capability which is not found in GKS. A device-independent package must be able to construct complex, possible disjointed figures on any graphics device. Area-filling operations are becoming more common in hardware but these operations are heavily device-dependent and, for non-intelligent devices, require special emulation software support.
  Areas with holes which need several separate polygons to be defined are widely used in application software, despite the relative complexity of the task involved. A common example of disjointed figures are the shaded (polygon) fonts frequently used in presentation graphics

- Opague or transparent overplotting.

  CRT's, inkjet and electrostatic plotters allow you to specify how two polygons should overlap. The raster technology simplifies the removal of hidden surfaces considerably, and complicated algorithms for hidden lines are therefore no longer necessary. On the other hand, very many vector devices are still in use and these cannot be neglected. The objective for portability is not met if the software is restricted to a specific type of output device.

- Cross-hatching.

  Hatching the interior of the polygon is a feature which may not be present in a GKS implementation. If available, GKS does not allow the application programmer to control the pattern.

A program written for one GKS implementation will therefore not always produce an identical output on another implementation. The GKS standard leaves too many important issues open to the developer of a GKS implementation. More specific rules are required in the standards. Further, because of the irritating restrictions in GKS software vendors are adding new functionalities to their GKS implementation, which are far beyond the scope of the original specified standard.

GKS, a good starting base

As a graphics system GKS is not perfect. It is now over a decade since its basic design and five years since its last significant change. In that time computer graphics has come a long way. This is especially true in the case of the modern engineering work- stations, with sophisticated image processing and advanced 3D capabilities.

Proposals for enhanced standards would need a design which contains additional primitives and attributes to handle these systems and their functionality. GKS, however, was a good starting base for the understanding of graphics theory.

Graphics standards seem to negate the very advantage that personal workstations offer

Graphics is increasingly being used on workstations which have limited memory and disk space, yet offer the advantage of very fast, usually bitmapped graphics. Graphics standards seem, however, to negate the very advantage that personal workstations offer. They are large, take up a lot of memory during execution and a lot of disk space, and are slow. Attempts to establish higher-level graphics standards for the personal workstations have therefore so far failed. If an intervening level of standard is inserted, system performance becomes unacceptable. So de-facto standards like X-window with its support of low-level functions will become a dominating graphics system in these environments.

The arrival of the new family of PS/2 workstations and the OS/2 operating system will create a new de-facto graphics standard; Windows Graphics Presentation Manager from Microsoft. Windows is an easy-to-use programming environment for graphics in OS/2. Special routines for menus, dialog boxes, and scroll bars are included which fully utilize the graphics capabilities of the hardware. Essentially, Windows' graphics interface will be made compatible with IBMs GDDM graphics system. Programmers someday will be able to recompile their OS/2 Windows program to run on an IBM Mainframe system. The conclusion is that IBM is creating its own de-facto graphics standards.

The efficiency problem

The efficiency question is particularly important in graphics. Many implementations of standards are built on top of other graphics packages or even other standards. For example, IBMs implementation of PHIGS (graPHIGS) is implemented on top of the local graphics system GAM for support of the popular 3D IBM workstation 5080. Users familiar with this workstation and GAM have complained about the slow performance generated by an additional software layer.

IBM's GKS implementation is another example, built on top of the IBM graphics de-facto standard package GDDM. Performance is reduced by 50-60% for applications developed for GKS instead of GDDM. Why use GKS when writing in GDDM would be more efficient? The 5080 could also in theory be programmmed in a 2D environment by GKS through GDDM-graPHIGS-GAM.

Many other implementations of GKS are built on top of another de-facto standard implementation of X-window. These graphics standards will always be large and inefficient compared to what might be achieved in a given computer graphics environment.

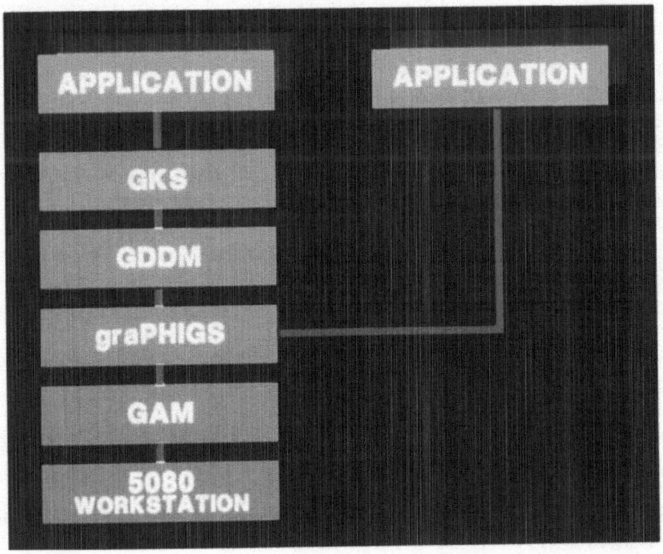

Figure 1: The three-dimensional 5080 workstation from IBM can in theory be supported by GKS through these graphics packages.

	GKS	GKS-3D	PHIGS	PHIGS+	CGM	CGI
OUTPUT	X	X	X	X	X	X
INPUT	X	X	X	X		X
WORKSTATION MODEL	X	X	X	X		(X)
BITBLK						X
SEGMENT	X	X	(X)	(X)		X
HIERARCHICAL DATA BASE			X	X		
MODELLING DATA EDITING			X	X		
3D		X	X	X		
HLSR			X	X		
LIGHTING MODELS				X		
SHADING				X		
GEOMETRIC				X		

SUPPORTED
MORE PRIMITIVES AVAILABLE
DEPENDENT ON LEVEL
NOT STANDARD

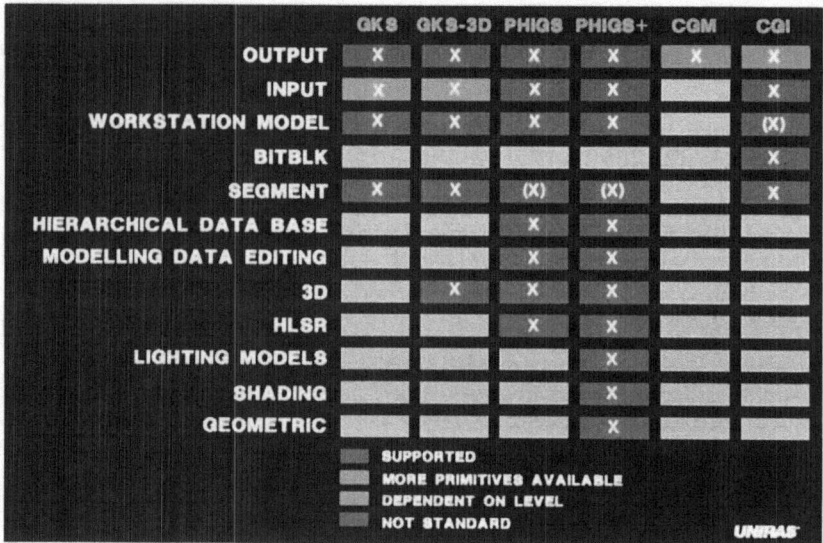

Figure 2: The functionality of the graphics standards.

The PHIGS will become the three-dimensional standard

The specification of GKS only defines a flat two-dimensional (2D) graphics system. Work is currently in hand to develop three-dimensional standards, GKS-3D which will extend the GKS standard and PHIGS.

GKS-3D is a proposed standard that is intended to provide a strict extension of the capabilities of GKS to support 3D functionality. As such it will allow existing GKS programs to operate in a 3D environment.

Many technical and scientific computer graphics application programmers have expressed dissatisfaction, including poor utilization of advanced hardware, slow response, inefficient data structures, and poor data structure manipulation facilities. The PHIGS standard is being developed by people involved in the ANSI standardization process, who felt that some users required a more powerful interface to write highly interactive applications.

PHIGS intends to satisfy the needs for the entire 3D environment. PHIGS has therefore been designed to address the needs of dynamic, highly interactive graphic applications, which include the following:

- definition, display and manipulation of geometrically related objects (i.e. hierarchically defined).

- a high degree of interactivity which necessitates frequent dynamic modification of graphical entities.

In short, PHIGS is designed to be the interaction toolset for graphical model building and manipulation.

PHIGS was originally not intended to compete with GKS-3D, but simply to provide better support for particular 3D environments. But standards need to be compatible, and compatibility between PHIGS and GKS-3D has been a high priority for the standard organizations to solve. However, PHIGS is not yet compatible with GKS-3D, and some people on the PHIGS committee claim that the existing GKS standard is not a suitable base for compatible extensions to serve the needs on which they have focused. PHIGS is now defined well enough for us to know that it is almost certainly not going to be compatible with GKS-3D.

The hierarchy and editing features of PHIGS are so important for CAD applications that GKS-3D will probably never be very successful as a standard. Since CAD constitutes such a large part of the computer graphics market place, vendors will be reluctant to build hardware that efficiently supports GKS-3D. PHIGS is likely to become attractive to the users when it is effectively supported on high performance workstations.

PHIGS has obvious appeal to chip and board vendors who would instantly gain a relatively painless compatibility with much of the important code in the engineering workstation industry. Software developers however, have still been reluctant to participate. They have seen other graphics standard proposals arrive, only to fail against the harch requirements of interactive performance. These vendors want to see first if PHIGS will deliver on its promises.

The result is a deadlock. Hardware vendors are hesitant to commit additional parts to a PHIGS implementation that does not support their latest 3D display technology and which may not be used. Software vendors are hesitant to use PHIGS until it is more widely accepted.

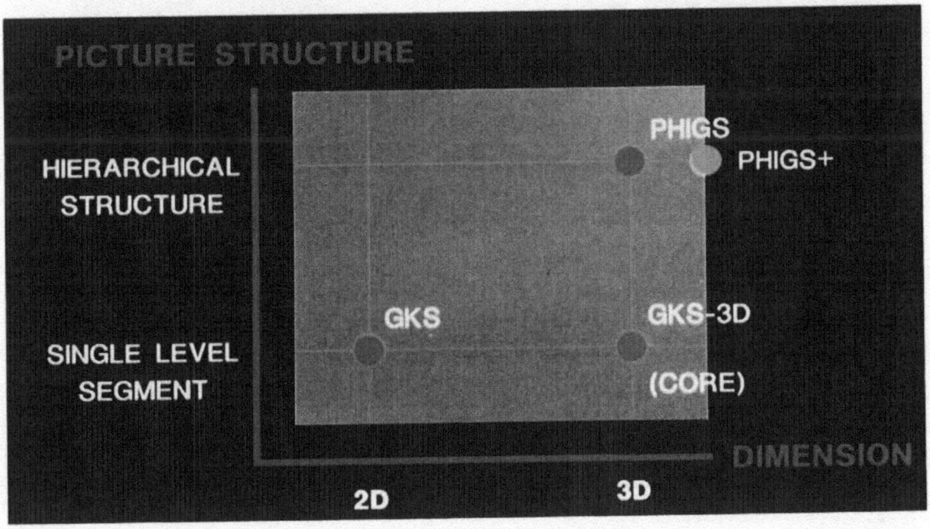

Figure 3: The dimension and level of database in the graphics standards.

The State-of-the-art standard is now being designed by the hardware vendors themselves

Technology has advanced considerably in the seven years PHIGS has been under development. The progression of the developing standard through the official standard-making bodies is never rapid, but in recent years the process of joint development of standards within ISO and in the U.S. has slowed the progress even more.

It has been apparent for some time that there are a number of weak areas in PHIGS, areas which have been passed over in the standardization process for various reasons. There is a need to display realistic 3D images in color and to visualize the effect of different parameters on a 3D surface. Figures 4 and 5 show examples of applications which cannot be processed with any existing standard although existing hardware technology now is capable of doing it.

Figure 4: The aircraft surface is divided into a very large number of small panels, and the pressure on each of these panels is calculated and visualized in this 3D display.

The super-workstation vendors have now formed an unofficial working group to address the need for a standard which fully utilizes the state-of-the-art hardware technology. This PHIGS+ committee was formed in the fall of 1986 and is composed of about 30 representatives of which a majority represents hardware vendors like Stellar Computer, SUN, Apollo, HP, IBM, and Digital Equipment.

The PHIGS+ proposed standard extensions address the capabilities of the new generation of high-performance workstations that will become widely available in late 1987 and 1988. These workstations will have the performance necessary to interactively in real-time, support such tasks as geometric transformation, lighting and shading of 3D bodies.

The emphasis in the development of PHIGS+ has been the display of realistic 3D images which require:

- new primitives for spline curves and surfaces
- lighting models
- shading models

It will probably be at least several years before PHIGS + work becomes officially recognized by the standard committees, but it is expected that PHIGS+ will be widely reflected in high-end graphics workstation products in the near future. Hundreds of thousands of workstation users will soon be developing applications for the workstations in a PHIGS+ environment, thus creating another de-facto standard.

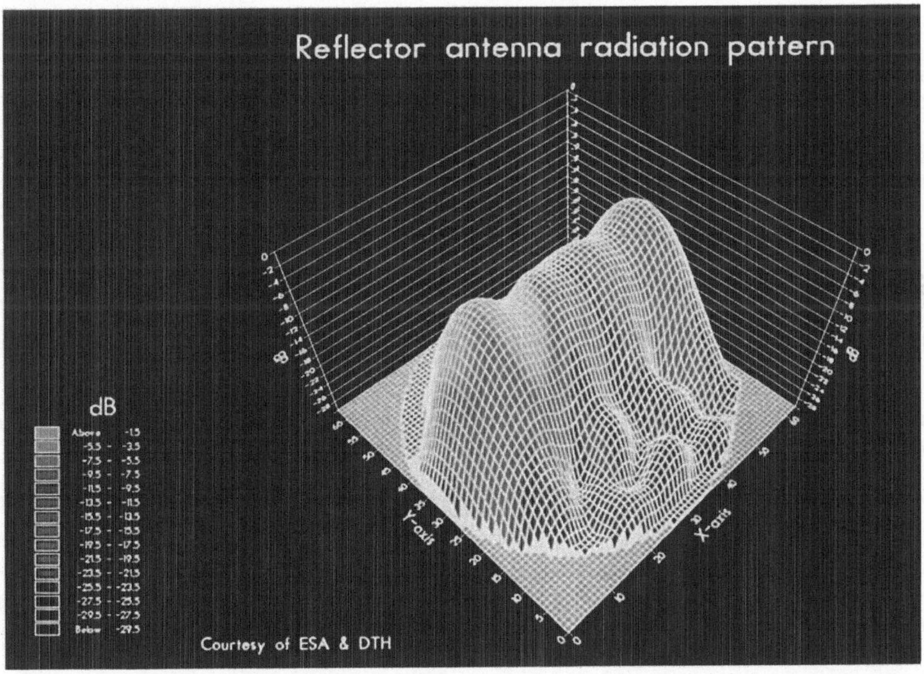

Figure 5: A 3D image showing the 3D radiation pattern around a microwave antenna. The signal strength (height) is visualized together with the amplitude (color on the surface).

Functionalities beyond the emerging standards

While standardization efforts proceed, it is important to accumulate experience by considering the practical aspects of planning, implementing and using real systems in real environments.

By 1989 most graphics workstations will provide around 20-30 MIPS and will most likely be capable of real-time 3D graphics using 32 or 64-bit floating point operations. The lighting modules in PHIGS+ is applied on a primitive by primitive basis and does not allow any interaction between objects such as shadows or reflections which are required in animation. Ray tracing algorithms which have produced some of the most spectacular results in in computer-generated images will be implemented in hardware on the next generation of workstations.

All emerging graphics standards (except CGI) lack the low-level functionality possible on raster-based devices. Graphical output cannot be displayed using the BitBLT functions. The application programmer is not allowed access to the underlying raster operations so prevalent on modern workstations.

Finally, it must be stressed that the real importance of GKS and emerging graphics standards is that they have drastically opened up the discussion in the computer graphics community, and created an increased interest in computer graphics in general. However, the alphabetic soup of graphics standards and the battle between various proposals has also caused great confusion among the users.

At least three years away

While the momentum toward graphics standardizing is currently strong, a standard like PHIGS+ is not expected to be completed until beginning of the 1990s. UNIRAS is now in the process of evaluating its applications performance in a PHIGS+ environment. It is becoming clear that UNIRAS intends to make PHIGS+ the interface to all of its 3D applications in the future. UNIRAS' commitment to PHIGS+ will help the acceptance of this now emerging graphics standard.

References

ANSI/X3H31 "Programmer's Hierarchical Graphics system", ANSI, NewYork, Aug, 1985.

G. Enderle, K. Kansy, G. Pfaff, "Conputer Graphics Programming", Springer-Verlag, Berlin, Heidelberg, NewYork, Tokyo 1984

Eurographics Association, "The GKS Review", 25-27 September 1987, Disley Manchester, UK.

ACM SIGGRAPH, "PHIGS+ Functional Description" Revision 2.0, July 20, 1987, c/o Conference Management Office, 111 East Wacker Dr., ste 600, Chicago, IL 60601.

Chapter 5

Computer Graphics in Medicine and Sciences

Molecular Graphics: A New Tool in Computer-Assisted Chemistry

J. Weber, P.-Y. Morgantini, J.-P. Doucet, and J.-E. Dubois (Switzerland and France)

Abstract

Molecular graphics (MG) is nowadays an essential component of the basic tools used in computer-assisted chemistry. As such, it is employed in numerous applications where its role consists not only in building and visualizing chemical models, but also in simulating complex situations resulting from the dynamic properties of chemical systems. This paper presents several basic techniques used in MG by reviewing some applications developed in our laboratories in the following areas: (i) modelization of molecular architectures; (ii) real time animated representation of dynamic processes; (iii) construction and visualization of molecular properties such as electron densities and intermolecular interaction potentials.

Introduction

It would be difficult nowadays to find a single application in chemical research and development where computers are not involved to some extent. Even in conventional areas of chemistry such as synthesis and analysis, the use of computers has led to a significant improvement of the techniques employed so far, as exemplified by the development of computer-assisted snythesis planning systems (1) or by the indispensable use of computerized data acquisition systems in chemical laboratories (2). In addition, specific applications of computer-assisted chemistry have presided to the birth of new disciplines of utmost importance in contemporary chemistry such as computational quantum chemistry (3), molecular dynamics simulations (4), molecular graphics (5), etc.

Molecular graphics may be defined as the application of computer graphics to study molecular structure, function and interaction, by using models describing the behavior of single molecules. Indeed, whereas experiments are performed at the macroscopic level, involving roughly 10^{23} molecules, most of the models used in chemistry are based on the microscopic aspect of this science, i.e. they aim at describing the structure and properties of a single molecule or the possible reaction mechanisms between two molecules. A basic component of any MG system is thus its ability to build or retrieve from a data base the 3D architecture of a given compound, i.e. the cartesian coordinates of its constituting atoms, and then to allow the chemist to manipulate in real time the corresponding model by applying simple transformations such as rotations, translations, scale factor, etc. It is also important to manipulate several molecular models so as to simulate the details of the formation of molecular complexes in terms of their most favorable bonding conditions. This is particularly relevant for drug-receptor interactions, where a simulation of the docking of the drug on the active site of the protein is a prerequisite in drug design applications.

Another important aspect of MG lies in the calculation and representation of molecular properties such as electron densities, intermolecular interaction potentials, solvent accessibility, etc. Represented conventionally as color-coded dots on the molecular surface on calligraphic systems, or as 3D solid models on raster equipments, these properties allow to readily estimate the chemical stability and reactivity of both known and unknown species, which helps in turn to understand, and in some cases predict, reaction mechanisms between these compounds. It is therefore not surprising that MG has become an indispensable tool used intensively by pharmaceutical and chemical industries in various areas, such as the search for new drugs or novel catalytic materials, where the economical consequences of the design of new chemicals with appropriate properties are enormous.

In this communication, we would like to briefly review some basic MG applications developed in our laboratories and illustrated in a video tape (6) to be projected during CG International 88 held May 1988 in Geneva. In addition, some very recent developments in the calculation and representation of approximate intermolecular potentials for large compounds will be presented. They should allow to rapidly estimate and visualize the possible catalytic properties of the important class of compounds known as organometallics.

Static and Dynamic Structural Models

Simple models of complex molecular architectures may be represented on graphic displays: in addition to ball-and-stick models, space-filling representations may also be generated (Fig. 1). They consist of intersecting atomic spheres represented using solid modeling algorithms on raster systems

Figure 1. Molecular modeling: the structure of a trioxane derivative represented as ball-and-stick (left) and space-filling(right) models (AED 512).

or of mesh or "chicken-wire" spheres on calligraphic systems. With respect to conventional mechanical models, the advantages of using molecular models generated on a graphic display are obvious: accurate, reproducible representations of 3D structures are easily obtained and it is possible to manipulate them interactively so as to examine every detail. In addition, several structures may be simultaneously displayed and independently manipulated, which allows: (i) to superimpose them and to rapidly evaluate their similarities and differences as well, and (ii) to find the most favorable conditions for the approach of reactive species over a substrate, as exemplified by the interactive docking of an inhibitor onto an enzyme (7). In all these applications, however, the geometrical structures of the molecules are rigid, i.e. the relative positions of their constituting atoms are kept unchanged during the modelization steps.

Another, though more elaborate, possibility is to perform dynamic modeling: as the assembly of atoms constituting a molecular skeleton never remains rigid or frozen in normal conditions, real time modeling of the relative atomic motions within the structure leads to a much more realistic representation. MG is indeed an ideal tool through which to visualize the changes of a system as a function of time: provided a suitable data base, made of successive sets of atomic coordinates as a function of time, has been calculated, it is possible to carry out graphic animation of dynamical chemical processes. Calligraphic and high quality raster systems as well have proved excellent for representing complex mechanisms such as structural fluctuations in large biological molecules and concerted deformations

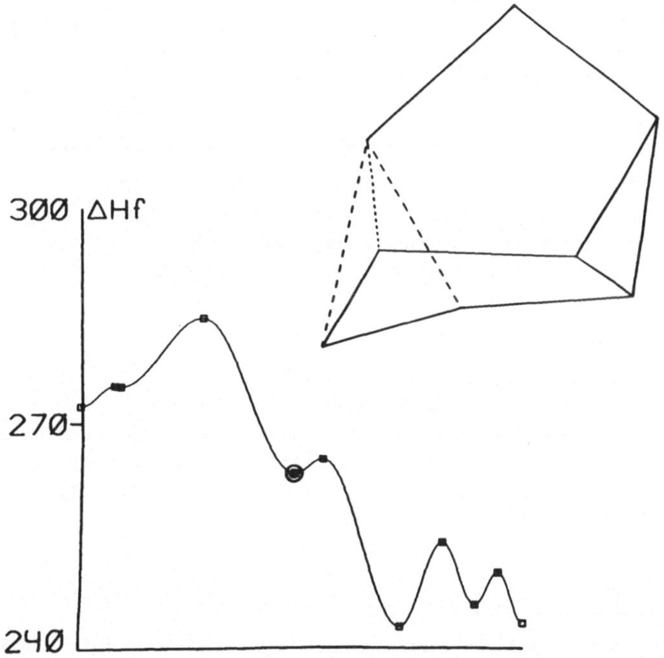

Figure 2. Rearrangement of the $C_8H_9^+$ cation: structure of a reaction intermediate together with the associated energy curve. The energy of the displayed structure is indicated by the position of the cursor on the curve (VG 3400).

encountered in molecular vibrations and rearrangements. As examples, two elaborate unimolecular dynamic processes, namely the rearrangement of a polycyclic carbocation (Fig. 2) and the pseudo-rotation of a seven-membered heterocyclic compound (Fig. 3) have been recently reported (8,9) and they

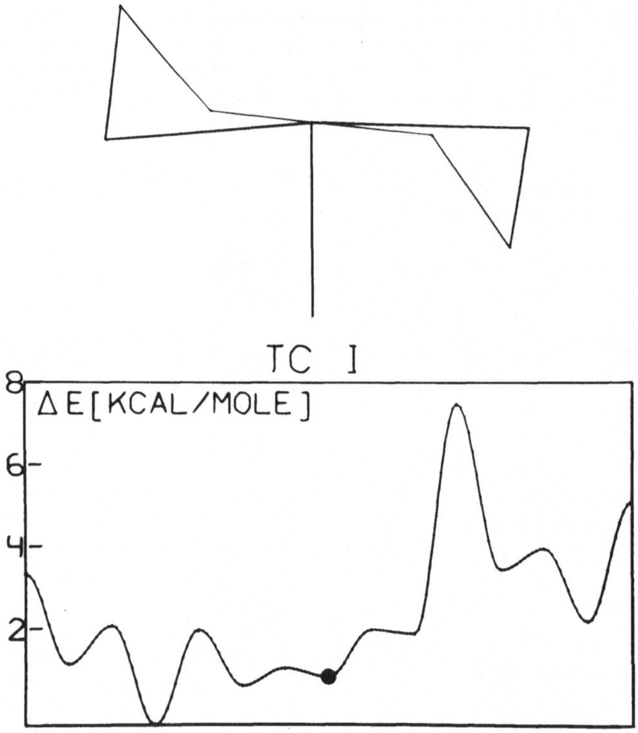

Figure 3. Twist-chair isoclinal (TCI) conformation of S-methyl-thiepanium, an intermediate along the pseudo-rotation reaction path. Curve and cursor as in Fig. 2 (VG 3400).

are illustrated in the video tape. In addition, the stereochemical aspects of a bimolecular reaction of Diels-Alder type have been illustrated by computer graphics animated models (Fig. 4) (10), in an application enabling the user to visualize step by step the detailed features of the reaction mechanism, which also underlines the great potentials of MG for teaching chemistry.

Models of Molecular Properties

As sophisticated as they might be, the different representations of static or dynamic structural models would be incomplete without the capability to superimpose electronic properties such as electron densities, interaction potentials for possible associations with reagents, reactivity indices, etc. Indeed, structural architectures are only part of the complex, multi-faceted aspects of molecular structures and electron densities are

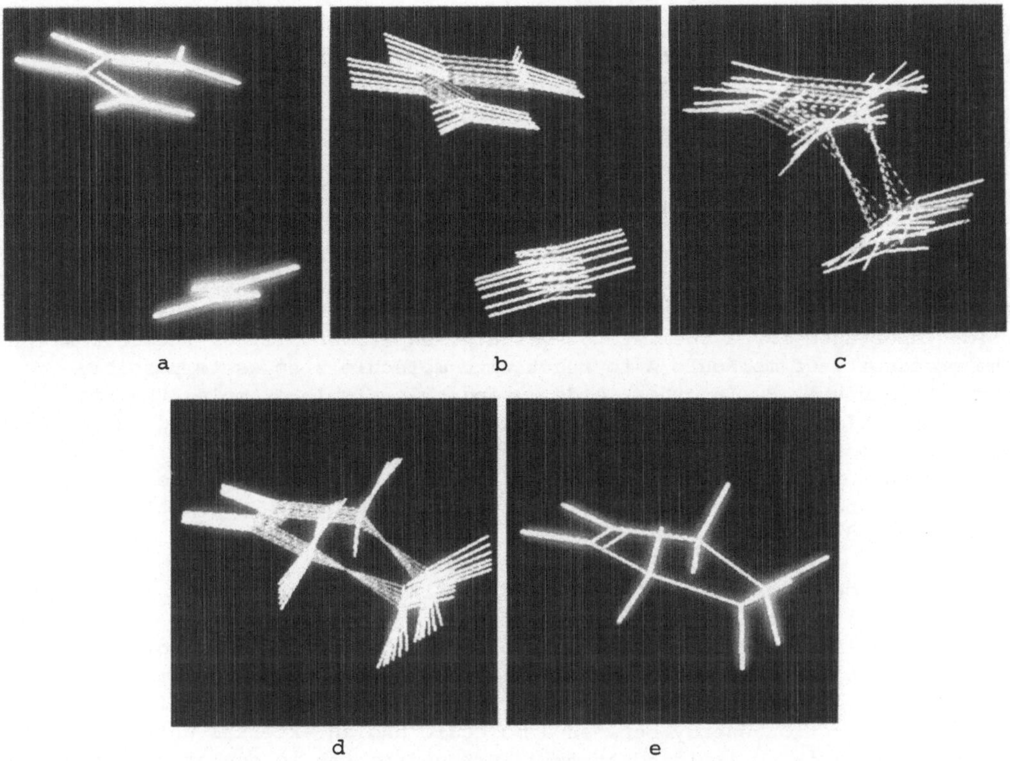

Figure 4. Sequences of the Diels-Alder model cycloaddition of ethylene on butadiene: a) initial reactants: ethylene (lower part) and butadiene (upper part); b) intermediate conformations; c) transition state; d) formation of cyclohexene adduct; e) final product: cyclohexene (AED 512).

the "flesh" surrounding the "bones" which correspond to chemical bonds. The fuzzy clouds representing electron densities are thus of primary importance as they lead to a good description of molecular shapes and polarities: intermolecular interactions involve the intermingling of these clouds and for a favorable drug-receptor interaction, the electron-deficient sites of one partner should match the electron rich ones of the other. The matching of structural shapes, i.e. the well-known key and lock image, is therefore not the only effect governing drug-receptor interactions.

In order to evaluate molecular properties, various methods of computational quantum chemistry have to be used. Their degree of sophistication and reliability depends on the size of the compound under study: because of the huge amount of computer time they require, which increases very rapidly as a function of the number of atoms, accurate, state-of-the-art models can only be used for small molecules (i.e. made of 10-20 light atoms), whereas approximate methods have to be employed for larger compounds. In MG applications, adequate representations of these properties are generated using graphic procedures and algorithms leading to 2D contour maps, 2D color-filled contour maps (11), or more sophisticated 3D representations (11-13). However, the MG imagery rapidly reaches a high level of complexity as several objects with different structures are now to be displayed. The graphic capabilities of modern modeling systems allow to solve this problem by offering the possibility to represent interactively and manipulate complex images made of several hundreds of thousand vectors or dots.

Molecular reactivity is a basic concept in chemistry. Indeed, chemists have always been interested in using molecules as building blocks in order to synthesize novel compounds with specific properties. It is therefore of prime importance for a chemist to evaluate, experimentally or theoretically, the propensity of molecule A to react with molecule B so as to possibly form the product AB. In other words, using this simple example, the rate of the reaction $A + B \rightleftharpoons AB$ is a key data if one is interested in obtaining the product AB from simple reactants A and B. In addition, it is important to know the structural features of AB complex formation, i.e. which sites of A and B are responsible for the formation of new chemical bonds between A and B.

Using techniques recently developed, MG is able to bring answers to these questions, at least from a qualitative or semi-quantitative point of view. A significant fraction of intermolecular interactions is governed by electrostatic forces between essentially unperturbed molecules: molecular electrostatic potentials (MEPs), which represent the electrostatic (Coulombic) interaction energy between a molecule and an external unit positive charge, are easily calculated as maps surrounding the molecular skeleton, using quantum chemical methods (14) and then conveniently represented on graphics systems. MEP minima (i.e. the most negative regions) correspond

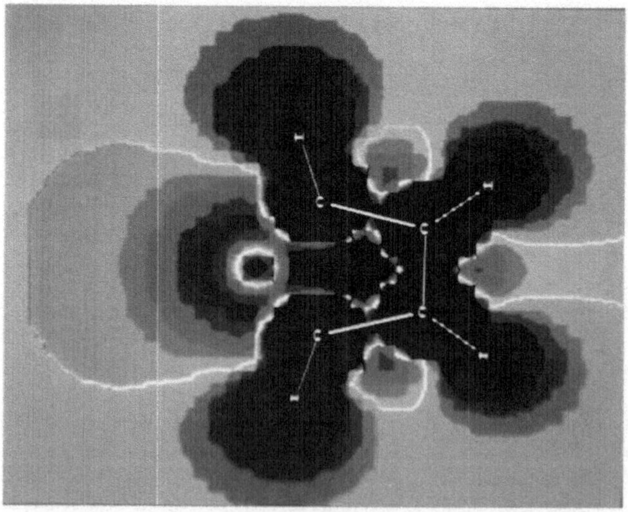

Figure 5. Color-filled contour levels of the MEP calculated for the molecule of benzvalene in a plane containing four carbon atoms. The most reactive sites for cationic attack are depicted by the dark red zones (AED 512).

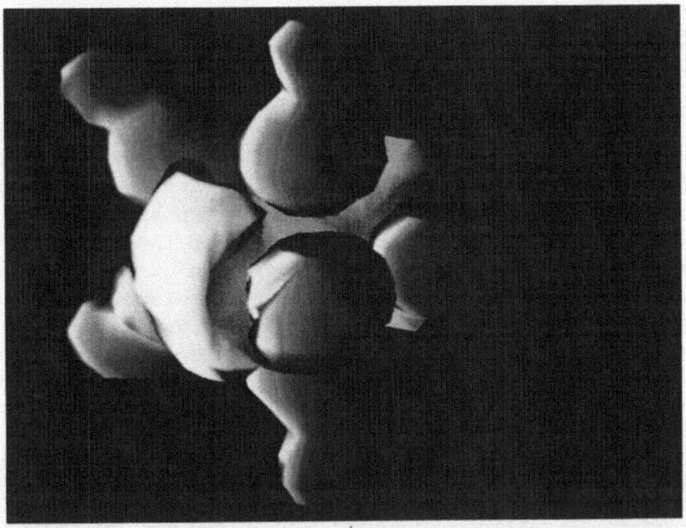

Figure 6. 3D solid model of the MEP calculated for the benzvalene molecule. Reactive sites for cationic attack correspond to the central yellow lobe (AED 512).

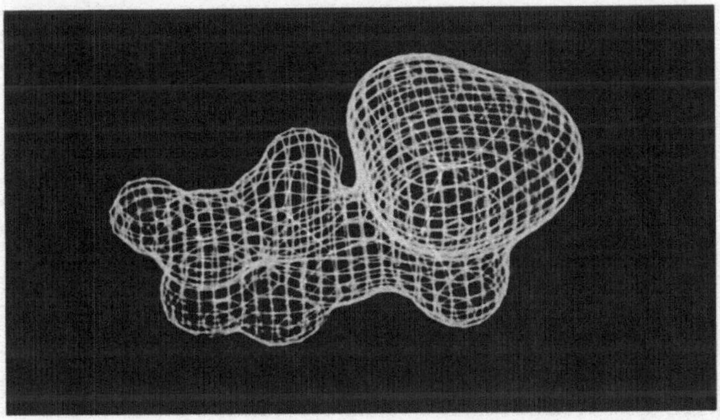

Figure 7. 3D mesh surface of the positive part of the MEP of hallucinogen mescaline (MPS, Evans & Sutherland).

to the most favorable sites for an attack by a positively charged, or an electron acceptor, reactive whereas MEP maxima on the molecular surface are characteristic of sites easily attacked by a negative, or electron donor, reactive. The most reactive sites of a given compound are therefore immediately deduced from an inspection of the MEP, which can be represented as: (i) 2D color-filled contour levels (Fig. 5), or (ii) a 3D solid model (Fig. 6), or (iii) an isometric 3D mesh surface (Fig. 7). These computer-generated images are of considerable help to the chemist as they allow to attribute reactivity indices to the molecules under study.

However, electrostatic energies represent only one of the components of intermolecular potentials: at large distances from the molecule, i.e. beyond the molecular surface usually built as the union of intersecting van der Waals spheres (Fig. 1), electrostatic interactions are indeed predominant and the MEP model is a good approximation. At shorter distances, other components of the interaction potential should be taken into account, namely charge transfer, polarization, exchange repulsion and dispersion energies (15). We have recently developed a theoretical model allowing to evaluate these different components (16) within the framework of the so-called extended Hückel formalism (17). Its main advantage lies in the small amount of computer time it requires, which makes it possible to calculate in a few minutes on the VAX-11/780 a complete map of interaction energies for organometallic compounds made of 20-50 atoms. An example of modelization of these interaction energies, represented as colored dot surfaces, is found in Fig. 8, where it is seen that the site of cationic attack on $Fe(CO)_5$ is located on the carbonyl groups in the MEP model and on the central metal atom according to the total interaction potential. The results of the

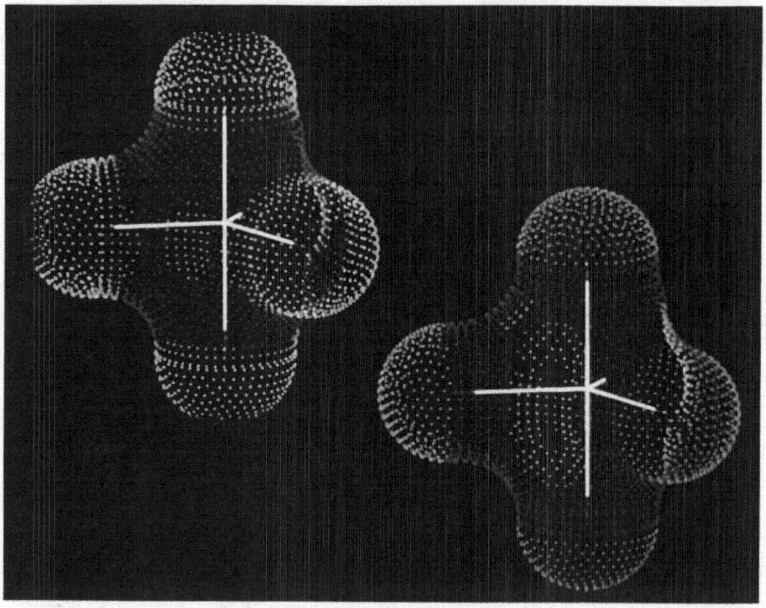

Figure 8. Interaction energies calculated for the $Fe(CO)_5$ molecule and represented as a colored dot surface: electrostatic part (MEP, left) and total interaction potential (right). The most reactive regions for cationic attack correspond to red zones (PS-390, Evans & Sutherland).

MEP model should thus be taken with caution in the case of transition metal complexes. However, from the point of view of graphics only, the advantages of this type of representation are that dot surfaces are transparent, which allows to simultaneously visualize the molecular skeleton, and that the image may be rotated and clipped in real time (13). Preliminary results obtained using this model have shown that this new MG tool is of great interest for modelizing inorganic and organometallic species such as novel homogeneous catalysts.

Conclusion

Undoubtedly, the spectacular development of MG techniques, which are now extensively used in several research applications, is due to the visual grasping of fundamental chemical concepts in a condensed from using simple and appropriate models. The potentials of MG are indeed enormous, as chemistry is a science where it is essential to build and manipulate models of molecular architectures and their major physico-chemical properties. In fact, most problems in molecular structure and dynamics, conformational analysis and chemical reactivity can nowadays be tackled by using computerized models which considerably facilitate interpretation and understanding.

In this paper, we have presented some basic applications of MG which provide the chemist with an efficient tool for an in-depth study of molecular structure and reactivity. However, these applications represent only a few of the multiple capabilities of MG and several other spectacular developments have been recently reported (18), which underlines the increasing role played by this new approach in computer-assisted chemistry. When applied to problems such as drug design, protein engineering, the search for novel catalysts and new biologically active molecules, the study of reactions on solid surfaces, etc., these techniques are now an indispensable tool for chemists and biologists working in different areas of molecular research.

Acknowledgements

This work has been supported by the Fonds National Suisse de la Recherche Scientifique (Project 2.806-0.85) and the Association pour la Recherche contre le Cancer (ARC).

References

1 R. Barone and M. Chanon, in "Computer Aids to Chemistry", G. Vernin and M. Chanon (eds), Ellis Horwood, Chichester (1986), p. 19

2 I.E. Frank and B.R. Kowalski, Anal. Chem. 54, 232R (1982)

3 S. Wilson, "Chemistry by Computer", Plenum, New York (1986), p. 41

4 M. Karplus and J.A. McCammon, Scient. Amer. 254, 30 (1986)

5 J.E. Dubois, D. Laurent and J. Weber, Visual Computer 1, 49 (1985)

6 J. Weber, M. Roch, J.P. Doucet and J.E. Dubois, "Imagery and Graphic Animation in Chemistry", 16mm film, Université Audio-Visuel, Ecole Normale Supérieure, F-92211 Saint-Cloud, France (1986)

7 C.D. Selassie, Z.X. Fang, R.L. Li, C. Hansch, T. Klein, R. Langridge and T.B. Kaufman, J. Med. Chem. 29, 621 (1986)

8 C.W. Jefford, J. Mareda, J.J. Combremont and J. Weber, Chimia 38, 354 (1984)

9 J. Weber, M. Roch, J.J. Combremont, P. Vogel and P.A. Carrupt, J. Mol. Struct. Theochem 93, 189 (1983)

10 J. Weber, D. Mottier, P.A. Carrupt and P. Vogel, J. Mol. Graphics 5, 126 (1987)

11 J. Weber and M. Roch, J. Mol. Graphics 4, 145 (1986)

12 W.G. Richards and V. Sackwild, Chem. Britain 18, 635 (1982)

13 M.L. Connolly, Science 221, 709 (1983)

14 E. Scrocco and J. Tomasi, Advan. Quantum Chem. 11, 115 (1978)

15 K. Morokuma, Acc. Chem. Res. 10, 294 (1977)

16 J. Weber, P. Fluekiger, P.Y. Morgantini, O. Schaad, C. Daul and A. Goursot, J. Comp. Aided Mol. Design, submitted for publication

17 R. Hoffmann, J. Chem. Phys. 39, 1397 (1963)

18 H. Frühbeis, R. Klein and H. Wallmeier, Angew. Chem. Int. Ed. Engl. 26, 403 (1987)

Molecular Graphics and Modeling on the PC

H. van de Waterbeemd, P.-A. Carrupt, and N. Huijsmans (Switzerland)

ABSTRACT

In recent years a number of computerized graphical tools appeared on the market which are of great importance for the chemist, biologist, pharmacologist and toxicologist for the rational molecular design of bioactive compounds such as drugs. In the present paper we want to review several molecular graphics and modeling programs which can be run on microcomputers. An overview is given of available programs discussing of each its possibilites and shortcomings. In particular we introduce a new program named Waalsurf which is a high-quality molecular graphics facility which can be installed on a low-cost PC.

INTRODUCTION TO MOLECULAR GRAPHICS AND MOLECULAR DESIGN

The design of bioactive molecules such as drugs, agrochemicals and flavours is a highly sophisticated and expensive process. Many active compounds were discovered from systematic screening on particular test systems. More rational approaches became possible with the rapid development of the computer era. Indeed, computer-assisted methods are now widely and successfully used in the field of drug design (Vinter, 1985; Burgen et al, 1986; Marshall, 1987). Four main areas may be defined were computer-technology plays a crucial role:

- Quantitative Structure-Activity Relationship studies (QSAR)
- Molecular graphics and modeling
- Computational chemistry
- Data base management

Molecules are three-dimensional objects with spatio-temporal properties (Van de Waterbeemd and Testa, 1987). Chemists have used several mechanical devices for the representation of molecules, such as Dreiding and CPK models. Computers shift molecular models from the work-bench to graphics displays (Langridge et al, 1981). Moreover, computers allow that conformational behaviour and electronic properties can be calculated. With the introduction of graphical tools making it possible to display and manipulate molecules and computational results, an enormeous breakthrough was realized in the field of molecular design. All large drug companies and many universities and other research institutes have equipped themselves with some molecular graphics facility. Such system consists mostly of a high-resolution graphics display and molecular graphics and modeling software. The total investment of these systems is considerable, so that up to now many smaller institutes could not afford this progress. On the other hand, the expensive workstations are generally not used by each medicinal chemist in his daily work. However, over the last few years a number of programs appeared on the market offering molecular graphics and modeling possibilities on personal computers. Of course such programs have severe limitations when used as a stand-alone program. When they can be linked to a main frame computer and some other software, they become increasingly more useful. PC molecular graphics (Hubbard, 1983, 1986) may also be the first step to become familiar with these techniques before going to work with a larger system. The main advantage is that each medicinal chemist or pharmacologist can use it on his own PC. In analogy with graphics applications in other fields this type of work for the chemist has been named desk-top chemistry. Allthough limited in possibilities, even simple programs running on a PC might guide the molecular designer in his decisions.

In the present paper we will define some general molecular graphics and modeling characteristics and we will give an overview of a number of available programs on a rapidly growing market for PC users. Finally we introduce a new program developped on a personal computer but taking advantage of the graphics possibilities on a PGA card. This program named WAALSURF has remarkable interactive high-quality graphics but can be installed on a low-cost PC system.

MOLECULAR GRAPHICS

By a molecular graphics system we mean a facility that allows to display molecules as realistic as possible and in several commonly accepted representations such as ball-and-stick, Dreiding and space-filled. Color-coding is another essential point. Since molecules are three-dimensional objects, a number of techniques are generally used to obtain a depth effect. Surfaces can be shaded and color intensity can decrease with the distance, which is called depth-cueing. Zooming and clipping are two other techniques used in molecular graphics. Depth illusions are also obtained with real-time rotations. Stereoperception can be obtained by displaying twice the same molecule some distance apart and seen under a slightly different angle. Various devices exist to see such stereoimages, such as red-green glasses and the use of polarization filters and an aluminium screen.

MOLECULAR MODELING

The simple display of a molecule can give the drug designer some general idea about its sterical properties, in particular in comparison with other molecules. However, it is of interest to have the possibility to manipulate the molecule in several ways. Manipulations, modifications and calculations on molecules are termed together as molecular modeling.

The information to build a molecule for display and manipulation may come from various sources. An important data collection exists of X-ray crystallographic data in the Cambridge and Brookhaven data banks. Many programs are capable to read directly data from these banks. When no crystallographic data are available a so-called model builder can be used. This module consists of a set of standard fragments which can be assembled on the screen. The final molecule can often be refined. This can be done by changing certain interatomic distances and angles or by using a conformation minimizer. Molecular mechanics calculations are frequently used to obtain rapidly a "reasonable" conformation. Molecular modeling involves operations including:

- docking
- least-squares atom-to-atom fit
- interatomic distance and angle measurements
- conformational analysis
- molecular electrostatic potential and interaction calculation

The last two approaches can only be done in an approximative way on a microcomputer and require more sophisticated programs running on mainframe (mini and super) computers.

PROGRAMS FOR THE MICROCOMPUTER

Representations of molecular structures are an important way for chemists to transfer information to other chemists. This task has been facilitated by a number of computer-assisted molecular representation programs available on the market for various computers. Among many others, we briefly mention some examples.

On the Macintosh computer, the MACDRAW program has been proposed (Whitesell, 1985) for drawing chemical structures, and recently a chemical template addition called CHEMPLATE has been reported (Hwu et al, 1987). A most useful program for molecular structure drawing on the Macintosh is called CHEMDRAW, alternatives are CHEMINTOSH and CHEMPANION. Similar in approach and possibilities for the IBM PC, HP-150 and compatibles is MPG (Molecular Presentation Graphics). Another versatile program for drawing organic chemical structures is WIMP (Wisconsin Interaction Molecule Processor) for the IBM PC, PC-XT and PC-AT. A highly developed tool for drawing molecules is also integrated in the wordprocessor CHEMTEXT (Gerson and Love, 1987) and the data base program CHEMBASE for IBM PC and PS/2 series. These programs can also read molecular structures from the larger data management progams MACCS-II and REACCS.

The above mentioned programs are in use mainly for the drawing of molecules. Below a number of programs are described which are usually designated as molecular modeling programs. In Table 1 an overview is given of the programs discussed in this section.

Table 1. Molecular graphics and modeling software for personal computers.

Program	Distributor
ALCHEMY	Tripos
CAMSEQ/M/PC-ORTEP	Weintraub
CHEMDRAW	Cambridge Scientific Computing
CHEMINTOSH-CHEMPANION	SoftShell Company
CHEMNOTE	Polygen-Léonard
CHEMTEXT-CHEMBASE-CHEMTALK	Molecular Design Ltd
MACDRAW	Apple
MOLCAD II	TH Darmstadt, Brickmann
MOLECULAR EDITOR	Kinko's Graphics
MOLECULAR GRAPHICS PACKAGE	Chemdata Ltd
MOLGRAF	Elsevier-Biosoft
MOLIDEA	Compudrug
MPG	Hawk Scientific Systems
PC-CHEMMOD	U-Micro
PC-MCE-MGM-MSA	Areli
PC MODEL	Academic Press, Henkel and Clarke
WAALSURF	Leiden University, Softarts-Actimol
WIMP	Aldrich

MOLGRAF is a molecular graphics program for the IBM PC or Apple II. It allows rotations and superpositions of molecules. The program also provides information on bond lengths, bond-angles and torsion angles. A data base of a number of common pharmacological agents is included. In the same category falls the program PCMODEL developed by Henkel and Clarke. For the IBM PC-XT or PC-AT and compatibles the integrated package MOLIDEA is another alternative for simple molecular modeling. The molecular structure input of this program is even non-graphic. The program calculates atomic Cartesian coordinates, represents molecules as wire-frame and space-filled models and allows rotations around a bond or X, Y or Z axes.

A series of three molecular PC programs have been developped for IBM PC or Olivetti/AT&T. The low-price program PC-MCE (Molecular Chemical Education) allows visualisation of molecules with a maximum of 500 atoms and some simple manipulations. PC-MGM (Molecular Graphic Manipulation) and PC-MSA (Molecular Structure Analysis) are two higher priced programs. PC-MGM can visualize molecules upto 1000 atoms, or two molecules of 500 atoms. Several representations are offered, including skeleton, real volume balls, Van der Waals dot surface and space filling cross hatching.

Three-dimensional effects are obtained by continuous movement of the molecules. PC-MSA explores conformational energy space for molecules with a maximum of 200 atoms.

Several PC molecular modeling programs derive directly from larger software packages. Among these we discuss here CHEMNOTE, CAMSEQ/PC, ALCHEMY and PC-CHEMMOD.

CHEMNOTE works on the IBM PC computer or compatibles and is in fact a "front-end" for the VAX-based molecular modeling programs CHARMM and HYDRA and users of CHEMNOTE should be familiar with these two programs.

CAMSEQ/PC and CAMSEQ/M are PC software products having their origin in the 1970s. The original CAMSEQ (Conformation Analysis of Molecules in Solution by Empirical and Quantum techniques) program was one of the first integrated molecular modeling systems. The microcomputer-based versions have an open structure and can communicate with several external programs such as MM2, SYBYL, MACCS, CHEMBASE-CHEMTEXT. CAMSEQ/M controls the input and storage as well as the various display features. CAMSEQ/PC is a molecular mechanics-based conformational analysis in a simulated solution environment module. CAMSEQ/M/PC has numerous options. In the same package the ORTEP-II program is included which is an additional molecular representation mode.

One of the best-known molecular graphics and modeling programs is SYBYL. An interesting derivative for PC users is ALCHEMY, which can read and write SYBYL mol.files. It can be installed on an IBM PC in the CGA or EGA configuration and requires only 256 kB. A hard disk and 8027 co-processor are recommanded. The program contains an electronic Dreiding kit to build molecules and has a conformation optimization procedure. Atomic distances and angles can be measured and changed, and molecules can be colorcoded and superimposed by a least-squares atom-to-atom fit. ALCHEMY is also able to assign the absolute configuration to asymmetric centers. Molecules can be rotated and translated interactively. The molecular size is only limited by the available memory. A poor and time-consuming space-filled reprentation is offered which cannot be rotated in an interactive way.

PC-CHEMMOD is launched as "real" molecular modeling for the IBM PC and is a daughter of the workstation-based program CHEMMOD. It brings in colour-graphics real-time rotations and translations. A range of molecular representations is included varying from stick and spacefill to stereoview. Stereoview is offered by a red green pair. Molecules can be build up from fragments and a fast conformation optimizer is included. Charges can be calculated by the Del Re procedure. Conformational behaviour can be explored and displayed in torsion angle and Ramachandran plots. PC-CHEMMOD supports molecules of upto 250 atoms. Along with the PC-CHEMMOD program comes a Vector Graphics Processor (VGP) taking up one expansion slot and dedicated to fast graphics. Furthermore a co-processor 8027/80287 and 640 kB RAM are required.

For the Commodore Amiga users the program MOLCAD II is under development at the Technical University of Darmstadt by Brickmann and collaborators. The following features are announced: data input from PDB-files, representation of 5 molecules simultanously, interactive rotation, translation, zoom in/out, measurement of interatomic distances and angles, least squares fit of superimposed molecules, molecule builder and dotted Van der Waals surface.

A second program mentioned in the literature for use on the Amiga is WAALSURF (Huijsmans et al, 1987), which will be presented in the next section.

WAALSURF

Waalsurf is a molecular graphics representation program in which in particular attention is paid to the graphical aspects. It makes full use of the filled circle primitive on the IBM Professional Graphics Controller using the PGA norm. The program has been developed in Turbo-Pascal, while an Amiga implementation was programmed in C. A full technical description has been given elsewhere (Huijsmans et al, 1987).

Graphical aspects

The display controller board used by WAALSURF has rather high-level graphic primitives. Display generation is speed up by relegating many tasks to this controller using a temporal priority approach. The graphic elements used are line segments for the binding structure (Dreiding models), shaded spheres for the ball-and-stick model and intersecting shaded spheres for the Van der Waals surfaces. When a spherically depicted atom is illuminated by a single light source close to the observer, the projected pattern is a concentric set of color shades. With a limited discrete set of color shades per atom, this concentric intensity pattern is obtained when a nested set of concentric filled circles is displayed from back to front. This temporal priority method to display shaded spheres can easily be extended to the display of intersecting spheres. The display memory of the PGC is 8 bit deep. For the docking of two molecules, 4 bit can be used for each molecule.

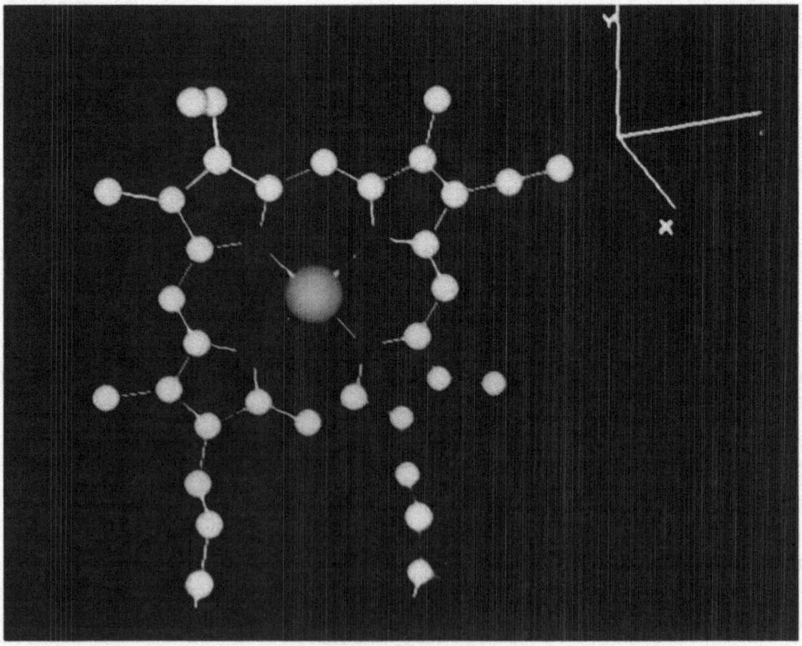

Figure 1. A heme-group in ball-and-stick representation (program Waalsurf, generated on IBM PC/AT with Matrox PG640A graphics board).

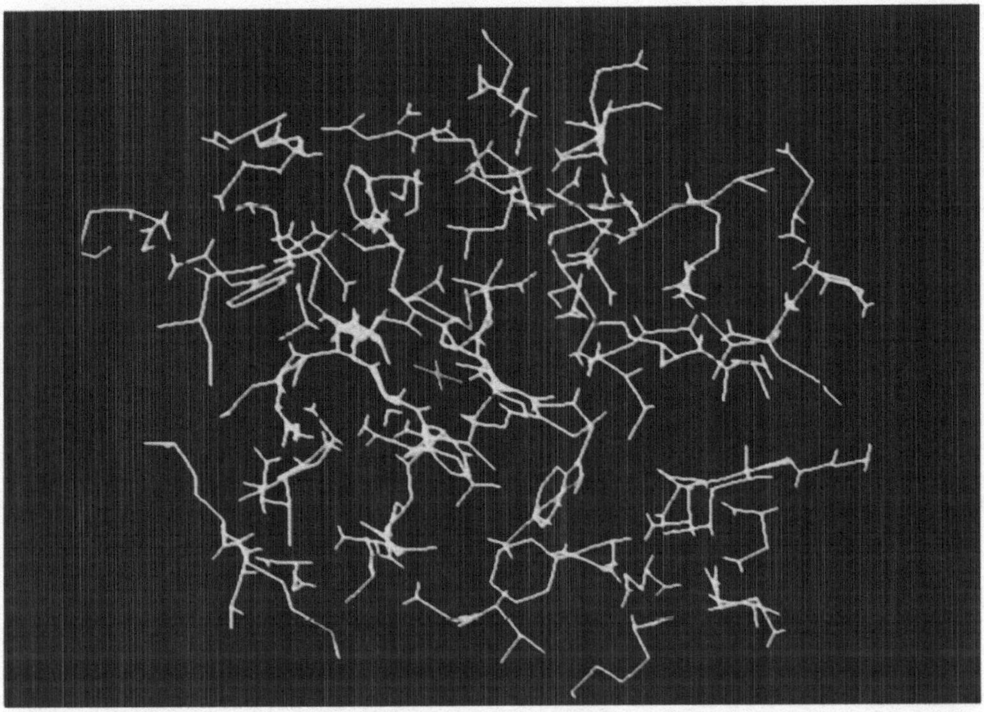

Figure 2. A Dreiding bond skeleton model of a cytochrome protein with the heme-group in the middle (program Waalsurf).

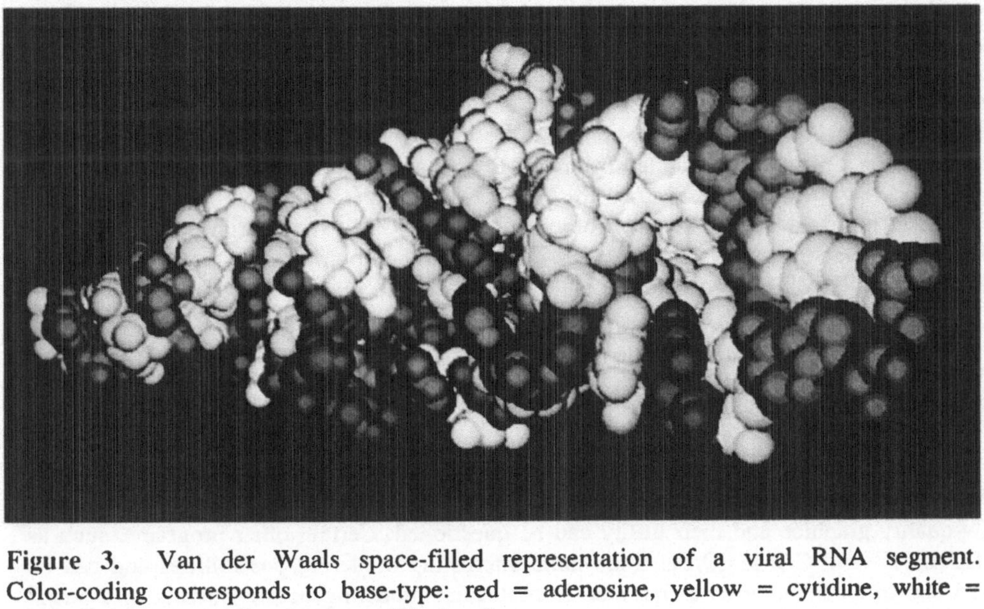

Figure 3. Van der Waals space-filled representation of a viral RNA segment. Color-coding corresponds to base-type: red = adenosine, yellow = cytidine, white = guanosine, blue = uridine (program Waalsurf).

Features

WAALSURF is keyboard-driven and uses a hierarchical tree of menus. A pointing cursor in 2D and 3D is provided to interact with the displayed molecule. The program handles a molecule of up to 2500 atoms or simultanously two molecules of up to 1250 atoms each. From atomic coordinates the module MAKEBOND calculates bondstructure and generates a connectivity matrix. Molecules can be displayed in ball-and-stick representation (Fig. 1), as Dreiding models (Fig. 2), and as space-filled Van der Waals surface (Fig. 3). The viewing angle, the size and the amount of perspective can be changed. Flexible color-coding is available to highlight certain properties, e.g. backbone structure, polar groups or hydrophobic fragments. Various labels can be stored. The molecules with all information on color, labels, etc, can be stored at any moment during the seesion for later use. The module WAALFILM is included for making sequences of images to be used in conferences or for educational purposes. Interatomic distances, bond-angles, and torsion-angles can be measured. Molecules can be rotated and translated in any representation mode in real time. WAALSURF has an option to make hard copies on an IBM or HP inkjet color-printer.

Display speed

With a PC-AT2 (6 Mhz), a ball-and-stick image of about 75 atoms with 5 circles per atom is redisplayed in 1 second. A Van der Waals representation of a 1000 atom molecule with 10 circles per atom takes about 1 minute. Even better results are obtained with the PC-AT3 (8 or 10 MHz). It is also possible to work in low resolution to speed up the operations, and in high resolution only for the final images.

Interfaces

WAALSURF is developed as a molecule representation program and is not a stand-alone program for e.g. conformational analysis. Therefore a number of interfaces are and will be developed to other programs. At present WAALSURF is able to read data files from various origin, in particular from the Brookhaven protein data bank (PDB-files). Interfaces have also been written to MACROMODEL (Still) and to the molecular dynamics program GROMOS (Groningen University). A versatile communication program between the graphics of WAALSURF and a number of quantum chemical programs is DESMOL (Data Exchange Support for MOLecular modeling).

CONCLUSION

Molecular graphics and modeling programs are available at different price-levels. Most programs are orientated towards the IBM PC and compatibles. Some programs offer low-quality graphics and their utility can be questioned. Certain other programs, such as ALCHEMY and CAMSEQ/PC offer some interesting modeling possibilities and can be used e.g. in teaching or as a first step to molecular modeling before moving to a larger system. High-quality graphics on a PC-based computer can be realized when a special graphics card is used. This approach is offered by PC-CHEMMOD and WAALSURF. The program WAALSURF demonstrates that molecular graphics with rather advanced features with acceptable time performance can be run on low-cost microcomputers. PC molecular graphics programs give the chemist a realistic image of his molecules and can be useful when they can be linked to a main-frame on which all kind of calculations can be run. Desk-top chemistry seems to become more and more a reality and PC programs have certainly their role to play (Morffew, 1983; Hubbard, 1983; Gross and Duane, 1986).

ACKNOWLEDGEMENT

The authors are indebted to H.R. Kottmann of Molecular Design Ltd for a copy of CHEMTEXT.

REFERENCES

Burgen, A.S.V., Roberts, G.C.K. and Tute, M.S. (eds), Molecular Graphics and Drug Design, Elsevier, Amsterdam (1986)

Gerson, C.K. and Love, R.A., Technical word processors for scientific writers, Anal. Chem. 59, 1031A-1048A (1987)

Gross, E. and Duane, J., Protein graphics: historical development, future directions and microcomputer applications, Comput.Appl.Biosci. 2, 173-179 (1986)

Hubbard, R.E., Colour molecular graphics on a microcomputer, J.Mol.Graphics 1, 13-16 (1983)

Hubbard, R.E., Molecular graphics on microcomputers. In: Molecular Graphics and Drug Design, Burgen, A.S.V., Roberts, G.C.K. and Tute, M.S. (eds), Elsevier, Amsterdam, (1986), pp. 57-73

Huijsmans, D.P., Van Delft. A., Kuip, C.A.C., Waalsurf, molecular graphics on a personal computer, Computers and Graphics 11, 449-458 (1987)

Hwu, J.R., Wetzel, J.M. and Robl, J.A., ChemPlate and Hopkins, a template and font for drawing molecular structures with the Macintosh computer, J. Chem. Educ. 64, 135-137 (1987)

Langridge, R.L., Ferrin, T.E., Kuntz, I.D. and Connolly, M.L., Real-time graphics in studies of molecular interactions, Science 211, 661-666 (1981)

Marshall, G.R., Computer-aided drug design, Ann.Rev.Pharmacol.Toxicol. 27, 193-213 (1987)

Morffew, A.J., Where do we go from here? A personal view on the future of molecular graphics, J.Mol.Graphics 1, 83-87 (1983)

Still, C., Columbia University, USA

Van de Waterbeemd, H. and Testa, B., The parametrization of lipophilicity and other structural properties in drug design, Adv. Drug Res. 16, 85-225 (1987)

Vinter, J.G., Molecular graphics for the medicinal chemist, Chemistry in Britain, 32-38 (1985)

Whitesell, J.K., MacDraw, J.Amer.Chem.Soc. 107, 6140-6141 (1985)

PC MOLECULAR GRAPHICS SOFTWARE DISTRIBUTORS

ALCHEMY, Tripos Associates, 6548 Clayton Road, St.Louis, MI 63117, USA (1986).
CAMSEQ/PC, Weintraub Software Design Associates Inc., PO Box 42577, Cincinnati, OH 45242, USA (1987).
CHEMDRAW, Cambridge Scientific Computing, PO Box 2123, Cambridge MA 02238, USA.
CHEMINTOSH-CHEMPANION, SoftShell Company, PO Box 632, Henrietta, NY 14467, USA.
CHEMNOTE, Polygen, 200 Fifth Avenue, Waltham, MA 02254, USA.
CHEMTEXT-CHEMBASE-CHEMTALK-MACCS-REACCS, Molecular Design Ltd, 2132 Farallon Drive, San Leandro, CA 94577, USA.
DESMOL, Softarts-Actimol, Chemin de Maillefer 37, CH-1052 Le Mont/Lausanne, Switzerland.
MOLCAD II, Brickmann, J., TH Darmstadt, Physikalische Chemie I, Petersenstrasse 20, D-6100 Darmstadt, FRG.
MOLECULAR EDITOR, Kinko's Graphics Academic Courseware Exchange, 4141 State Street, Santa Barbara, CA 93110, USA.
MOLGRAF, Elsevier-Biosoft, 68 Hills Road, Cambridge CB2 1LA, UK.
MOLIDEA, Compudrug Ltd, Fürst Sandor u.5, H-1136 Budapest, Hungary (1987).
MPG, Hawk Scientific Systems Inc, PO Box 316, Bloomingdale, NJ 07403, USA.
PC-CHEMMOD, U-Micro, Winstanley Industrial Estate, Long Lane, Warrington, Cheshire, WA2 8PR, UK.
PC-MCE/MGM/MSA, Areli, Monte Carlo, Princedom of Monaco.
WIMP, Whitlock, H.W., University of Wisconsin, Madison, Wisconsin, USA; and Aldrich Chemical Company (1986).
WAALSURF, Softarts-Actimol, Chemin de Maillefer 37, CH-1052 Le Mont/Lausanne, Switzerland; and Computer Science Department, University of Leiden, PO Box 9512, NL-2300 RA Leiden, The Netherlands (1988).

MOPIC: An Advanced Molecule Rendering Program for Microcomputers

F. T. Marchese and S. Reda (USA)

ABSTRACT

MOPIC (MOlecular PICtures) is a microcomputer implementation of molecular graphics software. It is designed for chemists and students, with no computer training, who need to manipulate and display molecules but do not require dedicated high performance systems. Moreover, since its graphics is patterned after vector display systems, MOPIC produces stick and dot sphere images of molecules which communicate a degree of visualization far superior to present microcomputer software.

1. INTRODUCTION

We have developed a microcomputer-based molecular graphics system for non-computer oriented scientists and students. It allows them to enter, manipulate and display molecules within minutes. Beyond this, it provides rendering capabilities and a degree of visualization superior to present microcomputer software and comparable to vector display graphics systems.

In the following section we discuss the background behind the development of our molecular graphics software. Subsequent sections present a description of the software, summary and conclusion.

2. BACKGROUND

The vast majority of molecular modeling and graphics systems are implemented on mini or larger computers, supporting the manipulation of tens to hundreds-of-thousands of atoms (Pique 1987). If high performance vector displays are attached, such as the Evans and Sutherland PS300 series, razor-sharp images of molecules can be manipulated in real-time.

These tools give researchers unprecedented insight into molecular structure and function and, as a result, have become integral components of research efforts ranging from molecular biology to drug design (Fetterich 1986). However, all this insight comes at a price! The expense of computer hardware and the long learning curves for associated software prevent placement of such sophisticated systems on every chemist's desk.

Current attempts at microcomputer implementations of molecular modeling systems succeed in emulating many attributes of the dedicated systems including: structure manipulation, computation of geometric information (e.g. bond lengths, angles and dihedral angles), even animation. However, many programs suffer from weak user interfaces and all have poor image quality (Turbe 1988).

User interfaces are critical components of microcomputer molecular graphics packages. Most chemical researchers and students are not computer oriented and use these packages only intermittently. As a result, an easy-to-use interface, with short start-up time, is essential to productivity.

The type of image displayed has as much to do with the visualization process as the quality of rendering. Ideally, the image should convey enough geometric information about the molecule that the viewer develops an intuitive sense for the structure's spatial characteristics. Much of this can be achieved on microcomputer systems with stereoscopic projections, animation and the appropriate choice of molecular representation.

There are three basic ways to represent a molecule: stick figures, ball and stick displays or space filling images (Max 1983). Stick figures are most common and easiest to display. From this representation, a chemist determines the bonding network for a molecule. In contrast, space filling models portray the overall shape and steric properties of the molecule, but it is sometimes difficult to see the relative placement of atoms. Ball-and-stick figures are a compromise between stick and space filling and allow display of some spatial and geometric information. The latter two representations fare poorly on microcomputer systems; using ball-and-stick models, even for moderate size molecules, on small, low resolution raster screens results in poor image quality, while outline and shaded disk representations of space filling models often fail to convey significant three dimensional shape.

In contrast, on vector displays, space filling models are represented by spheres whose surfaces are composed of dots. Each dot position is defined by three cartesian coordinates, presenting explicit three dimensional depth information. Moreover, the translucent quality of dot spheres permits viewing a superimposed stick figure on the molecular backbone (Bash 1983).

Dot spheres can be adapted easily to raster displays with little loss of image quality. As a result, they should be adaptable to microcomputer graphics systems.

Thus, recognizing the limitations of current microcomputer graphics systems, we designed a package which exploits the strong user interface capabilities of microcomputers and the rendering methods of vector displays. The program, called MOPIC (MOlecular PICtures), is discussed below.

3. MOPIC

MOPIC is a microcomputer based molecular graphics program specifically designed for scientists and students who require the rendering capabilities of a dedicated workstation in a less dedicated way. Therefore, development of MOPIC focused on a strong user interface and high visual quality rendering.

MOPIC was implemented on an IBM PC/XT with 640K, a math coprocessor and hard disk drive in Turbo Pascal. There are 3500 lines of code, approximately two-thirds of which are associated with the user interface.

Since MOPIC's users are expected to be non-computer oriented, a fault-tolerant interface has been designed to prevent program destruction and maintain data integrity. Menus and submenus are used to access all MOPIC's features. The structure of this interface minimizes learning time so a new user performs productively within a few minutes.

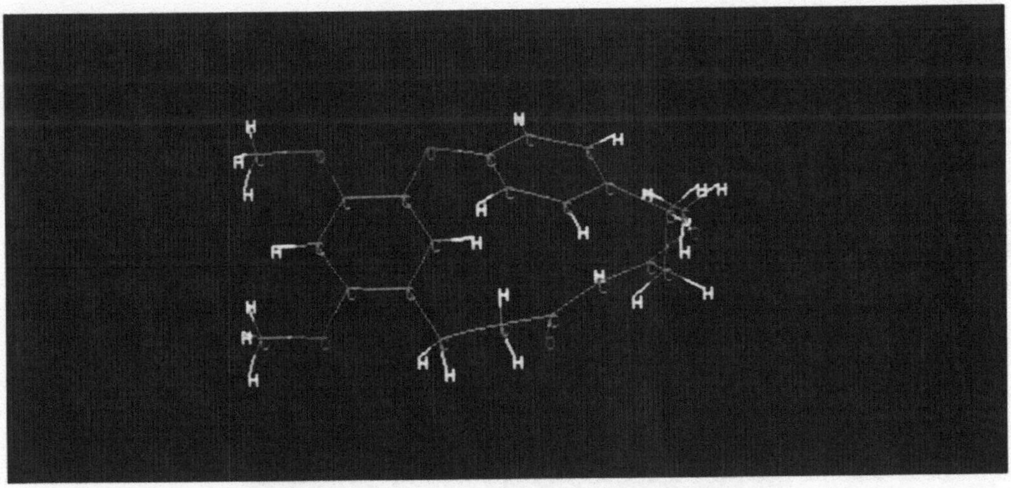

Fig. 1 Dreiding model of Garuganin-I with atom labeling. Color is used to designate atom type (carbon (green), oxygen(red), and hydrogen (white)).

MOPIC accommodates as many as 1000 atoms in any combination of molecules up to the 1000 atom limit. It can display several molecules simultaneously and perform three dimensional transformations, such as translation and rotation on individual molecules, as well as on all shown on the screen. In addition, it calculates standard geometric indices, including bond distances, angles and dihedral angles.

The graphics capabilities of MOPIC emulate vector display systems. The basic rendering representations are the stick figure (also known as a Dreiding model) and the dot sphere.

A stick figure is displayed with or without atom labeling and/or numerical position in the data structure. Figure 1 depicts the Dreiding model of Garuganin-I, an antibiotic derived from plants. Notice color is used to represent atom type (e.g. carbon (green), oxygen (red) and hydrogen (white)).

Dot spheres are used to delineate the overall shape and steric properties of the molecule. Each atom is represented by a sphere, the size of which is characteristic of the atom's van der Waals radius, a measure of the atom's size. In the screen display of the molecule, each atom dot sphere is oriented along a bond and clipped according to its intersection with other atoms. Figure 2 displays a dot sphere rendering of 9-anilino acridine where intensity depth cueing is used to enhance depth perception. In simultaneous display of Dreiding models and dot spheres, the translucency of the dot sphere allows the user to see the bond network. For example, in chloramphenicol (Fig. 3), all bonds are clearly visible through the dot sphere.

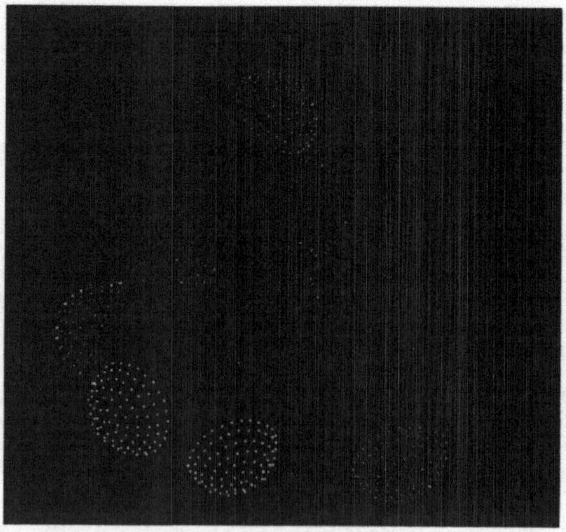

Fig. 2 Dot sphere image of 9-anilino acridine. Intensity depth cueing is used to enhance depth perception.

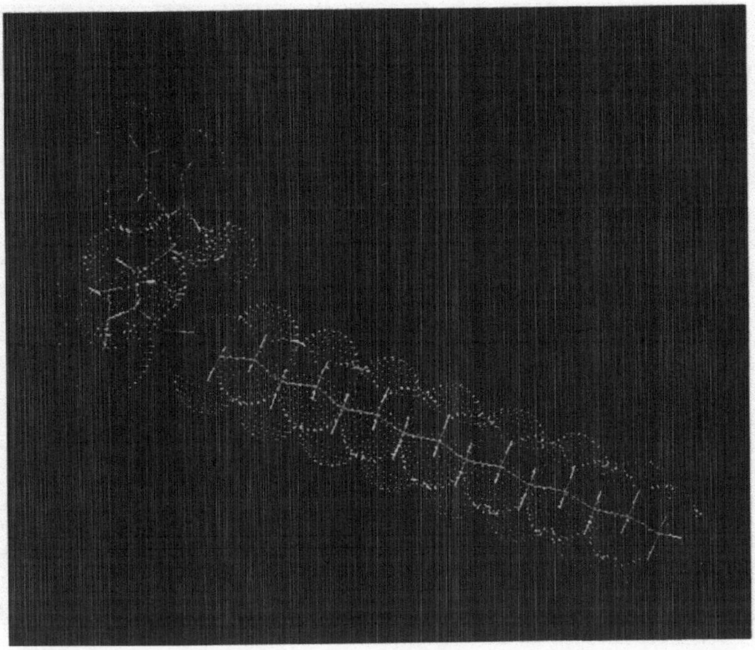

Fig. 3 Superimposed Dreiding model and dot sphere plot of chloramphenicol.

Further detail is achieved through z-clipping of dot spheres which results in molecule "slicing". Figure 4 shows the z-clipped exposed bond network of the guanine-cytosine dimer. Clipping away nearly all dots exposes the three hydrogen bonds between the two DNA bases and portrays explicitly the anticipated overlap between van der Waals spheres.

Depth perception is refined with stereoscopic views of displays. In addition, the color of individual atoms or entire molecules can be changed to highlight stereochemically important features. Figure 5 depicts a stereo view of the bis-p-nitrophenylphosphate ion with carbon and hydrogen atoms rendered in white, phosphorous atoms in orange, nitrogen in blue, and oxygen red. By drawing carbon and hydrogen atoms in white, the various functional groups (phenyl (white), nitro (red and blue), and phosphate (red and orange)) become visually distinct entities.

MOPIC's animation feature provides real-time rotation of the Dreiding model around each of the three orthogonal axes. Animation can be stopped, the molecule examined and animation restarted along another axis at any time. Whenever the motion is stopped, the molecular coordinates are saved as the current coordinates. As a result, the animation feature can be used to quickly find the best viewing orientation.

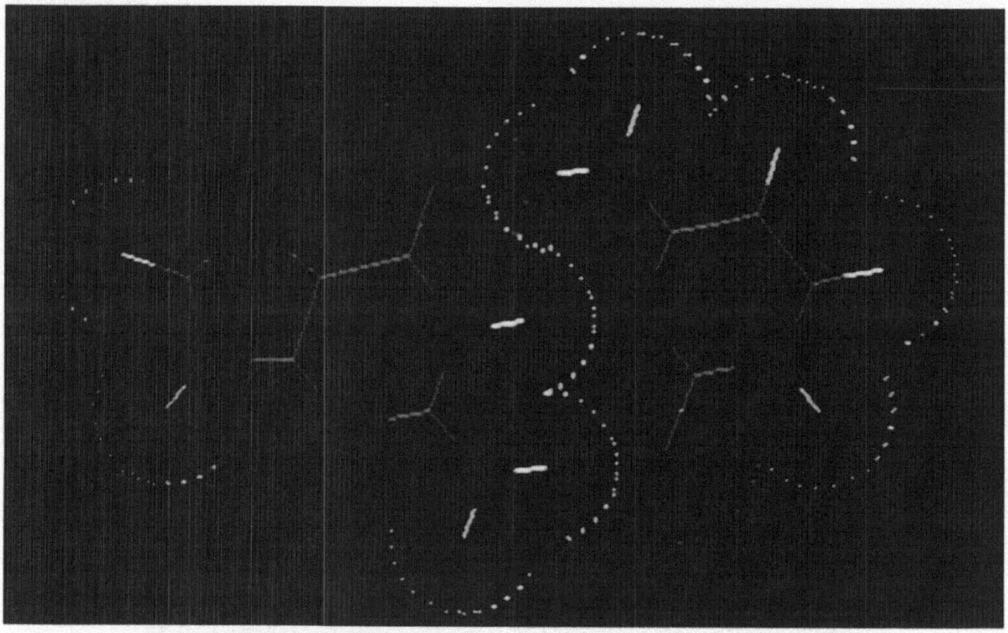

Fig. 4 Z-clipped dot sphere plot of the DNA base pair guanine-cytosine.

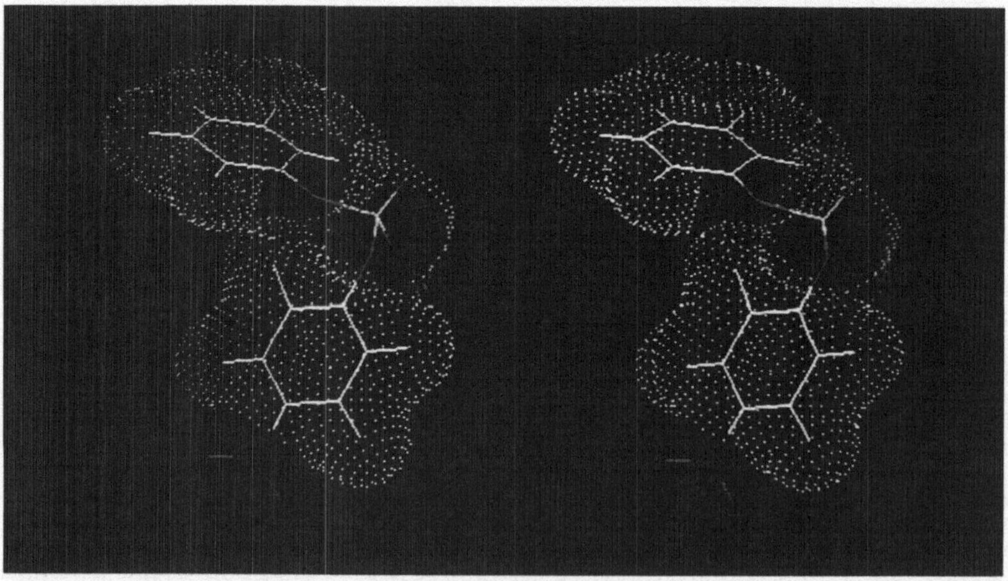

Fig. 5 Stereoscopic view of superimposed dot sphere and stick figure of bis-p-nitrophenylphosphate. Carbon atoms are rendered in white to enhance detail.

Any image MOPIC renders on the screen can be drawn on a plotter (Fig. 6). Since chemists must be able to place the results of graphics sessions into their laboratory notebooks for future reference, this becomes a very important program feature. Furthermore, black and white hardcopy can be used as figures for manuscripts or easily reproduced as foils. Clearly, the communication of information does not end when a chemist completes a microcomputer session.

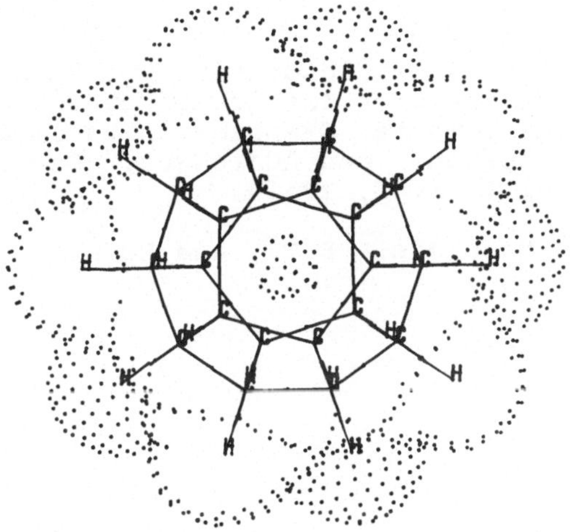

Fig. 6 Plotter output of z-clipped dot sphere image and Dreiding model of dodecahedrane.

4. SUMMARY and CONCLUSIONS

We have presented a new microcomputer based molecular graphics program designed to be easy to use and to produce high quality rendering of molecules. Since this graphics module is patterned after vector display systems, it is possible to produce stick and dot sphere images of molecules which communicate a level of three dimensional space visualization vastly superior to present microcomputer software. Moreover, the menu driven user interface is designed for scientists with no computer training and allows them to construct and display molecules within a few minutes. Finally, because this is a microcomputer based system, it is inexpensive to assemble, maintain and enhance and permits a portability not normally found on dedicated, high performance systems.

AVAILABILITY

MOPIC is presently in beta-test and should be available within six months. Before the package is released, the graphics interface will be modified to accommodate standard color graphics adaptors (e.g. EGA, PGA, VGA). The anticipated cost of MOPIC will be under $200.00.

REFERENCES

Bash, P.A. (1983), Pattabiraman, C., Huang, C., Ferrin, T.E., and Langridge, R., Science, Vol. 111, pp 134.

Fletterich, R. (1986) and Zoller, M., eds. "Computer Graphics and Molecular Modeling," Cold Spring Harbor Laboratory, NY.

Max, N. (1983), IEEE Computer Graphics and Applications, Vol. 3, pp 21.

Pique, M. (1987) and Thorraldsdottir, H., " The University of North Carolina and Research Institute of Scripps Clinic List of Known Molecular Computer Graphics Installations: Equipment Survey, Contact Person, and Addresses," Dept. of Computer Science, Chapel Hill, N.C., 27514.

Turbe, N. (1988), Marchese, F.T., and Reda, S., Manuscript in preparation.

Computer Graphics and Complex Ordinary Differential Equations

F. Richard (France)

1. Introduction

This paper describes the graphical part of a broader project consisting of the resolution of algebraic linear and homogeneous differential equations in the complex domain.

In order to represent the solutions of such equations, two major problems have to be solved: the first is entirely mathematical and consists of obtaining the solutions themselves. The second is entirely *computer graphical* and is the problem of representing complex functions of a complex variable. Such representation is particularly difficult to achieve because these functions are **four dimensional** in nature.

Without entering into all the details, the paper will first present the mathematical context of this work. It is important to realize that there is not just one calculation method for the solutions, and so we wish to compare different methods and to determine their respective regions of stability or instability. Obviously a graphical representation can facilitate the search for an efficient calculation tactic. It is also important to know that the functions which are being studied have exponential behaviour in general. Thus they have drastic variations of modulus which must be taken into account.

Two representation methods were studied and programmed. The second, and major, part of this paper will be devoted to their development.

The first method consists of representing in the complex plane the set of image-points obtained when the variable describes a curve in the domain. In our case, the possible curves are naturally circles centered on a particular singularity, which enables us to study the variation of the function around the singularity. By reducing the number of parameters to be displayed, it is also possible to reduce the representation to **two dimensions**.

This method has been explained in detail in a previous paper [1], but its principles will be reviewed and two significant examples of the **curves** obtained will be given to illustrate the possibilities offered by the software.

Much emphasis will be placed on the description of the second method, on the difficulties encountered during its development and on the results obtained. In this method the four dimensions have been simulated by representing the functions as **three-dimensional shaded surfaces**. More precisely, the relief of the modulus of the function is shaded according to the argument of the image-points. Specific problems will be emphasized: the circularity of the colour table, the refinement of some facets into smaller sub-facets and the possibility of truncating the surface.

To conclude this paper the two methods will be compared and constrasted. In fact they are **complementary** and, indeed, the first method is a tool which makes the second possible.

2. Mathematical context

This work has been motivated by recent work in three domains:

- in pure mathematics: research carried out by B. Malgrange and J.P. Ramis led to new results concerning the classification of Ordinary Differential Equations (*théorèmes d'indice Gevrey* [2]) and to the introduction of a class of divergent series, the k-summable series, which have interesting properties of resummation. This research had practical repercussions in applied mathematics since it has formed the basis for great strides in the two following domains.

- in formal calculus: a team of research workers at Grenoble worked out developments in algebraic programming, which enable the calculation of the formal invariants of the differential equations studied. The algorithms are regrouped in a solver (the solver DESIR), which computes a **basis of formal solutions** in the neighbourhood of any point, even if it is a regular or irregular singularity.[3,4]
- in numerical analysis: the series that appear in the formal solutions given by the solver DESIR in the neighbourhood of a regular point or a regular singular point are **convergent**, but in the neighbourhood of an irregular singularity the series are generally **divergent**. Numerical methods of resummation have been worked out by J. Thomann at Strasbourg, using results from k-summability theory. Consequently it is also possible to find the *actual* solutions by two methods:
  a) transformation of the divergent series into convergent **generalized factorial series**. [5, 6, 7]
  b) spectral decomposition.
  If $\hat{f}(z)$ is 1-summable (a state to which a k-summable series can be reduced), its Borel transformation
  $$\hat{\phi}(t) = a_1 + \frac{a_2}{1!}t + \frac{a_3}{2!}t^2 + \ldots + \frac{a_{n+1}}{n!}t^n + \ldots$$
  is convergent in a disk centered at the origin and its sum $\phi(t)$ extends analytically in all directions except, at most, in a finite number of singular directions, which can be determined. One can thus calculate the sum $f(z)$ of $\hat{f}(z)$ as:
  $$f(z) = \frac{1}{z}\int_0^{e^{i\theta}\infty} \phi(t)e^{\frac{-t}{z}}\,dt.$$
  The analytical extension of $\phi(t)$ can be represented in different ways, particularly by approximations of Padé-type $\left[\frac{L-1}{L}\right]$ of $\hat{\phi}(t)$ which can be decomposed into simple components
  $$\frac{A_1}{t-c_1} + \frac{A_2}{t-c_2} + \ldots + \frac{A_L}{t-c_L}.$$
  Thus, $f(z)$ can be decomposed as the sum:
  $$f(z) = \sum_{i=1}^{L} \frac{A_i}{z}\int_0^{e^{i\theta}\infty} \frac{e^{\frac{-t}{z}}}{t-c_i}\,dt,$$
  that is, a sum of exponential integrals which can be calculated by optimal formulas (Gauss-Laguerre, continued fractions, ...).

In the first version of the solver DESIR, the results were only displayed on the screen and there was no automatic connection between the formal resolution and the numerical resolution. Now the results of the solver DESIR are written in the form of FORTRAN subroutines, dependent on the studied equation, which are compiled and linked with the main program of resummation and graphical representation. Thus we solved the problems of interface between the formal part of the software, written with REDUCE and the numerical one, written in FORTRAN.

In the following we will deal as an example with the Bessel equation $z^2y'' + zy' + (z^2 - \nu^2)y = 0$, where we choose $\nu = 0$. This equation has two singularities: 0 is a regular singular point and ∞ is an irregular one.

The solver DESIR computes the n first terms (n arbitrary) of the following formal solutions by induction:
near 0:

$$f_1(z) = \sum_{k=0}^{\infty} \frac{(-z^2/4)^n}{n!\Gamma(n+1)} \qquad \text{and} \qquad f_2(z) = f_1(z)log(z) + f_2^2(z)$$

Note that $f_2^2(z)$ is not given explicitly because $f_2(z)$ is not used in the following.

near ∞:

$$g_1(z) = z^{-1/2}e^{iz}\sum_{n=0}^{\infty} a_n z^{-n}, \quad \text{where } a_0 = 1; \quad a_n = \frac{(-i)^n}{8^n n!}\prod_{k=0}^{n-1}(2k+1)^2, \quad n \geq 1,$$

and $$g_2(z) = z^{-1/2}e^{-iz}\sum_{n=0}^{\infty} b_n z^{-n}, \quad \text{where } b_0 = 1; \quad b_n = \frac{i^n}{8^n n!}\prod_{k=0}^{n-1}(2k+1)^2, \quad n \geq 1.$$

f_1 is identified as the classical solution J_0, a solution which can be found again in the neighbourhood of ∞ by a linear combination of g_1 and g_2. We will see just later that the first method of representation is particularly suited to the study of the problem posed by the choice of the linear combination, which is well known as the connection problem. It is also ideal for emphasizing the Stokes phenomenon: the coefficients of the linear combination depend on the sector in which the function is computed.

3. First representation method

The purpose is to represent the image under the considered function of a circle or a circular arc around the studied singularity z_0. In other words image of sets of the type:

$$A_\rho = \{z = z_0 + \rho e^{i\theta}, \theta \in \mathrm{I}\},$$

are to be constructed. This requires fixing the parameter ρ and letting θ move in I (any given finite segment of $\mathbf{R}$).

Without representing the domain, the *co-domain* is then plotted in the complex z-plane, that is, in two dimensions.

Each point $f(z)$ is displayed on the screen with a colour corresponding to the argument of its corresponding point z, chosen in a palette of up to 256 different colours (which are more than enough for this type of plotting). These 256 colours are distributed on the interval $[0, 2\pi]$ in a fixed way, which enables the user to associate automatically each colour with an argument: for instance blue corresponds to 0, red to $\frac{2\pi}{3}$, yellow to π, and so on.

For more details about the possibilities offered by the software - the drawing of several A_ρ on the same graph, the zoom, the storage of curves which the user finds interesting - see [1].

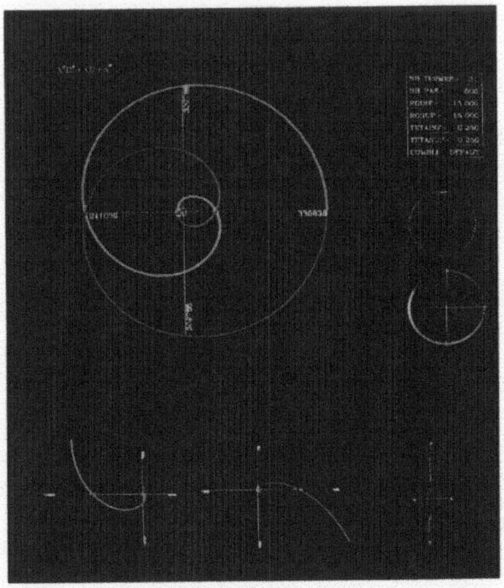

Figure 1: *a montage of the image of $A_{15,0}$, with $I = [\frac{-\pi}{2}, \frac{\pi}{2}]$ and three successive zooms of the region near the origin. It illustrates the principle of the representation and will be used later for the comparison between the two methods exposed. For more details about the menu displayed in the upper right part of the screen, see [1].*

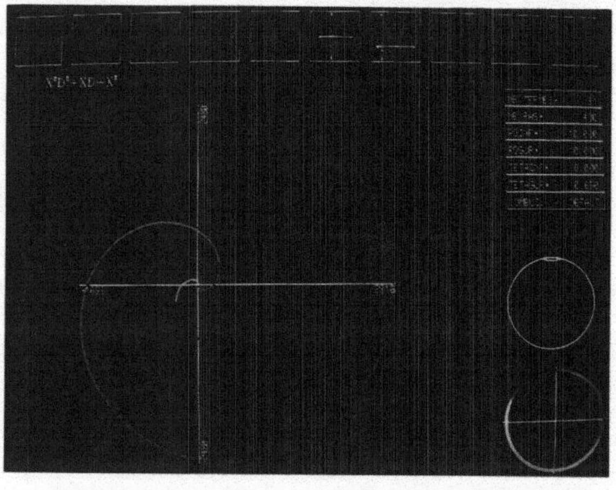

Figure 2: *illustration of Stokes phenomenon.*

In this figure the first small curve stored represents the image under J_0 of $A_{10,0}$, where $I = [0.0, 0.65 * 2\pi]$. The function is computed by the convergent series f_1. The small set of green points that are the images of points of argument greater than π are plotted on top of the pink ones that are the images of points of argument slightly greater than 0. The second small curve is a zoom of the previous one: the green points are more clearly seen. The main graph represents the image of the same circular arc under J_0 computed by three methods, the different curves obtained with each method can be identified by the type of line:

- *by the convergent series f_1: it is the curve plotted with a dotted line. This curve is hidden by the curve plotted with a continuous line.*
- *by a linear combination of g_1 and g_2, computed by spectral decomposition: it is the curve plotted with a dashed line.*
- *by the same linear combination, where g_1 and g_2 are computed by generalized factorial series. This curve is plotted with a continuous line.*

In the two last cases, the green points do not hide the pink ones. But it is not because of a lack of precision, it is due to the Stokes phenomenon: the linear combination of g_1 and g_2 giving J_0 in the domain $|Arg(z)| < \pi$ is not available if $Arg(z) > \pi$. This explains why the curves are merged only for points of argument smaller than π.

4. Second representation method

4.1 Principle of the representation

The function f is computed at each point of a circular network, defined by its minimum and maximum radius, its starting and ending angles, the number of facets per radial sector and per turn. Next the 3D surface is created by all the facets whose vertices are the points $(\rho cos(\theta), \rho sin(\theta))$ at the height $|f(\rho e^{i\theta})|$. To emphasize the relief, vertical walls are added at the sides of the surface: an internal wall along the circle of minimum radius, an external wall along the circle of maximum radius, a starting wall along the starting angle and finally an end wall along the ending angle.

We take advantage of the 3D hardware capabilities of the terminal (Tektronix 4128) to display the wire-frame of the created object without removing hidden lines. Thus one can choose the projection easily and quickly by using the function keys of the terminal. The subsequent processing is limited to the case of an orthogonal parallel projection. Considering the visualized 3D-object fixed, the user can move the projection plane. That is, he can modify its origin point V.R.P. (View Reference Point) and its perpendicular vector V.P.N. (View Plane Normal).

When the user is satisfied with the shape of the wire frame, the program recovers the projection parameters stored by the terminal, computes the corresponding projection matrix and displays the projected surface in 2D. The hidden parts are erased and the facets are shaded according to argument.

In order to illustrate the steps in the second representation method, the function J_0 will be put aside momentarily. The function $f(z) = log(z)$ will be used instead since it is simple yet produces an esthetically pleasing result. In any case it falls within the class of functions which were studied since it satisfies $zy'' + y' = 0$ for which the basis of the formal solutions supplied by DESIR is $h(z) = 1$ and $f(z) = log(z)$. Moreover it is a typical example of a multiform function $f(z) \neq f(z + e^{2i\pi})$. On the following photos f is calculated on the cicular network defined by `ROINF = 0.05, ROSUP = 1.5, TETAINF = -0.55 (turn), TETASUP = 0.55.`

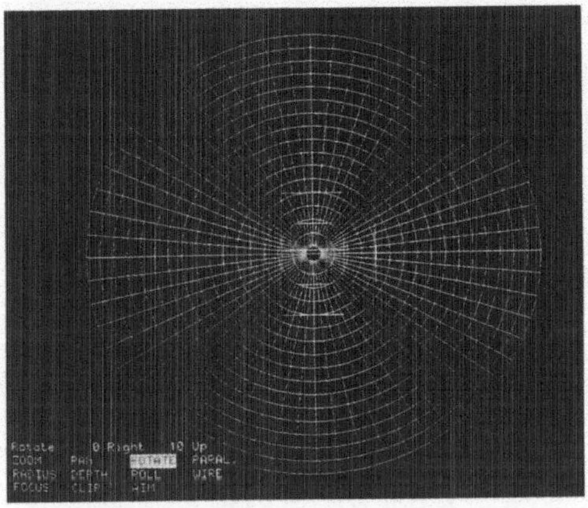

Figure 3: *First the created surface is always viewed from infinity on the z-axis. In the lower left part of the screen one can see the local functions that permit choosing the parameters of projection.*

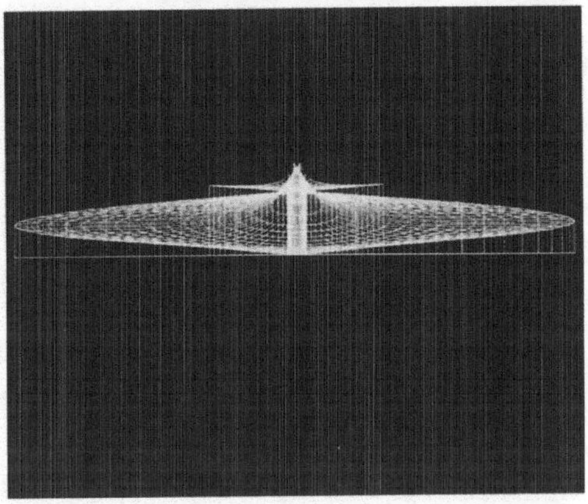

Figure 4: *moving the V.R.P. slightly gives the user the impression that the surface slopes. The relief appears. Here the view direction is parallel to the x-axis.*

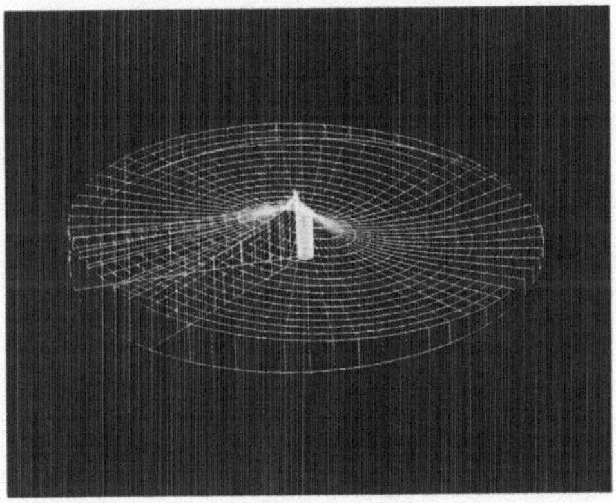

Figure 5: *this view is chosen to be shaded.*

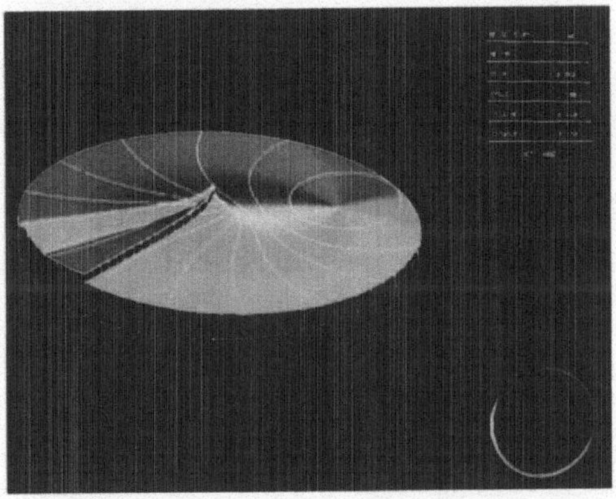

Figure 6: *the surface is shaded with the previous defined projection.*

4.2 Display of the 2D surface

4.2.1 Hidden surfaces

Consider first a surface whose network describes at most one turn (`TETASUP - TETAINF` $\leq 2\pi$). In this case, there are no facets which intersect or which interlace. On a raster device, the problem of hidden surfaces is reduced to the classification of the facets from the farthest to the nearest, the back facets will then be overlayed by the closer ones that hide them (completely or partially). Moreover, except for the vertical walls, no two points of the surface are on the same vertical. The order or proximity of the points is then the same as that of their projection in the (x, y) plane.

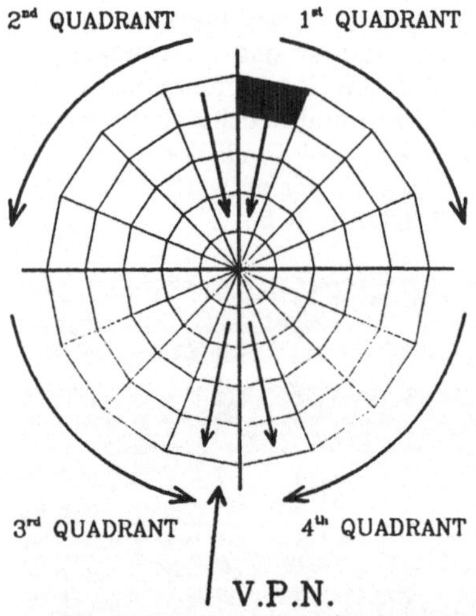

The farthest facet is determined in a very simple manner, it is the farthest away in the direction indicated by the projection of V.P.N. However, if the projection of V.P.N. is null, (if V.P.N. is perpendicular to the (x, y) plane), any display order is suitable. Once the farthest facet is determined, it is a matter of displaying the surface by quadrant, sector by sector (clockwise or anti-clockwise according to the quadrant), and each sector facet by facet; from outside toward inside in the first two quadrants, from inside toward outside in the final two. Alternatively each quadrant could be displayed annulus by annulus, from outside to inside in the first two quadrants, from inside to outside in the other two, while within each annulus, the facets are displayed in the order defined for sectors.

To preserve correct display order when the walls are added, the display order previously defined cannot be generalized for the vertical facets. For instance, in the first quadrant, suppose that the external wall is considered as an extra annulus of the surface. The display order would be the following: the facet of the external wall of the first sector, then the first sector, then the facet of the internal wall, then the facet of the external wall of the second sector. Now, if the surface is viewed from above, the bottom part of this second wall facet could partly hide the first facet of the first sector of the surface.

The display order which respects the criterion of proximity is as follows: in both first quadrants, display of the whole external wall (which does not hide any part of the surface, whatever the view direction), display of the surface in the previous display order, and display of the whole internal wall (which must not be hidden by any piece of surface).

On the other hand, as we have chosen the display order by sector, the starting and ending walls can be taken as extra sectors of the surface. If we had chosen to display the surface by annulus, the external and internal walls should have been considered as annuli of the surface and the starting and end walls would have required special treatment.

Finally, if the network on which the function is to be represented describes more than one turn, the sectors, which include more than one stratum of surface, must be specially treated. That is, for each facet projection, it must be determined in which order the corresponding facets in the space are to be displayed. Furthermore, to preserve the accuracy of display, either the facets of two strata must not intersect, or they can only intersect along an edge.

4.2.2 Shading according to argument

For this purpose an existing subroutine was used, based on an algorithm which obtains contour lines of a parameter known at each vertex of a 2D quadrilateral, by linear interpolation on the sides [8]. More precisely, the display of the quadrilateral is carried out by

```
CALL GSURF7(X,Y,Z1,PAS,IM,ICODE)
```

where:

`X,Y,Z1`: array of four real numbers. `X,Y` are the coordinates of the vertices. `Z1` is the array of values used to determine the colour.

`PAS`: calculation increment for contour-lines (from 0).

`IM`: index in the colour-table of the range where `Z1` varies between 0 and `PAS`. The following ranges correspond with the following indices in the colour-table.

`ICODE`: parameter giving the type of filling.

-3: draw contour-lines only, space between lines filled in black.

-2: as for -3, plus draw the quadrilateral sides.

-1: draw sides of the quadrilateral which is then filled in black.

0: fill space between contour lines with different colours.

1: as for 0, plus drawing of the sides.

2: display of the different colours, of the contour-lines which delimit them and of the sides of the quadrilateral.

3: as for 2, without the sides.

4: draw the contour-lines only, without erasing what was previously displayed.

5: as for 4, without the sides.

So, combined with a projection computation, GSURF7 allows the shading of a surface according to a parameter different from the height.

$$\texttt{X,Y,Z} \xrightarrow{\textit{projection}} \texttt{X1,Y1}$$
$$\texttt{X1,Y1,Z1} \xrightarrow{\texttt{GSURF7}} \text{colour display}$$

In our case, the simplest use of GSURF7 permits shading the surface according to argument by assigning to $\texttt{Z1}(k)$ the argument of $f(\texttt{X}(k)+i\texttt{Y}(k))$. To be consistent with the first representation method, the colour-table is filled in order to obtain, when the argument varies from 0 to 2π, the same gradual range of colours as in the case of curves, from blue to magenta, red, yellow, green, cyan, back to blue. But other kinds of filling are possible: the surface can for instance be displayed with only the contour-lines of modulus, or only the contour-lines of the argument corresponding to $k\pi/6$.

Codes 4 and 5 do not solve the problem of hidden surfaces, they must be combined with another call to GSURF7. But then, they allow the most interesting and the most complete filling: the contour-lines of the modulus can indeed be superimposed on the surface shaded according to argument.

$$\texttt{X,Y,Z} \xrightarrow{\textit{projection}} \texttt{X1,Y1}$$
$$\texttt{X1,Y1,Z1} \xrightarrow[\texttt{ICODE=0}]{\texttt{GSURF7}} \text{colour according to the argument}$$
$$\texttt{X1,Y1,Z} \xrightarrow[\texttt{ICODE=4}]{\texttt{GSURF7}} \text{contour-lines of the modulus}$$

Figure 6 illustrates the two previous paragraphs and employs this last type of filling.

4.3 Specific problems

4.3.1 Colour-table

Previously it has been explained that the surface is shaded according to argument by a call to GSURF7 with $\texttt{Z1}(k) = Arg(f(\texttt{X}(k) + i\texttt{Y}(k)))$, $k = 1,4$. This implies that a range must be chosen for the argument. Here the range 0 to 2π was chosen. If no precautions are taken, the results obtained on some facets are aberrant. Consider a facet where the argument is close to 0 nearly everywhere, but where its value at each vertex is either slightly greater than 0, or slightly smaller than 2π. For such a facet, the values of Z1 calculated by linear interpolation on the sides will describe the whole interval $[0, 2\pi]$, so the associated colours will include the complete gradual range of colours, whereas the desired result is a facet that is blue.

To remedy this error, the argument is locally modified on each facet in the following way: consider that the values of the argument at each vertex are distributed on the unit circle and thus they define four arcs, whose length is calculated. The greatest boundary of the longest arc is chosen as the smallest argument, that is, the smaller arguments are incremented by 2π.

In this way, arguments greater than 2π are obtained. Now an argument θ is associated with the index $\texttt{N} = [\theta/\texttt{PAS}] + \texttt{IM}$ in the colour-table. To obtain the right colour for arguments greater than 2π, the colour-table should be duplicated. That is, the same colours should be assigned to two ranges of indices, the first one corresponding to the arguments between 0 and 2π, the second one corresponding to the arguments between 2π and 4π. This solution is not satisfactory, since it takes more space than necessary in the colour-table. It was better to add a parameter to GSURF7, which does not exist in the initial subroutine and does not appear in the description given in the previous paragraph. In the modified GSURF7, the index N is replaced by $\lfloor \theta/\mathtt{PAS} \rfloor$ *mod* N1+IM, where N1 is the additional parameter giving the number of colours used to describe $0, 2\pi$. Note that this modification does not introduce any error, if GSURF7 is used in a standard way, as long as N1 is assigned to any value greater than the number of colours used ($= \lfloor max\ \mathtt{Z1/PAS} \rfloor$). The following figures (7, 8, 10) prove that this modification has had the desired effect and has correctly solved the problem.

4.3.2 Selective refinement of facets.

This possibility has been introduced to improve the precision in some regions of the network by creating smaller facets within the facets previously defined. For this purpose the surface is first displayed with a direction of projection parallel to the z-axis. Then the user can pick two points with the graphic cursor to define the region to be refined. One of these points determines the minimum annulus radius and angle and the other gives the maximum annulus radius and angle. All the facets of the defined region will be sub-divided in smaller facets, whose number is determined by giving the number in the radial direction and the number in the circumferential direction.

The parameters associated with the sub-facets are retained, and they are taken into account when the surface is later displayed with a non-trivial projection. The following figures illustrate the advantage of this capability, which improves simultaneously the precision of the contour-lines of the modulus and of the colour ranges of the argument.

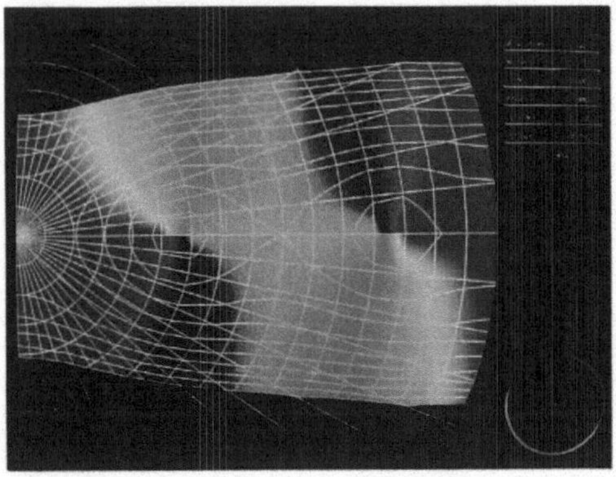

Figure 7: *before facet refinement*

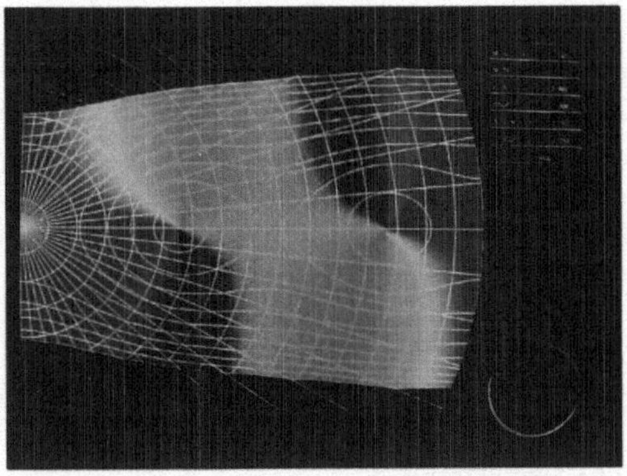

Figure 8: *after facet refinement of two sectors on each side of the real axis. Each facet of this region is sub-divided in 11 sub-facets in the radial direction and 5 sub-facets in the circumferential direction. The high number of sub-facets in the radial direction permits moving aside from real axis the colours different from blue and yellow. (Recall that $J_0(x) \in \mathbf{R}$, if $x \in \mathbf{R}$). It is important to note that the precision is sufficient on the other facets, and that there is no need to have extra detail there.*

4.3.3 Truncation

This procedure has the same role as zoom in the first representation method. It has the identical goal which is to emphasize the small variations of modulus, which are flattened when the complete surface is displayed.

Take the example of the function J_0, on a circular network defined by ROINF=0.0, ROSUP=7.0, TETAINF=0.0, TETASUP=0.6. The modulus varies between 0.0 and 300.0. It is quite obvious that small variations along the real axis of order 1.0, will be invisible. One solution consists of truncating the surface at a height ZMAX given by the user. That is, all higher points are reduced to this limiting height.

By such a rough procedure, the limit facets (those, that have at least one vertex on the actual surface and at least one on the truncated part) do not take the exact shape of the surface. To obtain satisfactory results, they must be split in two parts: one part is horizontal (truncated) and the other is entirely on the surface. This split is inspired by the same principle as GSURF7, since the purpose is to determine the contour-line ZMAX on the limit facets. In fact this contour-line is approximated by a segment of a line joining the points that are on the sides at the height ZMAX (determined by linear interpolation).

When the surface is displayed, a code is used to distinguish the *normal* facets that must be shaded, from the truncated one, that must be displayed in black and for which the sides of the quadrilateral must be shown, even if it is not the case on the surface. The partially truncated facets are treated as refined facets, and the same code enables the distinction between the sub-facet that belongs to the surface and the sub-facet that belongs to the truncated part.
Figure 9 gives an example of the result.

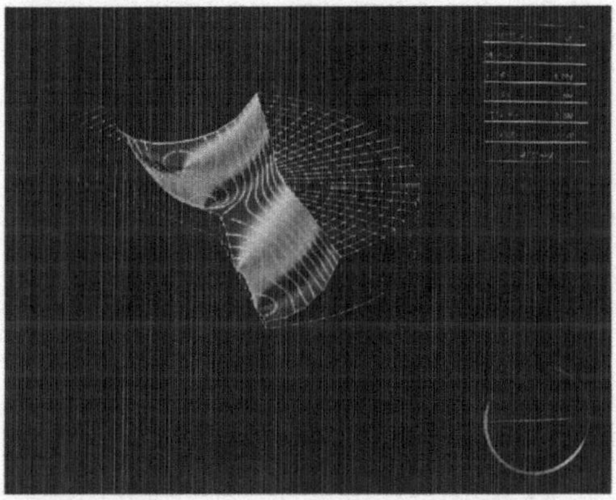

Figure 9: *example of a trucated surface. The function J_0 has been calculated on the circular network defined above and has been truncated at the height* 2.4. *The contour lines of modulus are plotted with* PAS=0.2.

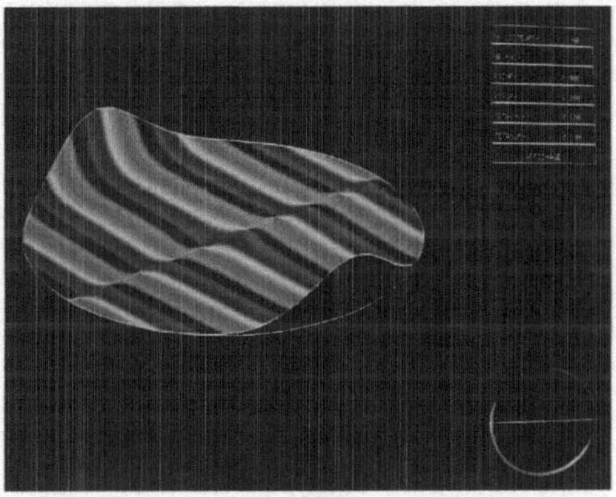

Figure 10: *the function J_0 has been calculated on the circular network defined by* ROINF = 0., ROSUP = 16., TETAINF = -0.5, TETASUP = 0.5.

5. Comparison of the two methods

To have a good understanding of the two representations, it is vital to keep the dual significance of colour constantly in mind. In the first representation the colour is associated with the argument of the *corresponding point*, whereas in the second representation the colour is associated with the argument of the *image-point*.

Now it is clear that the same phenomena are visible on the curves and on the surfaces, but not at all in the same way. Figures 1 and 10 have been made essentially to emphasize this point. The closure of all the curves representing J_0 when the variable describes half a turn in the domain is represented on the surface by symmetry about the origin. If one moves along the last annulus of the surface, from imaginary negative axis to imaginary positive axis, each time one crosses a blue strip this corresponds on the curve to a crossing of the real positive axis. More precisely, if one moves from real positive axis to imaginary positive axis, first one finds yellow points that correspond in fig. **1** with the points of the third zoom (real negative points on the curve are displayed in yellow on the surface). The first blue strip crossed corresponds with the crossing of the real positive axis on the second zoom (with violet points). The second blue strip corresponds with the crossing of the real positive axis on the main graph (with pink points). And finally, the blue strip, that is on the surface along the imaginary positive axis, corresponds on the curve with the pink end point (that is on the real positive axis). The results of the two methods are in accordance with each other.

But the differences between the two representations are obvious too. The first method is more a study tool, used to analyse the formal and numerical results, to determine the *good* methods of calculation according to the region. The second method is more a synthesized representation, using the information obtained from the curves.

If the second method seems less interesting for the study of the calculation methods, it gives on the other hand a better final representation of the studied function. To confirm this statement, recall the case of $f(z) = log(z)$: with the first representation, the image of A_ρ, where $I = [a, b]$, is a segment of a line of abscissa $log(\rho)$ and ordinates varying between a and b. The second representation, an attractive multicoloured surface, makes it much easier to visualize the function (fig. **6**).

6. Conclusion

Although this paper has used only two functions as examples, the software can be used with a wide range of functions. Formal solutions for any linear homogeneous equation with polynomial coefficients can be produced by DESIR. However the numerical and graphical parts are only applicable to such equations of order two or less, or for certain generic equations of higher order.

For equations that meet these criteria, the software provides useful tools for visualization. As pointed out by Jahnke and Emde in their pioneering work [9], graphical representation brings new understanding of the behaviour of functions. The great advantage of the present approach is that it adds the power of computer graphics to the task. The use of colour, choice of the region of calculation and representation, choice of view direction and zoom give the user the possibility of examining any area of interest in detail. In that respect, the computer graphics method gives excellent results.

1. F. Richard, "Graphical Analysis of Complex O.D.E. Solutions," *Computers Graphic Forum, Volume 6, Number 4,* December 1987.
2. J.P. Ramis, "Théorèmes d'indices Gevrey pour les équations différentielles ordinaires," *Memoirs of the American Mathematical Society, Volume 48, Number 296,* March 1984.
3. J. Della Dora and E. Tournier, "Formal solutions of differential equations in the neighborhood of singular points,", *SYMSAC 81, proceeding of the 1981 ACM Symposium on Symbolic and Algebraic Computation,* Edition Paul S. Wang.
4. J. Della Dora, C. Dicrescenzo and E. Tournier, "An algorithm to obtain formal solutions of a linear homogeneous differential equation at an irregular singular point," *Lecture notes in Computer Science,* Edited by J. Calmet, Springer-Verlag (1982), Computer Algebra, Eurocam'82 (European Computer Algebra Conference), Marseille, France, April 82.
5. J.P. Ramis, "Les séries k-sommables et leurs applications," *Springer Lecture Notes in Physics n° 126,* Springer-Verlag (1980).
6. J.P. Ramis, J. Thomann, "Some comments about the numerical utilization of factorial series," *Numerical Methods in the study of critical phenomena,* Springer-Verlag (1980).
7. J. Thomann, "Séries 1-sommables, séries de factorielles généralisées et approximants de type Padé," Séminaire IMAG n° 373, Grenoble (1981).
8. T. Wendlinger, "Construction, étude et représentation graphique de surfaces définies par des relevés de points," Thèse de 3° cycle, Strasbourg 1985.
9. Eugene Jahnke and Fritz Emde, *Tables of functions with Formulae and Curves,* Dover Publications, New-York, 4th ed. (1945).

During this work I received a scholarship from the C.N.R.S. and the Région Alsace. The software runs on the I.B.M. 3090 and the graphical equipment of the Centre de Calcul de Strasbourg.

Approximation of Missing Sections of CT-Image Sequences Using Binary Interpolation

V. Heyers, J. Dengler, and H.-P. Meinzer (Germany)

ABSTRACT

A method is described whereby computer tomograph (CT) image slices are interpolated, an important step in the 3D visualization process. The segmented components of the images are interpolated as binary structures and then reunited. This new method of binary interpolation interpolates coordinates. The interpolation lines are bound by the image pixels. This is an element not found in current triangulation techniques.

INTRODUCTION

An interpolation method for CT image slices is given. Interpolation is necessary for 3D visualization of a limited number of image slices. In order to minimize the patient`s x-ray exposure the number of slices is limited to 30-60 with a resolution of 256x256 per slice. A CT-image assigns a number to each point of the image. A range of numbers is characteristic for each component, whereby each number is a measure of density. That means at any given image point the corresponding number indicates e.g. muscles or bones.

REASONS FOR USING BINARY INTERPOLATION FOR GREYVALUE CT-IMAGES

For interpolation of two images it is not useful to take the average of their CT-values, as is usually done.
The average of two CT values $(a_{material1}+a_{material2})/2$ is usualy neither within the range of densities of material 1 nor of material 2.

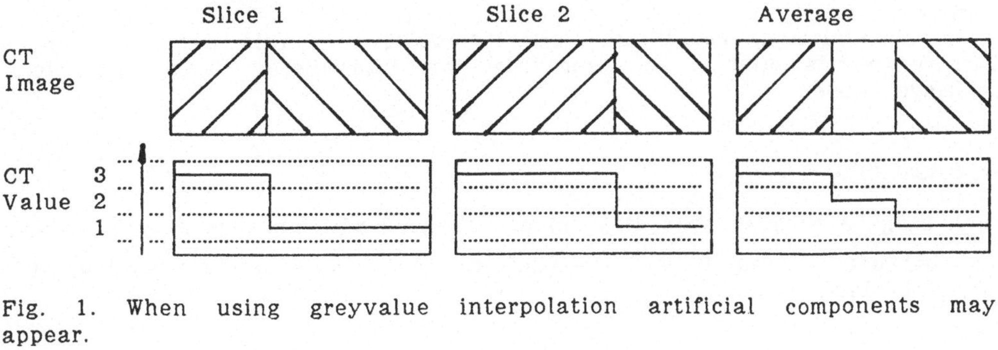

Fig. 1. When using greyvalue interpolation artificial components may appear.

THE ALGORITHM

Instead of trying to find a hypothetical absorption coefficient in the interpolated image slices, it is semantically more correct and computationally more efficient to decide for each component in the image (e.g. muscle, bone etc.), whether and where it should appear in the interpolated slices. (Fig. 2).

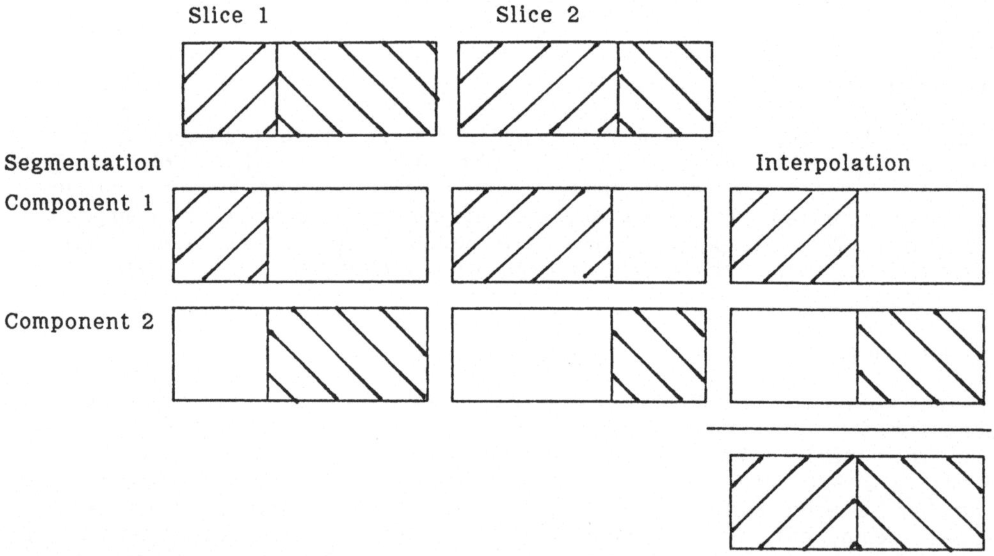

Fig. 2. Segmentation and binary interpolation does not lead to the appearance of artificial components.

The segmentation is performed by using the characteristic absorption coefficents.
Given one greyvalue sequence of n components, n binary image sequences will result after segmentation.
The triangulation method (e.g. Zsuppan and Réthelyi), often applied to binary interpolation is not recommended in the case of more than one surface (because of the problem of bifurcation, e.g. Fig. 11). It is complex and timeconsuming. A different method may be applied, described as follows:
As in triangulation, coordinates are interpolated in this new procedure. Contrary to triangulation the procedure uses interpolation lines bound by the image pixels.

THE BASIC IDEA

Given image A with an edge at $y_A(x)$ and image B with an edge at $y_B(x)$, the edge between A and B with respect to the y-axis is interpolated at $(y_A+y_B)/2$. (Fig. 3).

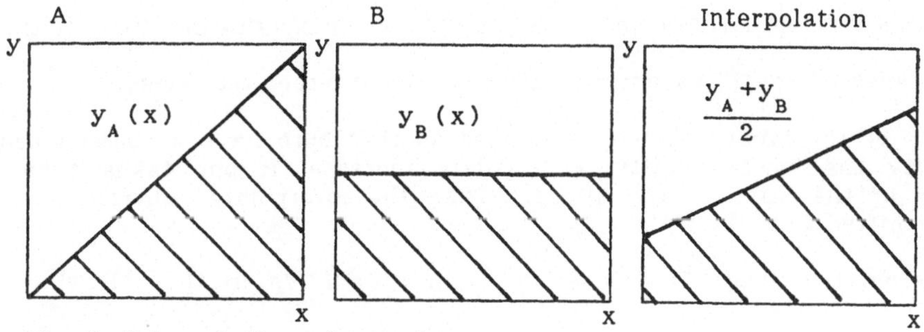

Fig. 3. Interpolation of an edge

Planes are interpolated in the same way.

HOW TO DESCRIBE PLANES

A convex plane can be characterized by four vectors ("edge depth vectors"). Each vector describes the distance between the object and the image boundary. (Fig. 4, Fig. 5).

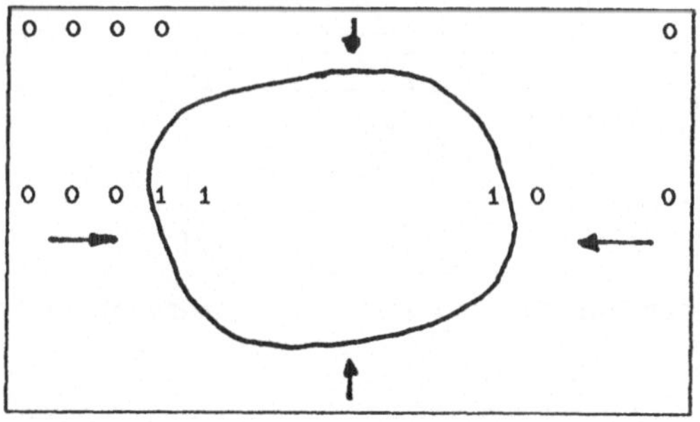

Fig. 4.

If the image is an n*m matrix, the result are four "edge depth vectors" (=: EDV). (Two of each dimension m and n.)

If there is no "1" in a column or a line the corresponding EDV element will be "0". (Fig. 5).

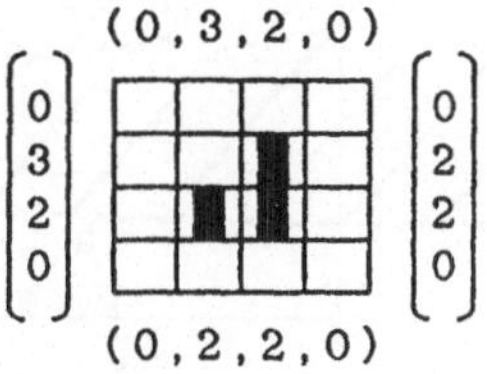

Fig. 5. Determination of an "edge depth vector".

A finer angular resolution is possible by using a hexagonal grid.

HOW TO CREATE THE INTERPOLATION SLICE WITH A SET OF EDGE DEPTH VECTORS

The averages of the EDVs are the EDVs of the interpolated image.

When one of the binary objects is shifted so that both have a common center of gravity the image quality will usualy increase, if one takes then the averages of the EDVs of the slices . Then the interpolated object slice has to be reshifted half way.

The interpolated image is created by using the EDVs in the following way (Fig. 6):

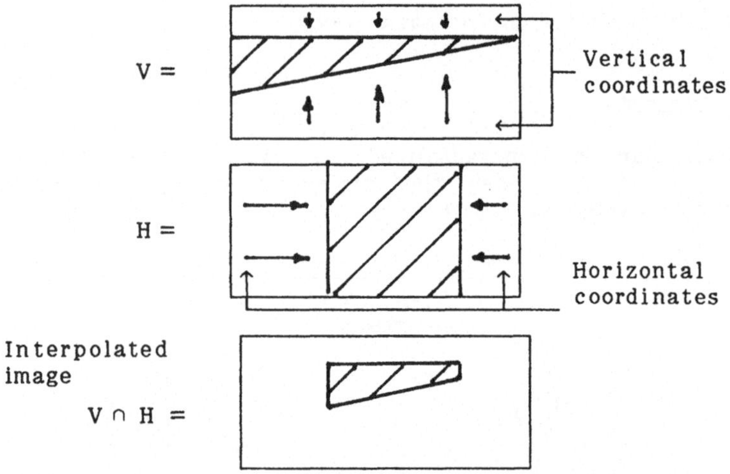

Fig. 6. The interpolated image is the intersection of V and H.

DIFFICULT REGIONS

There are also "difficult regions" (Fig. 7: $(x_{kA};x_{kE})$), when only one of the contiguous images has a coordinate and the mathematical average is physically inappropriate.

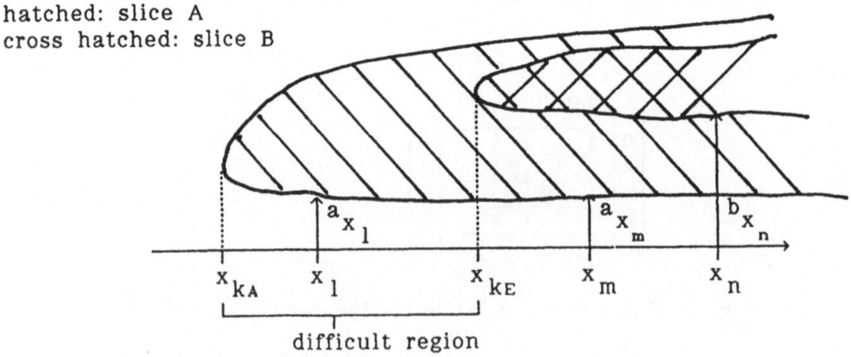

Fig. 7.

In this difficult region the coordinates for interpolation must be determined differently.

Some simple methods produce rather unsatisfactory results.

Example:

Interpolate slice A and B.

slice A

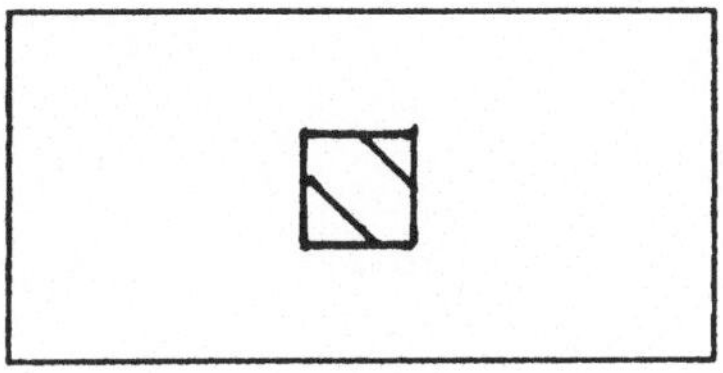

slice B

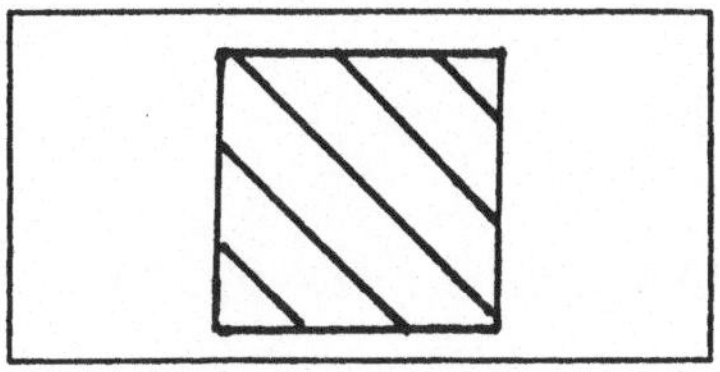

Method α: In the difficult region the only existing coordinate ($\neq 0$) is taken as the coordinate for interpolation.

Method β: In the difficult region there will be nothing in the interpolated image.

result
method α

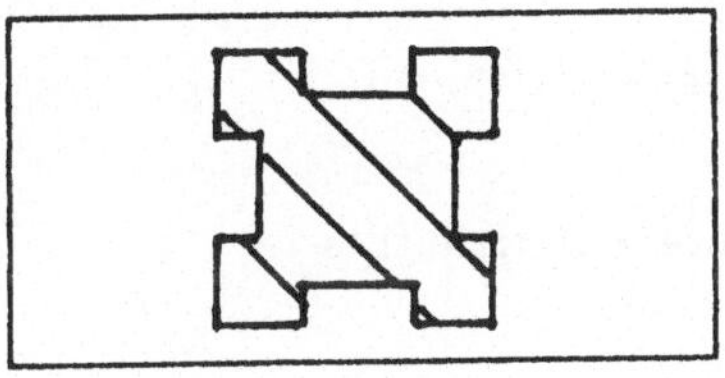

result
method β

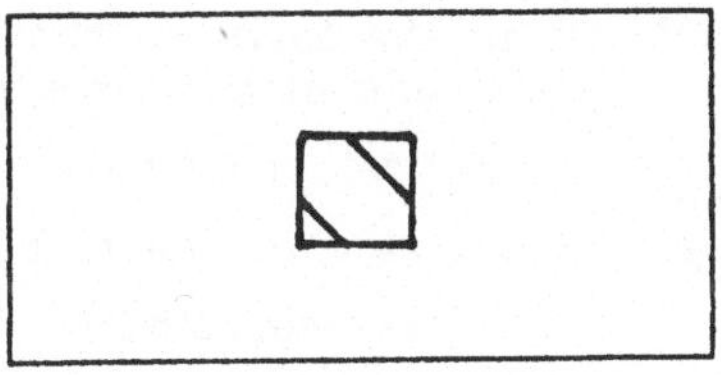

= slice A

Neither result is useful.

Satisfying results in the difficult region are achieved by the following method:

$\vec{a}$ is EDV of slice A:

$$\vec{a} = (0,0,\dots,0,a_i,a_j,\dots,a_l,0,0,\dots,0)$$

$\vec{b}$ is EDV of slice B:

$$\vec{b} = (0,0,\dots,0,b_i,b_j,\dots,b_\ell,0,0,\dots,0)$$

$\vec{m}_{A,B}$ is a mask:

$$\vec{m}_{A,B} = (0,0,\dots,0,1,1,\dots,1,0,0,\dots,0),$$

given by $m_i = 1$, if $(a_i+b_i)>0$
$m_i = 0$ otherwise

use the function f:

$$f(\vec{a}) = (a_i,a_i,\dots,a_i,a_j,\dots,a_l,a_l,\dots,a_l)$$

$$f(\vec{b}) = (b_i,b_i,\dots,b_i,b_j,\dots,b_\ell,b_\ell,\dots,b_\ell)$$

f replaces each "0" in the EDVs on the

- left side of the first coordinate $\neq 0$ with this first coordinate.
- right side of the last coordinate $\neq 0$ with this last coordinate.

EDV of the interpolated image becomes

$$\vec{k}_{A,B} := \vec{m}^{\,T}_{A,B} \; (f(\vec{a}) + f(\vec{b})) / 2$$

(Outside of the difficult region $\vec{k}_{A,B}$ is given by $\vec{k}_{A,B} = (\vec{a} + \vec{b}) / 2$, in agreement with the original definition.)

This method not only interpolates rectangles as expected, but circles are also satisfyingly interpolated.

COMPLEX STRUCTURES

The set of four EDVs doesn`t suffice for a complete description of complex structures.

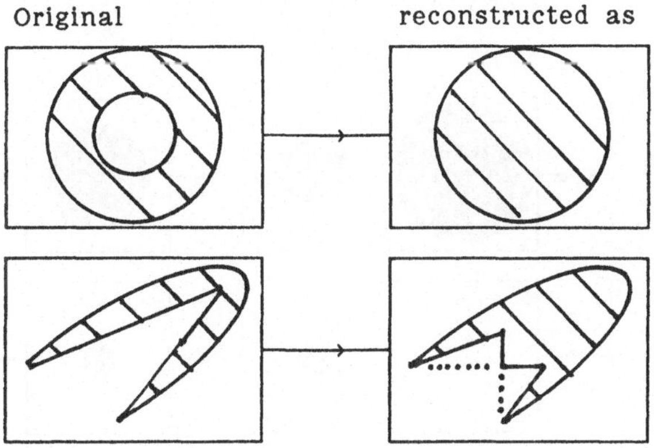

Fig. 8: The structures, which are reconstructed from the EDVs of the originals lack inner details.

Inner details must be described with the help of more sets of EDVs, if desired.

These EDVs of the inner structures can be obtained in the following manner:

As in the process of determining the EDVs one starts at the four edges of the original image. Each image pixel is changed from "0" to "1" until the first "1" appears in the image (Fig. 9. "filling").
The result is then inverted (Fig. 9. "inversion").

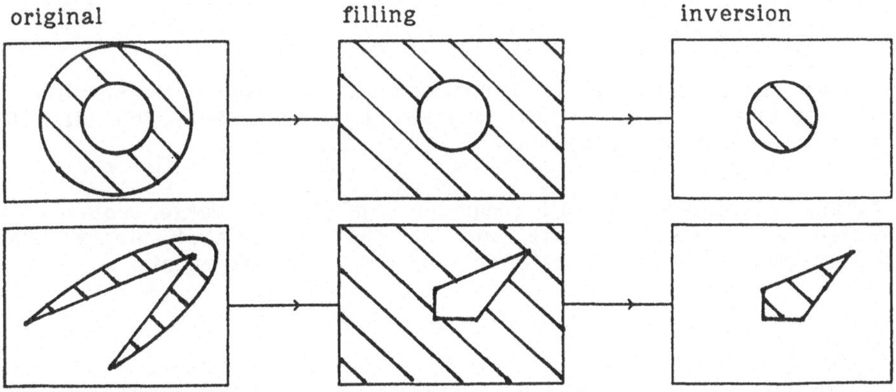

Fig. 9: Examples of determining the inner structure

Even complex structures fitted into one another can be described completely with some sets of EDVs.

EXAMPLE FOR INTERPOLATION OF COMPLEX STRUCTURES

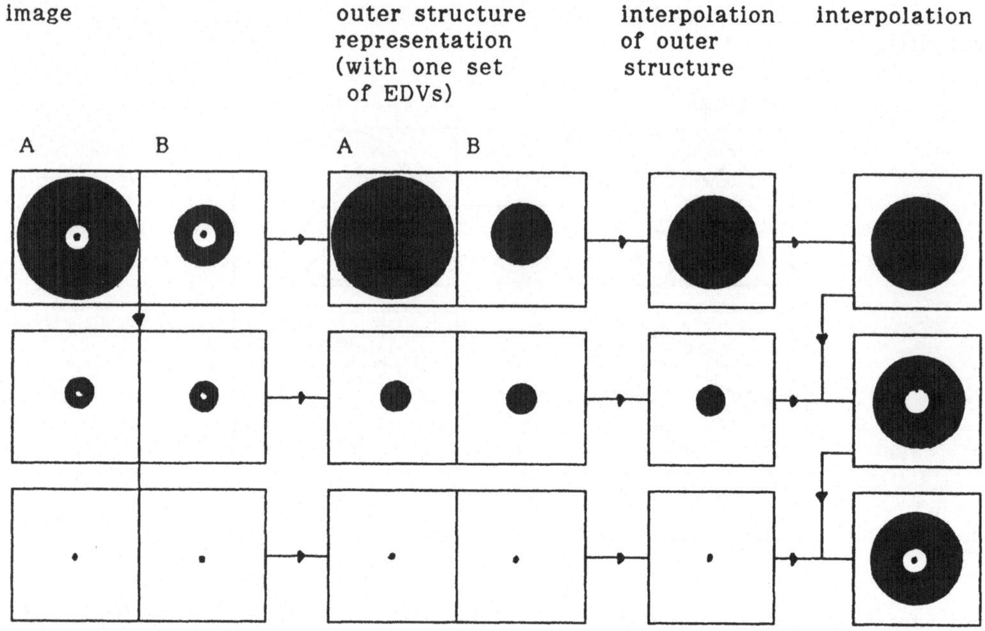

Fig. 10. Three iteration runs of the algorithm

Often a useful interpolation is already achieved after the first iteration run , if the result (R) of this run is corrected, where the following relations are not valid:

$$R \subset A \cup B$$

$$R \supset A \cap B$$

Where inner details are of no importance, it is useful to simplify the original images with morphological operations (Serra, 1982; Schmidt, 1987) in order to save many calculations.

After binary interpolation of all components of the CT image sequence, the interpolated CT images are the sum of the interpolated binary images multiplied by the absorption coefficients of the special material.

CONCLUSION

A new, reliable and time efficient method for interpolating CT-slices has been proposed. The interpolation slice will always coincide with at least one of the neighbouring segmented slices at each pixel, thereby largely reducing possible errors.

The slice of binary interpolation yields good results, when one of the two neighbouring object slices is part of the other. But even complex structures in images very different from each other are interpolated rather well (Fig. 11).
These results encourage the application of the method also for other image sequences, e.g. to achieve a smooth cloud movement in meteorological satellite images.

Slice A

Interpolation

Slice B

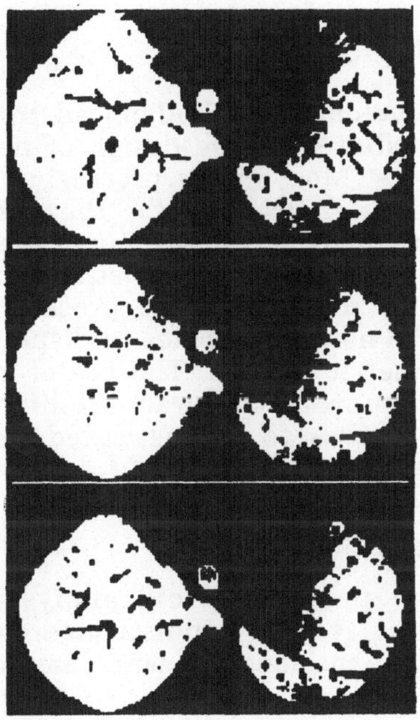

Fig. 11. Interpolation between two slices of lungs

REFERENCES

Schmidt, M.(1987): Erkennung komplexer Zellstrukturen mit Methoden der mathematischen Morphologie. 9. DAGM-Symposium, Proceedings, pp. 161-165

Serra, J.(1982): Image Analysis and Mathematical Morphology. Academic Press London

Zsuppán, F. and Réthelyi, M.(1985): Approximation of missing sections in computer reconstruction of serial EM pictures. Journal of Neuroscience Methods, No. 15, pp. 203-212

Computer Graphic Techniques Applied to Medical Image Analysis

O. Ratib (USA)

INTRODUCTION

The recent development of advanced computer graphic techniques has significantly contributed to the design of new image processing and image analysis algorithms. Most image processing workstations rely nowadays on sophisticated computer graphics for the simplification of user interactions and for the enhancement of the display of the results. In this paper we would like to outline some of the characteristics and advantages of graphic oriented user interfaces for medical image processing and analysis. Also we will review some of the new approaches in displaying complex analysis results in color coded parametric images. The use of graphics and color coded images can significantly improve the practicability of medical image analysis and allow an easier access to sophisticated quantitative algorithms for non computer-oriented clinicians.

GRAPHIC USER INTERFACE

Medical image processing and analysis have always been relatively complex tasks that require sophisticated programs, the use of which was usually limited to experienced users, familiar with computer handling and programming. There is however an increasing need to make this kind of technology more accessible to clinicians and physicians who are willing to use advanced quantitative analysis techniques but who cannot afford to spend too much time learning how to use complicated programs. Also, medical images are becoming more and more accessible through hospital's Picture Archiving and Communication Systems (PACS). There is therefore an increased demand for workstations where clinicians can display and process medical images. The trend leads toward networks of standalone workstations that allow local manipulation and analysis of medical images [1]. Often these analysis have to be performed on images from different imaging modalities (i.e. X-ray radiography, CT scans, Radionuclide scintigraphy), and clinically relevant decision are made from the combination of the results obtained from these different images. Therefore the design of a workstation must provide sufficient flexibility to allow the display and evaluation of images with different resolution and characteristics. We have recently developed an image analysis workstation based on a Macintosh II that allows simultaneous display of multiple images using overlaid windows, as well as text and graphics (see fig. 1). Images are transferred from a central PACS server through an Ethernet network. The PACS server is operational in a clinical environment and provides archiving and retrieval capabilities for different imaging modalities [2]. Images are accessible through different types of viewing stations available to the radiologists and clinicians, the Macintosh being one type that allows for more quantitative and numerical analysis of the images as opposed to simple display and viewing stations.

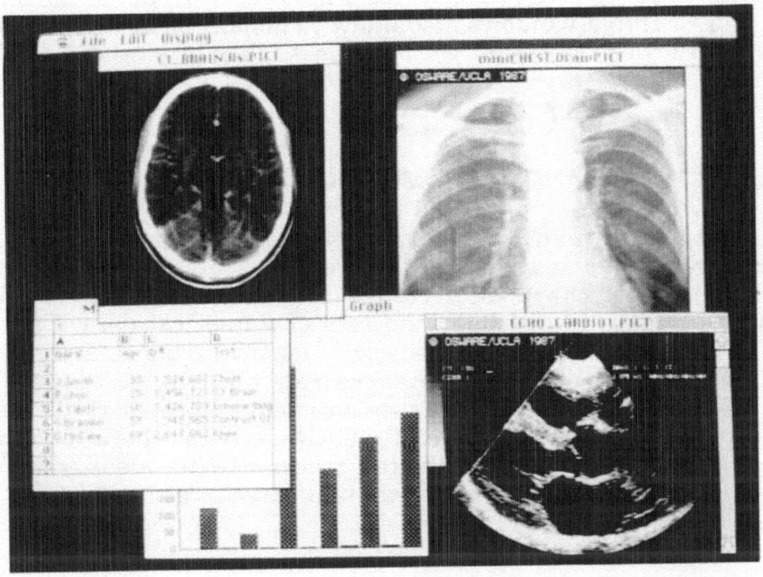

Figure 1: Example of a multiple-window graphic display on a Macintosh II computer showing images from different modalities (Brain CT scan on the left, chest X-ray on the upper right and a cardiac ultrasound image on the lower right) together with graphic and text in separate windows.

One of the major improvement in the design of a user-friendly interface was the introduction of a graphic-oriented display using multiple windows, icons and pull-down menus. This type of design has encountered a very large popularity among clinicians and medical researchers because of its ease of use and the reduced amount of training required to be able to use complex applications and programs. Initially provided by personal computers like Apple's Macintosh, graphic user interfaces are now becoming available on several other minicomputers and even on some mainframe operating systems. In general the use of a graphic oriented user interface is driven by an interactive pointing devise such as a mouse or a trackball and offers the following advantages [3]:

- **User-initiated actions:** The user, not the computer, initiates and controls the sequence of actions.
- **See-and-point (instead of remember-and-type):** Users select actions from alternatives present on the screen.
- **Direct manipulation:** Users have direct control on the actions on the screen and a direct access to the geographic distribution of the display.
- **Feedback and interactive dialogs**: Through overlaid dialog windows option selection and immediate controls can be manipulated by the user.

Another feature inherent to the use of graphic-oriented interface with windows is the possibility of resizing and tiling of the windows allowing to display simultaneous images of large sizes on screens that do not have necessarily the full resolution to display all the images side by side simultaneously. By assigning a separate window to each image, the user can directly access them by bringing selected windows in "front" of all the others. Scrollable and resizable windows also allow to display high resolution images on screens with lower resolution with the possibility to pan and scroll across the image.

Graphic Displays and Parametric Images

Graphic outputs of numerical results is extensively used to display in a visually comprehensive manner complex data resulting from quantitative analysis. Histograms, charts and curves are usually easier and faster to capture by the human brain than long sets of numerical data. This concept applies to data obtained from the analysis of medical images. A large number of analysis techniques of medical images rely on graphic outputs for the display of the results of quantitative measurements. Nuclear medicine images are the most suitable type of images for such analysis where topographic or temporal distribution of a radiolabelled tracer can be measured from the images and is usually plotted as a distribution curve or a time-activity curve.

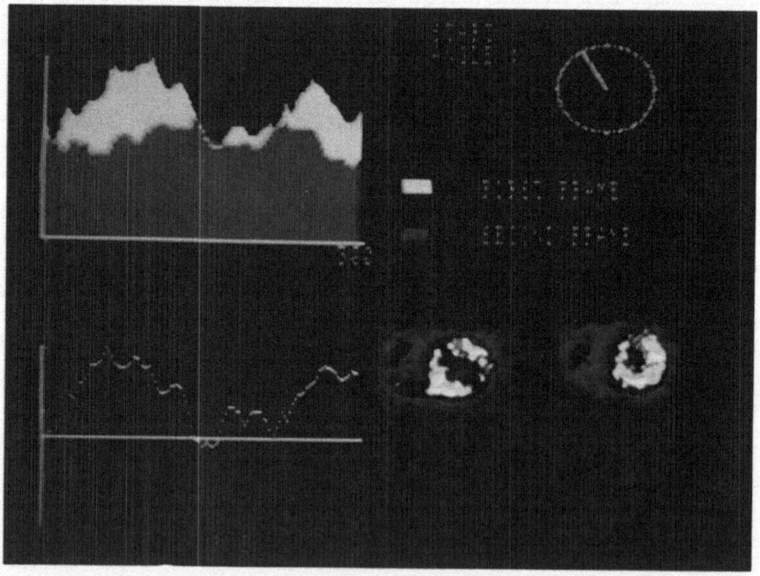

Figure 2: Results of a quantitative analysis of scintigraphic images of the heart. Regional tissue distribution of the radiotracer in the myocardium is displayed as circumferential profiles on the upper left of the image. Profiles are obtained from the two images on the lower right and displayed in two different colors (blue and yellow).

Another type of graphic output however, which is more specific to topographic and regional image analysis, is the concept of parametric images.

From functional images to parametric images: Functional imaging is the display of organ function using images. The creation of functional images may be as simple as the imaging of a compound known to behave in a way which characterizes the function of an organ (i.e. when using radionuclide tracers in conventional nuclear medicine) or as complex as the result of a mathematical function of a set of images. The rationale for functional imaging is to allow the extraction from the images of a characteristic parameter related to the function or the anatomy of an organ. Complex mathematical procedures are used to localize and highlight changes in a specific function of the organ that cannot be visually detected from the images. One could make a distinction between direct functional imaging, in which images of distribution of a particular tracer or die are used by themselves as functional images, and indirect functional imaging, in which the "parametric" images are formed by mathematical manipulations.

Direct functional imaging: Conventional radionuclide images are the best example of direct functional imaging. Such images allow the localization of radiopharmaceuticals distribution corresponding to one or more physiologic mechanisms of the explored organ. Similar approaches may be used in digital contrast angiography when the dye distribution is measured on the images and used as an index of the vascular flow. Videodensitometric measurement of cardiac volumes from contrast ventriculograms may also be considered as direct functional imaging since it does not imply mathematical transformations of the original images into resulting functional images.

Indirect functional imaging (parametric imaging): Indirect functional imaging (more correctly called parametric imaging) is accomplished by mathematical calculations from the original images. Results of these calculations are reported on parametric images representing a topographic map of the calculated parameter. The purpose of such calculation is to detect and to bring to light some property of the images which is usually not evident on visual inspection. The wide range of different kinds of parametric images my be separated into five basic types: 1. images formed from calculations on one image, 2. images formed from simple maneuvers involving more than one image (addition, subtraction , divisions, etc...), 3. images formed from the application of mathematics to temporal density curves of each point of the image, 4. images formed of more complex mathematical functions, and 5. color coded maps representing topographic or geographic distribution of a measured parameter in an image or in an organ in an abstract geometric shape that does not necessarely correspond to the exact shape of the organ.

1. Among the simplest image manipulations aimed to enhance some features that may not be obvious on the analog images are those involving contrast and color scale modifications. The human eye is not a linear instrument; it is logarithmic and has edge enhancement capabilities. In order for the brain to appreciate properly the image data, the data must be presented with a gray scale or color range that enhances the parts of the data that contain the information. The selection of a range of gray levels may also be used to highlight some special features. This latest procedure

is used in the so called "linear background subtraction" corresponding to a cutoff of the low intensity levels resulting in a better delineation of high intensity objects of an image.

2. There are a wide number of simple manipulations involving several to many images. The most common is image subtraction used for "mask" subtraction in images after injection of a contrast material by subtracting an image obtained prior to the injection. Successive subtraction of sequential images are also used for the visualization of the progression or changes in the contrast distribution as well as motion (mask mode imaging, time interval difference (TID), etc...). A typical example is shown in figure 2 where parametric images representing the blood flow distribution of the coronary arteries were generated by calculating the difference in intensity in five sequential images obtained from five consecutive heart beats at exact same time in the heart cycle [4]. This type of image manipulation have the advantage of being based on simple mathematical operations and could be performed at very high speed using hardwired image and array processors.

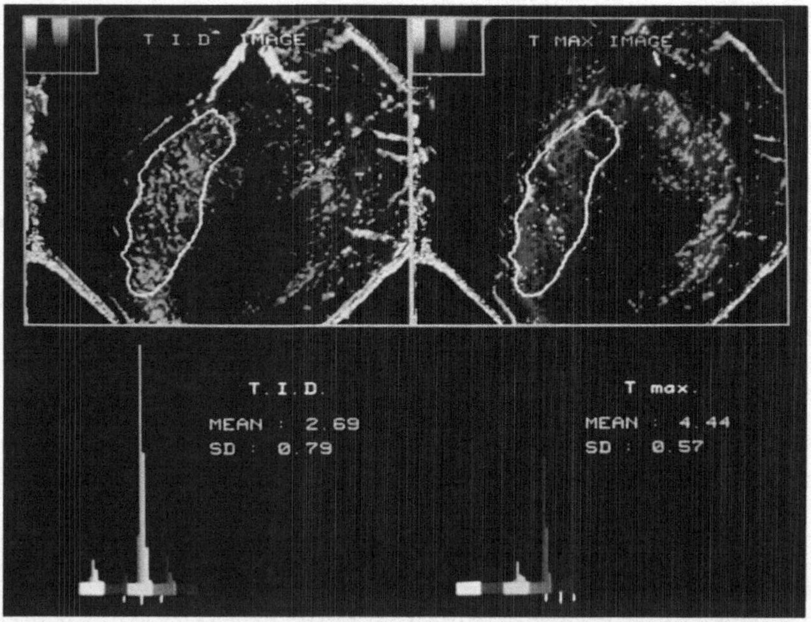

Figure 3: Parametric images obtained from a sequence of five digitized angiograms of the coronary arteries. The image on the left is obtained by the time-difference-interval (TID) technique where the difference between two successive images is obtained and displayed in a different color for each pairs of images. The resulting color coded image represents the time sequence of opacification of the vessels where white and red colors correspond to areas with early opacification and areas in blue and green correspond to late opacification. The image on the right represents in a similar fashion the time of the maximum intensity in each pixel. These images can be further analyzed by generating the histograms of the distribution of each parameter within a region of interest outlined manually.

3. Pixel by pixel evaluation of changes in intensity are used in dynamic sequential imaging modalities aimed to analyze temporal changes occurring in the image components. Results of such analysis techniques are then compressed into single parametric images which are usually color coded using predefined color scales. Several parameters describing the changes in intensity in each pixel can be displayed using this technique (Time of maximum intensity, max slope of increase or decrease in intensity, difference between maximum and minimum intensity, etc...). Resulting color coded parametric images greatly improve the detection and localization of regional changes in temporal behavior of the contrasted parts of the image. Such changes can usually not be detected by visual examination of the sequential images in cine mode.

4. Complex mathematical functions may be applied to analyze time/intensity curves of each pixel of the images. Such mathematical procedures include curve fitting, Fourier analysis, differential and factorial analysis. Examples of such a technique applied to cardiac images is presented in the next paragraph.

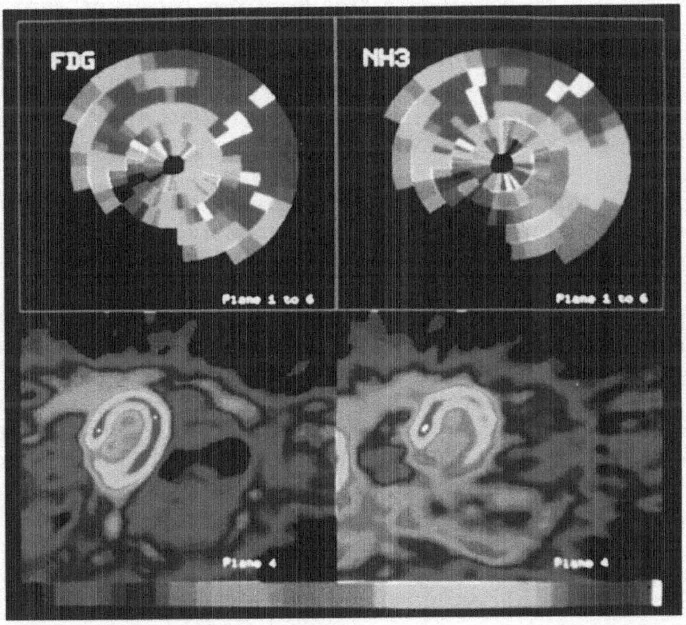

Figure 4: Polar maps showing the regional distribution of metabolic tracers in the myocardium obtained from positron emission tomography (PET) images of the heart. Each map on the top represents the geographic distribution of the tracer over the whole heart in six concentric rings corresponding to six slices across the heart. By convention the most inner ring corresponds to the apical an inferior level of the heart while the external rings correspond to the basal slices. The two maps shown here correspond to images obtained with two different tracers: the upper left showing the metabolic activity of the myocardium and the upper right showing the blood flow distribution. The two images shown in the bottom are representative images selected in one plane.

5. The last method of displaying parametric images is the generation of color coded maps representing the geographic or temporal distribution of a parameter measured from the images. A typical example is the generation of polar maps to display the distribution of a radiolabelled tracer in the heart obtained from tomoscintigraphic images. This technique is now commonly used in conventional nuclear medicine and an example of such a display is shown in figure 4 showing the regional distribution of radiotracers in the myocardium measured in images obtained from positron emission tomographic scans.

Typical applications in cardiac imaging: With the development of digital imaging techniques, dynamic images of the heart motion have become accessible to computer processing and analysis. Several cardiac imaging modalities benefit from digital recording, particularly the radionuclide angiograms, the contrast cine-angiograms, the echocardiograms and x-ray and magnetic resonance scans. All these images can be stored in digital form and processed by computer analysis programs. Such programs not only allow the extraction of morphological information about the heart structures but also permit a quantitative evaluation of the motion and function of the different regions of the heart. Image processing and analysis software can be divided into separate sets of algorithms that are image independent. Very similar methods can be applied to images from different sources (isotope, ultrasound, radiographic). Before the development of computer analysis techniques, the evaluation of dynamic images of the heart for example, could only be done visually by a highly trained cardiologist. In recent studies significant improvement in diagnostic accuracy when using dynamic analysis techniques for the evaluation of the heart motion has been well demonstrated.

Recent analysis techniques relying on a temporal evaluation of the heart wall motion are significantly more sensitive in detecting cardiac abnormalities than conventional global morphological parameters. Computer techniques offer a more objective and reproducible evaluation. The heart wall motion being a complex mechanism, conceptual models and mathematical algorithms are needed to adequately analyze the temporal sequence of changes occurring during the heart cycle. We have particularly studied the application of Fourier analysis methods for the evaluation of segmental cardiac motion. The application of Fourier transformation is based on the hypothesis that any periodic function can be represented as the sum of cosine and sine waves of different frequencies, each frequency characterized by a specific amplitude and phase. Expressed alternatively, Fourier analysis describes a signal in terms of its frequency content. Because cardiac contraction is generally a regular, recurrent event, it has periodicity and is well suited for the use of temporal Fourier analysis. The displacement of a point within the ventricle through the heart cycle can roughly be approximated with one sinusoidal wave at the fundamental frequency, the heart rate. This sinusoidal wave at the fundamental frequency is referred as the first Fourier harmonic. The first harmonic amplitude is an estimate of the total extent of motion. The phase shift of the first harmonic is a reasonably good approximation of the timing of the oscillation and can be used as a parameter to measure delays in wall motion between different regions of the heart. The changes in the first harmonic phase however does not differentiate between delays in the filling and in the emptying phase of the heart cycle.

Higher order harmonics provide more information about the motion profile in the different parts of the cycle but they are more sensitive to artefacts and noise interferences related to each imaging technique.

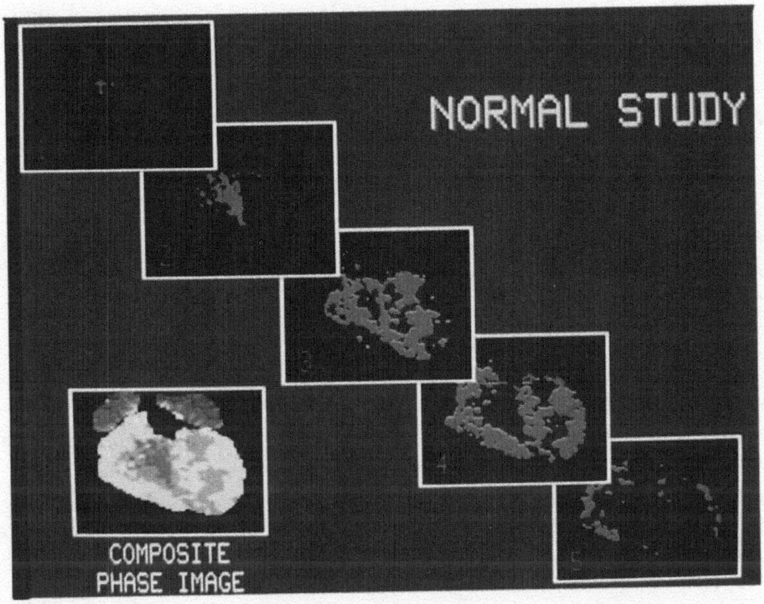

Figure 5: Results obtained by Fourier-phase analysis of cardiac wall motion from a radionuclide angiogram. The sequence of wall motion across the cardiac silhouette is shown in red on a green background in a sequence of five images. A composite color coded image in the lower left corner shows the same data on a single image where red areas are those contracting first and the areas in red and blue are those moving last.

The assessment of regional abnormalities in the temporal sequence of wall motion is of great interest for the clinical evaluation of heart diseases. It allows the detection of subtle changes of cardiac function in several types of cardiac disease before any changes in the global cardiac performance could be identified. Computer processing of digitized images not only allows functional parameters to be extracted from a sequence of images but also offers the possibility of displaying the resulting distribution on parametric or functional images representing a topographic map of the changes of the measured parameter in each point of the image. In fact, the advantage of parametric imaging is to enable the eye to easily detect regional changes in dynamics that are otherwise not readily apparent on visual inspection of the original data. We have applied the Fourier-phase analysis technique to images obtained from radionuclide images of the heart [5] as well as contrast cineangiographic images [6], and shown that significant improvement in diagnostic accuracy for the detection of cardiac wall motion abnormalities can be obtained. The result of such a technique applied to radionuclide angiogram is shown in figure 5, where the sequence of regional wall motion is highlighted over the cardiac silhouette in a sequence of parametric images.

CONCLUSIONS

The use of graphic user interface greatly facilitate the handling of complex image analysis programs by clinicians without or with little experience in computers. Also the use of color coded graphic outputs to generate parametric images allows the physicians to rapidly access the result of complex quantitative analysis algorithms that provide more objective and reproducible analysis of medical images.

REFERENCES

1. Gonzalez RC: Desktop Image Processing. Proceedings of *Electronic Imaging 87*, Boston, 1987.
2. Taira RK, Mankovich NJ, Boechat MI, Kangarloo H, Huang HK: Design and implementation of a picture archiving and communication system (PACS) for pedistric radiology. (in press), *AJR*: 1988.
3. Human Interface Guidlines: The Desktop Interface. Addison Wesley, 1987
4. Ratib O, Chappuis F, Rutishauser W: Digital angiographic technique for the quantitative assessement of myocardial perfusion. *Ann. of Radiology*, vol 28: 193-198, 1985.
5. Ratib O, Henze E, Schön H, Schelbert HR: Phase analysis of radionuclide angiograms for the detection of coronary artery disease. *Am. Heart J.*, 104: 1-12, 1982.
6. Ratib O, Righetti A, Brandon G, Rasoamanambelo L: A new method for the temporal evaluation of ventricular wall motion from digitized ventriculography. *Computers In Cardiology*, Seattle: p409-413, 1982.

Three-Dimensional Reconstruction Procedure Using GKS Primitives and Software Transformations for Anatomical Studies of the Nervous System

J.-P. Hornung and R. Kraftsik (Switzerland)

INTRODUCTION

The analysis of morphology or distribution of neurons in the brain requires sectioning of the brain which allows the cells to be viewed with a microscope, and which, moreover, is usually a requirement for the execution of the histological techniques needed to make the nerve cells visible. The section is thin relative to the size of the neuron (electron microscopy) or relative to regions of the brain (light microscopy) of interest in a particular study: Therefore, the spatial information is virtually reduced to a plane.

In order to restore the third dimension, it is necessary to combine the data from series of sections collected from the same block of tissue. Several approaches have been used to arrive at a 3D reconstruction. First attempts used simply cardboard, woodenware, or plastic plates of adjusted thickness cut out in the shape of the structure as seen in the series of sections and reassembled in appropriate fashion (this technique was already used in the late 19th century, but see also for example: Halliday and Törk, 1986; Sjöstrand, 1974; White, 1979). Recently, numerous computer graphic procedures were developed (e.g. Dürsteler et al. , 1977 (in our laboratory); and Kalia et al., 1985; Macagno et al., 1976; Mize, 1983; 1984; Stevens et al., 1980; Woodward et al., 1985). We describe here a procedure utilizing GKS (Graphic Kernel System) graphic primitives (cf. Enderle et al. 1984) combined with software computation for 3D transformations. The procedure can be applied to tissue sections prepared with different histological approaches and aimed at visualizing, in 3D, the morphology of a neuron or part of it, using electron microscopy, or the distribution of identified groups of neurons or axons within the brain, using light microscopy. This procedure may be combined with morphometry (see one example below).

DATA ACQUISITION AND DISPLAY

Light microscopic (human thalamus : Miklossy et al., 1987; human brainstem : Törk and Hornung, 1986) and electron microscopic (cat cortex : Törk et al., 1986; frog spinal cord : Antal et al., 1986) material was used. Serial sections of known thickness were collected and numbered so that the actual space between sections and their relative positions are precisely known.

Where light microscopic material was concerned, the sections are drawn on transparent paper using a camera lucida. Drawings are aligned with respect to one another according to landmarks found in the section. A set of reference points are added to the drawings, in order to orient properly the drawings on the graphics tablet. Outlines are digitized on a graphics tablet (Summagraphics MM1201) connected to the graphic system (Sigmex 6100) with echo on the screen. This system is linked to a Vax 750 minicomputer (Digital Equipment), and run with an interactive acquisition program written in FORTRAN 77 (Vax-11 Fortran, V3.0) using GKS graphic subroutines (Uniras, Denmark). The reference points are marked on the tablet, so that the drawings could be aligned before digitization. We have also tested a different interactive alignment procedure directly on the graphic screen, which was applied after the digitization of the sections, but for reasons discussed below we have preferred the former method.

The menu on the screen displays a choice of types of structures. An outline is recorded as a set of points. Each point is stored with its X- and Y-coordinates and a set of points, belonging to an outline, is preceded by a heading containing the number of points and a code identifying the type of structure. Correction is allowed for by two routines: (i) points can be deleted sequentially in reverse order of their entry (KILL function) or (ii) a whole set of points may be deleted at once (DELETE function). When an outline has been digitized, the data are written on disk either by adding a last point located over the first one, in order to display a closed outline (END function), or the set of points is written without adjunct, in order to be displayed as an open outline or as a series of points (END-OF-LINE function). Once all the outlines of a section have been digitized, selecting END a second time terminates the interactive session, and this procedure is repeated for the following sections.

In the case of electron microscopic preparations, the area of interest is photographed. From a montage of the micrographs of a section, the outline of the neurons is transferred by hand on a transparent paper along with landmarks used for alignment. The digitization is identical to that described above for light microscopic material. However, the reconstruction of a neuron, which is large relative to the magnification of the preparation, requires a different alignment procedure. When several portions of a neuron within one section are separated by a distance larger than about a third of the width of the total area reconstructed, each portion has to be aligned separately (micro-alignment), in order to compensate for the distortion due to the deformation of: (1) the section during the cutting with the ultramicrotome, (2) the section under the electron beam of the microscope, and (3) the photographic montage. Once properly aligned the sections are digitized. Micro-alignment is made while outlining the neuron on the transparent sheet, so that, at the time of digitization, the elements are aligned.

In order to generate a three-dimensional reconstruction, the program uses the content of the files sequentially to display the structure on the screen: first the section most distant with respect to the observer, and last the one that is the closest. The reconstruction of a volume in space is done using either polyline primitives ("wire model") or fill area primitives ("solid model"). In the "wire model", to remove the hidden lines, we use an artifice: when one outline is drawn over another, we first fill in the surface delineated by that covering outline in a color that is identical to the background (with a fill area primitive). This has the effect of masking the parts of the covered outline which are behind the outline to-be-drawn. We then draw the contour of the covering outline again (with a polyline primitive), and the resulting image is graphically equivalent to one which we would have obtained after applying an hidden line removal algorithm. The display of the sections in reverse order produces an mirror image of the opposite side. The location of relatively small elements, such as a neuron in a region of the brain, is labelled by dots. In a reconstruction, there may be one or several elements (e.g. one or several nuclei or neurons), each one made of several outlines belonging to a series of sections passing through this element. For the reconstruction, each element, identified by a code, can be individually selected for display. When several elements are drawn, the elements located further away are displayed first and the closest structures, covering the previous ones, are displayed last. Depending on the angle of view, the order of selection of the elements has to be adjusted. Since the order in which the different elements are displayed is critical with respect of the relative spatial location, this order can be selected interactively during the display session using a menu selection.

A third (Z-) coordinate is added to the points of each section. This coordinate corresponds to the distance separating the sections of a series. The three coordinates (X,Y,and Z) are used when the transformation matrix is applied. The matrix can handle rotation and translation along the 3 axis and scaling in respect of origin. The matrix is calculated using the parallel projection formulas. The display of a structure which has been modified by the transformation matrix is made by replacing the coordinate values of the points entered during digitization by those calculated with the matrix. The figures presented in this paper are close-ups taken from the Sigmex graphic screen.

RESULTS

A. Light microscopy

1. Distribution of serotoninergic neurons of the human brainstem

Serotoninergic neurons, innervating most parts of the brain, have their cell bodies confined to the brainstem, in nuclei close to the midline (the raphe nuclei). Brainstems from normal patient were collected postmortem. Serial frozen sections were reacted with an antibody specific for serotoninergic neurons. These neurons were plotted at 400 X using a light microscope outfitted with a camera lucida. The outlines of the brainstem was also drawn, but at a lower magnification. For the final display, files containing the location of the neurons were scaled down to match the size of the brainstem. We have reconstructed the entire human brainstem, in preparation of an atlas of the distribution of the serotoninergic neurons (Törk and Hornung, 1986).

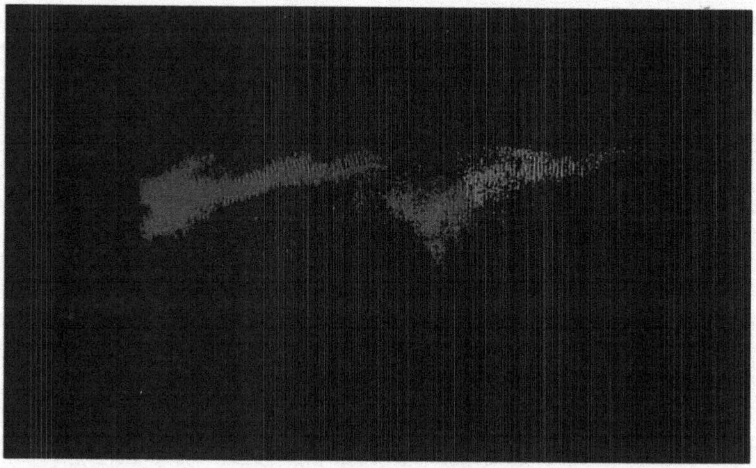

Figure 1: Antero-dorsal view of a human brainstem reconstructed from serial sections reacted for the immunocytochemical detection of serotoninergic neurons. The outline of the sections (in dark blue) is displayed from the caudal-most (at the right) to the rostral-most (at the left) using the hidden-line removal procedure. Each serotoninergic neuron is displayed by a dot. Note that serotoninergic neurons are grouped in several nuclei, each one coded with a different color.

The outline of the brainstem is displayed using the hidden-line-removal procedure and each serotoninergic neuron is represented by a dot (Fig. 1). The serotoninergic neurons are color-coded according to the nucleus to which they belong. Nuclei can be displayed individually or in any combination. Using lateral and dorsal views, it has been possible to define size and shape of each nucleus, which otherwise would be virtually impossible since each nucleus extends over many sections.

2. Pattern of axonal degeneration in the human thalamus

This study (Miklossy et al., 1987) describes the precise localization of degenerating axons in the thalamus of patients who have suffered from small brain injuries resulting in different forms of neglect. Thalami were collected postmortem and cut serially on a freezing microtome. Using a new method that involves examining a section in polarized light, even small sets of degenerating axons appeared as bright patches (Miklossy and Van der Loos, 1987). Outlines of the thalamus and its nuclei were entered from the same sections viewed in bright field microscopy.

Selected nuclei of the thalamus, the outline of the entire thalamus, and the area containing degenerating axons, have been selected for this display (Fig. 2). In selecting the appropriate nuclei and angles of view, it is possible to define the location of a lesion in the brain and thus to correlate precisely a particular neurological defect with its neuroanatomical substrata.

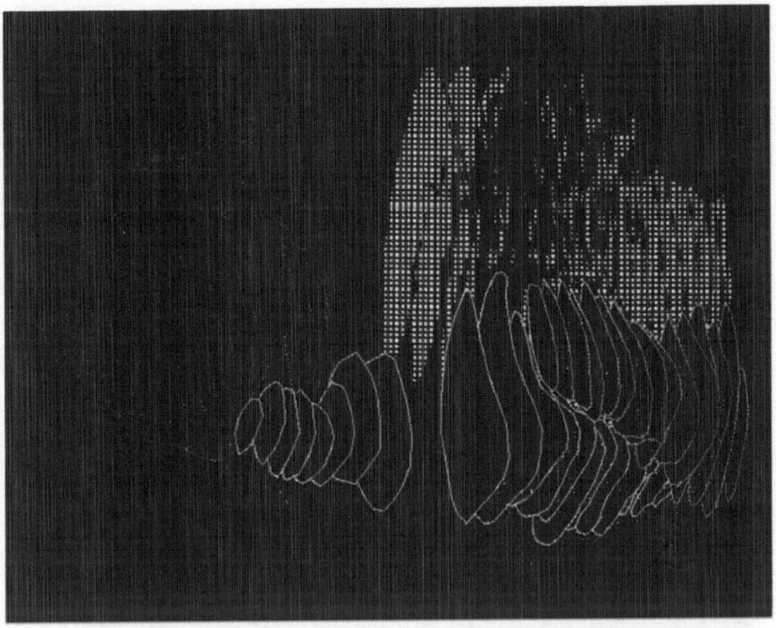

Figure 2: Postero-medial view of a human thalamus containing degenerating axons as a result of a local brain injury. The outline of the whole thalamus is represented in yellow. Three nuclei of the medial and posterior thalamus have also been displayed with different colored outlines. The regions of the thalamus containing degenerating fibers are displayed with a white dot pattern. The figure demonstrates the lesion was restricted to the antero-lateral nuclei of the thalamus.

B. Electron microscopy.

3. Serotoninergic axon terminals surrounding cortical neurons.

In cat cerebral cortex, cell bodies and proximal dendrites of certain neurons are surrounded by several serotoninergic axons forming a pericellular array, often referred to as a "basket". Combining immunocytochemistry and electron microscopy, we demonstrate that large varicosities of serotoninergic axons indeed form synapses with the surrounded neuron and that these terminals constitute a large proportion of its input (Törk et al., 1986).

Hundreds of serial ultrathin sections are viewed with the electron microscope. Every fourth section, the area of interest is photographed and prints were made at a final magnification of 15'000 X. The outlines of the neuron and of the immunoreactive axons were transferred from the electron micrographs to transparent paper, along with landmarks used for alignment. The cortical neuron or the serotoninergic axons can be displayed separately or simultaneously, and transformations such as rotation and zooming allow an analysis of the topographical relationship between the two structures (Fig. 3). With the same procedure, changing only the output primitive, the neuron can be displayed with a fill area whose intensity increases as its surface is closer to the viewer (Fig. 4), yielding a vivid 3-D impression of its shape.

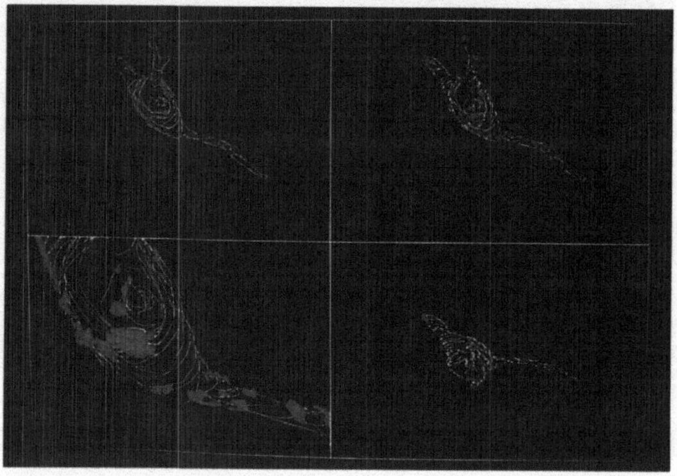

Figure 3: Four views of a cortical neuron reconstructed from serial ultrathin sections. The upper left panel shows the neuron alone. In the upper right panel, the same neuron is displayed with the labelled serotoninergic axons which surround it. In the lower left panel, the central part of the same view has been magnified and clipped, using GKS transformation routines. In the lower right panel, the same neuron is displayed with a rotation of 60 degrees around the X-axis. This set of views demonstrates the various treatments we can apply to the reconstruction in order to visualize the three-dimensional relationship between a neuron and axons that surround it.

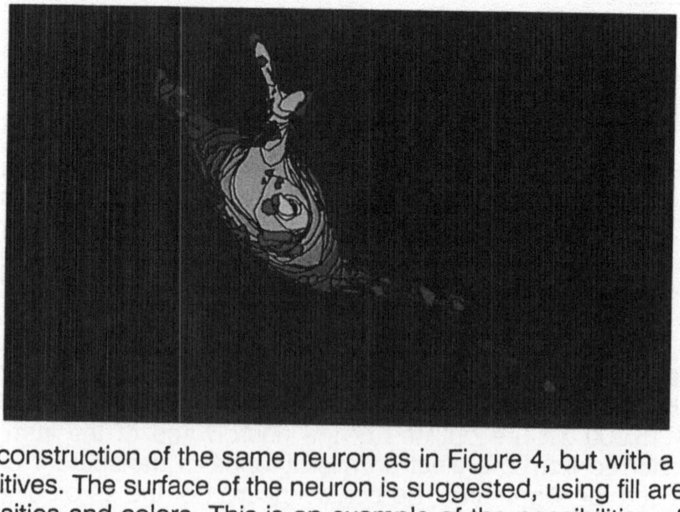

Figure 4: Reconstruction of the same neuron as in Figure 4, but with a different set of graphic primitives. The surface of the neuron is suggested, using fill area primitives of graded intensities and colors. This is an example of the possibilities of adaptation of the graphic output by changing only the GKS primitives.

4. Synaptic organization of dendritic trees of frog spinal cord motoneurons

Dendritic segments of motoneurons in frog spinal cord were reconstructed using serial ultrathin sections. This allowed the analysis of form, diameter, area and length of these segments, as well as of number,size and distribution of synapses impinging on them.

Initially, we used a monochrome graphic system (full refresh stroke display, Megatek) (Antal et al., 1986) which permitted us to visualize the synapses only in lateral views. The use of the raster color graphic system (Sigmex) enabled us to use the hidden-line removal for the dendritic contours (Antal and Kraftsik, 1987). To represent a structure (e.g. a synaptic contact) on the lateral surface of a dendritic segment, the space separating two adjacent sections can be filled in with a distinctive color. Details of the shape of the dendrite (Fig. 5), unexpected from light microscopic observations, were revealed: there was a succession of widenings and narrowings, and there were numerous thorn-like protrusions in close relationship with the synapses.

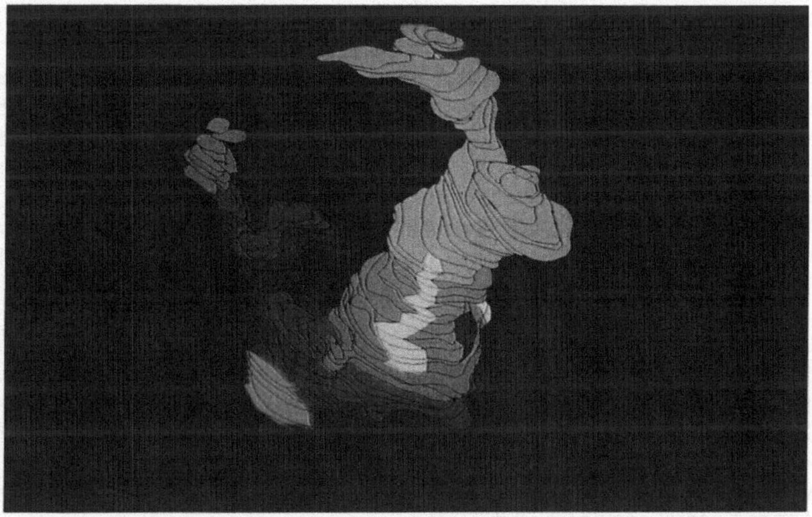

Figure 5: Reconstruction of a dendritic segment of a frog spinal motoneuron as analyzed with the electron microscope. This segment was rotated and scaled in order to demonstrate optimally the elements of the dendrite.The segment is produced filling in the inside of each dendritic outline with graded intensities and colors, in function of depth. The synaptic- surfaces are represented with fill areas. Different types of synapses are coded with different colors.

An outline, in this study, is divided in sectors which are of two kinds: synaptic contact or non-synaptic dendritic surface. The length of the sectors are used to calculate the area of the dendritic surface and synaptic contacts of a segment of motoneuron dendrite. They were approximated by the sum of the lateral side of each dendritic segment and of a synaptic sector respectively, in each section, which was obtained by multiplying the perimeter of profiles by the thickness of the section. The ratio between the total synaptic area and the total dendritic area was calculated to obtain an important parameter: "synaptic coverage". On the basis of these data, theoretical models of the function of these motoneurons can be developed and tested.

DISCUSSION

In recent years, with the increased use of computers in bio-medical laboratories, several groups have developed equipment and software for morphological studies in biology, including the neurosciences. One category of applications was oriented towards a global approach combining 3-D reconstruction, image analysis and quantitative analysis of the data (Cartos system: Macagno et al., 1976; CARP system: Woodward et al. , 1985). A second category of graphic systems aimed at a specific application on one type of biological specimen studied with one histological technique in the context of a given study (McGuire et al., 1984; Moens and Moens, 1981; Stevens et al., 1980; Tuohy et al, 1987).

Our attempt has been to generate a modular program for the acquisition, and display in 3-D of data derived from serial sections which are applied in our laboratory in the context of different neuroanatomical projects involving light or electron microscopy. Taking advantage of the flexibility of the GKS primitives, the display of the various reconstructions could be easily modified in order to obtain an optimal picture for any particular structure under analysis. In addition, the files containing the coordinates of the points can be used for geometrical measurements and quantitative analysis.

In developing our programs several options were taken so as to design a system which is simple to use and easy to modify in view of the diversity of the applications. First of all, the graphic tablet has been chosen as the digitizing interface for both light and electron microscope material. During this first step, it is also possible to align the drawings or the micrographs before they are digitized. This procedure is very simple and even faster than an alignment made interactively on the screen of the terminal after digitization. In addition, since electron micrographs require separate micro-alignments of different parts of the section, the procedure by hand is simple and quick, compared to automatic procedures.

Our graphic programs will be in the future implemented with routines for interactive editing of the display, allowing for zooming, clipping and lettering so that a final picture may be obtained, ready for projection or publication. We also consider creating other routines which allow to select specific regions of the display for the purpose of modifying parts of it or of quantitatively analyzing their contents.

In summary, we have presented a procedure for 3-D reconstruction of serial sections of nervous tissue applying basic routines which have three advantages: (1) they are device-independent, due to the use of GKS routines and to standard Fortran;

(2) they require only basic equipment (graphics tablet and display) used in conjunction with processing units ranging from Personal Computers to graphic workstations, thus making the system affordable even for individual laboratories; (3) the modular structure of the program and data files allow an easy adaptation of acquisition or display modules for new applications.

ACKNOWLEDGEMENTS

We are grateful to Prof. H. Van der Loos for critical reading of the manuscript and to Dr. J. Miklossy for the use of one figure. This work was supported by a Swiss NSF grant number 3.158.

LITERATURE REFERENCES

Antal M., R. Kraftsik, G. Szekely and H. Van der Loos (1986) Distal dendrites of frog motor neurons: a computer-aided electron microscopic study of cobalt filled cells. J. of Neurocytol. 15:303-310.

Antal M. and R. Kraftsik (1987) Synaptic organization of motoneuron dendritic trees in the frog spinal cord. Neuroscience letters Suppl.22:S93

Dürsteler M.R., C. Blakemore and L.J. Garey (1977) Uptake of Horseradish Peroxidase by Geniculo-Cortical Axons in the Golden Hamster: Analysis by Computer Reconstruction. Exp. Brain Research 29:487-500.

Enderle G., K. Kansy and G. Pfaff (1984) Computer graphics programming. GKS - The graphics standard. Springer-Verlag, Berlin.

Halliday G. and I Törk (1986) Comparative anatomy of the ventromedial mesencephalic tegmentum in the rat, cat, monkey and human. J.comp.Neurol. 252:423-445.

Kalia M., D.J. Woodward, W.K. Smith, K. Fuxe, T. Hökfelt and M. Goldstein (1985) Topographic distribution of catecholaminergic neurons in the rat medulla oblongata using quantitative three-dimensional reconstruction.In Quantitative neuroanatomy in transmitter research, L.F. Agnati and K. Fuxe eds., Macmillan, London, pp. 127-143.

Macagno E.R., C. Leventhal, C. Tountas, R. Bornholdt and R. Abba (1976) Recording and analysis of 3-D information from serial section micrographs: the cartos system. In Computer Technology in Neuroscience, P.B. Brown ed, Wiley, New York, pp. 97-112.

McGuire B.A., J.K. Stevens and P. Sterling (1984) Microcircuitry of bipolar cells in cat retina. J.Neurosci. 4:2920-2938.

Miklossy J., H. Van der Loos, J.P. Deruaz, J. Bogousslavsky and F. Regli (1987) Thalamic aphasia and neglect: cortical involvement as shown by anterograde axonal degeneration in the human brain. Abstract in the Symposium on Cellular Thalamic Mechanims, Verona, p 94.

Miklossy J. and H. Van der Loos (1987) Cholesterol ester crystals in polarized light show pathways in the human brain. Brain Research 426:377-380.

Mize R.R. (1983) A computer electron microscope plotter for mapping spatial distributions in biological tissues. J.of Neuroscience Methods 8: 183-195.

Mize R.R. (1984) Computer applications in cell and neurobiology: a review. International Review of Cytology 90:83-124.

Moens P.B. and T. Moens (1981) Computer measurements and graphics of three-dimensional cellular ultrastructure. J. of Ultrastructure Research 75: 131-141.

Sjöstrand F.S. (1974) A search for the circuitry of directional selectivity and neural adaptation through three-dimensional analysis of the outer plexiform layer of the rabbit retina. J.Ultrastructure Research 49: 60-156.

Stevens J.K., T.L. Davis, N. Friedman and P. Sterling (1980) A systematic approach ot reconstructing microcircuitry by electron microscopy of serial sections. Brain Research Reviews 2:265-293.

Törk I. and J.P. Hornung (1986) Topography and morphology of serotoninergic neurons in the human brainstem. Soc. Neurosci. Abst. 12:1023.

Törk I., J.P. Hornung, K.A. Mulligan and H. Van der Loos (1986) Synaptic connections of serotoninergic axons in the molecular layer of the cat's neocortex. Neuroscience letters Suppl. 26:S104.

Tuohy M., C. McConchie, R.B. Knox, L. Szarski and A. Arkin (1987) Computer-assisted three-dimensional reconstruction technology in plant cell image analysis: applications of interactive computer graphics. J. Microscopy 147:83-88.

White E.L. (1979) Thalamocortical synaptic relations: a review with emphasis on the projections of specific thalamic nuclei to the primary sensory areas of the neocortex. Brain Research Reviews 1:275-311.

Woodward D.J., W.K. Smith, D.S. Schlusselberg, S.A. Azizi and J.K. Chapin (1985) Tasks in computer-assisted neuroanatomy: data acquisition, imaging and database. In Quantitative neuroanatomy in transmitter research, L.F. Agnati and K. Fuxe eds., Macmillan, London, pp.25-40.

The Use of Three-Dimensional Dynamic and Kinematic Modelling in the Design of a Colonoscopy Simulator

A. Poon, C. Williams, and D. Gillies (UK)

Introduction

This paper addresses the problem of accurately modelling the motion of endoscope inside the human colon as the basis of an animated teaching aid. A problem arises from the difficulties that student endoscopists have in controlling the instrument. The human colon is a dynamically complex object capable of forming loops and changing shapes in response to the movement of the endoscope. Since the colon obviously cannot be seen from outside the inexperienced endoscopists can only rely on the TV display of the inside of the colon to deduce where the tip is. Under certain circumstances, when the colon forms into loop, no amount of pushing can advance the endoscope. A complicated manoeuvre is then necessary to straighten it to allow forward movement. At present learning the successful control of endoscopes in a colon examination is a difficult task requiring practice during hundreds of examinations. Moreover, patients can be put at risk when inexperienced endoscopists practise their skills. As a substitute for real patient, mechanical models of colon are available which are made of plastic, but they can damage the instrument. An alternative to these teaching methods is to replace them with a computer simulation. The objective would be to provide a graphical representation of the view as seen from the eyepiece of the endoscope coupled to endoscope controls similiar to an conventional endoscope. Additionally the simulator can, on command, provide views from outside the colon, readout of time elapsed, accuracy and instruction feedback to the users. The system needs to work in real time and, for wide distribution, be available on a microcomputer.

There are several ways in which the endoscope can be modelled. The simplest method is to represent the colon with a spline curve defined by an array of points fixed in space. The colon is drawn simply as a series of circles centred on and normal to the spline curve [8]. The view from the endoscope can easily be obtained by perspective projection from the position of the endoscope tip. This simple method suffers from the disadvantage that the configuration of the colon is fixed in space while in reality the colon can move under the influences of the endoscope within certain constraints. A more complex method is to treat the defining points of the spline curve as the joints of an articulated body with rigid linear links. The endoscope itself is also modelled by an articulated chain. This enables a kinematic and/or dynamic model to be used to specify its motion. At present the modelling method is based on the dynamic equations developed by Armstrong [1,2,3] which are derived from the Newton Euler formulation [6]. Acceleration of each link is calculated given the forces and torques acting on the link. Numerical integration is then used to find the velocity and positions of each link. A recursive method is used to obtain the solution of the equations efficiently.

Computational Modelling for 3D Animation

The process of computer animation can be divided into several phases [17]. First of all, an object model is needed to represent the real objects. This model is usually an approximation of the actual objects being modelled using primitives such as polygonal mesh, splines surfaces, rigid articulated bodies, or soft objects [23,24] etc. The motion of the objects, their trajectory, velocity, acceleration, must be specified next. If necessary, heuristic and/or dynamic approaches can be used to calculate the motion. Having decided on the motion specification, the behaviour of the camera needs be decided. The position and direction of view of the camera must be specified. The camera may move so therefore its trajectory, velocity and acceleration must be specified. Finally, the objects must be rendered to obtain realistic pictures. Picture quality can be improved with shading, textures, motion blur and in fact rendering has been the major area of graphic researches in recent years. It has been commented that too much emphasis is put on rendering and, at least as far as 3D animation is concerned, not enough in specifying motion. In this paper, we are primarily concerned with the first two steps that of devising an object model for the endoscope and colon and specifying its motion.

The main concern of computer animation systems is with what can actually be seen. However, the motion of an object must conform to physical laws in order that the motion looks natural. Therefore there are two approaches to simulation: heuristic, where a few simple rules are used and physical, where accurate physical laws are taken into account. Computers are most suitable for modelling geometrical shapes as demonstrated by the widespread uses of CAD applications. On the other hand, modelling natural objects such as clouds, fires, trees and water is extremely difficult and problematic. Physical model are almost impossible to produce because of the enormous number of factors that must be taken into account to produce realistic natural objects, or if a physical model is available, it is often too expensive for animation. Most researchers therefore opt for the heuristic approach for modelling natural objects.

In the modelling of the endoscope and colon, the priority is for production of a plausible graphic display that can convince the users that they are performing a real colonoscopy. This implies that an heuristic model can be used since the actual dynamics involving forces and torques do not have to be calculated, as opposed to controlling motion of robots, where dynamic analysis is necessary. However, the motion of the endoscope is very complex with great freedom, and so it is hard to specify heuristically the motion alone. With a physical model, it is easier to produce the required motion, especially when interaction with the environment is involved. Unfortunately the computation cost of a full dynamic model is prohibitive for real time simulation with modest hardware. Therefore, by combining both the heuristic and physical approaches, a compromise can be reached between efficiency and ease of control of motion and accuracy. The compromise between efficiency and accuracy is a common problem in computer graphic systems, particularly when real time simulation is required. As more details are displayed, more computation power is needed. Since the overwhelming majority of modelling is only an approximation of real life, there is no limit as to the accuracy that can be obtained. There are always more accurate or complete models to be found. The increase in accuracy invariably means heavier demands on hardware and many systems make use of heuristics or rules to simplify calculations. Examples are Particle systems [16], Soft objects [23,24], modelling of natural phenomena [5,7], anti-aliasing, and reflectance models.

Problems in Colonoscopy

The modern fibrescope consists of a head with eyepiece and controls, and a flexible shaft with a manoeuvrable tip (figure 1). The head is connected to a unit containing a light source and air/water supply. The shaft contains the fibre bundles and the control wires for tip movement and two or more operating channels allowing passage of flexible instruments such as biopsy forceps through the shaft to the tip. The shaft is torque stable so that when the head rotates, the rotatory movement is transmitted down the shaft to the tip. The tip can be bent by manipulating four control wires attached to the tip. Most modern endoscopes allow tip deflection of up to 180 degrees all round. The control wires are passed through the shaft from the tip to the head and connected to two control wheels. The fibre bundle is about 4 mm in diameter and contains thousands of fine glass fibres about 10 mm in diameter. The bundle is extremely flexible and capable of carrying visual information even if it is tied in knots. The image quality is, however, not as good as rigid lens system because of the fine mesh appearance of endoscopic images due to the optical properties of fibre bundle. However,the images are sufficiently clear for diagnosis and surgical purposes. The colon is somewhat like an elastic tube located inside the abdominal cavity. Depending on its condition, the colon can be long and tortuous when inflated or stretched, or much shorter and straighter when deflated or when an endoscope is passed through it and pulled back. The colon contains the following structures : rectum, sigmoid colon, descending colon, splenic flexure, transverse colon, hepatic flexure, ascending colon and caecum (figure 2). The rectum, the descending and ascending colons and the caecum are fixed in position relative to each other and bound down to various parts of the abdominal cavity. The rectum and the caecum are located at either end of the colon while the descending and ascending colons are straight and can be easily passed through by an endoscope. The sigmoid and transverse colons present more problems for computer modelling. They normally flop into a variety of positions and their movements are limited by their connections to mesenteries (mesocolon). The mesenteries are narrowed at the base at the pelvic brim which forms an inverted V shape. This structure allows easy rotation of the sigmoid colon around the narrow base to form the so called alpha loop. A similar loop may form by inadvertantly rotating the transverse colon and is termed the gamma loop.

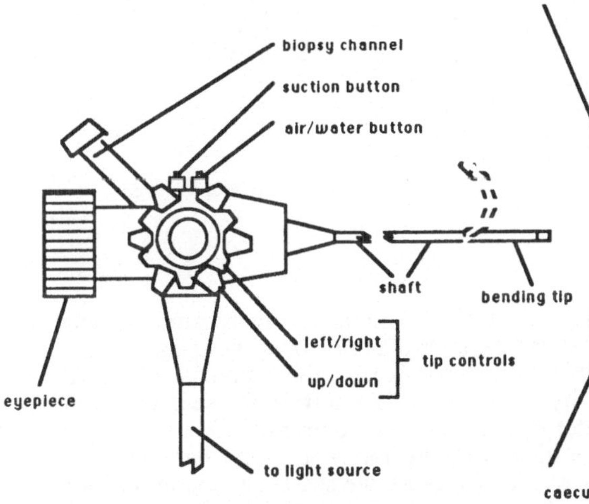

Figure 1: The Endoscope

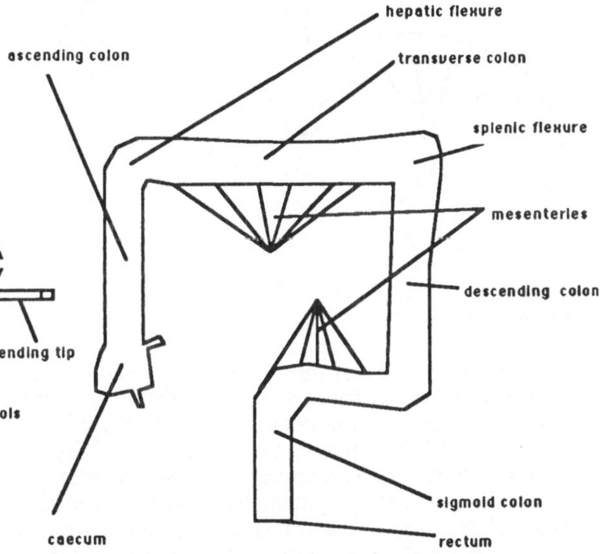

Figure 2: Structures of the Human Colon

The alpha loop is important because it removes the acute bend at the junction between the sigmoid and descending colon. When the endoscope passes through the sigmoid colon directly without forming an alpha loop, because of the direction the endoscope is pushed, the sigmoid colon tends to be stretched and bowed up and an acute hairpin bend results at the junction leading to the descending colon as shown in figure 3. This 'N' bend can be very difficult to negotiate, especially for inexperienced endoscopists. It can be removed either by pulling back to reduce the 'N' bend or with an alpha manoeuvre (figure 4), whereby the sigmoid colon is rotated anti-clockwise through 180 degrees. The endoscope can then slide through the junction smoothly and easily. Another feature of endoscopic manoeuvres is referred to as paradoxical behaviour. This is the apparent paradox that when the endoscope is pushed in, the view from the tip shows that it is moving backwards instead of forwards as expected or visa versa. This behaviour is caused by several configurations of the colon. The most common one is when the endoscope has reached the transverse colon and is within sight of the hepatic flexure. The transverse colon is looped downwards. In order to make progress the endoscope must be hooked around the transverse colon and by pulling back the endoscope the transverse colon can be lifted up and straightened. This straightening of the transverse colon also shortens it so that the tip appears to move forwards in relation to the colon. When the tip is pushed in again, it almost slides back to the original position but not quite. A little progress can be made each time and by repeating the above manoeuvre, the endoscope can inch its way to the hepatic flexure. For more details of the physical properties of the endoscope and colon see [22].

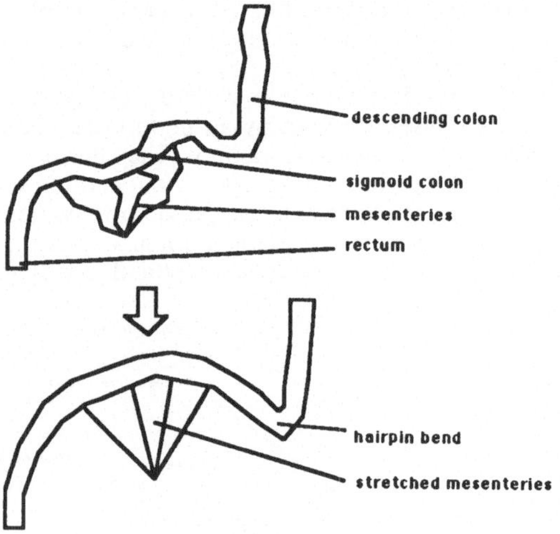

Figure 3: Formation of a hairpin bend

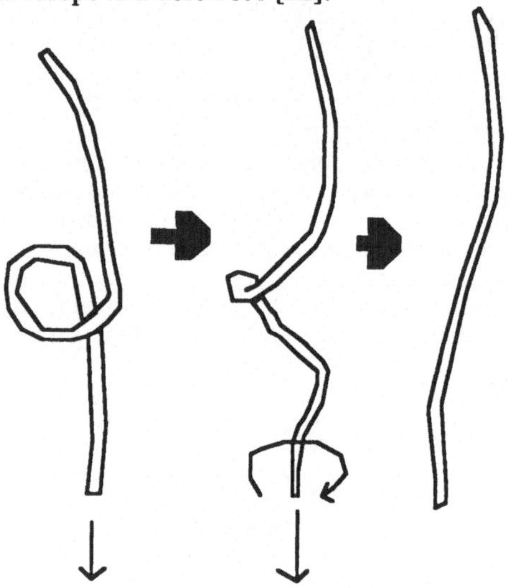

Figure 4: The Alpha Manoeuvre

The Model

Our proposed models of the endoscope and colon are based on kinematic and dynamic models of articulated bodies [6,13,4,9]. Both are represented by an articulated body with rigid linear links, but while the endoscope motion is calculated dynamically, the colon is modelled kinematically. The endoscope is represented by a dynamically controlled linear chain of articulated bodies. It is assumed that the diameter of the endoscope does not affect its motion significantly so each segment is modelled as a ideal straight line. Each joint has only two rotational degrees of freedom since the endoscope is relatively torque stable and therefore each link cannot twist freely with respect to its neighbours. The dynamic model is based on the Newton Euler formulation. The physical properties of the endoscope are not completely analogous to that of a linear chain. The endoscope is a non-rigid body which does not have distinct joints and segments. It can bend at any point, so a completely accurate model would need to divide it into point masses and calculate the kinematic and dynamic relationship between adjacent points. Since each point has three degrees of freedom, and an endoscope model should contain thousands of points, it is very expensive computationally. The proposed model therefore represents a compromise for efficiency. It is an approximation of reality. Each segment represents a number of point masses that are the same distance relative to each other.

The colon is represented by a linear articulated chain. At each joint a circle normal to the proximal segment is defined. This represents the bounding diameter of the colon at that point. The colon motion is calculated kinematically which means that the relationship among position, velocity and acceleration of each segment is taken into account, but not the mass, forces, and torques. The kinematic approach is chosen for the colon to reduce the amount and complexity of computation. It is likely that with two dynamically controlled chains the cost of computing their interaction would be too high. Each joint of the colon has three rotational degrees of freedom and one translational degree of freedom along the direction of the proximal segment. The latter is needed to simulate the elasticity of the colon when air is blown in or sucked out. The kinematic structure of the colon means that it only moves when the endoscope makes contact with it. Basically, the problem of finding the intersection between the colon and endoscope can be reduced to calculating the intersection(s) between a straight line (or curve if the endoscope is represented by interpolating with splines) and a cylinder representing a segment of the colon. The main problem is to distinguish the special cases, for example when the intersection is not a single point or when more than two intersections are found in a particular segment.

The joints in the endoscope and colon model cannot be completely free to move in any direction. For example, the segments cannot overlap each other, and the joints in either model cannot move beyond a certain angle otherwise the motion will appear unrealistic. Internal forces and torques must therefore be applied to the joints to prevent unrealistic movement. Internal damping forces are also important to avoid instability and oscillation which can occur in the dynamic model. These damping forces are usually modelled by spring and damper pairs and are proportional to the speed at the local degree of freedom. The constant of damping may be different for each degree of freedom and should be calculated separately. [19,20,21]

The colon model (as well as the endoscope) is constrained within a predefined volume representing the abdominal cavity. Since the colon is attached to mesenteries its movement within the abdominal cavity is also restricted. Forces are generated when the mesenteries are stretched to the limit and when the colon touches the abdominal wall. Frictional forces are generated when the endoscope touches the colon. The magnitude depends on the coefficient of friction and the direction is opposite to the motion. Lastly, the abdominal cavity is filled with other digestive organs such as small intestine and pancreas etc. To move the colon from its initial position requires work to be done to overcome the resistance from pressing against these other organs. It is assumed that the forces opposing the motion of the colon is proportional to the displacement from the initial position and against the direction of motion. These forces can be used to control the motion of the endoscope.

Kinematics and Dynamics of Articulated bodies

There are several approaches in formulating the dynamics equations of articulated bodies. The Langrangian [6,11] and Newton-Euler methods [2,6,18,15] are the best known and have been applied in graphic animation and simulation of robot arms. Recently, other methods have been proposed including Gibb-Appell [19,20], generalised d'Alembert [14], and Kane's formulations [12]. These dynamic formulations all give roughly the same result, and the choice depends on the nature of the articulated bodies being modelled and the applications. The motion equations obtained relate the acceleration of the links with the forces and torques acting on the link. These equation can be used to find the acceleration given the forces and torques, and hence the velocity and position of the articulated bodies by integration. Alternately, for robotic control, the inverse problem must be solved and forces and torques are calculated which produce the given acceleration.

Newton-Euler Formulation

The Newton-Euler formulation [2,6,18,15] is based on Newton's Second Law and d'Alembert Principle. It is more efficient than any other method mainly because of its use of a local vector representation and the recursive nature of the solution method. The formulation has a cost of O(n) where n is number of degrees. Each link is attached to a separate local co-ordinate system which moves with the link. Certain quantities, such as the moment of inertia tensors, are invariant under this condition, which simplifies calculation considerably. The Newton-Euler formulation consists of a set of forwards recursive equations which propagate kinematic information such as velocity and acceleration, and a set of backwards recursive equations propagating dynamic information such as the forces and torques acting on successive links. The structure of the equations is less elegant than Langrange formulation since they involve vector cross product terms which do not stress the relationship between the form of the equations and the articulated bodies. Despite this, computational efficiency makes the Newton-Euler formulation the best suited to real time control or simulation purposes. Since the Newton-

Euler formulation is based on moving local co-ordinate systems, which are called frames, it is necessary to understand how they relate to each other and a fixed inertial co-ordinate system.

Moving Co-ordinate Systems

Here we are interested in the relationship between moving frames, and especially the problem of finding the position, velocity and acceleration of the vector w.r.t to the fixed frame given the velocity of the moving frame and the vector w.r.t the moving frame as shown in figure 5, where r is fixed in the primed co-ordinate system which is moving.

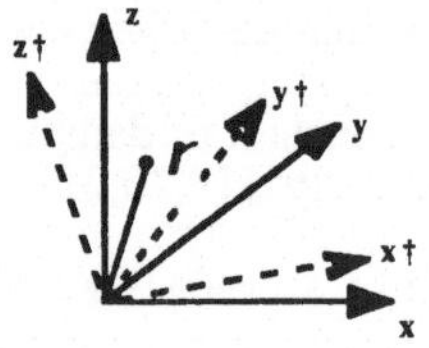

Figure 5: Moving Coordinate Systems

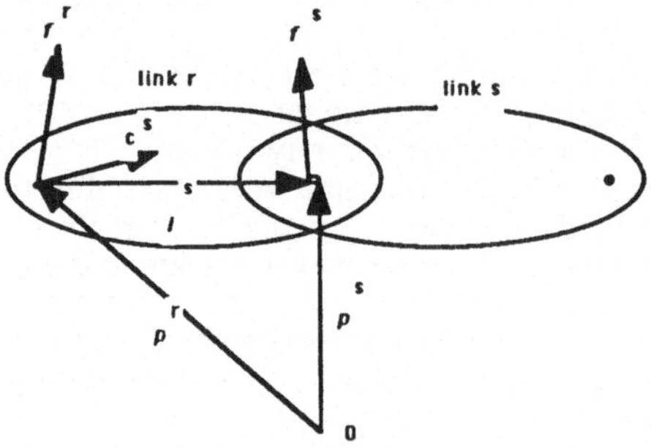

Figure 7

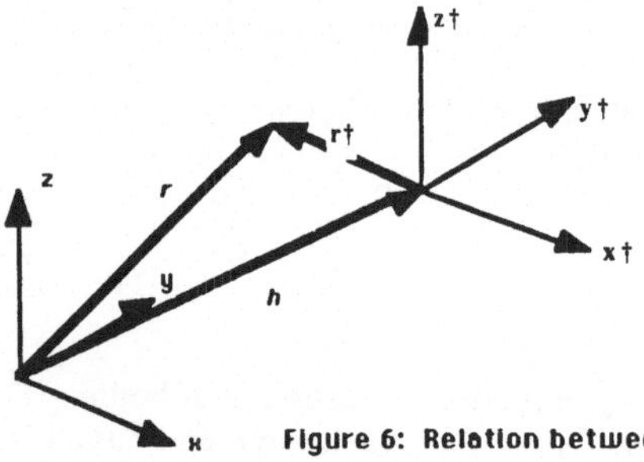

Figure 6: Relation between coordinate systems

The fundamental equation describing this behaviour is derived as:

$$dr/dt = d^{\dagger}r/dt + w \times r$$

To obtain the acceleration we differentiate again:

$$\frac{d2r}{dt2} = \frac{d^{\dagger}2r}{dt2} + 2w \times \frac{d^{\dagger}r}{dt} + w \times (w \times r) + \frac{dw}{dt} \times r \qquad (1)$$

Equation (1) is called the coriolis theorem. The second term is the coriolis acceleration and the third term is the centripetal acceleration.

If the frames do not share the same origin, as shown in the figure 6, then:

$$r = r^{\dagger} + h$$

velocity

$$dr/dt = dr^{\dagger}/dt + dh/dt$$
$$= d^{\dagger}r^{\dagger}/dt + w \times r^{\dagger} + dh/dt$$

acceleration

$$\frac{d2r}{dt^2} = \frac{d2r^{\dagger}}{dt^2} + \frac{d2h}{dt^2} = \frac{d^{\dagger}2r^{\dagger}}{dt^2} + 2w \times \frac{d^{\dagger}r^{\dagger}}{dt} + w \times (w \times r^{\dagger}) + \frac{dw}{dt} \times r^{\dagger} + \frac{d2h}{dt^2}$$

Our dynamical model for the endoscope is derived from the basic Newtonian force and torque equations for each section (figure 7).

force equation: $m_r \, ac_r = R_s \, f_s - f_r$

torque equation:

$$J_r \, dw_r/dt + w_r \times (J_r w_r) = R_s g_s - g_r - c_r \times f_r + (p_r - p_s + c_r) \times R_s f_s$$

The derivation is similar to that found in Armstrong [1,2], and produces a final equation relating force and acceleration:

$$f_r = R_s f_s - m_r w_r \times w_r \times c_r - m_r dw_r/dt \times c_r - m_r a_r + RI_r^T (fe_r + m_r a_g)$$

and a torque equation:

$$J_r dw_r/dt = - w_r \times (J_r w_r) - g_r + R_s g_s - c_r \times m_r ac_r + l_s \times R_s f_s$$

$$+ RI_r^T ge_r + m_r c_r \times RI_r^T a_g + pe_r \times RI_r^T fe_r$$

Lastly, the equation relating the accelerations at successive hinges is:

$$R_s a_s = w_r \times (w_r \times l_s) + a_r - l_s \times dw_r/dt \qquad (2)$$

The notation in the above equations is as follows. Matrices are represented by upper case letter while vectors are in lower case. Furthermore, link p refers to the parent link of link r (nearer the root link or link 1) and link s refers to the son link of link r. The following quantities are represented in the frame of link r unless otherwise stated.

fc_r= force acting on the centre of gravity of link r
gc_r= torque acting on the centre of gravity of link r
m_r = mass of link r
ac_r= linear acceleration at centre of mass of link r
J_r = inertia matrix of link r
dw_r/dt = angular acceleration at proximal hinge of link r
w_r = angular velocity at proximal hinge of link r.
f_r = force link r exerts on its parent at its proximal hinge.
g_r = torque link r exerts on its parent at its proximal hinge.
c_r = position vector from proximal hinge of link r to its centre of gravity.
p_r = position vector of the proximal hinge of link r represented in inertia frame.
a_g = acceleration due to gravity represented in inertia frame.
l_r = hinge to hinge vector from proximal hinge of link r parent to proximal hinge of link r represented in the frame of parent.
fe_r= external force acting on link r at point per represented in inertia frame.
pe_r= vector from proximal hinge of link r to point of application of force fe_r.
ge_r= external torque acting on link r represented in inertia frame
R_r = rotation matrix converting from representation in frame r to representation in the frame of the parent link.
RI_r= rotation matrix converting from representation in frame r to representation in inertia frame.
RI_r^T = inverse (transpose) of RI_r

Solution of Dynamic Equations

Armstrong [1,2] proposes a solution method based on the following linear relationship:

$$dw_r/dt = K_r a_r + d_r \quad (3)$$
$$f_r = M_r a_r + f'_r \quad (4)$$

The above equations hypothesise that there are linear relationships between dw_r/dt, the angular acceleration and ar the linear acceleration, and between f_r, the reactive force acting on the parent link through link r, and a_r. The coefficients K_r, M_r, d_r and f' can be calculated by equating the coefficients with the corresponding motion equations, which are arranged into similar form. Once the recursive coefficients have been computed for each link with a backwards pass towards the root, the acceleration at the root link can be calculated using equation (4) because the force on the parent is zero since there is no parent. Equation (2) and (3) can then be used to obtain the acceleration at successive links with a forwards pass from the root. The position and velocity of each link can be calculated by integrating the acceleration, ie. multiplying the acceleration vector with the time step between each iteration. Armstrong's formulation is the most efficient dynamic formulation available for articulated bodies at the moment. The disadvantages of it is that the type of joint is limited to revolute joint with 3 degrees of freedom. However it is possible to constrain the joint to 1 or 2 degrees of freedom, as required by our application, with some extra computation cost.

Other Formulations

The general motion equations derived from the Langrange formulation [6] are a set of n second order coupled nonlinear differential equations, where n is the number of degree of freedom, when effects of gear friction is ignored. The solution of the equations is usually obtained by numerical matrix inversion which can be highly inefficient. The derivation of the dynamic equations depends on the homogeneous representation of vectors and transformation matrices relating successive links and the Langrange-Euler equation which minimises the difference in the kinetic and potential energy of the articulated bodies.

$$\frac{d}{dt}\left[\frac{\partial L}{\partial(dq_i/dt)}\right] - \frac{\partial L}{\partial q_i} = r_i \qquad \text{for } i = 1, 2, .., n$$

where
L = K (kinetic energy) - P (potential energy)
q_i = generalised co-ordinates (translational or angular)
r_i = generalised forces (forces or torques)

The cost of the classical Langrange formulation is $O(n^4)$ which means real time uses are almost impossible. The main advantages of this approach is that the equations obtained is mathematically elegant and the structure of the equations reflect the physical nature of the articulated bodies. Hollerbach [11] suggested a recursive formulation of langrange equation which is O(n) ,although it is still less efficient than Newton-Euler formulation and the simplicity of the form of the equations is lost.

This formulation is based on the Gibbs formula [19] which describes the energy of acceleration. For articulated bodies of n links :

$$G = \sum_{k=1}^{n} \left[1/2\, m_k a_k^T a_k + 1/2\, \alpha_k^T I_k \alpha_k + \alpha_k^T (w_k \times I_k w_k) + f(w_k) \right]$$

where

α_k = angular acceleration
m_k = mass of link k
Ik = inertia tensor

w_k = angular velocity
a_k = acceleration at centre of mass
f(wk) = scalar which disappears after differentiation

The actual dynamics equations are found by partially differentiating the Gibbs formula with respect to the local acceleration relative to each degree of freedom. An equation is obtained for each degree of freedom relating the local acceleration with the generalised forces or torques acting on that degree of freedom. The cost of this formulation is O(n4). The main advantage is that the forces, torques, mass, configuration, and velocity information are partitioned neatly and elegantly. It is easy to alter any of them without affecting other variables which facilitates experimentation in motion control of complex bodies.

The general d'Alembert formulation [14] is similar to Langrange-Euler formulation in that both produce closed form non-linear differential equations that describe the behaviour of articulated bodies, and share the same advantage that the equation is mathematically elegant. However, General d'Alembert has a cost of $O(n^3)$ which is better than Langrange-Euler; the efficiency is obtained by changing the kinematic representation of L-E from 4x4 homogeneous to position vectors and rotation matrices used in N-E formulation. Kane's formulation [12] generates dynamic equations in explicit and efficient form, but it is mainly applied in the dynamic analysis of robot manipulators and is not well suited for simulation.

Conclusion and Future Works

The main concern of the endoscope simulator is with the balance between efficiency and accuracy. At one extreme, a totally physical model, correct in all dynamic details, is too expensive. In this case, a hardware solution, probably using parallel architecture [25], is appropriate. This approach could provide an interesting research project, and recently Armstrong has proposed a parallel algorithm for his dynamic equations [3]. At the other extreme, a totally heuristic model has several disadvantages. First motion specification is laborious because it has to be done either by inbetweening, which needs manual intervention, or by simple heuristic rules which alone are not adequate to specify the complex motion of colon and endoscope. Therefore we feel that a combination of the two different approaches should yield the best result in terms of efficiency while maintaining enough realism for graphic display purposes. In the proposed model, the colon is controlled by heuristics while the endoscope is controlled dynamically. Currently, the dynamic model of the endoscope has been programmed. The Armstrong equations were used, modified to take into account the torque stability of the endoscope. The results give a reasonable behaviour, though currently the computation time using C on a 80386 based computer is still too long for animation. This problem may be avoided by paying more attention to the fundamental algorithms used. The next step in the development of the model will be to investigate the interactions between the colon and endoscope in the real world in details and then applying this knowledge to fine tune the behaviour of the overall model.

Acknowledgement

The authors would like to express their thanks to the Cancer and Polio Research Fund Ltd. who have provided the financial support for this research.

References

[1] W.W. Armstrong, "Recursive Solution to the Equation of Motion of an N-Link Manipulator," ASME Proc. of the fifth World Congress on theory of Machines and Mechanisms (1979).

[2] W.W. Armstrong, M.W. Green, "The Dynamics of Articulated Rigid Bodies for the Purposes of Animation," The Visual Computer, (1985) 1: pp. 231-240.

[3] W.W. Armstrong, M. Green, R. Lake , "Near Real Time Control of Human Figure Models," IEEE CG&A, June 87, pp. 52-61
[4] N.I. Badler, K.H. Manoochehri, G. Walters, "Articulated Figure Positioning by Multiple Constraints," IEEE CG&A, June 87, pp. 28-38
[5] J. Bloomenthal, "Modelling the Mighty Maple," Siggraph 85, Vol.19, No. 3, pp. 305-311.
[6] K S Fu, R.C. Gonzales, C.S.G. Lee "Robotics : Control, Sensing, Vision, and Intelligence." McGraw Hill (1987).
[7] G.Y. Gardner, "Visual Simulation of Clouds," Siggraph 85, Vol.19, No.3, pp. 297-303.
[8] D. Gillies, C. Williams, "An Interactive Graphics Simulator for the Teaching of Fibrendoscopic Techniques," Eurographics' 87, G. Marechal(Editor), Elsevier Science Publishers B.V. (North-Holland).
[9] M. Girard, A.A. Maciejewski, "Computational Modelling for the Computer Animation of Legged Figures," Siggraph 85, Vol. 19.No.3, pp. 263-269
[10] R. Hall, "A Characterization of Illumination models and shading techniques," The Visual Computer (1986) 2: pp. 268-277
[11] J.M. Hollerbach, "A Recursive Lagrangian Formulation of Manipulator Dynamics and a Comparative Study of Dynamics Formulation Complexity," IEEE Trans. on Systems, Man and Cybernetics. Vol. SMC-10, No. 11, Nov. 80, pp. 730-736.
[12] T.R. Kane, D.A. Levinson, "The Use of Kane's Dynamic Equations in Robotics," The International Journal of Robotics Research, Vol. 2, No. 3, Fall 1983, pp. 3-21.
[13] J.U. Korein, N.I. Badler, "Techniques for Generating the Goal-Directed Motion of Articulated Bodies," IEEE CG&A, Oct. 82, pp. 71-81.
[14] C.S.G. Lee, B.H. Lee, R. Nigam, "Development of the Generalized d'Alembert Equations of Motion for Mechanical Manipulators," Proc. od the 22nd Conference on Dicision and Control, Dec. 14-16,1983
[15] J.Y.S. Luh, M.W. Walker, R.P.C. Paul, "On-line Computational Scheme for Mechanical MAnipulators," Transactions of ASME, Journal of Dynamic Systems, Measurement, and control, June 80, Vol. 102 pp. 69-67
[16] W.T. Reeves, "Particle Systems - A Techniques for Modelling a Class of Fuzzy Objects," Siggraph 83, Vol.17, No.3, pp. 359-376.
[17] D. Thalmann, O. Ratib, N. Magnenat-Thalmann, A. Righetti, "A Model for the Three-dimensional Reconstruction and Animation of the Human Heart," The Visual Computer, (1985) 1: pp.241-248
[18] M.W. Walker, D.E. Orin, "Efficient Dynamic Computer Simulation of Robotic Mechanisms," Transactions of ASME, Journal of Dynamic Systems, Measurement, and control, Sep. 82, Vol. 104 pp. 205-211
[19] J. Wilhelms, B.A. Barsky, "Using Dynamic Analysis to Animate Articulated Bodies Such as Humans and Robots," Proc. Graphics Interface 85, Canadian Information Processing Soc., Toronto, May 85, pp. 97-104
[20] J. Wilhelms,"Using Dynamics Analysis for Realistic Animation of Articulated Bodies," IEEE CG&A, June 87, pp. 12-27.
[21] J. Wilhelms, "Toward Automatic Motion Control," IEEE CG&A, Apr. 1987, pp. 11-22.
[22] C. Williams, P. Cotton, "Practical Gastrointestinal Endoscopy," London, Blackwell Scientific Publication 1980,1982
[23] G. Wyvill, C. McPheeters, B. Wyvill, "Data Structure for Soft Objects," The Visual Computer, (1986) 2: pp. 227-234.
[24] B. Wyvill, C. McPheeters, G. Wyvill, "Animating Soft Objects," The Visual Computer, (1986) 2: pp. 227-234.
[25] Y.F. Zheng, H. Hemami, "Computation of Multibody System Dynamics by a Multiprocessor Scheme," IEEE Trans. on Systems, Man, and Cybernetics, Vol. SMC-16, No. 1, Jan/Feb 86

Chapter 6

Applications of Computer Graphics

A Hierarchical Simulation Environment for VLSI

M. Bourgault, J. Cloutier, C. Roy, S. Fauvel, and E. Cerny (Canada)

Abstract

In order to aid the debugging of complex circuits, our multiple-window hierarchical object-oriented simulation environment for VLSI circuits provides powerful features for navigation in the cell hierarchy of the simulated circuit. The environment mimics this hierarchy in that each cell (instance) is treated as an object which can show its structure (static) and simulation state (dynamic signal values, probes, etc.) in its own screen window. The structural description is obtained from a circuit database. The dynamic description is accessed by interposing virtual cell simulation objects between the interface and the simulator. These objects map the possibly flattened simulation structure back onto the structural hierarchy and provide a homogeneous access for controlling the simulator and for observing the simulation results in every cell. The parallel object hierarchies of structure, dynamic descriptors and interface windows allow easy replacement of objects in a simulation at multiple levels of abstraction, and it can be adapted for a distributed simulator.

Introduction

Simulation is still the prevailing technique for verifying the behavior of digital ICs. For managing the ever increasing complexity of VLSI circuits, modern design methodologies use hierarchical decomposition of the circuit into smaller, more easily understandable, modules called cells. At each hierarchical level, the cells thus consist of interconnections of other lower-level cells, etc., until atomic elements such as transistors, gates or some other functional modules are reached. The lower-level cells are treated as black boxes, represented by their external geometry, I/O ports and function. The internal details are hidden. At the same time, however, the circuit debugging process can become tedious, because it may be difficult to navigate in a complex cell hierarchy and to pinpoint the source of error. This is especially true if the simulator presents the designer with the hierarchy flattened. Therefore, most modern simulators provide a powerful user interface that allows more subtle forms of interaction than the usual post-mortem analysis of waveforms. For instance, the interfaces of THEMIS [Dosh84] or Edisim [Hill83] are good examples, however, the navigational features are not sufficiently developed, and also the interface can be difficult to adapt to new forms of simulators and circuit models, which may be in part due to the structure of the simulator itself.

Modern integrated CAD systems must provide means for managing the cell hierarchy of VLSI designs, while encouraging the exploration of design alternatives. Top-down and bottom-up design should be supported. We reported an approach to the organization of such a system in [Deme86, Deme87]. A simulator which is to function in such an environment must support multiple levels of abstraction, provide simple cell-model replacement and communicate with the user in a way which allows to operate naturally in the hierarchical circuit structure the user created and to observe the behavior at any hierarchical level. This implies that each cell (simulator) must have internal autonomy in its implementation and form of interactions, yet externally it must integrate with the rest of the system through a uniform interface. As shown in [Deme87], this can be achieved by treating cells as objects (abstract data types), all having similar interfaces but possibly different internal details. The approach lends uniformity to both the software design and user interactions.

Our multiple-window hierarchical environment for an event-driven simulator provides flexible navigational tools beside the usual signal observation/editing/analysis features. Furthermore, the interface is structured in such a way that it is in great part independent of the type of the event-oriented simulator used, thus making easier to adapt to different simulators. It is aligned with the underlying philosophy and integration mechanisms of our object-oriented VLSI design environment CHESHIRE [Deme86,87], and to some extent by our object-oriented simulator [RoyC85, Clou86a].

Organization of the Environment

The simulation environment is constructed around three parallel object hierarchies, as illustrated in Fig. 1: Circuit structure, simulation state, and viewing windows. As will be seen, the last hierarchy is usually only partial.

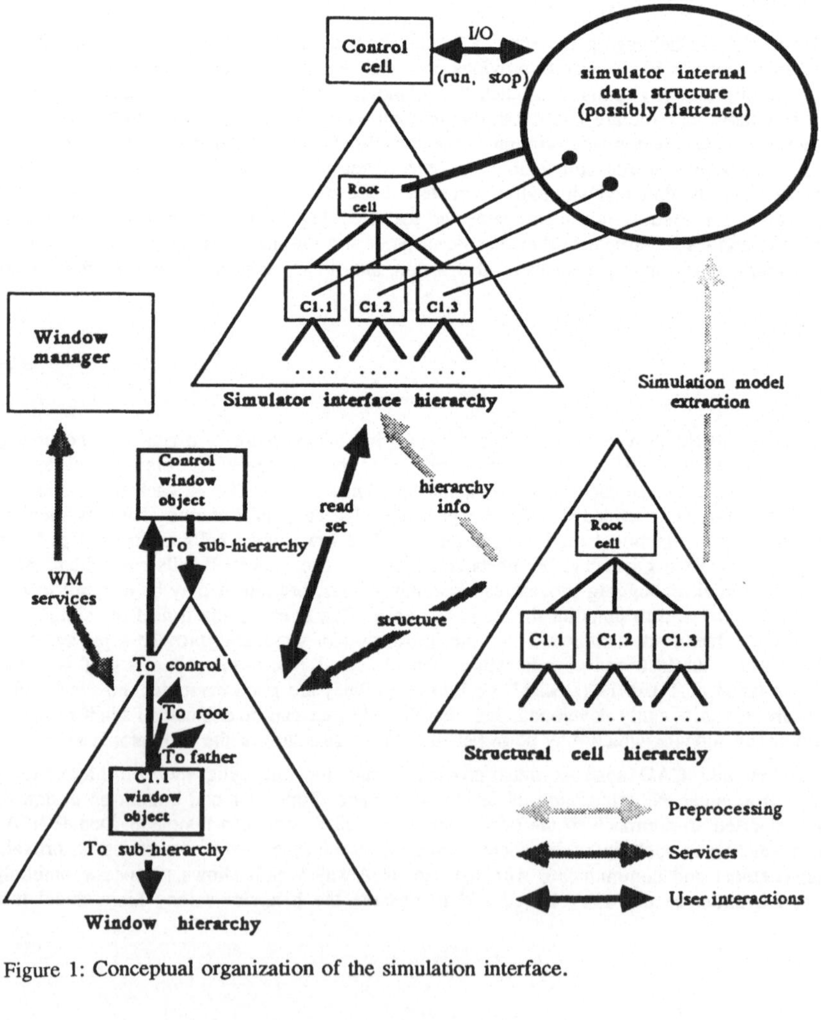

Figure 1: Conceptual organization of the simulation interface.

Structural Hierarchy

We assume that a hierarchical design methodology is used when designing the circuit to be simulated. Each cell consists of an interconnection of lower-level cells, until atomic elements such as transistors or gates or behaviorally described modules are reached. We recognize two types of cells: Leaf cells, which consist only of an interconnection of atomic elements or contain a behavioral description of the cell in some description language, and Composite cells, which consist of interconnections of other composite cells or leaf cells. In the actual implementation of our event-driven simulator [RoyC85, Clou86a], the leaf cells are modelled at the switch level, or their behavior can be described in terms of communicating processes, each of which is a program module. The structural circuit hierarchy is implied by the cell-object database, whose contents were created by the circuit designer.

For efficiency reasons, most simulators do not preserve the circuit hierarchy explicitly in the data structures describing the simulated circuit, that is, the hierarchy is flattened and internal circuit nodes are assigned uniform internal identifiers. There are translation tables which allow to reconstruct the complete node name (name of the cell instance in which the node occurred, its location in the hierarchy, and the node's local name). These tables are then used to interpret the simulation results. Relating these long names to the actual location of the node in the circuit is not easy for the designer, it is much more convenient if the system does the association automatically by making a link with the structural hierarchy. The problem lies then in how to organize this link in an efficient and structured way, in order that the user could browse through the circuit, examining the signals, setting local break-points, probes, etc. It is exactly this problem our simulation environment tries to resolve by constructing the other two object hierarchies.

Simulation State Hierarchy

This hierarchy of objects mimics the structural hierarchy in that there is a one-to-one mapping between an object here and a circuit cell instance in the structural hierarchy. Each such object contains the necessary information (tables of names and pointers) to access the simulation state of the corresponding circuit cell within the possibly flattened simulator's data structures.

Furthermore, each simulation state object has a well defined and identical set of access primitives (methods) which allow to examine the state of a given node or an I/O port in the cell, set its initial values, set break-points, and establish observation probes. The nodes or ports are referred to using only its local names, since the position of the object in the cell hierarchy determines its context.

A purely textual user interface could be easily attached directly to this object hierarchy, in order to control the simulation. Although its usage would still be quite cumbersome, it is useful and sufficient for debugging purposes. The uniform primitives used at the interface of the state objects allow interacting with different kinds of simulators in which the control operations may be implemented in different ways, *i.e.*, the state objects hide these differences from the higher interface layers and the user.

Viewing Windows Hierarchy

This hierarchy is related to the particular visual presentation of the user interface. In our case, within the system CHESHIRE, the user interface is based on the desk-top paradigm, consisting of multiple (overlapping) windows which then may contain graphics regions, static and pop-up menus, activation button, etc.

Each object in this hierarchy corresponds at the same time to an open screen window object, to a cell instance in the circuit hierarchy, and to its simulation state object. An object in this hierarchy is created only when the user opens a window for examining the structure and simulation state of a given cell. There are means provided (to be described later) for navigating in the circuit cell hierarchy. The object is destroyed whenever the user closes its viewing window.

Each viewing object makes a link between the simulation state and the structural description, and projects this information on the screen in the corresponding window. The simulation control primitives provided by the state object and intercell navigation commands are made accessible/visible through menus, activation buttons, etc.

Overall Simulation Control

In order to provide means for starting the simulator, applying the input stimuli, controlling progress of the simulation, observing the circuit responses on primary outputs, etc., in short to emulate the environment — the test bench — of the simulated circuit, an overall simulation control window with its associated objects is placed above the root cell of the circuit. This window appears whenever simulation is requested and stays open throughout the entire simulation. It also contains the entire abstracted circuit hierarchy, acting as a selection menu for opening new cells — windows, as described below.

Intercell Navigation

The objective is to provide a means for the user to freely navigate through the circuit hierarchy, not necessarily following the hierarchical links, and not having to keep open all the windows — cells on the path from the root (not to clutter the screen and workspace with useless windows). Since the simulator usually runs as a single process, implementing the objects described in the previous sections as processes would be quite costly. A simpler way which provides similar features, but in addition a simple access to shared variables, is available through the use of coroutines. Coroutines, like processes, have their own local stacks for preserving context. Therefore, it is possible to transfer control among them in any order, unlike procedures in which exiting transfers control to the calling procedure. Upon receiving control a coroutine will start execution at the point where it left off previously. Our window management for the CHESHIRE system uses coroutines for passing control between the windows and the manager. It is then a simple matter to make the association between the window object, and the corresponding structural and simulation state objects inside the coroutine which is attached to the window object. This mechanism is simple and provides the necessary means for transferring control between any currently open cell windows, and for closing them (thus destroying the associated coroutine and objects).

In order to be able to open new cells (windows), an abstracted form of the structural circuit hierarchy is shown in all the currently open cell windows. More specifically, it is sufficient that only the sub-hierarchy starting at the current cell which is displayed, since the higher levels can be accessed from any other higher-level open cell or from the main simulation control window. This abstracted hierarchy acts as a selection menu for creating the corresponding cell — windows. Although this provides complete flexibility for opening new cells, a more rapid way is provided for accessing (and possibly opening) the root, father and child cells of the current cell by means of buttons. This is illustrated in Figures 1 – 2.

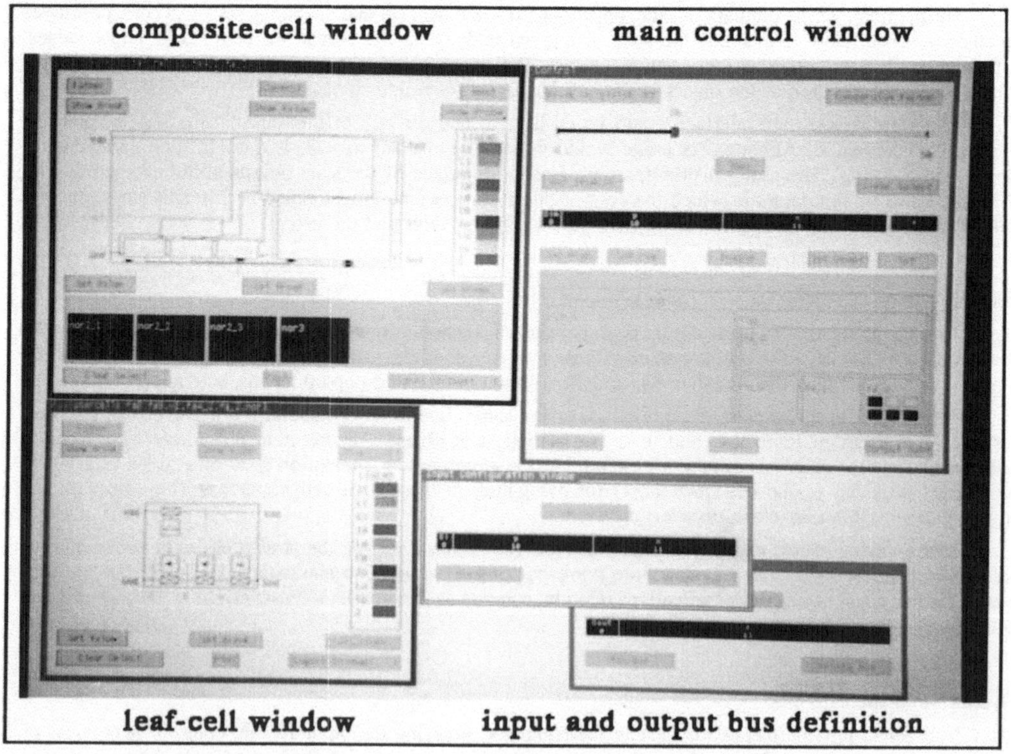

Figure 2: Overall window organization.

Visual Presentation

The visual layout of windows attempts to minimize the hand and eye movements of the user needed to accomplish a given operation. An overall picture of the control, composite and leaf-cell windows is shown in Fig. 2.

In all cases the simulation control is in the upper part of the window. The control window contains buttons for advancing the simulation, specifying the termination time which could be an exact time instant or a directive that the simulation should proceed until the stabilisation of all signals (*i.e.*, until the event queue(s) is (are) empty).

The simulation can be started either in interactive mode or in batch mode. In the former case, the user can specify the primary input signal values to be applied at the current simulation time, and the simulator executes until the specified stop condition is reached. At that point the resulting signal values are displayed in color on the primary I/O ports and on wires/ports in all open cells — windows. In the batch mode, the user specifies the file which contains a sequence of input stimuli, which is executed until a stop condition is reached. This condition can be either a particular time instant, a break-point condition or the end of the stimuli file. The input vectors in the file can be associated either with its time of application relative to the time of application of the preceding input, or with a marker that indicates that the circuit should reach a stable state before the next input is to be applied.

In either the batch or interactive mode all circuit responses on primary I/O ports and on specified probe points are stored in a trace file which has the same format as the input stimuli file. This means that the response file could be used as input stimuli for some other circuit. Also, at any point in the simulation, the contents of the file can be displayed graphically as waveforms in a window.

One important feature which aids the interpretation of signals is the possibility to regroup related primary I/O ports to form busses. The signal values can then be specified or read in other radices than just binary. The user defines the busses using two additional windows in which he/she can specify the desired permutations and grouping of the individual ports. This definition can be dynamically changed during simulation and the displayed signal values adapt to the new definition.

The middle section of all cell and control windows contains the menus, pop-ups and buttons for reading/setting of signals, probes, initial values, delays and break-points. As mentioned, whenever applicable the display of information is done by color-coding wires in the structural view of the cell located in this area of the window. Currently, the leaf cells contain a symbolic layout of the circuit in terms of transistors, contacts and wires. We are completing the implementation of the leaf-cell window for behavioral cells, in which case it will contain an identification of the underlying processes and their communication links.

Finally, the menus and buttons for opening/closing of windows and for the transfer of control are located at the bottom of the window. For obvious reasons only the composite cells contain the selection menu of the underlying sub-hierarchy.

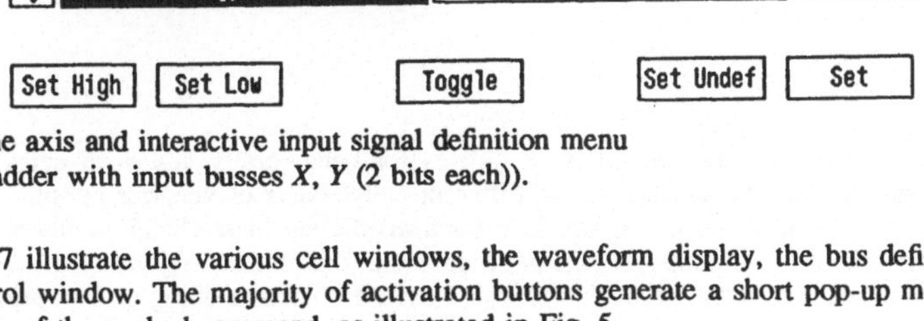

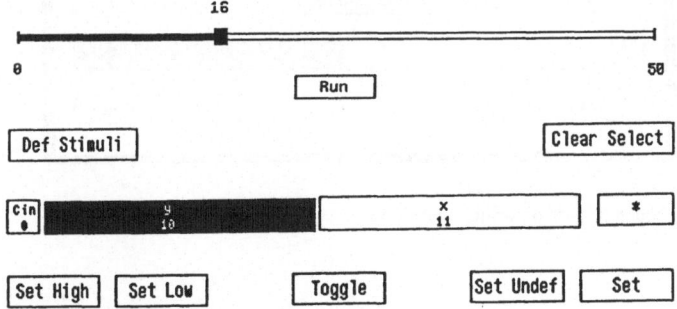

Figure 3: Main time axis and interactive input signal definition menu
(for an adder with input busses *X*, *Y* (2 bits each)).

Figures 3 – 7 illustrate the various cell windows, the waveform display, the bus definition windows, and the main control window. The majority of activation buttons generate a short pop-up menu for specifying the exact nature of the evoked command, as illustrated in Fig. 5.

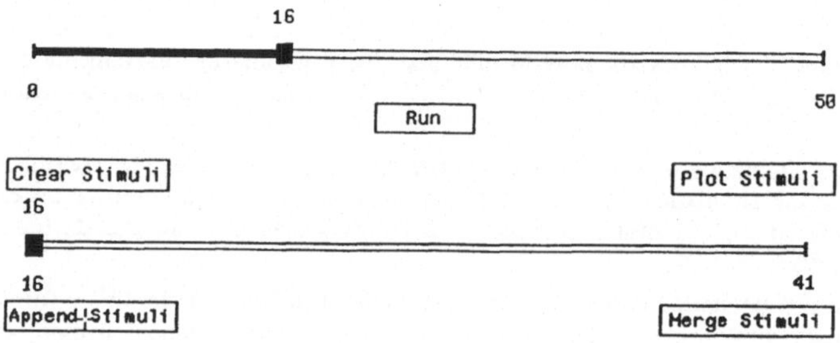

Figure 4: Main time axis and batch simulation time axis.

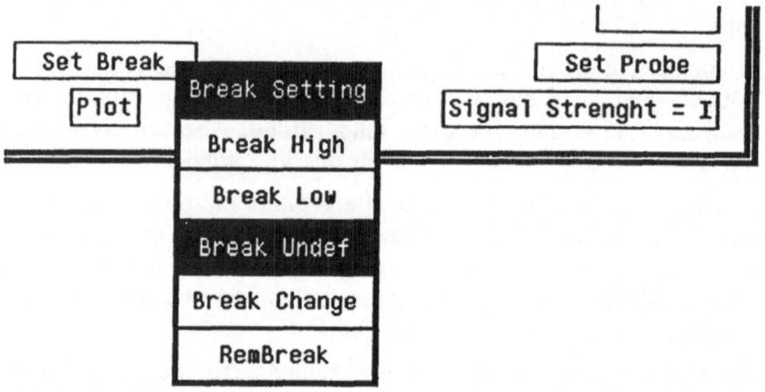

Figure 5: Defining break-points in composite and leaf-cell windows.

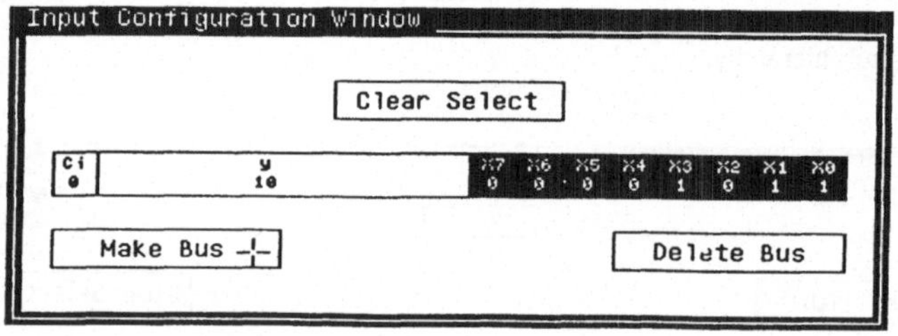

Figure 6: Bus definition window.

Conclusion

Currently, we are completing the interface objects for behaviorally described cells. The hierarchical nature of the interface makes the substitution of different cell models or versions possible. The same structure also simplifies the construction of an interface for a distributed hierarchical simulator operating over a communication network (*e.g.*, [Clou86b]). This is because the (distributed) objects of the dynamic descriptor hierarchy can communicate over the network with the interface objects residing on one processor.

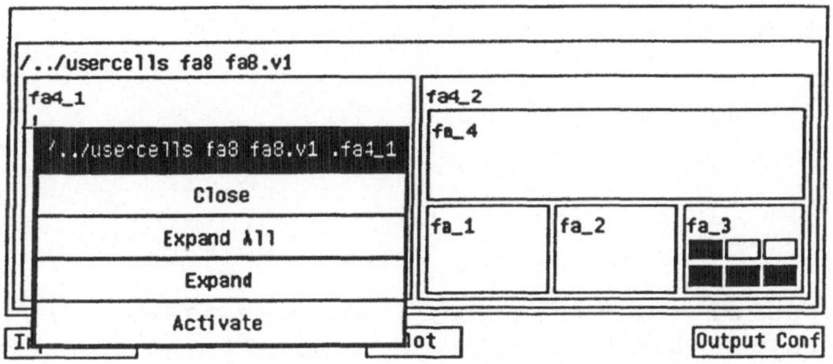

Figure 7: Intercell navigation menu and pop-up related to an activated entry.

The entire system CHESHIRE is implemented in the MAINSAIL language (T.M. of Xidak, Inc.), and consists of approximately 80 000 lines of code, of which the interface contributes about 10 000.

Acknowledgments

The work was partially supported by NSERC Canada grant G-1582 and FCAR Quebec grant No. 86-AS-2208. The authors express their appreciation to Denise St-Michel for careful preparation of the manuscript.

References

[Clou86a] J. Cloutier, M. Bourgault, S. Fauvel, C. Roy, E. Cerny, and J. Gecsei, "An Object-Oriented Mixed-Mode Hierarchical VLSI Simulator", *Proceedings of the 1986 Canadian VLSI Conference*, Montreal, October 1986.

[Clou86b] J. Cloutier, C. Roy, and E. Cerny, "A Distributed Mixed-Mode Hierarchical Simulator", *Proceedings of the 14th IASTED Conference on Simulation and Modelling*, Vancouver, June 1986.

[Deme86] L.-P. Demers, G. Bois, P. Jacques, and E. Cerny, "An Integrated VLSI Design System with Symbolic Layout Tools", *Poster Session, International Workshop on Symbolic Layout and Compaction*, Chapel Hill, November 1986.

[Deme87] L.-P. Demers, P. Jacques, S. Fauvel, and E. Cerny, "CHESHIRE: An Object-Oriented Integration of VLSI CAD Tools", *Proceedings of the 24th Design Automation Conference*, Miami, June 1987.

[Dosh84] M.H. Doshi, R.B. Sullivan, and D.M. Schuler, "THEMIS Logic Simulator — A Mix Mode, Multi-Level, Hierarchical, Interactive Digital Circuit Simulator", *Proceedings of the 21st Design Automation Conference*, Las Vegas, June 1984.

[Hill83] D.D. Hill, "Edisim: A Graphical Simulator Interface for LSI Design", *IEEE Transactions on Computer-Aided Design of Integrated Circuit and Systems*, Vol. CAD-2, No. 2, April 1983.

[Roge85] W.A. Rogers, and J.A. Abraham, "CHIEFS: A Concurrent, Hierarchical and Extensible Fault Simulator", *Proceedings of the 1985 International Test Conference.*

[RoyC85] C. Roy, L.-P. Demers, E. Cerny, and J. Gecsei, "An Object-Oriented Switch-Level Simulator", *Proceedings of the 22nd Design Automation Conference*, Las Vegas, June 1985.

3-D Geometric Modelling in Design and Manufacturing of Furniture Parts

F. Zhang, S. Cai, Y. Wang, and Z. Ju (China)

Abstract

Three types of furniture parts and modelling method in FCAD system (Computer Aided Design for Furniture Structure), is introduced. Some interactive functions for modifying part models and deriving a variety of practical parts are described. Finally, the application of the modelling method to computer aided manufacturing of furniture parts is prospected.

1. Introduction

Geometric modelling plays a very important role in a CAD/CAM system. The geometric model is often used to generate engineering drawings for design as well as data for manufacturing. Thus, geometric modelling affects directly the quality and efficiency of design. A good geometric model should meet the following demands:

(1) Completeness. The model must contain a variety of information on which various functions can be performed.

(2) Simplicity. The model can be created in a simple, straight forward way. No special requirements to hardware are assumed.

(3) Efficiency. The model can be operated easily and efficiently. And a fast response is often appreciated.

(4) Openness. The model can also provide sufficient information when system functions are extended.

In the recent years, many solid modelling techniques have been developed attempting to meet the above criteria[1-3]. In this paper, a solid modelling method for the design of furniture structure in our FCAD system is introduced.

2. System Overview and Modelling Consideration

2.1 System Overview

FCAD is a computer aided furniture structure design system based on a 16-bit microcomputer, the IBM PC/AT with a 640x400 graphical monitor. Its low cost configuration allows a widespread usage. The FCAD software can be clasified into three categories: main programs, system files and utilities. It was developed with MS-DOS as its operating system, Source codes are writen in PASCAL and assembly language. Program size is about 40 K lines of statements. Aseembly language is only used to write device drivers, making it easy to convert FCAD onto other machines.

FCAD has been used by Nanjing Woodwork Factory to redesign the model 8101 and used by Taichou Woodwork Factory to design a new style of furniture. The design results have showed the drawings it produced are as good as of manual design (see

Fig. 8) but the design speed is as 6-10 times fast as of manual design.

FCAD system is based on the 'library supported, top-down decomposition and bottom-up composition' design methodology. That means the design of parts is the bases of the design of furniture.

The main goal of FCAD system is to produce engineering drawings of furniture structure and various material lists.

Engineering drawings of furniture structure are fully dimensioned orthographic three-view drawings. They are sectioned views with hidden lines removed. The sectioned view can reveal some details of the complicated assembly or furniture.

Material lists are used to support later manufacturing. They include block material list, board material list, and linker (e.g. hinge) list. Among them, the block material list gives tree species, usages and sizes of block shaped parts, the board material list gives species and sizes of board shaped parts. With these material lists, the supply department can properly cut raw materials, and the parts can then be produced in processing workshop.

2.2 Modelling Consideration

In order to build powerful and efficient models, we follow four guidelines listed bellow:

(1) 3-D solid models of furniture parts must be created so that various sectioned orthographic projection views can be easyly obtained.

(2) To lower system costs, only 2-D graphical input devices are used to create 3-D solid models of parts.

(3) The construction of part models must be simplified. Part models can communicate with its geometry in a popular and lucid way.

(4) The modification of part models can be done easily. All the required parts can be acquired by modifying or deriving from standard parts.

3. Modelling Furniture Parts

Observing a variety of furniture parts, we can find that they can be classified into three types: rotating objects, sweeping objects, and free-form objects.

3.1 Definitions and Conventions

(1) Line element

Three kinds of line elements are defined in FCAD system. They are POLYLINE, ARC, and SPLINE.

A POLYLINE is specified by a group of sequential vertices P1,P2,...,Pn (n>=2), denoted by POLYLINE (P1, P2, ..., Pn). It is a sequence of end-to-end connected straight lines.

An ARC is specified by a start point As, a passing point Ap, and an end point Ae, denoted by ARC (As, Ap, Ae).

A SPLINE is specified by a set of sequential control points S1, S2,..., Sm (m>=4), denoted by SPLINE (S1, S2, ..., Sm). It is a HERMITE-like curve passing through these points. It is continuous and also has continuity of tangent vector.

(2) Line string

Line string is a sequence of end-to-end connected line element. A line string is not allowed to intersect itself.

(3) Line ring

If and only if the start point of the first line element coincides with the end point of the last line element, this line string is named as line ring. So line ring is a closed line string.

3.2 Model of Rotating Object

Generally speaking, a furniture part produced by a lathe is a rotating object. It can be obtained by spinning a line string about an axis (Fig. 1a).

To simplify the construction of the rotating model, we assume y-axis is the rotating axis, the rotating generatrix is defined as a line string on xy-plane. Thus, the following characteristic data must be addressed in the rotating object models:

. Rotating Generatrix: a line string defined on xy-plane.
. Rotating Axis: y-axis, defaulted.

3.3 Model of Sweeping Object

When a planar surface sweeps over some distance along a certain direction, a solid part can be acquired. The sweeping object shown in Fig. 1b is obtained by sweeping a polygon along the direction perpendicular to the polygon plane.

To simplify the construction of the sweeping model, assume z-axis is the sweeping direction, the sweeping surface is defined by its surronding line ring on xy-plane. Besides, linear scaling of sweeping surface is allowed during sweeping procedure. With the same scaling factor, different positions of the scaling center can result in different objects. Thus, the following characteristic data must be addressed in the sweeping object models:

. Sweeping Surface: a line ring defined on xy-plane.
. Sweeping Direction: positive z-axis direction, defaulted.
. Sweeping Length: a real number.
. Scalling factor: a real number.
. Scalling Center: a vertex on xy-plane.

Assume Ps(Xs,Ys) is a point on the sweeping surface, Sc(Xc,Yc) is the scaling center, S is the scaling factor, then the corresponding point Pe(Xe,Ye) on the swept surface can be obtained by the following equations:

$$Xe=(Xs-Xc)*S+Xc$$
$$Ye=(Ys-Yc)*S+Yc$$

Obviously, when scaling factor S equals to 1, the scaling center will not affect the sweeping.

3.4 Model of Free-Form Object

The parts which can not be represented by the above two models fall into the third type: free-form objects. Usually, it is very hard to represent them using geometric rules. Legs are the most common free-form objects in furniture(Fig. 1c). In FCAD system, free-form objects are defined by a set of characteristic sections. A section is obtained when a horizontal plane intersects the free-form object. A set of characteristic sections are selected in such a way by which the geometric shape of a free-form object can be determined.

A section contour can be represented by a ring defined on the cutting plane when a coordinate system is properly selected. The following are the characteristic data in free-form object models:

. Section Normal: y-axis, defaulted.

. Section i (i=1, 2, ..., n)

.. Height of Section i: hi--a real number.

.. Contour of Section i: ci--a line ring defined on Y=hi plane.

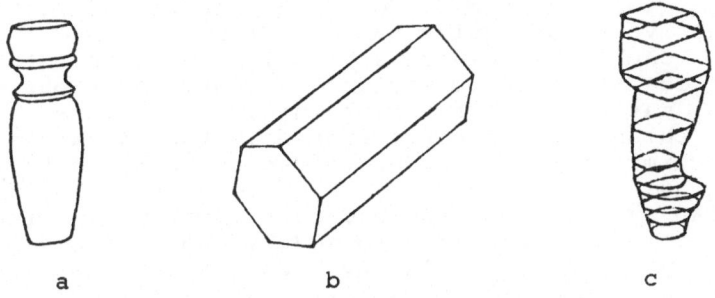

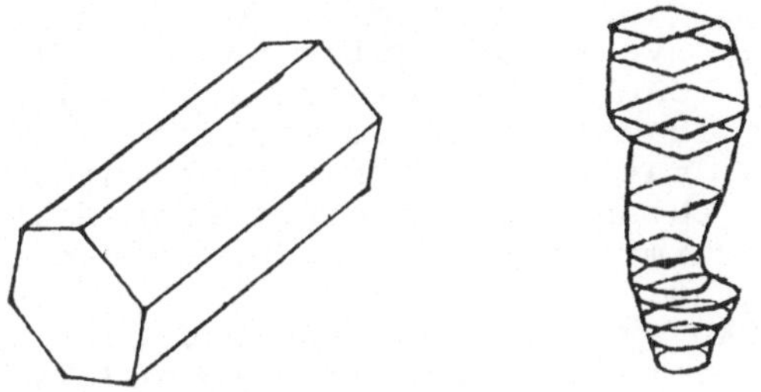

Fig. 1 Three types of furniture parts

3.5 The Data Structure of Furneture Assembly

The above characteristic data can be used to describe the geometric shapes of three types of furniture parts. In this aspect, the information is complete. However, to display the orthographic projection views of parts, a great deal of calculation must be done. To get a fast response in assembling parts into a piece of assembly or furniture, FCAD system generates the orthographic view data of a part

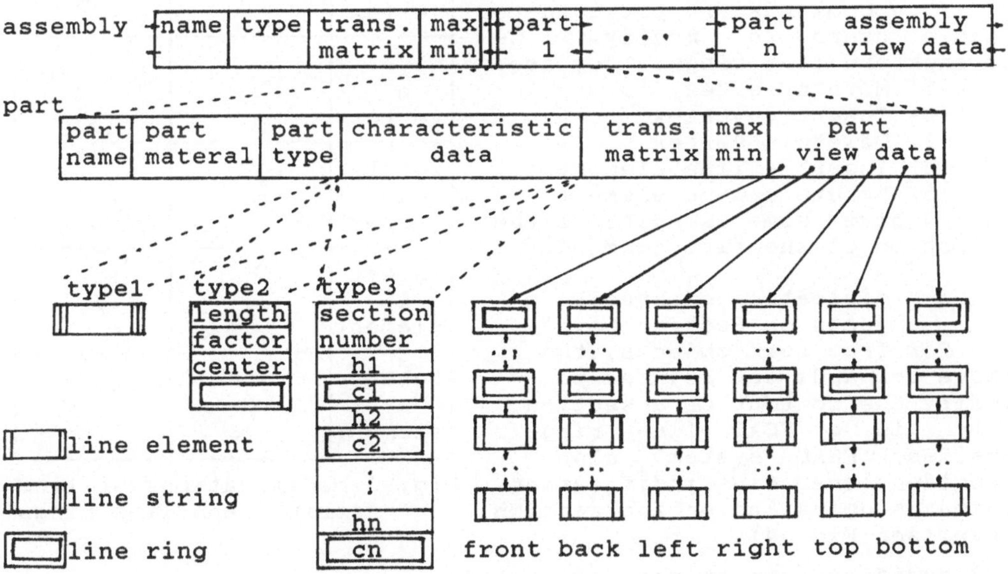

Fig. 2 The data structure of a furniture assembly

immediately after it has been designed or modified. Therefore the view data is also included in the model. Besides, the model data must contain part attributes (e.g. part name, material, etc.) to meet the requirements of preparing production documentation. Fig. 2 shows the data structure of a furniture assembly consisting of several parts.

4. Interactive Modification and Derivation of Part Models

Besides model input facilities, the system also provides some modification functions. So the designers can modify model data interactively to acquire suitable part.

For a CAD system having a part library as its design support, it is attempted to include sufficient parts in the library to satisfy with a variety needs of designs, on the other hand, the number of parts stored in the library should be within some limitation in order to reduce cost and to speed up the processing.

In FCAD system, a standard part library is created. A group of functions is provided to modify the part model data or to change a part as a whole. By these functions, a standard part can be modified to satisfy an application. So a standard part represents a set of practical parts. In this way, the utility of the part library is improved, and the number of indispensable parts stored in the library is also reduced considerably.

4.1 Modifications on the Characteristic Data Level

Modifications on this level change the characteristic data of a model directly.

4.1.1 Modification of Line Strings and Line Rings.

Five commands are provided to enable users to modify line strings and line rings. They are:

(1) Move a vertex
(2) Insert a vertex
(3) Delete a vertex
(4) Insert a line element
(5) Delete a line element

Fig. 3 gives some examples of the execution of the five commands.

4.1.2 Modification of Free-Form Objects on Section Level

For free-form objects, the above commands can be used to modify the contour of a section, which is a FCAD line ring. Besides, FCAD system also provides other five modification commands operating on the section level(see Fig. 4).

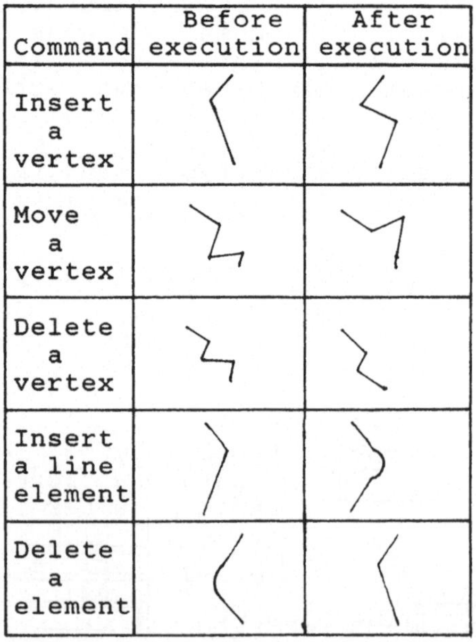

Fig. 3 Modifications of line strings and line rings

4.2 Modifications on the Part Level

Formally, modification on this level changes a part as a

whole. But actually it changes the model data of the part directly or indirectly. The provided commands include: rotation, scalling, mirroring and extension.

(1) Rotation: By rotation, a correct assebmling orientation is acquired.

(2) Scaling: Some of parts can be obtained by scalling the standard parts in three directions properly, the final dimensions of the parts can be specified by designers.

(3) Mirroring: Applying this operation to a part, we can obtain a symmetric part. Thus only one of a pair of symmetrical parts is stored in the part library. Fig. 5 shows a pair of legs.

(4) Extension: Most frames (e.g. doorframe, windowframe) in furniture are composed of two basic parts illustrated in Fig. 8a. Their lengths may vary when used in different furniture. But their widths, thickness and dimensions at notchs and bulges on the parts are generally remain the same. So the simple scaling function will not work in this case. For this reason, FCAD system provides another command named EXTENSION which splits a standard part at an appointed position and then joins a segment onto it, the resulting length is specified by designer(see Fig. 6b).

Command	Before execution	After execution
Change a gap	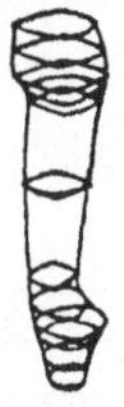	
Move a section	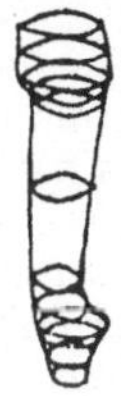	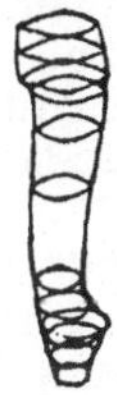
Insert a section		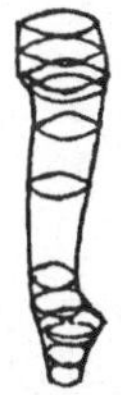
Copy a section	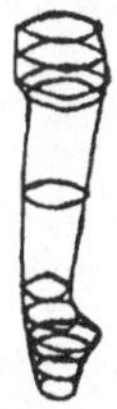	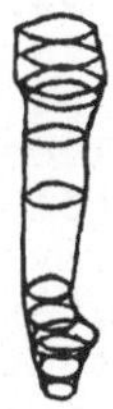
Delete a section	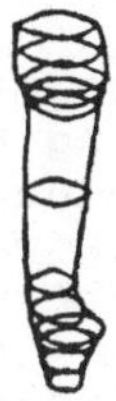	

Fig. 4 Modification on the section livel

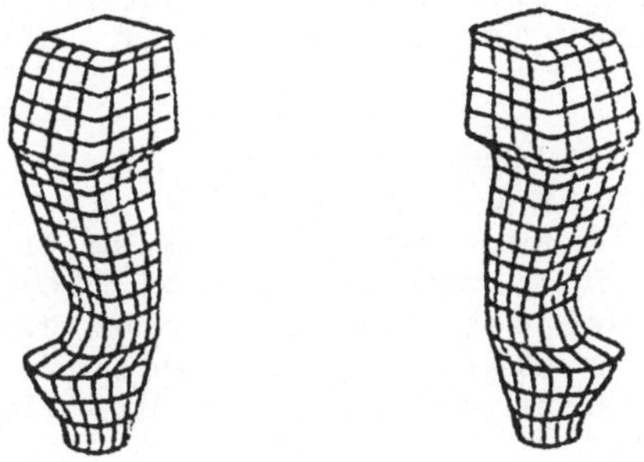

Fig. 5 A pair of symmentric legs

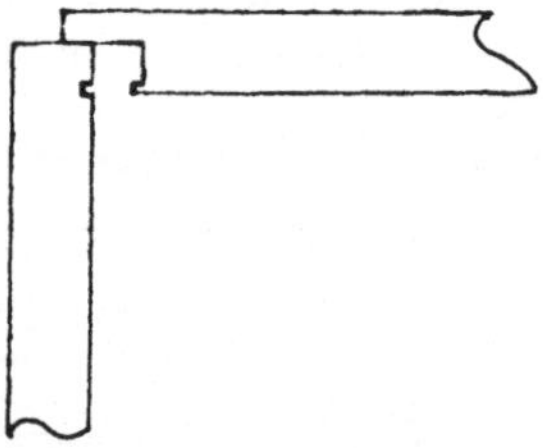

Fig. 6a Two parts of a frame

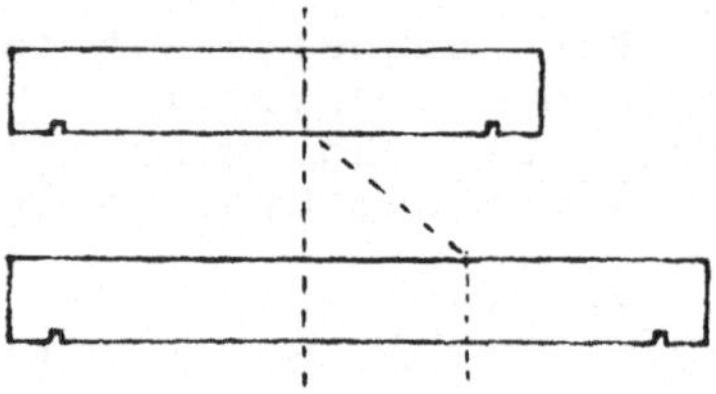

Fig. 6b Extension operation

5. Application Prospects of the Model for CAM

At present, wooden furniture parts are generally produced manually or by human controlled machine tools. Thus the efficiency and quality can not be guaranteed.

The solid modelling technique used in FCAD gives an unambiguous geometric shape for each part, and provides sufficient data for the computer aided manufacturing.

5.1 FCAD models support material cutting

In manufacturing processes of wooden furniture, the cutting process proceeds first. Cutting operations include sawing tree into cuboid-shaped blanks and board cutting. In this aspect, the size of a part blank is provided by the FCAD part model directly or indirectly.

The item 'maximal and minimal coordinates' in part model stores the initial size of the part. All the transformations (e.g. scaling, rotating and translating) made during modifying and assembling are accumulated in a transformation matrix stored in the part model (when operating on the part) or in the assembly model (when operating on the assembly to which the part belongs). The final size of a part is obtained by multiplying these matrices to the initial size.

5.2 The rotating generatrix is provided

Recently, the rotating parts are produced by manual controlled lathes. The accuracy and quality of products are heavily depending on the skill of operators. Therefore they are not guaranteed and the efficiency is low. It will be improved a great deal (in accuracy, speed and safety) if a lathe produces parts following the rotating generatrix contained in the rotating part model.

5.3 The profiling machine can be substituted

The profiling machine which has been using recently is a good tool to produce free-form parts of furniture. Because the profiling machine works depending on the profiler made of iron, the styles of parts to which a furniture designer can refer are limited and the creation of a new style of iron model is expensive and time-comsuming. It is worth very much to use the electric model to substitute iron model.

Suppose a free-form object is specified by k sections, and m well distributed rays(orientation lines) parallel to xz-plane are drawn from the center of section i. The intersections of the orientation lines and the contour of the section constitute a set of orientation control points {Cij} (i=1,2,...,k, j=1,2,...,m). Then the SPLINE(C1j,C2j,...,Ckj) is named as orientation boundary.

Between the bottom section and the top section, using n equal-interval planes parallel to xz-plane to intersect m orientation boundaries respectively, we have a matrix of n x m intersection points, denoted by S:

$$S = \begin{bmatrix} S11 & S12 & S13 & \dots & S1m \\ S21 & S22 & S23 & \dots & S2m \\ & & \vdots & & \\ Sn1 & Sn2 & Sn3 & \dots & Snm \end{bmatrix}$$

in which, Sij is the intersection of the No. i plane and the No.j orientation boundary.

Matrix S determines the side surface of a free-form object (Fig. 7a).

The curve SPLINE(Si1,Si2,...Sim, Si1) forms a contour of the intersection between the No. i plane and the boundaries of free-form object (Fig. 7b). When n and m are chosen properly, Matrix S can be used to control a milling machine in producing free-form parts.

6. Conclusions

Basically, three types of part models provided in FCAD system have covered all kinds of furniture parts. The system also provides some special functions such as making tenon, drilling hole to complement some details of models in order to reduce the complexity of the model. Both characteristic data and view data are included in the model, it speeds up the response of part transformations and furniture assembling. In addition, characteristic data and attributes can be used effectively in computer aided manufacturing of furniture parts.

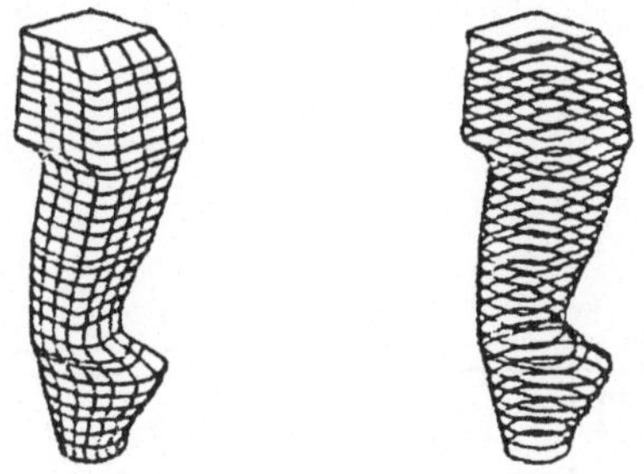

(a) (b)

Fig. 7 Surface generation of a leg

References

[1] George Allen, An introduction to solid modelling, Computers & Graphics, 8:4(1984).

[2] A. A. G. Requicha and H. B. Voelcker, Solid Modelling: A Historical Summary and Contemporary Assessment, IEEE CG&A, 2:3(1982).

[3] M. J. Pratt, Solid Modelling and the Interface between Design and Manufacture, IEEE CG&A, 4:7(1984).

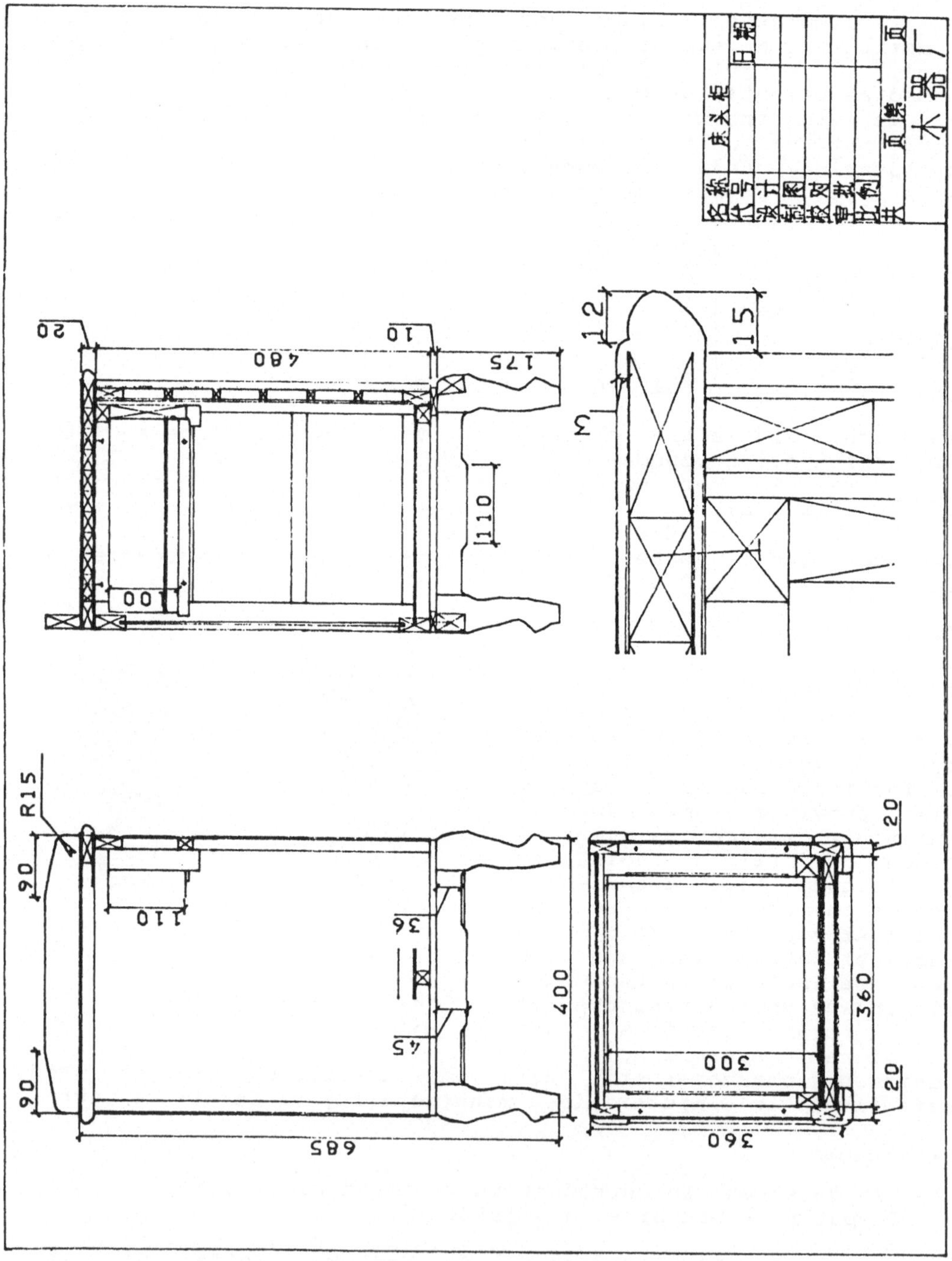

Fig. 8 The drawing of bedside cupboard

Computer-Assisted Color Conversion[sm]

D. M. Geshwind (USA)

INTRODUCTION

The process of adding computerized color to black and white motion pictures and television programs has been hailed as "an ingenious technological breakthrough" and derided as "cultural butchery". Businessmen see it as a means of breathing new life into unsaleable media properties while the original filmmakers (who do not share in the new income) see it as "vandlism" of classic works of art.

While it is a matter of opinion as to whether colorization is a good idea in and of itself, it is clear that bad colorization is not. The current products available for broadcast and home video have been almost uniformly washed out, over-simple and unsubtle. Film critic Gene Siskel observes,

> "There's a certain timidity about the colors used, lot's of pastels, as in ... Topper. The coloring of Yankee Doodle Dandy is a visual mess. In some scenes everything is awash with blue except the skin tones, which are the same for every actor. So much for the actors' individuality ... The coloring is even more laughable in the classic It's A Wonderful Life ... And the classic gaffs; look at Frank Sinatra in Suddenly, 'Ol' Blue Eyes' is back ... as 'Ol' Brown Eyes'."

His cohort Roger Ebert continues,

> "They tend to pick light blues, light greens, pinks, violets, yellows ... in the 30s Cagney looked like he was going out to commit murder, colorized he looks like he's going out to play golf."

These defects are not inherent in our colorization process. Nor does the work now being done at commercial colorization facilities have to be so poor. The low quality of current colorization services is a matter of economics and poor design, not technological limitations.

To understand the trade-offs, one must realize that the popular notion - that an 'artist' colors only one frame of a scene and the 'computer' colors all the rest - is a gross exageration. Artificial intelligence and pattern recognition has had limited success in being able to extract known objects (e.g. armored tanks) in restricted situations (e.g. sitting out in the open). Tracking and extracting multiple, unfamiliar, moving objects, that mutually overlap, in contexts that change every few seconds with each camera shot, is beyond the current state-of-the-art. This research may one day result in an affordable, fully automated colorization technology but, for the forseeable future, continual human judgement and interaction is still a necessary component of computerized colorization systems.

Although the process is highly computer assisted, and much more efficient than hand painting each frame, it is still very labor intensive. The colorization operator must outline each separately colored object in a very large proportion of the film's frames. And, since labor is the most expensive element of the process, the fewer distinct objects and the fewer colors in a scene, the less colorization costs. Mimicing the visual complexity inherent in a 'real' color scene is very expensive.

The choice of washed-out pastels is made for a different reason. With thousands of frames to paint, colorizers can afford to spend little time getting the details correct on each one. And the computer process that 'colors' the intervening frames is not always accurate. The greater the movement in the scene, the more these problems are apparent. Siskel notes,

> "Coloring also stumbles when the actors move. Look at the color bleeding in the dance scenes of Yankee Doodle Dandy."

The inaccuracies in the placement of colors are much less noticable if the colors are less saturated. In some converted films the colors are so washed-out they can barely be seen - but, then neither can the mistakes. However, in the current market it is not visual quality which is important but simply the ability to reclassify a film as color for legal or marketing purposes. Says Ebert,

> "It's a story about money, not about art".

NEW APPROACH

We have developed a newly patented technology for film colorization that has a number of advantages over current techniques. The underlying principle of our approach is to maintain the new color information as a separate component until very late in the process. This allows us to apply various data compression techniques when creating and processing the color component, without degrading the original black and white image information in any way.

The human visual system is less sensitive to color detail than to black and white detail. Detection of edges, perception of shading and other detail functions depend primarily upon the luminance rather than the chrominance aspect of a visual scene. Thus, when a low information density color overlay signal is combined with a high density luminance signal the result is percieved as a high density full color image.

One application allows for the production of colorized product in virtually any format with only moderate processing requirements. Current systems transfer the black and white film to videotape as a first step and thereby immediately discard as much as 90% or even more of the original information. A color signal is generated, also at video resolution, and the two are combined electronically. Therefore, color converion production is limited to videotape product. Scaling the entire system up to high-definition video is not now economically practical and would still not produce results suitable for theatrical projection. However, our approach allows us to create a color overlay film at moderate resolution and optically combine it with the original black and white film as the finaly step. In this way, a composite film can be produced economically, that will be perceived as both full color and high definition.

This same technique can be applied to a computer assisted system that will permit economical restoration of faded or damaged color film.

When colorizing for video product we can reduce the data density of the color signal even further, permitting very economical production on relatively low-tech systems. By applying these techniques, the amount of computer processing time, human interaction, storage, and overall, the need for highly complex high-speed systems, can be greatly reduced. All these factors result in making the process much more economical.

This reduction in operating costs makes it economically feasible to take the time needed to colorize with more care and subtlety and with more sophisticated design.

DATA COMPRESSION

We can generate a low information density signal by compression of the digital representation of the color specification in any combination of three ways:

Spatial Compression: the color information is not specified at all points on a given frame. This may be as straightforward as working with uniformly larger pixels, or may involve the creation of a low detail representation, such as a polygonal outline of objects.

Temporal Compression: the color information is not

specified for every frame. The same color frame information may simply be repeated for a sequence of several black and white frames, or shape interpolation (inbetweening) may be applied to the color areas.

Color Choice Compression: the amount of information used to specify color at each pixel may be reduced uniformly throughout by restricting the 'color space' within which the image exists. Alternately, a single color specification may be applied to a large group of pixels, such as within a polygonal area.

Visable anomalies may result from compression or undersampling; spatial defects include 'the jaggies'; temporal defects include jerkyness, doubling or strobing; color choice defects include contouring or 'flatness'. The perception of these defects can be reduced or eliminated by various antialiasing techniques; inbetweening or cross-dissolving in the temporal domain; digital or analog low-pass filtering or optical defocusing for spatial and contouring defects. Also, to counter a uniform 'flat' look to objects, additional variation to the color information may be added, as detail, at a later stage in the process.

TYPICAL SYSTEM OPERATION

What follows is a practical comparison of the requirements for coloring a one second sequence of film using both straight-foward digital image processing and our approach. We will assume that the scene is a non-action scene where the motion of objects is moderate, as is typical with much black and white motion picture material.

By straight-foward digital image processing, if theatrical film output is desired, scanning rates would have to be in the range of at least 1500 lines per frame and data depth of about 24-bits per pixel to accomodate full color variation. This results in:

1500 lines x 1500 lines = 2.25 million pixels/frame

x 3 bytes/pixel = 6.75 million bytes/frame

x 24 frames/second = 162 million bytes/second.

Assuming that ten objects are to be separately colored in each frame, and that an artist can paint these ten objects in two minutes, 48 minutes of operator time will be required to paint these 24 frames.

Using our approach, we will be leaving the high density luminance information in the film domain. We will therefore be creating chrominance information at a more moderate resolution of 500 lines/frame. Color specificaiton will be limited to 8-bits per pixel which will allow for many separately tagged objects with some variation within objects (e.g. 32 objects with up to eight hue variations within each object).

Operator outlining of objects will be limited to one out of six frames. The intervening even numbered frames will be created by inbetweening the positions and shapes of the objects; all odd numbered frames will be created by cross-disolving the color information of the two adjecent even frames during optical printing. Storage requirements are:

500 lines x 500 lines	=	.25 million pixels/frame
x 1 bytes/pixel	=	.25 million bytes/frame
x 12 (even) frames/second	=	3 million bytes/second.

The operator requires 8 minutes to 'paint' four frames. We will assume that it will require an additional 4 minutes to check the interpolated frames and hand correct for one or two objects that moved too erratically for inbetweening to work completely.

By applying these techniques a 54-fold decrease in information creation and storage requirements has been achieved and a savings of 75% of the human labor.

Variations on the process may provide additional efficiencies of operation or add subtleties to the composite image. For example, the availablity of high-speed polygon rendering hardware makes it possible to create, store and process only the object outline data, on the order of a kilobyte per frame, rather than the full-density, pixel oriented, color information, which is 100s or 1000s of kilobytes per frame. The outline data is then fed to one of these 'rendering engines' for at, or near, real-time display and recording.

In another implementation, the luminance information is scanned in at the same low information density as the chroma information. Although this version of the luminance information will ultimately be discarded, to be replaced by the original high density version, it is used to modulate the chroma information. The hue of individual image areas may be varied on a pixel by pixel basis to avoid a 'flat' unrealistic look. For example, rather than color a person's face a single uniform pink hue, the highlights might be made more yellow and the shadows slightly blue to give the effect of sunlight.

CASE STUDY

Figures 1 through 5 show the various elements, and stages of compositing, for a typical colorized frame. The images were all generated on our prototype colorization system which was built around an IBM-PC/AT look-alike, a 512 x 512 pixel by 32-bit digitizing and display board, and our own custom software, writen in 'C'.

Figure 1 shows a black and white image digitized from a standard video source. The image is from the movie "King Kong" which is copyrighted to RKO Studios and is used here for illustration purposes only.

Figure 2 shows a background element that may be used for a large number of frames, so long as the camera position remains the same. It was created by an operator using "paint system" software and is one of several color-only elements that is composited with the black and white image to create the final full-color image. It is a "direct color" element in that color information (hue and, optionally, saturation) is derived from this color element alone, without regard to the black and white image (Fig. 1).

Figure 3 shows a foreground element which will be used for a single or small number of frames. It is an "indirect color" element and was created by the computer from a combination of an outline generated by an operator, the luminance information contained in the original black and white image (Fig. 1) and a color look-up table associated with this object in the scene. For each pixel within the operator generated outline, the computer consults the corresponding pixel in the original black and white image (Fig. 1). This luminance value, in turn, provides an index into the look-up table where color information is derived for that pixel of the foreground color element (Fig. 3).

The range of color values in the look-up table associated with the foreground "Kong" element were designed as follows. It was intended to "color" Kong basically black, but to overlay a hint of colors to distinguish shadows and highlights. As explained above, the look of natural sunlight can be achieved by adding a yellowish tint to highlights and a blueish tint to shadows. A color look-up table was thus constructed to range smoothly from a blue/purple for dark values to a yellow/tan for light values. Desaturated colors were chosen so as to add just a hint of color to Kong in the final composite image (Fig. 5). Although subtle, this looks very different than leaving Kong completely uncolored.

Figure 4 shows how the color-only elements from Figs. 2 and 3 have been combined (along with a "direct color" element for a figure in the lower right corner) to create the composited color-only image. In addition, a low-pass digital filter has been applied to the composite to soften or blur the edges between the various elements.

Figure 5 shows the final full-color composite image. It was obtained by using the information in the original black and white image (Fig. 1) to modulate the luminance and saturation

Fig.1

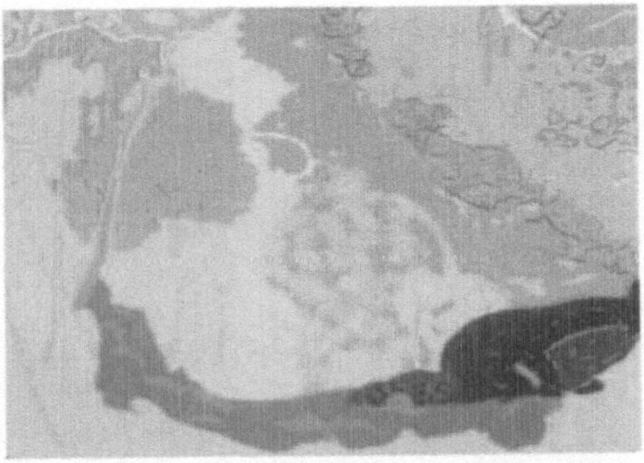

Fig.2

Fig.3

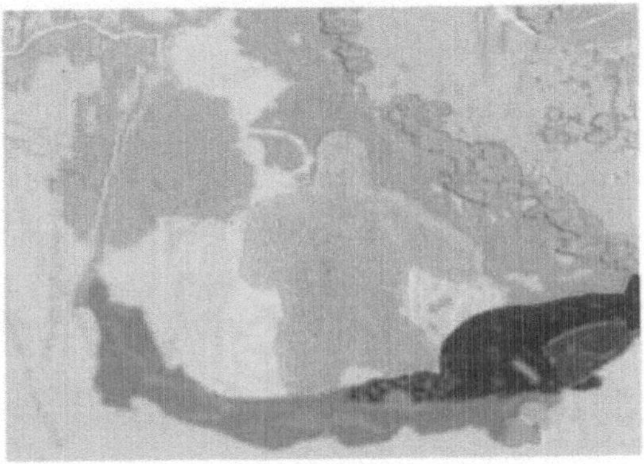

Fig.4

Fig.5

of the information in the color-only composite image (Fig. 4) on a pixel-by-pixel basis. Several other algorithms were then applied to the final image to adjust the contrast and brightness of the final image and to compensate for "flicker" in the original black and white film.

IN CONCLUSION

Improved colorization technology will increase production quality and satisfy many of the critics of the process as it is currently practiced. However, purists argue that any colorization process is a desecration of pristine classics.

It should be noted that films, particularly when shown on television, are hardly maintained as originally intended. Edited to fit time slots, interupted by commercials, displayed on a small, high-contrast CRT, and bandlimited to a fuzzy 4 MHz; home viewing is vastly different than the theater experience. But it is tollerated as a way to secure wide and continued distribution for a large and varied catalog of films.

There are many older films that are equally worthwhile but which are effectively non-existent because it is not economically viable to broadcast black and white, and because large sections of the audience shun black and white programs even when they are shown. Colorization makes these films available again and, for a significant portion of the population, increases their enjoyment of these programs.

Analysis of Urban Geographic Queries

P. Boursier (France)

ABSTRACT

Basic concepts of urban data management and processing are introduced. Applications, types of data and operations are reviewed.

Geographic queries are analysed in the context of urban data management and processing. Elementary operations are extracted, both from the access to objects and geometric computation points of view.

A set of queries is designed, based on these sets of elementary operations, and measurements to be done on these queries are discussed. This constitutes a first step towards the definition of benchmarks that could be used to measure the ability and the performance of data management systems for handling and processing urban data, and graphics-oriented data in general.

1. INTRODUCTION

As data base management systems have shown their limits for handling non-traditional data, performance evaluation has been mostly concerned with business-oriented applications. The best-known benchmarks are the Wisconsin benchmark [Bitton, Dewitt and Turbyfil, 84], designed to measure the performance of relational DBMS, and the TP1 benchmark [Anon et al., 85], designed to measure transaction throughput. More recent work has focused on engineering applications, trying to measure the response time for simple object-oriented applications [Rubenstein, Kubicar and Cattell, 87].

We are here concerned with geographic-oriented applications, and more precisely with urban data management. The specificity of urban data, and geographic data in general, comes from their geometric and graphic dimensions, unknown with traditional business data. The problems they raise also appear with CAD data and applications. This is more generally the problem of pictorial or spatial data management [COMPUTER, 81].

Very few experiments have been led to measure the ability of a DBMS to fulfill the requirements of this kind of applications. In the geographic domain, a very practical and pragmatic approach is followed by Goodchild [Goodchild and Rizzo, 86], whereas Marble's work is more theoretical and closer to traditional DBMS benchmarking [Marble and Sen, 86]. Also related to performance evaluation, older results only concern the compaction of maps and images, and the design of specific data structures and algorithms [COMPUTER, 81; Boursier and Scholl, 82; Samet, 84], or the analysis of spatial indexing techniques [Roussopoulos, 86].

We think that urban data management constitutes a good representative of graphics-oriented multimedia applications, and consequently we chose it as a test application. What we want to measure is the *response time to geographic queries*. Now, benchmarking a graphics-oriented DBMS requires to define:

- a set of data, either actual or synthetic,
- a set of queries,

both representative of the applications.

Within this framework applied to urban data management, two main problems have to be solved:
(i) find the good parameters that characterize urban data, so as to be able to design and build synthetic data bases,
(ii) analyse typical geographic queries, so as to classify them, extract the elementary operations and deduce from this what should be measured.

We only face the second problem in this paper.

In the following of the paper, we introduce in section 2 urban data management and we explain the specificity of urban data and urban data processing. In section 3, we characterize geographic queries and we extract elementary operations from basic geographic queries. Then, we specify in section 4 a set of significant benchmark queries derived from the set of elementary operations previously defined. We conclude in section 5 by discussing future work to be done for benchmarking urban and geographic, and more generally graphics-oriented DBMS.

2. URBAN DATA MANAGEMENT

2.1. Applications

Urban data management is mainly concerned with daily current works, such as the management of land survey, underground networks (water, gas, electricity, telephone) and urban heritage in general (administrative buildings, monuments, urban furniture). Characteristic of these applications is the volume of information, due to the want of a good precision for a large scale cartography. Typical scales are in french cities 1/200 th for detailed maps of networks and topography (1 cm on the map for 2 meters on the ground) , and 1/1000 th to 1/5000 th for land survey and less detailed topography (1 cm for respectively 10 and 50 meters). The processing of these data consists most of the time in selecting a limited geographic area and querying for the display of descriptive (numerical or textual) and possibly graphical informations qualified by some selection criteria.

Typical queries look like the following:

Q1. *"Which land parcels belong to non city residents ?"*
Q2. *"What is the perimeter of parcel number 327 ?"*
Q3. *"What is the average surface of parcels in a given block ?"*
Q4. *"Which parcels are located less than 100 meters from an hydrant ?"*
Q5. *"Which parcels are located in front of 15, Baker Street ?"*
Q6. *"What are the streets without any hydrant ?"*
Q7. *"Which blocks do not contain any electricity closet?"*
Q8. *"Where does the electricity network precisely crosses the water network ?"*

An other kind of applications concern urban decision making, or *urban planning*. The objective is then to study the feasibility and the impact of such projects as the construction of a supermarket, the opening of a new bus line or fittings to the electricity network. These applications usually do not require large scale maps. But they require new functionalities, also typical of CAD applications, since they take time into account. We will not consider in this paper this second class of applications.

2.2. Urban data

Urban data come from multiple sources. The most important are:
- *maps*, that require a digitization process so as to extract and exploit the information consisting of *geographical entities or GEs*, namely parcels, buildings, hydrants, monuments, traffic lights or pieces of networks,
- *census data*, political, socio-economic or demographic, and attached to geographic locations,
- *aerial photography*, processed by photo-interpretation to extract geographic objects.

Urban data can be classified depending on their origin and utilization:
- *cadastral data*, that concern the geographic location, identification and characteristics of land parcels (type, surface, presence of buildings), as well as the identification of the owners,
- *topographical data*, including the crossroads and streets divided into pieces,
- *networks*, concerning for example the distribution of gas, electricity or water,
- *thematic data*, covering various subjects, such as land use, tourism, pollution or politics.

They can also be classified, depending on their nature:
- *factual data*, for the descriptive part of information, namely objects identifiers and characteristics (surface, height, througput, for example),
- *textual data*, for the expression of town planning rules. This kind of information may sometimes appear under the form of maps, to demarcate constructible zones, for example,
- *graphical data*, to record the geographic location, the course or the contour of geographic objects. The problem of storing these non traditional data is discussed in section 3.

From a geometric point of view, we may distinguish between:
- *point data*, for locating road signs, telegraphic poles, or even trees,
- *linear data*, showing for example the course of rivers or networks,
- *polygonal data*, to indicate the contour of buildings and land parcels, or administrative limits.

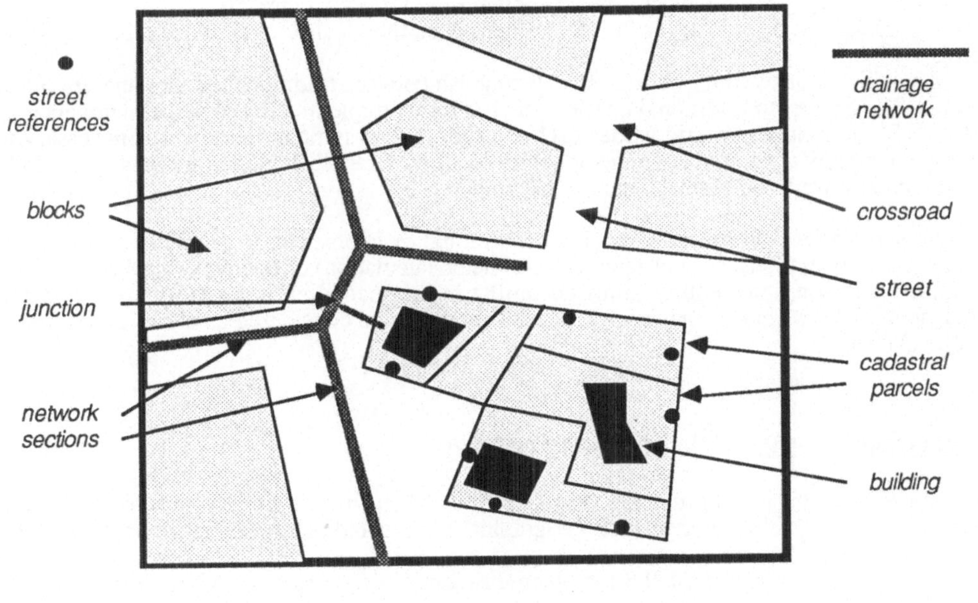

Figure 1: *Sample cadastral sheet with geographic entities*

Figure 1 shows a portion of a sample cadastral sheet, traditionally used in french cities, with electricity and water networks superimposed. This kind of document is used for extracting geographical entities (digitization process). *Blocks* appear on this sheet, separated by *streets* that can be decomposed into *street sections* and *crossroads*. Blocks contain *parcels*, that in turn may sometimes contain *buildings* .

2.3. Urban data processing

Two types of queries have to be considered:
- *traditional queries*, which could be handled by a traditional DBMS,
- *geometric queries*, that require extra query processing since specific geometric computation have to be done after accessing the objects.

If we consider the sample queries given in section 2.1:
(i) query **Q1** ("Which land parcels belong to non city residents ?") is a typical traditional query, since it does not require any additional computation after the relational query processing phase,

(ii) queries **Q2** ("What is the perimeter of parcel number 327 ?") and **Q3** ("What is the average surface of parcels in a given block ?") may be considered as traditional ones if the perimeter and surface of parcels have been precomputed and stored as simple attributes. If not, these values must be computed on graphical data, and the queries become simple geometric ones,

(iii) queries **Q4** to **Q8** are a particular case of geometric queries involving *spatial relationships* between objects. [Orenstein, 86; Peuquet, 86]. Therefore, they are called *spatial queries*. Three kinds of spatial relationships may be distinguished:
- *distance* between geographical entities. It happens for queries **Q4** ("Which parcels are located less than 100 meters from an hydrant ?") and **Q5** ("Which parcels are located in front of 15, Baker Street ?"),
- *inclusion* between objects, for such queries as **Q6** ("What are the streets without any hydrant ?") and **Q7** ("Which blocks do not contain any electricity closet?"),
- *intersection* of objects, as in **Q8** ("Where does the electricity network cross the water network ?").

About query answering, we may also distinguish between traditional queries and *graphical queries*. The answer to traditional queries consists for example in a list of parcel numbers (**Q1**, **Q4** or **Q5**), or simply numeric values (**Q2** and **Q3**). For graphical queries, it is necessary to display the graphical component of geographical entities. Graphical queries are thus specified by using such keywords as "display" instead of "find".

To summarize, queries may be either traditional or geometric. If geometric, they can be simple (unary operations, such as length or perimeter calculation) or complex (binary operations: distance, inclusion, intersection), thus becoming in the second case spatial queries. From an other point of view (query answering), queries may also be considered as either traditional or graphical ones.

3. ANALYSING URBAN GEOGRAPHIC QUERIES

Since we want to measure the response time of an information system to geographic queries, we have to characterize such geographic queries and determine more precisely what should be measured.

We have shown in section 2.3 that geometric queries require a two-phase processing that consists in:
a) finding the objects concerned by the query,

b) executing some specific spatial data processing that depends on the query (calculation of length or surface, for example).

We are interested in measuring the time to access the objects (phase a)). But finding the objects that satisfy spatial geometric queries also requires to execute specific geometric functions. This will be for example the case for query **Q7** where blocks-related data have to be retrieved and tests of inclusion made to see if any electricity closet is contained in these blocks.

Then, the response time will be affected by the data structures and algorithms used to store and retrieve the graphical part of objects. Consequently, it will be necessary to distinguish between data access and geometric processing when measuring the response time. That is the goal of the present section. We first define graphical objects as the non-traditional graphical part of geographic entities. Then, we go into more details concerning geographic queries and try to extract elementary operations from basic geographic queries.

3.1. Geographic entities and graphical objects

As we previously mentioned, urban data are a subset of geographic data. As such, they may contain, in addition to traditional attributes, a *geographic location attribute*. This peculiar attribute records the graphical representation of a geographic entity (GE). Then, to each GE will be associated a *graphical object* or *GO*.

We will distinguish between three kinds of graphical objects, related to the three kinds of data defined in section 2.2:
- *point-like objects* or *SGOs* (S for simple), used for point data, associated to point-located GEs,
- *linear objects* or *LGOs*, for linear data,
- *polygonal objects* or *PGOs*, for polygonal data.

Depending on the data structure used, GOs will be stored either as a list of pair of coordinates (vector-based methods), or as a list of picture elements or pixels (grid-based and raster-based methods) [Nagy and Wagle, 79; Boursier 84]. Derived from these generic methods, many data structures have been designed, among which hierarchical methods such as quadtrees [Samet, 84]. In the following, we will consider that a GO is recorded as a list of pair of coordinates, relatively to a coordinate system. For most french cities, the "Lambert III" system is used.

3.2. Deriving elementary operations from geographic queries

First, we will introduce three kinds of access to geographic entities:
- *primary access*, based on primary keys used to uniquely identify the objects,
- *secondary access*, based on other traditional factual attributes (street or city name, height, length or surface if pre-computed and stored),
- *geometric access*, based on the geographic location attribute and requiring the use of geometric operations.

We will now review the different kinds of geometric queries, so as to extract the basic elementary kinds of geometric accesses and geometric operations:

(i) *simple geometric queries* first imply to retrieve the wanted objects. This is done by using primary or secondary access. Then, they require simple unary operations to compute the length of a piece of network, the perimeter or the surface of a land parcel (if not pre-computed). Two elementary operations are therefore necessary: length calculation and surface calculation. These queries should be compared to traditional ones using aggregate functions in relational DBMSs,

(ii) *distance-based queries* can be classified into six categories, depending on the kinds of GOs concerned:

- find the distance between two SGOs,
- find the minimal distance between two LGOs,
- find the minimal distance between two PGOs,
- find the minimal distance between a SGO and a LGO,
- find the minimal distance between a SGO and a PGO,
- find the minimal distance between a PGO and a LGO.

From an algorithmic point of view, three different algorithms are necessary:
- distance between two SGOs,
- minimal distance between SGO-LGO or SGO-PGO,
- minimal distance between LGO-LGO, PGO-PGO or LGO-PGO.

From an access point of view, all kinds of *distance-based queries* require to "find the objects such as the distance between a given object and candidate objects ranges between given values" (primitive **D1**).

(iii) twelve kinds of *inclusion-based queries* may be differentiated, if we consider all kinds of potentially interesting combinations of graphical objects. Among these, only six are really interesting ones:
- find the SGO(s) contained in a given PGO,
- find the PGO(s) contained in a given PGO,
- find the PGO(s) that contain a given SGO,
- find the PGO(s) that contain a given PGO,
- find if a given PGO contains a given SGO,
- find if a given PGO contains another given PGO,

These six kinds of inclusion-based queries fall into two classes:
- those which try to find objects containing a given object or contained in a given object. Processing such queries first implies to look for candidate objects, and then to execute specific algorithms to verify if the candidate objects satisfy the query.
- those which try to know if a given object contains or is contained in an other given object. For this second class of queries, referenced objects are first retrieved, and the inclusion algorithm is then applied.

From an algorithmic point of view, we shall consider two different algorithms:
- inclusion of a SGO into a PGO,
- inclusion of a PGO into another PGO.

From an access point of view, the six kinds of inclusion-based queries also fall into only two classes, plus a specific case for retrieving a single object containing a given point:
- **I1:** "find the objects contained into a given object",
- **I2:** "find the objects that contain a given object",
- **I3:** "find the minimal object containing a given point".

(iv) eighteen different kinds of *intersection-based queries* could be differentiated. Fifteen are interesting ones, that fall into three classes:
- those which look for the object(s) resulting from the intersection of two given objects,
- those which look for the object(s) intersecting a given object,
- those which only try to know if two given objects intersect.

From an algorithmic point of view, we will define five algorithms:
- intersection of two SGOs,
- intersection of two LGOs,
- intersection of two PGOs,
- intersection of a LGO and a SGO,
- intersection of a LGO and a PGO.

From an access point of view, all kinds of intersection-based queries imply to "find the objects intersecting a given object (primitive **J1**)".

To summarize, processing geometric queries requires five different geometric access primitives:
-**D1**: "find the object(s) such as the distance between a given object and candidate objects ranges between given values",
- **I1**: "find the objects contained into a given object",
- **I2**: "find the objects that contain a given object",
- **I3**: "find the minimal object containing a given point",
- **J1**: "find the objects intersecting a given object".

Measures of the response time to geographic queries should be decomposed, according to these elementary operations.

4. DESIGNING A SET OF BENCHMARK QUERIES

We have defined a set of queries to measure the performance of a data management system for multimedia urban data. They are based on the set of elementary operations defined in section 3, and designed to perform on the synthetic database defined in section 4.3, as well as on actual urban databases.

This set contains traditional retrieval queries requiring primary and secondary access to objects. It also contains simple geometric queries and more complex spatial queries, more significant and specific of urban data processing.

On the other hand, this set does not contain neither insertion nor update queries. Such operations may be very complex in the context of geographic data processing and were not to be considered here.

Primary access queries:
- **P1:** "find a land parcel, given its identifier "p" "

Such a query is refered to as name lookup in [Rubenstein, Kubicar and Cattell, 87]. It looks for a single object, given its identifier.

- **P2:** "find all the parcels that belong to block "b" in section "s" "

This second query looks for a group of objects, from its primary key. It corresponds to range lookup.

- **P3:** "find all the parcels of the territory"

Variant of the previous one, this query looks for all objects of type "land parcel" contained in the database on the territory under study.

Secondary access queries:
- **S1:** "find the parcels which pre-calculated surface is less than 1000 square meters"

This kind of query searches objects selected by the values of one descriptive attribute. As P2 and P3, it corresponds to range lookup, on a secondary attribute this time.

- **S2:** "find the buildings built on parcels which pre-computed surface is less than 1000 square meters"

For this query and the next one, we use the descriptive attribute that links parcels and buildings, indicating for each parcel if a building is present, giving its identifier if so. This is not a geometric query since the inclusion relationship is explicit and not only geometric. Such a query is refered to as reference lookup, since it implies to retrieve in a first time the parcels corresponding to the selection criterion, and then the buildings linked to these parcels.
- **S3:** "find the parcels containing buildings which ground surface is greater than 500 square meters".

This operation is called group lookup. It is the reverse of the previous one, since it requires to retrieve first the buildings that satisfy the selection criterion, and then the parcels that contain these buildings. This query is more difficult to deal with than the previous one, as no explicit link is stored from buildings to parcels.

Geometric queries:

- **G1:** "find the parcels bordering parcel "p" "

This distance-based spatial query looks for parcels bordering a given parcel (distance = 0). It illustrates access primitive D1.

- **G2:** "find the buildings distant from the drainage network by more than 100 meters "

This is another kind of distance-based query that looks for buildings within a certain distance from network sections.

- **G3:** "find the address location points (street references) corresponding to parcel "p" "

This is an inclusion-based spatial query of type I1. It implies to retrieve the identifier of a point-like object(s) contained in a given polygonal object.

- **G4:** "find the parcel which postal address location is "15, Baker Street" "

Opposite to query G4, this inclusion-based spatial query of type I2 implies to retrieve the polygonal object that contains a given point-like object identified by a descriptive attribute.

- **G5:** "find the parcel spotted on screen or identified by geographic location (X,Y)"

This geometric query looks for one single parcel geometrically located. It is an inclusion-based spatial query, since it requires a test of inclusion between a point object (precise geographic location) and candidate polygonal objects (cf. primitive I3).

- **G6:** "find the network section having a connection to building "b" "

This constitutes an intersection-based spatial query (cf. primitive J1). It successively looks for building "b", the junction connected to it (if any), and the corresponding network section.

- **G7:** "find the buildings having no connection to the drainage network"

This is another kind of intersection-based query. It implies to geometrically verify for each building (using the geographic location attributes) if any junction arrives to it.

5. CONCLUSION

Database benchmarking aims at measuring the performance of a data management system in a given environment, for a pre-defined set of data and queries. In the case of urban data management, we have shown that measuring the response time to spatial queries requires to consider both the time to access the objects and the time to process geometric operations.

Spatial indexing will have to be considered, since the data structures and access methods used for graphical data can have a sensitive influence on the searching and processing times.

Now, an other important aspect has not been tackled. It concerns the possibility, that occurs more and more frequently and especially for engineering applications, to store data on a *server* and to express queries and receive results on a *workstation*. This possibility raises two additional questions and requires:

(i) to decide whether the geometric operations will be processed either on the server or on the workstation. This could lead to important variations in the response time, especially if specialized processors are used on the workstation,

(ii) to consider the time to transfer data between the server and the workstation.

Measures will be done on two kinds of data sets:
(i) on synthetic data, generated from a model which is currently under design and test,
(ii) on actual urban data coming from french large cities (more than 100 000 inhabitants).

The combination of these two kinds of experiments will allow to validate the model and determine which are the good parameters that have an influence on performance in accessing geographic objects. Among these, we will consider the graphical type of objects (point, line, polygon), their dimensions (length, perimeter, surface), and "fuzzier" ones such as the shape, the regularity or the texture of the objects.

REFERENCES

[Anon et al., 85]
Anon et al., "A measure of transaction processing power", *Datamation*, April 1985.

[Bitton, Dewitt and Turbyfil, 84]
D. Bitton, D.J. Dewitt, C. Turbyfil, "Benchmarking database systems: a systematic approach", *Proc. VLDB Conf.*, October 1983.

[Boursier and Scholl, 82]
P. Boursier, M. Scholl, "Performance analysis of compaction techniques for map representation in geographic databases", *Conputers and Graphics, 6-2*, 1982.

[Boursier, 84]
P. Boursier, "Computer-Assisted Regional Planning with a small computer", *COMPCON FALL, Arlington (USA)*, October 1984.

[COMPUTER, 81]
"Special issue on Pictorial Information Systems", *IEEE Computer, Vol.14, No.11*, November 1981.

[Faloutsos, Sellis and Roussopoulos, 87]
C. Faloutsos, T. Sellis, N. Roussopoulos, "Analysis of object-oriented spatial access methods", *Proc. ACM-SIGMOD Conf.*, San Francisco, May 1987.

[Goodchild and Rizzo, 86]
M.F. Goodchild, B.R. Rizzo, "Performance evaluation and workload estimation for geographic information systems", *Proc. 2nd Int. Conf. on Spatial Data Handling*, Seattle, July 1986.

[Marble and Sen, 86]
D.F. Marble, L. Sen, "The development of standardized benchmarks for spatial database systems", *Proc. 2nd Int. Conf. on Spatial Data Handling*, Seattle, July 1986.

[Nagy and Wagle, 79]
G. Nagy, S. Wagle, "Geographic data processing", *ACM Computing Surveys, Vol.11, No.2*, June 1979.

[Orenstein, 86]
J.A. Orenstein, "Spatial query processing in an object-oriented database system", *Proc. ACM-SIGMOD Int. Conf. on Management of Data*, Washington, May 1986.

[Peuquet, 86]
D.J. Peuquet, "The use of spatial relationships to aid spatial database retrieval", *Proc. 2nd Int. Conf. on Spatial Data Handling*, Seattle, July 1986.

[Rubenstein, Kubicar and Cattell, 87]
W.B. Rubenstein, M.S. Kubicar, R.G.G. Cattell, "Bechmarking simple data base operations", *Proc. ACM-SIGMOD Conf.*, San Francisco, May 1987.

[Samet, 84]
H. Samet, "The quadtree and related hierarchical data structures", *ACM Computing Surveys, Vol.16, No.2*, June 1984.

GQL: A Graphical Database Language Using Pattern Images

H. Du and M. Azmoodeh (UK)

Abstract: GQL is a graphical formal query language for manipulating 'a database. By providing a set of pattern images, the language allows users to draw pattern graphs against the graphical schema of the database. This paper describes various aspects of GQL: the underlying model, the pattern images and graphs, and the representation of database operations.

1. Introduction

Database query languages proivide users with mechanisms of manipulating a database. Graphics is one of the techniques used to support an "easy-to-use" language with a two dimensional syntax. Much research has been done in this area (QBE, ISIS [Kenn 85], SNAP [Bryc 85], etc). As more sophisticated graphics facilities are available in computer systems, the implementation of graphical query languages becomes less expensive and such languages become more comprehensive.

Many existing graphical query facilities are prototype systems (GUIDE [Wong 82], SNAP, etc) and lack full consideration of various aspects of a query language, i.e. qualification and quantification of data, specification of query operators, and representation of operations for making queries. Therefore they have limited expressive power. Languages such as QBE and BRMQ [Azmo 85] still have a textual syntax though they are amenable to graphical representations. Queries in SNAP and GUIDE are represented as a highlighted segment of the database schema. Since the schema only shows the conceptual structure of the database, it is not a sufficient tool to represent database manipulations. SNAP and GUIDE tried to attach qualification conditions on the segment graph, but both of them run into difficulty when considering quantifications such as "for all" and "exist some".

This paper presents a Graphical Query Language (GQL) which is defined on a subset of first order predicate calculus. The language defines a set of pattern images which are used to construct pattern graphs. GQL also develops a graphical mechanism for general operations. To make a query in GQL, users merely use the GQL pointer device to draw pattern graphs and activate necessary operations against the database schema network displayed on the terminal screen. The paper describes the language as follows. Section 2 introduces its underlying data model and the graphical representation of the model. Section 3 defines the basic set of pattern images, pattern graphs, and their underlying semantics. Section 4 discusses GQL forms of representing and performing database operations. Section 5 shows how to specify an example query with GQL.

2. The Underlying Data Model and Its Graphical Representation

The GQL underlying data model is a semantic data model developed on a similar line as E-R model [Chen 76], SBRM [Azmo 84], QBRM [Jian 85] and IFO [Abit 84]. The model describes the real world as *objects* and various *relationships* among objects. An object represents an element in the world and a relationship represents a property of an object.

2.1. Objects and Relationships

Every object has a unique value and belongs to a particular object type. An object is either an *atom* which is a string, an integer, a floating number or a boolean, or a *structure* which is composed of some atomic objects and/or other structures. All object values of the same type form the *domain* set of that type. The domain of a structured object type is a set of abstract identifiers which refer to the actual structures. Every object type is named by the user.

The model uses binary relationships to describe associations between two objects. A relationship can act as an object and take part in further associations. Relationships with the same conceptual meanings are grouped into a relationship type which abstractly represents a type of associations between two types of objects.

Binary relationships are used to represent different categories of conceptual associations. Some relationships compose a structured object and define "aggregation_of" hierarchies between the structured object and its component objects. The components are known as the attributes of the structured object. Binary relationships can directly represent the functional dependency between two objects. The model uses nested binary relationships ([Jian 85]) for the dependencies among several objects. Nested binary relationships are the relationships whose arguments can be relationships, e.g. R1 (R2 (x, y), z). Some binary relationships represent "is a subtype of (IS_A)" hierarchy between objects, along which objects have property inheritance. Binary relationships (the simple and the nested) represent operations (functions) as mappings from the argument objects to the results.

In logic terminology, object type P defines a "member" predicate P(x). P(x) is true iff the term x refers to an object in the domain of P; otherwise P(x) is false. A relationship corresponds to a predicate R (x, y) which is true iff the relationship exists in the database. The logical meaning of a qualified binary relationship R1 (R2 (x, y), z) is that predicate R1 (R2 (x, y), z) is true iff predicate R2 (x, y) is true and term R2 (x, y) makes R1 (R2 (x, y), z) true.

2.2. Graphical Representation of the Model

Nodes and arcs are the two basic components of a graph. They respectively represent objects and relationships. Based on this criteria, we define a variety of node and arc images to graphically represent different conceptual items of the model (Fig. 1).

A dot, an oval and a rectangle represent an object, an atomic object type and a structured object type respectively. We define a table for showing the domain of an object type or the instances of a relationship type. The table is single-columned for an atomic object type, multiple-columned for a structured type and double-columned for a relationship type. Table forms for nested relationships are also nested. The images of relationships for composing structures and for representing functional dependencies are single-line directed arcs whose arrows show the directions of the mappings. In order to differentiate these two types, users can define special names for the former or use the default naming facility of the model: using the concatenation of string "Has_" and the name of the attribute object type to which the relationship points. The images for nested binary relationships are the nesting of arcs for simple relationships. The image for "IS_A" relationship is a heavy-line directed arc whose arrow indicates the mapping from a subtype to its supertype. We shall discuss the graphical images for operations in section 4. All images for object and relationship types have type names as labels.

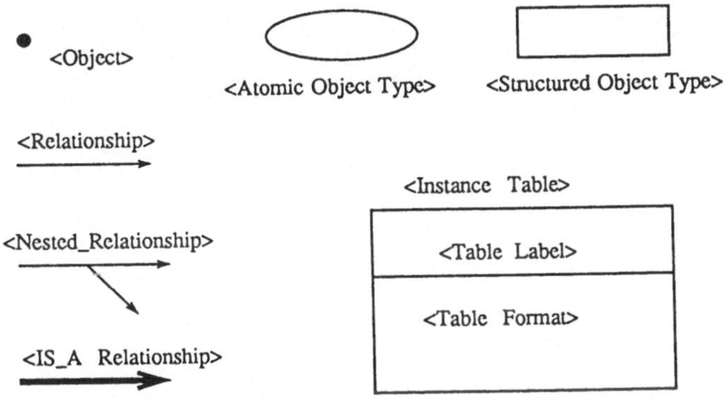

Figure 1. Graphical Images for the Underlying Data Model

The database schema is designed in terms of the graphical representation of the underlying data model. Figure 2 gives a sample database schema which describes the supplies and employment information of a company.

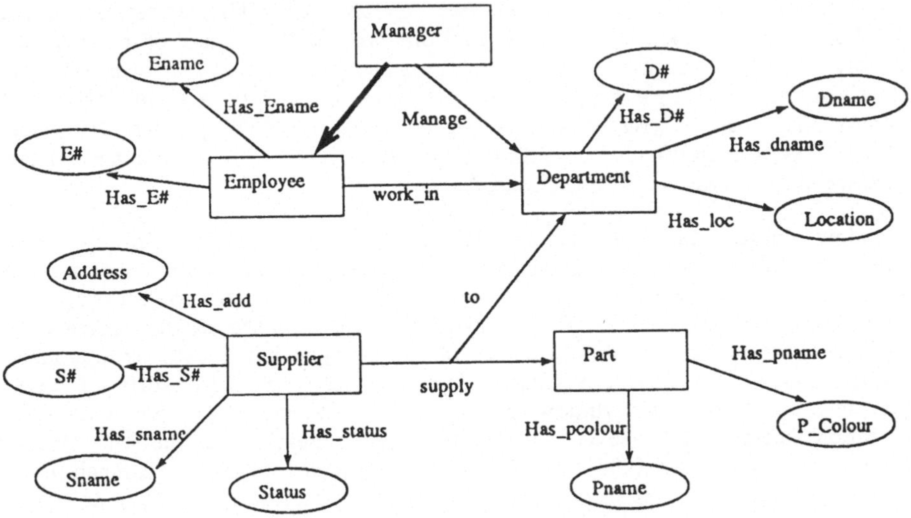

Figure 2. A Sample Database Schema

3. Overview of GQL

Before describing GQL in details, we first introduce the concept of GQL pointer. GQL pointer is a two dimensional locator. It is an abstraction of devices such as cursor, light pen and mouse. Associated with a set of access keys, the pointer is used for specifying data types, drawing pattern images and activating operations.

3.1. Basic Pattern Images

GQL defines a set of basic pattern images for representing the specifications to objects and relationships. Figure 3 lists some of them where P and R stand for an object type and a relationship type respectively. The rest are to be introduced in later sections.

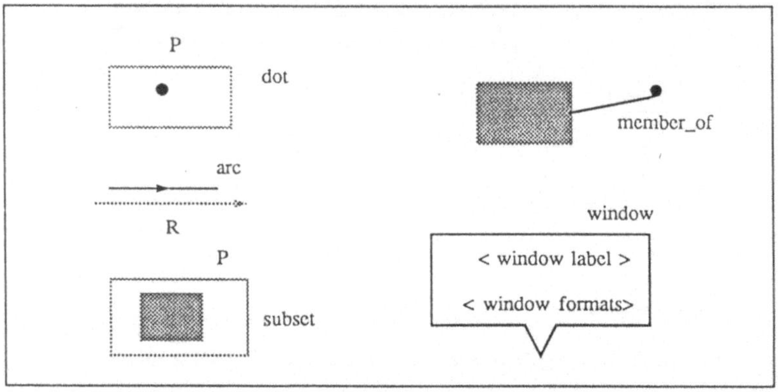

Figure 3. GQL Basic Pattern Images

The dot image denotes an object x such that $x \in P$. The arc image specifies a particular relationship R(x, y) if the arc links two dots, or a set of relationships R(x, y)s if the arc links to a subset (see section 3.2). The subset image defines subset $P' \subseteq P$. The membership image shows that subset P' consists of objects such as x (a dot). Window images are designed for specifying operations over objects and relationships, and therefore associated with the images for objects and relationships. A pattern image can be created and erased by using the GQL pointer with "specify" and "abort" keys respectively. In addition, a window can be opened and closed by the pointer with access keys "open" and "close".

Of window images, the most frequently used are the windows for qualification/quantification to objects and relationships (Q/Q windows). The window created on an object image has a menu format. It takes the name of the object type as the window label and the names of the attribute object types as the entries of the menu. The window for an atomic object takes the type name both as the label and the only menu entry. Users textually input values and the results of functions against menu entries. The window on an arc has format "____rel_name____". A qualification operator (QL) over the relationship is applied to the left underlying position and a quantifier (QN) on the second argument of the relationship, to the right. The window format for a structured object makes it possible to specify a query on the structure without going further down to its attributes. Qualification

QL on the structured object is distributed into the qualifications to its attribute objects QL1, ..., QLn, and QL ≡ QL1 Λ ... Λ QLn. There is no Q/Q window image for an IS_A arc due to its nature. The formats of Q/Q windows are illustrated in Fig. 4.

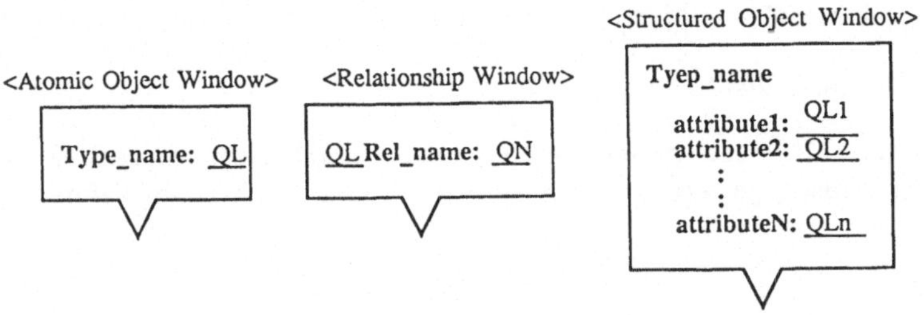

Figure 4. Formats of Q/Q Windows

Creating/closing a Q/Q window defines a new qualification/quantification. Opening/closing a Q/Q window provides a way of viewing or modifying the current qualification/quantification. Opening or creating a Q/Q window followed by aborting it discards the current qualification/quantification.

3.2. Pattern Graphs

Let us assume that we have :-

1) objects x and y, and object types X and Y where x∈X and y∈Y;
2) relationship type R defined from X to Y;
3) qualification function Qual() applied on y through a window, specifying a subset Y'⊆Y; and we require subset X' of X.

Basic Pattern Graphs

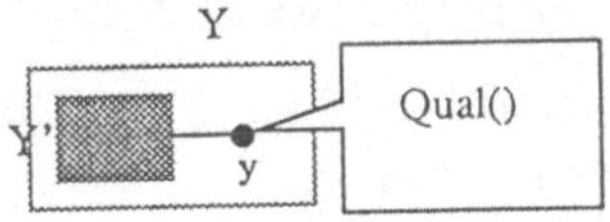

Pattern 0: The specification of objects

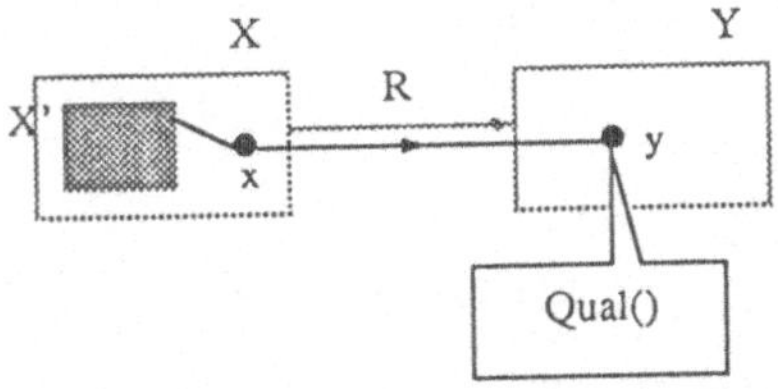

Pattern 1: Existential reference to objects (∃)

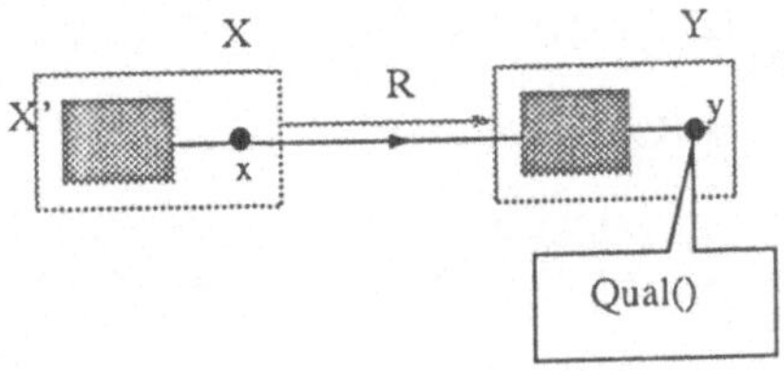

Pattern 2: Universal reference to objects (∀)

The semantics of the patterns are listed as follows.

Pattern 0: $Y' = \{y \mid (y \in Y) \wedge Qual(y)\}$
Pattern 1: $X' = \{x \mid (x \in X) \wedge (\exists y)((y \in Y) \wedge Qual(y) \wedge R(x, y))\}$
Pattern 2: $X' = \{x \mid (x \in X) \wedge (\exists y)((y \in Y) \wedge Qual(y)) \wedge (\forall y)((y \in Y) \wedge Qual(y) \rightarrow R(x, y))\}$

Note that pattern 2 takes the natural semantics from a natural language, assuming Y' is not an empty set. For example, the query "find suppliers who supply all red parts to a department" would return no answers if there is not any red part.

Generalised Pattern Graphs

In order to generalise the pattern graphs and extend their expressive powers, two alternative generalised pattern graphs, patterns 3(a) and 3(b), are defined.

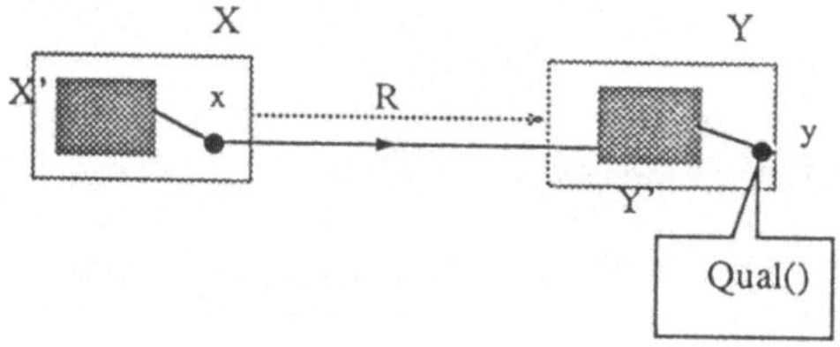

3 (a)

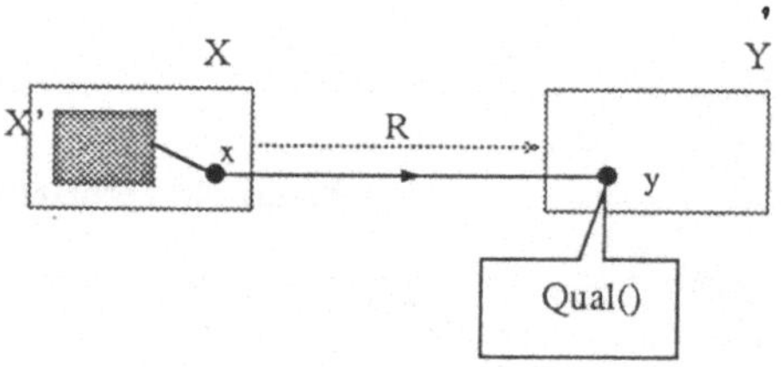

3 (b)

In pattern 3(a), object x refers, through R, to one or a collection of the objects in Y' which satisfy Qual(). Dot y in Pattern 3(b) may now represent a *collection* of objects. Through the window on arc R, quantifiers "∃" and "∀" can be assigned to QN, and operators "Not" and "Only", to QL. To keep the consistency with the previous patterns, 3(a) and 3(b) treat "∀" and "∃" as the default cases of QN respectively. GQL defines extended quantifiers "at_least(N)", "at_most(N)" and "exact(N)" with the following meanings.

at_least(N): $X' = \{x \mid (x \in X) \wedge Count(\{y \mid (y \in Y) \wedge Qual(y) \wedge R(x,y)\}) \geq N\}$
at_most(N): $X' = \{x \mid (x \in X) \wedge Count(\{y \mid (y \in Y) \wedge Qual(y) \wedge R(x,y)\}) \leq N\}$
exact(N): $X' = \{x \mid (x \in X) \wedge Count(\{y \mid (y \in Y) \wedge Qual(y) \wedge R(x,y)\}) = N\}$

where function Count(S) returns the number of elements in set S. Quantifiers can be associated with Operators "Not" and "only".

"Not" with "for all":

$$X' = \{x \mid (x \in X) \wedge \neg(Y' \neq \{\} \wedge (\forall y)((y \in Y) \wedge Qual(y) \rightarrow R(x,y)))\}$$
$$= \{x \mid (x \in X) \wedge (Y' = \{\} \vee (\exists y)((y \in Y') \wedge Qual(y) \wedge \neg R(x,y))\}$$

"Not" with "exist some":

$$X' = \{x \mid (x \in X) \wedge \neg(\exists y)((y \in Y) \wedge Qual(y) \wedge R(x,y))\}$$
$$= \{x \mid (x \in X) \wedge ((Y' \neq \{\} \wedge (\forall y)(((y \in Y) \wedge Qual(y)) \rightarrow \neg R(x,y))) \vee Y' = \{\})\}$$

"Only" with "for all" and "exist some" (represented by Q):

$$X' = \{x \mid (x \in X) \wedge (Qy)((y \in Y) \wedge (Qual(y) \leftrightarrow R(x,y))\}$$

The association of "Not" and an extended quantifier causes the negation to predicate P(Count({}), N) where P refers to a comparison operator. The associations of "Only" and any extended quantifiers are not meaningful and therefore not allowed in GQL.

Pattern Graphs with Nested Arcs

Pattern graphs for nested arcs can be constructed by nesting pattern graphs for the component binary arcs, and have corresponding semantics. This is evident from pattern 3 and the semantics of nested binary relationships (see section 2.1), and the applications of different qualification operators and quantifiers.

Pattern Graph Construction

The pattern graphs that we have discussed can be applied to construct a complex graph for a query. Using the GQL pointer, a user can either draw the whole pattern graph "part by part" in a sequence, or specify different parts separately and then link them together. These two construction criteria are known as *sequential construction* of different parts and *piecemeal construction* of sub-queries.

4. GQL Representations of Operations

Operations useful for making queries are defined as built-in operators and functions in GQL. They are classified according to object types and presented in menus. Users can call them by typing in their textual names against Q/Q window entries. GQL also provides graphical methods, operational windows and operational arcs, for representing and performing the operations. Using the GQL pointer, users can select an operation from a menu, obtain an operational image and apply the image to a query pattern graph.

4.1. Operational Windows for Query Operators

Query operators include "retrieve", "insert", "delete", and "update" for manipulating the database, and "define_new" and "define_derived" for defining a new and a derived data type. The operators are listed in a global operation menu. When users select them, the windows with the formats listed in Fig. 5 are obtained.

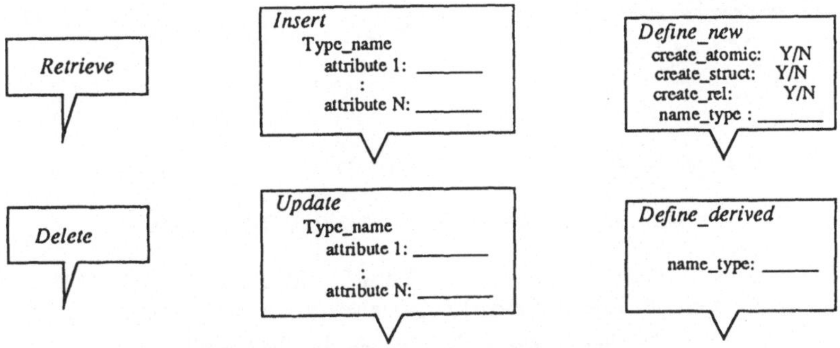

Figure 5. Operational Windows for Query Operators

All the windows take the operators as labels. The windows for manipulating operators can be applied to a dot, a subset and an arc for manipulating an object, a set of objects and a relationship. If a "retrieve" or a "delete" window is applied to a subset image, all the objects that satisfy the query condition are selected or deleted. In "insert" and "update" windows, the new data values are the phrases against entries of window menus. ">>" operator in the two windows allows users to go to the next "page" of the window and specify the next data item if the windows are applied to subset images. A "define_new" window has three alternative commands for creating a data type image and a command for naming it. The window is applied to the appropriate place in the schema network where the type image is due to appear. A "define_derived" window is applied to a type image from where the new type is derived. "Define_derived" results in the generation of an object or a relationship type and an IS_A link from the derived to the original type.

4.2. Operational Arcs

Figure 6(a) lists operational arcs for logical, comparison, set, and arithmetic operators. The arcs for logical, set and arithmetic operators represent functions with result values. They should be applied to images for appropriate items.

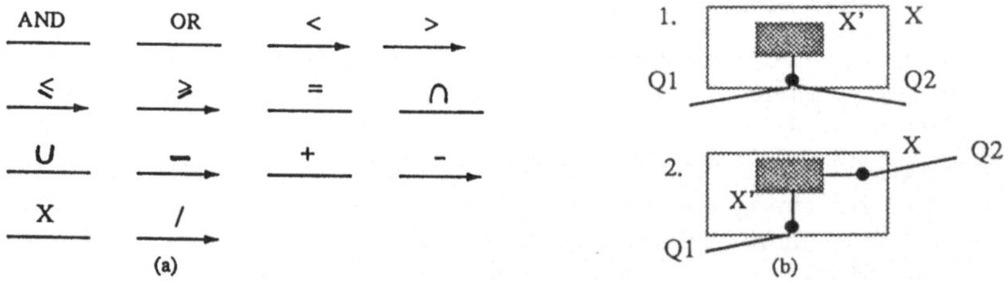

In (b), in case 1, $X' = \{ x \mid (x \in X) \wedge Q1(x) \wedge Q2(x) \}$; in case 2, $X' = \{ x \mid (x \in X) \wedge (Q1(x) \vee Q2(x)) \}$

Figure 6. GQL Operational Arcs and Default Graphs For "And" and "Or"

For convenience, GQL provides a default way of representing logical "and" (Fig. 6(b).1) and "or" (Fig. 6(b).2) in pattern graphs. Logical, set and arithmetic operators can be nested for representing complex logical, set and arithmetic connections (e.g. Fig. 7). A comparison arc can be nested with an arithmetic arc, signifying that the result of the arithmetic operation satisfies the comparison.

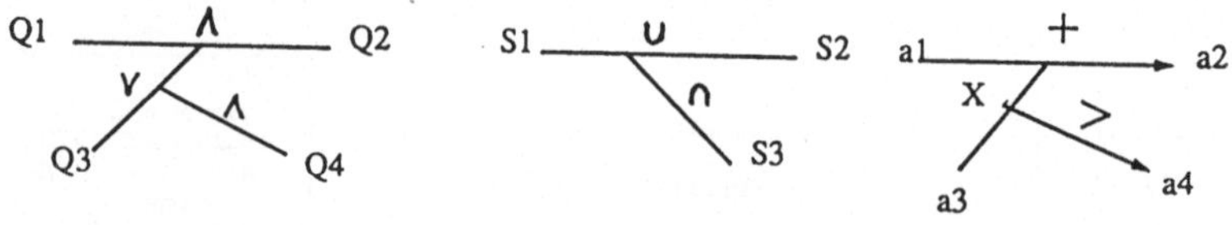

$((Q1 \wedge Q2) \vee Q3) \wedge Q4$ $(S1 \cup S2) \cap S3$ $(a1 + a2) \times a3 > a4$

Figure 7. Some Examples of Complex Calculations

Aggregate functions "Count", "Average", "Total", "Minimum" and "Maximum" are applied to a collection of objects (mostly numeric-type), and return a single numeric value. GQL represents an aggregate function as an operational arc which links an image for a collection of objects (including object type images) to a dot. Here is an example of using aggregate function "Maximum". The query is "*Find employees who earn the highest salary*".

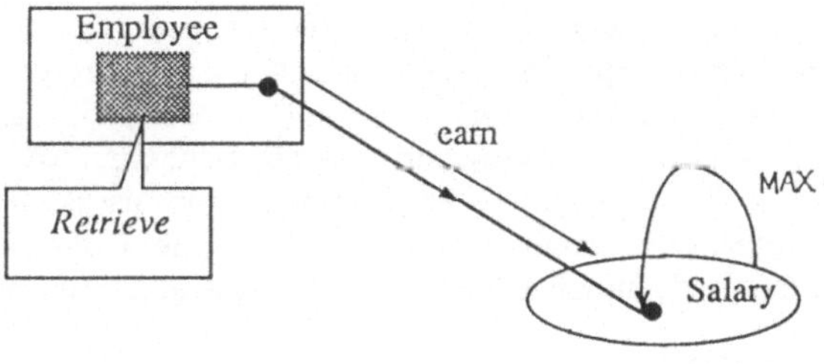

5. Example Session

We present a query example based on the database schema in Fig. 2, and explain how a user describes the query in GQL. The query is "*Find a supplier which supplies at least one red pen to all departments on the second floor*".

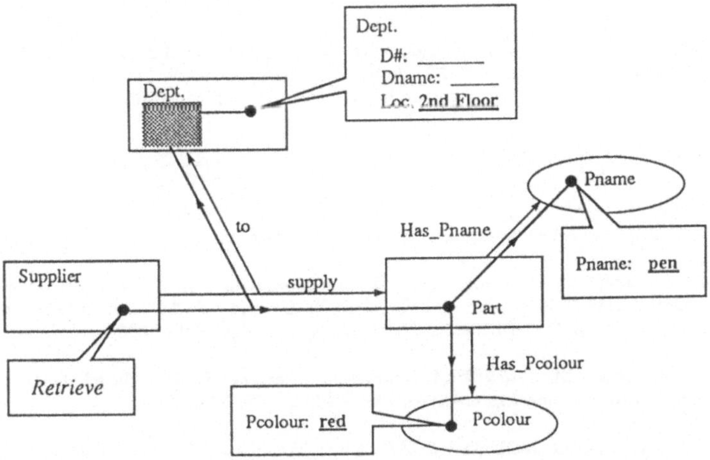

First, the user draws a dot against box "supplier", and from that dot, draws an arc along relationship type "supply" to box "part". The user then creates a dot connected to the arc, opens a window against the dot, and specifies the part to be "red" with name "pen". Then the user draws a nested arc along relationship type "to" to box "department", and creates a subset image with a "member_of" link to a dot. By opening a window against that dot, the user specifies "location" on "2nd floor". Now the user moves the pointer back to the dot on "supplier", opens the "retrieve" operational window. The query is now complete.

6. Concluding Remarks

GQL defines a natural graphical method of making queries. The language is a descriptive formal query language based on a subset of a first order predicate calculus. It provides a set of basic pattern images in which pattern graphs are constructed for queries. It defines a graphical mechanism for database operations.

GQL is supported by an interpreter which checks the syntax grammar of GQL as users draw pattern graphs, translates a legal pattern graph into an underlying logical expression, and evaluates it. The query evaluation is prompted by GQL built-in command "run_query". Answers are returned to users in the format determined by query operators. The implementation of GQL interpreter requires support from advanced graphics facilities for drawing, enlarging, shrinking, copying and highlighting various pattern images and graphs. Sophisticated icon, window and menu facilities provide a good language environment for users. The implementation of a prototype GQL interpreter is now undergoing in the University of Essex. It is built on top of PROLOG and under UNIX* + SUN3/suntool window package.

Future works on GQL include the management of the database schema and the representation of transitive closures. New built-in operators and their graphical representations will be defined to handle the schema management operations such as traversing, duplicating, extracting, etc. GQL will consider transitive closures as recursive rules that are supported by the underlying logic. The language needs new mechanisms for representing recursions in graphical forms.

Acknowledgements: We would like to thank Dr. Y. J. Jiang for his very useful comments on this paper. Special thanks should go to IFS group, especially Mr. R. Brown, in the department for providing computer facilities and technical assistance for the implementation of GQL.

REFERENCES

[Abit 84] Abiteboul, S. and Hull, R., "*IFO: A Formal Semantic Database Model*", Proc. ACM SIGACT-SIGMOD Symp. on Principles of Database Systems, April, 1984, pp119-132

[Azmo 84] Azmoodeh, M. Lavington, S. H. and Standring, M., "*The Semantic Binary Relationship Data Model of Information*", 3rd BCS and ACM Symposium on Research and Development in Information Retrieval, Cambridge, July, 1984

[Azmo 85] Azmoodeh, M., "*BRMQ: A Data Base Interface Facility Based on Graph Traversals and Extended Relationship on Groups of Entities*" CSM-78, Sept. 1985

[Bryc 86] Bryce, D. and Hull, R., "*SNAP: A Graphics-based Schema Manager (Extended Abstract)*", IEEE International Conf. on Data Eng., Los Angeles, Feb. 1986

[Chen 76] Chen, P., "*The Entity-Relationship Model — Toward a unified view of Data*", ACM Trans. on Database Syst. Vol.1, No.1, Mar. 1976, pp9-36

[Jian 85] Jiang, Y. J. and Lavington, S. H., "*The Qualified Binary Relationship Model of Information*" BNCOD-4, July, 1985

[Kenn 85] Kenneth, J. G. etl, "*ISIS: Interface for a Semantic Information System*" ACM, SIGMOD, Vol.14, No.4, Dec. 1985

[Wong 82] Wong, H. and Kuo, I., "*Graphical User Interface for Database Exploration*", Proc. of 8th Inter. Conf. on VLDB, Mexico City, Sept. 1982

* Trademark of Bell Laboratories

Computer-Aided Sail Section Drawing

L. P. Vidal (Spain)

Abstract : Sail cutting is presently a trial and error procedure, as performed by most manufacturers. In this paper, a first approach to computer aided sail pattern drawing is presented. To derive the aerodynamic sections of sails circle interpolations are used, and subsequent refinements are allowed because the development and the resulting implementation are highly modular.

Keywords : Surface modelling, sail design, sail patterns.

1 Introduction

Sail cutting is usually performed in a very empirical fashion by most sail-makers,although some developments point into the direction of computer-assisted design of many parts of the aero-hydrodynamic complex that constitutes a ship.

This paper will present an initial approach to the drawing of sail sections with assistance of a small microcomputer. A GKS interface with graphics is used and this makes the programming of the drawings very easy.

Circle interpolation will be used to approximate the aerodynamical flow-lines of the sail.

2 Background

Sailing ships have been completely outphased by powered vessels for commercial transportation of goods and passengers. But sail manufacture has continued and it has undergone a steady evolution [Nordbok 83] in many areas: the quality of sailcloth, or the study of aerodynamic shapes [Banks 80], for instance, have significantly improved in these last years. The fluid interactions between hull and water, on one side, and between sails and air, on the other side have been accurately studied [Marchaj 79], together with the possible interconnections between the four parts of this complex system. An interesting application of surface modelling with interpolation functions to the problems of sail definition can be found in [Haw 85]. In a similar fashion, this paper presents a methodology to solve the problem of sail section development, that is to say: the distribution and shape of the sections will be defined with the computer.

3 Definitions

This section will give idea for those not familiar of sailing terminology, and describe the hypothesis, restrictions and assumptions used to reach the final results expected from the algorithm.

3.1 Sail shape

Sailing ships to-day usually work on two triangular (or Marconi)sails: the mainsail, with one side tied up to the ship's mast, and the jib sail (or genoa), hung on the stay, a cable that supports the mast from the bow (or front) of the ship's structure.This paper will deal only with triangular sails.

The main parts of triangular sails are:

Luff: the fore side of the triangle by which the sail is attached to the mast, if it is the mainsail, or to the stay, if it is the jib.

Leech: the aft side of the triangle.

Foot: the inferior side of the triangle, which in the main sail is attached to a yard called the boom.

Head: the upper vertex of the triangle.

Clew: the aft vertex of the triangle

Tack: the fore vertex of the triangle.

3.2 Sail sides

To simplify the problem the sides of the sail are supposed to be straight. Hence there will be no roach: slight convex round or concave hollow made on either of the three sides for varied reasons.

The back effects due to the aerodynamic pressure on the free side of the sail, the leech, will neither be considered. Normally, this side undergoes a torsion, called twist, which consequence is that the aerodynamic sections of the sail point gradually more towards the wind direction as they are looked upon from the foot to the head. These effects should be taken into account when defining the desired shape of the sail. This means that to specify the sail one can work from the construction plan of the sail [Baader 82] on which one can give either the perimeter or the various aerodynamic curves.

3.3 Sail curvature

The determination of the surface of the sail is outside the scope of this paper. We will suppose that, after an aerodynamic study has been done, or out of experience the spatial shape of the sail has been defined. Usually this is translated into the specification of the aerodynamic cross-sections at several heights. The aerodynamic cross-section at any height can then be interpolated from these original data.

Aerodynamic cross-sections can take a very wide variety of shapes.As yet, no universally accepted optimal curve has been defined and each designer uses which he deems best. Most authors think that, for light winds, a section with the belly centered is the best bet, whereas for fresh and strong winds the belly must be placed farther forward, until the point placed at 30% of the chord. In accordance with this opinion, in this paper a curve has been used that is the union of two arcs of circle (fig. 1). This kind of curve is smooth enough to become a good aerodynamic flow-line, and it allows the continous displacement of the maximum thickness point along the chord line. Nevertheless, the algorithm has been designed to allow an easy introduction of other analytic curves by the addition of other routines with the definition of the shape. For curves formed by the union of two arcs of circle, the thickness of the foil can be determined from the angle of incidence. Namely, for the case of one simple arc of circle (see fig. 1):

$$\frac{f}{c} = \frac{1 - cos\alpha}{2.sen\alpha} \tag{1}$$

And, for the union of two arcs of circumference (fig. 2):

$$\frac{f}{c} = \frac{1 - cos\alpha}{sen\alpha} \cdot \frac{p}{100} \tag{2}$$

where α is the angle of incidence, p is the relative position (in percentage) of the belly and f/c is the thickness of the foil The appropriate expression will be used to perform the computations. In short the

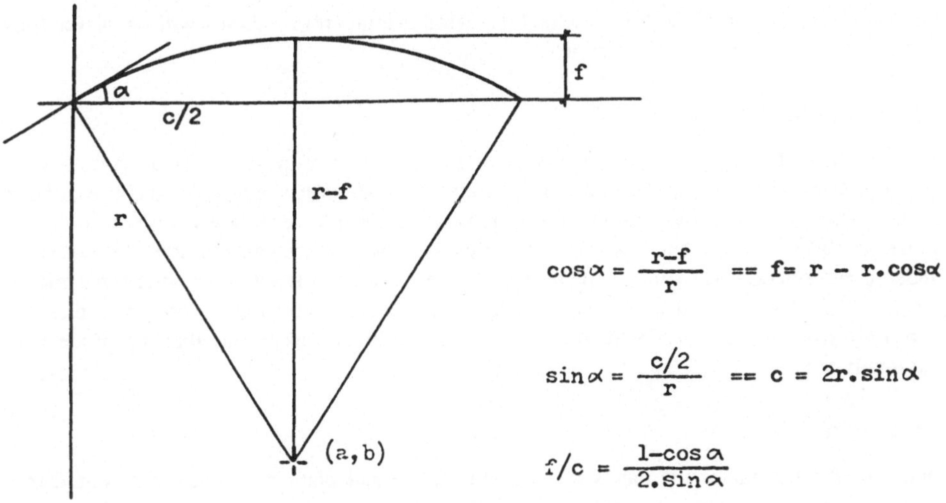

Figure 1: Relationship angle of incidence-belly. Arc of circumference.

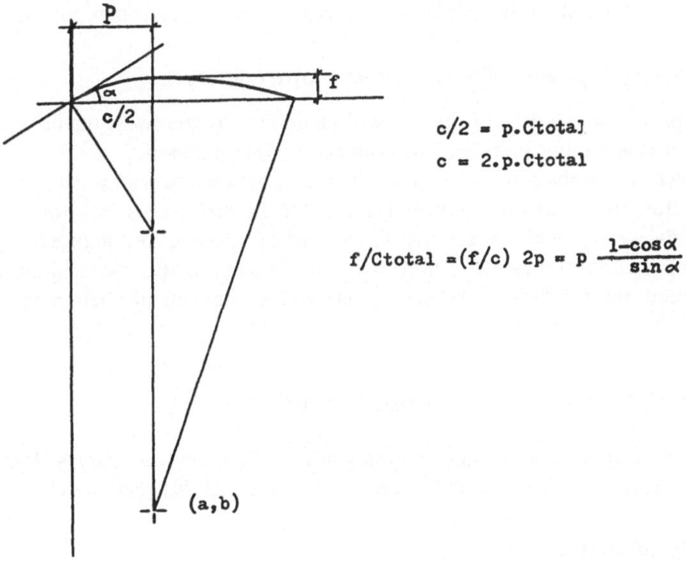

Figure 2: Relationship angle of incidence-belly. Union of two arcs of circumference.

designer knows the layout of the sail in which the aerodynamic cross-sections will be curves formed with the union of two arcs of circumference.

3.4 Elasticity of the sail

The new synthetic fibers have allowed a relative stability of present-day sails as compared with old cotton or linen sails.Most important among these fibers are polyester tissues manufactured with polyethilene tetraphtalate, known commercially as Dacron, though there have been new additions to the choice of fibers available such as Mylar and Kevlar. These improvements notwithstanding, sails still undergo deformations (of course smaller than before) that are a function of wind force and angle of incidence. The designer will be supposed to have taken these effects into account beforehand, and therefore they will not be considered in the present algorithm. This means that the tissue will be deemed totally stable.

3.5 Cut style

Cut styles, or the lay out of the bands of tissue inside the sail plan, have been very varied in history:vertical, radial, solar, etc. Nowadays, most sails are made with a horizontal cut. The reason is quite simple and was discovered by Ratsey and Lapthorne of Cowes in the nineteen tens [Banks 80]. A roll of tissue is made with two different groups of yarns: the warp yarn, running lengthwise and the weft yarn, running breadthwise. The warp is the least yielding thread. The leech is the most stressed side of the sail, because there is no support to it, and therefore, the warp should be aligned to the leech. This is easy to achieve cutting the rolls of fabric normal to the leech, in what is called the horizontal cut. Throughout this paper we will only consider horizontal cut sails.

3.6 Plane development of a double-curvature surface

It has been previously stated that the sail will be defined by the aerodynamic cross-sections at several heights and that any other point will be obtained by interpolation.

If the leech side of the sail was vertical, the seams between the sail sections would be approximately horizontal. But, since this does not hold, there will be differences in positions and heights between the ends of the seams. This means that it will not be possible to obtain exactly the desired surface, with the proposed development method. What this assures is that the position of the seams in space is that required and the rest of the sail panels will be defined by their properties as a developable surface.

4 Formulation of the proposed solution

The following is an abstract of information gathered from several sources [Banks 80] [DoCarmo 76] [Gutelle 79] [Haw 85] [Howard 83] [Marchaj 76] [Marchaj 79] [NaPu 81].

4.1 Study of surfaces

The reader is referred to [DoCarmo 76] for the formulations concerning the geometric properties of ruled surfaces, and non-cylindrical surfaces. Among ruled surfaces, developable surfaces play an important role. A developable surface is the union of patches of surfaces of cylindric, conic and tangent definition.

4.2 Geometry of the sail

If a sail has to be manufactured with rolls of sailcloth, supposed to be not elastic, they will have to be divided into developable surfaces.

Division following the aerodynamic cross section We can, first, suppose that the position of the maximum camber of the foil and the belly (camber to chord ratio) is constant from the foot to the head of the sail (fig. 3), a natural division can be established taking the aerodynamic profiles at the ends of the sail section. Thus, the directing curves would be the aerodynamic profiles defining the sail sections, and the generators would be the segment from each point to its homologous at the aerodynamic profile in front. Thus, there would be a set of conic surfaces which would form, once patched together, exactly the desired sail,if linear interpolation is used to determine aerodynamic cross-sections between those given. The next step is to suppose that only the position of the maximum camber (but not its amount, neither absolute nor relative) is constant from foot to head of the sail, then we have to study how to divide the sail. If the method described in [DoCarmo 76] is applied, then the resulting surface is not developable. Three generators have to be considered: a straight segment joining the maximum camber points at contiguous aerodynamic cross-section, and two other segments joining the corresponding ends of the sections. Then we find that:

- At the maximum camber point, the surface is developable since the normals to the surface at both ends of the generator are equal, as well as along the generator.
- At the straight segment joining the fore extreme points of the sections (luff), the normal is different at the ends of the generator: To define the tangent plane at these points, we take the generator and the tangent to the aerodynamic cross-section, we see that this tangent is different at each end (because of the different bellies and therefore different angles of incidence).
- At the straight segment joining the aft extreme points of the sections (leech) the same as before applies.

Division by horizontal cut The problem becomes more complicated because the division of the sail in sections has not to be made following the aerodynamic cross-sections. Instead, it has to be made normal to the leech (horizontal cut condition).

In the first hypothesis (constant position and value of the belly), the surface would be developable only if the edges of the section were placed between two consecutive aerodynamic cross-sections.In this case the edges would be curves of the same kind and constructing the generators as before we would have a conic surface. This can not be taken for granted on different conditions.

We propose to solve the problem considering smaller developable surfaces, since we have already defined the edges of the section, though not their positions, and the generators have been determined by the design of the sail.

To determine the edge curves of a sail section we will use a sufficiently large set of points on these curves. We will consider two consecutive pairs of points (we understand by pair two points, one at the upper edge and the other at the lower edge). With the four points we construct a quadrilateral in space. In the cases above mentioned, where we had a developable surface we would have obtained a trapezoid (conic surface) or a rectangle (cylindric surface). In the cases where we did not have a developable surface, these figures are not on a plane, because the upper and lower sides of the quadrangle (those joining consecutive points at the same edge) are not in the same direction. To simplify the description, we could say that the trapezoids have been twisted to allow the bases to point to different directions.

We can divide each of these pseudo-trapezoidal surfaces in two triangles. The two triangles share a common side which is the previously non-existant diagonal (fig. 4). We obtain a surface divided

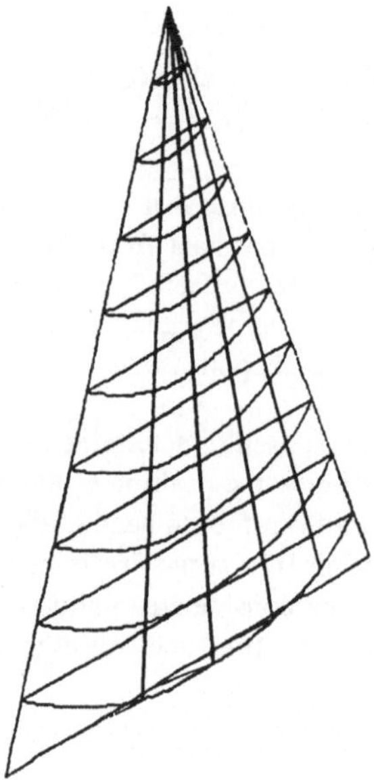

Figure 3: Division of the sail following the aerodynamic sections with constant thickness (f/c).

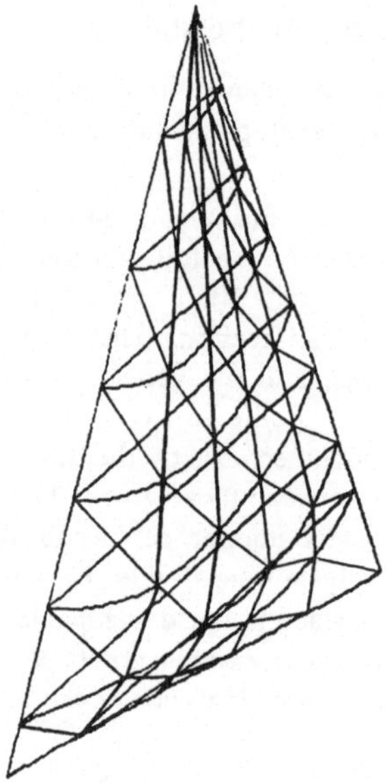

Figure 4: Division of the sail following the horizontal cut, and subdivision into triangles. The separation between points is exagerated.

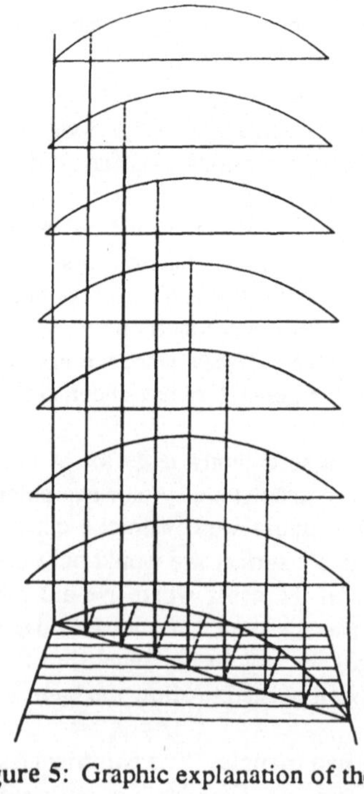

Figure 5: Graphic explanation of the interpolation.

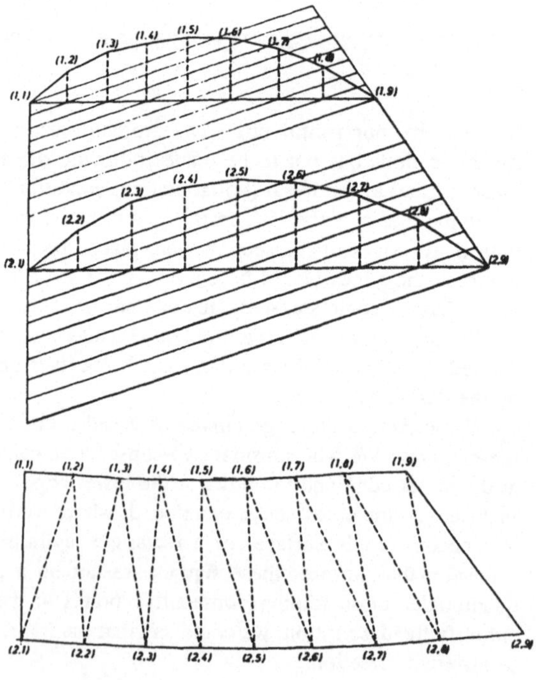

Figure 6: Graphic explanation of the triangulation.

into acute triangles. The difference of orientations between the planes defined by these triangles is the angle between the tangent planes at the extremes of the generators. The closer the surface will be to a developable surface (locally), the closer that angle will be to zero. In the case where the surface was developable the angle would be zero and the two triangles would form a true plane trapezoid. If we had to carry a discrete study (with a limited number of points) of a developable slice we should divide the slice into trapezes; conversely, if the slice was non-developable, it shoud have to be divided into triangles. The closer the chosen slices will be to a developable surface, and the closer the data points on the edge curves will lie, then the smoother will be the transition between each of these triangles and its neighbouring ones.

On the other hand, although the elasticity of the sail has been deliberately omitted from the realm of this paper, it might contribute to smooth out possible theoretical discontinuities in the transitions between triangles.

5 Implementation of the proposed solution

The solution to the problem exposed is implemented in a program written in FORTRAN: From an input consisting of a set of design parameters we obtain the drawings to scale of the sail sections we have to cut to obtain the final desired product.

5.1 Problem analysis

The problem is solved by the repetitive application from the head of the sail to the foot, section by section of the following steps:

- 1. Definition of the curves in space of the upper and lower edges of the sail section, by means of NPOIN points in each one(fig. 5), which involves: 1a. On the x-y plane, a straight line is drawn normal to the leech, and NPOIN regularly spaced points are placed between the leech and the luff. 1b. The NPOIN aerodynamic profiles correspondidng to the points of paragraph 1a are computed and the depth z at the point is deduced. 1c. The profile at the edge is formed by joining with straight segment the NPOIN points calculated. It has to be noted that NPOIN is a refinement parameter supplied by the user.
- 2. Development of the sail section by successive triangulation betwen two points of one edge and one of the opposite edge (fig. 6).The process starts at the leech and proceeds until the luff is reached.
- 3. As a function of the sail panel breadth, validate that panel, or recompute the lower edge, correcting the separation from the upper one, until the breadth is between 90% and 100% of the breadth of the fabric roll.

5.2 Results

The results have been drawn in several renderings:

- Result 1: A textual summary of data and results.
- Result 2: Drawing of the desired distribution of aerodynamic cross-sections (fig. 7).
- Result 3: Drawing of the resulting division of the sail into sections with the inclusion of the fold down of the curves in space of the edges of the sections(fig. 8).
- Result 4: General drawing of the developed panels (fig. 9)
- Result 5: Individual drawing of the development of each panel (fig. 10)

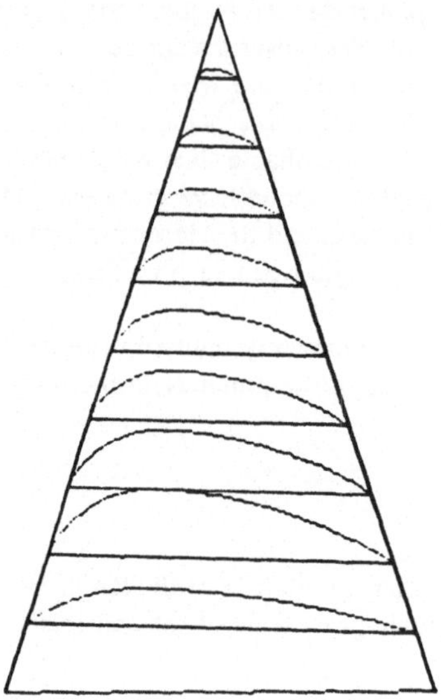

Figure 7: Distribution of aerodynamic cross-sections in straight projection.

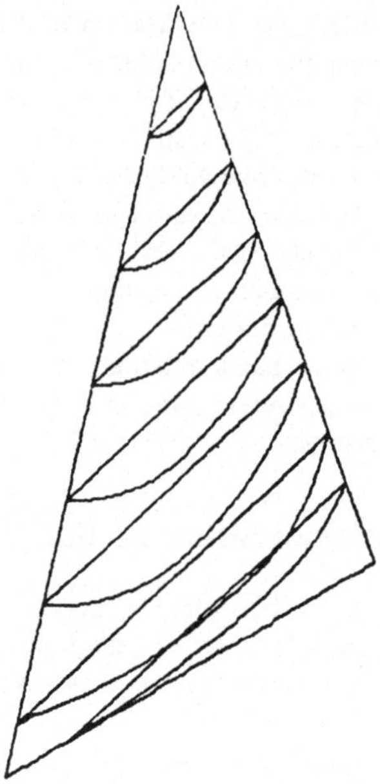

Figure 8: Distribution of sail sections in isometric projection.

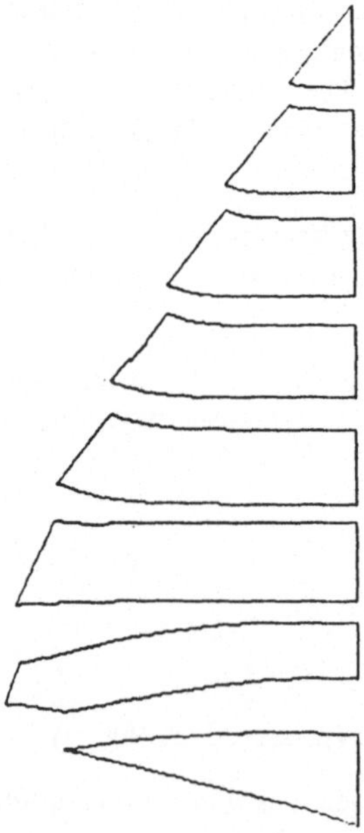

Figure 9: General developement of sail sections.

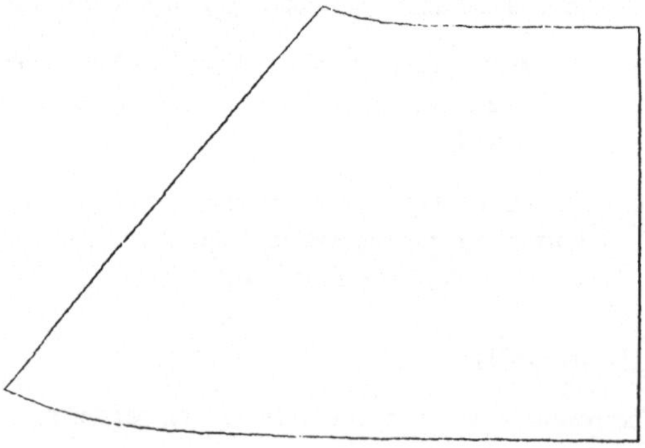

Figure 10: Detailed developement of an intermediate sail section.

6 Further improvements and developments

Some restrictions,described in section 3, have been introduced. This leaves several lines open for further study.Here are some of them:

Splines We have proceeded from the assumption that the aerodynamic cross-sections are formed by the union of two arcs of circumference; this might easily be not sufficiently accurate for a sailmaker or for a sailor wishing to study carefully the behaviour of slightly different sails.

A particularly good choice to define any kind of curve with only one routine is the use of splines with a convenient set of data points. Splines have the property of joining the points with a maximally smooth curve, very convenient for aerodynamic purposes. Splines could also be used to interpolate the coordinates of the aerodynamic sections along the sail.

Roach Roach is very often used by sailmakers, sometimes with very large rounds and hollows. Leech roach yields a much larger sail surface. Battens are then used to confere some rigidity to the trailing edge of the aerodynamic foil.The rounds and hollows at the luff and foot of the sail are used to give some extra belly at the fore side of the sail, using the greater flexibility of modern construction masts and booms. It would be worthwhile to study the problem of curved sides of the triangular sail,first; and later,the possibility of the curved sides not being coplanar. Splines could again be used for the definition of the spatially-curved sail edges.

Different cut styles Although the horizontal cut is the most widely used technique among sailmakers we might be interested in other types of cut.Windsurfing sails, for instance, are lately cut with a vertical cut; this does not contradict the reasonement developed to explain the alignment of the weft yarn with the leech of the sail: windsurfing sails are exposed to much smaller stresses than full-fledged ocean racing sails. Another example of special cut is the spherical shape of spinnakers.Consequently, the possibility of introducing different cuts should be studied in the future.

Other kinds of sails As in the preceding paragraph, we have chosen to study the most common sail in use in contemporary sailing (Marconi or triangular), but there is still a small minority of square-rigged craft which could be considered.

Exactness of the final shape The final surface does not conform exactly with the desired shape in the areas where we have defined the aerodynamic cross-sections, and the algorithm ensures only that the edges of each panel belong to the desired shape.A study could be undertaken to determine the absolute and relative differences between the desired aerodynamic cross-sections and the obtained surface.

7 Conclusions

The study and the solution to the problem of the determination of the shape of the sail panels to obtain a given surface have been presented.The consideration of the amount of wasted material has also been taken into account.

A Computing time

The programs to draw sail section patterns have been implemented on an IBM PS-2 model 30, with 640KB of main memory and a 20MB hard disk to store intermediate files. This model is equipped, as standard, with a CGA graphics card which allows monochrome drawings with a resolution of 640x200 points. To perform all the computations of a particular sail, we have run a program that takes a mean time of 335 seconds to execute.

Then, according to the expected results, we have the following process times: programs:

- Result 1.Mean run time: 52.45 seconds.
- Result 2. Mean run time: 53.06 seconds.
- Result 3. Mean run time: 118.07 seconds.
- Result 4. Mean run time: 166.86 seconds.
- Result 5. Mean run time: 87.33 seconds.
- Result 6. Mean run time: 27.47 seconds.

References

[Baader 82] BAADER, Juan *Lo sport della vela* U. Mursia editore, S.p.A. Milano,1982.

[Banks 80] BANKS, Bruce; KENNY, Dick *Las Velas. Diseño, manejo y comportamiento* H. Blume Ediciones Madrid, 1980.

[DoCarmo 76] DO CARMO, Manfredo *Differential Geometry of Curves and Surfaces* Prentice Hall Inc., Englewood Cliffs, New Jersey, 1976.

[Forsythe 77] FORSYTHE, G. *Computer Methods for Mathematical Computations* Prentice Hall, Inc.- Englewood Cliffs, New Jersey, 1977.

[Garioni 75] GARIONI, Giacomo *Barche olimpiche e level class* Istituto Geografico De Agostini, Novara, 1975.

[Gutelle 79] GUTELLE, Pierre *Voiles et gréements* Editions Maritimes et d'Outre-mer, Paris, 1979.

[Haw 85] HAW,R.J. *An application of geodesic curves to sail design* Computer Graphics Forum Vol4 No2 June 1985 pp.137-141

[Howard 81] HOWARD-WILLIAMS, Jeremy *Cuidado y reparación de velas* Ediciones Lidiun, Buenos Aires, 1981.

[Howard 83] HOWARD-WILLIAMS, Jeremy *Sails* Granada Publishing Limited, Herts, 1983.

[IAS 81] INSTITUTE FOR ADVANCEMENT OF SAILING *La regolazione delle vele* U. Mursia editore, S.p.A., Milano, 1981.

[Langevin 82] LANGEVIN, Sylvestre *Los veleros de regatas* Mundo científico, no.17 Ed. Fontalba Barcelona, octubre,1982.

[Marchaj 76] MARCHAJ, C.A. *Teoria e pratica della vela* U. Mursia editore S.p.A., Milano, 1976.

[Marchaj 79] MARCHAJ, C.A. *Aero-Hydrodynamics of sailing* Granada Publishing Limited, Herts, 1979.

[Nordbok 83] NORDBOK, AB *Las artes de la vela* Editorial Raíces Santander,1983.

[NaPu 81] NAVARRO, Vicente;PUERTA, Fernando *Geometría y teoría de campos* CPDA, ETSEIB, Barcelona, 1981.

The Effect of Format on Information Processing Using Graphics

L. Gingras, L. Harvey, M.-C. Roy, and F. Cloutier (Canada)

ABSTRACT

This is a study to determine whether the characteristics of a graphic and the position of its elements affect an individual's efficiency in information processing. The study, which deals with bar graphs, compares the rules put forward by Tufte for constructing graphics with results obtained on multidimensional stimuli in cognitive psychology.

INTRODUCTION

Graphics have become increasingly popular in the organizational environment as graphic software has become more affordable. Graphics are a good way to increase management efficiency because they synthesize information and make comparisons easier. Moreover, the graphic presentation of information decreases the time required to process that information (Bertin, 1983). However, although graphics maybe very promising in an organizational context, it is still important to know how to construct them so that they provide the desired advantages.

Studies of information systems often try to determine whether graphics perform better than tables, performance being measured by the results obtained during decision making (Lucas, 1981; Lucas and Nielsen, 1980; Benbasat and Dexter, 1985). A variable that has rarely been analyzed in such studies is the format of the graphic. A given graphic constructed differently might give different results, as some ways of showing information might be more favourable to information processing than others.

In an effort to determine the effect of format on processing efficiency before decisions are made, this study concentrates particularly on what the individual does when performing an information processing task using graphics.

THE PROBLEM

Rules for constructing graphics are numerous and varied, but they are rarely based on empirical studies. This causes doubt as to the format that the graphic should follow. The situation is only aggravated by conflicting

Tufte's principles are in opposition with the current tendency of graphic software to generate redundancy. The effects of Tufte's graphics principles have not been analyzed empirically. His theory, however, can be challenged when looked at from a different perspective of perceptual organization, that of "chunks."

THE ORGANIZATION OF INFORMATION BY CHUNKING

The term "chunk" was first used by Miller (1956) to describe "the organization of an input string into coherent groups" (Kintsch, 1977). The gathering of elements into superior units or "chunks" appears to be an efficient means of increasing an individual's memory capacity. "Chunks" can also be processed more quickly than each of their elements taken individually, "the time to process a chunk being less than the time to process its constituent chunks (Rosenbloom and Newell, 1982)."

In his studies on the capacity of information transmission channels, Miller made certain recommendations that aimed at increasing that capacity. One of those recommendations originated from Eriksen, and stipulates that redundancy of elements, at least when using simple signals, increases the capacity of a channel (Eriksen and Hake, 1955), facilitates the formation of "chunks", and improves processing.

A graphic representation permitting an individual to better gather data into "chunks" should therefore lead to more efficient processing. Considering that "chunks" are the result of a visual communication process, it is possible to arrange the format of graphic in order to favour "chunking." However, the perceptual organization principles governing "chunk" formation are not yet sufficiently understood, so the effect of graphic format cannot be predicted. The principle simply says that "perceptual organization tends to move in the direction of a regular, simple, meaningful, and stable percept" (Kintsch, 1977). Eriksen and Hake (1955) demonstrated that the use of multidimensional stimuli increases an individual's ability to discriminate. The multidimensional stimuli strategy, when applied to graphics, is reflected by the use of several elements representing the data. A graphic comprising several elements should therefore produce a format that would facilitate the formation of "chunks", making the graphic easier to process.

HYPOTHESES

Tufte's recommendations lead to graphic presentation formats that are very different from those suggested by Eriksen and Hake's recommendations. According to Eriksen and Hake, redundancy of elements facilitates the formation of "chunks", thereby increasing the capacity of the channel. Graphic forms displaying redundancy of information therefore have a positive effect on processing efficiency. Tufte, however, feels that information redundancy should be avoided in graphics. He says that graphics displaying minimal redundancy are more efficient. This difference reports on the impact of presentation formats on performance (Lucas and Neilsen, 1980; Jarvenpaa, 1986). It is therefore imperative that presentation formats be found that will be properly processed by the individual.

The search for rules for constructing graphics involves several fields of study, from cognitive psychology to decision making, and also touches such technical considerations as global density. Cognitive psychology claims to avoid information overloads (Bertin, 1983; Ives, 1982) and to select and summarize the information to be presented (Mitchell, 1983). It also respects the individual's reference framework by presenting information in a form that is compatible to him, in accordance with his expectations (Rasmusen, 1983; Gaines, 1978).

Communications theory emphasizes language principles: integrity of meaning must be assured for messages sent from the person who transmits the information to the one who receives it (Foley and Wallace, 1974; Simcox, 1984). It also emphasizes psychological principles: psychological obstructions must be avoided (Foley and Wallace, 1974). Certain studies have shown that the optimal global density (i.e. the number of characters used over the total number of characters possible) for graphics designed to be presented on monitor screens is around 25% (Tullis, 1983).

FIG. 1

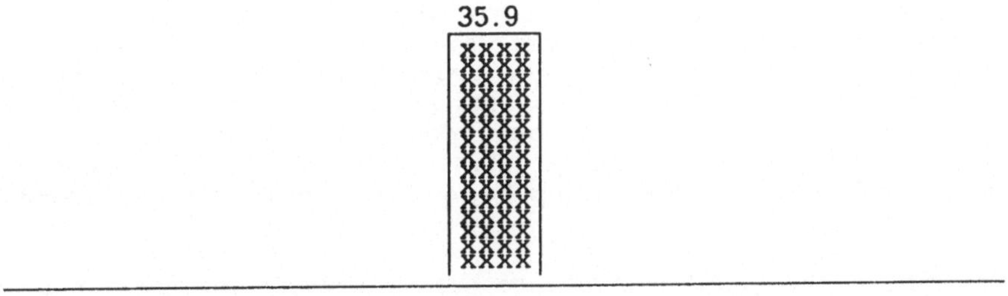

THE SIX REPRESENTATIONS OF A BAR GRAPH

TUFTE'S THEORY

Whereas all the above mentioned theories suggest rules for constructing graphics, they do not lead to any formal theory. Tufte (1983), on the other hand, put forward a theory for constructing graphics which permits information to be communicated clearly, precisely and efficiently. A bar graph may represent information in six different ways: the height of the left vertical line, the height of the right vertical line, the height of the shading, the position of the horizontal line, the position of the numeral, and the value of the numeral (see Fig. 1). Tufte suggests that only one of these elements be used, as the others are redundant. He says that the graphic should draw attention to the information's meaning and substance, and not to ornamentation. Redundancy of information must be avoided at all costs.

in opinion engenders the following question: which graphic format can be processed most efficiently, the one displaying minimal redundancy, or the one containing several redundant elements?

Tufte's principles lead to the conception of supposedly better graphic forms. In this study, a graphic form was considered more efficient than another when the time required to process it was shorter (Bertin, 1983). Both the underlying action of information processing and the effect of graphic format on processing efficiency could be determined by measuring the length of reaction time required to execute a task. Reaction time corresponded to the length of time measured between the presentation of the graphic and the subject's response.

Eriksen and Hake's empirical results lead us to believe that the number of elements that permits the best processing is superior to one. This leads us to our first hypothesis:

HYP1: There are significant differences in processing time for graphics containing different numbers of elements.

There is another factor that influences the processing time for a graphic: the difficulty of the task. Such difficulty can be attributed to the vertical distance separating two targets to be compared, to their horizontal distance, and to the type of task. In this experiment, vertical distance (i.e. the difference in height) was maintained constant while horizontal distance (i.e. the position of the targets) varied. The task, which consisted in comparing two targets, remained constant. Considering that no other similar study had ever been done, it was impossible to predict the effect of the position of the targets. Such positioning, however, could affect processing time. Our second hypothesis therefore is as follows:

HYP2: There are significant differences in processing time for graphics where targets to be compared are located at different positions.

METHOD

The graphic form used for this experiment was the bar graph. The six elements defined by Tufte and described above lead to 63 possible combinations. The left and right vertical lines lead to symmetrical combinations. All combinations with the right vertical line were eliminated, as they were symmetrical to those with the left vertical line: 47 combinations were therefore retained for this experiment. Table 1 shows the number of combinations retained in relation to the number of elements.

Apart from the number of elements, we also investigated the position of the two targets to be compared. Three different positions were used: the targets were separated by one, three, or five columns. This procedure was sufficient for determining whether position affects processing efficiency. Considering that each bar graph contained seven columns, the third position implied that the targets were located one at each end. Three graphics were made for each combination of elements, for a total of 141 graphics (see example in Fig. 2).

TABLE 1

Number of elements	1	2	3	4	5	6	
No. of combinations	5	11	14	11	5	1	47

COMBINATIONS RETAINED IN RELATION TO NUMBER OF ELEMENTS

The seven values of each bar graph were generated at random, and were set between 10 and 20 inclusively. Columns on the bar graphs were separated by blank spaces that were equivalent to 30% of the total width occupied by a column and a blank space. The horizontal line under the columns was retained; the vertical axis was eliminated. The letters identifying the columns were located under the horizontal line, at the center of each column. The letters "A" to "H" were used, except for the letter "B" which was dropped because of its resemblance to the number "8". The positions of the letters "A" to "H" were determined randomly, but with the condition that the letters "A" and "C" respect the three positions studied. The absolute difference between the values of A and C was maintained constant and equal to three, with a probability of 50% that A would be greater than C. Each graphic was presented to the subjects with a tachistoscope linked to a mini computer which recorded reaction times.

FIG. 2

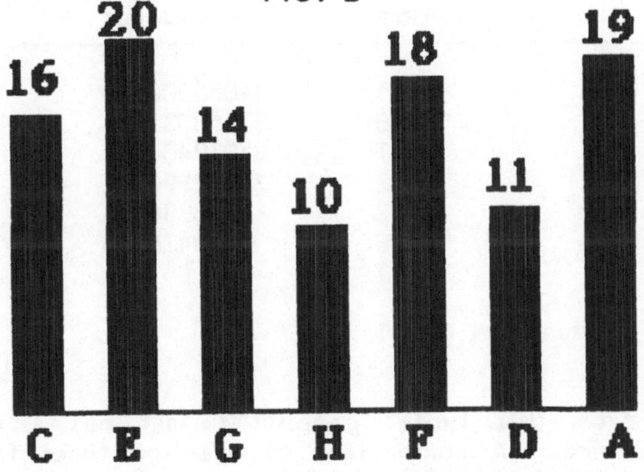

EXAMPLE OF A SIX ELEMENT GRAPHIC

The task that subjects had to accomplish on each graphic was to compare the columns identified A and C, and to indicate which was greater. This task was chosen because one of the strengths of graphic representation is that it permits information to be compared (Tufte, 1983; Zelazny, 1985).

Subjects participated at two experimental sessions of approximately 40 minutes each, on two different days. Each session comprised of a familiarization period to allow subjects to get used to the machines, followed by the passage of a block of 141 graphics, a one minute break, and a second passage of the same 141 graphics. The order of apparition of the graphics was determined at random, and was different for the two sessions. Twenty-two subjects participated in the experiment, an adequate number in studies using reaction time (Townsend, 1984). The subjects were either university students or graduates, aged between 20 and 34 years old. There were 13 men, and 9 women. Each subject provided reaction times on 4 blocks of 141 graphics for a maximum total of 564 readings per subject. Of the 12 408 readings recorded, some had to be eliminated because of technical errors.

RESULTS

Using a completely randomized factorial design (Kirk, 1982), two variance analyses were performed in order to determine the variables that influence reaction time (RT). The first took into account the graphic factor, whereas the second classed the graphics according to the number of elements they contained, analyzing the element factor. Table 2 shows the results of the first analysis.

TABLE 2

VARIANCE ANALYSIS OF REACTION TIME

Source	Degrees of Freedom	Sum of the Squares	F Value
Subject	21	2440540066.8	*2289.13
Graphic	46	322580318.3	*17.45
Session	1	670194544.6	*1667.34
Position	2	232325905.2	*289.00
Graphic*Position	92	167783988.3	*4.54
Graphic*Session	46	21434380.8	1.16
Session*Position	2	6527.0	0.01

* Significant at 0.001

As can be seen from this table, graphic format has a very significant effect on reaction time. A comparison of reaction times for each graphic using Scheffe's test (Kirk,1982) enabled us to determine which graphics which were significantly different from the others, where alpha = 0.001. A more in-depth analysis of the elements comprising the ten graphics showing the fastest reaction time (Table 3) indicated that "shading" was the most frequent element (90%), followed by the left vertical line (70%). The least frequent element was the value of the numeral (40%). The number of elements varied between 2 and 5, with an average of 3.5.

TABLE 3

THE TEN GRAPHICS SHOWING THE FASTEST REACTION TIMES

Graphic #	LVL	RVL	HL	SH	POS	VAL	Number of Elements
21	X	X		X			3
34	X			X			2
9	X	X	X	X			4
37			X	X			2
6	X	X		X	X	X	5
15	X	X			X	X	4
29			X	X		X	3
17	X	X		X	X		4
14			X	X	X	X	4
11	X		X	X	X		4
Total	7	5	5	9	5	4	35

KEY:

LVL	Left Vertical Line;	RVL	Right Vertical Line
HL	Horizontal Line;	SH	Shading
POS	Position of Numeral;	VAL	Value of Numeral

The element analysis of the ten graphics showing the longest reaction time (Table 4) indicated that "shading" was almost always absent. (The right vertical line could not be used to interpret the graphics because certain figures had been eliminated at the outset). The two elements "position" and" value of the numeral" were present in these graphics 60% and 50% of the time respectively. The number of elements varied between 1 and 3, with an average of 2.

This type of analysis by graphics brings to light the phenomenon that elements do not all have the same effect. They can therefore not be chosen arbitrarily. "Shading", which came up the most often, corresponds to Tufte's intuitive choice, where shading was the only element retained. However, analysis by graphics does not enable us to discern either the impact of the number of elements or the phenomenon that would explain the overall results. We therefore performed a second variance analysis on the number of elements.

Table 5 shows the results of this analysis. The three variables identified here--session, position, and subject--were also identified in the first variance analysis in Table 2.

The results of the two sessions showed a difference in average reaction time (RT) of 466.1 ms (Table 6). The inferior average RT in the second session can be attributed to the fact that subjects had learned how to use the equipment, and had become accustomed to the task and to the graphic formats.

TABLE 4

THE TEN GRAPHICS SHOWING THE LONGEST REACTION TIMES

Graphic of #	LVL	RVL	HL	SH	POS	VAL	Number Elements
19	X	X				X	3
44			X				1
27	X			X	X		3
40					X	X	2
35	X				X		2
28			X		X	X	3
41			X			X	2
42			X		X		2
47					X		1
45						X	1
Total	3	1	4	1	6	5	20

KEY:

LVL	Left Vertical Line;	RVL.	Right Vertical Line
HL	Horizontal Line;	SH	Shading
POS	Position of Numeral;	VAL	Value of Numeral

The results for the number of elements is also significant at 0.001. Fig. 3 shows the relation between reaction time and the number of elements. Note that reaction time decreases with the number of elements in a graphic. These results refute the null hypothesis and confirm our first hypothesis.

TABLE 5

VARIANCE ANALYSIS OF REACTION TIME WITH THE ELEMENT VARIABLE

Source	Degree of Freedom	Sum of the Squares	Value of F
Subject	21	2440540066.8	*279.70
Graphic	1	668635379.7	*1557.42
Session	5	93567723.2	*43.59
Position	2	232653488.2	*270.95
Graphic*Position	5	446886.9	0.21
Graphic*Session	2	7401.3	0.01
Session*Position	10	16372241.2	*3.81

* Significant at 0.001

Moreover, the results clarify the contradiction between Tufte's statement and Eriksen and Hake's results. Tufte's principle requiring that all redundant information be erased is refuted by the results of our study. In fact the opposite is true, as the use of several elements guarantees a more efficient and more rapid processing.

Variance analysis also indicates that the position variable - the distance between the two targets to be compared - is very important to reaction time. Such significant results confirm our second hypothesis. The best reaction time was obtained with position 3, where the two targets were at each end of the graphic, whereas position 1, where the targets were separated by a single data, resulted in the longest reaction time. These results can be explained by the shorter time required to identify a base for comparison when elements are located at the extremities of a bar graph rather than within.

TABLE 6

AVERAGE REACTION TIME PER SESSION

	Session	Average RT (ms)
1	6187	2951.6
2	6163	2485.5
	Difference:	*466.1

* Significant at 0.01

As the interaction between the position variable and the element variable (Table 5) was found to be significant, subsequent trend analyses between reaction times and the number of elements were done independently for each level of the position factor. Those analyses showed that the linear trend predominates in all positions.

This trend indicates that reaction time decreased as the number of elements was increased. In other words, we observed a redundancy gain in every position. The interaction is explained by the fact that this gain is more accentuated when the targets are in the third position (at the extremities of the bar graph).

In short, the results of this experiment confirmed both hypotheses, and supported the following propositions in cases where reaction time is used to measure performance:

1- The format of a bar graph significantly influences processing efficiency. The choice of elements is important. Shading proved to be a common element (90% ofthe time) in the ten most efficient graphics. But, shading alone is not enough.

2- The number of elements used to represent information in a bar graph significantly influences processing efficiency. In general, using six elements is more efficient than using only one.

3- The position of targets to be compared significantly influences processing efficiency. Targets that are easy to locate might take less time to process.

FIG. 3

RELATION BETWEEN REACTION TIME AND NUMBER OF ELEMENTS

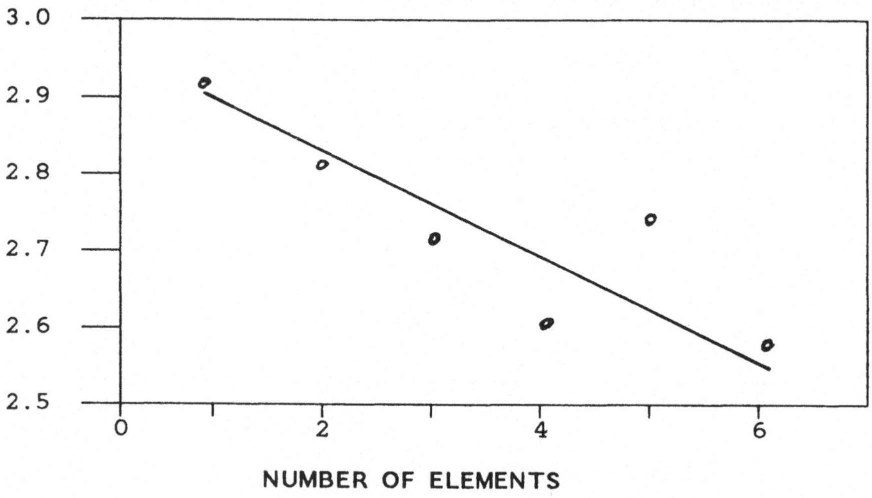

CONCLUSION

This laboratory study determined the validity of several rules stemming from theories on constructing graphics. The results indicate that the different forms of that a bar graph can take, whether considered individually or in groups classified according to the number of elements or to target position, are all significantly linked to processing efficiency.

Practically speaking, the results of this study seem to suggest a certain number of rules: -the use of several elements in a graphic guarantees more efficient processing; -the difficulty of a task where graphic items are to be compared is more a result of the location of those items than of the horizontal distance separating them.

Redundancy of information should therefore be emphasized, and- items to be compared should be located so as to make it easier for the decision maker to identify them. In further studies, a model for graphic information processing should be developed and verified to take into account such things as colour, which was not looked at in this study. Furthermore, it would be interesting to increase the number of sessions included in this experiment in order to eliminate possible interference caused by subjects learning how to perform the ask.

BIBLIOGRAPHY

BERTIN, Jacques, Semiology of Graphics, translation by William J. Berg, Wisconsin, Wisconsin Press, 1983.

ERIKSEN, Charles W., HAKE, Harold W., "Multidimensional Stimulus differences and Accuracy of Discrimination", Journal of Experimental Psychology, vol. 50, no.3, pp. 153-160, 1955.

FOLEY, James D., "The Art of Natural Graphic Man-Machine Conversation", Proceedings of the IEEE, vol. 62, no. 4, pp. 462-471, 1974.

IVES, Blake, "Graphical User Interfaces for Business Information Systems", MIS Quarterly, Special Issue, pp. 15-46, 1982.

JARVENPAA, Sirkka-Liisa, An investigation of the Effects of Choice Tasks and Graphics on Information Processing Strategies and Decision Making Performance, Abstract and General Results, Doctoral Dissertation, University of Minnesota, Minnesota, 1986.

KINTSCH, Walter, Memory and Cognition, New York, John Wiley & Sons, 1977.

KIRK, R.E., Experimental design: Procedures for the Behavioral Sciences, Belmont, Brooks / Cole Publishing Company, 1982.

LUCAS, Henry C. et NEILSEN, Norman R., "The Impact of the Mode of Information presentation on Learning and Performance", Management Science, vol. 26, no. 10, pp. 982-993, 1980.

LUCAS, Henry C., "An Experimental Investigation of the Use of Computer-Based Graphics in Decision Making", Management Science, vol. 27, no. 7, pp. 757-768, 1981.

MARTIN, James, Design of Man-Computer Dialogues, New Jersey, Prentice Hall, 1973.

MILLER, George A., "The Magical Number Seven, Plus or Minus Two: Some Limits on our Capacity for Processing Information", The Psychological Review, vol. 63, no. 2, pp. 81-97, 1956.

MITCHELL, Christine M., "Design Strategies for Computer-Based Information Displays in Real-Time Control Systems", Human Factors, vol. 25, no. 4, pp. 353-369, 1983.

NEWELL, A., SIMON, H.A., Human Problem Solving, New Jersey, Prentice Hall, 1972.

RASMUSSEN, Jens, "Skills, Rules, and Knowledge: Signals, Signs, and Symbols, and Other Distinctions in Human Performance Models", IEEE Transactions on Systems, Man, and Cybernetics, vol. 13, no. 3, pp. 257-266, 1983.

ROSENBLOOM, Paul S., NEWELL, Allen, "Learning by Chunking Summary of a Task and a Model", Proceedings of the AAAI, The National Conference on Artificial Intelligence, Pittsburg, 1982.

SIMCOX, William A., "A Method for Pragmatic Communication in Graphic Displays", Human Factors, vol. 26, no. 4. pp. 483-487, 1984.

TOWNSEND, James T., "Uncovering Mental Processes with Factorial Experiments", Journal of Mathematical Psychology, vol. 28, pp. 363-400, 1984.

TUFTE, Edward R., The Visual Display of Quantitative Information, Connecticut, Graphics Press, 1983.

TULLIS, Thomas S., "The Formatting of Alphanumeric Display: A Review and Analysis", Human Factors, vol. 25, no. 6, pp. 657-682, 1983.

ZELAZNY, Gene, Say It With Charts, Illinois, Dow Jones Irwin, 1985.

Development of an Integrated Computer Art System

M. King (UK)

Abstract

An 'Integrated Computer Art System' is described which offers the computer artist, illustrator and designer a much wider range of 2D manipulations than in conventional paint systems. The system allows non-programmers to explore a range of techniques based on computer geometries and algorithms, including certain types of fractals, in an interactive fashion, while still giving full control down to the pixel level. The system is under development, but already shows potential for generating new computer imagery not belonging to the now 'conventional' world of 3D photo-realism.

Introduction

Computer graphics has long been associated with 3D scene simulation, with increasing compute-power devoted to the techniques of photo-realism. For the artist, illustrator and graphic designer these methods have limited use, and they have found the 2D paint system, with all its limitations, to be more suited to their budgets, needs and abilities. Paint systems have a well established nature by now, and do not receive the intensive research effort that photo-realism is still receiving. In my proposed 'Integrated Computer Art System' (ICAS) I am trying to redress the balance by extending the paint system concept with an increased functionality that addresses the needs of the non-programming computer artist and designer. ICAS, in brief, provides a mixture of paint and object-oriented techniques with additional features including pattern-making, tesselations and interactive fractals. The range of facilities have been selected by a careful consideration of what the computer can offer to the artist and designer working in two dimensions, based on a range of old and 'new' geometries. The system can also be used to create three dimensional imagery, but not based on the usual computing techniques of photo-realism. These are too restricting to the artist, for whom a personal feel for depth, light, shade and perspective is what gives their work a unique character.

1) The concepts behind ICAS

In a paper entitled 'Towards an Integrated Computer Art System' (King 1987) I outlined the basis for ICAS, building on my PhD research (King 1986), while this paper presents the results of implementing some of those proposals. The PhD thesis concluded that the computer provides for a range of new media in the visual arts, and that their user interfaces are an essential part of the media. In the thesis I developed a taxonomy of computer art media, and some new terms which describe concepts that I feel are important in this area, and I will briefly summarise these here.

The first distinction that I have made is between interactive and scripted systems. In interactive systems the user is not required to program the system, and most of the image-making involves a high level of hand-eye feedback, as in a paint system. Scripted systems, in contast, imply the creation of a program script, usually text-based, and its subsequent execution for the realisation of the imagery. Feedback is thus through a write - execute - rewrite cycle.

The creation of imagery in either type of system is by synthesis from primitives, except where image processing or equivalent techniques are used, in which case a degree of image analysis is also needed. The concept of synthesis from primitives is a very important one in this context, and is what makes art and design applications of computers unique. Most computing applications revolve around information retrieval and analysis, with the reduction of a large data base into a few concise conclusions a frequent goal. Alvey Ray Smith (1984) recgnised this when he coined the term ´data base amplification´ for the techniques behind a range of computer generated imagery. The creative and synthetic aspects of computer art and design systems has not received a large amount of attention however, and the concepts that I am introducing here should help to make a more detailed discussion of these applications possible.

In the context of synthesis from primitives I make a second important distinction: between arbitrary and algorithmic synthesis from primitives, and indeed much of what follows depends on this distinction. Arbitrary synthesis from primitives involves a sequence of operations on the medium that derive from the artistic whim or intuition of the user - the machine has no ´understanding´ of the sequence or control over it. Algorithmic synthesis involves a sequence of operations governed by a set of rules that are communicated to the machine and encapsulated in a machine-executable algorithm. As a simple example the incorporation of set or coloured pixels following a free-hand curve in a paint system is arbitrary, while the incorporation of pixels in a (Bresenham) straight line is algorithmic. One of the challenges of any art medium is the balance between algorithmic and arbitrary techniques, and I believe it to be especially so with computer art. In looking at algorithms used by computer artists and computer graphics researchers since the sixties to generate imagery, I have realised that these can all be considered as embodiments of different types of geometry. Looking more closely at these algorithms or geometries, it seemed that they could conveniently be classified as ´classical´ or ´recursive´ geometries, and I have listed a ´computer artist´s geometrical toolkit´ under these two headings:

The Computer Artist´s Geometrical Toolkit

CLASSICAL GEOMETRIES
. geometries of parallel lines, triangles, rectangles and polygons
. the conic sections: circle, ellipse, parabola and hyperbola
. nets, bands and tesselations
. non-recursive functions
. Lissajou´s figures, cardioids and cycloids
. parametric curves

RECURSIVE GEOMETRIES

. iterative functions (recurrence relations)
. random numbers
. recursive patterns
. fractals and graftals
. particle systems
. growth models
. linear and array grammars
. Markov chains

2) Proposed structure of ICAS and progress to date

The proposed structure of ICAS, outlined in King (1987), was a two-level system, with an object-oriented or drafting level from which one could ´descend´ into a paint level. The drafting level was to provide the usual object-oriented manipulations, but greatly extended in terms of pattern-making, tesselations and fractals (recursively substituted shapes). The paint mode allows for pixel-editing of the output from the drafting mode, raster-based cut and paste, and more gestural and expressive free-hand work.

In the object-oriented or drafting mode the intention was to implement a wide range of the geometries listed above in the ´toolkit´. However, because one can never anticipate all the possible needs of the user, and because some geometries are difficult or clumsy to control interactively, it is intended that ICAS should include a scripted component, which would manipulate the image through the creation of small ´scripts´ or programs.

Development effort so far has concentrated on the integration of a drafting medium and a paint system. The drafting aspect has allowed for a comprehensive range of manipulations not easily provided for in paint systems, and also the implementation of the sophisticated pattern-making facilities, and some interactive fractals. The system is written in C and runs on IBM PC compatibles driving an Io Research Ltd 8 bit per pixel frame store. The data structure for the drafting mode is a doubly-linked list of nodes, each containing a field identifying the primitive (line, poly-line, rectangle, filled rectangle, circle etc), and fields containing the variables of instantiation (position, size and colour). The sequence of the linked list determines the order of drawing, so that for the user to change the layering the sequence has to be changed by changing the pointers in the list. Superimposed on the list is a tree-structure reflecting the hierarchy that the user imposes on the drawing by creating groupings. The tree-structure is implemented using grouping nodes that are pointed to by the elements in the group, and that point back in turn to the elements. The group nodes also contain information on the extents of the group. An individual group is manipulated by recursively descending its structure until primitives are reached.

3) Work-table philosophy

Normally in a paint system all the user´s input is stored as a modification to the array of pixels in a frame buffer, and recovery from the latest modification is only possible if multiple picture planes are available (these are expensive and give only limited recovery). Scaling up or down results in a sampling effect and picture degradation, and hence the full screen tends to be in use for the image in a paint system. Whatever the resolution, the user is unlikely to want to give up portions of the screen ´real-estate´ to menus, palettes, and icons representing various ´tools´. These tend to be stored off-screen and blitted onto the screen when required. This means that spare frame-buffer capacity is required for interactive systems, and is of course expensive. One of the tricky parts of designing a paint system on a limited budget, is that often there is little spare memory.

With an object-oriented or drafting system the problems of scaling up and down are reduced because of the underlying (vector) description of the picture. In the design of ICAS I have therefore used only some 80% of the screen for the image in drafting mode, while using the entire screen for paint mode. The advantage of working in the drafting mode is that all the tools are at hand, as illustrated in Fig. 1.

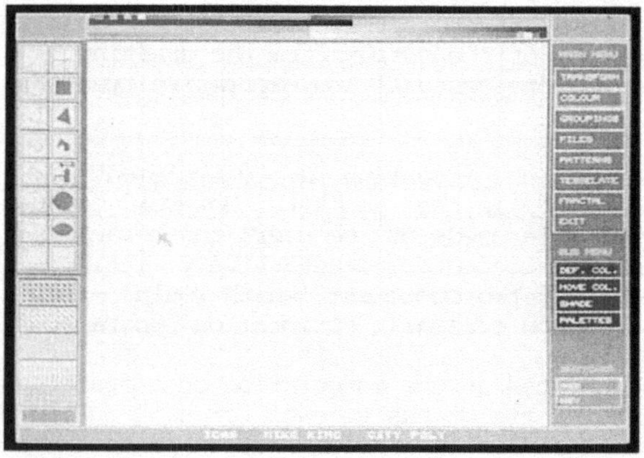

Fig. 1 Screen layout of the ICAS ´work-table´

I call this a ´work-table´ approach, because it more closely parallels a traditional artist´s work table, on which one would have to hand brushes, paints, geometrical instruments and so on. The paint system approach of blitting up the palette and menus for every single change of colour, brush and operation is a bit like keeping all these items in a drawer under your table, with the added complication that opening the drawer obscures part of the art-work! This is not to be taken as a criticism of windows in general - it is just an awkward way to work in this particular application. Coming back to the work-table philosophy, the work area can in fact be used to store many motifs, scraps of design and so on. The ability to reduce a fragment down and place it in a corner for later use adds greatly to the power of the system. While the work table is useful in the construction of an image, it is a nuisance in that the shapes and colours in the menus and palettes are distracting from the overall composition and effect of the created image. Artists get round this by pinning a work in progress to a blank wall where one can more easily judge the composition. In ICAS this need is taken into acount by a facility that removes the surrounding menus and palettes and re-draws the image to full scale - as it would be seen on exit to paint mode. A press of a key then returns the user to the work table with the reduced image for further manipulation. One would typically go in and out of the work table a number of times in the creation of a finished product, in order to judge its progress.

4) Design and motif creation

The basic techniques while in drafting mode are similar to those found in Macdraw - a drafting system for the Apple Macintosh. The common techniques of rubber-banding, dragging, and echoing the selection of an item by highlighting are provided, along with a method for capturing items for manipulation as a group. Because the palette is always visible, smooth shaded polygons can be easily created by selecting a new colour between vertices. Flood-fills are provided, and can be individually deleted by traversing a stored list of them which highlights them in turn. Figures 2 to 9 show the sequence of creation of some images, and also illustrates the range of imagery that the system is capable of. Some of the images contain lines that have been ´roughened´ by a function provided within the fractal menu (described later).

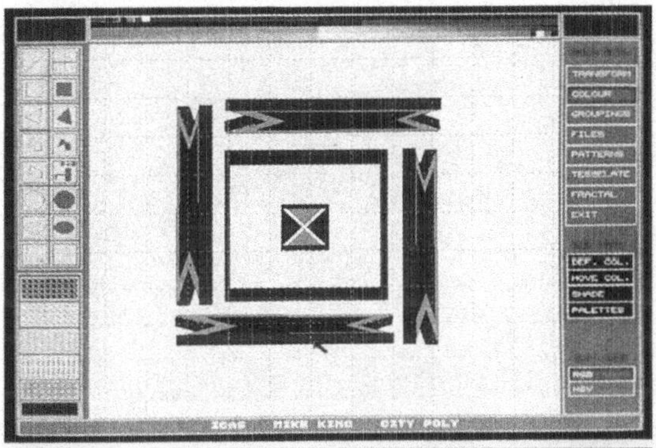

Fig. 2 First part of a design created using mirror, rotate and copy

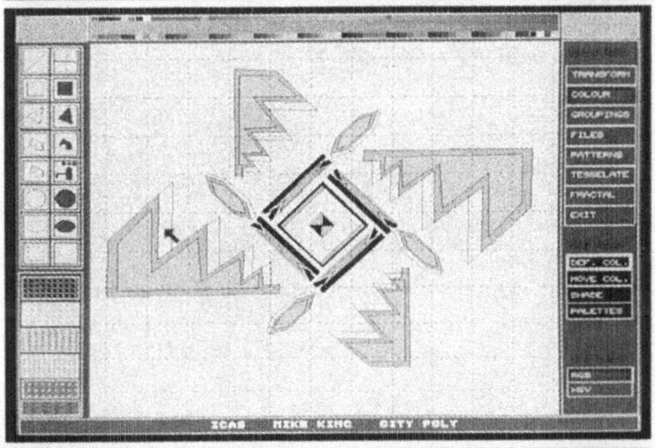

Fig. 3 Design reduced and rotated and more elements added

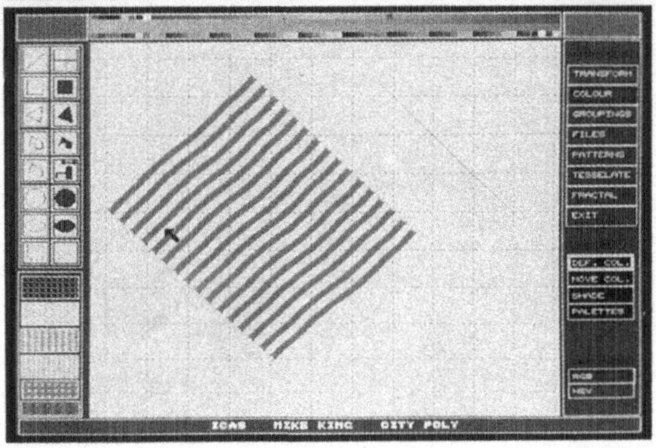

Fig. 4 A series of ´roughened´ lines are created

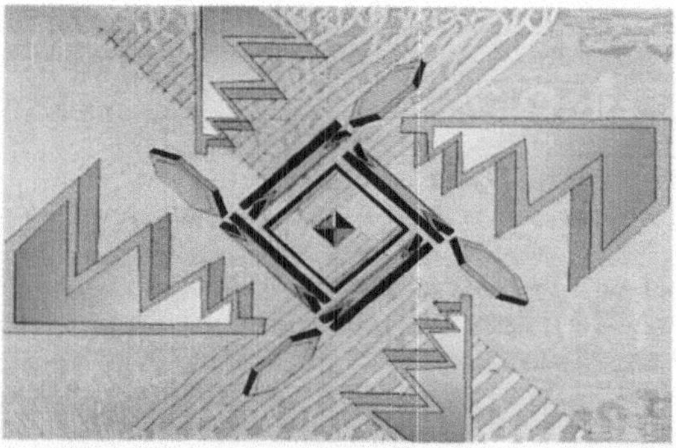

Fig. 5 The previous designs are combined using cut and paste, and free-hand elements added in paint mode

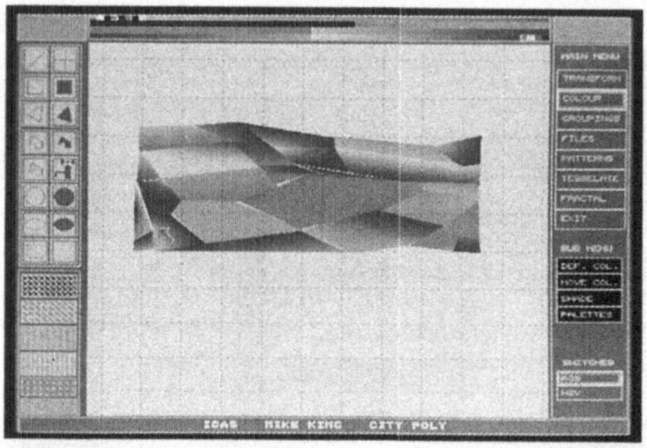

Fig. 6 First stage of a design using shaded polygons

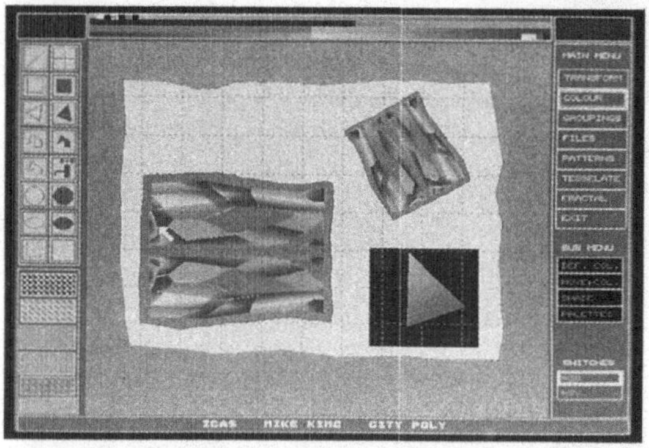

Fig. 7 The polygons are grouped as a whole, scaled, mirrored and rotated, and other elements added

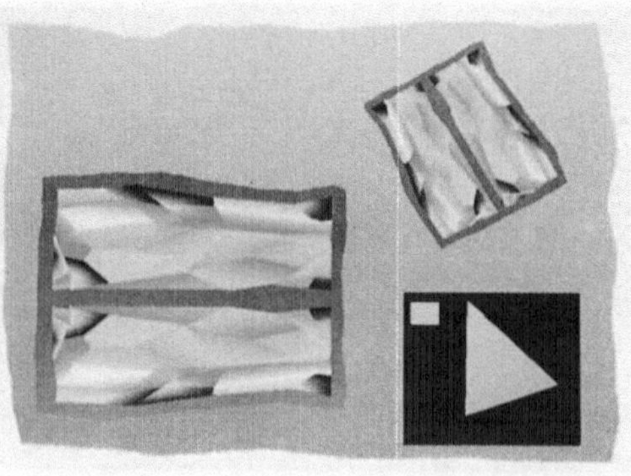

Fig. 8 The final image cut and pasted in paint mode

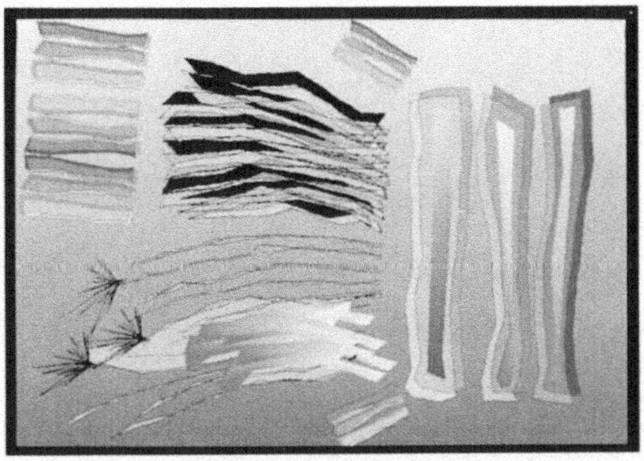

Fig. 9 Mostly drafting techniques are used in this abstract composition

5) Pattern-making

I regard pattern-making as one of the classical computer geometries, and an obvious area for exploitation by computers in art and design. At present various arrangements of motifs can be displayed, based loosely on a classification in MacGregor and Watt (1984). The user designs a motif, usually to a large a scale as possible, and then scales it down for repeating. Because of the data-structure underlying the motif the scaling down can be safely performed, secure in the knowledge that it will scale up perfectly. The work-table philosophy comes into play again with pattern-making, because only the currently selected grouping is patterned. The pattern covers the entire screen, the work-table at first disappearing. On the work-table can be any number of motifs and scraps of design, and of course these all re-appear on return to drafting mode. Figure 10 shows the ICAS work-table with some motifs and the following figures show some sample patterns.

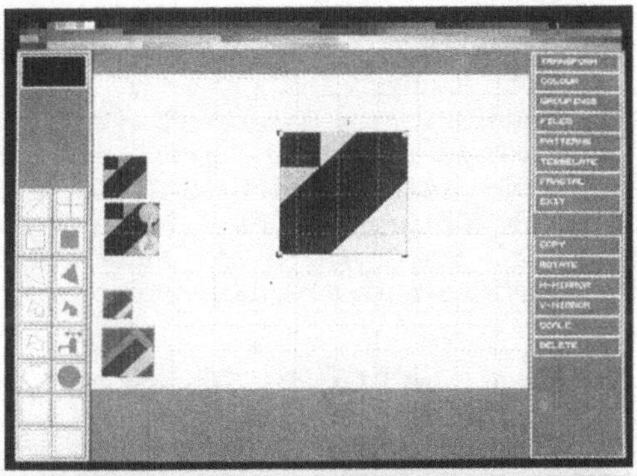

Fig. 10 ICAS work-table with some motifs for patterning

Fig. 11 A simple pattern

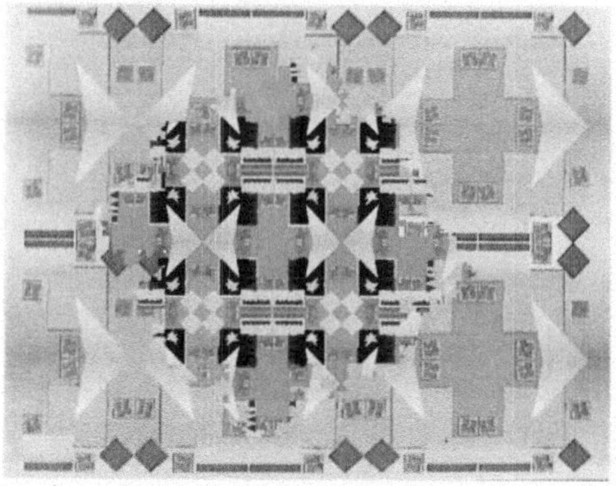

Fig. 12 A combination of patterns

The system has been used by myself and a few students so far, and it is surprising how fast one can experiment with different motifs and groupings. Important elements of pattern-making are rapidly made apparent: the difference of the final effect with the same motif but with different groupings, and for any given motif and grouping the arising of ´emergent forms´. These are shapes created by the gaps between the elements of the motif, and also the longer thrusts of pattern, which range from harmonious to disturbing in their overall effect.

Tesellations are not yet implemented, but will again be done at the drafting level. A tesselation differs from the patterns created through the 17 network groups in a few essential ways. The key to a tesselation is its outline, not just its orientation. One can think of a tesselation as consisting of a plane covered with identical blank tiles, whose outlines fill the plane without gaps, and whose outlines mark out the image. A form that tesselates may vary from a rectangular tile to the intricate figurative shapes of Escher, and may or my not be decorated with motifs. If the form for tesselation is decorated with a motif there is no requirement that the motif should interlock - it is just the outline that is important. Figure 13 shows the basis on which ICAS will provide interactive tesselations. As with patterns the tesselation will be generated full-screen for exit to paint mode, or, on return to the work-table, the complete tesselation can be incorporated into the data-structure for subsequent manipulation.

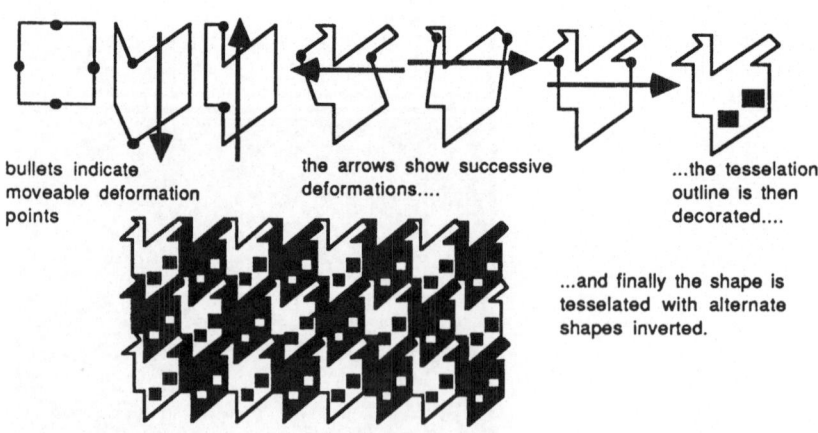

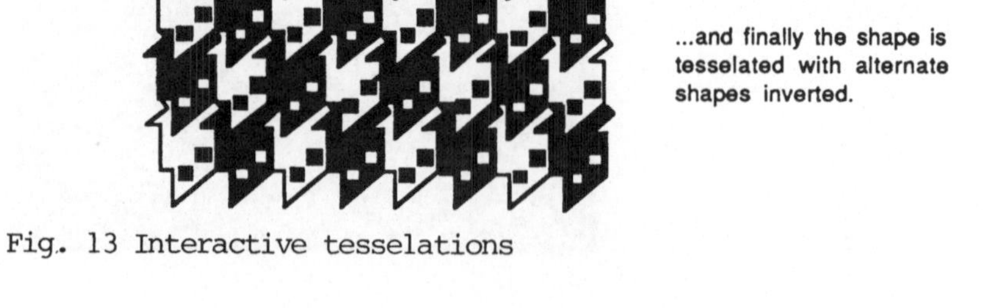

bullets indicate moveable deformation points
the arrows show successive deformations....
...the tesselation outline is then decorated....
...and finally the shape is tesselated with alternate shapes inverted.

Fig. 13 Interactive tesselations

6) Interactive fractals

All the previous facilities so far described are based on what I have called the classical geometries. I have also introduced some recursive geometries into the system with the provision of some simple fractals. These are based on the recursive substitution of a collection of line segments (called the generator) into another collection of line segments (initiator). At its simplest this is provided by a function called ´roughen´ which uses a simple built-in generator consisting of 3 line segments. More interesting fractals can be created by the use of user-defined generators however. As with pattern-making and tesselations the system ´goes out´ to full screen to draw the selected fractalised initiator. The resulting image depends on the sense of both initiator and generator - i.e whether they are drawn clockwise or anticlockwise, leading in the case of the Von Koch snowflake to the normal or anti-snowflake (see Mandelbrot, 1982). The generated fractal image can be ´incorporated´ on return to the work-table, for manipulation in ways already described. Figure 14 shows some examples.

Fig. 14 Fractal trees cut and paste with recursive rectangles

As with most algorithmic synthesis from primitives, once the degree of data base ´amplification´ goes over a certain (fairly low) level, the results (first time) are unpredictable, though deterministic. The nature of the results can be anticipated with experience, and it is exactly this experience that ICAS can so rapidly provide to the artist and designer, both with classical and recursive techniques.

7) Exit to Paint

On ´exit to paint´ the palettes and menus are removed and the image drawn full-scale, or, in the case of patterns, tesselations and fractals, the current selection only is ´patterned out´ to full size. The image is now manipulated at a paint level, with the normal low level of editing. Colour and look-up table manipulation is provided, and indeed the paint component of ICAS is full-functioned enough to be sufficient for the needs of many artists. I have found with some of my students that both classical and recursive geometries hold little interest for them at first; they find the expressive capabilities of TV resolution 8-bit painting quite sufficient, and sufficiently different from conventional media to be exciting. However, the point of ICAS is to extend the paint system to include techniques that are unique to the computer, either because the technique allows increases of orders of magnitude in speed of execution (object-oriented manipulations, pattern-making and tesselations), or because the technique is in practice impossible to realise by hand (for example fractals).

8) The next step: constraint-driven geometries

The concept of using constraints to describe geometrical problems to the computer goes back to Sketchpad, through Smalltalk (Byte 1981) and ThingLab (Borning 1979) to Greg Nelson´s Juno system (Nelson 1985). I plan to make a constraint-solver the scripted component of ICAS. I conceive the scripted component of ICAS to be closely integrated with the rest of the system and to look very little like a conventional high-level programming language. The ideas put forward by Greg Nelson and his forerunners will be the starting point, with the interesting challenge of developing constraint-driven recursive geometries. Imagery from chaotic functions (one of the recursive geometries in my classification) could be generated by scripts of a few lines.

Conclusion

ICAS is something like half-way towards fulfilling the original concept and has already shown interesting results, not just in term of the range of imagery produced with the system, but also in terms of user interface design. I believe that the development of such systems, taking place outside the research thrust into photo-realism in computer graphics, will have an impact on the visual language of a new generation of artists and designers. By extending the paint system with increased control over both old and new geometries, the non-programming artist has direct access to a new world of imagery.

References

Borning 1979
Borning, Alan, "Thinglab - a Constraint-Oriented Simulation Laboratory" SSL-79-3, Xerox PARC, Palo Alto CA July 1979.

King 1986
King, M.R., "Computer Media in the Visual Arts and their User Interfaces" PhD thesis, Royal College of Art, London 1986.

King 1987
King, M.R., "Towards an Integrated Computer Art System" in Earnshaw, R.A. and Lansdown, R.J., (eds.) "State of the Art in Computer Art and Animation" conference proceedings, Springer-Verlag, 1987.

MacGregor and Watt 1984
Macgregor, J. and Watt, A., "The Art of Microcomputer Graphics" Addison-Wesley Publishing Co., 1984.

Mandelbrot 1982
Mandelbrot, B.B., "Fractals: Form, Chance and Dimension" W.H.Freeman and Company.

Nelson 1985
Nelson, G., "Juno, a constraint-based graphics system" Computer Graphics, Volume 19, Number 3, 1985, pp. 235-243.

Smith 1984
Smith, A.L., "Plants, Fractals and Formal Languages" SIGGRAPH ´84, pp. 1-10.

Improving the Programmability of Robotic Workcells

G. Carayannis and A. Malowany (Canada)

Abstract

In this paper we briefly describe WRAP (Workcell ReAl-time Programming) which provides an integrated run-time/programming environment for a distributed robotic workcell. A robotic workcell is a distributed system consisting of a variety of elements such as multiple robots, multiple sensors and other factory machines. To synchronize and coordinate the concurrent operations of these elements WRAP uses a user defined state formalism. A sample idealized assembly application programmed under WRAP is also discussed to illustrate the programming methodology, the power and the flexibility of the system. The assembly workcell consists of two six degree of freedom robots, a linear stage, an overhead camera and a infrared range sensor mounted on one of the robots.

1. Introduction

Robots have evolved since their introduction in industry; both their electrical and mechanical characteristics have improved, and microprocessor technology has provided the computing power needed for path control. Recent sensor technology has made available a wide variety of contact (touch, force) and non-contact (vision, range) sensors at reasonable cost With these advances robotic applications have become more and more demanding; starting from pick-and-place in the 1970s they have grown to require the cooperation of multiple robots, sensors and other factory equipment (conveyor belts, milling machines, etc.) in order to perform complex operations such as assembly, inspection and repair.

Unfortunately such complex systems are very hard to program. Even when the technology exists it is hard to use due to system programming and integration problems: one has to be an expert in each and every aspect of the system in order to be able to cope with its complexity. For the same reasons, existing robotic workcells tied to a specific application cannot be easily adapted to new applications, which defeats the very idea of flexible manufacturing. In order to be able to change this situation, robot and sensor manufacturers should start dealing with the integration aspects at both the hardware and the software levels This has already started with the adoption of MAP [6] as a communication standard within a factory and the development of robot systems which support a host computer link eg. the Unimation VAL II controller In addition a sophisticated workcell programming environment is required that will allow the programmer to think in terms of programming the operations of the complete workcell instead of programming each individual element.

1.1 Robotic Workcell: Elements and programming requirements

This paper deals with the problem of programming a complex robotic system, a *Robotic Workcell* Using our terminology, such a system consists of *Manipulating Elements* (eg. robots, XY-stage), *Sensing Elements* (eg. vision, force), and *Knowledge Elements* (eg. data base, expert system) that are coordinated to perform a given task. For efficiency these elements should operate concurrently, exchange information for synchronization and coordination purposes and consult a database to find information about the 'world around them' and about each other. Elements in these three classes are called *Active* because they perform intended operations. Into a fourth class we place *Passive Elements* such as tools, jigs, trays, feeders and other fixtures.

Associated with each active element there is a 'controller' The 'controller' should not always be viewed as a 'separate box' It could be a 'control process' running on a multiprogrammed computer The level of sophistication of these 'controllers varies according to the complexity and capabilities of the controlled element Supervising the element controllers is the *workcell controller*. This hierarchical structure allows the application programmer to think in terms of operations at the workcell level without being too much concerned about actions at the element level such as the particular path that the robot is going to follow unless this kind of control is desirable The purpose of a robot programming environment is to allow the programmer to alter the operations of the workcell by reprogramming the workcell controller There are some rather important issues to be faced during the design of an environment for robot programming These are

- *Application independence* A knowledgeable programmer should be able to build different application packages using the functions provided by the system.
- *Expandability of the workcell*. It should be easy to integrate new elements into the system in order to expand it or improve the performance of the application.
- *Range of users* The programming environment should provide a natural, high level (ie. robot and sensor independent) interface to the naive user without restricting the experienced robot system programmer.
- *Increased productivity*. The programming environment should help minimize application development time.

- *Error treatment*. The fact that a robotic system interacts with the real world makes errors quite unpredictable. Furthermore, error conditions could be hard to reproduce. The system should be able to deal with hardware or software problems and should know how to to detect and, in the best case, avoid accidents (eg. collisions) [14].

1.2 Robot programming: what has been done to make it achievable

In recent years, a lot of effort and energy has been put into designing more and more sophisticated robot languages in order to allow robot users to easily program more and more complicated robot applications This has resulted in a significant number of robot programming systems and languages developed either by robot manufacturers or research institutions. It is beyond the scope of this paper to detail all these efforts but two good surveys are [7, 15]. It was said that there are as many robot programming languages as robots, and this might not be far from being true. Robot programming languages can be classified in three general classes: *point to point* motion languages, *manipulator* level languages and *task* or *object* level languages With a point to point language the manipulator arm is lead through a sequence of motions which is recorded and then played back at execution time. At the manipulator level, the programmer describes the task as a sequence of positions and orientations of the robot's end effector. Here, the structure of a robot language resembles assembly language. Manipulator level languages provide limited for sensor interaction. This implies that, in general, positions are fixed rather than computed at run time. The third class includes languages that have been the dream of robot programmers Here the programmer deals with intended actions of the manipulator rather than motions of its end effector. Perhaps the best known example of an attempt to develop a *task* level robot language is AUTOPASS, a system for automatic mechanical assembly that was designed at IBM in the late seventies. Task level languages are able to control multiple robots, interface with sophisticated sensors and provide a *high level* robot programming environment.

In general, three approaches have been taken in the design of robot languages. The traditional one is to focus on the semantics of the robot control system. Then, additional language constructs (ie. conditional branching, subroutine calls etc.) are developed on top of the syntax that describes robot motions The design of most robot languages followed this approach. The next approach is to start with an existing general purpose language and extend it by adding the necessary robot control primitives. The advantage here is that the basic language and programming tools already exist. Following this approach RAPT was based on the APT language, and RCCL [17] on C. ADA has also been used as the basis of yet another robot language. The third approach, followed by IBM in the design of the AML language, is to design a new general purpose language, instead of using an existing one, and to extend it with robot control functions. The justification is that certain compromises are already made in existing general purpose languages while design trade-offs in the new language will be selected having the robotics extensions in mind.

Several robot programming systems have been developed and discussed in the robotics literature. Perhaps the most complete one is the hierarchical robot control system, designed and implemented at the Industrial Systems Division of the National Bureau of Standards (USA) by Albus and his co-workers The project started in the seventies [4], but its first realistic application was not reported until 1984 [16]. Each of the seven levels of hierarchy in the NBS Automated Manufacturing Research Facility is divided into a sensor, a world model and a task decomposition part, so that the system can be viewed as three separate hierarchies. a task decomposition hierarchy, a world model hierarchy and a sensor processing (feedback) hierarchy To program the system in a simple way, the three hierarchies implemented as finite state automata The system is programmed using state transitions tables instead of traditional procedural robot programs Each of the seven levels has a pre-defined set of commands. For each command a State Transition table is built this table decomposes the command into a sequence of commands for the level below, and controls their execution [3].

Baird and his colleagues at the RCA laboratories proposed a two level hierarchy to control a robotic workcell, with a cell controller (a PDP 11/34A running RSX-11M) executing a device coordination program to control the workcell devices through dedicated serial link [5] A communication subsystem was implemented using the message passing primitives available in RSX (mailboxes)

Kak and his colleagues at Purdue University have developed an automated assembly cell with two levels of control: a Supervisor, and a Motion Controller as well as a Sensory system. Two databases, the Global Knowledge Base, that stores static information and the Current World Model that stores dynamic information are used to maintain *a priori* knowledge about the world The Supervisor is responsible for generating plans and passing action requests to the Motion controller. The Motion Controller handles the execution of action requests and controls several Motion Execution Units, described as 'augmented versions of a Robot Controller [18].

In the "Laboratoire d'Automatique et d'Analyse des Systèmes du CNRS" in Toulouse (France) R Alami and his colleagues have developed NNS, a LISP-based environment for the integration and setting up of *Flexible Assembly Cells (FACs)* [2]. NNS consists of a two level hierarchy, with a *Master Module (MM)* controlling a set of *Specialized Modules (SMs)*. A SM is a complete software and hardware system that can recognize a set of commands, perform the corresponding activities and return a result. Communication between the MM and the SMs is in terms of Remote Procedure calls. Programming NNS involves writting a Master Module. The user has to worry about the coordination of the operations of the Specialized Modules using a mechanism based on SIGNAL and WAIT primitives. In more recent publications of the same group the problem of programming a FAC is discussed and the concept of a "workcell state" is introduced [1]

Maimon developed the "activity controller" theory to coordinate multiple robots and other automated machines. The system associates a resource supervisor with every shared system resource [20, 21] A resource supervisor prevents access to non free resources, checks the eligibility the requests, and queues and prioritorizes them. SIGNAL and WAIT primitives are used to achieve mutual exclusion. The software is organized as two groups of processes runing on a VAX computer under UNIX, communicating through shared memory; the first is the activity controller and the second a set of communication programs that pass commands to the controlled elements (robots, machines etc).

We have developed WRAP, a flexible, application independent runtime environment for programming robotic workcells. WRAP hides the burdensome details of the workcell elements from the application programmer allowing him to think in terms of programming the operations of the complete workcell instead of programming each individual element. A state formalism is used to relieve the programmer from concerns about synchronizing and coordinating the parallel execution of active workcell elements. This is more sophisticated than the 'resource manager' method proposed by Maimon. Our interprocess communication method is more general than the 'mailbox' method proposed by Baird. Although it is based on the UNIX TCP/IP inter-process communication protocol it can be easily adapted to a different environment.

This paper will briefly present the WRAP environment and describe its first application in the programming of a multi-robot multi-sensor workcell to perform an idealized assembly operation.

2. The WRAP environment: a brief presentation

2.1 Programming Methodology

This section describes the WRAP environment and how it can be used for workcell programming. WRAP uses a state formalism to achieve the coordination of concurrent operations of active elements within a workcell. Initially the application is decomposed into a set of logical 'steps', called *activity blocks* which must satisfy the following requirements:

1.) All activities (ie. 'units of work') in an activity block are to be executed by one active element.

2.) All assumptions about the required state of the workcell environment to enable the activities are made once at the beginning.

3.) The state of the workcell is redefined before the execution of the activity block terminates.

If we look at an activity block from an operating system point of view, it has to request and be granted permission to 'modify' the status of a set of elements and parts in the robot world. The system treats the status of an element or part as a resource. Points 2 and 3 are now equivalent to requesting all necessary resources before execution of a process can start and relinquishing them before execution can terminate. Since all necessary resources are requested at the same time and are relinquished at the end of the block, deadlocks due to indefinitely waiting for a resource are prevented.

To satisfy requirement 2, we associate an enabling a pre-condition with each activity block A precondition is a hypothesis about the state of the workcell environment. Pre-conditions are associated with the status of workcell elements and cannot be directly associated with objects manipulated by the workcell (which we call parts) This choice was made because parts are dynamic entities; they enter the workcell, move from one place to another and then exit. For the runtime system to be efficient the definition of pre-conditions had to be static Pre-conditions are defined as conjunctions of binary valued condition variables Condition variables are hypotheses about the status of a workcell elements and are introduced to indirectly reference the state of parts in the workcell. Condition variables are user defined, take binary values and are associated with workcell elements. Condition variables take their values from functions defined by the user The value of a condition variable is automatically re-evaluated by the system every time the status of its associated element is changed. The introduction of condition variables increases the programming flexibility and power of the WRAP Environment.

The programmer may associate one or more state modifications with each activity. A state modification indicates the new value that a state variable takes after the execution of the activity. Not every activity is required to cause a state modification, since the concept of a 'state' is only important for active element coordination and synchronization purposes. WRAP offers the programmer a database which maintains a representation of the workcell. The database can be accessed either to retrieve the data needed to execute an activity or modify data, to include information returned by sensing element. More details about the database are published elsewhere [9, 11].

After the application is decomposed into blocks, the user creates the input program. A mouse driven graphic interface has been designed to facilitate this task [12]. Activity blocks are displayed as nodes and conditions as arcs; pre-conditions and state modifications are comprised of conditions. For each activity block the user is prompted to enter the enabling pre-condition, the set of activities and their corresponding state modifications. Using the mouse the user edits the program and identify activity blocks and conditions. Finally, the system validates the consistency of the user's input and creates a Constraints Net that describes the application problem. Each node in the net represents an activity block as defined above. The net is analyzed and the input program to the WRAP Environment is created by SAGE, a sequencing/optimization system based on Petri Nets [10]. SAGE generates only deadlock free programs.

A sample list of WRAP robot activities is given in Table 1. WRAP offers the programmer the flexibility to add new user-defined activities to the existing ones through a simple procedure. This means that WRAP is adaptable to any application. Hence Table 1 is presented here as an example rather than as a list of necessary and sufficient robot commands; clearly such a list depends upon the particular application. New devices are also easy to incorporate into WRAP. The programmer, as part of the initialization, declares the logical name of the required devices. At startup WRAP consults a table of known devices and creates the appropriate control tasks which will be described in the next section. This mechanism gives WRAP additional flexibility and makes it independent of a particular application, since each application can use a different set of workcell elements and/or activities but still be executed under the same environment.

2.2 Software Architecture

In the remainder of this section we present the software architecture of the environment. WRAP is implemented as a logically distributed system, consisting of a set of concurrent processes which have no shared memory and communicate solely by message passing. WRAP processes, execute on a set of machines connected with a Local Area Network (LAN). A set of communication primitives that allow both blocking and non-blocking message passing over the LAN is used [13].

Figure 1 shows the different processes (called tasks) that constitute the WRAP Environment. These tasks are: the *Workcell Interpreter (WI)*, the *Data Base Manager (DBM)*, and a set of *Virtual Device Control (VDC)* tasks, each being associated with one active element. These tasks are further discussed in the following sections. We call the input I to the WI task a *workcell program*: it consists of two parts: a declaration part ID and an action part IA. The latter is a partial ordering of activity blocks: $IA = \{ \ldots B_i \prec B_j \ldots \}$. The WI, as its the name implies, interprets the workcell program and coordinates its execution. Initially the declarations are processed. Here the programmer specifies the environment (passive and active elements) and the parts that will be manipulated. After the declarations are processed, the WI consults a table that relates active elements with VDC functions (that can be either system or user defined), and creates the VDC tasks and a set of FIFO (first-in first-out) queues one associated with each VDC task The queues are managed by the WI. Each VDC task communicates with the WI and the DBM tasks As the input program is interpreted the queues are loaded. If the pre-condition associated with the block at the top of the queue is true, the activity block is processed and removed from the queue. As a result of this processing a set of VDC commands are generated and passed to the VDC task

The *Data Base Management (DBM)* task is responsible for managing the workcell database We consider the database to be a very important part of the system. The more 'intelligent' a robotic system is, the more important the knowledge stored in the database becomes. WRAP's database stores information about workcell elements and parts (such as current positions and orientations, current values of attributes eg weight, object models etc.). A database 'object' can either be a 'system defined' workcell element or a 'user defined' (ie. application dependent) part (such as a printed circuit board of a given type, an IC, a capacitor, etc.) [9, 11].

The key part of the WRAP environment is the State Table that maintains a representation of the physical status of all the workcell elements and parts in the workcell. The State Table is maintained by the *State Table Administrator (STAdm)* which, in the current implementation of WRAP is not a separate process but runs as part of the DBM. The STAdm is responsible for evaluating pre-conditions in order to decide whether all resources necessary to execute an activity block are available. For the current activity block B_i at time t the WI passes the pre-condition as the query $q(pc_i, t)$ to the STAdm. The STAdm evaluates the pre-condition and responds with a binary valued answer $r(t)$.

If the pre-condition is false, the virtual device is considered *blocked* and the WI proceeds to the next queue which is associated with a non-blocked virtual device. If a pre-condition is true, then all state variables whose values are altered by the execution of activities in the block are marked undefined and the VDC commands $c_i^k(t)$ are passed to the appropriate virtual device. The 'undefined' marking of a state variable provides a locking mechanism for the database entry: while its state variable is undefined, an entry can only be updated (say by a sensing device) but cannot be read. Later, as each activity is executed, the state variables that it modifies are updated, and therefore re-defined. This is important as it guarantees that the system will not introduce deadlocks; in other words, a deadlock-free program will not deadlock due to the synchronization mechanism used by the WRAP Environment. As mentioned earlier, this has an analogy in an operating system where in order to avoid deadlocks a process is forced to either request all resources it will require at the same time, or if it needs additional resources to first release those previously allocated and then submit a new request.

The *State Table* also maintains the 'history' of all workcell states since the activation of WRAP for a given application. This information can, at a later time, be used for debugging or error recovery purposes. In the latter case the WI or a separate *Error Recovery Expert* could generate new VDC commands to drive the workcell from the error state to one that would allow the application program to continue.

There is a *Virtual Device Control (VDC)* task associated with each virtual device. Its purpose is to provide a generic interface to the workcell elements of a specific class (eg. robots) by handling the commands and error messages to and from each one. Typically, the VDC task associated with virtual device k decomposes the ith 'complex' command c_i^k (such as *LOCATE_OBJECT*) into $N \geq 1$ 'primitive' ones (such as *GRAB_FRAME, THRESHOLD, etc.*) The virtual device acknowledges the termination of a command with a multi-valued response, with values ranging over the following output set:

$$O(response) = \{response_1,\ response_2,\ \ldots,\ response_n\}$$

After the response is received, the VDC task passes the state modifications $\{\ sm_i^k(t)\ \}$ to the STAdm task to re-define one or more undefined state variable Before the WI task generates a VDC command c_i^k, it sends requests q_i to the DBM to translate abstract descriptors and to provide the low level information r_i needed for the execution of the command. After the execution of a command by a virtual device, the corresponding VDC task generates a list of 'world' changes and updates the world model stored in the database.

2.3 On the Coordination of workcell operations

The coordination of workcell operations requires explicit knowledge of all points of synchronization. Synchronization is required under two conditions: (i) the sharing of passive elements such as a jig, and (ii) the satisfying of precedence constraints. To deal with both sources of synchronization, the user defines a state representation of the workcell and then associates **pre-conditions** of operations with **workcell states**.

The **state vector** therefore defines the status of the workcell. It consists of a set of **state variables** which indicate the current status of all passive workcell elements and parts in the workcell. State variables are therefore associated with passive workcell elements and with parts in the workcell. In every case, the state variable has been defined and is stored in the database as part of the system's knowledge about the passive element or the part, ie. is part of the data structure that the system uses to represent a part.

The current implementation of WRAP recognizes four types of state variables: Boolean eg. JIG A ('OCCUPIED or 'EMPTY'), Arithmetic eg number of workpieces remaining in a feeder; Enumerative eg

BOARD 1 ('INSPECTED', 'REPAIRED', etc.), Frame, a Homogeneous Transform that describes a position and orientation in 3D space.

Pre-conditions are used to coordinate and synchronize the operation of the active workcell elements. A **pre-condition** is associated with each group and must be true in order for the activities in the group to be performed eg. to pick-up a board from a jig, there should be a board in the jig already! A pre-condition is a conjunction of binary **condition variables** c_k; condition variables are derived from state variables For example, one could have: c_1 *becomes* $TRUE$ *when* $status(JIG\_A) = OCCUPIED$

c_2 *becomes* $TRUE$ *when* $status(R1.tool) = ON$

Remember that associated with a condition variable is a binary valued function. This function is evaluated by WRAP to determine the new value of a condition variable. Whenever a state variable changes value, WRAP re-calculates the values all the condition variables associated with it. The system provides some basic functions used to relate state to condition variables. The user can define and use additional functions specific for the application. These functions can access the database and take decisions based on the status of the workcell environment.

State and condition variables can be either *defined* or *undefined*. The 'undefined' marking implies that a workcell operation is in progress which will modify the state variable. A 'defined' condition variable is strictly boolean (TRUE or FALSE), while a 'defined' state variable, as previously explained, can be of boolean arithmetic, enumerative or frame type.

2.4 The Organization of the WRAP Database

In this section, we describe the DBM/STAdm task implementation. From our point of view, integrating a database within the WRAP environment is advantageous for several reasons:

1.) It provides a standard way of arranging, maintaining and retrieving knowledge about the workcell environment. As a result the consistency of the software that will be developed to control the robots and interface with the sensors and the other active workcell elements, will increase.

2.) It simplifies robot and sensor programming by providing a standard way to map abstract descriptors used by the programmer (eg. peg@input_tray.pos) into low level information used by the run-time system (eg. the position and orientation of the peg on the input_tray).

3.) It maintains the *state variable* associated with each workcell element and part. This state representation is used to synchronize and coordinate the operation of the workcell.

4.) It maintains the *history* of the workcell, in terms of old values of state variables This information can be used for error recovery as well as to identify the reason for the failure. This 'history' can also serve for analyzing the productivity of the workcell and help improve its efficiency by providing a feedback to SAGE.

Conceptually, the database is organized in two hierarchies, a **Model** hierarchy and an **Object** hierarchy; all *models* are part of an *entity* called *MODELS*, while all *objects* are part of either an *entity* called *WORLD* or of another object, referred to as the *PARENT*. Objects are instances of models. Models (or Templates) are identified by their **class** while objects are identified by their **name**. There are many fields associated with each database entry: the *name* field uniquely identifies the entry; the *class* field identifies a model or the model corresponding to an object; the *part_of* field identifies the parent of the entry; the *position* field describes the position and orientation of the object in the workcell; the *state_variable* field maintains the representation of the user-defined status of the object. Finally the *attribute* field associates user-defined attributes with workcell objects.

WRAP 'sees' the database as having three parts: a *dictionary* of models, a description of the *workcell environment* and a *state table*. A Database Manager (DBM) was written to interface WRAP to the database and manipulate the data structures. The DBM provides functions to **create** and **delete** objects **define** and **undefine** state variables, **add attributes** (each one with class, qualifier and data fields) etc. In the next section, each of these functions will be briefly discussed.

The database can also maintain geometric (or shape) information about objects. A bounding volume representation of each divisible object is maintained and functions are provided to alter it when a sub-object is attached or removed from it. For indivisible objects together with the bounding volume representation the system keeps a more detailed hierarchical geometric model At the lower level we have edges that are combined to define polygonal surfaces. Surfaces are then translated and rotated in 3D space to define solids One or more solids can be combined to define objects Since geometric information associated with indivisible objects is static, it is defined as part of the object model Finally, a set of functions is provided to display objects on a graphics display system.

During the operation of the workcell, the database is memory resident. This favors high speed interactions and is possible due to its small size. At the end of a session, the information stored in the database can be saved in a file, which we call the 'database file', that can be read back later to start a new session The database file is an ASCII file, so it can be generated and/or modified using a standard editor

3. Using WRAP to program a multi-robot multi-sensor workcell

The objectives of this application were to demonstrate the modeling and programming facilities of WRAP and evaluate its run-time performance. Figure 2 shows the configuration of the workcell. We used two robot arms, a Unimation PUMA 260 six degree of freedom revolute robot and a MICROBO ECUREUIL six degree of freedom cylindrical robot. A linear stage is used to move parts from one robot to the other. Two sensing elements are used to locate the parts; an overhead CCD camera and a infrared range detector mounted on the end-effector of the PUMA robot. Two jigs are used in the application. Randomly oriented pegs appear on the 'input jig' while the completed assembly is moved to the 'workcell output'.

To demonstrate the distributed capabilities of WRAP the environment was configured to run on a set of computers. Two MICROVAX II computers connected through a 10Mb/sec Ethernet LAN were used. one to control the PUMA and the other to run the vision software. An INTEL dual CPU (80286/8086) system running the iRMX operating system was used to control the MICROBO robot and the linear stage [19]. The two robot virtual devices were implemented in RCCL.

To demonstrate the operation of the WRAP environment, an idealized multi-robot assembly task is programmed. The PUMA robot is used to pick-up a peg (using information from the range sensor) and insert it into the hole of an assembly base, a cylindrical object, located on the linear stage. The exact position of the hole is found using the overhead camera. After the peg is inserted the complete assembly is moved to the MICROBO which moves it to the 'workcell output' jig. Then the linear stage moves back under the camera and this completes a cycle. We assume that while the linear stage is moving from the MICROBO to the PUMA area, a new assembly base is placed on it. This is done by a human operator

Since the camera is used to locate the hole of the assembly base part a calibration has to be performed to establish the correspondence between the coordinate system of the camera and the coordinate systems of the two robots. Once this is done a calibration matrix, which relates the x_{camera}, y_{camera}, z_{camera} coordinates of a point in the camera's field of view, to the x_{robot}, y_{robot}, z_{robot} coordinates, is derived.

To write the workcell program, we first identified the 'logical steps' that would constitute the activity blocks, for each of the active elements involved. Then we associated a pre-condition and a set of resulting changes to the workcell environment with each one. The pre-conditions were then defined as conjunctions of condition variables and the condition variables and functions were defined. Thus we have:

VISION sensor:

- **pre-condition:** stage at PUMA_AREA and NEW assembly base part is on the stage
  activity: grab image
  state change: assembly base part under camera becomes PICTURED
  activity: process image to identify base part and locate the center of the hole
  state change: assembly base part under camera becomes IDENTIFIED and the location of the center of the hole passed to the database

RANGE sensor:

- **pre-condition:** 'input jig' is SCANNED
  activity: process range image to find if peg is present
  state change: if a peg is detected a, new peg entry is created in the database and its status becomes NEW. The status of the 'input jig' becomes EMPTY or OCCUPIED
- **pre-condition:** peg on the 'input jig' is SCANNED
  activity: process range image to locate peg
  state change: peg becomes LOCATED and its position is stored in the database

LINEAR stage:

- **pre-condition:** base part is ASSEMBLED and stage is at PUMA AREA
  activity: move stage from PUMA_AREA to MICROBO_AREA
  state change: stage at MICROBO_AREA
- **pre-condition:** stage is EMPTY and stage is at MICROBO_AREA
  activity: move stage from MICROBO AREA to PUMA_AREA
  state change: stage at PUMA AREA stage becomes OCCUPIED, a database entry for a new assembly base part is created and its status becomes NEW

MICROBO robot.

- **pre-condition:** base part is ASSEMBLED and stage is at MICROBO AREA

activity: pick_up assembly from stage
stage change: stage becomes EMPTY
activity: move base part to 'workcell output'
state change: base part becomes PROCESSED

PUMA robot:

- **pre-condition:** 'input jig' is EMPTY
  activity: perform a fast scan to look for new peg on the 'input jig'
  state change: status of the 'input jig' becomes SCANNED
- **pre-condition:** 'input jig' is OCCUPIED and 'peg' is NEW
  activity: perform comprehensive scan of 'input jig' to get a detailed range image of the 'peg'
  state change: status of the 'peg' becomes SCANNED
- **pre-condition:** status of 'peg' is LOCATED
  activity: pick_up 'peg'
  state change: status of 'peg' becomes PICKED-UP, status of 'input jig' becomes EMPTY
- **pre-condition:** assembly base part on the stage is IDENTIFIED
  activity: insert 'peg' into the hole
  state change: status of base part becomes ASSEMBLED status of 'peg' becomes INSERTED

For the complete syntax and the semantics of the workcell program, the interested reader is referred to [8]

4. Conclusions

This paper presented the Workcell Real-time Programming (WRAP) environment developed at the McGill Research Center for Intelligent Machines at McGill University. WRAP provides an integrated environment for programming a distributed multi-robot/multi-sensor workcell. The workcell programmer enters the program in the form of 'logical steps' using a graphics user interface. For each 'step' the programmer is prompted to enter an enabling hypothesis about the state of the workcell needed to successfully perform the operations in the 'step' as well as a set of changes to the state of the workcell resulting after the successful execution of the 'step'. This input is then analyzed and processed and finally an time optimal workcell program is generated and downloaded to the run-time environment.

WRAP is implemented as a logically distributed system. A database manager process maintains a representation of the workcell environment and a user defined state representation which is used to coordinate and synchronize the parallel operations of the workcell elements. We described a sample application of WRAP in the programming of an assembly workcell consisting of two robots, one linear stage and two vision sensors, one based on intensity and the other on range data. In the future we plan to expand the environment in the areas of collision detection with static and non-static objects in the environment and deal with the problem of error detection and recovery.

The authors wish to acknowledge the financial support of FCAR and NSERC.

Table 1 Sample list of robot activities for pick-and- place operations.

Activity	Parameters required
move_absolute	destination (hom. transform equation)
move_relative	displacement (hom. transform)
change_speed	new speed
change_motion_mode	new mode (ie. joint, cartesian)
move_object	object, source, destination
switch_tool	tool state
pickup_object	object, source
deposit_object	object, destination
change_tool	new tool
operate_tool	tool state

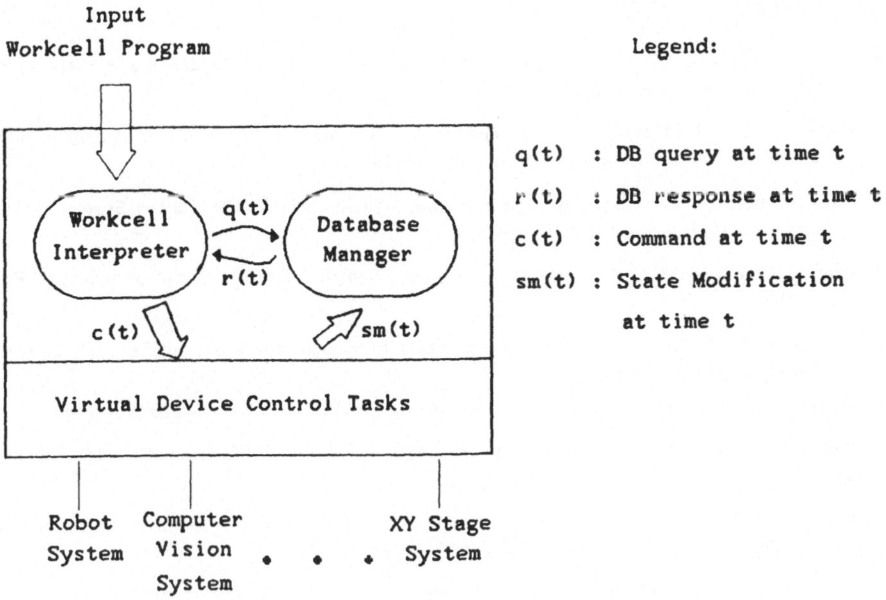

Figure 1 Software architecture of a run-time workcell programming environment.

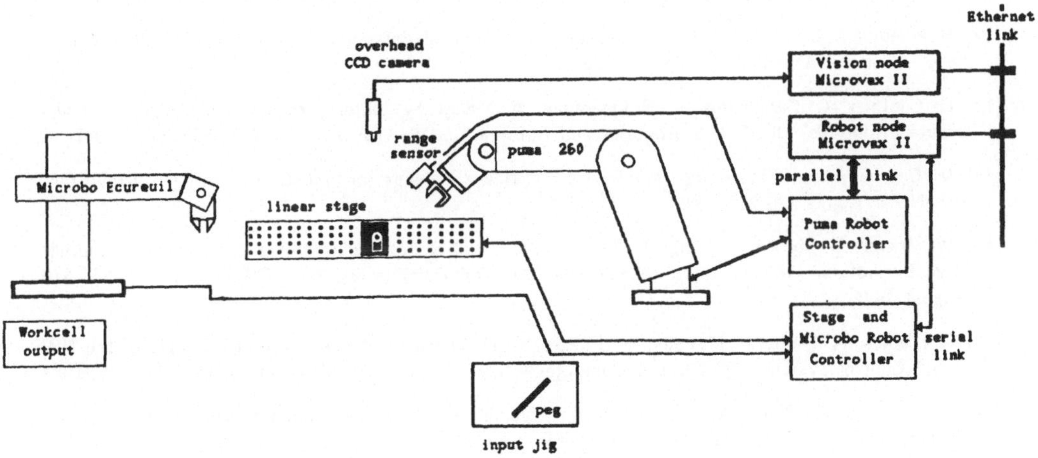

Figure 2 Workcell architecture for the peg-insertion application

5. References

[1] R. Alami, H. Chochon, "Programming of Flexible Assembly Cell: Task Modeling and System Integration" IEEE Conf. on Robotics and Automation, 901-907, 1985.

[2] R. Alami, "NNS: A LISP-Based Environment for the Integration and Operating of Complex Robotics Systems", IEEE Conf. on Robotics and Automation, 349-353, 1984.

[3] J. Albus, A. Barbera, M. Fitzgerald, "Programming a Hierarchical Robot Control System", 12th Int. Symp. on Industrial Robots, 505-517, 1982.

[4] J. Albus, J. Evans, "A Hierarchical Structure for Robot Control", 5th Int. Symp. on Industrial Robots, 231-237, 1975.

[5] H. Baird, E Wells, D. Britton, "Coordination Software for Robotic Workcells", IEEE Conf. on Robotics and Automation, 354-360, 1984

[6] N Beale "The MAP initialive", Computer Aided Eng J., Vol. 3, no. 3, 79-82, June 1986

[7] S Bonner, K. Shin, "A comparative study of robot languages", IEEE Computer, Vol. 15 no 12 December 1982.

[8] G. Carayannis, A. Malowany, "A Framework for a Robot Workcell Run-time Environment", Technical Report, McGill Research Center for Intelligent Machines, 1988.

[9] G. Carayannis, B. Blais, A. Malowany, M. Levine, "A Real-Time Database for a Robotics Workcell Programming Environment", IEEE Pacific Rim Conf., 141-144, 1987.

[10] P. Freedman, A. Malowany, " The Analysis and Optimization of Repetition within a Robot Workcell Sequencing Problems", Proc. IEEE Int. Conf. Robotics and Automation, 1988.

[11] P. Freedman, C. Michaud, G. Carayannis, A. Malowany, "A Data Base Design for the Runtime Environment of a Robotics Workcell", Robotics and Computer Integrated Manuf J. Spring 1988.

[12] P. Freedman, G. Carayannis, A. Malowany, "A Graphical Perspective on Robot Workcell Programming", Graphics Interface '88 Conf., 1988.

[13] D. Gauthier, G. Carayannis, G. P. Freedman, A. Malowany, "Interprocess Communication for Distributed Robotics", IEEE J. of Robotics and Automation, Vol. RA-3, no. 6, 493 -504, Dec. 1987.

[14] M. Gini, G. Gini, "Recovering from Failures: A New Challenge for Industrial Robotics", IEEE COMPCON Fall Conf., 220-227, 1983.

[15] W. Gruver, B. Soroka, J. Craig, T. Turner, "Industrial Robot Programming Languages: A Comparative Evaluation", IEEE Trans. on Systems Man and Cybernetics, Vol. SMC-14, no. 4, 565-570, August 1984.

[16] L. Haynes, A. Barbera, J. Albus, M. Fitzgerald, H. McCain, "An Application Example of the NBS Robot Control System", Robotics & Computer Integrated Manufacturing, Vol. 1, No. 1, 81-95, 1984.

[17] V. Hayward, R. Paul, "Manipulator Control using the "C' Programming Language under UNIX", IEEE Workshop on Languages for Automation, 3-10, 1983.

[18] A. Kak, K. Boyer, C. Chen, R. Safranek, H. Yang, "A Knowledge-Based Robotics Assembly Cell", IEEE Expert, Vol. 1, no. 1, 63-83, Spring 1986.

[19] D. Kossman, A. Malowany, "A Multi-Processor Robot Control System for RCCL under iRMX", IEEE Int. Conf. on Robotics and Automation, 1298-1306, 1986.

[20] O. Maimon, "A Multi-Robot Control Experimental System with Random Parts Arrival", IEEE Conf. on Robotics and Automation, 895-900, 1985.

[21] O. Maimon, Y. Nof, "Activity Controller for a Multiple Robot Assembly Cell", Winter Annual Meeting of the American Society of Mechanical Eng., 267-284, 1983.

Simulation and Teaching Techniques for Interactive Robot Programming: ROPSE

S. Elbaba, A. Troncy, and M. Martinez (France)

ABSTRACT. ROPSE, is a friendly unified system for both programming and robot guiding assistance. It constitutes the user interface in the industrial version of ACRO modular robots. ROPSE, implemented in Pascal on PC-AT micro computer, realizes full driving of the operator by interactive graphical means based on the tree-structured rolling menus principle and accessible by a logical mouse. Actions are selected on the screen for actual robot driving or easy and fast robot off-line programming. The system offers a set of complementary debugging tools : off-line graphical simulation, step-by-step robot on-line driving, and a teaching by showing module that proposes unconventional solutions.

1. INTRODUCTION

Programming of industrial robots often do leave the choice only between two methods : textual programming or teaching by showing. The first one is generally not accessible to the workshop personnel. The second, teaching by showing, is still today the most common robot programming mode because of its low-cost implementation, and its simple running principle. Meanwhile, it presents high limitations such as slowness in program development, and a difficulty to take into account outside information. Furthermore, when the actuators are not driven conventionally by a close-loop analogic servo-control, the teaching process is almost impossible to implement inexpensively.

In this paper, **ROPSE** (**RO**bot **P**rogramming **S**ystem **E**nvironment) an assistance module for both robot programming and driving is presented. It uses graphical and interactive techniques [DOM 86][DUE 86] and includes teaching by showing, while answering its limitations. This system environment constitutes the industrial version of the robot user interface of ACRO project robots [MAR 87], whose main characteristic is their modular design.

The hardware architecture of the ACRO robots command system supporting ROPSE, is presented together with the axis-controllers it drives. The system of program generation and robots driving is then described and its interactive feature is pointed out. Its advantages and limitations are discussed. Finally three program debugging tools are presented : a graphical simulation in step-by-step mode, an on-line driving in step-by-step mode, and a teaching by showing module. For the design of this last tool, it has been developped an unconventional technique for the utilization, as actuators, of digitally open-loop controlled stepping motors.

2. ACRO SYSTEM FOR MODULAR ROBOTS

The ACRO system is composed of a hardware multiprocessor system and of a robot command software including the ROPSE programming environment presented here. The goal of the ACRO project is the study, design and realization of robots that are entirely modular from the very mechanical structure downto the computer-based command system. By defining standardized components, essentially arm-modules and axis-modules (a joint integrating a stepping motor, a reducer and the associated computer-based controller), it becomes possible to create or modify, from these elements, any custom-designed manipulator according to the application specification. The advantage naturally consists in the obtention of a low cost flexible production tool and also in the possibility of constituting a manufacturing manipulator set which utilization mode and overall control are unified.

Structure of the control system

Design specifications for the ACRO computer-based control system are :

- the possibility of undertaking in a flexible way all, or at least a wide range of, mechanical configurations,
- performances that are not very sensitive to the structure complexity,
- a user interface as independent as possible of the same configuration.

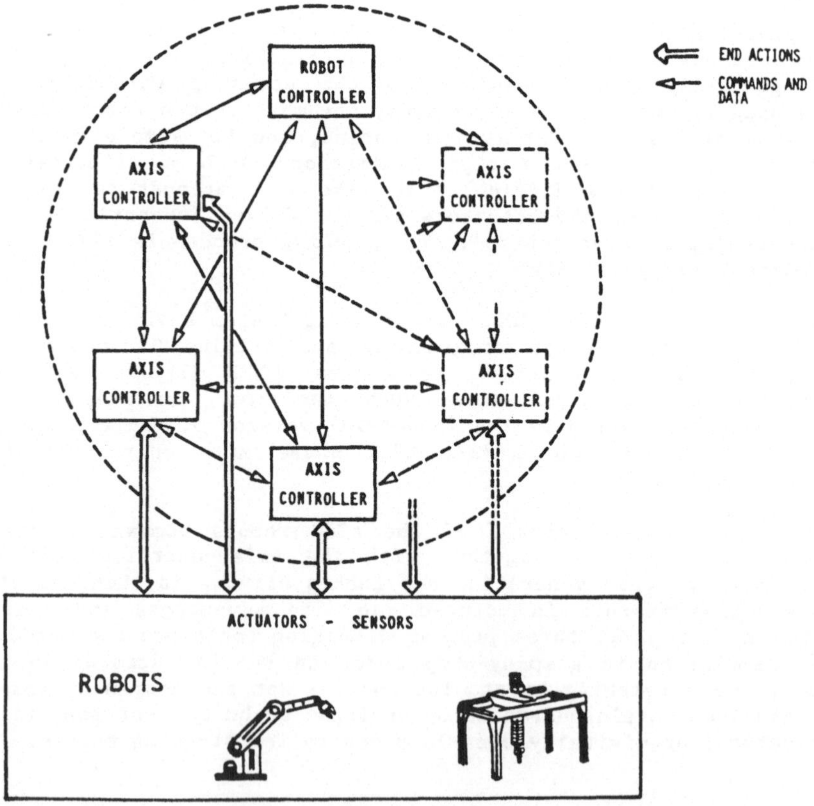

Figure 1 : Logical Structure of the ACRO Control System

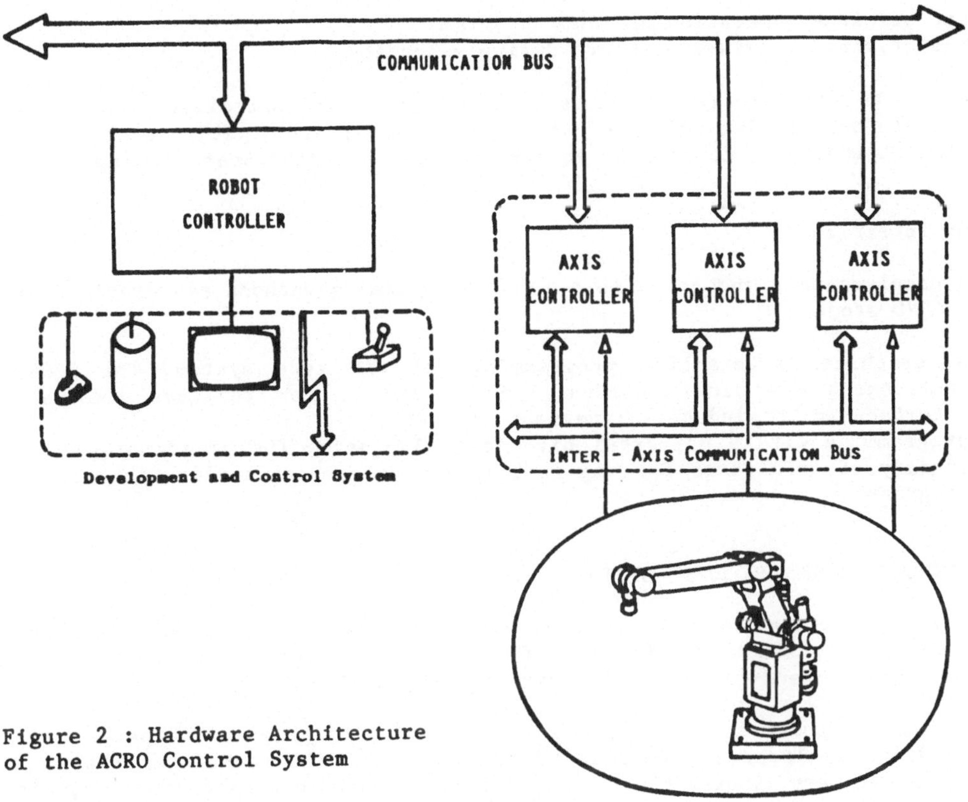

Figure 2 : Hardware Architecture of the ACRO Control System

These constraints lead to the elaboration of a control system whose main characteristics are :

- an open logical structure including the robot controller and n axis controllers, one for each axis (Fig. 1),
- a multiprocessor hardware architecture (Fig. 2). The adjunction of an extra axis simply implies the adding of an extra (micro-)processor to the structure.

Axis-controller

Each axis-controller (Fig. 2), implemented on one microprocessor, realizes the control of one articulation. It entirely manages :

- inter-communication using messages (data and commands),
- generation of joint movements (acceleration, displacement, breaking, stopping),
- inter-axis synchronization.

The move command message include an address, the move instruction code, a number of steps, a speed, the direction, and control indicators.

Robot Controller

The robot controller is a set of cooperating modules in charge of :

- the off-line generation of robot program,
- the driving of axis-processors during execution.

Due to the hardware multiprocessor structure, axis-controllers carry out in real parallelism most of the cycle management. This enabled to implement the robot controller in a PC-AT type microcomputer running at 10 Mhz.

User interface

Two complementary and compatible robot programming methods are provided in the ACRO project :

- a graphical interactive programming, of CAD type system. The ROPSE environment has been implemented first and it now realizes the user interface in the industrial version of ACRO,
- programming with a universal high level language. The programming of a library of primitives for the realization of complex applications is in progress.

3. STRUCTURE OF THE ROPSE SYSTEM

The ROPSE environment is a unified system for both robot programming and guiding which, thanks to its specifications, provides the preference and safe access to end-users little aware of programming :

- dialogue through non-textual means, especially of graphical type,
- guidance as large as possible of the operator. The techniques that are preferred are those that offer choice among coherent options, in opposition with those that let the initiative of the actions to the operator and then verify their coherency later,
- security in the running and debugging of industrial applications,
- compatibility with the received techniques in industrial robotics, such as teaching by showing for example.

The ROPSE specialized modules (Fig. 3), are activated by a command interpreter, based on the tree-structured rolling menu principle, and whose interactive aspects were very carefully handled. Via a logical mouse, the operator selects among the command groups :

- creation / modification of the robot program,
- management of the programs library,
- translation / teleloading of object programs,
- simulation of the cycle,
- starting / control of the cycle,
- teaching by showing,
- utility tools.

Among these modules, the basic tool is the specialized editor that operates on the same principle of interactivity and "a priori" coherence.

4. PROGRAMMING

Programs are interactively created or modified under continuous control of

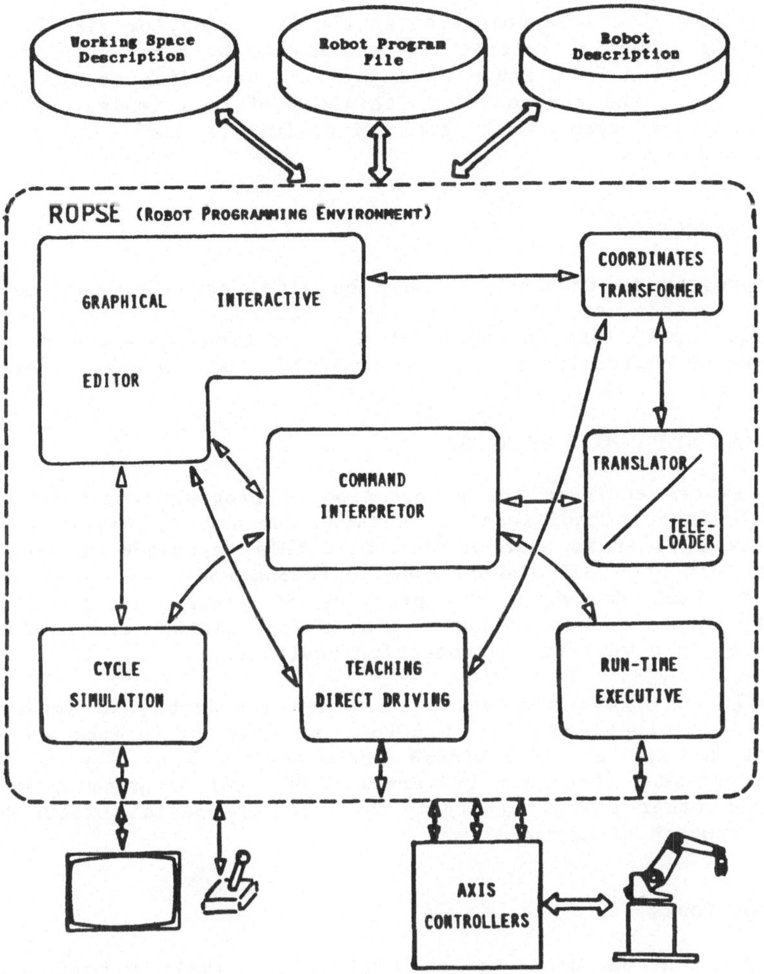

Figure 3 : Structure of the ROPSE system

the editor. The user selects from the menu, via a mouse as well, the required command or option :

- move on a straight line or via intermediate points,
- actuators move,
- terminate tools actions,
- wait,
- teaching by showing option,
- cycle control.

Next the system requires optional necessary parameters such as : a set speed, the passing through points or stop points. It verifies continuously actions coherency. The manipulator is permanently graphically displayed on a window of the standard screen, the third dimension being shown on a separate window. The move operation in the free mode, or via the passing-through-points mode, is implicit. It is achieved by robot off-line driving (Fig. 4), specified by a mouse or a joystick according to configuration. In the same way, the eventual uncertainties of positioning, of an elbow for example, are removed. Program windowing is implicit or achieved through cursor keys.

5. PROGRAM EXECUTION

Once the program is created, it must be first translated by means of a coordinate transformer, into n object programs that are teleloaded towards axis-controllers in charge of the execution. Once the run start is over, the robot controller is usually available for any other operation.

6. ADVANTAGES AND LIMITS OF ROPSE

The ROPSE system achieves the elaboration of programs whose structure is essentially linear. Conditional structures can not be easily taken into account [LOZ 83]. It is also obvious that this technique of "guiding" is sufficient only when all the desired positions and motions are known at programming time. Meanwhile the practice of manufacturing applications shows that, in their large majority, these applications are equivalent to simple cycles in a well-known production environment.

To take all cases into account, it is then reasonable to implement the dual system mentioned earlier : ROPSE, to give preference to economic development by non computer-minded end-users, and a library of robot primitives accessed through a universal high level programming system for the possible other cases. According to this, a special effort has been devoted to program debugging.

7. DEBUGGING TOOLS

Three tools can be used at the debugging level, according to the complexity or precision of the application : off-line simulation of the cycle, "on-line" execution in step-by-step mode, and teaching by showing.

Graphical simulation

The simulation module includes different tools for off-line simulation of the cycle. It enables interpretation of a robot program previously created under editor. The operator can initiate either a continuous simulation or a step-by-step simulation for more accurate verification, with correction and then recovery possibilities.

On-line execution in the step-by-step mode

This option is activated under the simulation module in the step-by-step mode. The robot is graphically simulated and simultaneously on-line driven. For this purpose, every instruction to which is added a compulsory stop at the end of each movement, must be handled by the translate-teleload-execute treatment. When needed, the operator can interrupt the

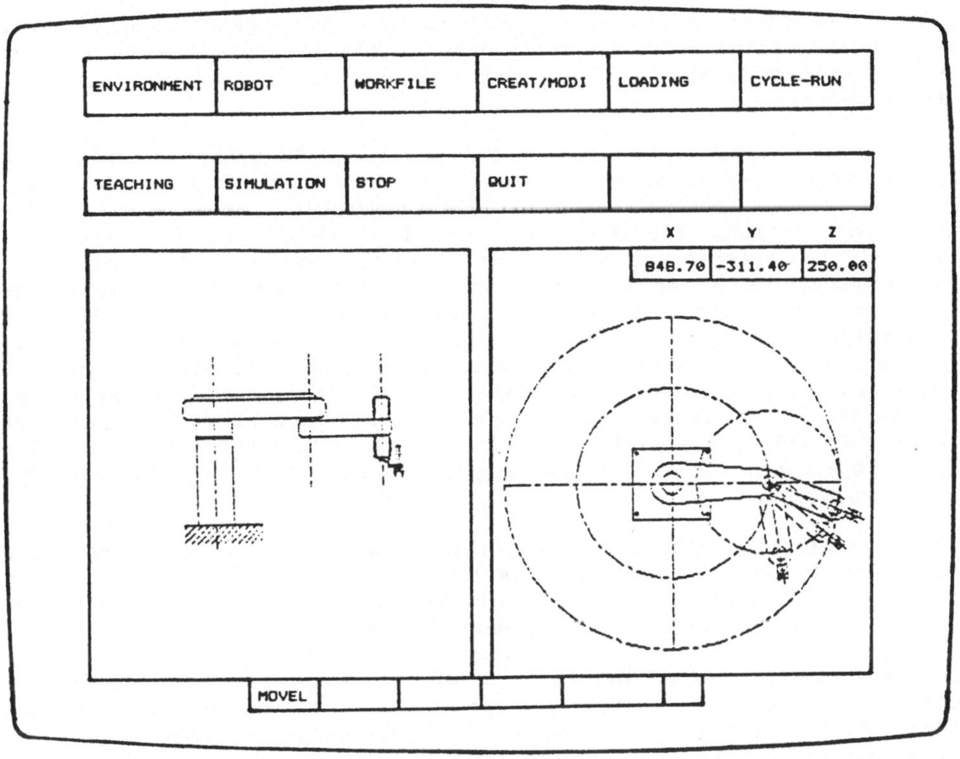

Figure 4 : Layout of the ROPSE graphic display

cycle via the keyboard (the special problem set by the stoppage of the stepping motor is seen later). The simulation module allows a return to the latest position, or to the initial position, and then recover after correction.

It must be noted that the juxtaposition of step-by-step sequences naturally cannot presume of the manipulator dynamic behaviour.

Teaching by showing

Teaching by showing, or guiding [LOZ 83], is a simple mean for acquiring coordinate frames (i.e. in the case of ROPSE cartesian frames). This technique, although not very productive, remains valuable for debugging in some critical cases [KOD 86], and must be industrially proposed if the experience accumulated in this field by the operators is to be taken into account [DIL 86][SEL 83]. ROPSE proposes for this a teaching by showing module in which the robot is driven by means of a joystick. It has been verified that this method for position specification is more natural and reliable than any other, for example a teach-box device or its simulation from a keyboard.

Teaching by showing cannot be implemented here following the usual technique : in almost all existing command systems, the joystick level inclination is interpreted by a computer device that sends to the servo-control a calculated target position to be reached before the next sampling. The close-loop analogic servo-control then generate a voltage, inversely proportional to the remoteness of the target. It is a driving technique with "a posteriori" corrections, performed by the servo control of the actuators.

In the present study, the command is completely "a priori". The use of stepping motors in robotics is full of promises because of their precision. Those motors are actually controlled in open-loop for inexpensive control. The speed of stepping motors can be varied by modifying the emission frequency of command impulses. Each of these impulses generates a one step rotation. Accelerations and decelerations follow laws that are not very well established. The determination of maxima values is complex and in practice must be experimentally precised. The axis-controller realizes the numerical command of the motor : maximal acceleration ramp, constant speed level, deceleration ramp, and stopping, all this from a reference (n_i,v_i) where n_i is the number of steps to be accomplished and v_i the maximal speed to reach. The difficulties to solve for the implementation of the **Teaching by showing module of ROPSE** were due to the open-loop control :

- the determination of the precise distance necessary to reach the speed reference at maximal motor acceleration,
- the non-interruptibility of the micro-movement in order to avoid the generation of too important management problems,
- the necessity to continuously provide the stepping motors with set points during all motor motion, in order to prevent the fall-out of step with total loss of torque and position. The sampling period must therefore be variable, which implies very dissuasive management problems when computed by the robot controller,
- the determination of angular coordinates once the desired position is reached.

Solutions to these problems rely on the following principles or choices :

- positions coordinates are computed, with a precision of one motor step, by the robot controller and sent as reference to axis-controllers,
- sampling period management is done by committing the axis-controllers the charge of determining the sampling times. In parallel to its main work of move management, the axis-controller verifies each time if it will be still capable to control the motion till the end position and wake the robot controller up for the next position sampling request within the requested time. The sampling period is then favourably proportional to the difference between instantaneous speed and the reference speed,
- each axis-controller permanently computes the instantaneous joint position of the motor and sends it on demand of the robot controller for recording the end-position.

8. RESULTS

The system described was tested in the field of education on two robots already constructed at the Lyon IUT. It shows a very simple and fast program development. End-user adaptation to ROPSE system appears short. The open-loop axis-controllers software allows maximal motor speed execution without any find out step-falts until today.

9. CONCLUSION

In this paper we described ROPSE, a unified programming and robot control system, accessible to workshop technicians. Treatments interactivity and user guidance are privileged by the use of graphical techniques and of a CAD programming mode, associated to a set of debugging tools. A solution to teaching by showing implementation is developped for the open-loop control of actuators. The open modular design of the control system allows the use of low-cost equipement (microprocessors and microcomputers of PC-AT type) and present day performances look very promising. The software, written in Pascal and which uses techniques that require reasonable computer power, show when tested the advantage of this system with an increase in the programming throughput and a very important decrease in the time of end-user adaptation as regards to classical programming systems, and easy and quick cycle driving.

REFERENCES

[DIL 86] R. Dillmann, B. Hornung, M. Huck : Interactive Programming of Robots Using Textual Programming and Simulation Techniques, Proc. of the 16th International Symposium on Industrial Robots, Brussels sep 1986.

[DOM 86] E. Dombre, A. Fournier, C. Quaro, P. Borrel : Trends in CAD-CAR systems for robotics, 1986 IEEE Intern. Conf. on Robotics and Automation San Francisco, Apr 1986 pp 3.1913-1918.

[DUE 86] G. Duelen, U.Kirchoff, M. Vucobratovic, D. Stokic : Software System for Programming and Control synthesis of Robots, Proc. of the 16th International Symposium on Industrial Robots, Brussels sep 1986.

[HAU 83] A. Haurat, M.C. Thomas : LMAC a language of Industrial Robots, 13th Intern. Symp. on Industr. Robots, Chicago Apr 1983 pp. 1269-1278.

[KOD 86] N. Kodaira, M. Oshita, H. Maruyama, M. Umetsu, K. Miura : An Off-Line Programming System for Spot Welding Robots, Proc. of the 16th International Symposium on Industrial Robots, Brussels sep 1986.

[LOZ 83] T. Lozano-Perez : Robot Programming, Proc. of the IEEE, Vol. 71, No 7, July 1983.

[MAR 87] M. Martinez, A. Troncy, S. El Baba, C. Hugues : Modularity Concept in Robot mechanical and Control system - ACRO Project, II WBC Conf on Adv. Tech. in Design and Manufacturing, Dec 14-18, 1987.

[SEL 83] M. Selfridge, A. Levas : Teaching Robots By Example, Proc. of the 13th International Symposium on Industrial Robots, Chicago Apr 1983.

[TAY 83] R.H. Taylor, D.D. Grossman : An integrated robot system architecture, Proc. of the IEEE, Vol. 71, No 7, July 1983.

[TRO 88] A. Troncy, M.T. Martinez, S. El Baba, C. Hugues : Modular Robots - Graphical Programming, IEEE Conf. on Robotics and Automation, Apr. 24-28, Philadelphia, 1988.

[YAM 86] N. Yamamoto, T. Ogasawara : A Multiprocess-Based Runtime Monitoring System for Intelligent Robots, Proc. of the 16th International Symposium on Industrial Robots, Brussels sep 1986.

5. CONCLUSION

Conference Committees

Conference Chairperson N.Magnenat-Thalmann Professor, Université de Genève, Switzerland and HEC Montréal, Canada

Honorary Committee

President	T.L. Kunii President of the Computer Graphics Society, Professor and Director, University of Tokyo, Japan
J.Doré	Maire de Montréal, Canada
J.C.Favez	Recteur, Université de Genève, Suisse
D.Föllmi	Conseiller d'Etat, Genève, Suisse
J.Guertin	Directeur, HEC Montréal, Canada
C.Haegi	Maire de Genève, Suisse
A.Rondeau	Directeur de la Recherche, HEC Montréal, Canada
J.R. Scherrer	Directeur Division Informatique Médicale, Université de Genève, Suisse
P.Tschopp	Doyen S.E.S., Université de Genève, Suisse
B.Vittoz	Président, Ecole Polytechnique Fédérale de Lausanne, Suisse
P.Welhauser	Président du Conseil d'Etat, Genève, Suisse

Computer-Generated Film Festival

President:	N.Magnenat-Thalmann Université de Genève, Suisse and HEC Montréal, Canada
D.Kochanek	National Film Board, Canada
J.M.Moser	Ecole Polytechnique Fédérale de Lausanne, Suisse
X.Nicolas	Sogitec, France
Ph.Quéau	Institut National de l'Audiovisuel, France
D.Thalmann	Université de Montréal, Canada

International Program Committee

President	D.Thalmann Université de Montréal, Canada
P. Brunet	Ecole Polytechnique de Barcelona, Spain
R.A. Earnshaw	University of Leeds, UK
H. Fuchs	University of North Carolina, USA
G. Hégron	INRIA / IRISA, France
T. L. Kunii	University of Tokyo, Japan
Th. Liebling	Ecole Polytechnique Fédérale de Lausanne, Switzerland
N.Magnenat-Thalmann	Université de Genève, Switzerland and HEC Montréal, Canada
J.F.C. Mortelmaans	University of Leuwen, Belgium
A. Nait Abdallah	University of Western Ontario, Canada
E. Nakamae	University of Hiroshima, Japan
A. Righetti	Hôpital de Genève, Switzerland
D.F. Rogers	US Naval Academy, USA
G. Toussaint	McGill University, Canada
J. Weber	Université de Genève, Switzerland
M. J. Wozny	Rensselaer Polytechnic Institute, USA
B.Wyvill	University of Calgary, Canada

Local Organization Committee

President:	G.H.Ducry	Ducry (D & S), Suisse
J.M.Bloch	JMB Publicité, Suisse	
H.W.Bosshard	Ecole des Arts Décoratifs, Genève, Suisse	
G.Garcia	Ecole Polytechnique Fédérale de Lausanne, Suisse	
S.Jeandrevin	Ecole Polytechnique Fédérale Lausanne, Suisse	
R.Messerli	CERN, Suisse	
J.Stark	Coopers Lybrand, Suisse	
D.Thalmann	Université de Montreal, Canada	
Secretariat:	C.Bahl, E.Kohl, M.Lê Dinh, M.Morin, M.Rigo	

Authors' Addresses

Varol Akman
Centrum voor Wiskunde en Informatica
Amsterdam, THE NETHERLANDS

Ibrahim Al-Qattan
Basic Engineering Program
Tennessee Technological University
Box 5002
Cookeville, Tennessee 38505, USA

Mario de Angelis
MIRALab, HEC
5255 Décelles
Montréal H3T 1V6, CANADA

Masaki Aono
Tokyo Research Laboratory
IBM Japan, Ltd.
5-19 Sanbancho
Chiyoda-ku, Tokyo 102, JAPAN

Jacqueline Argence
Ecole des Mines
Département Informatique Appliquée
158 Cours Fauriel
Saint-Etienne Cedex 42023, FRANCE

Bruno Arnaldi
IRISA
Campus Universitaire de Beaulieu
Av. du Général Leclerc
Rennes Cedex 35042, FRANCE

Emako Aso
Department of Information Science
Faculty of Science
University of Tokyo
7-3-1 Hongo, Bunkyo-ku
Tokyo 113, JAPAN

Nadim M. Aziz
Clemson University
College of Engineering
110 Lowry Hall
Clemson
South Carolina 29634-0911, USA

Manoochehr Azmoodeh
Dept. of Computer Science
University of Essex
Wivenhoe Park
Colchester CO4 3SQ, U.K.

Didier Badouel
IRISA
Campus Universitaire de Beaulieu
Av. du Général Leclerc
Rennes Cedex 35042, FRANCE

Meurig Beynon
Dept. of Computer Science
University of Warwick
Coventry CV4 7AL, U.K.

M. Boano
CERN Data Division
CH-1211 Genève 23, SWITZERLAND

Kadi Bouatouch
IRISA
Campus Universitaire de Beaulieu
Rennes Cedex 35042, FRANCE

Martin Bourgault
Dép. d'informatique et de recherche opérationnelle
Université de Montréal
C.P. 6128, Succ. A
Montréal, Québec, H3C 3J7, CANADA

Patrice Boursier
Domaine de Voluceau
B.P. 105 - Rocquencourt
Le Chesnay Cedex 78153, FRANCE

Achille Braquelaire
Université de Bordeaux I
Dép. de mathématique et informatique
351 Cours de la Libération
33405 Talence, FRANCE

R. Brazioli
CERN Data Division
CH-1211 Genève, SWITZERLAND

Shijie Cai
Computer Science Dept.
Nanjin University
Nanjin, CHINA

Gregory Carayannis
McGill University Research Centre for Intelligent Machines
Department of Mechanical Engineering
817 Sherbrooke St.W.
Montréal, Québec, H3A 2K6, CANADA

Pierre-Alain Carrupt
Softarts-Actimol
Consultants in Computer-Assisted Molecular Design
Chemin de Maillefer 37
1052 Le Mont sur Lausanne, SWITZERLAND

R. Caubet
Laboratoire L.S.I. Langages et Systèmes Informatique
Université Paul Sabatier
118, route de Narbonne
Toulouse Cedex 31062, FRANCE

Eduard Cerny
Dép. d'informatique et de recherche opérationnelle
Université de Montréal
C.P. 6128, Succ. A
Montréal, Québec, H3C 3J7, CANADA

Narayanaswami Chandrasekhar
School of Engineering
Electrical, Computer, and Systems Engineering Dept.
Rensselaer Polytechnic Inst.
Troy, New York 12180, USA

N. Chater
EdCAAD, Department of Architecture
University of Edinburgh
20 Chambers Street
Edinburgh EH1 1JZ, U.K.

Yong C. Chen
Department of Mathematical Sciences
Purdue University Calumet
Hammond, IN, 46323, USA

Luigi Ciminiera
CENS and Dipartimento di Automatica e Informatica
Politecnico di Torino
Corso Duca degli Abruzzi 24
10129 Torino, ITALY

Françoise Cloutier
Département Systèmes d'information organisationnels
Faculté des sciences de l'administration
Université de Laval
Cité universitaire
Québec, G1K 7P4, CANADA

Jocelyn Cloutier
Dép. d'informatique et de recherche opérationnelle
Université de Montréal
C.P. 6128, Succ. A
Montréal, Québec, H3C 3J7, CANADA

E.L. Dagless
Dept. of Electrical and Electronic Engineering
University of Bristol
Bristol BS8 1TR, U.K.

Joachim Dengler
Deutsches Krebsforschungszentrum
Institut für Epidemiologie und Biometrie
Abteilung: Medizinische und Biologische Informatik
Im Neuenheimer Feld 280
D-6900 Heidelberg 1, WEST GERMANY

Akio Doi
Tokyo Research Laboratory
IBM Japan, Ltd.
5-19 Sanbancho
Chiyoda-ku, Tokyo 102, JAPAN

Jean-Pierre Doucet
Institute of Topology and System Dynamics
CNRS Associated LA34
University Paris 7
1, rue Guy de la Brosse
75005 Paris, FRANCE

Hongbo Du
Dept. of Computer Science
University of Essex
Wivenhoe Park
Colchester CO4 3SQ, U.K.

Wen-Hui Du
Groupe Image (C46)
Département Images
Ecole Nationale Supérieure des Télécommunications
46, rue Barrault
75013 Paris, FRANCE

Jacques-Emile Dubois
Institute of Topology and System Dynamics
CNRS Associated LA34
University Paris 7
1, rue Guy de la Brosse
75005 Paris, FRANCE

N.D. Duffy
Heriot-Watt University
Dept. of Electrical and
Electronic Engineering
31-35 Grassmarket
Edinburgh EH1 2HT, U.K.

Andrew W.G. Duller
Dept. of Electrical and Electronic Engineering
University of Bristol
Bristol BS8 1TR, U.K.

Georges Dumont
IRISA
Campus Universitaire de Beaulieu
Av. du Général Leclerc
Rennes Cedex 35042, FRANCE

Y. Duthen
Laboratoire L.S.I. Langages et Systèmes
Informatique
Université Paul Sabatier
118, route de Narbonne
Toulouse Cedex 31062, FRANCE

Sami Elbaba
Université Claude Bernard
Inst. Universitaire de Technologie II
17, rue de France
69100 Villeurbanne, FRANCE

Hossam El Gindy
McGill University
School of Computer Science
805. Sherbrooke St.West
Montréal, Québec
H3A 2K6, CANADA

Hirohisa Enomoto
Department of Information Science
Faculty of Science
University of Tokyo
7-3-1 Hongo, Bunkyo-ku
Tokyo 113, JAPAN

Sylvain Fauvel
Dép. d'informatique et de recherche
opérationnelle
Université de Montréal
C.P. 6128, Succ. A
Montréal, Québec, H3C 3J7, CANADA

S.M. Fisher
Rutherford Appleton Laboratory
Chilton
Didcot OXON OX11 OQX, U.K.

Leila De Floriani
Istituto per la Matematica Applicata
Consiglio Nazionale delle Ricerche
Via L.B. Alberti, 4
16132 Genova, ITALY

Wm. Randolph Franklin
School of Engineering
Electrical, Computer, and Systems
Engineering Dept.
Rensselaer Polytechnic Inst.
Troy, New York 12180, USA

Norma Fuller
Department of Computer Science
University of Regina
Regina, Saskatchewan, S4S 0A2 CANADA

V. Gaildrat
Laboratoire L.S.I. Langages et Systèmes
Informatique
Université Paul Sabatier
118, route de Narbonne
Toulouse Cedex 31062, FRANCE

Cristina Gambaro
Dipartimento di Matematica dell' Universita' di
Genova
16132 Genova, ITALY

Michael Gervautz
Technical University Vienna
Karlsplatz 13/180
1040 Vienna, AUSTRIA

David Geshwind
Digital Video Systems
111 Fourth Avenue
New York 10003, USA
Latent Image Development Corp.
Two Lincoln Square
New York 10023, USA

Duncan Gillies
Department of Computing
Imperial College of Science and Technology
180 Queensgate
London SW7 2BZ, U.K.

Lin Gingras
Département systèmes d'information
organisationnels
Faculté des sciences de l'administration
Université Laval
Cité universitaire
Québec, G1K 7P4, CANADA

Pascal Guitton
Université du Québec à Montréal
Dept. de mathématique et informatique
CP 8888, Succ. A
Montréal H3C 3P8, CANADA

Koichi Harada
Faculty of Engineering
Hiroshima University
Saijo
Higashi-hiroshima 724, JAPAN

Keith Harrison
University of Sheffield
Department of Computer Science
Hicks Building
Hounsfield Road
Sheffield, S3 7RH, U.K.

Léon Harvey
Département systèmes d'information organisationnels
Faculté des sciences de l'administration
Université Laval
Cité universitaire
Québec, G1K 7P4, CANADA

Gérard Hégron
IRISA
Campus Universitaire de Beaulieu
Av. du Général Leclerc
Rennes Cedex 35042, FRANCE

Roger D. Hersch
EPFL
Lab. de microinformatique
Av. de Cour 37
1007 Lausanne, SWITZERLAND

Volker Heyers
Deutsches Krebsforschungszentrum
Institut für Epidemiologie und Biometrie
Abteilung: Medizinische und Biologische Informatik
Im Neuenheimer Feld 280
D-6900 Heidelberg 1, WEST GERMANY

Minh Hong Tong
MIRALab, IRO
Université de Montréal
C.P. 6128, Succ. A
Montréal H3C 3J7, CANADA

Jean-Pierre Hornung
Institute of Anatomy
University of Lausanne
9, rue du Bugnon
1005 Lausanne, SWITZERLAND

Nies Huijsmans
Department of Mathematical and Computer Science
University of Leiden
PO Box 9512
NL-2300 RA Leiden
THE NETHERLANDS

Masayuki IIzuka
Department of Electrical and Computer Engineering
Nagoya Institute of Technology
Gokiso-cho, Showa-ku, Nagoya 466, JAPAN

Masa Inakage
The Media Studio
3-5-17 Aobadai, Apt.201
Meguro-ku
Tokyo 153, JAPAN

Mikael Jern
V.P. Technology
Uniras A/S Copenhagen
376 Gladsaxevej
DK-2860 Soborg, DENMARK

Zhengwen Ju
Computer Science Dept.
Nanjin University
Nanjin, CHINA

Chu Kai-Ching
Inst. of Systems Science
National Univ. of Singapore
Heng Mui Keng Terrace
Kent Ridge, Singapore 0511 SINGAPORE

Mohan Kankanhalli
School of Engineering
Electrical, Computer, and Systems Engineering Dept.
Rensselaer Polytechnic Inst.
Troy, New York 12180, USA

Nami Kin
Department of Information Science
Faculty of Science
University of Tokyo
7-3-1 Hongo, Bunkyo-ku
Tokyo 113, JAPAN

Mike King
Computer Graphics
City of London Polytechnic
100 Minories
London EC3N IJY, U.K.

Hiroaki Kobayashi
Department of Information Engineering
Faculty of Engineering, Tohoku University
Sendai 980, JAPAN

Rudolf Kraftsik
Institute of Anatomy
University of Lausanne
9, rue du Bugnon
1005 Lausanne, SWITZERLAND

Tosiyasu L.Kunii
Department of Information Science
Faculty of Science
University of Tokyo
7-3-1 Hongo, Bunkyo-ku
Tokyo 113, JAPAN

Wolfgang Leister
Department of Computer Science
University of Karlsruhe
D-7500 Karlsruhe, WEST GERMANY

Kevin Linder
McGill University Research Centre for
Intelligent Machines
Department of Mechanical Engineering
817 Sherbrooke St.W.
Montréal, Québec, H3A 2K6, CANADA

Nadia Magnenat-Thalmann
Centre Universitaire d'Informatique
12 rue du Lac
1207 Genève, SWITZERLAND

Alfred Malowany
McGill University Research Centre for
Intelligent Machines
Department of Mechanical Engineering
817 Sherbrooke St.W.
Montréal, Québec, H3A 2K6, CANADA

Francis T. Marchese
Dept. of Computer Science
Pace University
New York, NY 10038, USA

M.T. Martinez
Université Claude Bernard
Inst. Universitaire de Technologie II
17, rue de France
69100 Villeurbanne, FRANCE

Thomas Maus
Department of Computer Science
University of Karlsruhe
D-7500 Karlsruhe, WEST GERMANY

Hans-Peter Meinzer
Deutsches Krebsforschungszentrum
Institut für Epidemiologie und Biometrie
Abteilung: Medizinische und Biologische
Informatik
Im Neuenheimer Feld 280
D-6900 Heidelberg 1, WEST GERMANY

David A.P. Mitchell
University of Sheffield
Department of Computer Science
Hicks Building
Hounsfield Road
Sheffield, S3 7RH, U.K.

Paolo Montuschi
CENS and Dipartimento di Automatica e
Informatica
Politecnico di Torino
Corso Duca degli Abruzzi 24
10129 Torino, ITALY

Pierre-Yves Morgantini
Laboratory of Computational Chemistry
University of Geneva
30, quai Ernest Ansermet
1211 Genève 4, SWITZERLAND

Heinrich Müller
Department of Computer Science
University of Karlsruhe
D-7500 Karlsruhe, WEST GERMANY

Seiichiro Naito
Information Science Research Laboratory
NTT Basic Research Laboratories
3-9-11 Midori-Cho, Musashino-Shi
Tokyo 180, JAPAN

Eihachiro Nakamae
Faculty of Engineering
Hiroshima University
Saijo
Higashi-hiroshima 724, JAPAN

Tadao Nakamura
Department of Information Engineering
Faculty of Engineering
Tohoku University
Sendai 980, JAPAN

Burkhard Neidecker
Department of Computer Science
University of Karlsruhe
D-7500 Karlsruhe, WEST GERMANY

Bruce G. Nichol
Schlumberger Well Services
Austin Systems Center
8311 N.F.M. 620
P.O. Box 200015
AUSTIN, TX 78720-0015, USA

Tsukasa Noma
Department of Information Science
Faculty of Science
University of Tokyo
7-3-1 Hongo, Bunkyo-ku
Tokyo 113, JAPAN

Paolo Palazzi
CERN Data Division
CH-1211 Geneva, SWITZERLAND

Caterina Pienovi
Istituto per la Matematica Applicata del C.N.R
via l.b. alberti 4
16132 Genova, ITALY

Luis A. Pineda
EdCAAD, Department of Architecture
University of Edinburgh
20 Chambers Street
Edinburgh EH1 1JZ, U.K.

Daniel Pletinckx
Research and Development Department
Barco Industries Creative Systems
Barco Industries
Th. Sevenslaan 106
8500 Kortrijk, BELGIUM

Andrew Poon
Department of Computing
Imperial College of Science and Technology
180 Queensgate
London SW7 2BZ, U.K.

Thierry Priol
IRISA
Campus Universitaire de Beaulieu
Rennes Cedex 35042, FRANCE

Przemyslaw Prusinkiewicz
Department of Computer Science
University of Regina
Regina, Saskatchewan, S4S 0A2 CANADA

Werner Purgathofer
Technical University Vienna
Karlsplatz 13/180
1040 Vienna, AUSTRIA

Osman Ratib
UCLA
Div. of Medical Imaging
Dept. of Radiological Sciences
and the Laboratory of Nuclear Medicine (DOE)
Los Angeles, CA 90024, USA.

Said Reda
Dept. of Computer Science
Pace University
New York, NY 10038, USA

Françoise Richard
Institut de Mathématique
7, rue René Descartes
67000 Strasbourg, FRANCE

James R. Rose
Director, Basic Engineering Program
Tennessee Technological University
Box 5002
Cookeville, Tennessee 38505, USA

Christian Roy
Dép. d'informatique et de recherche opérationnelle
Université de Montréal
C.P. 6128, Succ. A
Montréal, Québec, H3C 3J7, CANADA

Marie-Christine Roy
Département systèmes d'information organisationnels
Faculté des sciences de l'administration
Université Laval
Cité universitaire
Québec, G1K 7P4, CANADA

Francis J.M. Schmitt
Groupe Image (C46)
Département Images
Ecole Nationale Supérieure des Télécommunications
46, rue Barrault
75013 Paris, FRANCE

Manoj Seshan
School of Engineering
Electrical, Computer, and Systems Engineering Dept.
Rensselaer Polytechnic Inst.
Troy, New York 12180, USA

Adrian Sfarti
Evans and Sutherland
1808 Stierlin Road
Mt View CA 94043, USA

Paul Sharp
University of Otago
Dept. of Computer Science
Box 56 Dunedin, NEW ZEALAND

Yoshiharu Shigei
Department of Information Engineering
Faculty of Engineering
Tohoku University
Sendai 980, JAPAN

Richard Storer
Dept. of Electrical and Electronic Engineering
University of Bristol
Bristol BS8 1TR, U.K.

Achim Stösser
Department of Computer Science
University of Karlsruhe
D-7500 Karlsruhe, WEST GERMANY

Tokiichiro Takahashi
Visual Media Laboratory
NTT Human Interface Lab.
1-2356, Take
Yokosuka-shi, Kanagawa, 238-03 JAPAN

Toshinitsu Tanaka
Visual Media Laboratory
NTT Human Interface Lab.
1-2356, Take
Yokosuka-shi, Kanagawa, 238-03 JAPAN

Chua Tat Seng
Inst. of Systems Science
National Univ. of Singapore
Heng Mui Keng Terrace
Kent Ridge, Singapore 0511 SINGAPORE

Daniel Thalmann
Laboratoire d'Infographie
Département d'Informatique
Ecole Polytechnique Fédérale de Lausanne
1015 Lausanne, SWITZERLAND

Godfried Toussaint
McGill University
School of Computer Science
805. Sherbrooke St.West
Montréal, Québec
H3A 2K6, CANADA

A. Troncy
Université Claude Bernard
Inst. Universitaire de Technologie II
17, rue de France
69100 Villeurbanne, FRANCE

Sakae Uno
Tokyo Research Laboratory
IBM Japan, Ltd.
5-19 Sanbancho
Chiyoda-ku, Tokyo 102, JAPAN

Naoki Urano
Tokyo Research Laboratory
IBM Japan, Ltd.
5-19 Sanbancho
Chiyoda-ku, Tokyo 102, JAPAN

Adriano Valenzano
CENS and Dipartimento di Automatica e Informatica
Politecnico di Torino
Corso Duca degli Abruzzi 24
10129 Torino, ITALY

Lluis Pérez Vidal
Départament de Métodes Informatics
ETSEIB-UPC
Diagonal, 647
E-08028 Barcelona, SPAIN

Wong Wai-Hung
Inst. of Systems Science
National Univ. of Singapore
Heng Mui Keng Terrace
Kent Ridge, Singapore 0511 SINGAPORE

Yulan Wang
Computer Science Dept.
Nanjin University
Nanjin, CHINA

Han van de Waterbeemd
Softarts-Actimol
Consultants in Computer-Assisted Molecular Design
Chemin de Maillefer 37
1052 Le Mont sur Lausanne,
SWITZERLAND

Alan H. Watt
University of Sheffield
Department of Computer Science
Hicks Building
Hounsfield Road
Sheffield, S3 7RH, U.K.

Jacques Weber
Laboratory of Computational Chemistry
University of Geneva
30, quai Ernest Ansermet
1211 Genève 4, SWITZERLAND

R. Michael White
Institute for Geodesy and Photogrammetry
Swiss Federal Institute of Technology
ETH Hönggerberg
8093 Zürich, SWITZERLAND

Christopher Williams
Department of Endoscopy
St Marks Hospital
City Road
London EC1v 2PS, U.K.

George Wolberg
Dept. of Computer Science
Columbia University
450 Computer Science Bldg.
New York 10027, USA

Brian Wyvill
Department of Computer Science
University of Calgary
2500 University Drive N.W.
Calgary, Alberta, T2N 1N4, CANADA

Geoff Wyvill
University of Otago
Dept. of Computer Science
Box 56 Dunedin, NEW ZEALAND

Tetsushi Yamamoto
Department of Information Science
Faculty of Science
University of Tokyo
7-3-1 Hongo, Bunkyo-ku
Tokyo 113, JAPAN

John Yau
Heriot-Watt University
Dept. of Electrical and Electronic Engineering
31-35 Grassmarket
Edinburgh EH1 2HT, U.K.

Edward Yung
Dept. of Computer Science
University of Warwick
Coventry CV4 7AL, U.K.

Fuyan Zhang
Computer Science Dept.
Nanjin University
Nanjin, CHINA

W.R. Zhao
IHEP Academia Sinica
P.O.Box 918
Beijing, CHINA

Paul Zsombor-Murray
McGill University Research Centre for
Intelligent Machines
Department of Mechanical Engineering
817 Sherbrooke St.W.
Montréal, Québec, H3A 2K6, CANADA